American Jewish Year Book

The American Jewish Committee acknowledges with appreciation the foresight and wisdom of the founders of the Jewish Publication Society (of America) in the creation of the AMERICAN JEWISH YEAR BOOK in 1899, a work committed to providing a continuous record of developments in the U.S. and world Jewish communities. For over a century JPS has occupied a special place in American Jewish life, publishing and disseminating important, enduring works of scholarship and general interest on Jewish subjects.

The American Jewish Committee assumed responsibility for the compilation and editing of the YEAR BOOK in 1908. The Society served as its publisher until 1949; from 1950 through 1993, the Committee and the Society were co-publishers. In 1994 the Committee became the sole publisher of the YEAR BOOK.

American

Jewish

Year Book 1998

VOLUME 98

Editor
DAVID SINGER
Executive Editor
RUTH R. SELDIN

THE AMERICAN JEWISH COMMITTEE
NEW YORK

ISBN 0-87495-113-5

Library of Congress Catalogue Number: 99-4040

PRINTED IN THE UNITED STATES OF AMERICA
BY THE HADDON CRAFTSMEN, INC., BLOOMSBURG, PA.

Preface

This year's volume features four special articles, two relating to the 100th anniversary of the founding of the Zionist movement, and two to the 50th anniversary of the creation of the State of Israel. Shlomo Avineri and Anita Shapira present fresh insights into the origins of the Zionist movement, with Avineri focusing on the career of Theodor Herzl, and Shapira on Zionism in the context of the political and social upheavals of the 20th century. Yossi Klein Halevi and Arnold Eisen review the monumental achievements of Israel's first 50 years, reflecting on what Jewish statehood has meant, respectively, for Israel's citizens and American Jewry. A special photo insert augments this section.

Jewish life in the United States is treated in three articles: "National Affairs" by Richard T. Foltin; "Jewish Communal Affairs" by Lawrence Grossman; and "Jewish Culture" by Berel Lang.

Peter Hirschberg provides detailed coverage of events in Israel. Reports on Jewish communities around the world include Canada, Mexico, Argentina, Great Britain, France, the Netherlands, Italy, Switzerland, Germany, Austria, East-Central Europe, the former Soviet Union, Hong Kong, Australia, and South Africa.

Updated estimates of Jewish population are provided—for the United States, by Jim Schwartz and Jeffrey Scheckner of the Council of Jewish Federations and North American Jewish Data Bank; and for the world, by Sergio DellaPergola of the Hebrew University of Jerusalem.

Carefully compiled directories of national Jewish organizations, periodicals, and federations and welfare funds, as well as religious calendars and obituaries, round out the 1998 AMERICAN JEWISH YEAR BOOK.

We gratefully acknowledge the assistance of our colleagues Cyma M. Horowitz and Michele Anish of the American Jewish Committee's Blaustein Library.

THE EDITORS

Contributors

SHLOMO AVINERI, Herbert Samuel Professor of Political Science and director, Institute for European Studies, Hebrew University of Jerusalem, Israel.

GISELA BLAU, Journalist and publicist; Zurich, Switzerland.

HENRIETTE BOAS: Journalist; Amsterdam, Holland.

GREG CAPLAN, Doctoral candidate in history, Georgetown University.

ADINA CIMET, Lecturer, YIVO–Columbia University Yiddish summer program; consultant, Columbia–Barnard Urban Policy Center.

SERGIO DELLAPERGOLA: Professor and head, Division of Jewish Demography and Statistics, Avraham Harman Institute of Contemporary Jewry, Hebrew University of Jerusalem, Israel.

ARNOLD M. EISEN: Professor and chairman, religious studies, Stanford University.

RICHARD T. FOLTIN: Legislative director and counsel, Office of Government and International Affairs, American Jewish Committee.

ZVI GITELMAN: Professor, political science, and Preston R. Tisch Professor of Judaic Studies, University of Michigan.

MURRAY GORDON: Adjunct professor, Austrian Diplomatic Academy, Vienna, Austria.

LAWRENCE GROSSMAN: Director of publications, American Jewish Committee.

RUTH ELLEN GRUBER: European-based American journalist and author, specialist in contemporary Jewish affairs; Morre, Italy.

MIRIAM HERSCHLAG: Free-lance journalist; Hong Kong, China.

PETER HIRSCHBERG: Senior writer, *The Jerusalem Report*; Jerusalem, Israel.

YOSSI KLEIN HALEVI: Senior writer, *The Jerusalem Report*; Jerusalem, Israel.

IGNACIO KLICH: Lecturer, Latin American history, Faculty of Law, Languages and Communication, University of Westminster, London, England.

LIONEL E. KOCHAN: Historian; Wolfson College, Oxford, England.

MIRIAM L. KOCHAN: Free-lance journalist and translator; Oxford, England.

BEREL LANG: Professor of humanities, Trinity College.

COLIN L. RUBENSTEIN: National policy chairman, Australia/Israel and Jewish Affairs Council; senior lecturer, politics, Monash University, Melbourne, Australia.

JEFFREY SCHECKNER: Research consultant, Council of Jewish Federations; administrator, North American Jewish Data Bank, City University of New York.

JIM SCHWARTZ: Research director, Council of Jewish Federations; director, North American Jewish Data Bank, City University of New York.

MILTON SHAIN: Professor, Hebrew and Jewish studies, and director, Kaplan Centre for Jewish Studies and Research, University of Cape Town, South Africa.

ANITA SHAPIRA: Ruben Merenfeld Professor for the Study of Zionism and head, Yitzhak Rabin Center for Israel Studies, Tel Aviv University, Israel.

MEIR WAINTRATER: Editor in chief, *L'Arche*, the French Jewish monthly, Paris, France.

HAROLD M. WALLER: Professor, political science, McGill University; director, Canadian Centre for Jewish Community Studies, Montreal, Canada.

Contents

OTHER COUNTRIES

DIRECTORIES, LISTS, AND OBITUARIES

Special Articles

Herzl's Road to Zionism

BY SHLOMO AVINERI

THEODOR HERZL'S MOST QUOTED statement, surrounded by an almost prophetic aura, is undoubtedly the entry in his diary written after the conclusion of the first Zionist Congress in Basel in 1897, "In Basel I have founded the Jewish state." To this he added wistfully: "Were I to state this loudly today, the response would be universal derision. Perhaps in five years, certainly in fifty years, all will admit it." Fifty-one years later, in 1948, Israel gained its independence under the leadership of David Ben-Gurion.

For all its almost mystical bravura, the famous statement conceals more than it reveals: Herzl's first choice was not Basel, nor did he initially intend to convene a public congress. As his diaries clearly show, his original policy options were quite different, and only a combination of failures, contingencies, and sheer serendipity—those inscrutable building-blocks of so much of history's tortured process—led him to Basel and to what eventually became a winning strategy of Zionist politics and diplomacy.

First, as to the venue: When Herzl became aware that only a public—and well-publicized—world gathering of Jews might grant him the breakthrough he was seeking for his ideas, his first choice was Munich, a major metropolis in powerful Germany, not a mid-size provincial town in Switzerland. At that time, Munich boasted a vibrant artistic, intellectual, and architectural life, and was also conveniently located for easy railway access to most areas in Central and Eastern Europe, from where most of the delegates were to come. It also had a sizeable Jewish community.

Ironically, however, it was the rabbis and leaders of the Jewish Kultus-gemeinde of Munich who foiled Herzl's attempt to inscribe the name of Munich in the annals of Jewish history. But for their refusal to have the congress meet in their city, Herzl's statement would probably have been: "In Munich I have founded the Jewish state."

The reason the worthies of the Jewish community of Munich recoiled in horror from being involved in any way in Herzl's project can well be understood. Wealthy and prosperous, viewing themselves as proud Jews as well as ardent German subjects, the Jewish community leaders of Munich found it offensive and imprudent to be even indirectly associated with the outlandish idea of a political movement calling for the return of

3

Jews to Zion—it might cast aspersions on their German patriotism and their loyalty to the recently unified German Reich; it could even raise the disturbing specter of double loyalty. It is to these considerations that the Zionist movement owes its luck of not being associated with a city that would have its own symbolic resonance in other, far darker chapters of modern European and Jewish history.

Having been singed by this rebuttal, Herzl lowered his sights and, rather than looking for an alternative major metropolitan center in a major country, began looking for a less visible venue. Switzerland presented itself as a viable alternative—again, due to its centrality regarding train connections, but also due to its political marginality. By this time Herzl was already treading carefully, and, as his correspondence and diary suggest, he passed over the obvious choice, Zurich, fearing a similar rejection from the leaders of what was then—as it is now—the major Jewish community in Switzerland.

There was, however, another reason. Zurich, with its cosmopolitan atmosphere, had over decades been the magnet for revolutionaries from around the world, who found its atmosphere congenial as a place of refuge and asylum (Lenin was to spend some time there later); it thus became known as a hotbed of anarchism and sedition. Herzl was adamant in presenting his nascent movement as eminently respectable and unthreatening to the powers-that-be, unconnected in any way with the seedy political refugees, suspicious-looking revolutionaries, and bomb-throwers associated with the émigré culture of Zurich. Hence the choice of laidback Basel. Even its Jewish community, one of Herzl's correspondents wrote him, was insignificant: "It cannot help us much—but neither can it hurt us," wrote the Zurich lawyer David Farbstein, one of Herzl's earliest supporters.

Herzl was also satisfied that, despite its small Jewish population, Basel did possess a kosher restaurant, which would make it possible to draw observing Orthodox Jews to the congress. While himself wholly nonobservant (during the congress itself he complained about having to eat the unpalatable kosher food offered in what was obviously an indifferent eating house), Herzl was respectful of the symbolic meaning of religious traditions and understood that in order to succeed, the Zionist movement would need at least some support from Orthodox quarters. How important this symbolism was to Herzl is also evident from his decision to go to the synagogue in Basel on the Sabbath preceding the opening of the congress. He was honored with an *aliyah* to the Torah, and though never a synagogue-goer, he did confide to his diary that the occasion moved him deeply—even more than his own speech at the opening of the congress the next day.

Having become the venue for the first Zionist Congress through a series of unlikely causes, Basel eventually developed into the virtual capital of the Zionist movement in its first phrase. Out of the eleven Zionist congresses that met before the outbreak of World War I, seven met in Basel; at one point Herzl even contemplated asking one of his associates, the well-known architect Oscar Marmorek, to draw up plans for a "Congress Hall" in Basel, but the idea never materialized.

Yet convening a congress was not, in the first instance, the way Herzl imagined promoting and achieving his ideas. When Herzl set himself the task, in the summer of 1895, of addressing "the Jewish Question," he was at first utterly at a loss how to go about it. As the evidence of his diaries suggests, he initially played with the idea of writing a popular novel about the plight of the Jews and their deliverance in a Jewish state. He started collecting material and making notes for it, hoping to reach a wide audience through a literary medium. (Eventually, Herzl carried out another version of this idea in his utopian novel *Altneuland* ["Old-New Land"], but by then the Zionist movement had already been launched.) Basically Herzl thought that he would achieve his goal of creating a Jewish commonwealth by attracting to his vision the European Jewish moneyed aristocracy. These were the heads of the Jewish merchant banking houses whose influence and financial power stood at that time at their pinnacle, even as they evoked (and Herzl was well aware of this) the kind of anti-Semitism which claimed that, through their money, the Jews ruled the world.

Herzl had in mind primarily two banking magnates: Baron de Hirsch, known for extending to the Ottoman Empire the credit that made, among other things, the building of railways there possible, and who was already involved in Jewish philanthropy, mainly by supporting the establishment of Jewish agricultural settlements in Argentina; and the Paris Rothschilds, who were already known for their support of some of the first Jewish villages in Palestine, which they had rescued from bankruptcy.

Herzl's initial plan was to present himself before these financiers and convince them that he held the only key to the solution of the Jewish problem: the establishment of a Jewish commonwealth, preferably in Palestine (though at that time, mainly in deference to Hirsch's philanthropic projects in Argentina, he did not rule out South America as an option).

As these ideas were being formed in Herzl's mind in 1895, he was about to return to Vienna after a few years' stay in Paris as the correspondent for the prestigious Viennese liberal newspaper *Neue Freie Presse*. He was also known as a playwright, some of whose plays had been performed, to modest acclaim, in Vienna. Yet he was not a public figure, had as yet no organization or financial support behind him, and was basically speaking for himself. The idea that he could just walk into Hirsch's or Rothschild's gilded chambers and charm them into following his plans was totally unrealistic, even ridiculous, and was obviously doomed to fail. Nor did Herzl, for all his political acumen, realize that the last people likely to get involved in such a revolutionary scheme were Jewish financiers, pillars of the economic and political international order, who would do nothing to upset it or their role in it. They might contribute handsomely to Jewish philanthropies, as they did; but the last thing they would dare to get involved in was Jewish independent politics.

Yet Herzl failed to perceive this. He thought that his idea could be launched if a significant number of Jewish bankers would form a "Society of Jews" to finance the enterprise, or if a Jewish Council of Notables could be convened. He did gain access to Baron de Hirsch in his Paris mansion, but the outcome was embarrassing. Herzl had prepared a lengthy oration, and the baron, who probably expected another Jewish petitioner for another Jewish philanthropic cause, was taken aback and cut him off virtually in mid-sentence; Herzl was politely shown the door. He continued to bombard Hirsch with memoranda, but never got another chance to present his case.

For a proposed meeting with the Rothschilds he prepared himself in a more organized way. Herzl hoped to be able to address the whole House of Rothschild at one of their estates, but his attempts to arrange an audience never succeeded. However, out of the careful notes he prepared as the basis for his "Address to the House of Rothschild," he put together most of the material he would use in his brochure *Der Judenstaat* ["The Jewish State"], which he published the following year and which became the founding manifesto of the Zionist movement.

When the attempt to gain the attention and support of Jewish merchant bankers failed—as did a similar attempt to enlist the support of Vienna's chief rabbi—Herzl moved to an equally unsuccessful attempt to gain the support of major world leaders. His diaries for 1895–96 abound in feverish correspondence with a host of personalities, Jewish and non-Jewish, some eminently respectable, others less so, aimed at getting him access to the major courts and chancelleries of Europe and the Ottoman Empire. All these attempts failed, as they were doomed to. What serious statesman or king would deign to listen to a little-known journalist and playwright who thought that he and he alone knew how to solve one of Europe's most vexing problems, the so-called Jewish question? As many entries in his diaries attest, Herzl was aware that many of his interlocutors may well have considered him a crackpot, if not a confidence man; nonetheless, he tried again and again—in vain.

It was only after he had failed to get access to the powers-that-be that he decided to go public and try to build up a popular movement. Herzl's failures with Jewish bankers and world leaders convinced him that as a purely private person he was powerless and destined to remain so. Being a journalist and a chronicler of European political life, Herzl eventually realized that he needed public support—an organization, a funding source (until then all his efforts had been financed by his own and his father's limited resources). He had to speak for a movement, for an organization, for masses of people; only then would he be taken seriously and be listened to. Thus the idea of convening a congress came into being.

It is also significant that in the course of his frantic and futile attempts to reach Jewish magnates and world leaders, Herzl's own network of friends, supporters, and useful contacts constantly widened. To his own surprise, he learned that he was not the first to invent the Zionist wheel, that in Eastern Europe there already existed a network, albeit small yet with some resonance, called Hovevei Zion ("The Lovers of Zion"), that was supporting the few Jewish agricultural settlements already established in Palestine. He now also became aware for the first time of the Hebrew Enlightenment movement (Haskalah) in Eastern Europe and the literary revival of the Hebrew language among some members of the Jewish intelligentsia in Galicia, Lithuania, and southern Russia.

Thus the Zionist Congress was born, and the idea became flesh. Herzl himself commented ruefully that if the rich Jews would not follow him, the masses would. Strictly speaking, the masses never did flock to Herzl's movement. However, out of the failure of his attempt to enlist the rich and the powerful, there grew the Zionist movement as we know it—based on voluntary membership, developing representative and elected institutions and fund-raising structures, engaging in education, propaganda, and political lobbying—in short, "the state in the making" *(ha-medinah ba-derekh)* that was to become the World Zionist Organization and as such the underpinning of the eventual structure of the State of Israel. In this sense the statement "In Basel I have founded the Jewish State" transcends its boastful bravura intent. The entity created in Basel—paradoxically owing its genesis to the failures of Herzl's initial strategies—did indeed become the foundation of the very institutional structures that made possible the emergence of the Jewish state and determined to a large extent the contours of the representative, democratic, liberal, consensus-seeking, and coalition-building nature of Zionist and eventually Israeli politics.

The first Zionist Congress was not an elected body but a gathering of individuals who came in response to Herzl's invitation. Although he was still merely a private person, Herzl's name had become moderately known in Jewish circles due to the publication of *The Jewish State* in 1896. But the lawyers, doctors, writers, journalists, poets, and intellectuals who met in the staid and stuffy bourgeois atmosphere of the Basel Civic Union, known as the *Stadt-Casino,* felt that, even though they were not elected, they were doing something quite revolutionary and representative of the

Zeitgeist: they were reconstituting Jewish political life. The members of the congress saw themselves—and Herzl's diary entries attest to this repeatedly—as a Constituent or National Assembly, creating, by its very existence, something that Jews had not possessed for a long time, a Jewish political will institutionalized. The painting by Menachem Okin of the opening of the congress, melodramatic and stylized in the way it pictures Herzl in front of the delegates, clearly suggests an Assemblée Nationale, a Reichstag—the rebirth of a nation.

With this in mind, the delegates set out to create both the infrastructure and the legitimacy of the movement they called into being by their very meeting. The next congress was already elected on the basis of a voluntary membership fee, the symbolic shekel, evoking memories of the contributions made by Jews all over the Roman Empire to the coffers of the Temple in Jerusalem during the Second Commonwealth. This form of payment became both the initial financial basis for the organization as well as a symbol of its legitimacy and a mark of participation and membership in the newly created national enterprise. Every Jewish person paying the shekel—whose cost was computed in every country in its own currency—was entitled to vote in elections for delegates to the congress, which was to meet annually. At the Second Congress, meeting once again in Basel in 1898, an overwhelming majority decided that women who paid the shekel would have equal rights to vote and be elected to the congress—this at a time when women did not yet enjoy the suffrage in any European country or in the United States.

The organization of the congress and the nascent Zionist movement followed in the best traditions of European parliamentary life. Congress debates were public, and verbatim reports of the debates of each congress were published soon after its adjournment; in addition to plenary sessions, committees (on finance, education, membership, etc.) were established; between annual congresses an elected executive ran the affairs of the organization. Herzl himself was elected president of the congress and of the movement. Early on, factions emerged, first informally and later in a more structured form, giving rise to the eventual political parties that contested elections for congress—"general" (i.e., liberal) Zionists, socialist Zionists of various stripes, religious Zionists (Mizrachi), and so forth. The politics of coalition-building and inclusion gave rise to the need for political compromise, especially on issues like religion, with the Zionist movement—basically secular and nonobservant—nonetheless expressing respect for religious sentiments and traditions. Last but not least, as recently shown in Michael Berkowitz's perceptive study, this amalgam of modernity and tradition gave rise to the grammar of a modern Jewish national culture, encompassing literature, festivals, symbols, ceremonies, visual arts, and political procedures and activity. The line from Basel to the present achievements and tribulations of Israeli political life and culture is clear.

The Roots of Herzl's Zionism

Any assessment of Herzl's historical stature must, of course, try to respond to a fundamental question regarding the very core of his intellectual odyssey: what made Herzl, a successfully integrated cultural figure in fin de siècle Vienna, move from his initial liberal-integrationist position—one shared with so many other acculturated, comfortable Jewish intellectuals of his generation in the German-speaking world—to what at the time surely looked bizarre, advocacy for a Jewish state? In fact, this trajectory had already been followed before Herzl, but with hardly more than a ripple effect on the course of history, by such disparate people as Moses Hess and Leo Pinsker. Yet the specifics are always intriguing, in the case of Herzl even more so than most people are aware of, including those versed in Zionist history and myth.

The conventional wisdom is that what triggered Herzl's Zionist trajectory was the Dreyfus Affair. Herzl was present in Paris as a correspondent for his Viennese newspaper during the first phase of the protracted affair. He reported, with indignation and obvious pain, on the travesty of justice visited upon the hapless captain; he was present and reported again, with barely suppressed anger, on the public degradation of Dreyfus, when he was deprived of his commission after his first guilty sentence—his epaulets removed, his sword symbolically broken—all in a public military ceremony intended specifically to humiliate and degrade. Yet, on the evidence of Herzl's own diaries and correspondence, it would be wrong to see the Dreyfus Affair as responsible for his quest for a national solution to the plight of the Jews and for his despair over the fate of the European liberal dream.

The picture is more complicated, and the reasons for Herzl's change of heart are multiple. Though Herzl did report frequently about the first phase of the Dreyfus Affair (the later and politically much more stormy stages occurred when he was already back in Vienna and after he had launched the first Zionist Congress), there is hardly any reference in his reports and dispatches to the Jewish angle of the matter. What Herzl stressed in his reports (which he later also published in the collection of his articles from the Paris period in the volume *Palais Bourbon*) was the general xenophobia and chauvinism characterizing French public life; its rabid anti-German revanchism (for many French nationalists Dreyfus was primarily an Alsatian, with a suspect sympathy for Germany, which had annexed Alsace-Lorraine in the wake of France's defeat in 1870–71); the venality of the French press; the corruption of French parliamentary life; the unholy alliance among politicians, churchmen, and generals; the travesty of military justice; the vulgar populist outpourings of French politicians; and the masses' quest for a sacrificial lamb. Dreyfus's Jewishness is hardly mentioned by Herzl.

Moreover, the perusal of Herzl's diaries, covering hundreds of pages for the period 1895–1904, fails to come up with more than a couple of mentions of Dreyfus's name. His release from Devil's Island hardly merited more than half a sentence in the diaries, and even this was tucked away in a passage about a conversation with an Austrian politician.

This should not come as a surprise to anyone familiar with 1890s Vienna, or to any sensitive reader of Herzl's diaries. The sources of Herzl's skepticism about the failure of European liberalism and its internal fragility are deeply engraved in his own biography. The diaries reveal how much it was the development of politics and culture in his native Austro-Hungarian ambience, rather than French affairs, that left an indelible mark on his assessment of European politics and the future of the Jews. Incidentally, the number of Jews in France at that time was around 100,000, while more than two million Jews lived in the lands of the Habsburg Empire, encompassing not only Austria and Hungary proper, but also such centers of Jewish population as Bohemia, Slovakia, Galicia, Transylvania, and Bukovina.

After all, it was in his student days at the Law Faculty of Vienna University that Herzl found himself, like many other Jewish students, excluded from the local student fraternities (the *Burschenschaften*), because the Austrian fraternities, under the influence of anti-Semitic politicians and writers like Schoenerer and his Pan-German movement, were the first to exclude "non-Aryans" from their midst. It was the Vienna of the 1890s that also saw the emergence of a populist-nationalist movement, the Christian Social Party, led by Dr. Karl Lueger, whose xenophobic and anti-Semitic politics catapulted him, by popular choice and against the express wishes of the liberal government of Emperor Franz Joseph, to the post of mayor of Vienna—the first time an avowedly anti-Semitic politician was elected to public office in open, free elections anywhere in 19th-century Europe. It was in Vienna, not in Paris, that Herzl saw the collapse of the liberal, integrationist dream under the pressure of populist rabble-rousers, using the vote and the representative system to transfer political power from liberal to conservative politicians.

Herzl acknowledged this over and over in his diaries and correspondence: "I will fight anti-Semitism in the place it originated—in Germany and in Austria," he said in one letter. He identified the genealogy of modern, racist anti-Semitism in the writings of the German social scientist Dr. Eugen Duehring in the 1890s; it was here, in the intellectual discourse of the German-speaking lands, to which the names of Dr. Wil-helm Marr and Prof. Heinrich Treitschke have to be added, that Herzl saw the seeds of the destruction of European culture. It was not thugs coming out of the gutter or effluvia of social marginality, but stars in the intellectual firmament of German and Austrian spiritual and social life who were responsible for introducing, for the first time, racial criteria into modern intellectual, scholarly, and political discourse.

To this Herzl's diaries add an awareness of the brittleness and vulnerability of what appeared to many liberals — and primarily Jewish liberals — as the best political guarantee against bigotry and intolerance: the multinational Habsburg Empire, in whose lands Jews enjoyed equal rights, religious tolerance, unprecedented economic prosperity, and social mobility and protection under the law, all presided over by the patriarchal yet liberal symbolism of the Old Emperor.

Herzl devoted innumerable entries in his diaries to evidence suggesting that this benign, liberal empire was about to unravel, due to the combined pressures of competing social and national movements. It was these ethnic hatreds, coupled with a populist social radicalism, that were, according to Herzl, about to overcome the benevolent attempts at compromise and tolerance identified with the politics of the Habsburgs.

Lueger's victory in Vienna and the restructuring of the student fraternities along "Aryan" lines were only two examples: Herzl's diaries contain descriptions of the ethnic tensions (now totally forgotten except by experts and the descendants of those involved) between ethnic Germans and Czechs in Bohemia and Moravia, as well as in the Parliament in Vienna. Herzl followed the development of these tensions, which were reaching their climax around the turn of the century and were beginning to undermine the stability of the government in Vienna, as parliamentary life was becoming increasingly overshadowed by the extreme bickerings between nationalist German and Czech deputies in the Imperial Diet in Vienna. Herzl followed the intense struggle over questions of language in schools in Bohemia, and on many occasions reported listening to the laments of Austrian ministers (many of liberal Polish and Czech background) about the systemic crisis enveloping political life in the empire and eroding its stability. He reported similar developments from Galicia and Hungary, where ethnic and linguistic strife between Poles and Germans, and among Hungarians, Croats, and Slovaks, was endangering the survival of the tolerant, multi-ethnic empire.

To Herzl, all this had a specific Jewish angle: in Bohemia, for example, most Jews, especially in the capital, Prague, historically gravitated toward an identification with the German-speaking population, since emancipation and integration meant for them integration into the dominant German-language culture. When ethnic German parties and organizations adopted an "Aryans only" policy in the 1890s, many Jewish intellectuals and professionals found themselves excluded from what they considered their spiritual home; Herzl mentioned a number of personal tragedies ensuing from this development. When some of these Jews, now excluded from German-speaking associations, turned toward Czech groups, some Czech leaders loudly hooted them out, rightly pointing out that it was only German anti-Jewish attitudes that made those Jews embrace Czechdom. As a consequence, many Jews found themselves excluded from both German and Czech identity, thrown, so to speak, out of modern society and thrown back, sometimes against their own will, on their Jewish identity. Herzl enumerated additional instances from other regions of the Habsburg Empire.

There is a surprising amount of material in Herzl's diaries dealing with the political ascendancy of exclusivist ethnic nationalism in the Austro-Hungarian Empire. Herzl maintained close contacts with Austrian liberal politicians who tried to stem the tide of emerging nationalism, and on one occasion even prepared a draft for a compromise on school language policy at the request of the Austrian prime minister, Count Badeni (himself a Polish aristocrat from Galicia, with whom Herzl had numerous meetings dealing with, among other matters, the national and social plight of Jews in that province). Yet all was to no avail, and Herzl followed with a sinking sensation the gradual disintegration of the policies of tolerance and the ascendancy of the shrill calls for an ethnocentric politics marked by intolerance and xenophobia.

It was this awareness on Herzl's part that the era of the Good Old Emperor was drawing to a close in *Mitteleuropa* that propelled him to the realization that Jewish life in Central and Eastern Europe was in danger of being swept into the vortex of conflicting ethnic hatreds—with the Jews in the cross fire, with nowhere to escape to. That Jewish masses were suffering in Czarist Russia or Romania was common knowledge, but now that Herzl began to feel the Austro-Hungarian Empire itself beginning to unravel, he saw the Jewish tragedy moving to Central Europe, to the lands in which liberalism and tolerance were supposed to guarantee a safe Jewish existence and allow the Jews to lead decent lives and to prosper.

Herzl was one of the first to realize that this was about to happen, at a time when most commentators still believed in the longevity of the Central European equivalent of Victorian liberalism and in its capacity to survive and reform. His frantic search for a way out for the Jews ("out of the quarrels and battles of Old Europe," as he put it) was an outcome of this realization.

Herzl's road to Zionism was thus premised not on an emotional response to an individual tragedy in the West, emblematic as it might be, but on a structural analysis of the malaise of European politics in general at the turn of the century—with anti-Semitism only one ingredient in a new grammar of politics which Herzl discerned and correctly identified as being, alas, the wave of the future. In this cultural ambience of Central and Eastern Europe lay the seeds of the collapse of the European 19th-century balance of power and its accompanying liberalism, leading to the cataclysms of World War I and eventually to World War II. It was in Vienna, after all, only ten years later, as ethnic clashes intensified, that a young and not too successful painter was swept into the eye of the storm of these hatreds, out of which he wove together his own destructive brand of racism and anti-Semitism. Yet well before Hitler ever heard the names of Schoenerer and Lueger, Herzl's political sensibilities and understanding alerted him to the rumblings of the coming earthquake.

The Holocaust was only one—the most murderous—consequence of the collapse of the Austro-Hungarian Empire and the demise of a dream of a multi-ethnic, multi-religious, and tolerant Central Europe. The social and economic tensions in the Russian Empire, of which Herzl became gradually aware once he was launched on his Zionist politics, similarly alerted him to the collapse of the traditional mode of Jewish existence even in the less hospitable lands of the czars. Because of the Russian government's exclusionary politics, Jews were constantly pushed toward revolutionary activity, and the Jewish salience among revolutionaries further ignited anti-Semitism and xenophobic politics.

Herzl's Zionism, combining the best traditions of European liberalism and a modern, basically secular interpretation of the Judaic heritage, was at its root a critique of the failure of European culture, an awareness of the coming crisis in European politics, and an almost uncanny deciphering of the writing on the wall that exploded into the terrible European series of wars and massacres starting in 1914 in Sarajevo. That this dark chapter of European history has not been totally exorcised became dramatically evident with the siege of Sarajevo and the massacre at Srebrenica in the 1990s.

Few followed Herzl's call; not many were ready to internalize the cultural pessimism that informed Herzl's liberal and humanitarian vision of a Jewish state based on the principles of equality and justice. Yet Herzl's tragic achievement in successfully deciphering the hieroglyph of history is emblazoned on the world's map by the existence of a Jewish state in the Land of Israel—a state encompassing almost 5 million Jews, home to a vital, if contentious, modern Jewish culture, based on a not always easy combination of Judaic tradition, modern Hebrew language, and modern science and technology. The tragedy is that so few followed his prescient clarion call. Had many more Jews listened to his dramatic and tragic reading of modern history, it might have been otherwise.

Contemporary Echoes

Paradoxically, some of Herzl's analysis regained relevance almost a hundred years later, when Israel did already exist, with the collapse of the Soviet Union and the onset of a set of civil wars in the Horn of Africa. One of the reasons why hundreds of thousands of former Soviet Jews chose to leave for Israel was that, with the collapse of the Soviet regime and the emergence of new nation-states from the ruins of the former USSR, questions of nationalism and ethnic identity again came to the fore. Jews who had earlier viewed themselves under the Soviet system as *homo Sovieticus* faced a novel challenge as new identities linked to historical ethnic and religious ties came to dominate much of public discourse. In newly independent Ukraine, for example, many Jews who historically identified with Russian rather than Ukrainian culture, and who were more conversant with the Russian than with the Ukrainian language, found themselves having to adopt a new identity, and in many cases learn a new language. Having to relate to Ukrainian historical memories was for many of them not only an alien but also a painful experience, given the complexity of Ukrainian-Jewish relations.

Similar challenges were faced in the Muslim Central Asian republics as well as in the Baltic states, where most Jews were Russian speakers and identified with a Soviet rather than with a local identity. In some cases, as in Estonia and Latvia, many Jews were denied citizenship rights by the newly emergent legislatures, as they were lumped together with other Russian-speakers as "aliens" and even "colonizers." It is not an accident that immigration to Israel today from the former Soviet Union comes primarily from these areas—to which Moldova and Belarus could also be added—where Jews are often caught in the cross fire of ethnic, national, and religious clashes over identity and sovereignty.

A similar fate befell the small remnant of the Jewish community in Sarajevo, itself one of the components of the historical multi-ethnic and multi-religious mix that has characterized Bosnia for generations. Despite its small numbers, this community also constituted an important ingredient in the Titoist construction of Bosnia. With the demise of Yugoslavia, it found itself stranded on the alien sea of ethnic and religious warfare among Serbs, Croats, and Muslims, and most Jews left the country, going mainly to Israel. The handful of Jews in Grozny, the capital of Chechnya, were similarly evacuated to Israel during the bloody Russian attack on the independence-seeking Chechen region.

The massive exodus of Ethiopian Jews to Israel occurred under somewhat analogous circumstances reminiscent of the Herzlian thesis regarding Jewish survival under conditions of ethnic strife. The civil war in Ethiopia toppled not only the Communist regime of Mengistu, but also the Amharic hegemony inherited from the Ethiopian imperial heritage of Haile Selassie. The overthrow of Communism in Ethiopia was also an ethnic conflict over hegemony in multi-ethnic Ethiopia, and it was this that made the tenuous position of the Beta Israel communities even more precarious. While focusing primarily on East-Central European Jewry, Herzl was aware, incidentally, of the existence of black Jews, and this subject even came up in his meeting with the king of Italy, which at that time annexed neighboring Eritrea.

When viewed in this perspective, Zionism appears historically as one of the Jewish responses to the challenge of modernization and to the various transformations it caused in the uneasy equilibrium that made Jewish life in Europe possible, if not always easy. The emergence of modern Arab nationalism in the 20th century similarly threatened Jewish life in the Arab lands. Herzl's awareness of the dangers inherent in some aspects of modernity—and especially the consequences of the emergence of contending nationalist movements within the multi-ethnic area stretching from the Baltic to the Black Sea—makes his analysis a powerful witness to a malaise in Europe and in world history which is, alas, still with us. By focusing on the plight of the Jews in these changing circumstances, Herzl brought his humanist and universal vision to bear on one specific aspect of modernity and its discontents, thus making Zionism an inseparable part of modern and contemporary history.

Zionism and the Upheavals of the 20th Century

BY ANITA SHAPIRA

DISCUSSION OF HISTORICAL phenomena always involves the element of time. Thus, with regard to Zionism, one may ask: Why did it emerge when it did, rather than sooner or later? For an answer to this question, attention needs to be given to the broader historical framework within which Zionism arose.

Jacob Talmon characterized Zionism as "a Jewish response to the most effective factor in the modern world—nationalism." For his part, Gershom Scholem labeled Zionism "the Jews' utopian return into history." Different though these perspectives are, they share a sense of Zionism as a phenomenon anchored in a concrete historical context. Zionism did not emerge in an autonomous spiritual domain, as Jewish history in the Diaspora is depicted by some. Nor was it simply a natural result of the age-old yearning for Zion, as others tend to describe it. Rather, Zionism was a product of its time, a response to historical developments that demanded a new dialogue between Jews and the societies in which they resided.

A common view holds that the Zionist movement was late to appear and late in achieving its goals. Two phenomena are mentioned in this context: the emergence of an Arab national movement and the Holocaust of European Jewry. Had Zionism appeared 50 years earlier, according to the "late" school of thought, it would have preceded the rise of Arab nationalism and avoided a clash with the Palestinians. By the same logic, Herzlian Zionism intended to provide a solution to the Jewish problem in Europe in its existential sense. In this regard it failed, being late in creating the safe haven envisioned by Herzl: The Holocaust preceded the Jewish state. The State of Israel did not prevent the destruction of the Jews, since it was established only in its wake.

Historians have a difficult time coping with the question of unrealized options in history. However, the argument that Zionism missed a better opportunity to realize its goals 50 years earlier is ahistorical. Just as certain elements may have existed then that would have been more accommodating to Zionism, other factors might have made Zionism's very appearance utterly implausible to begin with.

The argument presented here is that there is an inseparable connection between the history of the 20th century and the realization of the Zionist idea; that absent certain key characteristics of the 20th century, it is doubtful whether Zionism could have achieved its aims. Just as it is doubtful that Zionism could have appeared before its time, it is equally doubtful that its realization could have occurred at a later date. A direct response to the question, "Can one imagine a project like Zionism being put into effect in today's world?" is "no." Why this is so has everything to do with unique circumstances of the 20th century that helped facilitate the realization of the Zionist idea.

The present fin de siècle has elicited comments and assessments by intellectuals and politicians attempting to appraise the past century. Isaiah Berlin has labeled the 20th century the "most terrible century in Western history," while Eric Hobsbawm has titled his book on the 20th century *The Age of Extremes*. The conspicuous element in all attempts to characterize the 20th century is the element of instability, of ideological and political extremes, of a world cut loose of its moorings. This was the world in which Zionism charted its special path.

Zionism as an ideology and political movement sought to undermine the status quo, challenging the existing division of the world, established society, and the prevailing power structures. As such, it was closely tied to the political, social, and cultural- ideological upheavals of the 20th century.

The Political Dimension

In examining the political developments which constitute key turning points in the Zionist saga, the connection between the convulsions experienced in the 20th century and the transformation of Zionism from idea to concrete reality is strikingly evident. For all his energy and imagination, Herzl was unable to obtain the desired charter for Palestine, because he was operating in a stable European world. The great change in Zionism's fortunes came about as a result of what Mark Sykes described as the "thawing of the frozen sea of international politics," i.e., the outbreak of World War I and the subsequent division of the Ottoman Empire. The Balfour Declaration, a major turning point in the history of Zionism, was surely the product of a series of misconceptions on the part of the British, all of which bore the imprint of the age. British statesmen, particularly those who came from the ranks of the aristocracy, tended to treat the world as their private playground, which they could do with as they pleased. This tendency gave birth to the fantastic idea that it would be interesting to allow the Jews to settle in Palestine, to see what they might make of it. It was this same approach that led T.E. Lawrence to devise his scheme to undermine the Ottoman Empire by manipulating the national aspirations of the Arabs, which led to the creation of modern Iraq and the Kingdom of Transjordan.

In the years immediately following World War I, the international order was still dominated by Europeans, who operated on a Eurocentric basis. It was a fleeting moment in time, one that appeared to embody the apex of European world domination, but that actually contained the seeds of its own destruction as a result of the nationalist demons which Britain unwittingly set free. The Zionist movement took advantage of this brief moment, even though it was cognizant of the risks involved in an alliance with declining European power.

The sea of international politics froze over once again in the early 1920s. The next window of opportunity for the Zionist movement coincided with World War II, which saw the decline of Britain and France and the rise of the United States and the Soviet Union as superpowers. It was the division of spoils following this war that allowed for the creation of the State of Israel. Britain's military and economic bleeding in the wake of the war made it increasingly dependent on the United States and led to the disintegration of the British Empire. In the United States, the problem of Jewish refugees caused by the war served as a rallying point for Jewish and general public opinion in support of a Jewish state. Even the Soviet Union's otherwise surprising support for the establishment of the State of Israel makes sense in the context of the emerging cold war and the Soviet Union's attempt to penetrate the Middle East at the expense of Great Britain.

In 1948, in the aftermath of World War II, revolutionary changes were still possible on the global scene. Around the same time that Israel achieved statehood, India obtained its independence in a bloody civil war; Mao Tse Tung established his hold on China; the Communists took over Czechoslovakia; and the Soviet Union's threat to Western Europe appeared real enough to lead to the Marshall Plan. In contrast, in the second half of the 20th century, the world was divided into two great nuclear camps, making for a situation of stalemate. Changes in the status quo became all but impossible prior to the 1990s, which saw the collapse of the Soviet Union and the disintegration of the Communist empire. These developments opened once again a window of opportunity in the Middle East.

So much for Zionism's link to the upheavals of the 20th century in the political realm. Let us now turn to the social, and then to the cultural-ideological, aspects.

The Social Dimension

Zionism wished to transform a diaspora minority people into a sovereign nation ruling its own territory. From a social point of view, this ambition entailed a process of migration and resettlement in Palestine of a group that had been largely European for hundreds of years. In myth and literature, the Jew has often been depicted as a wanderer—the old Jew carrying his bundle on his back—moving from country to country. In reality, however, Jews had been almost entirely stationary from the 16th century through the final quarter of the 19th century. It was only then that Jews joined the general European movement of mass migration that sent millions of Germans, Italians, Irish, English, Poles, and others to the lands of colonization across the ocean. The growing awareness of Russian Jews that the authorities were no longer willing to guarantee their physical safety led to the snowballing of transoceanic migration.

The collapse of East European Jewry's traditional frameworks of life in the wake of mass migration is powerfully captured in S.Y. Agnon's classic novel *A Guest for the Night*. Jewish towns were being emptied of their young people, leading to the decline of an entire culture and the realization that there was no turning back. In the wake of World War I and the Bolshevik revolution, this process was greatly accelerated, and it continued during the interwar period. Not surprisingly then, those Jews who were young and daring often chose to leave. Itzik Manger's famous song "A Tree Stands on the Path" reflects this reality.

The phenomenon of European-wide migration as a legitimate, accepted, option in time of need encouraged Jews to give it serious consideration. It is true that emigration to lands of white colonization, and to the United States in particular, remained the preferred option. Still, once emigration itself was viewed as acceptable, the way was cleared for a revolution in thinking that could lead to the decision to emigrate to Palestine.

The change in direction—in favor of Palestine—that occurred in the flow of Jewish emigration from the mid-1920s on was related more to world events than to ideological conviction. The closing of the gates to the United States in the early 1920s reflected incipient isolationist trends. The world economic crisis that began in 1929 reinforced these trends worldwide. At the same time, the situation of the Jews in Europe suffered a severe decline with the rise of the Nazis in Germany and protofascist regimes in Poland, Romania, and Hungary. At this point, the Zionist solution became the only viable one open to Jews, not because it was superior or more righteous, but simply because the other solutions were no longer available. This became all the more evident in the wake of the Holocaust.

Mass migration of Jews continued during the first decade following World War II. Thus, the Communist takeover of Eastern Europe sparked a movement of refugees westward. For its part, the decline in the status of Jews in Islamic countries following the establishment of Israel brought about the departure of entire communities.

The flight of refugees from east to west was not unique to Jews; millions attempted to flee. Indeed, the willingness to take a chance and change one's destiny rather than accept a limiting reality is one of the 20th century's defining characteristics. The realization of the Zionist idea simply cannot be understood without this mental paradigm shift with regard to emigration.

The life stories of countless Jewish families provide dramatic evidence of the results of Jewish migration in this century. Consider, for example, a 60-year-old Jew living in Venezuela. His parents were born in Bukovina to a large, poor, and pious family, some of whose members chose to emigrate to South America, but many of whom remained in Europe and perished in the Holocaust. He himself was born in Venezuela, is a successful professional, has a secular outlook, but maintains a connection to his Jewishness. He has children living in both Israel and Venezuela. There are millions of such stories.

The Cultural-Ideological Dimension

Perhaps the most fascinating aspect of Zionism's link to the convulsions of the 20th century is the ideological dimension. The 20th century, as Yehudi Menuhin put it, "raised the greatest hopes ever conceived of by humanity, and destroyed all illusions and ideals." This was an age in which conflict between the superpowers was not limited to the political realm, but also involved a clash of worldviews, pitting radically opposed ideologies against each other. Capitalism vs. Communism, democracy vs. dictatorship—these were the battle lines of the 20th century. While the competing ideologies were fundamentally secular in nature, many related to politics in terms of total redemption, creating an "all or nothing" mentality. Jacob Talmon took note of this in pinpointing "political messianism" as a key factor of 20th-century life, seeing it in constant conflict with a pragmatic, secular, evolutionary, and tolerant trend.

Two redemptive political ideologies, in particular, played a crucial role: nationalism and socialism. The former sought the salvation of the nation, while the latter strove for the salvation of humanity as whole. Both movements emerged in late 19th-century Europe, but eventually spread throughout the world. In doing so, nationalism and socialism acted as agents of modernization and Europeanization, offering alternatives to classical religion as a source of explanation of the past and hope for the future, as well as a focus for social solidarity and political activity. On the face of it, nationalism and socialism were polar phenomena. The former emphasized that which separates people—a unique culture and a shared past—and strove to preserve these differences. The latter sought to create a new social order in which the nation-state was discarded together with other elements of the dead past. In reality, however, there was considerable affinity between nationalism and socialism in the messages they conveyed to their followers. This is particularly true in the case of nations subjected to foreign rule; under such circumstances, the idea of national redemption was often bound up with social and economic change. National liberation movements, non-European ones in particular, often adopted a socialist agenda and saw themselves as part of the revolutionary left.

Zionism belonged to the cultural-ideological world in which the lines of demarcation between national redemption and human redemption were blurred. In Zionist thinking, the concept of *"tikkun olam"* and the correction of the generations-long injustice done to the Jewish people seemed to go hand in hand, as part of one and the same march toward a glorious future. Even those trends within Zionism that were not captivated by the socialist ideal per se tended to see Zionism as an ideology striving not only to change the Jewish people's political status, but to establish in Palestine a model society based on social justice. One need only refer to Herzl's *Altneuland* in this context. For second-generation Zionists — those born in the 1880s and after — a constant grappling with the socialist idea, and its synthesis with the Zionist idea, were central components of their worldview.

For members of that generation, impending revolution was a constant presence in daily lives. When a poor, young Jewish orphan in early 20th-century Warsaw would weep on his pillow after an arduous day of work in the company of vulgar and violent men, his friend would stroke his head and comfort him: "Don't cry, Slutzkin, the revolution will come soon!" (Both men later spent the majority of their lives on a kibbutz in the Jezreel Valley.) Confidence in imminent redemption granted spiritual meaning to daily acts. The spiritual energy generated by the sense of participation in history's culmination served as Zionism's propelling force, just as it did for revolutions from Beijing to Northern Africa.

In their efforts to recruit followers, the Zionists had to wage ongoing battle against other redemptive ideologies that made claim to Jewish youth, such as Communism and Bundism. Zealousness, the demand for total loyalty, and intolerance were the accepted weapons in this confrontation. Even within the Zionist camp, incessant battles were waged to win the loyalty of those belonging to the right and the left. Ideological deviation was viewed as the worst of sins, for which the most severe punishment was denunciation and removal from the fold. In a voluntary society, in which belonging was of primary importance, this punishment was akin to the rite of excommunication practiced by Jews in earlier ages.

Like other revolutionary movements, Zionism sought the creation of "a new man," a new Jew, who would differ in fundamental ways from his forebears. The belief in the possibility of human engineering and the readiness to reshape human nature were characteristic of the age, in which leaders did not hesitate to make decisions that determined the destinies of nations in a single blow. Faith in the possibility and justice of forcing grand solutions onto reality, regardless of costs, was accepted by "enlightened public opinion." The current generation was viewed as the sacrificial element needed to grease the wheels of history. It was for this reason that the young—the generation of the future—were considered so important.

The cult of youth accompanied the Zionist movement along its entire path. "Do not listen, son, to the morality of your fathers, and to the teachings of your mother pay no heed," wrote David Shimoni in a poem that became the anthem of the Hashomer Hatza'ir (Young Guard) movement. (The addition of the word *tza'ir*—"young"—to the names of all manner of social and cultural organizations is itself testimony to the cult of youth.) The rejection of the past meant rejection of the Diaspora, of the entire former Jewish way of life. Rejection also entailed a distancing from the petit-bourgeois lifestyle, and the acceptance of the burden of life in an unfamiliar land, under conditions of extreme hardship. In order to bring this about, young men and women needed the supportive framework of indoctrination that granted meaning and value to their suffering, and indeed bestowed upon them the crown of national redeemers.

Zionist history in the 20th century took place in the shadow of the major events of the age—as their object, not as a driving force in history. Zionism did not play a role in the eruption of World War I, nor was it a factor in World War II. It was not involved in the outbreak of the 1929 economic crisis, the Bolshevik revolution, or the collapse of the Soviet Union. But each and every one of these events was fateful for the history of Zionism. Most importantly, while nearly all the ideologies of the age ended up as colossal failures, Zionism proved to be a stunning success. The visionary element in Zionism was necessary in order to mobilize the human energies required for the fulfillment of the Zionist ideal. Without it, it is doubtful whether the spiritual strength and the hard core of activists needed to turn the idea into reality could have been generated. But in the final reckoning, Zionism was able to maintain its humane instincts. Although challenged by extremists, pragmatism—the art of the possible—served ultimately as Zionism's principal guideline.

Conclusion

If Zionism were to arrive on the scene today, could it realize its goals? This is, as noted above, an ahistorical question. However, it seems fair to say that Zionism could not succeed in the current context. Only in an age in which all of society's anchors were being uprooted, in which all traditional values and all guarantees of existence appeared to be in doubt—only at such a historical moment could Zionism have seemed a plausible approach to the Jewish problem. Furthermore, only in a period that emphasized dedication to the collective, when hopes for total redemption were rampant, when many peoples risked all they had for the sake of a better future—only at such a time could Zionism have channeled the spiritual energy of its followers and created the active vanguard so essential for its success.

Today, the power of collective ideals has dissipated. Zionism, like other "isms," is suffering the symptoms of aging. Its ideological fervor has been dampened; its recruiting abilities have declined considerably. Israeli society today reflects the dominant spirit of contemporary Western culture. Were Herzl to state today, "If you will it, it is no legend," he might well be regarded as nothing more than a writer of science fiction. Still, in the framework of the convulsions of the first half of the 20th century, Herzl's Zionist dream became the reality of Israel.

Israel at 50: An Israeli Perspective

BY YOSSI KLEIN HALEVI

IN 1945, THE JEWISH PEOPLE faced oblivion. Eastern Europe, the major center of Jewish religious and ethnic creativity, was gone; the Western Jewish communities lacked vitality and self-confidence; and several million Soviet Jews were being forcibly assimilated. The most intact Jewish communities existed in the Muslim world; but their golden era had long passed, and they now faced a shattering encounter with modernity and physical threat in post-colonialist Third World states.

Psychologically, the Jews were a defeated people. Perhaps the most devastating long-term trauma of the Holocaust was the Jewish sense of aloneness, of exclusion from humanity, just as the Nazis had insisted. The old stigma of Jewish cowardice had also seemingly been validated. And no amount of apologetic literature, of books with titles like "Jews Fight Too," could erase that shame and even self-loathing; for surely there must be something terribly flawed in a people that was so singularly hated and so passive in the face of assault.

Finally, Judaism—which identified Jewish history as the arena in which God's power and presence would be manifest—had, in the eyes of many Jews, been discredited by reality. Judaism's deepest vision, the redemption of history, was threatened with a fatal irrelevance. The Nazis had proven far more successful at imprinting their vision on history: choosing the Jews—but for a demonic fate, ingathering them from the four corners of Europe—but not for redemption. How many Jews in 1945 could believe in the all powerful God of Israel?

The State of Israel's role as post-Holocaust rescuer addressed the Jewish people's physical, psychological, and spiritual crises.

By salvaging fragmented and endangered diasporas, Israel began the difficult, sometimes traumatic process of restoring the Jews from separated communities back into a people. The ingathering of the exiles has occurred in three great waves, which may be compared to concentric circles gradually being absorbed into Israeli society: Holocaust survivors, Jews from Muslim countries, and immigrants from the former Soviet Union. Israel fulfilled the post-Holocaust Jewish commitment to rescue endangered Jews in any part of the globe, no matter how inaccessible. Saving Jews in "countries of distress"—the official Israeli designation for persecuted Jewish communities—remained a central goal of the state, be-

25

ginning with Yemenite Jewry in 1948 and culminating with Ethiopian Jewry in 1991. Perhaps the single greatest cause for celebration in Israel's 50th year is that, thanks to the Jewish state, the concept of "countries of distress" has become almost obsolete. (Iran, with an estimated 15,000 or more Jews, remains the lone "country of distress.")

Psychologically, Israel saved the Jewish people from the dissipation of its will to live. By restoring the Jews to the community of nations and creating the symbols of national normalcy—a parliament, a flag, army marching bands—Israel offered them reassurance of their membership in the human race, a premise not at all taken for granted by survivors after Auschwitz. Likewise, by re-arming the Jews and proving that they were no less willing and able to defend themselves than any other people, Israel restored their self-esteem. The fact that, only one generation after the Holocaust, Jews no longer need reassurance of their ability to fight and even feel a certain unease with power, confirms how successful Israel has been in healing the trauma of Jewish defenselessness.

Finally, by challenging the ingathering into Auschwitz with the ingathering into Zion, Israel salvaged the credibility of Judaism. For many Jews, Israel's existence restored faith in the God of Israel. For if Jews could see the Holocaust as proof that God had abandoned his people, then the sudden restoration of Jewish power meant that he had returned to them.

Inevitably, each of Israel's "rescue missions"—ingathering diasporas, psychologically healing the Jews, and re-empowering Judaism—has generated unforeseen dilemmas, which threaten to undermine those remarkable achievements. Israel has yet to successfully complete the transition from state-building to nation-building. Instead, it remains a fragile federation of "tribes" divided over the most basic understanding of Israeliness. Despite the astonishing resurrection of Hebrew and the emergence of the only dynamic secular Jewish culture left in world Jewry, Israel has yet to resolve its increasingly pressing identity questions. We endure government crises over defining who is a Jew, but we have yet to begin defining who is an Israeli. Fifty years into statehood, we still cannot agree on our external borders, or on the internal borders between Israeliness and Jewishness, democracy and faith.

The Concentric Circles of Ingathering

Of the three great immigrations to Israel, the quarter of a million Holocaust survivors who arrived in the late 1940s and early 1950s were the most successfully absorbed. The extent of that success is evident among their children. Unlike the Diaspora, Israel has scarcely produced any organized "second generation" activity to collectively confront a sense of dislocation. Partly that is because, until recently, Israeli society did not encourage introspection, valuing instead a stoical pragmatism. But the more important reason is that children of survivors easily entered the economic, cultural, and military elites, becoming virtually indistinguishable from the children of the pioneers. The survivors' success is so taken for granted by Israeli society that it is hardly invoked. Yet when the survivors first arrived, they were received with indifference, even hostility. Survivors were seen as the antithesis of Zionism's "new Jew," passive victims who threatened the daring spirit on which Israel's birth and continued survival depended, as if they carried a contagious weakness. Survivors—whom sabras derisively nicknamed "sabon," soap—were even accused of having been collaborators, their very survival suspect.

In part, survivors succeeded despite the hostility because Israeli society was familiar enough for them to absorb its codes. Unlike Sephardim, or immigrants from Arab countries, who came expecting the Holy Land and discovered instead a secular socialist state, survivors did not experience a drastic disorientation. Israel's ideological obsessions and schisms, and almost all its political parties, were rooted in pre-Holocaust Eastern Europe. The fact that at least some survivors had acquaintances among those who had immigrated before the war and now occupied positions within the state bureaucracy further increased their advantage over Sephardim.

But the decisive factor in the survivors' integration was their ability to see in Israel's struggles and triumphs a projection and a vindication of their own lives. Far from being an enervating influence, survivors infused Israeli society with the certainty that failure was not an option, that Israel's role was to deprive the Nazis of the final word on Jewish history. The survivors' grim optimism, coupled with the naive vigor of the native-born, insured that Israel would overcome the external threats and internal chaos of its early years. Together with the sabras, survivors formed the core of an emerging Israeli identity.

The process of absorbing the Holocaust itself into Israeli identity began with the 1961 Eichmann trial, the first time Israelis collectively confronted the Final Solution. Unlike the earlier trial involving wartime Hungarian Zionist leader Rudolf Kastner, suspected of collaborating with Adolf Eichmann and thereby confirming sabra stereotypes about survivors, this time the murderers rather than the victims were in the dock.

The 1967 Six Day War freed Israelis from any lingering insecurities about Jewish passivity; the 1973 Yom Kippur War, which nearly ended in Israeli defeat and produced televised images of Israeli POWs with padlocked hands, enabled Israelis to identify with the vulnerability of Europe's Jews. A more mature Israel confronted the Holocaust without the need for heroes and myths; Holocaust Memorial Day commemorations stopped focusing obsessively on partisans and ghetto fighters and allowed the nation to mourn its dead. Survivors were finally celebrated as a national resource. For many young secularists, the Holocaust became the most compelling part of their Jewish identities—ironic, given the initial sabra contempt for Holocaust victims as the antithesis of Israeliness.

The final chapter in Israeli reconciliation with the Holocaust and its victims began with the 1977 election of Likud leader Menachem Begin, the first Israeli prime minister to have spent at least part of the Holocaust years in Europe (as a prisoner in the Soviet Gulag). As if deliberately overcompensating for the imposed silence of the state's early years, Begin incessantly invoked the Holocaust, citing it as justification for his hardline policies.

Crucially, Begin broke the Holocaust's ethnic barrier, expanding the circle of mourning to include Sephardim and transforming the Holocaust from a dividing to a unifying factor. Until Begin, many Sephardim saw the Holocaust as an "Ashkenazi," rather than a "Jewish," trauma. No real effort had been made by the Labor Party's Ashkenazi leadership to draw Sephardim into a common grief. By becoming the first Ashkenazi politician to acknowledge the social wrongs done to Sephardim, championing their grievances and emotionally embracing them as fellow Jews, Begin enabled Sephardim to reciprocate and vicariously share his trauma. In opening up Holocaust memory to all Jews, Begin reinforced national cohesiveness and accelerated the integration of Sephardim into Israeliness.

THE SEPHARDIM

Unlike Ashkenazim, who moved to Israel singly or as constricted nuclear families, the nearly one million Sephardim constituting the second great immigration wave came en masse, as extended families and communities. The Jewish state rescued ancient diasporas that faced almost certain uprooting and disintegration in the post-colonialist era, retrieving them from the peripheries of the Jewish world back to its Israeli center.

Within Israel itself, though, Sephardim were largely relegated to the nation's physical and cultural peripheries. Many were brought without consent to isolated border settlements with little hope of economic advancement; in schools, Sephardi children were routinely shunted onto trade rather than academic tracks. An entire culture was dismissed by the Ashkenazi Labor establishment as primitive and irrelevant to Israeli reality. Sephardi music was not played on the radio; Sephardi history was not taught in schools. A generation of young Sephardim were raised in shame and self-loathing.

Even more than economic and social dislocation, Sephardim suffered a spiritual trauma: In fulfilling their deepest religious myth of return to Zion, they experienced their first mass religious breakdown. In the early years of the state, an active policy of secular coercion was aimed at the bewildered Sephardi immigrants. Young people were sent to kibbutzim where they were forced to work on Shabbat and eat nonkosher food; the sidelocks of Yemenite children were cut by absorption officials. There were instances of parents being denied employment for not sending their children to secular schools. Though no conclusive proof has emerged to substantiate persistent charges that Yemenite children were kidnapped by government officials in the state's early years and adopted by Ashkenazim, the "stolen children" serve as a useful metaphor for the cultural fate of an entire generation.

The Labor establishment—which had, after all, initiated the rescue and resettlement of the Sephardim—meant well. Its intention was to hasten the integration of Sephardim by turning their children into its vision of model Israelis. In the prestate years, Labor's Ashkenazi leaders had assumed they were preparing the infrastructure for the eventual absorption of the masses of Jews they had left behind in Europe; after the Holocaust, though, the masses who appeared in Zion were Sephardim. They were the "wrong" Jews: mystical, poorly educated, lacking socialist enthusiasm. In its awkward and ultimately counter-productive way, Labor tried to remake them into the "right" Jews.

Labor leaders were riveted to what they saw as the two essential dramas of Zionism: the transition from "Holocaust to rebirth" and the creation of a socialist state. In both those dramas, Sephardim were largely extraneous. And so they became extraneous Israelis.

In recent years, though, Sephardim, who today form about half the population, have made some significant inroads. Membership in the mainstream is no longer defined by ethnicity but class: Sephardim who make it into the middle class are considered fully "Israeli." Increasingly, Israeli culture, especially popular music, is becoming a fusion of East-West influences, replacing Western dominance. Politically, Sephardim occupy half the cabinet positions in the Netanyahu government, an unprecedented achievement. Within the Labor Party too, chairman Ehud Barak is attempting to open party leadership to activists from "the neighborhoods"—the Israeli euphemism referring to working-class Sephardi areas. Barak's 1997 public apology to Sephardim for Labor's old patronizing attitude was a courageous attempt to heal ethnic bitterness; not since Menachem Begin had any Ashkenazi politician spoken so movingly about the traumatic Sephardi experience of homecoming.

Tragically, however, just as Israeli society is finally becoming openly pluralistic, increasing numbers of Sephardim are opting for ultra-

Orthodox separatism. With its ten parliamentary seats, the ultra-Orthodox Sephardi Shas has become the country's third-largest party. Its short-term goal is leading the tradition-minded but religiously flexible Sephardi working class into ultra-Orthodox separatism; its long-term goal is transforming Israel into a theocracy. By emphasizing religion over peoplehood as the essential criterion for defining Jewishness, Shas excludes its constituency from a mainstream Israeli identity. Shas's network of elementary schools stresses religious, not secular, studies, insuring that its graduates will remain economically marginal. (Those schools also ignore the Holocaust, undermining Menachem Begin's achievement of drawing Sephardim into Holocaust memory.) Increasing numbers of Shas's young men opt for yeshivah deferments from the army, depriving them of another key entry point into the Israeli mainstream.

Shas has succeeded politically because it addresses the Sephardi longing for a return to their lost Diaspora intactness, for a way to the elusive Holy Land. Shas is the inevitable backlash, one generation later, against Labor's cultural coercion, the counter-revolution against secular Zionism. Ultra-Orthodox Yemenite rabbi Amnon Yitzhak, who has inspired thousands of Sephardim to abandon secularism, likes to end his revivalist-style rallies by cutting off young men's pony tails—avenging the shearing of Yemenite children's sidelocks in the state's early years. And yet, however understandable, the Shas backlash poses one of the most serious threats to Israeli cohesiveness, joining Ashkenazi-Sephardi tensions to the far more explosive secular-religious divide.

THE SOVIET JEWS

While Israel saved Sephardi communities from potential physical threat, its rescue mission of Soviet Jews preempted their cultural and spiritual disappearance. The very existence of Israel saved Soviet Jewry from oblivion: Without the decisive pull of Zionist pride to counter the forced assimilation of Soviet Jewry, that last repository of Eastern European Jewish genius would have been lost to the Jewish people, and its disappearance almost certainly made irreversible by the time the Communist regime fell. For most Soviet Jews, raised in an atmosphere of militant atheism, Judaism was inaccessible; and so the Soviet Jewish renaissance focused instead on national identity. Israel and its military victories, especially the Six Day War, emboldened thousands of young Jews to form the Soviet Union's only mass, nationwide, dissident movement.

The immigration of one million Soviet Jews—nearly 200,000 in the 1970s and the rest since 1989—completes a historical process begun a century ago, when the first Zionist pioneers set out from Russia and prepared the foundation for a Jewish state. No group of immigrants has been absorbed more quickly into the Israeli economy than the former Soviets; no other immigration has brought with it such prosperity and cultural abundance. The economic boom of the 1990s was largely generated by the new immigrants, who included a significant segment of the Soviet elite, its scientists and engineers and classical musicians.

And yet no immigration faces as problematic an absorption into Israeli identity. Seventy years of enforced Soviet assimilation have produced the least Jewishly identified and most heavily intermarried of any Israeli immigration. Indeed, many newcomers lack an instinctive empathy with Zionism's most basic myths—including the myth of "ingathering the exiles," the very motive for Israel opening its doors to them. "The Russians," as all immigrants from the former Soviet Union are known, are the mirror image of the Sephardim: While Sephardim arrived poorly equipped to adapt to a modern society but with an instinctive Jewish sense of belonging, Russians tend to be highly educated secularly but almost completely ignorant Jewishly. Sephardim came seeking the Jewish homeland; Russians came seeking the West. The result is that the two groups have experienced opposite absorption problems. Many Sephardim lag economically but retain an organic connection to Israeliness; indeed, it is hard to find another group anywhere so loyal to a state that had treated its members as second-class citizens. And while Russians are rapidly entering the Israeli middle class, many remain ambivalent about their relationship to the state.

Ironically, Russian absorption might have benefited from the kind of concerted attempt to educate immigrants into an ideological Israeliness that Sephardim experienced so traumatically in the 1950s. The collapse of an officially approved "ideal Israeli" has left Russians without a clearly defined identity to aspire to. The result is a growing assertiveness of a separatist Russian culture.

That trend toward self-ghettoization is reinforced by frequent Israeli stereotyping of Russian immigrants as mafiosi and prostitutes. All immigrant groups are subject to stereotyping: Successive waves of immigration have so frequently and profoundly altered Israeli society that stereotyping becomes a psychological survival tool, a way of managing excess diversity. But precisely because so many Russians are severed from Jewish identity, they are especially vulnerable to the stereotypers' message that they do not belong. So far, Israeli society has failed to convey to the Russians that their presence among us is a miracle, that they have come home to be healed from their Jewish amnesia.

Perhaps the most difficult impediment to absorption is the large percentage of non-Jews within the Russian immigration. The failure of the

Orthodox rabbinate to relax its stringent standards and enable Russian non-Jews to convert may further encourage Russian separatism from the Israeli mainstream. An alternative scenario is that the tens of thousands of non-Jewish Russians who have entered the secular Israeli educational system and the army will join the mainstream and transform it, making Israeli identity less automatically synonymous with Jewishness.

ETHNIC-RELIGIOUS DIVERSITY AND NATIONAL IDENTITY

Israel has ingathered the Jewish world's most concentrated ethnic diversity. Part of the adventure of the Israeli experience has been expanding the limits of national identity, discovering new, unimagined components of the Jewish people. Only a few decades ago, many Israelis were not even aware of the existence of Ethiopian Jews; now they live among us (though still largely as strangers). In recent years, Israel has begun absorbing its first Far Eastern "Oriental" immigration: several dozen ethnically Burmese families, members of the Christian Shinlung tribe on the Indian-Burmese border, who believe they are descendants of the Israelite tribe of Menashe and who have undergone rigorous Orthodox conversion. (So far, some 5,000 Shinlung out of a tribal population of two million identify as Jews.)

The ingathering of exiles has reversed the Diaspora concept of ethnicity: For Diaspora Jews, ethnicity means Jewishness; for Israelis, it is defined by the countries we abandoned. We are not just "Ashkenazim" and "Sephardim" but Indians and Yemenites and Russians and South Africans. Israelis would be perplexed by Diaspora jokes that end with the punch line, "Funny, you don't look Jewish." In Israel, there is no such thing as "looking Jewish." Nostalgic memories of grandparents and "Jewish" foods do not unite Israelis, as they do American Jews, in a common Jewishness, but divide us in our varied ethnicities.

Beginning in earnest in the 1980s, ethnic and ideological "tribalism" has grown, partly as a backlash against the imposed uniformity of the state's early years, and partly in response to the decline of the socialist Zionist ideology that was supposed to unite us into a single people. The intensifying debates over the future of the territories and the place of religion in public life have further encouraged the emergence of distinctive "tribes." There is an ultra-Orthodox Sephardi tribe and an ultra-Orthodox Ashkenazi tribe, a religious Zionist tribe and a secular left-wing "Tel Aviv" tribe, a Russian tribe and an Arab Israeli tribe. Though they live in such close proximity, those tribes manage to maintain a remarkable level of mutual ignorance, often defining each other by the most negative stereotypes. Israel's diversity can either enrich a common national identity, or it can destroy any hope of fashioning an Israeli people sharing the same myths of origin and committed to common goals.

ULTRA ORTHODOX JEWS AND ISRAELI ARABS

Among all of Israel's cultural and political communities, the two least assimilable into a common Israeliness are the ultra-Orthodox Jews and the Israeli Arabs. Neither identifies itself as Zionist; neither sends its young men for military service, a key factor in defining Israeli identity. Together they form 25 percent of Israel's population of six million (18 percent Arab, 7 percent ultra-Orthodox). And they maintain higher birthrates than any other Israeli community.

In recent years, however, each community has been absorbed into a particular kind of Israeliness—sectoral, rather than national. Ultra-Orthodox Jews increasingly identify with right-wing Israel, Arab Israelis with left-wing Israel. The result is a conditional Israeli identity, the emergence of a new category of "almost Israelis."

Except for a persisting anti-Zionist minority, the ultra-Orthodox community has moved from prestate anti-Zionism, to disinterested non-Zionism, to far-right nationalism (though acceptance of Zionism is de facto, not theological). Menachem Begin, the first Israeli prime minister to repeatedly invoke God and religious symbols, enabled ultra-Orthodox Jews to feel at home within the right-wing coalition. That process culminated in the 1996 elections, in which the ultra-Orthodox united around Benjamin Netanyahu, the first time the community endorsed a secular Zionist candidate.

Still, the ultra-Orthodox remain deeply ambivalent about their relationship with Israeli society. On the one hand, the fact that most ultra-Orthodox routinely speak Hebrew among themselves—reversing earlier insistence on maintaining Hebrew as the language of devotion and Yiddish as the language of the street—is a tacit acknowledgment that Zionism won. Indeed, there are increasing signs of ultra-Orthodox accommodation to Israeli reality. Even members of the anti-Zionist Eidah Haredit, for example, are now volunteering for the police department's civil guard, once considered anathema. And yet at the same time, the growing strength and self-confidence of the ultra-Orthodox community is leading to increased autonomy: Separate ultra-Orthodox towns and shopping malls and bus lines are reinforcing the community's self-ghettoization.

What Menachem Begin was to the ultra-Orthodox, Yitzhak Rabin was to Arab Israelis—the first prime minister to incorporate them into some form of Israeli identity. The Rabin government attempted to redress decades of discrimination by intensively investing in the Arab community (especially in education); de-emphasizing the Jewish aspects of Israeli identity; and initiating the Oslo process, which promised to make peace between the Israeli and Palestinian components of Arab Israeli identity.

Arguably, a majority of Arab Israelis want to be absorbed into Israeli identity—but an ethnically neutral one, emptied of Jewish resonance. The deeper problem in fashioning a common identity for Arabs and Jews is that the two groups perceive the very founding of the state in opposite ways: For Jews, 1948 means redemption; for Arabs, disaster. Some Arab Israeli leaders even contemplated commemorating Israel's 50th anniversary with a day of mourning for the Palestinian "holocaust." For Arabs and for Jews, then, the meaning of Israel's founding myth—"from Holocaust to rebirth"—is essentially reversed.

Any attempt at circumventing that fundamental clash of memory by creating a dejudaized Israeli identity embracing Arab Israelis will inevitably exclude that other "conditional Israeli" community on the opposite side of the cultural and political spectrum, the ultra-Orthodox. Conversely, any attempt to draw the ultra-Orthodox closer to the mainstream by emphasizing Israel's Jewishness will exclude Israeli Arabs. Both outsider communities are poised between accommodation and alienation; the tragedy for Israeli society is that integrating one community almost certainly means alienating the other.

The Psychological Transformation of the Jews

After the Holocaust, it could have taken the Jews generations, if at all, to break free from the self-image of victim. Yet, in a single generation Israel has transformed the Holocaust from raw wound to historical memory. Thanks to Israel's military victories—and also to the traumatic experience of becoming occupiers—arguably most Israelis outside of the hard right no longer perceive themselves as victims.

A crucial step in helping the Jews to place the Holocaust behind them and internalize their transition from victimhood to normalization was David Ben-Gurion's audacious decision to accept reparations from West Germany in the early 1950s. Menachem Begin, who led the violent opposition to reparations, was proven right by events that Israel was opening the way to German-Jewish reconciliation; yet that process was necessary to convince the Jews that the creation of Israel decisively ended the experience of exile. Only Israel had the moral authority to impose a peace process with Germany on the Jewish psyche.

Zionism intended not only to return the Jews to the land of Israel but to the community of nations. The gradual lifting of the diplomatic siege against the Jewish state has reinforced Israelis' psychological integration into humanity, breaking the stigma of the Jews as a people eternally set apart. One of the cruelest weapons used by the Arabs in their war against Israel was the isolation and demonization of the Jewish state, which evoked for Jews their aloneness during the Holocaust—and helped reinforce the rise of the right in the 1970s and '80s. Israel's diplomatic successes in the early '90s, along with the repeal of the "Zionism=racism" resolution in the UN General Assembly, restored Israeli confidence in the promise of Zionism to end Jewish ghettoization—and helped create a positive atmosphere enabling the Rabin government to initiate the Oslo process.

Young Israelis are less inclined than ever before to divide humanity into "*goyim*" and Jews. The very word *goyim*, suggesting a homogeneous Gentile world united by its antipathy to Jews, sounds increasingly ludicrous in modern Hebrew. Becoming a nation among nations means accepting human diversity beyond a simplistic division of the world into "us and them." The extraordinary desire among Israelis to travel to the most remote places is one indication of their growing ease in the world (along with a desperate need to periodically escape the pressures of Israeli life).

In certain basic ways, Israel has transformed the Jewish character beyond recognition. The relief of homecoming, of becoming a majority, has allowed us to relax into ourselves—or, if not quite relax, to at least be fully ourselves without self-consciousness. Jewish timidity has given way to a brash, even arrogant exuberance. That transformation is evident in the way seemingly any Israeli child will spontaneously and effusively speak in public gatherings or before a TV camera, in the way teenagers celebrate Independence Day by bopping strangers over the head with plastic hammers—and also in the way we shout at each other in public places and do not care how "pushy" or obnoxious we appear on lines at the bank or the post office.

The re-formation of the Jews into a nation has shattered some cherished self-images. Jews, we have discovered, are child-molesters and rapists and murderers—just like any other people. No doubt that was always so; but where we once tried to hide our flaws from hostile eyes, now we broadcast them on the front pages of our newspapers. That lack of self-consciousness may also have tempered somewhat the Jewish drive for excellence. Indeed, Israeli education is often disappointingly mediocre. One Russian immigrant offered this insight: "When I came to Israel I was amazed to discover dumb Jews. In Moscow all the Jews I knew were high achievers. At first it made me very depressed. But then I realized: In Russia we were a minority that had to constantly prove itself. Here, we are a people."

A NATION OF SOLDIERS

Israel's most profound impact on the Jewish character has been in altering its relationship to army service. In their prestate debate with Labor Zionists, the right-wing Revisionists insisted that the essence of the Zionist revolution would be transforming the Jew not into a farmer or worker but a soldier; and the Revisionists won. The ongoing Arab siege turned the Jews from a people lacking the most minimal military skills into a permanently mobilized nation in which the borders between civilian and military life are often blurred. An ironic measure of Zionism's success is that traditional anti-Jewish stereotypes have been reversed: from cowards to militarists, from wandering Jews to usurpers of another people's land.

In a nation that was born resisting invasion and has never known the absence of threat, that marks its history by the years in which wars were fought, and whose enemies offer mere recognition as their major concession in peace talks, the army inevitably dominates. Military service is never far from people's consciousness—whether it is the fate of a son or a neighbor's boy in Lebanon, or the more mundane intrusion into daily life of the plain brown envelope in the mail announcing reserve duty, a periodic reminder of the illusion of a citizen's sovereignty.

The impingement of the military on civilian life also works in reverse: Israel's citizen army is remarkably relaxed, especially in the reserves, where officers are not saluted and are routinely called by their first names. The intimacy between civilian and military sectors has helped keep the army committed to government authority and to democracy. During the *intifada*, for example, the army became the arena where the Jewish people confronted itself; each unit serving in the territories became in effect a mini-parliament debating the limits of security and morality.

The army has been the prism through which has passed a random, even anarchic, assemblage of fierce individualists, divided and subdivided by background and ideology, and has emerged resembling a people. Wave after wave of immigrant recruits has been imprinted with a common experience and mission. The unit I served in for my basic training, for example, contained new immigrants from 18 countries. Most of us were in our 30s, indelible civilians in ill-fitting uniforms. And yet, toward the end of our training, when we were formally sworn in and handed Bibles in a ceremony attended by our families—including kibbutzniks and West Bank settlers and Ethiopian women with blue tattoos on their foreheads—we were somehow transformed into a unit. Afterward, we painted the flags of our countries of origin on our bunk walls, as though we were leaving behind something of our old identities.

The experience of sharing the same tent with soldiers from radically different backgrounds has tempered the intensity of Israel's internal divisions. Though Israeli society is one of the most heavily and casually armed in the world, and its life-and-death political debates are passionate and unrestrained, only two instances of politically motivated murder among Jews, however traumatic, have occurred since the War of Independence: the grenade attack on a Peace Now rally in February 1983 that killed demonstrator Emile Grunzweig, and the assassination of Prime Minister Yitzhak Rabin in November 1995.

Repeated warnings of civil war—between Sephardim and Ashkenazim in the early 1980s and between leftists and rightists after the Rabin assassination—have proven unfounded. The one real danger of civil war among Jews, or at least of total estrangement, is the conflict between ultra-Orthodox and secular Israelis—which only reinforces the point that Israelis who serve together in the army are unlikely to fight each other on the streets. It is largely because the ultra-Orthodox lack that shared Israeli experience of all-night border patrols and summer desert maneuvers that their disputes with secularists turn so easily from resentment to hatred.

The army has established the emotional parameters of Israeliness. When a Russian immigrant soldier named Nicolai Rappaport was killed in Lebanon in early 1998, he was mourned by the nation as one of its heroes even though he was not halakhically a Jew (only his father was Jewish); when Rappaport's body was returned to Russia for burial, partly because he would have been denied interment in a Jewish cemetery, even many traditional Israelis felt outrage and shame. Rappaport, after all, had fulfilled the ultimate mitzvah of Israeli citizenship; and he belonged to the national consensus far more than the ultra-Orthodox rabbis who would have denied him burial.

And yet, inevitably, as the country distances itself from its collectivist beginnings and gropes toward a Jewish and Middle Eastern version of normalcy, the army's charisma is lessening. The peace process, consumerism, the decline of ideology, the burdens of occupation—all have encouraged the "civilianization" of Israel and undermined Israelis' patience for the endless demands of life in a besieged fortress. Increasing numbers of reservists opt for easily obtained exemptions; according to one astonishing report, only 30 percent of eligible men now serve in reserve units. And while 18-year-old recruits in the standing army continue to vie for places in elite combat units, the primary motive for most of them has shifted from Zionism to self-fulfillment, the need to test oneself against experience (though patriotism certainly reinforces the desire to serve). Only religious Zionists, who are increasingly prominent in elite combat units and the officers' corps, and who have replaced kibbutzniks as the army's ideological elite, continue as a group to be primarily motivated by Zionist values.

With each successive war, the army has lost a little more of its glow. The Six Day War was the last conflict to produce victory albums; the Yom Kippur War, the last to produce rousing battle songs. Israelis' attitude toward the army is a mixture of affection and resentment and wry acknowledgment of its human limitations: the army, for better and worse, is us.

We no longer delight, as we did in the early years of statehood, in martial prowess and military parades, no longer require proof of our own vitality, our radical break with Jewish fate. We no longer wrestle with the ghosts of the Holocaust but with the very real dilemmas of how to secure the long-term existence of a Jewish state in the Arab world.

The shift in Israelis' relationship to the army is best expressed on Yom Hazikaron, Remembrance Day for the Fallen. On Yom Hashoah, Holocaust Memorial Day, we mourn the consequences of powerlessness; on Yom Hazikaron, we mourn the consequences of power. School and community services emphasize not the glory but the pain and loss of war. The TV documentaries are not about battles but individuals: three brothers who died in the 1948 War of Independence, the Holocaust survivor who lost two sons in the Yom Kippur War, a widow who every night writes letters to her dead husband. Those who fell are recalled not as patriots and martyrs but as fathers, sons, friends. Love of country and heroism under fire are valued, but always defer to personal grief. In the sad songs that play relentlessly on the radio, no enemies are invoked to unite the country except death itself.

PREOCCUPATION WITH SURVIVAL

Despite the shift in Israelis' relationship with the army, security remains a central concern. Fifty years into statehood, we still cannot take permanence for granted. Israel has empowered the Jews with the will and means to resist their enemies; but it has not ended our preoccupation with survival. Israel is the only country in the world that provides gas masks for every citizen, one of the few countries in the post-Cold War world that faces a real prospect of nonconventional warfare. According to a recent poll, fully 57 percent of Israelis are not sure the country will survive in the long term, citing both external threats and internal divisions. We live between fear of destruction and sudden reprieve, moving from the ecstasy of 1967 to the despair of 1973 and back again to the euphoric relief of the Entebbe rescue of 1976. Emotionally, the trajectory of Israel's history is not from Holocaust to rebirth but repeated wavering over the ultimate fate of the Zionist experiment.

Beginning with the Lebanon War and intensifying with the *intifada*, large numbers of Israelis came to believe that their government was at least partly to blame for the absence of peace; and so the security threat shifted from uniting Israelis to further dividing them. In recent years, Israel's apocalyptic fears have been increasingly internalized, directed toward rival political camps rather than the Arab enemy. Both leftists and rightists agree about this: that if their ideological opponents prevail, the country will not be merely diminished but destroyed. Leftists argue that time is on the Arabs' side, and that an Israel under permanent siege will eventually fight one war too many; and so the right, by blocking any opening for peace, is dooming the country to destruction. Rightists counter that only by convincing the Arabs of Israel's resolve will it secure peace, and that vital territorial concessions will expose the country to a final assault; and so the left, by encouraging enemies who have not genuinely accepted Israel's existence, is fatally undermining its security.

Apocalyptic fears, however subtly, also animate the secular-religious debate. Secularists see in the growing power of the religious parties the threat of a Jewish theocracy, which would alienate most American Jews and eventually the U.S. Congress and result in Israel's total isolation. At the same time, Israel's secular elite, which maintains the army and the high-tech companies and the universities and the science labs, would flee en masse, depriving the country of its crucial edge over the Arabs and eventually leading to its destruction. Ultra-Orthodox Jews counter that secular hedonism is a provocation against God, who twice before exiled the Jews for not fulfilling his commandments and who will certainly do so again if we continue to spiritually pollute the Holy Land.

The result of all those mutually exclusive apocalyptic scenarios is the inability of Israeli society to create a civic culture of tolerance—and more profoundly, a sense of common purpose crucial to a cohesive national identity. When both sides are convinced that the other's positions threaten the nation's existence, real tolerance or national unity is impossible. Inevitably, then, when either a left-wing or right-wing government comes to power, the opposition feels not just disenfranchised but desperate, as if the country has been usurped by mad adventurers. That despair is reinforced by the overlapping of political and cultural agendas: The right not only destroys the peace, as the left sees it, but draws theocracy closer; the left not only fatally weakens the country physically, as the right sees it, but also spiritually, by dejudaizing Israeli identity.

The extremes of the right and the left tend to demonize opponents. Hard-line religious rightists often refer to leftists as *"erev rav,"* the Gentiles who joined the Israelites going out of Egypt and whom some rabbinic traditions blame for instigating the construction of the Golden Calf and corrupting Jewish purity. For its part, the hard-line left often labels its opponents as fascists and even Nazis. One columnist in the left-wing daily *Ha'aretz*, denouncing an innocent billboard campaign featuring mainstream left- and right-wing leaders smiling together and urging tolerance, mockingly wrote, "What Jewish glue can create a bond between the fascist and the humanist? How about billboards emblazoned with the visages of Josef Goebbels and Thomas Mann?"

The country's security pressures, then, affect its social intactness in paradoxical ways. On the one hand, the shared army experience reinforces a common Israeliness. Yet the mutually exclusive positions on how to save the country undermine the emergence of an Israeli people whose factions perceive each other as partners in preserving Israel rather than as its potential destroyers.

Security pressures affect the Israeli psyche in basic ways. Everyone is engaged in the national debate; even elementary-school students passionately argue about the peace process. Everything matters; little buffer exists between politics and daily life, public and private domains. When police cordon off a public area to examine a "suspicious object," we do not flee what may be a bomb but press against the barricades for a closer look. We drive with contempt for each other and for our own safety, a nation of soldiers intimate with killing machines and unable to respect the lethal potential of mere cars. We do not simply go on vacation abroad, we escape; the intensity of living on the edge is alternately exhilarating and unbearable.

The intimacy in which Israelis live with danger and death, the repeated reversal of the natural order whereby parents bury children in military cemeteries, has created a deep spiritual need, an urgency among many to know if there really is a God and a soul and a life after death. Some explore the plethora of "new age" and eastern religious movements, which are thriving in Israel; others turn to Orthodox Judaism. (A growing hedonism is yet another response to the spiritual crisis.) The "return to Judaism" movement has been energized by war. One wave of "penitents" came after the 1973 Yom Kippur War, when Israel glimpsed its own mortality; another followed the 1991 Gulf War, when 39 Scud missiles fired at Israeli cities claimed only one fatality, convincing many Israelis of God's protection. The seemingly endless conflict, along with Israel's unique status as a country whose right to exist is still unresolved, reinforces the appeal of ultra-Orthodoxy's theology of despair, which insists that only Torah observance and Divine intervention can save the Jews.

The security situation's ongoing domination of the national agenda also empowers religion politically: Both Labor and the Likud are willing to defer to the sectarian demands of religious parties in exchange for support on the territorial issue. The result has been the corruption of both democracy and faith.

The Transformation of Judaism

By empowering Judaism's essential myths of the return to Zion and the ingathering of the exiles, Israel inspired a worldwide Jewish religious revival. That revival did not begin immediately with the founding of the state, when Jews were still too stunned by the Holocaust; instead, it was deferred until the biblical-like victory of the Six Day War, which seemed to shatter Israel's mundane facade and reveal the country's miraculous essence. 1948 revived the Jewish body, which reveled in its physical resurrection; 1967 revived the Jewish soul.

For many Jews, the abrupt transition from absolute powerlessness to military mastery was too overwhelming to be processed in mere political terms. The result was the first outburst of messianic enthusiasm among Jews in centuries. The religious Zionist camp became the center point of redemptive expectation, with largely negative consequences. By focusing their messianic hopes on the retention of Judea and Samaria, religious Zionists subtly displaced the theological centrality of Jewish peoplehood with the land of Israel — culminating in the assassination of Yitzhak Rabin by Yigal Amir, who violated the unity of the people to preserve the unity of the land.

Many religious Zionists, inspired by messianic fervor, have become more religiously stringent and distanced from secular culture, undermining the community's traditional moderation and its crucial role as bridge between Orthodox and secular Israelis. Rabbis have assumed increasingly central roles in the religious Zionist community, which once insisted on restricting their authority to halakhic issues. The 1995 ruling by 15 leading religious Zionist rabbis forbidding soldiers to participate in any West Bank withdrawal attempted to impose rabbinic over military authority and threatened Israel's key unifying institution.

Yet since the Oslo process, and especially the assassination of Rabin, redemption has quietly faded from the religious Zionist theological agenda; the community is far more preoccupied with apocalyptic fears than with messianic hopes. And religious Zionists have finally begun a long-deferred debate over their commitment to democracy and their relationship to the secular mainstream. The consequences of that debate could be an historic schism between Orthodox democrats and theocrats, with the former drawing closer to the Israeli mainstream and the latter to the ultra-Orthodox separatists.

Besides inadvertently triggering a messianic movement, Israel restored Orthodox Judaism, nearly destroyed in the Holocaust, to centrality in Jewish life. Orthodoxy became the state religion, its rabbis incorporated into government bureaucracy and granted a monopoly over marriage, divorce, and conversion. For Orthodox and even many non-Orthodox but traditionally minded Israelis, some form of religious control over public life is essential for granting "Jewish legitimacy" to the state. Until it assumed political form in the late 19th century, the dream of return to Zion was inseparable from the dream of returning Judaism to Zion. Along with the Jewish people, Judaism too was in exile. Only in the land of Israel could it be completely fulfilled, its commandments and prayers attuned to the seasonal and spiritual rhythms of the Holy Land. Most of all, only in Israel could Judaism resume its classical role as the state religion of the Jewish people. And so what seem like acts of religious coercion to many secularists—for example, banning public transportation and commerce on Shabbat—are perceived by Orthodox Jews as the logical, indeed inevitable, expression of Jewish statehood.

Zionism won the loyalty of the Jews in part because it offered to fulfill their contradictory longings: to be chosen, and to be like everyone else. Zionism simultaneously actualized biblical myth and created a normal nation-state. Israel has tried to mediate between its people's opposing desires by devising the so-called "status quo," which allowed some measure of religious control in an essentially secular society. Israel is not a theocracy; it is, rather, a democracy burdened by an official state faith and by religious legislation.

Initially at least, secular leaders like Prime Minister David Ben-Gurion saw the creation of statist Orthodoxy as a magnanimous gesture to Jewish unity, a concession by a triumphant secular Zionism to a defeated Orthodox minority. In allowing its democracy to be compromised by religious intervention, Israel insured the passionate loyalty of religious Zionists and also neutralized anti-Zionist theology in the mainstream ultra-Orthodox community.

And yet, as the power of statist Orthodoxy has grown, augmented by legislation and coalition politics, secular resentment has grown along with it. The result is that at least some secularists have become alienated from the most basic Jewish identity. Though dogmatic secularists represent only a small minority, they include a large part of the Israeli cultural elite, and their influence far exceeds their numbers.

In recent years, the Israeli paradox of a secular state in Zion has begun to unravel. Increasing numbers of both Orthodox and secular Israelis are dissatisfied with the status quo's inevitable compromise of both the state's democratic and Jewish identities, and want Israel to unequivocally decide between the two. The danger is that any decision resolving that ambiguity in favor of either the Judaists or the absolute secularists will alienate the losing side from Israeli identity.

Though most Israelis are more ambivalent than dogmatic on religion-state issues, two growing constituencies on opposite sides of the divide could determine Israel's future character. If the Russian immigration continues at its current steady pace of 60,000 a year, Russians will eventually form a pivotal voting bloc, one of whose key issues will be ending rabbinic control over marriage and divorce. And if Shas continues to grow at its phenomenal rate, pressure will increase to expand the power of statist Orthodoxy. The result will be a Russian-Sephardi confrontation further linking ethnic to religious tensions.

Ultimately, the greatest damage committed by statist Orthodoxy has been to Judaism itself. By expropriating Judaic authenticity, statist Orthodoxy has divided the nation into artificial "secular" and "religious" identities. Though most Israeli Jews believe in God, circumcise their sons, give their children bar and bat mitzvahs, place mezuzahs on their doorposts, celebrate the Passover seder, and fast on Yom Kippur (70 percent last year, according to polls), anyone who is not Orthodox is automatically categorized as secular. Even the Hebrew language has conspired to reinforce the Orthodox monopoly on Judaism: the Hebrew word for "Orthodox" and "religious" is identical — *dati*.

The message that Judaism belongs to the Orthodox alone has spiritually disenfranchised non-Orthodox Israelis, who are made to feel self-conscious and inadequate around religious ritual and study. As a result, Judaism in Israel remains the Judaism of the ghetto, the rigid faith of an embattled minority.

The promise of Zionism for Judaism was to restore it to majority status. Only a Judaism that belonged to the entire people would feel self-confident enough to risk innovation. Yet Zionism brought the Jews home from exile, but not Judaism. In its rituals and prayers, Israeli Judaism scarcely reflects this century's convulsions of Holocaust and homecoming — the most intense Jewish experiences since the destruction of the Second Temple, and perhaps since the Exodus from Egypt. Statist Orthodoxy's theology of separation from the Gentiles remains appropriate for a persecuted minority, not for a majority confronting its own non-Jewish minorities. Ironically, Judaism, the religion of history, has become ahistorical, frozen in an earlier time. So long as Judaism remains in exile, it will lack the freedom and vitality to evolve into its next, Israeli, stage. And Israeli society will remain caught in a no-win clash between a rigid Orthodoxy imprisoned by the past and a spiritually depleted secularism incapable of creating a Jewish future.

The Future of Israel

The main work of the coming decades will be imprinting Israeli society with a national identity that respects diversity but offers shared values, myths, and goals.

Israel has yet to fully implement the essential message of the Zionist revolution: that the Jews are no longer disparate communities but a people again. Peoplehood requires each of its components to respect the inviolate needs of the other, precluding mutual secession. In the Diaspora, Hassidic sects or the Reform movement can adopt any decision or life style without needing to consider each other's reactions. But in Israel, no community is entirely self-referential; anything done by one part of the people resonates in the whole national body.

Perhaps Israeli society needs to redefine Zionism: Acts that reinforce a national Israeli identity are "Zionist," acts that undermine it, "anti-Zionist." In the recent debate over "Who is a Jew?" for example, the government-appointed Ne'eman Commission offered a "Zionist" compromise that respected the bottom-line needs of each side: Israel would empower Conservative and Reform rabbis to teach Judaism to potential converts but would leave the actual conversion in Orthodox hands. In contrast, those Orthodox Jews who rejected the Ne'eman Commission's attempt to reconcile Halakhah with Jewish unity were acting like a separatist community without responsibility to the Jewish people as a whole. By that same measure, the American Reform movement's recognition of patrilineal descent as a way of defining Jewishness placed denominational over national Jewish interests. (Not coincidentally, the Israeli Reform rabbinate rejected patrilineal descent, which would preclude marriage between Orthodox and Reform Jews.) Both Orthodox opposition to the Ne'eman Commission and Reform advocacy of patrilineal descent were in effect "anti-Zionist" positions.

Too often, Israeli governments make crucial decisions without considering their effects on the nation's cohesiveness. When the Begin government embarked on the 1982 Lebanon War, and when the Rabin government recognized the PLO in the 1993 Oslo accord, neither bothered to address the most basic concerns of its opposition; and so those two radically different approaches to the Palestinian problem ruptured the nation and produced at best inconclusive results. Israel can succeed in war or peace only when its leaders seek broad consensus.

A Zionist approach to Israel's left-right schism would acknowledge the legitimacy of both sides: that the right's insistence on wariness of our enemies' intentions, and the left's insistence on respect for our enemies' humanity, equally invoke truths learned from Jewish history. That acknowledgment does not mean obscuring the debate between them with a false unity or avoiding the necessity of making difficult political choices. But by creating an atmosphere of minimal mutual respect, we can begin defusing the apocalyptic fears we direct at each other and realize, perhaps, that dividing the Jewish people into irreconcilable camps poses far greater danger to Israel's survival than the victory of either right or left.

Another crucial step toward healing Israeli society is replacing statist

Orthodoxy with religious pluralism. Expanding the possibilities of Jewish observance will help avert Israel's descent into two warring cultural camps—a superficial secularism that sees little of value in Judaism, a xenophobic Orthodoxy that sees little of value outside Judaism. Along with Israeli Judaism, Israeli national identity needs to become more expansive.

Israel lives with an increasingly untenable irony: that a Diaspora Jew who has no intention of ever moving to Israel can feel far deeper affinity with the country than an Arab citizen born and raised in it. The de facto exclusion of the Arab minority from Israeli identity was, perhaps, initially inevitable. Preoccupied with refashioning a people from a bewildering diversity of immigrants and defending the country from external threat, Jewish Israel had little psychic space for a minority that identified emotionally, if not tangibly, with its enemies. Indeed, so long as the Arab-Israeli conflict persists, mutual suspicions between Israel's Arabs and Jews will impede full Arab integration.

Still, no society can remain healthy when a large percentage of its citizens are emotionally disenfranchised from the national identity. And while there are no definitive solutions for resolving the place of Arabs in Israeliness, Jewish society and the nation's institutions can encourage a process of gradual identification—for example, by ending formal discrimination in government funding and implementing some form of national (nonmilitary) service for young Arab men, reinforcing the concept of "equal rights for equal responsibilities."

In fact, the Arab community is itself ambivalent: Arab Israelis increasingly feel nationally Palestinian but culturally Israeli. Many non-Jews—Russian immigrants as well as Arabs—speak fluent Hebrew and live, at least on some level, according to the Jewish year cycle. Devising ways of incorporating them into Israeli identity is an opportunity to further the psychological transformation of the Jews from embattled minority to relaxed majority.

While Israeli peoplehood can no longer be entirely synonymous with Jewish peoplehood, the national identity must remain connected with the country's founding Jewish myths. Only a self-consciously Zionist state would have dispatched planes in the midst of an Ethiopian civil war to extract thousands of barefoot African Jewish tribesmen and turn the rescue into a national celebration. An Israel that is no longer in some sense Jewish would cease to motivate its own people, who, more than citizens in any Western country, are expected to sacrifice for the nation.

The consequence of ingathering the exiles is that no one group, no single political or cultural vision, has been allowed to monopolize Israeli identity. And so there is deep unease. Secular Jews fear a theocratic Israel, while Orthodox Jews fear a hedonistic Israel that is losing its soul;

leftists anguish about the collapse of the peace process, rightists about the collapse of their biblical dream. All sides share a growing sense of tenuousness, of "their" Israel slipping away, a fear of homelessness.

The Israeli experience proves that there are no absolutist solutions, no single ideology capable of effectively addressing the nation's crises. Instead, solutions will come when each group is allowed to see something of itself, its ideal Israel, in the nation's reality—and when those groups abandon hopes of hegemony over Israeli identity. That means accepting the inevitability of our paradoxes: that we are at once an Eastern and a Western people, a democratic and a Jewish state a secular entity and a holy land.

The logical conclusion to the ingathering of the exiles is the emergence of a multifaceted Israeli personality, absorbing the society's contradictions and embracing paradox as the vitalizing force of Israeliness. The creation of an integrated Israeli culture, reflecting the varied traditions and insights Jews have brought with them back home, will finalize Israel's transition from rescue to renaissance.

Israel at 50: An American Jewish Perspective

BY ARNOLD M. EISEN

IN EXAMINING THE IMPACT of the State of Israel on American Jewry over the past half century, one is struck repeatedly by the resort made by thoughtful observers to a series of striking and recalcitrant paradoxes.

Israel's creation is one of the most important events in all of Jewish history. The sense of the miracle in Israel's existence is palpable and widespread. Yet it proves rather difficult to define in specific terms what Israel's existence has meant for American Jews.

Studies old and new confirm that Israel is central to the public life of American Jewry, but in terms of the private lives of American Jews, Israel remains by and large a far-off, unknown place; in fact, two-thirds of American Jews have never been there.

Though positively regarded and emotionally powerful, Israel is also profoundly disconcerting to a segment of American Jews. On a day-to-day basis, it is apparently without much consequence.

Events in Israel, both political and religious, fill the pages of the Jewish and the general press. The attention given to Israel in America seems excessive, out of all proportion. The "peace process" and the debate over "Who is a Jew?" give rise to serious conversation in Palo Alto, no less so than to serious arm-twisting in Washington. Israel makes itself felt in every American election cycle and looms large in every American Jewish fund-raising campaign. Yet, with few exceptions, Israel has been a non-subject in American Jewish literature and remains marginal to American Jewish religious thought. As Alvin Rosenfeld noted recently: "What are we to make of the obvious distance that our most serious and accomplished writers have put between themselves and the astonishing successes of political Zionism?"[1]

My purpose in this essay is threefold. To begin with, I want to probe the peculiar combination of closeness and distance that characterizes the relationship of American Jews to Israel. Second, I wish to focus on the

---

[1]Alvin Rosenfeld, "Promised Land(s): Zion, America, and American Jewish Writers," *Jewish Social Studies*, n.s. 3, no. 3, Spring/Summer 1997, p.121.

role that Israel has played in American Jewish religious thought. This is an area of special interest to me, and one where Israel's marginality perhaps tells us most about the meaning that Israel *does* have for American Jews. Finally, in keeping with this essay's title, I want to capture through a somewhat more personal perspective what Israel at 50 means for the individual American Jew. My hope is to express in essay form the combination of joy and apprehension, illumination and perplexity, transcendent faith and satisfaction in the everyday that I myself feel toward Israel as it — and I — approach a half-century of life.

The analysis presented here is far from dispassionate, but then again, American Jews as a whole are not dispassionate in their attitudes and behavior toward Israel. That is so even when, or perhaps especially when, American Jews work hard to keep Israel at a safe emotional distance. The pattern of their relationship to Israel is bound up with the most basic ground rules and assumptions of modern Diaspora existence. It is rooted, too, in the deepest loyalties and fears of an American Jewish community still living in the shadow of the Holocaust. Most American Jews are profoundly grateful for Israel's existence, and many understand its importance to their own existence. For them to draw closer to Israel, however, would require a degree of distinctiveness from Gentile America and an intensity of engagement with the burdens of Jewish history and traditions that the majority of American Jews are simply unwilling to undertake. Such Jews will likely not draw much closer to Israel any time soon, barring catastrophe there or here, not because Israel means too little to them, but, paradoxically, because it means too much — in complex ways, and for deeply felt reasons, which this essay aims to describe.

Distant Relations

A. M. Dushkin, a leading Jewish educator in the United States, speculated in an essay published at the very moment of Israel's creation about seven outcomes that might result from the renewal of Jewish sovereignty: renewed faith in the possibility of life; vindication of biblical prophecy; enhancement of Jewish dignity and self-assurance; concretization of modern Judaism inside the Jewish homeland; new content to Judaism as religion and civilization; a new impetus to the renewal of Hebrew; and a new ideal of service for Jewish youth.[2] Commenting on Dushkin's essay eight years later, Arnold Band argued that the first and the last of

---

[2]Alexander Dushkin, "Implications of the Jewish State for American Jewish Education," *Jewish Education* 19, no. 2, Spring 1948, pp. 2–5.

Dushkin's seven potential outcomes should be eliminated from consideration. "Faith in the possibility of life is too subjective a concept and too contingent upon innumerable imponderables to be detected with any certainty," Band maintained. As for the ideal of service to Israel, Band indicated that it "was doomed to a rapid disintegration." Band focused his attention on Dushkin's five other possible outcomes, but after applying them to a study of Jewish schools in Boston, concluded that "there have been no radical changes which have been inspired by the new State."[3]

Ironically, I would argue that it is the two possible outcomes that Band ruled out, for the reasons that he correctly ruled them out, that have proven of greatest moment in shaping Israel's impact on American Jewry. We will therefore examine each of them in turn—faith in the possibility of life, and a new ideal of service for American youth—the better to understand the dynamics of American Jewry's simultaneous drawing near to and self-distancing from Israel.

Consider the comments made at a symposium held in 1968 to ponder "The Impact of Israel on American Jewry: 20 Years Later."[4] Rabbi Irving Greenberg argued that the Six Day War had such an enormous impact on Jews in the United States because it confirmed the traditional view of the Jews as a chosen people—a people singled out by God or history. Greenberg and the other symposium participants also took note of a new confrontation with the prophetic dimensions of Jewish existence (Dushkin's second point), and the fostering of a general sense of positive Jewish self-acceptance in the United States (Dushkin's third point) in the wake of the Six Day War. It was left to Marshall Sklare, however, to observe that the outpouring of concern for Israel's existence in 1967 had less to do with attachment to the state per se than with a reliving of Jewish history from the 1930s onward—the "cataclysmic history" from which Jews in the United States had remained exempt and which the threat to Israel in May 1967 had seemed to revive. Elie Wiesel seconded this in noting that American Jews, as they listened to the speeches at the United Nations threatening Israel, had suddenly all become children of the Holocaust.

This exchange highlights what I take to be Israel's most fundamental meaning to American Jews, whether in 1948, 1956, 1967, or 1998: *the triumph of life over death.* Israel signifies the Jewish people's mysterious survival against all odds for over two millennia, a renewed lease on life rarely

---

[3]Arnold J. Band, "Trends in the Jewish School System. Boston: A Case Study," *Jewish Social Studies* 21, 1959, pp. 7, 12.

[4]*The Impact of Israel on American Jewry: 20 Years Later* (American Histadrut Cultural Exchange Institute, New York, 1969), pp. 7–9, 39, 58, 72.

granted nations in this world. In 1948 Jewish sovereignty was restored in the Holy Land. A small group of Jewish fighters defeated a powerful enemy, defying near impossible odds. No less amazing, the world saw fit to recognize the new state; Israel's flag flew proudly at the United Nations. And all this happened a mere three years after six million Jews were murdered in Europe. If deserts were blooming in the Jewish homeland, exiles were streaming to build new cities and a new life in the old/new national center, and Jews were singing and dancing again almost everywhere, this was clear testimony to the triumph of life and blessing.

By 1998, of course, these images are utterly trite in their familiarity. I rehearse them nonetheless because their impact on American Jewry has been overwhelming, and because they retain much of their mythic power even today. Israel remains a source of enormous pride to American Jews, who thrill at its vitality, strength, and accomplishments. This is all the more true when Israelis manage to combine strength with compassion, military prowess with achievements in realms such as agriculture and computer technology, excellence in music along with muscle. This is the synthesis of "Athens" and "Sparta" at which Saul Bellow marveled[5]— speaking for many, I think—in *To Jerusalem and Back*, a synthesis which, coming so soon after the death camps, touches Jews the world over at the very core and elicits dedicated efforts aimed at securing Israel's survival.

But Israel has also compelled an anxious confrontation with the perilous facts of Jewish history. Life and death seem to hang in the balance repeatedly where Israel is concerned. Hence a repetition of the age-old nightmares that occur, paradoxically, at the very same moment when Israel enables Jews both inside the state and in the Diaspora to confront the Holocaust in a way that would have been impossible without the margin of safety that Israel provides. Renewed Jewish power and vitality, for all that they remain threatened, have permitted Jews, for once, to contemplate the terrors of Jewish life and history from a standpoint of relative security—on the far shores of the dream, in possession of the Promised Land.

And yet, Jews in the United States have not found ways other than philanthropy, organizational activity, and lobbying, all practiced from afar, to involve themselves in Israel's miraculous new lease on life. That is not in any way to diminish the importance of these modes of service to the state. They have actively engaged tens of thousands of Jews over the past five decades and have elicited philanthropic sums far beyond all expectations. Nonetheless, American Jews have arguably not conceived an "ideal of service" to Israel applicable in moments not characterized by

---

[5]Saul Bellow, *To Jerusalem and Back: A Personal Account* (New York, 1976).

life-and-death emergency. Most certainly, they have not found ways to make Israel's day-to-day routines an integral part of their own lives. The gap between the relationship to Israel on the mythic level of death and rebirth, and the nonrelationship that predominates on the day-to-day level, is enormous. One reason for it surely lies in the simple fact that one can know or, better, imagine a myth from afar, whereas reality, complex and always changing, requires a firsthand acquaintance that is in this case woefully lacking. Few American Jews know Hebrew, and not many of those who do not know the language take the trouble to read Israeli literature in translation.[6] Millions of American Jews of course follow newspaper headlines and television reports concerning the peace process and Israeli religious strife, but not many thousands make the effort to acquire a detailed knowledge of Israeli life. In a 1995 survey, a majority of American Jews did not know that Benjamin Netanyahu and Shimon Peres belong to different parties.[7]

The significant structural differences between the two Jewries further impede mutual understanding, despite shared religious and cultural traditions, a common history, and familial connections. Consider, for example, the ethos of daily life in Tel Aviv, Carmiel, or Jerusalem, which — to the degree that it has not been universalized by pop culture, McDonald's, and the worldwide patterns governing professional and personal life — is as different from the ethos in White Plains or Chicago as is the landscape. Israel's ethnic diversity, too, within and beyond the Jewish population, is not that of America. The experience of war and army service, utterly formative to Israelis, is unknown to most American Jews of this generation. Israel's political system is — for good reason — as perplexing to Jews in the United States as its mix of state and synagogue is disturbing. Finally, the preoccupation of Israeli Judaism with land, messiah, and power, all foreign to American Jews, is cause for serious perplexity and possible concern.[8]

Charles Liebman and Steven Cohen, explicating the differences between the American and Israeli Jewish outlooks in *Two Worlds of Judaism*, point to an additional set of divergent orientations that work to distance the two communities.[9] Jewish history and peoplehood are primary commitments for Israelis, salient in daily experience and featured

---

[6]Alan Mintz, "Israeli Literature and the American Reader," *AJYB 1997*, pp. 93–114.

[7]*American Jewish Attitudes Toward Israel and the Peace Process: A Public Opinion Survey* (American Jewish Committee, New York, 1995).

[8]For a more detailed presentation of this argument, see my essay *A New Role for Israel in American Jewish Identity* (American Jewish Committee, New York, 1992).

[9]Charles S. Liebman and Steven M. Cohen, *Two Worlds of Judaism: The Israeli and American Experiences* (New Haven, 1990). See especially chaps. 5–6.

prominently in the culture and the schools. American Jews, for the most part, have far less awareness of Jewish history and a much weaker sense of connection to Jews elsewhere. This is so, in large measure, because Jewish allegiances in America are personalist and voluntarist. They must be chosen, one family, indeed one person, at a time. In Israel, group loyalties come with the territory, and Jewish identity is part of a collective experience that is conveyed and reinforced by the very language in use and the history that decisively shapes one's life. American Jews align themselves more with universal values and see Judaism as propagating those values. Overwhelmingly, they identify Jewish values with liberalism. Israelis are more particularist, and their view of the world, like their state, is characterized by borders not always easy to cross. Liberalism is not central to the Israeli outlook.

All of this makes for distance as a rule, with Orthodox Jews on both sides of the divide constituting the single notable exception. Because Jewish religious observance is so central to their lives, and that observance determined by a Halakhah recognized as authoritative in both countries, Orthodox commonality is increased from the outset. It is further enhanced by higher levels of Jewish learning and Hebrew proficiency among Orthodox Jews in America, and by the tradition of yeshivah study in Israel for American Orthodox young people. Still, some differences between the two Orthodox communities remain. These differences serve to highlight the degree to which, for American Jews as a whole, only the myth of Israel—which foregrounds the state's very existence, rather than the details of actual life there—brings near what is distant.

One suspects, for a variety of reasons, that many American Jews prefer it this way. The distance they maintain from Israel, alongside their relation to it, well suits the implicit contract that they, following a pattern set by other Jewries in the modern West, have made with the state and society of which they are a part. Certainly the mode of American Jewish relation to Israel is as old as American Zionism. This is the case whether one considers the political Zionism first championed by Louis Brandeis in this country or the cultural Zionism popularized in the United States by such figures as Solomon Schechter and Mordecai Kaplan.

American Zionism

Brandeis, in the course of making Zionism an option for himself and American Jews like him, stripped the movement as conceived in Europe and Palestine of two related and fundamental elements—the critique of Diaspora existence and the insistence that Zionism constitutes a path to self-fulfillment. It was clear to Brandeis from the outset that American

Images of History

The Haganah ship *Exodus,* defying British naval blockade, arrives outside Haifa, July 21, 1947. Its 4,500 refugee passengers are forcibly returned to Europe.

Standing beneath a portrait of Theodor Herzl, David Ben-Gurion proclaims Israel's independence (May 14, 1948)

President Harry Truman greets
Chaim Weizmann, Israel's first
president, in Washington
(May 25, 1948)

Israel's flag is raised for the first time at
UN headquarters, Lake Success, N.Y.
(May 12, 1949), with Foreign Minister
Moshe Sharett (r.) and Israeli representa-
tive Aubrey (Abba) Eban (l.) assisting

The 1950s . . . Israel's soldier-farmers build the new state and defend its borders.

UNITED JEWISH APPEAL

ISRAEL GOVERNMENT PRESS OFFICE

Gen. Moshe Dayan briefs colleagues on the progress of the 1956 Sinai Campaign

AP/WIDE WORLD PHOTOS

Between 1948 and 1958, Israel absorbs over 850,000 immigrants. Yemenite *olim* being fed after long flight from Aden (May 1950)

Former SS officer Adolf Eichmann, tried for crimes against the Jewish people, stands for the reading of the verdict in a Jerusalem court (Dec. 11, 1961)

AP/WIDE WORLD PHOTOS

The Six Day War . . . Gen. Uzi Narkiss, Defense Minister Moshe Dayan, and Chief of Staff Yitzhak Rabin enter the Old City of Jerusalem through the Lions' Gate (June 7, 1967)

ISRAEL GOVERNMENT PRESS OFFICE

Israeli paratroopers at the Western Wall, the *kotel,* shortly after the capture of the Old City

Prime Minister Golda Meir, with Chief of Staff Lt. Gen. David Elazar (l.), visiting frontline forces in Egypt during the 1973 Yom Kippur War

Israeli armored vehicles crossing the Suez Canal (October 1973)

President Anwar Sadat, President Jimmy Carter, Prime Minister Menachem Begin, at the White House . . . the signing of the Camp David Accords with Egypt (March 26, 1979)

Israeli soldiers overlooking Beirut
during the 1982 war in Lebanon

Between 1984-1990, Labor and
Likud shared power in a series of
national unity governments. Here,
Shimon Peres, prime minister, and
Yitzhak Shamir, foreign minister,
exchange positions (Oct. 20, 1986).

Anatoly (Natan) Sharansky, released
from Soviet prison and reunited with
his wife, Avital, in Israel, with Minister
of Industry and Trade Ariel Sharon
(Feb. 1986)

Intifada . . . mass violence erupts in Gaza and
the West Bank, as Palestinians protest Israeli
occupation (Dec. 1987)

The Gulf War forced Israeli families into sealed rooms, wearing gas masks, as Iraqi missiles caused extensive damage and personal injury, primarily in the Tel Aviv area (Jan.-Feb. 1991)

Prime Minister Yitzhak Rabin, President Bill Clinton, and PLO chairman Yasir Arafat, at the White House . . . the signing of a "Declaration of Principles" (Sept. 13, 1993)

Prime Minister Yitzhak Rabin, President Bill Clinton, and King Hussein of Jordan, on the Israel-Jordan border . . . the signing of the Israel-Jordan peace treaty (Oct. 26, 1994)

Peace rally in Tel Aviv at which Prime Minister Yitzhak Rabin was assassinated (Nov. 4, 1995)

World leaders attend the funeral of Yitzhak Rabin on Mt. Herzl in Jerusalem (Nov. 6, 1995)

Likud prime ministerial candidate Benjamin Netanyahu, who successfully challenged incumbent Shimon Peres, casts his ballot in Jerusalem (May 29, 1996)

Jews were not homeless or in exile; that they were not fated to encounter an inevitable anti-Semitism. Jewish existence in the United States, he maintained, was to be celebrated and enhanced rather than critiqued or abandoned. The aim of Zionism in America, therefore, was to secure a comparable homeland in Palestine for the millions of Jews who needed it; the means for accomplishing this task were political and philanthropic. Emigration was not to be expected or urged. American Zionists did not envision being "built up" by the land of Israel as they helped to build up that land, on the ground. Indeed, they hoped to export an American version of fulfillment—including such "prophetic" ideals as freedom, equality of opportunity, individual responsibility, and technological know-how—to Palestine. This has of course remained the American Zionist credo until the present day.

No less so, Schechter and the other communal leaders who transplanted cultural Zionism to American shores made significant alterations in the doctrine set forth by the leading European theoretician of that school of thought, Ahad Ha'am. They agreed that Jews in America, as elsewhere, all too often languished in spiritual exile; that knowledge of Jewish history and acquaintance with the Hebrew language were at a low level; and that religious practice was giving way to secularization and assimilation. Schechter and Kaplan followed Ahad Ha'am's lead in arguing that the immediate aim of Zionism should be the establishment of a "spiritual center" in Palestine, which would nurture the development of a revived Jewish culture that could then be exported to Jews throughout the world. However, Schechter stressed the need for a spiritual center in Palestine precisely so that Jewish culture—and with it Jewish religion—could be renewed in the United States, no less than in Palestine. With the assistance of the new center in Palestine, Schechter maintained, a religious flowering of Judaism could take place in the United States.

The center was to serve its periphery. Ahad Ha'am too had envisioned this, but he had not imagined that religion could "trump" culture in the way that Schechter and others in America argued. This too is a point of view that has endured, as evident in Kaplan's stunning reformulation of the purpose of Zionism in 1955: "Zionism has to be redefined so as to assure a permanent place for Diaspora Judaism." Israel's role, Kaplan continued, should be "based on the desire to provide the setting in which the Jewish People could become a fit instrument of this-worldly salvation for every Jew, wherever he resides."[10]

A distinctive American variant of Zionism found expression in a vari-

---

[10]Mordecai M. Kaplan, *A New Zionism* (New York, 1955), pp. 41, 119.

ety of ways. For example, when the Zionist Organization of America adopted a platform in 1918, it stressed progressive principles of pluralist democracy and a mixed public-private economy. Similarly, Arthur Goren has indicated how the ideal of the *halutz*, the pioneer, was Americanized for promotion here.[11] The dominant image became that of the young intellectual or professional who left a promising career in order to redeem the land and build a moral society. In institutional terms, the Young Judaea movement rejected pioneering elitism in favor of an "all-Jewish program" addressed to the masses of Jews, while Habonim declared itself in favor of a Zionism born of individual choice. The decision to become a *halutz*, it was argued, should be private, reached without coercion, and undertaken for positive reasons. Such distinctively American permissiveness and pluralism, Goren observes, ran counter to European Zionist notions of party discipline and ideological collectivism. "Limited halutziut," rather than emigration, became the order of the day—service to Israel through summer camps, study programs, and the like.

American Jewish responses to the Zionist idea reflected genuine national feeling and a strong Jewish commitment. At the same time, it is clear that American Zionists took their cue from the American scene. Zionist, and later Jewish communal, leaders, have consistently striven to strike the proper balance between minority citizenship in a developing American democracy and Jewish loyalties arising out of common history, shared religious commitments, and an enduring sense of Jewish peoplehood. As part of the effort to harmonize these two commitments, the Jews in Palestine were for a long time depicted as people not unlike those in the United States, committed to ideals not unlike those that animated Americans, but not yet fortunate enough to enjoy the full blessings of America. The job of American Jews was not to join them there, but to help them from here; to change Jewish history rather than to change American Jews, much less America.

The famous agreement reached in 1950 between Israeli prime minister David Ben-Gurion and American Jewish Committee president Jacob Blaustein gave classic expression to an understanding of the proper relationship between citizenship in the United States and membership in the Jewish people. Ben-Gurion wrote in his letter:

> The Jews of the United States, as a community and as individuals, have only one political attachment and that is to the United States of America. They owe no political allegiance to Israel. . . . We, the people of Israel, have no

---

[11]Arthur Aryeh Goren, "'Anu banu artza' in America: The Americanization of the Halutz Ideal," in *Envisioning Israel: The Changing Ideals and Images of North American Jews*, ed. Allon Gal (Jerusalem, 1996), pp. 83–88, 95, 104, 109.

desire and no intention to interfere in any way with the internal affairs of Jewish communities abroad. The Government and the people of Israel fully respect the right and integrity of the Jewish communities in other countries to develop their own mode of life and their indigenous social, economic and cultural institutions in accordance with their own needs and aspirations.

In his response, Blaustein paid tribute to Israel's great progress and expressed confidence in the new nation's ability to overcome the difficult problems it still faced. On behalf of the American Jewish Committee, he promised: "We shall do all we can to increase further our share in the great historic task of helping Israel to solve its problems and develop as a free, independent and flourishing democracy."[12]

In line with the Ben-Gurion–Blaustein agreement, American Jewish public life would concern itself in part with voluntary assistance to Israel, and for the rest with the welfare of the American Jewish community. Both elements were important to the assertion of collective Jewish identity in the United States and contributed mightily to the maintenance of Jewish distinctiveness. For many Jews in America, over an extended period, communal commitments focused on Israel defined the essence of their Jewishness. Still, as far as American Jewry as a whole was concerned, Israel was not in the forefront of consciousness or of Jewish public life prior to 1967. Neither Israel nor the Holocaust was even mentioned in the questions posed in an August 1966 *Commentary* symposium on "The State of Jewish Belief," and none of the respondents saw fit to bring them up.

After 1967—with the Six Day War's traumatic reminder of the singled-out Jewish condition, followed by Israel's miraculous deliverance—Israel took center stage in American Jewish public life, a position it held for over two decades. The mythic meaning of Israel to American Jews, operating at the deepest level of personal existence, became joined to the dominant communal agenda, operating at the most visible level in newspapers, meetings, and philanthropy. In this context, the unity of the Jewish people and the centrality of Israel to Jewish life became key elements in Jewish civil religion. Jewish giving to Israel increased dramatically. Jack Wertheimer points out that American Jews gave over $100 million in the two-week period between May 22 and June 10, 1967, and have since donated about $6 billion to Israel via the United Jewish Appeal alone.[13] Parallel to this, Israel's place on the agenda of Jewish organizational life has grown enormously. As Wertheimer indicates:

---

[12]*In Vigilant Brotherhood: The American Jewish Committee's Relationship to Palestine and Israel* (American Jewish Committee, New York, 1964), pp. 54–55.

[13]Jack Wertheimer, "Jewish Organizational Life in the United States Since 1945," *AJYB 1995*, pp. 48–49.

In the 1970s, then, sectors of the organized community that previously had paid scant attention to Israel-related matters now threw their energies and resources into such lobbying. The Council of Jewish Federations formed an Israel Task Force, and the community relations field shifted much of its personnel and budget to the task of explaining Israel's needs to the American public. In the early 1970s, for example, NJCRAC estimated that 65 percent of its budget was spent on activities for Israel and Soviet Jewry. The American Jewish Committee spent between 25 and 50 percent of its budgets on Israel-related programs, while the ADL allocated 30 percent to Israel programming. . . .[14]

There is some evidence that in the last few years Israel's importance for American Jews, both mythic and public, has diminished somewhat. The policies of the current Israeli government are far less popular in the United States, both among Jews and in Washington, than those of its predecessor, and the continuing attempts by Orthodox Jews in Israel to delegitimate and exclude other forms of Judaism have made the situation worse. Moreover, these developments have coincided with an American Jewish communal agenda increasingly focused on "continuity," with funding priorities shifted to "local needs" such as education.

At the same time, American Jews are expressing more interest than ever before in spirituality and/or religion, and are more inclined than ever toward "universalist" and "personalist" aspects of Jewishness rather than the "ethnic" dimensions of Jewish existence. They are correspondingly less inclined than in past decades to award Israel a significant role in their Jewish emotional loyalties. Asked in a recent survey by Steven M. Cohen whether they agreed that Israel is "critical to sustaining American Jewish life," just over half of a representative sample of American Jews agreed that it was; asked "how emotionally attached are you to Israel?" only 27 percent said they were "extremely" or "very" attached (down from 37 percent as recently as 1988), while 42 percent said they were "somewhat attached" and over 25 percent said "not attached." About a third saw Israel as extremely important to their own sense of being Jewish — fewer, Cohen notes, than "those who said the same for the Torah, High Holidays, the Jewish family, American anti-Semitism, the Jewish people, and the Holocaust (where, for each, about half the sample answered in like fashion)."[15]

I would contend that the disengagement indicated by these developments is not merely the effect of current Israeli government policy or of recurring conflicts over "Who is a Jew?" Rather, it represents still another

---

[14]Ibid., pp. 54–55.

[15]Steven M. Cohen, "The Fall of Public Judaism: The 1997 JCCA Survey of American Jews" (unpublished manuscript), p. 24. For earlier figures and the conceptualization employed here, see Cohen and Liebman, *Two Worlds of Judaism.*

attempt to fine-tune the pattern of distance and relationship that has always characterized the American Jewish approach to Israel. An examination of Israel's place in American Jewish religious thought will provide further insight into the dynamics of this process.

God, Torah, Israel, and the State

Scholars of contemporary Judaism have made much of the fact that Abraham Joshua Heschel, without question one of the most profound and influential Jewish thinkers to have worked in the United States in the century, conceived of Judaism as a religion that "sanctifies time rather than space." Heschel certainly did not intend this as an argument on behalf of the Diaspora or against a territorial homeland. His point had much more to do with the distinction between Sabbath and weekday, the actual context in which he used the phrase, or, in a larger sense, between spirit and normalcy—between the demand for justice and the practice of business as usual. Heschel's contrast between space and time somewhat matches the categories of Joseph Soloveitchik, the leading American Orthodox thinker, who distinguishes between the world of "majesty" and the world of "covenant." We misunderstand Heschel and Soloveitchik if we read them as dismissing the importance of the land or State of Israel. But we also misread them if we fail to see that neither they nor other American Jewish religious thinkers have placed land and state at the center of their thought. Here, too, both distance and relationship are apparent.[16]

Consider, for example, a passage in the only work by Heschel in which he deals at any length with the State of Israel—*Israel: An Echo of Eternity*—written, not coincidentally, in the wake of the Six Day War. Heschel offers praise to Jerusalem, surveys its role in Jewish faith, and traces the Jewish people's "covenant of engagement" to the land of Israel over the ages. He then enlarges on the centuries-long story of Jewish longing for return to the land of Israel, and argues that, while the creation of the State of Israel is in no way an "answer to Auschwitz," it does "enable us to bear the agony of Auschwitz without radical despair." Then comes the following passage:

> Our imperishable homeland is in God's time. We enter God's time through the gate of sacred deeds. The deeds, acts of sanctifying time, are the old an-

---

[16]See Abraham Joshua Heschel, *The Sabbath*, in *The Earth Is the Lord's and The Sabbath* (New York, 1966), and Joseph B. Soloveitchik, *The Lonely Man of Faith* (New York, 1992). For a more extensive discussion of these issues see my book *Galut: Modern Jewish Reflection on Homelessness and Homecoming* (Bloomington, 1986), pp. 156–80.

cestral ground where we meet Him again and again. The great sacred deed for us today is to build the land of Israel.[17]

In this passage, "homeland" remains a metaphor until the final sentence. It is imperishable—eternal rather than temporal, spiritual rather than material, and as such necessarily attainable in every time and place. Zionism and the State of Israel enter this passage only through the category of the sacred deed, a paramount sacred deed to which Jews in this time are called. Thus Heschel chastises American Jews for having taken Israel's existence for granted until the Six Day War. Israel's rebirth is cause for wonder and celebration, though not for *aliyah*, which is nowhere recommended. Israel's existence should be taken as "a challenge . . . an urging for spiritual renewal, for moral re-examination," but not as the reason for any larger questioning of the fundamentals of Jewish life in the United States.

A similar pattern is evident in the work of Soloveitchik, who barely mentions Israel in most of his writings and deals with it extensively only when Israel's status as a sign of God's continuing providence over the Jewish people is the issue. In his classic essay "Hark, My Beloved Knocks," published in 1956, Soloveitchik argued that the establishment of the State of Israel was proof that the hiding of God's countenance in the Holocaust had come to an end: "Let us not view this matter lightly! It is the voice of my Beloved that knocketh!"[18] In this case, the response demanded apparently is *aliyah*, though the word is never used. But note that Soloveitchik urges participation in a divine rather than a human project. Moreover, he goes on to argue that the building of the Jewish homeland, if it is to retain God's blessing, must follow the dictates of Torah. In a series of addresses to Orthodox Zionist audiences, Soloveitchik chastised Orthodox Jews for not appreciating and joining in the divine activity under way in Israel.[19] At the same time, he made it clear that only Jews loyal to the Torah were fit to direct those efforts on the ground. Note too the following declaration in an essay by Soloveitchik offering support to Israel's religious parties:

> I understand the greatness, value and importance of the State, the wonder of its establishment and preservation, only from the point of view of the

---

[17]Abraham Joshua Heschel, *Israel: An Echo of Eternity* (New York, 1967), pp. 127–28.

[18]Joseph B. Soloveitchik, "Hark, My Beloved Knocks," in *Torah and Kingship*, ed. Simon Federbush (Hebrew) (Jerusalem, 1961), pp. 11–44. For partial English translation, see Soloveitchik article in *Theological and Halakhic Perspectives: Reflections on the Holocaust*, ed. Bernhard Rosenberg and Fred Heuman (Hoboken, 1992), p. 76.

[19]Joseph B. Soloveitchik, *The Rav Speaks: Five Addresses* (Jerusalem, 1983), pp. 26–36, 73–77; see also pp. 155–56, 198.

uniqueness of the people of Israel and its relation to the God of Israel. As a secular-historical entity that is not animated by any covenantal goal, the State does not excite me. . . . And I cannot imagine any tie between the Jews of the Diaspora and a State insofar as it is secular.[20]

As American Jewish thinkers, both Heschel and Soloveitchik devoted the bulk of their efforts to strengthening Judaism in the United States, rather than to deepening the relation of American Jews to Israel. Both thinkers, moreover, articulated the place that the land and state occupy—central and yet peripheral; mythic in focus rather than everyday—in consonance with their larger views about God, Torah, and Jewish peoplehood, the last of these also of course known as Israel. Finally, both fended off the challenge posed by Israel to the personal decision not to live there; not to participate firsthand in the ingathering for which they prayed daily; not to observe the commandments that could only be observed in the land; not to contribute every day and directly to a project that they believed to be somehow in accord with, or even directed by, divine providence.

Jewish religion here not only trumps Zionism, but also contextualizes its claims, thereby limiting them. By legitimating Diaspora Judaism, Heschel and Soloveitchik silence competing Jewish claims which, if heard loud and clear, might well cast doubt on the adequacy or feasibility of Jewish religious life in the United States.

I want to offer some further examples of this same pattern selected from American Jewish religious thought of the last few years—the *Commentary* symposium of 1996[21] and a sampling of recent volumes by prominent American Jewish religious thinkers.

Contributors to the *Commentary* symposium fall into a number of categories on the subject of Israel. Some did not mention the state at all, despite a question this time around on how the Holocaust and Israel—paired by the editors, as they are often joined in popular consciousness—had influenced faith, religious identity, and observance of the respondents. Others did discuss Israel, but only in the mythic terms of life after death, miracle, hope, "Zion." Israel's function as a proof for divine providence, or of God's renewed presence in history, was mentioned frequently. Only Blu Greenberg, however, declared that Israel was a thrilling miracle that engaged her more than any other Jewish involvement. Few

[20]Joseph B. Soloveitchik, "Concerning Love of the Torah and Salvation of the Soul of This Generation," in *In Aloneness, In Togetherness*, ed. Pinchas Peli (Hebrew) (Jerusalem, 1967), p. 430.

[21]"What Do American Jews Believe? A Symposium," *Commentary* 102, no. 2, Aug. 1996, pp. 18–96.

contributors ascribed importance to Israel in terms of their own Jewish lives without an immediate qualification that returned the emphasis to America. None, of course, advocated *aliyah*. All in all, the *Commentary* symposium gives expression to much love of and pride in Israel, while treating it as a distinctly minor element in terms of theological reflection.

Recent volumes of Jewish religious thought differ in degree but not in kind from the thrust of the *Commentary* symposium. For example, Daniel Gordis, in a popular work on Jewish spirituality, *God Was Not in the Fire*, indicates that he will not be treating the subject of Israel, because his topic does not demand it.[22] In a second volume, this one dealing with contemporary Jewish existence as a whole—*Does the World Need the Jews?*—Gordis does raise the subject of Israel, but only in order to refute the claim that it should occupy center stage in current Jewish life.[23]

Arthur Green, in a work rooted in the Jewish mystical tradition, *Seek My Face, Speak My Name*, deals with Israel briefly in the section on redemption.[24] A new Judaism is being articulated in Israel, Green contends, "one that involves land and language more than it does observance of tradition." This stress, Green is aware, makes American Jews uncomfortable, but they can profit from it, because Diaspora Jews have become too urbanized and too intellectualized to "take cognizance of divinity in our natural surroundings."

Judith Plaskow, in *Standing Again at Sinai: Judaism from a Feminist Perspective*, builds on the traditional structure of God, Torah, and Israel and focuses on the State of Israel in a chapter entitled "Israel: Toward a New Concept of Community."[25] The redefinition of the people of Israel, Plaskow argues, necessarily involves consideration of the state, because "the human difficulties in dealing with difference, the social implications of traditional attitudes toward difference, the continuities between the modern Jewish construction of difference and historical Jewish treatment of others all emerge with special vividness in the context of the State of Israel." Considered in these terms, Plaskow maintains, Israel's treatment of both the Palestinians and gender inequality in the country needs to be critiqued: "It seems that the Jewish experience of oppression has led not to the just exercise of power by Jews in power, but to the Jewish repetition of strategies of domination." Plaskow, then, draws a negative lesson from Israel about what Jewish life should be like in the United States.

---

[22]Daniel Gordis, *God Was Not in the Fire* (New York, 1995).
[23]Daniel Gordis, *Does the World Need the Jews?* (New York, 1997).
[24]Arthur Green, *Seek My Face, Speak My Name* (Northvale, N.J., 1992), p. 176.
[25]Judith Plaskow, *Standing Again at Sinai: Judaism from a Feminist Perspective* (San Francisco, 1990), pp.107–19.

Two other recent works oriented neither to feminism nor to spirituality do accord Israel more sustained and complicated treatment, though neither moves very far from the themes enunciated in this essay thus far. Irving Greenberg's *The Jewish Way*, organized according to the cycle of the Jewish calendar, ends with a chapter on Israeli Independence Day that carries the title—using the mythic terms with which we are familiar—"Resurrection and Redemption."[26] Greenberg labels Zionism "the new exodus," and sees it, with the help of Soloveitchik's "Hark, My Beloved Knocks," as a providential counterpoint to this century's "Egypt," the Holocaust. "The creation of the state was a deeply human act," Greenberg claims, yet nonetheless "an act of redemption of biblical stature. . . . The Bible insists that the human role in redemption in no way reduces the divine intentionality and responsibility for the outcome of events."

Greenberg is also concerned to underscore the "end of *galut* (exilic) Judaism" that has occurred by virtue of Israel. The state has placed that power in Jewish hands, thereby transforming Jewish history and Judaism. Thanks to Israel's creation, Jews can now "serve God in the joy of victory," raising the question of exactly how Yom Ha'atzmaut—unquestionably a religious holiday, in Greenberg's eyes—should be celebrated. Greenberg endorses the recitation of Hallel, and includes the marking of Yom Hazikaron, the day before Independence Day, which in Israel is devoted to remembrance of fallen soldiers.

Eugene Borowitz, in *Renewing the Covenant*, relates to Israel in a variety of contexts—perhaps the greatest single innovation in this regard. Not surprisingly, he deals with it in terms of the Holocaust, noting that Israel offers Jews a personal experience of "God's saving power." Borowitz continues: "The State of Israel appeared a model of moral politics; it also became the shining symbol of our people's transpolitical, instinctive, life-affirming answer to Hitler's nihilism, giving it a numinosity, a sacred aura that even a secularized generation could not ignore." Still, Borowitz stresses that the state cannot be the answer to the quest of American Jews for a "substitute absolute" capable of replacing lost faith in modernity. "Despite all that the State of Israel means to us and has done for us, there is a compelling Jewish and human distinction between its claiming our deep devotion and serving as our actional absolute." Borowitz returns to the subject of Israel in dealing with what he calls "the sparks of chosenness," i.e., the meaning of the covenant linking the Jewish people to God. Israel's existence, Borowitz observes, "has

---

[26]Irving Greenberg, *The Jewish Way: Living the Holidays* (New York, 1988), pp. 373–404.

intensified the possible effects of our people being chosen," since "a culturally self-determining Jewish community provides the Jewish people corporately with the optimum situation in which to work out its God-oriented destiny." Here too Borowitz adds a qualifier, noting that Diaspora Jews normally have closer contact with Gentiles on a personal level and can thus more easily carry out this particular aspect of Jewish chosenness, once called "mission."[27]

Israel figures in one additional context in Borowitz's book, namely in attempting to apply the classical "covenant-ideal" of living as a nation in the world of realpolitik and "within the tensions of survival/sanctification." At the same time, the challenge for Diaspora Jewry, in Borowitz's view, is to determine "what it might mean to be an enfranchised self as a believing Jew."

A survey of the prayer books in use by American Jews, conducted by historian David Ellenson, has found that there too, as in the works summarized above, "even when the territoriality of Jewish existence in the state is recalled and the presence of the Jewish people in the Land is acknowledged, the universal elements in the tradition remain highlighted." The state is "refracted specifically through the prism of a universalistic ethos." National memory in the prayers uttered by American Jews is joined to personal spiritual quest, and the "linked myth" of Holocaust and Redemption is repeatedly canonized by the liturgy. "The present-day reality of a secular Israel . . . [is] far removed from the vision of the Jewish state presented in these liturgies. Simply put, the State of Israel embodies a religious, not a secular nationalist, reality for the adherents of these American Jewish religious denominations" [Reform, Conservative and Reconstructionist].[28]

Orthodoxy presents a rather complicated picture. Although the prayers uttered in Israeli and American Orthodox synagogues are virtually identical, some differences in religious outlook remain, as expressed in a recent symposium on the subject of Israel in the Orthodox journal *Tradition*.[29] Wariness continues concerning the messianism evident among many Orthodox Israelis of the younger generation, and Americans are far less comfortable than their Israeli counterparts with legislation imposing Orthodox control of marriage, divorce, and conversion. Finally, opinions differ among modern Orthodox Jews in America regarding the

[27]Eugene Borowitz, *Renewing the Covenant: A Theology for the Postmodern Jew* (Philadelphia, 1991), pp. 44, 77–78, 196.

[28]David Ellenson, "Envisioning Israel in the Liturgies of North American Liberal Judaism," in *Envisioning Israel* (see note 11), pp. 126–34, 145–47.

[29]See "Reflections on the Six-Day War After a Quarter Century," *Tradition* 26, no. 4 (Summer 1992), pp. 8–24.

recitation of Hallel on Israeli Independence Day—a practice not only universal among modern Orthodox Jews in Israel, but a strong marker of identity that distinguishes them from traditionalist Orthodox Jews unwilling to accord the state this mark of Jewish legitimacy.

The non-Orthodox American Jewish thinkers surveyed above, and the rabbis who compose the prayer books in use by non-Orthodox American Jews, are in one crucial respect similar to the handful of Jewishly knowledgeable and committed writers of fiction who of late have created a spate of exceptions to Rosenfeld's generalization about non-interest in Israel.[30] All are subject to the need for self-justification vis à vis the existential claims that Israel makes, the need for a cogent response to Israeli challengers who argue that American Jews too will in the end succumb to the forces of assimilation and/or anti-Semitism, that authentic Jewish life and creativity are possible only in Israel, that for Jews who care deeply about being Jewish there is really only one place in the world to live. Consider the remarkable series of Israeli characters, and dialogues on Israeli and Israel-Diaspora themes, in Philip Roth's recent novels *The Counterlife* and *Operation Shylock*. Even if the rabbis, theologians, and fiction writers are not, like all of Roth's personae, avowedly secular, and even if they are not, like the Roth double in *Shylock*, avowed "diasporists," American thinkers nonetheless have to answer the difficult question that Roth's characters seem compelled time after time to answer: How can American Jews not want to live in the Jewish state?

"One can play a role in history without its having to be obvious," Nathan tells his brother Henry, newly relocated to a Gush Emunim settlement on the West Bank. "It may be that flourishing mundanely in the civility and security of South Orange, more or less forgetful from one day to the next of your Jewish origins but remaining identifiably (and voluntarily) a Jew, you were making Jewish history no less astonishing than theirs, though without quite knowing it every moment, and without having to say it."[31] If one can flourish transcendently in South Orange, thanks to the Jewish religious tradition; if one does remember Jewish origins in prayer, communal activity, study, and ritual; if one thereby remains not only identifiably Jewish, but substantively so—the claim to be making Jewish history, and the knowledge that one is doing so, come still more easily.

---

[30]See, on this point, Andrew Furman, *Israel Through the Jewish-American Imagination: A Survey of Jewish-American Literature on Israel, 1928–1995* (Albany, 1997), pp. 3–4, 188–200. Cf. Rosenfeld, "Promised Land(s)," p. 120.

[31]Philip Roth, *The Counterlife* (New York, 1988), p. 146, cited in Rosenfeld, "Promised Land[s]," p. 125. For the diasporist argument, see Philip Roth, *Operation Shylock* (New York, 1993), especially pp. 44–47, 156–58, 200–01.

The acknowledgement of the claims of Israel and the decision not to live there underscore yet again the combination of relationship and distancing at the heart of the American Jewish response to Israel.

The Claims of the Center

Having brought the argument this far, I wish to speak in more personal terms as an American Jew who has made *aliyah*, and returned from *aliyah*, and has written books and essays about Jewish thought in which the subject of Israel is rarely in the foreground for very long.

I remember wondering more than once as a teenager, and actually asking the question aloud one Friday evening at an *oneg shabbat* at my synagogue, why all those American Jews who cared about being Jewish had not long since moved to Israel. There seemed to be so much life there, so much sheer vitality, whereas most of American Judaism seemed confined to the doldrums of synagogue and Hebrew school and the petty concerns of organizational life. When my wife and I made *aliyah*, it was, I think, the fullness of Jewish life possible in Israel that attracted us more than anything else. In Israel life was rich, with the most mundane activities bound up in the most transcendent of human projects. We did not leave the United States because of any disappointment with this country, or any experience of anti-Semitism, or any conviction that America was not as much a home as human beings can know on this earth. And we did not come back to the United States for any but personal reasons. There was no disappointment with Israel, no sense that the promised land had failed to live up to any of its promises, no exchange of Zionist commitments for "diasporism."

And yet, for all that, if one chooses to live in the United States rather than in Israel, one imagines Jewish life primarily in terms that can be put into practice here. An ethic of aspiration, even if it remains an ideal far beyond one's grasp, must nonetheless be close enough to stimulate aspiration, not so far removed as to preclude reaching for it. The Torah that holds American Jews, in all their varieties of Jewish commitment, is a Torah that can be lived where they live. What is more, that Torah, because it calls upon Jews to transform all human projects everywhere in accordance with the will of God, will almost inevitably trump Israel's centrality for Jewish existence. Judaism itself thus removes Israel from the foreground most of the time, just as "Israel" in its classic sense— the Jewish people as a whole—always encompasses, and so limits, the claims of Israel as land or state. This is so despite the fact that many of the most important Jewish realizations for the minority of American Jews who are deeply involved with the Jewish state occur in Israel and because of Israel. Let me enumerate a few of these realizations, which I believe are widespread among committed American Jews of this generation.[32]

Consider the experience of Jewish peoplehood that comes, for example, when riding an Egged bus. The physiognomies of those on board are many and various, and yet we know immediately that they belong to the same "family." We recognize that all have come from far away to be in this place, the only place on earth where we could meet them all, and meet them on what is for all home turf. The sense of shared peoplehood is increased when we reflect on the gratitude felt for the soldiers riding on the bus. Their guns protect us from people who consider us enemies simply because of who and what we are. "Us" and "them" come clearly into view. A similar realization may stem from turning the dial on the radio late at night and hearing only Arabic, except for the Voice of America, the BBC, and the station of the Israeli Defense Forces. These lessons of "us" and "them" are difficult for young American Jews, heirs to Vietnam-era antipathy toward military force and skeptical of cold-war rhetoric about the enemy. One often does not want to know that history is inescapable. The realization alters politics and confirms identity.

Like many other American Jews, I became convinced of the centrality of Israel in contemporary Jewish life not from paying attention to the interminable debates on the subject but by sitting in Jerusalem—specifically, in my case, at the Cinemateque during a showing of *Because of That War*, a film about and starring two young Israeli rock musicians, both the children of Holocaust survivors. When the lights went up after the film that day, disputes on the issue of centrality suddenly seemed academic. It was clear that Israel represents the principal continuation of Jewish history in this century and into the future. For all that American Jews too have the potential to write a major chapter in the history of the Jewish people, Israel is the place where the fate of the Jews stands most exposed to view and is most on the line. One is grateful to know Hebrew at such moments, because it makes possible the direct absorption of lessons such as this one without the need for subtitles, and enables one to discuss it in the language which, like the Jewish people, is alive again, thanks to Israel. This is a source of much pleasure, as is physical contact with the land of Israel: the natural features such as wadis and hills, and the layers upon layers of history still visible on the surface of the land or recently excavated from beneath it.

One also learns important things about God and Torah in Israel. Pil-

---

[32]For more on these matters, see my book *Taking Hold of Torah: Jewish Commitment and Community in America* (Bloomington, 1997).

grimage becomes vivid on a Shavuot morning in Jerusalem when, after participating in an all-night study session, we join the throngs streaming from every direction toward the common center, the Western Wall. There and elsewhere in Israel the appeal of sacred space becomes compelling, as the spell of sacred time is sensed in the stillness of the streets on Yom Kippur. One learns what it means to testify with one's feet and to live by a calendar that moves to Jewish rather than Gentile rhythms.

Prophecy too can come into fuller view, and not only because a scroll of Isaiah discovered at Qumran is on permanent exhibit at the Shrine of the Book. Sitting near the Wall or on the Temple Mount, looking out at the same expanse of desert that filled Isaiah's vision, it becomes easier to understand the prophet's conviction that human beings are all caught between the sky above and the rock beneath, dazzled and overwhelmed by the light. We reside in a place where everything matters, subject to a responsibility from which there is no escape. Indeed, "Holy, holy, holy is the Lord of Hosts. The whole earth is full of His glory."

In Israel everything does seem to matter, all the time, to the point that one wishes for some levity, and is all the more disappointed when it comes from debates in the Knesset. History matters and is of ultimate importance. Perspective, for better and for worse, seems to vanish at times, as foreign and domestic policy issues of the moment are debated in terms of a tradition that is centuries old.

Nor is Torah any longer confined to the prophetic critique of power delivered from the sidelines. Judaism in Israel must now engage power, because Israelis wield power, the situation mandating an interplay of state and religion that is unnerving to American Jews, whose ability to be Jews rests on a constitutional separation between state and religion. The political disputes recounted in the biblical books of Numbers or Kings take on new significance as one observes the analogous struggles of contemporary Israelis to fuse the age-old claims of covenant with the pressing demands of political reality. It is no wonder that the Israeli civil religion seeks to confer the sanctity of divine covenant upon political decisions that now, as in the Bible, are the subject of great controversy.[33] Nor is it a surprise when God and Torah are invoked by religious Israelis to justify beliefs or behavior that other Israelis find reprehensible, likewise because of God and Torah.

All of this proves perplexing to American Jews upon first encounter, and for many it remains troubling no matter how well they come to know Israel. Yet, power is not inimical to virtue, a point that Emil Fackenheim,

---

[33]Charles S. Liebman and Eliezer Don-Yehiya, *Civil Religion in Israel* (Berkeley, 1983).

Irving Greenberg, and other Jewish religious thinkers in North America have emphasized against the background of Israel's existence.[34] Indeed, power makes many good deeds possible and prevents some bad deeds that stem from the desperation of powerlessness. The many fine uses of Jewish power in Israel these past five decades prove this. But it is also true—as Isaiah Leibowitz, David Hartman, and other Israeli thinkers have stressed—that power puts ethical and religious ideals to the test, and that Jews, like others, do not always pass, whether in their relations to the Palestinians or to one another.[35] Hence the recent critiques of Zionism ventured in the name of Jewish or Zionist ideals.[36] That seems an inevitable consequence of the Zionist dream and the achievement of "normalization," at times on view far more than either Israelis or American Jews would wish. Jewish living in Israel is unshielded by the minority status and relative powerlessness of Diaspora Jewish life, where the moral refuge of standing on the sidelines is always available and often made use of.

These are some of the palpable meanings that Israel carries for those privileged not only to be alive at a time when the state exists, but also to know its reality close up. And this is to say nothing of the mythic aspects of Israel, which remain as potent as ever. One cannot walk the streets of Israeli cities, see the faces of Ethiopian immigrants, hear Russian all around, and not marvel at the "ingathering of the exiles," an exhilarating example of a prayer that has actually come true. Moreover, the Zionist account of modern Jewish history—particularly as amended in recent years to take account of Diaspora achievement on the one hand and Zionist or Israeli failings on the other—is far more persuasive than Diaspora versions that minimize the extent of anti-Semitism or the threat of assimilation.

American Jews, for all that they benefit from living with what is distinctive to the 20th-century United States, do seem subject to the same "rules" that have governed all of modern Jewish history. We too negotiate loyalties, depend on shifting coalitions of interests, know the fragility of our success. The Israelis are right to insist on this, even as we are right

---

[34]See Emil Fackenheim, *To Mend the World* (New York, 1982), and *The Jewish Thought of Emil Fackenheim*, ed. Michael L. Morgan (Detroit, 1987). See also Greenberg, *The Jewish Way*, chap. 11.

[35]See Isaiah Leibowitz, *Judaism, Human Values, and the Jewish State*, ed. Eliezer Goldman (Cambridge, 1992), and David Hartman, *Conflicting Visions: Spiritual Possibilities of Modern Israel* (New York, 1990).

[36]See the summary by Amos Elon, "Israel and the End of Zionism," in *New York Review of Books* 43, no. 20 (Dec. 19, 1996), pp. 27–28; and Menachem Brinker, "The End of Zionism?" in *Dissent* 32, no. 1 (Winter 1985).

to remind them that a tiny state located where Israel is located is not exactly in the best position to claim that it has secured the future of the Jewish people. Nor are Israelis, for all the advantages of public Jewish time and space and immediate access to Hebrew, entitled to the prideful boast that they, unlike us, have secured the future of Judaism.

The Jewries of the United States and Israel, then, however one stands on the contested issue of the true Jewish center(s), and for all the differences between the two communities that I have enumerated, seem in this sense at least to be on parallel tracks. Israel represents one of the two options for Jewish survival and Jewish thriving that have proven viable in the modern world—life inside a sovereign state protected by its army. The United States represents the most promising case yet of the other option—minority existence in a Diaspora democracy, in which Jews take the risk that they can maintain the economic and political clout necessary to guarantee their rights and can secure the resources needed to maintain and transmit the Jewish way of life. Both Jewries seek, in language that we have used repeatedly in this essay, to marry normalcy and covenant—to meet the needs of survival, the demands of the everyday, as well as the demands of the highest values that Jews know: God and Torah.

These basic facts of the modern Jewish situation are unlikely to change in the next half-century, even as Israel quickly overtakes the United States in its Jewish population and eventually contains the majority of the world's Jews. Shared Jewish interests, then, regardless of principles that may or may not be shared, would seem to require that Jews in Israel and the United States be open to the lessons that each bears for the other, as well as the challenges that each poses to the other. These fall into two categories.

It has long since become a commonplace that Israel and Diaspora require each other for their physical survival, and that the Jewish people, for its survival, requires both. Israelis are obviously dependent on U.S. governmental assistance, and this in turn depends in part on the support of a united American Jewry. However, American Jews likewise benefit in a host of ways from Israel, albeit intangibly. Dignity and self-respect—and so achievement—are bound up, to a degree we cannot and should not wish to test, in the existence of a sovereign and successful Jewish state. This dependence is implicitly acknowledged, I believe, in the anxiety that Israel always live up to the highest moral ideals and never get far out of sync with the policies of the U.S. government. American Jews naturally want Israel to help them feel good about being Jews. Interests and principles, normalcy and covenant, work together in this respect.

The interdependence of the two Jewries in the cultural and religious spheres is less widely acknowledged, but is, in my view, no less serious.

Jewish thought here and there, for all its differences, is nourished by the same sources, classical and modern, and developments in both countries sooner or later have an impact on the other. Experiences in Israel such as those I pointed to play a crucial role in the Jewish journeys of many of the most committed American Jews. The myth of Israel continues to help secure the identification of those less committed. Jewish artists and scholars in the two societies are utterly interdependent; American synagogues, their liturgies barely altered by Israel's existence, have been greatly enlivened through music imported from Israel, as American homes and ritual observances have been beautified by imported art objects. Israelis for their part have not only been significantly affected by American popular culture that in turn bears the imprint of American Jewish experiences, but are increasingly feeling the impact of developments, whether feminist or Orthodox or "new age" or Conservative or Reform, that first took place and took root in the United States. This cross-fertilization too is likely to continue, regardless of population shifts, and will likely grow among the minority in each country that cares deeply about Jewish peoplehood and tradition.

It seems pointless to me to argue any longer, as Jews have often argued over the past five decades, over whether Israel deserves to be considered the political center of the Jewish people, or whether it has earned the right, culturally or morally, to be considered the spiritual center. Nor, I think, should Jews here or there any longer insist on the word "Zionist" to describe activities better and more simply designated as Israeli or Jewish, whether these be organizational, economic, or educational. Complete fulfillment of the tasks set for political Zionism by Herzl and other founders — the ingathering of all the world's Jews to Palestine, with a resultant end to anti-Semitism — must await the coming of the messiah, just as Ahad Ha'am said a century ago. Complete fulfillment of the tasks set by Ahad Ha'am and other spiritual Zionists — the renaissance of Jewish culture throughout the world — must likewise await the messiah. In the meantime, Israel need not be the "light unto the nations" to be worthy of American Jewish interest, but only what it is: a thriving Jewish society where various visions of Jewish life jostle with each other and compete for the allegiance of Israelis, in ways that are directly relevant to Jews in the Diaspora. Israel's pursuit of normalcy should concern American Jews as much as its pursuit of covenant. I assume that efforts to reach a settlement with the Palestinians will remain a source of concern on both counts — and should constitute added reason for involvement in Israel by American Jews, rather than for disengagement from it.

For reasons that should by now be apparent, I do not expect the two communities as a whole to turn toward one another in the next 50 years of Israel's existence. Most American Jews will continue to rely on myth, while keeping the reality of Israel at a safe distance. The Israeli government will often assist them by its actions, as will proponents of one or another form of Judaism not shaped by the very different conditions of America and so not receptive to the reigning American pluralism. What is written about Israel and Zionism, here or there, will have a lot less effect on how American Jews perceive and relate to Israel than the facts of what Israelis make of their country in coming years. Efforts toward peace, just treatment of Israel's minorities, and acceptance of differing forms of Judaism will yield positive outcomes.

That is not to say, however, that organized Jewry could not do more to bridge the gap between the two Jewish populations. On the contrary, it could with not much effort expand the set of joint projects already under way, for which I would henceforth reserve the term "Zionism." *Aliyah*, and the knowledge of Israel that is the prerequisite to *aliyah*, will of course remain a part of this continuing Zionism, though emigration to Israel from the Western Diaspora will probably remain at low levels. The emphasis, however, will likely fall on projects through which thousands of American Jews can get to know Israel and Israelis more intimately, and vice versa. Money has already begun to flow through investments and hands-on involvement rather than merely via philanthropy. Information and ideas are flowing not only through books but through television and the Internet.

Visits to Israel, and not only by young people, are more and more devoted to meeting ordinary Israelis and getting to know Israeli society in all its complexity, rather than taking the form of "missions" focused on meetings with government officials and confronting only the Israel packaged so as to maximize excitement and donations. Hebrew literacy, currently possessed by very few American Jews, would certainly increase access to Israeli reality as well as to the classical sources of Jewish tradition. Most important of all, perhaps, are projects such as "Partnership 2000," an initiative sponsored by the Jewish Agency, which joins local Jewish communities in the United States with specific cities and towns in Israel and puts the Jews of those communities to work, in partnership, on tasks of education and development both in Israel and in the Diaspora. The program has recently been expanded to include study groups that link American Jews and Israelis in the common exploration of Jewish history and tradition. All of these activities make each of the parallel tracks more vivid to the other and are likely to have an impact on the pursuit of both normalcy and covenant.

Heschel, then, was not wrong: Israel is a place of "great sacred deeds" in which American Jews can join, even if, as a living Jewish state, it is also a place of much profane reality. Nor was Kaplan wrong: Israel has helped to assure a "place for diaspora Judaism" in America, a Diaspora which, for all its failings, represents an achievement undreamed-of when Israel was born half a century ago. One shudders to think what American Jewish life would be like in the absence of Israel. Grateful for the immensity of what has been and what is, one looks forward to the next 50 years with enormous expectancy—and no small measure of hope.

Review
of
the
Year

UNITED STATES

United States

National Affairs

DURING THE SECOND HALF of 1996 and through the year 1997 the Jewish community battled to avoid retreat on a number of issues on its traditional agenda, even as new and largely unexpected ones came to the fore. Welfare and immigration, both of great concern to the Jewish community, were the subjects of far-reaching reform laws that many in the community opposed but that were nevertheless enacted in the second half of 1996. Events on the international front also had an impact on the national agenda, chiefly changes in Israeli policy following the election of Benjamin Netanyahu in May 1996, fresh initiatives seeking compensation for Holocaust survivors, and revelations about Swiss actions during World War II.

THE POLITICAL ARENA

The Presidential Election

As the presidential campaign of 1996 moved through the summer conventions and toward its conclusion, there was no real question as to which candidate would garner a majority of the Jewish vote. The historic ties between American Jews and the Democratic Party were not about to be swept aside in 1996 any more than in previous election years. The contest was, instead, for the swing vote. Could enough Jewish voters be brought over to the Republican side of the ballot to make the difference in a close election?

Thus, as the campaign got under way in earnest, beginning with the conventions at which their respective parties formally nominated President Bill Clinton and former senator Bob Dole, Dole set out to woo the Jewish vote. Dole had some resistance to overcome in this regard, both with regard to Jewish concerns that the religious right was calling the agenda of the Republican Party and, more specifically, with the fact that the Republican presidential candidate had something of a mixed record on Israel. On the latter issue, Dole pointed to his recent success in pushing through Congress, over the Clinton administration's objection, legislation that recognized Jerusalem as the capital of Israel. As to the socially conservative wing of his party, he made efforts that seemed to many (certainly not solely for the benefit of the Jewish community) to create some perception of distance.

The selection of former congressman and cabinet secretary Jack Kemp as Bob Dole's running mate was seen as good news by many in the Jewish community. Apart from his positions on abortion and church-state relations, which were contrary to those of the organized Jewish community, the combination of his strong pro-Israel stance, his historic (if, of late, somewhat compromised) commitment to immigration and civil rights, and—perhaps most importantly—a level of personal familiarity and comfort led many in the Jewish community to regard Kemp as a friend. In September, however, Kemp ran into a contretemps when, on two separate occasions, he spoke favorably of Louis Farrakhan's philosophy of self-help for the black community, even as he called on Farrakhan to renounce anti-Semitism. Kemp's comments provoked criticism not only from the partisan National Jewish Democratic Council (NJDC), which asserted that "you can't separate the message from the messenger," but also from nonpartisan quarters. Even a spokesman for the Republican-affiliated National Jewish Coalition made the wistful comment that he wished Kemp "could find a better example to prove his point."

The Democrats had a much less difficult job of persuasion. The primary message coming out of their convention was a litany of the terrible things that might happen under a Dole presidency (an attack on church-state separation, the barring of abortion, uncertainty as to the future of U.S.-Israeli relations), while reminding Jewish constituents of the common perspective they shared with the president on a slew of domestic policy issues and the strength of his record on Israel. Even on issues where some in the Jewish community had been critical of Clinton, such as his signing of the 1996 welfare reform law, the president's advocates had the advantage of being able to say that Dole would be even worse, and that the president was committed to dealing with some of the problems in that bill.

As the election approached, it appeared that the national race would be no real contest, and even more so with respect to the Jewish vote, of which, polls indicated, Clinton was likely to garner at least 80 percent. Thus, by late October, the research director of a Republican-aligned polling firm was commenting that "both candidates are ignoring the Jewish vote. [Since] this election is not as close as past elections [and the Jewish vote receives more attention in close elections], the Jewish vote will play less of a role in the presidential election." In sharp contrast to 1992, when Clinton had assiduously courted Jewish voters up until Election Day, reports indicated that only the toss-up state of Florida was receiving close attention in the form of a series of rallies set up by the Clinton-Gore Jewish Outreach office. But, commented journalist Matthew Dorf in covering the campaign, "If Clinton is taking the Jewish vote for granted, it appears that the Dole campaign is letting him." There was little attention to Jewish voters from the Dole side, even in states where Dole could not prevail without reducing Jewish support for the Clinton-Gore ticket.

In the end, there were no surprises. President Clinton was reelected with a comfortable plurality of over 49 percent and a margin of victory of approximately 8 percent; if not the majority for which he had hoped, the election results provided the president with the basis on which throughout 1997 he was able to claim support for the centrist, pragmatic approach he had adopted in 1995 and 1996. The Jewish vote was more or less as predicted, overwhelmingly in favor of Clinton. A leading exit poll service showed Jews voting 78 percent for Clinton, 16 percent for Dole, and 3 percent for third-party candidate Ross Perot.

Congressional Elections

If the presidential race saw little attention to the Jewish vote, that was certainly not the case on the congressional side during the 1996 campaign. Republican and Democratic candidates in a number of close races were very much focused on Jewish voters who they thought could make the difference, both in votes and in contributions of time and money. Thus, by some reckoning, New Jersey's Jewish voters—constituting more than 5 percent of the electorate—were likely to be the deciding factor in the race between Rep. Robert Torricelli, Democrat, and Rep. Dick Zimmer, Republican, to replace outgoing Democratic senator Bill Bradley. And neither candidate was shy about looking for ways to appeal to the Jewish constituency. Another race of interest, in Minnesota, featured a rematch between two Jewish candidates as former senator Rudy Boschwitz, a Republican, sought to regain the seat he had lost in 1990 to Democrat Paul Wellstone, now the incumbent. In a state with a small population, the expected closeness of the race nevertheless led the two candidates to vie—as they had in 1990—for the Jewish vote.

In the end, Wellstone and Torricelli were reelected and elected, respectively, by comfortable margins, margins that were even wider among Jewish voters. Jewish observers suggested that in races where neither party could make the case that its candidate was more steadfast in support of Israel, Jewish voters were more likely to look at social issues, such as welfare and immigration policy, in considering how to cast their votes. Wellstone, it was noted, was the only senator facing reelection who voted against the 1996 welfare reform law that so many in the Jewish community had opposed.

On the House side, it was hard to miss the racial acrimony in the race between Rep. Cynthia McKinney, the incumbent African-American Democrat, and John Mitnick, her Jewish Republican challenger. Mitnick accused McKinney of ties to Nation of Islam leader Louis Farrakhan, while McKinney's father—also angry at a U.S. Supreme Court decision that led to the redrawing of the lines for his daughter's district so as to include substantially more whites and Republicans—called Mitnick a "racist Jew." Following these latter comments, McKinney kicked her father off the campaign and denounced his comments and the anti-Semitism and racism of Farrakhan. She went on to win reelection by a comfortable margin. Following the election, American Jewish Committee southeast area director Sherry Frank commented that McKinney "will need to begin the healing process [with the Jewish community] so that she is able to effectively represent the 7 percent of her population which is Jewish." In two other House races of interest, both in Texas, former Republican congressman Ron Paul—who had last served in Congress 12 years before and who had written articles in the intervening period that some characterized as racist and anti-Israel—was returned to office. Freshman Republican Steve Stockman, who had come under criticism for his ties to the militia movement, was defeated in his bid for reelection.

When the smoke had cleared, and assorted runoffs, recounts, and challenges were concluded, Republicans continued to control the House, but by a somewhat reduced margin. The Senate, in contrast, saw Republicans strengthen their hold with a net gain of two seats. The changes in numbers and, to some extent, the turnover in seats to new faces, even where the party holding a given seat remained the same, led to the expectation that the House would be somewhat more moderate on issues of concern to the Jewish community, while the Senate would be more conservative and ideological than before.

In terms of Jewish members, Senators Carl Levin (D., Mich.) and Paul Wellstone (D., Minn.) were reelected, leaving the Senate with its *minyan* (prayer quorum) of ten. In the House, 25 Jews were elected to the 105th Congress, the same as at the start of the prior Congress. All 22 Jewish incumbents who sought reelection were successful. Of the remaining three, one retired (Anthony Beilenson of California), one ran for the Senate midterm and won (Ron Wyden of Oregon), and one ran for the Senate at the end of his term and lost (the above-mentioned Dick Zimmer of New Jersey). The three Jewish newcomers, all Democrats, were Steve Rothman of New Jersey, Brad Sherman of California, and Robert Wexler of Florida. Tough reelection fights were won by freshman Republican Jon Fox of Pennsylvania, whose 10-vote election night margin grew to a grand 84 votes by final tabulation, and Democrats Jane Harman of California and Sam Gejdenson of Connecticut.

The congressional voting pattern of the Jewish population, taken overall, was similar to the presidential vote. Exit polls showed Jews favoring Democratic House candidates over Republicans by a margin of 74 to 26.

Following the 1996 election Jewish advocates began to consider how they might cultivate a moderate center of Republicans and Democrats in the 105th Congress, to fend off the drastic budget cuts and conservative social initiatives that had been on the agenda in the 104th. To the surprise of some, 1997 turned out to be relatively uneventful on the legislative front (see below).

Two studies appearing toward the end of 1997 provided a coda for the 1996 elections. First, it was announced in November that a forthcoming issue of *Fortune* magazine would name the American Israel Public Affairs Committee (AIPAC) as the second most powerful interest group in Washington. The ranking was based on a survey of Washington policy analysts and rated AIPAC high for "the votes it can deliver."

Later that month, the Washington-based Center for Responsive Politics issued a study revealing that pro-Israel donors continued to favor Democrats by a 2-1 margin: some $4.2 million from pro-Israel PACs going to Democrats as compared to $1.5 million given to Republicans. However, there was a rise in giving by Jewish donors to Republican candidates compared to the previous congressional election, and a decline in contributions to the Democratic side. The study also showed a 17-percent decline in overall Jewish giving from 1994, perhaps reflecting a general drop in giving by younger Jews to established Jewish organizations as well as a distaste for politics arising out of the ongoing campaign finance scandals.

As 1997 closed, the Jewish community awaited argument before the Supreme Court in a case with substantial political implications. Just about one year earlier, in December 1996, the full U.S. Court of Appeals for the D.C. Circuit had ruled that the American Israel Public Affairs Committee, AIPAC, should be regulated as a political action committee (or "PAC") because it had ostensibly been involved in raising funds for candidates for public office. Notwithstanding its acronym, AIPAC is organized not as a political action committee but as a nonprofit organization engaged in lobbying. It strongly denies that it has been involved in activity that should bring it under the jurisdiction of the Federal Election Commission. In June 1997 the U.S. Supreme Court agreed to hear AIPAC's appeal from the ruling.

The Religious Right

Following Election Day 1996, leaders of the religious right—the Republican Party's socially conservative constituency—who had made no secret of their unhappiness over Bob Dole's lack of enthusiasm for their agenda even as he mouthed support, refused to accept any blame for his defeat. Instead, asserted Ralph Reed, executive director of the Christian Coalition, "Conservative evangelicals had provided the fire wall that prevented a Bob Dole defeat from mushrooming into a meltdown all the way down the ballot." On the Sunday prior to the election, the Christian Coalition distributed 46 million voter guides to 125,000 churches covering local races and Congress. This and other similar efforts were said to have made the difference in reelecting a Republican Congress for the first time in 69 years.

Adversaries of the religious right, on the other hand, were quick to point out that the 1996 election was hardly a reaffirmation of the conservatives' agenda, neither in the presidential race (whatever the right's disenchantment with him, Bob Dole was clearly the candidate of preference) nor in congressional races, in which the most conservative candidates had a mixed record, at best. Of the Republican incumbent representatives defeated in 1996, more than half were among those most highly rated by the Christian Coalition. On the other hand, the Senate took on a markedly more socially conservative cast.

However 1996 was interpreted, it remained certain that the religious right would remain heavily engaged in the political process, with Christian Coalition founder Pat Robertson already promising that religious conservatives would not again accept in 2000 a "peripheral" role in the presidential race. And even before the election Ralph Reed stressed the priority that conservative Christians would continue to place upon local races. "I'd rather have a thousand school board members and 2,000 state legislators than a single president," he said. Commented Mark Melman, a Democratic pollster, "In race after race, they nominated their candidate for Congress, for Senate, for state legislature. That's real power in the political process, and we ignore that power at our peril." Trying hard not to ignore that "peril," the Interfaith Alliance and the National Jewish Democratic Council undertook to distribute their own voter guides in 1996, albeit with a far more modest distribution. But Matthew Brooks, executive director of the Republican-affiliated National Jewish Coalition, asserted that the divergence between the Jewish community and the Christian Coalition had been overstated, commenting that "it's not in the Jewish community's interests to focus on what separates us," but on "ways to cooperate."

No such cooperation was in evidence when, in early February 1997, the Christian Coalition announced its "Samaritan Project," a package of priorities described as a "bold plan that shatters the color line and bridges that gap that has separated us from our African American and Latino brothers and sisters." The package's components included calls for tuition vouchers and church-run drug rehabilitation programs, initiatives that the coalition had long supported. This led Phil Baum, executive director of the American Jewish Congress, to call the project nothing but a "cosmetic rearrangement . . . under the guise of a new preoccupation with the plight of the disadvantaged minorities," and Rabbi David Saperstein, director of the Religious Action Center of Reform Judaism, to say that the Christian Coalition's "real priorities remain changing the Constitution to tear down the wall separating church and state." But Rabbi Yechiel Eckstein, president of the International Fellowship of Christians and Jews, disagreed, calling the project "good for our country and . . . good for the Jews."

At the same time, leaders of a number of "progressive" religious groups conceded at an April 1997 conference convened by the Religious Action Center of Reform Judaism that it was the Christian Coalition and others on the religious right who seemed to have persuaded the public that theirs was the voice of religious authority. Noting that the abolitionist, disarmament, and civil-rights movements all had been strongly associated with "progressive religion," Rabbi Eric Yoffie of the Union of American Hebrew Congregations questioned why today's political left no longer spoke in religious language. "Perhaps liberals are no longer religious. Perhaps we are lost without the towering religious figures we had in the past. Perhaps we've misunderstood church-state separation," he said.

In May 1997, as Ralph Reed announced his departure from the Christian Coalition for the world of private political consulting, it remained clear that neither he nor the socially conservative movement that he had led would remain long unheard from. The question for some observers was whether, without Reed, the coalition would become more ideologically "pure" and less likely to make the kinds of choices that Reed had made when he swung his support behind Dole in 1996.

The Clinton Administration

During a visit to Poland the first week of July 1996, First Lady Hillary Clinton visited the Auschwitz-Birkenau death camp. Shaken by the mountains of human hair and stacks of eyeglasses, shoes, and children's clothing displayed there, she condemned Holocaust denial and spoke of the need not to "let up for a minute in your condemning of extremism and intolerance." She traveled from the camp to Warsaw where she met representatives of the Polish Jewish community; at the other end of the emotional spectrum, she was treated to a serenade of Hebrew songs by children at a Jewish kindergarten.

Just after President Clinton's reelection in November 1996, Secretary of State Warren Christopher announced that he was resigning his post as of the upcoming second inauguration. The announcement was, by and large, met with praise for Christopher from the Jewish community for his efforts to move the peace process forward. Accolades came from, among others, AIPAC and the Conference of Presidents of Major American Jewish Organizations. But a dissenting voice was heard from the Zionist Organization of America, which pronounced Christopher a "major disappointment" for having "ignored Yasir Arafat's anti-peace behavior."

On December 5, 1996, President Clinton announced his new foreign policy team, designating Czech-born Madeleine Albright, the U.S. ambassador to the United Nations, as the next secretary of state. Although she was not Jewish, her parents had fled the Nazi occupation, leaving her with a family history of displacement with which many American Jews were familiar. An already high-ranking Jewish aide, Samuel Berger, was named as national security adviser. Retiring senator William Cohen, named to be secretary of defense, also had a Jewish connection: his father is Jewish, his mother is not; Cohen does not consider himself Jewish. But all of this was secondary to the positive response of most of the Jewish community to these appointments, based on the past performance of the officials and the sense that the administration would maintain continuity in its role in the Middle East.

In a surprising turn of events, the accession of Albright to the post of secretary of state quickly became a "Jewish story" in a very personal sense as she was confronted with evidence—soon after formally assuming the office on January 23, 1997—that at least three of her grandparents were Jewish. Those grandparents, as well as many other relatives, died in the Holocaust. Albright's parents, who fled Czechoslovakia in 1939 shortly after the Nazi invasion of that country, raised their daughter as a Roman Catholic and never told her about her Jewish background. Ironically, the story of her past, which came to light as the result of an investigation by the *Washington Post*, was published just as she was about to depart for her first visit to Israel as secretary of state. Later in 1997, she visited the Pinkas Synagogue in Prague where she found the names of her paternal grandparents inscribed on the walls together with the names of more than 77,000 other Czech and Slovak Holocaust victims. Afterward, Albright commented with clear emotion that in earlier tours of Prague she had been at that synagogue, but "I did not know my own family story then. Tonight, I knew to look for those names . . . . To the many values and many facets that make up who I am, I now add the knowledge that my grandparents and members of my family perished in the worst catastrophe in human history."

Some other high-ranking appointments during the latter half of 1996 and in the year 1997 had Jewish provenance that was less of a surprise. In January 1997, one-time Democratic Party official Steve Grossman resigned his position as chairman of the American Israel Public Affairs Committee to become national chairman of the Democratic National Committee, taking on the party position at a time when Democrats were wrestling with a host of illegal campaign-contribution issues. The appointment of Grossman, who had earlier served as AIPAC's president, was hailed by party colleagues, Jewish and non-Jewish alike.

A trio of high-ranking appointments of persons well known to the Jewish community were confirmed by the Senate in 1997. The Australian-born Martin Indyk, who had served from April 1995 to the fall of 1997 as the first Jewish U.S. ambassador to Israel, was confirmed in November 1997 to the position of assistant secretary of state for Near Eastern affairs. Daniel Kurtzer, an observant Jew with a long record in the foreign service, including duty with Dennis Ross in the peace process beginning in 1991, was confirmed as U.S. ambassador to Egypt. Kurtzer announced plans to keep the ambassador's residence kosher. And in June 1997 Stuart Eizenstat—who had served every Democratic president since Lyndon Johnson and had been the Clinton administration's point person on Holocaust restitution issues—was sworn in as under secretary of state for economic, business, and agricultural affairs. Kurtzer turned to Eizenstat for advice on keeping a kosher kitchen while on a diplomatic posting since Eizenstat, during his earlier term as U.S. representative to the European Union, had been the first U.S. ambassador to do just that.

In December, with the simultaneous celebration of Christmas and an unusually late Hanukkah, President Clinton, with children from an area day school in attendance, held a menorah lighting ceremony in the Oval Office on the Jewish festival's first night. He noted that the ceremony marked the start of a yearlong celebration of the 50th anniversary of the founding of the Jewish state.

1997 Elections

As usual, there was little electoral activity during an odd-numbered off year. Worthy of note, however, was the strength of the normally Democratic Jewish vote in New York in support of the reelection of Republican mayor Rudolph Giuliani—72 percent as compared to the 27 percent vote for his Jewish Democratic challenger, Ruth Messinger. In contrast, New Jersey Jewish voters favored State Senator James McGreevey, the Democratic challenger, over Governor Christie Todd Whitman, the Republican incumbent, by a margin of 55.7 percent to 40.2 percent. Governor Whitman squeaked by to win reelection by one percentage point.

Terrorism

In July 1996 Illinois governor Jim Edgar signed into law a state counterterrorism bill imposing criminal penalties for providing funds or other material support to groups engaged in international terrorist activity. There was also a flurry of activity at the federal level at the beginning of August as the House of Representatives passed a bill intended to supplement the omnibus antiterrorism legislation signed into law by President Clinton in April 1996. But that new bill, which included measures to enhance airport security, extend the Racketeer Influenced Corrupt Organizations Act (RICO) to terrorism offenses, and create a bipartisan "blue ribbon" panel on terrorism, was not taken up by the Senate and died with the close of the 104th Congress. Before it adjourned for the election season, Congress did, however, enact the Iran and Libya Sanctions Act, a bill directed at deflecting major foreign investment in those countries because of their support for terrorism.

In January 1997 the Anti-Defamation League wrote to Secretary of State Warren Christopher expressing disappointment that no designations had been made of foreign terrorist organizations, pursuant to the authority provided in the 1996 federal antiterrorism law. The naming of groups as foreign terrorist organizations would bar them from raising funds in, or having access to, the United States. In the fall, Secretary of State Madeleine Albright issued the long-awaited list.

Based on a provision of the new antiterrorism law that affords American citizens the right to seek civil damages against states that sponsor terrorists, in February 1997 Stephen Flatow, father of the 20-year-old American victim of an April 1995 suicide bombing in the Gaza Strip, announced that he would bring suit for $150 million against Iran. Islamic Jihad, a foreign terrorist group that receives considerable support from Iran, claimed responsibility for the fatal attack. Flatow, noting that he was "not a sovereign state" and could not "wage war," described his action as a way to seek justice. Another family's quest for justice came to a conclusion later that year when, in August 1997, the PLO settled the lawsuit that had been brought by the family of Leon Klinghoffer after he was murdered by Palestinian terrorists during a 1982 cruise on an Italian ship, the *Achille Lauro*. Even as it settled the case by paying an undisclosed amount to the Klinghoffer family, the PLO admitted no wrongdoing, maintaining as it had ever since the incident that the attack had been carried out by a renegade group.

Another U.S. case, that of Mousa Mohammed Abu Marzook, a Hamas leader and sometime-U.S. resident, was resolved in 1997. Marzook had been taken into custody when he tried to enter the country in July 1995 because of his suspected involvement in terrorist activity, which made him subject to deportation under domestic immigration law. Before the deportation proceeding could move forward, Israel requested his extradition. For over a year, Marzook, who denied that he had been anything other than a fund-raiser and a political organizer for Hamas, resisted extradition. Then, in January 1997 Marzook surprisingly announced that he would no longer fight extradition; four months later, Israel — fearing that an Israeli trial of Marzook would lead to an upsurge of violence by Palestinians — decided in April to drop its extradition request. As U.S. authorities began once again to prepare deportation proceedings, Jordan agreed to accept Marzook in what one report characterized as "a humanitarian gesture." An Israeli official was quoted as saying that deportation to Jordan was the "most convenient" way of handling the matter and that Israel trusted Jordan's King Hussein to "know how to contain Marzook's activities."

Left unresolved, probably forever, was the question of whether a 69-year-old Palestinian man's shooting of seven people (one fatally) and then himself atop the Empire State Building on February 23, 1997, was in any way politically connected. Police officials later reported that they found on Ali Abu Kamal's person two letters in English and Arabic condemning Zionism and the United States, France, and Great Britain for their supposed role in oppressing the Palestinian people. But Kamal's family asserted that he had no connection to militant groups, and it seemed likely that distress over financial losses had contributed to his action.

The Jewish community of Jacksonville, Florida, was astounded when, in March 1997, Harry Shapiro, the owner of a recently failed kosher butcher shop, was arrested for making a bomb threat against, and placing a bomb at, a local Conservative synagogue, hours before former Israeli prime minister Shimon Peres was scheduled to speak there. The bomb threat had been made by a caller identifying himself as affiliated with "American friends of Islamic Jihad." No sign of the bomb was found at the time, and Peres's speech went ahead on February 13 as scheduled. Nine days later the device was found on the premises by children and was destroyed by the police without harm to anyone. Shapiro, who later turned himself in, was said to be both very angry that his business had recently closed and opposed to Peres's policies on the peace process. In June Shapiro pleaded guilty to the federal crime of using an explosive to threaten a foreign official and guest of the United States and was sentenced to ten years in prison.

The potential for domestic terrorism hit home on April 24, 1997, during the week of Passover, when an envelope oozing "red liquid" was found in the mailroom at the Washington headquarters of B'nai B'rith International. The building — which also houses offices of the Council of Jewish Federations, the Hebrew Immigrant Aid Society, and the National Council of Soviet Jewry — was sealed, and all of the people inside quarantined for a period of several hours, while investigators and emergency personnel came onto the scene. A five-block radius was cordoned off, with traffic jams ensuing in downtown Washington into the evening rush hour, and some people trapped in neighboring buildings as well. By 8:30 P.M., authorities had determined that the substance in the envelope was not toxic and allowed everybody to leave. The Jewish Telegraphic Agency later reported that a letter contained in the envelope included a note that was "anti-Jewish" and made threats that were "not specific." For B'nai B'rith, the experience was an unsettling one of *deja vu*. Just over 20 years before, in March 1977, its staff had been held hostage when B'nai B'rith's offices were taken over by Black Muslim extremists.

In August 1997 Ghazi Ibrahim Abu Maizar, a Palestinian who had earlier been apprehended for illegally entering the United States, was arrested in Brooklyn for possession of at least two active suicide bombs in his apartment. Questions were immediately posed as to how he had been allowed to stay in the country, pending deportation, without his background being investigated, and whether he had been acting alone or as part of a conspiracy linking him to Mideast terrorist groups. Although no connection between Abu Maizar and Hamas was demonstrated, law enforcement officials were quoted as saying that the organization had raised tens of millions of dollars in the United States.

The week of Abu Maizar's arrest also saw a trial begin in a New York federal court of Ramzi Ahmed Yousef, charged as the mastermind in the 1993 World Trade Center bombing. A jury convicted Yousef on those charges in November 1997.

Soviet Jewry, Refugees, and Immigration

As the 104th Congress closed for business in October 1996, one of its final actions was the enactment of legislation providing for a major overhaul of federal immigration law. Having earlier succeeded in stripping out of the immigration bill provisions that would have substantially cut back on the number of "family preference" immigrants to be afforded visas, Jewish advocates spent much of July through October working to mitigate some of the remaining problems in the legislation. There were some successes. The bill that the president ultimately signed into law no longer included the so-called Gallegly Amendment, a provision that would have allowed states the option of denying free public education to undocumented children. Nor did it include provisions that would have denied legal immigrants benefits even beyond what had been done in the welfare law enacted earlier that year.

But the new immigration law still included provisions that could be harmful to persons arriving on these shores seeking asylum from persecution. One section subjects people traveling with irregular or no documentation to "expedited exclusion" at all ports of entry unless they can establish a "credible fear of persecution" in an on-the-spot interview with a low-level INS officer; another provision requires asylum seekers to file an asylum application within one year of arriving in the United States, with only very narrow exceptions.

On March 5, 1997, a coalition of ethnic, immigrant advocacy, and civil-rights groups held press conferences in Washington, D.C., New York, and Los Angeles calling on the federal government to make the naturalization process accessible to all immigrants who are eligible to become U.S. citizens. These press conferences—as well as similar events in other cities later that month—took place prior to hearings by the congressional Oversight Committee on Naturalization, which reviewed U.S. naturalization procedures used in recent years. The press conferences stressed the contribution immigrants had made to the United States and the importance of naturalization in binding the nation and immigrants to one another.

In 1997 Jewish advocates were also faced with a proposal by the administration to reduce the number of refugee "slots" to be made available to Jews and others fleeing from persecution in the former Soviet Union. In its initial proposal for fiscal year 1998, the administration announced its intention to allot 21,000 places for refugees from that group of nations, some 9,000 fewer than the previous year. But, as the fiscal year began in early October 1997, the administration indicated that an additional 5,000 slots would be available, for a total of 26,000. "It's closer to the reality of the total flow," commented Martin Wenick, executive vice-president of the Hebrew Immigrant Aid Society. Even so, this represented a reduction from the previous year's figure of 30,000.

As Congress adjourned at the end of 1997, Jewish advocates succeeded (as they had done in 1996 for FY 1997) in extending for one more fiscal year—through September 1998—the so-called Lautenberg Amendment, which affords Jews and Pentecostal Christians from the former Soviet Union, among others, a reduced burden of proof in making the case that they should be granted refugee status by the United States.

Foreign Aid

As in previous years, maintaining U.S. aid to Israel remained a priority of the organized Jewish community. In 1996, $12 billion in U.S. aid worldwide was folded into the omnibus spending bill that was passed by Congress as it rushed to adjourn for the election season. The bill included $3 billion for Israel—with crucial provision for early dispersal—as well as $80 million for refugee resettlement and $50 million for antiterrorism efforts. It also provided for $2.1 billion in aid to Egypt, $75 million for the Palestinians in connection with the peace process, and the last installment on the forgiveness of Jordanian debt.

Final passage of the foreign-aid bill for fiscal year 1998 was also held up until the end of a congressional session, this time passing as part of a marathon session just before Congress adjourned at the end of 1997. As with the bill passed in 1996, the FY98 bill also fully funded Israel's foreign-aid program. It also included a ban on direct U.S. aid to the Palestinian Authority, an action largely seen as symbolic inasmuch as the $100 million in annual aid to the Palestinians was largely provided through nongovernmental agencies. Pursuant to an agreement with the White House, Israel returned $50 million of its $3 billion in aid, which was then paid to Jordan; Egypt also contributed $50 million toward a total U.S. aid package for Jordan of $225 million.

Sheinbein Extradition Case

A Maryland murder case took on unexpected international ramifications when one of two suspects in the crime, 17-year-old Samuel Sheinbein, fled to Israel in September 1997. Sheinbein's father had been born in British Mandate Palestine and received Israeli citizenship with the founding of the Jewish state in 1948, arguably bestowing Israeli citizenship on his American-born son as well. Israeli law forbids extradition of its citizens, although it does provide that a citizen may be tried in an Israeli court for a crime committed abroad. A furor erupted immediately as claims were made in the United States that Sheinbein might avoid prosecution through this "loophole."

With parties as diverse as the U.S. government and the Anti-Defamation League agreeing that a way should be found for Israel to extradite Sheinbein, Rep. Robert Livingstone (R., La.), chairman of the House Appropriations Committee, took a more extreme position. In a statement issued in October 1997 he indicated he would take steps to reduce the aid to Israel then pending in a bill over which his committee had jurisdiction if Israel did not extradite Sheinbein. Both the National Jewish Democratic Council and the Republican-affiliated National Jewish Coalition urged Livingstone not to link the Sheinbein affair to Israel's foreign aid, noting that Israel's hands might be tied by its own law. The crisis was defused somewhat when, later that month, Israel announced that it was rejecting Sheinbein's claim to dual citizenship and that it was, accordingly, prepared to extradite him to the United States, leading Livingstone to say that he intended to take no action with respect to aid to Israel. But, with an announcement that Sheinbein intended to challenge the Israeli government's decision and fight extradition, the expectation was that a U.S. trial might be years off.

Communal Implications of the Budget Process

On August 22, 1996, President Clinton signed the welfare reform bill into law, effectively dismantling the 60-year-old federal guarantee of assistance to any eligible poor American and placing the responsibility on the states to create and maintain their own welfare and work programs. Along with lifetime limits and work requirements that many in the Jewish community found problematic because they were not sufficiently flexible, the community devoted the greatest attention—and concern—to the law's implications for permanent legal residents who had not become citizens. Most legal immigrants, including those already in the country, were barred from Supplemental Security Income (SSI) and Food Stamps, and those arriving after the date of the law's enactment faced even more stringent cutbacks. In so doing, the welfare reform law stripped legal immigrants of benefits for which they had long been eligible on virtually the same terms as citizens and threatened to impose a harsh burden on social-service providers as they attempted to cope.

Jewish community workers strove to prepare their organizations and the populations they served for the conditions they would face as the new, state-based system went into effect, even as they advocated for restoration of those benefits. Jewish advocates in Washington and around the country, working with similarly minded communities, urged that states implementing the new system maintain the safety net—and urged Congress and the president to mitigate the unintended consequences of the welfare law on legal immigrants. These coalition efforts were spearheaded within the Jewish community by the Council of Jewish Federations.

Tens of thousands of Jewish immigrants were among those who lost nutrition benefits when food stamps were cut off on April 1 and faced the prospect of losing SSI benefits as of August 1. In a reprise of the Soviet Jewry rallies of the 1980s, thousands gathered on the steps of the U.S. Capitol in April 1997 to urge "Don't abandon our elderly and sick." Following up on the promise he had made at the reform law's signing—that he would seek to undo the provisions denying benefits to legal immigrants—President Clinton's 1998 budget proposed restoration of a portion of the benefits taken from legal immigrants. After a consensus emerged in Congress that there be at least some relief for legal immigrants, the budget finalized in the summer of 1997 included a substantial restoration of access to SSI benefits for legal immigrants.

The welfare reform "fix" failed, however, to restore food stamps for legal immigrants and refugees. Thus, as 1997 ended, the Council of Jewish Federations—working together with Jewish and non-Jewish coalition partners—was campaigning to have the administration include restoration of those benefits in the budget to be issued in January 1998. Speaking of Jewish elderly immigrants who had lost federal benefits, Diana Aviv, director of the CJF Washington office, said, "In our community, we're going to have death or starvation or serious crises in our emergency rooms."

In a related development, Jewish organizations applauded the Senate's defeat of the Balanced Budget Amendment in March 1997, a measure that they contended would have led to cuts in foreign aid and social programs.

ANTI-SEMITISM AND EXTREMISM

Assessing Anti-Semitism

In November 1996 the Federal Bureau of Investigation unveiled its annual report on hate crimes, in which it revealed that American Jews had overwhelmingly been the most frequent victims of hate crimes based on religion for 1995—some 1,085 incidents or 83 percent of all religion-motivated attacks. This figure also constituted some 13 percent of all hate crimes for the year. As is always the case, however, these reports were subject to the caveat that, because neither state nor local law enforcement reporting is obligatory, the absolute numbers of offenses and even their proportions provide only a partial picture.

The Anti-Defamation League's annual audit of anti-Semitic incidents released in February 1997 indicated a decline in incidents for the second year in a row: 1,722 incidents were reported to the ADL in 1996, a drop of about 7 percent from 1995. The report reflected the lowest figures since 1990 and stood in contrast to 1994's record high of 2,004 incidents. While incidents involving harassment or threat of assault dropped by about 15 percent as compared to the previous year, incidents of anti-Semitic vandalism in fact increased from 727 incidents to 781, a 7-percent rise. Despite this, the ADL greeted the results of its report as good news. "It tells us that the combination of law enforcement action and educational outreach is an effective one-two counterpunch that is reaping results in the traditional arenas where anti-Semites are active," said ADL national director Abraham Foxman.

The American Jewish Committee cautioned against reading too much into the relative decline of incidents as reported in the ADL audit. "Anti-Semitic incidents are only part of the package," said Kenneth Stern, AJCommittee's program specialist on anti-Semitism and extremism, noting that hate and antigovernment groups continued to present a threat to the "security of Jews and the vibrancy of American democracy." And both ADL and the Simon Wiesenthal Center viewed with alarm what Rabbi Abraham Cooper, the center's associate dean, described as an "absolute explosion of hate sites on the Internet." "We're looking at the emergence of a subculture of hate on the Internet," he added, "and that unfortunately means that the potential pool of young people into these particular groups is much broader."

In light of the ADL's reported decline in number of incidents, the American Jewish Committee's 1997 Annual Survey of American Jewish Opinion, released in May, held particular interest. It showed that American Jews continued to have an "ongoing sense of anxiety" about anti-Semitism, considering it a greater threat to Jewish life in the United States than intermarriage. This finding, asserted AJCommittee's director of research David Singer, reflected a "significant gulf between mass Jewish opinion" and findings in studies of the general population that do not reflect anti-Semitism to be as widespread as the Jewish perception. The AJCommittee study also found that American Jews who were intermarried were far more likely than those who were not to consider anti-Semitism to be a greater threat than intermarriage.

Acts of Violence

In the early morning of September 14, 1997, an Atlanta synagogue and cars in front of a senior citizens' facility at an Atlanta Jewish community center were spray-painted with anti-Semitic graffiti, including swastikas in red paint. It was not known whether the incidents were connected. Non-Jewish clergy and political leaders quickly rallied to condemn the actions, and a $4,000 reward for information leading to the arrest and conviction of the perpetrators was posted by area churches, a local homeowners' association, and the local Republican Party.

As the year closed, a task force of federal and local officials was at work in Los Angeles investigating two fires that broke out on December 28 at synagogues in the city's Fairfax district, both apparent arsons. The task force, set up following the 1996 burnings of black churches in the South, was charged with carrying out a preliminary investigation to be followed by a decision in Washington as to whether a formal civil-rights inquiry was appropriate. That same week also saw the vandalization of a publicly displayed menorah in Scarsdale, New York (three of the menorah's arms were torn off) and the spray-painting of a swastika on an Islamic star-and-crescent that was part of the seasonal display at the White House ellipse.

CROWN HEIGHTS RIOTS

On February 10, 1997, over five years after the anti-Jewish riots in the Brooklyn neighborhood of Crown Heights that claimed the life of Talmud scholar Yankel Rosenbaum, a federal jury convicted Lemrick Nelson, Jr., and Charles Price of violating Rosenbaum's civil rights in connection with that killing. Jewish leaders, who had been critical of an earlier state court verdict in which Nelson was acquitted of murder charges, hailed the federal verdict. "Justice at last has been done," said Howard Teich, president of the American Jewish Congress's Metropolitan New York Region. But Rabbi Avi Weiss, president of the Coalition for Jewish Concerns-Amcha, noted that "there was an entire mob that surrounded [Rosenbaum]" and called for further prosecutions.

As of year's end, sentencing of Nelson and Price had not yet taken place. Also still pending was a civil case brought against the City of New York alleging that the civil rights of Jews in Crown Heights had been violated because the city had not taken sufficient steps to protect them from the riots.

Other Anti-Semitic Incidents

In March 1997 *USA Today* reported on allegations that the Avis car rental company had an informal policy of discrimination against Jews in its rental practices. The matter emerged after one former employee provided an affidavit in a racial discrimination case against Avis asserting that Avis employees had been directed to avoid renting to "yeshivas," a code word for Hassidic Jews. Other former employees were quoted as saying that while at Avis they were on guard for customers with Jewish-sounding accents or names. Avis officials responded that the company had a strict policy against discrimination and that they intended to investigate the charges. In its report on the matter, the Jewish Telegraphic Agency noted that discrimination cases filed with the Equal Employment Opportunity Commission had risen to 319 in 1996, up sharply from 195 in 1990.

In September 1997, six Illinois Department of Public Health officials were directed by a U.S. district court to pay $250,000 to Sherwin Manor, a Jewish nursing home located in Chicago, for submitting false findings of federal and state violations by the facility during a routine certification survey. The district court's action followed a 1994 decision by the U.S. Court of Appeals for the Seventh Circuit, based on testimony about anti-Semitic remarks by the inspectors and substantial evidence refuting their charges against the nursing home, that Sherwin Manor's right to equal protection under the law had been violated by "verbal abuse accompanied by the imposition of a special administrative burden." In addition to falsely charging that the nursing home lacked no-smoking signs and that residents were not given a program of activities, the inspectors had assessed a violation against Sherman Manor because it failed to serve its residents pork, even though a varied diet of beef, chicken, and fish was available.

Legislative Activity

In June 1997 President Clinton announced a major initiative on race expected to take the form of a number of hearings and forums across the nation. In his announcement the president noted that the "classic American dilemma" of racism had become many dilemmas of race and ethnicity, and referred to "a resurgent anti-Semitism" that was present "even on some college campuses."

On November 10, 1997, more than 350 victims of hate crimes, law enforcement officials, educators, and representatives of advocacy groups participated in the daylong White House Conference on Hate Crimes at George Washington University, followed by an evening reception at the United States Holocaust Memorial Museum. Speaking at the conference, President Clinton termed hate crimes the "antithesis of the values that define us as a nation" and announced a number of new initiatives directed at hate-based violence, including plans to create hate-crimes working groups to be organized by the Attorney General at the national level and within the offices of the various U.S. Attorneys locally.

The president also took the occasion to endorse legislation introduced by Senators Edward Kennedy (D., Mass.) and Arlen Specter (R., Pa.), and with bipartisan support on the House side, that would extend the coverage of existing criminal civil-rights legislation. The legislation would encompass crimes based on gender, sexual orientation, and disability (crimes motivated by racial, religious, or national-origin animus being already covered) and expand the jurisdictional basis for such crimes to be prosecuted. Jewish groups, notably the ADL and the American Jewish Committee, had worked together with non-Jewish groups in helping to promote and craft the legislation as well as with the White House in planning the hate-crimes conference.

On the state scene, in February 1997 the New York State Assembly passed a state "hate crimes" law intended to heighten the degree of offense when acts of violence are motivated by bias and prejudice. The bill was defeated, however, in the New York State Senate.

INTERGROUP RELATIONS

Black-Jewish Relations

LOUIS FARRAKHAN AND THE NATION OF ISLAM

Louis Farrakhan and the Nation of Islam commemorated the one-year anniversary of the 1995 "Day of Atonement" in Washington, D.C., with a "World's Day of Atonement" rally in October 1996 in New York in which more than 30,000 people participated. Although some attending stressed that they were there to hear Farrakhan's message of black unity and not because of agreement with his anti-Jewish statements, his remarks—although critical of whites, the United Nations, and the United States—singled out only one ethnic group, the Jews. The Jewish Telegraphic Agency reported that "the minister's anti-Jewish rhetoric was . . . ardent and plentiful."

The 1996-97 period saw the Jewish community still in a quandary about how to respond to a racist and anti-Semitic movement that many respectable groups and government officials treated as legitimate. Following disclosure that a Nation of Islam representative had been designated by Washington, D.C., mayor Marion Barry as a member of the planning committee for a January 1997 D.C. "Day of Dialogue" on racial polarization, the ADL, the American Jewish Committee, and the American Jewish Congress announced that they would not participate in the event. Guila Franklin, director of the AJCongress's Washington area chapter, said that her organization's decision was made because "this was a day of dialogue that included a group that does not accept Jewish people and does not have respect for Jewish people."

In contrast, Operation Understanding, a Washington-based group dedicated to fostering communication between Jewish and black teenagers, and the National Conference (formerly National Conference of Christians and Jews) both indicated they would still participate. "I want to eradicate racism," said Cheryl Kravitz, executive director of the Washington office of the National Conference. "I'll do whatever it takes." In a similar vein, Philadelphia mayor Ed Rendell, a Jewish Democrat, invited—and then shared a podium with—Farrakhan at a local rally, with predictable adverse response from many Jewish agencies. The National Jewish Democratic Council commented that it was "saddened" by Rendell's action.

In July 1997 a federal district court ruled that a Nation of Islam-affiliated security firm would be allowed to proceed with its lawsuit against U.S. Representative Peter King (D., N.Y.) and New York State Assemblyman Jules Polonetsky, charging that they had conspired to deprive the company of its constitutional rights. The firm lost its contract to patrol a federally funded housing project in 1996, some two years after King and Polonetsky began urging termination of that contract on the grounds that the Nation of Islam was engaged in racial discrimination and that NOI security firm employees were using their positions to proselytize. The court's opinion reasoned, without reaching a conclusion on the merits, that the allegations as to King and Polonetsky's actions were, if true, sufficient to allow a judge or jury to find that the security firm was "retaliated against based on [its] association with the Nation of Islam and Farrakhan" or that the firm had been treated "selectively" on the basis of religion. American Jewish Congress legal counsel Marc Stern described the decision as "problematic" because government officials might be persuaded to "'just lay off'—it's too expensive and burdensome to bother with Farrakhan."

In another matter, the Nation of Islam was on the losing side when the Clinton administration announced in August 1996 that it would deny Farrakhan permission to receive a promised $1 billion in "humanitarian aid" from Libya. U.S. citizens may not engage in transactions of this nature with a state that has been found to support international terrorism, such as Libya, absent permission from the U.S. Treasury's Office of Foreign Assets Control. Officials of the Nation promised to seek redress in court, even as Jewish leaders hailed the decision.

A Farrakhan world tour at the end of 1997, including Israel and a planned meeting with Palestinian Authority chairman Yasir Arafat, posed some problems for Israeli officials. Initial consultations with American Jewish groups revealed a consensus that Israel should not bar Farrakhan from entering the country, because, in the words of Phil Baum, executive director of the American Jewish Congress, "it would appear that they fear him if they don't let him in." The American groups did, however, urge Israeli officials not to accord Farrakhan the respectability of an official visit with government officials, notwithstanding his expressed desire to discuss the Israeli-Palestinian peace process.

Although he had not been expected to arrive in Israel before mid-January, Farrakhan surprised Israeli officials when he crossed the border from Jordan to the West Bank in December. He left Israel after staying only one day, during which he met with officials of the Palestinian Authority, rather than going ahead with a visit to the Al-Aksa Mosque in Jerusalem. He cited security concerns, even though he had been assured by Israeli officials that they would see to his safety. Israeli officials had also made clear that they would not participate in any meeting with Farrakhan until he issued an apology for his anti-Semitic and anti-Zionist statements.

MAINSTREAM CIVIL-RIGHTS ORGANIZATIONS

The headlines garnered by the usual Jewish confrontations with the Nation of Islam hid to some extent the long-standing alliance between Jewish and black civil-rights organizations in the common cause of fighting hatred and combating discrimination. Jewish groups such as the ADL and the American Jewish Committee worked during 1996 and 1997 with the NAACP and the NAACP Legal Defense Fund, under the aegis of the Leadership Conference on Civil Rights (LCCR), to develop and promote new federal legislation directed at hate crimes (see above). And a number of Jewish organizations, such as AJCommittee, the National Council of Jewish Women, and the Union of American Hebrew Congregations, continued their work as members of the LCCR steering committee organized to defeat federal bills and state initiatives intended to prohibit the use of racial preferences in education and employment affirmative-action programs.

Jewish groups also became involved over the nomination of Bill Lann Lee, former director of an NAACP regional office, to the position of assistant attorney general for civil rights. When the nomination stalled in the Senate Judiciary Committee toward the end of 1997, they urged that the nomination be allowed to come to a Senate floor vote.

The makings of a fresh coalition effort began to emerge over an issue that had long been at the core of Jewish concerns — school vouchers. During 1997, as polls began to reveal increasing support for the voucher concept among African Americans, proponents of vouchers began to reach out to the black community for support. Thus, a press conference held by the Christian Coalition in February 1997 at the unveiling of its Samaritan Project (see "Religious Right," above) included a show of support by several black ministers. In a similar vein, representatives of the Union of Orthodox Jewish Congregations and Torah U'Mesorah: The National Society for Hebrew Day Schools came together with black advocates of vouchers, including Howard Fuller, professor of education at Marquette University and former superintendent of the Milwaukee public schools, at a July 1997 Capitol Hill press conference to announce the formation of a pro-vouchers coalition. "Once again," said Nathan Diament, director of the Orthodox Union's Institute of Public Affairs, "blacks and Jews are uniting in a common cause to secure hope and opportunity for all our children through excellent education." These efforts notwithstanding, mainstream organizations in both the Jewish and African-American communities remained adamantly opposed to vouchers, as reaffirmed in a resolution adopted by the NAACP at its annual convention that same month.

CIVIL-RIGHTS ISSUES

Even as several Jewish organizations joined with other civil-rights groups to turn back the assault on affirmative action taking place in Washington, they were also part of efforts to turn back state- and local-based initiatives to do the same thing. Thus, Jewish groups were part of the coalition that worked, unsuccessfully, to defeat the California ballot initiative, Proposition 209, barring government programs that include preferences based on race or gender. Exit polls following the November 1996 referendum showed Jewish voters opposing the initiative by a margin of 58-42, a sharp variance from the overall white vote favoring the proposition 63-37. (Blacks, Latinos, and Asians joined with Jews in opposing the initiative — by even wider margins.) One year later, the coalition formed to defeat an initiative to bar affirmative action in the city of Houston (with the active involvement of the Houston chapter of the American Jewish Committee) was more successful. Unlike Proposition 209, the Houston ballot proposition went down to defeat in November 1997.

In contrast to these efforts, Jewish and black groups differed in their responses to the case of *Piscataway Board of Education v. Piscataway.* That case, which was scheduled to be argued before the U.S. Supreme Court toward the end of 1997, involved a challenge to the laying off of a white schoolteacher by a New Jersey school board, while a black teacher with virtually identical credentials and seniority was kept on, in order to promote diversity. The school board, supported by a number of civil-rights groups in briefs *amici curiae*, defended its action as an appropriate application of affirmative action principles. Several Jewish organizations argued in a brief that the school board's action in *Piscataway* was a tenuous application of affirmative action principles. They joined others in the civil-rights community in welcoming the announcement in November 1997 that the New Jersey school board had settled the case out of court shortly before the Supreme Court was to hear argument. This resolution was made possible when a coalition of civil-rights groups agreed to pay 70 percent of the settlement fund rather than face the Court's determination of what they felt, agreeing on this point at least with the Jewish organizations, was a poor vehicle for the consideration of affirmative action principles.

OTHER MATTERS

With a keen eye to the parallel with the burning of synagogues in Germany in 1938, Jewish organizations quickly rallied in solidarity with some 40 black congregations whose churches had burned down in 1995 and 1996, many suspected to be racially motivated arsons. By July 1996 many agencies, both national and local, and synagogues were engaged in fund-raising drives — often in coordination with other faith groups — to rebuild the churches. By year's end, the Anti-Defamation League and the Urban League had presented more than a quarter-million dollars to the National Baptist Convention, representing black churches in the South, for this purpose. And the American Jewish Committee worked in partnership with the National Council of Churches and the National Conference of Catholic Bishops to administer an $8-million fund representing contributions from foundations and individuals as well as in-kind contributions. In other cases, Jewish youngsters and adults took a more direct hand, such as a group of black and Jewish teenagers who traveled from Washington, D.C., to Boligee, Alabama, to spend a July 4th holiday rebuilding that town's Mount Zion Baptist Church. Both Jewish and black leaders noted the silver lining in an otherwise troubling cloud, that these joint efforts allowed for strengthening of bonds between their communities that had been frayed by differences on other issues.

In a painful ending to these efforts, allegations began to surface in September 1997 that much of the money that had been paid to the National Baptist Convention to rebuild the burned churches never made its way to the affected communities. This followed reports that the Reverend Henry Lyons, president of the convention, had mishandled church money, a controversy that nearly led to his ouster. After an exchange of letters between Lyons's attorney and ADL, a portion of the money raised by ADL that had not yet been used to restore victimized churches, some $189,500, was returned to the Jewish group. In the meantime Florida prosecutors were looking into whether the handling of money by the National Baptist Convention violated the law. Lyons maintained throughout that he was innocent of any wrongdoing.

Other Ethnic-Jewish Relations

A matter that had been a minor irritant in Jewish-ethnic relations was resolved in September 1996, when the Anti-Defamation League settled a federal-class action suit that had been brought against it by a dozen ethnic organizations over alleged improprieties in ADL's information-gathering operation. The suit, which had been filed some three-and-a-half years earlier by Arab American, black, and Native American groups, as well as individuals, claimed that ADL's California offices had illegally spied on them and their members. While continuing to deny any wrongdoing, ADL agreed to pay $175,000 toward the plaintiffs' legal fees and to establish a $25,000 community relations fund. ADL also consented to a court-ordered limitation on certain information-gathering practices. Plaintiffs' attorney Peter Schey of the Center for Human Rights and Constitutional Law pronounced the settlement "fair," even as the ADL hailed it as "an appropriate way to put an end to what has been a particularly draining litigation."

The still tentative, but warming, relations between the Jewish American and Arab American communities that developed in the wake of Oslo and the peace process began to unravel almost as soon as the Netanyahu government was elected in May 1996. Approximately one month after the election, James Zogby, president of the Arab American Institute, was already asserting that Jewish Americans had "rolled over" in failing to protest changes from Labor policies. At an Arab summit held in Cairo in June, Khalil Jahsan, executive director of the National Association of Arab Americans—a group that had been engaged in dialogue and cooperative activity with the American Jewish Committee and the National Jewish Community Relations Advisory Council (NJCRAC)—called for a "freeze" in the normalization of relations with Israel. In a response typical of others in the Jewish community, Jess Hordes, Washington representative of the Anti-Defamation League, pronounced these statements "disturbing," calling them a reversion to "the old style of propaganda." NJCRAC associate executive vice chairman Martin Raffel called on Arab American leaders not to "prejudge" the new government. Nevertheless, Jahsan predicted that, given the difficulty American Jews would have in opposing Likud policies, "we will probably see a pulling away from these types of encounters where we have cooperative efforts."

Interreligious Relations

MAINLINE PROTESTANTS

In December 1996 and January 1997, Churches for Middle East Peace, a coalition of 15 liberal church groups that includes the National Council of Churches (an umbrella organization encompassing some 52 million people belonging to 33 mainline Protestant and Orthodox communions) ran ads in the *New York Times* and *Roll Call*, a Washington political newspaper, calling for shared control of Jerusalem by Israelis and Palestinians. The effort to influence U.S. policy toward Israel reflected by these ads was viewed by many in the Jewish community as part of a pattern of one-sided criticisms of Israel. And for some they reflected something more. The "constant criticism of the State of Israel," said Rabbi Leon Klenicki, interfaith affairs director of the Anti-Defamation League, "is the new way of theological anti-Judaism, of the teaching of contempt. Before they denied us a role in God's plan and now they want to deny us a place in history." The ADL issued an "open letter" condemning the ads, while the American Jewish Committee sent a letter to the ads' signatories—17 leaders of Christian communions and religious orders—elaborating on that organization's concerns.

Nevertheless, the mainline churches' perspective on Israel stood, as it had done for many years, in stark contrast to the cooperative relationship between those churches and Jewish organizations on such domestic policy matters as church-state separation and social-justice issues. And, it was announced in January 1997, Jewish leaders and national Protestant leaders had come together earlier that month to find at least some common ground on the Middle East by developing a joint statement supporting the Middle East peace process and the Oslo accords.

EVANGELICAL CHRISTIANS

The positions of evangelical Christians on the organized Jewish community's chief concerns presented a mirror image of the positions taken by the mainline Protestant churches. Thus, at a conference jointly convened in February 1997 by

Fuller Theological Seminary, a prominent Los Angeles evangelical school, and the American Jewish Committee, it was quite clear that evangelicals held differing views from their Jewish interlocutors on such domestic concerns as church-state separation and social policy—even as the ongoing evangelical Christian support for Israel was much in evidence. But more than policy disputes were on the agenda.

Some Jews at the conference questioned the purpose of dialogue when evangelical Christians believe they hold the only path to God's grace and make conversion of Jews a priority; conversely, some evangelical Christians questioned whether sharing a platform with Jews might not compromise their "position on evangelicism." Nevertheless, the Committee's interreligious affairs director, Rabbi A. James Rudin, stressed that the conference was a necessary step in the long-range effort to convince evangelicals that they should cease supporting "deceptive missionary activity." And, in a statement published later in 1997 in *Christianity Today*, Fuller president Richard Mouw asserted that while he had "a nonnegotiable commitment to evangelicism," he opposed "treating Jews as if they were only 'targets' for evangelism" and that evangelical Christians "must cooperate with Jews in working for the health of society."

The tensions between Jews and evangelical Christians on the issue of singling out Jews for missionary work had arisen earlier at the 15th National Workshop on Christian-Jewish Relations, held in November 1996 in Stamford, Connecticut, and attended by over one hundred leading Jewish and Christian clergy, including representatives of all four Jewish movements, Catholics, and Protestants (as well as at least one Muslim). This event was the first time that a high-ranking official of the Southern Baptist Convention was to meet with Jews since the convention's adoption earlier that year of a resolution explicitly making the missionizing of Jews a priority. A panel discussion featuring Philip Roberts, director of the convention's Interfaith Witness Department, and Jewish and Catholic clergy, extended to nearly three hours in what one observer called a "tumultuous" discussion as both Christians and Jews spoke out against the theology and the strategy represented by the resolution. AJCommittee's Rudin said that the Christian critique of the Southern Baptist position as being "a misreading of Christianity" was "heartening and validating."

At the same time, there was ample evidence during 1997 of the strong support for Israel to be found among many in the evangelical community. Thus, Israeli prime minister Benjamin Netanyahu was warmly received by some 3,000 people, mostly evangelical Christians, during an April 1997 visit to Washington. The conference was convened by Voices United for Israel, a group of "pro-Israel Jewish and Christian organizations" that seeks to build support for "a safe and secure Israel." Among those attending were Pat Robertson, Ralph Reed, and Jerry Falwell, who also met privately with Netanyahu. Responding to the criticism that Jews should not legitimize a group largely composed of organizations committed to proselytizing Jews, Voices United founder Esther Levens asserted, "The fact that the Prime Minister came and spoke is validation enough for what we are trying to accomplish, which is to have a very broad grass-roots support for the State of Israel."

And later that year, in September, the International Fellowship of Christians and Jews announced that it expected to be contributing some $5 million from 60,000 individual donors, mostly evangelical Christians, to the United Jewish Appeal—nearly doubling the contribution made by the fellowship the previous year. The funds would be designated mostly for costs associated with absorbing the large numbers of Jews from the former Soviet Union who immigrated to Israel, reflecting the contributors' belief that they were helping to fulfill biblical prophecies that the ingathering of Jews to Israel would precede the Second Coming. The growth in support by evangelical Christians was met with no little ambivalence by UJA officials, with the leadership directing that fund-raisers not be "proactive" in seeking funds from the evangelical community, even while "we say 'thank you' for what they are doing." Bernie Moscovitz, executive vice-president of UJA, explained, "Some of our leadership think it is perfectly all right to accept money even if their motivation is not identical to our own, and others think that it is better for Jews to take care of themselves."

CHURCH-STATE MATTERS

The period from midyear 1996 through the end of 1997 saw a confluence of issues and events relating to the proper relationship of church and state in a pluralistic and avowedly secular (but not secularist) state, an issue at the forefront of American Jews' concerns.

Judicial Action

In June 1997 the Supreme Court made two significant church-state decisions. One struck down the Religious Freedom Restoration Act; the second was in *Agostini v. Felton*, when, by a 5-4 vote, it overturned a 1985 ruling that barred public-school teachers from providing remedial instruction on-site at parochial schools. The decision dealt with a narrowly proscribed issue and was itself narrowly reasoned; nevertheless, it immediately opened the door to debate as to whether other types of public aid to parochial schools would now be able to win the Court's sanction. Within a month of the decision the Department of Education issued guidelines for public-school administrators as to how to carry out remedial programs in parochial schools while avoiding church-state entanglement. The guidelines—which are not binding—provided that parochial-school classrooms should be free of religious symbols when public-school teachers were providing instruction, and that those teachers should neither be engaged in "team teaching" with parochial-school teachers nor become involved in the parochial school's religious activities.

Both sides of the vouchers debate found ground for comfort in the *Agostini* decision, but it was far from clear how the Supreme Court would rule on the constitutionality of vouchers. During 1997, appeals courts in both Wisconsin and Ohio struck down local voucher programs as violating state constitutional provisions barring the use of state funds to support religious institutions. Both decisions were subject to further appeal to the high courts of the respective states in which they were rendered.

Alabama was a notable battlefield in the church-state debate. Thus, during 1997, a federal court struck down a 1993 state law that permitted student-initiated prayer; this followed a lawsuit by a public-school vice-principal who had unsuccessfully tried to stop the practice of prayer before sporting events and the handing out of Bibles in the classroom. The federal court also issued an order barring vocal prayers at school sporting events and Bible readings on school grounds. One of the counties affected by this ruling refused, with the support of Governor Fob James, to comply with the ruling. The Alabama attorney general asked that there be a delay in enforcing the decision pending appeal, claiming that the order violated students' free-speech rights.

In February 1997 Alabama state judge Roy Moore was directed by a superior court to remove a wooden carving of the Ten Commandments from his courtroom. At the time of the order, Alabama governor James announced that he would call out the National Guard and state troopers to prevent removal of the plaque. "The display of the Ten Commandments in Judge Moore's courtroom, in context and intent," said the American Jewish Committee in a statement that reflected the sentiment of many in the Jewish community, "clearly promotes religion. It is wrong for a court to suggest that people who might subscribe to a particular code, as represented by the tablets, may receive preferential treatment and those who do not might be looked upon with disfavor."

The controversy was compounded when, in early March, the U.S. House of Representatives voted 295-125 to adopt a "sense of Congress" resolution affirming that the Ten Commandments represent a "cornerstone of Western civilization and the basis of the legal system here in the United States" and supporting the placement of the Ten Commandments in courtrooms and government offices. The House resolution, although it was without binding effect and made no mention of the Alabama case, was seen as disturbing by many Jewish groups, not only on religious liberty grounds but also because it implicitly supported defiance of a court order.

And in August 1997 the American Civil Liberties Union filed a federal lawsuit on behalf of a Jewish family who alleged that their three school-age children, the only Jewish children in a rural Alabama school district, had been the target for several years of anti-Semitic slurs, proselytizing, and ridicule, often by school officials. In one instance, the suit claimed, a child's head was physically forced down during a school prayer service. Another child was said to have been directed to write an essay on "why Jesus loves me." Governor James acknowledged in a statement that "if any part of what is alleged in this lawsuit is correct, it is absolutely unacceptable."

In a case that could set important guideposts as to how courts should handle custodial disputes involving the religious upbringing of the children of divorce, the Massachusetts high court ruled in December 1997 that a lower court had acted within the law when it forbade a fundamentalist Christian father from taking his three children to church or enrolling them in Sunday school. Their mother, from whom he is divorced and who has custody of the children, is an Orthodox Jew. An appeal to the U.S. Supreme Court may be in the offing.

In May 1997 New York State's highest court struck down as unconstitutional the New York State legislature's second effort to provide a special school district for the Hassidic community of Kiryas Joel, an area in Rockland County that had earlier been designated as a separately incorporated suburban village, as a way to provide state-funded remedial education to Hassidic children outside of the usual public-school venue. An earlier effort to create this district had been struck down by the U.S. Supreme Court in 1994 as unconstitutional, immediately following which a new law was enacted purporting to create a more neutral basis upon which such a district could be established. But the New York high court's May ruling upheld the determination of an intermediate appellate court that the new law was a "subterfuge" designed to benefit Kiryas Joel. The Supreme Court's *Agostini* decision in June 1997 (see above) led some to speculate that the Kiryas Joel dispute was now moot because the state would be able to send public-school teachers into the Jewish schools to provide remedial services. But that did not happen. In August 1997—post-*Agostini*—New York State created a separate Kiryas Joel school district for the third time.

And in July 1996 a federal appellate court sitting in California ruled that the city of Beverly Hills had engaged in an unconstitutional establishment of religion when it allowed Chabad to erect a menorah in a public park while denying other groups permission to place religious symbols at the site. While not questioning the city's right to set a uniform policy of not permitting the placement of large unattended objects on public property, the court found that Beverly Hills had erred in this case by affording special treatment to one particular religious group. The suit challenging the city's action had been filed by a local chapter of the American Jewish Congress.

Finally, in December 1997, the federal court of appeals for the Tenth Circuit upheld a lower court's dismissal of the lawsuit brought by Rachel Bauchman, a Jewish high-school student in Salt Lake City who claimed that her constitutional rights had been violated when she was required to sing religious devotionals in her choir class and perform at churches and religious gatherings. She also claimed that her objections to these practices were ignored and led to harassment and death threats, and that the school made no attempt to stop these actions. Bauchman had been supported in her appeal by an array of Jewish and Christian groups, including the American Jewish Congress, the American Jewish Committee, the Anti-Defamation League, and the Union of American Hebrew Congregations. In the *amicus* brief filed on her behalf in 1996, several of these groups argued that the lower court's imposition of extraordinary procedural obstacles merely to get into court "clearly signals that those who would seek to preserve their religious liberties . . . will receive an unwelcome reception in the courts within [the Tenth Circuit]." A further appeal to the U.S. Supreme Court was expected.

Legislative Activity

To nobody's surprise, the 105th Congress saw a reprise of earlier initiatives to provide public funding for low-income families to be used toward tuition at private sectarian and nonsectarian schools. Perhaps more surprising, 1997 closed without any of these voucher initiatives having been passed by the Congress.

Proposals for a "religious freedom" constitutional amendment were not quick to emerge in the 105th Congress, reportedly because of disagreements that had emerged among pro-amendment factions in the previous Congress. Hearings had been held on proposals for such an amendment in July 1996 before the House Judiciary subcommittee on the Constitution. In the end, amendment proponents did not resolve their differences. There was no vote, either in committee or on the floor, before Congress recessed for the 1996 election.

The logjam showed some sign of breaking when it was revealed in May 1997 that the National Association of Evangelicals (NAE) had decided to endorse a new version of the amendment unveiled by Rep. Ernest Istook (R.,Okla.). Hearings on the revised Istook proposal were held before the subcommittee on the Constitution in September 1997. (The hearings were delayed for several days after Rep. Jerrold Nadler (D., N.Y.) and several Jewish groups alerted the chairman that he had inadvertently set the hearings for the Jewish holiday of Shemini Atzeret.) In November the initiative was sent on to the full committee by a strictly party-line vote. Notwithstanding that vote, along with endorsement by the House leadership and an impressive list of 150 cosponsors, there remained a strong sense that the bill was unlikely to achieve the two-thirds majority of the House, much less the entire Congress, necessary to send it on to the states for ratification.

Most Jewish groups remained adamant in their opposition, attacking the initiative as unnecessary and dangerous. "It's a catch-all problematic initiative that would mean vouchers and prayer in school with teacher participation and religious symbols in the heart of government," said Michael Lieberman, assistant director and counsel in the Anti-Defamation League's Washington office. There was some fall-off, however, as the initiative began to move forward. The Union of Orthodox Jewish Congregations (O.U.), despite its support for vouchers, had earlier joined a coalition that formed to oppose a constitutional amendment, based on a fundamental concern with any tampering with the First Amendment. But in 1997 the O.U. pulled out of the coalition, taking no position on the newest manifestation of the measure. "We're sort of caught in the middle," Nathan Diament, director of the union's Institute for Public Affairs told the Jewish Telegraphic Agency. "While we don't like the concept of constitutional, organized school prayer, we are in favor of the concept of school vouchers or other government programs being available on an equal basis to religious institutions and individuals."

The 1996 welfare reform law included a provision intended to direct tax dollars to religious institutions that, as with vouchers, highlighted a split in the Jewish community. That provision, termed "charitable choice" by its chief advocate, Sen. John Ashcroft (R., Mo.), allows religious institutions to provide the social services funded by the welfare law. The Orthodox supported the measure, but many in the Jewish community objected to the lack of appropriate safeguards against religious discrimination and to the use of public money for sectarian purposes. During the rest of 1996 and through 1997, Senator Ashcroft continued efforts to include similar provisions in other social-service legislation pending in Congress.

"Free-Exercise" Developments

Advocates of religious liberty suffered a severe setback when, on June 25, 1997, the U.S. Supreme Court issued a 6-3 ruling in *City of Boerne v. Flores,* striking down the Religious Freedom Restoration Act (RFRA) as unconstitutional, at least as applied to the states. The measure was enacted in 1993 to protect religious practice from government interference, and the Court's new decision left Jews and practitioners of other minority religions vulnerable to legislators and government officials who might sometimes be oblivious to the impact of their actions on religious observance. "Neutral laws regarding the drinking age and medical procedures could be enforced against Christian communion and Jewish circumcision rituals," the Anti-Defamation League commented. Almost immediately members of Congress began to consider, in consultation with legal scholars and advocates, what options might be available to reinstate at least some of the provisions of the RFRA, but by year's end, no revised version had been introduced in Congress.

There was some better news on other free-exercise fronts. On August 14, 1997, President Clinton formally issued Guidelines on Religious Exercise and Religious Expression in the Federal Workplace, a document that had been developed in consultation with a broad-based assemblage of religious and civil-rights groups including the American Jewish Congress, the Christian Legal Society, and People for the American Way. The guidelines, applicable only to federal employees, allow for a broad range of religious expression while recognizing that coercive proselytizing and religious harassment of employees on the job is not to be countenanced. The guidelines also establish a workable standard for accommodation of religious practice, such as Sabbath and holy day observance and the wearing of religiously required garb, in the workplace.

Progress was made, as well, in an ongoing effort to enact legislation that would expand workplace protections for religious employees in the private sector and at the state and local government level. The Workplace Religious Freedom Act (WRFA) was introduced in the Senate by John Kerry (D., Mass.) and in the House by Bill Goodling (R., Pa.), with Sen. Dan Coats (R., Ind.) and Rep. Jerrold Nadler (D., N.Y.), who had long promoted the need for this legislation, as the chief cosponsors in their respective houses. This reflected the first significant bipartisan support for the initiative. In another first, a hearing on workplace religious accommodation was held before the Senate Labor and Human Relations Committee on October 21, 1997, chaired by Senator Coats, a senior member of that committee. Witnesses included American Jewish Committee legislative director and counsel Richard Foltin, who chairs a coalition of over 30 religious and civil-rights groups that support WRFA, and John Kalwitz, an Orthodox Jewish resident of Indiana who lost his job when his employer refused to allow him to be excused from working on Saturdays.

HOLOCAUST-RELATED MATTERS

Holocaust Reparations

Allegations that Holocaust victims and their survivors had been wrongly denied access to money deposited in Swiss banks prior to and during World War II were very much at the fore at the end of 1996 and throughout 1997—and with a marked U.S. involvement. Following closely upon a call by the World Jewish Congress for Switzerland to establish a $250-million fund to provide compensation for misappropriated Jewish assets, Senate Banking Committee chairman Alfonse D'Amato (R., N.Y.) led the charge on the American political scene, holding hearings of his committee on the issue in December 1996. Shortly thereafter, outgoing Swiss president Jean-Pascal Delamuraz aroused accusations of "shocking insensitivity" from Jewish critics when, on New Year's Eve, he asserted that demands for such a fund in advance of the close of an internal investigation were "nothing less than extortion and blackmail." By mid-January 1997, Delamuraz—now Switzerland's economics minister—had apologized for offending the feelings "of the Jewish community at large," and negotiations between Swiss officials and Jewish representatives were said to be back "on track."

Another controversy emerged almost simultaneously. Christopher Meili, a security guard at a Swiss bank, rescued two binfuls of World War II-era documents from destruction and turned them over to the Zurich Jewish community organization, the Cultusgemeinde. The bank acknowledged that it had made a "deplorable mistake" in slating the documents for shredding, but nevertheless suspended—and then fired—Meili from his job, because turning bank papers over to a third party was said to violate Swiss bank secrecy laws. Meili received financial help from Swiss and American Jewish organizations, and in August 1997 he was granted asylum by the United States. As the Meili story was breaking, reports surfaced of a newly declassified 1946 American intelligence report that revealed that Switzerland had been actively involved in shipping looted gold for Nazi Germany.

During the rest of 1997, the Swiss government swung back and forth between efforts to put the best face on its earlier actions and present response, and defensive statements reflecting irritation at the way in which it was being depicted. Thus, in February the Swiss government announced that it would create a Holocaust Memorial Fund to benefit needy Holocaust survivors, not necessarily including those who were entitled to the proceeds of Swiss bank accounts, to be set up in cooperation with Swiss banks and insurance companies. In February the government also announced the creation of a foundation, subject to approval in a national referendum and by the nation's Parliament, to assist victims of the Holocaust and other catastrophes. But neither the Swiss government nor, for that matter, the United States or virtually any other of the World War II allies and neutrals was spared the harsh light of a U.S. government report, issued in May 1997, on the wartime role of those nations in dealing with gold looted by the Nazis. The report was prepared under the direction of Stuart Eizenstat, an American Jew who during the course of the report's preparation had been confirmed by Congress as under secretary of state for economic affairs.

A high point came in July when Swiss banks began to publish the names of titleholders to dormant accounts, welcoming those with a possible claim to those accounts to file applications. But even while the Jewish community continued its negotiations with Switzerland and the Swiss banks at year's end, matters were complicated by a class-action lawsuit brought against the banks by Holocaust survivors in a New York court and by the threat of American sanctions by state and local government actions directed at the Swiss. In December the United States, joined by the Swiss banks as well as by the World Jewish Congress and Israel, agreed on the need for a global settlement of all Holocaust-era claims, a move that up to that point the Swiss government had resisted. Edgar Bronfman, president of the WJC, had earlier suggested that a payment by Switzerland of billions of dollars would be required to close all of the pending matters, including claims having to do with dormant bank accounts and the Swiss purchase of looted gold from the Nazis.

In an effort to provide an example to other countries singled out by the Eizenstat report, in October 1997 Rep. James Leach (R., Iowa) introduced legislation authorizing the United States to pay $25 million in contributions to organizations serving Holocaust survivors residing in this country and calling for the return of art works looted by the Nazis to survivors of the original owners.

The U.S. Congress weighed in during 1997 in support of the efforts of the Conference on Jewish Material Claims Against Germany to have Germany pay reparations to Holocaust survivors living in Eastern Europe and the former Soviet

Union who had received little or no compensation (compared to survivors residing in the West who had received more than $54 billion since World War II). In August, 82 senators signed a letter to German chancellor Helmut Kohl, circulated by Senators Christopher Dodd (D., Conn.) and Kay Bailey Hutchison (R., Tex.), calling on Germany to make immediate payments to the survivors in the former Eastern bloc. This followed on the Senate's action the prior year in passing a resolution, sponsored by Senators Alfonse D'Amato and Daniel Inouye (D., Hawaii), to significantly expand eligibility for Holocaust survivor compensation. The August 1997 letter was placed in advertisements taken out in a range of national and international publications by the American Jewish Committee.

The matter received increased attention with the revelation that Germany was paying pensions to thousands of former SS and Nazi police veterans residing outside of Germany, even as it declined to pay reparations to a large group of Holocaust survivors. President Clinton raised the question with Chancellor Kohl earlier in 1997 during a visit by Kohl to the United States. Discussions between Jewish and German officials followed, giving rise to hope of a successful resolution. But as the year ended it was still unclear that the German government was prepared to make a financial contribution to those called by Rabbi Andrew Baker, director of European affairs for the American Jewish Committee, "the forgotten survivors." German officials cited concerns that any such payment would open the door to claims by hundreds of thousands of non-Jewish survivors of Nazi persecution still living in Eastern Europe. Negotiations were still under way at year's end to obtain compensation for about 27,000 survivors in Western countries, including the United States, who were not eligible because they did not meet the criteria of an annual income of less than $14,000 combined with having spent at least six months in a concentration camp or 18 months in a ghetto.

A federal class-action lawsuit filed in New York in April 1997 accused European insurance companies of failing to honor life and property insurance policies purchased prior to World War II by Jews, many of whom later perished in the Holocaust. The companies had offered a number of justifications for refusing to pay under the policies: that beneficiaries had not provided proof of death of the insured; that they (the companies) could not locate the policies or that they had expired when the insureds failed to make premium payments; or that Nazi-controlled or postwar Communist governments had compelled the companies to turn over the insurance holdings. Plaintiffs' attorney Edward Fagan asserted that the insurance companies "did not have the right to turn over the property of foreign nationals to those governments." And, referring to the issue of the lack of proof of death, another plaintiffs' attorney commented, "They knew full well that Auschwitz didn't issue death certificates." By one estimate the class action would involve more than 10,000 claims which, with average claims in excess of $75,000, would total in the billions of dollars. Shortly after the lawsuit was filed, one German insurance company—Allianz A.G., Europe's largest—announced its intention to investigate any claims and to honor its obligations under the wartime policies.

OSI ACTIONS

The Justice Department's Office of Special Investigations continued its work in seeking to identify, denaturalize, and deport Nazi war criminals who had entered the United States in the years following World War II. Thus, as 1996 wound down, OSI moved to revoke the American citizenship of Kansas City resident Michael Kolnhofer, accused of serving as an SS guard at the Sachsenhausen and Buchenwald concentration camps. That proceeding ended abruptly when the 80-year-old Kolnhofer died in March 1997, following a December 31 shoot-out with police that ensued after reporters had gathered at his house in the wake of OSI's filing.

At the end of January 1997—following the trial in a denaturalization proceeding in Cleveland—a federal judge directed that Algimantas Dailide be stripped of his citizenship because of his role in the persecution of Jews while serving as a member of the Nazi-linked Lithuanian security police force. In December 1997 a federal judge ordered the deportation of Johann Breyer, a resident of Philadelphia and a native of Slovakia, following his admission that he had served as an SS guard at Buchenwald and Auschwitz.

OTHER HOLOCAUST-RELATED MATTERS

In December 1997 the Canadian government—which had been criticized for not diligently tracking down suspected Nazi-era war criminals who made their way to that country—announced that former OSI director Neal Sher had been appointed as a consultant to Canada's war-crimes unit. Noting Sher's impressive record during his 12 years as head of OSI, Prof. Irving Abella, chairman of the Canadian Jewish Congress's war-crimes committee, hailed the development. "It is a sign," he said, "that the government does indeed realize that time is running out and that they must take whatever measures necessary to bring to justice the perpetrators of heinous crimes committed during World War II."

Jonathan Pollard

Jonathan Pollard, with the support of many American Jews and Israelis (including Israeli prime minister Benjamin Netanyahu), continued to seek early release from prison after serving ten years of a life sentence for spying on the United States on behalf of Israel. As the second half of 1996 began, President Clinton announced his decision to reject Pollard's pending clemency appeal, asserting through his press spokesperson that the "enormity of Mr. Pollard's offenses, his lack of remorse, the damage done to our national security, the need for general deterrence and the continuing threat to national security" had warranted the original life sentence, and that any shortening of that sentence would be "unwarranted." Proponents of the pardon were quick to express strong disappointment in the decision.

But this was far from the end of advocacy for Pollard's release. In May 1997 an unusual joint letter from Rabbi Eric Yoffie, head of the Union of American Hebrew Congregations, and Rabbi Raphael Pollard, head of the Union of Orthodox Jewish Congregations, called on President Clinton "to show mercy to Jonathan Pollard and commute his prison sentence." On October 29, 1997, Pollard petitioned Israel's High Court of Justice to direct the Israeli government to acknowledge that he had acted on behalf of the state, a petition still pending as of the end of 1997. In December 1997 the Knesset passed a resolution calling for his release. Also during the last weeks of 1997, Israel's absorption minister, Yuli Edelstein, and its communications minister, Limor Livnat, made visits to Pollard in prison, with Livnat delivering a message from Prime Minister Netanyahu expressing hope for Pollard's early release. During the latter visit, in remarks broadcast on Israeli television, Pollard apologized for his actions. "I am extremely sorry for what happened," he said. "My motives may have been well and good, but they only serve to explain why I did what I did. They certainly do not serve as an excuse for breaking the law."

RICHARD T. FOLTIN

Jewish Communal Affairs

Events in Israel from July 1996 through the end of 1997 profoundly affected American Jewish life. Benjamin Netanyahu was elected prime minister of Israel in May 1996, defeating incumbent Shimon Peres, who had taken office after the assassination of Yitzhak Rabin. Netanyahu's subsequent formation of a Likud-led right-of-center governing coalition, including the 23 Knesset members from the Orthodox parties, gave many American Jews grounds for concern. Not only was the new government likely to slow down if not halt the Rabin-Peres peace process, but it was also expected to press for legislation to reaffirm Orthodox hegemony over Israeli Judaism. Both the peace process and Jewish religious pluralism would be major matters of interest to American Jews over the next year and a half.

ISRAEL-RELATED MATTERS

Netanyahu and American Jews

Media interest was intense when the new prime minister of Israel arrived in the United States in July 1996, and he did not disappoint. In the words of the front-page story in the *New York Times* (July 11), Netanyahu "put his deep knowledge of American politics and lingo to work today, moving with verve through the stations of official Washington and spreading his message of Israeli self-confidence and skepticism about Arab intentions." Both in his talks with political figures and in meetings with Jewish groups in New York, Netanyahu promised that he would continue the peace process that the previous Labor government had begun, but said that he would be a tougher negotiator than his predecessors and insist that the Palestinians keep their commitments under the Oslo accords.

A poll of American Jewish opinion released by the Israel Policy Forum upon Netanyahu's arrival indicated that the community was favorably disposed to the new Israeli government: 81 percent of American Jews supported the Rabin-Peres peace process; 95 percent believed that its continuation was important for the United States; 59 percent said that they would have voted for Peres instead of Netanyahu, but 62 percent had a favorable view of the new prime minister; 64 percent felt that he was sincerely interested in continuing the peace process; and 85 percent thought that the process would continue under his government, albeit at a slowed pace. All in all, said Jonathan Jacoby, IPF executive vice-president, the results showed that American Jews viewed Netanyahu as a moderate.

Even so, Netanyahu's victory, capped by the successful U.S. visit, buoyed those elements of American Jewry that had been suspicious of the peace process all along. Morton Klein, president of the Zionist Organization of America (ZOA), expressed pleasure that "Arafat's violations of the peace accords" would now become "a central theme for achieving a real and durable peace." When Netanyahu took questions at a meeting of the Conference of Presidents of Major American Jewish Organizations, loud hissing greeted the executive director of Americans for Peace Now when he asked about Palestinian national aspirations; this was followed by sustained applause for the prime minister's reply that his concern was "the national aspirations of the Jews."

The centrist Jewish organizations, which had generally supported the Rabin-Peres peace policies, took a wait-and-see attitude. Thus David Harris, executive director of the American Jewish Committee, suggested that Netanyahu's "youthful vigor and communication skills" had made a positive impression on American Jews. But it remained to be seen, he said, whether the prime minister could count on the passionate support of grassroots American Jewry in times of crisis. Netanyahu, declared Harris, "remains a work in progress."

The first real test of American Jewish sentiment came in September, when the Israeli government opened a new entrance to an archaeological tunnel in East Jerusalem. Amid Muslim assertions that this act constituted desecration of their holy places directly above the tunnel, Palestinian rock-throwers took to the streets. When Israeli troops sought to quell the rioters, they were fired upon by Palestinian Authority police, who killed 14 Israelis. Although the Israeli casualties guaranteed an American Jewish consensus in denunciation of Palestinian violence, there were clear differences of opinion about the underlying issues. According to the mainstream groups, whatever questions might be raised about the wisdom of opening the tunnel, Palestinian resort to violence was grossly disproportionate to the alleged offense. Distinctively dovish groups, on the other hand, saw the tunnel opening as a needless provocation and placed the burden for reducing tensions on the Netanyahu government. Those organizations that had all along distrusted Palestinian intentions interpreted the firing upon Israelis as proof that the Oslo accords, if allowed to go forward, would lead to disaster for Israel. Indeed, members of the Zionist Organization of America, the most outspoken of the hawkish organizations, did not hesitate to criticize Israel's Likud government for insufficient zeal in Israel's cause. In October, Eliahu Ben-Elissar, Netanyahu's ambassador to Washington, was booed and heckled at a ZOA fundraiser in New York for saying that, since his government was committed to the territorial concessions contained in the Oslo accords, "not everything can be saved."

In October, ZOA president Morton Klein attacked the Anti-Defamation League for inviting *New York Times* columnist Thomas Friedman to address its annual dinner-dance in Los Angeles, scheduled for December. Accusing Friedman of repeatedly defaming Israel in his columns, Klein listed 13 statements and actions by Friedman that he considered anti-Israel. Getting no satisfaction from the ADL, Klein sent out an "action alert" calling for a mass protest of Friedman's appearance at the event. ADL national director Abraham Foxman, inundated by what seemed to be an organized campaign of phone calls, faxes, and e-mail messages urging him to disinvite the *Times* columnist, retorted that Friedman's comments on Israel had always been stated within a context of support for the Jewish state. "We don't need this kind of thought police," said Foxman of Klein, and urged his expulsion from the organized Jewish world since "he has lowered the discourse to a new level of personal intolerance."

Klein then charged that Foxman had violated a 1995 agreement to maintain civility of debate in Jewish organizational life and urged the Conference of Presidents to reprimand the ADL leader. The Israeli government entered the fray when David Bar-Illan, Prime Minister Netanyahu's communications director, seconded Klein and asserted that Friedman should not be given a platform by "any organization that purports to be Zionist." Cooler heads eventually prevailed: Friedman addressed the ADL dinner-dance; a committee of the Conference of Presidents expressed regret that the ADL-ZOA contretemps had hurt the Jewish community; Foxman acknowledged that "some of my statements were inappropriate, and I apologize for them"; and Bar-Illan explained that his criticism of Friedman was his own personal view, not that of his government.

The decision of the Israeli cabinet in mid-December to build more homes in West Bank settlements at the same time that negotiations were going on for an Israeli withdrawal from Hebron caused new strains in the relationship with the United States. President Clinton—just reelected overwhelmingly to a second term and therefore no longer dependent on the Jewish electorate—publicly criticized the move at a December 16 news conference. On the same day, newspapers published the text of a letter to Prime Minister Netanyahu from eight former senior U.S. diplomats—including three former secretaries of state—urging him not to expand the settlements. American Jewish leaders, eager to head off any crisis in U.S.-Israeli relations, got only the vaguest of signals from Jerusalem, as Israeli ambassador Ben-Elissar sought to minimize the importance of the decision to build in the settlements and assured American Jewry that relations between the two countries remained strong. With Israel's long-term strategy unclear, and President Clinton enjoying considerable credibility in the Jewish community for supporting Israel during his first term, mainstream American Jewish organizations reacted cautiously. The Conference of Presidents, the American Israel Public Affairs Committee (AIPAC), the American Jewish Committee, and the Anti-Defamation League all refrained from issuing statements, though their top officials told reporters of their concern that Clinton had, for the first time, gone public with criticism of Israeli policy. In contrast, Americans for Peace Now and Project Nishma, Jewish groups that were critical of the Netanyahu government's slowdown of the peace process, praised Clinton's remarks.

Further tough challenges to Israeli policy and its American Jewish defenders were to come. On December 21, the *New York Times* ran a full-page ad sponsored by Churches for Middle East Peace that called on Israel to give up its claim to all of Jerusalem. Among the groups signing on to the ad were many of the largest and most influential mainline Protestant churches, member organizations of the National Council of Churches, with whom Jewish groups often cooperated in support of liberal domestic causes. Conspicuously absent from the ad's sponsor list were the National Conference of Catholic Bishops and the evangelical Protestant denominations. The ad—which included a coupon for readers to send to the Senate Foreign Relations Committee, urging adoption of "the concept of a shared Jerusalem"—was intended to kick off a broader campaign to influence public opinion and U.S. government policy. The ad was reprinted in *Roll Call,* the Capitol Hill newspaper, on January 20, 1997, Inauguration Day, and 25,000 copies were given out to government officials.

Organized American Jewry reacted vigorously, with public denunciation of the ad and letters of protest to its signatories. A meeting between a delegation from the Conference of Presidents and the National Council of Churches aimed at finding some common ground on the issue did not succeed. Rev. Joan Brown Campbell, NCC general secretary, refused to retract the group's support for a shared Jerusalem.

American Jewry greeted announcement of the Hebron redeployment agreement in mid-January with satisfaction, not only as a substantive step on the road to Middle East peace, but also as the first indication that Netanyahu's self-proclaimed strategy of slowing down the peace process did not mean bringing it to a halt. Martin Raffel, associate vice-chairman of the National Jewish Community Relations Advisory Council (NJCRAC) said, "What happened will serve to alleviate concern by some that this Israeli government's approach to the peace process would lead to deadlock." An opinion survey conducted by the Israel Policy Forum found 64 percent of American Jews in favor of the Hebron agreement, with over 80 percent approving the role that the Clinton administration played in securing it.

On December 19, 1996, as the Hebron accord was being negotiated, the television show "60 Minutes" ran an exposé about Dr. Irving Moskowitz, a wealthy American Jew who gave large amounts of money to Jerusalem institutions. Ostensibly charitable donations and therefore tax-exempt, much of the money was actually used to buy up Arab property in East Jerusalem, furthering the ideological aim of bringing Jerusalem's Muslim Quarter into Jewish hands. Dovish American Jews joined with Arab American groups in calling for a probe of Moskowitz's activities, and there was some concern in the mainstream Jewish community that such questionable use of philanthropic funds could bring closer government scrutiny of legitimate donations to Israeli causes. But despite a wave of media attention to the Moskowitz story, he continued to finance his projects unhindered.

Har Homah

At the beginning of March 1997, the Israeli government announced plans to build a new Jewish neighborhood in Har Homah in southeastern Jerusalem. Palestinians charged that this was their land. Israel countered that two-thirds of the area had actually been expropriated from Jewish owners, and also that, since the area was part of the municipality of Jerusalem, not the West Bank, Israel was legally entitled to build there. Though not explicitly condemning the plan, President Clinton said he would prefer that the decision had not been made. The Conference of Presidents announced that its 53 member organizations unanimously backed Israel's right to build in Jerusalem, but did not mention any specific building project by name. Indeed, the wisdom of building on Har Homah was publicly questioned by the more dovish members of the conference. Conference executive vice-chairman Malcolm Hoenlein denounced UN debate on the Israeli decision to build, calling it "a platform for one-sided criticism of Israel." While American Jews expressed gratitude to the administration for exercising its veto in the Security Council to stop a resolution denouncing the construction plan as illegal, President Clinton's original statement questioning Israel's move raised fears in the Jewish community about American Middle East policy.

Even more alarming was the administration's decision to send an American representative to a meeting of foreign diplomats in Gaza in mid-March that was convened by Yasir Arafat and to which Israel was not invited. AIPAC, which was able to get more than 100 members of Congress to publicly criticize this move, sent a letter to the president cautioning that "the willingness of the people of Israel to take risks for peace is based on their confidence in the support and friendship of the United States," a confidence diminished by U.S. participation in the Gaza meeting. Once again, as had happened in the wake of the Jerusalem tunnel opening, only Americans for Peace Now and Project Nishma voiced unequivocal support for the president's stand.

With Har Homah as their grievance, Palestinians again took to the streets in violent demonstrations against Israel, and on March 21 a suicide bomber killed three women and wounded more than 40 people in Tel Aviv. American Jewish organizations, following the lead of the Israeli government, charged that Arafat had violated the peace accords by giving a green light to violence. On March 26, with violent demonstrations still going on in the West Bank, and the Arab League urging its members to resume the economic boycott of Israel, a Conference of Presidents delegation had a very difficult meeting with Secretary of State Madeleine Albright in Washington. The Jewish leaders blamed American policy for the setback to peace: by criticizing the Har Homah project while not insisting that Arafat clamp down on violence, Washington, they argued, had virtually encouraged the Palestinian side to use force.

Two days later, on March 28, the American Jewish Committee ran a full-page ad in the *New York Times* asking: "Chairman Arafat, Which Will It Be? Peace or

Jihad?" It quoted a Hamas leader, released from a Palestinian jail ten days before, telling a cheering crowd in Gaza on the very day of the bombing that Jerusalem would only be liberated through holy war.

Prime Minister Netanyahu arrived in Washington on April 7 and met with the president and the secretary of state. While both agreed with Netanyahu that negotiations could only resume with the renunciation of terrorism, the Americans did not budge on the inadvisability of building at Har Homah. Using the language of formal diplomacy, Clinton told reporters afterwards: "We had a very specific, frank, candid, and long talk." White House spokesman Michael McCurry put it a bit differently: The president, he reported, "gave the prime minister some serious things to think about." Netanyahu did better later that day with some of his other American audiences. The 2,000 people at AIPAC's policy conference cheered him enthusiastically, as did the 3,000 evangelical Christians who heard him address the annual conference of Voices United for Israel.

In May the Israeli government moved to improve its relations with U.S. officials and with the American Jewish community by appointing two American-born Israelis to major diplomatic posts. Dore Gold, till then Netanyahu's political advisor, was named ambassador to the UN, while Leonard Davis, who had headed AIPAC's Israel office, would become deputy chief of mission at the Israeli embassy in Washington.

Coping with Pressure

There was another suicide bombing at the end of July at a busy Jerusalem market, which killed 15. Convinced that the peace process would peter out without a significant push from the United States, Secretary of State Albright announced a new American initiative. In an address to the National Press Club on August 6, Albright challenged both Israelis and Palestinians to speed up the process by "marrying" discussions of interim agreements with talks on final-status issues. Her speech contained repeated calls to the Palestinian Authority to do more to contain violence: "There can be no winks, no double standards, no double meanings, and, with respect to the imprisonment of terrorists, no revolving doors." And Albright rejected any moral equivalency between building projects and killings. Not surprisingly, many American Jewish leaders expressed pleasure with the speech when they first heard it. Nevertheless, a careful reading of the text (reprinted in full on two pages of the August 8 *New York Times,* the space paid for by the Center for Middle East Peace and Economic Cooperation) made it clear that Albright was not backing down on previous American opposition to "unilateral acts" by either side that affected the peace process—i.e., Har Homah—and that Washington expected Israel to fulfill its obligations under the peace accords to carry out further withdrawals from the West Bank.

This delighted the Israel Policy Forum (recently merged with Project Nishma), which sponsored a "Thank You, Secretary of State Albright" ad in the *New York*

Times (August 10, 1997). But American Jewish groups in the center and on the right wondered what would happen if the Palestinians restrained further violent acts long enough to convince the Americans that Arafat was keeping his side of the peace bargain. Would the immense force of the U.S. government and American public opinion be directed against Israel for its "unilateral acts" and reluctance to hand over more territory to the Palestinian Authority?

On September 4, just a few days before Secretary Albright's first visit to the Middle East, there was another suicide bombing in Jerusalem; it killed five Israelis and wounded some 200 others. During her stay in Israel, September 10 and 11, Albright extracted a pledge from Arafat to crack down on terrorism, but she also stated publicly that Israeli policies had caused "suffering" to the Palestinians. Her call to Prime Minister Netanyahu for a moratorium on settlement expansion fell on deaf ears. The Israel Policy Forum sponsored a survey of American Jewish opinion immediately after the Albright mission (conducted by Penn and Schoen, President Clinton's pollsters) that found overwhelming support for U.S. policy: by a 9–1 margin, American Jews wanted the administration to take an "even-handed" approach to the Israel-Palestinian dispute; 84 percent felt that both Arafat and Netanyahu should be subject to American "pressure"; and 79 percent backed Albright's request for a moratorium on Israeli settlements in the territories.

The apparent growth of dissatisfaction with the Netanyahu government in American Jewish circles did not go unnoticed in the White House. On October 6, President Clinton, Vice-President Gore, and Secretary of State Albright held a "working dinner" with a small group of American Jews that lasted for three hours. Unlike such meetings in previous administrations, the guest list was not arranged by the Conference of Presidents of Major American Jewish Organizations; rather, the names were individually selected by the White House. Leaders of the mainstream Jewish organizations were there, but no noted "hawks." Conspicuous by their presence were three dovish activists: Jack Bendheim of the Israel Policy Forum, S. Daniel Abraham of the Center for Middle East Peace and Economic Cooperation (neither organization belonged to the Conference of Presidents), and Sara Ehrman, a close personal friend of the Clintons who was on the board of Americans for Peace Now. Also at the dinner was the visiting president of Israel, Ezer Weizman. While few of the participants were willing to say much about the discussion afterward, the clear impression conveyed to the administration was that the American Jewish community supported an active American role in bringing peace to the Middle East. Furthermore, at least Clinton and Albright came away from the session convinced that Jews were not unanimously enamored of Israel's current government, held diverse views about the specific matters in dispute between Israel and the Palestinians, and would not necessarily react with outrage if Washington gently pressured Israel to make concessions for the sake of peace.

The White House dinner, coming on the heels of the IPF survey, encouraged those elements in American Jewish life that considered the Israeli government insufficiently flexible on peace. In a widely noted *New York Times* column (October 9, 1997), Thomas Friedman declared: "The White House knows there's a new mood out there among American Jews," many of whom felt, he wrote, that Israel's leaders had "more in common with Larry, Moe and Curly than with David Ben-Gurion, Menachem Begin and Yitzhak Rabin." He urged Jews to channel their philanthropic dollars only to those Israeli institutions that were pluralistic and supported the Oslo process, and he proceeded to list them.

American Jewish advocates for Netanyahu's policies, eager to demonstrate that there was actually little public backing for U.S. pressure on Israel, countered with two opinion surveys—one of American Jews, the other of the broader American population—sponsored by the *Middle East Quarterly* (*MEQ*) and carried out by Arthur J. Finkelstein and Associates, which had previously done media work for Netanyahu. According to the *MEQ* data, a large majority of both Jews and other Americans felt that Israel should not continue peace negotiations until terrorism was halted, that Jerusalem should remain under undivided Israeli control, and that the establishment of a Palestinian state was unlikely to bring an end to terrorism.

The U.S. administration, however, proceeded on the assumption that neither the Jewish community nor other Americans would be averse to pressure on Israel so long as there were no outright threats. When Netanyahu visited the United States in late November, President Clinton could not find the time to meet with him, though he did have time to confer well-publicized honors on Leah Rabin, widow of Yitzhak Rabin, the prime minister who had pioneered the peace process, and on Shimon Peres, his successor. American Jewish leaders downplayed the snub, even after Netanyahu told CNN that he considered Clinton's "unbecoming" conduct insulting to the State of Israel.

Notified that the administration might go public about its differences with Israel over the peace process unless the Israeli government showed some willingness to meet its withdrawal obligations under Oslo, the Conference of Presidents agonized over the wording of a letter to Clinton. A consensus within the conference did not view the administration's actions as undue pressure on Israel. The letter sent to the president called for strong U.S.-Israeli relations, cited the need to get both Israelis and Palestinians to move toward peace, and did not criticize the administration. Diverging from this consensus, the ZOA attacked Clinton's initiative, as did, somewhat surprisingly, the usually left-leaning AJCongress, which called it "bad tactics and bad strategy." But the dovish elements in the Jewish community saw the moderately worded letter to Clinton as a major victory. Mark Rosenblum, political director of Americans for Peace Now, commented, "Netanyahu very much wants the American Jewish community to pull his chestnuts out of the fire, and that ain't happening."

As Washington stepped up its diplomatic offensive to pry territorial concessions out of Netanyahu, administration officials kept in touch with American

Jewish leaders to make sure that the Jewish community did not misconstrue American intentions. On December 10, Martin Indyk, assistant secretary of state for Near Eastern Affairs, and Dennis Ross, special Middle East coordinator, participated in a conference call with Jewish leaders, assuring them that the administration was working with Israel, not against it, and that the issue of Palestinian terrorism was not being subordinated to the question of Israeli redeployment. Building on the precedent set by the White House "working dinner" in October, the Jews chosen to be on the conference call were all supporters of the Oslo peace process.

In a conference call of his own the next week with the Conference of Presidents, Netanyahu sought to assure the American Jewish community that he was sincerely striving to move the peace process forward, in cooperation with the United States. Meanwhile, his ambassador in Washington, Eliahu Ben-Elissar, went over the heads of the official Jewish leadership and sent a letter to 2,500 American rabbis cautioning that American Jewish criticisms of Israel and diplomatic pressure by the U.S. government had the effect of raising Palestinian expectations and thereby undermining chances for peace.

Pluralism in Israel

If the election of Netanyahu in May 1996 heightened American Jewish concerns about the fate of the peace process, it positively alarmed the non-Orthodox community in the United States about the threat to prospects for religious pluralism in the Jewish state. A 1995 decision of the Israel Supreme Court had opened the way for the recognition of non-Orthodox conversions in Israel (those performed outside the country were already recognized) but left it up to the Knesset to pass a law to that effect. The new government, however, beholden to the religious factions, would surely try to sidestep the decision by passing contrary legislation, enacting into law the old informal status quo that withheld recognition from non-Orthodox conversions performed within the state.

Such an outcome might well alienate Reform and Conservative Jews—who far outnumbered the Orthodox in America—from Israel. The very prospect of such a scenario reverberated in the world of Jewish philanthropy even before the Israeli election, since some 80 percent of donors to federations and UJA called themselves Reform or Conservative. Reacting to speculation about a non-Orthodox backlash if Netanyahu won, the United Jewish Appeal sought to preempt dissension by issuing a letter right after the election. Signed by leading rabbis of all the denominations, it endorsed the UJA campaign as a nonpolitical cause that helped Jews in need, one which should not be held hostage to the religious pluralism debate. But several influential rabbis, including Simeon Maslin, president of the Central Conference of American Rabbis (Reform), Sheldon Zimmerman, president of Hebrew Union College (Reform), and Jerome Epstein, executive director of the United Synagogue of Conservative Judaism, refused to sign. While most of the recalcitrant rabbis said that they continued to endorse the UJA campaign, they hesitated to commit themselves in writing until they saw how Netanyahu intended to proceed. The implied financial threat was calculated to induce the massive American Jewish fund-raising apparatus to throw its weight behind religious pluralism. As Rabbi Eric Yoffie, president of the Union of American Hebrew Congregations, put it, "We want the federations to take a more assertive stance."

Prime Minister Netanyahu's first visit to the United States in July 1996 did nothing to clarify his intentions on the religious pluralism front. After a day spent meeting with administration officials in Washington, Netanyahu arrived in New York City on July 11 for three days of talks with Jewish groups and business leaders. New York Jews, especially the non-Orthodox, were primarily interested in what he would say about religious pluralism. Chancellor Ismar Schorsch of the Jewish Theological Seminary told a *New York Times* reporter (July 11, 1996): "The issue that concerns American Jewry is the status of Reform and Conservative Jews. They constitute overwhelmingly the majority of American Jews." But all Netanyahu would say publicly was: "We said we'd preserve the status quo. We stand our ground. We'll keep the status quo." He did not say whether his definition of status quo included the recent liberalizing Supreme Court decision.

In September, at least a dozen Reform rabbis around the country suggested in their High Holy Day sermons that congregants give to Reform institutions in Israel rather than to UJA, on the grounds that UJA funded Orthodox institutions in Israel that denied the legitimacy of Reform, while giving only pennies to Reform causes. Other Reform rabbis, unwilling to boycott the UJA completely, urged members to reduce their UJA pledges by some percentage, and donate the difference to Reform institutions. UJA's defense—that the disparity of allocations between Orthodox and non-Orthodox recipients was based, not on bias, but on the far greater number of Orthodox institutions in Israel—fell on deaf ears.

CONVERSION BILL PROPOSED

By mid-November 1996, when American Jewish leaders gathered in Seattle for the annual General Assembly (GA) of the Council of Jewish Federations (CJF), the Orthodox Shas Party in Netanyahu's coalition had already drawn up, but not yet submitted to the Knesset, a bill stating that no conversion to Judaism performed in Israel would be recognized without the approval of the chief rabbinate. It would also bar such conversions outside Israel for residents of Israel, thus preventing Israelis from evading the requirement for Orthodox conversion by quick trips outside the country. While such legislation would offend the non-Orthodox by effectively circumventing the Supreme Court, Prime Minister Netanyahu sent a message to CJF leaders prior to the GA pledging to "oppose any legislation which will change the status quo regarding conversions outside Israel." Since these would remain valid for non-Israelis no matter who performed them, the pending bill could be construed as making no change that would affect American Jewry.

Despite Netanyahu's assurance, and against the wishes of Orthodox groups that urged the federation world not to get involved in what they considered a domestic Israeli issue, the GA passed a resolution calling on Israel not to "change the current situation regarding recognition of conversions" either in Israel or elsewhere. By "current situation" most of the delegates had in mind the recognition of non-Orthodox conversions in Israel, as propounded by the Supreme Court. Netanyahu, who canceled a scheduled visit to Seattle to address the GA, spoke by satellite and reiterated his rather different understanding of the "status quo": only Orthodox conversions in Israel, recognition of all conversions done abroad.

Conservative and Reform rabbis argued that, even if all the proposed legislation did was enshrine in law the previous unwritten practice of an Orthodox monopoly inside Israel, a message was being sent that the non-Orthodox, wherever they lived, were second-class Jews. In the wake of the GA, American anger at the prospect of the conversion bill mounted. Rabbi Gordon Tucker, an influential figure in the Conservative movement, expressed the feelings of many when he wrote that "this means that the Jewish state will have declared the Judaism my congregants and I practice to be inauthentic as a matter of law." As for the argument that the Israeli political system would only begin to take the non-Orthodox seriously when there were enough Conservative and Reform Jews in the country to constitute a potent voting bloc, Tucker replied that religious pluralism was a matter of "civil rights and freedom of belief and conscience," not politics, and therefore the size of the disenfranchised group was irrelevant (*Jerusalem Report,* January 23, 1997).

A delegation of 50 Reform rabbis flew to Jerusalem at the end of January 1997 to warn the prime minister and other Israeli leaders of the dire consequences of what they considered the delegitimization of the bulk of world Jewry. Netanyahu listened politely and explained that the realities of coalition politics dictated passage of the conversion bill. Rabbi Ammiel Hirsch, executive director of the Association of Reform Zionists of America, told reporters that the legislation might lead non-Orthodox Diaspora Jews, acting on their own and without any formal denominational policy, to "disengage" from Israel, a step that would shrink philanthropy to the Jewish state and possibly weaken its political strength in the United States as well.

Reform and Conservative leaders met with Netanyahu again in February when he visited New York, with the same result. He told them that he was bound by preelection commitments to support the conversion bill. And if any proof were needed that the prime minister was beholden to the Orthodox, he refused permission to photograph the meeting, lest he be shown in the Israeli media in the company of non-Orthodox rabbis. In contrast, another meeting held the same day with Orthodox leaders was photographed.

The NJCRAC plenum in February addressed the issue of religious pluralism in a session cautiously titled "Challenges to the American Jewish-Israel Relationship." Julius Berman, past chairman of the Conference of Presidents, representing the Orthodox view, objected to umbrella organizations such as CJF and NJCRAC involving themselves in religious issues that pertained to Israel. Israelis, he noted, showed minimal interest in non-Orthodox Judaism and should not have it foisted upon them by American Jewry. Shoshana Cardin, also a past chairwoman of the conference and current chairwoman of the United Israel Appeal, spoke of her personal resentment at the delegitimization of the non-Orthodox in Israel, but argued that nothing could realistically be done about it, and that any punitive cutoff of funds would only injure innocent needy Jews.

In late February, at the same time that the Israeli media were uncovering bribe-taking by two rabbis for facilitating Orthodox conversions—casting serious doubt on Orthodox claims that non-Orthodox conversions were uniquely bogus—another delegation of prominent American Jews arrived in Israel. These were members of the board of governors of the Jewish Agency; they met in Jerusalem with influential political leaders, most notably the ministerial committee on Diaspora affairs, chaired by Natan Sharansky, minister of trade and industry. One member of Sharansky's committee, a Shas minister, walked out when he realized that a Reform rabbi was in the room. Meanwhile, a dozen Reform and Conservative activists held a vigil outside. The official upshot of the session, in the words of Sharansky's office, echoed Netanyahu: The minister wanted to prevent the erosion of Reform and Conservative rights, but also recognized the Israeli political reality. Commented Dr. Conrad Giles, CJF president: "The Israeli politicians don't have a clue going in as to the impact of their actions on the Diaspora."

Meanwhile, the Jewish Agency board, at its regularly scheduled meeting at the Dead Sea, set up its own "committee on the unity of the Jewish people." Orthodox representatives, who favored the pending conversion law, insisted that support for "unity" not be interpreted as acceptance of pluralism. But Rabbi Eric Yoffie reiterated the warning that passage of the conversion bill would adversely affect fund-raising for Israel in the United States, and urged local federations to follow the CJF lead and pass resolutions opposing the legislation.

Perhaps chastened by the critical response that greeted Reform coolness to the UJA campaign the previous fall, Yoffie was careful not to give the impression that his movement was actually calling for a cutoff of philanthropy. Yoffie, along with other non-Orthodox American rabbis, signed a public letter—surely urged upon them by the fund-raising establishment—stating: "It is important to every Conservative and Reform Jew to support klal Yisrael by making a meaningful gift to the 1997 federation/UJA campaign."

At the beginning of March, JTS chancellor Ismar Schorsch suggested a far-reaching plan to foster greater religious pluralism in Israel: some $100–$150 million would be taken "off the top" of the UJA campaign to fund Conservative and Reform institutions in Israel. In Schorsch's eyes, this would help compensate for the sums already allocated to the Orthodox. While unwilling to endorse the specific sum that Schorsch proposed, Reform's Yoffie backed the concept, calling it "affirmative action." But the professional head of Conservative Judaism's congregational wing, United Synagogue executive director Rabbi Jerome Epstein, dissented from such a strategy, and Richard Wexler, UJA national chairman and a Conservative layman, called Schorsch's idea "reprehensible" since it would take money away from "the needs of our people" just to "build up the coffers of the movements." Schorsch insisted that it was precisely those aided by UJA's humanitarian activities—the Russian immigrants to Israel, for example, many of whom were denied Orthodox recognition as Jews—who would benefit most from a heightened non-Orthodox religious presence in Israel.

On March 22, with the Israeli cabinet about to finalize the conversion bill, the *Los Angeles Times* reported that the Union of Orthodox Rabbis of the United States and Canada was planning to declare Reform and Conservative forms of Judaism as "not Judaism." A relatively obscure organization reporting a membership of over 500, the union had been founded in 1902 to represent the Orthodox rabbinate, which, at that time, was predominantly European-born and Yiddish-speaking. Since its inception, however, the group had been gradually marginalized within Orthodoxy by the emergence of Americanized Orthodox rabbis. Spokesmen for the group explained that their statement was timed to buttress the supporters of the conversion bill in Israel. On March 31, leaders of the organization held a heavily attended press conference at the New York Hilton where they stressed that they were not reading any Jew out of Judaism, but simply pointing out the inauthenticity of the forms of Judaism practiced by the non-Orthodox. The *New York Times* headline was "Jewish Group Casts Out 2 Main Branches" (April 1, 1997).

The non-Orthodox movements reacted with predictable disdain. Other Orthodox organizations—the moderate Rabbinical Council of America and Union of Orthodox Jewish Congregations of America (UOJCA), and even the pro-*haredi* Agudath Israel—criticized the union's action for eroding Jewish peoplehood and making solutions to religiously divisive issues even more difficult. Significantly, however, not even the moderate Orthodox bodies affirmed the Jewish authenticity of the non-Orthodox movements that the union statement had denied. Perhaps the oddest reaction to the affair was the full-page ad in the *New York Times* (April 15, 1997) suggesting that the "80 to 90 percent of American Jews" newly delegitimated might want to find out more about Jews for Jesus.

CONVERSION BILL PASSES FIRST READING

The Israeli cabinet approved the conversion bill, angering the non-Orthodox movements even more. Criticized by Reform and Conservative leaders for not doing enough to head off the legislation, the American fund-raising bodies could only express anguish. The Council of Jewish Federations issued a statement declaring "that any legislative amendment that has the potential to form a wedge between Israel and Diaspora Jewry is unacceptable." UJA chairman Wexler said that the Israeli situation was "frustrating for the national system and the campaign." On April 1 the bill passed the first of the required three readings in the Knesset. A few hours later, Prime Minister Netanyahu told reporters that some Reform and Conservative leaders were deliberately misleading their movements about the bill, making it seem to delegitimize their Judaism when all it did was formalize the old status quo. Talk of cutting off philanthropy, Netanyahu charged, came from "uninformed circles, or, worse, from informed circles who know the truth and still threaten."

The Reform and Conservative movements responded with a joint statement urging their synagogues to withhold speaking invitations from any Knesset member who voted for the bill's final passage. And while expressing continued support for federation and UJA campaigns, the statement called for pressure on the fund-raising bodies to allocate more money to Reform and Conservative institutions in Israel. JTS chancellor Schorsch went further. He issued a letter calling for "dismantling" the Israeli chief rabbinate, since it had "not a scintilla of moral worth," and charging that the Union of Orthodox Rabbis' statement represented a mood of intolerance reminiscent of the rhetoric that led up to the Rabin assassination. Schorsch also suggested boycotting any Jewish philanthropy that backed the Orthodox monopoly in Israel, a step that would, in effect, eliminate the funding of virtually all Orthodox institutions. The Reconstructionist movement agreed unequivocally, asserting that Jews should "restrict their Israel-oriented gifts to organizations actively committed to religious pluralism."

Despite the tough rhetoric on all sides, rumors swirled about a possible deal: The government would shelve the conversion bill, and the Reform and Conservative movements in Israel would freeze the lawsuits they had earlier initiated against the religious establishment in the hope of inducing the Supreme Court to strike down, in explicit terms, Orthodoxy's monopoly on legal recognition.

American Jews first heard about the plan when Netanyahu visited the United States in early April. Although the prime minister minimized the significance of the conversion law in a nationally televised press conference, and angered Reform Jews by canceling a scheduled meeting with their Religious Action Center—Rabbi Eric Yoffie called it "a deliberate affront"—Netanyahu held a closed-door meeting on the evening of April 7 with leaders of the Reform and Conservative movements, UJA, and CJF. Netanyahu acknowledged the need to find "creative solutions," and deputized MK Alexander Lubotsky and Bobby Brown, adviser on Diaspora affairs, to remain in the United States for a few days to continue talks with Jewish leaders on resolving the crisis. What ensued was a strange game of "chicken," with Netanyahu's representatives urging the non-Orthodox movements to drop their Supreme Court litigation as the first step to a settlement, and the Conservative and Reform leaders insisting that the conversion bill be dropped first. Brown described the sensitivity of the situation: "Anything done on either side to heat up the issue makes it harder to come to mutually acceptable conclusions."

Negotiations dragged on in New York and Jerusalem. By the end of May, there was still no progress, and the Orthodox parties were calling for a second reading of the conversion bill. On May 30, the American Jewish Committee ran a full-page ad in the mass circulation *Yediot Aharonot* newspaper urging rejection of the legislation, since it would "question the legitimacy of the religious life of the overwhelming majority of American Jews." On the holiday of Shavuot— June 11—ultra-Orthodox attacks on Conservative men and women praying together at the Western Wall—many of whom were Americans—further exacerbated tensions. The victims claimed that they had been pelted with human excrement.

NE'EMAN COMMISSION FORMED

The next week, after three days of marathon meetings in Jerusalem between non-Orthodox leaders and government officials, an agreement was reached along the lines that had been bruited about for a month and a half: a simultaneous moratorium on the conversion bill and on the Reform and Conservative court challenges. This would buy time for an interdenominational committee of Israelis, chaired by Finance Minister Ya'akov Ne'eman, to devise long-term solutions to the problem. August 15 was set as the date for the committee to complete its work. While many were skeptical about the committee's prospects, Bobby Brown suggested that its very creation was "one of the greatest victories" because "people will be talking to each other."

The committee began its deliberations on June 30. The Jewish Agency Assembly was meeting in Jerusalem at the same time, and Netanyahu used the occasion to explain to the Americans in attendance that religion-state issues in Israel could only be handled by "ad hoc compromises," and that an accommodation was made more difficult by "hammer blows" from the Diaspora. And he pointed out that American Reform Jews, who had unilaterally introduced a patrilineal definition of Jewishness, were not in a position to complain that Israel had not consulted them about the conversion bill. "I urge people to tread very lightly on this very fragile ground," he said.

At the insistence of the Reform and Conservative movements, however, the Jewish Agency Assembly tackled the issue of religious pluralism. Annual allocations to the Reform, Conservative, and modern Orthodox religious movements in Israel were doubled to $5 million, and Israeli authorities were called upon to act against violence at the Western Wall. At the insistence of the Orthodox, the word "pluralism" was not used in any official assembly statement, replaced by euphemisms such as "Jewish unity" and "religious freedom."

At the beginning of August, the conflict over pluralism was heightened when the Supreme Court ruled that a Reform woman had the right to serve on a local religious council. And, on August 11, four days before the Ne'eman Commission's projected deadline, on the fast of the Ninth of Av, which commemorates the destruction of the two Temples, there was another incident at the Western Wall. Some 150 Reform and Conservative Jews—men and women praying together, in contravention of Orthodox tradition—were chased away, not, this time, by the ultra-Orthodox, but by the police. While police officials said that this was necessary to head off a potentially violent confrontation, the non-Orthodox activists claimed that the police action proved that Israeli officialdom had become a tool of the extreme Orthodox. "They're symbolically, and more than symbolically, driving us out of the gates of Jerusalem," commented Rabbi Uri Regev.

Meanwhile, the anticipated recommendations of the Ne'eman Commission were leaked to the Israeli press: A joint conversion school representing all the denominations would be established, but the actual conversion procedure would be performed by an Orthodox rabbinical court according to Halakhah. But August 15 came and went with no report from the committee. According to people privy to its deliberations, a combination of the Supreme Court decision on religious councils, the incident at the Wall, and the premature news leak caused a breakdown in the talks. But the committee resolved to keep meeting.

With another High Holy Day season on the horizon, the American Jewish fundraising establishment—fearing the specter of rabbinic boycotts once again—took steps to insure that Reform and Conservative anger over religious pluralism did not have a catastrophic effect on philanthropy. Already, UJA was feeling the pinch. While the 1997 annual campaign was now expected to bring in $15–$16 million more than in 1996, this was still some $20 million less than what had been projected originally. In fact, said Bernard Moscovitz, UJA's CEO, donations had been 8.5 percent ahead of 1996 until the Union of Orthodox Rabbis' statement and the Knesset's first reading of the conversion bill heated up the religious pluralism issue in the spring. Perhaps equally demoralizing, a number of prominent Jews in the entertainment industry—actor Billy Crystal and executives Lew Wasserman and Bram Goldsmith, for example—were so upset about the conversion bill that they were refusing to participate in planned public celebrations of Israel's 50th anniversary in 1998. Even the downturn in American Jewish tourism to Israel in 1997 was widely attributed to anger over the treatment of the non-Orthodox movements.

The fund-raisers developed a strategy to save the campaign. UJA and the Council of Jewish Federations offered to raise up to $10 million each for the Reform and Conservative institutions in Israel, on the understanding that these funds would come from gifts over and above the regular campaign; negotiations were begun with the Union of Orthodox Jewish Congregations to provide the same service for modern Orthodox institutions. In addition, UJA and CJF brought eight members of the Israeli Knesset to America for a week of visits to local communities, so that they might see for themselves how important religious pluralism was for American Jewry. All eight returned home resolved to oppose the government's conversion bill, should it come to a vote. In another step to assuage American ire, Natan Sharansky spoke via satellite to the quarterly CJF meeting in early September, but the result was not what CJF leaders expected. Sharansky promised that the government would protect the rights of all Jews to worship at the Western Wall, but, he added, this did not cover people who "incite." When former CJF president Maynard Wishner pointed out that Southern blacks had also been accused of incitement for exercising their rights, Sharansky replied that making prayer into "a political demonstration" could threaten the work of the Ne'eman Commission.

Prime Minister Netanyahu's September 15 address in Jerusalem to UJA leaders from America produced similar dissatisfaction. Devoting himself mainly to peace-process issues before an audience concerned primarily with religious pluralism, Netanyahu reaffirmed the unity of all Jews, gave no indication of when the Ne'eman Commission would finish its work, and suggested that the non-Orthodox movements were to blame for the crisis because they had taken their claims to the Supreme Court. The Americans felt that he had evaded the issue.

Four days later, Ya'akov Ne'eman spoke to a closed-door meeting of the Conference of Presidents in New York. His ostensible topic was the Israeli economy, but he spent most of the time fielding questions about his religious pluralism commission. While reluctant to go into specifics, Ne'eman spoke of the earnest desire of the group to reach a solution, warned that failure could strike a catastrophic blow at the unity of the Jewish people, and urged American Jews to be patient.

But with the Jewish New Year approaching, little patience was in evidence. Four Orthodox organizations—Agudath Israel, the National Council of Young Israel, the Rabbinical Council of America, and the Union of Orthodox Jewish Congregations—issued a joint statement insisting on the maintenance of the religious status quo in Israel and charging that American Jewry's "political, economic and social pressure" on Israel "created a climate of ill-will and anger." The statement added, for good measure, that prayer at the Western Wall had always been conducted according to Orthodox tradition, and that it stood to reason that local religious councils, which administer religious services to the community, should be run by those who subscribe to accepted religious precepts.

The American Reform and Conservative movements, for their part, urged rabbis to devote their sermons to the drive for religious pluralism in Israel and to solicit money from their congregations for their movements' institutions there, in addition to appealing for the standard donations to UJA and Israel Bonds. Some rabbis went further. The Harvard students who reported to Prof. Ruth Wisse that their rabbis had sermonized on Yom Kippur about Israel's "repressive policies" toward non-Orthodox Jews (*Forward*, October 17, 1997) were not the only American Jews to hear that message from the pulpit. The New Israel Fund, dedicated to the promotion of democracy and pluralism in Israel, published a 90-page resource book on religious pluralism for non-Orthodox rabbis. A good number of rabbis asked their congregants to contribute to the fund, which then ran a series of eye-catching full-page ads in the *New York Times* and the Anglo-Jewish press with such headlines as: "The Torah should be used to bring the Jewish people together. Not pull us apart"; "No government has the right to decide how someone should lead a Jewish life"; and, more provocatively, "Imagine a Jew in this country being told how to practice religion. That's exactly what's happening in Israel."

The results of the elections for delegates to the World Zionist Congress, announced October 9, gave additional evidence of the raised consciousness of Reform and Conservative Jews. Together, the slates put forward by the two movements committed to the cause of religious pluralism in Israel received 73.7 percent of the vote. While the Orthodox, who garnered only 10.8 percent, charged that the heavy non-Orthodox vote reflected an expensive get-out-the-vote campaign rather than the true feelings of American Jewry, Reform and Conservative leaders took the result as a mandate to try to dismantle the Orthodox monopoly in Israel. And since the American delegation would constitute 29 percent of the World Zionist Congress, scheduled to meet in December, the non-Orthodox movements would surely increase their influence over the allocation of funds of the Jewish Agency for Israel, a partner of the World Zionist Organization.

With the Knesset due to reconvene on October 27, the Ne'eman Commission was dealt a serious blow by Sephardic chief rabbi Eliyahu Bakshi-Doron, who declared that converts processed through a multidenominational board "would not be real converts." Then the Shas Party threatened to quit the government if it did not push through the pending conversion bill that would bar the recognition of non-Orthodox conversions performed in Israel, as well as another law that would ban non-Orthodox from membership on religious councils. The Reform and Conservative leaders, declaring they were no longer bound by earlier promises to restrain themselves, threatened to resume their litigation before the Supreme Court. On October 26, Netanyahu convinced the Orthodox parties to hold back on the new legislation, but the Reform and Conservative forces insisted on pressing their legal cases, infuriating the influential Natan Sharansky, who accused Reform of fomenting the crisis. On October 28, the non-Orthodox groups, under heavy pressure from Israeli legislators, suspended the litigation, and the Ne'eman Commission went back to work with a new mandate to craft a solution within three months.

REFORM AND CONSERVATIVE CONVENTIONS

Both the Reform and Conservative movements in the United States held national conventions in November 1997. At the biennial convention of the Union of American Hebrew Congregations, the Reform rhetoric was uncompromising. Speeches and resolutions that called for ending the Israeli chief rabbinate and instituting religious pluralism drew enthusiastic ovations. Israeli ambassador Eliahu Ben-Elissar was a lone voice in opposition, urging Reform Jews to move to

Israel if they wanted to influence policy. So incensed was the ambassador when a speaker compared his government's stance on religious pluralism to China's human-rights policies that he walked out in protest.

The tone at the biennial convention of the United Synagogue of Conservative Judaism was quite different. Both Israeli chief rabbis had publicly distinguished Conservative from Reform Judaism, viewing the former as more acceptable since it was committed to Halakhah, albeit in modernized form. Was this the harbinger of a divide-and-conquer strategy whereby the Orthodox establishment, through the Ne'eman Commission, would coopt the Conservatives by granting them some form of recognition, leaving Reform, the avowedly nonhalakhic movement, out in the cold? And, if so, should the Conservatives take the bait? Opinions differed. Stephen Wolnek, the new president of the United Synagogue, said: "We would not allow the Reform movement to veto a solution within the Ne'eman Commission that we find acceptable." But Rabbi Reuven Hammer, a leader in the Israeli Conservative movement, insisted that Conservative Jews should hold out for equal rights for Reform. More evidence that the Conservative movement spoke with several voices on this issue came a few weeks later, when Prof. Jack Wertheimer, provost of the Jewish Theological Seminary, published a blistering attack on those non-Orthodox leaders seeking to influence Israeli policy by withholding philanthropy (*Commentary,* December 1997). This, he wrote, would balkanize the Jewish people, destroy the federation system, and punish needy Jews.

CJF GENERAL ASSEMBLY, AGUDATH ISRAEL, ZIONIST CONGRESS

The Reform and Conservative conventions were but preludes to the Council of Jewish Federations' General Assembly, held in Indianapolis in mid-November. Though many issues were on the agenda, religious pluralism was paramount. As Martin Kraar, CJF executive vice-president, put it, "This isn't about conversions in Israel. It's about where Israel-Diaspora relations will go in the future."

When Prime Minister Netanyahu arrived to address the delegates on November 16, some wore signs saying "Israel: Don't Write Off 4 Million Jews." Five well-known liberal Jews handed out flyers outside the hall urging delegates only to applaud politely at the beginning and end of the prime minister's speech, and no more, so as to demonstrate respect for his office but a lack of enthusiasm for his policies. In his address, Netanyahu underscored the unity of the Jewish people and urged support for the work of the Ne'eman Commission. In an oblique jab at the non-Orthodox movements, he declared: "Let us stop looking at each other as enemies. Let those who would divide us go elsewhere." (In fact, Netanyahu had expressed himself even more strongly at an earlier private dinner for UJA's big givers, accusing certain "elements" of trying to sabotage the Ne'eman Commission.) Reporter J. J. Goldberg noted that Netanyahu got "the chilliest reception ever given to an Israeli prime minister by U.S. Jewish leaders" (*Jerusalem Report,* December 11, 1997). On the other hand, Ehud Barak, leader of the opposition Labor party, pledged to the delegates that he would oppose any legislation limiting the validity of non-Orthodox conversions, and he was roundly applauded.

Under severe pressure from the rest of American Jewry, the moderate Orthodox ran an ad in *USA Today* on November 18, "A Call for Jewish Unity," in which the Rabbinical Council of America, the Union of Orthodox Jewish Congregations, and three other centrist Orthodox organizations backed the Ne'eman Commission, while decrying financial pressure on Israel and the overheated rhetoric on all sides. And a week later, Rabbi Norman Lamm, president of Yeshiva University, the preeminent modern Orthodox institution of higher learning, announced that he, too, wished the Ne'eman Commission to succeed. He was committed to Halakhah, Lamm asserted, but "communal peace is also a principle of Judaism." And he insisted that, from an Orthodox perspective, Reform and Conservative efforts to encourage traditional religious practices were praiseworthy.

But these signs of Orthodox moderation raised the possibility of conflict with the traditionalist Orthodox. The same weekend that Lamm made his conciliatory speech, the annual convention of Agudath Israel denounced any compromise with the other movements and resolved to spend $2 million for a public-relations campaign in Israel and the United States to convince Jews that non-Orthodox forms of Judaism spelled disaster for the Jewish people. One prominent Agudah rabbi went so far as to call Rabbi Lamm a "hater of the Lord." No one at the convention protested, nor was any apology forthcoming afterward.

Reform leaders, meanwhile, began to worry that if the Ne'eman Commission failed, the Israeli government might make Reform the scapegoat and blame it for disrupting Jewish unity. To head off this possibility and to persuade Jewish public opinion that Reform was not striving for anything unreasonable, in early December the movement issued a seven-page statement spelling out its demands: a cooperative conversion program (even if only Orthodox rabbis actually signed the conversion document); the right of any rabbi to perform marriages (even if these had to be only marriages allowed by Jewish law and the two witnesses had to be Orthodox); and an announcement by Prime Minister Netanyahu publicly withdrawing the conversion bill. The Reform statement also urged its activists to continue exerting influence on federation decision makers not to acquiesce in any deal unacceptable to the Reform and Conservative movements.

Meeting in Jerusalem later in December, the Zionist Congress—with its large Reform and Conservative delegations—overrode the objections of Orthodox delegates and officially espoused religious pluralism. It issued a statement calling on Jewish leaders to help insure the success of the Ne'eman Commission. In the event that body failed, delegates insisted that no legislation on the Law of Return or any similar religious matter that involved the Diaspora should be carried out unless with "wide approval and by bearing in mind the support of all parts of the Jewish people in Israel and the Diaspora."

RELIGIOUS AFFAIRS IN U.S.

Although the major battleground for interdenominational strife was Israel, American Jewish communities felt the aftershocks. Denominational cooperation was clearly in decline. The statement of the Union of Orthodox Rabbis delegitimizing Reform and Conservative Judaism was almost matched by the less publicized assertion by Rabbi Simeon Maslin, president of the Central Conference of American Rabbis, that "aside from devotion to Jewish learning, Orthodoxy offers little to American Jewry in the 21st century." Reports from around the country indicated that non-Orthodox Jews were cutting back on their philanthropic giving to Orthodox institutions. With Orthodox rabbis increasingly reluctant to allow the use of *mikvehs* (ritual baths) for non-Orthodox conversions, Conservative congregations were building their own, even though it usually made no economic sense to support two in the same locality. The Jewish antihunger organization Mazon, hoping to get all the religious bodies of American Jewry to support its 1997 fund-raising campaign to feed the needy of all religions, was rebuffed—at the last minute—by the Union of Orthodox Jewish Congregations, which wanted priority to go to the Jewish hungry. Even an interdenominational initiative to get all Jews to observe a special Sabbath on Friday night, April 4, 1997, in whatever way their denomination prescribed, could not be officially endorsed by the Orthodox Union, since it might imply the legitimacy of non-Orthodox Sabbath observance. Local boards of rabbis—which fewer and fewer Orthodox rabbis were joining anyway—found it more difficult than ever to operate effectively, largely due to acrimony over religious pluralism in Israel. In both New York and Washington, D.C., carefully crafted joint letters urging interdenominational cooperation and forbearance failed to garner the support of a significant minority of local rabbis, who felt that the statement was either not specific enough about religious pluralism or was too specific.

To be sure, not all interdenominational bonds were severed. Orthodox bodies worked with their non-Orthodox counterparts in writing to President Clinton on behalf of imprisoned spy Jonathan Pollard; and the interdenominational New York Board of Rabbis raised money to help repair two synagogues in Israel, a Reform and a Conservative, that had been damaged by ultra-Orthodox vandals. Also, a Shas Party proposal that the Orthodox break away from the Jewish Agency for Israel and create a separate entity that would fund only Orthodox projects aroused no interest in the United States. In addition, regular closed-door discussions between Reform, Conservative, and modern Orthodox rabbis went on in such major communities as New York, Chicago, and Los Angeles. Yet so palpable was the downturn in relations that two close friends, Orthodox rabbi Marc Angel, a former president of the Rabbinical Council of America, and Reform rabbi Sheldon Zimmerman, president of Hebrew Union College, felt compelled to issue a public joint plea to their colleagues "to work together, to build a future together, to retain our sense of family togetherness" (*New York Jewish Week,* November 28, 1997).

Unique among the nondenominational Jewish organizations, the American Jewish Committee sought to bring together representatives of the various religious groups in the hope of developing common ground. The Committee hosted two conferences toward the end of 1996, one on the state of Jewish peoplehood one year after the Rabin assassination, the other on the prospects for American Jewish continuity (see below, "The Continuity Debate"). And in late 1996, AJC hosted a delegation of Jerusalem high-school principals for ten days of exposure to American-style religious pluralism through visits to different kinds of American Jewish schools.

Denominational Developments

The crescendo of interdenominational conflict was related to developments within the religious movements, each heavily influenced by its own institutional needs and internal politics.

ORTHODOX JUDAISM

The assertiveness of the more extreme, or sectarian, Orthodox, who sought to keep outside cultural contacts to a minimum, continued to influence their more moderate Orthodox counterparts.

September 28, 1997, was a banner day for the sectarian Orthodox, largely represented by Agudath Israel. It was the tenth *siyum hashas,* completion of a cycle of study of the entire Talmud, celebrating the accomplishment of those able to stick to the regimen of learning a page a day for seven-and-a-half years. This program of daily study, which united thousands of men studying the same page all over the world, began in Poland in 1923. The steady growth and new self-confidence of American Orthodoxy since the 1960s had made Talmud study increasingly popular, and the 1997 celebration was the largest ever: 20,000 people filled Madison Square Garden for the main ceremony, with an estimated 50,000 more around the world participating by satellite hookup. To be sure, many involved in the celebration had not actually reviewed a daily page for 7,211 days, but were rather demonstrating solidarity with the project and esteem for those with the fortitude to complete it. In any case, this large-scale religious event reinforced sectarian Orthodoxy's conviction that its form of Torah scholarship, by immunizing practitioners against the values of secular society, was the key to Jewish survival.

The high status given to religious study in these Orthodox circles had, however, brought on new problems. Males were increasingly expected to spend years developing talmudic expertise rather than preparing to earn a living; meanwhile, the priority given to childbearing militated against their wives pursuing careers. As a result, large numbers of fervently Orthodox Jews were dependent on government aid. This came to the attention of the American public in November 1997 when a Hassidic woman reached New York mayor Giuliani on his call-in radio show and told him that the burden of coping with two-year-old twins and two-month-old triplets had led her to contemplate suicide. Giuliani swiftly provided her with the necessary help. Her husband, readers of the *New York Times* learned (November 8, 1997), "earns little as a nursery school teacher and, like many Hasidic men, often spends time away from his wife and children to study the Talmud."

Faced with growing financial pressures, the temptation to cut legal corners sometimes proved too great to resist, and some rabbis and educational institutions were accused of fraud and theft; there was even a case of money-laundering for drug rings. The media pounced on these cases, causing tremendous shame in heavily Orthodox neighborhoods. Rabbi Abraham Pam, the head of a leading rabbinical school, addressed the problem openly, in Yiddish, from the podium at the Agudath Israel convention in November 1996. He stressed the *hillul hashem,* the desecration of God's name, that Orthodox Jews create by financial misdeeds. He went on to castigate, as well, husbands who extorted huge sums of money from their wives as the price for granting them a *get,* the Jewish divorce document.

Yet such abuses did not begin to challenge the prevalent notion in sectors of the Orthodox community that withdrawal from the American mainstream was proof of greater Jewish authenticity, a tendency that was even spilling over into modern Orthodoxy. The 1996 convention of the Union of Orthodox Jewish Congregations of America, held over Thanksgiving weekend, reflected the defensiveness of moderate Orthodoxy under siege by more stringent interpretations. A major address by sociologist William Helmreich spelled out how the proponents of Orthodox insularity had gradually undermined older assumptions that Orthodoxy could mesh comfortably with the outside world. Helmreich cited the high number of sectarian Orthodox employed as teachers in modern Orthodox day schools, the culturally narrowing impact on American young men and women of a year or more of study in Israeli Orthodox educational institutions, and, most significantly, a loss of self-confidence among those in the Orthodox camp who were ideologically sympathetic to modern values. Helmreich cautioned that, no matter how closely the modern Orthodox tried to mimic the sectarians, they would never achieve total acceptance: "We will always be a paler shade of black."

Others at the convention did not share Helmreich's viewpoint, and, in fact, expressed admiration for those who distanced themselves from the corrosive influences of contemporary America. Dr. Bernard Lander, the president of Touro College in New York City, which provides vocational courses for yeshivah students so they would not have to be exposed to the liberal arts, told the convention that secular universities were "the crematorium of our people." The sectarian Orthodox *Jewish Observer* (February 1997) ran a five-page response to "the Helmreich principle," arguing that what the sociologist saw as an unfortunate shift to the right was actually a return by partially secularized Orthodox Jews to the classical faith.

So powerful had this separationist motif become that it began to affect at least some Orthodox Jews attending an Ivy League university—the type of young Jews who in previous years would have been considered the most acculturated and least sectarian within Orthodoxy. In the fall of 1996, two Orthodox freshmen at Yale refused to abide by the university policy that all unmarried students reside in the dormitories. Deeming the coed dorms antithetical to their Jewish religious values, they paid the required housing fees in order to maintain their student status, but lived off campus. In December 1997, joined by three new Orthodox students to form the "Yale Five" (one subsequently married to exempt herself from the regulation), they sued the university, charging that Yale's housing policy violated their constitutionally protected freedom of religion.

A group of modern Orthodox rabbis who shared Helmreich's frustrations launched a new organization, Edah, in the fall of 1996, dedicated to the promotion of a reinvigorated synthesis of Orthodox Judaism and modernity. To inculcate this spirit into the rabbis of the future, Edah set up a training program for students of Yeshiva University. In April 1997, however, soon after a leading Talmud professor at Yeshiva publicly compared Orthodox liberals to the biblical Amalek, the school severed all ties with Edah and strongly discouraged rabbinical students from involvement with its training program. Rabbi Norman Lamm, president of Yeshiva and himself associated with the moderate wing of Orthodoxy, took no personal part in the controversy. Despite the rebuff from Yeshiva, Edah managed to secure sufficient funding by the fall to establish a formal office and run full-page newspaper ads setting forth its goals: commitment to Halakhah in both the ritual and interpersonal realms; Torah study along with secular wisdom; encouragement to "rabbinic leaders to apply the just, humane, and spiritually fulfilling values of Torah to contemporary circumstances"; recognition of the religious significance of the State of Israel; and "love for other Jews, no matter what their level of observance."

Of all the divisive issues within Orthodoxy, the role of women was the most explosive. On January 21, 1997, the Vaad Harabonim of Queens, New York, the local Orthodox rabbinical association, voted overwhelmingly to ban separate prayer groups for women. A number of other Orthodox communities had such services, which enabled women to participate actively in the ritual in a way they could not in the standard Orthodox synagogue, where the sexes sat separately and men conducted the services. The Queens rabbis refused to address the specific halakhic arguments of one of their colleagues, Rabbi Simcha Krauss, who found women's prayer groups to be within the guidelines of Jewish law. Citing a 1985 prohibition issued by five Yeshiva University rabbis, the Vaad declared not only the prayer groups but also women dancing with the Torah on Simhat Torah and women reading the Scroll of Esther publicly on Purim to be "breaking the boundaries of Jewish tradition" and therefore "prohibited."

If the decision represented a further intensification of Orthodoxy's adversarial posture vis-à-vis modernity, it also precipitated a backlash of protest from many moderate Orthodox men and women to whom it appeared to indicate that religious restrictions on women's roles—at least in this case—were based not on an objective reading of Orthodox legal sources but rather on the rabbis' personal preference for the traditionally passive role of women in ritual life.

Publicity generated by this controversy swelled the number of participants at the first-ever International Conference on Orthodoxy and Feminism, held in New York in February, from an expected 450 to over 1,000. Reporter Peter Steinfels, writing in the *New York Times* (February 22, 1997), pointed out how this gathering differed from other feminist events: "The meeting was notable for its seriousness about Jewish learning and tradition. No one denied that modern feminism had arisen outside Judaism, but the premise was that it had to be tested and incorporated within the framework of halakha." Among the issues discussed were the plight of women in broken marriages whose husbands refused to give them a *get,* ways of restructuring the Orthodox synagogue so as to give women a greater sense of participation while maintaining the traditional separation between the sexes, and the possibility of women eventually taking on some of the roles currently performed by rabbis, such as deciding points of Jewish law. Indeed, in the aftermath of the conference, two modern Orthodox rabbis announced the formation of a program to train women to answer halakhic questions, and the Union for Traditional Judaism—which had broken away from the Conservative movement when it began ordaining women, but which now occupied the space on the denominational spectrum between modern Orthodox and Conservative—began developing a degree program for women that would enable them to carry out many rabbinic functions, but without the title of rabbi.

So successful was the Orthodox feminist conference that it led, in July, to the formation of a new organization, the Jewish Orthodox Feminist Alliance. Projecting a first-year budget of $150,000, it began planning for a second conference in February 1998.

In December, Orthodox feminism achieved a milestone when two leading synagogues in New York City—Lincoln Square Synagogue and the Hebrew Institute of Riverdale—hired women to perform counseling and educational functions normally handled by rabbis. They would not, however, be called rabbis, nor would they perform ritual functions halakhically barred to women.

CHABAD-LUBAVITCH

When Israeli prime minister Netanyahu came to the United States in September 1996, his schedule was so tight that he was not able to see a number of important people. But one he did manage to meet, at least in spirit, was the late Rabbi Menachem Mendel Schneerson, head of the Lubavitch Hassidic movement, whose grave the prime minister visited. After removing his shoes at the site and saying a prayer, Netanyahu told reporters that Schneerson was "the most influential Jew of our time." American adherents of the Lubavitch sect expressed pride at this recognition of their leader, though the help Netanyahu had received from Israeli Lubavitchers in the recent election surely played a role in his decision to come to the cemetery.

But Lubavitch remained a movement in crisis. Though their rabbi had been laid to rest in 1994, not only had no successor emerged, but his followers were split between those willing to acknowledge that he was gone and those who insisted that he had not really died and would soon reemerge as the messiah. On July 9, 1997, the day after the third Jewish anniversary of his death, the mainstream movement opened a new center in Washington—the Living Legacy Institute—and ran a full-page ad in the *New York Times* announcing the event. But the messianists preempted them with a full-page *Times* ad the day before, announcing that "The third of Tammuz is not the Rebbe's yahrzeit," since he had never died; he had been "liberated from the limitations of corporeal existence," so as to complete the task of redemption.

CONSERVATIVE JUDAISM

The Conservative movement, while not riven by sharp ideological conflict, continued to face challenges to its position at the center of the denominational spectrum. The internal debate noted above about whether to maintain the alliance with Reform in the fight for religious pluralism in Israel, or to aim for a limited arrangement whereby Conservative rabbis would gain greater recognition from the Orthodox, was just one example of contradictory pulls on the movement from the left and the right.

In October 1996, soon after the Southern Baptist Convention called for evangelizing the Jews, Rabbi Harold Schulweis of Encino, California, suggested a Jewish campaign to convert others to Judaism, "a national or international Jewish movement to educate, invite, and embrace non-Jews into the fold." While such sentiments had been heard in the precincts of Reform, this was the first time that a prominent Conservative rabbi had given them voice. Schulweis pointed to the proselytizing activity of Jews in the Roman Empire and argued that there is much in Judaism that might appeal to spiritual searchers. He announced to his congregation that he would host a series of lectures on Judaism geared to non-Jews and asked families to host these non-Jews for Sabbath meals.

Schulweis's initiative triggered sharp debate. Not only did the Orthodox criticize him on theological grounds, but even Reform leader Rabbi Eric Yoffie felt that, on practical grounds, such outreach should be limited to the Gentile partners in mixed marriages. While some Conservative rabbis agreed with Schulweis, leaders of the movement, such as JTS chancellor Ismar Schorsch, did not. Schorsch found "proselytizing profoundly offensive. One religion is not better than another. . . . The superiority of Judaism lies in the fact that it doesn't try to sell itself" (*Jerusalem Report,* February 20, 1997). Despite the lack of any formal backing from his movement, Schulweis said that his call elicited a flood of inquiries from non-Jews.

Another issue emanating from the West Coast also affected the movement: the role of spirituality. In late 1995, the Los Angeles branch of the Seminary—the University of Judaism—split off and went its own way, on the stated grounds that the New York school's emphasis on textual study was ill-suited to the spiritual concerns of West Coast Jews. By 1997, however, attention to the spirit was clearly evident in JTS itself. Not only did the school sponsor a series of open lectures on "Spiritual Journeys," but rabbinical students themselves eagerly participated in two discussion groups, "What Do You Believe?" and "God Talk." While he could understand student demand for such activities, Chancellor Schorsch was clearly uneasy. He said: "It's much more subjective. It's much less subtle, and it is much more centered on the individual." He insisted that spiritual exercises should not crowd Jewish practice or textual scholarship out of the curriculum (*New York Times,* April 12, 1997).

In the fall of 1996, JTS released a major demographic survey of the Conservative movement, conducted by a team of researchers led by Prof. Jack Wertheimer. It encompassed data from Conservative synagogues, their adult members, recent bar/bat mitzvahs, and the Conservative sample in the 1990 National Jewish Population Study, which included many unaffiliated Jews who called themselves Conservative. The survey findings were initially interpreted positively. At a press conference in October at which the data were released, Chancellor Schorsch said: "The center is holding. The Conservative movement has stubbornly held on to its ideals." But closer inspection of the report revealed a mixed picture. The overwhelming majority of the movement fully accepted Conservative Judaism's position on equality of the sexes; at the same time, more than two-thirds agreed with the Reform espousal of patrilineal descent, and 28 percent wanted their rabbis to be willing to perform intermarriages. Observance patterns proved disappointing. Just 62 percent agreed with the central tenet of Conservative Judaism, that there was an obligation to follow Jewish law. Actual practice was even weaker: less than a quarter of Conservative Jews kept kosher, only 37 percent lit Sabbath candles, and just 29 percent attended services even twice a month.

According to the findings, younger Conservative Jews were much more Jewishly literate and somewhat more observant than their elders, probably reflecting the impact of the movement's educational system and summer camps. Yet that might not necessarily translate into future gains for the movement. As Rabbi Jerome Epstein, executive vice-president of the United Synagogue of Conservative Judaism, explained, many of the most motivated young Conservatives were joining Orthodox synagogues, because few Conservative congregations provided vibrant models of observant Jewish life. At the 1997 biennial convention of the United Synagogue, Epstein suggested the creation of "magnet congregations" to attract Jewishly serious singles and young marrieds.

REFORM JUDAISM

On October 31, 1996, Rabbi Sheldon Zimmerman was officially installed as president of Hebrew Union College (HUC), the seminary that ordains Reform rabbis. Zimmerman—who had earlier expressed the wish to be called the institution's *rosh yeshivah,* the traditional honorific for the head of an Orthodox talmudic academy—used the occasion to reiterate his call for greater breadth and depth of Torah learning in the movement. Only thus, according to Zimmerman, would Reform attract Jews seeking "spiritual sustenance and meaning."

The trend toward greater traditionalism and spirituality among Reform leaders was evident at the 1997 biennial of the Union of American Hebrew Congregations (UAHC), a year after Zimmerman's inaugural address. Although no kosher food was available, for the first time in its history the UAHC offered *kippot* (skullcaps) to worshipers, and many donned them, as well as prayer shawls. Both of these items had been anathema to Classical Reform. Even three separate morning services were not enough, as worshipers spilled out into the hotel lobby. One prominent rabbi, addressing the delegates, called on the movement to restore the traditional doctrine of the afterlife, in its literal sense. Rabbi Eric Yoffie, UAHC president, decried the Judaic ignorance of all too many Reform Jews, "who can name the mother of Jesus, but not the mother of Moses." He challenged his followers to learn how to chant the Torah; to read and discuss at least four serious Jewish books each year; to study Jewish texts as part of temple committee meetings; to learn Torah as part of the regular Sabbath service; and to go back to the Orthodox custom of staying awake all night learning Torah on the eve of the Shavuot holiday, which marks the traditional date of the revelation on Mt. Sinai.

Another indication of the new winds blowing within Reform was the election of Rabbi Richard Levy as the new president of the Central Conference of American Rabbis (CCAR). The first president not to come from the ranks of the pulpit rabbinate or the administration of HUC, Levy had been a Hillel rabbi. Echoing Yoffie, Levy bluntly acknowledged that, in his experience, Reform students hesitated to join Hillel "because they fear they will not know enough to be able to participate without embarrassment." Calling for a return to traditional *mitzvot* (commandments), Levy challenged the notion that more observance meant capitulating to the Orthodox. On the contrary, he insisted, "if all Jews stood at Sinai, Reform Jews stood there too." And Levy announced that, at the 1999 convention, the Reform movement would be ready with a new official credo that would help "transform the nature of our private and our public days into holy lives" (*Reform Judaism,* Fall 1997).

Yet for all of the excitement among the movement's elite about recapturing religious meaning, much of the rank and file had more mundane concerns. Sociological reality put the issue of mixed marriage—specifically, the question of rabbinic officiation—near the top of the movement's agenda. With such marriages on the upsurge (young Reform Jews, according to the 1990 National Jewish Population Study, were intermarrying at a 62-percent rate), pressure was mounting to convince more rabbis to perform them. As things stood, the movement officially opposed officiation at mixed marriages, while at the same time upholding the principle of rabbinic autonomy. But a group of lay leaders, led by David Belin, wanted to erase the official opposition, claiming that some three-quarters of Reform Jews wanted their rabbis to perform mixed marriages. A proposal put forward by the Belin group at a UAHC board of trustees meeting in December 1996 urged rabbis to "resolve ambivalent feelings in favor of rabbinic officiation," and to devise new phraseology for mixed-religion ceremonies so as not to make the non-Jewish partner uncomfortable.

The Belin resolution was overwhelmingly rejected. This result had little to do with the trustees' feelings about rabbinic officiation, which most of them favored, but with the jurisdictional question of whether it was appropriate for the laity to dictate religious policy to the rabbinate. In the end, the lay people backed down from such a confrontation. Reflecting rabbinic resentment at lay pressure, Rabbi Eric Yoffie, president of the UAHC, told the trustees that he felt it wrong for congregations to hire a rabbi on the basis of whether he or she would perform mixed marriages.

Belin put forward his resolution once again at the UAHC biennial in October 1997. This time he was buttressed by a new survey of rabbinic attitudes toward intermarriage conducted by the Jewish Outreach Institute, which Belin chaired. Signaling a shift toward greater accommodation of mixed marriage, a majority of the non-Orthodox rabbis surveyed said that their congregations had more to gain than to lose by reaching out to these families; 36 percent of the Reform and 62 percent of the Reconstructionists said they performed intermarriages; and a surprisingly large minority of Conservative and even Orthodox rabbis who would not officiate at these weddings noted that they would refer mixed couples to other rabbis who did. (To be sure, representatives of these movements questioned the accuracy of the findings.) But the data did not help Belin's cause. Many of the UAHC delegates, viewing his suggestion as an insult to their rabbis, booed and hissed his presentation, and the proposal was not even considered.

The Jewish validity of another kind of marriage—between two people of the same sex—was on the agenda of the Reform rabbis. Already on record in favor of the civil marriages of gays and lesbians, in June 1997 the CCAR convention heard the report of its ad hoc committee on human sexuality that had been set up a year earlier. The committee recommended that Reform Judaism endorse, and its rabbis perform, same-sex Jewish marriages. Final action on the report was scheduled for the 1998 convention.

The CCAR also adopted—for the first time in its history—a "platform" on the meaning of the State of Israel. This document, seven years in the making, signified the final stage of the gradual Zionization of a movement that had been historically ambivalent, even hostile, to the idea of a Jewish state. The platform stated that Israel was obliged to embody the high moral standards of Judaism, with full rights for all citizens; that preserving Jewish lives came before the holiness of the land; that all Reform institutions should encourage the study of Hebrew; that while Israel was "the spiritual and cultural focal point of world Jewry,

Israeli and Diaspora Jewry are interdependent"; that American Jews should be encouraged to visit Israel and to settle there; and—in a clear reference to the fight over religious pluralism—that Israel would be better off "as a pluralistic, democratic society."

RECONSTRUCTIONIST JUDAISM

The smallest branch of American Judaism—barely 1 percent—Reconstructionism made something of a stir late in 1996 with the release of a survey of its members. True to its popular image of appealing to intellectuals, 41 percent of Reconstructionist households had at least one adult with a Ph.D., M.D., or law degree. Over half the sample had been raised in Conservative homes, 71 percent said they were drawn to Reconstructionism by the sense of warmth it exuded, and 65 percent said the inclusiveness and sexual egalitarianism of the movement were important to them.

In perhaps the most surprising finding, 34 percent of the Reconstructionists claimed that they kept kosher, even though the movement taught that this was simply a Jewish folkway. This was in contrast to the 24 percent of Conservative Jews who kept kosher, even though, for them, *kashrut* was a Torah requirement. This disparity led Rabbi Mordechai Liebling, executive director of the Jewish Reconstructionist Federation, to suggest that "voluntaristic Judaism works . . . exposing people to a rich, meaningful Jewish life and allowing them to bring their full cognitive faculties to bear leads them to choose to be more observant." Liebling also felt that the high percentage of conversions to Judaism of non-Jews married to Reconstructionist Jews—40 percent—vindicated the movement's policy of openness to the intermarried.

If, indeed, Reconstructionism was so successful for its adherents, why was it not catching on in the broader Jewish community? According to Rabbi Liebling, the essential doctrines first propounded by Rabbi Mordechai Kaplan, the founder of Reconstructionism—such as the centrality of Jewish peoplehood, Judaism as an evolving civilization—had quietly penetrated the other movements, to the point that "70 percent of American Jews are Reconstructionists at heart—they just don't know it" (*Moment,* June 1997).

The Continuity Debate

Someone looking only at the amount of activity within the denominations and between them would hardly suspect that in the eyes of many knowledgeable observers, American Judaism was in fact in danger of disappearing.

A *New York* magazine cover story (July 14, 1997) put the question bluntly: "Declining Birth Rates. Rampant Intermarriage. The 'Seinfeld Effect.' Are American Jews Assimilating Themselves Out of Existence?" Those Jewish leaders interviewed for the article by reporter Craig Horowitz tended to answer in the affirmative. With Jews successfully entering the mainstream of American life, concluded Horowitz, "it requires only a small stretch of the imagination to see an America 75 or 100 years from now in which the only readily identifiable Jews will be the Orthodox and the ultra-Orthodox. Everyone else will have assimilated themselves out of existence." Even attending the lectures and classes given by the most charismatic Jewish outreach activists gave Horowitz the "sense that it is time to circle the wagons, to turn inward, to huddle together." Writing in the *New York Times Sunday Magazine* (June 8, 1997), Ari Shavit asserted that "Jewish America seems to be engaged in a process of demographic suicide (average age, 39; average number of births per mother, 1.6; rate of intermarriage exceeding 52 percent)." Calling America "the most luxurious burial ground ever of Jewish cultural existence," Shavit suggested that the crisis would ultimately endanger Israelis as well: It remained to be seen "whether a meaningful non-Orthodox existence is possible in the third millennium; whether we can all avoid being the last of the non-Orthodox Jews."

There were some who felt that the problem was being exaggerated. Journalist J.J. Goldberg, for example, argued on the op-ed page of the *New York Times* (August 3, 1997) that the actual intermarriage rate was not the oft-cited 52 percent but 38 percent, that Jews who married non-Jews did not necessarily mean to abandon Judaism, that many mixed-faith couples were "open to raising their children as Jews," and that the crisis atmosphere had been artificially stimulated by political conservatives who wanted to get Jews to turn inward, "return to the ghetto," and abandon political liberalism. Goldberg hoped, by publicizing the lower intermarriage rate, to halt Jewish panic so that the community "could assume its role as a leading force for decency and tolerance in America."

Among the political conservatives Goldberg was seeking to refute was former assistant secretary of state Elliott Abrams, whose book *Faith and Fear: How Jews Can Survive in a Christian America* attracted considerable attention. Accepting the accuracy of the grim demographic data, Abrams argued that the erosion of the Jewish community was due to its espousal of liberal universalism and an extreme interpretation of the separation of religion and state. While such an outlook served Jewish interests in combating anti-Semitism and easing Jewish professional and business success, wrote Abrams, it also distanced Jews from their religious identity, leaving young Jews little reason not to marry Gentiles. Abrams believed that only a return to serious Jewish religious practice might save the American Jewish community. And, in his view, this would entail restoring religion to the American public square in alliance with the Christian right.

Abrams's stress on the religious dimension of Jewish survival—if not his denunciation of liberalism and his plea for cooperation with Christian conservatives—was echoed by many of the Jewish thinkers who participated in *Commentary*'s symposium, "What Do American Jews Believe?" (August 1996). The questions about God, the chosen people doctrine, the Holocaust, the State of Israel, and denominational relations elicited significantly more traditional responses than those expressed in the first such *Commentary* symposium 30 years before.

For some Jews, even a return to previously discarded beliefs and practices did not satisfy the urge for transcendence. Jewish "spirituality," in the sense of mystical communion with the supernatural, came into vogue, and not only among Jews. "Pop Goes the Kabbalah" was the title of a long article in *Time* (November 24, 1997). Younger Jews, it claimed, were discovering the treasures of medieval Jewish mystical literature, and so were Jewish and non-Jewish celebrities such as Madonna, Sandra Bernhard, and Roseanne, who said that Kabbalah was like quantum physics except that "you get it right away."

Quite another slant on the situation of American Jewry was provided by the well-known law professor Alan Dershowitz in his book *The Vanishing American Jew: In Search of Jewish Identity for the Next Century.* Dershowitz agreed with Abrams on the seriousness of the crisis, but proposed a diametrically opposite solution. Noting that the stimulus for this book was his son's marriage to a Catholic and the realization that his grandchildren would not be considered Jews according to traditional Jewish teachings, Dershowitz argued for the recognition of the Jewish authenticity of secular forms of Jewishness. By this he meant the acceptance of "compassion, creativity, contributions to the world at large, charity, a quest for education" as valid markers of Jewish identity. The alternative—the survival as Jews of only those relatively few who took the religion seriously—was not a prospect he relished.

Whatever diagnosis the intellectuals might propose, leaders of the Jewish community were faced with the practical task of grappling with intermarriage. It was no accident that a *Newsweek* report on mixed-religion families (December 15, 1997) focused primarily on Jews married to Gentiles. At some 2.5 percent of the population, an over-50-percent intermarriage rate threatened the very survival of the community, a fate that Christian denominations did not have to worry about. But the very ubiquity of the intermarried made it a difficult issue to discuss candidly; after all, even the assumption that mixed marriages constituted a problem might offend these couples. An American Jewish Committee poll in early 1997 documented the understandable tendency of mixed-marrieds not to view their status as an aberration. While 61 percent of American Jews thought that anti-Semitism was a greater threat to Jewish life in the United States than intermarriage, the figure rose to 82 percent among those with non-Jewish spouses.

In the formulation of communal policy, two conflicting positions had crystallized. One, often justified by the argument that the act of marrying a non-Jew did not necessarily indicate lack of interest in being Jewish, called for a heavy investment in outreach programs to intermarried families. The other view considered this a waste of precious communal resources on individuals who, in most cases, were too far removed from Jewish life to be positively affected anyway, and also a subtle signal that intermarriage was Jewishly acceptable. This school of thought preferred carefully targeted initiatives to strengthen the Jewish identification of people already at least peripherally involved in Jewish life.

In August 1996, proponents of the latter position—some 20 rabbis and academicians from across the denominational spectrum—issued a "Policy Statement on Jewish Continuity." It affirmed commitment to Torah and Jewish learning, Jewish peoplehood, and the concept of covenant. The statement affirmed the "plurality of religious expression in American Judaism," but insisted on maintaining "strong, visible religious boundaries between Jews and non-Jews," proposed outreach programs primarily for "the moderately affiliated," and urged that programs directed "toward those who have strayed furthest from Judaism" must not "siphon away funds urgently needed to strengthen Jewish life at its core. Nor should outreach give rise to ideological neutrality on core issues such as mixed marriage itself." (A subsequent somewhat revised statement, signed by 30 leading figures from all denominations, was published as "A Statement on the Jewish Future," in the *Jerusalem Report,* June 22, 1997.)

On December 5, 1996, the American Jewish Committee convened a consultation of community leaders—including proponents and opponents of the statement—to discuss "Strategies to Secure Jewish Continuity." The overall tone of the discussion was hostile to the statement—indeed, Peter Steinfels, who interviewed some of the critics a few days before the consultation, described their reaction as "cold fury" (*New York Times,* November 30, 1996). Several participants spoke movingly about their own relatives, who, they charged, were written off by the statement. Federation leaders explained that their mandate was to support the outreach projects of all segments of the community, rather than–like the statement—make value judgments about which were worthy and which not. Thus David Arnow, a vice-president of New York UJA-Federation, argued that instead of criticizing one form of outreach or another, the emphasis should be on the positive: "What do we have to offer people that they will find valuable?"

Of all the approaches urged over the previous few years to bolster Jewish continuity and reverse the demographic erosion of American Jewry, day-school education came to exercise a special fascination in 1996–97. But the push for day schools led to tensions in some communities.

One significant development was the decision of the Seattle-based Samis Foundation to subsidize tuition at the one Jewish high school in the city, which was run along Orthodox lines. As a result, beginning in the fall of 1996, the cost of sending a child to the school fell from $7,150 to $3,000. This was believed to be the first time that any foundation had granted a blanket subsidy to all students in any one Jewish school. The foundation's assumption that financial constraints had prevented many Jewish families from using the school proved correct: The size of the freshman class tripled, as even many non-Orthodox parents opted to send their children there. But this private help for the high school impelled the local federation to rearrange its allocations for Jewish education. It reduced funding for the high school and used the money to help other institutions.

The next community to confront the day-school issue was Chicago, where a coalition of yeshivah and day-school presidents organized to get more federation support. The facts were not in doubt: the Chicago Jewish Federation was giving just under $2.5 million to day schools, 18 percent of its total allocations, significantly higher than the national average of 12 percent, yet not enough to cover accelerating expenses. George Hanus, the president of a day school in the city, predicted that "the system will go bankrupt in the next decade unless we figure out a way to pay for families that can't afford it." But Steven Nasatir, executive vice-president of the federation, wondered where more day-school money would come from. "Do we take it from care of the aged? Care of the hungry in Chicago or in Russia? Do you take it from community centers, which is an informal educational experience which touches a lot of people?"

Chicago's day-school proponents, recognizing that the problem transcended the local community, announced the formation of a National Jewish Day School Scholarship Committee. Some 170 Jewish educators from around the country came to Chicago for the initial meeting of the committee on September 21, 1997. Representing Orthodox, Conservative, and Reform schools, they brought with them letters of support from the national leaders of their denominations. A highlight of the meeting was the release of a new study, *The Financing of Jewish Day Schools,* written by Marvin Schick and Jeremy Dauber, and funded by the Avi Chai Foundation. It argued that, on the whole, these schools were performing heroically under adverse conditions. Despite the dual program of Judaic and secular studies, the day schools' per capita expenditures were about the same as those of public schools offering only a secular program, and tuition payments in most of these schools covered no more than half the budget. Furthermore, confirming what the Samis Foundation had discovered in Seattle, parents choosing not to send children to day schools were most often deterred by the high tuition.

Momentum continued to build for more aid to day schools. Some help was found independent of the federation system. In October 1997, philanthropist Michael Steinhardt announced the formation of the Partnership for Excellence in Jewish Education. Twelve individuals, families, and foundations would each donate $1.5 million over five years. The money would go for the establishment of new elementary schools and the extension of some existing elementary schools into junior high schools; each school was required to raise at least the same amount from other nontuition sources as it got from the partnership.

Meanwhile, day-school proponents submitted resolutions to their local federations committing these bodies "to work diligently to make a quality Jewish day school education available to all Jewish children," a goal justified by invoking "the survival of the Jewish people." While only the Chicago federation officially endorsed it, the resolution was placed on the agenda of the General Assembly of the Council of Jewish Federations that met in November, where it was voted down. The federation leaders, many of whom said that they favored increased funding for day schools in principle, nevertheless feared that this resolution, if interpreted literally, might force them to channel all new campaign money into the day schools, to the exclusion of other needs. But the GA did set up a task force that would study the issue and report back at the 1998 meeting.

This did not satisfy the day-school enthusiasts. In December day-school proponents in Baltimore launched a public campaign with newspaper ads that called on the federation to spend more on these schools. And in Los Angeles, real estate developer Joseph Bobker announced that he was giving up on the federation system. He set up an independent United Jewish Education Fund, with its own professional staff, to raise money for the city's day schools. Infuriated federation officials charged him with "polarizing" the community.

Holocaust-Related Developments

There was continuing interest in the long-term legacy of the Nazi destruction of European Jewry 50 years earlier, as well as some surprising revelations. The fascination with the Holocaust stood in marked contrast to an almost total indifference (except for a scholarly conference at Harvard and an extensive symposium in the September 8–15, 1997, *New Republic*) to the 100th anniversary of Zionism.

The U.S. Holocaust Memorial Museum in Washington, which had opened its doors in 1993, continued to attract large crowds. While visitors in the early days had been mostly Jewish, the museum now estimated that the proportion of non-Jews had reached 62 percent. The museum was a standard stop for many student groups visiting Washington from all over the United States and abroad, and its Web site averaged over 50,000 hits a week.

The Museum of Jewish Heritage–A Living Memorial to the Holocaust, which opened in New York City in September 1997, differed from the Washington institution in placing the Holocaust within the broader context of 20th-century Jewish life, and in telling the story through the eyes of individual victims and survivors. "New York has struggled for 50 years to build a memorial to the Holocaust," wrote a *New York Times* critic (September 15). "And that goal has now been brilliantly realized."

Meanwhile, on the West Coast, Steven Spielberg's Shoah Foundation hired Michael Berenbaum, formerly director of the Research Institute of the Holocaust Memorial Museum, to take charge of the Visual History Foundation, whose mandate was to videotape interviews with tens of thousands of Holocaust survivors all over the world. The American public's interest in the Holocaust was in evidence once again when NBC-TV aired Spielberg's three-hour blockbuster movie *Schindler's List,* which had won seven Oscars in 1994, on February 23, 1997. The sole sponsor, the Ford Division of Ford Motor Company, agreed to no commercial interruptions. The ratings were enormous.

SWISS BANKS AND THE JEWS

Through 1995 and early 1996 there were revelations about Jewish funds deposited in Swiss banks before and during the Holocaust that had never been returned to survivors or their heirs. Largely due to the persistence of the World Jewish Congress, more and more details surfaced in late 1996 and through 1997, including the fact that there was gold in Swiss banks that had been confiscated from Jews by the Nazis. American Jews—especially the survivors and their families—insisted on restitution, and the American government, which had apparently not pushed the Swiss hard on the matter immediately after World War II, became embroiled in this complicated question as well. In January 1997 the Swiss ambassador to the United States was forced to resign upon the disclosure that he had advised his government that Switzerland had to win what he called this "war." At least three special commissions were investigating—one headed by former Federal Reserve chairman Paul Volcker, another by Under Secretary of Commerce Stuart Eizenstat, and the third appointed by the Swiss.

Among American Jews—most of whom were unfamiliar with the complexities of international banking, but quite aware that a massive injustice had been done—two important questions arose. One was purely tactical: should individual claimants sue the Swiss banks, or would that only hamper the efforts of governments and international Jewish bodies to negotiate an overall settlement? The other question was how aggressively to confront the Swiss. Some who urged caution believed that the Swiss would be more likely to settle if they did not feel that there was an international campaign to blacken their reputation. Others were concerned that Jewish emphasis on financial restitution might reinforce anti-Semitic stereotypes about Jews and money, while diverting attention from the human toll exacted by the Holocaust.

American Jews took to their hearts Cristoph Meili, a security guard at the Union Bank of Switzerland, who in January 1997 turned over to a Jewish institution archival material from the bank that was about to be shredded. As it turned out, these papers contained information about the assets of Holocaust victims. Meili was fired, and the Anti-Defamation League immediately set up a $36,000 fund to help him. In May Meili came to the United States and testified before the Senate Banking Committee, as Jewish organizations arranged numerous job offers. In July President Clinton signed a bill, unanimously passed by Congress, granting Meili and his family permanent residency status.

By July American newspapers were printing lists released by Swiss banks of unclaimed accounts from the Holocaust period. In December a three-day conference in London, attended by delegates from 40 countries, set up a new international fund to help Holocaust survivors, and each nation pledged to research and account for what it had done during the Holocaust.

MADELEINE ALBRIGHT

For American Jews, the most startling revelation related to the Holocaust was the disclosure of the Jewish origins of Madeleine Albright, the new secretary of state. In February 1997 Albright acknowledged the accuracy of a report in the

Washington Post that her Czech parents were actually Jews who converted to Catholicism after escaping from the Nazis to England in 1939—but who never told their children about their religious roots or the fact that two of their grandparents perished in Auschwitz. In July Albright paid an emotional visit to Prague, where she toured the Jewish cemetery and the old synagogue where her paternal grandparents' names were among those of 77,000 Holocaust victims inscribed on the walls. In apparent response to skeptics who found it hard to believe that she had never before suspected her Jewish origins, Albright told reporters that, though she had visited this synagogue a year earlier with Hillary Clinton, she had not checked the names because "I did not know my own family story then."

American Jews had conflicted feelings about the Albright revelation. Those who thought that she might have known all along that her parents had been Jewish feared that such a "self-hating Jew" would be biased against Israel; others suggested that even if she was genuinely surprised to find out the truth, she might now bend over backward in Middle East diplomacy to favor the Arab side, so as to prove that her Jewishness did not influence her policies. Optimists suggested that the centrality of the Holocaust to the circumstances of her upbringing might make her especially sensitive to Israel's plight as a lone democracy beset by hostile dictatorships. One by-product of the Albright story was the Jewish community's sudden realization that there were surely thousands of other people—mostly in Central and Eastern Europe—whose parents or grandparents converted or hid their Jewishness to save themselves. Some of the descendants had, like Albright, discovered their Jewish origins, while countless others remained in the dark.

Jewish Studies Controversy

At the beginning of July 1996, Prof. Thomas Bird, a Catholic scholar of Yiddish, was appointed director of Jewish studies at Queens College, a unit of the City University of New York. The choice was immediately attacked by some Jewish faculty members on the grounds that Bird did not have a Ph.D., did not know Hebrew, and, not being Jewish, could not provide a role model for Jewish students. In addition, some expressed the fear that the local Jewish community might withdraw support from the program under its new chairman. In his resignation letter sent two weeks after his appointment, Bird wrote: "It is impossible not to conclude that the attempt to trash my academic record and standing in the community through insinuation and omission is anything other than a fig leaf for objections to my being a Gentile."

Outside the Queens College faculty, Jewish sentiment overwhelmingly supported Bird and regretted his resignation. The American Jewish Committee—which gave Bird an award for his long-standing efforts on behalf of Soviet Jews—the American Jewish Congress, and the Anti-Defamation League all issued statements backing Bird and stressing that religion was an invalid criterion for an academic appointment. Many Jewish studies professors from other universities agreed. The president of Queens College announced the appointment of a search committee to find a distinguished Jewish studies scholar to take over the chairmanship; meanwhile, Bird and two others were named to administer the program jointly on an interim basis.

Fascination with Bible

Each Sunday for ten weeks, beginning in mid-October 1996, millions of Americans watched "Genesis" on PBS. Hosted by Bill Moyers, the show featured animated discussions between a shifting cast of Jewish and non-Jewish scholars about the first book of the Bible, from the creation of the world to the story of Joseph. Moyers, who had spent six years planning the project, got the idea from Burton Visotzky, professor of Midrash at the Jewish Theological Seminary, who had been conducting such discussion groups for a long time. Through "Genesis," many Americans, Jews and non-Jews, were exposed to Midrash, the traditional Jewish mode of scriptural exposition, which was far looser and more allusive than the literal approach to the Bible that most Americans were brought up on.

The popularity of "Genesis" and the publications it spun off was not an isolated phenomenon. Some half-dozen new translations and books interpreting Genesis also found interested consumers. Visotzky—the author of one of the books—believed that the issues dealt with in the first book of the Bible resonated with contemporary Americans: infertility, sibling rivalry, loneliness, greed, dysfunctional families. Others suggested that discontent with the spiritual bankruptcy of modernity and awareness of the impending end of the millennium induced a fascination among broad sectors of the population with the biblical and Judaic roots of Western culture.

Another aspect of the new fascination with the Bible was popular interest in "Bible codes." Unlike the Moyers series, whose targeted audience was liberal and highly educated, the codes fascinated Jews and Christians of a more fundamentalist stripe. Several writers in Israel and the United States claimed that predictions about the future are encoded in the Hebrew text of Scripture. That is, by counting a certain number of letters in sequence, one might find the names of later illustrious rabbis, as well as information about such major events as the Holocaust and the assassination of Prime Minister Rabin. (One of these writers even claimed to have warned Rabin.) In some Orthodox circles, Bible codes were used to prove the divine origin of Scripture to nonbelievers. Skeptics, however, pointed out that there is no agreement on the authentic text of the Bible, and that similar "codes" might be found, if searched for long enough, in any long book. No one, however, could disagree with Michael Drosnin, whose book *The Bible Code* was published by Simon and Schuster, that the public discussion "is tapping into the great hold that religion still has on the world."

Some geneticists enhanced the popular credibility of the Jewish Bible even further when they found that many *kohanim,* traditionally believed to be descendants of the biblical high priest Aaron, actually do share two distinctive markers on the Y chromosome that is only transmitted from father to son, which is indeed the way that priestly status was handed down through Jewish history. The results of this research were announced toward the end of 1996, and even many non-Orthodox Jews, whose denominations had long ago discarded the special religious status of *kohanim,* acknowledged being awestruck by the discovery.

Philanthropy

The complex network of American Jewish philanthropic agencies continued to raise extraordinary amounts of money. According to the 1996 report of *The Chronicle of Philanthropy,* the United Jewish Appeal ranked sixth among all U.S. charities, and 16 local Jewish federations made the top-400 list, along with a number of other Jewish organizations. Yet the weaknesses that had already become evident in American Jewish philanthropy—overreliance on a few large donors, doubts over the willingness of the younger generation of Jews to contribute as their parents had, controversy over aid to an Israel that did not recognize non-Orthodox forms of Judaism—remained. In late 1996 and through 1997, philanthropic agencies sought to address two interrelated challenges. These were, first, determining the relative priorities of aid to Israel and support for domestic Jewish concerns; and, second, satisfying the desires of many contributors who wanted a greater say in where their money was going.

How to divide up the philanthropic dollar between American and Israeli causes was a central theme in ongoing talks between the Council of Jewish Federations, primarily concerned with local Jewish needs, and the United Jewish Appeal, which, through the United Israel Appeal and the American Jewish Joint Distribution Committee, allocated money to Israel and other foreign Jewish communities. In recent years, as Israel came to be seen as a prosperous country no longer under direct military threat, federations put more money into local projects and sent less to Israel. A May 1996 proposal for outright merger had been rebuffed both because federation leaders felt that it threatened their autonomy, and because advocates of aid for Israel feared that there were insufficient guarantees of money to overseas causes. In July, a looser "partnership" was proposed: although the organizations would have one common board and executive committee, staffs and chief executives would remain separate. The joint board and executive committee would both be made up of an equal number of representatives from the UJA and the federations, presumably insuring that domestic and overseas needs would get equal consideration, but there were no requirements imposed on federations about how much they would allocate overseas. The plan was finalized in June 1997, when a majority of the federations voiced their approval.

Recognizing that the new system would provide no ironclad guarantees of funding for Israel, the UJA and the Jewish Agency for Israel—which receives and disburses the UJA money in Israel—made a concerted effort to convince American Jewry that Israel still needed its philanthropy for the absorption of immigrants and for Zionist educational programs, even though the country was thriving. Indeed, UJA chairman Richard Wexler virtually conceded that American Jewish support for Israel was important less for the money itself than for the bond it sustained between the two Jewish communities. But critics questioned whether the Jewish Agency, a highly politicized body, was spending the money from America efficiently and suggested that American Jews might help Israel more effectively by bypassing the Jewish Agency and directing their money to specific causes and institutions in Israel. This was already being done on a large scale (a total of some $700 million per year) by individual American Jews, and some felt that the time had come for the UJA itself to give to worthy Israeli institutions without the Jewish Agency as an intermediary. Dissatisfaction with the political and religious policies of the Netanyahu government intensified this impulse, as some federation leaders sought to direct money to Israeli organizations that promoted the peace process and religious pluralism.

The San Francisco federation was the first to break ranks. In March 1997 it subtracted $1 million from its annual UJA contribution: half would be allocated to local Jewish causes, the other half given directly to Israeli projects that promoted Arab-Jewish understanding and Jewish religious pluralism. Federation president Alan Rothenberg commented that "nowhere in the Talmud does it say write a check to the UJA." But UJA chairman Wexler, who went to San Francisco in a vain attempt to stave off this move, charged that elderly Jews in the former Soviet Union would now go hungry because the federation had cut back on its overseas aid. Nevertheless, the UJA itself, unable completely to ignore the new philanthropic individualism, set up a program whereby donors could specify where their money would go.

Donors' desires to control the allocation of their gifts were a concern in several communities beside San Francisco, affecting both money for Israel and domestic philanthropy. In New York, for example, UJA-Federation enabled donors especially interested in Jewish culture to earmark donations for specific projects of the National Foundation for Jewish Culture. In Louisville, one major donor was allowed to keep Israel from getting any of his large gift, despite the federation's standard practice of giving 40 percent to the UJA. In Oakland, California, givers were encouraged to donate, first, to the general fund, and then, to contribute to a choice of special funds for social justice, education, Israel, or spiritual renewal. As this trend toward customized giving spread, so did the misgivings of the fund-raising establishment. Martin Kraar, executive vice-president of the CJF, said: "You don't ensure that the greatest needs will be met that way . . . donors may not have all the information in the aggregate about where the money is needed."

Organizational Developments

The Conference of Presidents of Major American Jewish Organizations named Melvin Salberg, former ADL national chairman, its new chairman. The Jewish National Fund, buffeted by charges of mismanagement, chose Ronald Lauder as its new president. The Israel Policy Forum and Project Nishma, both dedicated to advancing the Middle East peace process, merged under the IPF name. The National Yiddish Book Center, a major repository of Yiddish literature, opened a permanent facility on the campus of Hampshire College in Amherst, Massachusetts.

LAWRENCE GROSSMAN

Jewish Culture

TOWARD THE END OF 1997, the YIVO Institute for Jewish Research sponsored a benefit dinner in New York City honoring two guests: the *Forward*, celebrating its hundredth birthday as a newspaper, and Philip Roth, who was receiving a Lifetime Achievement Award for the array of his writings that began in 1959 with the short stories of *Goodbye, Columbus* and to which he added his 22nd book in 1997, the novel *American Pastoral*. The principals on the dais at this occasion illustrate just how complex the idea of "American Jewish Culture" is.

First, YIVO—founded in Vilna in 1925 but, since the Holocaust, on location in New York City where it waits now to move into the new Center for Jewish History, joining there the American Jewish Historical Society, the Leo Baeck Institute, and the Yeshiva University Museum. The main preoccupation of YIVO now is to assemble and study records of Jewish life in Eastern Europe, a culture which, like the Yiddish language through which that life mainly expressed itself, was virtually destroyed in the Holocaust.

Second, the *Forward*—the socialist daily that emerged in response to East European Jewish immigration to the United States, achieving a peak circulation of 250,000 and surviving now, with none of its earlier competitors left, on the 25,000 readers of its weekly edition published in English and Russian versions, as well as the Yiddish original.

Third, Roth, whose early writings produced a rare consensus—openly hostile—within the American Jewish civic and religious establishments, but who has gradually acquired something like respectability even among those same critics. At least on this celebratory occasion, the onetime charges against Roth of Jewish self-hatred and vulgarity were set aside—although the author himself, still conceding little to the evening's premise that his writings were, after all, in some important sense Jewish, limited his response to expressing gratitude to YIVO, devoted as it was to Yiddish, for its willingness to honor him as "an English writer for achievement in English."

The cast of characters at the YIVO dinner makes it clear that no one definition of American Jewish culture will work easily. Indeed, one may ask why "American Jewish" to begin with, rather than "Jewish American"? And even more basically still: why attach any ethnic or religious labels to artistic or intellectual work?

As important as these questions are, they cannot be answered in a brief essay devoted to Jewish cultural expression in a single year, 1997. Suffice it to say that this essay will take as its terrain the meeting ground of the identifiably American and the identifiably Jewish—when the two mingle, yet continue to retain clear marks of their sources.

Jewish Studies

A key development in the Jewish cultural sphere in recent decades has been the growth of Jewish studies programs in colleges and universities across the country. Prof. Harry Wolfson retired in 1958 as the Nathan Littauer Professor of Jewish Literature and Philosophy at Harvard, and to look back at that event now calls attention to two startling aspects: first, the chair that Wolfson occupied for more than 30 years as a scholar of international renown was funded extramurally, outside the usual terms and conditions of chairs occupied by members of the Harvard faculty. The second point is that with Wolfson's retirement, there was at the time only one other chair in an American university that had the term "Jewish" attached to it—that held by Salo Baron, Professor of Jewish History, Literature, and Institutions (since 1930) at Columbia. Apart from "parochial" institutions like Yeshiva University, the Jewish Theological Seminary, and Hebrew Union College, 50 years ago there were no programs in Jewish studies in the United States. By contrast, a minimal estimate in 1997 places the number of such programs— including departments and interdepartmental majors—at 85, with ten universities offering Ph.D.'s specifically in Jewish studies, and some 20 others, M.A. programs in the field. Approximately a hundred chairs in various areas of Jewish studies have been endowed in colleges and universities across the country. The Association for Jewish Studies, founded in 1969 with fewer than 40 scholars, who were either affiliated with Jewish institutions or who taught in relative isolation in secular ones, now has 1,400 members.

This growth has undoubtedly benefited from the recent, more general emphasis on programs of cultural and ethnic studies, and the future of some of these initiatives seems less secure than others. But the communal support received by many Jewish studies programs—itself a recent phenomenon in American Jewish philanthropy—together with the participation in them of faculty with regular appointments in the standard disciplines, puts them in a relatively strong position. A noteworthy development in the same area was the completion in 1997 of a $2,000,000 challenge grant from the National Endowment for the Humanities to support the dissertation fellowship program in Jewish studies initiated by the National Foundation for Jewish Culture.

It is too early to judge what impact the development of Jewish studies programs will have on the American Jewish community. Lectures and courses sponsored by these programs are often open to the public, and it is possible that these offerings and the "Centers" of Jewish studies that have in some cases grown up around them may become as regular a feature of the American Jewish landscape as have religious institutions or community centers in their own different ways.

Another important development in recent years has been the proliferation of new, smaller-scale sites of Jewish learning unaffiliated with the standard religious or synagogue organizations or university departments. Examples of these are the Drisha Institute in New York and Ma'yan in Boston (both of these directed to women), versions in cities across the country of a communal and nondenominational "Bet Midrash," and weekly learning sessions, open to all comers, which under the sponsorship of Jewish student organizations have drawn increasingly large attendance at some of the major urban universities (Columbia, Pennsylvania, Yale). To be sure, the ostensible purpose of most such programs is to develop and transmit Jewish, not "American Jewish" learning. But both their settings and the methods and interests represented in these programs place them firmly within the current American intellectual context.

Holocaust

Predictably, the emphases of academic Jewish studies programs have mirrored those of the Jewish community at large. The focus on the Holocaust is an example of this, with that event almost as central in the Jewish studies curriculum as it has become in the communal institutions of American Jewish life. A Ph.D. program specifically in Holocaust studies, for example, has been initiated at Clark University. One of the most publicized academic controversies of 1997 concerned the proposed appointment to an endowed chair at Harvard of a Holocaust historian. Disagreement within the university about the person to be appointed and about the terms set for the chair resulted in a stalemate and then the deferral of the appointment.

Probably the best-selling American Jewish book of the year (although published in 1996) was Daniel Jonah Goldhagen's *Hitler's Willing Executioners*, which continued to draw attention and controversy to its sweeping allegation that German, rather than only Nazi, "eliminationist antisemitism" provided both a necessary and a sufficient explanation of the occurrence of the "Final Solution." Including translations abroad, that book's sales have exceeded 500,000 copies, a remarkable number for any scholarly work, especially one that had been sharply criticized by scholars in the field. It seems impossible to understand this popular response–accompanied by lectures and symposia in synagogues, community centers, colleges — without recognizing in it an impulse of collective memory in the American Jewish community that contrasts with the sense of mourning, even of victimization, that has been the dominant motif among the still-growing number of Holocaust memorials or monuments in the country. (Depending on how one counts, these memorials — which range from a single tablet in a cemetery commemorating a destroyed population in an Eastern European Jewish town to rooms set aside in community centers to specially commissioned sculptures in or outside communal buildings to the large United States Holocaust Memorial Museum in Washington — would number in the hundreds at one end of the spectrum and, even for "major" ones, more than 30.) In contrast to these motifs, Goldhagen's book can be seen as a monument to anger, even revenge — themes otherwise muted in most American Jewish writings and reflection on the Holocaust.

The year 1997 also saw, after a nearly 20-year history of starts and stops, the opening of the Museum of Jewish Heritage – A Living Memorial to the Holocaust in New York City, still with a notable emphasis on the Holocaust, although not as exclusively as had been envisioned in the earlier plans for it when New York City was still contending with Washington, D.C., over which of the two cities should become the site of the "national" Holocaust memorial.

Among the annual National Jewish Book Awards, a separate award is reserved for work on the Holocaust. The 1997 prize in this category went to Saul Friedlander for the first volume of his *Nazi Germany and the Jews*. (The more general award for nonfiction was given to Ruth Gay, for *Unfinished People: Eastern European Jews Encounter America*.) In their race against time, the two principal collections of survivor testimonies — the Yale University Fortunoff Video Archives and the Shoah Visual History Project, initiated and funded in part by Steven Spielberg — continued the process of taping those testimonies. The number of Holocaust "centers," which typically include a library and the sponsorship of lectures — some attached to educational institutions, some free-standing in cities — continued to increase. At the end of 1997, there were approximately 35 of these, the most recent addition the Hatikvah Center in Springfield, Massachusetts.

By the end of 1997, attendance at the United States Holocaust Memorial Museum, since its opening in spring 1993, totaled nine and a half million visitors. The estimate by the museum administration that more than half of these visitors have been non-Jewish is noteworthy in its bearing on the question of the impact and reception of Jewish themes in the broader American society. The museum is a national institution, a large part of its annual budget provided by the U.S. government. But it would be difficult for any visitor to miss the connections to Jews, to Jewish history, and to the American Jewish community, which have, by implication, become part of the broader contours of American society.

New Focuses of Interest

At the same time, however, the continuing public and scholarly attention to the Holocaust in the United States has evoked, even among those responsible for it, a reaction, a sense of an imbalance that emphasis on the Holocaust contributes to American Jewish identity, in its reinforcement of what the historians Cecil Roth and Salo Baron objected to more generally as the "lachrymose" conception of Jewish history. This criticism has undoubtedly indirectly influenced the emergence of competing interests in other topics — for example, aspects of spirituality (sometimes related to "New Age" thought outside the American Jewish scene) and the increased attention to other historical and topical issues in the Jewish past. The discernible move beyond a focus on Zionism and Israel, the Holocaust, and Soviet Jewry can be understood not so much as a rejection as a shift intended to bring the focus closer to home, a turning inward, principally to those problems and concerns that have appeared under the heading of Jewish "continuity" in America and to the shaping of positive Jewish identity.

Related to this was a spurt of interest in Bible study, with 1997 emerging as the "Year of Genesis." A widely viewed series of discussions on the biblical book of Genesis, produced and moderated by Bill Moyers—inspired by Burton L. Visotzky's *The Genesis of Ethics*—was carried on PBS television and then published as a volume; several much-noted translations of Genesis and commentaries also appeared during the year (for example, by Robert Alter and by Stephen Mitchell); other broader reflections or interpretations were also published, among them *Genesis: As It Is Written*, edited by David Rosenberg, in which a number of writers not otherwise known for their interest in traditional Jewish texts consider specific incidents and themes of Genesis, and Karen Armstrong's *In the Beginning: A New Interpretation of Genesis*. Although there is no reason to think that this focus on the "first" biblical text will go on to the books of Leviticus or Deuteronomy, even the one appearance suggests that something significant is taking place here. The search for a combination of historical roots and current meaning could find few more evocative sources than Genesis; that "beginning," furthermore, remains a text for which the disputed "Judeo-Christian" conjunction, so commonly overworked in characterizing Western religion and culture, seems less problematic than for others.

Still another trend on the cultural front has been the renewal of interest in Yiddish, epitomized in the opening in 1997 of the new building of the National Yiddish Book Center on the Hampshire College campus in Amherst, Massachusetts. Since its founding in 1980, the center has collected more than 1.3 million Yiddish volumes, almost entirely from American contributors; it has arranged for the duplicate copies and sets of these to be sold or contributed to institutions and private purchasers. The center now has plans to "digitalize" more than half the estimated 40,000 titles ever published in Yiddish; this will have the effect of enabling the republication of those volumes on demand.

At the same time, the center, together with YIVO and now also a number of universities, has found sufficient interest to support courses of study in Yiddish. Thirty colleges or universities now have regular sequences of such courses, with the number of institutions offering only individual courses more than double that. The likely extent of the Yiddish revival is limited; even its most optimistic devotees do not foresee a future for Yiddish as again a language of general usage or a source of new literary achievement.

The continuing use of Yiddish as the vernacular language among certain Hassidic groups (e.g., the Satmar, Bobover, Sqverer) is the one "natural" context in which Yiddish now survives. But even the apparent growth of these groups does not suggest any substantial effect on the future status of Yiddish as a living language. New textbooks and children's books have been written and published for this constituency (together with several weekly papers including *Der Yid* and *Die Tseitung*), but scholarly writing and significant records are generally written in Hebrew, and it is unlikely that the Yiddish taught and used in these groups will go much beyond the restricted, strictly functional role it now has.

Literature

American Jewish culture found significant literary expression in 1997. Philip Roth's *American Pastoral*— less intense than much of his previous work but no less evocative of the American (that is, Newark) Jewish initiation into American rites like baseball and summer trips to the seashore—has already been mentioned. 1997 also saw the publication, 11 years after his death, of an edition of *The Complete Stories* by Bernard Malamud, who, like Roth, had objected to being characterized as a Jewish writer (an objection which has somehow to be reconciled with the Yiddish epitaph— *"der ba'al ma'assios"* [the "teller of tales"]—on his Mt. Auburn cemetery gravestone in Cambridge). The Nobel Prize winner Saul Bellow published a novella in 1997, *The Actual*, that was awarded the National Jewish Book Award in fiction. Here, as in much of his earlier work, Bellow consistently balances his characters on the line between this- and other-worldliness without allowing his text ever to acknowledge openly the Jewish idiom animating that balance.

Neither Norman Mailer's still more ambiguous identification nor his reputation as a writer was made clearer by his publication during the year of *The Gospel According to the Son*. It may be that here, as in his earlier Egyptian novel, *Ancient Evenings*, Mailer comes as close to representing Jewish themes as he is willing or able to by evoking a near but quite distinct "other"—in this book, the original "Jewish-Christians" and most prominently, the first among them; it seems clear that he was closer to home, more at home, in "The March on the Pentagon" or in *An American Dream*.

Cynthia Ozick's long-awaited sequence of stories, *The Puttermesser Papers*, appeared to considerable critical acclaim. Leslie Epstein, recalled for his earlier and almost picaresque Holocaust novel *The King of the Jews*, published *Pandemonium*, another almost picaresque Holocaust novel, now set partly in Hollywood. Isaac Bashevis Singer's *Shadows on the Hudson* (translated from the Yiddish of its serial publication in the *Forward* in 1957) appeared on the cusp between 1997 and 1998 to mixed reviews. The principal character in this novel, Herz Grein, had lost his family in Poland in the Holocaust and then made his way in the United States as a Hebrew school teacher, but the novel's narrator insists that "Americanness had entered his bones." If there is a question about the Jewishness of some of the writers noted above, one might question the Americanness of Singer—another nuance in the complexity of American Jewish culture.

There can be little doubt that the award to Singer of the Nobel Prize in 1978 was a testimonial to him not only as a writer, but as a writer of Yiddish—the first and quite certainly the only Yiddish laureate. It seems clear, in any event, that for all the other writers mentioned above, their setting out from a Jewish "base" in their contemporary United States not only affects the themes and idiom of their work, but shows itself still more emphatically in the remarkable imaginative energy they give to (or get from) refracting the texture of a second culture.

Whether or not it is generally true, as the influential American Jewish literary critic, Harold Bloom, has claimed, that writers gain their strength by reacting against their predecessors, there can be little doubt of the impetus—the nerve— that the situation of being a "Jew in America" gave to writers like Roth and Bellow.

Their point of origin and much that follows it differ notably for a younger generation of American Jewish writers who published books in 1997 or whose work, which appeared a year or two earlier, still occasioned discussion. Among the latter are Allegra Goodman (*The Family Markowitz*, 1996), Rebecca Goldstein (*Mazel*, 1995), Tova Reich (*The Jewish War*, 1995), and Thane Rosenbaum (*Elijah Visible*, 1996). In 1997, David Mamet, better known as a playwright, published an historical novel, *Old Religion*, based on the Leo Frank case in Georgia; Jonathan Rosen, literary editor of the *Forward*, published *Eve's Apple*; and Francine Prose's children's book *The Angel's Mistake* appeared.

A substantial section of the November/December issue of *Tikkun* magazine was devoted to what it called "The Jewish Literary Revival," with the authors just mentioned prominent among those cited. Earlier in the year (Spring 1997), a special issue of the literary quarterly *Prairie Schooner* dealt with the theme "Jewish American Writers," including a still more diverse group of poets and fiction writers. Comparisons are always invidious, and predictions often end by defeating themselves, but even if one sets aside the differences in literary force between the "founding" generation of American Jewish writers and these younger authors, the shift in the range and selection of literary themes is noteworthy, as though the older writers, more alien in their surroundings, found larger (and broader) imaginative possibilities than their successors, who are much more "at home." The new force of the question of Jewish identity thus expresses itself in literary stresses as well.

Publication of the volume edited by Steven Rubin, *Telling and Learning: A Century of American Jewish Poetry*, demonstrates through the work included there of poets like Allen Ginsberg, Louise Gluck, Anthony Hecht, Stanley Kunitz, Denise Levertov, Philip Levine, Robert Pinsky (who in 1997 was named national Poet-Laureate), and Adrienne Rich how strong, if varied, a voice American Jewish poets have had. In the event, 1997 marked the deaths of Ginsberg and Levertov—the former especially recalling the historical turn in American poetry propelled by the "Beats." It is no small part of this that he would be remembered as much for his poem "Kaddish" as for his "Howl."

An increasingly important literary presence in American Jewish culture, however much it stretches the concept, is the appearance of books by Israeli authors in English translation. 1997 saw the publication, among others, of novels by Amos Oz (*Panther in the Basement*), A.B. Yehoshua (the paperback edition of *Open Heart*), and the mystery writer Batya Gur (*Forbidden Fruit*), together with a volume by the poet Yehuda Amichai (*The Common and Great Tranquility*). In addition, Israeli writers have assumed a prominent role as lecturers during American Jewish Book Week, held annually in November, usually at local Jewish community centers, where Jewish books are exhibited. An informal poll of the Jewish book exhibits in 1997 indicates that the best-selling books are not novels or works of history, but rather cookbooks and children's books, followed by inspirational works and memoirs. A memoir published in 1996 that continued to attract attention was James McBride's *The Color of Water: A Black Man's Tribute to His White Mother*. McBride's white mother, the daughter of an Orthodox rabbi who came to the United States from Poland, married an Afro-American minister and responded to the problem of interracial identity facing her children by depicting God as the "color of water." An American Jewish audience might understandably be drawn to this relatively uncommon but vivid example of "assimilation" as a new projection of their own sense of marginality.

Theater

As has traditionally been the case, theatrical productions during the year were centered in New York City. The most widely publicized of these was the new production of *The Diary of Anne Frank*, with a script adapted by Wendy Kesselman from the earlier one by Goodrich and Hackett. Kesselman attempted in her version to take account of objections to the earlier version, including what some critics saw as the unduly universalist and even redemptive features of the Diary itself. Tony Kushner's version of *The Dybbuk* was also produced in New York, while A Travelling Jewish Theatre of San Francisco adapted a two-character version of the original Ansky play. Also on the New York stage were Cynthia Ozick's version of her own novella *The Shawl*, Wendy Wasserstein's *An American Daughter*, David Mamet's *The Old Neighborhood*, Alfred Uhry's *Last Night of Ballyhoo*, which won the 1997 Tony Award, and Neil Simon's *Proposals*—the last two evoking an earlier and often nostalgic Jewish America. Two repertory Jewish theaters—the Jewish Repertory Theater and the American Jewish Theater—continued to bring productions to the stage in New York City, as did the Yiddish-language Folksbiene Theater.

Museums

The Jewish museum world, as recorded in the lists of the Council of American Jewish Museums, includes 52 institutions dispersed across the country—in Tulsa as well as in Los Angeles, in Jackson, Mississippi, as well as in Chicago. These are primarily art and historical museums (and apart from the primarily Holocaust museums and centers referred to above). In addition to their permanent exhibits, these museums also display temporary or traveling exhibits. Perhaps the most provocative of the latter in 1997—first mounted in 1996 at the Jewish Museum in New York City but then traveling in 1997 to Baltimore, Philadelphia, San Francisco, and Los Angeles—was the exhibition "Too Jewish: Challenging Traditional Identities." The "traditional identities" challenged by the work displayed in this exhibition (and further analyzed in essays published in the accompanying catalogue by authors including Sander Gilman, Linda Nochlin, and Margaret Olin) were Jewish stereotypes of features like "Jewish Noses" by Dennis Kardon; Jewish names, as in "Albert. Used to be Abraham" by Ken Aptekar; and "What Kinda Name Is That?" by Beverly Naidus; and the "Complex Princess," by Nurit Newman. This exhibition attempted to show how certain aspects of American Jewish cultural identity opened themselves to exaggeration—sometimes fruitfully, sometimes as self-caricature. Although some aspects of American Jewish culture presented in the exhibition seemed superficial or vulgar, clearly they had a social basis that any analysis of cultural identity would have to take into account.

Some of the same criticism directed at the "Too Jewish" exhibition was raised against the "Desert Cliche" exhibition that came to the Grey Gallery at New York University after having been shown earlier in Israel and in Miami. In this show, a group of Israeli artists held up to view as "cliches" certain central icons of Israeli life—images of the "Holy Land," the conventions of military heroism, the creation of the "Sabra," the former ambassador and foreign minister Abba Eban. In artistic terms, both this and the "Too Jewish" exhibition came closer to the satiric glosses of pop art than to more current trends in painting and constructivist art. But perhaps this lag—which was certainly not the case for abstract expressionism, in which American Jewish artists and critics were early and prominent—has to do precisely with the reinstatement of a social "subject," and a touchy one at that.

TV and Film

The most popular art media, television and film, are more difficult than other forms to place under the heading of American Jewish culture both because of the mass and diverse audiences they are designed to attract and because of the corporate process of their creation. According to the standard television ratings, "Seinfeld" was the most widely viewed regular program during 1997. Although this series could hardly be imagined except in relation to an American Jewish idiom or style, because none of the characters are identified explicitly as Jewish, and the program so thoroughly mingles (even confuses) ethnic elements, inclusion under the American Jewish rubric, even broadly defined, hardly fits.

Something similar might be said about Woody Allen's 1997 film *Deconstructing Harry*. A scene in which Harry's former wife sings the blessing over the Sabbath candles stands in splendid isolation in the film. In this area of popular culture, the choice seems to be between Seinfeld's "melting pot" style and Allen's multiple (and unmelted) selves–his own version of cultural pluralism.

Issues of Jewish identity appear in a more straightforward form in the annual Jewish Film Festivals, which have grown from a single festival in San Francisco less than a decade ago to more than 30 in 1997, taking place in almost all the major American cities and a number of smaller communities as well. The films typically shown over the course of a week or longer range from Yiddish films made in prewar Europe, to by-now classic Israeli films, to representations of Jewish life in exotic locales (to Americans, at least), like *Mendel*, set in Norway, or *Like a Bride*, set in Mexico. In film more than any other art medium—no doubt because of the importance of its visual effects—the focus on a Jewish subject seems to be a sufficient condition for identification as a "Jewish" film. An increasing number of such films—in particular, documentaries like *A Life Apart: Hasidism in America*, *Blacks and Jews*, and *Treyf*—have been directed to general as well as to Jewish audiences. Specific support for such productions has been provided since 1996 by a fund for Jewish Documentary Filmmaking, under the auspices of the National Foundation for Jewish Culture.

Periodicals

The number of periodicals addressed to an American Jewish audience, ranging from journals with specialized scholarly interests, to those more broadly representing belles lettres, to others that elaborate on current events or popular themes of community and social life, has also risen sharply. This development, too, suggests a growing confidence on the part of both writers and readers in their claims on the cultural context in which these publications appear. Examples of scholarly journals include *Jewish Social Studies*, *Prooftexts*, the *AJS Review*, *Israel Studies*, *Shofar*, *Jewish History*, and *Modern Judaism*. In the second group are *Judaism*, *Response*, *Kerem*, *Lilith*, and *New Menorah*, while the third group takes in *Commentary*, *Tikkun*, *Midstream*, *Jewish Monthly*, *Jewish Frontier*, *Congress Monthly*, and the *Hadassah Magazine*.

Without knowing exactly where to place them among these headings, the role should be mentioned of certain general-interest periodicals that devote disproportionate space to Jewish issues. The weekly *New Republic* is currently the most notable example of this (evidenced, for example, by its special double issue during 1997 on "Zionism at 100"); the focus is less emphatic but still apparent in the biweekly *New York Review of Books*.

So far as concerns the popular press, approximately 75 "Anglo-Jewish" newspapers are published, carrying mainly local news of Jewish community interest, in readership areas as small as New London, Connecticut, and as large as New York City or Los Angeles; these have a total circulation that one estimate puts as high as 2.3 million. Even allowing for a considerable margin of error in this figure, the presence indicated is significant. An analysis of this press would provide additional points of entry for understanding the popular culture of the American Jewish community.

Other Areas of Interest

The distinct Jewish feminist movement that has emerged in the last two decades has produced strong echoes in the cultural and intellectual spheres. Perhaps the most notable single event of 1997 in this sphere was the "Conference on Feminism and Orthodoxy" in New York in February, which drew an overflow crowd to the New York Marriott; the emphasis of that conference was on the issue of extending Orthodox women's participation in religious practice, but other issues raised by Jewish feminist groups have moved beyond that question to matters of leadership, of religious and scholarly teaching, and to the reexamination of the status of women in Jewish history.

The founding at Brandeis University of the International Research Institute on Jewish Women—and the two major conferences it sponsored in its first year—reflect the interest in reexamining the role of women in Jewish history. The Women's Caucus of the Association for Jewish Studies has also had an impact in this area. An important scholarly work written from a feminist perspective is the 1,500-page *Jewish Women in America: An Historical Encyclopedia*, edited by Paula Hyman and Deborah Dash Moore. Other recent works in this domain include *Talking Back: Images of Jewish Women in American Popular Culture*, edited by Joyce Antler; Laura Levitt's *Finding Our Way Home: Jews and Feminism, the Ambivalent Search for Home;* and *Making a Scene: The Contemporary Drama of Jewish-American Women*, edited by Sarah Blacher Cohen. *Rereading the Rabbis: A Woman's Voice*, by Judith Hauptman, professor of Talmud at the Jewish Theological Seminary, attempts to demonstrate the presence—sometimes explicit, more often tacit—of women in the classical religious texts.

The blending of political and religious responses to specific practical questions, which then ensue in cultural "practice," has also affected American Jewish culture. A number of environmental groups, for example, have sprung up that relate the environmental concerns of their members and audience to principles drawn from Jewish texts—the Teva Learning Center, Yetziah–Jewish Wilderness Journey, and the Coalition on the Environment and Jewish Life. Similarly, advances in medicine and the complex issues they raise find Jewish professionals attempting to bring the Jewish tradition to bear on broad societal problems. In 1997 the Eighth International Conference on Medical Ethics met in San Francisco, cosponsored by the Stanford University Medical School, and drew Jewish scholars, especially from the Orthodox community, as participants. While science might seem an unlikely arena for an American-Jewish conjunction, these developments suggest that still other unforeseen expansions of that phenomenon may yet be in the offing. The National Foundation for Jewish Culture, based in New York City, has become an increasingly important presence both in charting the course of such expressions and, through its collaboration with local community organizations, in fostering new ones.

Future Directions

It seems clear that the central problem recurring among the different levels and varieties of American Jewish cultural activity closely approximates the central issue facing the American Jewish community as such—how to sustain and elaborate Jewish identity in a context where multiculturalism has become the norm and where, as a consequence of this and other changes, Jewish identity itself becomes increasingly more problematic, internally as well as externally, as a social marker. While both Israel and the Holocaust will no doubt remain preoccupations of the American Jewish community, they increasingly appear insufficient as bases for either individual or group identity. As the distance increases from these two motifs in the American Jewish consciousness, it then becomes more urgent to identify other sources with the capacity to shape a full cultural or social identity that at once acknowledges the American context (diffuse and complex as this is), yet also fixes even the approximate lines of a distinctively Jewish space within it. The movement toward conservatism and stringency—in political terminology, to the right; more harshly, to fundamentalism—in many religious groups within the Jewish community (there are countercurrents as well, but the balance seems clear) can undoubtedly be understood as one response to this problem. This response emphasizes barriers and lines of demarcation, thus increasing the distance between the groups (Jewish as well as non-Jewish) that together constitute the American community. Such efforts are difficult to sustain and, if they were to succeed, would also exact a considerable price. But the alternative to it—a revived version of the "melting pot" ideal—faces difficulties no less severe, with its price the gradual assimilation and then disappearance of anything but vestiges of American Jewish culture as such. The sharp line between these two alternatives accounts for the uncertainty and ambivalence evident in so many of the expressions and representations of current American Jewish culture.

But the latter is itself a familiar pattern in Jewish history, as Jewish communities have rarely shown themselves of one mind about even the most pressing cultural or social concerns. Differences, ambivalence, and even unclarity can at times also provide a means to "be fruitful and multiply"—and if this prospect offers a challenge rather than assurance, that combination too has been a familiar presence in Jewish history.

BEREL LANG

Jewish Population in the United States, 1997

BASED ON LOCAL COMMUNITY counts—the method for identifying and enumerating Jewish population that serves as the basis of this report—the estimated size of the American Jewish community in 1997 was 6.0 million. This increase of 100,000 over last year's figure primarily reflects growth in several communities, documented by new demographic surveys and detailed below.

The new national figure for Jewish population is half a million more than the 5.5 million "core" Jewish population estimated in the Council of Jewish Federations' 1990 National Jewish Population Survey (NJPS).[1] The difference between the national and aggregated local figures is explained by definitional issues, disparate sample sources (e.g., organizational lists, often outdated; distinctive Jewish names; and random digit dialing), and the lapse in time, as well as a lack of uniformity in the methodologies used for research conducted at the local level.

The demographic results of the NJPS suggested that the population was growing slightly due to an excess of Jewish births over Jewish deaths during the late 1980s. However, extrapolation from the age structure suggests that, since the mid-1990s, the annual numbers of births and deaths have been balanced, and zero population growth is being realized. At the same time, some growth in numbers is achieved through Jewish immigration to the United States, particularly by refugees from the former Soviet Union.

The NJPS used a scientifically selected sample to project a total number for the United States, but could not provide accurate information on the state and local levels. Therefore, as in past years, in this article we have based local, state, and regional population figures on the usual estimating procedures.

While the Jewish federations are the chief reporting bodies, their service areas vary in size and may represent several towns, one county, or an aggregate of several counties. In some cases we have subdivided federation areas to reflect the more natural geographic boundaries. Estimates from areas without federations have been provided by local rabbis and other informed Jewish communal leaders. In still other cases, the figures that have been updated are from estimates provided in the past by United Jewish Appeal field representatives. Finally, for smaller communities from which no recent estimates are available, figures are based on extrapolation from older data. The estimates are for the resident Jew-

---

[1]See Barry A. Kosmin et al., *Highlights of the CJF 1990 National Jewish Population Survey* (New York, Council of Jewish Federations, 1991).

ish population, including those in private households and in institutional settings. Non-Jewish family members have been excluded from the total.

The state and regional totals shown in Appendix tables 1 and 2 are derived by summing the individual estimates shown in table 4, including communities of less than 100, and then rounding to the nearest hundred or thousand, depending on the size of the estimate.

Because population estimation is not an exact science, the reader should be aware that in cases where a figure differs from last year's, the increase or decrease did not come about suddenly but occurred over a period of time and has just now been substantiated. Similarly, the results of a completed local demographic study often change the previously reported Jewish population figure. This should be understood as either an updated calculation of gradual demographic change or a correction of a faulty older estimate.

In determining Jewish population, communities count both affiliated and non-affiliated residents who are "core" Jews as defined in NJPS. This definition includes born Jews who report adherence to Judaism, Jews by choice, and born Jews without a current religion ("secular Jews"). In most cases, counts are made by households, with that number multiplied by the average number of self-defined Jewish persons per household. Similarly to NJPS, most communities also include those born and raised as Jews but who at present consider themselves as having no religion. As stated above, non-Jews living in Jewish households, primarily non-Jewish spouses and non-Jewish children, are not included in the 1997 estimates presented in the Appendix below.

Enhanced Method

This year a new procedure has been instituted regarding duplicate counts within states and communities with boundaries that cross state borders. First, nearly all duplicate counts have been eliminated. Second, the population of a particular community is now listed under only one heading. An "N" following the name of a community refers the reader to the Notes section at the end of the article, where these areas are defined. The indented listings add up to the metropolitan total.

As a result of these changes, the population estimates for adjacent communities, particularly in urban states like Connecticut, are appropriately reduced. For example, the estimates for Stamford and Norwalk, Connecticut, have been reduced, as both communities previously included New Canaan and Darien in their counts. With communities that cross state borders, the numbers are appropriately divided and shown for each state. For example, Youngstown, Ohio, now shows a Jewish population of 3,800 instead of 4,000, and some 200 have been added to the communities of Sharon and Farrell, Pennsylvania.

As a result of this change in enumeration, the population estimates for the following communities are at least 100 less then last year's estimate, even though no demographic changes were reported by the community informants: Long Beach, California; Bridgeport, Danbury, Hartford, New London, Norwalk-Westport, and Stamford, Connecticut; Elgin, Joliet, and Southern Illinois, Illinois; South Bend, Indiana; Omaha, Nebraska; Elmira, New York; Cincinnati, Toledo, and Youngstown, Ohio; McAllen, Texas; Winchester, Virginia; Huntington and Parkersburg, West Virginia; and La Crosse, Wisconsin. The total for Portland, Oregon, would have decreased, since some of its population is now apportioned to neighboring Washington. However, the growth in this community more than offset the loss due to redistribution. In cases where the separated totals amount to less than 100, a listing is no longer provided. Such is the case for Quincy, Illinois, and the adjacent town of Hannibal, Missouri, which are no longer listed.

Finally, we now include at the end of the community listings in each state an approximation for "other places." This is simply a summing of all known communities under 100 that are not listed.

This more precise geographic reporting insures that the sum of listed communities within states more closely approximates the state totals shown in table 1.

Local Population Changes

The largest increase was in Las Vegas, Nevada, where a recent demographic study found 55,000 Jews, 35,000 more than the previously listed figure of 20,000 that had been reported for many years. This increase of 178 percent represents an actual increase in the Jewish population, mirroring rapid growth in the general population.

The second-largest reported increase, of over 29,000 people, was in Monmouth County, New Jersey, an increase of 88 percent. Though the Jewish population had been growing in this North Jersey shore suburban area for many years, it was only recently documented in a demographic survey. Most of the growth has occurred in the western area of the county, in towns such as Marlboro and Manalapan.

A recent survey in Los Angeles showed a slight increase of 18,000, up from the 501,000 indicated in the last survey, done 18 years ago. Several years ago there was a perception of slight decline, and the AJYB figure was accordingly reduced to 490,000. The new data suggest that this assumption was probably incorrect.

Based on informed estimates, the figure for Ventura County, which lies northwest of Los Angeles County, has been increased to 6,000, a growth of 67 percent.

Denver's recently completed survey documented an increase to 63,000 since its 1983 study, a growth of 17,000, which is equivalent to a rise of 37 percent.

Based on new survey results, the estimate for Cleveland, Ohio, was raised to 81,000, an increase of 16,000, 25 percent more than the previous 1987 study figure. The geographic area covered in the new survey includes some outlying regions, such as portions of Summit, Lake, and Geauga counties, which were not included in the earlier research. Further, an improved survey methodology, based on a greater percentage of random digit dial calls, projected larger numbers than previously estimated. Still another factor contributing to the growth is immigration, particularly from the former Soviet Union.

Dallas, Atlanta, and Boston each posted gains of over 5,000. The latter two were documented in new demographic surveys. The growth in Boston was mainly in the near western suburbs, while declines occurred mainly in the city, the northeastern suburbs, and the North Shore area. Though smaller in number than previously, Newton and Brookline remain the most densely populated Jewish areas.

Most of the other reported gains were in the South and West: Vail, Colorado; Sarasota and Boca Raton–Delray Beach, Florida; Columbus, Georgia; Columbia-Howard County, Maryland; the Portland, Oregon–Vancouver, Washington, area; and Spokane, Washington. Growth outside of these regions occurred in Pittsfield–Berkshire County, Massachusetts, and Kenosha, Wisconsin. The increase in the latter is partly due to the inclusion of outlying areas.

The largest decline was reported in the Philadelphia area, a loss of 18 percent, documented by a new communal survey. The drop here of 44,000 people occurred since the last study, done in 1983. Most of the loss was in the city of Philadelphia proper and in Delaware County. There was some growth, however, in Chester and Bucks counties.

Two South Florida communities, Broward County and Miami-Dade County, showed losses of greater than 10,000. A new study by the combined Jewish Federations of Ft. Lauderdale and South Broward (now collectively referred to as Broward County) documented a population reduction of 17,000. As with Dade County, which has experienced demographic decline for most of the past decade, the large elderly population in Broward is passing on, without sufficient replacement through birth or immigration for the population count to remain stable.

The Middlesex County, New Jersey, estimate is reduced by 6,000, reflecting perceived losses in northern parts of the county. The lower figures for Orange County and Bakersfield-Kern County, California, are corrections of faulty older estimates based on a new evaluation.

Data on Metropolitan Areas

In addition to the detailed Jewish population figures by community, region, and state, this year we have provided information for 40 metropolitan areas, rank-ordered by Jewish population (table 3). Included in this table are the Jewish percentage of each particular metropolitan area, its share of the U.S. Jewish population, and the cumulative share of total Jewish population for communities up to that ranking. As in 1995, when this table was last provided, there are only a few noteworthy changes in order of communal listing. Las Vegas moved from 31st to 16th place, Buffalo ascended from 37th to 27th, Philadelphia fell from 4th to 6th position, and Pittsburgh declined from 18th to 21st place. New in the ranking is Sarasota, Florida, in 38th place, replacing Columbus, Ohio, which had appeared on the 1995 list.

One obvious finding established in table 3 is the continued concentration of Jews within a few specific areas. One-third of the nation's Jewish population live in the tristate New York–Northern New Jersey–Long Island metropolitan area, which encompasses parts of New York, New Jersey, and Connecticut. It should be noted, however, that, as recently as 45 years ago, more than half of U.S. Jews were concentrated there.

Cumulatively, about half of all U.S. Jews reside in the top three metropolitan areas: New York–Northern New Jersey–Long Island, Los Angeles–Anaheim–Riverside, and Miami–Fort Lauderdale. To reach three-quarters of the U.S. Jewish population, 12 communities have to be included; for 90 percent of the total, 36 communities. This pattern reflects the fact that the Jewish population is generally concentrated in large metropolitan areas. By contrast, for the U.S. total population, the 34 largest metropolitan areas are needed to encompass half the population and all 309 of the nation's metropolitan areas include only about 80 percent of the nation's inhabitants.

The Jewish proportion in particular locales is of interest. The metropolitan area with the highest percentage of Jews remains West Palm Beach–Boca Raton, Florida, at 16 percent. New York–Northern New Jersey–Long Island and Miami–Fort Lauderdale, Florida, are the only other metropolitan areas with a Jewish population density of greater than 10 percent. In only one other area, Boston–Lawrence–Salem, are Jews more than 5 percent of the population; in four communities they exceed 4 percent of the total: Los Angeles–Anaheim–Riverside, Baltimore, New Haven–Meriden, and Atlantic City.

Future Research

Recognizing that numerous ongoing changes affect the size and profile of the Jewish population, the Council of Jewish Federations has begun preparations for a new national survey. To be conducted concomitant with the U.S. Census 2000, the National Jewish Population Survey will provide the Jewish community with reliable national data, updating the 1990 survey and making it easier to determine national trends that heretofore could only be guessed at.

The 1990 survey is the standard against which all other surveys of the Jewish community are measured. It provides the baseline information upon which NJPS 2000 will build, enabling trend analyses, projections, and more opportunities for study of subgroups. The desired sample size for the new survey will be 5,000, over twice that of the 1990 sample. This larger sample will permit more reliable and extensive examination of data on many subgroups for which limited data were available in 1990, e.g., young singles, Sephardic Jews, and the Orthodox, as well as more contrasts by geographic regions.

Among the questions it will answer are: How large is the Jewish population, and how is it changing? Where do Jews live, and where are they moving to? What regional differences exist? Have recent efforts to improve Jewish education had a measurable impact? Is the trumpeted increased religiosity among American Jews true? How successful are the Jewish denominations in attracting and retaining members? What is the intermarriage rate, and how is it changing? Is the impact of Israel and Zionism diminishing? What changes are occurring in the economic profile of American Jewry? What are the philanthropic patterns of Jewish baby-boomers? Is the nature of the American Jewish family changing?

The professional quality of this research undertaking will be assured by the internationally acclaimed demographers and other social scientists who comprise the National Technical Advisory Committee. NJPS 2000 will become the new definitive source of data about the American Jewish community.

JIM SCHWARTZ
JEFFREY SCHECKNER

APPENDIX

TABLE 1. JEWISH POPULATION IN THE UNITED STATES, 1997

State	Estimated Jewish Population	Total Population*	Estimated Jewish Percent of Total
Alabama	9,000	4,273,000	0.2
Alaska	3,000	607,000	0.5
Arizona	72,000	4,228,000	1.6
Arkansas	1,700	2,510,000	0.1
California	956,000	31,878,000	3.0
Colorado	68,000	3,823,000	1.8
Connecticut	97,000	3,274,000	3.0
Delaware	13,500	725,000	1.9
District of Columbia	25,500	553,000	4.7
Florida	620,000	14,400,000	4.3
Georgia	84,500	7,353,000	1.1
Hawaii	7,000	1,184,000	0.6
Idaho	500	1,189,000	(z)
Illinois	269,000	11,847,000	2.3
Indiana	18,000	5,841,000	0.3
Iowa	6,500	2,852,000	0.2
Kansas	14,500	2,572,000	0.6
Kentucky	11,000	3,884,000	0.3
Louisiana	16,500	4,351,000	0.4
Maine	7,500	1,243,000	0.6
Maryland	214,000	5,072,000	4.2
Massachusetts	279,000	6,092,000	4.6
Michigan	107,000	9,594,000	1.1
Minnesota	42,000	4,658,000	0.9
Mississippi	1,400	2,716,000	0.1
Missouri	62,000	5,359,000	1.2
Montana	800	879,000	0.1
Nebraska	7,000	1,652,000	0.4
Nevada	57,000	1,603,000	3.6
New Hampshire	9,500	1,162,000	0.8
New Jersey	461,000	7,988,000	5.8
New Mexico	10,000	1,713,000	0.6
New York	1,653,000	18,185,000	9.1
North Carolina	23,500	7,323,000	0.3

State	Estimated Jewish Population	Total Population*	Estimated Jewish Percent of Total
North Dakota	700	644,000	0.1
Ohio	145,000	11,173,000	1.3
Oklahoma	5,200	3,307,000	0.2
Oregon	20,000	3,204,000	0.6
Pennsylvania	282,000	12,056,000	2.3
Rhode Island	16,000	990,000	1.6
South Carolina	9,000	3,699,000	0.2
South Dakota	350	732,000	(z)
Tennessee	18,000	5,320,000	0.3
Texas	124,000	19,128,000	0.6
Utah	4,400	2,000,000	0.2
Vermont	5,700	589,000	1.0
Virginia	75,500	6,675,000	1.1
Washington	34,500	5,523,000	0.6
West Virginia	2,400	1,826,000	0.1
Wisconsin	32,500	5,160,000	0.6
Wyoming	400	481,000	0.1
U.S. TOTAL	**6,005,000	265,284,000	2.3

N.B. Details may not add to totals because of rounding.
* Resident population, July 1, 1996. (*Source:* U.S. Bureau of the Census, *Current Population Reports,* series P-25, no. 1106.)
** Exclusive of Puerto Rico and the Virgin Islands, which previously reported Jewish populations of 1,500 and 350, respectively.
(z) Figure is less than 0.1 and rounds to 0.

TABLE 2.   DISTRIBUTION OF U.S. JEWISH POPULATION BY REGIONS, 1997

Region	Total Population	Percent Distribution	Estimated Jewish Population	Percent Distribution
Midwest	62,082,000	23.4	705,000	11.7
East North Central ..	43,614,000	16.4	572,000	9.5
West North Central .	18,468,000	7.0	133,000	2.2
Northeast	51,580,000	19.4	2,811,000	46.8
Middle Atlantic	38,229,000	14.4	2,396,000	39.9
New England	13,351,000	5.0	415,000	6.9
South	93,098,000	35.1	1,255,000	20.9
East South Central ..	16,193,000	6.1	40,000	0.7
South Atlantic	47,616,000	17.9	1,068,000	17.8
West South Central ..	29,290,000	11.0	147,400	2.5
West	58,523,000	22.1	1,233,000	20.5
Mountain	16,118,000	6.1	213,000	3.5
Pacific	42,406,000	16.0	1,020,000	17.0
TOTALS	265,284,000	100.0	6,005,000	100.0

N.B. Details may not add to totals because of rounding.

TABLE 3. RANK-ORDERED METROPOLITAN STATISTICAL AREAS, BY JEWISH POPULATION, 1997

Metro Area	Estimated Jewish Population	Jewish % of Total Population	% Share of U.S. Jewish Population	Cumulative % Share of Jewish Population
1. New York-Northern NJ-Long Island*	1,969,000	10.6	32.8	32.8
2. Los Angeles-Anaheim-Riverside*	631,000	4.1	10.5	43.3
3. Miami-Ft. Lauderdale*	354,000	10.4	5.9	49.2
4. Chicago-Gary-Lake County*	265,000	3.2	4.4	53.6
5. Boston-Lawrence-Salem*	241,000	5.6	4.0	57.7
6. Philadelphia-Wilmington-Trenton*	231,000	3.9	3.9	61.5
7. San Francisco-Oakland-San Jose*	216,000	3.3	3.6	65.1
8. Washington, DC-MD-VA	166,000	3.7	2.8	67.9
9. W. Palm Beach-Boca Raton-Delray Beach	153,000	16.0	2.6	70.4
10. Baltimore	107,000	4.4	1.8	72.2
11. Detroit-Ann Arbor*	99,000	1.9	1.7	73.9
12. Cleveland-Akron-Lorain*	86,000	3.0	1.4	75.3
13. Atlanta	77,000	2.3	1.3	76.6
14. San Diego	70,000	2.7	1.2	77.8
15. Denver-Boulder*	63,000	2.9	1.1	78.8
16. Las Vegas	55,500	2.3	0.9	79.7
17. St. Louis	54,000	2.1	0.9	80.6

Metro Area	Estimated Jewish Population	Jewish % of Total Population	% Share of U.S. Jewish Population	Cumulative % Share of Jewish Population
18. Phoenix	50,000	2.0	0.8	81.5
19. Dallas-Fort Worth*	50,000	1.1	0.8	82.3
20. Houston-Galveston-Brazoria*	43,000	1.0	0.7	83.0
21. Pittsburgh-Beaver Valley*	41,000	1.7	0.7	83.7
22. Minneapolis-St. Paul	40,500	1.5	0.7	84.4
23. Tampa-St. Petersburg-Clearwater	40,000	1.9	0.7	85.0
24. Seattle-Tacoma*	30,500	1.0	0.5	85.6
25. Milwaukee-Racine*	26,000	1.6	0.4	86.0
26. Hartford-New Britain-Middletown*	26,000	2.3	0.4	86.4
27. Buffalo-Niagara Falls*	26,000	2.2	0.4	86.8
28. New Haven-Meriden	25,000	4.8	0.4	87.3
29. Cincinnati Hamilton*	24,000	1.3	0.4	87.7
30. Rochester	22,500	2.1	0.4	88.0
31. Sacramento	21,500	1.3	0.4	88.4
32. Norfolk-Virginia Beach-Newport News	21,500	1.4	0.4	88.8
33. Orlando	21,000	1.5	0.3	89.1
34. Tucson	20,000	2.7	0.3	89.4
35. Albany-Schenectady-Troy	19,500	2.2	0.3	89.8

Metro Area	Estimated Jewish Population	Jewish % of Total Population	% Share of U.S. Jewish Population	Cumulative % Share of Jewish Population
36. Kansas City	19,000	1.2	0.3	90.1
37. Providence-Pawtucket-Fall River*	17,500	1.6	0.3	90.4
38. Sarasota, FL	17,000	3.3	0.3	90.7
39. Atlantic City	16,000	4.8	0.3	91.0
40. Portland-Salem, OR	15,500	0.8	0.3	91.3

N.B. Details may not add to totals because of rounding.
Sources: U. S. Bureau of the Census General Population Estimates for Metropolitan Areas, 1996, Report #CPH-S-1-1. Designations for the metropolitan areas are in accordance with the 1990 U.S. Census boundary definitions. Areas marked * = CMSA (Consolidated Metropolitan Statistical Area); otherwise unit is PMSA (Primary Metropolitan Statistical Area). Jewish figures are for 1997.

TABLE 4. COMMUNITIES WITH JEWISH POPULATIONS OF 100 OR MORE, 1997
(ESTIMATED)

State and City	Jewish Population	State and City	Jewish Population	State and City	Jewish Population
ALABAMA		**ARKANSAS**		*Napa County	950
*Birmingham	5,200	Fayetteville	150	Oakland (incl. in	
Decatur (incl. in		Hot Springs	130	Alameda County,	
Florence total)		**Little Rock	1,100	under S.F. Bay Area)	
Dothan	150	Other places	300	Ontario (incl. in	
Florence	150			Pomona Valley)	
Huntsville	750	**CALIFORNIA**		Orange County[N]	
**Mobile	1,100	***Antelope Valley	700		60,000
**Montgomery	1,300	Aptos (incl. in Santa		Palm Springs[N]	9,850
Sheffield (incl. in		Cruz total)		Palmdale (incl. in	
Florence total)		Bakersfield-Kern		Antelope Valley)	
Tuscaloosa	300	County	1,600	Palo Alto (incl. in	
Tuscumbia (incl. in		Berkeley (incl. in		South Peninsula,	
Florence total)		Contra Costa County,		under S.F. Bay Area)	
Other places	250	under S.F. Bay Area)		Pasadena (incl. in	
		Carmel (incl. in		L.A. area)	
		Monterey Peninsula)		Petaluma (incl. in	
ALASKA		*Chico	500	Sonoma County,	
*Anchorage	1,600	Corona (incl. in		under S.F. Bay Area)	
*Fairbanks	540	Riverside area total)		Pomona Valley[N]	6,750
Juneau	285	*Eureka	500	*Redding area	150
Kenai Peninsula	200	Fairfield	800	Redwood Valley	200
Ketchikan (incl. in		Fontana (incl. in		Riverside area	2,000
Juneau total)		San Bernardino total)		Sacramento[N]	21,300
Other places	200	*Fresno	2,500	Salinas	750
		Lancaster (incl. in		San Bernardino area	
		Antelope Valley)			3,000
ARIZONA		Long Beach[N]	14,000	*San Diego	70,000
Cochise County	260	Los Angeles area[N]		San Francisco Bay	
*Flagstaff	350		519,000	Area[N]	210,000
Lake Havasu City		*Merced County	190	Alameda County	
	200	*Modesto	500		32,500
*Phoenix	50,000	Monterey Peninsula		Contra Costa County	
Prescott	250		2,300		22,000
Sierra Vista (incl. in		Moreno Valley (incl. in		Marin County	18,500
Cochise County)		Riverside total)		N. Peninsula	24,500
*Tucson	20,000	Murrieta Hot Springs		San Francisco	49,500
Yuma	125		550	San Jose	33,000
Other places	400				

[N]See Notes below. *Includes entire county. **Includes all of two counties. ***Figure not updated.

State and City	Jewish Population	State and City	Jewish Population	State and City	Jewish Population
Sonoma County 9,000		*Grand Junction ... 250		Norwalk[N] 9,100	
S. Peninsula ... 21,000		Greeley (incl. in		Norwich (incl. in	
*San Jose (listed under		Fort Collins total)		New London total)	
S.F. Bay Area)		Loveland (incl. in Fort		Rockville (incl. in	
*San Luis Obispo		Collins total)		Hartford total)	
.... 1,450		Pueblo 250		Shelton (incl. in	
*Santa Barbara ... 4,500		Steamboat Springs . 160		Bridgeport total)	
*Santa Cruz 4,000		Telluride 125		Southington (incl. in	
Santa Maria 700		**Vail 650		Hartford total)	
Santa Monica (incl.		Other places 200		Stamford 9,200	
in Los Angeles area)				Storrs (incl. in	
Santa Rosa (incl. in		CONNECTICUT		Willimantic total)	
Sonoma County,		Bridgeport[N] 10,000		Torrington area ... 580	
under S.F. Bay Area)		Bristol (incl. in		Wallingford (incl. in	
Sonoma County (listed		Hartford total)		New Haven total)	
under S.F. Bay Area)		Cheshire (incl. in		Waterbury[N] 3,800	
*South Lake Tahoe		Waterbury total)		Westport (incl. in	
.... 150		Colchester 300		Norwalk total)	
Stockton 1,000		Danbury[N] 3,200		Willimantic area... 700	
***Sun City 200		Danielson 100		Other places 200	
Tulare and Kings		Darien (incl. in			
counties 300		Stamford total)		DELAWARE	
Ukiah (incl. in Redwood		Greenwich 3,900		Dover (incl. in Kent	
Valley total)		Hartford[N] 25,200		and Sussex counties	
Vallejo area 900		Hebron (incl. in		totals)	
*Ventura County[N]		Colchester total)		Kent and Sussex	
.... 15,000		Lebanon (incl. in		counties 1,600	
Visalia (incl. in Tulare		Colchester total)		Newark area 4,300	
and Kings counties)		Lower Middlesex		Wilmington area . 7,600	
Other places 200		County[N] 1,600			
		Manchester (incl. in		DISTRICT OF COLUMBIA	
COLORADO		Hartford total)		Washington D.C.[N]	
Aspen 450		Meriden (incl. in		 25,500	
Boulder (incl. in		New Haven total)			
Denver total)		Middletown 1,300		FLORIDA	
Breckenridge (incl. in		New Britain (incl. in		Arcadia (incl. in Port	
Vail total)		Hartford total)		Charlotte-Punta	
Colorado Springs 1,500		New Canaan (incl. in		Gorda total)	
Denver[N] 63,000		Stamford total)		Boca Raton-Delray	
Eagle (incl. in Vail		New Haven[N] ... 24,300		Beach (listed under	
total)		New London[N] ... 3,800		Southeast Fla.)	
Evergreen (also incl. in		New Milford (incl. in		Brevard County.. 5,000	
Denver total) 250		Waterbury total)		Broward County	
*Fort Collins 1,000		Newtown (incl. in		(listed under	
		Danbury total)		Southeast Fla.)	

State and City	Jewish Population	State and City	Jewish Population	State and City	Jewish Population

***Crystal River ... 100
**Daytona Beach . 2,500
Ft. Lauderdale (incl. in
Broward County,
under Southeast Fla.)
**Ft. Myers 5,000
Ft. Pierce....... 1,060
Gainesville 1,600
Hollywood-S. Broward
County (incl in
Broward County,
under Southeast Fla.)
**Jacksonville.... 7,300
Key West 500
Lakeland....... 1,000
*Miami-Dade County
(listed under
Southeast Fla.)
Naples-Collier County
.... 3,500
New Port Richey (incl.
in Pasco County)
Ocala-Marion County
.... 500
Orlando[N]...... 21,000
Palm Beach County
(listed under
Southeast Fla.)
Pasco County ... 1,000
**Pensacola....... 650
Pinellas County . 24,200
**Port Charlotte-
Punta Gorda 900
*St. Petersburg-
Clearwater (incl. in
Pinellas County)
**Sarasota 17,000
Southeast Florida
.... 507,000
Boca Raton-Delray
Beach..... 86,000
Broward County
.... 220,000
Miami-Dade County
.... 134,000

Palm Beach County
(excl. Boca Raton-
Delray Beach)
.... 67,000
***Stuart-Port St. Lucie
.... 3,000
Tallahassee 1,640
*Tampa........ 15,000
Venice (incl. in
Sarasota total)
*Vero Beach....... 300
Winter Haven..... 300
Other places...... 100

GEORGIA
Albany.......... 190
Athens 400
Atlanta Metro Area
.... 77,000
Augusta[N]...... 1,400
Brunswick 100
**Columbus 1,100
**Dalton 180
Macon 900
*Savannah....... 2,800
**Valdosta........ 100
Other places...... 250

HAWAII
Hilo 280
Honolulu (incl.
all of Oahu).... 6,400
Kauai........... 100
Maui 210

IDAHO
**Boise 220
Lewiston (incl. in
Moscow total)
Moscow 100
Other places...... 150

ILLINOIS
Aurora area 500

Bloomington-Normal
.... 230
Carbondale (incl. in
S. Ill.)
*Champaign-Urbana
.... 1,300
Chicago Metro Area[N]
.... 261,000
**Danville 100
*Decatur 130
DeKalb 180
East St. Louis (incl.
in S. Ill.)
Elgin[N]........... 500
Freeport (incl. in
Rockford total)
*Joliet........... 450
Kankakee........ 100
Moline (incl. in
Quad Cities)
*Peoria.......... 800
Quad Cities-
Ill. portion 550
Rock Island (incl.
in Quad Cities)
Rockford[N]...... 1,100
Southern Illinois[N]
.... 650
*Springfield...... 1,060
Waukegan 400
Other places...... 250

INDIANA
Bloomington.... 1,000
Elkhart (incl. in S.
Bend total)
Evansville........ 400
**Ft. Wayne...... 950
**Gary-Northwest
Indiana 2,220
**Indianapolis .. 10,000
**Lafayette 700
*Michigan City 300
Muncie.......... 160
South Bend[N] 1,950

State and City	Jewish Population

*Terre Haute 250
Other places 250

IOWA
Ames (also incl. in Des
  Moines total) 200
Cedar Rapids 420
Council Bluffs 150
*Davenport (incl. in
  Quad Cities)
*Des Moines 2,800
*Iowa City 1,200
Quad Cities-
  Iowa portion 650
**Sioux City 520
*Waterloo 170
Other places 300

KANSAS
Kansas City area-
  Kansas portion[N]
  12,000
Lawrence 100
Manhattan 425
*Topeka 500
Wichita[N] 1,300
Other places 100

KENTUCKY
Covington-Newport
  area 500
Lexington[N] 1,850
*Louisville 8,700
Other places 150

LOUISIANA
Alexandria[N] 350
Baton Rouge[N] . . . 1,500
Lafayette (incl. in
  S. Central La.)
Lake Charles area
  200
Monroe (incl. in
  Shreveport total)

**New Orleans . . 13,000
**Shreveport 1,070
***South Central La.[N]
  250
Other places 150

MAINE
Augusta 140
Bangor 1,000
Biddeford-Saco (incl. in
  S. Maine)
Brunswick-Bath (incl.
  in S. Maine)
Lewiston-Auburn . . 500
Portland (incl. in
  S. Maine)
Rockland area 180
Southern Maine[N]
  5,500
*Waterville 200
Other places 150

MARYLAND
Annapolis area . . 1,800
**Baltimore 94,500
Columbia (incl. in
  Howard County)
Cumberland 265
*Frederick 900
*Hagerstown 325
*Harford County
  1,200
*Howard County
  10,000
Montgomery and
  Prince Georges
  counties 104,500
Ocean City 100
Salisbury 400
Silver Spring (incl. in
  Montgomery County)
Upper Eastern Shore[N]
  130
Other places 100

MASSACHUSETTS
Amherst area 1,300
Andover[N] 2,850
Athol area (incl.
  in N. Worcester
  County)
Attleboro area 200
Beverly (incl. in
  North Shore, under
  Boston Metro Region)
Boston Metro Region[N]
  233,000
Boston 18,400
Brockton-South
  Central 32,500
Brookline 20,000
Framingham . . 20,800
Near West 37,500
Newton 28,000
North Central . 22,900
Northeast 7,500
North Shore . . 19,600
Northwest 15,300
Southeast 10,200
Brockton (listed under
  Boston Metro Region)
Brookline (listed under
  Boston Metro Region)
Cape Cod-Barnstable
  County 3,000
Clinton (incl. in
  Worcester-Central
  Worcester County)
Fall River area
  1,100
Falmouth (incl. in
  Cape Cod)
Fitchburg (incl. in
  N. Worcester County)
  300
Framingham (listed
  under Boston
  Metro Region)
Gardner (incl. in N.
  Worcester County)

State and City	Jewish Population

Gloucester (incl.
N. Shore, listed
under Boston Metro
Region)
Great Barrington (incl.
in Pittsfield total)
*Greenfield 1,100
Haverhill 800
Holyoke 600
*Hyannis (incl. in
Cape Cod)
Lawrence (incl. in
Andover total)
Leominster (incl. in
N. Worcester County)
Lowell area 2,000
Lynn (incl. in N. Shore,
listed under Boston
Metro Region)
*Martha's Vineyard
. . . . 260
New Bedford[N] . . . 2,600
Newburyport 280
Newton (listed under
Boston Metro Region)
North Adams (incl. in
N. Berkshire County)
North Berkshire
County 400
North Worcester
County 1,500
Northampton. 850
Peabody (incl. in N.
Shore, listed under
Boston Metro Region)
Pittsfield-Berkshire
County 3,500
Plymouth area 500
Provincetown (incl. in
Cape Cod)
Salem (incl. in N.
Shore, listed under
Boston Metro
Region)

Southbridge (incl. in
S. Worcester County)
South Worcester
County 500
Springfield[N] 10,000
Taunton area . . . 1,300
Webster (incl. in S.
Worcester County)
Worcester-Central
Worcester County
. . . . 11,000
Other places 150

MICHIGAN
*Ann Arbor 5,000
Bay City 150
Benton Harbor area
. . . . 450
**Detroit Metro Area
. . . . 94,000
*Flint 1,800
*Grand Rapids . . . 1,600
**Jackson. 200
*Kalamazoo 1,100
Lansing area 2,100
Midland 120
Mt. Clemens (incl. in
Detroit total)
Mt. Pleasant[N]. 100
*Muskegon 220
*Saginaw 150
Other places 500

MINNESOTA
**Duluth 485
*Minneapolis . . . 31,500
Rochester 550
**St. Paul 9,200
Other places 150

MISSISSIPPI
Biloxi-Gulfport . . . 140
**Greenville. 160
**Hattiesburg 130

**Jackson. 550
Other places 450

MISSOURI
Columbia 400
Kansas City area-
Missouri portion[N]
. . . . 7,100
*St. Joseph. 265
**St. Louis 54,000
Springfield 300
Other places 200

MONTANA
*Billings. 240
Butte 100
Helena (incl. in
Butte total)
*Kalispell. 150
Missoula 200
Other places 100

NEBRASKA
Grand Island-Hastings
(incl. in Lincoln total)
Lincoln. 800
**Omaha. 6,350
Other places 50

NEVADA
Carson City (incl. in
Reno total)
*Las Vegas 55,600
**Reno 1,400
Sparks (incl. in
Reno total)

NEW HAMPSHIRE
Bethlehem 100
Claremont area . . . 140
Concord 450
Dover area 600
Exeter (incl. in
Portsmouth total)

State and City	Jewish Population	State and City	Jewish Population	State and City	Jewish Population
Franconia (incl. in Bethlehem total)		North Essex...	15,600	New Brunswick (incl. in Middlesex County)	
Hanover-Lebanon .	500	South Essex...	20,300	Northeastern N.J.[N]	
*Keene..........	300	West Orange-Orange	16,900	....	384,000
**Laconia	270	*Flemington	1,250	Ocean County (also incl. in Northeastern N.J. total)	9,500
Littleton (incl. in Bethlehem total)		Freehold (incl. in Monmouth County)			
Manchester area .	4,000	Gloucester (incl. in Cherry Hill-S. N.J. total)		Passaic County (also incl. in Northeastern N.J. total).....	15,000
Nashua area	1,890				
Portsmouth area...	950	Hoboken (listed under Hudson County)		Passaic-Clifton (incl. in Passaic County)	
Rochester (incl. in Dover total)		Hudson County (also incl. in Northeastern N.J. total).....	12,200	Paterson (incl. in Passaic County)	
Salem..........	150				
Other places......	100	Bayonne.......	1,600	Perth Amboy (incl. in Middlesex County)	
		Hoboken	1,100		
NEW JERSEY		Jersey City.....	6,000	Phillipsburg (incl. in Warren County)	
Asbury Park (incl. in Monmouth County)		North Hudson County[N].....	3,500	Plainfield (incl. in Union County)	
**Atlantic City (incl. Atlantic and Cape May counties) .	15,800	Jersey City (listed under Hudson County)		Princeton area...	3,000
				Somerset County (also incl. in Northeastern N.J. total).....	11,000
Bayonne (listed under Hudson County)		Lakewood (incl. in Ocean County)			
Bergen County (also incl. in Northeastern N.J. total).....	83,700	Livingston (listed under Essex County)		Somerville (incl. in Somerset County)	
		Middlesex County (also incl. in Northeastern N.J.)[N]	45,000	Sussex County (also incl. in Northeastern N.J. total)	4,100
Bridgeton........	200				
Bridgewater (incl. in Somerset County)				Toms River (incl. in Ocean County)	
Camden (incl. in Cherry Hill-S. N.J.)		Monmouth County (also incl. in Northeastern N.J.)	63,000	Trenton[N]	6,000
Cherry Hill-Southern N.J.[N]	49,000			Union County (also incl. in Northeastern N.J. total)....	30,000
		Morris County (also incl. in Northeastern N.J.)........	33,500		
Edison (incl. in Middlesex County)				Vineland[N]	1,890
Elizabeth (incl. in Union County)		Morristown (incl. in Morris County)		Warren County ...	400
		Mt. Holly (incl. in Cherry Hill-S. N.J.)		Wayne (incl. in Passaic County)	
Englewood (incl. in Bergen County)				Wildwood........	425
Essex County (also incl. in Northeastern N.J. total)[N]....	76,200	Newark (incl. in Essex County)		Willingboro (incl. in Cherry Hill-S. N.J.)	
East Essex	10,800			Other places......	250
Livingston	12,600				

State and City	Jewish Population

NEW MEXICO
*Albuquerque 7,500
Las Cruces 525
Los Alamos 250
Rio Rancho (incl. in
  Albuquerque total)
Santa Fe 1,500
Taos 300
Other places 100

NEW YORK
*Albany. 12,000
Amenia (incl. in
  Poughkeepsie-
  Dutchess County)
Amsterdam 150
*Auburn. 115
Beacon (incl. in
  Poughkeepsie-
  Dutchess County)
*Binghamton (incl. all
  Broome County)
  2,600
Brewster (incl. in
  Putnam County)
*Buffalo 26,000
Canandaigua (incl. in
  Geneva total)
Catskill. 200
Corning (incl. in
  Elmira total)
*Cortland. 150
Dunkirk 100
Ellenville 1,600
Elmira[N] 900
Fleischmanns 120
Fredonia (incl. in
  Dunkirk total)
Geneva area 310
Glens Falls[N] 800
*Gloversville 380
*Herkimer 180
Highland Falls (incl. in
  Orange County)

*Hudson 500
*Ithaca area 1,700
Jamestown 100
Kingston[N] 4,300
Kiryas Joel (incl. in
  Orange County)
Lake George (incl. in
  Glens Falls total)
Liberty (incl. in
  Sullivan County)
Middletown (incl.
  in Orange County)
Monroe (incl. in
  Orange County)
Monticello (incl. in
  Sullivan County)
Newark (incl. in
  Geneva total)
Newburgh (incl. in
  Orange County)
New Paltz (incl. in
  Kingston total)
New York Metro Area[N]
  1,450,000
Bronx. 83,700
Brooklyn 379,000
Manhattan. . . 314,500
Queens. 238,000
Staten Island . . 33,700
Nassau County
  207,000
Suffolk County
  100,000
Westchester County
  94,000
Niagara Falls 150
Olean 120
**Oneonta 300
Orange County
  15,000
Pawling (incl. in
  Poughkeepsie-
  Dutchess County)
Plattsburg. 260

Port Jervis (incl. in
  Orange County)
Potsdam 200
*Poughkeepsie-Dutchess
  County 3,600
Putnam County. . 1,000
**Rochester. 22,500
Rockland County
  83,100
Rome 150
Saratoga Springs . . 600
**Schenectady. . . . 5,200
Seneca Falls (incl. in
  Geneva total)
South Fallsburg (incl.
  in Sullivan County)
***Sullivan County
  7,425
Syracuse[N] 9,000
Troy area 800
Utica[N] 1,100
Walden (incl. in
  Orange County)
Watertown 120
Woodstock (incl. in
  Kingston total)
Other places 450

NORTH CAROLINA
Asheville[N] 1,300
**Chapel Hill-Durham
  3,100
Charlotte[N] 7,800
Elizabethtown (incl. in
  Wilmington total)
*Fayetteville. 320
Gastonia 210
Goldsboro 120
*Greensboro 2,500
Greenville. 240
*Hendersonville 200
**Hickory 110
High Point (incl. in
  Greensboro total)

State and City	Jewish Population	State and City	Jewish Population	State and City	Jewish Population

Jacksonville (incl. in
Wilmington total)
Raleigh-Wake County
. . . . 5,500
Whiteville (incl. in
Wilmington total)
Wilmington area . 1,200
Winston-Salem. . . . 485
Other places. 450

NORTH DAKOTA
Fargo 500
Grand Forks 130
Other places. 100

OHIO
**Akron 5,500
Athens 100
Bowling Green (incl.
in Toledo total)
Butler County 900
**Canton 1,580
Cincinnati[N] 22,500
Cleveland[N]. 81,000
*Columbus 15,600
**Dayton 5,500
**Elyria 175
Fremont (incl. in
Sandusky total)
Hamilton (incl. in
Butler County)
Kent (incl. in Akron
total)
*Lima. 185
Lorain 600
Mansfield. 180
Marion. 125
Middletown (incl. in
Butler County)
New Philadelphia
(incl. in Canton total)
Norwalk (incl. in
Sandusky total)
Oberlin (incl. in
Elyria total)

Oxford (incl. in
Butler County)
**Sandusky 130
Springfield 200
*Steubenville 125
Toledo[N] 5,900
Warren (incl. in
Youngstown total)
Wooster 135
Youngstown[N]. . . . 3,800
*Zanesville. 100
Other places. 400

OKLAHOMA
Norman (incl. in
Oklahoma City total)
**Oklahoma City
. . . . 2,300
*Tulsa 2,750
Other places. 100

OREGON
Ashland (incl. in
Medford total)
Bend. 175
Corvallis. 175
Eugene 3,000
Grants Pass (incl. in
Medford total)
**Medford 1,000
Portland[N]. 14,500
**Salem 530
Other places. 200

PENNSYLVANIA
Allentown (incl. in
Lehigh Valley)
*Altoona 525
Ambridge (incl. in
Pittsburgh total)
Beaver Falls (incl. in
Upper Beaver County)
Bethlehem (incl. in
Lehigh Valley)

Bucks County (listed
under Phila. area)
*Butler. 175
**Chambersburg . . . 125
Chester (incl. in
Delaware County,
listed under Phila.
area)
Chester County (listed
under Phila. area)
Coatesville (incl. in
Chester County, listed
under Phila. area)
Easton (incl. in
Lehigh Valley)
*Erie 850
Farrell (incl. in Sharon
total)
Greensburg (incl. in
Pittsburgh total)
**Harrisburg. 7,000
Hazleton area. 300
Honesdale (incl. in
Wayne County)
Jeannette (incl. in
Pittsburgh total)
**Johnstown 400
Lancaster area. . . 2,500
*Lebanon. 350
Lehigh Valley . . . 8,500
Lewisburg (incl. in
Sunbury total)
Lock Haven (incl. in
Williamsport total)
McKeesport (incl. in
Pittsburgh total)
New Castle. 200
Norristown (incl. in
Montgomery County,
listed under Phila.
area)
**Oil City 100
Oxford-Kennett Square
(incl. in Chester

State and City	Jewish Population
County, listed under Phila. area)	
Philadelphia area[N]	206,000
Bucks County	34,800
Chester County	10,100
Delaware County	15,700
Montgomery County	58,900
Philadelphia	86,600
Phoenixville (incl. in Chester County, listed under Phila. area)	
Pike County	300
Pittsburgh[N]	40,000
Pottstown	650
Pottsville	225
*Reading	2,200
*Scranton	3,150
Shamokin (incl. in Sunbury total)	
Sharon	250
State College	550
Stroudsburg	400
Sunbury[N]	200
Tamaqua (incl. in Hazleton total)	
Uniontown area	250
Upper Beaver County	180
Washington (incl. in Pittsburgh total)	
***Wayne County	500
Waynesburg (incl. in Washington total)	
West Chester (incl. in Chester County, listed under Phila. area)	
Wilkes-Barre[N]	3,200
**Williamsport	350
York	1,500
Other places	900

State and City	Jewish Population
RHODE ISLAND	
Cranston (incl. in Providence total)	
Kingston (incl. in Washington County)	
Newport-Middletown	700
Providence area	14,200
Washington County	1,200
Westerly (incl. in Washington County)	
SOUTH CAROLINA	
*Charleston	3,500
**Columbia	2,500
Florence area	220
Georgetown (incl. in Myrtle Beach total)	
Greenville	1,200
Kingstree (incl. in Sumter total)	
**Myrtle Beach	425
Rock Hill	100
*Spartanburg	330
Sumter[N]	160
York (incl. in Rock Hill total)	
Other places	500
SOUTH DAKOTA	
Sioux Falls	175
Other places	150
TENNESSEE	
Bristol (incl. in Johnson City total)	
Chattanooga	1,350
Kingsport (incl. in Johnson City total)	
Knoxville	1,650
Memphis	8,500
Nashville	6,000
Oak Ridge	250
Other places	200

State and City	Jewish Population
TEXAS	
Amarillo[N]	150
*Austin	10,000
Bay City (incl. in Wharton total)	
*** Baytown	300
Beaumont	500
*Brownsville	450
***College Station-Bryan	400
*Corpus Christi	1,400
**Dallas	45,000
El Paso	4,900
*Ft. Worth	5,000
Galveston	800
Harlingen (incl. in Brownsville total)	
**Houston[N]	42,000
Kilgore (incl. in Longview total)	
Laredo	130
Longview	150
*Lubbock	480
Lufkin (incl. in Longview total)	
Marshall (incl. in Longview total)	
*McAllen[N]	450
Midland-Odessa	150
Port Arthur	100
*San Antonio	10,000
South Padre Island (incl. in Brownsville total)	
Tyler	400
Waco[N]	300
**Wharton	100
Wichita Falls	260
Other places	500
UTAH	
Ogden	150
*Salt Lake City	4,200
Other places	100

State and City	Jewish Population	State and City	Jewish Population	State and City	Jewish Population

VERMONT

Bennington area. . . 300
*Brattleboro. 350
**Burlington. 3,000
Manchester area. . . 250
Montpelier-Barre . . 550
Newport (incl. in
  St. Johnsbury
  total)
Rutland 550
**St. Johnsbury 140
Stowe 150
Woodstock 270
Other places 100

VIRGINIA

Alexandria (incl. in
  N. Virginia)
Arlington (incl. in
  N. Virginia)
Blacksburg 100
Charlottesville. . . 1,000
Chesapeake (incl. in
  Portsmouth total)
Colonial Heights (incl.
  in Petersburg total)
Fairfax County (incl.
  in N. Virginia)
Fredericksburg[N] . . . 500
Hampton (incl. in
  Newport News total)
Harrisonburg (incl. in
  Staunton total)
Lexington (incl. in
  Staunton total)
Lynchburg area . . . 275
**Martinsville 100

Newport News-
  Hampton[N] 2,400
Norfolk-Virginia Beach
  19,000
Northern Virginia
  35,100
Petersburg area . . . 400
Portsmouth-Suffolk
  (incl. in Norfolk total)
Radford (incl. in
  Blacksburg total)
Richmond[N] 15,000
Roanoke 950
Staunton[N] 370
Williamsburg (incl. in
  Newport News total)
Winchester[N] 270
Other places 100

WASHINGTON

Bellingham 400
Ellensburg (incl. in
  Yakima total)
Longview-Kelso (incl.
  in Vancouver total)
*Olympia 450
***Port Angeles. . . . 100
*Seattle[N] 29,300
Spokane 1,400
*Tacoma 1,250
Tri Cities[N] 300
Vancouver 600
**Yakima 110
Other places 350

WEST VIRGINIA

Bluefield-Princeton 200
*Charleston 975

Clarksburg 110
Fairmont (incl. in
  Clarksburg total)
Huntington[N] 250
Morgantown 160
Parkersburg 110
**Wheeling 275
Other places 350

WISCONSIN

Appleton area 400
Beloit 150
Fond du Lac (incl. in
  Oshkosh total)
Green Bay 320
Janesville (incl. in
  Beloit total)
*Kenosha 350
La Crosse 100
*Madison 4,500
Milwaukee[N] 25,500
Oshkosh area 170
*Racine 375
Sheboygan 140
Waukesha (incl. in
  Milwaukee total)
Wausau[N] 240
Other places 300

WYOMING

Casper 100
Cheyenne 230
Laramie (incl. in
  Cheyenne total)
Other places 100

Notes

CALIFORNIA

Long Beach—includes in L.A. County: Long Beach, Signal Hill, Cerritos, Lakewood, Rossmoor, and Hawaiian Gardens. Also includes in Orange County: Los Alamitos, Cypress, Seal Beach, and Huntington Harbor.

Los Angeles—includes most of Los Angeles County, but excludes the eastern portion as well as those places listed above that are part of the Long Beach area. Also includes eastern edge of Ventura County.

Orange County—includes most of Orange County, but excludes towns in northern portion that are included in Long Beach.

Palm Springs—includes Palm Springs, Desert Hot Springs, Cathedral City, Palm Desert, and Rancho Mirage.

Pomona Valley—includes Alta Loma, Chino, Claremont, Cucamonga, La Verne, Montclair, Ontario, Pomona, San Dimas, and Upland.

Sacramento—includes Yolo, Placer, El Dorado, and Sacramento counties.

San Francisco Bay area—North Peninsula includes northern San Mateo County. South Peninsula includes southern San Mateo County and towns of Palo Alto and Los Altos in Santa Clara County. San Jose includes remainder of Santa Clara County.

COLORADO

Denver—includes Adams, Arapahoe, Boulder, Denver, and Jefferson counties.

CONNECTICUT

Bridgeport—includes Monroe, Easton, Trumbull, Fairfield, Bridgeport, Shelton, and Stratford.

Danbury—includes Danbury, Bethel, New Fairfield, Brookfield, Sherman, Newtown, Redding, and Ridgefield.

Hartford—includes most of Hartford County and Vernon, Rockville, Ellington, and Tolland in Tolland County.

Lower Middlesex County—includes Branford, Guilford, Madison, Clinton, Westbrook, Old Saybrook, Old Lyme, Durham, and Killingworth.

New Haven—includes New Haven, East Haven, Guilford, Branford, Madison, North Haven, Hamden, West Haven, Milford, Orange, Woodbridge, Bethany, Derby, Ansonia, Quinnipiac, Meriden, Seymour, and Wallingford.

New London—includes central and southern New London County. Also includes part of Middlesex County and part of Windham County.

Norwalk—includes Norwalk, Weston, Westport, East Norwalk, Wilton, and Georgetown.

Waterbury—includes Bethlehem, Cheshire, Litchfield, Morris, Middlebury, Southbury, Naugatuck, Prospect, Plymouth, Roxbury, Southbury, Southington, Thomaston, Torrington, Washington, Watertown, Waterbury, Oakville, Woodbury, Wolcott, Oxford, and other towns in Litchfield County and northern New Haven County.

DISTRICT OF COLUMBIA

Washington, D.C.—For a total of the Washington, D.C., metropolitan area, include Montgomery and Prince Georges counties in Maryland, and northern Virginia.

FLORIDA

Orlando—includes all of Orange and Seminole counties, southern Volusia County, and northern Osceola County.

GEORGIA

Augusta—includes Burke, Columbia, and Richmond counties.

ILLINOIS

Chicago—includes all of Cook and DuPage counties and a portion of Lake County.
Elgin—includes northern Kane County and southern McHenry County.
Rockford—includes Winnebago, Boone, and Stephenson counties.
Southern Illinois—includes lower portion of Illinois below Carlinville.

INDIANA

South Bend—includes St. Joseph and Elkhart counties.

KANSAS

Kansas City—includes Johnson and Wyandotte counties. For a total of the Kansas City metropolitan area, include Missouri portion.
Wichita—includes Sedgwick County and towns of Salina, Dodge City, Great Bend, Liberal, Russell, and Hays.

KENTUCKY

Lexington—includes Fayette, Bourbon, Scott, Clark, Woodford, Madison, Pulaski, and Jessamine counties.

LOUISIANA

Alexandria—includes towns in Allen, Grant, Rapides, and Vernon parishes.
Baton Rouge—includes E. Baton Rouge, Ascension, Livingston, St. Landry, Iberville, Pointe Coupee, and W. Baton Rouge parishes.
South Central—includes Abbeville, Lafayette, New Iberia, Crowley, Opelousas, Houma, Morgan City, Thibodaux, and Franklin.

MAINE

Southern Maine—includes York, Cumberland, and Sagadahoc counties.

MARYLAND

Upper Eastern Shore—includes towns in Caroline, Dorchester, Kent, Queen Annes, and Talbot counties.

MASSACHUSETTS

Andover—includes Andover, N. Andover, Boxford, Lawrence, Methuen, Tewksbury, and Dracut.

Boston Metropolitan region—Brockton-South Central includes Avon, Bridgewater, Brockton, Canton, East Bridgewater, Easton, Foxborough, Halifax, Randolph, Sharon, Stoughton, West Bridgewater, Whitman, and Wrentham. Framingham area includes—Acton, Bellingham, Boxborough, Framingham, Franklin, Holliston, Hopkinton, Hudson, Marlborough, Maynard, Medfield, Medway, Milford, Millis, Southborough, and Stow. Northeast includes—Chelsea, Everett, Malden, Medford, Revere, and Winthrop. North Central includes—Arlington, Belmont, Cambridge, Somerville, Waltham, and Watertown. Northwest includes—Bedford, Burlington, Carlisle, Concord, Lexington, Lincoln, Melrose, North Reading, Reading, Stoneham, Wakefield, Wilmington, Winchester, and Woburn. North Shore includes—Lynn, Saugus, Nahant, Swampscott, Lynnfield, Peabody, Salem, Marblehead, Beverly, Danvers, Middleton, Wenham, Topsfield, Hamilton, Manchester, Ipswich, Essex, Gloucester, and Rockport. Near West includes—Ashland, Dedham, Dover, Natick, Needham, Norfolk, Norwood, Sherborn, Sudbury, Walpole, Wayland, Wellesley, Weston, and Westwood. Southeast includes—Abington, Braintree, Cohasset, Duxbury, Hanover, Hanson, Hingham, Holbrook, Hull, Kingston, Marshfield, Milton, Norwell, Pembroke, Quincy, Rockland, Scituate, and Weymouth.

New Bedford—includes New Bedford, Dartmouth, Fairhaven, and Mattapoisett.

Springfield—includes Springfield, Longmeadow, E. Longmeadow, Hampden, Wilbraham, Agawam, and W. Springfield.

MICHIGAN

Mt. Pleasant—includes towns in Isabella, Mecosta, Gladwin, and Gratiot counties.

MISSOURI

Kansas City—For a total of the Kansas City metropolitan area, include the Kansas portion.

NEW HAMPSHIRE

Laconia—includes Laconia, Plymouth, Meredith, Conway, and Franklin.

NEW JERSEY

Cherry Hill-Southern N.J.—includes Camden, Burlington, and Gloucester counties.

Essex County—East Essex includes Belleville, Bloomfield, East Orange, Irvington, Newark, and Nutley in Essex County, and Kearney in Hudson County. North Essex includes Caldwell, Cedar Grove, Essex Fells, Fairfield, Glen Ridge, Montclair, North Caldwell, Roseland, Verona, and West Caldwell. South Essex includes Maplewood, Millburn, Short Hills, and South Orange in Essex County, and Springfield in Union County.

Middlesex County—includes in Somerset County: Kendall Park, Somerset, and Franklin; in Mercer County: Hightstown; and all of Middlesex County.

Northeastern N.J.—includes Bergen, Essex, Hudson, Middlesex, Morris, Passaic, Somerset, Union, Hunterdon, Sussex, Monmouth, and Ocean counties.

North Hudson County—includes Guttenberg, Hudson Heights, North Bergen, North Hudson, Seacaucus, Union City, Weehawken, West New York, and Woodcliff.

Somerset County—includes most of Somerset County and a portion of Hunterdon County.

Trenton—includes most of Mercer County.

Union County—includes all of Union County except Springfield. Also includes a few towns in adjacent areas of Somerset and Middlesex counties.

Vineland—includes most of Cumberland County and towns in neighboring counties adjacent to Vineland.

NEW YORK

Elmira—includes Chemung, Tioga, and Schuyler counties.

Glens Falls—includes Warren and Washington counties, lower Essex County, and upper Saratoga County.

Kingston—includes eastern half of Ulster County.

New York metropolitan area—includes the five boroughs of New York City, Westchester, Nassau, and Suffolk counties. For total Jewish population of the New York metropolitan region, include Fairfield County, Connecticut; Rockland, Putnam, and Orange counties, New York; and Northeastern New Jersey.

Syracuse—includes Onondaga County, western Madison County, and most of Oswego County.

Utica—southeastern third of Oneida County.

NORTH CAROLINA

Asheville—includes Buncombe, Haywood, and Madison counties.

Charlotte—includes Mecklenburg County. For a total of the Charlotte area, include Rock Hill, South Carolina.

OHIO

Cincinnati—includes Hamilton and Butler counties. For a total of the Cincinnati area, include the Covington-Newport area of Kentucky.

Cleveland—includes all of Cuyahoga County and portions of Lake, Geauga, Portage, and Summit counties. For a metropolitan total, include Elyria, Lorain, and Akron.

Toledo—includes Fulton, Lucas, and Wood counties.

Youngstown—includes Mahoning and Trumbull counties.

PENNSYLVANIA

Philadelphia—For total Jewish population of the Philadelphia metropolitan region, include the Cherry Hill-Southern N.J., Salem, Princeton, and Trenton areas of New Jersey, and the Wilmington and Newark areas of Delaware.

Pittsburgh—includes all of Allegheny County and adjacent portions of Washington, Westmoreland, and Beaver counties.

Sunbury—includes Shamokin, Lewisburg, Milton, Selinsgrove, and Sunbury.

Wilkes-Barre—includes all of Luzerne County except southern portion, which is included in the Hazleton total.

SOUTH CAROLINA

Sumter—includes towns in Sumter, Lee, Clarendon, and Williamsburg counties.

TEXAS

Amarillo—includes Canyon, Childress, Borger, Dumas, Memphis, Pampa, Vega, and Hereford in Texas, and Portales, New Mexico.

Houston—includes Harris, Montgomery, and Fort Bend counties, and parts of Brazoria and Galveston counties.

McAllen—includes Edinburg, Harlingen, McAllen, Mission, Pharr, Rio Grande City, San Juan, and Weslaco.

Waco—includes McLennan, Coryell, Bell, Falls, Hamilton, and Hill counties.

VIRGINIA

Fredericksburg—includes towns in Spotsylvania, Stafford, King George, and Orange counties.

Newport News—includes Newport News, Hampton, Williamsburg, James City, York County, and Poquoson City.

Richmond—includes Richmond City, Henrico County, and Chesterfield County.

Staunton—includes towns in Augusta, Page, Shenandoah, Rockingham, Bath, and Highland counties.

Winchester—includes towns in Winchester, Frederick, Clarke, and Warren counties.

WASHINGTON

Seattle—includes King County and adjacent portions of Snohomish and Kitsap counties.

Tri Cities—includes Pasco, Richland, and Kennewick.

WISCONSIN

MILWAUKEE—INCLUDES MILWAUKEE COUNTY, EASTERN WAUKESHA COUNTY, AND SOUTHERN OZAUKEE COUNTY.

Wausau—includes Stevens Point, Marshfield, Antigo, and Rhinelander.

Review
of
the
Year

OTHER COUNTRIES

Canada

National Affairs

AFTER NARROWLY SURVIVING the 1995 Quebec referendum on independence, Canada enjoyed increasing economic performance and political stability during 1996 and 1997. Still, the specter of another referendum before the turn of the century lurked in the background and influenced governmental actions at both the federal and provincial levels. Economically, growth was good, the high unemployment rate dropped to below 10 percent, and inflation was minimal.

A federal election was held on June 2, 1997. Prime Minister Jean Chrétien's Liberals returned to power, albeit with a reduced majority in the House of Commons, 155 of the 301 seats. The Reform Party, led by Preston Manning, achieved Official Opposition status for the first time with 61 seats, while the Bloc Québécois (BQ) dropped to 44. The Progressive Conservatives and New Democrats recovered somewhat from their disastrous performances in 1993, winning 21 and 20 seats, respectively.

Five Jews, including three newcomers, were elected as Liberal MPs: Herb Gray and Elinor Caplan in Ontario; Sheila Finestone, Raymonde Falco, and Jacques Saada in Quebec. Falco and Saada are both Francophones who were born in France and Tunisia, respectively. Gray, the most senior MP, was appointed deputy prime minister, the first Jew to reach that position. Elinor Caplan's former seat in the Ontario legislature was filled in a by-election by her son David. In Quebec, Howard Galganov ran as an independent for the House of Commons in Sheila Finestone's district, but did not really threaten her incumbency. Galganov was an outspoken antiseparatist (see below).

Among the issues of greatest salience to Canadian Jews were the preservation of national unity, rapid progress in actions against accused war criminals, social issues, and foreign policy in the Middle East. Although conservative commentators David Frum and Hugh Segal, speaking at the Toronto Jewish Book Fair in November 1996, had exhorted Jews to vote more conservatively because of the importance of tradition and values, Jewish voters appeared to persist in their long-standing support for the Liberal Party. Jews and other federalists took some comfort from the fact that the Bloc Québécois received only 38 percent of the vote in Quebec, suggesting a decline in support for secession.

In November 1997 Reform's Manning confronted his party's image problem with Jews and other minorities in an address to Montreal's Jewish Business Network. He pledged to insure that racists and anti-Semites would be excluded from the party. Also in November, former Quebec premier Jacques Parizeau elaborated on his remarks on the night of the October 1995 referendum, when he had blamed the defeat on "money and the ethnic vote." In a speech in Calgary, he specifically named the Greek, Italian, and Jewish minorities in Quebec as the culprits. (Representative bodies of the three groups formed a unity coalition several years ago.) Jack Jedwab, executive director of the Quebec region of Canadian Jewish Congress (CJC), denounced the comments as reprehensible, asserting that "his motivation was obviously pernicious."

In a major reform of municipal government, Ontario consolidated the several constituent cities of Metropolitan Toronto into one megacity. Mel Lastman, the longtime mayor of North York, won the mayoralty of the new Toronto. Among the new city councillors were Howard Moscoe, Mike Feldman, Milton Berger, Norm Gardner, and David Shiner.

Canada's Immigration and Refugee Board (IRB) was confronted with contradictory decisions of the Federal Court over the issue of whether Jewish refugee claimants ought to be denied entry automatically because they were entitled to immigrate to Israel under the Law of the Return. In a 1995 decision the court had affirmed that view; however, it reached the opposite conclusion in a May 1997 case involving Lioudmila Katkova, who fled the Ukraine but did not want to settle in Israel. Finally, in November 1997 the IRB's deputy chair, John Frecker, announced that the availability of Israeli citizenship would no longer be a factor in the board's decisions on Jewish applicants.

In November 1996 Quebec's lieutenant-governor, Jean-Louis Roux, decided to resign after it was revealed that he had worn a swastika during a 1942 anticonscription demonstration. After announcing his resignation, he met with Jewish community representatives and asked for forgiveness for his "lack of judgment."

Israel and the Middle East

Canada-Israel relations suffered a severe setback in the wake of the Mossad's abortive attempt to kill Hamas leader Khaled Mashaal in Amman in September 1997, when it was revealed that the agents carried forged Canadian passports. Canadian officials were furious over the matter and recalled Ambassador David Berger from Israel for consultations. Prime Minister Chrétien denounced the use of the passports as "completely unacceptable." Eventually Israel apologized, promising not to use Canadian passports again, and Berger was allowed to return to his post. But the affair and Prime Minister Benjamin Netanyahu's apparent lack of contrition left residual anger in Canadian foreign policy and political circles. Foreign Affairs Minister Lloyd Axworthy went to great lengths to emphasize that Canada had no role in the matter, despite some claims to the contrary by former ambassador to Israel Norman Spector, and stressed his view that the peace process should continue. While reiterating his government's desire to maintain good relations with Israel, Axworthy also declined to rule out the possible imposition of sanctions on Israel. After things began to settle down, Axworthy visited Israel in mid-November and met with Foreign Minister David Levy and Netanyahu. He received a written guarantee that the security services would not use Canadian passports in the future.

The Mashaal affair marred what had been a positive period in terms of bilateral relations, highlighted by the signing, ratification, and implementation of the Canada-Israel Free Trade Agreement, which took effect on January 1, 1997. The document was signed in an elaborate ceremony in Toronto on July 31, 1996, by Minister of International Trade Art Eggleton and Minister of Industry and Trade Natan Sharansky of Israel. The pact, Canada's first with a country outside North America, is comprehensive and designed to bolster bilateral trade very quickly. It also includes the Palestinian Authority within its scope. Sharansky hailed the signing as "a historic occasion which further solidifies the long-standing relationship" between the two countries. The ratification process in the two houses of Parliament produced some opposition, largely directed toward general Israeli policies rather than the deal itself, but the required bill passed handily.

To follow up on the momentum produced by passage of the legislation, Eggleton led a trade mission to Israel in February 1997, accompanied by some 60 business executives representing 49 companies, the largest group of Canadian business leaders ever to visit. During the trip a bilateral research and development program was extended for three years. As a result of the free trade treaty, trade between the two countries grew at a rapid pace, increasing by 38 percent during the first eight months of 1997, compared to the same period in 1996. Canadian exports to Israel were particularly strong, vindicating the Canadian government's determination to have such a treaty.

Israel was also involved in enhancing its relations with Quebec. During the April 1997 visit to Israel of Intergovernmental Affairs Minister Sylvain Simard, he and Education and Culture Minister Zevulun Hammer signed an agreement of cooperation in the fields of education, culture, and science.

Canada's general foreign policy orientation toward the Middle East came under scrutiny in 1996 and 1997. Axworthy expressed concern during the fall of 1996 that the peace process had lost momentum after the election of Netanyahu and advocated an interventionist posture for Canada, saying that "somehow we've got to get things back on track." However, Canada's orientation was called into question by the Foundation for Middle East Studies, which analyzed 21 United Nations General Assembly resolutions dealing with the Middle East that were passed in 1996 and generally opposed by Israel. Research Director David Goldberg pointed out that Canada voted in favor of 15 of the resolutions, abstained on five, and was on the same side as Israel on one (supporting the peace process). The other 20 resolutions were hostile to Israel's positions on a number of key issues, including Palestinian self-determination, Jerusalem, the Golan Heights, the UN committee on the Palestinians, Israeli settlements in the territories, nuclear weapons, and refugees. The pattern continued in March and July 1997 votes on resolutions regarding construction at Har Homah in Jerusalem, which Canada also supported. In a separate move, after a bombing in Jerusalem in July 1997, Axworthy wrote directly to Palestinian Authority (PA) chairman Yasir Arafat, asking him to act more forcefully against terrorism.

Jewish leaders delivered their own message on terrorism directly to Axworthy in a meeting in September 1997 at which B'nai Brith Canada (BBC), the Canada-Israel Committee (CIC), the Canadian Zionist Federation (CZF), and the Canadian Jewish Congress (CJC) were represented. They urged him to be more active on the terrorism issue and criticized Canada's UN voting record, claiming that there was "too much emphasis" on Israel at the world body and not enough on the failure of the PA to fulfill its obligations.

Norman Spector made several public comments that created a stir. The former ambassador to Israel charged in an August 1996 column in the Toronto *Globe and Mail* that there was "political" opposition to the Free Trade Agreement in the Department of Foreign Affairs. However, he praised the prime minister for not being swayed by advice from such sources. "Mr. Chrétien's demonstration of independence upset, but did not vanquish the Arabists," who had not "given up on trying to derail the agreement. . . ." He provided no specific names, but his remarks caused a furor within the department. Ultimately, Minister Axworthy defended his colleagues in a letter, rejecting the suggestion that there was an anti-Israel bias. Spector then produced another column escalating the attack by charging that Arabists had urged Jews in the department to make their careers elsewhere. That produced outraged statements and letters from former officials, such as Erik Wang, director-general of the Middle East Branch, who accused Spector of "an irresponsible slur." However, some backing for Spector was found in comments reported in the *Canadian Jewish News* by Richard Cleroux. He cited career foreign-service officer Aharon Mayne, who claimed that there was discrimination against "visible" Jews. "When it comes to the treatment of visible Jews around here, none is still too many," asserted Mayne, who charged that the department did not post Jews to Israel, even though people born in other countries could be posted to those countries. Spector kept up the pressure by renewing his charges in a February 1997 speech at a Toronto synagogue. He added that Canada's input on the Middle East was both "relatively ineffectual" and "counterproductive," and that Foreign Affairs bureaucrats displayed a "systematic bias" in favor of Arab positions. The opposition to Israel, according to Spector, was "strong, evident, consistent, and sustained."

Another sensitive issue involved refugee claimants from Israel. Any recognition by Canada that a purported refugee had reason to flee from Israel raised hackles in that country and among Israel's supporters in Canada. As a result of sustained pressure on the issue, only 92 refugees from Israel were accepted in 1996, the lowest total since 1990. Most were from the former Soviet Union. Eighty of them were admitted in Montreal, where officials were more sympathetic. The acceptance rate dropped from about 50 percent in 1994 to 7.5 percent in 1996. Chen Ivry, speaking for the Israeli embassy, expressed his dismay at Canada's acceptance of refugees from Israel.

David Sultan, Israel's ambassador to Canada, assumed his duties in 1996, succeeding Yitzhak Shelef.

Anti-Semitism and Racism

A number of individuals accused of anti-Semitic activities were involved in various types of proceedings. One of the most prominent was James Keegstra, whose case began in 1984, when he was accused of promoting hatred against Jews in his high-school classroom. After the Supreme Court of Canada finally upheld his conviction in September 1996, he was fined $3,000, given a one-year suspended sentence, and ordered to perform 200 hours of community service.

Holocaust-denying publisher Ernst Zundel benefited from a legal loophole when Federal Court judge Darrell Heald ruled in July 1996 that the Security Intelligence Review Committee could not consider accusations that he was a security risk because it had already come to the conclusion that he was a "radical right-wing racist" and thus could not be open-minded. The judge did not rule on the question of whether Zundel, a permanent resident, was a security risk, an issue that arose in connection with his application for Canadian citizenship. As a result of the decision, the government would have to find another way to evaluate the security risk matter.

Later in the year, Zundel's Web site was under review by the Canadian Human Rights Commission (CHRC), which asked a special tribunal to determine if it contained hate material. Zundel questioned the jurisdiction of the commission over international computer networks, because the server for the Web site was located in California. The jurisdictional challenge was turned down by the Federal Court, and the tribunal proceeded to hear evidence in October 1997. The League for Human Rights of B'nai Brith Canada accused Zundel of being "one of the leading purveyors of materials that expose Jews to hatred and contempt." In opening arguments, CHRC lawyer Ian Binnie asserted that the material on the Web site was "simply anti-Semitism and hate propaganda wrapped up in the flag of freedom of speech." The case would likely take years to resolve, especially because of the legal question of whether communications over the Internet are covered by the Human Rights Act.

In July 1996 a Canadian Judicial Council tribunal found that Judge Jean Bienvenue of Quebec Superior Court had displayed poor judgment in making comments from the bench to the effect that Jews had not suffered while dying in Nazi gas chambers. It recommended that he be removed from office because of a lack of sensitivity, a refusal to change his behavior, and because he had abused his power by injecting personal beliefs into the discharge of his official duties. Four of the five tribunal members agreed that he had violated the "duty of good behavior" required of judges and was unfit to serve. The judge decided to retire in September, before the government could act on the council's 22-7 recommendation that he be removed, a move that was hailed by Jewish community-relations bodies.

Raymond Villeneuve, a convicted terrorist who advocated Quebec's secession and had threatened violence against opponents, was the subject of a number of actions. In a September 1996 issue of *La Tempête*, the newsletter of his Mouvement de libération nationale du Québec, Villeneuve accused Ashkenazic Jews of playing a leading role in the opposition to separation and language laws. He went on to name several individuals, implying that they might face retaliation after independence was achieved. He also suggested on the radio to leaders of the English community that "it could come to bombs, or more simple methods like Molotov cocktails." As a result, CJC formally complained of incitement to the federal and Quebec attorneys-general. CJC Quebec Region chairwoman Reisa Teitelbaum declared his remarks to be "a clear incitement to violence." The Quebec Liberals proposed a motion condemning Villeneuve in the National Assembly, but the Parti Québécois (PQ) government blocked it by insisting that it also denounce Anglo-rights activist Howard Galganov, who was one of the Jews specifically attacked by Villeneuve. Liberal leader Daniel Johnson accused Villeneuve of "intolerance in its ugliest and most repulsive excess," but PQ premier Lucien Bouchard, while personally condemning him, wanted any formal motion to "eradicate the intolerance in all political camps, and in particular that of Mr. Galganov." The attempt to equate Villeneuve and Galganov infuriated Jewish spokespersons, especially since Galganov's tactics had always been peaceful and he had not advocated violence. (Although he was widely admired at the grassroots level, the Jewish elite tended to be uncomfortable with Galganov, finding him too confrontational.)

The incident only served to accentuate the gulf between Montreal's Jewish community and the ruling PQ. In a highly qualified clarification, Villeneuve blamed the Jews for not distancing themselves from the "provocateurs" among them and reproached the community for its "monolithism." Jack Jedwab, Quebec executive director of CJC, rejected the attempt to mitigate his earlier remarks: "He's just making his anti-Semitism and racism obvious." In March 1997 the Canadian Radio and Telecommunications Commission turned down a complaint about the radio broadcast but cautioned the station that Villeneuve's remarks had been at "the limit of acceptable comment." Villeneuve was not deterred. In a July 1997 interview in the tabloid *Vice,* he compared the Quebec national liberation movement to the Irgun. He claimed that he had no hatred of Anglophone Jews, "but when they place their interests on the side of the oppressors, they act as enemies of the Quebec people."

Columnist Doug Collins of British Columbia's *North Shore News* faced a provincial Human Rights Tribunal hearing concerning one of his 1994 columns, which criticized the Jewish role in the entertainment industry and questioned the veracity of historical accounts of the Holocaust. McGill University ethnic studies chair Morton Weinfeld testified that the piece had reinforced "several well-known and well-documented anti-Semitic stereotypes" by accusing Jews "of being dishonest and untrustworthy . . . , of being motivated mainly by greed and money, of controlling the media and Hollywood, and of using the media for deliberate 'Jewish' objectives." The issue before the tribunal was whether the column had contravened antihate provisions of the British Columbia Human Rights Act, and whether it was covered by federal constitutional protections of free expression. The tribunal, in a decision announced in November 1997, found that the column was indeed anti-Semitic and was likely to encourage anti-Semitism among readers, but did not constitute hateful material that required a remedy under the law's definition.

In Ontario, teacher Paul Fromm was terminated in February 1997 by the Peel Board of Education after BBC informed them that he had attended meetings and participated in programs of white supremacist and anti-Semitic groups. Fromm, who had a history of such involvements, had been reprimanded for his actions in 1992.

Racist agitator George Burdi continued to encounter legal problems. In February 1997 the Ontario Court of Appeal upheld a one-year jail term for his "severe and cowardly" attack on a female antiracist demonstrator in 1993. The court found that it was Burdi's intent "to incite his neo-Nazi followers to a frenzy of hatred." Then in April police in Windsor and Detroit raided the offices of his company, Resistance Records, which distributed racist music and other materials. The Detroit police seized 200,000 compact discs and cassettes. It was reported that Burdi's Detroit operation was designed to skirt Canadian antihate laws. Nevertheless, he and two followers were charged in September with conspiracy and willfully promoting hatred.

The 1996 Audit of Anti-Semitic Incidents, compiled by B'nai Brith's League for Human Rights, reported 244 incidents, down from 331 in 1995. While vandalism incidents were virtually unchanged at 81, anti-Semitic harassment dropped substantially, from 259 to 163. About 40 percent of all the incidents occurred in the Toronto area. Toronto, Ottawa, and Montreal all experienced declines in incidents, while smaller Ontario communities showed increases.

The 1997 Audit showed a further decline in anti-Semitic incidents, with 58 cases of vandalism and 154 of harassment, a total of 212—the lowest since 1992. Again, Toronto experienced the greatest share of incidents, but there was a drop in the number of incidents in smaller Ontario communities.

Among the incidents that occurred during 1996 and 1997 were the desecration of a cemetery in Victoria in June 1996, a July 1996 break-in at a North York home in which the vandals smeared swastikas and anti-Semitic slogans on the walls, and graffiti on a suburban Montreal synagogue in May 1997.

There were also instances of anti-Semitism in the media, including early 1997 articles in Arabic newspapers that denied the Holocaust and suggested that Jews were planning a holocaust against North American Arabs, an on-air gaffe in July 1997 by CBC sports announcer Bob Tallman, who used the word "Jewed" to describe a monetary transaction, and a story in Montreal's *La Presse* in May about a "Jewish criminal organization" that ran a money-laundering operation.

In December 1997 some 100 prominent Jews received anti-Semitic letters mailed anonymously from the United States. The eight-page diatribes were described by CJC's Bernie Farber as "the most extensive hate mail campaign I've seen."

Nazi War Criminals

The need to proceed with all deliberate speed against alleged Nazi war criminals living in Canada remained one of the highest priorities of Jewish community organizations, as it had been over the decade since the Deschenes Report recommended procedures for dealing with former Nazis in Canada. Faced with the dilatory pace of legal actions, the community looked for ways to speed up the process and keep the pressure on the courts and the government. After the Finta decision in 1994, which effectively ruled out criminal prosecutions, the government's strategy was to seek to strip war criminals of their citizenship (on the grounds that they obtained it fraudulently) and then deport them.

Generally the accused resisted vigorously, resulting in lengthy legal proceedings. The government did appear to be stepping up the pace, with over a dozen deportation cases under way or resolved. The government won a key procedural ruling in December 1997 from Federal Court Justice Marc Noel, who held that constitutional protections against self-incrimination did not apply in citizenship cases. Noel also criticized the government for not proceeding quickly enough. Moreover, in the same month, Neal Sher, former head of the Office of Special Investigations in the United States, was appointed as a consultant to Canada's war-crimes unit to provide "strategic advice."

One case that was brought to a successful conclusion involved Konrad Kalejs, who was accused of being an accomplice to war crimes and crimes against humanity. His Latvian Arajs Kommando (AK) unit operated in Russia in 1942. After hearings that began in May 1996, immigration adjudicator Anthony Iozzo concluded in August 1997 that because Kalejs was commander of guards at the Salaspils concentration camp, he was indeed an accomplice to war crimes. On the other hand, Iozzo discounted evidence about participation in murder with the AK. Kalejs was quickly deported to Australia, where he had previously become a citizen.

The highest profile case of the period was that of Helmut Oberlander, Erichs Tobiass, and Johann Dueck. It attracted considerable notoriety because of improprieties by government officials and judges that jeopardized the continuation of the proceedings. After it was revealed in 1996 that the assistant deputy attorney general had met with the chief judge of the Federal Court in order to persuade him to speed up the trial, the judge handling the case withdrew, and the new judge granted a stay in the proceedings because of the "serious breach of judicial independence." The government appealed, and finally the Supreme Court of Canada, in a unanimous ruling, held that the case could continue despite the imprudent actions. The gravity of the crimes and Canada's standing in the international community were cited as reasons for proceeding expeditiously. The Court criticized Federal Court Associate Chief Justice James Jerome, who had been on the case, for his "inordinate and arguably inexcusable" delays, behavior that "defies explanation." David Matas, speaking for BBC, welcomed the decision, adding that given the ages of the alleged war criminals, "we just can't afford to let these cases take the 10 years they looked like they were going to take." With the Supreme Court clearing the way, the cases could now be heard on their merits, though Tobiass died late in 1997.

Joseph Nemsila, a permanent resident whom the government was seeking to deport, died in April 1997. He had commanded a unit of the Hlinka Guard in Slovakia, which was accused of murdering hundreds of Jews. From a legal point of view, his case helped to establish the principle that domicile in Canada obtained through fraud or deception (i.e., failing to divulge wartime activities) was not a barrier to deportation, although the appeals of that ruling had not been exhausted.

Another suspected war criminal who died was Antanas Kenstavicius, who succumbed to cancer in January 1997, just as his deportation hearing was getting under way. The government claimed that in his capacity as a police official in Lithuania he participated in atrocities against Jews.

In the case of Ladislaus Csizsik-Csatary, the accused decided not to contest denaturalization and thus had his citizenship revoked by the cabinet in August 1997. He had been an officer of the Royal Hungarian Police who exercised authority inhumanely in a brickyard camp and also rounded up Jews for deportation to Auschwitz. Less than two months after the cabinet action he voluntarily departed from Canada and was barred from re-entry. Csizsik-Csatary was only the second suspected war criminal to be stripped of his Canadian citizenship.

Denaturalization hearings began in 1997 in cases involving a number of individuals: Vladimir Katriuk, for his role in the atrocities committed by his police battalion in Ukraine and Belarus between 1942 and 1944; Wasily Bogutin, accused of being a member of a Ukrainian police unit that collaborated with the Nazis and of involvement in the execution of a Jewish family in 1941; Peteris Vitols, who allegedly served in the Latvian police and the Waffen SS and was associated "with organizations actively engaged in atrocities against the civilian population"; Mamertas Rolland Maciukas, who belonged to Lithuanian police and Schutzmannschaft battalions, accused by the government of collaboration and participation in the mass killing of Jews and Gypsies in Belarus and Lithuania; Serge Kisluk, accused of collaborating with the Nazis in Ukraine and participating in war crimes and atrocities; Michael Baumgartner, originally from Hungary, who allegedly served as a guard at Sachsenshausen and Stutthof concentration camps and was a member of the Waffen SS; and Wasyl Odynsky, charged with being a guard at labor and concentration camps in Poland.

In addition, CJC and private investigator Steve Rambam accused Josef Kisielatitis of being a member of a Lithuanian unit that murdered thousands of Jews. He came to Canada after the war, then moved to the United States in 1962, but returned to Canada in 1985, just two days before a U.S. deportation hearing was scheduled to begin.

Early in 1997, in an assessment of the ten years since the Deschenes Report, Arnold Fradkin, former deputy director in the War Crimes Unit of the Justice Department, lamented the slow pace and lack of results up to the beginning of 1997. "It is not justice for Nazi war criminals and collaborators to find a safe haven in Canada." But, he warned, unless cases are moved forward with dispatch, "justice delayed will most certainly result in justice denied." He noted that Deschenes had recommended investigating 224 individuals, with 20 of them considered urgent. Yet 10 years later, only 13 proceedings had been undertaken, with only one of them successfully concluded. In an address at a Montreal synagogue in September 1997, Paul Vickery, head of the War Crimes Unit, claimed that his group was doing as well as could reasonably be expected and was "pressing forward as quickly as possible."

One factor that helped to increase the pressure on the government was the work of Steve Rambam, an independent investigator from New York, who located 157 alleged war criminals in Canada and interviewed 62 of them, on occasion even obtaining admissions of responsibility on tape. Rambam described himself as a free-lancer who undertook the investigations because he believed in the cause.

The effort to proceed more rapidly garnered support from a wide-ranging group of religious leaders, who met with Justice Minister Allan Rock in May and urged him to accelerate proceedings as a "moral imperative."

Holocaust-Related Matters

Plans were announced in February 1997 for the addition of a Holocaust gallery to the Canadian National War Museum in Ottawa, but opposition arose from some veterans' groups, who objected to diverting attention from the Canadian military, which is the focus of the museum's program. Consideration was being given to building a separate Holocaust museum.

Responding to questions about a possible Canadian role in laundering Nazi gold during the war, the Bank of Canada appointed a historian, Duncan McDowall, to investigate the matter. In his report issued at the end of November 1997, McDowall found that gold transferred to Canada was not connected with the Nazis and that none of the Nazi gold that passed through Switzerland made its way to Canada.

Demography

The number of Jews in Canada, based on the 1991 census, was 356,315.[1] Ottawa's Jewish population continued to grow rapidly, doubling from 7,000 to 14,000 between 1984 and 1996. Already growing at a faster rate than any place other than Toronto, it was likely to soon pass Winnipeg to become the third-largest Jewish community in the country. In contrast, Winnipeg continued to decline in Jewish population, with a drop of some 18 percent between 1971 and 1991. On the brighter side, the number of Jewish children under age 14 increased 3.7 percent during the second half of that period.

Montreal's Jewish community continued to be beset by uncertainty. A 1996 survey by Federation CJA showed that about one-quarter of Montreal's Jews were unsure where they would be living in five years, with only about half still expecting to be living in Montreal. Anecdotal evidence suggested that the atmosphere after the 1995 referendum was producing increased emigration, but community officials claimed that indicators such as the number of campaign contributors, immigration, and day-school enrollment had remained steady between 1995 and 1996. Some two-thirds of the respondents to the survey also were generally pessimistic about the outlook for the next five years—a higher level of pessimism than was expressed in a similar survey in 1991. The major reasons given for contemplating departure from Quebec were politics and economics.

Communal Affairs

Ground was broken in September 1997 for the expanding Jewish Community Campus in Ottawa, responding to demographic shifts and population growth. The $13-million campus will include a large building for the council and community center, a day-school building, a home for handicapped adults, and eventually a senior-citizen residence. In Winnipeg, the new $28-million Asper Jewish Community Campus opened in September 1997. Larry Hurtig, president of the Winnipeg Jewish Community Council, described the new campus as "the most important" project in the community's history.

Montreal also announced plans for a new campus in the Snowdon neighborhood that will integrate existing buildings that house the YM-YWHA, the Saidye Bronfman Centre, the Jewish Public Library, and Federation CJA. The $23-million expansion would be, according to Federation CJA president Stanley Plot-

---

[1]See Jim L. Torczyner and Shari L. Brotman, "The Jews of Canada: A Profile from the Census," AJYB 1995, pp. 227–60.

nick, a concrete "message to ourselves, to our city, and to all Quebecers and Canadians alike that our future is here." Community leaders expressed the hope that other organizations would move into the completed quarters, a key feature of which would be expanded senior-citizen facilities.

Another major project of the Montreal community, launched in 1996, was Operation Montreal, an effort to build an endowment fund of $30 million—to fund programs to help retain Jews in Montreal and to provide coverage for shortfalls in annual campaigns. Combined Jewish Appeal chairman Robert Vineberg said that the project was fueled by "the anxiety the community feels about its future." That anxiety was addressed directly in a *cri de coeur* by Plotnick in the *Canadian Jewish News* in April 1997, which followed by a few weeks Edgar Bronfman's statement quoted in the *Toronto Star* that "if I was a young person, I wouldn't stay in Quebec." Plotnick reminded Jews across Canada of the unique stress faced by his community due to the Quebec political situation. While lamenting threats to individual rights, language restrictions, the decline of Montreal, families watching children move away, and the deterioration of the economic structure, he confirmed the commitment of the community's leadership to deal with the issues and maintain "an exemplary Jewish community."

Toronto's Sephardic community celebrated the opening of the $16-million Sephardic Kehila Centre in Vaughan, just north of Metro Toronto, in September 1997. Israeli foreign minister David Levy was the guest of honor. The new building, which will house a synagogue, social hall, mikveh, swimming pool, and offices, will serve the approximately 15,000 Sephardim in greater Toronto.

Early in 1997 there was some talk of restructuring the Canadian Jewish Congress and moving its headquarters from Montreal to Ottawa, an action that would be perceived as a further indicator of the declining importance of the Montreal community. There were no further developments on this in 1997.

Israel-Related Matters

The Canadian Zionist Federation (CZF) decided to cancel the elections for the World Zionist Congress in Jerusalem in December 1997 and instead allocated the seats by agreement among the constituent organizations. In addition to saving the cost of an election, CZF president Kurt Rothschild claimed that the 25,000 members "don't have the stomach" for a vote. He was also sharply critical of the elections held in the United States.

El Al decided to move its Canadian head office from Montreal to Toronto in 1997 in order to tap the greater tourist potential in the Ontario market. The move was also designed to situate El Al more favorably to compete with the new service to Israel provided by Air Canada.

The Canadian team at the Maccabiah Games in Israel in July 1997 recorded its best showing in the history of the competition. It won three gold medals (hockey, men's basketball, and men's softball) and two silver medals (water polo and men's tennis doubles). Individual members of the team also won numerous medals in most of the sports.

Religion

Sephardic Jews in the Greater Toronto area formed the Sephardic Rabbinate of Ontario in mid-1996 under the leadership of Chief Rabbi Armand Assayag. The rabbinate, grouping 13 affiliated synagogues and organizations, was housed in the new Sephardic Kehila Centre. Rabbi Assayag, along with five other Canadian rabbis, was active in the newly formed Association of Sephardi Rabbis of North America. At the 1997 annual meeting in September in New Jersey, the group approved initiatives to better serve the religious needs of Sephardim.

The March 1997 declaration of the Union of Orthodox Rabbis of the United States and Canada, which denied the legitimacy of non-Orthodox movements within Judaism, had little impact in Canada, as several Orthodox rabbis took pains to dissociate themselves from it. Rabbi Dow Marmur (Reform) termed the announcement "pathetic," while Rabbi Baruch Frydman-Kohl (Conservative) lamented the inability of the Agudath Harabonim "to accept the historical reality of religious pluralism. . . ." Montreal's chief rabbi, Pinchas Hirschprung (Orthodox), was named as one of the supporters of the statement but denied signing it. Other rabbis were unsparing in their criticism.

In September 1997 Rabbi Reuven Bulka (Orthodox) brought 13 Canadian rabbis from diverse backgrounds together to form Kol Hakovod, Voice of Dignity, under the auspices of CJC. Its objective was to combat divisiveness and promote respect and cooperation. Rabbi Philip Scheim (Conservative) commented that the group reflected a community consensus that it was necessary "to find a way to acknowledge our differences and move forward together."

A survey of Montreal Jewry for the Montreal federation by Charles Shahar and Randal Schnoor showed much higher levels of religious observance than anywhere else in North America, with 85 percent fasting on Yom Kippur, 98 percent holding a Passover seder, about half observing kashrut at home, and about a quarter attending synagogue services on a regular basis. Some 63 percent belonged to a synagogue. The likelihood of religious observance was significantly higher among Sephardim than among Ashkenazim.

At its biennial convention in Toronto in November 1996, the Canadian Council for Reform Judaism decided that children of interfaith couples should not be allowed to enroll in Reform religious schools or participate in life-cycle events if they were also receiving formal education in another religion.

The first synagogue in Canada to be oriented toward gays, Congregation Keshet Israel in Toronto, introduced a "degenderized" prayer book in which all of the Hebrew text is also transliterated.

The Coalition of Jewish Women for the Get produced a documentary film, *Untying the Bonds . . . Jewish Divorce*, which premiered in Montreal in December

1997. The film, directed by Francine Zuckerman and written by Marsha Levy, Evelyn Brook, Marilyn Bicher, and Norma Joseph, was designed to increase awareness of the Jewish divorce issue by profiling three women who experienced difficulties in obtaining a *get* from their husbands. It also contains interviews with rabbis who condemn men who use the divorce situation to extort material benefits from their wives. In the film, Rabbi Reuben Poupko calls upon rabbis and the community as a whole to "use their moral authority" to combat "blackmail or mental torture."

Education

After years of legal and political battles, the struggle to obtain funding for Ontario's Jewish day schools appeared to have reached a dead end. The Supreme Court of Canada decided in November 1996 that the provincial government was not required to fund private denominational schools, even though Roman Catholic schools did receive support. In a 7-2 ruling, the Court rejected constitutional claims based on the religious equality section of the Charter of Rights and Freedoms. The decision affirmed earlier rulings that the funding of Catholic schools was based on a unique agreement at the time of Confederation in 1867, which meant that equal treatment arguments would not prevail. The Court took the view that as long as parents could avail themselves of the opportunity to send their children to religious schools there was no constitutional defect. The decision was a blow to the hopes of the Jewish community, which had been pressing the government intensely for 12 years to emulate the support for Jewish schools that was available in a number of other provinces. Henry Koschitzky, chairman of the Ontario Jewish Association for Equity in Education, said that "the message religious minorities take home is that here in Ontario, all are equal, but some are more equal than others." Protestant groups with day schools also criticized the decision sharply. For the advocates of funding, the only course of action that remained, and that had been tried frequently in the past, was the political route, to try to persuade the government to legislate a solution.

Some progress was made in August 1997 when a meeting between government officials and a delegation from the Working Group on Educational Equality, representing both Jews and Protestants, produced a statement from the executive assistant to the parliamentary assistant to the Minister of Education, saying that "parents are entitled to public economic support in the choice they make for their children's education." However, the government had yet to produce any money.

Montreal's Jewish schools, which had been publicly funded for nearly 30 years, were concerned that at some point those grants, currently about $20 million per year, might be eliminated. A report from an inquiry into Quebec's educational system recommended in October 1996 that the support be gradually reduced. Felix Melloul, executive director of the Association of Jewish Day Schools, expressed great concern and promised that his group would be prepared to do battle politically to protect its standing as part of the over 200 other private schools that presently received subsidies. The government funding allowed Montreal's Jewish schools to charge tuition at about half the rate paid by Toronto parents. Even so, the Jewish schools were hurting because of a 3.2-percent drop in government support in 1996–97 and a further 9.3-percent reduction in 1997–98. Melloul said that "it's going to be a question of survival for some schools."

Community and Intergroup Relations

Montreal's Jewish community and the Quebec government renewed their immigration agreement in 1996 for a third biennium. The program had already brought several hundred ex-Soviet Jews to Montreal since 1992.

In the aftermath of the flap over kosher Passover products in Quebec in the spring of 1996, the Office de la langue française (OLF) and the Quebec Region of Canadian Jewish Congress negotiated an agreement to prevent a recurrence. The OLF would recognize the Jewish community's right to import Passover foods that did not meet French-language labeling requirements and allow an annual 68-day period for such products to be sold. The CJC, the Vaad Ha'ir, and the Communauté Sépharade du Québec (CSQ) agreed to keep kosher importers aware of the requirements. There was no OLF interference with the distribution of kosher products during the 1997 Passover season.

The Quebec language police targeted a cemetery monument business in Montreal in December 1997 over a 50-year-old sign. The tombstone maker, L. Berson & Fils, was told to change the sign, in which the Hebrew word *matzevot* (monuments) was more prominent than the French word *Monuments*, or face penalties. After a public outcry, adverse media coverage, and backtracking by the minister in charge, the French language commission withdrew the threat.

In the aftermath of Quebec's 1995 referendum on sovereignty, tensions increased between some separatists and Jews. For example, Howard Galganov, a leader of the antiseparatist Quebec Political Action Committee, which garnered considerable publicity, made remarks that angered independence supporters (see above). In September 1996, Bloc Québécois leader Michel Gauthier called upon CJC to denounce him. Congress officials were astonished that they had been asked to intervene simply because Galganov happened to be Jewish. BBC's League for Human Rights attacked Gauthier's "ethnocentrism and chauvinism," while the CSQ's president, Maryse Ohayon, accused him of "intolerable extremism." Galganov was also attacked by journalist Gilles Paquin in *La Presse* because of his involvement with the Jewish Defense League on behalf of Soviet Jewry around 1970. Paquin denounced him as someone "who went to school in the JDL, an outlawed racist movement in Israel." In an October appearance at a Montreal synagogue, Galganov vowed not to keep quiet because of a fear of antagonizing non-Jews.

La Presse was the source of other articles that raised hackles among Montreal

Jews. In May 1997 the paper ran a story about a money-laundering scheme in which seven Jews, as well as 24 non-Jews, were accused. The depiction of the group as a "Jewish criminal organization" led CJC spokesman David Sultan to denounce the piece as "pernicious, tendentious and insensitive." The article and an accompanying sidebar contained references to Meyer Lansky and Bugsy Siegel and suggested that Jews were prominent among criminal elements because of their "financial power and especially their invaluable contacts in almost every country of the world." In November 1997 the newspaper ran a story that distorted the purposes of Federation CJA's new endowment fund, Operation Montreal.

A group of Jewish federal civil servants went to court to obtain paid leave on the High Holy Days on the grounds that such leave on Christian but not Jewish holidays was discriminatory. They were turned down in May 1997 by a 2-1 majority in the Federal Court of Appeal. The employees were allowed to use vacation days or accumulated overtime to be off on Rosh Hashanah and Yom Kippur. The dissenting justice argued that it should be possible to accommodate their needs, but the majority found that practical considerations and labor contracts precluded granting the relief sought. The Supreme Court declined to hear the case.

Culture

Both Montreal and Toronto had festivals celebrating the multifaceted dimensions of European Jewish culture. Toronto's Ashkenaz, held in August 1997, featured theater, dance, poetry, music, and film and included several premieres. Some 67,000 attended the weeklong event. KlezKanada was held for several days at a camp in the Laurentian Mountains north of Montreal in August 1996 and again in 1997. The focus was on klezmer music, with groups and personalities brought in from the United States to supplement local talent. The audience came from as far away as Israel and Latin America. The 1997 program expanded to include events dealing with film and theater as well as music.

Toronto documentary filmmaker Simcha Jacobovici and his co-producer Elliott Halpern won Emmy Awards in both 1996 and 1997. The first award was for *The Plague Monkeys*, which is about the Ebola virus. The second was for *The Selling of Innocents*, which deals with the exploitation of young girls in India. Their next film, *Hollywoodism: Jews, Movies, and the American Dream*, premiered in Toronto in November 1997.

None Is Too Many, a play based on the book about Canada's wartime immigration policy by Irving Abella and Harold Troper, was produced at the Western Jewish Theatre in Winnipeg in March 1997. Jason Sherman's script focused on the efforts of CJC's Saul Hayes to persuade bureaucrats to admit Jewish refugees fleeing Nazism. Sherman's *Reading Hebron*, which opened in November 1996 at the Factory Theatre Mainstage in Toronto, was a controversial work dealing with Baruch Goldstein's Hebron massacre.

Former prime minister Kim Campbell collaborated with Hershey Felder on the musical *Noah's Arc*, which premiered as a work in progress at UCLA in June 1997. The play raises questions about the Holocaust through the story of Noah and the flood.

Arnold Bennett directed his own play, *The Failure,* in a production in St. John's, Newfoundland. It is based on the poetry and prose of the Canadian Jewish writer A.M. Klein. Bennett suggests that Klein's quest for a personal messiah in his poetry was unsuccessful, and that he gave up writing after failing to resolve his questions about God and the Holocaust.

Montreal's Yiddish Theatre presented a musical adaptation of Mordecai Richler's *The Apprenticeship of Duddy Kravitz*, entitled *Duddy!* The play, directed by Bryna Wasserman in July 1997, was the first project of the new Dora Wasserman Endowment Fund for Jewish Culture, which is designed to insure the financial continuity of Yiddish theater in Montreal.

Among the films with Jewish themes that were exhibited at the Toronto International Film Festival in September 1996 were *A Tickle in the Heart* by Stefan Schwietert, *Holy Week* by Andrzej Wajda, *To Speak the Unspeakable: The Message of Elie Wiesel* by Judit Elek, *The Substance of Fire* by Daniel Sullivan, and *The Arena of Murder* by Amos Gitai. Among those shown at the 1997 festival were *Best Man* by Ira Wohl and *Exile Shanghai* by Ulrike Ottinger.

Some of the more important entries at the May 1997 Montreal Jewish Film Festival were *Chants de Sable d'Etoile* by Nicolas Klotz and *Nothing to Be Written Here* by Wendy Oberlander. The corresponding Toronto festival featured *Exodus 1947* by Elizabeth Rodgers and Robby Henson, *The Italians Are Coming* by Eyal Halfon, and *As Tears Go By* by Eitan Green. Daniel Petrie's *The Assistant*, based on Bernard Malamud's novel, premiered at the Montreal World Film Festival in August 1997. Among the five Israeli films at the festival was the Arabic-language film *Milky Way* by Ali Nassar.

Montreal's Italian Cultural Institute held a colloquium in September 1997 to mark the tenth anniversary of Primo Levi's death. Academics from Canada, the United States, Italy, and France presented papers on Levi's work.

Canada's National Library marked the centennial of the Canadian Jewish press with an exhibition in Ottawa in the fall of 1997. The curator was Cheryl Jaffee.

Publications

The protagonist of Mordecai Richler's tenth novel, *Barney's Version*, an aging television producer, looks back on his experiences in Jewish Montreal and in Paris in the 1950s. The novel chronicles his life and loves in Richler's characteristically funny, even outrageous, fashion. The book won Richler the Giller Prize, Canada's top literary award.

In Anne Michaels' first novel, *Fugitive Pieces*, two stories related to the Holocaust are contrasted. Both involve survivors or their children and convey with great depth of feeling the events and implications of that terrible period.

Growing Up Jewish, edited by Rosalie Sharp, Irving Abella, and Edwin Goodman, comprises essays by 26 prominent Canadian Jews recounting memories of the past. William Weintraub recalls the old days in what was then Canada's largest and most open city in the prize-winning *City Unique: Montreal Days and Nights in the 1940s and 1950s.*

Allan Nadler, who had been doing battle with at least part of the hassidic world for some time, produced *The Faith of the Mithnagdim.* Benjamin Freedman published *Duty and Healing: Foundation of a Jewish Bioethic* (on the Internet). Abraham Boyarsky wrote *The Laws of Chaos;* Yakov Rabkin and Ira Robinson edited *The Interaction of Scientific and Jewish Cultures in Modern Times.*

Anthony Bianco chronicles the business successes and failures of one of Canadian Jewry's wealthiest families in *The Reichmanns: Family, Faith, Fortune and the Empire of Olympia and York.* Conservative activist and writer Hugh Segal published his autobiography, *No Surrender,* as well as *Beyond Greed: A Traditional Conservative Confronts Neoconservative Excess.* Irene Burstyn focuses on the lives of women in *Picking Up Pearls.* Linda Frum remembers her mother, the renowned broadcaster, in *Barbara Frum.* Other works of biography and autobiography include *Various Positions: A Life of Leonard Cohen* by Ira Nadel and Shlomo Efrat's autobiographical *The Black Shofar.*

Felicia Carmelly produced the first comprehensive history in English on the slaughter of most of Romania's Jews: *Shattered! 50 Years of Silence — Voices from Romania and Transnistria.* Robert Jan van Pelt and Deborah Dwork wrote *Auschwitz: 1270 to the Present.* Frank Bialystock, in *Delayed Impact: The Holocaust and the Canadian Jewish Community 1945–1985*, deals with the issue of what he calls "collective amnesia," a condition that led to a lack of communication between Canadian Jews and the survivors who settled among them. Other Holocaust-related works include *Hitler's Silent Partners: Swiss Banks, Nazi Gold and the Pursuit of Justice* by Isabel Vincent; *Open Your Hearts: The Story of the Jewish War Orphans in Canada* by Fraidie Martz; and Elaine Kalman Naves's *Journey to Vaja: Reconstructing the World of a Hungarian Jewish Family.*

The critical early years of Canada's relationship with the new Jewish state are examined by Zachariah Kay in *The Diplomacy of Prudence: Canada and Israel, 1948–1956*, with particular emphasis on the Nobel Peace Prize-winning work of Lester B. Pearson. In *The Israeli-American Connection: Its Roots in the Yishuv, 1914–1945,* Michael Brown focuses on six Zionist leaders and how they gradually oriented Palestinian Jewry toward America. Also published was *Dawn of the Promised Land: The Creation of Israel* by Ben Wicks.

New translations from the Yiddish include *Stories by Yiddish Women Writers*, edited by Frieda Forman, Ethel Raicus, Sarah Silberstein Swartz, and Maggie Wolfe, and two works by Yehuda Elberg, *Ship of the Hunted* and *The Empire of Kalman the Cripple.* Ruth R. Wisse compiled the *I.L. Peretz Reader.*

New religious works include *The Haftorah Commentary* by Rabbi W. Gunther Plaut, and *Renew Our Days: A Book of Jewish Prayer and Meditation* by Rabbi Ron Aigen.

Some new works of poetry are *Funken in Zhar* (Sparks in Embers) and *A Song Will Remain* by Simcha Simchonovitch; *A Seed in the Pocket of Their Blood* by Rafi Aaron; *Selected Poems: A.M. Klein,* edited by Zailig Pollock, Seymour Mayne, and Usher Caplan; *Clusters* by Kenneth Sherman; *David and Jonathan: A Story of Love and Power in Ancient Israel* by Stephen Schecter; and *Jacob's Ladder* by Joel Yanofsky.

Gabriella Goliger won the Journey Prize for her short story "Maladies of the Inner Ear," which appeared in *Parchment*. Among the winners of the 1997 Canadian Jewish Book Awards were Anne Michaels, Roger Nash, Seymour Mayne and Glen Rotchin, Manny Drukier, Felicia Carmelly, Simcha Simchovitch, Mervin Butovsky and Ira Robinson, Steven Saltzman, Yves Lavertu, and Fraidie Martz.

Personalia

A number of Canadian Jews were appointed to the Order of Canada. Officers: Avie Bennett, Peter Bronfman, Barnett Danson, Jack Granatstein, Jane Jacobs, Ernest Samuel, Frank Shuster, Harold Seigel, Samuel Solomon, and George Rosengarten. Members: Thomas Beck, Jenny Belzberg, Simma Holt, Edith Jacobson Low-Beer, Richard Margolese, Sarah Paltiel, Bernard Snell, Al Waxman, Irving Zucker, Dorothy Reitman, Sigmund Reiser, Joseph Zatzman, and Leslie Dan.

Barry Carin was appointed High Commissioner to Singapore; David Levine became Quebec's Delegate-General in New York; Ronald Berger joined the Alberta Court of Appeal; Gerry Weiner became president of Quebec's Equality Party; Barbara Berger and Joel Moss were appointed to the Immigration and Refugee Board.

Norman Spector was appointed vice-president of Imperial Tobacco but subsequently took the position of president and publisher of the *Jerusalem Post*. Lorrie Goldstein became editor of the *Toronto Sun*.

Myron Scholes was awarded the Nobel Prize in Economics for 1997; Dr. Victor Dirnfeld was elected president of the Canadian Medical Association; Mark Wainberg was chosen as president-elect of the International AIDS Society; Barry Levy became the first Jewish Dean of Religious Studies at McGill University; and David Novak was appointed the first occupant of a chair in Jewish studies at the University of Toronto.

Several Jewish writers and scholars received the gold medal of La Renaissance Française: Alexis Nouss, Paul Sidoun, Regine Robin, Michel Vaiss, and Gerard Etienne. Gad Soussana won a silver medal.

Several Jewish organizations selected new presidents: Naomi Frankenberg at JNF Canada, Joseph Steiner at UJA Federation in Toronto, and Stanley Plotnick at Federation CJA in Montreal. Danyael Cantor was appointed executive vice-president of Federation CJA and Maxyne Finkelstein executive director. Bernie Farber became executive director of CJC's Ontario Region, succeeding Manuel Prutschi, who became the executive vice-president of the Sephardic Educational Foundation and the World Sephardic Educational Centre. Rabbi Irwin Witty retired as the executive director of the Board of Jewish Education in Toronto and was succeeded by Rabbi Jeremiah Unterman. Michael Briks became executive director of Jewish Immigrant Aid Services, and Lawrence Waller was appointed executive vice-president of Canada-Israel Securities. Brenda Gewurz was elected president of Montreal's Jewish Education Council. David Moss was appointed director of the Saidye Bronfman Centre for the Arts.

Among the deaths suffered by the community during the second half of 1996 were those of Harold Greenberg, in July, aged 66, a leader in the Canadian film and television industry and founder of Astral Communications; former Olympic wrestler Fred Oberlander, in July, aged 82; retired Senator H. Carl Goldenberg, in July, aged 82, one of the country's foremost labor lawyers and mediators; Albert Rose, in August, aged 78, a social work professor and expert on housing issues; Manya Lipshitz, in July, aged 89, Yiddish educator, writer, and political activist; former executive vice-president of JIAS and community leader Joseph Kage, in September, aged 84; Jack Reitman, co-founder of a national retail clothing chain, in October, aged 86; and Peter Bronfman, businessman, philanthropist, and co-founder of the Edper Group, in November, aged 67.

Members of the community who died during 1997 included Salah Mukamal, in January, aged 82, founder of Toronto's Iraqi Jewish Federation; bookstore chain co-founder Jack Cole, in January, aged 76; retired editor of the *Canadian Jewish News* Maurice Lucow, in March, aged 78; medical ethicist Benjamin Freedman, in March, aged 45; Isidore Pollack, businessman and patron of the arts, in April, aged 83; Irvin Strub, founder of the pickle company bearing his name, in May, aged 86; Ben Dunkelman, a leading member of Machal in Israel's War of Independence, commander of an armored brigade in the Galilee, in June, aged 83; former Ontario Progressive Conservative leader and cabinet member Larry Grossman, in June, aged 53; theatre director, drama teacher, and playwright Basya Hunter, in July, aged 85; Rose Goldblatt, concert pianist and professor, in September, aged 84; saxophonist and music professor Gerald Danovitch, in December, aged 65; and Gordon Schwartz, community fund-raiser and Maccabiah activist, in December, aged 55.

HAROLD M. WALLER

Latin America

Mexico

National Affairs

T<small>HE YEAR</small> 1997 <small>SAW</small> M<small>EXICO</small> emerging with some sense of dignity and achievement from the political upheavals that marked the preceding years, even as the country's political, economic, and moral structures were widely regarded as still shaky. In this period, the Mexican political system was remaking itself— from the centralized control of one-party government (the Revolutionary Institutional Party, PRI) to a new government composed of multiple parties of diverse ideological persuasions. One sign of the changing order was the death of the iron-fisted ruler of the Mexican labor branch of the PRI, the largest confederation of labor unions in the country, Fidel Velázquez, at the age of 97. Since 1941, and with only a three-year hiatus, Velázquez had been elected and reelected ten times to a position that some considered the second most important in the country. It could be said that his life and career symbolized the old authoritarian system and its demise.

The changes in the political arena were dramatically highlighted by the national and state elections of July 1997, which were monitored by the new Federal Electoral Institute (IFE), an independent organization headed by José Woldenberg. On July 6, 30 million Mexicans (an electoral participation rate of 58 percent) changed the political balance of power and ended 70 years of one-party rule. The PRI lost control of the Congress when two opposition parties, the left-wing Party of the Democratic Revolution (PRD) and the conservative National Action Party (PAN), together won over 50 percent of the seats in the Chamber of Deputies, the lower house. Also significantly, the first election ever for mayor of Mexico City (previously an appointed position) was won by PRD leader Cuauhtémoc Cárdenas Solórzano, and two out of six state governorships (Nuevo León and Querétaro) went to the National Action Party.

In December, when the mayor of Mexico City announced his cabinet choices, many minority representatives were included, a welcome "mouthful of fresh phonetics" enthused the writer Carlo Coccioli. Four Jews—Clara Jusidman, Roberto Eibenschutz Hartman, Rene Druker, and Jeny Saltiel Cohen—were invited to be

211

part of the new team, although not yet confirmed at year's end. Only one of the four, Jusidman, was currently affiliated with the Jewish community.

Although the economy was severely hurt by the bungled devaluation of the Mexican peso in December 1994, which unleashed perhaps the worst economic crisis since the Depression, some signs of recovery were evident. As a result of political changes, foreign money rushed back into the Mexican markets, strengthening the peso against the dollar. Yet more than a quarter of the workforce remained unemployed or underemployed; the already alarming lack of personal security in Mexico City, as well as in other large urban centers, was overwhelming; and the economic difficulties affected large segments of the middle class. The challenge to the government was clearly to listen to those seeking reform while not abandoning a commitment to economic modernization.

Israel and the Middle East

Israel and the Middle East remained topics of interest and strong opinions in the country. Despite the success of specific exchange programs between Israel and Mexico—academic, political, economic, and cultural—media reaction to Israel and its policies was often negative. Coverage of the September 4 terrorist attack on Ben Yehudah Street in Jerusalem was generally sympathetic; however, it was eclipsed by the death of Diana, Princess of Wales. Moreover, sympathy for Israel and Israelis was short-lived and had no effect on the generally lukewarm or negative attitudes that permeated the press. Discussions in the press by journalists who systematically analyze the Middle East and Israel, in particular after the failed Israeli attempt to assassinate a Hamas leader in Jordan in September, mostly expressed solidarity with the Arab position. In such cases it was left to committed Jewish journalists to explain and argue the case for Israel in the national press.

Since the mid-1970s, when Mexico voted for the "Zionism is racism" resolution in the UN and expressed sympathy for Yasir Arafat and the PLO, relations between Israel and Mexico had been somewhat strained. The visit to Israel of Dr. José Angel Gurría in February 1997, the first by a Mexican foreign minister in 22 years, helped to improve the atmosphere. Gurría had meetings with President Ezer Weizman, Prime Minister Benjamin Netanyahu, and Foreign Minister David Levy, as well as leaders of the opposition, business representatives, and even old acquaintances, such as Prof. Jacob Frenkel, whom Gurría knew from their joint work for the International Monetary Fund. Gurría's schedule included visits to universities and research institutes and the promotion of cultural exchanges between the two countries. The visit provided an opportunity for the Mexican ambassador to Israel, Dr. Jorge Alberto Lozoya, to give a lecture on "Mexico's Foreign Policy for the 21st Century," and for the Mexican government to host a reception at the Hebrew University in Jerusalem to inaugurate the Rosario Castellanos Chair in Literature, in memory of the deceased Mexican ambassador and writer.

Minister of Health Dr. Juan Ramón de la Fuente visited health institutions in Israel to discuss the renewal of exchanges of information and technology. Other sectors in Mexico, including agriculture, technology, and medicine, continued to exchange information and products with Israel. For example, Kibbutz Eilon proposed a project for the automatic canning of peppers and tomatoes on Mexican farms. The visit to Israel of Mexican deputy minister of international trade negotiations Jaime Zabludovsky highlighted the $100 billion in bilateral trade between the two countries. His visit was followed by that of a group of bankers and entrepreneurs seeking to continue and expand economic exchanges between the countries. In the arts, the visit of Itzhak Perlman with various Klezmer musician groups and that of Zubin Mehta with the Israel Philharmonic Orchestra were major events in the artistic life of Mexico City in August 1997. Israeli cellist Zvi Plesser performed in Mexico in May, under the sponsorship of Keren Hayesod, and Mexican pianist Jorge Federico Osorio went to Israel to perform in the festivities of Jerusalem 3000.

Perhaps the largest area of exchange was in various academic fields — medicine, engineering, feminist studies, literature, and philosophy. The Hebrew University, Tel Aviv University, Bar-Ilan University, and Ben-Gurion University of the Negev carried out exchanges with the major universities in Mexico: the UNAM (National Autonomous University), UIA (Iberoamerican Autonomous University), and other specialized institutes of higher learning. The Center for Judaic Studies of Iberoamerican University and Tribuna Israelita sponsored a colloquium on Judaic studies, February 27–March 3, 1997. Participants from Israel included professors Haim Avni, Nahum Megged, Shlomo Ben Ami, and David Bankier; a special guest was Argentinian Jewish writer Dr. Marcos Aguinis. Prof. Ephraim Meir, head of Bar-Ilan's philosophy department, participated in a colloquium on the philosophy of Emmanuel Levinas in June, joined by Mexican academicians Enrique Dussel, Silvana Rabino-Vick, Márcio Costa, Gabriela Traveso, and Fabián Giménez of UNAM and UIA. Also in June, Dr. David Galinsky, Israeli specialist in geriatric medicine, addressed a conference organized by the newly formed association of Mexican Friends of Ben-Gurion University and also spoke at the Centro Deportivo Israelita (Jewish Sports Center). The Health Ministry of Mexico joined Tel Aviv University in organizing a symposium in November on "Developments in Biomedicine." It was coordinated by Dr. José Halabe Cherem, who was elected to the presidency of the Mexican Council of Internal Medicine. Minister of Health Juan Ramón de la Fuente was present, as well as the representatives of all the institutions involved.

Israeli institutions hosted Mexican specialists, including Prof. Josefina Z. Vázquez of the Colegio de México and Prof. Leopoldo Zea of UNAM, at a Tel Aviv University conference on "Latin American Thought" in November 1996.

The Mexico-Israel Cultural Center, led by new director Monica Dinner, prepared an extensive and varied program to celebrate the 50th anniversary of the State of Israel. A sculpture competition, an exhibition by the renowned sculptor Sebastián (Enrique Carbajal), concerts, conferences, a photographic exhibit of works by Rafael Rodríguez Barrera, and a music festival were all scheduled.

Scholarships were given by the Weizmann Institute to allow three Mexican students from the Instituto Educativo Olinica, Colegio de Ciencias y Humanidades, and Preparatoria Pedro de Alba to travel to Israel. The Hebrew University provided scholarships in agricultural studies.

JEWISH COMMUNITY

Demography

The Mexican Jewish community, an estimated 40,000-strong, maintained its demographic stability. Most of Mexico's Jews lived in Mexico City and its suburbs, while the rest (about 2,500) resided in the cities of Guadalajara, Monterrey, and Tijuana.

Suburban developments built over the last ten years had become the residential areas of choice of Jewish families, and now included some schools, communal organizations, and institutions that decided to follow their constituencies.

Communal Affairs

Although the effects of the country's economic crisis were felt by most social classes, the community took emergency measures to help its most needy members. Schools provided large amounts of scholarship aid for parents who could not pay full school tuition, and holiday food baskets were provided to needy families. Specific subcommunities even went so far as to purchase cars to organize taxi services, in order to provide work for the jobless. Many areas of community life, however, continued to function as before.

The political turbulence of the country was mirrored in a dramatic and unprecedented upheaval within the community: the Ashkenazi Kehillah Nidkhei Israel, the central institution of Ashkenazi Jewry since 1958, was officially dissolved in October 1997, in what was effectively a coup. The activists who carried out the coup announced the formation of a new organization, under new leadership, to be called the Ashkenazi Community Council.

The Kehillah, which represented the 50 percent of Mexican Jewry who are of Ashkenazic origin, was an umbrella organization encompassing a wide range of ideologies, bridging the political and religious differences of the Bundist, Orthodox, and Zionist Jews who had joined forces to create the organization. Sephardic Jews, divided into several subcommunities, have their own communal structures and institutions.

Under Shimshon Feldman, who took over leadership of the Kehillah soon after its creation and remained its central leader and most powerful figure until his death in 1989, the organization was responsible for and controlled virtually every domain of Ashkenazic Jewish communal life—synagogues and religious rites from birth to death (all Orthodox), cultural affairs, food supervision (Kashrut), internal legal courts for conciliation and arbitration (which managed to enforce their verdicts mostly through the charismatic power of Feldman), modern religious education (Mizrachi), support for secular Jewish schools (Vaad Hachinuch), Zionist organizations, the management of the old-age home's facility, and ORT (Organization for Rehabilitation Through Training).

While the Kehillah that Feldman managed was officially democratic in structure, it had evolved into a bureaucracy autocratically controlled by Feldman and a small cadre, in which ideologies had ceased to play any major role, dissent was mostly silenced, and the injection of new ideas was discouraged. While this style benefited the leadership, it became increasingly anomalous as society at large moved to embrace democratic ideals and practices.

After Feldman's death, his son, Israel, stepped into what some regarded as an inherited post. Although the younger Feldman had spent many years in training and learning about the management of the institution, he was less charismatic than his father and saw his role as essentially managerial. The weakening of the venerable position held by the father offered an opening to those in the community who were seeking change. Individual congregations saw an opportunity to achieve more freedom, to reduce accountability to a central body, and to reconfigure positions of prestige and authority within the community.

The initiators of the coup were a small group, mostly from the Ramat Shalom Congregation, a new Orthodox congregation in the suburbs of Mexico City that now surpassed in size and wealth the Kehillah's main congregation in the city, Nidkhei Israel (founded 1922). Guided by Dr. Hugo Yoffe, a psychologist and consultant on organizational behavior, the group spent nearly a year developing a blueprint for change and maneuvering behind the scenes—trying to build support and testing possible internal resistance. None of this activity was known in the larger Jewish community.

The group made its takeover plan public at a meeting on October 13. A notice published in the local Jewish press had announced that a meeting would take place at which elections would be held. The meeting drew a small attendance of about 100, many organizations were not represented, and no vote was taken. But the meeting was the occasion for an announcement of a fait accompli: the Kehillah was officially dissolved, and its functions would be assumed by a new organization, the Ashkenazi Community Council. The new leadership group consisted of 12 men, mostly self-appointed activists but including Israel Feldman, who had evidently decided to let himself be coopted, with Yoffe as executive advisor. The new group presented itself, at the meeting and later in the local media, as "a true outgrowth of democracy, modernity and consensus" within the community, whose goal was to create a more inclusive body than had existed previously. Significantly, nothing was said about making the body more democratic, nor was any substantive program put forward.

Religious identification and control of religious life played an important role in the takeover, highlighting the declining importance of Zionism and other secular ideologies among Mexican Jews. A challenge mounted to the traditional positions of religious authority led to the dismissal of the only Mexican-born rabbi, Abraham Bartfeld, the rabbi of the Kehillah synagogue. At the same time, other Orthodox congregations within the Kehillah asserted new independence, taking advantage of the changes that had occurred in the urban geography and economic status of their constituencies. Acknowledging the growth and increasing influence of the Conservative Congregation Bet El, whose membership was several fold larger than that of the Orthodox congregations, the new leadership indicated willingness to include it as a constituent (a step that the Orthodox Kehillah did not allow during the life of Feldman and avoided for a time following his death). However, the largely self-sufficient Bet El apparently did not perceive any practical gain to itself from "official" recognition.

The coup met with no dissent, nor did it require public acquiescence to gain legitimacy. The Ashkenazi Community Council opened new offices in an effort to establish its separate identity, and moved to consolidate new alliances while distancing itself from old ones. As it began to exert authority, it clearly faced problems—the disgruntled feelings of some of its members, internal power conflicts not yet manifest to outsiders, and the tensions inherent in the unfulfilled promise of eventually uniting all organizations. The president of the new body is Bernardo Waiss; presidential advisor is Jaime Bernstein; vice-presidents with various portfolios are Isaac Friedman, León Waisser, Samuel Schuster, Sergio Abush, Israel Feldman, Mario Duke, Bernardo Broitman, Luis Epelstein, and Alejandro Kampler; general secretary is Max Wornovitzky. No women were given or attained positions of importance.

The Jewish Central Committee remained the chief representative body of Jews in Mexico, including all subgroups, Sephardic and Ashkenazic, as well as the communities in Guadalajara, Tijuana, and Monterrey. Isaias Gitlin was the group's current head, under its two-year rotating presidency. The Central Committee took on added importance in light of the changes taking place within the Ashkenazic segment of the community.

The Monte Sinaí community, made up mostly of Jews originating in Damascus, celebrated over 80 years of communal activity. The Maguen David community, made up of Jews from Aleppo, undertook to rebuild its community center, to include a synagogue, educational halls, youth centers, and other facilities. The project was launched only after a long campaign to gain consensus for the enormous project, during which all relevant issues were fully aired. Despite the current difficult economic climate, the majority decided in favor, and a substantial sum of money was raised the same evening as the vote.

Three new mikvehs (ritual baths) were opened in Mexico City, one by Ashkenazim, one by Sephardim, and one by the Conservative Bet El Congregation.

The Eishel of Cuernavaca, the old-age home sponsored by the Kehillah, celebrated renovation of its facilities with a series of activities, including visits by leaders of the Kehillah, by Rabbis David Tabachnik, Marcelo Rittner, and Rafael Spangenthal, and various women's groups, and concerts for the elderly. Retorno, an organization providing emotional support and guidance for persons addicted to drugs and/or alcohol, continued its work. Kadima, the advocacy group for the disabled, sought to raise its profile by expanding the range of its services and by increasing consciousness-raising activities. A new membership group for homosexuals, Shalom Amigos, was described in the communal press as the first Latin American Jewish organization of its kind.

FEMUJ, the Mexican Federation of Jewish University Students, was about to get permanent offices at the Kehillah building, at no cost, as part of a reorganization. Some 80 young people attended the 1997 national seminar, held in Puebla. The group planned to participate in the International Congress for Jewish Youth in Cuernavaca in 1998.

Jewish women's voluntary organizations continued to support projects of the Mexican Red Cross such as the Hospital of Naucálpan, the Hospital for Physical Medicine and Rehabilitation in the northern part of Mexico City, and the expansion of medical services at the Itzjak Rabin Center for Community Development. They also worked at Isla Marias in providing social rehabilitation for ex-inmates.

Circumciser *(mohel)* Nissim Michan traveled to Cuba to perform ritual circumcisions on 21 males ranging in age from 3 months to 42 years old.

Israel-Related Activity

In November 1996 the community organized several ceremonies in remembrance of Israeli premier Yitzhak Rabin, murdered two years earlier. The main event, organized by the Central Committee, was attended by Mexican dignitaries, representatives of the State of Israel, and members of the community. At Anahuac University, a student-initiated memorial service was held the same month.

A now well-established annual program of the Mexican Friends of the Hebrew University in February brought four distinguished female academicians from Israel to interact with the Jewish community and with specialists in their own fields in Mexico. This year's lecturers were Tamar El-Or, an anthropologist; Batsheva Keren, a geneticist; Yehudith Birk, an agriculturalist; and Elisheva Simchen, a public health physician.

Education

The network of communal day schools, the hallmark of the community, which encompassed about 70 percent of all Jewish children, was expanding despite economic problems and difficulty in recruiting and retaining teachers of Yiddish and/or Hebrew. Responsibility for this area of communal life, specifically all secular Jewish education, was completely in the hands of women, who continued to be excluded from other communal positions.

To the already impressive list of existing day schools (Colegio Israelita de México; Nuevo Colegio Israelita I.L.Peretz; Escuela Yavne; Colegio Hebreo Tarbut; Colegio Bet-Hayeladim; Tarbut Sefaradí; Colegio Monte Sinaí; Colegio Maguen David; Yeshiva Emuna; Colegio Atid) was added a new school, Gan Montessori, with an enrollment of about 30 children. Launched by four women teachers, the school teaches in Spanish and celebrates the Jewish holidays as part of Jewish culture. This represents a departure from the rest of the community day schools, which are not necessarily religious in orientation but which teach Judaic subjects in Yiddish and/or Hebrew. Another exception is Atid, which teaches mostly in English and has minimal Judaic instruction.

The list of schools does not include all the afternoon religious schools, adult education, or kolels (adult yeshivahs) that proliferated in the last decade, nor the activity of the Universidad Hebráica, which offers adult education in Judaic studies.

Community Relations

With the changes in the political system and the new saliency of electoral politics, Jewish communal leaders and heads of the Central Committee met with government officials, including President Ernesto Zedillo, as well as with opposition leader, now mayor of Mexico City, Cuauhtémoc Cárdenas, to discuss issues of concern to the Jewish community. Jews joined with others to protest the crime wave that threatened to engulf the capital city and the lack of police protection.

The ORT organization continued to expand its technical training programs in the capital and also in the interior states of Coahuila, Baja California, Nuevo León, Jalisco, Guanajuato, and Zacatecas. Its more than 50 centers cooperated with the Iberoamerican University, the Instituto Politécnico Nacional, and the Tlaxcala University.

Culture

One of the last events organized by the Ashkenazi Kehillah before its reconstitution was a colloquium of journalists, mostly but not exclusively engaged in writing in the Jewish-Mexican press. It was held at the Kehillah building in September. Participating were journalists from all the Jewish-Mexican news media as well as independent journalists and representatives of communal organizations. Among the topics discussed were whether the internal communal press should be institutionally controlled or independent, and how writers should deal with efforts at communal censorship. Another discussion focused on encouraging non-Jewish journalists to write about Jewish issues as a means to combat the latent anti-Semitism in the country.

Among established activities in the cultural life of the community, the Aviv Israeli Dance Festival, sponsored by the CDI (Sports Center), continued to draw large audiences. Held in March, the event is a highly professional undertaking that features the participation of large numbers of children and adolescents. In the larger cultural world, a short film by Ariel Gordon, *Adios Mamá,* the only entry submitted by Mexico, received a prize at the Cannes Film Festival.

Jewish-Christian Relations

As it had been doing every two or three years, Mexican B'nai Brith organized a "Friendship Seder" on May 8, 1997, at the Bet-Itzjak Synagogue in Mexico City. Among the distinguished guests were Norberto Rivera Carrera, the archbishop of Mexico; Ernesto Corripio Ahumada, the cardinal emeritus of Mexico; Sergio Carranza, bishop of the Anglican Church; Lic. Rafael Rodríguez Barrera, deputy minister of the interior; and Moshe Melamed, ambassador of Israel to Mexico. Hosting the event were Jose Kably, president of the Judeo-Christian Commission of B'nai Brith, and Manuel Taifeld, president of the Spinoza Lodge. Rabbi Samuel Lerer of the Bet-Israel Congregation also took part.

The Center for the Study of Religions (CEREM), the Secretaría de Gobernacion, and the Universidad Americana of Acapulco cosponsored a symposium in July on "The Role of the Churches in Mexico Today." An attempt was made to analyze the implications of the changes taking place at the national level in the political, economic, and social spheres.

Publications

Noteworthy works published in 1997 included Salomón Amkie Cohen's *Sabiduría Popular de los Judíos de Alepo* (Popular Wisdom of Aleppo Jews) and Alicia Hamui de Halabe's *Identidad Colectiva: Rasgos Culturales de los inmigrantes Judeo-Alepinos en México* (Collective Identity: Cultural Characteristics of Aleppan Jewish Immigrants in Mexico). *Ashkenazi Jews in Mexico: Ideologies in the Structuring of a Community,* by Adina Cimet, was published in the United States.

New works of fiction included Manuel Levinsky's *Alex, Perfil de joven sin rumbo* (Alex: Profile of a Youth Without Direction); Gildy Bardavid's *Parábolas para trascender* (Parabolas to Transcend); Luis Feher's *El Bostezo* (The Yawn); and Silvia Hamui Sutton's *Huellas Plasmadas en el Espacio* (Prints Left in Space).

Two distinguished works by Mexican Jews about Mexican history and culture were published this year. One was historian Enrique Krauze's *Mexico: Biography of Power, A History of Modern Mexico, 1810–1996,* which was translated almost simultaneously into English. The second was a volume compiled and edited by Boris Rosen, a respected left-wing intellectual, of writings by Guillermo Prieto. This volume is part of a series of modern editions of the works of 19th-century classical Mexican thinkers.

The Documentation Center of the Kehillah received a grant from the National

Council for Science and Technolology (CONACYT) for publication of a study of Mexican policy during World War II: *El Convenio Ilusorio: Refugiados de Guerra en México* (The Illusory Agreement: War Refugees in Mexico). *Eslabones,* a semiannual journal of regional studies sponsored by UNAM, published an issue on religions that included material on the Jewish community in Mexico.

Personalia

The election of architect Sara Topelson de Greenberg as president of the International Union of Architects (1997–99), an organization representing more than a million architects around the world, was greeted with excitement in the Jewish community. Topelson was also named Woman of the Year for 1996 by the National Anthropological Museum. A similar cause of pride was the induction of Margo Glantz into the Mexican Language Academy—a noteworthy achievement for a woman and for a minority member in particular. Glantz, a professor of literature at UNAM and winner of many literary prizes, is the daughter of the immigrant poet Jacobo Glantz, whose work has not been translated and is therefore largely unknown in Spanish-speaking circles.

After a 27-year career as a newscaster, Jacobo Zabludovsky, the foremost figure in television (and press) in Mexico—the Walter Cronkite of Mexico—announced his retirement. Zabludovsky was clearly identified as a Jew but had no specific links to Jewish communal activity. Although some suggested that his long, successful career was due in part to the Televisa network's close ties to the government, no one denied his professional abilities and his contribution to modernizing newscasting in Mexico.

Marcos Moshinsky, a nuclear physicist at UNAM, was awarded a 1997 UNESCO Prize at a ceremony in Paris for his contributions to world science. At UNAM, Dr. Bertha Fortes was honored at a special convocation for her work as a clinical psychologist and professor.

Dr. Teodoro Cesarman, an eminent cardiologist and well-known personality within the Jewish community and the country at large, died in September 1997 at the age of 74.

ADINA CIMET

Argentina

National Affairs

During the period 1995–1997, the Justicialists (PJ) continued to rule Argentina under President Carlos Menem, the country's chief executive since 1989; he was reelected in May 1995 for a four-year term under the country's 1994 reformed constitution. The PJ also outperformed former president Raúl Alfonsín's Radical Civic Union (UCR) in the 1995 legislative elections, while a left-of-center front (FREPASO) also did well on that occasion. However, in the legislative elections of October 1997, the PJ fared poorly and was likely to be dependent on UCR participation in setting a parliamentary agenda. Reverses for the PJ nationally and in some key local elections signaled the public's dissatisfaction with high levels of unemployment and the electorate's heightened perception of corruption, exacerbated by the belief in a judiciary subject to pressures by the ruling party.

The 1996 rate of economic growth was 4.4 percent, almost a fifth higher than that predicted by a host of forecasters, with an inflation rate of 0.054 percent being the country's lowest for over half a century; a year later the estimated rates of GDP growth and inflation were 8 percent and 0 percent respectively. While those securely employed continued to benefit from the end of hyperinflation under Menem, the heavy social cost of the government's economic policies was impossible to ignore. Unemployment increased from 16.4 percent in 1995 to 17.3 percent in 1996. With some government officials candidly admitting abroad that it might take generations to lower the rate of joblessness significantly, the decrease in the official level of unemployment to 13.7 percent, as recorded during 1997, was largely due, among other things, to a World Bank and government-funded scheme providing six-month-jobs for those prepared to work for $200 (U.S.) monthly. Moreover, foreign investment in the first five months of 1997 was nearly equivalent to the annual average for 1990–95, with official forecasts for that year of $8 billion being exceeded by a confirmed influx of $12 billion.

In 1997, seeking to close a dark page in Argentina's recent history, the government offered the sum of $200,000 as compensation, payable in bonds, to each of the 7,000 families of those who were abducted and killed during the 1976–83 military regime. Inasmuch as the package's terms entailed acknowledgment by the bereaved families that their loved ones were in fact dead, without necessarily knowing what happened to them post-disappearance, some refused the compensation. Among them was the founding leader of the Mothers of Plaza de Mayo, the human-rights group established by relatives of the military regime's victims.

Israel and the Middle East

Under Foreign Minister Guido di Tella's stewardship, the Menem government continued its close alignment with the United States—the foreign-policy counterpart of Argentina's commitment to neo-liberal economic policies. The country's international realignment since Menem was voted into the Casa Rosada, the presidential palace, which resulted in the United States granting Argentina extra-NATO ally status in 1997, also led Argentina to adopt an increasingly pro-Israel line, while attempting to retain a measure of independence.

The acknowledged improvement in Argentine-Israeli relations under Menem largely survived intact the transition from a Labor to a Likud-led government in Jerusalem in 1996. Even as the peace process lost momentum, Foreign Minister Di Tella made no apologies for Argentina's moderation, which he described as reflecting domestic considerations.

Considerable controversy swirled about Israel's ambassador, Yizhak Aviran, who was reprimanded on at least one occasion by Argentine officials. Such a dressing down took place in November 1996, following one of Aviran's not unusual forays into Argentine domestic affairs. Speaking at a vandalized Jewish cemetery, the Israeli envoy was quoted in *La Nación* (October 28, 1996) as saying, "We see nothing but darkness, more attacks, more threats, more hatred, and less security." Mincing no words, the outspoken ambassador's speech also affirmed that it was no longer enough "to be told that something is being done." Angered by what was generally seen—not just in Argentine government circles—as yet another undiplomatic statement representing "an interference in domestic affairs," Foreign Minister Di Tella had his deputy, Andrés Cisneros, meet with the Israeli envoy; an official communiqué let it be known that Aviran had been apprised of Menem's and Di Tella's "surprise and malaise" at this outburst.

Over the years Aviran's behavior generated a degree of resentment among Argentine Jews and others. His vitriolic attack on Supreme Court member Ricardo Levene, Jr., late in 1995 and call for the investigation of the Israeli embassy bombing to be taken away from the country's highest court in March 1997, or his criticism of the Catholic Church and government responses to anti-Jewish attacks in 1996, would undoubtedly long since have resulted in harsher measures in any other country. There were in fact calls for stronger action against the envoy. During 1997 a right-wing lawmaker, Guillermo Fernández Gill, declared himself in favor of Aviran being declared persona non grata for "grave intromissions in our internal affairs" that injured "national sovereignty," as well as for his "disrespect towards ministers of a democratically elected government." This last was a reference to Aviran moving away from where Interior Minister Carlos Corach, Foreign Minister Di Tella, and other officials were standing at the third anniversary commemoration of the AMIA bombing in July 1997. For their part, four Justicialist senators—Angel Pardo, Osvaldo Sala, Alberto Tell, and one-time Menem brother-in-law Jorge Yoma—urged the president to bring to Jerusalem's attention that Aviran's attitude was inconsistent with "the most elementary principles of international law" and deserved "the Argentine government's strongest protest," an implicit call on Israel to replace its long-serving diplomat in Buenos Aires.

The tilt in Jerusalem's direction went hand-in-hand with gestures designed to create the impression of a degree of evenhandedness toward the Arab world in general and the Palestinians in particular. For instance, Interior Minister Corach's visit to Tel Aviv in March 1996 yielded a bilateral agreement with the Israelis on terrorism, and a complementary draft accord with the Palestinians on the exchange of information on the same subject, which he ordered after meeting with the Palestinian National Authority (PNA) president in Gaza. Moreover, while Yasir Arafat failed to get Menem to intercede with Jerusalem to lift its ban on Palestinian workers, the Argentine government presented the PNA with a building for its diplomatic representation in Buenos Aires. This was an unpleasant reminder to opponents of Palestinian national aspirations that, no matter who ruled in Jerusalem, Argentina was on the side of those who viewed the PNA as an inevitable Palestinian state in the making. This was not the sole instance where Argentina's distaste for some Likud government policies coexisted with a commitment to a pro-Israel foreign policy orientation. Argentina unashamedly backed the UN General Assembly's condemnation of Israeli settlement activity in April 1996 and called for a halt of the Jebel Abu Ghneim/Har Homah project in Jerusalem.

Conditional support for Israel was also now generally endorsed by the two main opposition parties, as seen, for example, in multipartisan initiatives in Congress "to energetically repudiate" the assassination of Prime Minister Yitzhak Rabin in November 1995 and Hamas's three suicide-bombing attacks on Israeli civilians in March 1996. Both government and opposition reproached Israel for the civilian casualties in Lebanon in April (Operation Grapes of Wrath), and expressed concern over Israel's legalization of the use of torture in November.

A pro-Israel stand by the ruling party, along with Argentina's alignment with the United States under Menem, may have been factors in the traumatic bombings that wrecked the Israeli embassy in February 1992 and the Jewish community's AMIA headquarters two years later, with a combined toll of over 120 dead and several hundred wounded. This assessment can be gleaned from the conclusions of the multipartisan congressional commission monitoring official probes into both terrorist attacks, which were released in December 1997. Although the committee's fractiousness resulted in three different sets of conclusions—by mainstream Justicialists, opposition party members, and a Justicialist dissident— they all stressed, among other things, that changes in the country's international relations were not accompanied immediately by accommodation in the security and intelligence apparatus. The implication was that the attackers were able to exploit the weakness in the security and intelligence areas caused by that lag.

Despite the existence of antiterrorism agreements stemming from Interior Minister Corach's 1996 visit to the Middle East, and the confirmation by Rubén Beraja, the president of Argentine Jewry's representative body (DAIA) in October 1996 that Israel's Mossad continued to cooperate with Argentina's State Intelligence Secretariat (SIDE), officials feared that Argentina could still witness a third terrorist megabombing. Neither all Argentine officials nor all Jews, however, shared Ambassador Aviran's certainty that Iran and the armed wing of Lebanon's Hezballah were the "intellectual authors of the [two previous] attacks."

European advice to avoid incurring Iranian wrath and a reluctance to give up the country's foremost Middle East export market—one which, according to Iran, yielded an accumulated surplus in Argentina's favor of over $10 billion since 1984—had long been seen as compelling explanations for Argentina's unwillingness to sever relations with Tehran, as urged by Israel and some quarters in the United States. After the AMIA bombing in July 1994, Argentina had downgraded links with Tehran to the level of chargé d'affaires, but it resisted efforts to take stronger measures, especially after a former Iranian intelligence operative who had implicated Iranian diplomats in the attacks in Buenos Aires was discredited.

Foreign policy was clearly a consideration in the decision by government to give a piece of prime real estate in Buenos Aires to Saudi Arabia for a Sunni mosque and Islamic center. (Iran had supported the construction of the city's one existing mosque in the 1980s.) Apart from the rejection of the proposal by the Radical bloc in the lower house of the legislature, the Catholic primate of Buenos Aires, Antonio Cardinal Quarracino, expressed distaste for the project in the largest circulation Argentine daily, Buenos Aires's *Clarín* (March 27, 1996), in which he referred to Islam as a great heresy, and portrayed the prophet Muhammad as the descendant of "degraded idolaters from savage Arabia." Protest of the cardinal's words was minimal, and came chiefly from the Iranian cultural attaché, Hojjatulislam Mohsen Rabbani, who took serious issue with Quarracino in print. If Quarracino's view could be seen as emblematic of the Argentine Catholic hierarchy's pre-Vatican Council outlook, the deafening silence on the part of other parties vis-à-vis the country's aggrieved Muslim and Arab-descended citizens clearly reflected the prejudices of Argentine society. Responding to this, Argentines of Arab descent, especially the Muslim minority among them, were moved to increased assertiveness. In April the Buenos Aires Council of Islamic Institutions (CEIBA), called for an immediate halt to "anti-Arab and anti-Islamic racism; anti-Muslim discrimination and defamation; baseless accusations, e.g. the [Israeli] embassy and AMIA [bombings]; and media censorship."

By August 1996 the foundation stone of the future mosque and educational center—a project valued at $40 million that was likely to become the city's foremost Muslim prayer house—was laid in an official ceremony attended by, among others, the Wahabite kingdom's minister of Islamic affairs, Abdullah al-Turki, and his Argentine counterpart, Foreign Minister Guido Di Tella (whose portfolio also covers religious affairs), as well as Mayor Fernando de la Rúa, whose record as a Radical senator had included being the sole upper house opponent of the government's gift. Before the end of 1996, Congress also sanctioned draft legislation first introduced in July 1995 that declared the Islamic new year and two other festivals as nonworking days for the country's Muslim inhabitants. The number of Muslims was variously estimated but was undoubtedly less than the upper-ceiling self-estimate of 650,000. Moreover, nearly a century after the first Druze arrivals in Argentina, this Muslim group was recognized as a separate faith in December 1997.

Holocaust-Related Matters

Argentina's efforts to disengage from the image it earned during the Nazi era, still perceived as a hurdle in the way of optimized relations with the United States, translated, among other things, into Supreme Court endorsement of government efforts to cleanse the country of war criminals, a presidential decision to release records of past gold bullion transactions, and the setting up of a commission to look into the number of war criminals and stolen assets that may have come to Argentina.

None of these actions pleased the country's officially marginalized ultranationalists. However, because of the country's antidiscrimination legislation, they were unable to give vent to their sentiments in mass circulation publications, rather than their diminishing number of fringe newsletters. A possible exception was the case of Ayer y Hoy, a recently established and seemingly well-endowed Buenos Aires-based publishing house responsible for some quality publications that convey their coded message, while so far carefully managing to avoid provoking legal action. Among Ayer y Hoy's catalogue of publications is the magazine *La memoria argentina,* whose third issue was entirely devoted to Adolf Eichmann in Argentina, as well as a separate biographical volume entitled *Martin Bormann.* Both publications skillfuly exploit, among other things, important factual errors and exaggerations made by Nazi hunter Simon Wiesenthal over the years, in a clear attempt to discredit the man and, by implication, the cause of Nazi hunting. Ayer y Hoy also focused attention on Israel's infringement of Argentine sovereignty when kidnapping Eichmann in May 1960 and argued that Argentina altogether "bears no responsibility for Nazi crimes."

NAZI GOLD

In light of the fact that Argentina was among several Latin American states long suspected of holding Nazi assets in custody or serving as trans-shipment points for these—including gold plundered from the exchequers of countries invaded by the Third Reich and that taken from its Jewish victims—there was considerable interest in the U.S. interagency study of the subject, the so-called Eizenstat report, released in May 1997. The report's conclusion that there was no hard evidence among U.S. archival materials that plundered gold ended up in Buenos Aires would, if independently verified, neatly puncture the rationale for some of the blanket condemnation long directed at Argentina.

Argentina's decision to set up its own commission of inquiry into the influx of Nazis and tainted gold was viewed as a necessary step toward understanding the country's contemporary history. It was preceded by other steps taken by Menem and the ruling party's opponents in Congress. In December 1996 Ricardo Mercado Luna, a UCR lower house member, introduced draft legislation designed to create a special inquiry commission that would investigate any illegal Third Reich gold transfers to Argentina's Banco Central. According to a report in *Clarín* (December 8, 1996), Mercado proposed that such a commission should include legislators, journalists, and representatives of the Argentine Academy of History, the World Jewish Congress, and the Wiesenthal Center. Concurrently with this, an initiative of Radical senator Javier Meneghini set its sights on legislation that would declare illegitimate any former Third Reich assets still in the country. Three months earlier, President Menem had already agreed to subject Banco Central documents to public scrutiny, and in November 1996 Martín Lagos, the bank's vice-president, handed over to an interested party records of transactions in gold bullion since the 1930s. Moreover, in a December 1996 meeting between an American Jewish Committee (AJC) delegation and Foreign Minister Di Tella, Chief of Cabinet Jorge Rodríguez, and presidential secretary general Alberto Kohan, Di Tella requested whatever data the AJC might have on the entry of Nazi gold. Ultimately, Argentina's recent record on the Nazis was recognized by the London-based Inter-Parliamentary Council Against Antisemitism. Led by Greville Janner, a Labor MP, the council welcomed President Menem to membership in June 1997, as well as Foreign Minister Di Tella a few months later.

NAZI WAR CRIMINALS

In November 1995 a convincing though not unanimous Supreme Court supported Judge Leónidas Moldes's decision to grant Italy's extradition request of former SS captain Erich Priebke. Moldes's extradition order had been overturned in August by an appellate court on the strength of Argentina's statute of limitations for cases of homicide. While the Supreme Court was asked to consider Priebke's situation, a German extradition request was filed, presumably as a fallback position in case the Italian request collapsed. In its ruling the Supreme Court noted that the charges against Priebke did not amount to homicide, but represented prima facie a case of genocide and crimes against humanity for which no statute of limitations applied. The ruling also broke new ground by giving precedence to peremptory norms of general international law over bilateral treaties, in this case an Argentine-Italian treaty, that conflict with such norms. This last was regarded as a significant decision that could prove valuable in future cases involving extradition requests. Priebke's extradition also resulted in the interior ministry-decreed suspension of three federal policemen for embracing the suspected Nazi war criminal after escorting him from his home in San Carlos de Bariloche, Neuquén province, to the airport.

Later, the government took measures to preempt any return of the temporarily freed former SS officer. In August 1996, as soon as the Italian military tribunal's ruling on the former SS officer became known—guilty of participation in the March 1944 German reprisal execution of 335 defenseless civilians, including 75 Jews, in the Ardeatine caves, but freed on the grounds that his was a homicide case, which had since lapsed—Interior Minister Corach and Foreign Minister Di Tella jointly announced that, irrespective of Priebke's fate, his return to Argentina would not be countenanced under any circumstances. (See "Italy," elsewhere in this volume.)

An international conference on "War Criminals and Nazism in Latin America Fifty Years Later," organized by B'nai B'rith at Washington's United States Holocaust Memorial Museum in October 1996, heard about the presumed Argentine abode of Dinko Sakic, a commander of the Jasenovac concentration camp of Croatia's Nazi puppet government. Despite a July 1995 request by B'nai B'rith to the Croatian head of state to have Sakic brought to justice, and the latter's attendance at a veterans' meeting in the Croatian capital two months earlier, President Franjo Tudjman's reply that this would have to wait until the former Yugoslavia's conflicts in which his own country was involved were over essentially meant that Sakic remained at large, whether in Croatia or Argentina. Although reportedly on the U.S. Justice Department's watch list, neither Croatia nor the countries with legislation claiming jurisdiction in such cases showed active interest in Sakic's prosecution.

HOLOCAUST MEMORIALS

In May 1996 the national legislature approved the construction of a monument for Jewish victims of the Nazi genocide, to be erected on the square opposite the legislature in Buenos Aires. As publicized in the *Boletín Oficial,* draft legislation to this effect was introduced by Claudio Mendoza, a ruling PJ lower house member, and was sponsored by another 14 parliamentarians from the three main parties, including such luminaries as the UCR's lower house bloc leader, Federico Storani, and FREPASO's Graciela Fernández Meijide. A winner of the B'nai B'rith Human Rights Award in 1994, Mendoza was earlier behind the building of a similar monument in the northeastern provincial capital of Resistencia, Chaco province, "because there is always a need to remember, increase awareness and educate to prevent the recurrence of such a moral catastrophe as the Holocaust." The monument's design will be chosen through a competition organized by Argentina's Culture and Education Ministry.

Anti-Semitism

A recorded increase in anti-Jewish manifestations could be attributed to a combination of conditions conducive to the growth and spread of racism, xenophobia, and anti-Semitism. Among those were peak levels of unemployment since 1995 and inequality in the distribution of income; the intensified perception of corruption; the discrediting of key institutions; and the long-festering sequels of Argentina's imperfect transition from military to elected rule, i.e., without a thorough cleansing of the former regime's main security agencies.

Rodolfo Barra, a former minister of public works and Supreme Court justice, named justice minister in 1994, was ousted from the position two years later when it was revealed that he had a record of association with right-wing and anti-Semitic groups since his high-school days. As a law student he participated in an ultra-nationalist forum and was a devout follower of Leonardo Castellani, a Jesuit intellectual and unsuccessful parliamentary candidate for the anti-Semitic National Liberation Alliance (ALN) in 1946. Although Barra was more recently identified with the Opus Dei, a Spanish-created conservative Catholic organization, which cannot legitimately be accused of being a neo-Nazi outfit, by June 1996 he had lost the confidence of a section of Argentine society. Whereas DAIA vice-president Luis Steinberg declared that if Barra had once been a Nazi "he has now shown himself a democrat, and this is praiseworthy" — a view supported by his co-authorship with Interior Minister Corach of a book on Argentina's reformed constitution of 1994 — the average Jew found it "inadmissible that Barra should continue in charge of a ministry," and the DAIA was forced to revise its approach. Appointed temporarily to handle the justice portfolio was Barra's deputy, Elías Jassán, a one-time solicitor in the Menem brothers' law firm and a man active in the tiny Jewish community in La Rioja province. He thereby joined Corach as the second Jewish cabinet member in the present PJ administration.

While the U.S. State Department regarded Barra's fall from grace (in its human rights report for 1996) as evidence of "the government's desire to accommodate the sensitivities of the Jewish community," it could also be viewed as confirmation that the country's organized Jews had achieved a degree of political clout. Barra's departure in disgrace was above everything a sign of Jewish frustration at the complete failure of the investigation into the Israeli embassy bombing and meager achievements of the probe into the AMIA attack. The explanation for other former ultra-nationalists still holding office probably had to do with their lack of jurisdiction over the investigations, as well as their more convincing break with their ultra-nationalist past. In Barra's case, there was no evidence of his present attachment to an ultranationalist ideology or group and, not surprisingly, he was subsequently appointed as a congressional legal adviser.

Since 1991, Buenos Aires Jewish cemeteries had been vandalized seven times, including three attacks on the main burial ground in the greater Buenos Aires district of La Tablada — twice during 1996 and once in December 1997. Other Jewish cemeteries in greater Buenos Aires and throughout the country were also targeted during 1996–97. The vandalism of the Ciudadela Jewish cemetery, under the jurisdiction of the Buenos Aires provincial police jurisdiction, happened a few days after the third attack against La Tablada. The Jewish cemetery of Rosario, Santa Fe province, witnessed the desecration of 14 tombs and destruction of three tombstones in October 1997; its Villa Clara counterpart, in the province of Entre Ríos, was attacked in November 1996 and July 1997. In September 1996 a total of 66 tombs were defiled in two different attacks against Córdoba's new Jewish cemetery, in the neighborhood of San Vicente, the first of these on the Jewish New Year. Also during 1996, the Jewish cemetery of Salta, in the northwestern province of the same name, was vandalized. Like the Buenos Aires cases, the provincial ones all awaited clarification. While it was tempting to attribute the poor police work to political unwillingness on the part of the national and/or provincial governments concerned to get to the bottom of these cases, natural impatience with lack of results led many to ignore the difficulty of such cases — as witness the fact that it took longer, in fact several years, for the more experienced French to solve the vandalization of the Carpentras Jewish cemetery.

A few days after the first La Tablada attack in October 1996, when 100 tombs were defiled, some with graffiti reading "Holocaust, the great Jewish lie," a caller to the capital city's Jewish hospital, Ezrah, proclaimed that a National Dignity commando was responsible. Federal police cooperating with the Buenos Aires provincial police force in the investigation (the latter not entirely above suspicion of anti-Semitism and in the middle of a process of self-cleansing), produced some immediate results. Four people, all of them alleged members of a self-proclaimed Catholic ultra-nationalist Truth and Justice group, were detained and accused of the first attack. Their hatred of Jews was substantiated by their possession of hate pamphlets and publications that had been previously distributed among judiciary and university authorities in the greater Buenos Aires district of Morón. Among the four, Ricardo Russo, a PJ activist, had served as head of the foundation that promoted the creation of the University of Morón during the four previous years. Judging by press reports, the link between the detained and the attack was not their anti-Semitic literature but possession of aerosol paint similar to that used for the swastikas daubed at La Tablada. Whereas DAIA president Beraja initially said that it was too early "to be sure that the detained are directly linked with this attack," by November 1996 the four detainees were charged. However, because of the flimsiness of the evidence, they were to be tried for the dissemination of anti-Semitic literature rather than the attack on La Tablada.

In 1997, 35 tombs were destroyed at La Tablada, with over half as many damaged at Ciudadela, though unlike earlier attacks, however, no swastikas and/or anti-Jewish inscriptions were found in La Tablada and Ciudadela this time. As with previous attacks, the vandals went undetected, though former Buenos Aires policemen (and perhaps even other elements associated with that police force) were under suspicion. Since 1991, especially after the embassy and AMIA bombings, some 6,000 corrupt and otherwise unsuitable policemen had been purged from the 47,000-man Buenos Aires provincial police force, with some 500 dropped during 1997 alone. At the same time, the provincial legislature had extended the emergency legislation legitimizing such purges, though limited this time to the highest ranking officers. A willingness by some police officers to engage in activities aimed at sabotaging the reform effort had to be considered a possibility.

Reacting to the 1996 vandalization of La Tablada, President Menem issued his "most energetic repudiation of such an attack," while Interior Minister Corach declared himself overcome by "an admixture of horror, indignation and shame" and proclaimed that the authors of the outrage were "barbarians." Corach, Chief of Cabinet Rodríguez, and Menem's personal physician, Alejandro Tfeli (like the head of state, the descendant of Syrian Muslims), visited La Tablada to express government solidarity with Argentine Jewry, while the Buenos Aires provincial vice-governor, Rafael Romá, offered assurances of his administration's "profound desire to turn existing clues into results." Likewise, the 1997 attacks were described as "deeds, shameful to all Argentines" by Interior Minister Corach, who also offered the central government's undivided "collaboration and backing" to punish the perpetrators. In parliament and in the Buenos Aires provincial legislature, the 1996 vandalization of La Tablada evoked statements by UCR as well as PJ legislators demanding punishment of the vandals and swift police action. These and other expressions of solidarity with Argentine Jewry, though unlikely to bring about concrete results, at least indicated sympathy for the Jewish community and a resolve to address social tensions generally.

JEWISH COMMUNITY

Demography

A revised estimate by demographers of the Hebrew University's Institute of Contemporary Jewry (ICJ) put the size of Argentine Jewry in 1994 at 208,000, making it the world's seventh-largest Jewish community outside Israel. According to the same source, 180,000 Jews—some 90 percent of the country's total—lived in Buenos Aires, making it the third-largest Diaspora metropolitan area outside the United States. There were smaller Jewish concentrations in Córdoba, Rosario, Santa Fe, and Tucumán, among other Argentine provincial cities, most of which had lost population to Buenos Aires.

The Institute of Contemporary Jewry's figure for Argentina was disputed by some Jewish leaders as being too low, perhaps by as much as 20 percent. The ICJ's Sergio DellaPergola urged the launching of a new demographic study of Argentine Jewry.

Jewish-Christian Relations

The Catholic Church's record during the period of military rule was the subject of a meeting of the plenary assembly of the Catholic Episcopal Conference in April 1996. Nearly 13 years after the restoration of elected governments in Argentina, it approved a consensus document that lamented Catholic participation in human-rights violations and admitted that all it had done "was insufficient to prevent so much horror." The document was criticized by Monsignor Miguel Hesayne, bishop emeritus of Viedma, Neuquén province, and a human-rights campaigner, for the absence in the document of "gestures of repudiation of violence."

Following the series of cemetery vandalizations, Monsignor Casaretto, bishop of the greater Buenos Aires district of San Isidro, addressed a letter to the Masorti affiliated Bet El temple expressing the Catholic church's sympathy for the attacks the Jewish community had suffered. Though not written on behalf of the Episcopal Conference, news of the letter was leaked by Monsignor Guillermo Leaden, chairman of the Conference's Christian-Jewish dialogue sub-commission, in October 1996, after the Israeli ambassador chided the Catholic Church for its "silence" on the "reawakening" of anti-Semitism in Argentina.

Father Rafael Braun, a Catholic theologian, was among the recipients of the B'nai B'rith Human Rights Award in December 1996. The cleric was honored for his indefatigable efforts in behalf of Christian-Jewish dialogue, in which, he declared in May 1997, he always started by acknowledging the Catholic Church's "centuries-old anti-Semitic attitudes."

In May 1997 a permanent mural commemorating the Jewish victims of World War II, as well as those killed in the Israeli embassy and AMIA attacks, was placed in the Metropolitan Catholic Cathedral. It was inaugurated by Cardinal Quarracino at a public function attended by Interior Minister Corach, Buenos Aires mayor De la Rúa, former Polish president Lech Walesa, and an array of Jewish and other leaders. The project was undertaken at the initiative of the Argentine House in Israel, an institution created by a former Jewish school teacher in Buenos Aires and later successful entrepreneur abroad, Baruch Tenenbaum. Some objections were raised to the mural's implied equivalence of the Holocaust and the bombings in Buenos Aires.

In November 1997, AMIA, B'nai B'rith Argentina, and the Buenos Aires Arch-diocese organized their third annual walk on behalf of the disabled. Three months earlier, the same institutions sponsored a two-day series of workshops titled "Together We Can," which brought together some 2,000 secondary school students with special needs for a variety of artistic, sport, and dialogue-based activities.

Publications

Yiddish and other foreign-language newspapers were no longer published in Argentina, but three longtime Spanish-language Jewish periodicals — *La Luz,*

Mundo Israelita, and *Nuewa Sión*—showed a remarkable degree of resilience. *Comunidades* and *Masorti,* also weekly papers, began publication during the past ten years. Conservative Judaism's *Majshavot,* the Latin American Jewish Congress's *Coloquio,* and the Latin American Sephardic Zionist Federation's *Sefárdica* are quasi-academic journals providing, periodically, the fruits of historical and other research and critical essays. The most recent issue of DAIA's *Indice* was on the 60th anniversary of the Jewish umbrella organization (1995), and the WZO published an issue of *Controversia de ideas sionistas* in 1996.

Radio, television, and other media had eroded the importance of journalism in print and become a dynamic presence in the Jewish community. Most noteworthy are the Chai (transliterated in Spanish as Jai) radio station and the Alef cable television channel.

Several recent collections of scholarly essays are noteworthy. Among them, *German and Italian Jewish Scientists in Argentina and Brazil (Ibero-Amerikanisches Archiv 21: 1-2)* includes a unique reconstruction of Albert Einstein's visit to Argentina in 1925 (hitherto one of the father of relativity's least studied international trips), and devotes attention to the important contributions of the scientists who settled there in the 1930s and 1940s. Another collection— *Discriminación y racismo en América Latina* (Buenos Aires 1997), with an English-language selection appearing as two monographic issues of *Patterns of Prejudice* in 1996-97—contains proceedings from a conference at the University of Buenos Aires sponsored by, among others, the Latin American Jewish Studies Association, the Institute of Jewish Affairs, the Agudat Mechkar Amerika Halatinit, the Argentine Senate, and the Argentine Foreign Ministry. Like other collections of academic papers, these include important contributions by non-Jewish authors, attesting to a noteworthy and stimulating development. Whereas topics of Jewish concern were in the past the exclusive province of Jewish scholars, chroniclers, and publicists, there is heightened interest in such subjects among researchers and academics of various nationalities and ethnic-religious affiliations, one that translates into a healthy and enriching debate.

Among new works of fiction published in 1995 was *El fantasma del Reich* (The Ghost of the Reich) a collection of horror stories by the young writer and poet Marcelo di Marco, winner of an Antorchas Foundation award. The title story is a hair-raising account of ultra-nationalist Jew-baiting in the country, as fantastic as it is reminiscent of some of the goings-on in Argentina's secondary schools of the 1950s, 1960s, and 1970s. A noteworthy anthology of out-of-print works by poet César Tiempo (Israel Zeitlin's permanent nom de plume)—*Buenos Aires esquina sábadoc* (At the Crossroads of Buenos Aires and Sabbath)—artfully selected, annotated, and introduced by Eliahu Toker—was attractively published in 1997 by the Archivo General de la Nación (AGN), Argentina's national archive. Interior Minister Corach hailed the publication, saying that "remembering its best sons is part of any country's permanent debt with itself, one seldom settled," reflecting, perhaps, Toker's concluding comment that "hitherto, no Buenos Aires street or square bears his [Tiempo's] name."

A best-selling novel of 1997 was Marcos Aguinis's latest work, *La matriz del infierno* (The Womb of Hell). Aquinis is a former Latin American Jewish Congress deputy associate director and secretary of culture in the Alfonsín administration. The novel, which takes place in Buenos Aires and Berlin in the 1930s and is described as "a biography of an epoch," had three South American editions, which opened the way for a German-language translation, another feather in the cap of this multiprize-winning author.

Personalia

Late in November 1995 Alejandro Orchansky and Gerardo Belinsky were designated as Israeli honorary consuls. They were among 42 Argentine citizens approved by the lower house to act as honorary consuls, vice-consuls, and consular agents for 23 different countries. The list also included Luis Svatetz Eichenberger and Saúl Breitman, put forward by Honduras and the Dominican Republic, respectively.

Evidence that the Argentine foreign service, once an exclusive redoubt of the country's patrician families, was undergoing transformation was the designation in 1997 of Diego Guelar, a former ambassador to the European Community and Brazil, as the country's top diplomatic envoy to the United States. That Guelar — a one-time member of a Masorti community youth group and PJ lawmaker — was not an exception was highlighted by the presence of other politically appointed Jewish diplomats. More importantly, two Jewish gold medalists graduated from the Instituto del Servicio Exterior de la Nación, the training ground for Argentina's aspiring career diplomats: Luis Levitt (1991) and Claudio Rozencwaig (1996), the latter the winner also of the Elena Holmberg Prize for excellence in diplomatic theory and practice.

Writer Ricardo Feierstein, formerly in charge of the AMIA-initiated Milá publishing house, was among the winners of a 1996 essay competition on the role of the country's different immigrant groups in the development of Argentina. The competition was organized by the popular history magazine *Todo es Historia* (with funding from the Argentine education ministry's culture secretariat).

Legal counsel Esther Labatón was among the 1996 recipients of the B'nai B'rith Human Rights Award, for campaigning from her wheelchair for the right of the disabled to become fully integrated in society. A recipient of the 1989 Alpi Prize, Labatón was chairwoman of the Argentine bar association's commission on the disabled.

IGNACIO KLICH

Western Europe

Great Britain

National Affairs

A DRAMATIC CHANGE of government and a major organizational restructuring in the Jewish community were among the key events of late 1996 and 1997.

In May 1997, 18 years of Tory rule ended with a spectacular defeat for the Conservative Party and Prime Minister John Major. The Labor Party, headed by Tony Blair, came to power with 43.1 percent of the popular vote and an overall majority of 177 seats in the House of Commons—the largest majority of any party in the postwar era. The Conservatives, who polled their smallest share of the vote since 1832 (31.4 percent), were left with 165 seats in the House. The center-left Liberal Democrats more than doubled their representation to 46 seats, all the gains being made at the expense of the Tories. The upset was predicted by the pollsters, all of whom up until the actual election gave Labor a lead of more than 15 points.

The Tory defeat, coming at a time of falling unemployment and growing prosperity, had little to do with economics. Obviously, after 18 years of Toryism, sentiment favoring change was a strong factor. But this was powerfully reinforced by multiple examples of sleaze among Conservative MPs, deception of Parliament by ministers, and above all, a perception that Premier John Major had traded national leadership for increasingly desperate attempts to maintain some sort of party unity between Europhiles and Europhobes in his cabinet.

The Labor Party, by contrast, not only displayed a greater degree of skill in its presentation of policies but was also careful to promote an image that promised change, especially in respect to education and the national health service, while still pledging to remain within spending totals set by the Tories and not to raise the income tax. Only weeks after the election, new chancellor of the exchequer Gordon Brown transferred the power to set interest rates from the Treasury to the Bank of England, a historic move that removed politics from monetary policy.

At the Labor Party conference in September, Premier Blair proclaimed his aim of presiding over "one of the great radical reforming governments of our history." This took the form initially of winning referenda for devolution in Wales and Scotland, reducing benefits for single parents, and deferring a decision on whether to participate in the European Monetary Union until a referendum early in the next Parliament (due in 2002). The reason given was that the British economy had not yet converged sufficiently with those of the other likely participants. There was some concern that party unity might not survive the exigencies of reform of the welfare state: in December, 47 Labor MPs voted against the bill to reduce benefit payments to single parents. This was part of a welfare-to-work program, the full dimensions of which had yet to be revealed.

The far-right British National Party (BNP) did not fare well in the May 1997 general election. It fielded more than 50 candidates (thus qualifying for a TV election broadcast), but garnered only some 40,000 votes nationally. Most BNP candidates received less than 1 percent of the poll in their respective constituencies.

Israel and the Middle East

Following Labor's victory in May 1997, there was little to distinguish its Middle East policies from those of its Tory predecessors, though Labor, said Foreign Office minister Derrek Fatchett, was ready to become more actively engaged in regional diplomacy. Returning from his first official visit to the Middle East the following month, Fatchett spelled out Labor policy: "We believe in the principle of land for peace; we support the United Nations resolutions; and we are passionately committed to the peace process."

Both parties saw a major role for Britain in this process. As negotiations jolted from one crisis to the next, Britain pressed constantly for speedier implementation of the Oslo accords, at times tending to blame Israel for delays. In September 1996 both Foreign Secretary Malcolm Rifkind and Labor's shadow foreign secretary, Robin Cook, called on Israel to take immediate steps to redeploy its troops in Hebron. In October 1996 Rifkind described Netanyahu's policies as "primarily" responsible for introducing recent uncertainty into the peace process.

Jewish settlements in the territories were "illegal and an obstacle to peace," said a Foreign Office spokesperson in September 1996, when news broke that 900 houses were being built at Kiryat Sefer, just inside the West Bank. In February 1997 Rifkind was urging the Israeli government not to proceed with plans to build Jewish homes at Har Homah in southeast Jerusalem, which in his view could only detract from the positive atmosphere created by the Hebron agreement. In December 1997 Robin Cook, now foreign secretary, described the peace process as in stalemate, indicating that he attributed much of the blame to the Israelis. "We will make it clear to all parties—but specifically to Mr. Netanyahu—that they are bound by the Oslo accords, which have the status of an international treaty," he declared.

Israel's periodic closure of the territories also caused concern. In September

1996 both Rifkind and Cook called on Israel to suspend measures causing economic hardship to the Palestinians. "Any restrictions that are not legitimate on grounds of security should not be there," Rifkind said in October. Foreign Office minister Baroness Chalker, visiting Israel and Palestinian self-rule areas in January 1997, stressed British unhappiness with closure: it harmed the Palestinian economy and hampered aid workers seeking to enter Gaza. She announced that direct British aid to the Palestinian Authority would continue at an annual rate of some £10 million, to fund a water and infrastructure project in Hebron and to train Palestinian police.

Criticism notwithstanding, the Foreign Office's Fatchett insisted that Britain was not partisan. "We believe passionately in security for Israelis as we do in justice for Palestinians," he said in July 1997. He criticized both the Israeli government and the Palestinians: the former for failure to make some key commitments to the Palestinians, such as the release of prisoners and further troop redeployments, and the latter for human-rights violations and suspected financial corruption.

In May 1997 Foreign Secretary Cook said that he favored European action to help resuscitate the stalled negotiations between Israel and her Arab neighbors. In December he pledged that saving the peace process would be a "very high" priority when Britain took over the European Union presidency in January 1998.

Britain's active role was demonstrated by a series of diplomatic visits during the period under review. In September 1996 and November 1997 Netanyahu was in London; in November 1996 Rifkind was in Israel, and Israeli defense minister Yitzhak Mordechai, Syria's foreign minister, and King Hussein of Jordan visited London; and in February 1997 Israeli president Ezer Weizman enjoyed a spectacular state reception in his honor when he visited London. In July 1997 Palestinian Authority president Yasir Arafat had talks in London with Prime Minister Tony Blair, who reiterated British support for Arafat's work "in the cause of peace in the Middle East."

During Weizman's visit in February 1997, Prime Minister John Major talked of the "unprecedentedly close ties" between Jerusalem and London that began with the launching of the peace process. This was underscored by the Queen's speech at the opening of Parliament in May promising that the government would promote efforts for a durable peace in the Middle East. An event expressing the strength of the relationship took place in December 1997, when Prime Minister Blair lit the first Hanukkah candle at his constituency home in Sedgefield, Durham, to mark the start of Israel's 50th-anniversary celebration.

OTHER MATTERS

In October 1996 the British-Israel parliamentary group wrote to the Iranian embassy urging the Teheran government to give "a definite statement on the current state" of Ron Arad, the Israeli airman held captive since 1986. In May 1997

Foreign Office minister Derrek Fatchett called for Arad's release when he met with Arab leaders during his Middle East visit. The Foreign Office, he said, viewed the case as a serious violation of human rights.

Also in May, the National Lottery Charity Board gave £280,000 to the New Israel Fund for preschool education for Bedouin children, and more than £400,000 to three London-based charities aiding Palestinian causes: Friends of Bir Zeit University, Friends of the Spafford Children's Center of Jerusalem, and Medical Aid for Palestine.

Anti-Semitism and Racism

Traditional expressions of anti-Semitism in Great Britain continued to decline, according to the 1997 *Antisemitism World Report*, published by the Institute for Jewish Policy Research (JPR) and the American Jewish Committee. "Jews in Britain do not experience the same levels of racism as other, more visible, ethnic groups," the report noted, but warned that the threat from Islamism and terrorism still existed. Figures in the report, based on statistics collected by the Community Security Trust (CST), which replaced the Board of Deputies Communal Security Organization, showed recorded anti-Semitic incidents falling for the third consecutive year in 1996 to 227, an 8.1-percent decrease over 1995. The report attributed the decreased harassment of the Jewish community and the reduced threat of racism to effective action by the police and judicial authorities against racists and neo-Nazis.

Nevertheless, in October 1996 CST warned that the police and other authorities thought the Jewish community to be at risk. "There is a clear and present danger," with the main threat posed by Islamist and Arab terrorists and right-wing groups such as Combat 18 and the British National Party. The police believed these dangers would persist for the foreseeable future.

In July 1996 JPR reported on the growing use of cyberspace by far-right propagandists, which it judged particularly dangerous as an effective device for Holocaust deniers and because it enabled violent groups to coordinate activities. The report recommended inter alia that the Internet be subject to the same laws as other publishing processes. In November 1996 CST urged Jewish organizations to take precautions when using the Internet lest they disclose sensitive information.

The Board of Deputies continued to press for tighter legislation, especially against Holocaust-denial material. In June 1996 Prime Minister John Major told board president Eldred Tabachnik that he understood the concern but preferred to combat such material by education and use of the Public Order Act. The October Labor Party conference in Blackpool adopted a motion that had been proposed by Poale Zion (the Labor-affiliated Zionist group), calling on the future Labor government to make Holocaust denial a criminal offense. In January 1997 a private member's bill to outlaw Holocaust denial was given an unopposed first reading in the House of Commons, passed its committee stage in the House of Commons in March, but failed to make it into the statute books.

In July 1996 the director of Public Prosecution decided not to act on Holocaust-denial leaflets sent to schools, finding them "not insulting in the meaning of the Public Order Act." The same month the Crown Prosecution Service decided against prosecuting Dr. Mohammed al-Massara, a London-based Saudi dissident who called for the annihilation of the Jews.

Not all racial actions went unpunished. In November 1996 Aston Villa goalkeeper Mark Bosnich was fined £2,000 and warned about his future conduct, after he gave a Nazi-style salute to Tottenham Hotspur fans at a football match a month earlier. In January 1997 the parents of children who six months earlier caused damage estimated at £37,000 to tombstones at Rainsough Jewish cemetery, north Manchester, were fined £750. In April three youths were sentenced to custody terms of between three and six years at London Crown Court for attacks on Orthodox Jews in Stamford Hill, North London. In August plans for a large neo-Nazi music festival in South Wales were foiled by police action. In September a Feltham trash collector, Mark Atkinson, was jailed for 21 months for publishing two issues of *Stormer*, a magazine of Combat 18.

The new Labor government acted quickly to implement promises made in its election campaign and in the Queen's speech at the opening of Parliament in May 1997. A Crime and Disorder Bill that would strengthen existing laws against racial discrimination was announced by Home Secretary Jack Straw (Labor) in October, on the release of a Runnymede Trust report on problems facing British Muslims. The bill, which would make racial violence a specific offense and increase sentences for crimes where racism was a factor, received its second reading in the House of Lords in December. The government also intended to give racism priority when it took over the presidency of the European Union in January 1998.

Militant Islamic groups were increasingly frustrated in their campus activities. Manchester University Islamic Society withdrew a heavily contested anti-Zionist motion in October 1996; the same month, the Committee of University Vice-Chancellors and Principals set up a working group to advise colleges on ways to crack down on extremism and to confront groups inciting racial, religious, or political hatred. In September 1997 supporters of the militant Muslim group Hizb ut-Tahrir were ejected from Manchester student fairs for breaching bans imposed on their campus activities.

Off campus, local councils in Harrow and Brent canceled Muslim rallies in July 1996 because promotional literature denounced Israel and Jews. In November Home Office minister Timothy Kirkhope rejected a call to instruct the police to clamp down on Hizb; however, he reiterated the government's commitment to insuring that police had full powers to deal with any racially motivated crime. The same month Nottingham City Council canceled a Hizb meeting because the organization held "extremist views" offensive to Jews, women, and homosexuals.

In March 1997 Hackney Council in North London passed a motion describing the local presence of Louis Farrakhan's Nation of Islam as an "unacceptable threat to the building of bridges between the borough's communities." Farrakhan supporters should be made as unwelcome as the local BNP, it averred.

There was an effort to bridge the racial divide in July 1996 when Jewish, Asian, and black representatives launched a Commission for Racial Equality program, "Roots of the Future," designed to promote acceptance of Britain as a multiracial nation. In October 1996 soccer coach Glen Hoddle backed a "Let's kick racism out of football!" campaign, initiated by the Commission for Racial Equality in conjunction with the Professional Footballers' Association. In January 1997 Sir Sigmund Sternberg and British Muslim leader Dr. Zaki Badawi launched a forum for Muslims, Christians, and Jews, to promote dialogue and understanding in London. In February the Union of Jewish Students (UJS) joined forces with the National Black Alliance to counteract the threat from the BNP. In March the National Union of Students' Blackpool conference passed a motion introduced by Jewish and black leaders, backed by Labor students, urging students to campaign against racism on campuses and condemn activities by far-right political organizations.

Nazi War Criminals

The first case brought in Britain under the 1991 War Crimes Act ended in January 1997 when the jury at the Old Bailey found 86-year-old Szymon Serafimowicz unfit to plead. Serafimowicz, charged with the murder of Jews in Nazi-occupied Belarus between 1941 and 1942, died in August 1997.

In September Andrzej Sawoniuk, a retired British Rail worker from Bermondsey, East London, became the second man charged under the act. Accused of murdering five Jews in Domachevo, Belarus, between September and December 1942, Sawoniuk was remanded on conditional bail when he appeared at Bow Street magistrates court in November. The trial, at which the prosecution planned to call some 20 witnesses from Belarus and Israel, was expected to open at the end of March 1998. Sawoniuk denied all charges.

JEWISH COMMUNITY

Demography

The estimated number of Jews in Great Britain was 300,000. The steady decline in synagogue marriages since 1990 was reversed in 1996, according to the Board of Deputies Community Research Unit. The total number of marriages rose 9 percent to 947 in 1996 from 866 the previous year, with rises recorded in all groups except the Progressive sector, which continued to decline. The number of religious divorces completed in 1996 rose to 272, an 18-percent increase over the 1995 figure but still below the 1991 level. Burials and cremations under Jewish auspices fell 2 percent to 4,167 in 1996 from 4,233 in 1995. The unit estimated that 3,013 Jewish births took place in 1995, as compared with 2,377 in 1994.

Communal Affairs

In July 1997 Yasir Arafat met with leaders of the Jewish Board of Deputies, who pledged their support for the peace process. This caused Likud-Herut G.B. (British branch of the Israeli Likud Party) to accuse the board of undermining communal unity, even though communal unity was not, in fact, greatly in evidence. Benjamin Netanyahu's two visits to London—in September 1996 and November 1997—were accompanied by conflicting action by British Jewry, demonstrating the polarized sympathies within the community. In October 1996 British Friends of Peace Now called for a candlelight vigil outside London's Israeli embassy to press Netanyahu's government to move ahead with the peace process, while both left-wing opponents and right-wing sympathizers wrote to him to express their contradictory views. In November 1997 two letters with multiple signatures appeared in the *Jewish Chronicle*: one backed Netanyahu's tough stance; the other, attacking his conduct of the peace talks, was placed by the British Friends of Peace Now, who also demonstrated outside a United Jewish Israel Appeal (UJIA) event addressed by the Israeli premier.

A report by the Institute for Jewish Policy Research (JPR), based on a detailed analysis of its 1995 communal survey, found that the sense of attachment to Israel had weakened among young Jews since the assassination of Yitzhak Rabin in November 1995. Far from being a source of cohesion and consensus, Israel was becoming a source of division.

MAJOR ORGANIZATIONS MERGE

A merger took place in January 1997 between Jewish Continuity, the national fund-raising program for education, and the Joint Israel Appeal (JIA), the community's leading Israel funding body, significantly changing the landscape of Anglo-Jewry's fund-raising. "There will basically be two major organizations, ourselves and Jewish Care," said Brian Kerner, chairman of the board of directors of the new organization.

Efforts to preserve Jewish Continuity as an independent entity failed in June 1996, purportedly due to right-wing Orthodox opposition to its broad, cross-community orientation. Launched amid high hopes in 1993 to promote and strengthen Jewish education, Continuity was plagued by contention. In November 1996 representatives of Continuity and the Joint Israel Appeal (JIA) voted to merge, starting in January 1997.

Officially inaugurated in September 1997, the new body had a new name—the

United Jewish Israel Appeal (UJIA); new leadership—Jonathan Kestenbaum, former director of the Chief Rabbi's Office, who replaced Clive Lawton as chief executive; and a new structure. Instead of its predominantly Israel-oriented activity, UJIA now planned a two-pronged campaign: one would focus on "rescue," continuing support for new immigrants to Israel; the other on "renewal," domestic projects, though retaining Israel as a key element in educational initiatives. Each of the two branches had its own lay and professional officers, both supervised by Kestenbaum.

Funding was adjusted to reflect the two-way split. Half the proceeds of UJIA's 1997 Kol Nidre Appeal supported the immigration to Israel of Jews from the former Soviet Union, and half was allocated to domestic causes, which received only 30 percent in 1996. Operating policy also differed from Continuity's: UJIA planned to fund only selected programs that fit into its overall strategy, rather than make numerous small grants. It would try to work in partnership with existing organizations rather than launch its own projects. Its program emphasized consolidation and development rather than innovation. Lastly, it would work across the whole religious spectrum. "We raise funds across the community," Kestenbaum said. "We will work impartially across the community."

In October 1997 UJIA received its biggest single donation, £1.5 million from the Ashdown Charitable Settlement, earmarked for its leadership program. It will be used to create UJIA Ashdown Fellowships, "the first of their type," said Kestenbaum, "built exclusively for the British community, through British Jewish graduates and with British Jewish money." Also in October it was announced that UJIA's Kol Nidre Appeal had raised over £1 million.

OTHER MATTERS

In November 1996 a merger between Jewish Care and the Brighton and Hove Jewish Home was approved by the Charities Commission. In April 1997 Jewish Care opened a residential home in Finchley, North London, for 120 frail, elderly, infirm, and disabled Jews with an average age of 90. As of June 1997 Jewish Care encompassed 10 charities and 54 centers, with an annual budget of nearly £32 million, according to chairman Michael Levy. In December 1997 chief executive Melvyn Carlowe warned that Care faced a £1.4-million shortfall in its 1998 social-service budget because of cutbacks in local authority spending.

Mergers in the interest of increased efficiency and reduced duplication and waste dominated the communal scene. In July 1996 Manchester's two major social-service organizations, the Jews' Benevolent Society and Jewish Social Services, agreed to merge. In December Norwood Childcare and the Ravenswood Foundation formally merged to form Norwood Ravenswood, with 65 buildings, 6,000 clients, and an £18-million budget. In September 1997 Norwood Ravenswood announced plans to spend over £6 million on a series of pioneering housing projects around London, to provide small, homey accommodation tailored to the needs of individual residents. In April 1997 the B'nai B'rith Housing Society and the JBG Housing Society merged to form the BBJBG Housing Association, the largest provider of sheltered housing in the Jewish community.

In May 1997 the first shelter in England (and in Europe) for battered Jewish women and their children became operational, after a five-year campaign by Jewish Women's Aid.

Efforts on behalf of foreign Jews primarily concentrated on Eastern Europe. World Jewish Relief (WJR) was involved in a number of projects: renovating a Jewish community center in Sofia, Bulgaria; sending aid worth over £400,000 to Jewish communities in former Yugoslavia; raising over £65,000 to provide eye-testing and glasses for impoverished elderly Jews in Odessa in the Ukraine; providing Passover help for Ukrainian Jews in the form of food parcels, and also, in conjunction with the League of Jewish Women, gifts of material goods. In July 1997 WJR announced that it would concentrate its overseas program on Jewish communities in the Ukraine, spending some £400,000 on providing food parcels and, in conjunction with the American Jewish Joint Distribution Committee, building welfare centers in Vinnitsa and Lvov. In December 1997 WJR went a step further, shedding its domestic responsibilities entirely in order to concentrate on specific areas of need among Jews abroad.

Religion

Synagogue membership in the United Kingdom declined over 8 percent in 1996 from 1990 levels, according to a report by the Board of Deputies Community Research Unit. Some 93,684 households belonged to 365 synagogues in 1996, as compared with 102,144 members and 356 synagogues in 1990. Membership loss mainly occurred in the mainstream Orthodox (United Synagogue) sector, which accounted for 61 percent of total membership in 1996. Other groupings either increased or were stable. Some two-thirds of total synagogue membership belonged to 193 Greater London synagogues.

In January 1997 seven United Synagogue (US) synagogues were seeking full-time rabbis. In June 1997, after the US's budget of £220,000 for the chief rabbinate was cut by £50,000, it was announced that Chief Rabbi Jonathan Sacks would preach part-time at the Western-Marble Arch Synagogue, Central London. Payment for his services would be made directly to the Chief Rabbi's Office.

Relations between Orthodox and Progressive Jews hit a new low in August 1996 following the death of Rabbi Hugo Gryn, president of the Reform Synagogues of Great Britain (RSGB), senior rabbi of West London Synagogue, a Holocaust survivor, and a nationally respected television personality. After new US president Elkan Levy was criticized by RSGB executive director Rabbi Tony Bayfield for lack of Orthodox representation at Gryn's funeral, Levy apologized; he paid tribute to Gryn's "unique contribution" to communal life and represented the US at a packed memorial service for Gryn in December 1996. But Chief Rabbi

Jonathan Sacks continued to ride an unhappy line between the left and right wings of his constituency. Hoping to appease the Progressives, Sacks agreed to attend a memorial meeting for Gryn in February 1997, organized by the Board of Deputies and the Council of Christians and Jews (CCJ). This brought an accusation of *"hillul Hashem"* (profaning God's name) from *Dayan* Yisroel Lichtenstein, head of the Federation of Synagogues' Bet Din (rabbinic court).

Notwithstanding, Sacks attended the meeting in his role as a CCJ president, praising Gryn without referring to his rabbinic status. Hopes of communal unity evaporated in March 1997 when the *Jewish Chronicle* leaked a letter from Sacks to *Dayan* Chanoch Padwa, head of the Union of Orthodox Hebrew Congregations (an umbrella body of right-wing communities), describing Gryn as one of "those who destroy the faith" and Reform as "a false grouping." Progressive leaders knew, wrote Sacks, that they had "no enemy and opponent equal to the Chief Rabbi." In May Reform, Liberal, and Masorti leaders called on CCJ to appoint a second Jewish president alongside Sacks and its five Christian presidents. It also invited the US to discuss establishing a representative structure that would be a "fair, effective and a truthful reflection of our community." Although there was no official response to this request, it was announced in June that US, Progressive, and Conservative leaders would hold informal discussions to try to heal the rift over the chief rabbi's role.

In June 1996 all communal factions concerned with the plight of *agunot* ("chained women" whose husbands refuse them a religious divorce) welcomed the passage by the House of Commons of the Family Law Bill, which contains a clause enabling a spouse to ask a judge to defer granting a civil divorce until a *get* (religious divorce) is provided. The same month it was reported that of 80 couples seeking authorization from the Chief Rabbi's Office to marry in May and June, 33 signed the Prenuptial Agreement (PNA) introduced in April. A year later, in April 1997, the Union of Liberal and Progressive Synagogues (ULPS) introduced a document resembling a *get*, called *Sefer Keritut* (document of release), to meet "people's growing desire to have some sort of ceremony to mark the end of their marriage," said ULPS rabbinic board chairman Rabbi Harry Jacobi.

Although the government had agreed in September 1994 to permit Britain's first *eruv* (Sabbath boundary marker) in North-West London, subsequent legal challenges prevented implementation. In August 1996 a prestigious Leverhulme Trust grant enabled Prof. David Cesarani to undertake a study of the controversy.

In September 1996 Reform rabbi Elizabeth Sarah had to cancel a decision to officiate at a Jewish lesbian wedding. Her support for such ceremonies did not reflect RSGB policy, Rabbi Bayfield stressed. In March 1997 Rabbi Sarah resigned as RSGB program director. In June, a working group set up by RSGB's Assembly of Rabbis to examine the question of same-sex commitment ceremonies in relation to Jewish tradition deferred its findings to 1998; in August, the assembly set up a Responsa Committee to examine controversial issues and advise on policy.

In July 1996 Blooms, Britain's leading kosher food company, sold its manufacturing rights to Gilberts Kosher Foods after a deal with Greenspan Continental Meats fell through. In November a High Court judge found against managing director Michael Bloom in proceedings he initiated for a legal review of the London Bet Din's decision to revoke his *kashrut* license in December 1995.

In the wake of the scare over "mad cow disease" (BSE) and a concomitant 45-percent drop in kosher beef consumption, in July 1996 the London Board for Shechitah, London's main kosher meat supplier, dismissed 10 of its 45-strong workforce. At the same time, after consulting its rabbinic authorities, the board opposed the decision of Manchester's Kashrus Authority to license the import of frozen Argentinian beef.

In September 1996 Radlett and Bushey Reform Synagogue in Hertfordshire joined the increasing number of United Kingdom Progressive congregations offering support to emerging communities in the former Soviet Union, when it twinned with the Menorah community of Grodno in Belarus and organized a visit by its members to Belarus in November 1997. In February 1997 Andrew Goldstein, rabbi of Northwood and Pinner Liberal Synagogue, was appointed honorary rabbinic adviser to Bejt Simcha congregation in Prague.

Education

News that Carmel College, Britain's only Jewish boarding school, located in Wallingford, Oxfordshire, was to close in July 1997 shocked the community. Pleading falling enrollment and mounting debts, the school's governors planned to sell the 80-acre riverside campus to property developers. Indignant parents mobilized into a "Save Carmel College Campaign" (SCCC), but in July Carmel's governors rejected the group's plan to keep the school open. In August the site was sold for £4 million to the Sephardic Exilarch Foundation, which, said founder-trustee Naim Dongoor, would use it for communal, notably educational, purposes.

In July 1997 Chief Rabbi Sacks announced a review of the future of Jews' College, the Orthodox educational and rabbinic training center in London. Without a more clearly defined role, he said, it would be difficult to raise the college's annual budget of £500,000.

Jewish studies at universities expanded. In June 1996 the School of Oriental and African Studies (SOAS) announced plans to teach Yiddish, with instructors supplied by the Oxford Institute for Yiddish Studies. In October 1996 the Oxford Centre for Hebrew and Jewish Studies launched a £5-million appeal to mark its silver jubilee. The same month, a center for Jewish studies was launched at Leeds University. In June 1997 the University of Wales established a Judaism chair and appointed Progressive rabbi Dan Cohn-Sherbok as its first incumbent. In August 1997 Mark Geller, professor of Semitic studies at University College, London (UCL) was appointed Jewish Chronicle Professor of Jewish Studies at UCL. The same month Bernard Jackson, Queen Victoria Professor of Law at Liverpool University, was appointed to the Alliance Chair in Modern Jewish Studies at Manchester University.

In January 1997 eminent Yiddishist Dovid Katz left his job as research director of the Oxford Institute for Yiddish Studies, which he co-founded in 1994, after a bitter split with the Oxford Centre for Hebrew and Jewish Studies. In August Katz took the institute to an industrial tribunal, claiming racial discrimination and unfair dismissal, but withdrew his plea during the hearing.

Publications

Binjamin Wilkomirski, a Swiss-based professional musician, won the £4,000 *Jewish Quarterly* award for nonfiction in 1997 for *Fragments, Memories of a Childhood, 1939-1948*. The fiction award was divided between W.G. Sebald for *The Emigrants* and Clive Sinclair for *The Lady with the Laptop*, a collection of short stories.

New works of poetry included *The Flying Bosnian* by Miroslav Jancic; *The Skin Off Your Back* by Michael Rosin; *Rhymes at Midnight* by Fran Landesman; *Odd Mercy* by Gerald Stern; *Selected and New Poems 1980-1997* by Lotte Kramer; *Sugar-Paper Blue* by Ruth Fainlight; *Poems* and *Adolphe 1920* by John Rodker; *Poems* by Ellis Sopher; *Erotika or the Banquet of Love* by Gordon Jackson; *The POW! Anthology* edited by Michael Horovitz and Inge Elsa Laird; and *Daylight* by Elaine Feinstein. Jon Silkin published *The Life of Metrical and Free Verse in 20th-Century Poetry*; and two books appeared on Hugh Manning: *Hugh Manning: Poet and Humanist* by Ivan Savidge, and the *Selected Poetry of Hugh Manning*.

Books on religious subjects included *1,001 Questions and Answers on Rosh Hashanah and Yom Kippur* by Rabbi Dr Jeffrey Cohen; *The Politics of Hope* by Chief Rabbi Dr. Jonathan Sacks; *Beyond the Graven Image* by Lionel Kochan; and *Fountain of Blessings* by *Dayan* Pinchas Toledano, devoted to laws concerning Shabbat, festivals, and the High Holy Days, the second volume in his *Code of Jewish Law* series. *Mourning Becomes the Law* by Gillian Rose is a work of philosophy.

Books on Zionism included *Western Jewry and the Zionist Project, 1914-1933* by Michael Berkowitz; and *Theodor Herzl and the Zionist Dream* by Julius H. Schoeps.

Works on the Hebrew and Yiddish language and literature included *A History of the Hebrew Language* by Angel Saenz-Badillos; Joseph Perl's *Revealer of Secrets*, possibly the first Hebrew novel, translated and edited by Dov Taylor; *New Women's Writing from Israel*, edited by Risa Domb; and *The Oxford Book of Hebrew Short Stories*, edited by Glenda Abramson. Dovid Katz published *Oxford Yiddish III*.

Some new studies of anti-Semitism were *East London for Mosley: The British*

Union of Fascists in East London and South-West Essex (1933-1940) by Thomas P. Linehan; *A Pariah People: The Anthropology of Antisemitism* by Hyam Maccoby; and *The Accused: The Dreyfus Trilogy* by George R. Whyte.

Works of autobiography and biography included *Accidental Journey: A Cambridge Internee's Memoir of World War II* by Mark Lynton; *Life in Three Cities* by Fred S.Worms; *A Very British Subject* by Barnet Litvinoff; *I Remember, I Remember Chaplin in Brick Lane* by Michael Chapman; and *Odyssey of a Jewish Sailor* by F. Ashe Lincoln.

The corpus of Holocaust literature continued to expand. Survivors' accounts included *The Children Accuse,* edited by Maria Hochberg-Marianska and Noe Gruss; *Lost in Labyrinth of Red Tape* by Armin Schmid and Renate Schmid; *The Darkest Chapter* by David Ben-Dor; and *The Diary of Dawid Sierakowiak: Five Notebooks from the Lodz Ghetto,* translated by Kamil Turowski, edited by Alan Adelson. *The War After: Living with the Holocaust,* is by Anne Karpf, the daughter of Holocaust survivors; *The Boys* by Martin Gilbert, is about Holocaust survivors whom the CBF brought to England in 1945. Other works are *Nazi Germany and British Guilt* by Cecil Genese; *The Chosen People: The Story of the "222 Transport" from Bergen-Belsen to Palestine* by A.N. Oppenheim; *Blood Money: The Swiss, the Nazis and the Looted Billions* by Tom Bower; *Murder in Our Midst: The Holocaust, Industrial Killing and Representation* by Omer Bartov; *Alfred Wiener and the Making of the Holocaust Library* by Ben Barkow; and *The Myth of Rescue: Why the Democracies Could Not Have Saved More Jews from the Nazis* by William D. Rubinstein. *Belsen in History and Memory* by Jo Reilly, David Cesarani, Tony Kushner, and Colin Richmond is a collection of papers given at a conference in 1995 to commemorate the liberation of the concentration camp.

Historical works included *The Kidnapping of Edgardo Mortara* by David Kertzer; *British Policy and the Refugees, 1933-1941* by Yvonne Kapp and Margaret Mynatt; *Those Wonderful Women in Black: The Story of the Women's Campaign* by Daphne Gerlis; *A History of the Jews in the English-Speaking World: Great Britain* by W. D.Rubinstein; *A World Apart: The Story of the Chasidim in Britain,* by Rabbi Harry Rabinowicz; and *The Jews of Lithuania* by Masha Greenbaum. *Lions of Judah* by John Colvin contains accounts of Jewish fighters or fighting Jews.

New works of fiction included *The Cast Iron Shore* by Linda Grant; *My Affair with Stalin* by Simon Sebag Montefiore; *The Slow Mirror and other Stories: New Fiction by Jewish Writers,* edited by Sonja Lyndon and Sylvia Paskin; *The Days of Miracles and Wonders* by Simon Louvish; *Visitors* by Anita Brookner; and *The Knot* by Eva Figes.

Among new books on Israel were *Germany and Israel: Moral Debt and National Interest* by George Lavy; *Sharing the Promised Land: An Interwoven Tale of Israelis and Palestinians* by Dilip Hiro; and *War and Peace in the Middle East: A Concise History* by Avi Shlaim.

New works of literary criticism included *Realism, Caricature and Bias: The Fic-*

tion of Mendele Mocher Sefarim by David Aberbach; *Seriously Funny* by Howard Jacobson, a dissection of comedy through the ages; *Between "Race" and Culture: Representations of "the Jew" in English and American Literature*, a series of essays edited by Bryan Cheyette; and *A Home Within: Varieties of Jewish Expression in Modern Fiction* by Leon Yudkin. In *The Birth of Shylock and the Death of Zero Mostel*, Arnold Wesker describes the trials and tribulations of trying to stage his play.

Personalia

Peerages were awarded to advertising tycoon Maurice Saatchi, responsible for some Tory campaign material; Sir Peter Levene, Prime Minister Major's adviser on efficiency and effectiveness; Michael Levy, Jewish Care chairman and a key Labor Party fund-raiser; Greville Janner, former Labor MP; film producer Sir David Puttnam; Andrew Stone, Marks and Spencer joint managing director; Sir Anthony Jacobs, chairman of the Liberal Democrats' federal executive; and Michael Montague, former English Tourist Board chairman. Knighthoods went to Guenter Treitel, Oxford University's Vinerian Professor of Law; Jack Baer, former chairman of the Society of London Art Dealers, now a member of the Museums and Galleries Commission; physicist Michael Berry, Bristol University research professor; Jeremy Isaacs, for services to broadcasting and the arts; Judge Stephen Tumim for his work as chief inspector of prisons; Prof. David Goldberg, director of research and development at the Maudsley Hospital's Institute of Psychiatry; and former foreign secretary Malcolm Rifkind. Richard "Dickie" Arbiter, commercial radio court correspondent, was appointed Lieutenant of the Royal Victorian Order (LVO), a personal honor from the Queen.

Prominent British Jews who died in the second half of 1996 included Barnet Litvinoff, author, who edited Chaim Weizmann's writings, in London, in June, aged 78; Peter Montefiore Samuel, Viscount Bearsted, philanthropist, in London, in June, aged 84; Rabbi Robert Shafritz, minister of Wimbledon Reform Synagogue, in London in July, aged 51; Alfred Marks, comedian, in London, in July, aged 75; *Dayan* Joseph Apfel, senior member of Leeds Bet Din, in Leeds, in August, aged 87; Prof. Albert Neuberger, internationally renowned biochemist and Zionist, in London, in August, aged 88; Abram Games, graphic designer, in London, in August, aged 82; Louis Mindel, grand old man of the United Synagogue, in London, in August, aged 103; Hugo Gryn, Holocaust survivor and nationally acclaimed and respected Reform rabbi, in London, in August, aged 66; George Levy, antiques dealer and chairman of the Jewish Museum executive committee, in London, in September, aged 69; Jacob Gewirtz, former executive director of the Board of Deputies defense and group relations committee, in London, in September, aged 70; Sylvia Daiches Raphael, French scholar and translator, in Kingston, Surrey, in October, aged 82; Berthold Goldschmidt, musician, in London, in October, aged 93; Robert Carvalho, pillar of London's Sephardic community, in London, in October, aged 89; Geoffrey, Lord Finsberg, former Tory minister, in Stockholm, in October, aged 70; Gerda Charles, novelist, in London in November, aged 81; S. Herbert Frankel, economist, in Oxford, in December, aged 93; Alma Baroness Birk, one-time Labor minister, in London, in December, aged 79; Raphael Samuel, English social historian, in London, in December, aged 62; Sefton David Temkin, Jewish historian, in Manchester, in December, aged 79; and Arthur Jacobs, musicologist, in Oxford, in December, aged 74.

British Jews who died in 1997 included Nora Beloff, journalist, in London, in February, aged 78; Abraham Marks, Board of Deputies secretary 1966-1976, in London, in February, aged 74; David Segal, Yiddish actor, in London, in February, aged 95; Fred Zinnemann, film director, in London, in March, aged 89; Jack Wolkind, author of the working party report on the Board of Deputies, in London, in March, aged 77; Sydney Bunt, major worker for Jewish youth, in London, in March, aged 71; Peter Murray, Lord Taylor of Gosforth, only the second Jew to be Lord Chief Justice of England, in London, in April, aged 66; Schneier Levenberg, former London Jewish Agency representative, in London, in May, aged 90; Maurice Joseph Golomb, US's burial minister, in London, in May, aged 65; Victor Lucas, communal leader and US president 1984-87, in London, in May, aged 80; Rabbi Pesach Braceiner, *dayan* of the Federation of Synagogues Bet Din, in London, in July, aged 86; Rabbi Avraham Unterman, in London, in August, aged 87; Henry Kotlowski, prominent Zionist and communal figure, in London, in September, aged 90; Aron Dov Sufrin, Lubavitch education director, in London, in September, aged 67; Joseph Dollinger, cantor, in London, in September, aged 90; Reuben Goldberg, left-wing opponent of racism, in London, in October, aged 45; David Pela, former managing and deputy editor of the *Jewish Chronicle*, in London, in October, aged 78; Barry Marcus, director, Stepney Jewish community center, in London, in October, aged 54; Wilfred Josephs, composer, in London, in November, aged 70; Harry, Lord Kissin of Camden, patron of Israeli arts, in London, in November, aged 85; Jon Silkin, poet, in Newcastle-upon-Tyne, in November, aged 66; Sir Isaiah Berlin, internationally renowned scholar and thinker, in Oxford, in November, aged 88.

MIRIAM & LIONEL KOCHAN

France

National Affairs

FRANCE'S TROUBLING SOCIAL situation and political malaise persisted throughout the second half of 1996 and 1997, despite a dramatic election upset in May–June 1997. France had been in the grip of doubt and uncertainty for several years. Neither the left nor the right offered simple solutions to unemployment, international competition, immigration, and urban violence—all of which contributed to a faltering sense of national identity. The National Front (NF), the far-right party led by Jean-Marie Le Pen, took advantage of the situation by trying to attract dissatisfied voters and presenting itself as an "alternative" to the two main political streams. It talked about defending "national values," rejected "globalization," and was hostile toward immigrants.

President Jacques Chirac, a man of the right, supported by a right-wing majority in the National Assembly and a government led by Prime Minister Alain Juppé, concentrated on restructuring public finances, not on fighting social breakdown. While these measures were considered essential in the context of the integration of European economies, citizens whose primary concerns centered on social problems were disappointed, and the acclaim that greeted the right on taking office was short-lived. The personal style of the prime minister, whose culture and intelligence sometimes went hand in hand with a lack of tolerance for the weaknesses of others, did not add to the government's popularity.

The NF kept working to solidify its position, focusing especially on infiltrating trade unions and organizations and slowly developing a broader base. Previously, "Le Pen-ism" had been a far-right ideology limited to small groups of extremists. Now, however, there was also a new "reactionary Le Pen-ism" prevailing among people who felt disappointed by a right they deemed too modern, as well as a "leftish Le Pen-ism" appealing to people dissatisfied on social issues who found no outlet for their views in the parties on the left.

On February 9, 1997, the NF won the municipal election in Vitrolles, a city with a population of 35,000 in the south of France, near Marseille. The new mayor of Vitrolles was Catherine Mégret, wife of the party's delegate-general and second most important figure, Bruno Mégret. In reality Mme. Mégret was a figurehead, a stand-in for her husband, whose candidacy had been invalidated because of technical infractions committed during the previous election. This victory was a major success for Bruno Mégret, who, despite some internal opposition, was considered the most likely person to eventually succeed Jean-Marie Le Pen at the head of the NF.

The National Front's election victories along with public debates about immigration issues revealed a deep-seated uneasiness in French politics, which the Juppé government was not able to dispel. Nevertheless, people were surprised when President Chirac announced in April 1997 that he was exercising his constitutional right to dissolve the National Assembly and hold new legislative elections. Although elections were not required until the following year, the president hoped a new legislative mandate would breathe new life into his policies and make it possible for the government to conduct some long-term planning.

The result was catastrophic. In the first round of voting on May 25, the right received 36 percent of the vote as against 44 percent for parties from the left. This was the right's weakest showing since Charles de Gaulle established the Fifth Republic in 1958. In the end, voters in the second round on June 1 elected a National Assembly with a clear majority from the left: 320 deputies from the left compared to 256 from the right and the NF. As a result, Chirac nominated the leader of the Socialist Party, Lionel Jospin, as prime minister. The new government contained a large majority of Socialists, plus three Communist ministers and some representatives of other smaller parties. Once again, as had occurred twice during François Mitterrand's presidency, France was governed under a "cohabitation" arrangement in which power was shared between the popularly elected president and the prime minister.

The Jewish community counted both President Chirac, a Catholic, and Prime Minister Jospin, a Protestant, as genuine friends. No one could doubt their sincere determination to combat all forms of racism and anti-Semitism. The only question mark remained the National Front and its impact on the political situation.

Although some politicians foresaw an alliance of the NF and the parliamentary right, the leaders of the two main right-wing political parties, the Rally for the Republic (RPR) and the Union for French Democracy (UDF), categorically maintained their opposition to such an arrangement. On August 30, 1997, *Le Monde* quoted the president of the RPR, Philippe Séguin, as saying, "As long as I am with the party, there will be no alliance with the National Front." And the secretary-general of the UDF, Claude Goasguen, told the Jewish monthly *L'Arche* in November 1997, "There will never be an alliance between the UDF and RPR with the NF."

Still, by the late 1990s, the National Front, formerly relegated to the margins of political life, had become a force to be reckoned with, even though it was still publicly rejected by majority opinion in the other parties. More disquieting than its actual direct influence was the "Le Pen-ization of thought"—the increasing importance given by politicians and parties that ostensibly opposed the NF to certain themes championed by that party, specifically, an attempt to link immigrants with urban crime and loss of jobs, a call for fighting (legal or illegal) immigration and expelling unwelcome immigrants, and a tendency to limit the rights of foreigners living in France.

Israel and the Middle East

The changes that occurred in the domestic arena in 1997 did not affect France's relations with Israel, where continuity was the rule. This was true partly because Jacques Chirac, Alain Juppé, and Lionel Jospin were all longtime, genuine friends of Israel, although, at least in Chirac's case, there was also a desire to keep close to the Arab world. In addition, foreign policy fell within the president's "special domain," where the president is considered personally responsible for action, and the prime minister — from whatever party — is expected to work in harmony with the president.

The French diplomatic corps continued to behave toward Benjamin Netanyahu's government with a combination of courtesy and reserve. France's legislators, on the left and on the right, repeatedly stressed their ongoing support for the Israeli-Palestinian peace process as defined by the terms of the Oslo agreement. In this regard, the actions of the Israeli government elicited increasing impatience from French politicians, sometimes bordering on — or even crossing the line into — irritation.

A revealing incident occurred during Jacques Chirac's visit to Jerusalem on October 22, 1996. While walking in East Jerusalem, the French president expressed an interest in conversing with some Arabs on the street. Israeli security personnel, citing strict instructions regarding his personal protection, prevented him from making any such contact. Chirac was furious. "What do you want?" he yelled at the person in charge of security. "Do you want me to get back on the plane? This is a provocation." Members of the president's entourage filed an official complaint with the Israeli authorities, who apologized. The incident was declared closed before Chirac returned to France, but it gave him an opportunity to express his personal views, according to which "Jerusalem should remain an open city — open to Christians from Palestine as well as Christians from all over the world; open to all religions, naturally."

The president of the Representative Council of Jewish Institutions of France (CRIF, Conseil Représentatif des Institutions Juives de France), Henri Hajdenberg, who accompanied the French president on his visit, made a declaration on their return in which his discomfort showed through: "I personally do not doubt Jacques Chirac's intentions, but his approach was misguided. It was decided to create a diplomatic spectacle to make France's presence felt in the Middle East. It is a risky type of diplomacy, because once this kind of incident occurs, it can take on huge proportions" (*Le Monde,* October 27, 1996). "Showing the French flag in the Middle East" is in fact one of the most problematic aspects of what has been called for many years "France's Arab policy." According to this doctrine, it is essential that France maintain a special relationship with certain Arab countries based on, among other factors, local use of the French language, trade, military sales, and political influence.

In late 1997 Prime Minister Jospin used two separate occasions to express his feelings about Israel. On November 29 he attended CRIF's annual dinner, as is the custom for French prime ministers. The date had been chosen deliberately, and in his remarks Jospin spoke of the 1947 United Nations decision to partition Palestine and create a Jewish state. While recalling his "long-standing and vigorous support for Israel," he also commented on his "concerns about the policies Israel's leaders are currently pursuing."

On December 23, in an unprecedented gesture, Jospin received Israeli ambassador Avi Pazner, the diplomatic corps (including U.S. ambassador Felix Rohatyn), and representatives of France's Jewish community in his official residence at the Hôtel Matignon, to mark the start of Israel's 50th anniversary celebrations. After noting that it was the eve of Hanukkah (although there was no candlelighting, out of respect for the secular character of the state), Jospin referred to the birth of Israel as a "tremendous and wonderful lesson of hope." He emphasized "the right of the people of Israel to make their homeland in a place with which they have never ceased to have a unique connection." He added, "For France, the birth of Israel represented first and foremost the correction of a terrible injustice begun at the time of the Roman Empire, perpetuated all through European history and brought to a horrible climax with the Holocaust— especially since this was a horror in which French people, and the regime in charge at the time, played their part." Then the prime minister affirmed, "France hopes that the government of Israel, building on the openings created at Madrid and Oslo, will resolutely continue negotiations with Yasir Arafat on the future of the occupied territories."

The Jewish community focused on the first part of Jospin's remarks, notable for their warmth and sympathy. In its report, Agence France-Presse emphasized the second part of the speech, which expressed concerns shared by all French leaders regarding the situation in the Middle East. Both parts accurately expressed the reality of Franco-Israeli relations.

Anti-Semitism and Racism

According to most observers, when National Front leader Jean-Marie Le Pen talked about his favorite targets, immigrants and Jews, his remarks not only reflected his personal views but were also part of a strategic plan. Thus, on August 30, 1996, Le Pen declared, "Yes, I believe in the inequality of the races, yes of course, it's obvious. All of history demonstrates this." He was without a doubt expressing his deep personal conviction, but he was also sending a signal to the far-right activists who were the basis of his movement and who worried that their message would be watered down in the quest for a wider following. And he was discouraging those "tacticians" tempted by the idea of an alliance between the far right and the traditional right wing in France. For all that, this racist rhetoric was not translated into action. Racially motivated attacks remained rare in France, and they were almost never attributed to NF militants.

In the period under review, two racially motivated murder cases were tried in court, more than two years after the murders took place. Three young men were accused of throwing an immigrant from Mali into a Paris canal on July 13, 1994; at the trial in Paris in November 1997, one of the three was found not guilty, one was given a suspended prison sentence, and one was condemned to 12 years in prison. In the second case, two young men were convicted of having pushed an Arab immigrant into the harbor at Le Havre, where he drowned on April 18, 1995. One of the two culprits flew to his native Portugal, where he was put on trial in July 1997; the other underwent trial in Paris in December 1997. Both were condemned to 18 years in prison. In both cases the perpetrators were on the margins of society, traveling in the same circles as the "skinheads" and combining a taste for violence with hatred of blacks and Arabs.

Although these were isolated events, and most of the actual violence came from juvenile delinquents, there was nevertheless a clear connection between them and the climate of intercommunal tension that had its epicenter in "difficult" neighborhoods where immigrant populations coexisted as best they could with "old stock French." The tension was unquestionably linked to the economic crisis from which the country had not yet completely emerged, but it also reflected the difficulties France had experienced in absorbing an unprecedented wave of immigrants, primarily from Africa and predominantly Muslim.

In a poll conducted in September 1997 by SOFRES, France's leading market and opinion research organization, for the weekly *Figaro Magazine,* 85 percent said that immigration constituted a "very important" or "fairly important" problem; 50 percent felt that France should "not allow new immigrants into France," and another 15 percent wanted to "return a substantial number of immigrants to their home countries." Most people (58 percent compared with 36 percent) had the impression that immigrants made "little effort" or "no effort at all" to assimilate, although a small plurality (50 percent compared with 43 percent) believed that "most immigrants living in France can be integrated into French society."

While many French perceived the problem as one of cultural rather than racial differences, in some quarters a hostile attitude toward immigration translated into racist behavior. Jean-Marie Le Pen's comments on the "inequality of the races," mentioned above, were surely premeditated. By contrast, those of the new NF mayor of Vitrolles, Catherine Mégret, appear to have been spontaneous. In an interview with the German newspaper *Berliner Zeitung,* on February 21, 1997, she attributed insecurity in Vitrolles to residents of the city who came from North Africa and announced her intention to encourage them to leave. Her remarks led to legal action, and in September 1997 a court in Aix-en-Provence handed out a three-month suspended prison sentence to Mme. Mégret (whose father is Jewish) for "complicity in provoking racial hatred." She refused to retract her words, however, arguing that they belonged in the realm of "public debate and political opinions."

Episodes such as this, while perhaps contributing to the NF's political isolation, had very little effect on its sympathizers. On September 10, 1996, Prime Minister Juppé accused Le Pen of being "racist, anti-Semitic and xenophobic." The next month his minister of justice, Jacques Toubon, prepared a bill (which ultimately was never brought to a vote in the National Assembly) significantly strengthening France's legislation against racist speech. None of this, however, appeared to seriously threaten the NF. Le Pen and his associates typically responded to such efforts by denouncing the "media lynching" of which they were victims.

The NF's stance toward Jews illustrates the gap between the electoral rhetoric and its stronger, more "hard-line" language, reserved for its activists. According to a poll conducted by SOFRES for RTL radio, the leading commercial network, and Le Monde in March 1997, 25 percent of all French people, and 88 percent of those who identified themselves as potential NF voters, approved of Le Pen's comments about immigrants. On the other hand, Le Pen's denunciation of "Jewish influence over political life in France" received approval from only 4 percent of all French people and met with disapproval from 84 percent of the population. Among potential NF voters, only 19 percent agreed with Le Pen on this issue, compared with 63 percent who did not. Even among NF activists, 33 percent agreed with their leader's comments about Jews while 50 percent did not. These results indicated that rhetoric directly addressing the issue of immigration was "politically useful," while more ideologically based racism, such as attacks on Jews, did not go over well, even among people close to the NF.

While the far right's anti-Jewish preoccupation was usually only voiced internally in activist circles, occasionally it was expressed in action. One such occasion was the desecration of the Carpentras cemetery, an incident that was finally brought to a close in 1997 after occupying public attention for seven years.

It began on May 10, 1990, when someone discovered 34 vandalized graves in the Jewish cemetery of Carpentras, a city in the south of France. The vandals had exhumed the body of a man who had recently been buried, Félix Germon, and set up his body as if it were impaled. Emotions ran high. On May 14, more than 200,000 people, including President Mitterrand, marched silently in Paris to protest the act. The minister of the interior, Pierre Joxe, blamed the incident on "racism, anti-Semitism and intolerance," thus clearly pointing to the National Front. In response, Le Pen denounced what he called "an attack organized from on high."

The investigation dragged on far too long. Rumors suggested that the incident involved young people from well-to-do Carpentras families who had engaged in a macabre game, with no political agenda. The NF continued to denounce what it called a frame-up designed to hurt it. On November 11, 1995, NF activists marched in Carpentras to demand an apology for what Le Pen called a "state lie."

On July 30, 1996, however, a former militant from a far-right group—separate from the NF—made a spontaneous confession that led to the arrest of three other young people who moved in the same circles. The four vandals, whose profiles closely matched those of the other racist aggressors described earlier, admitted that their action had been motivated by anti-Semitism. Yannick Garnier, the first to repent, declared in court, "I was a racist and anti-Semite because I needed a scapegoat. Since then I have made peace with myself." The four were tried in Marseille in March 1997 and given prison sentences ranging from 20 months to two years.

The primary current manifestation of anti-Semitism in France was Holocaust denial. Its main representative was Robert Faurisson, a former professor of literature who called the Jewish Holocaust a "fiction." Use of Holocaust denial to spread anti-Semitic messages under the guise of historical research had led to legislative measures, despite some reservations about this course of action. The Gayssot Law of July 13, 1990 (named for its author, a Communist deputy and as of 1997 a minister in the Jospin government), defined the "questioning of crimes against humanity"—that is, Holocaust denial—as itself a crime.

Several cases of "questioning of crimes against humanity" were dealt with in the courts in recent years. The writer Roger Garaudy was prosecuted for his 1995 book *Les mythes fondateurs de la politique israélienne* (The Founding Myths of Israeli Politics), as was Robert Faurisson for a text called "Les visions cornues de l' 'Holocauste' " (Horned Visions of the "Holocaust"), distributed on the Internet in 1997 by an American service provider. In April 1997 a mathematics professor in a country high school, who had already been found guilty of distributing tracts denying the reality of the Holocaust, was barred from teaching in a public institution because of his denial activities.

On December 5, 1997, it was Jean-Marie Le Pen's turn to broach this subject during a press conference in Munich, Germany. "I say and I will say again at the risk of being sacrilegious," the NF leader affirmed, "that the gas chambers are simply a historical detail of the Second World War." And he added, "There is nothing dismissive or contemptuous in these words. If you take a 1,000-page book about the Second World War, which led to 50 million deaths, the concentration camps will take up two pages and the gas chambers 10 to 15 lines. That is what's called a detail."

These remarks were not impromptu. They were an almost word-for-word repetition of a declaration he had made a few months earlier to a special correspondent for the *New Yorker.* In fact, Le Pen had used the characterization of the gas chambers as a "detail" as far back as September 1987. At the time, several organizations brought him before a civil court (the Gayssot Law was not yet on the books), which ordered him to pay damages along with the cost of publishing the judgment in the newspapers.

Again after his Munich speech, organizations brought complaints to civil court, and on December 26, Le Pen was ordered to pay symbolic damages along with 300,000 francs ($50,000) to publish the decision. Criminal proceedings were also brought against Le Pen under the Gayssot Law. Once again, the political commentators questioned the NF leader's motives: simple repetition of a strongly held belief, or deliberate provocation to reaffirm his party's hard-line stance?

A booby-trapped package was sent to the *Jewish Tribune* on December 4, 1996. No one knows whether the package, which was defused before it could go off, was sent by an Islamic group (as a letter sent later seemed to indicate) or by the far right.

In December 1997 the trial of Illitch Ramirez Sanchez, alias Carlos, came to an end. Carlos, a "defender of the Palestinian cause" who was responsible for several assassinations around the world, was charged with the murder of three men in Paris in 1975. Before being sentenced to life in prison, he embarked on an incoherent monologue that combined an attack on "the Zionists" with a tribute (which would not be out of place in a National Front document) to "the true France that has lost its voice." It was an opportune reminder of the links that had always existed between the anti-Zionism of the ultra-left and the most traditional forms of anti-Semitism.

Holocaust-Related Matters

In July 1996 a commission chaired by historian René Rémond reported its findings on the "Jewish file" that had been found in the archives of the Ministry of Veterans Affairs in 1991. The commission had been appointed to perform two tasks: to determine the nature and origins of the file and to recommend what should be done with it.

With respect to the file's origins, experts concluded that it was actually a hybrid dossier, put together during the German occupation. The dossier contained excerpts from the general census of the Jewish population carried out at the time, along with lists of people interned in camps awaiting deportation to Germany. A majority on the commission recommended that the file be transferred to the National Archives. But the president of the Central Consistory (the central Jewish religious organization), Jean Kahn, wanted to see it at the Center for Contemporary Jewish Documentation, the CDJC (Centre de Documentation Juive Contemporaine), a Jewish institution in Paris devoted to study of the Holocaust. In October President Chirac decided in favor of Kahn. The file, now a symbol of the French administration's collaboration in Nazi persecution of Jews, would be given to the CDJC, to be housed in the Memorial to the Unknown Jewish Martyr in Paris, which stands in the CDJC building, in a section placed under the authority of the National Archives.

The episode highlighted the discrepancies between the memory of the war held by the general French population and that of French Jews. Half a century after the events in question, the issues remained unresolved. Pieces of information that were previously ignored or forgotten were only beginning to surface. Most recently, questions were being raised about the fate of Jewish property that was confiscated between 1940 and 1944, either by the Germans or by the French. Of the roughly 300,000 Jews living in France at the time, some 75,000, or 25 percent, disappeared in the Holocaust, and the process of restitution that followed the liberation was far from systematic. This is why, as a result of information published in Brigitte Vital-Durand's 1996 book *Domaine privé* (Private Domain) and in response to public questioning, the city of Paris established a commission of inquiry to study the history of some buildings inherited by the city after the war.

Art constituted another area of concern. During the four years that they occupied France, the Germans virtually plundered the country's museums and private collections. At the time there was also an "art market" where one could obtain works stolen from Jews or sold by Jews at artificially low prices because of their situation. Some restitution was later made, but the journalist Hector Feliciano demonstrated in his 1995 book *Le musée disparu* (The Vanished Museum) that national museums still held stolen works. The resulting debates, which continued through 1996, only intensified the prevailing distress.

Subsequently, additional questions were raised, such as the fate of businesses that were "Aryanized" by the pro-German Vichy government led by Marshal Pétain or the status of Jewish bank accounts regarded as heirless by French banking officials.

While many of these issues were addressed after liberation, doubts persisted as to how open and thorough the investigations actually were. That is why, in early 1997, in response to a demand by CRIF, Prime Minister Alain Juppé established a "working group" on the plundering of Jewish property by the Nazis and the Vichy regime. He appointed Jean Mattéoli, president of the Economic and Social Council, an official advisory body, to lead the group. A 74-year-old former member of the Resistance, Mattéoli was well respected and widely viewed as independent. Over the course of the year, other subjects were added to the group's agenda, most notably the fate of gold recovered by France and complaints filed in New York against French banks.

All of this was followed closely by Jewish leaders in France—so much so that the national press largely began to echo the Jewish point of view in these matters. But statements made by the president of the Jewish Agency, Avraham Burg, elicited active protests. Burg declared that the "next target" of Jewish organizations on the question of restitution would be France itself, even if that meant "carrying on regardless of reservations on the part of the French Jewish community, which fears stirring up passions and anti-Semitism" (*Journal de Genève et Gazette de Lausanne,* December 22, 1997). The president of CRIF, Henri Hajdenberg, immediately expressed "shock and indignation" and affirmed that he "did not need any lessons" on the subject, especially since Burg "has no real knowledge of the dossier." Clearly this issue would remain on the agenda, both national and international, for the foreseeable future.

Papon Trial

In September 1996 a court in Bordeaux announced that Jacques Papon, accused of "complicity in crimes against humanity," would have to appear in criminal court. This decision was confirmed in January 1997 by the French Supreme Court; the trial began nine months later on October 8.

The French justice system had already tried one Frenchman on the same grounds: Paul Touvier, who was in charge of information services for the Lyon militia during the occupation. But Touvier (who was sentenced in April 1994 to life in prison and died in prison on July 17, 1996) was not a prominent man, and by any standard was at the margins of French society.

Maurice Papon, on the other hand, was a rising young civil servant between 1942 and 1944, serving as secretary-general of the Gironde prefecture. More than that, he later had an extremely successful career in government and in the ranks of the Gaullist party, and even held a cabinet portfolio between 1978 and 1981. He was accused of having taken part in the arrest and deportation of more than 1,500 people as part of his duties with the Gironde prefecture, in the city of Bordeaux, between June 1942 and August 1944. The legal proceedings, launched by the victims' families, began in 1981.

The accused maintained that he had always acted as an underling, carrying out decisions taken by his superiors in the Vichy administration under constant German pressure. The plaintiffs and the government argued, to the contrary, that Papon showed tremendous zeal in carrying out orders, did nothing to slow the roundups and deportations of Jews, and at times even took the initiative, going beyond what had been ordered. In the absence of living witnesses, the court's only basis for making its decision consisted of administrative documents from the time. Many of the arguments focused on the distribution of authority within the hierarchy of the prefecture, on what information people had in 1942 about the fate of Jews who were deported, and on the correct interpretation of copies of letters bearing Papon's signature.

The initial sessions of the trial were devoted to the personality of the accused and the historical period in question. Some uncomfortable reminders of the past came out of this stage of the trial. For one, leading Gaullists were testifying as character witnesses for a person accused of collaborating with the Germans; furthermore, it appeared that Papon had been associated with the Gaullist movement from the liberation on, even though he had no proof of having taken any real action to serve the Resistance. Other testimony dealt with the period during which Papon was prefect of police under President de Gaulle. During this period, on October 17, 1961, a demonstration of Algerians was severely repressed, under circumstances that were never clarified.

The Gaullists felt as if they were under attack. Philippe Séguin, president of the Gaullist party, the RPR, heatedly condemned "the trial of General de Gaulle and Gaullism, and the trial of France," and denounced what he called a "climate of collective expiation and permanent self-flagellation." Interior Minister Chevènement also attacked the "climate of national masochism."

The trial—marked by incidents in the audience, conflicts among lawyers, and the accused's health problems—did not proceed easily. Initially scheduled not to go beyond the end of 1997, it dragged on and seemed as if it would have to last through 1998. The media continued to cover the trial in exhaustive detail, and although sections of the public sometimes became impatient with remembering these long-ago events, the process seemed to have an educational effect on a generation that had not experienced the occupation. Even those who were somewhat uncomfortable with seeing an old man of 87 judged according to criteria that were laid out half a century after the events took place acknowledged that people today needed to be familiar with this far-off time. As *Le Monde's* reporter at the trial put it, "Before we can turn the page, we need to read everything that's on it."

FRANCE FACING THE HOLOCAUST

Beyond the guilt of one man, the Papon trial called into question the behavior of an entire country. In a way, Maurice Papon symbolized a France that had lived through this period under the dual authority of German officials and the Vichy government—a France more or less voluntarily complicit in policies that included the persecution of Jews.

Even a few years earlier, trying a case of this sort would no doubt have been impossible. The French were not psychologically ready. But President Chirac had already broken a taboo in July 1995 when—unlike his predecessors from Charles de Gaulle to François Mitterrand—he solemnly recognized France's responsibility in the "Vél' d'Hiv' roundup" of July 16 and 17, 1942, in which more than 13,000 Parisian Jews were arrested and turned over to the Germans.

Lionel Jospin, at that time leader of the opposition, endorsed Chirac's move. On July 20, 1997, Jospin, as prime minister, commemorated the Vél' d'Hiv' roundup by reiterating Chirac's remarks of two years earlier. He repeated Chirac's use of the word "irreparable" to describe the behavior of the French government and administration, which turned over the Jews to the Germans. And he declared, "This crime should mark our collective conscience."

Another symbolic declaration was issued soon afterward. On September 30, Bishop Olivier de Berranger read a "declaration of repentance" for the behavior of the Catholic Church toward the Jews between 1940 and 1944. He read the declaration at the site of the camp at Drancy—which is located within his diocese of Saint-Denis—the place where the victims of the Vél' d'Hiv' roundup were taken, and the main camp where Jews were brought together before being deported to Auschwitz. The document represented a position taken by all of France's bishops and was signed by those whose dioceses included the sites of the major internment camps where Jews were held under the German occupation.

Speaking in the name of the Catholic Church, the bishops solemnly asked for "pardon" for the church's silence in the face of the persecution carried out by the Vichy regime. In the same document, they acknowledged the Christian roots of anti-Semitism, noting the "tradition of anti-Judaism" with which "Christian doctrine and teaching" were infused. "This was the compost," they said, "that nourished the poisonous plant of Jew-hatred." The declaration of repentance was widely and sympathetically covered in the media, and the chief rabbi of France, Joseph Sitruk, hailed it as a sign of "heroism." The declaration also served as a reminder that the church's collaboration with the Germans was far from monolithic. Bishops protested against anti-Semitic measures, and priests and many Christians risked their lives to save Jews. The only negative responses to the declaration of repentance came, predictably, from the far right.

The bishops' statement awakened other people's consciences. A week after the Drancy declaration, one of France's major police unions, the SNPT (Syndicat National des Policiers en Tenue), sent a delegation to the Memorial to the Unknown Jewish Martyr in Paris, where it issued a statement condemning its "predecessors' unspeakable acts" and asking for "pardon" for the role that police officers played in the roundups of Jews. On October 11, Prof. Bernard Glorion, president of the Ordre des Médecins, the body that regulates the ethical behavior of all physicians in France, recalled the exclusion of Jewish doctors under the occupation and said he "regrets and solemnly and humbly disavows" the acts that were committed at that time.

Other institutions also undertook a discreet process of internal reflection. Some people, however, reacted negatively to all this self-criticism. The SNPT's apology was contradicted by other police unions and even by Jospin's minister of the interior, Jean-Pierre Chevènement, who invoked the same argument that Charles de Gaulle and François Mitterrand had used: all the evil was committed by the Germans and by a few French people acting directly under their orders.

The Papon trial clearly gave new life to old arguments. For a variety of reasons, many French people were not ready to allow crimes committed in the name of their country to be remembered. They stuck to the traditional version, according to which "Vichy was not France," because the real France was in the Resistance or in London with General de Gaulle. Hence no acts of repentance or requests for pardon were needed.

On November 2, 1997, President Chirac gave an indirect reply to this version of history in his message at the inaugural ceremony for a memorial near the city of Thonon in the department of Haute-Savoie, close to the Swiss border. The memorial was dedicated by the Central Consistory to the tens of thousands of "Justes," righteous Gentiles who saved Jews during the occupation. "Two years ago," Chirac said, "I insisted on solemnly acknowledging the responsibility of the French state in the arrest and deportation of tens of thousands of Jews. Yes, betraying the values and the missions of France, the Vichy government acted, sometimes zealously, as the occupier's accomplice. Fifty years later, our country has to assume all of its history—the bright with the dark, the moments of glory with the shadows."

Chirac addressed the subject again on December 5, when he participated in a ceremony in which the "Jewish file" was deposited at the Memorial to the Unknown Jewish Martyr in Paris, in conformity with his decision of October 1996 (see above). After recounting the fate of the Jews under the occupation, Chirac said, "Good and evil alike have to be recognized and assumed. This is the least we can expect of an adult people, who have made the struggle for liberty and human dignity their highest mission. . . . At this very moment, the entire nation is accomplishing a difficult task of memory that has been put off for too long."

JEWISH COMMUNITY

Demography

In the absence of reliable statistical data on Jews in France, there is one generally accepted benchmark: in a variety of surveys taken over the last quarter-century, the proportion of French people who define themselves as Jews has always been around 1 percent. Since France has a population of just under 60 million, these surveys validate the common view that the number of Jews in France is in the neighborhood of 600,000.

Communal Affairs

The community celebrated the 40th anniversary of ASH, Social Action Through Housing (Action Sociale par l'Habitat). The celebration took place in Paris, on October 15, 1996, with the participation of André Périssol, at the time the minister of housing in the Juppé government. French law requires every employer to pay an annual assessment to an agency providing housing for social cases. The Jewish community established ASH in October 1956 in order to receive funds from this assessment, to be used for what was then one of the community's leading priorities: housing refugees from Egypt and North Africa. ASH collected 20 million francs (at the time, the franc was worth about US $0.0025) from this assessment, to which was added a grant of 25 million francs from the American Jewish Committee and a loan of 25 million francs from the French branch of the Jewish Trust Corporation. This was the beginning of a program that now involved managing 1,600 dwellings and providing technical and financial assistance to a variety of Jewish organizations working in related areas: retirement homes, student housing, children's homes, apartments for youth, shelters for the homeless, and the like. The current president of ASH was Joël Rochard, a senior civil servant in the Finance Ministry.

In December 1996, with then Prime Minister Alain Juppé in attendance, FSJU, the United Jewish Philanthropic Fund (Fonds Social Juif Unifié), which serves as the umbrella organization for Jewish community services, officially opened its new headquarters, in a building called Espace Rachi (Rashi Place), located in Paris's fifth arrondissement, not far from the Latin Quarter. In addition to FSJU, a number of other institutions also have their head offices in the building: the

United Jewish Appeal of France; CRIF; Coopération féminine (Women's Coop-eration); Jewish community radio; and the monthly magazine *L'Arche.* Mindful of the bombing of the headquarters of Jewish organizations in Buenos Aires in 1994, those responsible for the building worked with French police to install un-usually rigorous security precautions.

Community Relations

France's national debate on immigration and nationality had a significant im-pact on the Jewish community—even though it took place outside the commu-nity and Jews were barely mentioned in that context.

Under the provisions of an immigration bill introduced in November 1996 by Interior Minister Jean-Louis Debré, a French person could be arrested for shel-tering a foreigner without making a declaration to that effect. A collective of film-makers and other artists launched a protest movement that quickly mushroomed. The obligation to declare the presence of a foreigner was compared to the de-nunciation of Jews under the Vichy regime, and during a demonstration against the Debré Law, demonstrators were seen symbolically carrying suitcases outside the Paris railroad station from which Jews had once been deported.

While many Jews condemned exaggeration of this sort, they were clearly con-flicted, whatever their political tendencies. Many Jews had themselves immi-grated from Eastern Europe between the two world wars and had been in France without proper documents, and Jews who came from North Africa in the 1950s and 1960s had intimate experience of the tragic aspects of immigration. Chief Rabbi of France Joseph Sitruk, who generally had little inclination to get involved in the political sphere, noted that "a Jew cannot be indifferent toward the stranger." In this, the chief rabbi was in harmony with representatives of other religious communities, most of whom had taken a very "advanced" position on the immigration question.

Protests and problems of conscience didn't stop the Debré Law from being passed on February 27, 1997. Inevitably, Jews were invoked as witnesses in a drama in which they were, in a way, involved. A few days after the vote on the bill, President Chirac received representatives of the Jewish community at the Élysée Palace. The occasion was the 190th anniversary of the Grand Sanhédrin, the body convened by the Emperor Napoleon to formalize the entry of France's Jews into the French nation. In his speech at this celebration, Chirac used the ex-ample of the Jews to uphold "the ideal of integration." He also affirmed that clan-destine immigration had to be treated with "great firmness."

The president's remarks, no doubt motivated by the best of intentions in pre-senting the Jews as a positive example of integration, were viewed as a double-edged sword. Jews could no doubt pass for "good" immigrants in French public opinion, setting an example that immigrants from black Africa or North Africa should follow. However, at a time when immigration was regarded as a problem, the comment also reminded French people who might have forgotten that many Jews were immigrants too.

The parameters of the debate changed with the election of a Socialist majority in the National Assembly in the spring of 1997. The new prime minister, Lionel Jospin, commissioned two reports from a sociologist, Patrick Weil, one dealing with immigration and the other with the right to nationality. The bills that came out of these studies were regarded as too lenient by the right and too strict by elements of the left, but they were passed in late 1997. In the course of the debate, in a long interview in *Le Monde,* the philosopher Jacques Derrida recalled his own childhood experience as an Algerian Jew deprived of nationality by the Vichy government. He used this experience to support his proposition that "there can be no culture or social ties without a principle of hospitality."

Israel-Related Activity

France's Jewish community traditionally took a "legitimist" attitude toward successive Israeli governments. The community avoided taking a position on subjects on which Israeli society was divided. At the same time, when the Israeli government was attacked in French political circles or — more often — in the press, it loyally defended the government and often questioned the motives of those behind the attacks.

The election of Benjamin Netanyahu in May 1996 was greeted in the same spirit. While most Jewish leaders supported the peace process begun at Oslo, they refused to question the new prime minister's intentions. CRIF president Henri Hajdenberg met with Netanyahu in Israel in early August 1996. The weekly *Actualité juive* described the atmosphere as "cordial" and emphasized that the Israeli prime minister had "clearly" explained to his French visitors "that he intended to pursue the peace process" — on the condition, of course, that the Palestinians respected the agreements. A meeting was arranged for late September, when Netanyahu was scheduled to be in Paris. The newspaper added, "He accepted the invitation to address the Jewish community within the framework of CRIF."

In coordination with the Israeli embassy, CRIF sent out invitations for the evening of September 25 for the meeting with the prime minister, who would effectively be in Paris for just one day. A week before the event, however, it was learned that Netanyahu would spend that evening at a banquet organized by his own party, the Likud; CRIF was offered a one-hour meeting in the afternoon instead. The reaction was one of shock followed by anger. "I regret," Hajdenberg said, "that the prime minister of Israel has chosen to attend the evening meeting organized by a marginal group that represents a clique." The affair became front-page news in the Paris newspapers, with Likud-France president Jacques Kupfer making statements that cast doubt on how representative CRIF itself was. (His own organization was a member of CRIF, through the Zionist Federation.)

The CRIF leaders considered boycotting Netanyahu's visit completely, but a compromise was reached, and Hajdenberg met with Netanyahu privately. Agence France-Presse declared that "the incident is closed" and quoted Hajdenberg as saying, "I believe that the prime minister of Israel has understood very well who the representatives of the Jewish community of France are. He has committed himself to coming to the next CRIF dinner the next time he is in Paris." In the event, Netanyahu's meeting with the CRIF steering committee took place in Israel a few months later, in December.

It would be an exaggeration to reduce the relations of France's Jewish community with Israel to matters of protocol, but incidents of this kind clearly leave their mark, especially if they are seen as indicating a state of mind. Geographically, France and Israel are not far apart. Many Jewish families that left Eastern Europe after the Holocaust have members in both France and Israel. The same is true of families that left North Africa after decolonization. More than two thousand French Jews settle in Israel every year, one of the highest levels in the world, with the exception of the special case of the former Soviet Union. As a result, Israel is an integral element of the personal identity of French Jews.

On the institutional level, however, the Jewish community felt slighted by Israeli representatives. The language barrier is not a full explanation, especially since, while few Israeli leaders speak French, a growing number of Jewish leaders in France speak Hebrew. Thus, most of the activity conducted in support of Israel by the Jewish community, both internally and on the broader public stage, was the result of local initiatives and not developed jointly with Israel.

Religion

There was a major innovation in French religious life: the establishment of a labor union at the Paris Consistory, the venerable institution that manages Jewish religious life in the Paris region and is the main component of the Central Consistory (the national body). The Paris Consistory's finances were openly in crisis starting in the spring of 1996. The problem was at least partly related to the deep split on the group's board of directors, which was divided between 13 representatives of the ACIP-2000 slate led by Benny Cohen, president of the Consistory from 1989 to 1993, and 13 representatives of the AVEC slate led by the new president, Moïse Cohen. This "Cohen versus Cohen" conflict—a delight to religious columnists in the national press—did not facilitate sound management, especially since relations between the two camps were extremely strained. The new team accused the old one of having emptied the Consistory's coffers over a period of several years by embarking on an "extravagant" investment policy and "irresponsible" commitments.

The Consistory's deficit was accentuated by a substantial loss in revenue from kosher meat slaughter and supervision. This was related to the fear that "mad cow disease" would spread to France from its origin in the herds of Britain, which led to a drop in French beef consumption in 1996. When the president of the Consistory announced budget cuts, which meant that some people would have to be laid off, employees established a "defense committee" of ten people, five of whom were rabbis. This committee gave rise to a union local, affiliated with one of France's three major union confederations, Force Ouvrière, with a rabbi as the secretary of the local. *Le Monde* reported a threat of militant union activity, including "a burial and wedding strike." Fortunately, a compromise was found. The union local and Consistory management signed a collective agreement in which the employees agreed to a pay cut in exchange for keeping the work force at its existing level. The local continued its activities, publishing a newsletter in which articles about the Consistory's internal problems appeared side by side with rabbinic decisions on "Judaism and trade unionism" taken from the *Hoshen Mishpat,* a 14th-century compilation of Jewish law. Throughout this period, the leaders of Force Ouvrière acted with great discretion, giving Consistory employees advice on ways of managing the crisis with as little publicity as possible so as not to harm the image of the Jewish community.

However, the Paris Consistory's financial problems were not resolved, and alarming reports continued to circulate throughout 1997. With elections for 14 of the 26 seats on the board scheduled for late 1997, the preelection climate accentuated the anxiety. Meanwhile, personnel changes were announced in management: Moché Cohen took charge of Consistory activities with the new title of secretary-general, while Péguy Lévy became assistant secretary-general.

The appointment of Lévy represented a first step in the "feminization" of the Consistory; a more important one was to follow. In the November 1997 elections — in which for the first time people voted for individual candidates rather than slates — the three highest vote-getters were women, as was the fifth-place winner. This result led to a brief and ultimately inconsequential rabbinic debate on whether women were eligible to sit on the board. Moïse Cohen, who shortly afterward was reelected president of the Consistory, said he was happy with the feminization of the organization. This breakthrough, along with the unionization of personnel, would mark 1997 as a year of change in the Consistory's annals.

In other developments, the Synagogue de la Victoire, which in its architecture and history (although not in the size of its membership) was the most prestigious synagogue in Paris, appointed a new rabbi, Gilles Bernheim, in September 1997. The Liberal Jewish Movement of France, the MJLF (Mouvement Juif Libéral de France), published a new prayer book, compiled by Rabbi Daniel Farhi and entitled *Taher Libénou.* The MJLF also welcomed a new rabbi — Gabriel Farhi, son of Rabbi Daniel Farhi.

Education

The 1996 Zalman Shazar Prize, an Israeli prize for achievement in Jewish education and culture in the Diaspora, was awarded to two civil servants responsible for developing Hebrew-language education in France, Jacques Kessous and

Joseph Cohen. Kessous was the supervisor of Hebrew teaching for the French Ministry of Education at the national level; Cohen, based in Lyons, was the regional supervisor for the south of France.

After France and Israel signed cultural agreements in 1959, Hebrew became an official modern foreign language in French schools. The Education Ministry's programs provide for the teaching of Hebrew both as a language of communication and as a language of Jewish culture and heritage. There were currently about a hundred Hebrew teachers, accredited and paid by the government, in French schools; more than 5,000 students were enrolled in Hebrew classes, and each year nearly 1,500 chose Hebrew as a modern language in various examinations. Hebrew was also accepted as a foreign language in the highly competitive entrance examinations for some of France's most prestigious specialized post-secondary institutions (*grandes écoles*).

Some 25,000 children were enrolled in 110 Jewish day schools, in which secular instruction was paid for by the government, while the community supported Hebrew and Jewish studies. A community agency, the André Neher Institute, trained teachers and principals specifically for these schools, from kindergarten to university entrance level. This training, which complements general studies pursued through French institutions of higher learning, leads to a diploma recognized by the national education system. In September 1997 the Neher Institute began offering a course by videoconference from Bar-Ilan University in Israel.

The Jacob Buchman–Mémoire de la Shoah Prize, administered by the Fondation du Judaïsme Français (French Judaism Foundation), was awarded jointly in 1997 to Jean-François Forges's book *Éduquer contre Auschwitz* (Educating Against Auschwitz) and to *Fragments d'une enfance 1939–1948* (Fragments of a Childhood 1939–1948), a French translation of a German work by the Swiss writer Binjamin Wilkomirski. Forges, who is not Jewish, teaches history in a secondary school in the Lyons area. His book was published as part of a collection of educational studies intended for teachers and was based on his experience of teaching the Holocaust to young students.

Finally, a new Jewish day high school was opened in Paris in 1997: the École Georges Leven, under the aegis of the Alliance Israélite Universelle.

Culture

A large gathering called "Judéoscope," which brought together 10,000 people under the aegis of CRIF on February 2, 1997, was the occasion for a series of debates on Jewish identity, Israel, and the problems of French society, with a variety of participants including politicians from all parties except the National Front.

On the whole, increasingly varied images of Jews were presented in the media and the arts in France—for better and for worse. One of the most successful French films at the box office in recent years was Thomas Gilou's *La vérité si je mens!* (The Truth if I Lie!). Gilou, who is not Jewish, offers a humorous sketch of the Sentier neighborhood of Paris, a center of the wholesale garment trade carried out mostly by North African Jews. In the film, Jewish actors play non-Jewish characters and vice versa, although some Jews also play Jews. Many French moviegoers, Jews and non-Jews alike, found the result amusing, though the image of the Sentier and its residents was criticized by some as a caricature.

A film that made the "Jewish question" a focus of discussion in French cinematic circles was Claude Berri's *Lucie Aubrac,* starring Daniel Auteuil and Carole Bouquet, released early in 1997. It tells the true story of Raymond Aubrac, a French Jew who was one of the leaders of the Resistance, and his non-Jewish wife, Lucie, who organized his escape in 1943 after he fell into German hands. Raymond and Lucie Aubrac are still alive and very active. The release of the film sparked new interest in this period in French history along with the beginnings of a controversy about the exact circumstances of Aubrac's arrest and escape. For Berri, this was a return to the subject matter of his very first film, *Le vieil homme et l'enfant* (The Old Man and the Child), the semiautobiographical story of a Jewish child hidden by a French anti-Semite during the war.

Another film with a Jewish theme released in 1997 was Abraham Ségal's *Enquête sur Abraham* (Inquiry into Abraham), a documentary on the various ways the story of the common ancestor of the Jewish and Arab peoples is told. The film was based on Ségal's own book, *Abraham, enquête sur un patriarche* (Abraham: Inquiry into a Patriarch), published in 1995. Arnaud des Pallières's film *Drancy Avenir* (Drancy Future), which came out late in 1997, is devoted to remembering Drancy, the city near Paris from which Jews were transported to Auschwitz. Des Pallières, who is not Jewish, considers it "a scandal" that the task of remembering the Holocaust, which should be "shared by the whole community," had been "abandoned to the Jews themselves." Another film released in 1997, Charles Najman's *La mémoire est-il soluble dans l'eau?* (Is Memory Soluble in Water?), portrays the way a woman (Najman's mother, who played herself) relates to her past during the Holocaust and her desire to go on living. Finally, from October 25 to November 3, 1996, the Mediterranean film festival in Montpellier presented a retrospective of the work of Israeli director Uri Zohar.

In the theater, two new works deserve special mention. *Adam et Ève,* by Jean-Claude Grumberg, the most explicitly Jewish of contemporary French playwrights, opened early in 1997. It tells the story of two elderly Jewish Communists in France. In Enzo Cormann's *Toujours l'Orage* (Ever the Storm), staged in Toulouse and then in Paris in 1997, a young theater director struggling with his Jewishness meets a Shakespearean actor who survived Terezin.

In September 1997 the French choreographer Maurice Béjart, director of the Béjart Ballet in Lausanne, staged a version of S. An-Ski's *The Dybbuk* in Paris. Béjart, who was brought up as a Catholic but converted to Sufi Islam, was careful to use authentically Jewish elements in his production, taking his inspiration from the version he saw performed by the Habimah Theater of Israel in 1957. He even used the voice of the great Israeli actress Hanna Rovina in the soundtrack. An international encounter entitled "La traversée des musiques juives" (The Course of Jewish Music) was held in late July 1996 in a setting familiar to all Parisians: Parc de la Villette and Cité de la Musique. Organized by the percussionist Youval Micenmacher, this event lasted an evening, a day, and an entire night. American, Israeli, and French musicians performed Jewish music from Eastern Europe, Yemen, Georgia, Ethiopia, Morocco, Tunisia, and elsewhere.

In late 1996 the historian and art critic Itzhak Goldberg presented an exhibition entitled "Signes de terre" (Signs of the Land) at the prestigious Seita museum-gallery in Paris. The exhibition consisted of works by two Israeli artists: one Muslim, Asim Abu-Shakra (1961–1990), and the other Jewish, Avi Trattner (born 1948).

Finally, the sixth congress of the International Federation of Secular Humanistic Jews was held at the Sorbonne in Paris in October 1996.

Publications

The renewed interest being shown in the classic novel form in France had not had much impact on Jewish literature. Works of fiction dealing with Jewish subjects were fairly rare and of uneven quality. A few worth mentioning are Patrick Modiano's *Dora Bruder,* a fictional inquiry into the disappearance of a young Jewish girl during the occupation; Michèle Kahn's *Shanghaï-la-juive* (Jewish Shanghai), a novel about the influx into Shanghai of Jews fleeing Nazism; and Marc Weitzmann's *Chaos,* a largely autobiographical work in which Weitzmann's cousin, the writer Serge Doubrovsky, figures prominently.

Historical writing remained the strong point of publishing on Jewish themes in France. During the period under review, the following noteworthy historical works were published: *Un antisémitisme ordinaire, Vichy et les avocats juifs (1940–1944)* (Ordinary Anti-Semitism: Vichy and the Jewish Lawyers, 1940–44), by former justice minister Robert Badinter; Esther Benbassa's *Histoire des Juifs de France* (History of the Jews in France); Mireille Hadas-Lebel's *Le peuple hébreu* (The Hebrew People); François Fejtö's *Juifs et Hongrois* (Jews and Hungarians); Régine Azria's *Le judaïsme* (Judaism); Gérard Nahon's *La Terre sainte au temps des kabbalistes* (The Holy Land in the Time of the Kabbalists); Carol Iancu's *Les Juifs en Roumanie (1919–1938)* (The Jews in Romania, 1919–38); Maurice Blanchot's *Les intellectuels en question* (Intellectuals in Question), a reflection on the Dreyfus affair; Pierre Pachet's *Conversations à Jassy* (Conversations in Jassy), a return to the author's father's native town in Moldova, which in 1941 was the scene of a terrible pogrom; *Un Juif nommé Jésus* (A Jew Named Jesus) and *Le Juif Jésus et le Chabbat* (Jesus the Jew and Shabbat) by the Catholic writer Marie Vidal; and a collection edited by Yves Plassereaud and Henri Minczeles, *Lituanie juive, 1918–1940* (Jewish Lithuania, 1918–40).

Another well-represented category was biography and autobiography: Roland

Goetschel's *Isaac Abravanel, conseiller des princes et philosophe* (Isaac Abravanel: Adviser to Princes and Philosopher); Myriam Anissimov's *Primo Levi, la tragédie d'un optimiste* (Primo Levi: The Tragedy of an Optimist); *Examen de conscience* (Examination of Conscience) by August von Kageneck, a German journalist who had been a young Wehrmacht officer on the eastern front; Pierre Assouline's *Le fleuve Combelle* (The Combelle River), on the friendship between a young Jewish journalist and a former Nazi collaborator; Serge Moscovici's *Chronique des années égarées* (Chronicle of My Lost Years), a memoir; Georges Waysand's *Estoucha*, a biography of his mother, a Jewish Communist; and Maurice-Ruben Hayoun's *Moïse Mendelssohn* (Moses Mendelssohn).

A number of works on Judaism were published, among them *Les rites de naissance dans le judaïsme* (Birth Rituals in Judaism) by Patricia Hidiroglu; *Le Sicle du Sanctuaire*, an annotated French translation by Charles Mopsick of *Shekel ha-Kodesh*, a 13th-century kabbalistic work by Moses de Leon; Rabbi Gilles Bernheim's *Un rabbin dans la Cité* (A Rabbi in the City); Raphaël Draï's *Freud et Moïse. Psychoanalyse, Loi juive et Pouvoir* (Freud and Moses: Psychoanalysis, Jewish Law and Power); Théo Klein's *Le guetteur* (The Sentry); *Un judaïsme dans le siècle, dialogue avec un rabbin libéral* (Judaism in the Secular World: A Dialogue with a Liberal Rabbi) by Rabbi Daniel Farhi with Francis Lentschner; *La tendresse de Dieu* (The Tenderness of God) by Chief Rabbi René-Samuel Sirat with Martine Lemalet; and Alain Finkielkraut's *L'humanité perdue, essai sur le XXème siècle* (Lost Humanity: A Reflection on the 20th Century).

La démocratie d'Israël (Democracy in Israel), a study by the French-born Israeli constitutional expert Claude Klein, was published in France.

Finally, the appearance of two CD-ROMs, *Histoires du ghetto de Varsovie* (Stories of the Warsaw Ghetto) and *Histoire de la Shoah* (History of the Holocaust), is worth noting. Clearly, Jewish cultural output remained heavily influenced by events that occurred half a century ago.

Personalia

In 1997 France's Jewish community added another name to the long list of Jewish Nobel laureates. Claude Cohen-Tannoudji, who received the Nobel Prize for physics jointly with Steven Chu and William D. Phillips, was born in Constantine, Algeria, in 1933. In an interview with *Le Monde* in October 1997, he noted that because he grew up in Algeria he was able to escape "the deadly fate that Nazi ideology held in store for us." He explained in the same interview that working as both a researcher and a teacher allowed him "to remain faithful to the long-standing Jewish tradition of text study and commentary, detailed analysis of the range of possible interpretations, and transmission of knowledge to succeeding generations." Cohen-Tannoudji was not the first French Jew to win a Nobel Prize; however, his inclination to lay claim to his Jewish heritage and the ready audience he found for this avowal in the French media are worth noting. (As early as 1992, when Georges Charpak won the Nobel Prize in physics, the story of his coming to France as a Jewish immigrant child from Poland was widely reported in the press.)

Art historian Pierre Rosenberg was elected to the Académie Française in November 1996. Biologist and 1965 Nobel laureate François Jacob was elected to the Académie Française in November 1997. Physicist Claude Cohen-Tannoudji (see above) was named an officer of the Legion of Honor. Franco-Israeli poet Claude Vigée received the grand prize for poetry of the Académie Française (and was named an officer of the Legion of Honor). Rabbi Charles Liché and magistrate Myriam Ezratty were named commanders of the Legion of Honor; Léon Masliah, executive director of the Central Consistory, and Maurice Lévy, president of the Publicis advertising firm, were named officers of the legion; and Roger Bennarosh, founder and president of the Liberal Jewish Movement of France, the MJLF, was named a knight of the legion.

Prominent French Jews who died in the second half of 1996 included businessman and community leader Sylvain Kaufmann, 82, in August; businessman and community leader Claude Kelman, 88, in September; rabbi and educator Léon Askénazi ("Manitou"), 74, in Israel, in October; businessman and community leader Jean-Paul Elkann, 75, in November; businessman and community leader Michel Topiol, 86, in December; filmmaker Michel Mitrani, 66, in December; and Daniel Mayer, 87, Resistance fighter and Socialist leader, in December.

Prominent Jews who died in 1997 included Yiddish journalist and writer Léon Leneman, 89, in January; doctor and community leader Lucien Bouccara, 65, in February; lawyer Paul Garson, 76, in March; Moussa Abadi, 86, theater critic and former Resistance fighter, in September; Laura Margolis-Jarblum, 93, widow of the French Zionist leader Marc Jarblum, in Boston, in September; doctor and community leader Marcel Goldstein, 66, in October; journalist Jacques Derogy, 72, in October; the great French singer Barbara, 67, whose original name was Monique Serf, in November; banker Edmond de Rothschild, 71, in November; sculptor Michel Milberger, 75, in December; Léon Poliakov, 87, historian of anti-Semitism, in December.

MEIR WAINTRATER

The Netherlands

National Affairs

THE NETHERLANDS DURING the latter half of 1996 and 1997 enjoyed political stability and remarkable economic prosperity. Despite a number of minor crises, the government—a coalition of Labor (PvdA), the Liberals (VVD), and the Centrum—left Democrats 1966 (D'66)—was never really in danger, and Labor premier Willem Kok was generally praised for his pragmatic approach.

The extreme right, represented mainly by the Centrum Democrats (CD) was, in contrast to rightist parties in Belgium and France, unsuccessful. It had three of the 150 seats in the Second Chamber of Parliament and none in the 75-member Senate. Only one CD representative, Hans Janmaat, was known to the public. The other more extreme right-wing parties—CP'86 (an offshoot of the CD), the VNN (Volks Nationalisten Nederland), an offshoot of CP'86, and the Nederlands Blok, led by Joop Glimmerveen, had no seats in Parliament.

The main social problems confronting the Netherlands during the period under review were the environment, in particular in connection with the possible expansion of Schiphol Airport; drugs, including the use of Holland as a transit center; and crime.

The economy grew by over 3.4 percent, and inflation by only 2.8 percent. The Amsterdam Stock Exchange broke all records a number of times. Unemployment decreased by over 100,000 to some 350,000 and stood at about 5 percent of the working population. Most of those unemployed were the so-called hard core of unskilled and *allochthones*, i.e., recent immigrants from Third World countries. Privatization continued of hitherto government enterprises, such as the Telephone Services and the railways. The exception to the general prosperity was the Fokker Aircraft Factories, which went bankrupt and could find no buyers.

Israel and the Middle East

During the first six months of 1997, when the Netherlands held the presidency of the European Union (EU), Holland had more contacts than usual with Israel and the Palestinian National Authority. Generally, the Netherlands adhered to the policies of the European Union in these relations.

Israeli foreign minister David Levy visited The Hague January 28–30, 1997, where he met with Premier Kok and Foreign Minister Van Mierlo. Levy also met with representatives of the Jewish community in the Netherlands.

Yasir Arafat visited The Hague February 2–4 and met with Premier Kok and

Foreign Minister Hans Van Mierlo, following which they gave a joint press conference. Arafat emphasized that Europe could play an important role in the peace process in the Middle East, supplementary to the role of the United States. He stressed the importance of a seaport in the Gaza Strip and accused Israel of intentionally blocking its construction. He criticized Israel for the continued closure of access to the West Bank which, he claimed, caused an economic catastrophe of some $7 million daily. Arafat also met with the parliamentary foreign affairs committee and representatives of the construction firms connected with plans for the harbor in Gaza, for which the Netherlands had donated about $20 million.

A few weeks earlier Van Mierlo had written a letter to Arafat, but not to the Israeli prime minister, with guarantees of the EU that the Oslo agreements would be fully implemented. Van Mierlo also said he did not want to visit Israel if he could not, during his stay there, visit Orient House, a disputed Palestinian building in East Jerusalem.

During a stopover at Schiphol Airport on his way to the United States, on February 12, Israeli prime minister Benjamin Netanyahu met for an hour and a half with Premier Kok, followed by a brief press conference. The Gaza harbor was on the agenda of this meeting as well. To allay Israel's fear that arms could be imported through the harbor, Kok promised to give Israel special safety equipment for detecting weapons.

The parliamentary chairman of the Liberal Party (VVD), Frits Bolkestein, visited Israel in the second week of February to attend the meeting of the Liberal International Union, of which he was chairman. He also visited Arafat in Ramallah. Bolkestein urged that the EU limit itself to a supplementary role to that of the United States; he also opposed a visit of Van Mierlo to Orient House. He was received by President Ezer Weizman and met with Defense Minister Yitzhak Mordechai and opposition leader Shimon Peres.

Benjamin Netanyahu, accompanied by Mrs. Netanyahu and their two children, visited the Netherlands April 8–9. This time his visit was intended in particular to promote economic relations between Israel and Holland. To this end the Netherlands-Israel Chamber of Commerce arranged a meeting for him with Dutch captains of industry to discuss cooperation in high technology and other fields. Netanyahu also met with Premier Kok, who later called the meeting "frank," with Foreign Minister Van Mierlo, and with the members of the parliamentary foreign affairs and defense committees of both the Second Chamber and the Senate. An official dinner was given in his honor.

On April 10 Foreign Minister Van Mierlo visited Arafat in Gaza. Mrs. Suha Arafat visited Holland at the end of May, at the invitation of the representative of the Palestinian Authority in The Hague. Together with the wife of Premier Kok, she visited an Institute for the Blind and with the wife of the Dutch Minister of Agriculture the flower auction in Aalsmeer, where Palestinian flowers are auctioned.

King Hussein and Queen Noor of Jordan visited the Netherlands June 10–11 as guests of the Dutch royal couple, who were friends of long standing.

Queen Beatrix and Prince-Consort Claus paid an official visit to Egypt November 17–19. The visit was first planned some years ago, but was postponed because of security risks. Ironically, on the very morning of the royal couple's arrival in Cairo, fundamentalist Muslims carried out a terrorist attack on tourists in Luxor. Although the Dutch royal couple decided to continue the trip, so as not to appear to be insulting their hosts, the visit was limited to Cairo and its immediate surroundings.

A 35-year-old Palestinian, Imad Sabi, a member of the Popular Front for the Liberation of Palestine, who had spent 20 months in administrative detention in Israel, arrived in Holland on August 28, after having been released by Israel the previous day. The purpose of his visit was to study at the Institute for Social Studies in The Hague, which had granted him a stipend for 15 months. To obtain his release, he had to promise that during his stay abroad he would refrain from anti-Israel activities and would stay away from Israel for four years.

On February 7, the last Friday of Ramadan, some 600 Muslim fundamentalists including many women and children, demonstrated in The Hague—as they had in past years—against Israel and the United States. Many carried portraits of Iranian leaders. The mayor of the city gave permission for the demonstration provided it did not pass the American and Israeli embassies and that the banners had slogans only in Dutch so that they could be checked by the police. The demonstration received little publicity. On the following Monday representatives of the Jewish community expressed their concern to the mayor.

As in previous years pro-Iranian Muslims demonstrated in front of the Israeli embassy in The Hague on several occasions. On July 11 some 250 of them protested against the poster distributed in Hebron by an Israeli woman on which Mohammed was shown with a pig's head. The police did not interfere as the demonstration was directed against Israel but was not anti-Semitic.

Leadership of the Netherlands-Israel Society passed from Dick Dolman, former chairman of the Second Chamber of Parliament, to Willem Deetman, the outgoing chairman of the Second Chamber of Parliament and currently mayor of The Hague.

The 1992 crash of an El Al Boeing cargo aircraft over the Bijlmer district in the southeastern tip of Amsterdam, which resulted in the deaths of three crew members, one woman passenger, and 39 Bijlmer residents, was still a matter of controversy. Among other issues, there were charges that residents of the district were ill from toxic substances released in the crash. The fifth anniversary of the disaster, on October 4, 1997, received wide coverage in the news media, though the official commemoration was attended by only a few hundred people, including many officials. Boeing had assumed full responsibility for the disaster and paid the next-of-kin of the victims, mostly poor recent immigrants from Ghana and the Caribbean, the enormous sum of over $50 million, in addition to compensation from the Amsterdam municipality. Following publication of a book on the disaster last year by journalist Vincent Dekker, another journalist, Pierre Heyboer, published a book containing accusations against El Al, which was still being sued. Mystery novelist Thomas Ross published a semifictional thriller based on the incident in which the Mossad plays an important role.

Anti-Semitism, Racism, Extremism

Racism was not a serious problem in Holland. A case that was originally considered to involve racism and that received enormous publicity in Holland and abroad, in particular in Turkey, eventually proved to emanate from private motives. On March 26, 1997, in a popular quarter in The Hague, an incendiary bomb was thrown through the letterbox into the apartment inhabited by the Közedagh family, Turkish Kurds, causing the deaths of the mother and five of her ten children. A Turkish government delegation arrived in The Hague to protest the attack, and in The Hague itself a large demonstration took place organized by "white" residents. The firebomb was eventually found to have been thrown by a nephew of the father, who bore a grudge against his uncle.

According to Jaap Donselaar, an expert on the extreme right in Holland, there were only some two hundred extreme right-wing activists in the country, and they were internally divided. Some maintained contact with neo-Nazi groups in Germany, Denmark, and Belgium and took part in their demonstrations.

Hans Janmaat was convicted by the district court of Zwolle in April 1997 of having shouted racist slogans during a demonstration in that city in February ("The Netherlands for the Dutchmen" and "One's own people first"). He was sentenced to four weeks' imprisonment, of which two weeks could be served on probation. He appealed. Questions were raised about whether such demonstrations should be forbidden in advance or whether the police should intervene only when illicit slogans were shouted or shown on banners. The mayor of Zwolle, himself a staunch antifascist, demanded clear instructions from the government.

A monument at the former concentration camp at Vught, near Bois-le-Duc, which had been smeared with swastikas two years earlier by unknown persons, was smeared again on the eve of Memorial Day on May 4, 1997, this time with swastikas and the letters KKK, standing for Ku Klux Klan. The new Auschwitz monument, in the Wertheim public garden in the center of Amsterdam, was rededicated officially on the last Sunday of January 1997. Two years earlier it had been damaged by a disgruntled drug-addicted employee of the glass-blowing firm that constructed it,

Holocaust-Related Matters

Material claims by Jews resulting from the Nazi occupation were again in the news, partly as a result of developments abroad, in particular in Switzerland.

The subject of Dutch gold in Swiss banks covers four distinct categories of property: (a) the monetary gold of the Netherlands State Bank (Nederlandse Bank, DNB) that was looted by the Nazis and partly transferred to Switzerland; (b) the gold that residents of the Netherlands were forced to sell to the DNB during the Nazi occupation; (c) gold that residents of the Netherlands, before and during the Nazi occupation, transferred to Switzerland privately; and (d) the gold that was taken by the Nazis from individuals, largely Jews, some of which found its way to Swiss banks. For the first two categories the Netherlands received partial compensation in 1952, in an agreement called a final settlement; for the last two categories it did not.

In May 1997 Minister of Finance Gerrit Zalm established a commission, headed by Prof. Jos van Kemenade, the present governor of the province of North Holland and a former cabinet minister of education. The commission, which included some financial experts of Jewish origin as members, was to investigate to what extent Jews and other Nazi victims could be compensated. It worked in consultation with the newly formed Committee of Jewish Organizations on External Matters (CJOEB). In December the commission announced that it would make Fl. 20 million available from compensation it had received, of which Fl. 19 million would go to Jews and Fl. 1 million to others, mainly Romanies (Gypsies) and homosexuals. In addition, the Dutch Treasury donated Fl. 20 million for the rehabilitation of Jewish Nazi victims in Eastern Europe.

In consultation with the CJOEB (and in contrast to the recommendation of the U.S. commission headed by Under Secretary of Commerce Stuart Eizenstat), it was decided not to distribute the funds to individual victims but to use the money for general Jewish objectives, such as the restoration of neglected Jewish cemeteries and tombstones. The decision was strongly criticized by some, including those survivors who wanted to receive the sums to which they were entitled, however small. Others pointed out that the CJOEB did not represent all the present Jews of the Netherlands, since only a minority were affiliated with any of its constituent bodies. And the Orthodox claimed that many Orthodox Jewish charities were not represented in the JMW, the Jewish Social Welfare Foundation, and would be excluded. The *Nieuw Israelitisch Weekblad* (Dutch Jewish weekly) was filled with letters on the controversy. At the end of the year, the matter had still not been resolved.

Two long lists with names of persons from abroad who had accounts in Swiss banks in 1940–45 were published in Dutch papers in July, but they contained almost no names of Jews from Holland.

A situation came to light at the end of the period under review that aroused enormous interest and emotion. The progressive weekly *De Groene Amsterdammer* reported on December 3 that students temporarily living in the building formerly occupied by the Amsterdam branch of the Ministry of Finance had found, in the attic, a number of archival lockers with a card file of some 3,000 cards from the records of the Lippman-Rosenthal Bank. This bank, owned by

Jews until 1940, had been taken over in 1941 by the Nazis, who compelled all Jews to transfer to it their bank accounts, property, and valuables. The cards (from an original file of 13,000 cards) contained the names and last addresses of the owners and lists of the possessions they were forced to hand over on their arrival at Westerbork transit camp, such as fountain pens, watches, rings, and bracelets. The lockers in the attic had been overlooked when the Amsterdam branch of the Treasury moved to other premises some years ago.

Another discovery concerned the fate of the confiscated property. It was found that, whereas most of the objects had been returned to the former owners or their heirs in the course of the years, a number of heirless items had remained at the Amsterdam offices of the Treasury. In 1968 it was decided that employees of this office could buy them at the estimated value of ten years earlier, which they did. Disclosure of this episode caused widespread indignation. A commission headed by retired State Comptroller Frans Kordes, a highly respected man, was appointed to investigate the matter.

As for the 3,000 Lippman Rosenthal (generally called LiRo) cards, they were given into the custody of the JMW, which in turn made them available for inspection in the Amsterdam Municipal Archives. The cards could be examined only by filling in a form on which the applicant indicated his or her relationship to the person named on the cards. The total LiRo archives were kept in the General State Archives (ARA) in The Hague.

A related case was the so-called Treasure of Almelo. A Canadian soldier who participated in the liberation of the eastern part of the Netherlands in April 1945 wrote a letter a few years ago to the Municipality of Almelo, a town that he had helped to liberate. He wrote that in April 1945 he found in a villa in that town, which had served as local German headquarters, a large suitcase full of Jewish ritual objects and other valuables, which he turned over to the Almelo branch of the Netherlands State Bank. Now he wanted to know what had happened to the find. The Almelo bank branch had long been closed, and various efforts to investigate were fruitless. A high-ranking police officer, Erik Nordholt, who retired in the fall of 1997 as Amsterdam chief commissioner of police, was appointed to conduct a thorough investigation.

Another case that emerged during the period under review, and whose solution was also likely to take several years, involved the ownership of the Goudstikker art collection. Jacques Goudstikker was a well-known Amsterdam Jewish art dealer who specialized in 17th-century Dutch masters. On May 14, 1940, after the Nazis invaded Holland, he managed to escape with his young wife, Vienna-born Desi von Halban Kurz, and their infant son, Edward, by boat; however, during a stroll on deck at night, Goudstikker fell into an open cargo hold and lost his life. He had made no special provisions for his paintings, which were later sold by two of his non-Jewish employees to Nazi leader Hermann Göring and other German art collectors. After the war, many of the artworks were traced and returned to Holland, confiscated by the state as enemy property, and distributed to several Dutch museums.

Mrs. Goudstikker and her son had emigrated to the United States, where she later married the former Amsterdam lawyer A.E. von Saher. Her son officially adopted the name of his stepfather and was baptized. After the war, Mrs. Goudstikker tried, and failed, to get the collection back. In 1952, in order to avoid further difficult and expensive litigation, she agreed to a settlement in which she waived her rights to the collection in return for the sum of Fl. 2 million ($1 million), which was far below the actual value of the collection. Both Mrs. Goudstikker von Saher and her son, Edward, died in 1996. Edward von Saher's widow, a former German skating champion, and their two daughters announced that they would file suit against the Netherlands for the return of the collection. Netherlands under secretary of culture Aat Nuis asserted that, since Mrs. Goudstikker had given up her rights to the collection in 1952, the claim had no legal basis, but the Von Sahers maintained their position.

OTHER MATTERS

In October 1996 Fred Ensel, the then chairman of JMW, the Jewish Social Welfare Foundation, and Isaac Lipschits, retired professor of modern history at the University of Groninguen and author of a history of the JMW, claimed that Dutch notaries-public still had bank balances of Jews who had perished during the years 1940–45. The Royal Fraternity of Dutch Notaries-Public announced on February 25, 1997, that a thorough investigation had shown that of the 1,200 or so notaries-public in Holland, only a few were involved, and that the total amount in their hands was only about Fl. 450,000 ($225,000)—mainly West German payments under the *Wiedergutmachung* to persons who had in the meantime passed away and whose heirs could not be traced. JMW had created the impression that the amount was much larger. The Fraternity of Notaries-Public and JMW reached a settlement with the Treasury by which these balances were transferred to JMW.

A new phenomenon was the claim for the payment of life insurance benefits to heirs of Jews who had taken out life insurance policies in 1940–42. The difficulty was that some claimants had no documents to substantiate their claims and that some insurance companies had in the interim merged with other firms. Still, several companies decided that if a claim was plausible the money would be paid. Claims were also made by holders of post-office savings accounts, often of very small amounts, and by heirs of subscribers to a burial fund that had never financed the burials, since the subscribers perished in Eastern Europe. In all these cases, those involved took an accommodating view.

The Anne Frank House in Amsterdam was visited in 1997 by over 700,000 persons, mainly tourists from the United States, Japan, Great Britain, and Germany.

To accommodate the large numbers, adjoining houses were being demolished to allow for expansion.

Steven Spielberg's Survivors of the Shoah Visual History Project completed its work in Holland in June 1997. A total of 1,066 persons recounted their wartime experiences in video-recorded interviews.

JEWISH COMMUNITY

Demography

No official statistics exist on the number of Jews living in the Netherlands, but it is estimated at about 25,000. Of these only about one-third are affiliated with any of the three main communities—Ashkenazic, Sephardic, and Liberal. According to the Jewish Social Welfare Foundation (JMW), there were also some 10,000 Israelis living in Holland, many with non-Jewish partners.

The Netherlands Ashkenazi Congregation (NIK) had 5,313 members at the end of 1996, some 200 less than the previous year. Of these some 3,000 were in Amsterdam and the Amsterdam suburb of Amstelveen, 340 in The Hague area, and 332 in the Rotterdam area. In Almere, a new satellite town of Amsterdam, a group of some 40 Jews was formed.

Communal Affairs

An important achievement in 1997 was the establishment, after much initial opposition, of the Committee of Jewish Organizations on External Matters (CJOEB), also called CJO, to represent the entire Jewish community. Members of the new body are the Netherlands Ashkenazi Congregation (NIK), the Sephardi Congregation (PIK), the Liberal Jewish Congregation (LJG), the Federation of Netherlands Zionists (FNZ), Jewish Social Welfare (JMW), and the CIDI (Center for Information and Documentation on Israel). The CJOEB was formed to enable the organized Jewish community to approach the Dutch government on matters of common Jewish interest with one voice instead of many. The recently established Federatie Joods Nederland, which consists of Orthodox Jews only, at first opposed the CJOEB, on the ground that the Liberal community (LJG) had members who were not Jewish according to Halakhah (Jewish law).

The Jewish Social Welfare Foundation celebrated its 50th anniversary in 1997 with several festive events, the largest, on March 2, attended by some 3,000 persons. Founded a year and a half after the liberation of the Netherlands to coordinate charitable activity among the survivors, it developed into a large professional organization. Since financial aid was provided mostly by the government, the JMW offered primarily social, psychological, and cultural services. One staff member was assigned to work with Israelis living in Holland, to try and keep them within the Jewish community.

The Ashkenazi communities of The Hague and Rotterdam now had a joint administration, located in Rotterdam, led by Hans M. Polak, the retired secretary of the Amsterdam Ashkenazi Congregation. Johan Sanders, who became secretary of the NIK in 1973, retired partly on August 1; he was to be succeeded by Ruben Vis.

Rabbi Pinchas Meijers, a Chabad Hassid, left The Hague for Antwerp, where he found the atmosphere more congenial. The only Orthodox rabbi left in The Hague was now his younger Chabad colleague, Dov Katzmann.

The new Beth Chiddush group of progressive young Jews, some from the United States and Great Britain, held an alternative Kol Nidre service on the eve of the Day of Atonement in 1997. The brief service was conducted by a woman rabbi from Great Britain.

The only kosher butcher in Rotterdam closed down, leaving the whole of the Netherlands with only two kosher butchers, both in Amsterdam.

In the Liberal Jewish Congregation of Amsterdam the longtime board retired. The new chairman, 52-year-old Lucas Stranders, stated that the advisory committee of nine members would propose a number of new policies.

The highly regarded Reverend Barend Drukarch, himself Ashkenazic, who had served for a long period as rabbi of the Sephardic community of Amsterdam, retired on the approach of his 80th birthday. Part of his position was assumed by the young Moroccan-born Moshe Enekar.

The Federation of Netherlands Zionists (FNZ) was much occupied with preparations for the elections to the World Zionist Congress in December 1997, in which the FNZ was entitled to three delegates. One delegate each was elected from Arza (the Liberal Zionist movement), Mizrahi, and Poale Zion.

In 1996 the United Israel Appeal in the Netherlands (Collectieve Israel Actie) raised over Fl. 12 million (over $6 million, $500,000 more than in 1995). In 1997 the appeal brought in over Fl. 15 million (over $7.5 million), of which well over half consisted of inheritances and legacies.

Culture

In May 1997 the Jewish Historical Museum (JHM) in Amsterdam celebrated both its tenth anniversary in its present building—the complex of former Ashkenazi synagogues in the center of town—and the 65th anniversary of its founding in its former modest premises. The museum, which received over 100,000 visitors a year, is largely subsidized by the government, which appoints and pays its staff. On the occasion of the jubilee, the JHM organized an Open Day on May 11, which was attended by some 3,000 persons. Eighteen authors—Jewish or with some Jewish background—read selections from their works, and "Jewish" pastries were served. The JHM also opened a temporary exhibition of Jewish ritual textiles that had been expertly restored, with an exhibition catalogue, in English, titled *Orphaned Objects*. Other temporary exhibitions were "Jews in Berlin," a smaller version of the large exhibition on the same subject held in Berlin, and "Vriendelijk Bedankt" (Thank you very much), some 150 of the 1,100 objects that had been donated to the museum during the past five years, most of which could not be permanently exhibited.

The JHM also issued a CD, "Chazzanuth in Prewar Amsterdam," containing rare recordings of Chief Cantor Isaac Maroko and the choir of the Great Synagogue in Amsterdam, conducted by S.H. Englander. Maroko, most of his family, and most of the choir members perished in the Shoah.

Though there were few Yiddish-speaking Jews left in Holland, there was considerable interest in Yiddish. On November 30, 1997, the centenary of the Bund, which had not more than a handful of members left in Holland, was celebrated by the Yiddisje Krais group, with the participation of the Haimish Zajn choir. Klezmer music was prominently featured in the International Jewish Music Festival, held November 13–30, 1997, in different towns.

As in previous years, numerous courses and lectures on Jewish subjects were given in Amsterdam and throughout the country, intended for the general public as well as for Jews. The University of Amsterdam's extension department offered a course on "Changing Identities in Modern Judaism," with well-known Jewish speakers from the United States, such as Arthur Hertzberg, Michael Meyer of the Hebrew Union College, Daniel Boyarin of the University of California-Berkeley, and Paula Hyman of Yale University.

The Netherlands Society for Jewish History, which is sponsored by the Netherlands Royal Academy for Arts and Sciences, held its annual symposium in Amsterdam in November 1997. It was devoted to "Contributions of Jewish Artists to European Civilization," with papers by speakers from Holland, Israel, and other countries, all of them, as it happened, women.

In connection with the symposium, there was an award ceremony for the biennial Hartog Beem Prize, named for the Dutch-Jewish historian and given for an M.A. thesis on a Jewish subject that was completed at a Dutch university during the past two years. Eight theses competed for the prize, all of them, according to the judges, of high quality. The prize went to Mirjam Alexander for her paper on Hebrew inscriptions on paintings by 17th-century Dutch painters.

American-born Judith Frishman was appointed professor of Talmud at the Roman Catholic Theological Institute in Utrecht (KThU). This was in addition to her post as adjunct professor of Christian-Jewish relations in the Theological Faculty of the University of Leyden, where she received her doctorate. The chair was established about a century ago by a Protestant theological society.

Athalya Brenner was appointed professor of Old Testament at the (Protestant) Theological Faculty of the University of Amsterdam. Originally from Israel, Brenner had been living in the Netherlands for some years and specialized in feminist theology. Irene Zwiep, a specialist in medieval mystical Hebrew literature, was appointed a professor of post-Biblical Hebrew in the Literary Faculty of the University of Amsterdam. Some criticism was voiced at the selection of the last two over equally qualified male candidates.

In May 1997 Prof. Wouter J. van Bekkum delivered his inaugural address as "professor extraordinary" (adjunct) in modern Jewish history—a special chair funded by the Jewish Studies Foundation—at the University of Amsterdam. He succeeded Rena Fuks-Mansfeld, the first occupant of the chair, whose three-year appointment had come to an end. Van Bekkum, a full professor of medieval Hebrew poetry at the University of Groninguen, lectured one day a week in Amsterdam during a ten-week term. His courses, which began in December 1996, attracted mostly older students, both Jews and non-Jews.

The work of restoring defunct synagogues, at local non-Jewish initiative, continued. The buildings served as cultural centers, with special emphasis on cultural events of a Jewish character. In the restored synagogue in Bois-le-Duc, the capital of the province of North Brabant, an exhibition opened in December 1996 on the history of the Jews in that province. Part of the building was reserved for use as a synagogue, but too few male Jews were left in Bois-le-Duc to guarantee weekly services. In the former large synagogue in the Folkingestreet in Groninguen an exhibition on Jewish life around 1900 was organized by the Jewish History Foundation in that city. An illustrated book on the subject was published for the occasion, and five works of art were unveiled, depicting both the Jewish and non-Jewish history of the city.

Publications

Four books, all written by non-Jews who were born after or shortly before the Nazi occupation of the Netherlands, deserve special mention. Iddo de Haan's *Na de Ondergang* (After Destruction of Dutch Jewry: Memories of the Persecution of the Jews in the Netherlands 1945–1985) describes the different ways in which Jews and non-Jews remember the persecution of the Jews in the Netherlands. Regina Grueter's *Een fantast schrijft geschiedebnis. De affaires rond Friedrich Weinreb.* (A Beguiler Invents History: The Friedrich Weinreb Affair), originally a Ph.D. thesis at the University of Leyden, is the story of a Jewish swindler who sold phony exit permits to Jews during the war. Arie Kuiper's *Een wijze ging voorbij* (A Wise Man Passed) is a biography of Abel J. Herzberg (1893–1989), before 1940 a well-known Zionist leader, after 1945 a successful author who, though no longer active in the Jewish community, was frequently consulted as a media spokesman on Jewish issues. And Nanda van der Zee's *Om erger te voorkomen* (In Order to Prevent Worse) aroused controversy, suggesting that Queen Wilhelmina's departure in May 1940 to London enabled the Germans to install a civilian instead of a military administration, one that was far more unfavorable to the Jews and resulted in the high percentage of deportees.

Books by Jewish authors on their wartime experiences continued to appear in print. A fairly new phenomenon were novels by second-generation Dutch Jews on the impact of their parents' wartime experiences on their own lives. Among these were *Tralievader (Father Behind Bars)* by Carl Friedman (a woman.)

Jessica Durlacher—a daughter of the late author Gerhard L. Durlacher and the wife of the Dutch-Jewish author Leon de Winter, who herself earlier translated into Dutch Art Spiegelman's *Maus*—published *Het Geweten* (The Conscience), whose main character is called Edna Mauskopf. Two novels by Arnon Grünberg (born 1973, the son of Holocaust survivors, and now living in New York), *Blauwe Maandagen* (Blue Mondays) and *Figuranten* (Supernumerary Actors), enjoyed tremendous success in Holland and also abroad.

Gerhard L. Durlacher's *Collected Works* were published posthumously; three earlier published novels by Leon de Winter (*Hoffman's Hunger*, *Kaplan*, and *Supertex*) were issued in one volume.Salvador Bloemgarten wrote *Henri Polak,* a voluminous biography of the Dutch Jewish trade union leader and founder of the A.N.D.B., the Diamond Workers Union (1860–1943). Other new works included Marga Minco's *Nagelaten Dagen* (Posthumous Days); I.B. van Creveld's *Kille-zorg* (Three Centuries of Social History of Jews in The Hague); and, by Salvador Bloemgarten and J. van Velzen, *Joods Amsterdam 1890–1940*, a collection of historic postcards.

Personalia

Judith Herzberg, who was born in 1934, received the 1997 P.C. Hooft Prize, the highest Dutch literary honor, for her entire oeuvre, mainly poetry. Her father, the late Abel J. Herzberg, received the same prize in 1974.

Among prominent Dutch Jews who died in 1996–97 were Willem G. Belinfante, for many years a top official at the Ministry of Justice and the only surviving male member of the Sephardic community of The Hague, aged 92; Koos Caneel, who for many years after the war, together with his wife, was an itinerant Jewish teacher on behalf of the NIK, teaching Jewish children scattered over the countryside, aged 84; Yiddish singer Leo Fuld, aged 84; Leo Th. Keesing, retired director of Keesing's Publishing Company, which was founded by his father, aged 84; TV host and interviewer Jaap van Meekren, aged 73; Isaac Pais, longtime chairman of the Sephardic community of Amsterdam, aged 101; and journalist and filmmaker Sam Wagenaar, aged 89.

HENRIETTE BOAS

Italy

National Affairs

DURING THE SECOND HALF of 1996 and all of 1997, Italy's leftist government, which took office after the April 1996 general elections, consolidated its hold on power and implemented economic policy aimed at enabling it to join Europe's planned single currency. After Prime Minister Romano Prodi, an economist, assumed the premiership, Italy's deficit was cut by more than $57 billion. Gross Domestic Product for 1997 was estimated at above 2 percent, and the 1997 inflation rate was also estimated at around 2 percent. In December 1997 the International Monetary Fund praised Italy's efforts to overhaul the economy. The unemployment rate remained high, however — 12.4 percent nationwide in October 1997, with higher jobless rates in the south.

On the political front, calls for a more decentralized, federal form of government remained strong in the north, although the separatist Lega Nord (Northern League) dropped somewhat in support, partially due to grandiose gestures such as declaring the "independence" of a so-called "Padanian Federal Republic" in September 1996.

Gianfranco Fini, leader of the right-wing National Alliance Party, continued his efforts to distance his party from its Fascist roots. Part of this entailed his support for Holocaust commemorations and other Jewish causes. In December 1997 he called on the European Union to press for the restitution of Jewish property seized during World War II. The same month, he condemned the anti-Semitic laws introduced in 1938 by the Fascist government of Benito Mussolini, and he also condemned the so-called Salo Republic, a die-hard Fascist-run enclave set up by Mussolini in Nazi-occupied northern Italy after the Allied invasion in World War II.

Israel and the Middle East

Italy continued to maintain friendly relations with both Israel and the Palestinians. While supportive of Israel, Italian leaders did not disguise the fact that they disapproved of Israeli prime minister Benjamin Netanyahu's policies on Jewish settlements.

In September 1996 Italy sent emergency medical supplies to Gaza in response to an urgent telephone request from Palestinian Authority president Yasir Arafat to Italian foreign minister Lamberto Dini. The Italian Foreign Ministry said the five-ton shipment was organized with the agreement of Israeli authorities. Italy had already put $100,000 at the disposal of the Palestinian Authority for purchase of medicines and equipment, following the outbreak of clashes over the opening of a tunnel in Jerusalem. Also in September, on a one-day visit to Rome, Arafat met with Italian and Vatican leaders. He paid another brief visit to Italy a month later, stopping in Naples en route between Tunis and Paris to brief Italian leaders on the outcome of the Middle East summit in Washington earlier in the month.

Prime Minister Netanyahu met with Italian leaders during a brief visit to Italy in February 1997, one day after he had met with Yasir Arafat in Davos, Switzerland. Netanyahu discussed the peace process with Italian officials, who said that the Israeli prime minister seemed determined to make progress on Middle East peace efforts.

Prime Minister Prodi, during a visit to Syria in March 1997, spoke to reporters of his "concern" about Israel's decision to build housing in east Jerusalem.

A survey published in the spring of 1997, carried out by the Pragma organization, showed that Italians were divided as to whether Italy should defend Israel if it were in danger. They also overwhelmingly favored a Palestinian state—but only one that would coexist peacefully with Israel. In response to the question "If the existence of Israel were threatened, should Italy intervene together with American and European allies to defend it?" 25.3 percent said "certainly" and 27 percent "probably"; some 15.3 percent replied "certainly not"; and more than 11 percent said "probably not." Nearly 21 percent of respondents said they would be "doubtful" of such action. To the question "Do the Palestinians have the right to their own state?" 81.7 percent of respondents replied "yes, but only if such a new state coexists peacefully with Israel."

After talks with Lebanese president Elias Hrawi during a three-day visit to Lebanon in November 1997, President Oscar Luigi Scalfaro said that Italy—Lebanon's biggest trading partner and one of the main financial contributors to reconstruction efforts after the 1975–90 Lebanese civil war—backed a United Nations resolution calling for Israel's withdrawal from south Lebanon.

Italian leaders demonstrated support for Israel by participating in a public menorah-lighting ceremony on the first night of Hanukkah, in December 1997, inaugurating celebrations to mark the 50th anniversary of Israel. President Scalfaro, Prime Minister Prodi, Rome mayor Francesco Rutelli, and other VIPs took part in the ceremony, which was held at the Arch of Titus in the Roman Forum. A symbol of Jewish exile for nearly 2,000 years, the arch bears a carving of the menorah brought back to Rome by Roman conquerors as booty after the destruction of the Second Temple in 70 C.E.

A Palestinian convicted of taking part in the hijacking of the *Achille Lauro* cruise ship in 1985, who escaped in 1996 from a Rome prison, was extradited back to Italy from Spain in December 1996. In October 1997 a Libyan wanted in the 1986 bombing of the La Belle disco in Berlin that killed three people and injured 230 others was extradited to Germany from Italy, where he had been arrested in July after fleeing Germany.

Vatican-Israel Relations

The Vatican continued its "even-handed" approach to political events in the Middle East. At the same time, relations between the Vatican and Israel broadened and intensified in a manner that had practical as well as symbolic manifestations.

Yasir Arafat, on a one-day visit to Rome in September 1996, discussed the status of Jerusalem and difficulties in the Middle East peace process with the Vatican's top diplomats, Cardinal Angelo Sodano and Archbishop Jean-Louis Tauran, the person responsible for Vatican foreign relations. Arafat discussed Middle East issues, including the status of Jerusalem, with Pope John Paul II during another one-day visit to Rome in December.

Israeli prime minister Benjamin Netanyahu had a 20-minute meeting with the pope at the Vatican in February 1997, in which he reiterated Israel's standing invitation for the pope to visit Israel. The pope replied, "God bless Israel." In a weekly Sunday address from his Vatican window in March, Pope John expressed concern over Israeli policy, which, he said, could "seriously harm" the Middle East peace process. He appeared to be referring to the recent Israeli announcement that Jewish housing would be built in east Jerusalem. The same month, the Vatican announced that it would establish full diplomatic relations with Libya. In June the pope sent letters to both Netanyahu and Arafat expressing his deep concern over the deadlock in the Middle East peace process and urging the two leaders to overcome obstacles and resume dialogue.

In April Aharon Lopez arrived in Rome as Israel's second ambassador to the Holy See since diplomatic ties were established in 1994. He replaced Shmuel Hadas.

In November the two states signed an agreement regularizing the legal status of the Roman Catholic Church and its institutions in Israel. The accord was considered the most important step forward since bilateral relations were established.

On December 23, the first night of Hanukkah, a menorah was lit for the first time ever at the Vatican, a moving reminder of the positive changes that had taken place since the historic "Nostra Aetate" declaration of 1965. As the personal representative of Pope John, Edward Cardinal Idris Cassidy, president of the Pontifical Commission for Religious Relations with the Jews, lit the first candle. Archbishop Tauran also took part in the ceremony in the Vatican garden, which was attended by Israeli and Italian Jewish representatives.

Holocaust-Related Developments

There were a number of official state, regional, or local initiatives honoring Jews or commemorating the Holocaust. Rome mayor Francesco Rutelli presided at a ceremony in 1996 at Rome's town hall, the Campidoglio, marking the 53rd anniversary of the deportation of the Jews of Rome on October 16, 1943. In December 1996 a plaque was unveiled in Padova to honor Giorgio Perlasca, an Italian businessman who saved thousands of Jews in Budapest during World War II. In October 1997 a square in the town of nearby Teolo was named in Perlasca's honor.

In early 1997 several parliamentarians launched a move to have January 27 of each year, the anniversary of the liberation of Auschwitz, commemorated in Italy as a national day of remembrance of all people who were deported or persecuted by the World War II Fascist regime—victims of racism and political persecution as well as anti-Semitism.

In June 1997 Italy's Assicurazioni Generali insurance company announced that it would set up a $12-million fund for Holocaust victims. The fund was inaugurated with a ceremony at the Knesset, in Jerusalem, in November. The fund, which was established after Israeli legislators threatened to boycott the company if it did not honor policies held by Jews killed in the Shoah, would make payments in accordance with criteria that were to be determined by a committee headed by a retired Israeli Supreme Court justice.

At the same time, in setting up the fund, Generali reiterated its position that it had no obligation to honor individual policies of Holocaust victims, as its Eastern European operations had been taken over by post–World War II Communist governments. It was not known how many Holocaust victims held Generali policies. Generali, which was founded by Venetian Jews in 1830, had extensive operations throughout Central and Eastern Europe before World War II.

In August the Italian government handed over to the Jewish community five sacks of valuables and personal belongings plundered from Jews at the Nazi death camp of San Sabba near Trieste, the only death camp on Italian soil during World War II. The sacks were discovered lying in a Treasury vault earlier in the year. They had been taken by retreating German and Austrian troops at the end of the war, but brought back to Trieste later by the Allies and sent to Rome for safekeeping in 1962.

Reports surfaced in the summer of 1997 that the Vatican might have stored 200 million Swiss francs ($130 million), mostly in gold coins, for Croatian Fascists after World War II, in order to keep the money out of Allied hands. The reports were based on a previously classified U.S. document from 1946 that was made public by an American cable television network. The Vatican denied the reports and also said it had no plans to open its archives of the World War II period.

In May 1997 the pope approved sainthood for Edith Stein, a Polish Jew who converted to Catholicism in 1922 and became a nun before she was killed at Auschwitz in 1942. In November the pope beatified Hungarian bishop Vilmos Apor, who resisted Nazi occupation and helped Jewish deportees in his hometown of Gyor in 1944. He was shot to death by Soviet soldiers in 1945 while trying to save women refugees hiding in his church from being raped.

Nazi War Criminals

On August 1, 1996, a military court in Rome found former SS captain Erich Priebke guilty of having taken part in the 1944 massacre at the Ardeatine Caves south of Rome, but set him free because of mitigating circumstances and a statute of limitations. (See AJYB 1997, pp. 321–22.) The verdict, after a three-month trial, touched off a storm of protest. Friends and family of victims barricaded the courtroom. Priebke was rearrested eight hours later and jailed again pending a German request for extradition and expected appeals. Within a month, he had received more than 600 pieces of mail from well-wishers.

In October 1996 an appeals court quashed the verdict and ordered a retrial. Priebke went back on trial in April 1997, this time along with another former Nazi, Karl Hass. In July they were both found guilty but were given sharply reduced sentences. Hass went free, and Priebke ended up with about half a year to serve. He was allowed to serve his sentence under house arrest.

Anti-Semitism, Racism, Fascist Rehabilitation

At the end of December 1996, Jewish tombs in a Rome cemetery were desecrated, prompting condemnation from city officials as well as from Jews. On New Year's Eve, vandals spray-painted swastikas and racist and anti-Semitic slogans on walls and shutters of shops and banks in Mentana, a small town near Rome where no Jews live. In March 1997 a crude firebomb was hurled at Rome's main synagogue, causing minor damage to the entryway. The synagogue was empty at the time and no one was hurt. Police immediately detained a suspect, identified as a 34-year-old Egyptian who appeared to have been drunk or mentally disturbed.

Vittorio Mussolini, second child of Italy's World War II dictator Benito Mussolini, died in June 1997. In addition to family members and right-wing politicians, about 60 extremists, dressed in black shirts that recalled Fascist garb, gave the stiff-armed Fascist salute after the funeral in Rome. They waved a flag of the period, and a wreath bore the image of Benito Mussolini. Vittorio Mussolini, a dedicated Fascist who also had a career in the film business, was buried in the family tomb in Predappio, in north-central Italy.

The same month, it was announced that Villa Feltrinelli, on Lake Garda, Benito Mussolini's final residence before he was shot dead by partisans in 1945, would be turned into a luxury hotel. Developers of the project said the Mussolini connection would be a tourist draw, and that guests could even sleep in the bed occupied by the dictator and his mistress.

An exhibition on Benito Mussolini in the small Tuscan town of Seravezza caused controversy. The show, "Man of Providence: Iconography of the Duce, 1923–1945," presented a number of Fascist-era artworks that celebrated the wartime leader. Organizers received a flood of protests against it before the scheduled July 1997 opening and postponed the opening for six weeks. At around the same time, an exhibition opened in the town of Brescia about Mussolini's Jewish lover, Margherita Sarfatti.

JEWISH COMMUNITY

Demography

Some 26,000 people were registered as members of Italian Jewish communities, but since there were believed to be thousands of others who did not formally affiliate, the total number of Jews was generally estimated at 30,000 to 35,000. Most Italian Jews lived in two cities—Rome, with about 15,000, and Milan, with about 10,000.

About half of Italy's Jews were born in Italy, and half were immigrants who had come to Italy in the past few decades. Milan had a particularly diversified community, with Jews from a score of different national origins, including Iraq, Iran, and Lebanon. In November 1997 a ceremony at Rome's Campidoglio marked the 30th anniversary of the mass immigration to Italy of 2,000 Libyan Jews following a pogrom touched off by the Six Day War.

Communal Affairs

Although most Italian Jews were nominally Orthodox (following the Ashkenazic, Sephardic, or Italian rite), they were not strictly observant. The intermarriage rate was said to be 50 percent, and as many as 60 percent of Italian Jews were estimated to be either in mixed marriages or the children of mixed-marrieds.

At the same time, the composition and character of Italian Jewry was changing. Italian Jews, traditionally pluralistic and worldly, had become, following Emancipation in the mid- to late 19th century, highly assimilated. "Secular" Jews became prominent in politics, business, the professions, and the arts—and still are today. In the past few years, however, there was a move toward stricter Orthodoxy among a portion of the Jewish community, which resulted in some friction. A number of young people have sought identity in a return to religious Judaism, inspired by several younger, more rigorous Orthodox rabbis. In Milan, where the Jewish community is made up of immigrants from a variety of national backgrounds, many from Arab countries, some tension was caused by ultra-Orthodox Jews from these backgrounds asserting their role in the larger community. Chabad also had a growing presence in Italy; in Venice, Chabad opened a kosher restaurant just off the ghetto square in September 1996.

The delicate issue of conversion of children of mixed marriages was a particular catalyst for deep concern and sharply divided public opinion. The issue was seen as a symptom of the tension between the new conservatism and the traditional open Italian Jewish approach, broadening into a debate over "Who is a Jew?" and how Judaism should be practiced. The crisis erupted in the wake of a ruling by the Italian Rabbinical Assembly in October 1997 that the only children whose conversion would be permitted would be those whose mothers asked to convert at the same time. Rome's elderly chief rabbi, Elio Toaff, considered a liberal, did not hide his disagreement with this decision. Heretofore, it was standard practice to convert infants of mixed marriages at birth, even if the mother did not convert, if the family intended to raise the child as a Jew.

It was in Milan that the furor over the new ruling took on particular intensity when Milan chief rabbi Giuseppe Laras made it known that unconverted children of mixed marriages would not be permitted to attend Jewish schools. The case that triggered sharpest debate involved a Jewish father and a non-Jewish mother whose son had been converted at birth and was enrolled in the Milan Jewish nursery school. The now pregnant mother and her husband withdrew the boy from the school when they found out that the baby about to be born — who under the new ruling would not have the possibility of being converted — would not be allowed to go to the Jewish school. Jewish public opinion in Milan was sharply and loudly divided on the problem, which became the community's key internal policy issue. The local Jewish newspaper was inundated with letters and op-ed pieces on the conversion issue and the broader divisions it represented. Meetings and open discussions were held, and some Jews went so far as to predict that the central community organization would split — the question being, which faction would leave and which would stay

In Rome, community elections in May 1997 voted in a new leadership that was composed of many younger, more religiously conservative Jews, who were also much more militant in proclaiming a specific Jewish identity. This added to the polarization and led to accusations by liberals that the mounting fundamentalism sought to marginalize secular Jews in the community and narrow the horizons of Judaism. The conservatives, in turn, criticized more secular or liberal Jews for their attitudes toward the faith, which they considered too lax. Lia Levi, the founder and editor of the 30-year-old Rome Jewish community monthly, *Shalom,* and her husband, Luciano Tas, who was a lead writer on the paper, both quit *Shalom* because of what they said was pressure from the conservatives.

Under new income tax regulations, in 1997 Italians, regardless of their religion, were allowed to designate a tiny fraction (8 per mil) of their tax payments for the benefit of the Jewish community. This option had already long existed for some other religious organizations, including the Roman Catholic Church. The Jewish community carried out a publicity campaign, aided by testimonials from prominent Jews, to urge even non-Jews to contribute to the Jewish community, as a means of fighting racism and fostering democracy and pluralism in Italy.

Italian Jewish communities participated in international and interregional activities linking Italian Jews with Jews in other countries in Europe as well as with Israel. Many of these activities were coordinated through the European Council of Jewish Communities (ECJC). At Purim 1997, the ECJC arranged its first "Mifgash"—a singles weekend for Jewish adults in their 30s, which drew several dozen participants from six European countries.

The Venice Jewish community was awarded the 1996 "Venetian of the Year" award, sponsored by a local civic group, a local bank, and the Veneto region regional council. Venice's Jewish history is respected by Italians, and the Jewish ghetto of Venice is an important tourist attraction.

Jewish-Catholic and Jewish-Muslim Relations

In July 1996 the Union of Italian Jewish Communities sent a letter to the Israeli ambassador, for transmission to the Education Ministry and the Religious Affairs Ministry, deploring actions by some Israeli Jews in Hebron that deliberately insulted the Islamic religion and the prophet Mohammed.

In November 1996 Israeli singer Rinat Gabay joined two other singers—an Italian Catholic and a Muslim—in performing the song "The Tree of Faith and Peace" during celebrations at the Vatican marking Pope John Paul II's 50th anniversary as a priest.

During a brief visit to Sarajevo in April 1997, the pope awarded his International Peace Prize and $50,000 each to the Sarajevo Jewish community's social aid organization, La Benevolencija, and to three other Sarajevo-based religious humanitarian organizations—one Roman Catholic, one Muslim, and one Serbian Orthodox.

Also in April, the Vatican responded to Jewish protests over a stamp issued by the Vatican post office that shows Jews wearing the pointed hats of the medieval ghetto. A Vatican spokesman said no offense to Jews was intended by the stamp, which was part of a series reproducing miniatures from the 13th century. In one of the series, Jesus is shown speaking to an audience that includes people wearing headgear that identifies them as Jews.

During an 11-day visit to his native Poland in June, Pope John paid tribute to the millions of Jews who were killed in the Holocaust. He said that remembrance of their past tragedies and common heritage should spur reconciliation between Poles and Jews.

In July the Italian publisher Mursia withdrew a book about Jews and the Catholic church, following pressure from the Vatican and charges by Italy's Jewish leadership and others that it contained anti-Semitic historic revisionism. Italian Christian-Jewish friendship organizations also protested. The book, *Gli ebrei e la Chiesa* (Jews and the Church), was written by a priest, Vitaliano Mattioli, who teaches at two Roman Catholic colleges.

In September the Vatican issued a 300-page book for religious teachers to use with the Universal Catechism that urges them to pay particular attention to Judaism, to promote "tolerance, understanding and dialogue," and to educate against anti-Semitism.

The Vatican held an unprecedented closed-door symposium, October 30–

November 1, 1997, to examine "The Roots of Anti-Judaism in the Christian Environment." The meeting was attended by senior cardinals and other Vatican officials as well as about 60 Roman Catholic scholars and theologians. Representatives of other Christian denominations, including Protestant and Orthodox, also attended, but no Jews were invited. During the symposium the pope strongly condemned anti-Semitism and said long-standing anti-Jewish prejudice was responsible for the passivity of many Christians in the face of the Nazi persecution of Jews. The symposium did not produce a major papal document on anti-Semitism; however, a final statement at the conclusion of the meeting said that Christians who manifest anti-Semitism "offend God and the church itself."

Culture

A wide range of lectures, concerts, performances, classes, and other Jewish cultural events were programmed by Jewish communities and cultural centers in various cities. Rome and Milan featured several Jewish events virtually every week. In addition, many Jewish-themed events, including conferences and university study programs, were held outside the sponsorship of Jewish bodies, or were jointly sponsored by the Jewish communities and local civic authorities. Jewish events also drew an increasing audience of non-Jews. Amos Luzzatto, editor-in-chief of the Jewish intellectual journal *La Rassegna Mensile di Israel*, referred to this phenomenon as "an impressive growth of Jewish cultural interest in non-Jewish milieux."

Among exhibits on Jewish themes in 1997 was one of photographs of concentration camps by Erich Hartmann, in September, at the Palace of Expositions in Rome, one of the city's leading museums, and another in the town of Carpi, an exhibition on local Jewish history, in the spring.

There were several conferences and other events in 1997 marking the tenth anniversary of the death of Italian Holocaust survivor and writer Primo Levi, who died in April 1987, an apparent suicide. These were sponsored by civic institutions as well as by Jewish organizations.

Some noteworthy events under Jewish sponsorship were an international conference on "The Function of Jewish History and Culture Centers in Contemporary Society," organized by the Milan-based Center for Contemporary Jewish Documentation in February 1997, to inaugurate its newly remodeled premises. The same month, several Jewish organizations sponsored a symposium in Rome on "The Risorgimento and Religious Minorities."

Jewish music underwent a boom of popularity, particularly Klezmer music, and many mostly non-Jewish Italian Klezmer bands were formed. In the summer of 1996 and 1997 the city of Ancona hosted an International Festival of Klezmer Music, sponsored by a local youth organization. A Center for the Study of Jewish Music was founded in Milan in early 1997, and its director, Francesco Spagnolo, hosted a weekly program on Jewish music on a popular Milan radio station. In June 1997 the Venice municipality helped sponsor the city's second

Festival of Jewish Culture, and in September the Jewish Culture Center and the Rome municipality jointly organized a three-day festival on Roman Jewish culture. Jewish music and performance were featured at a number of other festivals around the country.

There was particular interest in Yiddish and East European Jewish culture. Yiddish courses were taught in Rome and Venice, and there were numerous concerts of Yiddish music in various cities. More than a dozen Yiddish films from the 1920s and 1930s were offered on video in Italy for the first time in 1996.

Jewish studies were taught at several universities, and in early 1997 a Jewish Studies Center was established at the University of Milan, thanks to a grant by a family foundation headed by Romanian-born Holocaust survivor Avram Goldstein-Goren, who has lived in Milan since the end of World War II.

Two major feature films and a documentary with Holocaust themes were released in 1997. *Memoria*, a documentary on Italian Holocaust survivors, was released early in the year. *La Tregua* (The Truce) is based on the memoirs of Primo Levi, and *La Vita e' Bella* (Life Is Beautiful) is a tragicomedy set in a death camp, directed by and starring one of Italy's top comedians, Roberto Benigni. The latter, released in December, was the biggest box-office hit of the Christmas–New Year season.

Conservation of Jewish monuments and heritage was a theme addressed by a conference in Rome in April 1997. Several historic synagogues in Italy were in various phases of repair or restoration. A Jewish museum opened in Ferrara in June 1997. A new seat of the Rome Jewish Community archive opened the same month, with Rome mayor Francesco Rutelli attending the inaugural ceremony.

Publications

Scores, if not hundreds, of books on Jewish themes—including fiction, history, biography, essays, Holocaust, religious works, and translations—were published by mainstream publishing houses as well as the Florence-based Jewish publisher, Giuntina. Menorah Bookstore in Rome, Italy's only Jewish bookstore, moved into new, larger premises and put its expanded catalogue on the World Wide Web.

Books on Jewish themes were given high exposure. The publication of the Italian editions of two books by Israeli author A.B. Yehoshua, for example, merited more than half a page in *La Stampa* newspaper in October 1996. A new book of essays by Nobel Prize-winning Jewish scientist Rita Levi Montalcini in November 1996 rated a full page of coverage in the newspaper *La Repubblica*. In September 1997 President Oscar Luigi Scalfaro took part in the ceremony launching a major new two-volume history of the Jews in Italy. Various political and cultural VIPs took part in events marking the publication of *L'Impostore*, the diaries of Giorgio Perlasca, the Italian businessman who saved thousands of Jews in Budapest during World War II.

A 22-year-old Jew, Mike Rabba, created a splash with his comic coming-of-age novel *Che differenza c'e tra una papera, un'anatra e un'oca?* (What Is the Difference Between a Duckling, a Duck, and a Goose?). Among other books of note were *La Parola Ebreo* (The Word Jew) by Rosetta Loy, a memoir by a non-Jew of the effects of the Fascist, anti-Jewish racial laws; *L'ebreo corrosivo* (The Corrosive Jew) by Moni Ovadia; *Un'Aringa in Paradiso* (A Herring in Heaven), an encyclopedia of Jewish humor by Elena Loewenthal; and two new volumes in a series of guidebooks to Jewish heritage in each Italian region.

In 1996 the Jewish intellectual journal *La Rassegna Mensile di Israel* issued a special two-volume edition on Yiddish. One volume included essays on Yiddish culture, and the other was a collection of Yiddish stories translated into Italian. In 1997 the magazine *Letteratura Internazionale* devoted an issue to Yiddish literature, and the Jewish publishing house Giuntina issued the first Italian translation of the works of Krakow Yiddish bard Mordechaj Gebirtig, who was killed in the Holocaust. The book was sold along with a cassette of Gebirtig's songs.

Personalia

Tullia Zevi, president of the Union of Jewish Communities in Italy and one of the most prominent women in Italy, received a number of honors. In May 1997 Rome mayor Francesco Rutelli awarded her the Premio Simpatia for "her commitment in working for peace and tolerance among peoples, without ever forgetting the tragedy of the Holocaust." In June she received the Artisti Uniti Prize in Florence for similar work, and she also received the Donna Roma Prize in Rome, an annual award given to outstanding women in the fields of culture, art, science, and public affairs. (Suha Arafat and Matilda Cuomo also received the award.) Also in June, the Italian government appointed Zevi to an unprecedented high-level commission charged with carrying out a probe of allegations that Italian troops had carried out brutal human-rights abuses when stationed in Somalia as peacekeeping forces between late 1992 and 1994.

At a ceremony in New York in October 1996, Prime Minister Romano Prodi was awarded the Appeal of Conscience Foundation's 1996 World Statesman Award.

Author Lia Levi won the 47th Castello Prize for children's literature in 1997 for her book *Una Valle Piena di stelle* (A Valley Full of Stars). In June 1997 journalist Fiamma Nirenstein was awarded the Ilaria Alpi Journalism Prize for her articles in various newspapers.

RUTH ELLEN GRUBER

Switzerland

National Affairs

IN THE POLITICAL LIFE of Switzerland, 1997 was the midterm year of the four-year national legislature. Elections in several of the 26 cantons and in a few major cities showed, with very few exceptions, the same pattern as the national elections in 1995: the Social Democratic Party on the left and the Swiss People's Party on the right (the latter established almost exclusively in the German part of Switzerland) were the winners. Both parties belong to the four-party coalition forming the Swiss government, with a balanced partisan spread of ministers: two Catholic, two Liberal, two Social-Democratic, one Swiss People's Party. This phenomenon has been dubbed the "magic formula," insuring political stability without a formal opposition.

The Social Democrats were increasingly a party of the liberal, middle-class, young to middle-aged, urban, educated professionals and managers, whereas some of the traditional Social Democratic voters, the workers, seemed to be drifting to the right, fearful of unemployment, foreigners, and economic crises. Often they opted for the People's Party, with its populist pro-Swiss agitation against foreigners.

The gains of the two big parties in local, regional, and cantonal elections highlighted the rapid decline of the traditional middle parties, including the religiously defined Catholic and Protestant parties. The Greens, the ecological party, were small but growing steadily.

Recession held Switzerland in a firm grip again in 1997 despite an optimistic outlook at the end of 1996. Unemployment rates, which were negligible up to the early 1980s, rose to an alarming 10 percent or more in certain parts of the country, the French- and Italian-speaking parts suffering more than the rest. Consumers stopped spending money, the National Bank did not help the situation by changing its restrictive money policy, and Switzerland almost reached deflation at the end of the year.

Tourism declined and picked up only at the end of the year, thanks to early snow in the mountains. The economic community was rocked at the beginning of December by the announced merger of two of the three big banks, Union Bank of Switzerland (UBS) and Swiss Bank Corporation (SBC), to form one of the largest banks in the world, together with the announcement that in Switzerland alone some 2,000 jobs would be eliminated. The outlook was dim. Apprenticeships for high-school graduates were scarce, inflicting fears of an increase in juvenile unemployment and related juvenile crime. Drugs were a big problem, although an experimental program of controlled dispensing of cheap heroin to selected addicts won international acclaim.

Switzerland was still not a member of the main international alliances, with the exception of the Organization for Security & Cooperation in Europe (OSCE), which it presided over for a year up to the middle of 1997. It accepted NATO'S invitation to the Partnership for Peace, however, and Swiss diplomats carried out missions for various international organizations such as the UN, the OSCE, and others. A contingent of "yellow caps" performed unarmed logistics duty in Bosnia, as they did in other countries upon UN request, and there were UN military observers in Swiss uniform serving in a few hot spots in the world. But the bilateral negotiations with the European Union were stalled. Many politicians in Switzerland urged that full membership in the EU and the UN be put before the people again, although both had been rejected in earlier polls.

Switzerland's absence from the EU meant that the country was excluded from the so-called Schengen agreement, regulating the movements of thousands of legal or illegal foreigners seeking refuge and a better life outside their native lands. The parties to the Schengen agreement could send foreigners back to the country of their first entry in Europe; Switzerland could not. Knowing this, bosses of criminal drug gangs sent their agents to Switzerland to conduct business, while they stayed clear of danger themselves.

HOLOCAUST-RELATED ISSUES

Underlying and overshadowing all events of the year 1997 was the ongoing debate about Switzerland's actions during World War II. Various issues had been raised and investigated on and off since the end of the war. Most of the questions centered on the role of Swiss banks and other financial institutions—specifically, the fate of the personal accounts opened by European Jews and others, and the gold and other assets plundered by the Nazis from conquered state treasuries and individuals and deposited in Switzerland. Both issues—the dormant accounts and the plundered gold—had long and tangled histories, but they came under the most intense scrutiny now, 50 years after war's end. During 1996 and 1997 there was considerable activity in regard to the former; the latter was also the subject of investigation.

A report issued in May 1997 by then U.S. Under Secretary of Commerce Stuart Eizenstat, on efforts to recover assets stolen or hidden by Germany during World War II, harshly criticized the actions of most Allied and neutral countries for failing to aid Holocaust victims both during and after the war. In a detailed account of Swiss financial dealings with Nazi Germany, the report suggested that, by acting as bankers for the Nazis, the Swiss helped to prolong the war. The Swiss Federal Council called the report "one-sided" and some of its conclusions "unfounded."

Dormant Accounts

The matter of unclaimed or heirless assets of survivors had been on the agenda of the Allies at the end of the war, but it took second place to the larger questions of reparations and refugee settlement. Efforts beginning in 1947 — both by individuals and by Jewish organizations — to identify heirless assets were hampered by Swiss bank secrecy regulations (ironically, the very laws passed in 1934 to help tax-evading French citizens that would also help to protect Jewish deposits from appropriation efforts by the Nazis). Survivors who knew of family assets in Switzerland met with numerous bureaucratic roadblocks in their searches, such as requirements that death certificates be produced for relatives killed in concentration camps.

The Swiss Jewish community began lobbying in the early 1950s for a change in the laws so as to facilitate the identification process. Everyone understood how formidable a task this would be, with many accounts untraceable due to the use of pseudonyms, numbers, or intermediaries. There was also some hesitation about publishing names of individuals who might be living in Iron Curtain countries, for fear that Communist governments would seize the assets or otherwise endanger those involved.

In 1962, after years of pressure by the Swiss Jewish community, the Parliament passed a law creating a central registry that would both identify and catalogue assets in dormant accounts and search out rightful owners who had been persecuted on political, racial, or religious grounds, or their heirs. A survey produced an inventory of assets worth more than 9 million Swiss francs (then about $2 million) held by banks, fiduciary companies, private administrators, and insurance companies, in 961 separate accounts. Of the 7,000 applications received, most were rejected on grounds of insufficient information; some 132 claims were approved, for 1.6 million Swiss francs; 151 accounts belonged to individuals in Eastern bloc countries, and no further action was taken in these cases; and 228 identified owners, most of them Jews, could not be located. At the end of the period 1966–77, during which this process took place, the unassigned assets, almost SF 2 million, were placed in a trust fund, 60 percent of which was given to the SIG (Schweizerischer Israelitischer Gemeindebund/Swiss Federation of Jewish Communities), and the balance to the Swiss Refugee Aid Society. The SIG decided to share its allocation with the American Jewish Joint Distribution Committee (JDC), which had helped Swiss Jews during the war to support Jewish refugees.

The 1962 process was viewed as only partially satisfactory. For one thing, there were loopholes in the law itself — which among other things allowed for no auditing or oversight of the banks' search procedures; for another, the implementation of the law was regarded as inadequate.

The persistence of individual claimants and Jewish organizations forced the Swiss to return to the issue in 1995. Early in that year, Rolf Bloch, president of the Swiss Federation of Jewish Communities, learned that the Federal Banking Commission had ordered the Swiss banks to look for accounts dormant for more than the legally required ten years. He asked the commission and the Swiss Bankers' Association (SBA) to widen the search to include accounts dormant longer than 50 years. (Paperwork may legally be destroyed after ten years, but records of accounts must be kept permanently.) A few months later, the World Jewish Congress (WJC) made the same request. In September 1995, the SBA, the Swiss Federation of Jewish Communities, and the WJC agreed that a search should be conducted for accounts opened between 1933 and May 8, 1945, the end of the war. It was further agreed that, starting in January 1996, the acting ombudsman of the Swiss banks would open a central information service to expedite all individual requests for searches.

In early February 1996, the SBA announced that its own internal investigation of Holocaust-era accounts had found 775 accounts containing some $32 million. The WJC criticized the search as inadequate, and its president, Edgar M. Bronfman, appealed to Sen. Alfonse D'Amato, chairman of the U.S. Senate's Banking Committee—which oversees foreign banks' activities in the United States—to look into the actions of the Swiss banks. D'Amato held the first of several hearings in April, during which Holocaust survivors testified to the difficulties they had encountered in trying to reclaim family assets.

In early May, with publicity and public pressure mounting, the SBA, clearly hoping to relieve the growing tension with the United States, agreed to set up a commission to investigate the status of Holocaust victims' assets. Signed on May 2 by the World Jewish Restitution Organization (WJRO) and the Swiss Bankers Association (SBA) in New York, the Memorandum of Understanding called for creation of a body of prominent individuals, to include Swiss non-Jews and Jews who were not Swiss, to oversee "forensic" audits of all the Swiss banks that were operating during the Nazi years, to be conducted by three internationally renowned auditing firms. The Independent Committee of Eminent Persons (ICEP)—whose expenses would be covered by the SBA—became known as the Volcker commission, for its American chairman, Paul Volcker, former head of the Federal Reserve Board, who was chosen by the other committee members. The ICEP audit was delayed in starting because the auditors wanted to be insured against possible future lawsuits. After a pilot audit in six banks, the major work in all the banks was set to begin in January 1998.

Meanwhile, in the course of 1996 and 1997, the ombudsman's office received 2,500 applications. Of these, 1,000 were excused from paying the required fee of SF 100 on humanitarian grounds. The SF 150,000 in fees collected from other claimants was donated to the private Foundation for Humanity and Justice headed by parliamentarian and university professor Gian-Reto Plattner in Basel. In 1997 the foundation disbursed SF 1 million in contributions to Holocaust survivors, Jews and Roma (Gypsies) alike, in Belarus and Latvia. While the donation by the ombudsman to Plattner's foundation was regarded as generous by some, others thought it inappropriate—a forced payment by survivors to help other survivors. Some 200 claims were submitted to the ombudsman through Senator D'Amato's office, for which no fees were paid. By June 1997, the ombudsman's office had uncovered SF 10 million, out of a claimed SF 17 million, belonging to nine Jewish victims. One Jewish individual alone, identity not revealed, claimed most of the SF 10 million.

In the early summer of 1997, after insisting for two years that they had no papers older than the legally required ten years, the banks began unearthing documents. The Union Bank of Switzerland (UBS) and the Swiss Bank Corporation (SBC) worked on their documents in various locations throughout Switzerland, using the knowledge and memories of retired personnel. Crédit Suisse (CS) brought truckloads of papers to Zurich, to an old warehouse, where they filled shelves 12 kilometers in length. These more aggressive searches were productive. On July 23, the SBA published newspaper advertisements in 28 countries and on the Internet listing 1,756 dormant accounts, along with names of owners and people with power of attorney. It was unclear, however, how many of these were Holocaust victims; also, two-thirds of the accounts were valued at less than $3,500. The total value of the accounts advertised was more than SF 60 million, roughly $42 million. The discrepancy between this and the $30 million reported earlier was explained by Swiss Bank Corporation as an error on its part—failure to report accounts because information was not transferred to a computer data base in the 1970s. Paul Volcker described publication of the list as only a first step in a much broader process.

On October 29, the SBA made public a new list of 3,687 dormant accounts opened by non-Swiss individuals prior to the end of World War II—with a total value of approximately $4 million. An expedited applications process was put into place, requiring a "relaxed standard of proof" from claimants.

As chairman of its claims resolution tribunal, in November 1997 the ICEP elected Jewish law professor Hans Michael Riemer, from the University of Zurich, an experienced judge. There was some concern at the end of 1997 that only 6 of the 15 arbiters had been selected, since the claims resolution process was scheduled to speed up in 1998. The board of trustees for the claims resolution tribunal was chaired by Volcker himself. The two other members were Israel Singer, secretary-general of the WJC, and Swiss law professor and senator René Rhinow.

Swiss Government Task Force

Only the Memorandum of Understanding of May 1996 had succeeded in "waking up the Swiss government," Swiss foreign minister Flavio Cotti said in an interview with the Swiss Jewish weekly *Jüdische Rundschau* in November 1996. Until then, the Swiss government had pretended that the issue was a private business matter of the banks, with no connection to Switzerland as a state.

A month earlier Cotti had established a task force within the Foreign Affairs

Ministry, under the chairmanship of Ambassador Thomas Borer, deputy secretary-general of the ministry, to investigate the Holocaust assets controversy. Borer represented Switzerland during numerous hearings in Congress and other bodies and acted as liaison to Jewish groups in the United States.

One of the task force's first achievements was the swift commissioning of serious historical research into the semi-secret contracts between Switzerland and Poland in 1949 and similar contracts later with Hungary, in which the Swiss agreed to turn over the dormant assets of Polish citizens in Swiss banks, in order to compensate Swiss citizens in Poland for their nationalized property. The Poles got some SF 600,000; the deal with Hungary was never implemented.

Humanitarian Fund

On January 1, 1997, Swiss government minister Jean-Pascal Delamuraz made a statement calling demands for the compensation of Holocaust victims by Swiss banks and threats to boycott Swiss banks "blackmail." (See more, below.) Jewish leaders in the United States, incensed by his comment and the failure of the Swiss government to repudiate it, withdrew from their ongoing negotiations. At the end of January, the City and State of New York threatened sanctions against U.S. affiliates of the Swiss banks. Quick to respond to these threats, on February 5, the big three Swiss banks agreed to set up a humanitarian fund of 100 million Swiss francs (around $70 million) to help needy Holocaust victims. Jewish leaders in New York responded positively a day later, saying they would not support a boycott of the Swiss banks. The fund was subsequently augmented by other Swiss banks, insurance companies, and businesses as well as by the Swiss National Bank. There was some fear that a contribution by the latter, which is almost entirely state-owned, could be challenged if put to a vote in Parliament. In the end, Parliament left it to the bank to decide on its own. With the addition of the SNB's SF 100 million, by the end of 1997 the fund totaled close to $200 million. The fund's board includes representatives of Jewish organizations and private Swiss citizens and is chaired by Rolf Bloch, head of the Swiss Jewish community; it is administered largely by the World Jewish Restitution Organization.

It proved difficult to disburse the money to former victims. The work was hampered initially by internal disagreements, with chairman Bloch insisting that all victims, not just Jews, benefit from the fund. It was agreed that the first recipients would be the so-called double victims in Eastern Europe, those who had suffered both from the Nazis and from Communism and had been ruined by the inflation after the collapse of the Soviet Union. It also became clear very quickly that the affiliated organizations of the World Jewish Restitution Organization could not deliver the necessary lists to the fund as quickly as originally hoped. The first recipients of $400 each were victims in Riga, Latvia. The next disbursement was made in Hungary to about 20,000 people.

It was subsequently decided that needy survivors in the United States, Israel, and Western Europe would receive the equivalent of SF 2,000 ($1,350). The first Roma (Gypsy) victims were given DM 2,000 in southern Germany at the beginning of the year; the Romani Federation turned over a list of some 16, 000 names and addresses to the fund administration. The problem in the Western world is that victims, even Jewish victims, are eligible only if registered with a survivor- or refugee-support organization linked to the WJRO. In Switzerland, there was some confusion about whether the approximately 400 members of a self-help group of survivors would have to have their eligibility verified by the WJRO— which they regarded as unnecessary—or could apply directly to the fund administration in Bern.

The fund's directors were concerned that its purpose could be misinterpreted and made sure to stress that it was not a fund for restitution—based on specific wartime experiences—but was a purely humanitarian gesture for all victims who had suffered in any way under Nazism. Chairman Bloch frequently explained that the fund's purpose was to demonstrate that the Swiss people cared about and com- miserated with the victims.

Proposed Solidarity Foundation

Early in March 1997 the Swiss government proposed revaluing its gold reserves to create a $4.7 billion solidarity foundation, the earnings from which would be used to help victims of natural catastrophes and oppression everywhere—pos- sibly including groups and projects of Holocaust survivors. The proposal for this foundation was subject to approval by parliamentary consent and national ref- erendums to be held in 1999 and 2000.

Independent Commission of Experts (Bergier Commission)

The Memorandum of Understanding had requested Switzerland to investigate its role during the Nazi years; however, it was not the government but Parliament that initiated legislation, in December 1996, creating a historians' commission, which began functioning in March 1997. Its members include American histori- ans Sybil Milton, from the U.S. Holocaust Memorial Museum in Washington, and Harold James of Princeton University; the Pole Wladyslaw Bartoszewski; and the Israeli historian Saul Friedlander, himself a child survivor. The research di- rector is Dr. Jacques Picard, author of the standard work *Switzerland and the Jews 1933–45*. The commission of experts, known as the Bergier Commission for its chairman, Prof. Jean-François Bergier, noted Swiss French historian, issued a pre- liminary report in December 1997 on the Swiss gold trade with Nazi Germany. According to statistics in the report, the Reichsbank shipped roughly $450 mil- lion worth of gold taken from the central banks of Nazi-occupied countries to Swiss banks during the war, and sent $146 million worth of looted individual as- sets to Switzerland (in today's dollars worth more than $4 billion and more than

$1.2 billion, respectively, not including interest). The report was prepared for an international conference convened in London that addressed the issue of the $70 million in so-called residual gold from World War II—gold plundered by the Nazis from occupied countries. The conference was organized by British foreign minister Robin Cook at the request of Lord Greville Janner. The conference commended Switzerland for the work it was doing in this area. Stuart Eizenstat, representing the U.S. government, proposed that the remaining millions of dollars of Nazi gold that the Western allies' tripartite gold commission had still not distributed to its original owners go into a fund for Holocaust survivors.

The historians' commission was also scheduled to research the flow of possible perpetrators' assets into Switzerland, the archives of firms conducting business with Nazi Germany or using slave labor in its affiliates just across the border in Germany, and Swiss refugee policy during the Nazi era.

The Meili Affair

On January 8, 1997, Christoph Meili, a night watchman in the Union Bank of Switzerland's headquarters on Bahnhofstrasse in Zurich found documents in the shredder room that he identified as dating from crucial wartime years. They were from the Eidgenössische Bank (Federal Bank), a big bank during that period that conducted business exclusively with Nazi Germany and its satellites, went broke after the war, and was taken over by the UBS. Meili knew that three weeks before, the new legislation creating a historians' commission contained a paragraph forbidding the destruction of all documents from the Nazi era. All the banks had issued even stricter orders a few days later, forbidding the destruction of any documents, no matter from what period. The documents he chose to save were a handwritten record book of loan grants during the 1920s, up to 1926, and account records from the 1930s up to the '70s, identifying properties in Berlin, with exact addresses, obviously in the possession of Eidgenössische Bank and later of UBS.

Meili took the papers home and decided to turn them over to a Jewish institution. Since he did not want to travel to Bern, to the Israeli embassy, or to send the papers by mail, he telephoned Information and asked for something "Israelitic." The operator gave him the first entry in the list, the Israelitische Cultusgemeinde Zürich (ICZ), the largest of the four Jewish community organizations in Zürich. After their security people received Meili and his papers and thanked him, Werner Rom, the ICZ president, and secretary-general Ada Winter decided to turn over the papers to the police.

Since it was a Friday, nothing happened until Monday morning, to the dismay of the ICZ leadership. On Tuesday morning, the district attorney, a former bank lawyer (with CS), allowed the UBS to issue a communiqué of its own about the matter, before publishing his own, which said that thanks to the full cooperation of the bank, the matter had been satisfactorily cleared up. Upon this, the ICZ called a press conference, where Meili, who had turned himself in to the police on Monday night, appeared and explained how and why he had saved the documents. He was a deeply religious person, he said. When God gave the papers into his hands, he felt called on to take action. The ICZ put its lawyer at his disposal when he turned himself in.

From that day on, Christoph Meili was an international media personality. News teams from all over the world went to see the young family every day in their modest house half an hour from Zurich. Sen. Alfonse D'Amato and his staff tried to convince him to come to the United States to appear before a Senate committee. After then UBS president Robert Studer accused Meili on TV of simply seeking publicity, Meili was asked by his supporters to put off going to the United States for a scheduled television appearance, so as not to play into the UBS's hands.

The ICZ paid to send the Meilis to a religious retreat, when they needed most to be incommunicado for a while. Their lawyer got them a secret phone number and a new mobile phone with a new number. The family received a few invitations for Friday night dinners and food baskets from Holocaust survivors. For Swiss Jews, and also for the rest of the population, Christoph Meili was a hero. The Parliament introduced a motion to protect people like Meili from being fired, a process that was not finished, in part because the Meilis left Switzerland secretly and sought refuge in the United States, which changed the Swiss public's opinion of him.

Meili had been suspended by his guard firm immediately after he removed the papers from the bank and was subsequently fired, with due notice. He got his full salary until the end of April 1997, and the ICZ pledged to help him over the months of unemployment if he did not find a job at once. Community leaders were in a difficult position: they could not risk appearing to be Meili's benefactors, for fear that people would believe they had bought his help. This was usually one of the first questions journalists posed to Meili: How much did the Jews pay you? The sinister assumptions and allegations never stopped, especially after Meili left Switzerland.

With some difficulty, the ICZ found a job for Meili, not a very good one, but at least something to fill in until he got something better. But before starting the job, as soon as his last bank salary payment arrived, Meili and his family left secretly for the United States. When they arrived there at the end of April, New York attorney Ed Fagan and Senator D'Amato took them under their wing. On June 4, 1997, the U.S. House immigration subcommittee voted to grant sanctuary to the Meilis.

The Zurich legal system took nine months to decide on whether or not to accuse Meili of breach of banking secrecy or not. The chief of the UBS archive, who was responsible for the unlawful destruction of relevant documents, was never in danger of being charged with breaking the federal law forbidding the destruction of wartime materials. So the book was closed on both cases in October.

Swiss Reaction

Many Swiss people started to feel uneasy as Switzerland's government and citizens found themselves increasingly in the limelight. Suddenly Switzerland was depicted as a wrongdoer, a war profiteer who dealt with looted and victims' gold from the Reichsbank, sold arms to Nazi Germany, and turned over Jewish refugees to the Gestapo. The Swiss banks were attacked as hoarders of dormant accounts belonging to Holocaust victims, demanding death certificates from their heirs.

The younger generations were better able to deal objectively with these accusations and to confront the past without prejudice than the deeply offended older generation that had struggled through World War II, the men standing guard at the borders, the women looking after farms, shops, and businesses. The discussions between historians, politicians, the people in the street, and in the media became heated. Some letters to the editor were openly negative or even anti-Semitic, and the general attitude toward Jews, Jewish organizations in the United States, and Israel was very angry. The controversy was ongoing, fueled almost every day by new revelations and discoveries of facts, documents, and deeds, the stream of historical and media reports, TV films, accusations, attacks, excuses, claims, complaints, statements, and interviews. Experts predicted at the end of 1997 that the debate would last for at least another two years, if not more, virtually guaranteeing a hostile environment in which to pursue justice for the victims. But fairness for Switzerland was demanded as well—an acknowledgement that the overwhelming majority of the population was anti-Nazi, helped to support Jewish refugees, and did not even know what their leaders did behind their backs. (The formula "justice for the victims and fairness for Switzerland" was first coined by Dr. Rolf Bloch, in a hearing of the U.S. House Banking Committee in December 1996.)

Anti-Semitism

Anti-Semitic slurs began at the very end of 1996 when a member of the Swiss Parliament's upper house said in all earnestness that Swiss Jews should ask American Jews to stop their continued attacks on Switzerland if they did not want to risk anti-Semitism here. To this expression of anti-Semitism in the guise of concern, Rolf Bloch, president of the Jewish community, merely responded that this was the wrong reproach to the wrong address.

The year 1997 was the worst for Swiss Jewry since the 1930s and World War II. It started immediately on January 1, when Economy Minister Jean Pascal Delamuraz, in interviews with two French-language newspapers in Geneva and Lausanne to mark the end of his one-year term as Swiss federal president, said that the money asked by the World Jewish Congress for a Holocaust victims' fund was blackmail and a demand for ransom. He said that there was an attempt under way to undermine the financial standing of Switzerland. Worst of all, he said that in view of all the attacks on Switzerland, he had to ask himself whether Auschwitz was in fact in Switzerland, not in Poland. His spokesman had demanded that this sentence be withdrawn from the printed interview; one paper complied, one did not.

There was instant outrage at his words—but also widespread approval. Delamuraz got hundreds of letters congratulating him. There were letters to the editor full of praise. Delamuraz declined for two weeks to apologize. When he did, in a letter to World Jewish Congress president Edgar M. Bronfman, he said only that he was sorry for the reactions his words had caused.

Delamuraz's words opened long-closed floodgates. The offices of the Federation of Jewish Communities, the communities themselves, and well-known Jewish personalities were besieged with hate mail for weeks, even months. It did not arrive anonymously, but mostly with names and addresses. After a while, positive mail started to arrive, too, in roughly equal amounts. But elderly Jewish men and women who had fled to Switzerland from anti-Semitic countries said that they felt as if they were reliving the 1930s.

A few swastikas were painted on community centers and Jewish shops and hastily removed. A Jewish journalist found a dead rat in her mail. Boys and men from the Orthodox community—who were easily identifiable by their skullcaps and traditional clothes—suffered abusive language in buses and in the street, with very few people coming to their defense. The members of the Orthodox community never complained officially, but more secular Jews stood up and talked back, especially the younger ones.

In the summer of 1997 a well-known Jewish lawyer received two murder threats, something unheard of in Switzerland. The first threat reportedly came from followers of a militant animal-rights activist, a man who agitates against ritual slaughter, which happens to be forbidden in Switzerland (all kosher meat is imported, with the exception of poultry) and publicly compares the kosher slaughter of animals to the Nazi destruction of the Jews. The lawyer, one of the best-known Jews in Switzerland, had to be protected by bodyguards when he went to court.

JEWISH RESPONSE

Swiss Jewry was thrown into an identity conflict. Long believing themselves well-liked and integrated into Swiss society, at the same time able to maintain their identity as Jews, they now saw themselves standing on thin ice. Early in the year, when the leaders of the Zurich community realized the degree of uneasiness Jews were experiencing, they organized an evening meeting at which people could openly express their fears and hopes. The big hall was packed as never before. It was, people commented, as if the Jews were seeking shelter in the flock. Jews of all ages felt they were being put to a severe test. Although anti-Semitism never quite vanished in 1997, it lost some of its earlier momentum. But hostile letters to the editor could be found in the press almost every day, especially after new verbal attacks were made on the Swiss banks by the World Jewish Congress or the Jewish Agency.

During this period, Jewish leaders expressed their opinions forcibly and they were listened to by political and other public figures and also by the general public. The churches came to their rescue, denouncing anti-Semitism sharply. The synod of the Protestant church of the canton of Zurich apologized publicly for not having played a more active role in rescuing refugees during the war. The churches pledged SF 250,000 to preserve and properly store the valuable archive of the Jewish refugee organization.

Many Swiss expressed their concern, denouncing anti-Semitism and invoking the harmony of their country, which is based on minorities bound together by a constitution that protects their different identities and cultures. Many Swiss took a new interest in the religion and culture of the Jews and showed solidarity in various ways. In the first six months of 1997, the Zurich Jewish community had to offer four times as many guided tours of its historic synagogue in the heart of the city as in the whole of 1996.

The strong wish of the Jewish community was not to repeat the mistakes of the past, when wartime Jewish leaders had not dared to stand up against the anti-Semitic policies of the government.

Extremism

A privately commissioned Jewish survey and a government study both showed that right-wing activity, such as by known skinhead groups, had increased, and it was mainly directed against foreigners, not Jews. Police departments in rural areas were often ill-prepared to handle the situation when a right-wing group rented space for a meeting in a restaurant or hall. The arrest and trial of such people often ended with sentences of probation. The Zurich police especially had been accused of turning a blind eye to right-wing activity, but some improvement was noted. The Jewish establishment was watchful, but not overly concerned.

Israel and the Middle East

The Swiss government enjoyed friendly relations with Israel, and Foreign Minister Flavio Cotti even announced plans to pay his long delayed visit to Israel in its 50th birthday year. Israel had come to accept the Swiss government's opening of low-level diplomatic relations with the PLO after the signing of the Oslo accords, and there were no diplomatic incidents. Attacks on Switzerland by Israeli politicians and the Jewish Agency for its wartime performance were always treated separately from the bilateral relations. For that reason, Swiss officials were offended when Israeli president Ezer Weizman canceled his visit to Basel for the Herzl centennial early in the year with a not very diplomatic excuse. It seemed clear that the change in plans was due to the tension over dormant bank accounts.

Switzerland agreed to provide a sizable army unit for background logistical support and additional protection if needed at the Herzl centennial in Basel in August, commemorating the first Zionist Congress in 1897. This friendly offer by the Swiss government was criticized in some non-Jewish quarters, due to the ongoing debate, but with so many Jewish and Israeli delegates coming to Basel, officials felt the extra security precautions were necessary. There were in fact threats beforehand from extremist circles, but no danger materialized.

JEWISH COMMUNITY

Demography

The Jewish population of Switzerland has long fluctuated around 18,000, augmented by many Israelis living and working in the country. Jews in the German part had largely come from Germany in the last century; some East European Jews came to the country early in this century, most since World War II as refugees. The Jewish population in the French part includes many French and a large community of Sephardic Jews, longtime residents of the country.

Most Jews, some 6,000–7000, live in the agglomeration of Zurich. The largest of the four Jewish communities in Zurich, the Israelitische Cultusgemeinde, had since the war become the largest German-speaking community in the world. A small number of Swiss Jews emigrated to Israel every year—largely professionals and yeshivah or university students.

Communal Affairs

The overwhelming flood of anti-Semitism and the ongoing Holocaust-era debate kept communal life in turmoil. In addition, most communities felt the grip of recession as individual Jews lost jobs or had reduced incomes. With decreased revenues, communities were hard-pressed to keep up with the rising costs of maintaining communal institutions and, in the larger communities, providing security arrangements. A few communities that were no longer able to pay their dues to the Federation of Swiss Jewish Communities ceased to be members, thus weakening the ability of that body to speak with one voice for all Jews living in Switzerland.

Also not part of the federation were the two Liberal communities of Zurich and Geneva, with a combined membership of about 1,000. Their mode of religious life was not acceptable to the Orthodox communities, which regarded the federation as primarily religious—not a political umbrella organization—in which membership was based on Halakhah, Jewish law. The only areas in which leaders of the federation were permitted to interact with the Liberal communities were security, anti-Semitism, and national political matters, and this degree of contact had only been approved by the delegates a few years earlier, after heated debate. The Liberals did not insist on membership for fear that this would cause the Orthodox communities to leave the federation and further weaken its role as the official voice of Swiss Jews.

The gala opening of the Assembly of Delegates in May 1997, in Basel, in honor of the Herzl centennial, was attended by the only woman and only Jewish member of the Swiss government, Ruth Dreifuss. Some Jews were offended when the government declined to send a member to the main Herzl centennial event in August and instead sent Judith Stamm, then president of the Parliament and technically in a position superior to that of a government minister. But Dreifuss agreed to attend a dinner during the celebration. Swiss Jews noted with pleasure Parliament's election of Dreifuss in December 1997 as vice-president of the Swiss confederation for 1998. She was slated to be federal president in 1999, and would be the first woman and the first Jew in that position.

The Jewish federation was working to modernize its structures as it looked toward the next century and millennium. A first position paper on the subject was rejected because it proposed, among other ideas, the inclusion of the Liberal communities, which was unacceptable to the Orthodox.

The situation with kosher meat was a difficult one. Imported meat was expensive, unaffordable in fact for many people, who were reduced to eating frankfurters on the Sabbath. At the same time, new eating habits, with less meat being consumed, meant reduced business for the two kosher butcher shops in Zurich, each supervised by one of the two Orthodox rabbis. There was some talk of a joint supervision arrangement, for economic reasons.

Culture

The Herzl centennial and the Holocaust debate were the impetus for widespread cultural activity, both for the Jewish community and for the general public. The Zionist centennial was the subject of many exhibitions, and the Holocaust debate produced several series of lectures in universities and popular universities, exhibitions, and performances. The biannual Jewish Culture Week in Zurich, organized by the Israelitische Cultusgemeinde, proved to be a big success with the non-Jewish audiences, featuring concerts by Klezmer and Israeli bands, theatrical productions, and exhibitions.

GISELA BLAU

Central and Eastern Europe

Federal Republic of Germany

National Affairs

National politics in the latter half of 1996 and 1997 continued along the path set for the Federal Republic by Chancellor Helmut Kohl. Under his leadership, the coalition government made up of the Christian Democratic Union/Christian Social Union (CDU/CSU) and the Free Democratic Party (FDP) made the changes in fiscal policy that it deemed necessary to bring the federal deficit below the 3.0 percent level set as a criterion for monetary union in the Maastricht Treaty. The final decision on which countries would participate in the Euro, the new European currency, was slated for March 1998. Unemployment continued to rise, topping 4 million—a new high in the post–World War II era. After having pledged to cut that figure in half by the year 2000, Chancellor Kohl acknowledged toward the end of 1997 that such a goal was not realizable.

Over the 18 months covered by this article, the major political parties began preparations for the 1998 federal elections. As a result, aside from a watered-down version of health-care reform, virtually no progress was made on such pressing issues as tax reform, the restructuring of state-funded pension plans, and educational reform. Coalitions in five of 18 state governments (Hesse, North Rhine-Westphalia, Schleswig-Holstein, Saxony-Anhalt, and Hamburg) of the Social Democrats (SPD) and the Greens, a leftist environmental party, fueled speculation that such a "red-green" coalition could displace the ruling federal government. Indecision within the SPD as to their candidate for chancellor also remained a major source of speculation. Party chief Oskar Lafontaine continued to control the party machinery, but centrist Gerhard Schröder, the minister president of Lower Saxony, enjoyed greater popular support. No decision was expected until after the March 1998 state elections in Lower Saxony.

Both the SPD and the CDU emphasized internal security, their rhetoric playing on public perceptions of insecurity at a time of high crime rates and sustained and increasing unemployment. Schröder demonstrated the willingness of even the traditionally civil liberties–oriented SPD to capitalize on popular anxiety when he announced that foreigners who proved to be a risk to the security of Germans would not be tolerated. In an effort to provide law-enforcement officials with increased means to combat organized crime, the federal government proposed a measure that would legalize the tapping of phones belonging to suspected criminals, with court approval. The primacy of civil liberties in postwar and unified Germany made this issue a topic of heated public debate.

Against this national backdrop, the Republikaner, an extreme right-wing political party, attempted to make themselves respectable, echoing those themes of the mass-based parties that meshed with their ideology. Their efforts proved largely unsuccessful, though, as the CDU/CSU and the right wing of the SPD were already satisfying the mainstream public's socially conservative inclinations. The German People's Union and the National Democratic Party of Germany, meanwhile, surpassed the somewhat more moderate Republikaner in importance on the extreme right, aiming their messages at the socially disaffected. Taken together, the membership of these three parties increased 5–6 percent in 1997 from the 1996 figure of 45,300.

The profile of right-wing voters had shifted in recent years from elderly veterans and former members of the Hitler Youth to young men with little education. Experts placed the potential right-wing vote on the national level between 10 and 20 percent.

Israel and the Middle East

Diplomatic relations between Israel and the Federal Republic were strained by developments in the Middle East peace process. Foreign Minister Klaus Kinkel's tenure in office had been marked by cordial relations with Israel and, in deference to the historical relationship between the two states, a reluctance to give advice to his Israeli counterparts. Developments in late 1996 and 1997, however, frustrated his efforts both to maintain a common foreign policy with his partners in the European Union (EU) and to achieve a balanced Middle East policy.

The Kohl government defended Israel on the international stage at a time when even the United States had become critical of Israeli policy. Kinkel blocked an attempt within the EU to impose sanctions against Israel in early 1997 in reaction to the settlements policy of Israeli prime minister Benjamin Netanyahu. On two separate occasions in the same year, in March and July, Germany voted against a United Nations resolution condemning the Netanyahu policy as contrary to the spirit of the Oslo accords. As these stands in defense of Israeli policy threatened to damage Germany's influence as an impartial supporter of peace in the Middle East, Kinkel traveled to the region in March 1997 and visited four Palestinian cities. When he stopped in Israel to see Foreign Minister David Levy on the same trip, officials described their meeting as "more than icy." After Kinkel warned Levy at a meeting at the UN in September that Germany could no longer protect Israel from the reproaches of the international community, Germany for the first time in its history voted against Israel in the UN General Assembly.

The Israeli Foreign Ministry continued to emphasize the strength of the friendship between Israel and Germany and the importance of the latter's role in the peace process. Indeed, in early December 1997, just weeks after President Bill Clinton would not find time in his schedule to meet with the Israeli head of state in Washington, Prime Minister Netanyahu looked to Chancellor Kohl for diplomatic assistance. Netanyahu traveled to Germany in December, to reaffirm the strong ties between the two countries and to capitalize on the influence Kohl exercised over his Western allies and Palestinian leader Yasir Arafat.

Official differences in policy toward "rogue states" in the Middle East remained an issue in German-Israeli relations. While both Israel and the United States attempted to isolate Iraq and Iran, the Kohl government persisted in its commitment to a "critical dialogue." Israel nevertheless toned down its criticism of this German policy after German and Iranian intervention led to the release in the summer of 1996 of an Israeli soldier who had fallen prisoner to Lebanese forces.

A new Israeli consul general, Miryam Shomrat, took office in Berlin in February 1997. Shomrat accepted the task of facilitating the transition of the embassy from Bonn to Berlin in anticipation of the official move of the government seat to the new capital of unified Germany. Although the majority of embassies will be located in the vicinity of the government district, the proposed building for the Israeli embassy is located in Wilmersdorf, a residential area of Berlin whose zoning laws would normally bar the opening of an embassy. The area was selected in part because the district is an historical center of Jewish life in Berlin. In recognition of that history and of the special German-Israeli relationship, Berlin officials were considering making an exception to the zoning laws.

A German musician touring Israel with the German Opera of Berlin provoked a public outcry when the media reported that he had signed a credit-card slip "Adolf Hitler." Apparently, Gerd Reinke used Hitler's name as a joke after having had a few drinks in a Tel Aviv hotel. The subsequent public reaction brought apologies from the German embassy and the ensemble with which Reinke was touring. Reinke himself was fired immediately and sent back to Germany; his efforts in the German courts to win reinstatement failed. The episode exemplified what Israeli scholar Moshe Zimmerman has referred to as the "schizophrenic" Israeli attitude: open, relatively positive relations with Germany at the governmental level, accompanied by more sensitive, problematic attitudes at the societal level.

Efforts were made to redress this discrepancy by means of academic cooperation, public festivals, and other activities. From April 27 to May 3, 1997, Mishkenot Sha'ananim, the guest house of the city of Jerusalem, was the site of the inaugural conference of an annual series entitled "The Mishkenot Encounters for Religion and Culture." Participants in the weeklong conference, organized by the Einstein Forum in Potsdam together with the Hebrew University, explored the theme "Visions of Paradise in Religion and Culture."

The two largest celebrations of Jerusalem Day 1997 in Germany took place in Berlin and Cologne. The street fair arranged by the Berlin Jewish community featured Israeli music, dance, and food and attracted 5,000 visitors. The 30-year anniversary of the reunification of Jerusalem was the theme of the festivities in Cologne. The participation of German officials in both Berlin and Cologne drew protests from Arab diplomats.

Anti-Semitism and Extremism

After decreasing in 1994 and 1995, the number of violent and nonviolent crimes committed by right-wing extremists increased in the last two years. Under the general category of punishable offenses, two-thirds of which were related to the display or dissemination of neo-Nazi symbols or propaganda, the Federal Office for the Protection of the Constitution counted 11,719 in 1997, up from 8,730 in 1996. The figure for violent crimes attributed to anti-Semitic or xenophobic motives rose slightly, from 781 in 1996 to 790 in 1997. Though these numbers fall short of the peak figures reached in 1992, they do indicate a mobilization of right-wing extremist groups. The number of potentially violent right-wing extremists in Germany rose from 5,400 in 1994 to 7,600. This trend is attributable to continued economic difficulties, a general increase in violent crime, and a growing skinhead music scene. Almost half (45 percent) of the violent crimes by right-wing radicals in 1997 occurred in the five states that made up the former German Democratic Republic (GDR), where just 17 percent of the German population lives. These states have a collective unemployment rate of 20 percent.

The rise in visibility of right-wing groups was not, however, limited to the five new states. In the September 1997 Hamburg election, the German People's Union (GPU) fell just 0.03 percent short of winning seats in the government of the northern German city-state. The GPU received as much as 19 percent of the vote in working-class districts hit hard by persistent unemployment. As mentioned above, the two radical right parties competing with the German People's Union, the Republikaner and the National Democratic Party of Germany, increased their membership significantly in 1997, each drawing support primarily from western Germany.

The number of skinhead concerts doubled from 35 in 1996 to 70 in 1997, drawing, on average, 1,500 participants. Young people were attracted to this scene not only because of ideology, but also because its allegedly apolitical musical style appealed to their tastes. The neo-Nazi music scene had developed into a profitable international industry that was difficult for German authorities to control.

In late October 1997 the police confiscated some 265,000 compact discs in raids in Hamburg and Kiel. The open borders within the European Union, however, allowed for a virtually unchecked supply of the music, for which there seemed to be strong demand. In Germany alone, there were at least 55 skinhead bands. The Internet, which was likewise beyond the reach of rigid state control, had also become a favored means of neo-Nazi communication and organization.

Activism on the Internet and the skinhead music scene reflected a broader trend on the far right toward small autonomous groups and Kameradschaften, the name given by the National Socialists to squads of Hitler Youth. After federal and state governments banned some ten neo-Nazi organizations in 1992 and 1993, the skinhead scene and the "youth troops" of the National Democratic Party grew in importance within the right-wing movement. Members of the now illegal neo-Nazi organization thus joined local Kameradschaften that stood beyond the reach of the government ban. At the beginning of December 1997 the Berlin police raided the largest of 11 Kameradschaften in the city. Their collective membership was approximately 120 neo-Nazis. Given the collection of knives, guns, and pipe bombs found during the raid (such weapons are illegal in Germany), experts feared a rash of right-wing violence in the pattern of the terrorist activities of the left-wing Red Army Faction in the 1970s.

Research conducted by the Moses Mendelssohn Center for European Jewish History and Culture at Potsdam University traced anti-Semitic crimes to the same population most prominent in the right-wing movement as a whole. Of the sample of perpetrators and suspects in cases involving anti-Semitic crimes between 1993 and 1995, 95 percent were men, and half were not yet 22 years of age. Of the violent anti-Semitic crimes perpetrated during the same period, 80 percent were committed by men under the age of 25. In contrast, "propaganda crimes" like the distribution of Holocaust-denial literature or threatening letters were committed by men of all ages, including unreformed Nazis in their seventies and men in their fifties who occupied leading positions in neo-Nazi publishing houses and associations.

On April 15, 1997, as part of its fight against right-wing extremism, the Federal Office for the Protection of the Constitution opened a public exhibition in Berlin. A display of the weapons and propaganda of the neo-Nazi movement documented the crimes committed by Nazis during the Third Reich and those of extremists in the postwar era. The title of the exhibit warned visitors that "Democracy Is Vulnerable."

EXTREMISM IN THE BUNDESWEHR

Defense Minister Volker Rühe (CDU) became embroiled in a scandal in the last months of 1997 that centered on right-wing extremism in the Bundeswehr, the German army. By the end of November, the Defense Ministry had already begun investigations into 126 cases of alleged extremist activities involving 161 soldiers. That figure represented a threefold increase from the number of incidents reported in all of 1996. In the face of almost daily revelations, Rühe steadfastly denied that the trend pointed to a failure on the part of the Bundeswehr to insure the commitment of its soldiers and officers to the democratic values of the state they are employed to defend.

The cases reported over the course of 1997 ranged from violent attacks on foreigners to the display of Nazi propaganda to a lecture at the Bundeswehr Academy given by a known neo-Nazi activist. In March nine drunken soldiers assaulted three young foreigners in Detmold. Two soldiers were among those arrested in August for setting fire to a shelter housing Italian construction workers in Dresden. In October a television news program aired neo-Nazi scenes from a videotape produced in 1994 by soldiers in Saxony. In November and December stories about Bundeswehr barracks in three different federal states hit the newsstands telling of right-wing publications, celebrations of Hitler's birthday and the anniversary of the beginning of World War II, and calls of "Heil Hitler!" and "Death to the Jews!"

The incident that finally led to a parliamentary investigation of extremism in the Bundeswehr was the revelation of ties with the neo-Nazi Manfred Roeder. The 1993 report of the Federal Office for the Protection of the Constitution devoted three pages to Roeder and his German-Russian Society, an organization for the promotion of German settlement in Northeast Prussia (a region in present-day Russia claimed by the Germans in both world wars). He was quoted in the report as lamenting the fact that Germans could not celebrate the anniversary of the opening of German-German borders on November 9, 1989, because the date was "reserved as a national day of repentance for a couple of synagogues that were set on fire in 1938." The reports of the same office in the following two years offered updates on Roeder's activities. Nevertheless, in accordance with its mandate to support "humanitarian" associations, the Defense Ministry provided the German-Russian Society access to Bundeswehr vehicles and tools. Furthermore, Roeder was invited in 1995 to give a lecture on the "Settlement of Russians of German Ancestry in the Königsberg Region" at the Leadership Academy of the Bundeswehr in Hamburg.

Defense Minister Rühe suspended the general responsible for the invitation. In response to calls for his own resignation, Rühe held his ground and complained of a rumor-mongering press. A parliamentary investigation into the affair was scheduled for January 1998.

GOLLWITZ

In September 1997, a village in the East German state of Brandenburg made headlines across Europe for its refusal to accept a group of between 50 and 60 Jewish immigrants from the former Soviet Union, as part of a state-mandated program. The mayor of Gollwitz, population 405, denied charges that anti-Semitism and xenophobia had motivated the decision.

Initial support for the villagers by the minister president of Brandenburg, Social Democrat Manfred Stolpe, provoked angry reactions from Ignatz Bubis, head of the Central Council of Jews in Germany, and Andreas Nachama, the president of the Berlin Jewish community. Bubis saw the affair not solely in terms of anti-Semitism but rather as an expression of a general fear of foreigners that had to be confronted by well-intentioned public officials like Stolpe. Upon further reflection, Stolpe came to the conclusion that the settlement of Jewish immigrants in Gollwitz was indeed an issue of surmounting xenophobia and the acceptance of historical responsibility.

Over the next few months, hundreds of journalists traveled to Gollwitz to question the villagers on their attitudes toward Jews and other foreigners. Efforts by the state and by local social workers to engage the local inhabitants in a discussion with the Jewish community of Potsdam and with residents of a nearby village that had successfully integrated 19 immigrants the previous year had little effect. The villagers and their representatives held fast to their conviction that the introduction of a group of foreigners into the community would bring about undesirable and intolerable changes in the town's way of life. As Gollwitz became a national symbol of xenophobia in Germany, a group of leftist and antifascist activists arranged a protest demonstration in the village on November 9, the anniversary of *Kristallnacht* (Night of Broken Glass).

Holocaust-Related Matters

WEHRMACHT EXHIBIT

An exhibit documenting the participation of the German army in crimes against humanity during World War II became the focus of national controversy in the winter of 1996–97. More than 130,000 visitors in 16 different cities had viewed "War of Extermination: The Crimes of the Wehrmacht 1941–44" since its Hamburg opening in March 1995. When the exhibit arrived in Munich in February 1997, the ruling Bavarian Christian Social Union (CSU) protested what it perceived to be the "disparagement of German soldiers." The party newspaper, the *Bayernkurier,* went so far as to label the photodocumentation of Wehrmacht soldiers massacring unarmed men, women, and children a "moral campaign of extermination against the German Volk."

At the time of the exhibit's opening in 1995, Peter Gauweiler, the CSU chief in Munich, labeled Hannes Heer, the curator of the exhibit, incompetent because of Heer's past association with the German Communist Party. Gauweiler also charged that the exhibit was filled with forgeries. CDU officials in Frankfurt made similar arguments the following month. These claims called into question the long accepted scholarly consensus on the German army's complicity in the murder of Jews on the Eastern Front. The refusal of the governing political parties to distance themselves from the right-wing extremists who also objected to the exhibit raised the intensity of the controversy. Even the conservative newspaper *Frankfurter Allgemeine Zeitung* recognized the campaign against the exhibit as a populist appeal to right-wing voters that threatened to poison German political discourse.

The national media spectacle created by these protests brought the issue to the floor of the Reichstag in mid-March of 1997. Members of all political parties participated in an emotional debate, many wrestling openly with their personal histories—the service of their fathers, brothers, and uncles in an army committed to defending and supporting a criminal regime. Though no agreement was reached on the wording of a resolution addressing the role of the Wehrmacht in crimes against humanity, many observers commended the seriousness and honesty with which the German parliamentarians confronted the questions raised by the exhibit.

The controversial exhibit attracted 90,000 visitors in Munich before moving on to Frankfurt in April 1997, where, as in other cities, there were protest demonstrations by right-wing groups and counter-demonstrations by the left. To avoid the security problems posed by demonstrations, the municipal government of Dresden chose to forbid them at the local opening of the Wehrmacht exhibit scheduled for January 1998.

Meanwhile, discussion of a permanent exhibit was already under way. Ignatz Bubis suggested the Bendler-Block as a possibility. The former headquarters of the Wehrmacht leadership in Berlin already housed the Museum of the German Resistance and offices of the German Defense Ministry. After Bubis's suggestion found little support, a representative from the western German town of Waldstadt proposed it as a permanent location. During the Nazi era, Waldstadt was the seat of the high command of the German army. The exhibit was scheduled to remain on tour, however, through the end of 1999, and no decision was expected on a permanent site within the near future.

RESTITUTION

After decades of silence about the company's activities during the Third Reich, the leaders of the Diehl armaments company initiated a dialogue with a group of women in Israel who had been forced laborers for the firm during World War II. Werner Diehl, the son of 90-year-old CEO Karl Diehl, traveled to Tel Aviv in December 1997 to meet with four women who were held as slave laborers in a Polish labor camp. Diehl announced plans to provide "voluntary support" for the women, who told of the participation of Diehl officials in the mistreatment, humiliation, and selection of prisoners. Representatives of Diehl made the important distinction between the voluntary measures to be undertaken by the company and compensatory payments, which would amount to an admission of responsibility for the wrongs inflicted upon the forced laborers.

The discussion came just days before the Nürnberg city council was to discuss a proposal by the Greens to withdraw an honor granted to the senior Diehl in 1996. With the support of the right-wing Republikaner, the council had voted in March 1996 to bestow honorary citizenship on industrialist Karl Diehl. Diehl published an open letter in his own defense before his son left for Tel Aviv. In the letter, Diehl called on historians to investigate his activities during the Third Reich and expressed his regret for the suffering of inmates who worked for his company. He also insisted that he was compelled by the Nazi state to use forced laborers, and that he gave them the best conditions possible under the circumstances. The timing of these events was significant in light of a November court decision concerning restitution for forced laborers. A district court in Bonn ruled that surviving inmates of concentration camps who had already received compensatory payments from the German government were not entitled to further restitution for lost wages.

The Berlin municipal government announced in November 1997 that it would no longer fund Esra, a social-services center providing psychosocial support for survivors of the Holocaust. Though Esra (Hebrew for "help") also received funding from the Conference on Jewish Material Claims Against Germany, the Berlin Jewish community, and the German Red Cross, the withdrawal of state financing would create serious problems for the center, which helped 150 patients yearly. The city justified its decision by arguing that Esra's patients "had no direct connection to the Holocaust," but the majority of its clients were in fact child survivors who were born in concentration camps or lived out the war in hiding.

At the end of 1997 talks continued between the Jewish Claims Conference and German officials over compensation for Holocaust survivors in Eastern Europe and the former Soviet Union. In 1995 the American Jewish Committee had compiled a list, country by country, of individual ghetto and concentration camp survivors in these areas. In January 1997 the parliamentary delegation of the Greens proposed applying reparations policies already in place for survivors living in the West to East European survivors as well. The Kohl government, however, showed no interest in addressing the matter. On May 7, 1997, the AJCommittee ran an ad in the *New York Times* showing a picture of a veteran of the Waffen SS alongside a photo of a concentration camp survivor. The text asked the reader to guess which of the two received a pension, and highlighted the injustice of Nazi veterans receiving pensions, while help was refused to some 18,000 surviving Holocaust victims. The issue was on the agenda when Chancellor Kohl visited President Clinton in Washington in June; soon thereafter Kohl received a letter signed by 82 U.S. senators requesting that pensions be paid to survivors in Eastern Europe. A commission was set up to study the question that fall.

The implementation of the German–Czech Friendship Treaty, meanwhile, made little progress over the course of 1997. Signed in January of 1997, the treaty provided for the establishment of a German–Czech Future Fund from which victims of Nazi persecution, including Jewish survivors in the Czech Republic, could seek redress. Disagreement about the makeup of the committee to oversee the fund was still unresolved at year's end.

HOLOCAUST MEMORIALS

Cities across Germany continued the work of memorializing the victims of past German crimes. In December 1996 Viennese artist Karl Prantl unveiled 14 five-foot-long blocks of granite placed alongside a church in the old city of Nürnberg in memory of the victims of National Socialism. Prantl used the same granite that inmates of concentration camps had to break with their own hands during the years of Nazi rule. The city of Brandenburg opened a memorial to the victims of the Nazi euthanasia program at the end of April 1997. In May the German railway company Deutsche Bahn laid the cornerstone at the Grunewald train station for a memorial to the 10,000 Jews deported to the east from that station. A public ceremony was scheduled for January 1998 for its dedication.

A hotly debated plaque in Hamburg was unveiled in June to remind passersby that a supplier of poisonous gas (Zyklon B) had formerly occupied the building now housing the Deutsche Bank. Later in the same month, a "site of memory" was unveiled on the plot of a former synagogue in the Berlin district of Kreuzberg. Empty stone benches stand among trees and bushes in the same layout as that of the pews in the synagogue that was destroyed on *Kristallnacht* in 1938. The memorial was designed by architect Zvi Hecker and artists Micha Ullmann and Eyal Weizman. In July the Bavarian city of Fürth dedicated a memorial in its New Jewish Cemetery to the Jews from the area who were killed by the Nazis. The Berlin municipal government approved plans for a memorial on Hausvogteiplatz, in the former textiles quarter of Berlin, to the Jews deported to their death in the east.

On November 9, 1997, the state of Brandenburg opened a museum in Barrack 38 of the former Sachsenhausen concentration camp, five years after neo-Nazis attempted to destroy it through arson. The permanent exhibit in the museum documents the experience of "Jewish Inmates in the Concentration Camp Sachsenhausen." The year ended on a disillusioning note as vandals ravaged the memorial to the murdered Jews of Berlin on the Grosse Hamburger Strasse in Berlin on December 30.

The debate surrounding the construction of a central Holocaust memorial in Berlin entered its ninth year. (See AJYB 1997, pp. 336–37.) The rejection by Chancellor Kohl and other critics in 1995 of the design selected originally for the memorial led to a standstill in the discussion for the better part of 1996. In October of that year, the three sponsors of the project—the federal government, the city of Berlin, and the Society for the Establishment of a Memorial for the Murdered Jews of Europe—announced that the cornerstone would be laid on January 27, 1999, the German Day of Remembrance for the Victims of National Socialism. Though they did not yet have a clear conception of how they were going to proceed, the sponsors reiterated their commitment to dedicating a memorial to the Jewish victims of the Holocaust and to the site for its construction just south of the Brandenburg Gate, thereby rejecting a call by prominent intellectuals to reconsider their stands on both questions. Three colloquia were held in early 1997 to discuss the why, where, and how of the proposed memorial. These meetings drew headlines in the press, such as "The endless debate continues," that reflected growing public exasperation with the issue.

In July 1997 the sponsors announced a second competition for the design of the memorial. Invitations to participate were extended to 25 artists and architects from all over the world. A panel consisting of James Young, an American authority on memorials; Stölzl Christoph, the director of the German Historical Museum in Berlin; the Berlin architect Josef Paul Kleihues; and art scholars Werner Hofmann and Dieter Ronte was commissioned to select the winning entry. These judges chose two designs for a final round of the competition, to which the sponsors added another two. The artists responsible for the four designs—the Paris-based Jochen Gerz; the American-trained, Polish-born architect responsible for the new Jewish Museum in Berlin, Daniel Libeskind; Berlin architect Gesine Weinmuller; and the American collaborators Peter Eisenmann and Richard Serra—were to be given the opportunity to introduce their ideas before the public in January 1998, as part of a series of public discussions leading up to a final decision. The decision was expected in March, with construction still scheduled to begin in January 1999.

JEWISH COMMUNITY

Demography

Immigration from the former Soviet Union continued to drive the growth of the Jewish community in Germany in 1996 and 1997. Between January 1, 1996, and January 1, 1998, 16,318 immigrants from the former Soviet Union (8,608 in 1996 and 7,710 in 1997) joined an official Jewish community. The total number of Jews registered with the member communities of the Central Council of Jews in Germany went from 53,797 on January 1, 1996, to 61,203 a year later, to 68,175 on January 1, 1998. Estimates of those Jews who either remained unaffiliated or were affiliated with communities outside the Central Council range from 20,000 to 30,000.

This growth in the national community was spread across Germany according to a formula worked out by the Central Council in negotiation with its member communities and the state governments. Ten new Jewish communities were founded since 1990, bringing the number of cities and towns in Germany with Jewish communities to 78. Only four of these had fewer than 50 members; 18 had more than 600.

The numbers of affiliated Jews in the largest communities were as follows for 1997 (with 1996 figures in parentheses for comparison): Berlin, 10,742 (up from 10,436); Frankfurt, 6,503 (up from 6,289); Munich, 6,194 (up from 5,726); Hamburg, 3,759 (up from 3,273); Cologne, 3,127 (up from 2,763). The growth in membership in state and regional associations of Jewish communities was as follows: Baden, 2,900 (up from 2,757); Bavaria, 4,848 (up from 4,184); Brandenburg, 392 (up from 299); Bremen, 751 (up from 654); Hesse, 3,417 (up from 3,118); Mecklenburg-Vorpommern, 534 (up from 402); Lower Saxony, 5,088 (up from

4,479); North Rhine, 9,554 (up from 8,184); Rhineland-Pfalz, 1,132 (up from 614); Saar, 759 (up from 656); Saxony, 529 (up from 449); Saxony-Anhalt, 593 (up from 503); Thüringia, 300 (up from 190); Westphalia, 5,239 (up from 4,599); Württemberg, 1,814 (up from 1,628).

Communal Affairs

Bavaria became the tenth German state to sign a state treaty with its Jewish community. The Protestant and Catholic churches had long had such agreements with the Bavarian government. The document, officially signed in mid-August 1997, creates the legal foundation for annual financial support from the state. Translated into numbers, the voluntary support given the Jewish community by the Bavarian state in the past amounted to roughly DM 1.2 million ($800,000) annually. The contract signed by Minister President Edmund Stoiber and Simon Snopkowski, the president of the Bavarian Association of Jewish Communities, provides for DM 3.7 million ($2.4 million) in 1998 and DM 4 million ($2.6 million) the following year. The funds will be devoted primarily to securing rabbis, cantors, and religious teachers for a Jewish population that increased by 40 percent in the last decade and now totaled 10,000.

On the local and regional levels, Jewish communities worked to create an institutional infrastructure that could accommodate their growing numbers. In January 1997 a new synagogue was dedicated in the western German town of Recklinghausen to serve the community of Bochum-Herne-Recklinghausen. The membership of this three-city congregation had grown from 85 members in 1989 to 1,139 in 1997. Amid the excitement of inaugurating the new house of worship, representatives of the Association of Jewish Communities in Westphalia acknowledged that conflicts over such issues as the distribution of power and use of scant community resources had resulted from the dramatic growth in membership. The Jewish community of Offenbach dedicated a new synagogue in November. In Duisburg a new community center with a synagogue was being built. In Kassel the synagogue was being enlarged, while the Jewish community of Wuppertal was making plans for a new one.

The combination of communal growing pains and the increased public visibility and assertiveness of Jewish personalities brought national press coverage to several intra-Jewish disputes. A conflict over finances led to the withdrawal of the Munich Jewish community from the Bavarian Association of Jewish Communities. The Baden Association of Jewish Communities, meanwhile, refused to recognize the establishment of several new congregations. In Hannover, the right of Russian-speaking immigrants to vote in communal elections became the subject of controversy. Finally, arguments developed in a number of places over how to define who is a Jew and thus who could be a legitimate member of the community.

At the meeting of the Central Council of Jews in Germany that took place in

Frankfurt am Main on November 11, 1997, the agenda was dominated by issues related to the transformation of the Jewish community through demographic and generational shifts. Social services and activities had demanded increasing attention over the last several years, as communities across Germany attempted to provide language training, job counseling, and general education to the more than 40,000 immigrants from the former Soviet Union. In order to provide a broader forum for the expression of grievances and the exchange of ideas relating to the problems of adjusting to the new conditions of Jewish life in Germany, council president Ignatz Bubis proposed that the Central Council hold a "Community Day" at the end of 1998.

Delegates expressed frustration with difficulties faced by many non-Jewish spouses and children in their search for a rabbi willing to preside over their conversions. Since there is no Beth Din (rabbinical court) in Germany, Orthodox rabbis in the country do not perform conversions, instead referring interested parties to the Beth Din in London. Some Liberal rabbis in Germany do perform conversions, but converts of non-Orthodox rabbis have often had problems having their status as Jews recognized by their local communities. One of the reasons many rabbis in Germany viewed conversion with disfavor had to do with the large number of non-Jews interested in becoming Jews. The motives of these would-be converts in the "land of the murderers" were often called into question. However legitimate this concern, it also exacerbated the frustrations expressed by the delegates at the meeting of the Central Council. Although Bubis showed sympathy for the concerns of the delegates, he insisted that the judgment of individual rabbis had to be respected and that the council was therefore in no position to impose a solution to the dilemma.

On the first day of Hanukkah 1997, the Central Council of Jews in Germany held its main observance in Munich at the site of a former synagogue. In front of an audience of public officials, church representatives, and journalists, President of Germany Roman Herzog lit the Hanukkah lights and affirmed his solidarity with the State of Israel as it embarked on its 50th year of existence. Leaders of the Munich Jewish community, politicians, and the German press all described the interfaith service in the former "capital of the [Nazi] movement" as a symbolic step forward in the process of reconciliation.

BERLIN

For the Berlin Jewish community, by far the largest in Germany, 1997 was a critical year. The communal elections held on June 1 brought about an important generational change in leadership. In a shift carrying as much symbolic import as practical substance, survivors of the Holocaust passed the presidency of the community to the first generation of Jews born in postwar Germany. The incumbent going into the elections, Jerzy Kanal, celebrated his 75th birthday in July 1996. Like most Jews living in Berlin after the war, he was born in Eastern Europe and came to Germany as a survivor of the Holocaust. His successor, historian Andreas Nachama, was born in postwar Germany as a child of survivors. He had been a public figure in Berlin for years, first as a cultural affairs official in the municipal administration and then as the director of the Topography of Terror, an exhibit documenting the bureaucratic infrastructure of the Nazi state. Under his leadership, the community took significant steps to further the integration of Russian-speaking Jews and to foster an official acceptance of religious pluralism previously unknown in the postwar era.

The shift in leadership was likely to speed up the transformation of communal institutions to reflect the demographic changes that had taken place within the Berlin Jewish community since the fall of the Berlin wall in 1989 and the subsequent influx of Jews from the east. Of the nearly 11,000 members of the community, almost two-thirds were Russian-speaking. Under the new leadership, the 1997 Rosh Hashanah annual report was published, for the first time, in German and Russian. The first issue of the community magazine appeared in January 1998 in bilingual form, with a completely new format targeted at the younger generation of Jews in Berlin.

In this new era of religious and ethnic pluralism, Jewish institutions in Berlin were flourishing. In May 1997, in two of the last significant events before the communal elections, the community opened the doors to its new gymnasium, and the Jewish junior high school (Realschule) awarded its first diplomas.

Though Nachama himself preferred to emphasize his work inside the Jewish community, he continued in the tradition of the postwar president of the Berlin community, Heinz Galinski, by maintaining a high profile in the German media, commenting publicly on all issues of importance to the Jewish community. His relations with the city government were not always harmonious. He even complained that non-Jewish German politicians treated him with less respect than his predecessors because he was born after the war. As he once put it, he felt that German policymakers gave him no "Auschwitz bonus."

AMERICAN JEWISH ORGANIZATIONS

Going back to the days of Allied occupation, denazification, and the transformation of the German economic infrastructure, American Jews had played a significant role in postwar Germany. Indeed, for more than 50 years, the American Jewish Committee (AJC) had committed energy and resources to the development and maintenance of a democratic Germany. Not until recently, however, did American Jews have a permanent institutional presence in the Federal Republic. During 1996 and 1997, the American Jewish Committee and the Ronald S. Lauder Foundation opened offices in Berlin, each to pursue goals related to its specific concerns. Together, however, they represent an important development in the relationship between the Jewish communities of Germany and America.

The first weekend of March 1997, in cooperation with the Central Council of

Jews in Germany and several organizations devoted to the trans-Atlantic partnership, the AJCommittee hosted a conference on "The Jewish Dimension in German-American Relations: Perceptions and Realities." The purpose of this "pre-opening" weekend, which featured the participation in panel discussions of prominent scholars, journalists, and politicians from the United States and Germany, was to investigate the perceptions held among Americans about Germany and those held by Germans about American Jewry. Speakers noted that the establishment of democratic institutions in West Germany and the restitution payments made by the Federal Republic to survivors of the Holocaust and to the State of Israel had facilitated the acceptance by Americans of Germany as a stable and reliable ally. Many American Jews, however, still viewed the successor to the Nazi state with fear and suspicion. On the other side, the German perception of American Jews evoked the image of an "East-coast establishment" that controlled the American press and exerted a disproportionate influence on Congress. Redressing the mutual misperceptions of Germans and American Jews was one of the primary goals of AJCommittee's Berlin director, Eugene DuBow. He and assistant director Wendy Kloke opened the committee's Berlin office for business in provisional quarters in July. The official opening of the permanent office was slated for February 1998.

To less fanfare but with no less significance for Jewish life in Germany, the Berlin office of the Ronald S. Lauder Foundation opened in October 1996. Inspired by the survival of Jewish life in Eastern Europe—despite the catastrophic events of World War II and the decades of Communist rule that followed—American businessman and former U.S. ambassador to Austria Ronald S. Lauder founded the organization in 1987 to "support and revitalize Eastern European Jewish communities." The Berlin office thus focused on helping to create the religious and educational infrastructure in Germany necessary for the integration of recently arrived Russian immigrants into an active Jewish community. Under the direction of Joel Levy, previously a career diplomat and the former head of the American Embassy Office in Berlin, the foundation offered a number of successful programs, such as a model matzah bakery, a Purim program for children, and the sponsorship of 40 children from Germany in the Jewish youth camp run by the Lauder Foundation and the Joint Distribution Committee in Szarvas, Hungary. The foundation also donated entire library collections with works in Russian, Hebrew, German, and English to the Jewish communities of Schwerin, Rostock, Erfurt, Leipzig, and Dresden, all cities in the former GDR. Another staff member worked on youth and outreach programs with the Jewish community in the western German town of Aachen. Still in the planning stage were four one-week day camps in communities in eastern Germany, at which a staff of six to eight instructors would introduce Jews of all ages to Jewish religion, rituals, and history.

Religion

Rosh Hashanah 1997 saw the first officially sanctioned egalitarian service in Berlin since the war. More than 200 worshipers attended the mixed-seating service and the *kiddush* reception that followed. With Berlin community president Nachama's approval, the community paid for the *kiddush* as well as for engaging a cantor. Two small egalitarian groups, one each in the eastern and the western parts of the city, had been meeting for years without official support. These groups were part of a larger Progressive Jewish movement in Germany (see below), and Nachama's open-arms policy toward them represented an important aspect of the new vibrancy of Jewish life not just in Berlin but throughout Germany.

The recognition in October 1997 of the traditional Adass Yisroel community by the state authorities in Berlin brought to an end a five-year legal struggle. The official Jewish community of Berlin had traditionally been organized as an Einheitsgemeinde, meaning that Liberal and Orthodox congregations coexisted within one inclusive institutional framework. The decision on the part of Adass Yisroel to remain outside this framework had its historical precedent in 1869, when a community of the same name seceded from the Einheitsgemeinde in order to lead a traditional Jewish life that it viewed as incompatible with membership in a broader community. For reasons relating to the public funding privileges that are granted to officially recognized religious communities, the present Adass Yisrael congregation had to convince the German courts that it deserved recognition as the successor community of the one that was founded in 1869 and dismantled by the Nazis in 1938. With legal disputes behind them, relations between the larger Berlin Jewish community and Adass Yisroel, the membership of which approached 1,000, reached a level of comfortable coexistence. Indeed, in a sign of its increased public acceptance, Adass Yisroel was invited to lead half of the religious ceremony at the unveiling of the Grunewald Holocaust memorial scheduled for January 1998.

The Progressive Jewish movement in Germany made great strides in 1997. During the Cold War, the presence of Jews among the Allied troops in Germany had insured the continued practice of a Judaism in Germany that was more Reform even than that of the minority of officially recognized Liberal congregations. The institutional void left by the withdrawal of foreign troops in the early 1990s was filled by the young Progressive movement in Germany, and indigenous egalitarian Judaism could be seen to be gaining momentum with each passing year.

The Liberal Jewish community of Munich, Beth Shalom, had played an important role in what its own annual report called "the rebirth of Progressive Judaism in Germany" since its founding in 1995. On June 27, 1997, the congregation celebrated the induction of Rabbi Dr. Walter Homolka as spiritual leader. Rabbi Homolka, the recently appointed head of Greenpeace Germany, was also a member of the European Beth Din of the World Union for Progressive Judaism.

The day of Rabbi Homolka's induction also witnessed the founding of the Union of Progressive Jews in Germany, Austria, and Switzerland. Under the chairmanship of Prof. Micha Brumlik of Frankfurt, member congregations in Munich, Cologne, Frankfurt, Kassel, Hannover, and elsewhere planned to provide a Liberal alternative to the Orthodox communities represented by the Central Council of Jews in Germany.

Beth Shalom also hosted the annual conference of the World Union for Progressive Judaism's European Region the first weekend in November 1997. The event marked the first time since 1928 that such a meeting had been held in Germany. On the first day of the conference, Rabbi Homolka dedicated a new cemetery for the Munich Liberal community. Though the Orthodox community had not given its official support to the Reform congregation, it welcomed the cemetery as a resolution of the difficult issues raised by the death of partners in mixed marriages and others who could not find their final resting place in the cemetery of the traditional community.

Israeli ambassador to Germany Avi Primor visited Beth Shalom twice in 1997. On his second visit, he addressed delegates of the World Union of Progressive Judaism on the opening evening of their conference. Primor praised the union's work and implicitly criticized the Orthodox domination of religious affairs in Israel. "Diversity is the essence of Jewish life," he declared.

Another noteworthy presence at the World Union conference was Andreas Nachama, whose father still served as cantor of the Pestalozzistrasse Synagogue in Berlin, a longtime member of the World Union. The presence of Nachama at the conference and his election to the board of governors of the Union's European Region caused tension in his relationship with Ignatz Bubis and the Central Council of Jews in Germany. Bubis questioned the propriety of Nachama's simultaneous membership in the Central Council and in the World Union, an organization that, in Bubis's words, "does not stand on the ground of the Halakhah." Nachama, in turn, expressed his frustration with the Central Council's resistance to the participation in community life of non-Orthodox Jewish groups. Approximately 40 congregations in Germany already functioned outside the Central Council's organizational framework.

Jewish-Christian Relations

With 77 local chapters and approximately 20,000 members, the Society for Christian-Jewish Cooperation (SCJC) was the central institutional site for interfaith encounters in Germany. The charter of the society called for the inclusion of representatives from the Protestant and Catholic churches as well as from the Jewish community on every chapter's governing council. Efforts in the direction of interfaith understanding, however, were rather one-sided in communities where the SCJC had founded a chapter despite the absence of an institutional Jewish presence.

German president Roman Herzog and the minister president of North Rhine-

Westphalia, Johannes Rau, spoke in Paderborn on March 2, 1997, at the opening ceremony of the annual SCJC Brotherhood Week. Lectures and panel discussions held throughout the week addressed Christian-Jewish dialogue, the peace process in the Middle East, and conditions in the former Yugoslavia. Hans Koschnik, a former administrator of the EU in Mostar, received the SCJC Buber-Rosenzweig Medal for his contribution to Christian-Muslim-Jewish reconciliation in the Balkans. Throughout the year, the Berlin chapter of the SCJC held lectures, film evenings, and roundtable discussions in cooperation with the Centrum Judaicum, the German-Israeli Society, and the Jewish Volkshochschule (School for Continuing Education). In the academic arena, scholars participating in a November conference in Duisburg, cosponsored by the Jewish Studies Department of the local university and the Evangelical Academy of Mülheim on the Ruhr, inquired into the present-day consequences of anti-Judaism in theology and art.

Education

Jewish educational institutions in Germany were thriving. In 1997 approximately 900 students attended the five Jewish elementary schools in Munich, Frankfurt, Düsseldorf, and Berlin (two). An estimated 240 students were enrolled in the Jewish secondary school in Berlin. The University for Jewish Studies in Heidelberg, which is affiliated with the Central Council of Jews in Germany, counted 160 students in 1997, among them an increasing number of Jews. Since its founding, university officials had bemoaned the fact that this new institutional infrastructure for Jewish education had drawn few Jewish students. Finally, schools for continuing education in Berlin, Munich, and Frankfurt offered adults a means of enriching their knowledge of Jewish history, religion, and languages.

The 1997–98 academic year was significant for the further development of Jewish studies at German universities as well. Prof. Michael Brenner, one of the most prolific historians of German Jewry in the 1990s, became the first scholar to occupy the chair for Jewish History and Culture at the Institute for Modern History of the Ludwig Maximilian University in Munich. On July 19, 1997, he delivered his inaugural lecture on the theme of "Jewish Historical Scholarship in German Universities." The Gerhard Mercator University in Duisburg inaugurated a Jewish studies program, granting both master's and doctoral degrees, at the beginning of the 1997–98 academic year. In October the Jewish studies department opened a Web site (http:\\www.uni-duisburg.de/FB1/JStudien/juedische__studien__in__deutschland.htm) listing more than a dozen Jewish studies departments throughout Germany, including two degree-granting programs in Yiddish, as well as several research institutes specializing in German-Jewish history. One of these research centers, the Institute for the History of German Jews, announced the establishment of the Hamburg Society for Jewish Family Research in October 1996.

At the end of November 1997 the Salomon Ludwig Steinheim Institute for

German-Jewish History held a conference at the Catholic Academy in Mühlheim on the Ruhr. Under the rubric of "Young Scholars of Jewish Studies on German-Jewish Culture and History," 20 German doctoral candidates gave papers and exchanged ideas on such topics as talmudic thought, Jewish history in the Middle Ages, and the limits of Jewish assimilation in modern Germany.

Culture

Interest in Jewish life before and after the Holocaust continued to be the focus of a wealth of cultural activities across Germany. Jewish cultural festivals continued to attract large audiences. The festival in Berlin alone, the theme of which was Jewish life in New York, featured 40 concerts, films, and lectures. Symbolically drawing public attention away from the horrors of the past and toward the richness of contemporary Jewish life, the two-week event begins annually on November 10, the day after the anniversary of *Kristallnacht.*

Several centennial anniversaries occurred in 1997, including the 100th anniversary of the first Zionist Congress. Museum exhibits, newspaper profiles, and a public lecture series in Munich invited the German public to examine the history of Zionism. On the occasion of the 100th birthday of Gershom Scholem, historian of Jewish mysticism, the Einstein Forum and the Institute for Advanced Study in Berlin, of which Scholem became the first fellow in 1982, held a December symposium on "Gershom Scholem as Writer." Additionally, public museums, libraries, and Jewish communal institutions all commemorated in some manner the 200th birthday of the German-Jewish poet Heinrich Heine, in spite of his ambivalent relationship to both Germany and Judaism.

In 1997 the Centrum Judaicum and the National Gallery in Berlin both featured the paintings of impressionist Max Liebermann in recognition of his 150th birthday. Without highlighting explicitly Jewish themes, museums in Berlin also displayed the work of dozens of Jewish artists forced into exile during the 1930s. Exile art was also the theme of "Lisbon 1933–1945: Refugee Station at the Border of Europe," an exhibit on display in fall 1997 in the Börne Gallery of the Frankfurt Judengasse Museum.

The blockbuster hit of the 1997 Christmas movie season, *Comedian Harmonists,* portrays the careers of one of the most famous German singing groups of the interwar period. Two of the members of the all-male sextet were Jewish, another was a baptized Jew, and a fourth had married a Jewish woman. The movie tells the story of the Comedian Harmonists from the group's beginning in 1927 through its struggle to continue performing in the Third Reich to the emigration of the three non-Aryan members in 1935.

In their 1997 documentary *Jeckes: The Distant Relations,* German filmmakers Jens Meurer and Carsten Hueck deal more directly with the history of Jews who were driven to flee Nazi Germany than did the Hollywood-esque Comedian Harmonists. The term "Jeckes" (or "yekkes") was a pejorative name given by East

European pioneers in Palestine, in the 1930s, to the urbanized, stiffly proper Jewish immigrants from Germany. The documentary consists of interviews with seven of these "Jeckes" and explores the meanings they attach to their German origins, their Jewish identities, and their lives in Israel. A documentary on the *Jewish Roundtable,* a group of Jewish intellectuals who fled Nazi Germany for New York, was one of the films featured in the 1997 Jewish Cultural Days in Berlin. The 1997 Berlinale, the world's third-largest film festival, featured films with Jewish themes from Germany, Norway, Italy, and Israel.

A conference arranged by the Einstein Forum at the end of June examined the place of Hannah Arendt's *Eichmann in Jerusalem* in the historiography of the Holocaust. Scholars from all over Europe, Israel, and the United States offered their thoughts on the legacy of Arendt's controversial work. The conference took on added interest in light of the controversies over the Wehrmacht exhibit and Daniel Goldhagen's book on the Holocaust (see "Publications," below).

Another important cultural happening was the opening in late 1996 in Potsdam of an exhibit on "German Jewish Soldiers" at the Office for the Research of Military History. The exhibit, which toured Germany after its initial run in Potsdam, documented the contribution of Jews to the military of the German states from the 18th through the 20th centuries. In the spring of 1997, under the title "And I Can Still See Their Faces," the Frankfurt Jewish Museum displayed a collection of 300 photos of Jewish life in Poland before the Holocaust.

JEWISH MUSEUM

Between the summer of 1996 and the end of 1997, the controversy over the Jewish Museum in Berlin, which had been going on for several years, gave rise to what some commentators called the worst crisis in relations between the Jewish community and the city government since 1945. Architect Daniel Libeskind had designed a post-modern extension to the baroque Berlin Museum, a section of which was to house the successor to the prewar Jewish Museum that was forced to close in 1938. However, serious differences existed between Reiner Güntzer, the director of the Berlin City Museum Foundation, and Amnon Barzel, the director of the Jewish Museum, over the nature and scope of the new institution. Barzel envisioned a museum that would fill the new wing and be independent financially and institutionally of the City Museum Foundation. Conceptually, he wanted the museum to reflect a Jewish perspective that could not be accommodated by the "integrative" concept advocated by the foundation. Güntzer, meanwhile, insisted that Barzel's project remain a department of the larger Berlin Museum, subject to the supervision of the Berlin Municipal Museum and occupying a small portion of the space encompassed by the Libeskind extension.

Though the sources of the conflict were many, observers of Jewish life in Germany viewed the debate chiefly in terms of a lack of mutual understanding and trust between the Jewish community and the Berlin government. A visiting delegation of the Israeli Knesset expressed dismay at the methods of the city administration, which one Knesset member described as counter to the spirit of democracy. The dispute between Güntzer and Barzel culminated in the latter's dismissal on the same June day in 1997 on which Andreas Nachama was to have his first meeting as the newly elected president of the Berlin Jewish community with Peter Radunski, the head of cultural affairs in the Berlin municipal government. Nachama compared Güntzer's unilateral dismissal of Barzel to the museum politics of the German government in the 1930s.

After several more months of acrimonious debate, some positive developments occurred in the last months of the year. At the end of October, the Berlin municipality intimated that the Jewish Museum would enjoy the institutional autonomy it had refused to cede to Barzel, though the substance of that autonomy remained a matter of dispute. Then, in the middle of November, a new museum director was appointed—an American, W. Michael Blumenthal, who served as U.S. secretary of the treasury under President Jimmy Carter. Blumenthal was born in Germany but had spent most of his life in the United States, where he had successful careers as an international economist and corporate CEO. Although virtually unknown to the German public before his appointment, his selection was welcomed by all sides in the debate, as well as the press, all of whom emphasized his energy, self-reliance, and willingness to make difficult decisions. Blumenthal's own words held out hope that the 18 months of tension might be at an end: "Old discussions do not interest me. I want to open a new chapter, and I believe that I can accomplish a lot for Berlin."

Publications

Three prominent Jewish public figures in Germany published books in 1996 and 1997. Ignatz Bubis recorded his life story in *"Damit bin ich noch längst nicht fertig." Eine Autobiographie* ("I Am Not Even Close to Finished": An Autobiography). In a second book entitled *Juden in Deutschland* (Jews in Germany), Bubis elaborated his views on the present state of the Jewish community and issued an admonition against forgetting history. Rafael Seligmann's *Der Musterjude* (The Model Jew) is the novelist's latest effort to provoke the German public—Jewish and non-Jewish alike—to talk, laugh, and joke about issues that have remained taboo since World War II. Micha Brumlik, leader of the Progressive Jewish movement in Germany, published his autobiography under the title *Kein Weg als Deutscher und Jude. Eine bundesrepublikanische Erfahrung* (No Way as German and Jew: A Federal Republican Experience). The title itself is a commentary, alluding to Jakob Wassermann's 1921 memoir *Mein Weg als Deutscher und Jude* (My Way as German and Jew).

Two Israeli public figures with ties to Germany published memoirs in 1997. Leah Rabin, the widow of the late prime minister Yitzhak Rabin, who herself was born in interwar Königsberg, toured Germany in the spring of 1997 in support of the German translation of her book *Our Life, His Legacy* (*Ich gehe weiter auf seinem Weg: Erinnerungen an Jitzchak Rabin*). As the first Israeli-born ambassador to serve in Bonn, Avi Primor developed a different relationship with Germany than those of his five predecessors. In *". . . mit Ausnahme Deutschlands." Als Botschafter Israels in Bonn* (". . . with the Exception of Germany": An Israeli Ambassador in Bonn), Primor tells how his preconceived image of Germany was belied by reality.

Several works on the Nazi gold controversy sparked the interest of the German reading public, among them Tom Bower's *Das Gold der Juden. Die Schweiz und die verschwundenen Nazi-Milliarden* (The Jews' Gold: Switzerland and the Lost Nazi Billions) and Michel Fior's *Die Schweiz und das Gold der Reichsbank. Was Wusste die Schweizerische Nationalbank?* (Switzerland and the Gold of the Reichsbank: What Did the Swiss National Bank Know?).

Among the memoirs of Holocaust survivors to stimulate public discussion in 1997 was *Die Mütze oder Der Preis des Lebens* (The Cap or the Price of Life), the German translation of Roman Frister's Hebrew original. In another popular memoir, *Der Ghetto-Schwinger* (The Ghetto Swinger), musician Coco Schumann recounts his experiences playing in a jazz band in Theresienstadt and how his music kept him alive in Auschwitz.

Even before the German translation of his work was released in August 1996, Daniel Goldhagen had sparked a new round of public debate concerning the Holocaust and collective guilt in Germany. In his book *Hitler's Willing Executioners,* Goldhagen, a political scientist at Harvard University, argues that an "exterminationist anti-Semitism" so pervaded German culture in the decades preceding the Nazi rise to power that ordinary Germans from all social and religious backgrounds were eager accomplices in the destruction of European Jewry. Goldhagen toured Germany in the fall of 1996, participating in roundtable discussions with scholars in front of standing-room-only audiences. The German translation became an instant best-seller. The German public, particularly the younger generation, rallied around Goldhagen, while a number of scholars criticized his methodology and conclusions. The books published in the wake of the Goldhagen debate demonstrate its magnitude as a German cultural event. Within days of the release of the German translation, a collection of already published reactions to the controversy appeared under the title *Ein Volk von Mördern? Die Dokumentation zur Goldhagen-Kontroverse um die Rolle der Deutschen im Holocaust* (A People of Murderers? The Documentation on the Goldhagen Controversy and the Role of the Germans in the Holocaust). In 1997, Wolfgang Wippermann, a German historian who had written extensively on the history of National Socialism, offered his own meditations on the meaning of the affair in the larger context of German confrontations with their past in *Wessen Schuld? Vom Historikerstreit zur Goldhagen-Kontroverse* (Whose Guilt? From the Historians' Debate to the Goldhagen Controversy). Finally, Siedler, the publisher of the German translation of *Hitler's Willing Executioners,* released in 1997 an addendum to the debate composed by Goldhagen himself. *Briefe an Goldhagen* (Letters to Goldhagen) is a collection of letters the author received from his readers and critics along with his responses.

Although the status of Goldhagen's contribution to the scholarship on the Third Reich remained in dispute, Saul Friedländer's *Nazi Germany and the Jews: The Years of Persecution 1933–1939* (Volume I) (1997) was almost universally well received. Another well-received work was the 1997 German translation of Henry Friedlander's *The Origins of Nazi Genocide: From Euthanasia to the Final Solution,* which appeared under the title *Der Weg zum NS-Genozid. Von der Euthanasie zur Endlösung.*

A number of important publications demonstrated a heightened interest in German-Jewish history before the Holocaust. Following the successful 1995 release of the sociolinguist Victor Klemperer's diaries from the Nazi years (see AJYB 1997, p. 347), the Aufbau publishing house brought out the remaining volumes of Klemperer's diaries. One two-volume set, entitled *Curriculum Vitae,* covers the years 1881–1918; another covers the years 1918–1932 and was published under the title *Leben sammeln, nicht fragen wozu und warum* (Collect Life, Do Not Ask Why and to What End). A single book released separately under the title *Und so ist alles schwankend* (Everything Remains Unsettled) documents the second half of 1945.

Aufbau also published for the first time Arnold Zweig's autobiographical *Freundschaft mit Freud* (Friendship with Freud), one of a planned 19-volume collection of Zweig's works. In *The Renaissance of Jewish Culture in Weimar Germany,* Michael Brenner highlights the German-Jewish exploration of Judaism after events during and following World War I left so many German Jews disillusioned with the quest for assimilation. Moshe Zimmerman, an Israeli historian, contributed the 43rd volume to the Oldenbourg Publishing series *Enzyklopëdie deutscher Geschichte* (Encyclopedia of German History) under the title *Die Deutschen Juden 1914–1945.* Historians Avraham Barkai, Paul Mendes-Flohr, and Steven M. Lowenstein cover the same time period in *Deutsch-jüdische Geschichte in der Neuzeit. Vierter Band: 1918–1945* (German-Jewish History in the Modern Era. 4th Volume: 1918–1945). Lastly, the *Archiv für Sozialgeschichte,* one of the most important German academic journals, devoted its 1997 volume to the history of "Jews in Politics and Society in the 1920s."

Personalia

In September 1996 President Roman Herzog bestowed the Officer's Cross of the Order of Merit of the Federal Republic of Germany on Eugene DuBow of the American Jewish Committee. Just months before moving to Berlin to open the committee's new office, DuBow accepted the award, given in recognition of his role in fostering German-Jewish relations, at a ceremony in New York at the office of German Consul General Erhard Holtermann.

A year after receiving the B'nai B'rith Gold Medal for Humanitarian Work, Chancellor Helmut Kohl received the 1997 Leo Baeck Prize of the Central Council of Jews in Germany. In conferring the honor, Central Council president Ignatz Bubis lauded Kohl's contribution to the reconciliation between Christians and Jews as well as between Germany and Israel. The 1996 Leo Baeck Prize went to the Frankfurt journal *Tribüne* for its 35-year record of fostering understanding of Judaism. B'nai B'rith chose another German citizen, magnate Frank Woessner, chairman of the board of the Bertelsmann Book Corporation, one of the world's largest publishing houses, as the recipient of its 1997 Gold Medal. As an expression of his commitment to German-Jewish culture, Woessner had overseen the publication of such unprofitable but important books as the collected works of Leo Baeck and the Liberal prayer book in Hebrew and German that was used for 1997 Rosh Hashanah services in the Beth Shalom congregation of Munich. (Siedler, a subsidiary of Bertelsmann, was responsible for the German translation of *Hitler's Willing Executioners* and the collection *Briefe an Goldhagen* that followed it.)

Goldhagen himself received an award in Germany in 1997. The *Journal for German and International Politics* bestowed its Democracy Prize on the American political scientist. For the occasion, the eminent German philosopher Jürgen Habermas delivered a speech in praise of Goldhagen.

Two important Jewish cultural figures who died in the second half of 1996 were Erika Milée, the former doyenne of the Hamburg Ballet, aged 88, and Erwin Leiser, documentary filmmaker of almost 50 works on the Nazi regime, aged 73.

Among prominent German Jews who died in 1997 were Rudolf Robert, a founding board member of the foundation "Help for the Victims of National Socialist Tyranny," aged 75; Simon Schlachet, president of the Aachen Jewish community from 1972 until his death, aged 85; East German novelist Jurek Becker, author of *Jakob der Lügner* (Jacob the Liar), a canonical work of Holocaust literature, aged 60; and Stephan Hermlin, another important GDR author, who died in April, just before his 82nd birthday.

GREG CAPLAN

Austria

National Affairs

I~n~ JANUARY 1997, Chancellor Franz Vranitzky, in a surprise move, resigned the chancellorship of Austria, explaining that "10 years are a sufficient spell" for the job. In stepping down, he handed over the government and leadership of the Social Democratic Party (SDP) to Finance Minister Viktor Klima. The coalition government, which had been formed by Vranitzky in March 1996, made up of the Social Democrats and the People's Party, continued in power through 1997 under Klima, differing little from the preceding government.

Vranitzky had taken office in June 1986, when the country was absorbing the shock of the election of Kurt Waldheim as president of Austria, the man who had fallen into international disgrace after being forced to acknowledge his wartime service in an infamous German army unit. At that time, the Freedom Party (FPO), which was controlled by its liberal faction, had been a junior coalition partner of the Social Democrats. When the far-right nationalist Jorg Haider gained control of the party in September 1986, Vranitzky dissolved the coalition. New elections produced a coalition government between the Social Democrats and the conservative, right-of-center People's Party in which Vranitzky served as chancellor until he stepped down from office.

During his term in office, Chancellor Vranitzky made an important mark on the country's foreign policy. In a bold move, he led his neutral country into membership in the European Union. He offered a helping hand to the neighboring countries in Central and Eastern Europe to adapt to the postcommunist period. In dealing with the Nazi past, he called on Austrians to come to terms with Hitler's legacy in their country.

Another major achievement was the normalization of relations with Israel. He was the first Austrian head of government to make an official visit to Israel and to acknowledge that Austrians, like Germans and others, were involved in crimes against the Jews during the Nazi era.

The coalition under Klima was badly shaken by the results of the vote in elections for the European Parliament in October 1997. The far right-wing Freedom Party (FPO), led by Jorg Haider, won almost 28 percent of the vote, less than 2 percent behind the Social Democrats. By its success at the polls, the Freedom Party consolidated its position as Europe's most successful far-right party. In a separate election, the Socialists also lost their overall majority in the Vienna City Hall, the country's most powerful regional assembly.

In his campaign, Haider struck a sympathetic chord among many Austrians with his tirades against immigration, which he openly associated with crime, charges of government sleaze, and most of all, his depiction of the European Union as an institution that would cost blue-collar jobs and lead to higher taxes. Like Euro-skeptics in Great Britain and elsewhere on the continent, he called for "a Europe of fatherlands," darkly warning that a united Europe would destroy national sovereignty. Haider could not be unmindful that the word "fatherland" has other associations in a land that welcomed Hitler's annexation in 1938. Many of Haider's supporters were blue-collar workers who in the past had voted for the Social Democratic Party. In attracting these voters, the leader of the FPO succeeded in tapping into growing disillusionment among Austrians over membership in the European Union and an austerity budget that cut welfare benefits and raised taxes and energy costs.

The success of the Freedom Party was a sharp setback to the complacency of the governing coalition, which had long assumed that Austrians would never go so far as to permit the far right to assume power. If the party were to make further gains in the next parliamentary election, it could conceivably be part of a new government or be given a mandate to form one. In a postelection editorial, the liberal daily *Der Standard* commented: "There has been a significant change in Austria's psychological and political landscape. This result shows voters are increasingly willing to put Jorg Haider in government."

Israel and the Middle East

Relations between Austria and Israel remained cordial, and contacts between the two countries at the political, cultural, scientific, and technical levels continued to develop. Underscoring these good ties was the visit paid to Israel by Chancellor Franz Vranitzky in September 1996, the first by a head of government or state to come to Israel since the election that brought the Likud government to power. The chancellor was received by Prime Minister Benjamin Netanyahu and President Ezer Weizman and met with other leading members of the new government. In a goodwill gesture, Vranitzky donated the $40,000 he received from a Fulbright prize to the Bruno Kreisky Forum, which sponsored a border-crossing project of youth from Israel, Jordan, and the Palestinian autonomous area. The 70 young people began their walk in Eilat, continued to Akaba, then to Amman, and ended in Bethlehem.

In May 1997 Vice-Chancellor and Foreign Minister Wolfgang Schussel made an official visit to Israel, where he had working sessions with Prime Minister Netanyahu, President Weizman, and Foreign Minister David Levy. In addition, he met with Palestinian Authority chairman Yasir Arafat. At these meetings there was an exchange of views on progress in the peace process and the political situation in the region. The meetings assumed added importance in view of Austria's scheduled assumption of the rotating presidency of the European Union in July 1998. Dan Tichon, Speaker of the Knesset, paid a four-day visit to Austria in May 1997 at the invitation of Dr. Heinz Fischer, the president of the Austrian Parliament.

Israeli prime minister Netanyahu made an official visit to Austria on September 21, 1997. In the course of the two-day visit—the first official visit by an Israeli prime minister to Austria—Netanyahu met with Federal President Thomas Klestil, Chancellor Klima, Foreign Minister Schussel, and National Parliament president Fischer. He also met with members of the Jewish community, including its president, Paul Grosz, and Chief Rabbi Paul Chaim Eisenberg. In an address before a large gathering in Vienna's Stadttempel, Netanyahu called on Austrian Jews to immigrate to Israel. He also delivered an address to the Second International Theodor Herzl Symposium, which was held at the Vienna City Hall (September 22–24, 1997), and attended the cornerstone-laying ceremony for the new Chabad school. Accompanied by President Klestil, Chancellor Klima, Foreign Minister Schussel, and other Austrian officials, Netanyahu paid a visit to the Mauthausen concentration camp, where many thousands of Jews and peoples of different nationalities were killed.

Talks between the chancellor and the Israeli prime minister centered around expanding trade between the two countries and the peace process, with the two leaders agreeing to establish a "hot line" so as to be able to carry on direct talks. Reflecting the positive nature of the discussions, Prime Minister Netanyahu invited Chancellor Klima to pay an official visit to Israel in 1998. A delegation of ten leading business people who accompanied Prime Minister Netanyahu met with 40 Austrian industrialists to lay out ways of doubling the volume of trade over the coming years. As part of this effort, the two sides agreed to revitalize the Austrian–Israeli Chamber of Commerce.

Bilateral trade between the countries amounted to roughly $250 million. Machinery and manufactured goods figured prominently in Austrian sales, while Israeli exports to Austria were largely manufactured goods, raw materials, and agricultural products. Both sides agreed that Israel needed to canvass the Austrian market more aggressively in order to increase its sales, for example, by being represented at trade fairs in Austria.

Austria named a new ambassador to Israel, Wolfgang Paul, who succeeded Herbert Kroll. A senior official in the foreign ministry, Paul had held ambassadorial posts in New Delhi, Sofia, and Prague.

CULTURAL AND SCIENTIFIC EXCHANGES

Austrian and Israeli officials signed a memorandum of understanding in Vienna in June 1996 to increase cultural contacts between the two countries. In pursuance of this understanding, a number of important cultural events took place during 1997. The Israel Philharmonic Orchestra, under the direction of Zubin Mehta, performed in the Musikverein in Vienna in February; the corps de ballet of the Staatsoper performed in Israel on May 14 and 15.

An exhibition of contemporary Israeli artists opened in Salzburg on June 23. The Kunsthistorisches Museum in Vienna mounted a special exhibition of artifacts from the Israel Museum, titled *Land der Bibel* (Land of the Bible), which ran from September 1997 to January 1998. On display were some 400 objects dating from the earliest paleolithic period to the scrolls of the Dead Sea, documenting the history of the Holy Land and Jerusalem and of the royal capitals of the ancient Near East. The exhibition was an exchange for the special exhibition at the Israel Museum in Jerusalem in June 1996 of artworks from the Kunsthistorisches Museum; this exhibition was held in honor of the 85th birthday of Austrian-born Teddy Kollek, the former mayor of Jerusalem.

Scientific exchanges between Austria and Israel continued to develop at the government and university levels. The Austrian Federal Ministry of Science and Transport sponsored scientific projects at Kibbutz Sde Boker. The Second International Austrian–Israeli Technion Symposium cum Industrial Forum— "Technology for Peace–Science for Mankind"—was held in Graz, June 4–6, 1997. Forty Austrian and 14 Israeli scientists heard papers on the topics of laser technology and space technology.

Holocaust-Related Matters

The special fund established by the Austrian government in June 1995 "for the victims of national socialism" had by June 1997 contacted all the estimated 27,000 people considered eligible to receive payments. The amount paid to each beneficiary was fixed at 70,000 schillings ($5,800), though in cases of special hardship this could be tripled. In 1996 the Ministry of Finance allocated 600 million schillings (approximately $50 million) to the fund and an equal amount for 1997. It was generally understood that the payments were to be seen as a good will gesture by the government and were not to be considered as reparations to the victims.

The legislation creating the fund set forth the conditions for eligibility. These included people who were persecuted because of their political beliefs, religion, nationality, sexual orientation, physical or mental disability, or were considered by the Nazis as asocial; people who were forced to flee Austria in order to escape persecution also qualified for payments. Other conditions included certification of Austrian nationality as of March 13, 1938, and proof of residence in the country. The regulations were subsequently eased to permit payment to the estate of an individual who died while his or her claim was being processed. As of June 30, 1997, the fund, which is headed by Hannah Lessing, made payments to 13,800 individuals in the amount of one billion schillings ($80 million). Payments were made to people in 52 countries, the largest number being from the United States (5,600), followed by Austria (2,400), Israel (1,800), United Kingdom (1,700), Australia (700), and Argentina (217). Thirty of the beneficiaries were 100 years old or older.

It had been the understanding that once all people eligible to receive payments were properly compensated, the fund would go out of existence. Meantime, however, consideration was being given to creating a permanent office to provide assistance to victims of National Socialism and their families.

A special exhibition, "Die Verbrechen der Wehrmacht 1941–1944" (Crimes of the German Army 1941–1944), opened in Graz in November 1997. Through pictures, letters, and official documents, the exhibition documented the complicity of the German army in carrying out the murder of countless Jews and other peoples during the war. The exhibition, which was shown in Vienna in the fall of 1995, had also been shown in a number of German cities.

ESRA, the social-service agency responsible for carrying out the Jewish community's welfare and social programs, sponsored a two-day symposium in Vienna, November 10–11, on the theme "Uberleben der Shoah–Und Danach" (Surviving the Shoah–and What After). The symposium, which was held in Vienna's City Hall, dealt with a range of issues relating to Holocaust-induced post-traumatic stress disorder. Experts from Austria, Germany, Israel, the Netherlands, and the United States attended the symposium.

WORLD WAR II GOLD RETURNED TO AUSTRIA

At a conference in Geneva in June 1997, Rabbi Marvin Hier, the executive director of the Los Angeles–based Simon Wiesenthal Center, demanded that investigations into the gold transactions of Switzerland and other neutral countries during World War II be expanded to include Austria. After the war, Austria received 50.5 tons of gold to compensate Vienna for its claim on 100 tons of gold the Nazis transferred to the German Reichsbank after Nazi Germany annexed Austria in 1938. Restitution of wartime losses for Austria was justified on the ground that at the 1943 Moscow Conference, the Allies decided to treat Austria as a victim rather than a perpetrator of Nazi aggression. Rabbi Hier asserted that Austria was not entitled to the gold because its people supported annexation, and more than a million Austrians fought in the German army and the SS. The Allied decision was outrageous, he said, because the gold belonged to victims of the Holocaust.

Related to this was the increasing interest being shown in securing monies owed to Jews by Austrian banks and insurance companies. This matter was first spotlighted with the publication in 1993 of Brigitte Bailer's book *Wiedergutmachung: Oesterreich und die Opfer des National-Socialismuss* (Reparations: Austria and the Victims of National-Socialism).

STOLEN ARTWORKS: AUERBACH COLLECTION AUCTIONED IN VIENNA

In October 1996, in Vienna, a two-day auction of artworks plundered from Jews by the Nazis raised $14.5 million. The 8,000 items for sale—including 19th-century landscapes and portraits, Old Master paintings and drawings, antique coins, sculptures, tapestries, and porcelain—all found buyers. Eighty-eight percent of the auction's proceeds would go to aiding victims of the Holocaust; the remaining 12 percent would aid non-Jewish survivors. The auction was conducted by Christie's of London, which agreed to forego its usual fee. A floral still life by 17th-century French painter Abraham Mignon yielded the highest price of the auction—$1.35 million—although it had been expected to bring in no more than $75,000. Paul Grosz awarded the Gold Medal of the Federation of the Jewish Communities of Austria to Chancellor Franz Vranitzky for his efforts in bringing about the benefit auction, as well as to Lord Hindlip, chairman of Christie's of London.

Most of the artworks had belonged to the 65,000 Jews who did not survive the Holocaust. At the end of the war, American soldiers found a large cache of art in a salt mine near Salzburg. Almost 10,000 of the works of art were returned to their owners or their relatives during the ten-year Allied occupation of Austria. In 1955, the departing U.S. Army instructed the Austrian government to return the rest of the items. Except for several hundred items that were claimed and returned, the roughly 8,000 remaining items were kept by the Austrian government and stored in a 14th-century monastery in Mauerbach, near Vienna. Austria's reluctance to own up to complicity in the Holocaust was thought to have played a role in the delay, expressed in limited efforts to advertise the works and a requirement that claimants show detailed proof of ownership. In 1995, the government, under strong international pressure, agreed to turn over the collection to Austria's Jewish community.

The net proceeds of the auction amounted to 130 million Austrian schillings ($10.1 million). This sum, minus the 12 percent set aside for the benefit of non-Jewish victims of the Holocaust, was distributed on a worldwide basis to needy Austrian Jewish victims of the Holocaust. The Federation of Jewish Communities in Austria, which had been assigned responsibility for distributing the funds under the law that authorized the Mauerbach auction, completed this task after intensive negotiations with its international partners—the Central Committee of Jews from Austria in Israel, the Committee for Jewish Claims on Austria, and the World Jewish Restitution Organization.

STOLEN EGON SCHIELE PAINTINGS

A dispute broke out in December 1997 over the ownership of two paintings by the famed Austrian Secessionist painter Egon Schiele. The paintings were part of a special exhibition, "Egon Schiele: The Leopold Collection," which was on display in the fall of 1997 at the Museum of Modern Art in New York City. The family of a Jewish Viennese art dealer, whose prize painting, "Portrait of Wally," by Schiele, was taken from her by the Nazis before World War II, asked the museum to hold on to it until the provenance could be determined. A second family, whose relative lost a Schiele work, "Dead City," displayed in the same exhibition, also requested the museum to retain the painting until ownership could be determined. The heirs of the owner of the work, Fritz Grunbaum, informed the museum that the painting had been taken from his collection without his consent by Nazi agents following the Nazi annexation of Austria in March 1938.

The paintings shown in New York all came from a collection of art owned by the Austrian government–financed Leopold Foundation. Dr. Rudolf Leopold, a 72-year-old Viennese ophthalmologist, began aggressively buying art in 1950. Over the years he amassed some 5,400 works. In 1994 his holdings were purchased by Austria and put in a private foundation, which is building a museum in Vienna. At the end of December, the Museum of Modern Art was deciding whether to honor its legal obligations to the Leopold Foundation to return the works, or to accede to the claimants' requests to retain the paintings.

HOLOCAUST MEMORIALS

The erection of the Vienna Holocaust memorial, which was designed by British sculptress Rachel Whiteread, remained mired in controversy. The project, initially proposed by Simon Wiesenthal to honor the memory of the 65,000 Austrian Jews who perished in the Holocaust, was to be placed in the Judenplatz in Vienna's first district. When it was discovered that the memorial was to be placed over the site of a recently discovered synagogue dating back to the 12th or 13th century, some members of the Jewish community had second thoughts about placing it there. The split in the Jewish community complicated the work of the Vienna City Council, which was expected to make a final decision in early 1998 on whether to site the monument in the Judenplatz. Also taking a stand on whether to have the monument in the Judenplatz was Archbishop of Vienna Christoph Schonborn, who expressed the view that the synagogue itself could best serve as a reminder of the horrible fate suffered over the centuries by many of the country's Jews. In 1420–21 many Jews committed suicide in the synagogue, and some 200 were burned alive at the hands of Christians who threatened to convert them to Christianity under pain of death. The statement provoked a strong reaction from Simon Wiesenthal, who asserted that the archbishop had overstepped his bounds by interfering in internal Jewish matters.

A memorial was dedicated to the victims of *Kristallnacht* and the Holocaust in Innsbruck, capital of the province of Tyrol. The design for the memorial was chosen from a competition conducted among the province's school youth.

JEWISH COMMUNITY

Demography

The Jewish community of Austria was undergoing changes in size, age, and composition. It was getting somewhat larger and younger and becoming more varied, though its growth was expected to slow, if not stop, due to recently enacted restrictive immigration and asylum laws. About 7,000 Jews were registered with the Israelitisch Kultusgemeinde (IKG), the official communal body, but knowledgeable observers claimed the actual number of Jews in the country was at least twice that.

Reflecting a long established pattern of Jewish population distribution, the overwhelming majority of Jews were concentrated in Vienna, with only about 300 to 400 making their homes in the large provincial cities of Salzburg, Innsbruck, Graz, and Linz.

With the virtual cessation of immigration from the former republics of the Soviet Union, the small but steady growth was now due to the increased fertility rate, mainly among the Sephardic and Orthodox Jews. It was generally agreed that the Sephardic Jews—most of them from the former Soviet republics of Georgia and Uzbekistan (Bukhara) and a smaller number from Tajikistan—would soon outstrip the Ashkenazic community in size.

A new building complex was dedicated on November 9, 1997, in Vienna's second district, which was becoming home to a growing number of the city's Jewish population. The complex has two residences for Jewish senior citizens and a home for students—as well as rental space for shops. The official date of the opening, November 9, was chosen both to commemorate *Kristallnacht* and to underscore the continuity and growth of Jewish life in the country.

Communal Affairs

In June 1996 Ariel Muzikant, a businessman, was elected to succeed Prof. Jacob Allerhand as president of the B'nai Brith chapter of Vienna. The new head of the organization, which numbered 82 members, said that it would develop programs around two policy objectives: combating neo-Nazism and far right-wing groups, and promoting greater understanding among the disparate groups within the Jewish community.

The Anti-Defamation League (ADL) established a new European regional office in Vienna in August 1997, to combat anti-Semitism and racism in Central and Eastern Europe. The office, headed by journalist Marta Halpert, was established through a grant from the Ronald S. Lauder Foundation. According to Abraham Foxman, the director of the ADL, the new office would work with government officials and Jewish community leaders in neighboring Eastern European countries to promote the rights of Jews and minorities in the region. As part of this effort, it would reach out to church groups and interfaith organizations.

ESRA, the agency that administers the community's wide array of social and welfare programs, continued to serve mainly people with Holocaust-related problems and the large Jewish immigrant population. Most of the aid was directed toward the elderly, youth, and families and included legal advice to recent immigrants; financial aid to people in need; housing and work for young people; and a psychotherapy clinic. Most of ESRA's budget was covered by grants from the federal government, with the Kultusgemeinde also contributing.

Christian-Jewish Relations

In a formal statement issued in November 1997, Archbishop of Vienna Schonborn acknowledged responsibility for the role of the Church in the persecution of Austrian Jews over the centuries and sought forgiveness for its actions. In this historic statement, the archbishop pointed to the great suffering of Vienna's Jewish community at the hands of Christians in 1420–21, which he described as a precursor of the fate that was to overtake Austrian Jewry in the 20th century at the hands of the Nazis. He stated that Christianity now recognized its guilt in the persecution of Jews and was asking for forgiveness. The statement attracted media attention, but no immediate response from the Jewish community.

The 1997 edition of *Das Judische Echo,* edited by Leon Zelman, was dedicated to the theme "Judaism and Christianity" (vol. 46, October 1997). Zelman, a survivor of the Mauthausen concentration camp and a leading figure in Austria's Jewish community, is the director of the Jewish Welcome Service—an Austrian government tourist office. He is a frequent speaker in Austrian public schools and civic organizations on the Nazi period, and an indefatigable worker in behalf of reconciliation between Austrian Jewry and the Catholic Church.

Culture

Among the several special exhibitions mounted by the Jewish Museum of Vienna in 1997, three attracted particular attention. One, "Neuland" (New Land), held March 14–May 4, focused on Austrian Jews who had emigrated to Palestine and participated in the cultural development of the State of Israel. The exhibition included writers, painters, photographers, architects, sculptors, fashion designers, actors, directors, and musicians. The second exhibition, "Masken: Versuch Uber die Schoa" (Masks: Approaching the Shoah), shown July 25–October 16, displayed the death masks of 29 murdered Jewish inmates of Nazi concentration camps. These masks were prepared in 1942 in the Anatomical Institute of Poznan by a Nazi official, at the request of the Anthropological Section of the Vienna Natural Historical Museum, which wanted skulls of Jews for its scientific research. The third exhibition, held November 7, 1997, to January 18, 1998, was in honor of the 150th birthday of the German-born impressionist painter Max Liebermann and featured works painted in the years 1900–1918.

Judische Kulturwochen (Jewish Cultural Week) in Vienna in November 1997 featured films, concerts, readings of poetry and literature, plays, and lectures.

The Second International Theodor Herzl Symposium, held at the Vienna City Hall, September 22–24, 1997, celebrated the centennial anniversary of the first Zionist Congress, which was convened on September 3, 1897, in Basel, Switzerland. A central theme of the papers read at the symposium was the historical achievements of Zionism and the Zionist movement. The year before, the City of Vienna organized an International Symposium on Theodor Herzl, to commemorate the centennial publication in Vienna of Herzl's *The Jewish State* (*Der Judenstaat*). In conjunction with this event, the *Illustrierte Neue Welt* (Illustrated New World), which was founded by Herzl in 1897, celebrated its 100th anniversary. The newspaper, a monthly publication, was under the editorship of Dr. Joanna Nittenberg.

Personalia

Viktor E. Frankl, famed Austrian psychiatrist and founder of logotherapy—which became known as the "third school" of Viennese psychotherapy—died on September 2, 1997, at the age of 92. In 1942 Frankl was arrested by the Nazi authorities along with other members of his family and deported. Only he survived the ordeal in which his father, mother, brother, and first wife all died in the camps.

During the three years he spent in four concentration camps, including Auschwitz, he came to the realization that those who gave meaning to their lives—perhaps by helping others through the day—were themselves more likely to survive. After his liberation, he wrote *Man's Search for Meaning,* describing his camp experience and how this led him to develop logotherapy, an approach that enabled many people to alter their lives when they might have given up. The book, which sold some nine million copies and was translated into many languages, had enormous influence. In the postwar period, Frankl practiced and taught psychiatry in Vienna for 25 years and spent 20 years in the United States as a visiting professor at Harvard and other universities. As a testament to his work, Frankl received honorary doctorates from institutions around the world.

MURRAY GORDON

East-Central Europe

T HROUGHOUT THE SECOND half of 1996 and all of 1997, Jewish communities in East-Central Europe continued the path of development and revival that was accelerated by the collapse of Communism in 1989–90. As the revival became more entrenched, emerging new communities took greater part in Europe-wide Jewish discourse and showed increasing self-confidence in demanding to be treated as equal members of the world Jewish community.

Several major issues dominated. One was the linked saga of property restitution and financial compensation to Holocaust survivors, particularly following new revelations about Nazi gold deposits, hidden Swiss bank accounts, insurance claims, and related matters. International aspects of the Nazi gold issue were the focus of a conference in London in December 1997.

Of pressing concern were efforts to obtain direct payments for aging Holocaust survivors in post-Communist states who, unlike survivors in the West, had never been compensated for their wartime losses. Jews in East-Central Europe increasingly demanded that their leaders or representatives participate in discussions on these matters. Some Jewish leaders from the region were outspoken in criticizing the World Jewish Restitution Organization (WJRO) and other international bodies for ignoring them.

Communities, as always, kept a vigilant eye on manifestations of anti-Semitism—and the Anti-Defamation League established an East-Central European office in Vienna in September 1997 to help in this area. However, the most pressing cross-border issues related to ways in which Jewish life could be strengthened—questions of Jewish identity, including how to deal with mixed-married couples and the children of mixed marriages; outreach to the unaffiliated; and the development of new communal leadership. Dealing with these issues influenced the agendas of local Jewish community structures as well as international Jewish organizations working in the region, such as the American Jewish Joint Distribution Committee (JDC), the Ronald S. Lauder Foundation, Chabad, and British-based World Jewish Relief.

The conference on "Furthering Jewish Life in Europe," held in Strasbourg at the end of June 1997 and sponsored by the European Council of Jewish Communities (ECJC) and the London-based Institute for Jewish Policy Research (JPR), brought Jewish representatives from Eastern and Western Europe and Israel together to discuss the issues on a pan-European level. Other organizations, such as the Europe Israel Forum, also sponsored meetings that brought Jews from Eastern and Western Europe together.

Jewish communities and organizations in East-Central Europe—like Jewish communities throughout the world—took increasing advantage of the Internet to air their views and maintain contact with each other. The London-based European Council of Jewish Communities played a special role in trying to facilitate communications and interaction among scattered communities, both by hosting a Web site with extensive intercommunity links and by organizing a variety of get-togethers, including conferences, study retreats, and singles' weekends. Jewish community centers or offices in most major cities in the region set up computer centers, often with the help of ORT or other organizations, from which community members could "surf the Net."

Albania

Devastating political, social, and economic turmoil swept the impoverished Balkan state in 1997. Albania's tiny Jewish community was caught up in the turmoil, and eventually many if not most Jews left the country either permanently or on a temporary basis. Some Jews were victims of the fraudulent pyramid investment schemes whose collapse touched off months of rioting, lawlessness, and anarchy in the country.

JEWISH COMMUNITY

Only about 60 Jews were known to live in Albania before the outbreak of violence and armed conflict in early 1997.

Just before Rosh Hashanah in 1996, about two-thirds of Albania's Jews gathered in the capital, Tirana, for a High Holy Day celebration organized by the Joint Distribution Committee. It was the first time the shofar had been blown in Albania in half a century. However, the JDC had to scrap its plans to send a young Italian Jew to Tirana to help celebrate Passover because of the dangerous situation there.

In March 1997 two former Albanian cabinet ministers—one Jewish and one married to a Jew—sought asylum in Israel. By the beginning of May, with the help of the JDC, at least half of Albania's Jews had left for Italy, Israel, or elsewhere, and fewer than 30 Jews were still in the country.

In May Israel donated 30 tons of flour to Albania. "This humanitarian aid is an act of solidarity with the Albanian people, and confirms the close relations that exist between the two peoples," the Israeli embassy in Rome said in a statement.

Bulgaria

Economic crisis swept Bulgaria in 1996 and 1997, sparking mass street demonstrations in early 1997 as incomes plummeted and basic commodities disappeared. The situation was so bad that Israel sent emergency medical aid, and the Joint Distribution Committee also sent help to old-age homes and orphanages serving the general public.

Following elections in November 1996, Petar Stoyanov took office as Bulgarian president in January 1997.

Holocaust-related developments: In March 1997 Jews, senior government officials, and Orthodox church leaders held a ceremony in the town of Kyustendil to honor Bulgarians who helped prevent the deportation of Jews to Nazi death camps during World War II. Specifically, they honored a delegation of five Bulgarians from Kyustendil, led by Speaker of Parliament Dimitar Peshev, who went to Sofia in March 1943 to appeal against the deportations ordered by Bulgaria's wartime ally, Germany. In conjunction with the commemoration, President Stoyanov ordered that Peshev's delegation be awarded posthumously the Order of Stara Planina, first class.

JEWISH COMMUNITY

Estimates of the Jewish population of Bulgaria ranged between 5,000 and 8,000, most of them in the capital, Sofia, and in Plovdiv.

The economic and political crisis hurt the country's Jewish population, especially elderly people living on fixed pensions, and it also induced many young Bulgarian Jews to emigrate to Israel. According to some reports, Bulgaria had the highest rate of Jewish emigration in the world, with some 300 to 400 making *aliyah* each year.

The community operated an elementary school and Sunday school in Sofia and a summer camp. Many activities took place in the Jewish community center, Beit Am, which was enlarged in 1997 to add space for classrooms and youth activities. The Jewish prayer book was translated into Bulgarian for the first time in 1996, and on Passover 1997 about 800 people attended community seders.

The magnificent domed synagogue in Sofia was rededicated in September 1996, after a full-scale restoration that took years. More than 1,000 Jews from around the world attended the ceremony, which was also attended by Bulgarian president Zhelyu Zhelev.

Czech Republic

In July 1997 the Czech Republic, along with Poland and Hungary, was invited to join NATO during the Western Alliance's Madrid summit. Vast floods devastated parts of the Czech Republic in the summer of 1997, causing extensive economic losses.

After months of economic and other problems, the government of Prime Minister Vaclav Klaus fell in late 1997. President Vaclav Havel named Josef Tosovsky as new prime minister in December. Havel himself suffered bouts of ill health, including an operation for lung cancer in December 1996.

In September 1997 President Havel made an official trip to the Middle East, visiting Lebanon, Jordan, Israel, and the Palestinian territories. He called for peace and urged Israelis to think twice about building new Jewish settlements.

There was mounting concern among Czechs over manifestations of racism, particularly those directed against Romanies (Gypsies), many of whom attempted to seek asylum in Canada and Britain. There were some anti-Jewish incidents, among them the vandalizing of seven tombstones in Lomnice u Tisnova in November 1996. In September 1997 some 80 tombstones were vandalized at the Jewish cemetery in Frydek Mistek, which had just been restored by a German organization.

Holocaust-related developments: Czech Jews were vocal about pressing Germany to start paying monthly compensation payments to Holocaust survivors in former Communist states. About 2,000 Jewish survivors lived in the Czech Republic.

In October 1996 the Federation of Jewish Communities in the Czech Republic announced that it would apply for the return to Jewish control of about 20 synagogues and Jewish cemeteries. This was based on a government decision in September to restore some buildings confiscated by the Communists to their original church owners. In November 1996 B'nai B'rith in the Czech Republic reacquired its pre-World War II headquarters, 57 years after the building was confiscated by the Germans.

In April 1997 an Interior Ministry spokesperson said that his ministry would help the Czech Jewish community find valuables stolen by the Nazis during the Holocaust. In May the President's Office established a commission to study the Holocaust era in Czechoslovakia.

In early 1997 it was revealed that Czech-born Madeleine Albright, formerly U.S. ambassador to the United Nations and the newly appointed U.S. Secretary of State, a woman known to be a practicing Christian, had in fact been born a Jew but was baptized and raised as a Catholic. After spending the war years in London during World War II, her family returned to live in Prague until 1948, when they fled Communism and settled in the United States, where Albright later converted to Episcopalianism. On an official visit to her native land in July 1997, now Secretary of State Albright visited Jewish sites in Prague, including the Pinkas Synagogue Holocaust memorial, where she found the names of three of her grandparents on the list of those killed by the Nazis. In September she visited the small town where her family came from and also Terezin (Theresienstadt), site of the ghetto concentration camp where her family members were interned. Albright's discovery of her Jewish roots as an adult spotlighted a fairly common situation in the Czech Republic and other former Communist states, where many Jews sought to conceal their Jewish roots or hide them from their children as a means of protecting them.

In late summer of 1997 Czech politicians joined Czech Jewish leaders in calling on Germany to prosecute Anton Malloth, 85, who had served as a guard at Terezin ghetto concentration camp. He was sentenced in absentia to death by a Czechoslovak court in 1948 and was discovered living in a Munich nursing home in 1997.

On September 7, 1997, a performance of Verdi's "Requiem" took place at

Terezin, under the patronage of President Havel and President Roman Herzog of Germany, performed by the German National Youth Orchestra and German and Czech choirs. Presented in memory of the victims, the concert also recalled performances of the mass by doomed Jewish musicians who were interned in the camp in 1943 and 1944.

On December 23, 1997, a German government spokesperson announced that Germany and the Czech Republic would sign an agreement setting up a 165-million mark ($93 million) fund for Czech victims of the Holocaust. The fund, part of a German-Czech reconciliation accord signed early in the year, would begin functioning on January 1, 1998. The money would be used for old people's homes and sanatoriums for 8,000 Jewish and non-Jewish survivors of Nazi camps and the resistance movement.

Nazi hunter Simon Wiesenthal received an honorary degree from Prague's Charles University in April 1997.

JEWISH COMMUNITY

An estimated 3,500 to 6,000 Jews lived in the Czech Republic, and possibly thousands more were of Jewish background. About half of the known Jewish population lived in Prague, with the others scattered in nine other communities, the two largest in Brno and Olomouc.

The revitalization of Czech Jewry, begun with the fall of Communism, continued, with the road to normality marked by expansion as well as internal diversity. In Prague, two non-Orthodox communities continued to function alongside the official Orthodox community. These were Bejt Praha, which called itself the Open Prague Jewish Community, and which was originally founded in the mid-1990s to appeal to foreign Jews living in Prague, and Bejt Simcha, founded by Sylvie Wittmann, who runs a Jewish travel agency in Prague. In addition, Chabad Lubavitch sent a representative to Prague in September 1996.

Bejt Praha, which became a member of the Federation of Czech Jewish Communities, held *kabbalat shabbat* (Friday evening) gatherings in the Jewish Town Hall building. It also sponsored nonreligious events marking Jewish holidays. Bejt Simcha remained outside the official Czech Jewish community organizations but was affiliated with the World Association of Progressive Jewry. (The Olomouc community, with about 180 members, also was Progressive.) Bejt Simcha held weekly *kabbalat shabbat* gatherings. Both groups scheduled lectures and meetings with visiting rabbis and other experts, generally conducted in English. A Jewish elementary school, sponsored by the Lauder Foundation, opened in Prague in 1997. It was the first such to be established in that city since World War II.

The Czech Jewish Museum in Prague celebrated its 90th anniversary in September 1996 with a ceremony attended by President Havel and other officials, during which Havel opened the museum's new Education and Cultural Center. The museum also started up an Internet Web site.

Numerous concerts, stage presentations, lectures, and other Jewish cultural events took place in Prague and elsewhere—some sponsored by the Jewish community, Bejt Praha, or Bejt Simcha, others part of the program of the Jewish Museum's new Education and Cultural Center. Still others were commercially sponsored as part of Prague's mainstream cultural offerings.

Concerts ranged from Yiddish song to classical performances to liturgical music. Theater included performances by the Jewish community's 14-member Jewish Children's Theater as well as professional performances. Among the latter was the September 1996 premiere of *Sweet Theresienstadt,* a Czech-language play based on a diary found in Terezin concentration camp, directed by American Damien Gray.

Restoration work began on the Spanish synagogue in Prague, and cemeteries and synagogues in various provincial towns were rehabilitated. Several new Jewish museums were opened, continuing a trend begun a year or two earlier. Associated with this, Jewish quarters in several provincial towns were in the process of renewal and restoration, and restaurants or cafes with Jewish-sounding names or Jewish-style decor opened in several of the old ghetto districts. In early 1997 an upscale kosher restaurant, Metzada, was opened by Israelis in Prague's Old Town. It changed hands later in the year and also changed the spelling of its name to Masaada. Bejt Simcha helped found a Jewish-style (nonkosher) restaurant called Sabra, at Terezin.

Hungary

Hungary continued the process of transition to a market economy, with more than 70 percent of the gross domestic product generated by the private sector. But inflation remained high—at least 24 percent in 1996—and about one-quarter of the population was estimated to live below the poverty line. The hardest hit were elderly pensioners (including thousands of Jewish elderly), Romanies, and dependent women and children.

A top priority of Prime Minister Gyula Horn's leftist-liberal coalition was readying Hungary for entry into NATO and the European Union. At the NATO summit in July 1997, Hungary, along with Poland and the Czech Republic, was invited to join the defense organization.

Hungary's relations with Israel continued to expand. Many Israeli tourists visited Hungary, and economic relations broadened. Trade between the two countries was about $100 million in 1996, and Israeli government figures showed that about 100 Israeli businesses had invested some $750 million in Hungary, mainly in the fields of telecommunications, computer software, and pharmaceutical products. In October 1996 a delegation of 160 Israelis attended the opening of Hungary's largest shopping mall, a huge facility in Budapest funded by Israeli and Hungarian investors. Israelis were investing in at least seven other malls in Hungary, including one in the eastern city of Debrecen, where some Israeli companies reportedly had been targets of anti-Semitic activities.

In January 1997 Hungarian foreign minister Laszlo Kovacs made a three-day official visit to Israel. While there, he met with senior Israeli officials and Israeli bankers, as well as with Yasir Arafat. Kovacs and Israeli foreign minister David Levy signed a technical cooperation agreement involving agricultural and other joint projects. In July 1997 the Israeli Ministry of Industry and Trade announced that Israel and Hungary had agreed on a trade pact to come into force on January 1, 1998, that would abolish duty on most imports. Duties on some other goods would be progressively abolished by the year 2000.

There were various incidents tinged with anti-Semitism (or perceived anti-Semitism) that involved ultra right-wing forces, either on the fringe of society or in the mainstream. In March 1997, as one instance, Deputy Speaker of Parliament Agnes Nagy Maczo, a prominent right-wing politician, caused a furor by calling attention to the Jewish origins of Matyas Rakosi, Hungary's much hated, hard-line Communist prime minister in the early 1950s.

Skinheads staged rallies on a number of occasions. After a rally by several hundred skinheads in Budapest on October 23, 1996, Budapest police questioned neo-Nazi leader Albert Szabo about his anti-Jewish speech, saying his statements could be interpreted as an incitement against a community. Szabo led a similar rally outside the U.S. embassy on March 15, 1997, Hungary's National Day.

On October 27, 1996, and on March 15, 1997, the extreme right-wing nationalist Hungarian Justice and Life Party, led by writer Isztvan Csurka, staged antigovernment rallies attended by tens of thousands of people.

In the wake of Jewish protests, Hungarian prosecutors in November 1996 banned the sale of a new Hungarian translation of *Mein Kampf.* The ban, however, touched off a debate on free speech. The new translation was by Aron Monus, a Hungarian émigré who had written anti-Semitic works of his own. Some of these were banned in Hungary in 1991, but the ban was overturned after Monus appealed on the basis of freedom of speech.

There were incidents of cemetery desecration, including the destruction of more than 200 tombs in a Jewish cemetery in Budapest in August 1996, and the destruction of a Holocaust memorial in the Jewish cemetery in Tatabanya, discovered in May 1997. On June 13, a Jewish cemetery in the northern town of Balassagyarmat was desecrated, the day before a scheduled Holocaust commemoration. Vandals damaged or toppled tombstones and also scrawled swastikas and Nazi slogans. In a statement, the Federation of Jewish Communities blamed the incident on the authorities' failure to make full use of the law against "anti-Semites and racists."

Holocaust-related developments: After years of negotiations, in the spring of 1997 the Hungarian government and the Jewish community set up a public foundation to oversee partial compensation of Hungarian Jews for community property seized during World War II. The Hungarian Jewish Heritage Foundation, with a 21-member board whose honorary president is Ronald Lauder, will administer a fund of four billion forints ($24 million) in compensation coupons given by the government. The government also turned over to the Jewish community seven state-owned buildings in Budapest (their rental income to be added to the fund) and ten valuable artworks once owned by Jews. Disbursements are to include a supplemental monthly pension of $20 to $30 a month to Holocaust survivors and support for Jewish religious, educational, and cultural activities.

Hungarian Jews, like others in former Communist states, also pressed Germany to compensate survivors. In February 1997 about 100 survivors staged a demonstration outside the Dohany Street Synagogue, which German president Roman Herzog was visiting during a three-day official trip to Hungary. Herzog met with the protesters and assured them that they would receive compensation.

JEWISH COMMUNITY

Hungary had as many as 100,000 Jews, but only a minority were affiliated with any communal or other Jewish institutions. About 6,000 were members of the Jewish religious community and about 20,000 had contact with Jewish organizations or facilities. About 90 percent of Hungary's Jews lived in Budapest, with the others scattered in more than two dozen smaller towns and cities. Regular prayer services were held in fewer than a dozen provincial towns.

The Federation of Jewish Communities in Hungary mainly represented Jews outside Budapest; the Association of Jewish Communities in Budapest represented the bulk of Hungarian Jews. Both organizations operated under a single joint executive director and were supported by the Joint Distribution Committee in carrying out religious, social-welfare, and education activities through the Jewish Social Support Foundation.

A large percentage of Hungarian Jews were elderly, many of them needy. The JDC underwrote cash grants, food-support programs, including meals on wheels, and other social-welfare services. More than 500 elderly Jews attended five adult day-care centers in Budapest and Szeged. Budapest had a Jewish hospital, and there were three Jewish old-age homes (two in Budapest and one in Szeged).

JDC increasingly sponsored activities aimed at making the Jewish community more self-sufficient, such as the Buncher program, which sent potential leaders for training in Israel.

In Budapest, there were about a score of active synagogues, plus kosher shops, two kosher restaurants, Talmud Torahs, Jewish publications, secular organizations, clubs, and other associations and institutions. Just before Rosh Hashanah in September 1996, Budapest's Dohany Street Synagogue, the largest synagogue in Europe, reopened with a gala ceremony after a years-long restoration. The Hungarian goverment contributed about $8 million of the $10 million cost. Among the 7,000 people attending the ceremony were Hungarian president Arpad Goncz and other government officials, former Israeli prime minister Yitzhak Shamir, and Budapest-born California congressman Tom Lantos, who celebrated his bar mitzvah in the synagogue in 1941.

Budapest had three Jewish schools, with a total enrollment of 1,500 pupils. In addition, about 200 children attended Jewish kindergartens. In September 1997 the Lauder Foundation opened a new Jewish kindergarten, with space for 62 children, as part of its Lauder Yavne Jewish Community School. Budapest was also the site of a rabbinical seminary (with fewer than a dozen students) and the Pedagogium Jewish teacher-training institute.

Budapest's Balint Jewish Community Center, which opened in 1994 as the first full-service JCC in East-Central Europe since the end of World War II, continued to offer a full monthly schedule of events ranging from educational activities to art shows, lectures, singles' parties, concerts, and holiday celebrations. Many of the center's cultural events were open to the public, among them an exhibition of lithographs by Marc Chagall held in October 1996 in cooperation with Protestant church groups. The three-week exhibit was coordinated with lectures, performances, and other events based on Chagall's work.

Cultural events on Jewish themes took place in other venues as well. Among them, a major exhibition, "Diaspora (and) Art," opened at the Jewish Museum in Budapest in March 1997. The show massed some 500 artworks by Jewish artists or on Jewish themes in an exploration of the changing position of Jews, artists, and intellectuals within Hungarian society. A conference relating to themes in the exhibit was held in May. The show inaugurated expansive new exhibition space for the museum, which hoped to create a higher profile both for the museum and Jewish culture among the general public in Hungary. In the fall of 1997 the two curators of the Diaspora exhibit, Levente Thury and Gyorgy Szego, were among the winners of a competition for East European Jewish artists held in London.

Poland

Along with Hungary and the Czech Republic, Poland was invited to join NATO at the Western Alliance's summit in Madrid in July 1997.

In parliamentary elections held in September 1997, AWS, an alliance of Solidarity and various rightist parties, defeated the leftist Democratic Left Alliance and formed a coalition government with the centrist Freedom Union (FU). Jerzy Buzek, from AWS, became prime minister, and the FU's Bronislaw Geremek, who is of Jewish origin, became foreign minister.

Poland's economic performance was one of the strongest of all post-Communist states. The gross domestic product grew by about 6 percent in 1997, and by mid-1997 Poland had attracted about $14 billion in foreign direct investment. Double-digit inflation remained a problem, though it fell to about 13 percent by the end of 1997 from 18.5 percent in 1996. The unemployment rate was 10.9 percent in August 1997. The economy suffered a severe blow from the extensive damage and losses caused by floods in the summer of 1997.

In January 1997 then Prime Minister Wlodzimierz Cimoszewicz made an official trip to Israel, the first ever visit to the Jewish state by a Polish premier. He visited Yad Vashem and met with top Israeli business and political leaders as well as with Yasir Arafat. As part of the visit, which was designed to foster economic and other bilateral relations, he took part in a ceremony at the Hebrew University in Jerusalem where he presented the 14th-century Wolf Haggadah to the Jewish National and University Library. The Haggadah, stolen from the Berlin Jewish community in 1938, was discovered by Russian troops in Poland in 1944. It was held in Poland until 1989, when a Montreal man claimed he had bought it and wanted a Swiss auction house to sell it. A court in Geneva seized it in 1990 to prevent the auction. The Polish government and the World Jewish Congress led a court battle to prevent the book from being auctioned, with the agreement that the Haggadah would be presented to Israel if successful. The final court decision preventing the auction came in October 1996.

In October 1997 the Polish government signed an agreement that paved the way to a $600-million antitank missile deal with an Israeli weapons manufacturer.

Political extremism and anti-Semitism remained on the fringes of mainstream discourse in Poland, and anti-Semitism played little role in the September 1997 election campaign. Still, there were manifestations of anti-Jewish attitudes. In November 1996 hundreds of skinheads and right-wing extremists staged Polish Independence Day demonstrations in several major cities. Some 1,200 marched in Warsaw, shouting "Poland for the Poles" and other slogans against Jews and foreigners.

On February 26, 1997, an arson attack on Warsaw's only Jewish house of worship, the Nozyk Synagogue, damaged the former main entrance and vestibule. Polish president Aleksander Kwasniewski condemned the attack as an act of barbarism, and government representatives as well as the U.S. and German ambassadors attended a special service the day after the attack.

There were also cases of Jewish cemeteries being vandalized, among them the cemetery in Oswiecim, the town adjacent to the Auschwitz death camp. Here, in the autumn of 1996, more than 40 tombstones were vandalized; police detained a 17-year-old skinhead who admitted the crime. (The cemetery, which is several kilometers from the Auschwitz camp, had been destroyed by the Nazis, but its stones were reerected in 1980.) In March 1997 a dozen tombstones were damaged in Krakow, and windows were smashed at a Jewish cultural center in Zary.

Rev. Henryk Jankowski, the Gdansk priest who was close to the Solidarity movement and former president Lech Walesa, again caused a furor, this time with anti-Semitic remarks made several weeks after the September 1997 elections, aimed at Foreign Minister-designate Geremek. He said in a sermon that he agreed with the view that "the Jewish minority should not be accepted in our government." Jankowski's superiors sharply rebuked him for these remarks, and he was suspended from priestly duties. In an earlier sermon in January, Jankowski had criticized the Polish government for giving in too much to the demands of Jews and the relatives of Holocaust victims. Less than a week earlier, he was formally charged with slandering Jews in a sermon in 1995, but legal action was later dropped.

In January 1997 Rabbi A. James Rudin, interreligious affairs director of the

American Jewish Committee, received the Figure of Reconciliation Award from the Polish Council of Christians and Jews, for his work in Catholic-Jewish and Polish-American relations.

Holocaust-related developments: In the wake of revelations about Swiss abuse of Nazi gold, Poland carried out an official probe into a 1949 arrangement under which Switzerland used Polish funds in unclaimed Swiss bank accounts as part of a compensation deal for assets seized by the Communists. In January 1997 Foreign Minister Dariusz Rosati said the probe showed that Poland's former Communist rulers had acted wrongly in using money left in Swiss banks by Poles who died in World War II, including Jews killed in the Holocaust, and announced plans to put matters right.

In February 1997 Parliament approved legislation regulating the relations between the Polish state and Jews. The legislation, which went into effect in May, mandated the return to Poland's Jewish community of some communal Jewish property, including synagogues, schools, and cemeteries. The legislation, which applies to property that belonged to Jewish communities on September 1, 1939— the day Nazi Germany invaded Poland—covers only properties nationalized by the government, not those currently in the hands of individuals. These government-owned properties include about 2,000 buildings and 1,000 cemeteries or sites of cemeteries. Foreign Jewish organizations criticized the bill, saying income derived from the sale or rent of these buildings, once returned, should also go to Polish Jewish Holocaust survivors and other Polish Jews who fled Poland after the war and far outnumber the Jews currently in Poland.

On March 5, 1997, representatives of international Jewish organizations and Polish authorities initialed an agreement for the long-term preservation of the Auschwitz-Birkenau death camp complex. The $100-million plan envisages linking Auschwitz and Birkenau (which are two miles apart) and instituting an exclusion zone around the site, where no commercial buildings may be erected.

In December 1997 eight wooden crosses and 11 wooden Stars of David were removed by Auschwitz Memorial Museum officials from a remote part of the grounds at Birkenau. A year and a half earlier, in July 1996, Elie Wiesel caused a furor in Poland when he called for removal of the crosses during his speech at ceremonies marking the 50th anniversary of the pogrom in Kielce. The crosses and stars had been placed at the camp in the mid-1980s by young Poles doing volunteer clean-up work. Jewish groups had protested the presence of the crosses— some (including Wiesel) protesting only the crosses for what they considered an attempt to Christianize Auschwitz, others protesting the presence of all specific religious symbols, including Stars of David, at the camp.

At the July 1996 Kielce anniversary ceremony, the Polish government apologized for that tragic episode. The apology was first expressed the previous spring in a statement by the foreign minister to a World Jewish Congress meeting and was "sanctified" at the anniversary ceremonies in July.

In October 1997 the final report of a five-year government probe of the pogrom was issued, confirming that army officers and Communist security men had taken part in the attack, in which 42 Jews were killed by a rampaging mob. The report also concluded that the authorities had not reacted quickly enough but found no evidence that the Communist government instigated the assault. Justice Minister Leszek Kubicki said it was clear that anti-Semitism was at the root of the violence.

Ceremonies were held in several Polish towns to dedicate Holocaust memorials or rededicate restored Jewish cemeteries. These included a monument erected in Wyszkow, near Warsaw, a collaborative effort by Polish officials, the U.S. government, and former Wyszkow Jews. The inaugural ceremony, held in mid-September 1997, was attended by the U.S. and Israeli ambassadors, Polish church and state representatives, dozens of Jewish survivors and other Jews, and local townspeople. In August 1996 a monument was dedicated at the site of the cemetery in Chelm.

In October 1996, 35 Poles were honored as Righteous Gentiles by Yad Vashem; 16 more Poles were awarded the honor in May 1997.

In April 1997 the annual ceremony to commemorate the Warsaw Ghetto uprising was held at the newly renovated Ghetto Heroes monument.

JEWISH COMMUNITY

Estimates of the number of Jews in Poland ranged from the 7,000–8,000 officially registered with the community or receiving aid from the Joint Distribution Committee, to 10,000–15,000, including people of Jewish ancestry who have shown interest in rediscovering their heritage, to a total of 30,000 to 40,000, which includes all persons of Jewish ancestry, whether or not they are aware of or open about it.

The Jewish Religious Community of Poland, funded by the JDC, maintained religious services in 15 localities and ran kosher canteens serving free meals to needy Jews in about half of those places.

The reins of leadership of Poland's Jews passed to the post-Holocaust generation in May 1997 when the newly elected board of the Union of Jewish Congregations in Poland chose 49-year-old Jerzy Kichler, from Wroclaw, as its president. Half the members of the board, elected earlier in May, were also born after the Shoah, as were three of the four other officers elected along with Kichler.

In October 1997 a local Jewish community organization was established in Warsaw. Prior to its creation, no official Jewish community operated in Warsaw; Jewish religious activities there were under the aegis of the Union of Jewish Congregations. Five of the new community's seven new board members were born after World War II.

In January 1997 more than 150 Jews of all ages and from various Polish cities held an unprecedented conference in Warsaw, sponsored by the JDC, on the future of Polish Jewry in the coming decade. The conference marked the first time that representatives of all major Polish Jewish organizations, including religious and secular Jews, old and young, gathered for such a purpose.

The Lauder Foundation expanded its operations as the major organizer of Jewish educational initiatives in Poland, including youth clubs, the Jewish school in Warsaw, and summer and winter camp programs. In 1997 the foundation installed a young rabbi as its representative in Krakow. Among other things, he ran a summer religious study program for adults. The Lauder Foundation and the JDC helped organize community celebrations of Passover and Hanukkah in communities around Poland.

The Seventh Festival of Jewish Culture took place in Krakow in June 1997. Also in Krakow, a month-long series of Jewish lectures and cultural events called "Bajit Chadasz" was presented in the fall of 1996 and again in 1997. In the spring of 1997, the Warsaw-based American-Polish-Jewish Shalom Foundation organized an essay competition on Jewish topics for Polish high-school students, for which the three winners would get free history tuition at Warsaw University and a trip to Israel. There were 800 entries.

Midrasz, a glossy Jewish monthly magazine edited by well-known journalist and writer Konstanty Gebert, began publication in Warsaw in April 1997, with Lauder Foundation funding.

Novelist Julian Stryjkowski, whose works portrayed a broad spectrum of Jewish life in Poland, died in August 1996 at the age of 91. Holocaust survivor Czeslaw Jakubowicz, the president of the Jewish Community of Krakow, died in March 1997. Chone Shmeruk, a pioneering Yiddish scholar, died in July 1997 at the age of 76, in Poland. Shmeruk, born in Warsaw in 1921, survived World War II in the Soviet Union and emigrated to Israel in 1949. In his later years he divided his time between Poland and Israel. He was buried in the Jewish cemetery in Warsaw.

Romania

Emil Constantinescu, the head of a center-right alliance, was elected president of Romania in November 1996, ousting a leftist government headed by Ion Iliescu. During the electoral campaign, right-wing nationalist extremists accused Iliescu and his allies of favoritism toward Jews and alleged that U.S. ambassador Alfred Moses, who is Jewish, was trying to make secret deals with Iliescu to foster Jewish interests. Anti-Semitic slurs were also aimed at presidential candidate Petre Roman, who is of partial Jewish descent.

The country continued a slow process of transformation to a market economy. The Iliescu regime had not moved fast on implementing economic, political, social, and judicial reforms but it did ratify a landmark friendship treaty with Hungary in September 1996, under which it guaranteed the rights of the large Hungarian minority. The economy grew by 4.5 percent in 1996, but inflation in 1996 was 57 percent. Declining living standards triggered strikes and other protests.

There were continuing efforts to rehabilitate wartime fascist leader Ion Antonescu, troubling people both within the Jewish community and elsewhere. In April 1997 ADL national director Abraham Foxman wrote to Constantinescu to protest the erection of a monument to the interwar fascist Iron Guard movement at the Black Sea resort town of Eforie Sud. The monument was put up following a summer camp organized by followers of the revived movement. Foxman said local authorities in Eforie Sud supported the project as a tourist attraction.

In November 1997 Senator Alfonse D'Amato and Congressman Christopher Smith of the United States protested to Constantinescu over the decision of Romania's prosecutor-general to start procedures for the posthumous judicial rehabilitation of members of Antonescu's wartime cabinet. In the wake of this protest, the Prosecutor-General announced that the process would be ended.

Israel and Romania maintained close relations, with a number of official visits and exchanges. After one of these visits, in June 1997, the PLO's UN observer expressed astonishment that Romania's foreign minister, Adrian Severin, had flown into an airport north of Jerusalem, in an area captured by Israel in the 1967 war, rather than Ben-Gurion Airport, near Tel Aviv. Addressing a meeting of the UN committee on Palestinian rights, he accused the Romanians of violating Security Council resolutions and resolutions of ICAO (the International Civil Aviation Organization) on Jerusalem.

At the beginning of November 1997 Prime Minister Victor Ciorbea made a one-day "unofficial visit" to Israel. In meetings with Prime Minister Benjamin Netanyahu and other officials, he discussed bilateral issues including trade relations, Israeli investments in Romania, the problem of Romanian guest workers in Israel, and the restitution of Jewish property.

The issue of Romanian guest workers in Israel was a thorny one. In September 1997 members of the Romanian Parliament's labor commission were told that up to 140,000 Romanians were working in Israel, many of them in construction, lured by Israeli salaries that were many times higher than Romanian wages. Romanian officials expressed concern over the exodus of cheap labor, and local Romanian media featured reports of bad working conditions and health care that had cost the lives of a number of workers. The problem was discussed by representatives of the labor ministries of both countries.

Holocaust-related developments: In a message to Romanian Jews in May 1997, President Constantinescu acknowledged Romanian complicity in the persecution and slaughter of Jews in the Holocaust. Iulian Sorin, secretary of Romania's Federation of Jewish Communities, praised him for being the first Romanian leader to speak so candidly. Constantinescu's message said, "Romanians participated with a criminal blindness in implementing the infamous Nazi project of the 'final solution. . . .' The sacrifice of hundreds of thousands of Jews on Romanian territory is a burden on all of us. . . . The killing of innocent people cannot be forgiven, put right or forgotten."

The president of the Federation of Jewish Communities in Romania, Nicolae

Cajal, at a news conference in June, defended the Romanian government against criticism by the WJRO that it was slow in implementing promises of restitution and compensation. The WJRO had singled out the Hungarian government for praise and said that Romania, Poland, and the Czech Republic were dragging their feet on the issue. In July, however, WJRO vice-chairman Naphtali Lavie praised the government after it ruled that people who had emigrated from Romania under the Communist regime were eligible to receive pensions. The ruling entitled Romanians "who have elected residence abroad to claim full length-of-service pension rights." About half of Romania's prewar Jewish population of 800,000 survived the Holocaust, and almost all subsequently emigrated to Israel.

In June Parliament approved a government decision to return to the Jewish community five properties confiscated during and after World War II. A nonprofit organization called Caritatea was set up by the World Jewish Restitution Organization and the local Jewish community to administer the returned assets. The group would also provide assistance to the Jews of Romania and carry out cultural and educational activities.

In December Romania's central bank confirmed that it had received sizable amounts of gold from Nazi Germany during World War II in payment for grain and oil shipments, but denied that it had any gold from Holocaust victims. A spokesperson said the gold bars received were smelted in the 1930s.

JEWISH COMMUNITY

About 14,000 Jews lived in Romania, more than half of them in Bucharest, most of them over the age of 60.

In September 1996 the Joint Distribution Committee—which supports the activities of the Federation of Romanian Jewish Communities—organized a study tour to Hungary by a delegation of Romanian Jewish community leaders, directors of old-age homes, social-service workers, doctors, and social workers. It was the first official Romanian Jewish delegation to visit neighboring Hungary since 1945. The aim was to show the Romanian group how Hungarian Jews, through the JDC and the Hungarian Jewish Social Support Foundation, operated medical and social services. It was also aimed at forging a professional relationship between Jewish leaders and social-service personnel in the two countries.

In the autumn of 1997 Rabbi Menachem Hakohen, 65, arrived from Israel to serve as acting chief rabbi. He replaced Rabbi Yezhekel Mark, who completed a two-year tenure. Hakohen was born into a rabbinical family in Jerusalem; before 1988 he served 14 years as a Labor Party member of the Knesset.

In late 1996, Bucharest's Jewish State Theater hosted the second Festival of Jewish Theaters, with groups from Ukraine, France, and Israel participating. Various other events—concerts, exhibitions, and performances with Jewish themes—took place during the period covered, and a number of books on Jewish topics were published.

Slovakia

Slovakia made significant progress in the transition toward a market economy, although 65 percent of the population considered living standards to be their greatest problem. Deep political and other divisions between supporters and opponents of nationalist, former Communist prime minister Vladimir Meciar polarized Slovak society. Some observers described it as a split between people who saw their future within a united Europe (the opponents of Meciar) and those who followed Meciar in seeking to isolate Slovakia from Western Europe. There were attempts to clamp down on the independent media, and reports of politically motivated dismissals of officials and intimidation of government opponents.

In the spring of 1997 controversy erupted over a teachers' manual published by the Slovak Education Ministry and funded by the European Union, which romanticized the Holocaust in Slovakia, making it appear, in the words of a Slovak Jewish leader, that "the Jews actually enjoyed themselves during World War II." The manual, "History of Slovakia for Slovaks," by Milan Durica, drew sharp protests from the Slovak Jewish community and others. The director of the Institute of History of the Slovak Academy of Sciences said it was a "dangerous falsification of history."

In April 1997 vandals destroyed or damaged some 70 tombstones in the Jewish cemetery in Kosice, in eastern Slovakia, and also damaged a Holocaust memorial there. At around the same time, a Jewish cemetery in Nove Zamky was desecrated. In response to these occurrences, the Jewish community issued a sharp statement warning against state-sponsored profascist activities, "laws tinged with racism," "anti-Jewish vandalism," and "the unwillingness of the Slovak justice system to implement a law against offenders guilty of anti-Semitic criminal acts."

The community also remained deeply concerned at continuing efforts by Slovak nationalists to rehabilitate the Nazi World War II puppet regime led by Rev. Josef Tiso. These included rallies honoring Tiso and, in October 1996, the opening of a Tiso "memorial room" in Banska Bystrica. In September 1997 the nationalist Slovak National Party (SNS), a member of the ruling coalition of Prime Minister Meciar, invited French rightist Jean-Marie Le Pen to Slovakia. Several hundred people staged a demonstration in Bratislava to protest the visit.

Also in September, Meciar assured visiting B'nai B'rith president Tommy Baer that anti-Semitism in Slovakia was a marginal phenomenon. Further, he said, Slovakia had been more diligent than some other former Communist states in restituting confiscated Jewish property.

Holocaust-related developments: The Jewish community was vocal in pressing for direct German compensation for Holocaust victims and was supported in this by the Slovak government. On the eve of the December 1997 conference in London on Nazi gold, the Foreign Ministry issued a statement "drawing attention" to the fact that Germany had so far neither compensated Slovak victims of the Holocaust nor paid compensation for "other forms of Nazi persecution."

Slovak Jews also had to press hard in order to get the Czech government to reverse its long-held position opposing compensation of Slovak Jews for gold seized during World War II, all of which ended up in Prague. After the breakup of Czechoslovakia in 1993, Slovak Jews demanded compensation for these losses. In July 1997 the Czech government announced that it would transfer the majority of the gold in its vaults to a Jewish foundation, the Czecho-Slovak-Israeli Foundation, which would use the funds to care for Jewish sites in Slovakia as well as for the 1,200 Slovak Jews who survived the Holocaust.

In October 1997, 18 Slovaks were honored as Righteous Gentiles by Yad Vashem during a ceremony in Bratislava attended by President Michal Kovac.

JEWISH COMMUNITY

About 3,000 Jews, mostly elderly, lived in Slovakia, about 800 of them in Bratislava, the capital, and about 700 in Kosice in eastern Slovakia. There were rabbis in both cities, and both cities had kosher restaurants, Jewish classes, clubs, and other activities. Smaller communities existed in about a dozen other towns, all functioning under the umbrella of the Union of Jewish Religious Communities in Bratislava. An Institute of Jewish Studies opened in Bratislava in 1996, and restoration work was going on at several Jewish cemeteries and synagogues around the country.

Bratislava's chief rabbi, Baruch Myers, was attacked by skinheads on December 6, 1996, the second such incident for the American-born Lubavitcher Hassid, who was roughed up shortly after taking up his post in 1993. This time, a 16-year-old skinhead was detained over the incident, which started with verbal abuse and culminated in a physical attack, which passersby intervened in to stop. The attack took place as Myers was putting the finishing touches on a 12-foot public Hanukkah menorah. At the public candlelighting, Bratislava mayor Peter Kresnek said the authorities were determined to root out all hate crimes. "The perpetrators of these crimes will be forgotten by history, relegated to insignificance, while the Hanukkah lights and their message will burn forever," he said.

FORMER YUGOSLAVIA

Bosnia and Herzegovina

Conditions in Bosnia-Herzegovina remained difficult as the country tried to forge ahead in the wake of the 1995 Dayton peace accord, which recognized Bosnia-Herzegovina as one state divided into two separate Serbian and Muslim-Croat entities that would eventually be integrated. The plight continued of thousands of people still classified as displaced persons, complicated by polarization between the Serbian Republika Srbska and the Croat-Muslim Federation, as well as political divisions within each of the two entities. Meanwhile, with the help of foreign donors, efforts went forward to repair the war's devastation, which, among other things, destroyed or damaged 60 percent of Bosnia's housing.

JEWISH COMMUNITY

The main Jewish community in Bosnia and Herzegovina was in Sarajevo, several hundred strong, but a community also existed in Mostar, a once beautiful town that was devastated during the war. Some 129 Jews lived in Mostar in 1992, but most moved away during the fighting. By mid-1997, fewer than 40 Jews lived in the town, almost all of them supported by social-welfare disbursements channeled through the Joint Distribution Committee. The 220-year-old Jewish cemetery, which was severely damaged during the fighting, was partially reconstructed after the 1995 Dayton agreement ended hostilities.

A small community with a few dozen members also existed in Tuzla, which after the Dayton agreement became the seat of allied peacekeeping troops. Two American rabbis who served as chaplains for the troops extended their role to help the local Jewish community, supplying it in 1996 with matzah, wine, Haggadahs and other Passover supplies. This created a renewed sense of organized Jewish communal life for a time. A meeting in Tuzla with a delegation from the Jewish Agency was attended by all adult members of the community—the first such in 20 years. Seven of the community's 13 children attended the JDC/Lauder Foundation summer camp in Szarvas, Hungary in 1996. As peace settled in, however, community involvement dropped, and several members left for Israel.

During a brief visit to Sarajevo in April 1997, Pope John Paul II presented the Pope John XXIII International Peace Prize to the Jewish aid organization La Benevolencija and to Roman Catholic, Muslim, and Serbian Orthodox charities. Each group received $50,000. This was the latest in a list of international honors for La Benevolencija, which worked during the Bosnian war as a key conduit of nonsectarian humanitarian aid. At Rosh Hashanah 1996, La Benevolencija was named "Newsmaker of the Year" by the *London Jewish Chronicle*.

Croatia

Croatia's economy was fairly stable and was developing, partly thanks to a dramatic revival of tourism. Inflation was low (around 3.5 percent in 1997). Gross domestic product grew by 4.2 percent in 1996; in 1997 it rose by 3.3 percent in the first quarter and 4 percent in the second. Still, the average wage was under $400 a month, and the unemployment rate was more than 15 percent. Although popular dissatisfaction with living standards was widespread, President Franjo Tudjman, who reportedly was suffering from cancer, was easily reelected to a third five-year presidential term in June 1997.

Tudjman's foreign policy caused some problems, however. The West accused it of not doing enough to promote the Dayton peace process. Only in October 1997, after months of pressure, did Croatia hand over 10 alleged war criminals to the Hague War Crimes Tribunal.

Croatia and Israel established diplomatic relations in September 1997, following years of delay. The move had been held up because of President Tudjman's allegedly anti-Semitic statements in an autobiographical book, as well as by the Croatian government's apparent attempts to rehabilitate the World War II Ustasha regime of Croatian fascists, which was a puppet of Nazi Germany. In October 1996, for example, 6,000 people attended a ceremony in which the remains of about 100 soldiers from Croatia's World War II fascist army were reburied alongside anti-Nazi partisan fighters at the seaside town of Omis, supposedly to promote reconciliation among Croats. An association of antifascist war veterans and the Simon Wiesenthal Center strongly protested the reburial.

Israel finally agreed to establish diplomatic relations in August 1997, after the Croatian government formally apologized to the Jewish people in a strongly worded statement that renounced Ustasha crimes. The statement was part of a document released jointly after high-level talks in Budapest between Israeli and Croatian representatives. It said, in part, "The new, free, and democratic Croatia . . . completely condemns Nazi crimes of Holocaust and genocide over Jewish people in many European states, including Croatia. Therefore, in the name of the Croatian people and the government we express to the Israeli people and the government our apologies and regrets for the crimes committed against Jewish people during the Nazi-time quisling regime [Ustasha]."

The establishment of relations drew criticism in some Jewish and Israeli quarters; Israel's *Ha'aretz* newspaper, for example, claimed that a military arms deal was involved in the decision. In November 1997 two Israeli opposition politicians attempted to block a planned visit to Israel by Tudjman, and Tudjman ended up postponing his trip. In fact, even before diplomatic relations were established, commercial and other links were well under way. In the summer of 1997, charter flights brought 250 Israeli tourists a week to the Adriatic coast.

Although Tudjman's government aroused criticism for its policies vis à vis the Ustasha, it had also long courted Jewish support. Few foreign Jewish representatives took part in a three-day celebration during Hanukkah 1996, organized by the Zagreb Jewish community to celebrate its 190th anniversary. Tudjman, however, attended the gala anniversary concert, and other senior officials attended the opening of a major museum exhibition on the opulent Zagreb synagogue, which was destroyed by the Nazis in 1941.

Several Jews held senior government posts, including Slobodan Lang, a close adviser to Tudjman, and Nenad Porges, president of the Jewish community from 1990 to 1993, who was named economy and trade minister, replacing another Jew in the post, Davor Stern.

Although anti-Semitism was regarded as less threatening than the rehabilitation of the Ustasha regime, several articles with an anti-Semitic slant appeared in some newspapers, and in May 1997 the Jewish cemetery in Karlovac was vandalized. A Croatian translation of the *Protocols of the Elders of Zion,* published in the summer of 1996, was on Croatian best-seller lists for months, with one-quarter of the first printing of 2,000 copies reportedly sold in a week. Publication of the Protocols was sharply criticized by non-Jews as well as Jews.

Holocaust-related developments: In April 1997 senior government officials attended an ecumenical service to commemorate victims of the World War II fascist prison camp at Jasenovac, where tens of thousands of Serbs, Jews, Romanies, and antifascist Croats died. Roman Catholic Croat, Serb Orthodox, Jewish, and Slav Muslim clerics took part in the ceremony at the Jasenovac memorial.

In September Croatia announced that it would cede the gold allocated to it by the Tripartite Gold Commission (established by the World War II Allies to distribute Nazi gold) to Holocaust victims. A government statement said that "[a]fter discussing the initiative of the World Jewish Restitution Organization, which urges the final distribution of the gold held by the Commission, the Croatian government has decided to renounce its share in favor of the Nazi Holocaust victims."

JEWISH COMMUNITY

About 2,200 Jews lived in Croatia, some 1,400 of them in the capital, Zagreb. A Jewish community center housed a prayer room, cafe and clubroom, auditorium, exhibition gallery, and computer center. An Israeli teacher, sponsored by the Joint Distribution Committee, taught Hebrew classes and led prayers.

Much smaller communities existed in Osijek, Split, Rijeka, and Dubrovnik. Like most communities in former Communist states, the Croatian Jewish community had undergone a revival in the past few years; however, it remained troubled by a number of problems, including an aging population (about half of its members were over 60, many poor and without family); a low birthrate; and the lack of a resident rabbi.

Identity was another issue: more than 75 percent of the community were either in mixed marriages or children of mixed marriages, and most children in the community were not Jewish according to Halakhah (Jewish law). The community took a definite decision to grant membership to people in this situation. The bloody breakup of Yugoslavia caused other problems, including a "brain drain" of younger Jews and the arrival of hundreds of Jewish refugees from Bosnia.

The celebration of the 190th anniversary of the Zagreb Jewish community in December 1996 was a major event, including a gala concert, symposium, and exhibition. The High Holy Days in both 1996 and 1997 saw the reopening of restored synagogues on the Croatian coast. A week before Rosh Hashanah in 1996, the nearly 500-year-old synagogue in Split was reopened after a restoration financed in part by the Split city council. Split has about 100 Jews.

At Rosh Hashanah 1997, the Baroque synagogue in Dubrovnik, which has a Jewish community of a few dozen, was reopened at a ceremony attended by

Croatian officials, the U.S. ambassador to Croatia, and a JDC delegation. Damaged by Serb shelling in 1992, the synagogue was repaired with funds raised by a non-Jewish couple from Washington, D.C.—Otto Reusch, a Jesuit-educated Swiss Catholic who is now an American citizen, and his wife, Jeanne—who had visited it in June 1996. Croatian Television featured the ceremony on evening news programs and in a documentary on the renovation.

In October 1996 Dubrovnik hosted an international academic conference on the history of Jews in the Adriatic, sponsored mainly by the government.

Yugoslavia

Yugoslavia continued to suffer fallout from the turmoil, economic hardship, isolation, and trauma associated with the bloody breakup of the former state. Unemployment was high, wages and industrial production low. At the end of 1996, it was estimated that a family of four would require more than twice the average wage just to purchase sufficient food.

At the end of 1996 and beginning of 1997, hundreds of thousands took to the streets in peaceful mass demonstrations against the regime of President Slobodan Milosevic. Organized by opposition political parties and university students, the demonstrations began after the government refused to accept opposition victories in some local elections, but expanded to become demands for an ouster of the Milosevic regime. Partly because of the lack of unity among the opposition, the protests eventually petered out, with little effect. Many members of the Jewish community took part in the rallies on a personal basis, but the community itself formally steered clear of political involvement.

In July 1997 the Federation of Jewish Communities warned of mounting intolerance fueled by Serbian nationalist politics and lingering political, social, and economic insecurity. A federation statement mentioned "several acts directed against persons and property not belonging to the majority nation or religion" and condemned "all instigation of national, religious and racial hatred and xenophobia in any form."

The statement received wide coverage in the media and won expressions of support from political and religious figures. While the statement did not use the term anti-Semitism, it was issued a few days after vandals damaged or toppled nine tombstones in the Jewish cemetery of Zemun, a suburb of Belgrade. Various public figures, including Patriarch Pavle of the Serbian Orthodox Church, condemned the vandalism. The statement was also prompted by highly publicized persecution of Croatian Catholics in Zemun, where Vojislav Seselj, one of Yugoslavia's most extreme Serbian nationalists, was elected mayor in late 1996.

Israel and Yugoslavia established diplomatic relations in late 1996, a year after the Dayton agreement put an end to four years of war in Bosnia and enabled the lifting of UN sanctions against Yugoslavia. The arrival of the new Israeli ambassador was given extensive publicity in the media. Even without formal diplomatic relations, Yugoslavia and Israel had maintained commercial links over the years, and the Yugoslav airline JAT had direct flights to Tel Aviv. Since the end of the war in Bosnia, a boom in Israeli tourism to Yugoslavia had developed.

JEWISH COMMUNITY

About 3,500 Jews lived in Yugoslavia, most over 60 years old. About 2,000 lived in Belgrade, where a well-equipped community center offered a wide range of educational, cultural, and social activities. There were smaller communities in Novi Sad, Sombor, Subotica, Zemun, and elsewhere, all linked in the Federation of Jewish Communities in Yugoslavia. The leadership of the Belgrade Jewish community was composed largely of "baby boomers" born after World War II, who played an active role in promoting Jewish community activities.

Rabbi Itzhak Asiel, who had been in his post since early 1995, following more than six years of training in Israel, continued to coordinate Jewish life on many levels, both in Belgrade, where he was based, and in smaller communities. Asiel took over most of the duties of Yugoslavia's longtime rabbi, Cadik Danon, who was elderly and in ill health. Asiel was widely credited with sparking a renewal of religious interest among Yugoslav Jews—conducting weekly Sabbath services in Belgrade's synagogue, a Sunday school for small children, clubs for teenagers and university students, regular young people's classes in religious customs and Hebrew, and Sabbath and other programs for all ages. He also oversaw programs to stimulate Jewish revival in small provincial communities.

The Belgrade community also had a choir that gave performances for the general public and a children's theater that put on at least two performances each year. In late 1996 the Belgrade community began work on plans for a new culture center to serve both Jews and the general public and a project to preserve Ladino, the Jewish language spoken by the traditional Serbian Sephardic community. In January 1997 the Belgrade Jewish Historical Museum helped organize a major exhibit on Belgrade's pre-Holocaust Jewish quarter, which drew big crowds and much publicity. The exhibit was mounted in a building used as an alternative culture center, which before the war belonged to the Jewish community.

RUTH ELLEN GRUBER

Former Soviet Union

National Affairs

Russia and some of the other states that emerged from the Soviet Union were plagued by social unrest and economic instability in late 1996 and 1997. The Communist-dominated Parliament voted early in 1997, 229 to 63, to remove President Boris Yeltsin from office, but the vote had no legal standing.

President Yeltsin appointed Anatoly Chubais, architect of the privatization of the early 1990s and the *bête noire* of Communists and their allies, as first deputy prime minister, in an effort to reenergize economic reform. At the same time, Boris Nemtsov, the 37-year-old governor of Nizhni-Novgorod province, which enjoyed a reputation as economically progressive and prosperous, was appointed the other "first" deputy prime minister. He was given responsibility for overseeing social programs, regulating monopolies, and supervising relations between the federal center and the regions. Another reformer, Yakov Urinson, was appointed economics minister.

In Russia, gross domestic product fell by 6 percent and industrial production by 6 percent in 1996. There were severe energy shortages in many areas, especially the Far East and Siberia. Millions were owed back pay, and in March 1997 about a million workers went on a nationwide strike to protest unpaid wages.

Corruption was said to be so endemic in most of the former Soviet republics that foreign businesses were loath to deal with them. This was especially true of Ukraine and, to a lesser extent, of Russia. It was estimated that about $100 billion was spirited out of Ukraine by local officials and business executives. Ukraine was the third-largest recipient of aid from the United States, following Israel and Egypt.

Sporadic fighting, bombings, and assassinations continued in Chechnya, the breakaway Caucasus region, but President Yeltsin signed a peace treaty in May 1997 with Chechen president Aslan Maskhadov, who had been elected in January on a platform of independence for "Ichkeria" (Chechnya). When the 21 months of fighting—involving 1.2 million soldiers—ended in August 1996, there were 25,000 to 60,000 civilian and 4,500 military dead, as well as half a million refugees and 798 Russians taken prisoner, with between 600 and 1,500 unaccounted for. The Chechen war contributed to the demoralization of the Russian military, which was severely underfunded.

In August 1996 the openly authoritarian president of Belarus, Aleksandr Lukashenka, presented a draft constitution that would extend his term of office and give him the right to annul decisions of local councils, set election dates, appoint judges, and dismiss Parliament. Demonstrations against these proposals were broken up by police. Belarus fined the Soros Foundation $3 million for alleged "currency violations" and expelled its American director. The foundation had contributed $13 million to education, science, and civic groups in Belarus. In February 1996 the International Monetary Fund suspended loans to Belarus due to that republic's lack of progress in implementing economic reforms. Belarus expelled the first secretary of the American embassy, who had observed a clash between police and nationalist demonstrators protesting Lukashenka's rule, and the United States retaliated by expelling a Belarussian diplomat.

In May 1997 NATO leaders and the Russian Federation president signed a "Founding Act" of mutual cooperation and security intended to reassure Russia that it need not fear NATO expansion into countries of the former Warsaw Pact. The act pledged Russia and NATO to consult on security issues and NATO not to deploy nuclear weapons on territories of new members.

In contrast to Soviet times, Jews had become prominent in Russian politics. Boris Berezovsky, who led the Russian negotiating team with Chechnya, was head of the National Security Council until dismissed by President Yeltsin in November. Berezovsky was head of the Logovaz conglomerate, which includes Russia's largest automobile dealership. He held major interests in Aeroflot — Russian International Airlines; Sibneft, one of Russia's largest petroleum companies; United Bank; and ORT, a public television network. Other prominent Jews included Aleksandr Livshits, former minister of economics and more recently the president's deputy chief of staff for economic issues; Yakov Urinson, Livshits's successor as minister of economics; Aleksandr Braverman, first deputy minister of state property; Boris Nemtsov, first deputy prime minister; and bankers Mikhail Frydman and Vladimir Gusinsky, both active in the Russian Jewish Congress.

Yukhym Zvyahilsky, former acting prime minister of Ukraine, who fled to Israel in 1994 after being charged with embezzling $25 million, returned to Ukraine in March 1997, presumably protected by his parliamentary immunity.

Israel and the Middle East

In October 1996 the Russian Ministry of Justice authorized the Jewish Agency for Israel to continue its operations as a local agency with 69 branches. This solved the dispute with the Russian government, which claimed that the Jewish Agency was operating illegally and had violated the terms of its charter. In addition to advocating and facilitating immigration to Israel, the Jewish Agency operated 236 Hebrew-language courses (*ulpanim*) in the former Soviet Union (FSU), with 18,150 students and 550 teachers.

Israeli prime minister Benjamin Netanyahu charged in August 1997 that Russia was helping Iran to develop guidance and delivery systems for long-range missiles. Some in the Israeli government advocated freezing economic cooperation with Russia. The Russian press admitted that Russia had $1 billion worth of military contracts with Iran, but Russian spokesmen, including Prime Minister Viktor Chernomyrdin, denied that Russia was helping Iran to build missiles. Foreign Minister Yevgeny Primakov went to the Middle East in October to lay the groundwork for Russia's renewed involvement in the region and took the occasion to deny again Russia's transfer of missile and nuclear technology to Iran. Primakov tried to bring Israel and Syria closer to peace talks and supported the "land-for-peace" formula for settling the dispute between the two countries.

Aleksandr Bovin resigned as Russia's ambassador to Israel in late 1997. He wrote in *Izvestiia* that Palestinian terrorism and the PLO's refusal to eliminate paragraphs from its charter calling for the destruction of Israel "caused shifts in Israeli public opinion that led to the fall of the Rabin-Peres government and enabled Netanyahu to hold up talks with the PLO" (no. 5, 1997). Azerbaijan deferred opening an embassy in Israel after a visit by Prime Minister Netanyahu in August 1997, who explored the possibility of Azerbaijani oil sales to Israel. Uzbekistan, however, opened an embassy that September.

In August 1997 Israel and Russia agreed on joint action to maintain security on flights between the two countries. Israel was the only country whose special services were allowed to enter Russia armed. Russia and Israel agreed to cooperate in combating organized crime and fighting terrorism. Immediately following the agreement, Grigory Lerner (Zvi Ben-Ari), an Israeli immigrant from Russia, was arrested in Israel and charged with 14 counts of extortion, bribery, and forgery in Israel. Russian deputy prime minister and minister of internal affairs Anatoly Kulikov went to Israel in connection with the case. Lerner was also accused of absconding with $85 million from Russia and with complicity in the murder of a Russian bank director.

Nationality Affairs

The Russian Federation (RF), which was still shaping its political structure, provided for national-cultural autonomy for the multiple peoples scattered over its territory. Thus, the second congress of Ukrainians held in Moscow in October 1997 drafted a program enabling Ukrainians in Russia to get an education in Ukrainian, publish a Ukrainian magazine, and have their own television channel—all to be financed from federal and regional budgets. Writing in the official newspaper, *Rossiiskiye vesti* (October 30, 1997), Emil Pain and Andrei Susarov concluded on the basis of an analysis of the 1994 "microcensus" that "many ethnic communities that had been thought to have been assimilated into kindred peoples are, in fact, retaining their ethnic distinctiveness and separate self-awareness."

Under a law of November 15, 1997, the nationality of a newborn child could be registered officially if the parents so desired, but there was no obligation to do so. A new provision was included whereby anyone could change his or her name starting at age 14 rather than 16, and authorization to do so would no longer be required from internal affairs agencies. Presumably, this would make it easier for people to disguise their ethnicity.

Another law proved highly controversial. As of October 1, 1997, nationality was no longer to be registered in one's internal passport (the "fifth paragraph"). This could prevent officials from taking account of nationality in admission to higher education, employment, and other decisions. While some welcomed this, particularly Jews and others who wished to keep their nationality private, the governments of Tatarstan and of several regions in the North Caucasus, as well as Communist deputies in the Duma, demanded that nationality be registered at least on a voluntary basis. Otherwise, they argued, the numbers of some nationalities would be artificially reduced in official calculations and reports.

Interestingly, a vice-president of the St. Petersburg Jewish Association, Aleksandr Frenkel, argued in a major newspaper that the nationality designation should not be dropped, since it "prevented the disappearance . . . of ethnic groups that were subjected to persecution and discrimination, and fostered conditions for their revival today" (*Nezavisimaya gazeta*, November 10, 1997). He suggested that nationality designation had also facilitated Jewish emigration and urged that it be kept because it "makes nationality a parameter of the relationship between the individual and the state" and enables peoples to demand state support of their cultures. Finally, designating one's nationality would prevent "unchecked pursuit of a policy of Russification." At year's end the matter was still being negotiated.

Anti-Semitism

Two contradictory trends marked the post-Soviet period. On one hand, in contrast to the Soviet regime, none of the post-Soviet governments in any of the successor states pursued explicitly anti-Semitic policies. On the other hand, spontaneous, grassroots anti-Semitism flourished, unchecked by governmental or social action. The main sources of anti-Semitism seemed to be, first, on the collective level, the sense of humiliation over the Soviet Union's loss of superpower status, and, on the individual level, the loss of jobs, income, and status. A second factor was the understandable inability of many to comprehend why their economic situation had declined so precipitously and why society seemed to be unraveling— with soaring crime rates, widespread pornography, and immoral and unethical behavior leading them to search for an explanation. As journalist Alessandra Stanley put it: "Frustrated with the wrenching economic and social upheaval that followed the collapse of Communism, and the Soviet Union, in 1991, and spurred on by politicians willing to tap their resentments, many people are returning to a traditional scapegoat, the Jews" ("Success May Be Bad for Jews as Old Russian Bias Surfaces," *New York Times*, April 15, 1997).

A third source of anti-Semitism was simply the anti-Jewish stereotypes and attitudes that had been transmitted from one generation to the next and continued to be so. Typical was the response by Vladimir Gudylev, a 41-year-old auto mechanic, to a question asked by a journalist on the streets of Moscow: "Today, what would you call the holiday Russia observes on November 7 [the anniversary of the Bolshevik Revolution, redubbed the 'day of peace and reconciliation']?" "It's a Jewish-Kike holiday. The Jews and the Masons are still in power" (*Moskovskii komsomolets*, November 6, 1997).

Institutionally, the sources of anti-Semitism seemed to be the Russian Orthodox Church, the Communist parties, and the extreme Russian, Ukrainian, Baltic, and other nationalists. The chief expressions of anti-Semitism, aside from insults and other face-to-face utterances, were destruction of Jewish property or monuments commemorating Jews and Jewish history; press and other media attacks on Jews, who were blamed for every evil imaginable; and physical attacks.

Recent examples of the first include swastikas and anti-Semitic slogans painted on the entrance to the only synagogue in Riga, Latvia, in December 1997 (while pamphlets were circulating calling Jews and Russians the main enemies of the Latvian people), and two desecrations in the summer of 1997, in Vilnius, Lithuania, at the site of the oldest Jewish cemetery. Tombstone desecrations were reported in Jewish cemeteries in Mogilev (Belarus), Smolensk (Russia), and Tallinn (Estonia). In July 1997 a memorial stone marking the site of the Vilnius ghetto during World War II was removed by vandals, an act condemned by Lithuanian president Algirdas Brazauskas. A less direct measure, perhaps not intended to be anti-Jewish, was the change made to a monument in L'viv, West Ukraine, in December 1997. Erected originally in tribute to Soviet troops in World War II, it was renamed to honor "fighters for freedom of Ukraine." These included the Organization of Ukrainian Nationalists (OUN), an explicitly anti-Semitic group in interwar Poland; the Ukrainian Insurgent Army (UPA), which for a time collaborated with the Nazis; and other "anti-Soviet" groups. Since the OUN and UPA were directly responsible for murdering Jews, the alteration of the monument was viewed by Jews as an ominous sign.

When Martin Scorsese's film *The Last Temptation of Christ* was shown on NTV (independent) in Moscow in November 1997, the Russian Orthodox Church condemned it as sacrilegious. Some called the television network "Tel Avivsion" and a "nest of Zionism." Pickets of NTV held up signs saying "Zionism will destroy Russia."

During the controversy over what to do with the physical remains of Tsar Nikolai II and his family, which had been going on for several years, Metropolitan Yuvenaly told a meeting of the Holy Synod: "Contemporary expert theological analysis of the notion of 'ritual murder' confirms the negative findings of the group of Russian Orthodox theologians who . . . testified at the Beilis trial in 1913. And analysis of the circumstances of the murder of the imperial family rules out any conclusion that it was ritual in nature" (Sergei Bychkov in *Moskovskii komsomolets*, November 12, 1997). Nearly 90 years after the world watched in amazement as a Russian court seriously considered a charge that a Jew had murdered a Christian child to use its blood for ritual purposes, not only were such beliefs still held, but a high-ranking church official was prepared to investigate the possibility that the act had occurred more than once.

Since the church's influence had grown tremendously—it now provided chaplains for the armed forces, spent huge sums on welfare activities, and constructed and reconstructed many churches, often with government funds—church attitudes toward the Jews were highly influential. This was a church that, unlike the Catholic Church, had not reconsidered its traditional teachings about Jews and whose attitudes toward Jews and Judaism were a throwback to centuries gone by. Curiously, even among the fast-growing neo-pagan churches in Ukraine, one writer found, the anti-Semitic motif was powerful. In a booklet issued by RUNvia, one such new religion, containing answers to 200 questions about its doctrines, *Izvestiia* reporter Yanina Sokolovskaya counted "up to 15 sections . . . dealing with the nature of the 'Yids' " (October 31, 1997).

A typical example of the way Jews were portrayed in some media is an article by one Anton Surikov in the newspaper *Zavtra*, in August 1997 (no. 33, p. 4). Entitled "The Collapse of Russia and the Jews," the article asserted that Boris Yeltsin's wife and daughter were Jewish (they are actually Russians). More importantly, Surikov stated baldly that "members of the Jewish community are in total control of the financial sphere and news media. That is, to all intents and purposes, the Jewish community governs Russia." In a bizarre twist, Surikov claimed that he learned this while on a trip to Israel, where officials expected massive pogroms to break out in Russia because Jewish control had aroused the righteous indignation of the populace. Israel was therefore preparing plans for the massive evacuation of the Jews. The United States, Surikov claimed, backed Deputy Prime Minister Chubais, a Jew (he is actually Russian), because "it is obvious that the Americans' ultimate goal is to de-industrialize Russia, reduce its population by 25 to 30 percent, and turn the country into a raw-materials colony of the United States, governed in U.S. interests by people like Chubais."

However absurd such statements may seem to outsiders, there was a considerable public in the former Soviet Union inclined to believe them. Certainly, most Jews continued to perceive the society in which they lived as riddled with anti-Semitism. It is striking that in a late 1997 survey of a quota sample of 500 Jews in Moscow and 300 in Ekaterinburg, Valeriy Chervyakov and Vladimir Shapiro of the Institute of Sociology, Russian Academy of Sciences, found that anti-Semitism was the single most important element in the formation of Jewish consciousness. In answer to the question "What was the greatest influence on the formation of your ethnic consciousness?" 56 percent of Muscovite Jews and 48 percent of those in Ekaterinburg said "anti-Semitism." Books, literature, and music were mentioned frequently as well, but anti-Semitism was reported more frequently than any other factor.

Significantly, when asked how they would like to have their "nationality" indicated in their passports, nearly half the respondents in both cities wanted either nothing registered or "citizen of Russia." They would not try to "pass" as

Russians" (*Russkii*)—only 1–2 percent would choose that—but only slightly less than half would choose to be registered as Jews, though at the time over 80 percent were so registered. Only about 60 percent would choose to be born Jewish if they could be born again. Clearly, to be known officially and publicly as Jews was still something many wanted to avoid, however positively they may have felt inwardly about their Jewishness. Nearly four out of five in both cities asserted that anti-Semitism was "very important" as a motivation for emigration.

According to Mark Krasnoselsky, director of the anti-defamation committee of the Russian Jewish Congress, there were about 50 "extremist organizations" and about 300–400 periodicals with circulations in the millions that carried anti-Semitic materials. While only 5 to 7 percent of respondents in opinion polls expressed explicitly anti-Semitic views, the "overwhelming majority" responded "don't know" to the question "What is your attitude toward Jews?" Indeed, the All-Russian Center for the Study of Public Opinion reported that the proportion of respondents claiming "no feeling one way or the other toward Jews" had gone from 26 percent in 1995 to 83 percent a year later (*Moskovskiie novosti*, April 20–27, 1997, p. 25). Krasnoselsky complained that legal measures against anti-Semitism were ineffective (*Nezavisimaya gazeta*, August 29, 1997). Indeed, in October 1997 the Duma rejected an amendment to the criminal code that would have banned public justification, approval, or praise of crimes committed by fascist regimes. Ironically, Nikolai Ryzhkov, a former Soviet premier, complained that such an amendment would allow suppression of dissidence. Russian Prosecutor General Yurii Skuratov said that his office, the Justice Ministry, and the Federal Security Service would set up an interdepartmental group to combat hate crimes. He told the Russian Jewish Congress that 49 criminal cases had been opened in the last two years on charges of inciting ethnic, racial, or religious hatred.

Nazi War Criminals

Past anti-Semitism continued to cast its shadow. In July 1997 the case against Aleksandras Lileikis, deported from the United States a year earlier for having covered up his role in massacres of Jews in wartime Lithuania, was suspended indefinitely because of his poor health. The Wiesenthal Center in Israel urged the Lithuanian government to arrest 89-year-old Kazys Gimzauskas, Lileikis's assistant, for war crimes. Charges against this former deputy director of the Vilnius region security police, 1941–44, were filed in November, and the law was amended to allow the trial of people who were in poor health. The posthumous rehabilitation of war criminal Petras Kriksciunas was revoked, the first instance of an abrogated rehabilitation. Sixteen similar cases were said to be pending.

In September 1997 Latvia declined to request the extradition of Konrad Kalejs, an Australian accused of war crimes who had been deported from the United States and Canada, because of "insufficient evidence."

Religion

The passage by the Duma in June 1997, in a 300–8 vote, of a law on religion was a dramatic development. The Federation Council approved the bill in September, and President Yeltsin signed it after having vetoed an earlier version in July. The law was strongly supported by the Russian Orthodox Church, because it would permit only those religions that had been active in Russia for over 50 years and that had branches in at least half of the federation's 89 regions to receive "all-Russian" (national) status. Religious groups operating even locally for fewer than 15 years could not be registered and were not legal entities. This deprived them of the right to own property or a bank account. The law was aimed at Catholics and Evangelical Christians, as well as groups such as Hare Krishna and Aum Shinrikyo, the Japanese cult responsible for the gassing of the Tokyo subway.

Polls showed that the Orthodox Church was the single most trusted institution in Russia — 54 percent named it as such, with the army being named by 42 percent and mayors by 35 percent. Nevertheless, the church had been trying to prevent other Christian and non-Christian groups from proselytizing in the Russian Federation. Yeltsin vetoed the original bill after Western protests; after it was slightly amended, he signed it. Protests by Western Christian groups continued.

JEWISH COMMUNITY

Demography

Emigration continued to erode FSU Jewry, whose low birthrates, aged population, and high mortality rates could not compensate for the outflow. The pace of emigration slowed somewhat in 1997, especially to the United States. In calendar year 1996 there were 19,497 immigrants to the United States from the FSU; between September 1996 and October 1997, there were 15,837. In the latter period, 41.5 percent of the immigrants came from Ukraine and 30 percent from the Russian Federation. Forty-seven percent had been in the labor force, and 69 percent of those were professionals. This was a lower proportion by far in the labor force than in any year since 1991. Following the pattern of previous years, 46 percent of the immigrants settled in New York City.

In 1997, 54,233 immigrants arrived in Israel from the FSU. According to the Israel Central Bureau of Statistics, 68 percent of immigrants arriving in 1996 registered themselves as Jews, the same proportion as had done so in 1994 and 1995.

Communal Affairs

Since the collapse of the Soviet Union, over 80 buildings that had once been Jewish communal property were returned to Jewish communities, and 67 others were in the process of being reclaimed. The American Jewish Joint Distribution Committee (JDC) ran seminars to train local Jews how to reclaim communal properties. There were 37 functioning Jewish community centers in 34 cities and towns, located in five republics, and most were housed in reclaimed properties.

The JDC supplied 145 Judaica libraries to Jewish schools, universities, cultural and religious societies, and synagogues in more than 75 cities. Five new libraries were opened in 1996.

According to estimates by the "Joint," a third of the Jewish population in the former Soviet Union were elderly, and between 200,000 and 300,000 were needy. About 70,000 of them received some sort of assistance. There were nearly 40 larger and a hundred smaller welfare ("Hasadim") societies in 127 localities, spread among five states that had emerged from the Soviet Union. About half were opened in 1996, eight of them in areas with a high proportion of Holocaust survivors. The latter were funded largely by the Conference on Material Claims Against Germany. About 1,700 volunteers in the former Soviet Union delivered food parcels, "meals on wheels," and medical equipment to those in need. The largest Jewish welfare organization in the FSU was "Hesed Avot" in Kiev, which provided hot meals to about 6,500 of the estimated 14,000 elderly Jews in the Ukrainian capital. The Joint sponsored an Institute for Communal and Welfare Workers in St. Petersburg, to create a cadre of social-work professionals for Jewish communal service.

The communal structures emerging in the FSU are typified by those of Odessa in Ukraine, Kishinev in Moldova, and Bishkek in Kyrgyzstan. Odessa, whose mayor was Jewish, had a Jewish Cultural Society, two Jewish schools, two kindergartens with 87 children, two synagogues, and a "children's home." About 600 people were studying Hebrew. It is estimated that of the nearly 90,000 Jews in and around Odessa, about a thousand emigrated each year. There were about 23,000 elderly, ill, and needy people, about 450 of whom received hot home meals. Kishinev had about 300 students in Hebrew courses, 13 small Jewish schools with about 1,180 students, about 30 Jewish organizations, and 133 elderly receiving home care. In Bishkek, the smallest of the three communities, the Jewish population had declined from about 9,000 in 1989 to 2,000, largely due to emigration. The communal organization called itself Menorah. There was a Sunday school with over 60 children, a day school with 20, a Jewish youth club with 60 members, a choir, and two dance groups. The local Jewish library held about a thousand volumes. The synagogue was attended mostly by "Bukharan" (Central Asian) Jews, whereas the Ashkenazim (European Jews) affiliated mostly with Menorah.

The Russian Jewish Congress signed an agreement with the Conference of Presidents of Major American Jewish Organizations and with the National Conference on Soviet Jewry to establish an "ongoing structured relationship." The Russian Jewish Congress signed a similar agreement with the World Jewish Congress, adding cooperation in restitution of Jewish property and in interfaith relations to their agreement.

In August 1996 a cornerstone was laid for a new synagogue in Almaty, capital of Kazakhstan. In January 1997, in Kazan, capital of Tatarstan in the Russian Federation, a century-old synagogue building was returned to the 10,000-strong Jewish community. A four-story building for the Jewish community of Tallinn, Estonia, was to be built in the center of the city. It was designed to include a synagogue, community center, and facility for the elderly. The World Union of Progressive Judaism claimed 30 affiliated congregations officially registered in the republics and three regional associations.

Culture and Education

In May 1997 a conference in Moscow on "The Lessons of the Holocaust and Contemporary Russia" featured over 60 speakers who presented scholarly analyses, personal recollections, and discussions of contemporary anti-Semitism and Holocaust education. Dr. Ilya Altman, director of a Holocaust center in Moscow, chaired the conference.

In September an international conference in Vilnius, Lithuania, discussed the legacy of the Vilna Gaon (the "Vilna Genius") on the 200th anniversary of the death of this outstanding rabbinic authority and leader of the Mitnagdic (anti-Hassidic) camp. The Association of Lithuanian Jews in Israel and the Simon Wiesenthal Center there called for a boycott of the conference, saying that Lithuania had done nothing to prosecute Lithuanians who had collaborated with the Nazis. The weeklong event was held nevertheless and included a ceremonial session of Parliament, a reception by President Algirdas Brazauskas, and the return of four Torah scrolls from Lithuanian archives to the one functioning synagogue in Vilnius.

Several groups representing American Jewish organizations visited Vilnius in 1997 in order to investigate the status of Jewish books and other artifacts stored in the Lithuanian capital. A delegation from the American Jewish Committee, YIVO Institute, and B'nai B'rith was followed by a group from Chicago, including Sen. Richard Durbin of Illinois. The Council of Archives and Research Libraries in Jewish Studies, supported by the National Foundation for Jewish Culture, also visited Vilnius in March to survey Judaica holdings. It recommended establishing an international commission to discuss preservation, restoration, archiving, and access. The groups found close to 125,000 volumes in the Judaica collection of the Bibliography and Book Center, of which fewer than a third had been catalogued and shelved. About 10,800 books were classified as "first editions" of Hebrew or Yiddish books published in Lithuania. Nearly 74,000 periodical volumes had been catalogued and were being microfilmed. The National Library's Judaica collection had some 370 Torah scrolls. The Beth Medrash Govoha of Lakewood, N.J., undertook an independent initiative and buried unusable Torah scrolls in Lithuania, claiming that it was a legitimate heir of Lithuanian Jewry (actually, this yeshivah originated in Belarus). The Telz Yeshivah, now in Cleveland but originally from the Lithuanian town of Telsiai, laid claim to many of the books and scrolls. The YIVO Institute, after years of negotiation, was receiving from Vilnius books and other materials that clearly had belonged to YIVO in Vilnius (then Wilno in Poland) and had survived the war. YIVO was to copy its own former holdings and return the originals to Lithuania.

Jewish education continued to expand in the former Soviet Union. The Conservative movement sponsored two day schools, in Odessa and Chernivtsi in Ukraine, the Orthodox movement many more. The JDC supplied educational materials to 45 day schools, 35 preschools, and over 200 Sunday schools. It claimed to supply a total of 296 schools that had 21,000 students enrolled. Educational publications included *Avot u'banim* (Parents and Children), a monthly journal in Russian for teachers, parents, and children, and *Evreiskaya shkola*, a professional educators' journal published by the Petersburg Jewish University. Twenty educators from the FSU attended the Melton Program for Senior Jewish Educators in Jerusalem, spending six months in intensive study.

A Hillel foundation, serving postsecondary students and young adults, opened in Minsk, the fourth such unit in the FSU. Hillel in Moscow, opened in 1994, counted 50 "activists," 300 "regulars," and up to a thousand occasional participants in its activities. For the first time, its members organized their own High Holy Day services, which were held in Moscow's Choral Synagogue.

In higher education, five Jewish institutions (the Jewish Universities in Moscow, St. Petersburg, and Minsk; Solomon University in Kiev; and Maimonides College in Moscow) claimed 850 students. Another 2,000 students were said to be taking courses in the roughly 50 Jewish studies programs at state and private universities. There were seven "people's universities," or institutes of adult Jewish education, involving some 1,600 people. For example, the Jewish Open University in Odessa claimed 80 students who met twice monthly in six-hour sessions. A similar pattern on a smaller scale was followed by the parallel institution in Vitebsk, Belarus.

Project Judaica—a joint program of the Russian State University for the Humanities, the Jewish Theological Seminary, and YIVO Institute—graduated 17 Judaic studies majors in 1996; in 1997, the Maimonides College in Moscow graduated ten students. It was projected that in 1998 Project Judaica would produce 15 graduates, the Jewish University of Moscow, 37, and Maimonides, 16. Sefer, the organization of academics involved in Judaica throughout the FSU, held its annual academic conference in February 1997, bringing together about 300 Jewish and non-Jewish academics.

ZVI GITELMAN

Hong Kong

National Affairs

ON THE NIGHT OF JUNE 30, 1997, the tiny Jewish community of Hong Kong greeted Britain's transfer of sovereignty to China with the same excitement and fascination its neighbors felt in witnessing this historic moment. While there was some measure of apprehension, few feared that the mainland would rule Hong Kong with an iron fist.

For years, the world had conjured a nightmare scenario in which China would shut down Hong Kong's stock exchange, arrest its democracy activists, censor the press, ban the English language, suppress religious worship, and expel the expatriate community. But Jews in Hong Kong, like the rest of the non-Chinese community, were cautiously optimistic. Like others, some sent their Chinese antiques abroad, in case Beijing decided to reclaim its national treasures. Others temporarily moved assets offshore. But virtually nobody expected religious persecution. Hong Kong's Jewish residents, who play integral roles in the fields of business, finance, and law, had good reason for confidence.

China had promised to preserve religious freedom as part of a commitment to "one country, two systems," the principle by which it pledged to rule Hong Kong. Some Christian groups, mindful of China's history of poor treatment of their coreligionists, were skeptical. But China had never singled out the small Jewish presence within its borders for ill treatment.

And indeed, the following months bore out the sanguine attitude of Jews and others in Hong Kong. China took a benign approach to its new sovereign role over what it called the "Hong Kong Special Administrative Region of the People's Republic of China," sometimes referred to as the SAR. The only time soldiers from China's People's Liberation Army were seen in large numbers on the streets of Hong Kong—in fact in any numbers at all—was in the dawn hours of July 1, when they rolled in to replace the departing British garrison.

In retrospect, an event with far greater immediate consequences for Hong Kong came just one day later and more than a thousand miles away, when Thailand floated its battered currency, the baht, and sent regional financial markets plunging. The economic downswing that followed was so profound, and came as such a great shock to many in Hong Kong, that the handover soon felt like a faint memory.

The era of seemingly limitless Asian economic growth had come to an end. Exporters were unable to compete with plunging prices in neighboring countries. Moves to ward off speculative attacks on the Hong Kong currency's link to the U.S. dollar brought sky-high interest rates, which in turn undercut the crucial banking and property markets. The stock market went into a tailspin. Hong Kong's finance houses with extensive investments in the shaky Southeast Asian markets were faced with crises that, in some cases, led to downsizing and even closure. Business and career plans were thrown into disarray. As 1997 ended, there was anecdotal evidence that a small but significant number of Jewish community members had either lost their jobs, feared they soon would, or had taken pay cuts.

While the Asian economic turmoil was assessed as the worst in 50 years and was expected to continue for some time, it did not cripple either Hong Kong or its Jewish community. Despite some casualties, there were also signs of resilience and an ability to adapt to the new austerity. When, in October, Hong Kong's Hang Seng Index began an unprecedented free fall, the English-language *South China Morning Post* ran pictures of ten businessmen who had initially suffered the greatest losses. The one non-Chinese face in the lineup was that of Michael Kadoorie, the Jewish community's most prominent member. Significantly, Kadoorie was also shown some days later when the *Post* listed those who had profitably rebounded.

Despite the economic turmoil and a distinction as possibly the most expensive place on earth to live and do business, Hong Kong was still viewed as having an excellent business and telecommunications infrastructure, a reliable monetary system, potential for entrée into the vast Chinese market, and attractive living conditions for expatriate employees.

Israel and the Middle East

Hong Kong's relations with Israel had always been strictly business, and that continued. While responsibility for external affairs reverted to China on July 1, Beijing and Israel signed an accord insuring that relations with Hong Kong would remain virtually unchanged after the handover. This included economic, legal, and cultural arrangements as well as mutual visa-free access for each other's passport holders.

Beyond retaining the existing ties, Hong Kong had a wide berth in continuing to shape its relations with Israel. For example, it was Hong Kong's secretary for economic services, not a Beijing official, who negotiated a civil aviation agreement with Israel's consul general in Hong Kong, Zohar Raz. The accord, which was already in effect in the latter half of 1997, was slated to be formalized in 1998. The introduction of direct flights from Israel increased the appeal of business travel and expanded possibilities for tourism.

Israel regarded Hong Kong as a fertile potential investment source. It actively courted Hong Kong business figures for major domestic projects such as the ambitious new Ben-Gurion Airport terminal, and sought joint ventures involving the many small Israeli startup firms. ZIM, Israel's national shipping company, had long had a presence in Hong Kong, and despite China's rejection of formal ties with Israel until 1992, some Israeli companies used Hong Kong as a launch pad into the mainland market. Chief among these was U.D.I., founded by the late Israeli industrialist Shaul Eisenberg. U.D.I.'s general manager in Hong Kong, Avishai Hamburger, also chaired the local Israel Chamber of Commerce. The chamber held regular luncheons for its 50 members and played a pivotal role in promoting trade with Israel.

Hong Kong was a substantial market for Israeli goods, receiving US$800-million worth of direct exports annually. The vast majority was in diamonds, bound for customers in Hong Kong and for re-export to other regional destinations. In the latter, leaner months of 1997, the market for luxury items shrank considerably, and the diamond trade took a beating. The growth of high-technology business, however, continued apace, with exports tripling toward the end of 1997.

Major Israeli high-tech firms including Orbotech, E.C.I., Scitex, and Rad had regional offices in the SAR. The growth of high-tech sharply increased the number of Israelis living in Hong Kong, roughly estimated at 300 households. (Accurate numbers are not available because reporting to the consulate is voluntary.)

Anti-Semitism

There were almost no external threats to the Jewish community of Hong Kong. Certainly none came from the Chinese residents of Hong Kong or from mainland China, which had no record of anti-Semitism.

Anti-Jewish sentiment could be found, however, among the British subjects who ruled Hong Kong. Colonialism stamped Hong Kong with an acute sense of class and status. For many years, the territory's bastion of highbrow hobnobbing, the Hong Kong Club, was closed to Jews and others deemed unsuitable. At least one top bank was known to have barred Jews from its board of directors in deference to Arab interests, and the territory's numerous, active Christian institutions at times also created an exclusionary atmosphere.

Still, it is hard to point to any tangible hindrance. Members of Hong Kong's Jewish community had reached great heights of wealth and social standing. At the beginning of the 20th century, Hong Kong had a Jewish governor, Sir Matthew Nathan. Earlier, the Sassoon and Kadoorie families carved out prominent places in the island's commercial foundation. More than a century later, in 1981, Lawrence Kadoorie would become Hong Kong's first peer of the British realm and would bear the title of Lord. Several Jews held prominent positions in the legal arena. "There have been occasions when anti-Semitism raised its ugly head, although fortunately infrequently," said Anne Godfrey, chairwoman of the Jewish Community Center's board of directors, whose husband, Gerald, sat on the Court of Appeals.

When, on several occasions in the autumn of 1997, Malaysian prime minister Mahathir Mohammed blamed Jews for the escalating market turmoil, Hong Kong's Jewish community was divided over whether and how to respond. Some members dispatched a letter of protest, while most preferred to play down or ignore the remarks. The incident raised concern over the absence of a framework for responding appropriately to anti-Semitism. Hong Kong's Committee of Jewish Organizations began discussions with the Anti-Defamation League about setting up an ADL branch in Hong Kong.

JEWISH COMMUNITY

Demography

At the end of 1997, some estimates put the number of Jews at about 3,000. Others went as high as 6,000. It was thought that many had no formal ties to Jewish institutions.

The makeup of the community was a tapestry of contrasting backgrounds, interests, and religious views. Its beginnings were in the mid- and late-19th century, when a number of merchant families of Baghdadi origin, including the Sassoons and Kadoories, came to set up outposts in their families' merchant empires. Their employees were other Jews, mainly from Bombay. Among the legacies of these two dynasties were giant corporations, leading philanthropic institutions, and Ohel Leah, the turn-of-the-century Sephardic synagogue that would eventually become a gold mine for the community.

After World War II, the small, close-knit community, which had endured Japan's occupation of Hong Kong, received a flood of predominantly Ashkenazic Jews from Shanghai who had survived the miseries of Japanese occupation. Most went on to Israel and other destinations, but some stayed and successfully rebuilt their lives and businesses in Hong Kong. In the postwar years, other business people began trickling in. By the early 1960s, Ashkenazic Jews outnumbered the Sephardim, but the community was still very small. The number of Jews began to increase considerably in the late 1980s, when economic slumps in the West and elsewhere made the prosperous territory an attractive destination.

Communal Affairs

The community grew up around one major institution, Ohel Leah, which was built in 1901. Predating the synagogue was a small Jewish cemetery above Happy Valley, its driveway flanked by Buddhist seminaries, its gravestones telling the story of a trickle of Jews who came—whether because of commerce here or calamity elsewhere—to this far-flung corner of the Orient. A Hevra Kadisha (Jewish burial society) made sure that funerals were handled properly. Some time around Shavuot of 1997 the society helped lay to rest the last Jewish resident of the China Coast Community, an ecumenical home for destitute, stateless, elderly people that was supported by the Jewish Benevolent Society.

The trustees of Ohel Leah (today known officially as the Incorporated Trustees of the Jewish Community of Hong Kong) were responsible for funding—often out of their own pockets—and administering various institutions. Among the community's earliest institutions was the Jewish Recreation Club, established in 1905, which provided a homey alternative to the often exclusionary clubs that still formed the backbone of Hong Kong's expatriate social life. For many years the Ezekiel Abraham School, founded in 1969, offered the only formal Jewish education, and was run on Sundays and afternoons by volunteers from the community. The Jewish Benevolent Society provided discreet no-interest loans to members in need.

The Jewish Women's Association (JWA), founded in 1947, took on the massive task of assisting the World War II refugees, while also contributing to Youth Aliyah. The JWA has continued its work till this day, raising funds in true Hong Kong style with a lavish annual Israel Independence charity ball. The group, which came to be dominated by Israeli women, continued to support a shrinking number of Shanghai refugees living out their last years in a nursing home in Israel and took on new charitable causes in Israel.

The status quo began to change in the 1980s, when religious controversy led to the formation of several new congregations. Ohel Leah's centrality receded, and a nonpartisan community center replaced the venerable yet time-worn Recreation Club. The impressive new Jewish Community Center of Hong Kong became the main focus of communal activity, a place where all members of the community could meet and interact—if not pray—on common ground.

JEWISH COMMUNITY CENTER

In the mid-1980s, the fund managed by the Incorporated Trustees was nearly depleted and unable to pay for legally required repairs to the supporting wall of the Ohel Leah Synagogue property. In solving this crisis, the Incorporated Trustees found themselves holding the strings to a purse of near-mythic proportions. In a deal rumored to have fetched at least US$150 million, the grounds of the historic synagogue were leased to a real-estate developer for 99 years. In 1992 twin luxury apartment towers were built on the land, which was on Robinson Road in the pricey Mid Levels residential neighborhood, where cramped three-bedroom apartments were renting for US$8,000 a month. A number of the units in the complex, named Robinson Place, were sold, at preferential prices, to the trustees and to community members. The first few floors of one of the towers became the home of the Jewish Community Center (JCC) of Hong Kong, equipped with a library, swimming pool, function halls, a kosher goods store, classrooms used by the Carmel Day School, and two kosher restaurants, meat and dairy.

JCC membership was automatically granted to anyone joining one of the three congregations recognized by the trustees. The 700 JCC member families came in nearly equal numbers from the Reform United Jewish Congregation, modern Orthodox Ohel Leah Synagogue, and Chabad-Lubavitch. (A 1996 poll of religious "sensitivities" showed that 35 percent of Hong Kong's affiliated Jews considered themselves Conservative, the one major Jewish stream with no institutional framework.)

A breakdown by nationality showed Americans far outnumbering others at 57 percent. Their ideas about Jewish life differed sharply from those of the once-dominant British subjects. American Jews were accustomed, for example, to the tripartite landscape of the Reform, Conservative, and Orthodox movements. For most British Jews, the Association of Orthodox Synagogues reigned supreme, regardless of whether they themselves were strictly observant.

Different tastes and expectations had to be reckoned with in determining the JCC's atmosphere. Some wanted the aura of an exclusive Hong Kong social club. The JCC was, after all, the offspring of the Jewish Recreation Club, whose members came together for the same games of tennis, croquet, and bowls played at all the finest social clubs. The marble walls, plush carpets, and elegant fixtures throughout much of the new center seemed to embody that approach, as did the center's rules prohibiting its own staff and members' maids from using the front entrance.

Others, coming from the American community-center tradition, with its mission of bolstering Jewish identity, preferred a less formal style, one emphasizing Jewish educational and cultural events. Programs became a major feature of the center, with a wide selection of social events, lectures, and classes on topics ranging from mah-jongg to medieval Jewish history, and visiting scholars-in-residence throughout the year.

Since 1996 the program director has been Jody Hirsh, a prominent U.S. Jewish educator with a strong arts background and an inclusive approach. Hirsh held a number of successful events and celebrations that brought the various synagogues and organizations together. In some cases, however, Orthodox leaders chose not to participate when they feared their presence would lend legitimacy to Reform Judaism. For example, attendance at a communal study day (Yom Limud) was reduced by a Chabad boycott because some classes were taught from a non-Orthodox perspective.

Other trends at the JCC included catering to the growing number of young children and providing more Hebrew-language programs, such as films, sing-alongs, and debates, to accommodate the large number of Israeli members. Israelis edged out the British as the second-largest group and constituted 18 percent of JCC membership. A JCC survey also showed that the number of singles had increased, and the community had become younger, with the largest group 30–39 years old. There were 450 children, nearly half of them between the ages of five and 12.

Apart from its regular members, the JCC also served the many travelers who came through, who helped to imbue Jewish life in Hong Kong with a sense of transience. Temporary sojourns, whether they lasted days or years, were the rule rather than the exception. The proud descendants of the Kadoories and Sassoons, who sailed in on the China trade over a century ago, remained key figures in a power elite that determined the success and shape of leading Jewish institutions, but they were few in number. Short-term visitors—tourists, business travelers, U.S. Navy personnel, or fund-raisers for Jewish religious institutions abroad—could count on a *minyan* for prayer and a kosher meal. Longer-term residents included young professionals spending three years on their way up the corporate ladder and entrepreneurs lured by uncharted Asian markets, living in the territory for ten or 15 years.

Looking toward the future, the community debated whether the Incorporated Trustees should continue heavily subsidizing the operations of the JCC and other Hong Kong institutions or require the members to take up more of the slack. Also, while the Jews of Hong Kong were blessed with a world-class building and facilities, they had yet to decide whether their JCC was simply a kosher recreation center for Jews or an institution with a Jewish cultural mission to fulfill.

Religion

Adjacent to the JCC stands the historic Ohel Leah Synagogue, with its white-washed facade, twin turrets, and vaulted roof. In keeping with the Sephardic style, seating is in horseshoe formation around a central *bimah,* with women's seating on the upper balcony. Entry to the grounds is through a guarded street-level portico and down cascading stone stairs, which also lead to the *mikveh* behind the synagogue. Despite periodic partial renovations over the years, the building reached such a state of cosmetic and structural disrepair that a thorough US$5-million restoration effort was launched in 1997.

While Hong Kong was a British colony, Ohel Leah had links with the Association of Orthodox Synagogues in the United Kingdom. England's chief rabbi was considered the community's top rabbinic authority and was accorded a dignitary's welcome on his annual visits. With the end of British rule, the nearly 250-member congregation, while self-described as modern Orthodox, ceased to have formal ties to any movement.

The welcoming atmosphere of the congregation, which includes a weekly Sabbath *kiddush* luncheon, was at times marred by internal strife, with some disagreements escalating into brawls of startling intensity. In summer 1997 a bitter fight over selecting a new rabbi divided the community and was fought in such an incendiary war of words, faxes, and fliers that it was reported in a full-page Sunday feature story in the local English-language paper, much to the chagrin of all involved.

The rift faded with the arrival of the energetic new rabbi, Yaacov Kermaier, whose previous job was as assistant rabbi at New York's Riverdale Jewish Center. "My goal is to establish Ohel Leah as a premier educational synagogue," said Rabbi Kermaier. The 28-year-old Yeshiva University graduate added that he wanted to "color the synagogue with a modern Orthodox character, to focus more on Zionism and to present to people a broader and more open-minded version of Orthodoxy than they might have been exposed to before."

If the past was any indication, Rabbi Kermaier faced some potholes on the road ahead. In fact, in the 1980s, Ohel Leah had seen several fissures that ran so deep they led to the formation of three new congregations.

CHABAD-LUBAVITCH

In 1985 a group of Hong Kong Jews, dismayed by what they felt was a deterioration of religious life, solicited help from a number of Orthodox organizations abroad. Chabad-Lubavitch was the only group to respond, and it did so by sending two young emissaries. One of them, the freshly ordained Mordechai Avtzon, served as Ohel Leah's rabbi for one year, then founded Chabad of Hong Kong and helped set up the Carmel School.

Rabbi Avtzon came to a community that barely managed to get a quorum at its weekly Saturday morning services and served a *kiddush* that was flagrantly unkosher. He overhauled the Jewish Recreation Club's kitchen and managed to increase attendance at Sabbath services and set up a daily *minyan*. At the same time, he failed to win over key community figures, who were uncomfortable with his brand of Orthodoxy and, in some cases, perceived his approach as coercive.

After a year—by then Avtzon had married and would soon start a family—the Ohel Leah trustees dismissed him. With support from a group of disaffected members, Avtzon moved operations to the Hilton Hotel. By 1997 he was working out of the five-star Furama Hotel in a deal that gave him dedicated space for a synagogue and special rates on rooms for the many religious business travelers he catered to.

Chabad in Hong Kong raised money through its worldwide movement and from local members. The economic slump of late 1997 hit the group relatively hard, dependent as it was on member contributions. It did receive some funding from the Incorporated Trustees, but, Avtzon said, it was far less than what Ohel Leah got and just one-fourth of what was allocated to the Reform UJC. Rabbi Avtzon was unequivocal about the Reform movement: "Judaism has only one denomination and that's Torah and Mitzvot. Anything else is simply not Judaism." "But," he hastened to add, "we were sent down in this world to be God's agents of Torah, not to be his policemen. Our job is to turn lights on, not to debate darkness and confusion."

Hong Kong had also become headquarters for a budding Chabad presence in Asia, with representatives in Bangkok, Singapore, and Japan.

UNITED JEWISH CONGREGATION

The United Jewish Congregation was formed in 1988 when Ohel Leah's rabbi refused to allow a bar mitzvah ceremony for a boy he considered not Jewish because the boy's mother had undergone a Reform conversion abroad. The father, angered over the decision as well as how it was handled, broke away along with a number of other congregants and founded the UJC, as it is known.

The UJC is affiliated with the World Union for Progressive Judaism, and while it had grown to 230 member families, it still faced difficulty in finding a rabbi able to make a long-term commitment. Just after Rosh Hashanah in 1996, Rabbi Levi Weiman-Kelman came to serve during a one-year sabbatical from Jerusalem's Kol Haneshama community. He was followed by Joel Oseran, director of education for the World Union in Jerusalem, also on a one-year stay. Like Ohel Leah's rabbi, the UJC rabbi is provided with a spacious apartment in the Robinson Place towers that house the JCC.

Services are held in an auditorium that belongs to the JCC and is in Robinson Place but that has no physical connection to the rest of the center. This is by design, in order to maintain the center as a strictly Sabbath-observing facility. The restrictions also mean that some UJC events are held at other locations in Hong Kong, such as the Hong Kong Country Club, the American Club, and—sometimes—at sea.

Rabbi Oseran said that his main focus was "helping people to maintain and to expand on their Jewish connection, and their sense of belonging to the Jewish community." He observed that many of those who became involved in the UJC had a minimal connection to their Jewishness and would probably not have joined a congregation in the United States.

In the latter half of 1997, the UJC launched a well-received Chavura program, creating 15 small groups for members to meet informally around common interests. The community also continued to raise funds for a development project in Shanghai administered by the American Jewish Distribution Committee. The funds assist Chinese residents of a neighborhood that harbored over 20,000 Jewish refugees from Nazi-dominated Europe in the 1940s.

OTHER SYNAGOGUES

Yet another breakaway synagogue, Shuva Israel, was founded by a group that accused Chabad of religious laxity. In 1990 Rabbi Avtzon and several parents started a nursery school, Torah Island, which, the following year, became the Carmel School. Operating in quarters rented from the Jewish Recreation Club, the school had open enrollment. To the dismay of some, this meant that many of the children were not Jewish under Halakhah, Jewish law. At the same time, some Sephardic members felt increasingly marginalized by the growing Ashkenazic presence. They founded their own nursery school, their own congregation, and, later, their own kosher restaurant, the Shalom Grill. By 1997, however, the Shuva Israel community was in decline: its founder had left to live in Israel, Chabad had arranged for a separate Sephardic service on the High Holy Days, and some members were interested in benefiting from services offered by the JCC.

Finally, there was Kehilat Zion Synagogue. Located in Kowloon on Hong

Kong's peninsular tip, it served the many business travelers who stay in that area. The rabbi, Netanel Meoded, was from Israel. Kehilat Zion was one of 48 synagogues worldwide established by Rabbi Sam Kassim, the head of a *haredi* (ultra-Orthodox) religious seminary in Jerusalem. At year's end, Kehilat Zion was applying to the Incorporated Trustees to be a member community in the JCC.

Education

For many, the community's day school was the most vibrant Jewish institution in Hong Kong. Carmel School had 120 students in preschool to fifth grade and another 40 enrolled in the nursery program. Founded in 1991 by Chabad's Rabbi Avtzon and a group of mainly non-Orthodox parents, Carmel was struggling to maintain a fragile balance between following the Orthodox approach mandated in its constitution and creating an atmosphere welcoming to Jews of all affiliations. Since Carmel was constitutionally independent of all other Jewish institutions in Hong Kong, and remained unaffiliated with any particular educational stream, it could pick and choose from the available British and North American Jewish curriculum materials. The current administration defined Carmel as modern Orthodox and Zionist, although admission was open to "any child whose family thinks the experience of a Jewish school would be of benefit." This policy extended to those who were not halakhically Jewish, such as the children of mixed marriages.

Jonathan Cannon, a modern Orthodox British educator who became executive director of the school in 1996, said that Carmel was "not in the business of negating one view or another," but rather promoted an approach that "acknowledges and validates" students' diverse backgrounds. He noted that, back in their home countries, many expatriate parents would not be sending their children to Jewish schools. They chose Carmel not only because most of the alternatives were Christian parochial schools, but because they were far away from extended families and community attachments. A school decorated with Hanukkah symbols rather than Christmas lights was a comforting haven for them, and many parents became deeply involved in supporting the school.

Over the years, parents and staff have navigated a number of disputes, including whether or not to teach about dinosaurs (they chose to teach), whether or not to allow a non-Jewish parent to head the PTA (they opted for allowing), and whether or not to let a Reform rabbi lecture in the school (they decided not to). Cannon said that, while the Jewish studies program would remain ever controversial, with challenges from both ends of the religious spectrum, parents were satisfied with the school's high level of academic excellence, which they viewed as a priority.

The school was housed in the Jewish Community Center, while remaining institutionally independent. It was planning to move to a larger facility provided by Hong Kong's Government Property Agency, which had categorized Carmel as a nonprofit international school. A loose five-year plan envisioned increasing the student body to 250, but, as with so much in Hong Kong, the precarious economic environment made it impossible to predict future developments.

Carmel's budget of roughly US$2 million was largely covered by tuition fees (up to 70 percent of the students had their US$9,000 tuition fees paid by parents' employers), with additional funds raised in an aggressive campaign by parents, and the rest subsidized by the Incorporated Trustees of the Jewish Community of Hong Kong, whose contribution included use of the building. The trustees made their continued support contingent on a goal of fiscal self-sufficiency. They were willing to fund the school during its startup years, but ultimately Carmel had to stand on its own. It was a principle that many in this business-driven town took for granted, one meant to deter irresponsible spending, but others worried that the school's potential could be limited by bottom-line considerations.

The trustees also continued to sponsor a Hebrew school, Ezekiel Abraham, which in 1997 had 90 students from a wide assortment of Jewish backgrounds. In addition to the Sunday program, there were after-school classes for Hebrew speakers and for those with minimal background, and a number of privately tutored students. Because the children of the more Jewishly committed families were placed in Carmel, Ezekiel Abraham had a high proportion of children with scant Jewish knowledge. Many of these children were seen as increasingly vulnerable because they were enrolled in the Hong Kong International School, with its American curriculum, high academic reputation, and what some parents described as Lutheran missionizing.

Culture

Preserving the community's past was the task of the Jewish Historical Society of Hong Kong. It was founded in 1984 by community members Dennis and Mary Leventhal and Anita Buxbaum, and S.J. Chan, an authority on the Jews of Kaifeng. The society's efforts included a catalogued Judaica library and several monographs on the Jews of Hong Kong, as well as assistance in the creation of the first Chinese version of the Encyclopedia Judaica, and service as liaison for academics engaged in Sino-Judaic studies. Near the end of 1997, a postdoctoral student at Hong Kong University began a two-year social history of the Jews of Hong Kong, funded in part by the Incorporated Trustees. There was also an effort to create the first inventory of the more than 300 people buried in the Jewish cemetery.

MIRIAM HERSCHLAG

Australia

National Affairs

MULTICULTURALISM, RIGHTS of the Aborigines, and immigration were key matters of public interest in the year and a half period ending December 1997.

Multiculturalism, a policy crystallized by the Liberal party while in government in the 1970s, recognizes the legitimacy of ethnic diversity, building upon it for the benefit of society as a whole, but within a framework of consensus and commitment to core Australian political and social values, such as the rule of law, parliamentary democracy, tolerance, freedom of speech and religion, and English as the national language.

The administration of Prime Minister John Howard initiated a review of the policy. In August 1997 the National Multicultural Advisory Council was appointed by Immigration Minister Philip Ruddock. In December the council released a paper designed to open debate on the issue, including areas in which the government could improve its performance and policies, as a prelude to producing its final report to the government due in mid-1998. The council's preliminary view was that multiculturalism was a success, and it pointed to a Newspoll in May 1997 showing that 78 percent of respondents viewed it positively. In launching the discussion paper, Prime Minister Howard embraced the cultural and ethnic diversity of Australia as "a remarkable success story," saying that "there is no place in the Australia that we love for any semblance of racial or ethnic intolerance. . . ."

Immigration to Australia dropped as the government gave more weight to skills criteria and less to family-reunion criteria, which the government claimed had resulted in increased unemployment. Knowledge of the English language also became a factor in the process. Overall, the annual immigration intake was reduced by 9,000 to 74,000 for the 1996–97 period.

The period under review also saw the end of the Special Humanitarian Migration Program, which had allowed between 7,500 and 8,000 Jews to immigrate to Australia from the former Soviet Union. The ending of the program had previously been agreed to by the Executive Council of Australian Jewry (ECAJ) and the Federation of Australian Jewish Community Services, with the Australian government.

Under Howard, the Liberal government continued a tight fiscal policy, with cuts to all departments except the Department of Defense. In education, substantial cuts to tertiary education were continued, and fee-based courses began to appear in universities across the country. (Fees for university education had been removed in the early 1970s by the then Labor government.)

The government's relations with Australia's Aboriginal people continued to be inflamed. Two issues dominated the debate. The first was the government's refusal to issue an apology for previous governmental policies that allowed Aboriginal children to be taken from their families and placed in Christian missions or with white families. A Human Rights Commission report on the issue of the "stolen children," published in May 1997, was highly critical of the policy. Jeremy Jones, director of community affairs for AIJAC, the Australia/Israel and Jewish Affairs Council, made the presentation to the National Reconciliation Convention on behalf of all faith communities, in his capacity as chairman of the Advisory Group on Faith Communities to the Council for Aboriginal Reconciliation.

The second issue was the government's proposed legislative changes that would effectively extinguish native title to lands occupied prior to white settlement and subsequently leased to farming and grazing interests. A High Court ruling in 1996, in what became known as the Wik decision, found that the pastoral leases did not eliminate native title. To counter this, the Liberal government proposed and began to pass legislation designed to effectively eliminate native title on pastoral leases. Unfortunately, some government members, embroiled in an electorally costly race debate, engaged in scare tactics, claiming that freehold titles — residential properties — were also under threat, a claim with no basis in fact.

The Australian Jewish community solidly opposed the government's policies both on the "stolen children" and Wik, supporting the Aboriginal rights in these matters. Gold-mining magnate and Lubavitch community leader Joseph Gutnick, a staunch Liberal supporter, derided the government and even stated at one stage that he would think about changing his vote if the government continued to enact prejudicial policies against the Aborigines.

The debate over Aborigines was also a factor in the rise of Pauline Hanson, the former Liberal Party candidate and now independent member of Federal Parliament, known for her racist views. In September 1996, in her maiden speech in Parliament, she asserted that Australia was being "swamped by Asians" and that indigenous Aborigines, who constitute less than 1 percent of the population, were not disadvantaged and did not deserve government assistance. Hanson attacked the process of reconciliation between the indigenous and nonindigenous populations, making numerous false claims about the ways in which Aborigines were advantaged over whites. Hanson also called for the dismantling of multiculturalism and for Australia to withdraw from the United Nations and all foreign treaties.

The effect of the speech and the refusal of newly elected prime minister John

Howard to explicitly repudiate and condemn her sentiments triggered a public outpouring of support for Hanson, with some opinion polls placing public support for her at 17 percent and above. Her celebrity lasted only several months, however, peaking with the formation of her own political party, One Nation, in April 1997. Her fortunes in the various political polls over the course of 1997 suffered a marked decline, except in her home state of Queensland.

In general, the Howard government won respect from the Jewish community for upholding the previous government's decision to reject Holocaust denier David Irving's visa application to visit Australia; for maintaining strong support of the private education sector and Jewish day schools; and for speaking out against racism and anti-Semitism.

Israel and the Middle East

The Howard government gave strong support to the Middle East peace process and Israel, as well as an unstinting opposition to terrorism. Prime Minister Howard accurately described himself as a "long-standing friend of Israel" and valued highly "the strong links between Australia and Israel." On key resolutions critical of Israel in the UN General Assembly, such as those passed in the Emergency Special Session during 1997 against Israeli housing construction in Jerusalem, Australia stood out from the flock. Apart from an initial vote against Israel on Resolution 51/223, in subsequent votes that were passed by large majorities, Australia voted with the minority abstaining. This was a significant change in Australia's voting pattern, reflecting the genuine empathy of the Howard government with Israel.

Federal Court Justice Marcus Einfeld continued his work with the Australian International Legal Resources (AILR) organization in Israel's occupied territories, under the control of the Palestinian Authority. AILR, an organization of lawyers, aimed to assist in building the rule of law in developing countries.

In April 1997, when a German court handed down its verdict holding Iranian leaders, including then President Rafsanjani, responsible for directing acts of international terrorism, Australia reacted along with most Western countries in withdrawing its ambassador from Iran. However, he returned only a couple of days later, arriving in Teheran on April 18. In an interview with the daily *Iran News*, Ambassador Hume said, "I met and briefed Foreign Minister Alexander Downer and Deputy Prime Minister and Minister for Trade Tim Fischer, who voiced their satisfaction, and it was decided that I should go back to Teheran." In the past, both Prime Minister Howard and Foreign Minister Downer had strongly denounced Iranian involvement in international terrorism. In mid-1996, Howard said that "Iranian involvement in terrorism is absolutely unacceptable." Complicating matters was the fact that, starting in 1991, Australia had maintained a line of credit of US $750 million to Iran and promoted a policy of "constructive engagement." Foreign Minister Downer stated in June 1997 that the government had not had the opportunity to review the line of credit to Iran (which had not yet been used), but would "certainly be happy to look at it." However, as of December the line of credit remained intact.

On December 23, 1997, Prime Minister Howard lit the first candle in the *hanukkiah* at the Sydney Jewish Museum at a function sponsored jointly by the Executive Council of Australian Jewry and the Zionist Federation of Australia. Due to Australia's position in relation to the International Date Line, Howard could quite rightly claim to be the first of many world leaders to light a Hanukkah candle in honor of Israel's 50th birthday. His words of friendship toward Israel at the time reflected his many years of close identification with, and support for, Israel.

Anti-Semitism and Anti-Zionism

In 1997 the Jewish community was able, for the first time, to judge the results of the federal antiracism legislation adopted late in 1995. Implementation of the law, which had been heralded as an effective means to deal with racist individuals and organizations in contemporary Australia, proved to be complex, time-consuming, and limited in effectiveness. Nevertheless, in certain cases the law had positive outcomes. In one instance, following a complaint lodged by the Executive Council of Australian Jewry against an Arabic newspaper, *El Telegraph*, published in Sydney, which had published an article citing the notorious *Protocols of the Elders of Zion* as if they were a factual document, the newspaper was required to publish a rebuttal in a form of a critique of the *Protocols,* in Arabic. The same newspaper also ran an article calling on Jewish and Arab Australians to work together against racism, co-written and signed by two leading members of the Jewish community. This outcome was achieved through conciliation by the Human Rights Commission, as mandated by the new law.

Other complaints, however, including instances of Holocaust denial on the Internet, were not so readily resolved. On a number of occasions, Jewish community leaders noted that the time between the commission of an act and its likely adjudication was so great as to render the process totally inadequate. In other cases, the perpetrators of anti-Semitic acts were anonymous, thus making complaint impossible.

During the calendar year 1997, 246 reports of incidents of anti-Semitism were recorded. These included violence, vandalism, and intimidation directed at Australian Jews and Jewish communal institutions around Australia. The reported figure represented an 18 percent decrease over 1996, but was 19 percent higher than the average over the previous seven-year period.

Typical of anti-Semitic incidents that occurred over the year were daubing of homes in Melbourne, Sydney, Brisbane, and Adelaide with anti-Jewish and Nazi graffiti, on some occasions associated with break-ins; damage to Jewish day schools from rocks thrown through windows of classrooms and fires deliberately lit; bomb threats against Jewish community organizations and schools; and telephone and mail threats.

The number of incidents of serious vandalism and significant personal injury was among the lowest since comparative records began to be kept. The comparative decrease in attacks on communal property could be attributed to greater awareness of communal security needs and the consequent increase in police protection and other measures. It is also relevant that the decreases in acts of harassment and intimidation that did occur were in population centers where the Jewish community had taken well-publicized legal action against prominent anti-Jewish propagandists.

There was a small increase in reports of physical harassment, and incidents of this type were reported at a rate of 17 percent above the average over the long term. Among reported cases of assault and harassment, most took place close to synagogues and were directed at Jewish families, or day-school students, easily identifiable by their school uniforms.

Some anti-Semitism was associated with events that drew public attention to the Australian Jewish community. Thus, for example, when four Jewish athletes were killed in a traumatic bridge collapse at the Maccabiah Games in Israel in July 1997 (see below), and more than 60 others were injured, the Australian media portrayed the events sympathetically, emphasizing that the athletes were Australian, not just Jewish. Still, letters to the editors of major Australian newspapers reflected a degree of anti-Semitism, one letter criticizing the right of Jews to have their own international sporting games.

EXTREMIST GROUPS

The Australian League of Rights—described by the Federal Government's Human Rights and Equal Opportunity Commission as "undoubtedly the most influential and effective, as well as the best organized and most substantially financed, racist organization in Australia"—continued to receive widespread but largely negative publicity. Media attention was aroused following the revelation in the *Australia/Israel Review* that Graeme Campbell, then ALP Member for Kalgoorlie, had not only addressed league seminars but used the platform to comment insultingly about the prime minister. Questions were raised about the league's attempts to influence public debate, the activities of racist groups in Australia, and the questionable judgment of public figures who participated in activities organized by and for extremist groups. Although not all political figures opposed contact with the League of Rights, there was unanimity in condemning its anti-Semitism. The league continued its extensive program of lectures and seminars aimed at equipping "actionists" around Australia with information to combat their Zionist, Fabian, and humanist enemies, and league material was regularly included in mail-drops of material encouraging hatred of Jews.

The Citizens Electoral Council (CEC), the front group of the Lyndon LaRouche cult, continued to operate in Australia during 1997, but at a much lower level than in previous years. The group persisted in its practice of spying on prominent members of the Australian Jewish community, intimidation of the Jewish community, and fraudulent fund-raising techniques.

The principal neo-Nazi group in Australia, Australian National Action, was less active during the period in review. Based in Adelaide, South Australia, with a substantial following in Melbourne, Victoria, National Action resorted to small-scale demonstrations against Asians, including some particularly distasteful abuse and assaults on schoolchildren.

Extremist publications, including *The Strategy*; *Lock, Stock & Barrel*; and *Nexus,* continued to promote the views of conspiracy theorists and the far right. U.S. militia leader Gerald "Jack" McLamb, a confederate of Bo Gritz and Mark Koernke, continued to receive substantial promotion in *The Strategy* following his 1995 tour of several cities and towns in Australia.

MEDIA BIAS

Incidents abounded of one-sided, unprofessional bias against Israel and insensitivity to Jews bordering on anti-Semitism, in both the print and electronic media. The most striking example came from the *Sydney Morning Herald*, which published an *Agence France Presse* report claiming that Israeli forces were dropping toy dolls in Lebanon to wound and kill Lebanese children. An investigation by the *Australia/Israel Review* proved that there was no evidence to substantiate the claims, and that the reporters involved were openly antagonistic to Israel.

The Melbourne *Herald Sun,* operated by Rupert Murdoch's News Corporation, published several letters highly critical of the Australian Jewish community during the year. One letter, by Nigel Jackson, a prominent anti-Semite and Holocaust denier, denounced attempts to bring Nazi war criminals to justice. The letter mentioned "the fanaticism of some powerful interests around the world" and cautioned the Australian government not to give in to a "noxious cabal of millionaires." Letters sent in response were not published.

Nazi War Criminals

There were further developments in the case of Konrad Kalejs, described as "a key officer in a unit that killed tens of thousands of innocents" by the U.S. Federal Court of Appeals in 1994. An Australian citizen since 1957, Kalejs had attempted to live in both the United States and Canada but had been deported by both. (For full background, see AJYB 1997, pp. 409–10.) Most recently, he had entered Canada in September 1995, was arrested by Canadian immigration officials at Pearson Airport in Toronto, and was detained but was then released on a promissory note to appear at a federal immigration hearing on May 1, 1996. Almost a year later, in August 1997, the Canadian immigration proceedings ended with a decision to deport Kalejs immediately to Australia. He arrived on August 20 to a media furor and a revived debate about whether war criminals were entitled to citizenship and residency in Australia. In the meantime, the Latvian government was seeking information about Kalejs's criminal activities from the records of the Australian, U.S., and Canadian governments in an effort to seek his extradition and prosecution in Latvia. At the end of 1997 it was not clear how far the process had advanced.

No action was taken in the case of Karlis Ozols, who was described in a 1992 brief for the Commonwealth Director of Public Prosecutions (DPP) as "the highest-ranking alleged war criminal living in Australia." As a senior member of the Arajs Kommando—with a higher rank, actually, than that of Konrad Kalejs—Lt. Col. Ozols commanded a company that assisted in the rounding-up, transportation, guarding, and execution of Jews in the Minsk and Slutzk ghettos in Byelorussia. The victims of Ozols's unit alone probably numbered more than 12,000. He was decorated with the German War Cross of Merit, which was rarely given to non-Germans, a sign that Ozols had distinguished himself in his duties.

Ozols arrived in Australia in 1949 as a displaced person, gained citizenship in 1956, and had lived in Melbourne undisturbed ever since. He was investigated by the federal government's Special Investigations Unit (SIU) throughout its five years of existence, 1987–92, and by mid-1992 a brief had found that there was a prima facie case against Ozols for committing genocidal war crimes.

The Jewish community remained deeply disturbed by the fact that Kalejs, Ozols, and other individuals, intimately linked to the Nazis' campaign of genocide, had been allowed to reside in and continually return to Australia. They urged amending the 1948 Australian Citizenship Act so as to permit removal of citizenship in cases of fraud or serious misrepresentation, even if that occurred prior to the ten-year period currently allowed. They also wanted the immigration minister to use his powers of discretion to remove citizenship from individuals whose involvement in and responsibility for war crimes and/or genocide were clearly established.

Leaders of the Australian Baltic community criticized Jewish protests over the presence of alleged Latvian war criminals in Australia, principally Konrad Kalejs and Karlis Ozols. On November 25, 1997, a letter signed by four leaders of the Australian Lithuanian community to the Lithuanian newspaper *Republika* asked the four leading candidates in the presidential elections whether they intended to apologize for Lithuanian participation in the murder of Jews during the Holocaust, or if they would "do so only when the President of Israel apologizes for the harm Jews did to Lithuanians—for illicit arrests, deportations, inquests, imprisonments, and massacres during the Soviet occupation."

JEWISH COMMUNITY

Demography

The Australian Jewish community continued to grow through immigration, particularly from the former Soviet Union and South Africa. Estimates for the total number of Jews in Australia ranged from 95,000 to 105,000, out of a total population of 18 million. There were believed to be hundreds of thousands of others with some ancestral connection to the Jewish community, the high number due largely to the predominantly male immigration of Jews to Australia in the early years of European colonization. Immigration from the former Soviet Union, South Africa, and, to a lesser extent, Israel, the United Kingdom, North America, and New Zealand more than compensated for loss of numbers due to natural factors and emigration to Israel.

The Jewish community was heavily concentrated in Melbourne and Sydney, with the Brisbane–Gold Coast representing the greatest growth area. Census figures (which are dubious, as the question on religion is not obligatory) indicate that between 10 and 15 percent of Jewish women and men currently had non-Jewish partners, although anecdotal evidence suggests the figure may be considerably higher. Another demographic feature of the community was the high percentage of elderly, which placed enormous stress on welfare and service agencies.

There were between 14,000 and 20,000 Jews from the former Soviet Union in Australia, with the overwhelming majority living in Sydney and Melbourne. Although the newcomers were successful in their general integration into Australian life, their lack of Jewish literacy made integration into the Jewish community a major challenge.

Communal Affairs

Personal relations between Australian Jews—one of the most pro-Israel Jewish communities in the world—and the State of Israel were severely tested during 1997 as a result of a tragic incident at the opening of the 15th Maccabiah Games in Tel Aviv. On July 14, two Australian Jewish athletes were killed and some 70 injured when the bridge they were crossing over the Yarkon River, leading into the stadium for the opening ceremony, collapsed. Two more athletes died later, most probably as a result of ingesting polluted water from the Yarkon River. The water was heavily contaminated with chemicals, some of which were reportedly sprayed by Maccabiah officials to keep mosquitoes away. Fifteen-year-old Sascha Elterman was still in a Sydney hospital at the end of the year, following numerous operations and suffering from an abscess on her brain as a result of her immersion in the Yarkon.

The images of Jewish athletes coming back to Australia in coffins greatly distressed the community and evoked enormous anger at the apparent incompetence of the Maccabiah Games' organizers and at the Israeli government itself. That the games' opening ceremony went on, even as bodies were being pulled from the Yarkon, also enraged many, although overriding security and rescue considerations understandably influenced the decision. At the same time, there was enormous admiration for the athletes who stayed on and competed in the games, bringing home to Australia dozens of medals from the competition. Leaders of the Australian Maccabiah organization, principally President Tom Goldman and

Tom Danos, and communal leaders like Australia/Israel and Jewish Affairs Council chairman Mark Leibler, traveled regularly to Israel to maintain the pressure on the Israeli government for compensation and a thorough investigation.

The official investigation, headed by Brig. Gen. (Res.) Yishai Dotan, refused to attribute specific blame for the collapse, although it became clear that the bridge was hopelessly substandard and that its builder had been selected because of an astonishingly cheap construction bid. (The bid from the Israel Defense Forces was $111, 200; the organizing committee accepted the Irgunit construction firm's bid of only $34,750; Irgunit kept about $7,700 and subcontracted the work to Ben Ezra Constructions for a cost of around $27,000.)

Goldman called for those responsible to resign from the Maccabi World Union or the subcommittee responsible for the games. In December he announced that Australian Maccabi would pull out of the world organization in protest. A meeting was convened between Jewish leaders, including AIJAC national policy chairman Colin Rubenstein and Zionist Federation president Ron Weiser, with Israel's ambassador to Australia, Shmuel Moyal, in an attempt to calm the situation. In August Israel had offered a $500,000 compensation loan to athletes, until insurance claims could be settled, but the money had not materialized by the end of the year.

After receiving the Dotan Committee's report (judged insufficient by many), Minister of Sports Moshe Peled concluded that there had been a chain of negligence including all parties involved in the collapse of the bridge. "The sequence of foul-ups began with engineer Micha Bar-Ilan, who designed the bridge, and continued with the Irgunit construction firm and its subcontractor Ben-Ezra Construction, and the Maccabiah organizing committee. . . . It symbolizes a deteriorating Israeli society in which amateurism and the notions of 'it'll be okay,' 'don't worry,' or 'trust me' are contributing to unnecessary deaths."

Following a rapid investigation, in December Israeli authorities filed charges of negligent manslaughter against five of those involved in the bridge collapse, including the contractor, the designer, and the chairman of the Maccabiah Games organizing committee. Families of the dead and injured indicated that they would file suit against the Israeli government and/or the Ramat Gan municipality, the Tel Aviv municipality, and the Maccabiah Organizing Committee. A survivor, Jason Steinberg, summed up the mood in the Australian Jewish community in an article in the national newspaper, *The Australian.* "What people clearly can't and may never understand is why in a country so respected and renowned for its efficient defense and security forces, could they not build a simple bridge to carry 5,500 Jewish athletes representing 50 countries over a small stretch of river?" he wrote.

Newspaper editorials became increasingly critical of Israel over time as the toll on the Australian athletes increased. The reactions of Australian Maccabiah officials, increasingly upset by apparent Israeli delays and insensitivity (some Israelis referred to the bridge collapse as an "accident," even as criminal charges were about to be laid against five of those responsible), became heated. This was reflected in the pages of the *Australian Jewish News* and also in the general media.

OTHER MATTERS

Australia/Israel Publications restructured in March 1997, becoming the Australia/Israel and Jewish Affairs Council (AIJAC). Mark Leibler, federal president of the United Israel Appeal, was appointed as national chairman of the organization. Dr. Colin Rubenstein became the national policy and editorial chairman, and Barry Smorgon, chairman in New South Wales. Michael Kapel remained as editor of the council's journal, the *Australia/Israel Review*. Jeremy Jones became AIJAC's director of international and community affairs, retaining his position as executive vice-president of the Executive Council of Australian Jewry (ECAJ), the elected roof body of Australian Jewry.

AIJAC marked its restructuring by establishing an historic affiliation with the American Jewish Committee, enabling the two to collaborate on key Jewish communal and national policy issues. The new partnership with the AJC and its Pacific Rim Institute seemed to highlight the Asia Pacific as an area of growing significance to the Jewish world, an area previously neglected by American and Australian Jewish organizations. This development coincided with the expansion of radical Islamic and Iranian activity in the Asia Pacific area, which had an obvious impact on those societies but would also inevitably affect Jewish communities throughout the region and have implications for Israel and the wider Jewish world.

Diane Shteinman of Sydney continued as president of the ECAJ. Ron Weiser continued in his position as president of the Zionist Federation of Australia. For the first time in well over a decade, the heads of the national representative organization of the Australian Jewish community and of the influential Zionist movement were both in Sydney, Australia's largest city. Nina Bassat continued in her post as president of the Jewish Community Council of Victoria (JCCV). Ron Samuel, a South African immigrant, succeeded Doron Ur as president of the Council of West Australian Jewry. Athol Morris was succeeded by Sue Doobov as president of the ACT Jewish community.

Isi Leibler continued as chairman of the governing board of the World Jewish Congress, a body with which the ECAJ was affiliated and worked closely.

Education and Culture

Government spokespeople, including Minister for Education David Kemp and Prime Minister John Howard, extolled the virtues of Jewish day schools on a number of occasions. Jewish schools, like all private schools, received government funding for their studies. Jewish day schools ranked as four of the top five schools in Melbourne for their final year results, continuing their exceptional record of the previous year, when they occupied all five top places. The only Jewish day school in Perth achieved the best results of any school in that state. While New South Wales did not publish similar comparisons, all Jewish day schools achieved outstanding academic results.

Storyteller Donna Sife of Sydney won first prize at the 1997 Australian national storytelling festival held at Macquarie University.

Kathy Temin was the youngest finalist in the inaugural contemporary art competition established by the Museum of Contemporary Art in Sydney.

The world premiere of *Hemispheres*, composed by Russian-Jewish Australian composer Elena Kats-Chernin, took place in Sydney, as did the inaugural performances of Barry Kosky's *Operated Jew*. A play on Jewish divorce difficulties, *Getting Your Man*, by Margie Fischer, was first performed in Adelaide.

Christian-Jewish Relations

The Uniting Church Assembly approved a document on the subject of its relationship with the Jews. In addition to the long and detailed statement, the group adopted a new action policy, which, among other things, encouraged all preachers, ministers, teachers, and others to take into account the theological implications of anti-Semitism and the Holocaust in their reading and interpretation of Scripture, and to study material on the church's historic role in promoting anti-Semitism. This policy emerged from five years of discussion and negotiation between Jewish leaders and the church.

The Jewish community continued to develop relations with the Catholic Church and the Lutheran Church, both of which had already adopted progressive policies on Jewish-Christian relations. The first formal meeting between Jewish community leaders and the Anglican Church took place in Sydney in December 1997.

The Jewish community worked closely with the mainstream churches, and with Islamic, Buddhist, Hindu, and Ba'hai groups on issues relating to indigenous peoples. Councils of Christians and Jews operated in most centers with significant Jewish communities.

Publications

The Fiftieth Gate by Mark Baker was published during 1997 to excellent critical reviews. So too were the *Last Walk in Naryshkin Park* by award-winning novelist Rose Zwi and essays on the experiences of European Jews by Lilly Brett called *In Full View*. Norman Rothfield published his autobiography, *Many Paths to Peace*.

Personalia

Sir David Smith, former assistant to the governor-general, was appointed a delegate to the Constitutional Convention; Rabbi John Levi, Melbourne University law lecturer Kim Rubenstein, and Eve Mahlab were unsuccessful candidates for election as people's representatives to the Constitutional Convention. Rabbi Levi, the first Australian-born rabbi, retired from his post as chief minister of Temple Beth Israel in Melbourne.

Ray Finkelstein QC was appointed as a Federal Court judge. Federal Court Justice Marcus Einfeld was one of only 100 Australians named as "national treasures" by the National Trust of Australia. Supreme Court Justice Howard Nathan retired from the bench during 1997. A colorful and beloved jurist, Justice Nathan was active within both the Jewish and wider communities.

Colin Rubenstein was appointed to the National Multicultural Advisory Council (NMAC). Michael Danby won Australian Labor Party preselection for the federal electorate of Melbourne Ports. If successful, he would become the only member of Federal Parliament to openly identify as a Jew.

Henry Burstyner, a Melbourne lawyer, won what was believed to be the first settlement with a Swiss bank over dormant funds deposited by a Nazi victim whose descendants had come to Australia after the war.

Jewish community benefactor, founder of the Sydney Jewish Museum, and prominent businessman John Saunders passed away in December 1997. His funeral was attended by numerous dignitaries, including Prime Minister John Howard and other prominent politicians from both sides of the aisle.

Other prominent community members who died in 1997 included Janet Simons, a local and international leader of the United Israel Appeal; respected community leader Mona Klein, widow of Jewish leader Louis Klein; Melbourne artist Jack Louis Koskie; Kurt Jacob, a patron of music with an international reputation for his expertise in harmonicas and accordions; Prof. Louis Goldberg, a leader in accounting, education, and research; Fred Gruen, a "Dunera" internee during World War II, who was arguably Australia's leading economic theorist; Zosia Mercer, president of WIZO; Ida Ferson, Holocaust survivor, activist, and renowned musicologist; David Martin, one of Australia's most prolific and talented writers; Rev. Isidor Gluck, emeritus cantor of Sydney's Great Synagogue; and Ken Weiner, long-serving leader of Sydney Jewry and prominent Liberal Party activist.

COLIN RUBENSTEIN

South Africa

National Affairs

THE PERIOD FROM MID-1996 to the end of 1997 saw the continuing transformation of South Africa in the post-apartheid era. The African National Congress (ANC) consolidated its power in the Government of National Unity (GNU) led by President Nelson Mandela, while the National Party (NP), under F. W. de Klerk, was the official opposition. In May 1997 Roelf Meyer, a leading member of the NP, left to start a new movement with Bantu Holomisa, formerly of the ANC. Three months later de Klerk retired from politics and was replaced as leader of the NP by Martinus van Schalkwyk. In September 1997 Meyer and Holomisa established a new party, the United Democratic Movement.

At the ANC national conference held in Mafikeng in December 1997, Nelson Mandela stepped down as president of the organization. He was replaced by Thabo Mbeki, widely respected as a pragmatist with a sound grasp of economic matters. President Mandela remained South Africa's president, scheduled to retire in 1999 when the country goes to the polls.

The ANC-led government introduced a new Growth, Employment and Redistribution policy (GEAR), as well as reforms in housing and educational policies in 1996. The special ministry responsible for the Reconstruction and Development Program (RDP) was abolished. Affirmative action gained impetus as the nation tackled past injustices. Nonetheless, huge discrepancies in wealth and living conditions remained. The economy grew by about 2 percent, and inflation decreased marginally to about 7.5 percent, the lowest in 24 years. Foreign investment remained unsatisfactory, notwithstanding the announcement by the government of new economic policies, including substantial privatization, fiscal discipline, and endorsement by the International Monetary Fund.

During the period under review, there was a substantial reduction in political violence across the country as a whole, although violence in KwaZulu-Natal Province continued. Criminal violence remained at a shockingly high level, against a backdrop of high unemployment, estimated at about 20 percent.

In his message to the Jewish community for the Jewish New Year in 1996, President Mandela praised Jews for their "major contribution to the well-being of South Africa in every sphere: enriching our culture, helping build our economy, and giving impetus to our intellectual achievements. The community has given our nation many who participated in the struggle for democracy, some at great cost and sacrifice. We know that we still face many challenges in transforming our country—it is my earnest plea that the Jewish community should continue to help us meet these challenges. It is my hope that the peace process in the Middle East will continue, and that it will bear fruit. Our experience has taught us that with goodwill a negotiated solution can be found for even the most profound problems" (*The Citizen,* September 14, 1996).

APARTHEID AFTERMATH

The Truth and Reconciliation Commission (TRC) began its task of investigating crimes committed under the apartheid regime. Under its provisions, individuals who applied for amnesty would not be brought to trial if they made a full disclosure of their actions since 1960. Investigators and researchers uncovered much new evidence to help complete the assessment of South Africa's history between 1960 and 1994. Such evidence includes the discovery of more than 260 secret graves, believed to be those of cadres of the armed wing of the ANC (Umkhonto we Sizwe), killed by apartheid security forces. A database of more than 14,000 human-rights abuses was compiled by investigative units, and thousands of victims received acknowledgment, counseling, and support.

Gesher, a social-action group based in Johannesburg, was the first Jewish organization to make a submission to the TRC, in January 1997. The submission was jointly compiled by Gesher chairman Geoff Sifrin, Rabbi Daniel Beller, and Steven Friedman (director of the Centre for Policy Studies, Johannesburg). The document, as outlined by its authors, provides "a particular view of Jewish tradition which, we believe, helps us better to understand the choices facing our society as it attempts reconciliation: we are concerned to show how elements of Jewish tradition can help South Africa deal with the important challenges it faces." The document went on to note that, in the South African situation, "people who have thought of themselves as bystanders must ask themselves how they ought to have acted, or in what ways they implicitly supported the apartheid system or failed to carry out their moral duty. They need to take appropriate responsibility for the system in which they lived, the atrocities committed under that system and for the process of reconciliation" (*South African Jewish Times,* February 7, 1997).

In March 1997 a minor storm erupted in the pages of the *Mail & Guardian* when Claudia Braude criticized the Jewish community's behavior under apartheid, in particular the role of Percy Yutar, a prominent Jew who prosecuted Mandela in the Rivonia Trial in 1963–64. Of particular concern was the refusal of the Board of Deputies' journal, *Jewish Affairs,* to publish Braude's article, which instead found its way into the *Mail & Guardian.*

A major oral submission was made to the TRC in November 1997 by Chief Rabbi Cyril Harris. He said: "We must examine the past, must admit failings for the past—those failings must prompt us all to move forward in some way, to do something now and in the years ahead to build a better country for the millions of our brothers and sisters who live in this country and hope for a better future." Harris welcomed the work of the commission, which he saw as giving "new meaning to wrongdoing and forgiveness." He acknowledged that most members of the community had in one way or another benefited from apartheid, although they had not initiated the apartheid system. Harris also reminded commissioners of the disproportionate role played by Jews in the struggle against apartheid. While acknowledging that many of the most prominent activists were not practicing Jews, he suggested that "they were moved by either Jewish and, more often than not, humanitarian motivations to speak out." Rabbi Harris also noted that in elections Jews voted against the NP "more so than any other white group," and had participated in various protest groupings such as the Five Freedoms Forum, Jews for Justice, and the Black Sash.

Notwithstanding the substantial anti-apartheid activism identified, Rabbi Harris confessed on behalf of the community "a collective failure to protest against apartheid." "The entire thrust of Jewish moral teachings," he said, "together with the essential lesson of Jewish historical experience, as the most consistent victim in the world, should have moved the community to do everything possible to oppose apartheid. Distancing oneself from the anguished cry of the majority and myopically pursuing one's own interests can never be morally justified."

Rabbi Harris went on to tell the commission about Tikkun, a Jewish communal program whose name means "repairing." "We are applying Jewish skills, resources, expertise and know-how to be of maximum benefit to the upliftment program," he said. (See "Community Relations," below.) Responding to a question put by a commissioner about a proposed wealth tax for whites, Rabbi Harris said he thought such a tax was reasonable and that he would be willing to put his weight behind it.

Israel and the Middle East

President Mandela's planned visit to Israel in August 1996 was postponed until October 1996, due to the president's tight schedule and on medical advice that August in Israel was too hot. Then, in the wake of increased tensions between the Israeli government and the Palestinian Authority, the visit was again delayed.

A high-level Israeli trade delegation visited South Africa in August 1996. Its members met with hundreds of local business executives to discuss investment and held talks with the government about a new trade agreement.

South Africa's new foreign policy, especially its self-proclaimed even-handed policy toward the Middle East, was a source of concern to Jewish leaders. When the government hosted Iranian president Ali Akbar Rafsanjani in September 1996, Seymour Kopelowitz, national director of the South African Jewish Board of Deputies (SAJBOD), made the community's feelings quite clear: "It's well known that Iran has sponsored terrorism against selected targets across the world and vehemently opposes the current Middle East peace process by giving support to Hizbollah and other organizations who wish to derail it." The board called on President Mandela "to urge President Rafsanjani to withdraw opposition to peace negotiations in the Middle East." Dialogue and not hostility between Muslims and Jews, argued the board, would advance peace everywhere in the world (*SAJT,* September 20, 1996).

City Press, a Johannesburg Sunday newspaper, was critical of the board's statement, claiming that the Jews in Israel "don't have a good record themselves. The Jewish community in South Africa must begin to owe allegiance to the country and start to think like everyone else in this country. They must not support President Mandela when it suits them and turn their backs when they think of Israel" (September 15, 1996). The board vigorously objected to *City Press* calling into question the Jewish community's allegiance to South Africa and pointed out that Jews had a democratic right to voice their opinions and to criticize the government. "Under no circumstances did the Board prescribe to President Mandela or the Government who he or they should see. Indeed, we asked the President to urge Rafsanjani to withdraw Iranian opposition to the peace process in the Middle East, knowing he and the South African government are firm supporters of the process" (*City Press,* October 6, 1996).

In a discussion with Jewish leaders, Mandela expressed understanding for Jewish concerns regarding relations with countries like Libya and Iran, but explained that he would not turn his back on friends who had assisted the ANC during the liberation struggle.

In December 1996 news broke of a 3-billion-rand (approximately $600 million) arms deal between the South African government and Syria. There was loud criticism from the National Party and the Democratic Party (DP), both of which considered the proposed deal counterproductive to Middle East peace and to South African foreign and economic interests. Speaking in Johannesburg, DP leader Tony Leon indicated surprise at the government's intention to supply arms to a country that "continued to violate internationally defined concepts of human rights." Both Syria and Israel should, he maintained, be subject to the same audit of human rights. "And equally, if it is found that, by introducing arms via Syria to that region it would destabilize the area, the same question must be asked about supplying arms to Israel. I'm not asking that special treatment be given to Israel. All I'm asking is that both countries be judged by objective criteria. And when that is done, Israel, warts and all, is going to be considerably ahead of the pack in the Middle East" (*SAJT,* March 7, 1997).

Acting Israeli ambassador Victor Hartel also condemned the proposed sale. He was joined by the South African Zionist Federation (SAZF), the SAJBOD, and the South African Union of Jewish Students.

The U.S. State Department informed the South African government that the American assistance program could be curtailed if the military sale went ahead.

President Mandela's spokesman, Park Mankahlama, said his government's policy would not be dictated by any country, no matter how powerful. The United States's enemies were not South Africa's enemies, he declared. Notwithstanding its tough public posture, the cabinet, fearing the anger of Washington, made its support for the arms deal conditional on the approval of Deputy President Thabo Mbeki. At the end of 1997, it appeared that the deal had been aborted.

The tilt of the government's Middle East policy was further evident in President Mandela's visit to Libya in November 1997. In Parliament, Tony Leon proposed a motion condemning the planned granting of the Order of Good Hope Award to Libyan leader Muammar Qaddafi. National SAJBOD chairwoman Marlene Bethlehem considered the award "offensive to the Jewish community because of Libya's dismal human rights record and also because of its involvement against both Israel and Jews."

Another source of tension for the Jewish community, indirectly related to the Middle East, was the emergence of a largely Muslim vigilante group, People Against Gangsterism and Drugs (PAGAD). The movement came to prominence in August 1996 when it was involved in the execution of a leading Cape Town gangster. Within a short while, concerns arose that more extreme elements within the group had agendas other than drug control, and that the group was in contact with radical Middle Eastern groups. When PAGAD leaders threatened to call in Hezballah and Hamas to assist them in their struggle against gangsters, the government issued a warning that outsiders would not be allowed to intervene in the internal problems of South Africa.

In February 1997 a radical Muslim group, Qibla, chanting "Death to America" and burning Israeli flags, marched on the Israeli embassy in Cape Town. A similar march took place in Johannesburg, organized by the Islamic Unity Convention. Ze'ev Luria, political counselor at the Israeli embassy, warned that vigilance against this small minority was necessary because of possible links to the Iranians.

On the eve of Yom Kippur 1997, Muslims held a pro-Hamas demonstration outside a Pretoria mosque and placed a full-page advertisement in the *Pretoria News* (October 10, 1997) criticizing the newspaper's "biased and one-sided version of events in the Middle East." The ad appealed to President Mandela to take account of the "facts" of hostile attacks on the people of Palestine.

In the wake of these tensions, Tony Leon warned Jews not to fall into the trap of believing that all Muslims were anti-Semites or fundamentalists. Speaking at a WIZO Fortnightly Forum in Johannesburg, he reminded Jews that they were better off under the new government than under the old. Jews, he noted, had the same problems as all other middle-class whites, relating to crime, economics, education, and health care. The threat to the Jewish community", contended Leon, "comes from within—from those who are leaving the country" (*SAJT*, March 7, 1997).

Following two suicide bombings in Jerusalem in May 1997, President Mandela sent a letter of condolence to Israeli president Ezer Weizmann, noting that the news "was received in South Africa with shock and despair. . . . We cannot condemn the act strongly enough and we trust that this tragic event will strengthen the resolve of all concerned to bring about a lasting peace."

In September 1997 Ben-Gurion University of the Negev conferred an honorary doctorate on President Mandela at a ceremony in Cape Town that was attended by parliamentarians, academics, and associates of the university.

There were new diplomatic assignments in this period. In September 1996 Frank Land, a career diplomat, replaced Malcolm Fergusson, South Africa's ambassador to Israel since May 1993. Uri Oren was appointed Israeli ambassador to South Africa in August 1997.

Anti-Semitism

Although anti-Semitism was of marginal significance in South African public life during the period under review, a number of troubling incidents occurred. These included repeated anti-Semitic remarks made by a senior lecturer at the Cape Technicon in Cape Town; a grotesque cartoon with anti-Semitic implications in an advertisement placed by the University of the Witwatersrand in a number of leading newspapers; anti-Semitic phone calls to call-in radio programs; graffiti with anti-Semitic sentiments; letters to various organizations warning of nefarious Jewish practices; Holocaust-denial letters; and anti-Zionist letters and comments that were often anti-Semitic.

Of greater concern was an emergent Islamism in which anti-Israel sentiment very often spilled over into blatant anti-Semitism. When a mosque was bombed in Rustenburg in January 1997, members of the Muslim community made statements suggesting that Israel's Mossad intelligence agency was behind the bombing. Anti-Semitic comments were regularly made on Radio 786, a Cape Town Muslim radio station. In September 1996, Lester Hoffman, chairman of the Cape Council of the Board of Deputies, noted that a special media subcommittee was monitoring all media reports and would take action where necessary. In March 1997, following a program on Radio 786 in which Dr. Ahmed Huber, interviewed in Switzerland, suggested that the Holocaust was exaggerated and the peace process in the Middle East an American Zionist swindle, the board complained both to the Minister of Telecommunications and to the Broadcasting Complaints Commission. In April an "out of court" settlement was arrived at: the SAJBOD would withdraw its allegations, and Radio 786 would publicize an apology in its newscasts.

A poster appearing in Hebron, in the West Bank of Israel, in July 1997, in which Muhammed was depicted by a Jewish extremist as a pig, had substantial repercussions in South Africa. In Pretoria, the Islamic community held a heated protest outside the Israeli embassy, and a stone was hurled at a passing car. In Cape Town,

Muslims protested in front of the Israeli embassy. Following the march, a Cape Town Jewish home that housed a Jewish Book Center was firebombed. Phone threats were also made against a Jewish old-age home and a synagogue. Widespread condemnation of this violence was expressed by the ANC, the Catholic Bishops' Conference, the Methodist Church of South Africa, Imam Rashied Omar, vice-president of the World Conference on Religion and Peace, and others. Omar claimed to speak on behalf of Cape Town's Muslim community. However, the Muslim Judicial Council, the official body representing Muslims, was silent. In a letter to Marlene Bethlehem, President Mandela promised that "the police are taking every possible step to deal with the incident."

JEWISH COMMUNITY

Demography

A national census was conducted in September 1996, but the results were not scheduled to be released until early in 1998. There were indications of stepped-up emigration of young Jews, but no definitive data. In July 1996 a lengthy article in *Rapport,* an Afrikaans Sunday newspaper, claimed the Jewish community had been reduced from 250,000 to 80,000. Jewish communal leaders reacted indignantly, pointing out that the Jewish population had, at its highest, in 1970, numbered only 118,000, and claiming (in an inflated estimate) that the figure in 1990 stood at 105,000. According to Mervyn Smith, president of the SAJBOD, crime and violence were driving young people out of the country. In Tony Leon's view, Jewish emigration was visible largely because it was highly qualified people in the professions who were leaving the country, and Jews were disproportionately represented in that category.

Communal Affairs

Crime, welfare, and the need to establish sound relations with the wider population dominated the Jewish communal agenda. At the Cape Conference of the Board of Jewish Deputies in August 1996, Cape Council chairman Lester Hoffman spoke of renewed waves of emigration among the youth against a backdrop of crime and a perceived shrinking job market associated with affirmative action. At the same conference, Raphael Smith stressed the need for the board to create a positive image of the new South Africa and advocated that young Jews be brought into "the Jewish community business" as full partners. National president Mervyn Smith considered rationalizing social welfare a priority, in particular incorporating different agencies into one fund-raising process.

In September 1996 the minister of Safety and Security in the Gauteng legislature, Mkhabela Sibeko, addressed the Gauteng Council of the SAJBOD about efforts to curb crime. Speaking on the same panel, Andrew Feinstein, member of the provincial legislature for the ANC, claimed that the government had had many successes in this area. Peter Leon, leader of the DP in the Gauteng legislature, disagreed with him, maintaining that crime had steadily worsened.

In an editorial titled "War on Crime," the *South African Jewish Times* questioned the government's ability to deliver on its plans to limit violence. "If a government cannot offer protection for its law-abiding citizens, for personal property and for environmental rights, and cannot ensure efficient law enforcement, then it is never going to succeed in other important tasks. Then economic prosperity will elude it and democracy will disappear into the mists of misery" (October 10, 1996).

In February 1997 a women's interdenominational meeting was held in Johannesburg under the auspices of the Union of Jewish Women (UJW), to protest the government's failure to provide security. In May the South African Union of Jewish Students (SAUJS) joined the ANC Youth League in a Johannesburg "Take Back the Night" march, in response to crimes of rape and violence against women.

In April 1997 an anticrime "Prayer, Protest and Plan" meeting was held by religious leaders in Johannesburg under the auspices of the Office of the Chief Rabbi, the Beth Din, the South African Rabbinical Association, and the Union of Orthodox Synagogues (UOS). Twelve hundred people attended. "We are living in a state of absolute anarchy," exclaimed Rabbi Yossi Goldman, chairman of the South African Rabbinical Association. "We are stretcher cases, ICU cases. Life support machinery is needed—and what does the Government give us? Plaster and Panado [bandaids and aspirin]!" Chief Rabbi Harris called for perpetrators of crime to be "shunned, outlawed, sent to Coventry" by their own families and communities. "We have to create a new and positive climate—an atmosphere that respects life, limb and property, which rejects and shuns each and every criminal as a damager of South Africa's chance of progress." A call was made for visible policing (*The Citizen,* April 8, 1997).

Tensions within the wider society were reflected in the Jewish community. A special project, Shalom Bayit (Peace in the Home), was established toward the end of 1996 to help deal with Jewish domestic abuse. Stanley Rothbart, honorary vice-president of the Society for the Jewish Handicapped, told a Jewish social-services conference in Johannesburg that the community had "recorded increased incidents of individual and family instability, substance abuse, divorce, loss of earnings and the impact of trauma on individuals and families." The increase in such traumas was confirmed by Brenda Solarsh, speaking at the 50th anniversary of Jewish Community Services in February 1997.

In January 1997 major donors and trustees of Jewish organizations in Johannesburg set up a commission of inquiry into the financial affairs of Jewish organizations and institutions. Known as Operation 2000, the commission included among its tasks an assessment of the viability and feasibility of Jewish day schools in Johannesburg. Sam Abrahams, formerly of the Arthur Anderson management firm, was appointed to head the commission.

In March 1997 a prominent communal leader, Russel Gaddin, criticized Jewish leaders who employed "scare tactics" to raise funds. In his view they were sowing "the seeds of despair" with their bleak and negative—and, he claimed, untrue—portrayal of the community's condition. However, in June, Selwyn Wald, chairman of the Society of the Handicapped, spoke of a situation of mounting peril for the underprivileged in the Jewish community, caused by the economic climate, draining emigration, and apathy.

Chief Rabbi Harris hit out at Jewish emigrants to countries such as Australia and Canada for abandoning their moral obligations to elderly parents and to the South African Jewish community. Doctors were especially criticized, since they had been educated at great cost to the government. Rabbi Harris suggested imposing a tax on Jewish emigrants to countries other than Israel, which would go toward maintaining the South African Jewish community. He recommended a figure of $250 per family per annum.

Notwithstanding communal concerns about security and welfare, Chief Rabbi of the Commonwealth Jonathan Sacks told the 39th national congress of the SAJ-BOD in August 1997 that the Jewish community would meet the challenges. "You will get through, because this country is strong and, more importantly, because you, as a Jewish community, are quite exceptional. There are very few, if any, Jewish communities in the world that have your warmth, your sense of loyalty to the Jewish heritage, the strength of your Jewish institutions, your commitment to the State of Israel and, above all, your sense of community."

At the same conference, Gesher chairman Geoff Sifrin called for the board to be more open to diversity, argument, dissent, and debate and to be a home for all sectors of the Jewish world. "In the past," he maintained, "the Board was not open to diversity and pluralism and gave a message that only certain narrow conservative attitudes to Judaism, Israel and South Africa would be tolerated," with the result that "many Jews felt alienated from the Board."

At the conference Rabbi Harris was presented with an award for outstanding leadership. Two months later, at a gala banquet in Cape Town marking the tenth anniversary of the chief rabbi's appointment, special tribute was paid to Rabbi Harris by President Mandela. "Chief Rabbi Harris is the spiritual leader of the community which has played an indispensable part in our national life. In years to come, when the history of our transition is written, his name will be among those leaders who lent a hand in the efforts to establish democracy, to heal divisions, and to start the process of building a better life" (*SAJT,* November 21, 1997).

A number of communal organizations celebrated anniversaries in the period under review: the Union of Jewish Women its 60th, Our Parents Home and Jewish Community Services their 50th, Magen David Adom its 50th year in South Africa, and Arcadia Jewish Children's Home its 90th year of caring for children.

Community Relations

The need for South African Jewry to reach out to the wider community was underscored by Chief Rabbi Harris when he introduced his booklet *Jewish Obligations to the Non-Jew* at a special gathering in Johannesburg in July 1996. In his remarks, Harris pointed out that the chief crime of South Africa's apartheid era had been separate development, and that the antidote was joint development. His booklet was "deliberately concise and concentrated," in order to stimulate debate on how the Jewish community could help build the New South Africa. The booklet was published under the auspices of Tikkun.

Speaking at the *South African Jewish Times* Business Achiever of the Year dinner in September 1996, Deputy Minister of Finance Gill Marcus called on the Jewish business community to share in a partnership with the government to "bring new life, a new vision, a new creativity" to the country, and to reach out to other groups that had not been as privileged as the Jews.

A number of community projects were initiated. Temple Israel in Johannesburg undertook to help support a day-care center in the inner city. The Union of Jewish Women started a project of providing clothing for rape victims who arrive at a district surgeon's office with their garments badly torn.

The South African Board of Jewish Education (SABJE) established a computer outreach program for pupils, teachers, and administrators at primary and high schools in Alexandria, a black township in Johannesburg. Gesher, a Jewish group promoting active involvement in South African society, continued to engage in social action.

Kim Feinberg established the Foundation for Holocaust and Tolerance Education in Johannesburg. Feinberg was South African coordinator for Steven Spielberg's Survivors of the Shoah Foundation.

In September 1997 the *Sunday Independent* ran a lengthy article on the possible Jewish roots of the Lemba ethnic group in the foothills of the Zoutpansberg mountains in Northern Province. This black group, according to anthropologists, had some customs that suggest a link to ancient Semitic cultures. A spokesman for the 40,000-strong South African Lemba community (there are 15,000 more in other parts of southern Africa) claimed that the group originated from a Jewish tribe in Sana'a Yemen (September 14, 1997).

Israel-Related Activity

Addressing the IUA-UCF (Israel United Appeal-United Community Fund) campaign opening in October 1996, Jewish Agency and World Zionist Organization chairman Avraham Burg warned Jewish leaders against putting local needs above those of Israel or assuming that Israel no longer needed financial aid. Raising funds for Israel prevented the growth of a "shtetl mentality" and actually enhanced the raising of money for local needs, he maintained. Burg announced the creation of a new program, Mabit, whereby Israelis could contribute funds to help preserve Judaism and unite Jewry. Speaking for the IUA-UCF campaign again in March 1997, Burg warned of a dangerous trend among Jews in South Africa and elsewhere to ignore the problems of Jews in the world and to focus only on their own concerns. In September 1997 Errol Goodman was appointed national director of the IUA-UCF.

South African Jews shared world Jewry's concern over efforts by Israel's chief rabbinate to delegitimate non-Orthodox Jews. In an editorial titled "Who Is a Jew?" the *South African Jewish Times* (June 13, 1997) condemned the exclusivity of the Israeli religious leadership: "Thus, at this point, for Israel to be a homeland for all Jews, it has to respect and protect the diversity of beliefs of all who live in the country, and by extension, the heterogeneity of a long heritage. In a democracy, a dictatorial attitude, however justly or legitimately felt, is bound to deepen divisions, rather than show a respect for religion per se."

The Mizrachi Organization of South Africa and Krok Vision, together with the International Institute in Israel, established a joint project, He'atid, the Future, in October 1995. It offered leadership training courses in Israel for carefully selected individuals concerned with social and economic development in their countries. Shirley Zar, head of town planning at the Witwatersrand Technikon, Johannesburg, introduced the Israeli "moshav" model of cooperative village in the black community. Her program was supported by the South African Associates of Ben-Gurion University and included a partnership involving the Israeli government, Ben-Gurion University, the local Jewish community (under the umbrella of Tikkun), the South West Gauteng Farmers' Cooperative, and Murray and Roberts Properties.

Aliyah 2000 was launched in August 1996 by the South African Zionist Federation, a project offering a wide range of information programs intended to present Israel as a viable alternative for Jews emigrating from South Africa, together with the inducement of attractive absorption packages. "We are concerned that so many of our community are leaving South Africa and so few are coming to Israel," explained Hertzel Katz, chairman of Telfed, the organization for South African immigrants in Israel.

A chair in criminal law was established at the Hebrew University of Jerusalem in the name of Justice Basil Wunsch, in tribute to his dedicated service as a jurist and to the South African Jewish community.

Religion

"Jews for Judaism" was established under the auspices of the Union of Orthodox Synagogues (UOS) in July 1996; it was affiliated with a group of the same name founded in the United States in 1985. Headed by Rabbi Craig Kacef, the organization was formed to combat the growing number of cults springing up in South Africa and to make the Jewish community aware of anti-Jewish missionary work.

Chief Rabbi Harris commended the government for passing the Divorce Amendment Act of 1996, which would help to rectify the plight of *agunot*, "chained women," and others whose spouses would not give them a religious divorce, even though the marriage was terminated civilly. The amendment provides that where a couple has undergone a religious marriage, the civil divorce may be withheld until a religious divorce has been arranged.

On Simhat Torah morning in 1996, 24 women assembled at a private home in Glenhazel, Johannesburg, where they took part in a women's Torah reading, without incident. One year earlier, a similar reading was disrupted by male members of the Jewish community.

In February 1997 Rabbi Ben Isaacson returned from Zimbabwe to serve the newly founded L.I. Rabinowitz Jewish Center in Johannesburg, named after a former chief rabbi of South Africa. The new congregation is committed to Halakhah but is not part of the UOS. Rabbi Isaacson said that he would abide by Beth Din rulings and that decisions would be made in consultation with Israeli and local rabbis. The center planned to concentrate on issues facing Jewish women within the framework of Jewish law, as well as "helping those staying in South Africa with the fears and burdens facing them on a daily basis, such as crime and emigration," said Rabbi Isaacson.

A new Orthodox synagogue, Emet Congregation, was founded in Johannesburg, and a new community center–synagogue was opened in George. Adath Jeshurun Congregation in Johannesburg, founded in 1936 by German-Jewish immigrants, followers of Rabbi Shimshon Raphael Hirsch, celebrated its 60th anniversary.

At the biennial conference of the UOS held in Johannesburg in May 1997, Rabbi Harris called for greater communal discipline, saying, "We are not in a normal situation, but we are in a threatening situation." He was referring to the fact that many synagogues that were no longer spiritually or financially viable insisted on hanging on instead of taking the obvious step of amalgamating with other synagogues in the area. Acknowledging that "shtieblech were indeed able to exert a high-level spirituality," Rabbi Harris said that Johannesburg was becoming full of "mini-shuls," to the detriment of the wider community. "Our community is far too fragmented and, in these difficult times, we must consolidate as much as possible." He also called for increased giving of charity, greater involvement in the broader community, and less pessimism.

South Africa's first woman rabbi, Bonnie Lee Leavy, from Pittsburgh, Pennsylvania, was appointed to serve Pretoria's Temple Menorah, under the auspices of the South African Union for Progressive Judaism.

In May 1997 the World Union for Progressive Judaism (WUPJ) held its 28th convention in Johannesburg and Cape Town, with over 350 delegates representing 26 countries attending. The theme of the conference was "Confronting Radical Change." Tribute was paid to President Mandela (who received the group's Humanitarian Award), to F.W. de Klerk, and to the local Jewish community for its support of the freedom struggle. In his opening address, WUPJ executive director Rabbi Richard Hirsch rejected the role of chief rabbis as obsolete and unnecessary, denounced Chief Rabbi Jonathan Sacks of Great Britain for refusing to attend the funeral of Rabbi Hugo Gryn, a distinguished Reform rabbi in London, and attacked the Israeli rabbinate's exclusivity. "If, as we declare long and loud, we are one people with one destiny, then we must have one world-wide policy. The winds of pluralism cannot prevail throughout the Diaspora and suddenly stop blowing when they reach the eastern shores of the Mediterranean," he said.

Education

The South African Board of Jewish Education (SABJE) announced a mid-1996 increase of 16 percent in school fees at King David School, Johannesburg. The chairman, Jeffrey Bortz, cited as reasons for the hike an increase in teachers' salaries and interest rates and the loss of pupils through emigration. Bortz pointed out that the SABJE needed to eliminate a large debt to the banks of approximately 10 million rand. A few months later Bortz indicated that the midyear measures had brought financial stability, helped by a 50-percent cut in the fee assistance program. In addition, the Hebrew Teachers' Training Seminary was to be phased out in three stages. There were further fee increases at the start of 1997.

Starting in 1997, Carmel College, Durban's only Jewish day school, was managed by Crawford Education Holdings, a private education company. This followed a general reduction in the number of Jewish pupils in the school. The Jewish character of the school was protected by frequent consultations between the Durban Hebrew Schools Association and Crawford.

In August 1996 the Isaac and Jessie Kaplan Centre at the University of Cape Town hosted an international conference on "Jewries at the Frontier." The conference was organized jointly by Professors Milton Shain (University of Cape Town) and Sander Gilman (University of Chicago) and attracted leading scholars from all over the world. In September 1997 the Kaplan Centre and the Institute for Contemporary Jewry at the Hebrew University held a joint international colloquium on "Zionism in the English-Speaking World—The First Hundred Years."

Culture

"The Jewish Sound," an hourlong program of Jewish music, drama, and phone-ins, hosted by Rabbi Yossi Goldman and sponsored by Chabad House, began airing on a community radio station in Gauteng Province in August 1996.

Moira Blumenthal Productions was the big winner at the First National Bank Vita Awards for its production of the play *Kafka Dances*. L. Rubin Booksellers, specializing in Jewish books and religious items, was forced into liquidation after 94 years in Johannesburg. The SAJBOD and Rand Afrikaans University hosted "The Dreyfus Affair: An Exhibition of Art, Truth and Justice" in August 1996.

The exhibition, which was also displayed at the Kaplan Centre for Jewish Studies at the University of Cape Town and at Rust en Vreugd in Cape Town, comprised material from the private collection of Dr. Lorraine and Martin Beitler of Miami, Florida.

Publications

Some noteworthy new publications of Jewish interest were *People of the Book* by Marcia Leveson; *Reverberations* by Phyllis Lewson; *Cutting Through the Mountain,* edited by Immanuel Suttner; *Last Walk in Naryskin Park* by Rose Zwi; and *Bibliography of South African Jewry* by Veronica Belling.

Personalia

Justice Richard Goldstone was installed as chancellor of the University of the Witwatersrand. Goldstone recently returned to South Africa after a two-year term as prosecutor of the United Nations War Crimes Tribunals for the former Yugoslavia and Rwanda. He continued as a judge on the Constitutional Court.

Meyer Kahn, a leading industrialist, was appointed chief executive of the South African Police Services for two years.

Justice Cecil Margo received an award from the Friends of the Israeli Defense Forces. In 1948 he responded to Ben-Gurion's urgent appeal for him to come to Israel to advise on the establishment and organization of the Israeli Air Force. Prof. Colin Tatz of Macquarie University in Australia received an honorary doctorate from his alma mater, the University of Natal.

Among prominent South African Jews who died between July 1996 and December 1997 were Etienne Mureinik, a distinguished legal academic specializing in constitutional and administrative law; Clive Menell, a leading industrialist and deputy chairman of the Nelson Mandela Children's Fund; Leonard Schach, lawyer turned theater director; Jack Penn, world-renowned plastic surgeon; Issy Sachar, prominent businessman and indefatigable Zionist worker; Sally Herbert Frankel, renowned economist; Ethel Aaron, founder of the famous Aarons, makers of *pletzlach, taiglach,* and other traditional Jewish confections; Tamar Smith, tireless Zionist and communal worker and humanitarian; Ronnie Bethlehem, a prominent businessman murdered by hijackers; Olga Kirsch, South African-born poet resident in Israel; Muriel Maisels, honorary life president of the World Zionist Organization of South Africa; and Rudolf Raphaely, a leader in South Africa's international trade, philanthropist, and Jewish communal worker.

MILTON SHAIN

Israel

THE 18-MONTH PERIOD FROM July 1996 to December 1997 was marked by a serious reversal in the Israeli-Palestinian peace process that negatively affected Israel's relations with both its Arab neighbors and the United States. It was also a period in which Prime Minister Benjamin Netanyahu appeared to be stumbling from one crisis to the next—at times on the domestic front, at times on the international scene.

After coming to power in June 1996, Netanyahu adopted a much more skeptical and hard-line approach to the peace process than that of his Labor predecessors. While he did sign the Hebron redeployment agreement in January 1997, in which he also committed to carrying out a further three withdrawals in the West Bank by mid-1998, it was one of the few bright spots in a period in which the Oslo agreements appeared to be on the verge of unraveling. Yasir Arafat's reluctance to clamp down on terrorist activity in the areas under his control served as a major stumbling block to progress, especially after Hamas suicide attacks in March 1997 in Tel Aviv, and in July and September in Jerusalem, which left a total of 24 dead.

The Mashaal affair—a botched attempt by Mossad agents to assassinate a senior Hamas official in the Jordanian capital of Amman in late September 1997—brought Israel's ties with the Hashemite Kingdom to the brink of collapse, and Israel was forced to pay a heavy price in the aftermath of the fiasco.

Finding himself embroiled in one crisis after another, Netanyahu displayed an uncanny ability to extract himself from seemingly hopeless situations. One close shave, the Bar-On affair—an influence-peddling scandal involving some of the country's leading political figures—almost brought his tenure to an abrupt end.

The period was marked by a significant economic slowdown as growth dropped off and unemployment rose dramatically. Netanyahu, though, was praised by many economists for pushing ahead vigorously with his privatization promises and for cutting government spending.

The end of 1997 found the prime minister facing three major hurdles: coalition wrangling over the proposed budget, the next phase of army redeployment in the West Bank, and the battle over conversion to Judaism, which pitted his religious coalition partners against the Conservative and Reform movements, backed by American Jews.

POLITICAL AND DIPLOMATIC DEVELOPMENTS

The Peace Process Falters

In the 18 months under review, the peace process experienced its worst setback since its inception in 1993, and the Israeli-Palestinian conflict assumed its old mantle of intransigence. During the campaign for the 1996 general election, Netanyahu had been evasive about his willingness to meet with Palestinian leader Yasir Arafat, were he to become prime minister, telling one interviewer that he would send his foreign minister to meet the head of the Palestinian Authority (PA). Indeed, in late July, Foreign Minister David Levy became the first senior member of the new government to meet with Arafat, a move that sparked strong criticism from right-wing militants. But Netanyahu continued to waver, refusing to give a clear indication of his own readiness for a face-to-face encounter with the Palestinian leader.

Through July and August the government did ease the closure of the West Bank and Gaza Strip that had been imposed by the previous Labor government after a spate of Hamas suicide bombings in February and March 1996 claimed 60 lives. But that did little to placate the Palestinians, who became increasingly angered over fresh developments. In late July the new government decided to place on the market 3,000 housing units in the West Bank that had been frozen by the Labor government under Yitzhak Rabin. Then, it announced in August that it would renew building in Jewish settlements in the territories. Following that, a day after the PA shut three of its offices in East Jerusalem — regarded as illegal by the Israelis — as a confidence-building gesture, the Likud-led municipality sent bulldozers into the Old City to demolish a Canadian-sponsored Palestinian youth club that had allegedly been built illegally.

Arafat also contributed to the growing tension with a number of inflammatory statements. He told a Gaza rally, for instance, in July, that the Palestinians were "obligated to all the martyrs who died for Jerusalem . . . till the last martyr, Yehiya Ayash" — a reference to the Hamas suicide mastermind known as "the Engineer," who was responsible for the deaths of dozens of Israelis and who was blown up and killed by a booby-trapped mobile phone in his Gaza hideout in January 1996. (Foreign papers reported that the operation was most likely the work of the General Security Services.)

Finally, after three months of sidestepping and procrastination, Netanyahu succumbed to U.S. pressure as well as to the entreaties of President Ezer Weizman, who told the prime minister, "If you don't meet with him, I will. . . ." On September 4, 1996, Netanyahu and Arafat exchanged handshakes and sat down for their first meeting, at the northern entrance to the Gaza Strip. It was clearly a historic moment: Netanyahu was breaking a right-wing taboo, talking with a man labeled by many in his camp as a murderer and a war criminal. While the prime minister described the meeting as "one of the toughest moments of my life," Arafat was more upbeat: "The door is open now for us to reactivate our negotiations at all levels," he said.

THE TUNNEL EPISODE

But the rapprochement proved to be fleeting. Only three weeks later, Israeli soldiers and Palestinian police were locked in bloody gun battles, and riots were breaking out in East Jerusalem and across the West Bank and Gaza. The deadly clashes were ignited by a decision to open a new exit—onto the Via Dolorosa—from an archaeological site, a tunnel that runs parallel to the Temple Mount and that opens out at the other end onto the Western Wall plaza. The decision in the early hours of September 24 to open the Hasmonean tunnel—an aqueduct that channeled water to the Second Temple 2,000 years ago—was taken by Netanyahu despite intelligence warnings that it could well result in widespread Palestinian violence.

The Palestinians, with Arafat setting the tone, charged that the construction of the exit threatened the Islamic holy structures on the Temple Mount; on September 25, pitched gun battles between Israeli soldiers and Palestinian policemen ensued. Five Palestinians died on the first day of clashes; several Israeli soldiers were wounded. "War in the Territories," trumpeted the front-page headline of one of the leading dailies. The army responded by sending large numbers of troops into the territories, but the violence escalated.

The very next day, September 26, a crowd laid siege to Joseph's Tomb in Nablus, attacking the compound where Israeli soldiers were holed up with rocks, gasoline bombs, and live fire. By the time the Israel Defense Forces (IDF) finally succeeded in extracting the soldiers, six were dead and another seven were wounded. The army's next move was to station tanks at the outskirts of West Bank towns to deter further violence. When the violence finally waned after a few days, 15 Israeli soldiers and around 70 Palestinians lay dead.

Three of Netanyahu's predecessors—Labor prime ministers Yitzhak Rabin and Shimon Peres, and even the Likud's Yitzhak Shamir—had resisted opening the tunnel exit on the advice of their intelligence experts. Now, intelligence reports indicated that the deadlocked peace process and the Palestinians' poor economic situation had raised frustration in the territories to the boiling point. Security chiefs suggested that the tunnel only be opened in conjunction with progress in the peace process so as to mute any potential for violence. But a combination of factors—inexperience, a poor reading of the situation, and political pressure from the right—appear to have led Netanyahu to ignore the advice.

IDF heads, along with Netanyahu, accused Arafat of exploiting the tunnel opening as a pretext for violence. Government officials insisted that the tunnel was simply a tourist site and that excavation and construction there posed no threat whatsoever to Islamic holy places. David Bar-Illan, a senior Netanyahu aide, said Arafat had to shoulder the blame, "wholly, solely and totally for the incitement." Bar-Illan, though, did admit that the government had "misread" its intelligence.

With the tunnel incident having brought the peace process to the brink of collapse, U.S. president Bill Clinton announced that he would host an emergency summit in Washington, on October 1–2, and immediately summoned both Netanyahu and Arafat. The prime minister refused to close the tunnel, but the two leaders completed their brief summit with a curious photo-op in which Netanyahu could be seen warmly shaking Arafat's hand.

The Hebron Agreement

The violence did not resume, and the two parties, with intense American coaxing, began the arduous process of negotiating the next stage of the Oslo accords—the IDF's withdrawal from the West Bank city of Hebron. Under the Oslo II accords, signed in September 1995, Israel had already withdrawn from six of the seven major West Bank cities, leaving them under Arafat's control. The handover of Hebron had been delayed by Shimon Peres after the Hamas suicide-bombing campaign in the early part of 1996 and had still not been carried out by the time Netanyahu won the election in May.

Hebron was unique. Unlike the other West Bank cities, it was the only place where Jews and Arabs lived together. Moreover, the city was home to the Cave of the Patriarchs, where Hebron's 500 Jews and many of its 120,000 Arabs prayed in adjoining halls. The negotiations see-sawed, agreement appearing at times to be at hand, only to slip away as new problems emerged. In mid-December hopes of concluding a deal were almost completely extinguished when Palestinian terrorists fired on the car of residents from the West Bank settlement of Beit El, killing a mother and her 12-year-old son. An incensed Netanyahu threatened to establish a new settlement in response to the attack. He was talked out of the idea by Defense Minister Yitzhak Mordechai and Foreign Minister Levy, after security chiefs warned that such a move could well ignite another violent showdown with the Palestinians and was sure to spur international disapproval. Still, the cabinet did decide to renew economic incentives to settlers that had been canceled by the previous Labor government.

Within months of the general election, the old Israeli-Palestinian cycle of mutual blame and mistrust had reemerged. Arafat suspected that Netanyahu would go through with the Hebron deal, bask in international acclaim for having concluded it, but then essentially freeze the Oslo process and begin expanding Jewish settlements. This was a major concern for the Palestinians, who feared that the new government planned to strengthen Israel's hold in the West Bank and loosen theirs ahead of any final-status talks. "They say Jerusalem is theirs forever," said Abu Ala, chairman of the Palestinian Legislative Council and a senior negotiator, in mid-December. "They say no to a Palestinian state, that settlements are to be expanded. I fear that the real Israeli policy is to kill the process." For his part, Netanyahu saw Arafat as lacking in credibility and believed the Palestinian leader would take all he could from the Oslo process and then continue to demand more, with the constant threat of violence in the background as a means of pressuring Israel. Netanyahu's aides also accused Arafat of deliberately dragging out the Hebron talks.

The talks were in jeopardy again on January 1, 1997, this time because of Jewish violence. Noam Friedman, a soldier doing his regular service, indiscriminately opened fire in the city's crowded vegetable market, wounding seven Palestinians before being overwhelmed by fellow soldiers. Miraculously, he did not kill anyone. The 19-year-old Friedman, from the settlement of Ma'aleh Adumim near Jerusalem, reportedly told police that his intention was to prevent the Hebron redeployment. "I fired to kill as many Arabs as possible," Friedman reportedly said. The Palestinians saw the incident as proof that they required increased protection from Jewish extremists; Netanyahu denounced the attack, saying "criminal acts" of this nature would not scuttle a Hebron deal. Terror struck again on January 9, when 12 people were injured by two bombs that exploded eight minutes apart at the old central bus station in Tel Aviv, but there were no serious injuries.

Talks continued despite the attacks, and after months of painstaking negotiations, a deal was reached on January 15. The next day, by 11 votes to 7, the cabinet approved the arrangement, which also provided for three further army redeployments by mid-1998. Science Minister Beni Begin, a fervent opponent of the agreement, announced his resignation, and some settler leaders accused Netanyahu of betraying them. While the left declared its support, Yitzhak Rabin's widow, Leah, sadly reflected that her husband had died because of opposition on the right to a pact that was now being entered into by a right-wing government. On January 16, the Knesset voted 87-17 (with one abstention) in favor of the Hebron agreement. The next day, when the army redeployed in the city, Benjamin Netanyahu became the first right-wing prime minister to forfeit West Bank land.

DEBATE OVER NEXT MOVES

The Oslo accords gave Israel the right to determine the size of each redeployment, but they also determined that the army should pull back to "specified military locations." According to right-wing critics, that definition could only be interpreted as referring to military bases, which would mean handing over close to 95 percent of the West Bank to the Palestinians by the end of the third withdrawal, thus leaving Israel with few cards to play going into final-status negotiations. Netanyahu, though, found support on the left. Labor MK Yossi Beilin argued that the phrase applied not only to military bases but also to strategic areas in the West Bank such as the Jordan Rift and settlements. Meretz MK Amnon Rubinstein also came to the prime minister's aid, writing in a letter to Netanyahu that withdrawal from up to 50 percent of West Bank land by the end of the third redeployment would be in line with Oslo stipulations.

The Hebron agreement threw the far right into turmoil. They had demonstrated fiercely against Rabin and worked strenuously to get Netanyahu elected. Now, "their" prime minister had not only given over West Bank land to the Palestinians but had signed a document including provisions for further withdrawals. Elyakim Ha'etzni, one of the settler leaders of the far right, described Hebron as "our Pearl Harbor." The Greater Israel protagonists, he said, "were taken completely by surprise. Netanyahu wrote one thing in his book [*A Place Among the Nations*], and then proceeded to do the exact opposite."

But the settlers appeared divided on how to proceed. Some, like Ha'etzni, supported the creation of a new Greater Israel political organization with a new leader and a strong campaign against Netanyahu and his government. The mainstream settler leadership supported a more moderate line, convinced that Netanyahu's government was the best they could hope for, and that it would be self-defeating to try to topple him. "We must be pragmatic and do all we can to save what can still be saved," said Pinhas Wallerstein, head of the Council of Jewish Settlements.

Talk of a national unity government surfaced periodically during this period, but never came to fruition. Shimon Peres met with Infrastructure Minister Ariel Sharon in December 1996 to discuss the possibility. But most observers estimated that Netanyahu, who had alluded to the idea of forming a government with the Labor Party, had only done so to clip the wings of his own recalcitrant ministers. In February 1997 there was renewed national unity talk, with Likud Knesset member Michael Eitan expressing strong support for the idea. He argued that Israel required a broad-based governing coalition in order to take the tough decisions that would be needed in final-status negotiations with the Palestinians. Eitan had already laid much of the ideological groundwork for a Likud-Labor alliance in a series of meetings with Labor's Yossi Beilin in which the two reached agreement on the outlines of a final settlement with the Palestinians. Ultimately, nothing came of the discussions and the national unity idea faded again.

The signing of the Hebron agreement had raised hopes that the peace process would move forward more smoothly. For Netanyahu, it won newfound international acclaim. At the annual World Economic Forum in Davos in early February, the prime minister was the center of attention as world leaders clambered to meet with him. Optimism was further fueled by the mid-February release of more than two dozen Palestinian women security prisoners from Israeli jails. (The previous Labor government had failed to free the women prisoners due to strong right-wing opposition over the fact that the group included convicted killers.)

HAR HOMAH AND THE FIRST REDEPLOYMENT

The thaw in Israeli-Palestinian relations did not last long. In late February the government gave the go-ahead for a Jewish housing project to be built at Har

Homah, a hilltop situated just outside Israel's pre-1967 border but inside present Jerusalem city limits, and in an area the Palestinians viewed as the site of the capital of their future state. The post-Hebron optimism evaporated as Har Homah became the new battleground in the struggle over Jerusalem and plunged the peace process into what would become an extended deadlock.

In the period leading to the Har Homah decision, Netanyahu found himself trapped between pressure from the United States and the Europeans, who were against the project, and elements in his own governing coalition who threatened to bring him down if he did not unleash the bulldozers. The Americans made it clear that the 6,500-unit development constituted a serious obstacle to peace. Jordan's King Hussein warned Netanyahu that the project could seriously endanger the peace process, and Arafat charged that it was "totally unacceptable . . . a violation of everything written and agreed upon." The Shin Bet security service warned of Palestinian violence if the development went ahead.

On the domestic front Netanyahu faced coalition members who threatened to topple him if he caved in to international pressure. They included members of the centrist Third Way Party, and especially a group of 17 right-wing Knesset members who had banded together to insure that Netanyahu did not make further concessions after Hebron, who threatened to absent themselves from crucial Knesset votes if he did not begin construction.

Domestic pressure prevailed, and the prime minister sent in the bulldozers. U.S. president Clinton was unimpressed: "I would have preferred the decision not to have been made because I don't think it builds confidence," he said. "I think it builds mistrust." But Netanyahu was defiant, insisting that Israel, like any other country, had an inalienable right to build in its capital. "Even if the whole world is against us," he announced, "we'll build in Jerusalem."

Arafat loudly denounced the Har Homah decision, warning that it had plunged the two sides into "the worst crisis" since the start of Oslo. The Israeli government, he charged, "is making us a laughing-stock. . . . I have no trust in Netanyahu. We are heading toward the abyss."

With the bloody aftermath of the September 1996 tunnel decision obviously still fresh in his mind, Netanyahu tried to temper Palestinian anger by promising to build 3,015 housing units for Arabs in ten different East Jerusalem neighborhoods. But Palestinian leaders were not impressed. They rejected Netanyahu's proposal as a fig leaf, pointing to the small number of housing units that had been built for Arabs in Jerusalem since 1967. (The statistics showed that while about one-third of East Jerusalem had been expropriated since 1967 to build almost 36,000 homes for Jews, fewer than 600 Arab homes had been built with government assistance in that same period.)

Palestinian leaders argued that the shortage of Arab housing in East Jerusalem was a separate issue from Har Homah, which in their eyes was connected to the future status of Jerusalem. "To have any hope of reaching a compromise on Jerusalem you have to keep some sort of continuity between east Jerusalem and the Palestinian areas, and this project cuts that continuity," said Ghassan Andoni, a physics professor at Bir Zeit University in the West Bank and one of the leaders of the battle against Har Homah. "Israel is telling the Palestinians that East Jerusalem is outside the negotiations, that the final status of Jerusalem has already been defined."

The strategic importance of the Har Homah project, for which two-thirds of the land had been expropriated from Jews and one-third from Arabs, was undeniable. A glance at a map confirmed that Har Homah would help fill in the line of Jewish neighborhoods on the capital's southeastern perimeter. In so doing, it would erect a barrier between the Arab population of East Jerusalem and Palestinian towns to the south, like Bethlehem, and would undermine Palestinian demands to turn the eastern part of the city into their future capital.

All attempts to find a compromise solution to the disputed hilltop project failed. Tension mounted further in early March when Israel demanded that the Palestinians close four offices they were operating in East Jerusalem. On March 10, chief Palestinian negotiator Abu Mazen handed in his resignation after another unsuccessful meeting with Foreign Minister Levy. Arafat rejected the letter, but there were reports that the Palestinian leader had become so disillusioned that he was considering leaving Gaza and relocating to Cairo.

(The UN General Assembly passed a resolution in April, and again in July, condemning the Har Homah project; the only two countries to support Israel were the United States and the tiny island of Micronesia.)

Further Redeployment

The situation deteriorated even further when the government made a decision on March 6 regarding the amount of territory to be ceded to the Palestinians as part of the first of three further phases of IDF redeployment in the West Bank. According to the agreement, Israel had the right to decide unilaterally on the scope of the withdrawal. When it did, the Palestinians were enraged—in part by the fact that they had not been consulted, but mainly because of the limited scope of the announced withdrawal. Arafat denounced the decision as a "trick and conspiracy against the peace process." He was referring to the fact that out of the total of 9 percent of West Bank land the government said it was transferring to full Palestinian control (known as "Area A" in the Oslo accords), about 7 percent was already under partial Palestinian control ("Area B"). Less than 2 percent of the proposed handover was territory under full Israeli control ("Area C").

Netanyahu, for his part, told the Knesset plenum that the decisions regarding both Har Homah and the redeployment had sent a clear message to the Palestinians. "I think they [the Palestinians] were convinced a Palestinian state would arise, with half of Jerusalem as its capital," he said. "And now, after the further redeployment and after Har Homah, they understand that this state will not be created."

In fact, no further redeployment took place in 1997. Arafat rejected the March decision on the ground that it was unilateral—even though this was Israel's right—and because the amount of territory designated by the government was too small.

SUICIDE BOMBERS RETURN

The rising Palestinian anger spilled over into violent protest on March 20, when demonstrators clashed with Israeli soldiers in Bethlehem. The protests soon spread to Hebron. Chief of Staff Amnon Shahak warned that if armed Palestinians participated in the demonstrations, "it won't be an *intifada* but a war."

A yearlong hiatus in suicide bombings came to an end on March 21 when a Palestinian bomber walked into the packed Cafe Apropo in downtown Tel Aviv and detonated an explosives-filled suitcase he was carrying. Three women were killed, and another 40 people were injured in the blast. An incensed Netanyahu accused Arafat of giving a "green light" to terror and immediately demanded that the Palestinian leader destroy the "terrorist infrastructure" in the areas under his control as a precondition for the continuation of the peace process. "They have to do a lot more than just rounding up the usual suspects, and then releasing them after a few days or weeks," he fumed.

Israel handed Arafat a list of Islamic militants it wanted behind bars, insisting that there would be no peace process if he did not move swiftly against the terrorists. But the Palestinians, angry over the Har Homah project and the redeployment issue, were loath to comply with Israel's demands. In response, Arafat exasperated his Israeli counterparts, as well as the Americans, by flying off on a tour of South Asia, where he offered his services as a mediator in the conflict between the Sri Lankan government and rebel Tamil Tigers. Jibril Rajub, the Palestinian Authority's security chief in the West Bank, declared that "security cooperation was buried with the first bulldozer that went up on Jabal Abu Ghneim (Har Homah)."

These and similar comments by leading Palestinian officials left the government with the impression that Arafat was tacitly condoning the use of terror as a weapon against Israel because of its decision at Har Homah. Both Shahak and the head of military intelligence, Moshe Ya'alon, backed Netanyahu's claim, saying that Arafat had indirectly signaled to Hamas and the Islamic Jihad that they had his blessing to renew terror attacks. On March 9, they said, Arafat had met with the heads of the Islamic movements after a long break and had also released Hamas militants from Gaza jails, including Ibrahim Makadme, a leading figure in the organization's military wing. Ya'akov Peri, a former Shin Bet (security services) chief, said that while Arafat had to bear the blame for easing up on the Islamic militants, it was not clear to what degree he was directly culpable. "From my experience, Arafat was always careful not to give direct orders—neither for bomb attacks nor for foiling attacks," he said.

A poll conducted in late March by the Palestinian Center for Public Opinion found that a full 49 percent of Palestinians supported the March 21 suicide bombing. In the territories, violent confrontations continued. Two Islamic Jihad suicide bombers blew themselves up near two Jewish settlements in the Gaza Strip on April 1; miraculously, no one was injured. Israeli security sources estimated that the intended targets were school buses transporting children from the settlements of Kfar Darom and Netzarim.

A week later, fierce rioting broke out in Hebron after a yeshivah student shot and killed a Palestinian near the Cave of Makhpelah (Cave of the Patriarchs), after he and a fellow student had some type of acid thrown in their faces. In the ensuing clashes with the army, two Palestinians were killed and a further 90 injured. Six Israelis were injured. The army poured troops into the area in an effort to quell the protests.

A few days later, Israeli security forces cracked a Hamas terror cell operating out of the West Bank town of Surif, which had been responsible for the killing of 11 Israelis in an 18-month period, including the Apropo bomb blast. It was also revealed that the group was responsible for the kidnapping and murder of Sharon Edri, 20, a soldier who disappeared seven months earlier. Members of the cell led the security forces to the spot where they had buried the young man.

With the peace process floundering, there was no progress on a host of other bilateral issues, including the opening of a safe passage for Palestinians between Gaza and the West Bank and the opening of a harbor and an airport in Gaza. After months of unproductive wrangling over the opening of the Palestinian Authority airport at Dahaniya, in Gaza, Israel finally granted Arafat permission to use the facility—but only for himself. Fearful that his people would view such an arrangement as a sellout to Israel, Arafat chose not to accept the offer.

In advance of an early April meeting with President Clinton, Netanyahu announced that Israel would not "succumb to the dictates and threats of terror" and would continue to build at Har Homah and in the territories. It was a line he adopted in his meeting with the U.S. president on April 8, insisting that Arafat take strong steps against the terrorists in the areas under his control and restore security cooperation with Israel. But he also said he was ready and willing to move quickly to final-status negotiations with the Palestinians, which would include the thorniest issues, like the future of Jerusalem, the Palestinian refugee problem, and the final borders of the Palestinian entity.

Addressing an AIPAC dinner in Washington after the meeting with Clinton, Netanyahu described his talk with the president as "excellent" and said that Israel had a "sure friend" in the White House. Clinton was markedly less enthusiastic, describing the talks only as "frank" and "candid." In their meeting, Clinton had reportedly made it clear to Netanyahu that he would not take kindly to any further unilateral Israeli moves like Har Homah.

Netanyahu's plan, it appeared, was to move quickly to final-status talks so that he would be able to skip the next two stages of West Bank redeployment that he had agreed to in the Hebron pact (the first stage, decided on in March, had still not been carried out). Senior U.S. officials questioned whether the prime minister was ready to make the painful concessions that would be required in such talks. Why, they asked, would it be easier to deal with the incredibly complex final-status issues when the two sides had encountered such great difficulty in tackling far less sensitive matters? In the Foreign Ministry in Jerusalem officials expressed concern that Washington, fed up with the lack of progress on the peace front, was beginning to disengage. They noted that new Secretary of State Madeleine Albright had displayed only moderate interest in the region since taking office in December 1996.

Middle East envoy Dennis Ross was back in Israel on April 16, trying to get the two sides talking again, and he returned a month later with the same mission. Around the same time, Foreign Minister Levy met with Albright in Washington in an effort to get the talks back on track. The round of diplomatic activity, however, produced few tangible results. In another effort to break the two-month deadlock, President Weizman met with Arafat at the Erez checkpoint in early May. "Bibi is the prime minister of Israel," Weizman reportedly told Arafat. "It doesn't matter if you love him or hate him, you have to talk to him. You must meet with him."

A Netanyahu-Arafat meeting did not follow. Reports emerged in late May that Netanyahu had rejected an American proposal whereby the Palestinians would renew security cooperation with Israel and fight terror in exchange for an Israeli commitment to cease settlement construction. Egypt's president Hosni Mubarak tried his luck at mediating a compromise over Har Homah when he met Netanyahu at Sharm el-Sheikh in the Sinai desert on May 27. After the meeting, Israeli officials announced that there had been progress, but the Palestinians said the talks had yielded nothing. The Egyptians were cautiously optimistic, with Foreign Minister Amre Moussa describing the talks as a "new start, not a failure. But there remains a wide gap between the positions of the two sides. . . ." In mid-June Infrastructure Minister Ariel Sharon met with Arafat's deputy, Abu Mazen—his first meeting with a top Palestinian official. This sparked fears among right-wing hard-liners that a deal was in the works, but the two sides still remained away from the negotiating table.

Meanwhile, the whole battle over land had taken on a new and ominous form. In May the PA made an alarming decision: Palestinians selling land to Jews, it decreed, would face the death penalty. Israeli leaders condemned the decision as barbaric, but Palestinian justice minister Freikh Abu Medein strongly supported the move. The sale of land to Jews, Palestinians argued, was not merely a real-estate transaction; it had clear and far-reaching political consequences. "They are isolated traitors, and we will act against them according to the law," Arafat said of the enactment of the death penalty over land sales. Shortly after the announcement, two Palestinian land-dealers were found brutally murdered in the West Bank city of Ramallah. In mid-June, 57-year-old Hakam Kamhawi, another land dealer, died in the hospital after having endured two weeks in Palestinian custody. It was unclear whether Kamhawi had been beaten to death, committed suicide, or suffered a heart attack.

While relations between the two sides remained deadlocked, Netanyahu continued to assert that the only way to move forward was to go directly to final-status negotiations. In early June he unveiled his "Allon-plus Plan," which bore some resemblance to a scheme once drawn up by former Labor leader Yigal Allon, who died in 1980. According to Netanyahu's blueprint, Israel would cede 50 percent of the West Bank to the Palestinians, annex the greater Jerusalem area and the Jordan Valley, maintain a buffer along the western edge of the West Bank, and retain control of the water sources in the territories. Arafat immediately rejected the plan, saying there was "nothing to talk about."

The Palestinians were further incensed when the U.S. House of Representatives voted on June 10 to officially recognize Jerusalem as the united capital of Israel and to budget $100 million to have the U.S. embassy moved from Tel Aviv to Jerusalem. Even though the Clinton administration said it would not support the measure, the vote drew strong criticism from the Palestinians and the Arab countries.

Rioting broke out again in Hebron in mid-June. In a week of clashes that evoked *intifada*-like scenes, with soldiers using tear gas and rubber bullets to disperse stone-throwing Palestinian youths, more than 100 Palestinians were injured. The rioting continued into July, and there were flare-ups elsewhere in the West Bank. Abu Ala, the chairman of the Palestinian Legislative Council, participated in a demonstration in the West Bank town of Ramallah on July 12 in which an Israeli flag was burned. After being condemned by government officials, the Palestinian leader said that he did not support flag burning, but the incident was a reflection of Palestinian frustration.

Tension in the West Bank town of Hebron rose again in late June when posters depicting the prophet Mohammed as a pig were pasted up in the city. Tatiana Susskin, a young women connected to the outlawed extreme right Kach movement, was arrested for allegedly having put up the posters. In late August, the 26-year-old Susskin was released from jail to house arrest, and she later underwent psychiatric testing. Susskin was convicted on December 30 of carrying out acts of racism and supporting a terror organization.

With the peace process teetering on the brink of collapse, raising fears of a descent into all-out violence, the army secretly conducted a simulation of a reinvasion of the territories that Israel had already handed over to Arafat. Senior officers carrying out the simulation of the contingency plan, aptly named "Field of Thorns," concluded that the IDF could rapidly retake Palestinian-controlled areas, but at a tremendous price. The projected cost: hundreds of Israeli soldiers and thousands of Palestinians would be killed, and thousands more on both sides would be injured. The IDF concluded that the most effective means of containing widespread Palestinian violence, and one entailing a far less devastating cost in human life than a full-scale invasion, would be a tight siege of the Palestinian cities, with the army blocking any movement between them.

Toward the end of July, with talk circulating of an imminent resumption of negotiations just ahead of a visit by Dennis Ross, Islamic militants struck again. On July 30, two suicide bombers, acting only seconds apart, blew themselves up in the crowded Mahaneh Yehudah market in Jerusalem, killing 15 people (one more died later) and injuring 170. When Arafat phoned Netanyahu to offer his condolences, the Israeli prime minister angrily rebuked him, demanding that he take immediate action to quell the terrorists. In public, Netanyahu lashed out at Arafat: "About 150 leaders of Hamas and Islamic Jihad were set free like savage animals . . . set free to prowl in our cities and our streets to commit these barbarous acts. . . ."

Government officials outlined a list of measures they insisted Arafat adopt immediately, including the confiscation of all illegal weapons, the extradition of terror suspects to Israel, and an end to the "revolving door" policy whereby his security forces arrested Islamic militants only for them to be quietly released a short time later. They also demanded that the PA chairman move against elements in his own Palestinian Authority who had encouraged attacks on Israel. The PA, said Likud MK and former deputy chief of the General Security Services (GSS) Gidon Ezra, had to make a "mental switch" and recognize that its enemy was not Israel but Hamas.

Government officials stressed that they would consider restarting talks only when they detected a fundamental change in Arafat's approach. "Unlike the previous government, we're making future talks conditional on them fighting terror," said Ezra. "You won't see us pressing on with the Oslo accords come what may, and talking about 'victims of peace.'" Still, Foreign Ministry officials were more optimistic that Dennis Ross would be back in the region within days in an effort to jump-start the talks.

Israel also adopted a series of punitive measures in the wake of the bombing, including sealing off the territories, which blocked tens of thousands of Palestinians from reaching their jobs in Israel. Netanyahu announced that certain tax revenues, which Israel collected for the Palestinians, would be withheld. Efforts were also made to persuade the United States to suspend funding to the PA, and there was talk of jamming the broadcasts of Palestinian TV and radio, which Israel said were rife with incitement. The government also gave the army the go-ahead to enter PA-controlled territory if it had information on a specific terror cell or suspect. In fact, only days before the bombing, an undercover Israeli unit had moved into the West Bank city of Tulkarm and snatched an escaped Islamic Jihad prisoner from a cafe there.

In the initial period after the bombing, Washington adopted Netanyahu's line, insisting that Arafat had to crack down on terror if the peace process was to move forward. "There can be no winks, no double meanings, no double standards, and with respect to the imprisonment of terrorists, no revolving doors," said Secretary of State Albright.

A seemingly tireless Dennis Ross headed back to the region in mid-August in an effort to push for progress in security cooperation between the two sides ahead of a planned late-August visit by Albright. The secretary of state, in comments on Middle East policy to the National Press Club in Washington in mid-August, said that, despite the prolonged strife, she had no doubt that there would ultimately be an agreement between the two sides. But she did warn of the dangers of prolonging the process. "The question today," she said, "is not whether the Israelis and Palestinians will reach a mutually acceptable agreement, but when. . . . The longer decisions are postponed, the more conflict and suffering will ensue."

With the Americans seemingly on the verge of getting the two sides together, Hamas struck again. On September 4, three suicide bombers blew themselves up on Jerusalem's Ben-Yehudah pedestrian mall, killing five Israelis and wounding scores of passersby. While Netanyahu dodged questions about whether the Oslo process was finally dead, the day after the bombing the cabinet announced that there would be no further redeployments in the West Bank until Arafat moved against the terrorists in the areas under his control. At the same time, in anticipation of Albright's visit, Netanyahu did decide to release 42 million shekels ($12 million) of the tax revenues that he had been holding back from the PA ever since the July 30 Jerusalem bombing. He also progressively eased the tight closure that had been clamped on the territories after the bombings.

The peace deadlock at times descended into tit-for-tat exchanges between Netanyahu and Arafat. "I would like to tell Netanyahu that he is still new to politics," Arafat said during an early August visit to Amman. "He does not know the Palestinian people and he's new in Israel as well, because his whole life he lived abroad." Netanyahu did not hesitate to respond to the personal attack: "I'm not new here," he retorted. "I understand what's going on here better than him. Arafat always falls into this trap. Whenever there's a crisis, he thinks the government is about to fall. I'm better than him at reading America as well. I say to him . . . you will not get 90 percent of the territory. I won't give it to you."

In mid-September, Madeleine Albright made her first visit to the Middle East since taking office. Before beginning talks with Netanyahu and Arafat, she traveled to Hadassah Hospital on Mount Scopus to visit those injured in the Ben-Yehudah bombing. When the diplomatic leg of her visit began, she told the Palestinians she wanted them to display "zero tolerance" for terror and to move forcefully against the Islamic militants. But she also had demands of Israel. She made it clear that the United States expected Netanyahu to stick to the Oslo accords and said she wanted a commitment that Israel would not take any more unilateral steps like the Har Homah project. She also asked Netanyahu to move forward with some long outstanding issues like the opening of a port and airport in Gaza.

Diplomatic observers wondered whether Albright's visit signaled a new American willingness to step back into the fray and play a more interventionist role than it had in previous months. That, certainly, was the advice of President Weizman. After he met with Albright, one of her aides let slip that the president had suggested to the secretary of state that she "bang Arafat's and Netanyahu's heads together," in order to get them to move forward with the peace process. (Albright might have been reminded of Weizman's advice when the government announced on September 25 that 300 new homes would be built at the West Bank Jewish settlement of Efrat. The announcement followed shortly after a phone call between herself and Netanyahu in which the Israeli leader made no mention of the construction plans.)

THE SECOND REDEPLOYMENT

Netanyahu was faced with an embarrassing situation when three Jewish families moved into two houses located in the Arab East Jerusalem neighborhood of Ras al-Amud on September 14. After the Har Homah episode, which had drawn worldwide condemnation, it was the last thing the beleaguered prime minister needed. Some senior ministers condemned the move. "These settlers," said Defense Minister Mordechai, "are hurting and weakening Israel."

The money for the purchase of the property came from Irving Moskowitz, a wealthy Miami businessman and close ally of Jerusalem mayor Ehud Olmert. For years, Moskowitz had donated large sums to purchase Arab property in East Jerusalem in an effort to settle as many Jews there as possible. He had also contributed money toward the restoration of the Hasmonean tunnel, and along with Olmert had pushed for the tunnel's opening in September 1996. The Ras al-Amud incident died down after the government reached a compromise with Moskowitz and the settlers, whereby the three families would leave and would be replaced by 10 yeshivah students who would guard and maintain the homes. But the basic goal of both Moskowitz and the settlers had been achieved: a Jewish foothold in a once Arab-only neighborhood in Jerusalem.

After a deadlock that was now six months old, Abu Mazen, Dennis Ross, and David Levy, who was one of the government's most vigorous advocates of the peace process, met on October 6 in Jerusalem in an effort to restart talks on implementing the interim accords of the Oslo agreement. Again there was no breakthrough, and an increasingly irate Arafat announced a few weeks later that if a final accord were not reached by 1999—the end of the five-year Oslo interim period—he would unilaterally declare a Palestinian state. In response, Netanyahu reportedly told members of the Tsomet Party, during a private meeting, that if Arafat went ahead with his threat, Israel would annex the sections of the West Bank that were still under its control at the time. But Likud hard-liner Ariel Sharon gave a sense of how fundamentally the thinking among certain sectors of his party had changed since the inception of Oslo, when he announced at a briefing in New York in November that "defining the Palestinian entity as a state is a foregone conclusion, and it won't be long before the Palestinians declare an independent state even if Israel opposes it."

By the end of November, the second phase of IDF withdrawal from the West

Bank—as agreed to under the Oslo II accords and reaffirmed by Netanyahu in the Hebron agreement—had come to dominate the agenda. Once again Netanyahu found himself trapped between U.S. demands to move ahead with the pullback and right-wing domestic pressure on him to freeze the process. On November 30, the government voted 16-0, with two abstentions, to carry out the second withdrawal. But the overwhelming support for the decision, including that of cabinet hard-liners, was due to the fact that it made no reference either to the scope of the pullback or to a date by when it was to be carried out. The ministers also conditioned the redeployment on the Palestinians fulfilling a long list of Israeli demands, including formally abrogating the clauses in the PLO covenant that call for Israel's destruction, clamping down on terror, and handing terror suspects over to Israel.

While Netanyahu was careful not to display any maps, according to press reports he was ready to cede between 6 to 8 percent of the West Bank to the Palestinians. But at a December 7 meeting in Paris, Madeleine Albright reportedly told the prime minister that he was not being generous enough and that she expected a double-digit offer. With American pressure intensifying, Netanyahu put together a four-man team, including Defense Minister Mordechai, Foreign Minister Levy, Infrastructure Minister Sharon, and himself, in order to come up with a map of Israel's "vital strategic interests," which would include those areas that would remain under Israeli control after final-status talks had been completed.

The problem for Netanyahu was that, with 27 percent of the West Bank already controlled by Arafat, and with the government demanding that two buffer zones were essential for Israel's defense—one in the east along the Jordanian border and another along the western edge of the West Bank—it had become extremely difficult for him to cede any more territory without beginning to isolate some of the Jewish settlements, leaving them hemmed in by Palestinian-controlled territory. Any more concessions in areas where many of the settlements were located, warned right-wing Knesset member Michael Kleiner, would "strangle these settlements. People will have to leave their homes in armored convoys." On December 17, the day before Netanyahu was to meet with Albright again in Paris, three of the most prominent settler leaders announced that if he went ahead with the redeployment before the Palestinians fulfilled all Israel's demands, they would work to bring him down.

When Netanyahu met with Albright the next day in Paris, the only map he showed her was the old Oslo map. There were reports, however, that he told U.S. officials that he would push through a decision to withdraw from at least 10 percent of the West Bank in early 1998. The reasons for the delay, he explained to his American counterparts, was that he did not want to risk a coalition rebellion that might sink the 1998 budget. The Americans agreed, and shortly after the Paris meeting, the White House announced that Clinton was inviting both Netanyahu and Arafat to Washington in mid-January. Both men, it seemed, would have to make some tough decisions by then—Arafat having to comply with strong American demands that he adopt an uncompromising attitude to terror and beef up security cooperation with Israel, and Netanyahu having to finally come up with concrete answers on the second pullback.

In the midst of the withdrawal debate, Israel and the Palestinians found something else to quarrel over—the PA's decision to include East Jerusalem residents in its first-ever census, starting on December 10 when 5,000 officials began counting Arab residents in the territories. Anxious not to be seen to be compromising in any way on the status of Jerusalem, the government rushed a law through the Knesset banning the census in the capital. The PA decided to postpone its counting in that area.

OTHER DIPLOMATIC DEVELOPMENTS

Relations with Egypt

The leaders of the Arab world had been both astonished and alarmed by Netanyahu's 1996 election victory. They had expected Peres to win. Now, unexpectedly, they had to contend with a hard-line Israeli leader who was skeptical about the peace process. The Egyptian press attacked Netanyahu almost immediately from the day he took office, accusing him of "beating the drums of war." Netanyahu's statement to Congress, during a July 1996 visit to the United States, about the need for the Arab states to embrace democracy, further fueled the vitriol in the Arab press and raised the ire of Egyptian president Hosni Mubarak and other Middle East leaders. After Netanyahu flew to Cairo to meet Mubarak on July 18, though, the two men emerged from their discussion sounding optimistic. The Egyptian leader expressed "much hope for the continuation of the peace process."

But relations had deteriorated again by September when Egypt threatened to cancel the third Middle East and North Africa economic summit scheduled for Cairo in early November, because of the paralyzed peace process. If Egypt went through with its threat, Netanyahu scoffed, it would be "cutting off its nose to spite its face," a remark that sparked an unrelenting tirade against him in Egypt. One Egyptian minister suggested that the Israeli prime minister needed to see a psychiatrist. No, wrote one Egyptian paper, he needed a "whole hospital." Ultimately the economic summit went ahead, but the seemingly interminable Hebron negotiations dampened the atmosphere, and Israel played a far less central role than it had in the two previous summits in Casablanca and Amman.

The arrest of Azzam Azzam, an Israeli Druze taken into custody by the Egyptians on the eve of the conference, also soured the atmosphere. Azzam, who was employed in an Israeli-run factory in Egypt, was accused of spying for the Mossad. Israeli leaders insisted that Azzam was innocent and demanded that he be released.

Early in 1997 the leading Egyptian newspaper, *Al-Ahram*, took the highly uncharacteristic step of apologizing for a report it had published, accusing Israel of injecting 305 Palestinian children with the AIDS virus. This marked the first-ever formal apology for a mistaken or false article about Israel by the Egyptian press. But the event was a one-time exception. With the peace process stalled, 1997 was marked by growing anti-Israel sentiment in Egypt, which found strong expression in regular media claims of Israeli espionage and sabotage, as well as constant attacks on Netanyahu. There was even a case (in September) in which the Egyptian press and cinema unions decided to investigate three individuals—a writer, a film director, and a political analyst—for visiting Israel.

When President Weizman visited Egypt in late September, in an attempt to thaw the frosty relations between Jerusalem and Cairo, Mubarak turned down his invitation to visit Israel, saying it would not happen until there was tangible progress in Israeli-Palestinian talks. "How is it possible to conduct such a visit in an atmosphere as electrified as the present one?" Mubarak asked his Israeli counterpart. "Any visit that does not bring results will complicate our relations even more."

Mubarak's criticism was often of a personal nature. In an April interview he painted a black picture of the peace between his country and Israel, which, he said, would "stay cold for a long time to come. You see, in the last three years, peace was beginning to work, alongside the progress made in the peace process with the Palestinians. But since Netanyahu came to power, everything has stopped. . . . Don't they understand they are ruining everything?"

While Israeli government officials acknowledged the worsening relations, they argued that the ailing peace process was not the root cause. They insisted that Egypt's criticism of Israel was really part of a strategy whereby Cairo intended to downgrade its relations with Jerusalem and boost its role in the Arab world. That process, they said, had begun when Rabin was still at the helm, with Mubarak turning down invitations to visit Israel even then. Egypt's excuse then, argued Netanyahu's aides, was Israel's refusal to sign the Nuclear Non-Proliferation Treaty. Now it was Netanyahu.

Another indication of the tense relations was the Egyptian's detention of Dvora Ganani, an Israeli businesswoman with considerable financial interests in Egypt, in mid-July 1997. Ganani was arrested and questioned for several hours and only freed after the intervention of Labor leader Ehud Barak, who was on a visit to Cairo.

Tension escalated further when an Egyptian court found Azzam Azzam guilty of espionage in early September and sentenced him to 15 years' hard labor. Israeli officials, who had consistently denied that Azzam was a spy and demanded his release, protested the court's decision. Netanyahu described the ruling as an "outrage" and called on Mubarak to exercise his constitutional powers to have Azzam released. But Mubarak, clearly not wanting to be seen to be capitulating to Israeli demands or to be seen to be undermining the Egyptian legal system, ignored the prime minister's requests. In a communiqué to Netanyahu, which was leaked to the press, he accused the Israeli leader of exploiting the Azzam affair for his own internal political needs. The Egyptian president was praised by the Egyptian media for his "tough reaction" to Israel's "arrogance and dictating." Later, Mubarak hinted that if the matter had been dealt with discreetly by Israel, it could have been settled differently. Israeli officials, however, were adamant that the Egyptians had convicted an innocent man and that Azzam had become an innocent victim of the change in relations. It was no coincidence, they said, that his arrest had come on the eve of the 1996 Cairo economic summit, and was intended to embarrass Israel and cool normalization. Once the media got hold of the story, they said, it became impossible for the Egyptian authorities to back down.

Relations with Egypt seemed bumpy on almost every front. On October 17, front-page headlines of the daily tabloids in Israel bellowed the news that Egypt's long-serving ambassador in Tel Aviv, Mohammed Bassiouny, was involved in a sex scandal with a belly dancer. According to the reports, an unnamed belly dancer from Ramat Gan had filed a complaint with the police against Bassiouny for having enticed her to the Tel Aviv apartment of a well-known local plastic surgeon in August, in order to have sex with her. The reports also revealed that Bassiouny, married with two children, had dismissed the allegations and accused the belly dancer of trying to blackmail him. The case had been kept quiet by court order, but became public when the State Attorney's Office decided not to pursue the matter after having questioned the dancer and having dispatched senior police investigators to speak to Bassiouny.

Relations with Syria

Talks between Israel and Syria had already broken down toward the end of Shimon Peres's term when President Hafez al-Assad refused to denounce the Hamas suicide bombings in early 1996, but relations between the two countries got steadily worse after Netanyahu came to power. While the Israeli leader made it clear that he would not agree to any preconditions for the renewal of talks, Syria demanded that the negotiations be restarted at the point they had been stopped with the previous Labor government. Netanyahu also indicated that he would not countenance a situation where talks between the two countries proceeded while the Iranian-backed Hezballah continued its assault, with Syrian consent, on Israeli soldiers in the south Lebanon security zone. Syria responded by trying to encourage other Arab states to halt normalization with Israel, and its state-run media compared Netanyahu to Hitler.

The Americans tried to get the two sides together in July 1996, but failed. Netanyahu's "Lebanon First" suggestion—that Israel and Syria try to reach a solution on Lebanon before commencing negotiations on the Golan Heights—also came to naught. With the rhetoric of mutual blame escalating and the deadlock seemingly unbreakable, relations reached a dangerous point in mid-

August, when the Syrians began moving some troops from Lebanon and redeploying them around Mt. Hermon, the strategic peak atop the Golan range. That was followed by large-scale Syrian infantry, armored, and air maneuvers, which also included ground-to-ground missile forces. Israeli papers quoted Arab sources as saying that Syria feared an Israeli offensive; inside Israel there was speculation that maybe Syria aimed to launch a limited offensive, with the aim of grabbing a piece of the Golan in an effort to smash the diplomatic impasse and force Israel to the negotiating table. The IDF went on alert in the north, and soldiers' leaves were canceled.

Tension increased, with the state-controlled Syrian media accusing Israel of "beating the drums of war." Rafael Eitan, the agriculture and environment minister and a former chief of staff, warned the Syrians that if they attacked Israel they would be "broken and bloodied" and possibly even "wiped off the face of the earth." Prof. Ze'ev Maoz, Syria expert of Tel Aviv University, spoke worryingly of a psychological switch in the Syrian military: "What was done over the past four years," he said, "the sustained effort, through lectures and other indoctrination, to prepare the troops for the shift to peace, has been turned around. Since Netanyahu came to power, the Syrians have been preparing the army psychologically for war."

Netanyahu and Defense Minister Mordechai sent soothing messages to Damascus via the Americans, making it clear that Israel had no hostile intentions. By September, though, Israeli troops had taken up defensive positions along the border and were carrying out exercises on the Golan. The Israeli press reported that 10,000 Syrian troops had been shifted from Lebanon and deployed in a defensive posture on the other side of the border. In October the IDF asked for emergency funding in case of a war with Syria—a scenario army intelligence said was no longer remote. It was not until November that the border tension subsided, but deputy Chief of Staff Matan Vilnai remarked ominously at the end of the year that the probability of war with Syria was higher than it had been two years previously. "The IDF," he said, "is now involved in a massive improvement of its deployment on the Syrian border and is increasing its readiness for a war scenario." Chief of Staff Shahak quickly toned down Vilnai's prognosis, saying it did not mean that war was imminent or inevitable at some future date.

Talks with Syria remained deadlocked throughout 1997, despite occasional reports of plans to revive them. Addressing a meeting of the Israel-America Friendship Association in February, U.S. ambassador to Israel Martin Indyk was candid about the price Israel would have to pay for a peace agreement with Damascus. He said he did not think there was "any possibility whatsoever . . . that he [Syrian president Assad] would be ready to sign a peace agreement with Israel, short of full withdrawal from the Golan."

At the beginning of 1997, Mordechai had said he expected peace talks with Syria to resume by the spring. Foreign Minister Levy also spread optimism about renewed talks with the Syrians. But Damascus continued to demand that the talks restart at the point they had broken down the previous year. The Syrians also claimed that this included a verbal commitment by Rabin to return the whole of the Golan Heights to Syria and withdraw to the 1967 pre–Six Day War lines. Netanyahu, however, insisted that he was not bound by any unwritten agreements, and the Americans backed him on this point. He discussed the Syrian track with Clinton during a mid-February visit to Washington, but nothing concrete followed. On a visit to Amman shortly afterward, Netanyahu commented that he could not "force the Syrians to come to the negotiating table. If they don't want to resume the talks," he said, "there is nothing I can do."

Clinton sent a special communiqué to Assad in early May in another ultimately vain effort to get the Syrian leader back to the negotiating table. By mid-1997, with progress looking increasingly remote, Shahak told the Knesset Foreign Affairs and Defense Committee that the Syrians were "preparing an offensive option."

A Knesset subcommittee report around the same time worryingly revealed that budget constraints had left the army unprepared for a future war. According to the report, the IDF's weaponry was aging, it had too few helicopters, and it suffered from too little training. Ephraim Sneh, a Labor MK and head of the subcommittee, remarked, "If Israel goes to war today, it will win, but it will pay a heavy price." Chief of Staff Shahak complained that the defense budget had created an "insufferable" situation with regard to the army's preparedness.

Probably the only encouraging sign was Assad's decision to allow a delegation of 50 Arab Israelis, including mayors and Knesset members—one of whom was a Druze officer in the IDF reserves—into Syria for a visit in early August. The delegation met with senior Syrian officials, as well as with Assad. But statements by some of the delegation members evoked anger inside Israel, especially comments by Knesset member Abd al-Wahab Darawshe to Palestinians in a refugee camp. "I swear to you before Allah," he told the 20,000-strong crowd, "that you will return to Palestine."

Yitzhak Rabin had defined a formula for an agreement with Syria, saying that the depth of Israeli withdrawal would be determined by the extent of the peace; Netanyahu redefined the formula in mid-August when he announced that the "depth of the peace" would be determined by the "depth of security arrangements" the two sides agreed to. "The type of peace that is possible here [in the region]," he added, "is peace based on power, where we nurture our power."

The IDF's analysis remained largely unchanged toward the end of the year, with Maj. Gen. Amiram Levine, head of the Northern Command, warning that Syria was "taking very fundamental steps to prepare for the possibility of the development of war." In early November the U.S. State Department confirmed that Mideast envoy Dennis Ross had been holding discussions with Syria and Israel in an effort to get the two sides back to the table. But by the end of the year there was still no sign of a thaw.

Relations with Lebanon

Lebanon remained Israel's only active war front, and in the period under review the number of Israeli soldiers who lost their lives or were injured there grew alarmingly. Despite a huge investment in increased safety measures and the unveiling of the elite Sayeret Egoz counterinsurgency unit, Israel's war of attrition with the Hezballah in south Lebanon continued. On December 24, 1996, two soldiers were killed by a Hezballah roadside bomb in Israel's self-styled security zone, bringing to 26 the total number of soldiers killed there in the course of that year; another 96 were injured.

Israeli casualties mounted in 1997, with 39 soldiers losing their lives — the highest toll since the creation of the security zone in 1985. (About 60 Hezballah fighters lost their lives in the course of the year.) The escalating confrontation also exacted a growing number of civilian casualties. In the course of August close to 20 Lebanese civilians were killed — caught in the cross fire between Israel and its South Lebanon Army (SLA) militia, and the Hezballah. In a series of tit-for-tat exchanges, the SLA indiscriminately shelled the Lebanese port city of Sidon, after two children of a senior SLA officer who had himself been killed by the Hezballah were killed by a bomb planted by the Iranian-backed Shi'ite organization. Eight civilians were killed in the Sidon shelling, and although Israel censured Gen. Antoine Lahad, head of the SLA, Hezballah guerrillas unleashed a Katyusha barrage on northern Israel. They fired 60 rockets into the Galilee, sending residents in the north scurrying into their bomb shelters.

Chief of Staff Shahak told politicians in the Knesset Foreign Affairs and Defense Committee in late October that it had become increasingly difficult to gather intelligence on Hezballah. The movement's fighters were better trained then ever and were receiving more and more sophisticated weaponry, such as night-vision equipment and upgraded antitank missiles. In October it was reported that about 50 planeloads of weapons, including Sagger and Faggot antitank missiles, had made their way from Iran via the Damascus airport to the Hezballah in Lebanon.

THE LEBANON DEBATE

Several disastrous events in the course of 1997 heightened public questioning of Israel's continued military presence in the security zone in southern Lebanon. One of these occurred on February 4, when two Sikorsky helicopters carrying Israeli soldiers to their bases in southern Lebanon collided in midair, killing 73 men. Ironically, the soldiers were being flown into Lebanon as a safety precaution, since Hezballah roadside bombs and ambushes made traveling overland too dangerous. The horrific pictures from the site of the crash — of bodies and of soldiers' personal possessions strewn across the ground — and the rows of the faces of the dead covering the front pages of the daily newspapers spurred calls for the army's immediate withdrawal from Lebanon.

Seven months later, in early September, Israel suffered another huge blow when a naval commando unit that had landed on the Lebanese coast late at night and moved inland toward a classified target walked into a Hezballah ambush. Twelve of Israel's top commandos were killed. Only days later, five soldiers burned to death in the security zone when they were unable to extricate themselves from a brushfire ignited by Israeli artillery shells fired at Hezballah positions.

In September and October, two soldiers were killed when their tanks took direct hits from Hezballah-fired antitank missiles. These Merkava II tanks, among the world's most advanced, on which the army had spent millions beefing up the protective armor, were thought to be almost impregnable, yet Hezballah had succeeded in penetrating them. To make matters worse, on October 8, a Hezballah squad succeeded in making its way undetected to a point some 150 meters from Israel's northern border where it attacked Israeli positions, killed two soldiers, and then melted away.

The Hezballah successes and the rising death toll fueled the public debate. After the helicopter crash, a group called "Four Mothers" sprang up; its members began agitating for an urgent withdrawal from Lebanon and called on the government to rethink Israel's presence there. A Tel Aviv University poll conducted in September 1997 revealed that, while 60 percent of the Jewish population favored staying put, a full 32 percent supported unilateral withdrawal—a figure once unthinkable. The latter received a surprising boost in November when the daily Ha'aretz ran a story revealing that the head of the Northern Command, Amiram Levin, had expressed views favoring a pullback, and there were other officers under his command who shared his opinion. Levin backtracked after the story was printed, but its impact could not be discounted.

Prime Minister Netanyahu and Defense Minister Mordechai, however, were adamant that the IDF could not unilaterally withdraw from Lebanon. After the defense establishment held an intensive three-week review of the IDF's position in south Lebanon, Mordechai made it clear that in his view a unilateral pullout would only make the situation worse. "There can be no adventurism at the expense of the lives of our citizens," he said in an October interview in the daily Ma'ariv, effectively backing up the argument that if Israel left south Lebanon without an agreement, Hezballah would be situated right on the northern border, clambering to get across.

But the Lebanon argument crossed the country's left-right political divide, with some government ministers talking of the need to contemplate withdrawal even in the absence of a comprehensive peace agreement with Lebanon's patron, Syria. Labor Knesset members were also divided over the question of whether to bring the troops back home. The "Four Mothers" got their strongest political backing from Labor MK Yossi Beilin, who started the Movement for a Peaceful Withdrawal from Lebanon. Beilin argued that Israel had become a hostage of Syrian president Assad in south Lebanon and that the time had come to withdraw unilaterally, redeploy strongly along the country's northern border, and warn the Lebanese government that it would be held responsible for any anti-Israel hostilities. As long as Israel remained in Lebanon, he insisted, its hands would be tied — both because the international community viewed its presence there as that of an occupier, and because of a set of U.S.-brokered accords that were negotiated after Israel's April 1996 Grapes of Wrath bombardment of Lebanon (in which 100 civilians were killed when Israeli shells ploughed into a UN base), which curtailed the scope of the IDF's activities.

The pro-withdrawal camp also argued that Hezballah's violent resistance was to Israel's presence in Lebanon, not to Israel's existence, and that it was unlikely to be directed southward after Israel departed from the zone.

But those opposing withdrawal argued strongly that the security zone was still fulfilling its intended function of stopping terrorist penetrations and light-arms fire across the border. They warned that if Israel departed from the zone, which was patrolled by 1,500 Israeli soldiers and some 2,500 SLA members, without a comprehensive agreement, a coalition of guerrilla groups would mobilize on the border and strike at residents in northern Israel. The result, they insisted, would be further escalation, forcing the IDF to go back into Lebanon to curb these attacks, having lost the advantage of a pro-Israel local militia and a partially supportive local population. "Hezballah openly declares its desire to help the Palestinians liberate Palestine," remarked Ephraim Sneh, one of the architects of the security zone. Without Syrian involvement in a deal, the anti-withdrawal camp argued, there simply could not be one. "More than ever before, Lebanon is under total Syrian control," said Uri Lubrani, Israel's veteran coordinator of government activities in Lebanon. "There is no Syrian bypass route."

The public debate in Israel over the IDF's continuing presence in south Lebanon generated disquiet among the residents in the security zone, especially those with ties to the SLA, who feared for their future once Israel departed. General Lahad gave vent to these fears when he warned in an October interview that were Israel to pull back unilaterally, part of his forces would likely defect to Hezballah, and the remainder might well evolve into another anti-Israel militia.

Relations with Jordan

Relations between Israel and the Hashemite Kingdom were rocky in the period under review. While King Hussein had been the single Arab leader who was not startled by Benjamin Netanyahu's victory — he congratulated the Israeli leader on his win — the honeymoon period was short-lived. Relations began to cool after the new government announced shortly after its formation that it planned to increase Jewish settlement in the West Bank. Crown Prince Hassan postponed a planned trip to Israel in September 1996 because of the deadlocked peace process. Then came the Jerusalem tunnel-opening incident, which severely shook relations.

Despite the diplomatic fallout, Hussein was especially angered by the fact that one of Netanyahu's aides had flown to Jordan to meet with him only hours before the tunnel opening, yet had mentioned nothing to him about the matter. Jordan also claimed that the tunnel opening was a violation of its peace treaty with Israel, which recognizes Jordan's special status with regard to Islamic holy places in Jerusalem. Israel's ambassador to Jordan was presented with an official complaint by the Jordanians.

Shortly after the early October emergency summit in Washington, Hussein issued an uncharacteristically harsh indictment of Netanyahu, warning that "if there was not peace in the region, then Prime Minister Netanyahu would have to carry a gas mask around with him, like in the days of the Gulf War." Two weeks later, the king made his first visit to the West Bank since 1967, meeting Arafat in Jericho and announcing that he was in favor of a Palestinian state. In early January 1997, though, Hussein did step in to help resolve the final hitches in the Israeli-Palestinian talks on Hebron.

The growing anti-Israel feeling inside Jordan was evident when 4,000 protesters clashed with policemen during the first Israeli trade fair in Amman, which took place on January 8, 1997. Demonstrators carried banners declaring that "Jordan is not the Zionist bridge to the Arab world." The efforts by Islamic fundamentalists to undermine the fair had the desired effect—only 70 of the 200 Israeli companies expected to turn up did so.

Angered by Netanyahu's decision to go ahead with the Har Homah project, the king sent the Israeli prime minister a furious letter in early March, in which he accused him of intentionally humiliating the Palestinians and of being bent on destroying the peace process. The tone of the letter, which was leaked to the press, was extremely harsh. "My distress," wrote Hussein, "is genuine and deep over the accumulating tragic actions which you have initiated as the head of the government of Israel, making peace—the worthiest objective of my life—appears more and more like a distant elusive mirage. I could remain aloof if the very lives of Arabs and Israelis and their future were not fast sliding towards an abyss of bloodshed and disaster, brought about by fear and despair. . . . I frankly cannot accept your repeated excuse of having to act the way you do under great duress and pressure. I cannot believe that the people of Israel seek bloodshed and disaster and oppose peace. . . . Your course of action seems bent on destroying all I believe in or have striven to achieve. . . ."

Days later, on March 13, a Jordanian soldier went on a murderous rampage at Naharayim on the Israeli-Jordanian border. Standing in a watchtower, he opened fire on a group of junior high school girls from the town of Beth Shemesh, then climbed down and chased the girls, still firing at them, until he was overpowered by his fellow Jordanians. Two girls died immediately; five more were pronounced dead on arrival at a nearby Jordanian hospital. Israeli medical teams were held back for a full 40 minutes by the Jordanians, before being allowed access to the scene of the attack.

Ironically, the 200-acre enclave had been referred to as the "Island of Peace," and was returned to Jordanian sovereignty when the peace accord was signed in 1994. Crown Prince Hassan strenuously condemned the attack, calling it a "black day" for Jordan, and a joint Israeli-Jordanian inquiry was set up. Foreign Minister David Levy, however, linked the incident to the king's irate letter, saying that comments of the kind included in the communiqué "created a psychological atmosphere that could lead to such tragic acts."

The killings resulted in a remarkable and highly moving visit by King Hussein to Israel. The monarch flew into Israel to visit the bereaved families in Beit Shemesh; in unprecedented scenes broadcast live on Israel television, he entered the homes of the families—wearing his traditional red keffiyeh—held their hands, embraced some of them, and offered his condolences. "I feel as if my daughters have been killed," he told one family. "I know there is nothing that is equal to your mourning," he told another, "but, believe me, I mourn with you."

But the tragic event failed to heal the diplomatic wounds. A joint Israeli-Jordanian memorial ceremony for the seven schoolgirls was canceled after a dispute broke out between the two countries in early May over water allocations to Jordan under the peace treaty between the two countries. Relations were strained further in early August when King Hussein canceled a planned meeting with Netanyahu and sent his brother, Prince Hassan, instead. On August 13 the two leaders did meet in Aqaba in an attempt to smooth relations. On September 20, however, two guards at the Israeli embassy in Amman were shot and lightly wounded in an attack for which the Islamic Opposition Front claimed responsibility. A week later, the Mashaal affair brought relations to an all-time low.

THE MASHAAL AFFAIR

The events that took place in broad daylight on an Amman street on September 25, 1997, were to trigger one of the worst diplomatic and intelligence debacles in Israeli history. At 10:35 A.M., two Israeli Mossad agents brushed past Khaled Mashaal, the head of the Hamas political bureau in Amman, as he was on his way to his office, and pressed a device to his ear that unleashed a fatal, untraceable chemical poison. The Mossad agents quickly climbed into a getaway car, but Mashaal's bodyguard gave chase in a taxi and collared the two men as they tried to switch cars. Jordanian police appeared on the scene as the agents struggled with the bodyguard, and the two Mossad men were taken into custody. The captured agents were carrying Canadian passports, but when the Canadian ambassador was summoned, it soon became clear they were not citizens of his country. Mashaal, who had begun to feel ill, was admitted to a hospital.

News of the failed operation quickly reached Mossad chief Danny Yatom, who immediately informed the prime minister, who in turn telephoned King Hussein to tell him that "we have a problem." Livid at Israel's attempt to carry out an assassination on Jordanian soil, the king threatened to cut off diplomatic ties. If

Mashaal died, he warned, the two Mossad agents would be tried and hanged. Yatom was hastily dispatched to Amman with the antidote for the poison injected into Mashaal, and his life was saved.

But it soon became clear that Israel would have to pay a heavy price for the bungled operation. In exchange for the release of its agents, Israel agreed to the release of Sheikh Ahmad Yassin, the spiritual leader of Hamas, as well as the release of dozens of Palestinian and Jordanian security prisoners in its jails. Canada condemned Israel for using its passports and recalled its ambassador.

On October 1, Netanyahu ordered the release of Yassin, and the Hamas spiritual mentor was immediately flown to Amman for medical treatment. Five days later he flew into Gaza where he was welcomed by over 10,000 ecstatic supporters. The same day, the two interned Mossad hit men were returned to Israel. (Among those security prisoners released in the embarrassing aftermath of the bungled operation were members of a terror squad who had landed on an Israeli beach in 1990 with plans to kill Jews in Tel Aviv.)

When opposition Labor politicians and leading political columnists called on Netanyahu and Yatom to resign, citing the huge damage to Israel's image and to its intelligence services, Netanyahu skillfully deflected attention from the negative fallout of the botched assassination, insisting that such operations were vital in what was a "just" war on terror. He also announced the creation of a commission of inquiry, but gave it no real judicial powers. (By the end of the year the commission was still deliberating.)

National Infrastructure Minister Ariel Sharon, highly regarded for his security credentials by many on the right, rallied behind Netanyahu. He described Mashaal as the "number one" figure in Hamas and also took over much of the behind-the-scenes negotiations with the Jordanians. Likud MK and former Shin Bet deputy chief Gidon Ezra justified the attempted hit on the grounds that there was no way of knowing that the Hamas suicide attacks in July and September in Jerusalem, in which 20 Israelis were killed, were the last. Israel, said Ezra, was acting "to stop the next terror attacks."

In the weeks following the debacle, more embarrassing operational blunders emerged. One of the most glaring was the failure by the Mossad operatives planning the hit to detect that Mashaal's driver doubled as a bodyguard and was trained in self-defense. More worrying was the negative fallout of the ill-fated mission, which had to be seen against the backdrop of the deadlocked peace process, Israel's shaky ties with its Arab neighbors, and frayed relations with the United States. The blow dealt to the country's once-vaunted Mossad agency and to the battle against terror also could not be ignored.

The release of the quadriplegic Yassin, who exerted a curious charisma despite his poor sight and hearing, created a new source of authority in the Gaza Strip, just when Yasir Arafat could least afford it. Yassin's release served to boost Hamas's prestige at a time when Arafat's image was already battered—by the floundering peace process, revelations of widespread corruption among his ministers, and rumors of his failing health.

The immediate anxiety over the threat from a strengthened Hamas momentarily threw Netanyahu and Arafat together, and the two leaders met on October 8 to discuss their mutual predicament, their first meeting in eight months. The two men reportedly discussed ways to improve security cooperation to contend with the new developments. Some hailed the meeting as a boost for the paralyzed peace process, but it proved to be no more than a short time-out in the ongoing deadlock. It was not long before Netanyahu was again accusing Arafat of not clamping down on terror and insisting that he would make no further concessions until he did so.

Around the time of Yassin's release, Arafat actually seemed to have begun to clamp down on Islamic militants and their institutions. But after the failed assassination attempt, he eased up again, releasing some of the new Hamas activists he had ordered arrested. The Mashaal affair and Yassin's release, observers said, had made it more difficult for an already reluctant Arafat to move against the Islamic fundamentalists. "If this was an action designed to fight terrorism, it has been damaging to that struggle," remarked Prof. Asher Susser, a Tel Aviv University expert on Jordan and the Palestinians. "For Arafat to crush Hamas when there is nothing in the offing for him—in terms of territorial and economic gains—turns him into a collaborator with Israel in his people's eyes."

In the weeks after his release, Sheikh Yassin spoke of the possibility of a ten-year cease-fire with the Jewish state—if Israel agreed to withdraw from all the territories it had conquered in 1967, made Jerusalem a Palestinian capital, and dismantled all the Jewish settlements. He also issued a number of uncompromising statements, such as "Israel as a Jewish state has to disappear from the map," in an October interview. He did add, however, that when "Israel stops killing us and conquering our land . . . we can stop the suicide attacks." (In a unique overture to the Hamas leader, in late October Israel's Sephardic chief rabbi, Eliyahu Bakshi-Doron, sent Rabbi Menachem Froman of the West Bank settlement of Tekoa to meet with Yassin in Gaza and present him with a letter. "We have to do whatever we can to stop violence," Bakshi-Doron wrote in the letter, "and the only way to do that is through dialogue. I am full of hope that Sheikh Yassin can solve this problem. I call on him as a [fellow] believer in God.")

For Jordan's King Hussein, the fact that Israel had tried to carry out an assassination on Jordanian soil was shocking evidence of Netanyahu's disregard for the special relationship between Amman and Jerusalem: the close intelligence understanding between the two countries—the only one of its kind Israel had with an Arab state, the carefully constructed strategic alliance that provided Israel with a security buffer on its eastern border and Jordan with security in the face of a threat from Iraq or Syria, as well as the prospect of economic benefits. What is more, the hit could not have been timed more badly in terms of internal Jordanian politics, coming just as the king was battling the influence of the Islamists in the campaign for parliamentary elections which they were set to boycott. "Israel showed no recognition of [King Hussein's] domestic sensitivity," observed Susser. "That was shocking for the King. . . . He feared that Jordanians would think he was conniving with Israel."

In the diplomatic community, some accused Israel of engaging in state terror. President Clinton, already frustrated by what he perceived as Netanyahu's foot-dragging in the peace process, in a telephone conversation with King Hussein at the height of the affair reportedly referred to the Israeli prime minister as "impossible."

For U.S. administration officials dealing with the Middle East, observed terror expert Ehud Sprinzak, the fiasco was "another indication of [Netanyahu's] poor judgement. They don't buy into the argument that you have to chase terrorists wherever." But Sprinzak also pointed out that Clinton could not ignore Congress, which was much more supportive of Netanyahu's "gung-ho" approach to fighting terror. "They buy into Netanyahu's line that the only way to fight terror is tooth and nail," he said.

Relations with Other Regional States

With the peace process frozen, there were few encouraging developments in Israel's relations with other Arab states. Following the tunnel opening and the ensuing gun battles, King Hassan of Morocco announced that his country would downgrade its ties with Israel.

Concerns also grew in Israel over Iran's efforts to obtain a nuclear capability, with the help of Russian scientists, and expert predictions that by the end of the decade Iran would have long-range surface-to-surface missiles capable of reaching Israel. There were also reports that Iran was trying to purchase technological know-how from South Africa's nuclear program, as well as some of its portable elements. (South Africa's nuclear program had been developed in the 1970s and 1980s under a partnership between Israel and the white South African government.)

When tension rose in the Persian Gulf region again in November 1997 over Saddam Hussein's refusal to allow the American members of the UN inspection team in his country entry to certain sites, Israelis began to wonder whether they were in for another Saddam missile fest. Most experts, though, predicted that Saddam would not strike at Israel. Western intelligence sources estimated that the Iraqi leader had engineered the crisis in an effort to safeguard his nonconventional weapons systems, which were important to him as a deterrent against Iran. Nevertheless, the IDF's gas-mask distribution stations registered a threefold increase in the number of people coming to renew their masks.

Once again the annual Middle East economic conference proved to be a disappointment as most Arab governments boycotted the mid-November event held in Doha, Qatar. Israel tried in vain to moderate the conference closing statement, which declared that peace between Israel and the Palestinians must be based on the land-for-peace formula.

Despite the stalled peace talks, Israel's Manufacturers' Association announced that trade with Arab states had grown in the first nine months of 1997. Exports were up by 23 percent to $59.5 million compared with the same period the previous year, and imports grew by 62.5 percent to $36.5 million. Most of the trade was with Egypt and Jordan.

Relations with the United States

U.S.-Israeli relations became increasingly chilly in the period under review as Netanyahu appeared to retreat from the obligations of the Oslo accords signed by his predecessors. When he arrived in the United States for his first meeting as prime minister with President Clinton in July 1996, the Americans were hoping that his hard-line preelection rhetoric would be replaced by a more flexible, pragmatic approach. But they were quickly disappointed as Netanyahu refused to commit to dates for both the Hebron redeployment and a meeting with Arafat. Moreover, the personal disharmony between Netanyahu and Clinton was reflected in the post-summit press conference. Asked why he had supported Shimon Peres so energetically during the Israeli election campaign, a slightly embarrassed Clinton replied that he did not think "it needed much explaining" — a clear reference to Netanyahu's strong criticism of Oslo. The prime minister had a much warmer reception when he addressed a joint meeting of the two houses of Congress. Promising that Jerusalem would remain forever the united capital of Israel, and pledging to do everything in his power to cut U.S. civilian aid to Israel, Netanyahu brought the audience to its feet on several occasions.

But the prime minister's repeated statements about settlement expansion, his delay in meeting with Arafat, and ultimately the tunnel opening fed the administration's suspicion. Clinton was careful, however, not to pressure the Israeli leader, for fear of alienating Jewish voters in the November U.S. presidential election, and the president's special envoy to the Middle East, Dennis Ross, was intensively involved in brokering the Hebron deal in January.

December saw the appointment of Madeleine Albright as the new U.S. secretary of state, and there was much speculation over whether she would choose to play a hands-on role in the peace process, or sit back and let the two sides stew for a while. In the first part of 1997, Albright appeared to have adopted the latter approach, but with the Hamas suicide bombings in the second half of the year, the Americans were forced to step in and play the role of active mediator once again.

Worrying signs of the increasing strain in U.S.-Israeli relations were evident in the second half of 1997. In the space of a few weeks, between September and October, the chairman of the Appropriations Committee, Rep. Bob Livingston of

Louisiana, twice held up aid to Israel over relatively minor misunderstandings. The first hold on aid came in late September and was sparked by Israel's failure to extradite a U.S.-born teenage boy accused of the brutal murder of a Hispanic youth in Silver Spring, Maryland. The boy had fled to Israel with the hope of being tried there for the crime, insisting that since his father was born in Israel, he was an Israeli citizen and so could not be extradited. U.S. officials, including Albright, pushed hard to convince Israel to send him back to Maryland for trial.

In late October, Livingston again suspended aid, this time over Israel's failure to produce the paperwork needed to process a months-old deal to shift $50 million in U.S. aid from Israel's $3-billion account to cash-strapped Jordan. Ultimately, both issues were resolved: Israel did provide the paperwork, and Israeli attorney general Elyakim Rubinstein ruled in late October that the teenager could legally be extradited to the United States.

While minor hiccups in U.S.-Israel relations were certainly not uncommon over the years, a suspension in aid—even if only temporary—certainly was. Veteran observers of U.S.-Israeli relations pointed to the two incidents as proof of the erosion in the special relationship between the two countries resulting from the stalled peace process. But beyond the policy differences, there was another problem—a growing mistrust of Netanyahu in the Clinton administration. After returning from his four-day visit to Washington in October, President Ezer Weizman told reporters that he was shocked by the extent of the hostility he observed.

A further sign of the tension was President Clinton's refusal to meet with Netanyahu during the prime minister's November visit to the United States. While the White House claimed that the president had "scheduling problems," at one point his plane and that of the Israeli leader were parked close to one another at Indianapolis airport, and Clinton did find time to meet with Shimon Peres, who was in the country to give talks to various groups. Back in Israel after his trip, Netanyahu, during a private meeting, alluded to Clinton's refusal to meet him, saying, "The Americans believe there is a Saddam of the East—the one in Iraq— and a Saddam of the West—me." An aide to the prime minister later said he had been joking.

The erosion in relations, diplomatic observers said, had to be seen not only against the backdrop of the ailing peace process, but also in light of the growing unwillingness of U.S. Jews to automatically spring to Israel's defense, this because of the conflict over the issue of religious pluralism. "The 'Who is a Jew?' issue is important because it has a potential to alienate much of the American Jewish community over this core issue of their identity," explained Richard Haass, a former Bush administration strategist and director of foreign policy studies at the Brookings Institution. "And that has the potential to do lasting damage to the relationship."

But not all viewed the bilateral relations in crisis terms. "People who say this is a crisis have very short memories," observed Samuel Lewis, a former U.S. ambassador to Israel. "Think about the strains during the latter days of the Shamir government, when the Bush administration was holding up loan guarantees. Think about relations between the Reagan administration and the Israelis at the time of the Lebanon war."

Toward the end of the year, Secretary of State Albright met with Netanyahu in Paris on two occasions (December 7 and 18), in an effort to get the prime minister to give her a commitment regarding a date for the second redeployment as well as the amount of West Bank territory he intended handing over to Arafat. By the end of the year, the Americans were still waiting for Netanyahu's reply, having given him a short reprieve so that he could get his budget passed before having to deal with the highly explosive issue of withdrawal.

One constant source of quiet, low-level friction was the ongoing saga of Jonathan Pollard, the naval intelligence officer serving a life term in a U.S. jail for spying for Israel. Pollard was back in the news in late April 1997, when he petitioned the Israeli Supreme Court demanding to know why the government refused to recognize him as an Israeli agent. Toward the end of the year, Pollard received separate jail visits from two high-level Israelis—Absorption Minister Yuli Edelstein and Communications Minister Limor Livnat.

Israel and American Jews

Once again the highly volatile "Who is a Jew?" issue put Israeli-Diaspora relations to the test. Toward the end of 1996 the ultra-Orthodox Sephardic Shas Party submitted a bill in the Knesset stipulating that conversions to Judaism performed anywhere in the world would have no legal validity in Israel unless they had the stamp of approval of the Orthodox-controlled Chief Rabbinate in Israel. For Conservative and Reform Jews—especially in the United States, where they constituted a majority, as opposed to Israel where they were a small minority—the bill was nothing less than a declaration of war. Essentially, if the law passed, it would render Conservative, Reform, or other non-Orthodox conversions performed in Israel or abroad invalid under Israeli civil law. The significance of that for the non-Orthodox was potentially devastating: Their converts would not be eligible for automatic citizenship under the Law of Return.

Netanyahu tried to allay the fears of American Jews by promising to oppose the proposed legislation that would change the status quo (in which non-Orthodox conversions performed abroad were recognized in Israel). But the prime minister's reassurances could not assuage the deep sense of insult felt by non-Orthodox Jews in America. In their eyes, the bill had a clear message: The country they supported politically and financially as the legitimate Jewish homeland was labeling their brands of Judaism invalid in that very homeland.

Netanyahu angered American Jews when he canceled a planned address to the Reform movement's annual public policy conference in Washington during a visit in early May 1997, but managed to keep a speaking engagement with a

group of Christian evangelists. "If he could find the time to meet with a fundamentalist Christian group that gathered here," said Rabbi David Saperstein, head
of Reform's Religious Action Center, "could he not find the time to meet with
key leaders and representatives of the largest segment of the American Jewish
community? To many of our people it makes the whole thing even more astonishing." Netanyahu did later meet with a group of Reform and Conservative rabbis in his hotel, but they came away unimpressed by what they heard. Speaking
later in Washington, Netanyahu remarked ruefully that it was "probably easier
to make peace with the Palestinians than to resolve this issue satisfactorily."

Reform and Conservative leaders across the United States began urging their
congregants and the local federations to donate their money directly to non-
Orthodox institutions in Israel, rather than placing it in the general United Jewish Appeal (UJA) pot. In an attempt to limit the damage to its campaign, the UJA
began discussions in mid-May with Reform and Conservative leaders on a proposal to jointly raise $20 million for the movements' institutions in Israel. A
week earlier the UJA had run a full-page advertisement in the *New York Times*
beseeching donors to separate between the pluralism debate and their support for
Israel. "Wherever you stand on the debate about religion in Israel . . . ," the ad
read, "don't make your federation and UJA the battlefield."

With the conversion issue still unresolved, toward the end of the year the leaders of the non-Orthodox communities in the United States began discussing a
massive lobbying campaign to defeat the Knesset legislation. Ideas included a
massive airlift of 500 to 1,000 American Jewish leaders to Israel to meet with ministers, Knesset members, and the chief rabbis, as well as a reverse airlift to the
United States of the whole Knesset, at UJA expense, so that they could hear firsthand from American Jews how they felt about the issue.

At the mid-November 1997 meeting of the Council of Jewish Federations, Netanyahu was given a distinctly lukewarm reception and received only polite applause—in stark contrast to the enthusiastic ovations afforded every other prime
minister from Menachem Begin to Yitzhak Rabin. During his address Netanyahu
expressed empathy with the American Jewish position, telling the audience that
he was "a friend who is deeply and acutely aware of your pain."

The disenchantment of U.S. Jews with Israel was fueled further by their discomfort with the Israeli government's hard-line approach to the peace process. A
poll of 700 American Jews, conducted by the Israel Policy Forum, revealed that
a full two-thirds of the respondents had supported the Hebron deal, while only
14 percent opposed it.

Other Foreign Relations

The flood of diplomatic visitors to Israel that had characterized the Rabin-
Peres period dried up under Netanyahu, largely because of the ailing peace
process. There were, however, a number of high-profile visitors who arrived in the

second half of 1996 and in the course of 1997. Japanese foreign minister Yuki-hiko Ikeda came in late August 1996, visiting Israeli sites and the Palestinian areas, where he announced that his country would transfer $12 million in aid to the Palestinian Authority. When French president Jacques Chirac visited Israel in late October, he traveled to Ramallah, where he became the first foreign leader to address the Palestinian Legislative Council. Chirac, who was seeking an increased role in the peace process, expressed support for the creation of a Palestinian state.

Despite the general deterioration in Israel's international standing, Niger renewed diplomatic ties with Jerusalem on November 28. The African state had cut off relations during the 1973 Yom Kippur War. And in late December, President Ezer Weizman made the first-ever official visit by an Israeli head of state to India.

Industry and Trade Minister and former dissident Natan Sharansky made a dramatic return trip to Russia starting January 26, 1997 — his first since being released from a Soviet prison in 1986. During his five-day trip, Sharansky visited the grave of human-rights activist Andrei Sakharov and toured the Christopol prison, where he had been interned for more than eight years.

On February 3, 1997, Prime Minister Netanyahu and his wife, Sara, visited the Vatican, where they met with Pope John Paul II, who accepted an invitation from the prime minister to visit Israel before the year 2000. In late February, Ezer Weizman became the first Israeli president to make a state visit to Britain. Weizman, who met with the royal family, had served as a Royal Air Force pilot in World War II. His visit came 80 years after Chaim Weizmann, his uncle, helped bring about the Balfour Declaration, which represented the British government's agreement in principle to a Jewish homeland in Palestine. Foreign Minister David Levy was also abroad in late February, visiting China to discuss both the Mideast peace process and the status of the Israeli embassy in Hong Kong during the handover of the city to Chinese rule.

Israel moved to disrupt a potential arms deal between South Africa and Syria in the first half of 1997, which entailed the sale of $641 million in arms to Damascus, including tank fire-control systems. Israel hoped that American pressure on South Africa would sink the deal.

Israel-Turkey relations improved dramatically in the course of 1997. The two countries signed an economic agreement on April 4, to expand the volume of trade between the two countries from $500 million to around $2 billion. A few days later, in Ankara, Foreign Minister Levy became the first Israeli minister to meet with Turkey's prime minister, Necmetin Erbekan, the head of the Islamic Welfare Party. But the most dramatic developments were on the military front, causing analysts to observe that the improved relations between the two countries represented the emergence of a new strategic alliance in the region. During his mid-December visit to Ankara, Defense Minister Mordechai was warmly welcomed. The strength of the emerging alliance was underlined by the fact that

Mordechai's visit took place at the same time as the Islamic summit was being held in Teheran.

As part of the new military agreements, Israeli fighter planes and helicopters began conducting training exercises in Turkey. On December 31, Ankara once again ignored criticism from the Arab world and awarded Israel with a second contract, worth $75 million, for the upgrading of its jets. It was also announced that Israel and Turkey had decided to hold their first joint naval exercise, with U.S. participation, in the Mediterranean Sea off the Israeli coast, in January 1998.

In early May 1997, President Ernesto Samper became the first Colombian head of state to visit Israel, despite requests from American diplomats that Israel not invite him because of his alleged links to the drug trade in his country.

In late August, Prime Minister Netanyahu flew to the Far East, where he visited Japan and South Korea in an effort to increase trade and boost diplomatic relations. Speaking to 35 heads of major Japanese companies, Netanyahu tried to convince his audience that peace was on the way and that they should invest in Israel. "It's true that the stock exchange of peace is on a downward trend," he noted, "but I have insider information I can reveal to you that we're going to make peace, and it's in your interest to invest now so you don't miss the boat." But the Japanese were not buying, and officials made it clear that their big companies would not invest in Israel as long as the diplomatic situation remained unstable. During a short stop in Beijing, Netanyahu also tried to persuade Chinese officials to stop supplying material to Iran for the building of a nuclear reactor.

In September Israel and Croatia announced that they would establish diplomatic ties, this after Croatian president Franjo Tudjman issued an apology for having questioned whether six million Jews had actually perished in the Holocaust, in a book he published in 1989. There were suggestions that Israel's eagerness to establish ties with Croatia was motivated by the potential for lucrative arms sales to the Baltic state.

Israel received a surprise visitor on December 14 when Nation of Islam leader Louis Farrakhan crossed the Allenby Bridge from Jordan on a tourist visa, with the Foreign Ministry still deliberating whether to allow him in or not. He headed for the Palestinian-controlled areas where he met with Yasir Arafat. Farrakhan announced that he would pray at Jerusalem's Al-Aqsa Mosque, but he abandoned his plans and departed after claiming that the Israeli government would not offer him security guarantees.

DOMESTIC AFFAIRS

Netanyahu's First 18 Months

Netanyahu's first 18 months in office were littered with crises, confrontations with many of his ministers, and increasing criticism and disillusionment with him inside his own party. A growing number of Likud members also began to question the prime minister's credibility and trustworthiness. So frequent were the controversies and so loud the criticism of the decision-making process in the prime minister's office, even from within the ruling coalition, that the British *Economist* magazine ran an October 1997 cover shot of Netanyahu with the headline "Israel's Serial Bungler." Even as political commentators often panned Netanyahu and his penchant for stumbling into crises, they marveled at his Houdini-like ability to extract himself from seemingly impossible situations and survive.

Already in the process of putting together his government, in June 1996, Netanyahu experienced his first crisis, when designated foreign minister David Levy threatened to reject the post if Ariel Sharon was not included in the cabinet. The mini-crisis dragged on for two weeks, and in early July, Levy issued an ultimatum. During a joint appearance in front of the TV cameras, Levy warned a stony-faced Netanyahu that if Sharon was not made a minister, he would resign. Within a few days Sharon was sworn in as head of the Ministry of National Infrastructure—a ministry created just to accommodate him.

The team of aides Netanyahu put together was largely inexperienced, and questions were raised about the wisdom of his choices when several of his appointments were forced to resign or left of their own volition during his first six months at the helm. By August the first minister in the cabinet had resigned. After Attorney General Michael Ben-Yair announced an investigation into allegations against Justice Minister Ya'akov Ne'eman for suborning a witness in the Deri case, Ne'eman resigned. (In November, Ne'eman was charged, but with having given false testimony to the Supreme Court regarding the matter.) Tsachi Hanegbi, a Netanyahu loyalist, replaced Ne'eman.

Throughout his first 18 months, Netanyahu clashed with various segments of the Israeli establishment, including the media, the judiciary, and the military. When the daily *Ma'ariv* reported that Oren Shehor, the military head of government activities in the territories, who was in charge of one of the negotiating teams with the Palestinians, had been meeting secretly with opposition leaders, including Shimon Peres, Likud leaders were outraged. Army regulations clearly stipulated that a uniformed officer who wanted to meet with a politician first had to obtain the permission of the defense minister. In early November, Netanyahu and Defense Minister Yitzhak Mordechai suspended Shehor from any further involvement in talks with the Palestinians. In late December, Shehor handed in his resignation.

The same month, relations between Netanyahu and the head of the General Security Services, Ami Ayalon, came to a head when the prime minister hinted in a TV interview that Ayalon was responsible for the decision to open the controversial tunnel in Jerusalem. Ayalon acknowledged that he had agreed to the tunnel opening, but had advised that it be done only if there was concrete progress in the deadlocked peace process. There were reports that Ayalon was on the verge of resigning, but he did not leave his post.

Netanyahu was also at loggerheads with the media, which became ever more critical as the crises mounted. In the 1996 national election campaign, the right had accused the press of being left-leaning; after his victory, the media-savvy Netanyahu continued to use the antipathy toward the press in some segments of the public to galvanize his supporters.

As if the political and diplomatic crises that dogged him were not enough, Netanyahu was also forced to contend with a number of embarrassing personal incidents connected to his wife, Sara. Toward the end of 1996, a 21-year-old South African immigrant named Tania Shaw, who had worked in the Netanyahu's home as a nanny, claimed she had been mistreated by Sara Netanyahu and that she had been unfairly dismissed and was owed money by the first family. She filed a $25,000 civil suit against the Netanyahus.

On the political front, Netanyahu was having a tough time with his ministers and his own party. After Benny (Binyamin) Begin resigned in January 1997 over the signing of the Hebron deal, he quickly became Netanyahu's most vocal critic within the Likud, attacking him for continuing with the Oslo process and for government impropriety over the Bar-On affair (see below). In May Deputy Finance Minister David Magen, a member of the Gesher Party, resigned over what he said was the prime minister's incompetence and poor leadership.

Within weeks it was the chance of the finance minister himself, when Netanyahu effectively engineered the resignation of Dan Meridor on June 18, ostensibly over a relatively minor alteration to foreign exchange-rate policy. The chemistry between the two men had never been good, and Meridor was one of Netanyahu's more vocal critics over the Bar-On affair. What is more, during the 1996 election campaign, when Netanyahu was trailing badly in the polls, reports emerged of a possible putsch being organized within the party, with Meridor as the leader of the rebellion.

Netanyahu's ousting of the highly regarded Meridor sparked criticism within the Likud and among coalition allies. Former Likud prime minister Yitzhak Shamir announced in a radio interview that he had lost faith in Netanyahu. But the prime minister was clearly counting on the matter soon disappearing from the headlines and on his coalition partners not wanting to bring him down for fear of new elections. "They can all scream their heads off, but they know that when they destroy Netanyahu, they'll destroy themselves," said Likud MK Reuven Rivlin.

Ya'akov Ne'eman, who had been acquitted on May 15 of giving false testimony to the Supreme Court, was sworn in as Meridor's replacement; Michael Eitan joined the cabinet as science minister. But the cabinet reshuffle left Likud powerhouse Ariel Sharon seething, since he had been Netanyahu's initial preference for the post of finance minister. A planned reconciliation meeting between the two lasted three minutes, ending when Sharon abruptly up and left.

One sign of the trouble within the ruling coalition was a July 21 no-confidence vote, which the opposition won 49-44. Still, the outcome was little more than a moral victory for the Labor-led opposition, since under the new election law an absolute majority of 61 MKs was required to bring down the government in a vote of no confidence. Shas spiritual mentor Rabbi Ovadia Yosef found his own way to express his dissatisfaction with the prime minister. "The Gemara gives a parable," he said during a July sermon. "When a shepherd is angry at his flock, when they cause him grief or trouble, don't walk straight, what does he do? He puts as their leader a little, blind nannygoat, who walks and falls. And they walk and fall. A blind nannygoat. Why does he do this? Because they are not right. . . . If we have as a prime minister someone who is not suited, it is our fault, not his." When the rabbi's implied criticism of Netanyahu became public, Shas politicians tried to explain that Rabbi Yosef's words were merely a parable, that he had not been criticizing Netanyahu himself.

Criticism in the Likud was also growing as party members became increasingly frustrated and disillusioned with the prime minister, whom they began to view as both incompetent and untrustworthy. "The Israeli people," Meridor said in the weeks after his resignation, "deserve more than a choice between Netanyahu and Labor." After the Mashaal debacle in late September (see above), the criticism got louder. "Every morning people turn on the radio asking what catastrophe is coming next," said David Re'em, a Likud MK and one of Netanyahu's most out-spoken critics in the party. After Netanyahu delivered his opening speech at the start of the Knesset's winter term, none of his ministers came forward to offer the traditional congratulatory handshake.

Netanyahu's ability to survive was not only due to his political instincts or his skilled use of the media, but was also the result of the new direct election law, which required an absolute majority of 61 in a vote to bring down both the prime minister and the Knesset. With Knesset members not eager to risk their seats, it was difficult to find 61 who would be willing to vote no-confidence in the gov-ernment. To bring about direct elections just for prime minister, but not for the Knesset, 80 members of parliament were required, also a seemingly unlikely prospect. Some observers did speculate, though, that the moment 61 votes could be found to support a no-confidence motion, it would only be a matter of hours before enough Knesset members—fearful of new general elections—came for-ward to complete the required 80.

There was also much speculation over a possible challenge to Netanyahu by Jerusalem mayor Ehud Olmert. Olmert, along with the American philanthropist Irving Moskowitz, had pressured Netanyahu over the tunnel opening and em-barrassed the prime minister with the Ras al-Amud housing affair. After a com-promise was reached over Ras al-Amud, political observers wondered where the Olmert-Moskowitz duo would strike next. They also wondered whether Olmert, with the financial backing of Moskowitz, was trying to outflank Netanyahu from the right in a bid to challenge him for leadership of the Likud and ultimately the prime ministership.

In late October, Netanyahu was in hot water again after reporters recorded him loudly whispering into the ear of Rabbi Yitzhak Kadourie, an elderly kabbalistic sage with strong influence among Sephardic Israelis, that the left had "forgotten what it means to be Jewish" and was willing to place the country's security in the hands of the Arabs. After Ashkenazic chief rabbi Yisrael Lau criticized the remarks for being divisive, the prime minister issued a "half-hearted" apology.

Netanyahu faced possibly the biggest threat to his tenure when his efforts to cement his control over the Likud sparked a mutiny. At the party convention in November, Netanyahu engineered the canceling of party primaries, all the while denying that he was behind the move. Many Likud ministers and Knesset members saw the change back to the previous system of picking the party Knesset list as a direct threat to them. No longer would they be elected by 200,000 Likud members, but rather by 2,700 central committee members, many of them Netanyahu loyalists. For them, the message was clear: Reverting to the old system was a way for Netanyahu to get rid of potential rivals within the party.

Likud leaders were also outraged by what they viewed as antidemocratic tactics at the convention. Before the vote over abolishing the system of primaries was held, ballot papers were handed out that had X-es preprinted on them in the appropriate boxes. After the convention, a freelance cameraman told the press that he had been hired by party hacks loyal to Netanyahu and his right-hand man, Avigdor Lieberman, to film those party members who opposed doing away with primaries. Even a Netanyahu loyalist, Silvan Shalom, said that it reminded him of "dark regimes."

With Netanyahu visiting the United States in mid-November, the rebellion gained momentum. The mutineers, including Meridor, Begin, Olmert, Tel Aviv mayor Ronni Milo, and Communications Minister Limor Livnat, reportedly met to coordinate moves to replace Netanyahu. The question was whether they could garner enough Likud members to support them. At a November 17 meeting of the Likud Knesset faction, speaker after speaker lambasted the prime minister and his party henchmen. Even Defense Minister Mordechai, whom some viewed as a potential rival to Netanyahu and who until then had tried to remain above party politics, announced that he was "considering his future."

But the rebellion petered out as quickly as it had sprung up. Olmert, Milo, and Meridor could not reach agreement on which of them would assume the leadership role, nor on how best to oust Netanyahu. There were also clear ideological differences between members of the rebel group, with Milo, for example, supporting Oslo and Limor Livnat much more hard-line. Many of the remaining Knesset members also feared that if new elections were held, the Labor Party might well sweep to power.

Milo fueled the rumor mill further when he announced in mid-November that "major changes" were about to take place in the traditional Israeli party structure. He was apparently referring to what political commentators had termed the

"Big Bang"—a fundamental reordering of the Israeli political map that would be brought about by the creation of a centrist party made up of politicians from both Labor and Likud.

When Netanyahu returned from abroad, he immediately set about to appease his critics in the party. He promised to hold a referendum among the 200,000 Likud members over the issue of primaries, and he also set up a committee to investigate any irregularities at the Likud convention. (By the end of the year, the committee had disbanded and talk of a referendum had receded.) Most significant was the November 23 resignation of Avigdor Lieberman as director-general of the Prime Minister's Office—the man who had helped Netanyahu conquer the Likud, had overseen the rebuilding of the party, and had helped engineer Netanyahu's win in the 1996 elections. Likud leaders had fingered Lieberman as the one who put Netanyahu's plan to do away with primaries into action and who had worked behind the scenes to insure the vote went his boss's way at the party convention. Netanyahu, political analysts observed, had now lost his closest and most loyal aide and had become even more isolated.

There was much speculation over Lieberman's future, some suggesting that he would continue to help Netanyahu from outside the Prime Minister's Office. There was even conjecture over whether the former Russian émigré would go into politics himself, using his popularity among Jews from the former Soviet Union as a springboard. In mid-December, Lieberman ended the speculation when he announced that he was entering the race for head of the World Likud—the party's international body—against the incumbent, Ronni Milo. Realizing that he had little chance of reelection because of his dovish views, Milo stood aside only days before the vote, and the more hard-line Livnat, an ally of his, stepped in. The scenes at the party convention became ugly when voting got under way, with members of the French Likud delegation, who were identified with Lieberman, physically blocking members from reaching the ballot boxes. After punches were thrown and several journalists and cameramen were beaten, the vote was called off. Netanyahu, realizing that the chaotic scenes were doing damage to him and the party, rushed to the convention to cool tempers. In overnight negotiations, the two camps agreed to back down and to elect a compromise candidate, Zalman Shoval, a former ambassador to the United States.

Already battered by the internal Likud wrangling, Netanyahu had to face yet another embarrassing episode concerning his wife. In December the daily *Yediot Aharonot* printed a lengthy article revealing that Sara Netanyahu maintained a private staff and two secretaries to which she was not entitled. The article also chronicled her abusive behavior toward those working for her. In one instance, the article alleged, she ordered bodyguards to clean up after her children. In another, she allegedly forced a staff member to taste a bottle of wine she had received as a gift to make sure it was not poisoned. And in yet another embarrassing encounter, she allegedly tossed her husband's shoes at a cleaning woman whom she felt had not polished them sufficiently. The Netanyahus did not file a libel suit against *Yediot*, but they did announce that they were canceling their subscription to the paper.

The 1998 budget debate provided Netanyahu with yet another bout of coalition worries. While he seemed to have secured the support of most of his coalition partners ahead of the December 31 vote, there were reports that Foreign Minister Levy was unhappy—both with the government's slowness on the peace front and what he said was the budget's lack of sensitivity with regard to social concerns and the poor. There were also reports that hard-line coalition members were making their support for the budget contingent on Netanyahu agreeing to put off the West Bank redeployment. Benny Begin had already announced that he would not support the budget because of Netanyahu's agreement to go ahead with the pullback. As it happened, the budget debate ran into 1998. (See "Economic Developments," below.)

The Bar-On Affair

On January 10, 1997, Jerusalem lawyer Ronni Bar-On was appointed attorney general. Bar-On's appointment to the country's top prosecutorial job had been brought to the cabinet meeting without prior warning and hurriedly pushed through by Netanyahu, who refused to accept his ministers' requests for a delay so that they could learn more about the candidate—a somewhat inconspicuous Jerusalem lawyer and a Likud party activist. The decision sparked an immediate wave of criticism. Law professors attacked the appointment ferociously, stressing not only Bar-On's close party affiliation, but, more importantly, his limited experience and the fact that he simply did not meet the accepted criterion for the office of attorney general—mainly the qualifications needed to become a Supreme Court justice. It also soon emerged that Chief Justice Aharon Barak had not given his approval to Bar-On's appointment when consulted by Justice Minister Tsachi Hanegbi.

When the appointment was challenged in the Supreme Court, Bar-On announced that he was resigning—after only 24 hours on the job and never having even entered his office. Netanyahu had reportedly asked Bar-On to stand down and end the embarrassment the appointment was causing the government. Hanegbi complained that Bar-On had been the victim of "a baseless witch-hunt." Bar-On was equally incensed: "The unjustified personal attack on me," he fumed, "has created an injustice toward me, the government and the person who stands at its head."

On the night of January 22, 1997, Israel Television's Mabat news program dropped a bombshell. Ayala Hasson, a relatively inexperienced reporter, revealed an incredible tale. According to information that she uncovered, Bar-On had been appointed as part of an influence-peddling scam that included some of the country's leading politicians. Reportedly, once he occupied the senior legal post, Bar-

On would accept a plea bargain for Arye Deri, the leader of the ultra-Orthodox Shas Party, who was facing corruption charges. In return, said Hasson, Deri promised to provide Netanyahu with the votes he needed in the cabinet to push through the Hebron agreement. (Hence, the scandal became known as the "Bar-On–Hebron Affair." The press also nicknamed the affair "Bibigate," and there were many columnists who drew comparisons with Watergate.)

All the protagonists in the story, including Netanyahu, Hanegbi, Deri, Avigdor Lieberman, and David Appel, a building contractor and Likud activist with close ties to Lieberman and Deri, strenuously denied any involvement, and some threatened legal action against Israel TV. Netanyahu, who initially dismissed the report as a "complete fabrication," soon became a little more cautious, saying it was "inconceivable" that any of his aides could have been involved in such a scam. His aides attacked the media, especially Israel TV, insinuating that it was biased toward the left and was out to topple the prime minister.

Israel TV stood by its story, insisting that the accusations in its report were "rooted in concrete." Several ministers expressed shock at the revelations and their potential ramifications, if proven accurate, and most of Netanyahu's cabinet colleagues refused to give him unequivocal public backing. Former Science Minister Benny Begin, the only one who had voted against Bar-On's appointment, called for Justice Minister Hanegbi to be fired for having allegedly misled the government when he presented Bar-On's candidacy. Yisrael B'Aliyah leader Natan Sharansky, a Netanyahu loyalist, announced that if there was "even 10 percent of truth in Israel TV's story, this government has no place in continuing to govern." There was much speculation over Hasson's sources. Most reports pointed to Deri's attorney, Dan Avi-Yitzhak, who at one point had been on Netanyahu's short list for the attorney general post. The suspicions were strengthened when Avi-Yitzhak resigned as Deri's lawyer and withdrew from the corruption case.

The upshot of Bar-On's resignation was that Netanyahu was ultimately forced to appoint the man who many had felt all along was the obvious choice for the job—Elyakim Rubinstein, who had served as cabinet secretary in both the Shamir and Rabin governments and was a sitting district court judge. Some suggested that Netanyahu had intentionally overlooked Rubinstein because he apparently viewed him as less pliant and as part of the legal establishment, which, along with many of the country's elites, he regarded as hostile to him. On January 29, Rubinstein, who had also participated in peace talks with Egypt, Jordan, and the Palestinians, was approved by the cabinet.

Under growing pressure, Netanyahu announced that the police would investigate the matter, and State Attorney Edna Arbel officially ordered one of the most sensitive police investigations the country had ever known. A somewhat dismayed public then watched as a procession of senior political figures, including Deri, Hanegbi, and Netanyahu himself, were questioned by the police.

Despite Israel TV's insistence when it initially broke the story that it had no evidence of Netanyahu's complicity in the scam, the prime minister was questioned in his office by police for four hours on February 18. It soon leaked out that Netanyahu had been cautioned by his interrogators that he might ultimately face criminal charges, making him the first Israeli prime minister ever to be questioned as a suspect. It also emerged that the prime minister had been evasive when questioned, answering "I don't know," or "I don't remember," to many of the questions put to him.

The day after he was questioned by police, Netanyahu appointed Ya'acov Weinroth, a leading criminal lawyer, to represent him. As much as giving Netanyahu private advice, Weinroth quickly mounted his client's public defense, giving a string of TV, radio, and newspaper interviews in which he strongly protested Netanyahu's innocence and rejected opposition calls for the prime minister to suspend himself until the investigation was over. In one interview he declared that Netanyahu would emerge completely unstained by "so much as a particle of a criminal act."

After weeks of investigation the affair reached another climax when it was leaked to the papers that the police had recommended to State Attorney Arbel that Netanyahu, Hanegbi, Deri, and Lieberman all be indicted for their roles in the Bar-On scandal. The country, and Netanyahu, waited with bated breath as Arbel and Rubinstein deliberated. On April 20 they gave their answer—and Netanyahu breathed freely again. Due to insufficient evidence, they announced at a televised news conference, the prime minister would not be indicted. Hanegbi, they said, would not be charged either. The only one who would face charges was Shas leader Arye Deri. But Arbel and Rubinstein's 75-page report was sharply critical of the prime minister and spoke of a "real suspicion" of criminal behavior at the highest political echelons.

Netanyahu was unbowed. In a carefully crafted six-minute address on television, he conceded that mistakes had been made regarding Bar-On's appointment but denied that there had been any illegalities. He also attacked the opposition parties and what he said were "leftists in the media" who were out to get him. "At the root of the whole affair," he continued, was not an attempt to subvert the country's legal system, but a campaign by "people who don't like me and want to delegitimize me as prime minister. . . . Some people, especially at Channel 1, are still not prepared to accept the voters' choice in the last elections. And almost every evening they try to undermine the legitimacy of the government."

Clearly Netanyahu was counting on the public not sifting through the whole report, much of it phrased in technical legal language. But the report in fact confirmed that much of what the press had revealed was correct. "Our conclusion," stated Arbel, "is that there is indeed a real suspicion that the prime minister proposed to his cabinet the appointment of attorney Bar-On as government attorney general only, or among other things, to please MK Deri, while aware of, or turning a blind eye to, the possibility of an improper connection between Deri and Bar-On." But, she concluded, she did not think that it would be possible to prove this "beyond reasonable doubt." Arbel noted that several members of her team had been in favor of charging both Netanyahu and Hanegbi. For his part, Rubinstein wrote that there had been "a real threat to the rule of law."

Netanyahu's coalition partners, some of whom had made far-reaching statements when the story first broke, heaved a sigh of relief when Arbel and Rubinstein announced they were not pressing charges against the prime minister. Avigdor Kahalani, the head of the centrist Third Way, had little difficulty in persuading the more militant members of his party to remain in the coalition. Sharansky, who had said that even if "10 percent" of the Bar-On story was true the government had no right to exist, made certain demands of Netanyahu—that he consult ministers more frequently and change the decision-making process in the government—but quickly made it clear that his party was not leaving the coalition.

Some leading Likud figures, like Finance Minister Dan Meridor, were openly critical of Netanyahu. "Instead of attacking the media, the police and the state prosecution," he said, "those involved would do better to ask themselves how this terrible failure occurred." But Meridor did not resign (he would do that a short time later, in June; see above). Members of the Labor Party, the left-wing Meretz, and the Movement for Quality Government all appealed to the Supreme Court in an effort to have the attorney general's decision not to indict overturned, but they were ultimately all overruled on June 15.

The fact that the Moroccan-born Deri, the head of the Sephardic Shas Party, was the only one singled out for likely prosecution evoked a wave of ethnic tension. In the eyes of Shas supporters, the decision was yet another sign of the prejudice toward Sephardim, in this instance by the Ashkenazi-dominated state prosecution. At a rally in a Jerusalem stadium attended by thousands of Shas supporters, Deri was lifted up and carried around like a conquering hero. "All the Ashkenazis got off. Only the Sephardi was blamed," railed Rabbi Ovadia Yosef, the spiritual leader of Shas. His son, David, charged that the country's legal system had lost its legitimacy, and Sephardic politicians on both the left and the right said the decision to single out Deri alone for indictment indicated a high degree of social insensitivity.

The Labor Party—Ehud Barak Takes Over

Even though Netanyahu appeared to be stumbling from one crisis to the next, the Labor opposition remained largely ineffective. This was due in no small measure to the fact that Shimon Peres, who had lost the 1996 election, remained at the party helm. Peres's criticism of the Netanyahu government was muted, maybe because he still harbored hopes that Netanyahu might invite him to join a national unity government. The fact that the party was gearing up for leadership primaries also limited Labor's effectiveness, as the various candidates invested time in their own personal campaigns. It was not until June 1997, a full year after Labor's defeat, that a new leader was chosen to head the party.

Four candidates put themselves up for election ahead of the June 3 party primary. The clear favorite was Ehud Barak, the former chief of staff who had served as foreign minister in the previous Labor government. With his military background—he headed Israel's elite Sayeret Matkal commando unit during his army career and was head of military intelligence before ultimately reaching the top post—Barak saw himself as the natural successor to Yitzhak Rabin, whose own military career and security credentials had enabled him to garner enough of the centrist vote in the 1992 elections to oust then prime minister Yitzhak Shamir. Barak, who had been Netanyahu's commander in Sayeret Matkal, focused his campaign largely on the issue of peace and security, a fact that led some in his own party to label him a "Bibi clone." The only candidate considered a remote threat to Barak was Yossi Beilin, a minister in the former Labor government and one of the architects of the Oslo accords. The only candidate who focused his campaign almost exclusively on social issues was Shlomo Ben-Ami, a former ambassador to Spain and a history professor. The Moroccan-born Ben-Ami argued that the Israeli-Palestinian conflict was in the process of being resolved and that the real issues on the agenda were now social ones. Only someone with his background, he insisted, could attract traditional Likud voters, many of them of Sephardi origin and from Israel's poorer areas. The dark horse was Ephraim Sneh, a former health minister and commander of Israeli forces in Lebanon and the West Bank.

In the months before the party primary, Barak was dogged by an episode from his past, the 1992 Tze'elim affair. As chief of staff, he was present when a fatal training accident occurred at the Tze'elim base: five members of the elite Sayeret Matkal commando unit were killed when a missile was accidentally fired at their position. A newspaper report in 1995 claimed that Barak had failed to assist the victims and had hastily left the scene in his helicopter before the injured were evacuated—allegations he vehemently denied. Barak was concerned that State Comptroller Miriam Ben-Porat, who had been working for almost two years on a report on the incident, would make her findings public just ahead of the party election. (In early July the state comptroller finally announced that she would not be investigating Barak's behavior with regard to the evacuation of the injured. She explained that she had encountered conflicting testimonies and did not have the tools to undertake such an inquiry.)

In mid-May Barak and Peres clashed over the role that the latter would continue to play in the party. Peres was prepared to accept what would be a newly created role of party president, if the position was vested with certain powers. Barak was also willing to accept the creation of a new post, but only so long as it was an honorary one, devoid of any real power. When the two went head-to-head at the May 13 party convention, Barak easily won a vote on the issue, and the idea of a party president was buried. For Peres the snub was humiliating. So was the reaction of the party members during his speech. "They call me a loser. I ask you, am I a loser?" he shouted from the podium. The answer was a deafening "Yes! Yes!"

As expected, Barak won an easy victory in early June, garnering just over 50 percent of the vote. Beilin placed second with a creditable 28 percent; Ben-Ami also did better than many had expected with 15 percent; Sneh got a mere 4 percent of the vote. Shortly after his election, Barak visited the Western Wall where he was jeered by some of the ultra-Orthodox worshipers. He then headed for the working-class Tel Aviv neighborhood of Kfar Shalem where he met with residents. The choice of locations for the two visits was not coincidental. In the May 1996 general election, Netanyahu had won almost wall-to-wall support in the religious community as well as massive support from the largely Sephardic working class. To have any chance of winning the next election, Barak knew that these were two of the key constituencies where he would have to chip away at Netanyahu's support.

In line with this strategy, Barak took the Labor Party convention to the Sephardic working-class town of Netivot in the Negev in late September—its first ever outside of Tel Aviv. Barak then did something no Labor leader before him had ever done. He asked the Sephardim for forgiveness for the "mistakes" made in absorbing immigrants from North Africa and Middle Eastern countries in the early years of the state. He apologized for the condescending treatment they had received, for the fact that the immigrants and their children had been dispatched to remote desert towns like Netivot, and for the fact that their culture had been shunned and their descendants made to feel embarrassed about their own traditions and roots. "Entire communities were uprooted," said Barak, "tradition was broken, the fabric of the family damaged. It wasn't done maliciously, but the result was a great deal of suffering. We didn't always know how to respect the wealth of the [Jewish] sources from which we draw. In my name and in the name of the Labor Party—I ask for forgiveness."

Some party old-timers were angered by the apology, but Barak's strategy was clear: not only was he asking for forgiveness, but he was also saying that he represented a new generation in the party, that since he had been a child in the early years of the state, he bore no direct responsibility for the humiliations for which he was apologizing. The apology, clearly part of Barak's strategy to break the right wing's hold on Sephardic voters, was also meant to distance Labor from the left-wing and ultra-secular Meretz Party, which many of the traditional Sephardim viewed as hostile to religion and as the ultimate representative of the Ashkenazi elite. Barak's remarks were met with some skepticism, especially in the press, but also among the general public. Some Sephardim, though, saw Barak's apology as a possible opening to a new relationship, but said they would take a wait-and-see approach.

Barak was criticized by his supporters in his first few months at the helm for being too stately in his criticism of the government and Netanyahu. But he adopted a more militant tone in his address to the Knesset at the opening session of the winter term, calling on Netanyahu to resign and accusing the prime minister of having "no judgement, no insight or ability, to lead us away from the tragedy he's pushing us into." In his first six months as party leader, however,

Barak did not seem to be winning over disillusioned Likud voters, despite the prime minister's many blunders. He struggled to find the right message and the right tone and, unlike Netanyahu, his television appearances were often awkward. Some senior Labor members also began to express dissatisfaction with the way Barak was running the party, and he was criticized for being too dictatorial at a late-November party convention. He also drew fire when he hinted that if early elections were called, there might not be sufficient time to have full party primaries for the Knesset list.

Barak continued to hold a healthy lead in the polls, hovering around the low-to-middle forties as opposed to Netanyahu's low thirties. Still, around 25 percent of the voters remained undecided, a crucial factor, since previous elections had shown that two-thirds of the floating vote traditionally went to the right.

Religion

THE CONVERSION BATTLE

The ongoing battle between the Orthodox and non-Orthodox denominations focused in this period on the issue of conversion to Judaism. The Knesset was considering legislation that would formalize the status quo, which gives the state-run Orthodox Chief Rabbinate exclusive jurisdiction over all conversions performed in Israel, thereby denying the legitimacy of conversions performed by non-Orthodox bodies. The conflict heated up on April 1, 1997, when the bill passed a first reading in the Knesset by a vote of 51–32. The vote sparked immediate recrimination between the Reform and Conservative movements, both of which had long been seeking recognition in Israel, and the Orthodox establishment, bent on denying them any legitimacy. Delighted with their victory, ultra-Orthodox Knesset members announced that their next mission would be to end state recognition of non-Orthodox conversions performed abroad. (The bill did not concern itself with conversions performed outside Israel.)

While a Knesset committee was given the task of searching for a compromise solution before the bill was brought for a final vote, religious politicians made it clear that if Netanyahu did not back the legislation, his political career would come to an abrupt end. "If Netanyahu wants to stay in power he has to keep his promises," said ultra-Orthodox Shas Knesset member Shlomo Benizri, referring to the coalition agreement the prime minister had signed with his party. "The Reform don't have any voting power in Israel."

The Conservative and Reform movements did however make progress on another front in their battle for recognition in Israel when the Supreme Court passed a ruling in mid-April that effectively forced the religious council in Netanyah to accept a Reform representative as a member. The decision was a major blow for the Orthodox establishment, which held exclusive control over the councils and the hundreds of millions of shekels in government funds they received to build synagogues, supervise *kashrut*, operate ritual baths, and provide other religious services in their areas.

The person at the center of the controversy was Dr. Joyce Rosman Brenner, a member of the Reform movement who had spent two years battling to get onto the Netanyah council. Despite a landmark 1994 Supreme Court decision that barred religious councils from disqualifying candidates because they were Conservative or Reform adherents, the Orthodox establishment had employed a series of delaying tactics in an effort to put off implementation of the ruling. (Hence the repeat ruling in April.)

Religious politicians, frantic to find a way to circumvent the ruling, suggested new legislation, or even dissolving the councils altogether. "Anything is better than having Reform and Conservative," remarked ultra-Orthodox MK Avraham Ravitz. On August 10, Netanyahu, acting as religious affairs minister (because the serving minister, Eli Suissa of Shas, refused to sign), was left with no choice but to sign the order making Rosman Brenner a member of the Netanyah religious council. When she arrived for the meeting, the council head angrily refused to start and demanded that she leave. When Rosman Brenner refused, he summoned the police. After much wrangling, she agreed to leave but vowed that she would be back the next time the council met.

Meanwhile, on the conversion front, there were attempts to broker a compromise. Conservative and Reform leaders did agree to freeze a petition to the Supreme Court demanding recognition of non-Orthodox conversions in Israel, as long as the Knesset legislation was frozen too. But the chances of a compromise looked remote, especially with ultra-Orthodox politicians refusing to budge. After Reform and Conservative leaders attended a session of the Knesset Law Committee in which compromises on the conversion bill were discussed, Moshe Gafni, a Knesset member of the ultra-Orthodox United Torah Judaism Party, said that sitting "in the same room as them is like watching a Torah being burned."

In an effort to find a way out of the conversion imbroglio, in June Netanyahu appointed prominent lawyer and former Justice Minister Ya'akov Ne'eman (he would become Finance Minister in July; see above) to head a committee to try and find a compromise on the conversion issue. Most observers thought that Ne'eman, an Orthodox Jew, would try to find a technical solution to the sensitive issue. But he went much further, endeavoring to shape a compromise of historic proportions—one that would accommodate Reform and Conservative Judaism within the halakhic framework. Ne'eman hoped that the compromise would prevent a major split between Orthodox and non-Orthodox, as well as between Israel and the Diaspora.

The seven-man committee—comprising five Orthodox members, one Reform member, and one Conservative member—held 40 sessions before reaching a compromise solution on both conversion and marriage that was acceptable to all but one of the members—a remarkable feat. The committee recommended setting up a conversion school to be attended by all potential converts, in which rabbis from all three denominations would lecture, but with the final conversion court being made up only of Orthodox rabbis. With regard to marriage, the committee recommended that the state also recognize marriages performed by Conservative and Reform rabbis, as long as they adhered to Halakhah and there were two representatives of the Chief Rabbinate present at the ceremony as witnesses. The key to the committee's approach was to offer the sides what they desired most—halakhic primacy for the Orthodox and recognition for the non-Orthodox.

But everything went sour in mid-October when Ne'eman met with Rabbi Ovadiah Yosef, the spiritual mentor of the ultra-Orthodox Shas Party, to present the emerging compromise. Shas Knesset members were present at what Ne'eman hoped would be a private discussion, and the details of the compromise were leaked to the media. Arye Deri immediately denounced it as "horrific." The rest of the Orthodox establishment—including the modern-Orthodox National Religious Party, which had always viewed Jewish unity as a primary value—followed suit, denouncing any compromise that would lend legitimacy to Conservative and Reform rabbis in Israel. Sephardic chief rabbi Eliyahu Bakshi-Doron, who had labeled Reform rabbis "clowns," referred to Reform Judaism as a fabricated religion (although he did say he might be willing to deal with Conservative leaders). Ironically, his comments came as he was trying to initiate a dialogue with the Islamic fundamentalist Hamas movement. "I'm ready to negotiate with any Jew as a Jew," he said. "As a brother. And the Reform are our brothers. But to negotiate with Reform leaders as rabbis, absolutely not! They got angry when I said that a Reform rabbi who conducts a marriage between two women is a clown. I repeat: One can negotiate even with Sheikh Yassin. He has his faith, I have mine. But if there are Reform rabbis who say they don't believe in God, isn't it absurd that these people head temples and lead prayers? As rabbis, they're clowns. The leader of the lesbian [Reform] community in San Francisco is also called a Reform rabbi. Does anyone think we can recognize her as a rabbi? We'd make a joke out of Torah."

In mid-October Shas officials met with Netanyahu to protest the recommendations of the Ne'eman committee, and the prime minister quickly announced that he would back the law effectively barring state recognition of non-Orthodox conversions carried out in Israel. The prime minister was in a bind, trapped between threats by the religious parties to bring down the government if he did not support their bill, and demands by the secular Third Way, Yisrael B'Aliyah, and Tsomet that he block the legislation. Not that Labor leader Ehud Barak had it any easier—having to choose between supporting the bill and losing face with his secular electorate as well as with American Jewry, and opposing the bill and endangering a possible future coalition with the religious parties.

Conservative and Reform leaders were incensed and threatened to return to the Supreme Court. But just as the sides appeared to have reached a dead end, the non-Orthodox were persuaded to reconsider, to accept a three-month time-out during which Ne'eman was supposed to find a way out of the morass.

Back in August, passions had reached the boiling point over another issue of disagreement between the two sides—the right to hold mixed prayer services at the Western Wall. On August 11, the Jerusalem police evicted a group of about 200 male and female members of the Conservative movement who had arrived at the Western Wall Plaza, on the eve of Tisha B'Av, to hold a joint prayer service. Police said they were acting to protect the Conservative worshipers from angry ultra-Orthodox Jews opposed to the gathering. Conservative members complained about police brutality and vowed to return to the Wall to hold mixed prayer services.

RELIGIOUS-SECULAR SHOWDOWN

The dramatic rise in the power of the religious parties in the 1996 general elections—they garnered more than a fifth of all Jewish votes—set the scene for a religious-secular showdown, and particularly a confrontation between large sections of the religious community and the liberal-leaning Supreme Court. One of the major battlegrounds was the issue of Shabbat—whether streets, shops, stores, and restaurants should remain open on the Sabbath. The first heated clash was over the ultra-Orthodox demand that Bar-Ilan Street, a major Jerusalem road passing largely through ultra-Orthodox areas, be closed on the Sabbath and on Jewish holidays. The Bar-Ilan standoff became violent in 1996 when ultra-Orthodox demonstrators gathered along the road during the Sabbath and hurled rocks and other projectiles at police and passing motorists. Activists of the secular left-wing Meretz Party also demonstrated, organizing convoys of cars to travel along the disputed road during the Sabbath.

When Transport Minister Yitzhak Levy of the National Religious Party decreed that the road would be closed on the Sabbath, secular activists petitioned the Supreme Court, which ruled in mid-August that the street should remain open and that a committee should be appointed by the government to investigate the matter. The decision was met by a furious ultra-Orthodox assault on the court. Chief Justice Aharon Barak was placed under 24-hour guard by the General Security Services after he was vilified in the ultra-Orthodox media. One newspaper described Barak as "a great danger to democracy and freedom," while another described a coup-like scenario in which Barak dissolved the government and instituted martial law. In mid-April 1997, when the Supreme Court ruled 6–1 again to keep the road open, the six affirmative judges were given round-the-clock protection. Passions finally cooled after a compromise solution was imposed whereby the road would be closed during prayer hours.

The secular neighborhood of Ramat Aviv Gimel in north Tel Aviv provided another flashpoint early in 1997, when Lev Leviev, the new ultra-Orthodox owner of the Africa-Israel Real Estate and Development Company, announced that a mall his company was constructing in the area would be closed on the Sabbath and all its restaurants would be kosher. (Construction on the mall had started before Leviev took over, and contracts had already been signed with restaurants.) Tel Aviv mayor Ronni Milo called on residents to boycott the mall if it closed on Saturdays and to organize a "Shabbat caravan" of vehicles to drive through the nearby ultra-Orthodox neighborhood of Bnei Brak. Ultra-Orthodox leaders jumped to Leviev's defense. One denounced his critics as "Nazis," and the ultra-Orthodox paper *Hamodia* began printing a blacklist of places that were open on the Sabbath and charged admission fees, calling on its readers to boycott them.

Under Shas labor minister Eli Yishai, Druze members of his ministry's Sabbath enforcement squad, which had ceased operating under the Labor government, began making rounds again. They handed out dozens of fines to stores doing business on Saturday.

There were other local conflicts between religious and secular Jews. The most severe confrontation, in Pardes Hannah, began in mid-1997 when a group of secular residents, who had recently moved into a town-house project in the area, discovered that mobile homes had been illegally erected on a nearby site to serve as an ultra-Orthodox learning center. The ultra-Orthodox also rented 30 apartments in the neighborhood and set up a synagogue in one of them. It was not long before the two sides were at loggerheads. The secular residents claimed that the ultra-Orthodox had cursed them, attacked them, and threatened their lives. The ultra-Orthodox residents, in turn, accused their secular neighbors of being intentionally provocative by playing loud music near the synagogue on the Sabbath. Both sides lodged complaints with the police.

On December 30, gasoline bombs were tossed into two of the ultra-Orthodox trailers that were being used as classrooms, leaving them badly damaged. Despite attempts by politicians from the ultra-Orthodox Shas Party and the secular Meretz Party to negotiate a compromise, at year's end the two sides were still refusing to budge.

The Maccabiah Bridge Disaster

The 15th Maccabiah Games in the summer of 1997 had been planned as a celebration of Zionism's 100th anniversary, but they turned into a nightmare even before the events got under way. As the Australian delegation made its way across a temporary bridge constructed over the Yarkon River to carry the athletes into the Ramat Gan National Stadium for the opening ceremony, the bridge gave way. Dozens of athletes were trapped in the twisted wooden planks and metal rods of the collapsed structure, while others were pushed under water. Soldiers and police nearby rushed into the river and dragged people to safety. Two Australian athletes were killed; others were rushed to hospital with broken limbs. In the days that followed, another two athletes died. In total, more than 60 were injured.

From their hospital beds, athletes related the horror of their experience. One thought he was "about to die" when he was pushed under the water and trapped by flailing limbs, before forcing himself to the surface. For viewers sitting at home watching the opening ceremony live on television, the scenes were bizarre. The camera panned back and forth between the festivities in the stadium, where spectators were unaware of the tragedy taking place just a short distance away, and the collapsed bridge, where divers were scouring the river bed, hunting for bodies.

After a day of mourning, the organizing committee decided to proceed with the games, and the Australian delegation decided to stay and compete. Recriminations began almost immediately, with questions raised over why the opening ceremony had not been called off once the extent of the disaster became clear. That argument quickly gave way to the more serious issue of why the bridge had not been sturdy enough to support the athletes. The Ministry of Education and Sport set up a commission of inquiry, which produced its report as the games closed. The findings revealed a scandalous picture of negligence—from faulty planning to incompetent execution in the building of the bridge—and laid the blame on the bridge designer and engineer, Micha Bar-Ilan, the construction company and its subcontractor, and the Maccabiah organizing committee. The commission cited failure to comply with the required standards for bridge building, the use of inferior materials, and a dismal lack of coordination between the construction companies and the organizing bodies. Moreover, they noted, the builders did not possess the required permit for constructing bridges.

It also soon emerged that the two athletes who died after the event were poisoned by the waters of the Yarkon, which were found to be highly contaminated. Many of the athletes fell ill after their immersion in the water, and a 15-year-old tennis player, Sasha Elterman, contracted meningitis. In December she was still in serious condition in a Sydney hospital.

The commission's findings were handed over to the police, who initiated a criminal investigation. Each of the parties cited in the report, however, denied blame for the disaster. The remarks sparked anger and frustration among the Australians, and those feelings grew as the investigation dragged on. Fears soon began to arise that the guilty parties would never be punished and that the athletes would not receive reparations or be compensated for medical expenses. Israel did set up a $500,000 fund in late August to provide compensation to the families of the athletes killed and injured in the disaster, with the money to be advanced as loans and returned once insurance claims were settled. But that did little to reduce the growing disillusionment. "As we see it, the Israeli system of justice is being tested, and we are worried that responsibility for the deaths and injuries will be whitewashed," said Colin Elterman, the father of Sasha. He was equally critical of the games' organizers: "We think the Maccabi World Union played a major role in what happened and we are fearful that the people who are really responsible will get away."

When the investigation had still not produced any concrete results by early November, some of the Australians, in desperation, suggested that the Australian government bar Israel from participating in the Sydney 2000 Olympics, unless those responsible for the disaster were brought to justice. Tom Goldman, the president of Maccabi Australia, who traveled to Israel in November to press the case, said that the whole affair had soured Australian Jews' view of Israel. "I wish that this tragedy had not impacted on Australian Jewry's love of Israel," he remarked, "but the cold, hard fact is that it has, and it will continue to do so until the questions are answered."

In mid-December the families of the four victims publicly called on the Israeli government to undertake a full public inquiry into the Maccabi World Union (MWU). If that did not happen, they threatened in a letter to sports minister Moshe Peled, "the pressure from ourselves and the Israeli people, together with years of litigation, will cripple the MWU, and Israel will be the big loser." In December the State Attorney's Office announced that five people, including the engineer, heads of the construction companies, and the head of the Maccabiah organizing committee, Yoram Eyal, would be indicted on charges of criminal negligence.

The Yehudah Gil Affair

The Mossad was still trying to recover from the Khaled Mashaal fiasco of September 1997 when it took another profound blow a few months later. This was the revelation in December that one of its veteran field agents, Yehudah Gil, had been feeding the organization fabricated intelligence material for almost two decades. The false information, it emerged, had almost plunged Israel into war with Syria on two separate occasions—and might have undermined chances for peace during the Rabin-Peres regime.

After Gil's longtime source, a senior officer in the Syrian military, retired, Gil allegedly began to deceive his superiors by providing them with information he thought they wanted to hear and that confirmed their own assessments. In this way, Gil reportedly reinforced the suspicions among some of his superiors and also army intelligence that Syria's intentions were warlike. The deception almost had disastrous consequences. IDF intelligence chief Moshe Ya'alon had warned Netanyahu in mid-1996 that Syria might strike. In August the Syrians moved their 14th Division to the Mount Hermon area, and Gil presented a report that supported the hypothesis of a surprise Syrian strike.

Fortunately, Defense Minister Mordechai did not rely on the intelligence assessments and decided against mobilizing the reserves. "A different defense minister and we could have been in trouble," said Meretz MK Ran Cohen. It was after this near miss that serious suspicion fell on Gil. He was indicted both for endangering state security and for theft, since money transferred to him to pay his Syrian source was missing. His trial began in late December.

There was much speculation over Gil's motives. Some pointed to his right-wing views—he served briefly as the secretary-general of the far-right Moledet Party—

while others suggested he may have been corrupted by the money. Gil's Mossad colleagues believed that he became desperate after his source dried up and acted out of a desire to safeguard his status in the organization.

Rabin Assassination Aftermath

The second anniversary of the assassination of Yitzhak Rabin, in November 1997, was marked by a renewed round of mutual recrimination between left and right over the responsibility for the murder. Attention was also focused on a spate of conspiracy theories that had been circulating since the assassination, including one claiming that Shimon Peres was involved in a plot against Rabin.

Much of the controversy centered around the role played by Avishai Raviv, a friend of assassin Yigal Amir and an informer for the General Security Services (GSS). The right claimed that Raviv was an agent provocateur, used by the GSS to blacken their name, and demanded that a secret annex dealing with Raviv in the report of the Shamgar Commission of Inquiry into the murder should be made public. Left-wing politicians argued that Raviv was a largely irrelevant factor in the assassination and that the right was trying to divert attention from its responsibility for the atmosphere of incitement that existed at the time of the murder.

When the government allowed the secret annex to be publicized, in November, it emerged that Raviv had been involved in numerous acts of violence and provocation during his eight years in the pay of the Shin Bet (GSS). The report described Raviv as a close friend of Amir's and said it was "astonishing that Raviv did not inform his handlers of Amir's bragging about his plans to kill the prime minister." But the Shamgar Commission report did make it clear that it had found no basis whatsoever for any of the conspiracy claims. Nevertheless, right-wing leaders called for Raviv and his handlers to be indicted. The Justice Ministry was still looking into the matter at year's end.

Margalit Har-Shefi, a friend of Yigal Amir, was charged on February 11, 1997, for failing to report that Amir had spoken to her of his assassination plans and for directing him to an arms store in the Beit El settlement where she lived. Her trial was still in progress at year's end.

A mass rally held the evening of November 8, in Tel Aviv's Rabin Square, to commemorate the slain prime minister, was an indication that the nation was still deeply divided. Two hundred thousand people poured into the square for one of the biggest rallies in Israel's history, but it was as much a protest against Netanyahu as a commemoration of Rabin. The crowd was predominantly left-wing and secular, and Meretz MK Yossi Sarid was loudly cheered when he lambasted the prime minister. "Go, go home!" he shouted. "We are fed up with the lying, the charlatanism and the running away from responsibility." By contrast, when Natan Sharansky—the only government representative present—stood up to speak, he was greeted with a chorus of boos.

Economic Developments

By the end of 1996 the economic indicators all pointed in the direction of a serious slowdown, and some observers were even suggesting that Israel could be headed for a recession in 1997. The increase in gross domestic product was 4.5 percent in 1996, as opposed to 7.1 percent in 1995; growth in industrial output dropped from 8.5 percent in 1995 to 5.5 percent in 1996, and the business GDP from 8.8 percent in 1995 to 5.2 percent in 1996. Export growth halved, rising only 5.0 percent in 1996, compared to 10.1 percent the previous year. The trade deficit (excluding ships, planes, and diamonds) was up to $10.4 billion, an increase of 3.8 percent. The increase in import growth was the lowest in the 1990s, and private consumption fell off as well, dropping to 5.2 percent versus 7.4 percent in 1995.

Inflation was up in 1996 as well. While it had been 8.1 percent in 1995, it again reached double-digit proportions, up to 10.6 percent for the year. The Bank of Israel (BOI) adopted a monetary policy of high interest rates in order to put the brakes on what, at one stage, looked like spiraling inflation. While the Treasury and the country's industrialists put heavy pressure on BOI governor Jacob Frenkel to lower the rates, he refused to bend and continued to use interest rates as a key anti-inflationary measure.

While the targeted deficit for the year had been 2.5 percent of GDP, the domestic budget deficit amounted to 15 billion shekels in 1996, or 4.9 percent of GDP. Most economic observers agreed that the economy had become overheated under the previous Labor government, that Labor finance minister Avraham Shohat had been too loose, and that collective measures would be required to rein in the deficit. In late July 1996 Netanyahu announced that his government would cut the budget for the coming year in order to reduce government expenditure, which was running ahead of budgeted figures. When the budget was finally passed at the end of December, seven billion shekels were slashed.

Frenkel did depart momentarily from his high interest rate policy in mid-June 1997, when he lowered rates by 1.2 percent. But when the consumer price index for June rose by a sharp 1.1 percent, he reverted to his old policy of keeping rates high. Despite pressure from the prime minister to lower the rates, Frenkel raised them by 0.7 percent on August 25. A disappointed Netanyahu insisted that the governor's high-interest-rate policy would serve to stymie new growth, and there were reports that the prime minister's aides might propose legislation to remove the setting of interest rates from the hands of the BOI governor. While Frenkel's conservative monetary policies prevented a devaluation of the shekel and kept inflation down, they had the adverse effect of depressing growth and pushing up unemployment.

While the economic slowdown continued in 1997, it was a year of contrasting economic developments. Inflation rose by only 7 percent, the lowest since 1969. What is more, the current account deficit fell by around $2 billion to $3.5 billion.

On the other hand, in 1997 there was a significant drop in the GDP growth rate—to 2.1 percent, compared with 4.5 percent the previous year. Unemployment was also up to around the 8 percent mark.

The marked slowdown in the economy was reflected by the balance of payments in 1997. Imports of goods and services grew by a mere 2.4 percent, while exports increased by 7.5 percent. The rate of increase in private consumption dropped appreciably in 1997, with per capita consumption increasing by only 0.9 percent. Experts attributed the slower rate of increase in per capita consumption to a fall in per capita disposable income.

The issue of budget cuts was back on the agenda in early September 1997 when the cabinet voted 11–6 in favor of a 2.3-billion-shekel ($660 million) Finance Ministry budget-reduction package, which included a 400-million-shekel ($114 million) cut in the defense budget and a 250-million-shekel ($72 million) cut in education. Economic observers predicted, however, that the cuts would not get ultimate Knesset approval later in the year.

When Netanyahu came to power in 1996, he promised to free Israel of the shackles of an over-centralized economy and introduce an unfettered free-market system through a program of widespread privatization. After his first 18 months in office he could point to some impressive sell-offs of government companies and state-owned monopolies, and many economic observers commended him for being ahead of schedule in his privatization plans. In 1997 alone, the government sold shares in Israel Chemicals, the Bezeq telecommunications company, and the Israel National Oil Corporation and collected over $2 billion from the sale of shares in three banks. Bank Hapoalim was sold to a group headed by Ted Arison, which paid $1.37 billion for a controlling interest in the bank.

Unemployment took on ominous proportions in 1997. The previous Labor government had succeeded in reducing it to around 6 percent, but by the end of 1996 the trend of declining unemployment was starting to reverse, with the jobless figure at 6.7 percent. In 1997 it continued to rise, reaching 7 percent by midyear and 8 percent at the end of the year, with no fewer than 15 towns registering an unemployment rate of over 10 percent.

The Negev town of Ofakim, with a jobless rate of over 14 percent, dominated the news in mid-December. With many of the residents on strike, demonstrating in the streets, and burning tires, politicians set out on the traditional pilgrimage southward to the unemployment hot spot. First it was the turn of opposition Labor party head Ehud Barak, who traveled to Ofakim—a traditional Likud stronghold—to meet with bitter residents. He was followed by the prime minister, who swept into town with several of his ministers, as well as with a list of 300 jobs that were being made available for the town's residents and promises of more to come. It soon became clear that fewer than 200 jobs were available, and the more than 2,000 unemployed in the town were left with few long-term answers. Economic observers pointed to structural changes in the economy, growing privatization, and the out-sourcing of textile production by Israeli companies to places like Jordan and Egypt, where labor costs were much lower, as the major reasons for the growing jobless rate. They predicted that the pool of unemployed was likely to expand further.

The 1998 budget debate provided Netanyahu with a major headache. By Wednesday, December 31, 1997—the technical deadline for the vote—Netanyahu appeared to have secured a slim majority for passing the 207-billion-shekel ($58 billion) budget after promising massive funding to West Bank settlers and ultra-Orthodox Jews. But the wrangling continued, and the budget debate spilled over into 1998.

State budgets had often resulted in embarrassing bouts of horse trading, but this time around the wrangling was particularly feverish because of the numerous special-interest groups in Netanyahu's coalition. The prime minister's pledges were thought to have won the support of coalition partners Yisrael B'Aliyah, representing Russian immigrants, as well as the various religious parties. The far-right Moledet Party, which was not part of the coalition, agreed to support the budget after Netanyahu promised funds for West Bank settlement and the establishment of a settler radio station.

While the Finance Ministry insisted that the price tag on the prime minister's pledges was below a billion shekels, opposition legislators put the figure at more than two billion shekels. The figure was particularly significant since the budget was intended to shave 2.3 billion shekels ($657 million) off state spending in 1998. The cuts, which were needed because of the economic slowdown, included some 400 million shekels ($110 million) from the defense budget and 200 million shekels ($55 million) from the education budget.

OTHER ECONOMIC DEVELOPMENTS

At the beginning of 1997, Israel's status was upgraded by the International Monetary Fund from that of developing country to that of industrialized nation, a move that was expected to help the country's credit rating.

In late July 1997, Claridge Israel—part of the Canadian-based Claridge group headed by Charles Bronfman—announced a $370-million deal for the purchase of a controlling interest in Koor, Israel's largest industrial holding company, with an annual turnover of $3.5 billion. The sale of Koor, by the U.S.-based Shamrock holdings, was one of the biggest in the country's history.

International telephone service was opened to competition in 1997 with two companies, Barak and Golden Lines, launching low-cost services.

Israel's tax authorities launched an investigation into Rupert Murdoch's News Datacom Israel, on suspicion of tax evasion to the tune of tens of millions of dollars.

Lev Leviev, a Tashkent-born ultra-Orthodox diamond dealer, paid $190 million to Bank Leumi for a 54-percent share of Africa-Israel Investments, the country's biggest real-estate company; he caused an uproar when he announced that a mall his company was building in the ultra-secular north Tel Aviv suburb of Ramat Aviv Gimmel would be closed on Saturdays (see above).

The Strauss dairy firm paid $62 million for control of Elite, the coffee and chocolate manufacturer.

Welfare statistics published in the course of 1997 revealed that 693,000 people were living below the poverty line in Israel; 301,000 of them were children.

According to statistics released in mid-1997, Israeli men earned 1.9 times more than Israeli women. While the average gross monthly salary for men was 6,113 shekels ($1,798), for women it was 3,225 shekels ($949).

THE HISTADRUT LABOR FEDERATION

The Histadrut Labor Federation had undergone major restructuring between 1994 and 1996. Many of its huge assets had been sold off, ridding the union of a major conflict of interest, the fact that it both employed workers as well as represented them. But its membership had shrunk, as a result, from 1.8 million to 770,000 at the end of 1996, and it remained in deep financial crisis. It was not surprising, then, that when it launched a major strike in late December 1996, at the height of the budget debate and arguments over social-welfare cuts, many predicted that it was the union's swan song.

But they were to be proved wrong. The strike was initially sparked by a government plan to eliminate a tax break for working women. Already furious over government plans for rampant privatization, workers at the ports and at other major state-owned enterprises put down their tools. When the unions ignored a government-obtained court order banning the strike at the ports, the police arrested Shlomo Shani, the Histadrut's number two man. Standing next to Shani in a police station, union head Amir Peretz made a single call on his cellular phone, and public-sector workers across the country went on strike.

The strike ended, though, with what appeared to be a victory for the ailing Histadrut and for Peretz. Not only was Shani released without being charged, but the Knesset buried the proposed women's tax change. The strike also went some way toward resurrecting the Histadrut's battered image among its members. But Shani was cautious, pointing out that one strike was not enough to prove that the Histadrut was again a force to be reckoned with. "We mustn't get carried away," he said. "If we don't prove ourselves tomorrow, then yesterday is worth nothing."

Public-sector workers were on strike again six months later, on July 24, when the Histadrut called for a nationwide walkout in sympathy with workers from Bezeq telecommunications who were protesting the sale of 12.5 percent of the company's shares to Merrill Lynch. The Bezeq workers were back on the job the next day after being promised that they would get a share of the proceeds of the privatization sale.

The major showdown between the Histadrut and the government came in early December 1997, when Peretz ordered a strike over the government's refusal to honor an election eve promise made by the Labor government with regard to workers' pension schemes. The immediate catalyst for the nationwide strike was a comment by Finance Minister Ne'eman, who attacked Histadrut workers already on strike. "We don't need outside enemies anymore. We don't have ticking bombs, we have homemade, exploding bombs," he said.

"He declared war and we have no choice but to fight back," declared Peretz in response, and 700,000 public-sector workers walked off the job. Planes were grounded at Ben-Gurion Airport, some areas of the country were without water, government offices were closed, as were banks, and telephone service was disrupted. As the strike dragged on, attempts were made to find a compromise, and President Weizman tried to mediate between Peretz and Ne'eman. The standoff finally ended after five days—with another victory for Peretz, as Ne'eman agreed to stick to the pension agreement.

The tourist industry showed decline in the period under review: In 1996, 2.36 million tourists visited Israel, compared with 2.22 million in 1995. In 1997 the number was 2.28 million. A clear indicator of the tourism crisis was the fact that the average occupancy in Jerusalem hotels over the High Holy Days was a mere 50 percent.

The Yemenite Babies Saga

The issue of the missing Yemenite babies moved in and out of the public eye in 1996–97, but conclusive proof regarding the claims by Yemenite activists that thousands of Yemenite babies were kidnapped in the early years of the state and sold for adoption, some of them to American Jews, remained elusive. (According to the authorities, children had not been kidnapped, but in the confusion and chaos of the state's early years, had died in hospitals and been buried without their parents' knowledge.)

The story hit the headlines at the end of December 1996, when four graves were opened which were said to contain the remains of missing children who, government authorities said, had died of natural causes. When opened, three of the graves appeared to be empty, though officials insisted that the procedure of digging up the graves had not been done professionally and that soil shifting may have made it difficult to find the remains. For those demanding answers to the mystery, the explanations were yet another example of an official cover-up.

The second, more dramatic, development was the case of Tsila Levine and Margalit Omessi. Levine, who had been adopted by kibbutzniks in the late 1940s and later settled in the United States, tracked down a woman named Margalit Omessi whom she believed to be her mother. In late August 1997, DNA testing confirmed that Omessi was in fact Levine's biological mother, and it seemed that for the first time there was incontrovertible proof that a Yemenite baby had been taken from her parents and illegally given away for adoption. "I dreamed of finding my daughter," Omessi exclaimed after the test results were revealed. "I was sure she was alive . . . people thought I was making it up." But the emotion-filled reunion was dampened when results of a second round of genetic testing were released on October 8, contradicting the earlier tests.

Crime

Crime rose sharply in the period under review, with worrying increases in both violent crime and theft. In the period from January to August 1997, crime rose overall by almost 14 percent compared with the same period the previous year. Murders were up by 13.4 percent to a total of 110 in the first eight months of the year; rape was up by 7.7 percent (350 cases); apartment break-ins increased by a staggering 32.1 percent; and car theft went up a full 26.5 percent (120 cars per day). The number of cases of husbands murdering their wives rose alarmingly. Crime experts did provide one comforting statistic, that the murder rate in Israel was still a fifth of that in the United States.

The spiraling number of car thefts was due in part to the withdrawal of the Israeli army from the Gaza Strip and areas of the West Bank. The Israeli cities that suffered the most were those close to the Green Line, the pre-1967 border. Palestinian thieves, sometimes working in tandem with Israeli felons, smuggled the cars into the autonomous areas for dismantling at chop shops, and Israeli police could no longer pursue them. Experts also attributed the increase in car theft to the rise in the standard of living in Israel over the past decade and the resulting growth in the number of cars on the road.

Demography

Israel's population stood at 5.9 million at the end of 1997, as opposed to 5.75 million at the end of 1996. The Central Bureau of Statistics (CBS) announced that the country's population would pass the six-million mark in 1998, its 50th year of independence. The CBS also announced that Israel's population growth was a remarkable 2.5 percent, far higher than that of most other developed nations, where growth was usually around 0.3 percent. About 60 percent of the population growth was due to natural increase, which was particularly high among Israeli Arabs and the ultra-Orthodox. The remainder was the result of immigration.

IMMIGRATION

The total number of immigrants to Israel in 1996 was 70,919, a drop of a full 8 percent compared with the previous year. In 1997 immigration was down again, to 65,982, a drop of around 7 percent, most of it due to the decline of immigration from the former Soviet Union. Immigration from the former Soviet Union dropped in 1996 to 58,900 and dropped even further in 1997, to 54,600.

Russian immigrants, who numbered some 700,000 by the end of 1997, continued to make their way in Israeli society, although many lived in a ghetto-like world with its own shops, theater groups, and Russian-language newspapers. By 1997 a full 80 percent owned their own homes, 90 percent had washing machines and TVs, and 50 percent had their own cars. Emigration was no more than 8 percent.

Not everyone, though, had succeeded. While the national unemployment rate reached just over 8 percent in 1997, among Russian immigrants it was around 10 percent. Significantly, about 43,000 Russian immigrant families (19.4 percent of all immigrants) were living below the poverty line in 1997.

Immigrant women, in particular, continued to suffer from certain social stigmas. In a poll published in 1997, 65 percent of the respondents (502 Israelis were polled) said that, overall, they had a negative impression of immigrant women; 44 percent said they believed many immigrant women were involved in prostitution. More than half of the respondents said they based their views on media reports.

A case that captured the media spotlight was that of Zvi Ben-Ari, the Hebrew name of Gregory Lerner, an immigrant millionaire who was accused of fraud, embezzlement, and bribery. Lerner, who was kept in jail for months without being charged, as police struggled to piece together a case against him, became a hero among some immigrants and placed fourth in a poll of the most popular immigrants in the Russian-language daily *Vesty*. He was indicted in September 1997.

A proposal in August 1997 by Avraham Ravitz of the ultra-Orthodox United Torah Judaism Party to amend the Law of Return angered members of Yisrael B'Aliyah. Ravitz moved to rescind a clause that granted eligibility for Israeli citizenship not only to those with a Jewish mother, but to anyone with a Jewish father, grandparent, or spouse as well. Ravitz was motivated by an article in the daily *Ha'aretz* which claimed that over half of the immigrants from the former Soviet Union who arrived in Israel in the 18-month period between January 1996 and mid-1997 were not Jewish. Ravitz said his aim was to block cases in which a "100 percent kosher goy, who has no intention of being anything else, discovers somewhere that he has a Jewish grandparent and exploits it to get into a Western country."

Yisrael B'Aliyah politicians, including Absorption Minister Yuli Edelstein, made it clear they would not countenance any tampering with the Law of Return. Any attempt by religious politicians to limit the number of Russian immigrants who did not meet the criteria of Jewish law from entering the country, warned Yisrael B'Aliyah's Roman Bronfman, would seriously jeopardize the coalition's future.

Environment

The Trans-Israel Highway was at the heart of a major debate involving conservationists, politicians, and planners in 1997. The environmentalists complained that the mega-highway, planned to run from Rosh Hanikra in the north to Beer-sheva in the south, would slice through Israel and gobble up vast sections of the country's scarce land reserves. The first 90-kilometer phase alone was expected to use up around 3,250 acres, with a projected price tag of $700 million. In mid-April, the highway's first interchange, at Ben Shemen, was completed. By midyear, bids from four separate international companies for the 90-kilometer stretch had also been received.

Opponents of the huge scheme, which had received the go-ahead after Yitzhak Rabin's election in 1992, argued that it would harm agriculture and was unlikely to relieve traffic congestion in the long run. Rather than invest vast sums in a mas-sive road project that would soon be outstripped by vehicle growth, they sug-gested, the government should invest its resources in mass transit, in the form of an extensive rail system.

But officials of the road company argued that, while a rail system was neces-sary, the traffic situation would reach catastrophic proportions without a major highway connecting northern and southern Israel—a development they claimed would also bring industrial opportunities to Israel's outlying regions. To justify the project, they produced traffic growth statistics showing that in the previous 25 years the number of cars in Israel had increased eightfold. By the year 2000, they estimated that around 1.7 million cars would be on the country's roads, and by the year 2010, Israel minus the sparsely populated Negev desert would have more cars per square kilometer than any other country in the world except Sin-gapore.

One continuing environmental eyesore—and danger—was Hiriyah, Israel's largest garbage dump, which had taken on mountainous proportions. The gov-ernment ordered the 82-meter-high dump, situated not far from Ben-Gurion Air-port, closed by December 31, 1997, after a similar order in December 1995 had gone unheeded. Despite warnings that Hiriya's height was resulting in a growing number of collisions between birds hovering around it and planes entering and leaving the airport, there was no guarantee that the year-end deadline would be met. There were reports of planes being damaged by the impact of the birds, as well as reports of planes having to change their landing paths at the last moment in order to avoid collisions with the birds.

While Transport Minister Yitzhak Levy threatened to shut the airport if the year-end deadline was not met, the local councils that unloaded their garbage at Hiriyah demanded that the government foot the added cost of transporting the waste down south to dumps in the Negev desert. But Environment Minister Rafael Eitan said he would cover only 70 percent of the cost, and by December 31 the dump had not been closed.

Sports

The period under review was not filled with great Israeli accomplishments on the world's playing fields. Probably the most noteworthy achievements belonged to Israel's swimmers, who turned in the best performance ever by an Israeli swim team at a major competition when they traveled to Seville, Spain, for the European Swimming Championships in August 1997. Eitan Orbach became the first Israeli swimmer to win a medal at a world-class competition when he took silver in the men's 100-meter backstroke event. The Israeli men's medley relay team also shone, placing fifth in the final, and two other Israeli swimmers also reached the finals in their events.

Once again Israel failed to reach the World Cup soccer finals, even though many observers believed the country had its best team ever and its best chance to qualify since Israel's only World Cup appearance in Mexico in 1970. Israel still had a chance of approaching the final qualifying games, after having beaten the powerful Bulgarian side at home and drawn with Russia. But the national team stumbled at the final hurdle, losing in Russia and Bulgaria, and the country's soccer fans were forced to put their World Cup dreams back in storage for another four years.

One sign of the improving standards, though, was the fact that a number of Israeli players were scooped up by foreign teams. The most notable was Eyal Berkowitz, who went to play in the English Premier Division for Southampton, and was then bought by West Ham United, another Premier Division team. By the middle of the 1997–98 season, Berkowitz had already been heralded by fans and observers alike as one of the leading midfielders in the English game.

An Israeli cricket team made an unprecedented trip to Malaysia, which had no diplomatic ties with Israel, to participate in a World Cup qualifying competition. Unhappy with the Israeli presence in their country, several hundred Islamic demonstrators turned out to protest. On the one occasion when demonstrators did manage to get inside a stadium and invade the pitch, it turned out they had picked the wrong venue, that the Israeli team was playing at another location across town.

Legal Matters

A number of high-profile legal cases involving white-collar or political crimes reached their conclusion in 1997.

Rafael (Raful) Eitan, the environment and agriculture minister, was acquitted on February 19 by a Haifa court; Eitan had been indicted for illegally obtaining information from a classified army data base and using it against a member of his Tsomet Party.

Israel announced on April 3 that it was dropping its request for the extradition of Hamas leader Mousa Abu Marzook from the United States; Israeli officials explained that putting Marzook on trial for involvement in terror attacks would have a negative impact on Israeli-Palestinian relations.

Hassan Salameh, 26, second-in-command of the Hamas military wing, was convicted by a military court on June 30 for planning three suicide attacks in 1996 that killed 46 people; Salameh told the judge he would not object to the death sentence.

Moshe Feiglin and Shmuel Sackett, heads of the extremist Zo Artzeinu group, were convicted of sedition in September for their protest activities against the Rabin government in 1995.

Ehud Olmert was acquitted by a Tel Aviv district court on September 28; the Jerusalem mayor and Likud MK had faced charges of financing fraud connected with the 1988 Knesset election campaign.

The conviction of former Jewish Agency head Simcha Dinitz for fraudulently charging thousands of dollars of personal purchases to Agency credit cards was overturned by the Supreme Court on October 14.

In November Ariel Sharon lost a libel suit against the daily *Ha'aretz* and journalist Uzi Benziman. A 1991 article in that paper claimed that the ex-defense minister had misled then prime minister Menachem Begin about the objectives of the 1982 Lebanon War.

Shas MK Raphael Pinhassi was given a 20,000-shekel ($5,700) fine and a one-year suspended sentence for conspiracy and making false statements regarding party finances, after he agreed to a plea bargain in December.

Rabbi Moshe Levinger of Hebron, one of the pioneers of the settler movement, was found guilty by a Jerusalem magistrate's court on December 14 of assaulting Arabs in the city and was sentenced to six months of community service and an 8,000-shekel ($2,300) fine.

Labor MK Avi Yehezkel, facing charges of breach of trust, fraud, and falsifying documents in the 1992 party primary elections while a Histadrut labor federation official, was acquitted in December.

Personalia

Among Israeli personalities who died in the second half of 1996 were Benjamin Halevy, 86, one of the judges who sentenced Nazi war criminal Adolf Eichmann to death in 1961; Yair Rosenbloom, 52, composer of the "Song of Peace," which was sung by Yitzhak Rabin and the participants in the rally at which he was assassinated; Rabbi Rafael Soloveichik, 70, who headed a long and partially successful battle against performance of autopsies in Israel; Nahum Tim Gidal, 87, Munich-born photographer who was one of the century's pioneer photojournalists and leading visual chronicler of the Zionist movement; Shmaria Guttman, 87, archaeologist who discovered the ancient Jewish city of Gamla on the Golan Heights; Michael Stieglitz, 48, a former military attaché in Moscow and brother-in-law of Natan Sharansky; Shmuel Meir, 42, Jerusalem deputy mayor, killed in a car crash outside the capital; Yusuf Abu Ghosh, 77, an Arab member of the prestate Lehi underground who helped former right-wing Knesset member Geulah Cohen escape from a British prison in Abu Ghosh; Azaria Rapaport, 73, veteran journalist and broadcaster; Yosef Milo, 80, actor, director, and founder of the Cameri and Haifa theaters, who won the Israel Prize in 1968; Rabbi Moshe Ze'ev Feldman, 67, former Knesset member and chairman of the ultra-Orthodox Agudath Yisrael; Manfred Klafter, 78, founder of Amcha, the Holocaust survivor support organization.

Former president of Israel Chaim Herzog died of pneumonia in Tel Aviv on April 17, 1997, at the age of 78. Herzog had spent much of his career in the military, first in the Haganah, then as an officer in British intelligence during World War II, and finally in the IDF, where he served in field commands, as the head of military intelligence, and as military governor of the West Bank after the Six Day War. The Belfast-born Herzog also served as Israel's ambassador to the United Nations, where he was remembered for ripping up the document equating Zionism with racism in front of the General Assembly.

Other personalities who died in the course of 1997 included Shoul Eisenberg, 76, billionaire businessman with extensive and far-flung interests in the United States, China, Korea, India, Hungary, and Israel; Anat Elimelech, 23, a model and TV personality, and her boyfriend, David Afuta, 38, a celebrity hairdresser, both killed in Jerusalem in an apparent murder-suicide; Avraham Stern, 62, National Religious Party MK; Yitzhak Rager, 64, who served as mayor of Beersheba from 1989; Netanel Lorch, 72, veteran diplomat and Knesset secretary 1972–83; Chone Shmeruk, 76, Hebrew University Yiddish professor, Israel Prize winner, who died in Poland, where he taught Yiddish literature; Shmuel Ya'akobson, 68, Knesset secretary for 14 years; Moshe Etzioni, 89, former Supreme Court judge; Ada Sereni, 92, Rome-born leader of illegal *aliyah* from Italy after World War II and founding member of Kibbutz Givat Brenner; and Uzi Narkiss, 73, general who led the IDF's capture of East Jerusalem and the West Bank in the Six Day War, later head of the Jewish Agency's Aliyah and Information Departments, in Jerusalem.

PETER HIRSCHBERG

World Jewish Population, 1996

THE WORLD'S JEWISH POPULATION was estimated at just above 13 million at the end of 1996.[1] The estimates for the various countries reported in this article reflect some of the results of a prolonged and ongoing effort to study scientifically the demography of contemporary world Jewry.[2] Data collection and comparative research have benefited from the collaboration of scholars and institutions in many countries, including replies to direct inquiries regarding current estimates. It should be emphasized, however, that the elaboration of a worldwide set of estimates for the Jewish populations of the various countries is beset with difficulties and uncertainties.

Since the end of the 1980s, important geopolitical changes have affected the world scene, particularly in Eastern Europe. The major event was the political breakup of the Soviet Union into 15 independent states. Similarly, the former Czechoslovakia and Yugoslavia broke down into several successor states. East and West Germany reunited after a political split of 45 years. The Jewish population has been sensitive to these changes, large-scale emigration from the former Soviet Union (FSU) being the most visible effect.

In spite of the increased fragmentation of the global system of nations, about 95 percent of world Jewry is concentrated in ten countries. The aggregate of these major Jewish population centers virtually determines the assessment of the size of total world Jewry, estimated at 13,025,000 persons at the end of 1996. The country figures for 1996 were updated from those for 1995 in accordance with the known or estimated changes in the interval—migrations, vital events (births and deaths), and identificational changes (accessions and secessions). In addition, corrections were introduced in the light of newly accrued information on Jewish populations. Corresponding corrections were also applied retrospectively to the 1995 figures for major geographical regions (see table 1), so as to allow adequate comparison with the 1996 estimates.

In recent years, new data and estimates became available for the Jewish populations of several countries through official population censuses and Jewish sponsored sociodemographic surveys. Several official sources have yielded results on

[1]The previous estimates, as of 1995, were published in AJYB 1997, vol. 97, pp. 513–544.

[2]Many of these activities are carried out by, or in coordination with, the Division of Jewish Demography and Statistics at the A. Harman Institute of Contemporary Jewry, the Hebrew University of Jerusalem. The collaboration of the many institutions and individuals in the different countries who have supplied information for this update is acknowledged with thanks.

Jewish populations, such as the population census of the Soviet Union held in 1989, the Swiss census of 1990, the 1991 and 1996 censuses in Canada, Australia, and South Africa, the 1991 census of Brazil, the Romanian and Bulgarian censuses of 1992, the sample census conducted in the Russian Republic in February 1994, and the Israeli population and housing census of November 1995. Independent large-scale studies include the 1990 National Jewish Population Survey (NJPS) in the United States and the Jewish sociodemographic surveys completed in South Africa and in Mexico in 1991, in Lithuania in 1993, and in Chile in 1995. Additional evidence on Jewish population characteristics emerged from the systematic monitoring of membership registers, vital statistics, and immigration records available from Jewish communities and other Jewish organizations in many countries or cities. Some of this ongoing research is part of a coordinated effort to update the profile of world Jewry in the later portion of the 1990s.[3]

The more recent findings basically confirm the estimates we reported in previous AJYB volumes and, perhaps more importantly, our interpretation of the trends now prevailing in the demography of world Jewry.[4] While allowing for improved population estimates for the year 1996 under review here, these new data highlight the increasing complexity of the sociodemographic and identificational processes underlying the definition of Jewish populations, hence the estimates of their sizes—the more so at a time of enhanced international migration. Consequently, as will be clarified below, the analyst has to come to terms with the paradox of *the permanently provisional character of Jewish population estimates.* Users of Jewish population estimates should be aware of these difficulties and of the inherent limitations of our estimates.

Presentation of Data

DEFINITIONS

A major problem in Jewish population estimates periodically circulated by various scholarly or Jewish organizations across the world is a general lack of coherence and uniformity in the definition criteria followed. Often, the problem of

---

[3]Following the 1987 international conference on Jewish population problems held in Jerusalem, initiated by the late Dr. Roberto Bachi of the Hebrew University and sponsored by the major Jewish organizations worldwide, the International Scientific Advisory Committee (ISAC) was established. Currently chaired by Dr. Sidney Goldstein of Brown University, ISAC aims to coordinate and monitor Jewish population data collection internationally. See Sergio DellaPergola and Leah Cohen, eds., *World Jewish Population: Trends and Policies* (Jerusalem, 1992).

[4]See Roberto Bachi, *Population Trends of World Jewry* (Jerusalem, 1976); U.O. Schmelz, "Jewish Survival: The Demographic Factors," AJYB 1981, vol. 81, pp. 61–117; U.O. Schmelz, *Aging of World Jewry* (Jerusalem, 1984); Sergio DellaPergola, "Changing Cores and Peripheries: Fifty Years in Socio-demographic Perspective," in *Terms of Survival: The Jewish World Since 1945,* ed. R.S. Wistrich (London, 1995), pp. 13–43.

defining the Jewish population is not even addressed. The following estimates of Jewish population distribution in each continent and country (tables 2–9 below) consistently aim at the concept of *core* Jewish population.[5]

We define as the *core* Jewish population all those who, when asked, identify themselves as Jews; or, if the respondent is a different person in the same household, are identified by him/her as Jews. This is an intentionally comprehensive approach, reflecting *subjective* feelings. Our definition of a person as a Jew broadly overlaps but does not necessarily coincide with *halakhic* (rabbinic) or other legally binding definitions. It does *not* depend on any measure of that person's Jewish commitment or behavior—in terms of religiosity, beliefs, knowledge, communal affiliation, or otherwise. The *core* Jewish population includes all those who converted to Judaism or joined the Jewish group informally and declare themselves to be Jewish. It excludes those of Jewish descent who formally adopted another religion, as well as other individuals who did not convert out but currently refuse to acknowledge their Jewish background.

We adopt the term *extended* for the sum of (a) the *core* Jewish population and (b) all other persons of Jewish parentage who are *not* Jews currently (or at the time of investigation). These non-Jews with Jewish background, as far as can be ascertained, include: (a) persons who have themselves adopted another religion, even though they may claim still to be Jews ethnically; (b) other persons with Jewish parentage who disclaim to be Jews. It is customary in surveys such as these to consider parentage only and not any more distant ancestry. Some censuses, however, do ask about more distant ancestry.

We designate by the term *enlarged*[6] the sum of (a) the *core* Jewish population, (b) all other persons of Jewish parentage included in the *extended* Jewish population, and (c) all of the respective further non-Jewish household members (spouses, children, etc.). For both conceptual and practical reasons, this definition does not include any other non-Jewish relatives living elsewhere in exclusively non-Jewish households.

Israel's distinctive legal framework for the acceptance and absorption of new immigrants is provided by the Law of Return, first passed in 1950 and amended in 1954 and 1970. The law awards Jewish new immigrants immediate citizenship and other civil rights in Israel. According to the current, amended version of the Law of Return, a Jew is any person born to a Jewish mother, or converted to Judaism (regardless of denomination—Orthodox, Conservative, or Reform). By decision of Israel's Supreme Court, conversion from Judaism, as in the case of some

---

[5]The term *core Jewish population* was initially suggested by Barry A. Kosmin, Sidney Goldstein, Joseph Waksberg, Nava Lerer, Ariella Keysar, and Jeffrey Scheckner in *Highlights of the CJF 1990 National Jewish Population Survey* (New York, 1991).

[6]The term *enlarged Jewish population* was initially suggested by S. DellaPergola, "The Italian Jewish Population Study: Demographic Characteristics and Trends" in *Studies in Jewish Demography; Survey for 1969–1971,* ed. U.O. Schmelz, P. Glikson, and S.J. Gould (Jerusalem-London, 1975), pp.60–97.

ethnic Jews who currently identify with another religion, entails loss of eligibility for Law of Return purposes. The law extends its provisions to all current Jews and to their Jewish or non-Jewish spouses, children, and grandchildren, as well as to the spouses of such children and grandchildren. As a result of its three-generation time perspective and lateral extension, the Law of Return applies to a wide population, one of significantly wider scope than the *core, extended* and *enlarged* Jewish populations defined above. These higher estimates are not reported below.

ACCURACY RATING

We provide separate figures for each country with approximately 100 or more resident *core* Jews. Residual estimates of Jews living in other, smaller communities supplement some of the continental totals. For each of the reported countries, the four columns in the following tables provide the United Nations estimate of mid-year 1997 total population,[7] the estimated end-1996 Jewish population, the proportion of Jews per 1,000 of total population, and a rating of the accuracy of the Jewish population estimate.

There is wide variation in the quality of the Jewish population estimates for different countries. For many Diaspora countries it would be best to indicate a range (minimum-maximum) rather than a definite figure for the number of Jews. It would be confusing, however, for the reader to be confronted with a long list of ranges; this would also complicate the regional and world totals. The figures actually indicated for most of the Diaspora communities should be understood as being the central value of the plausible range of the respective core Jewish populations. The relative magnitude of this range varies inversely to the accuracy of the estimate.

The three main elements that affect the accuracy of each estimate are the nature and quality of the base data, the recency of the base data, and the method of updating. A simple code, combining these elements, is used to provide a general evaluation of the reliability of the Jewish population figures reported in the detailed tables below. The code indicates different quality levels of the reported estimates: (A) Base figure derived from countrywide census or relatively reliable Jewish population survey; updated on the basis of full or partial information on Jewish population movements in the respective country during the intervening period. (B) Base figure derived from less accurate but recent countrywide Jewish population investigation; partial information on population movements in the intervening period. (C) Base figure derived from less recent sources, and/or unsatisfactory or partial coverage of Jewish population in the particular country; updated according to demographic information illustrative of regional demographic trends. (D) Base figure essentially speculative; no reliable updating procedure. In categories (A), (B), and (C), the year in which the country's base figure

---

[7]United Nations, Department for Economic and Social Information and Policy Analysis, Population Division, *World Population Prospects; The 1996 Revision* (New York, 1997).

or important partial updates were obtained is also stated. For countries whose Jewish population estimate of 1996 was not only updated but also revised in the light of improved information, the sign "X" is appended to the accuracy rating.

World Jewish Population Size

GLOBAL OVERVIEW

Table 1 gives an overall picture of Jewish population for the end of 1996 as compared to 1995. For 1995 the originally published estimates are presented along with somewhat revised figures that take into account, retrospectively, the corrections made in certain country estimates, in the light of improved information. These corrections resulted in a net decrease of 71,000 in the estimated size of world Jewry for 1995. This change resulted from downward corrections for Israel (-69,700); Estonia, Latvia, and Lithuania (-1,300 together); and Colombia and Venezuela (-1,000 each); and an upward correction of 2,000 for Australia. Some explanations are given below for the countries whose estimates were revised.

The size of world Jewry at the end of 1996 is assessed at 13,025,000. World Jewry constituted about 2.26 per 1,000 of the world's total population in 1996. One in about 443 people in the world is a Jew. According to the revised figures, between 1995 and 1996 the Jewish population grew by an estimated 27,000 people, or about +0.3 percent. Despite all the imperfections in the estimates, world Jewry continued to be close to "zero population growth," with the natural increase in Israel barely compensating for demographic decline in the Diaspora.

The number of Jews in Israel rose from a revised figure of 4,479,800 in 1995 to 4,567,700 at the end of 1996, an increase of 87,900 people, or 2.0 percent. In contrast, the estimated Jewish population in the Diaspora declined from 8,508,200 (according to the revised figures) to 8,457,300—a decrease of 50,900 people, or -0.6 percent. These changes primarily reflect the continuing Jewish emigration from the former USSR. In 1996, the estimated Israel-Diaspora net migratory balance amounted to a gain of about 34,700 Jews for Israel.[8] Internal demographic evolution produced a further growth of 53,200 among the Jewish population in Israel, and a further loss of 16,200 in the Diaspora. Recently, instances of accession or "return" to Judaism can be observed in connection with the emigration process from Eastern Europe and the comprehensive provisions of the Israeli Law of Return (see above). The return or first-time access to Judaism of some such previously unincluded or unidentified individuals has contributed to slowing down the pace of decline of the relevant Diaspora Jewish populations and some further gains to the Jewish population in Israel.

As noted, it is customary to correct previously published Jewish population estimates in the light of improved information that became available at a later date.

---

[8] Israel Central Bureau of Statistics, *Statistical Abstract of Israel 1997,* no. 48 (Jerusalem, 1997), p. 50.

TABLE 1. ESTIMATED JEWISH POPULATION, BY CONTINENTS AND MAJOR GEO-
GRAPHICAL REGIONS, 1995 AND 1996

Region	1995 Original Abs. N.	1995 Revised Abs. N.	1995 Revised Percent[a]	1996 Abs. N.	1996 Percent[a]	% Change 1995–1996
World	13,059,000	12,988,000	100.0	13,025,000	100.0	0.3
Diaspora	8,509,500	8,508,200	65.5	8,457,300	64.9	−0.6
Israel	4,549,500	4,479,800	34.5	4,567,700	35.1	2.0
America, Total	6,486,200	6,484,200	49.9	6,493,000	49.8	0.1
North[b]	6,052,000	6,052,000	46.6	6,062,000	46.5	0.2
Central	53,200	53,200	0.4	53,100	0.4	−0.2
South	381,000	379,000	2.9	377,900	2.9	−0.3
Europe, Total	1,741,300	1,740,000	13.4	1,691,700	13.0	−2.8
European Union	1,017,200	1,017,200	7.8	1,023,500	7.9	0.6
Other West	19,900	19,900	0.2	19,900	0.2	0.0
Former USSR[c]	600,900	599,600	4.6	546,600	4.2	−8.8
Other East and Balkans[c]	103,300	103,300	0.8	101,700	0.8	−1.5
Asia, Total	4,629,200	4,559,500	35.1	4,636,300	35.6	1.7
Israel	4,549,500	4,479,800	34.5	4,567,700	35.1	2.0
Former USSR[c]	59,100	59,100	0.5	48,400	0.4	−18.1
Other[c]	20,600	20,600	0.2	20,200	0.2	−1.9
Africa, Total	105,700	105,700	0.8	104,400	0.8	−1.2
North[d]	8,400	8,400	0.1	8,100	0.1	−3.6
South[e]	97,300	97,300	0.7	96,300	0.7	−1.0
Oceania	96,600	98,600	0.8	99,600	0.8	1.0

[a]Minor discrepancies due to rounding.
[b]U.S.A. and Canada.
[c]The Asian regions of Russia and Turkey are included in Europe.
[d]Including Ethiopia.
[e]South Africa, Zimbabwe, and other sub-Saharan countries.

Table 2 provides a synopsis of world Jewish population estimates for the 50-year period 1945–1995, as first published each year in the *American Jewish Year Book* and as corrected retroactively, incorporating all subsequent revisions. These revised data appear here for the first time. They introduce much needed corrections to the figures published up to 1980 by other authors and, since 1980, by ourselves. Thanks to the development over the years of an improved data base, these new revisions are not necessarily the same revised estimates that we published year by year in the AJYB based on the information that was available at each date; nor is it unlikely that further retrospective revisions will become necessary as a product of future research.

The revised figures in table 2 clearly portray the slowing down of Jewish population growth globally since World War II. Based on a post-Holocaust world Jewish population of 11,000,000, an estimated growth of 800,000 occurred between 1945 and 1955, followed by growths of 700,000 between 1955 and 1965, 242,000 between 1965 and 1975, 129,000 between 1975 and 1985, and 117,000 between 1985 and 1995, including a short period of actual decline during the late 1980s. While it took 13 years to add one million to world Jewry's postwar size, it took 38 years to add another million. The very modest recovery of the early 1990s mostly reflects the already noted cases of individuals returning to Judaism, especially from Eastern Europe, as well as a short-lived "echo effect" of the postwar baby boom (see below).

TABLE 2.   WORLD JEWISH POPULATION ESTIMATES: ORIGINAL AND CORRECTED

Year	Original Estimate[a]	Corrected Estimate[b]	Yearly % Change
1945	11,000,000	11,000,000	
1950	11,490,700	11,373,000	0.67
1955	11,908,400	11,800,000	0.74
1960	12,792,800	12,160,000	0.60
1965	13,411,300	12,500,000	0.55
1970	13,950,900	12,633,000	0.21
1975	14,144,400	12,742,000	0.17
1980	13,027,900	12,840,000	0.15
1985	12,963,300	12,871,000	0.05
1990	12,806,400	12,869,000	−0.003
1995	13,059,000	12,988,000	0.18
1996	13,025,000	–	0.28

[a]As published in *American Jewish Year Book,* various years.
[b]Based on updated, revised, or otherwise improved information.
Estimates for 1980 and after: The Avraham Harman Institute of Contemporary Jewry, Hebrew University of Jerusalem.

DISTRIBUTION BY MAJOR REGIONS

Just about half of the world's Jews reside in the Americas, with over 46 percent in North America. Over 35 percent live in Asia, including the Asian republics of the former USSR (but not the Asian parts of the Russian Republic and Turkey)—most of them in Israel. Europe, including the Asian territories of the Russian Republic and Turkey, accounts for over 13 percent of the total. Less than 2 percent of the world's Jews live in Africa and Oceania. Among the major geographical regions listed in table 1, the number of Jews in Israel—and, consequently, in total Asia—increased in 1996. Moderate Jewish population gains were also estimated for North America, the European Union (including 15 member countries), and Oceania. Central and South America, Eastern Europe, Asian countries other than Israel, and Africa sustained decreases in Jewish population size.

Individual Countries

THE AMERICAS

In 1996 the total number of Jews in the American continents was estimated at close to 6.5 million. The overwhelming majority (93 percent) resided in the United States and Canada, less than 1 percent lived in Central America including Mexico, and about 6 percent lived in South America, with Argentina and Brazil having the largest Jewish communities (see table 3).

United States. The 1989–1990 National Jewish Population Survey (NJPS), sponsored by the Council of Jewish Federations and the North American Jewish Data Bank (NAJDB), provided new benchmark information about the size and characteristics of U.S. Jewry—the largest Jewish population in the world—and the basis for subsequent updates.[9] According to the official report of the results of this important national sample study, the core Jewish population in the United States comprised 5,515,000 persons in the summer of 1990. Of these, 185,000 were not born or raised as Jews but currently identified with Judaism. An estimated 210,000 persons, not included in the previous figures, were born or raised as Jews but in 1990 identified with another religion. A further 1,115,000 people—thereof 415,000 adults and 700,000 children below age 18—were of Jewish parentage but had not themselves been raised as Jews and declared a religion other than Judaism at the time of survey. All together, these various groups

---

[9]The 1990 National Jewish Population Survey was conducted under the auspices of the Council of Jewish Federations with the supervision of a National Technical Advisory Committee chaired by Dr. Sidney Goldstein of Brown University. Dr. Barry Kosmin of the North American Jewish Data Bank and City University of New York Graduate School directed the study. See Kosmin et al., *Highlights,* and Sidney Goldstein, "Profile of American Jewry: Insights from the 1990 National Jewish Population Survey," AJYB 1992, vol. 92, pp. 77–173.

TABLE 3. ESTIMATED JEWISH POPULATION DISTRIBUTION IN THE AMERICAS, END 1996

Country	Total Population	Jewish Population	Jews per 1,000 Population	Accuracy Rating
Canada	29,680,000	362,000	12.2	B 1996
United States	269,444,000	5,700,000	21.2	B 1990
Total North America[a]	299,252,000	6,062,000	20.3	
Bahamas	284,000	300	1.1	D
Costa Rica	3,500,000	2,500	0.7	C 1993
Cuba	11,018,000	700	0.1	C 1990
Dominican Republic	7,961,000	100	0.0	D
El Salvador	5,796,000	100	0.0	C 1993
Guatemala	10,928,000	1,000	0.1	B 1993
Jamaica	2,491,000	300	0.1	A 1995
Mexico	92,718,000	40,700	0.4	A 1991
Netherlands Antilles	266,000	300	1.1	C 1996
Panama	2,677,000	5,000	1.9	C 1990
Puerto Rico	3,736,000	1,500	0.4	C 1990
Virgin Islands	106,000	300	2.8	C 1986
Other	20,515,000	300	0.0	D
Total Central America	161,996,000	53,100	0.3	
Argentina	35,219,000	205,000	5.8	C 1990
Bolivia	7,593,000	700	0.1	B 1990
Brazil	161,087,000	100,000	0.6	B 1991
Chile	14,421,000	21,000	1.5	A 1995
Colombia	35,444,000	4,000	0.1	C 1996 X
Ecuador	11,699,000	900	0.1	C 1985
Paraguay	4,957,000	900	0.2	B 1997
Peru	23,944,000	2,900	0.1	C 1993
Suriname	432,000	200	0.5	B 1986
Uruguay	3,204,000	23,300	7.3	C 1993
Venezuela	22,311,000	19,000	0.9	B 1997 X
Total South America[a]	322,305,000	377,900	1.2	
Total	783,553,000	6,493,200	8.3	

[a]Including countries not listed separately.

formed an extended Jewish population of 6,840,000. NJPS also covered 1,350,000 non-Jewish-born members of eligible (Jewish or mixed) households. The study's enlarged Jewish population thus consisted of about 8,200,000 persons. The 1990 Jewish population estimates are within the range of a sampling error of plus or minus 3.5 percent.[10] This means a range between 5.3 and 5.7 million for the core Jewish population in 1990.

Since 1990, the international migration balance of U.S. Jewry should have generated an actual increase of Jewish population size. According to HIAS (Hebrew Immigrant Aid Society), the main agency involved in assisting Jewish migration from the FSU to the United States, the number of assisted migrants was 32,714 in 1990, 35,568 in 1991, 46,083 in 1992, 35,928 in 1993, 32,906 in 1994, 24,765 in 1995, and 20,169 in 1996.[11] These figures include a small number of individuals who settled in Canada, and, more significantly, refer to the *enlarged* Jewish population concept, therefore incorporating the non-Jewish members of mixed households. The actual number of FSU Jews resettling in the U.S. was therefore somewhat smaller, yet quite substantial. It should be noted, however, that since 1992 the number of Jewish immigrants from the FSU to the U.S. has been steadily declining.

In retrospect, the influence of international migration between 1971 and 1990 was less than might have been expected. The first National Jewish Population Study, conducted in 1970–71, estimated the U.S. Jewish population at 5.4 million; the 1990 NJPS estimated a core Jewish population of 5.5 million, a difference of 100,000. However, since Jewish immigration contributed 200,000–300,000 in this period, it is clear that the balance of other factors of core population change over that whole 20-year period must have been negative. Detailed analyses of the 1990 NJPS data actually provide evidence of a variety of contributing factors: low levels of Jewish fertility and the "effectively Jewish" birthrate, increasing aging of the Jewish population, increasing outmarriage rate, declining rate of conversion to Judaism (or "choosing" Judaism), rather low proportions of children of mixed marriages being identified as Jewish, and a growing tendency to adopt non-Jewish rituals.[12]

A temporary increase in the Jewish birthrate occurred during the late 1980s, because the large cohorts born during the "baby boom" of the 1950s and early

---

[10] See Kosmin et al., p. 39.

[11] See HIAS, *Annual Report 1996* (New York, 1997). See also Barry R. Chiswick, "Soviet Jews in the United States: An Analysis of Their Linguistic and Economic Adjustment," *Economic Quarterly,* July 1991, no. 148, pp. 188–211 (Hebrew), and *International Migration Review,* 1993 (English).

[12] See Goldstein, AJYB 1992; see also U.O. Schmelz and Sergio DellaPergola, *Basic Trends in U.S. Jewish Demography* (New York, American Jewish Committee, 1988); Sergio DellaPergola, "New Data on Demography and Identification Among Jews in the U.S.: Trends, Inconsistencies and Disagreements," *Contemporary Jewry* 12, 1991, pp. 67–97.

1960s were in the prime procreative ages; however, by the mid-1990s this echo effect had faded away, as the much smaller cohorts born since the late 1960s reached the stage of parenthood. A surplus of Jewish deaths over Jewish births again prevailed among U.S. Jewry.

Taking this evidence into account, our estimate of U.S. Jewish population size at the end of 1996 starts from the NJPS benchmark core Jewish population of 5,515,000, and attempts to account for Jewish population changes that occurred since the later part of 1990, after completion of NJPS, through 1996. Assuming a total net migration gain of about 60,000 Jews from the USSR, Israel, and other origins for the whole of 1990, we apportioned 20,000 to the later months of 1990. Further Jewish population growth was estimated at 40,000 for 1991, 45,000 for 1992, 30,000 for 1993, 25,000 for 1994, and 15,000 for 1995. In 1996, as noted, the number of Jewish immigrants from the FSU to the United States continued to decline. At the same time, Israeli statistics continue to show moderate but steady numbers of immigrants from the United States. Between 1990 and 1996 a total of over 13,000 American Jews emigrated to Israel, and larger numbers of Israelis left the United States after a prolonged stay and returned to Israel.[13]

We estimate the total Jewish population increase in the United States at about 10,000 in 1996. This figure accounts for immigration net of emigration and for some attrition based on current marriage, fertility, and age-composition trends in the U.S. core Jewish population. We thus suggest an estimate of 5,700,000 Jews in the United States at the end of 1996.

The research team of the North American Jewish Data Bank (NAJDB), which was responsible for the primary handling of NJPS data files, also continued its yearly compilation of local Jewish population estimates. These are reported elsewhere in this volume.[14] NAJDB estimated the U.S. Jewish population in 1986 at 5,814,000, including "under 2 percent" non-Jewish household members. This closely matched our own pre-NJPS estimate of 5,700,000. The NAJDB estimates were later updated as follows, as against our own (ICJ) estimates (in thousands):

Source	1990	1991	1992	1993	1994	1995	1996
NAJDB	5,981	5,798	5,828	5,840	5,880	5,900	5,900
ICJ	5,535	5,575	5,620	5,650	5,675	5,690	5,700

---

[13]*Statistical Abstract of Israel,* vol. 48, 1997, pp. 141, 150, 159.

[14]The first in a new series of yearly compilations of local U.S. Jewish population estimates appeared in Barry A. Kosmin, Paul Ritterband, and Jeffrey Scheckner, "Jewish Population in the United States, 1986," AJYB 1987, vol. 87, pp. 164–91. For 1996 see Jeffrey Scheckner, "Jewish Population in the United States, 1996," AJYB 1997, vol. 97, pp. 215–37. The 1997 update appears elsewhere in the present volume.

Changes in NAJDB estimates reflect corrections and adaptations made in the figures for several local communities—some of them in the light of NJPS regional results or new local community studies. It should be realized that compilations of local estimates, even if as painstaking as in the case of the NAJDB, are subject to a great many local biases and tend to fall behind the actual pace of national trends. This is especially true in a context of vigorous internal migrations, as in the United States.[15] In our view, the NJPS figure, in spite of sample-survey biases, offered a more reliable baseline for assessing national Jewish population than the sum of local estimates.[16]

Canada. Results of the 1996 Canadian census provided new evidence for the estimate of the local Jewish population. As customary in Canada, this mid-decade census provided information on ethnic origins, whereas the 1991 census included questions on both religion and ethnic origin, besides information on year of immigration of the foreign-born, and languages. In 1996, 351,710 Canadians reported a Jewish ethnic origin, thereof 195,810 as a single response and 155,900 as one selection in a multiple response with up to four options.[17] To interpret these data it is necessary to make reference to the previous census and to the special processing by a joint team of researchers from McGill University's Consortium for Ethnicity and Strategic Social Planning, Statistics Canada, and Council of Jewish Federations Canada, under the direction of Prof. Jim Torczyner.[18]

The 1991 census enumerated 318,070 Jews according to religion; of these, 281,680 also reported being Jewish by ethnicity (as one of up to four options to the latter question), while 36,390 reported one or more other ethnic origins. Another 38,245 persons reported no religion and a Jewish ethnic origin, again as one of up to four options.[19] After due allowance is made for the latter group, a total core Jewish population of 356,315 was estimated for 1991—an increase of 44,255 (14.2 percent) over the corresponding estimate of 312,060 from the 1981 census. A further 49,640 Canadians, who reported being Jewish by ethnic origin but identified with another religion (such as Catholic, Anglican, etc.), were not in-

---

[15]See Uzi Rebhun, "Changing Patterns of Internal Migration 1970–1990: A Comparative Analysis of Jews and Whites in the United States," *Demography* 34: 2, 1997, pp. 212–213.

[16]While the NAJDB estimate for total U.S. Jewry in 1996 exceeds ours by 200,000 (a difference of 3.5 percent), over the years 1991–1995 we have estimated a Jewish population increase of 125,000 as against 102,000 according to NAJDB.

[17]The sum inconsistency appears in the original report: Statistics Canada, *Top 25 Ethnic Origins in Canada, Showing Single and Multiple Responses, for Canada, 1996 Census (20% Sample Data)* (Ottawa, 1998).

[18]Jim L. Torczyner, Shari L. Brotman, Kathy Viragh, and Gustave J. Goldmann, *Demographic Challenges Facing Canadian Jewry: Initial Findings from the 1991 Census* (Montreal, 1993); Jim L. Torczyner and Shari L. Brotman, "The Jews of Canada: A Profile from the Census," AJYB 1995, vol. 95, pp. 227–60.

[19]Statistics Canada, *Religions in Canada—1991 Census* (Ottawa, 1993). See also Leo Davids, "The Jewish Population of Canada, 1991" (paper presented at Eleventh World Congress of Jewish Studies, Jerusalem, 1993).

cluded in the 1991 core estimate. Including them would produce an extended Jewish population of 405,955 in 1991.

In comparison with the 1981 census, the 1991 data revealed an increase of 21,645 (7.3 percent) in the number of Jews defined by religion. A more significant increase occurred among those reporting a Jewish ethnicity with no religious preference: 22,610 persons, or more than twice (+144.6 percent) as many as in 1981. The increase was comparatively even larger among those reporting a partially Jewish ethnic ancestry and among ethnic Jews with another religion. Besides actual demographic and identificational trends, changes in the wording of the relevant questions in the two censuses possibly influenced these variations in the size of both the core and the ethnically (or, in our terminology, extended) Jewish population of Canada.[20]

Most of the 1981–1991 Jewish population increase was due to international migration—out of the total increase of 44,255 core Jews, 25,895 (59 percent) had arrived in Canada since 1981. The principal country of origin was the former USSR (6,230), followed by Israel (4,975), the United States (3,630), and South Africa (2,855).[21] Practically all the rest of the Jewish population growth consists of ethnic Jews who did not report a religion, including many whose reported Jewish ethnicity was only one among several others. The latter are quite certainly children of intermarriages, whose frequency indeed increased in Canada by about one-third over the 1980s.[22] All this implies that the 1981–1991 demographic balance of the Jewish population living in Canada was close to zero or slightly negative. Taking into account the increasingly aged Jewish population structure, we suggested that, in the years following the 1991 census, the continuing migratory surplus would have generated a modest surplus over the probably negative balance of internal evolution. For the end of 1995 we updated the 1991 baseline of 356,300 to 362,000.

The 1991 census equivalent of the 1996 census figure of 351,710 ethnic Jews (including those not Jewish by religion, but excluding those Jews who did not report a Jewish ethnic origin) was 349,565. Based on a similar criterion of ethnic origin, Canadian Jewry thus increased by 2,140 people over the 1991–1996 period. Though it should be stressed that the ethnic-origin definition is not consistent with our concept of a core Jewish population, the evidence of very slow Jewish population increase—notwithstanding continuing immigration—suggested keeping our 1995 estimate unchanged for 1996. The resulting figure of 362,000 makes the Canadian Jewish population the world's fourth-largest.

---

[20]The results of preceding censuses can be found in Statistics Canada, *1981 Census of Canada: Population: Ethnic Origin; Religion* (Ottawa, 1983, 1984); Statistics Canada, *Population by Ethnic Origin, 1986 Census: Canada, Provinces and Territories and Census Metropolitan Areas* (Ottawa, 1988).

[21]See Torczyner et al., *Demographic Challenges . . . , Appendices,* p. 22.

[22]Ibid., p. 20.

Central America. Results of the 1991 population survey of the Jews in the Mexico City metropolitan area[23] pointed to a community definitely less affected than others in the Diaspora by the common trends of low fertility, intermarriage, and aging. Some comparatively more traditional sectors in the Jewish community still contribute a surplus of births over deaths, and overall—thanks also to some immigration—the Jewish population has been quite stable or moderately increasing. The new medium Jewish population estimate for 1991 was put at 37,500 in the Mexico City metropolitan area, and at 40,000 nationally. Official Mexican censuses over the years provided rather erratic and unreliable Jewish population figures. This was the case with the 1990 census, which came up with a national total of 57,918 (aged five and over). As in the past, most of the problem derived from unacceptably high figures for peripheral states. The new census figures for the Mexico City metropolitan area (33,932 Jews, aged five and over, in the Federal District and State of Mexico) came quite close to—in fact were slightly below—our survey's estimates. Taking into account a modest residual potential for natural increase, as shown by the 1991 survey, but also some emigration, we estimated the Jewish population at 40,700 in 1996.

The Jewish population was estimated at about 5,000 in Panama, 2,500 in Costa Rica, and 1,500 in Puerto Rico.

South America.[24] The Jewish population of Argentina, the largest in Latin America and seventh largest in the world, is marked by a negative balance of internal evolution. Various surveys conducted in some central sections of Buenos Aires at the initiative of the Asociación Mutualista Israelita Argentina (AMIA), as well as in several provincial cities, point to growing aging and intermarriage.[25] Short of a major new survey in the Greater Buenos Aires area, the quality of the estimates remains quite inadequate. Since the early 1960s, when the Jewish population was estimated at 310,000, the pace of emigration and return migration has been significantly affected by the variable nature of economic and political

---

[23]Sergio DellaPergola and Susana Lerner, *La población judía de México: Perfil demográfico, social y cultural* (Mexico-Jerusalén, 1995). The project, conducted in cooperation between the Centro de Estudios Urbanos y de Desarrollo Urbano (CEDDU), El Colegio de Mexico, and the Division of Jewish Demography and Statistics of the A. Harman Institute of Contemporary Jewry, the Hebrew University, was sponsored by the Asociación Mexicana de Amigos de la Universisad Hebrea de Jerusalén.

[24]For a more detailed discussion of the region's Jewish population trends, see U.O. Schmelz and Sergio DellaPergola, "The Demography of Latin American Jewry," AJYB 1985, vol. 85, pp. 51–102; Sergio DellaPergola, "Demographic Trends of Latin American Jewry," in *The Jewish Presence in Latin America,* ed. J. Laikin Elkin and G.W. Merks (Boston, 1987), pp. 85–133.

[25]Rosa N. Geldstein, *Censo de la Población Judia de la ciudad de Salta, 1986; Informe final* (Buenos Aires, 1988); Yacov Rubel, *Los Judios de Villa Crespo y Almagro: Perfil Sociodemográfico* (Buenos Aires, 1989); Yacov Rubel and Mario Toer, *Censo de la Población Judia de Rosario, 1990* (Buenos Aires, 1992); Centro Union Israelita de Cordoba, *First Sociodemographic Study of Jewish Population; Cordoba 1993* (Cordoba, 1995).

trends in the country, generating a negative balance of external migrations. Between 1990 and 1996, over 6,000 persons migrated to Israel, while unknown numbers went to other countries. Accordingly, the estimate for Argentinean Jewry was reduced from 206,000 in 1995 to 205,000 in 1996.

In Brazil, the newly released results of the population census of 1991 show a Jewish population of 86,816, thereof 42,871 in the state of São Paulo, 26,190 in the state of Rio de Janeiro, 8,091 in Rio Grande do Sul, and 9,264 in other states.[26] The previous 1980 census showed a countrywide figure of 91,795 Jews, of which 44,569 in São Paulo, 29,157 in Rio de Janeiro, 8,330 in Rio Grande do Sul, and 9,739 elsewhere. Since some otherwise identifying Jews might have failed to declare themselves as such in that census, we adopted a corrected estimate of 100,000 for 1980, and kept it unchanged through 1995, assuming that the overall balance of Jewish vital events, identificational changes, and external migrations was close to zero. The new census figures apparently pointed to a countrywide decline of approximately 5,000 since 1980, most of it in Rio de Janeiro, where Jewish population estimates were, indeed, decreasing since 1960. On the other hand, regarding Brazil's major Jewish community, São Paulo, all previous census returns since 1940 and various other, admittedly rough, Jewish survey and register data were consistent with the widely held perception of a growing community, but the 1991 census figure contradicted that assumption.[27] A 1992 study in the state of Rio Grande do Sul and its capital, Porto Alegre, Brazil's third-largest community—unveiled an enlarged Jewish population of about 11,000.[28] Excluding the non-Jewish household members, the core Jewish population could be estimated at about 9,000, some 10 percent above the 1991 census figure. In the light of this and other evidence of a substantially stable Jewish population, though one confronting high rates of intermarriage and a definite erosion in the younger age groups, we preferred keeping the 100,000 estimate for 1991, extending it to 1996. Brazil's was the ninth-largest Jewish community in the world.

In Chile, a sociodemographic survey conducted in the Santiago metropolitan area in 1995 indicated an enlarged Jewish population of 21,450, of which 19,700 were Jews and 1,750 non-Jewish relatives, including persons not affiliated with any Jewish organization.[29] Assuming another 1,300 Jews living in smaller provin-

---

[26]IBGE, *Censo demográfico do Brazil* (Rio de Janeiro, 1997); Daniel Sasson, *A comunidade judaica do Rio de Janeiro; Metodologia da pesquisa* (Rio de Janeiro, 1997).

[27]Henrique Rattner, "Recenseamento e pesquisa sociológica da comunidade judaica de São Paulo, 1968", in *Nos caminhos da diáspora*, ed. Henrique Rattner (São Paulo, 1972); Claudia Milnitzky, ed., *Apendice estatistico da comunidade judaica do estado de São Paulo* (São Paulo, 1980); Egon and Frieda Wolff, *Documentos V; Os recenseamentos demográficos oficiais do seculo XX* (Rio de Janeiro, 1993–1994).

[28]Anita Brumer, *Identidade em mudança; Pesquisa sociológica sobre os judeus do Rio Grande do Sul* (Porto Alegre, 1994).

[29]Gabriel Berger et al., *Estudio Socio-Demográfico de la Comunidad Judía de Chile* (Santiago-Buenos Aires, 1995).

cial communities, a new countrywide estimate of 21,000 Jews was obtained. Previous lower estimates reflected results of the 1970 population census and a 1982–83 community survey, but probably overestimated the net effects of Jewish emigration. The new survey portrays a rather stable community, with incipient signs of aging and assimilation.

In Venezuela, preparations were being made for a new sociodemographic survey.[30] Preliminary work devoted to preparing a comprehensive list of households for sampling, along with compilation of death records, suggested that the local Jewish population estimate should be revised downward to a provisional figure of 19,000.

On the strength of fragmentary information available, our estimate for Uruguay was slightly reduced, that for Colombia was reduced to 4,000, and that for Peru was not changed.

EUROPE

About 1.7 million Jews lived in Europe at the end of 1996; 62 percent lived in Western Europe and 38 percent in Eastern Europe and the Balkan countries—including the Asian territories of the Russian Republic and Turkey (see table 4). In 1996 Europe lost 2.8 percent of its estimated Jewish population, mainly through the continuing emigration from the European republics of the FSU.

European Union. Incorporating 15 countries since the 1995 accession of Austria, Finland, and Sweden, the European Union (EU) had an estimated combined Jewish population of 1,023,500—an increase of 0.6 percent over the previous year. Different trends affected the Jewish populations in each member country.[31]

Since the breakup of the USSR, France has had the third-largest Jewish population in the world, after the United States and Israel. The estimated size of French Jewry has been assessed at 530,000 since the major survey that was taken in the 1970s.[32] Monitoring the plausible trends of both the internal evolution and external migrations of Jews in France suggested little net change in Jewish population size. A study conducted in 1988 at the initiative of the Fonds Social Juif Unifié (FSJU) confirmed the basic demographic stability of French Jewry.[33] The French Jewish community continued to absorb a moderate inflow of Jews from North Africa, and its age composition was younger than in other European coun-

[30]Sponsored by the two main Jewish community organizations, the Asociación Israelita de Venezuela and the Union Israelita de Caracas.

[31]See Sergio DellaPergola, "Jews in the European Community: Sociodemographic Trends and Challenges," AJYB 1993, vol. 93, pp. 25–82.

[32]Doris Bensimon and Sergio DellaPergola, *La population juive de France: sociodémographie et identité* (Jerusalem-Paris, 1984).

[33]Erik H. Cohen, *L'Etude et l'éducation juive en France ou l'avenir d'une communauté* (Paris, 1991).

TABLE 4.   ESTIMATED JEWISH POPULATION DISTRIBUTION IN EUROPE, END 1996

Country	Total Population	Jewish Population	Jews per 1,000 Population	Accuracy Rating
Austria	8,106,000	9,000	1.1	C 1995
Belgium	10,159,000	31,700	3.1	C 1987
Denmark	5,237,000	6,400	1.2	C 1990
Finland	5,126,000	1,300	0.3	B 1990
France[a]	58,365,000	524,000	9.0	C 1990
Germany	81,922,000	70,000	0.9	C 1996
Greece	10,490,000	4,500	0.4	B 1995
Ireland	3,554,000	1,200	0.3	B 1996
Italy	57,226,000	30,000	0.5	B 1995
Luxembourg	412,000	600	1.5	B 1990
Netherlands	15,575,000	26,500	1.7	C 1995
Portugal	9,808,000	300	0.0	C 1986
Spain	39,674,000	12,000	0.3	C 1991
Sweden	8,819,000	15,000	1.7	C 1990
United Kingdom	58,368,000	291,000	5.0	B 1996
Total European Union	372,841,000	1,023,500	2.7	
Gibraltar	28,000	600	21.4	B 1991
Norway	4,348,000	1,200	0.3	B 1995
Switzerland	7,224,000	18,000	2.5	A 1990
Other	815,000	100	0.1	D
Total other West Europe	12,415,000	19,900	1.6	
Belarus	10,348,000	23,000	2.2	C 1996
Estonia	1,471,000	2,600	1.8	B 1996 X
Latvia	2,504,000	12,800	5.1	B 1996 X
Lithuania	3,728,000	5,200	1.4	B 1996 X
Moldova	4,444,000	8,000	1.8	C 1996
Russia[b]	148,126,000	340,000	2.3	B 1996
Ukraine	51,608,000	155,000	3.0	C 1996
Total FSU in Europe	222,229,000	546,600	2.5	

TABLE 4.—(Continued)

Country	Total Population	Jewish Population	Jews per 1,000 Population	Accuracy Rating
Bosnia-Herzegovina	3,628,000	300	0.1	C 1996
Bulgaria	8,468,000	3,100	0.4	B 1992
Croatia	4,501,000	1,300	0.3	C 1996
Czech Republic	10,251,000	2,400	0.2	C 1995
Hungary	10,049,000	53,500	5.3	D
Poland	38,601,000	3,500	0.1	D
Romania	22,655,000	13,000	0.6	C 1993
Slovakia	5,347,000	3,500	0.7	D
Slovenia	1,924,000	100	0.1	C 1996
TFYR Macedonia	2,174,000	100	0.0	C 1996
Turkey[b]	61,797,000	19,000	0.3	C 1995
Yugoslavia[c]	10,294,000	1,900	0.2	C 1996
Total other East Europe and Balkans[d]	179,689,000	101,700	0.6	
Total	787,184,000	1,691,700	2.1	

[a]Including Monaco.
[b]Including Asian regions.
[c]Serbia and Montenegro.
[d]Including other countries.

TABLE 5.   ESTIMATED JEWISH POPULATION DISTRIBUTION IN ASIA, END 1996

tries. However, migration to Israel amounted to 7,500 in 1980–1989, and about 9,500 in 1990–1996. Since 1990, aging tended to determine a moderate surplus of deaths over births. In view of these trends, our French Jewish population estimate was revised to 525,000 in 1995, and 524,000 at the end of 1996.

Periodic reestimations of the size of Jewish population in the United Kingdom were carried out by the Community Research Unit (CRU) of the Board of Deputies of British Jews. Based on an analysis of Jewish deaths during 1975–1979, the population baseline for 1977 was set at a central value of 336,000.[34] A second national estimate by CRU, based mainly on an evaluation of Jewish death records

[34]Steven Haberman, Barry A. Kosmin, and Caren Levy, "Mortality Patterns of British Jews 1975–79: Insights and Applications for the Size and Structure of British Jewry," *Journal of Royal Statistical Society,* ser. A, 146, pt. 3, 1983, pp. 294–310.

in 1984–1988, suggested a central estimate of 308,000 for 1986.[35] A study of Jewish synagogue membership indicated a decline of over 7 percent between 1983 and 1990.[36] The vital statistical records regularly compiled by the CRU show an excess of deaths over births in the range of about 1,000–1,500 a year.[37] Further attrition derives from emigration (over 7,000 emigrants to Israel in 1980–1989, and nearly 4,000 in 1990–1996). Allowing for a continuation of these well-established trends, we adopted an estimate of 300,000 for 1991, reducing it to 292,000 for 1995. A new survey of British Jews conducted in 1995 indicated a significant rise in intermarriage (38 percent of all married men, and 50 percent among Jewish men less than 30 years old), implying increasing assimilatory losses.[38] Our revised Jewish population estimate for 1996 was 291,000 (sixth-largest worldwide).

In 1990, Germany was politically reunited. In the former (West) German Federal Republic, the 1987 population census reported 32,319 Jews. Immigration used to compensate for the surplus of deaths over births in this aging Jewish population. Estimates of the small Jewish population in the former (East) German Democratic Republic ranged between 500 and 2,000. While there is a lack of certainty about the number of recent Jewish immigrants from the FSU, according to available reports, over 60,000 settled in Germany since the end of 1989, including non-Jewish family members.[39] The following estimates for unified Germany include figures of Jews affiliated with the Zentralwohlfahrtstelle der Juden in Deutschland (ZJD),[40] and our own estimates (ICJ), which (a) allow for some time lag between immigration and registration with the organized Jewish community, (b) take into account a certain amount of permanent nonaffiliation, and (c) assume there are enough incentives for most newcomers to be willing to affiliate with the Jewish community:

Source	1989	1990	1991	1992	1993	1994	1995	1996
ZJD	27,711	28,468	33,692	37,498	40,823	45,559	53,797	61,203
ICJ	35,000	40,000	52,500	50,000	52,000	55,000	62,000	70,000

[35]Steven Haberman and Marlena Schmool, "Estimates of British Jewish Population 1984–88," *Journal of the Royal Statistical Society,* ser. A, 1158, pt. 3, 1995, pp. 547–62.

[36]Marlena Schmool and Frances Cohen, *British Synagogue Membership in 1990* (London, 1991).

[37] Marlena Schmool, *Report of Community Statistics* (London, yearly publication).

[38]Stephen Miller, Marlena Schmool, and Antony Lerman, *Social and Political Attitudes of British Jews: Some Key Findings of the JPR Survey* (London, 1996).

[39]See Madeleine Tress, "Welfare State Type, Labour Markets and Refugees: A Comparison of Jews from the Former Soviet Union in the United States and the Federal Republic of Germany," *Ethnic and Racial Studies* 21:1, 1998, pp. 116–37.

[40]Zentralwohlfahrtstelle der Juden in Deutschland, *Vierteljahresmeldung über den Mitgliederstand* (Frankfurt, 1997).

At the beginning of 1996, the number of applicants for Jewish migration to Germany from the FSU had surpassed 108,000.[41] While most of these applications were already approved, the actual number of immigrants was lower, as some of the applicants preferred to move to Israel or the United States, or to remain in their present places of residence. Nevertheless, the potential for growth of the Jewish population in Germany continues to be significant. Moreover, the comparatively younger age composition of immigrants could have some rejuvenating effects on the long-established deficit in the local balance of Jewish births and deaths.

Belgium, Italy, and the Netherlands each had Jewish populations ranging around 30,000. There was a tendency toward internal shrinkage of all these Jewries, but in some instances this was offset by immigration. In Belgium, the size of the Jewish population was probably quite stable, owing to the comparatively strong Orthodox section in that community. In Italy, membership in Jewish communities has been voluntary since 1987, a change from the previous, long-standing system of compulsory affiliation. Although most Jews reaffiliated, the new looser legal framework facilitated the ongoing attrition of the Jewish population. Recent Jewish community records for Milan indicated an affiliated Jewish population of 6,500, as against over 8,000 in the 1960s, despite substantial immigration from other countries in the intervening period. This evidence prompted a reduction in our national estimate for Italy to 30,000. In the Netherlands, a recent study indicated a growing number of residents of Israeli origin. This may have offset the declining trends among veteran Jews. The Jewish population was estimated at 26,500.

Other EU member countries have smaller and, overall, slowly declining Jewish populations. Possible exceptions are Sweden and Spain, whose Jewish populations are tentatively estimated at 15,000 and 12,000, respectively. Austria's permanent Jewish population was upwardly estimated at 9,000. While a negative balance of births and deaths has long prevailed, connected with great aging and frequent outmarriage, immigration from the FSU has tended to offset the internal losses. The small Jewish populations in other Scandinavian countries are, on the whole, numerically rather stable.

Other West Europe. Few countries remain in Western Europe that have not joined the EU. In 1996 they accounted for a combined Jewish population of 19,900. The estimate of Switzerland's Jewish population is based on the results of the 1990 census. The official count indicated 17,577 Jews, as against 18,330 in 1980—a decline of 4 percent.[42] Allowing for undeclared Jews, we put the estimate at 18,000.

---

[41]Pavel Polian and Klaus Teschemacher, "Jewish Emigration from the Community of Independent States to Germany" (paper presented at 3rd European Population Conference, Milan, 1995); Jewish Agency, Department of Immigration Absorption, internal report (Jerusalem, 1996).

[42]Bundesamt für Statistik, *Wohnbevölkerung nach Konfession und Geschlecht, 1980 und 1990* (Bern, 1993).

Former USSR (European parts). Since 1989, the demographic situation of East European Jewry has been radically transformed as a consequence of the dramatic geopolitical changes in the region.[43] The economic and political crisis that culminated in the disintegration of the Soviet Union as a state in 1991 generated an upsurge in Jewish emigration. After rapidly reaching a peak in 1990, emigration continued, slightly attenuated, throughout 1996. While mass emigration was an obvious factor in population decrease, the demography of FSU Jewry has been characterized for years by very low levels of "effectively Jewish" fertility, frequent outmarriage, and heavy aging. As a result, the shrinking of the Jewish population has been comparatively rapid.

Official government sources provide the fundamental basis of information on the number of Jews in the FSU. The Soviet Union's census and subsequent data distinguish the Jews as one in a recognized list of "nationalities" (ethnic groups). In a societal context that, until recently, did not recognize religious identification, the ethnic definition criterion could be considered comprehensive and valid. Data from the last official population census, carried out in January 1989, revealed a total of 1,450,500 Jews.[44] The figure confirmed the declining trend already apparent since the previous three Soviet censuses: 2,267,800 in 1959, 2,150,700 in 1970, and 1,810,900 in 1979.

Our reservation about USSR Jewish population figures in previous AJYB volumes bears repeating: some underreporting is not impossible, but it cannot be easily quantified and should not be exaggerated. The prolonged existence of a totalitarian regime produced conflicting effects on census declarations: on the one hand, it stimulated a preference for other than Jewish nationalities in the various parts of the FSU, especially in connection with mixed marriages; on the other hand, it preserved a formal Jewish identification by coercion, through the mandatory registration of nationality on official documents such as passports. Viewed conceptually, the census figures represent the core Jewish population in the USSR. They actually constitute a good example of a large and empirically measured core Jewish population in the Diaspora, consisting of the aggregate of self-identifying Jews. The figures of successive censuses were remarkably consistent with one another and with the known patterns of emigration and internal demographic evolution of the Jewish population in recent decades.

Systematic analysis of previously inaccessible data about the demographic characteristics and trends of Jews in the FSU has produced important new in-

---

[43]For the historical demographic background, see U.O. Schmelz, "New Evidence on Basic Issues in the Demography of Soviet Jews," *Jewish Journal of Sociology* 16, no. 2, 1974, pp. 209–23; Mordechai Altshuler, *Soviet Jewry Since the Second World War: Population and Social Structure* (Westport, 1987).

[44] Goskomstat SSSR, *Vestnik Statistiki,* 10 (1990), pp. 69–71. This figure does not include about 30,000 Tats (Mountain Jews).

sights into recent and current trends.[45] The new data confirm the prevalence of very low fertility and birthrates, high frequencies of outmarriage, a preference for non-Jewish nationalities among the children of outmarriages, aging, and a clear surplus of Jewish deaths over Jewish births. These trends are especially visible in the Slavic republics, which hold a large share of the total Jewish population.[46]

The respective figures for the enlarged Jewish population—including all current Jews as well as other persons of Jewish parentage and their non-Jewish household members—must be substantially higher in a societal context like that of the FSU, which has been characterized by high intermarriage rates for a considerable time. While a definitive estimate for the total USSR cannot be provided for lack of appropriate data, evidence for the Russian Republic indicates a high ratio of non-Jews to Jews in the enlarged Jewish population.[47] Nor can definitive information about the ratio between Jews and non-Jews in an enlarged Jewish population in the FSU be derived from the statistics of immigrants to Israel. Due to the highly self-selective character of *aliyah,* non-Jews constitute a relatively smaller minority of all new immigrants from the FSU than their share among the Jewish population in the countries of origin.[48] It is obvious, though, that the

---

[45]Mark Tolts, "Some Basic Trends in Soviet Jewish Demography," in *Papers in Jewish Demography 1989,* ed. U.O. Schmelz and S. DellaPergola (Jerusalem, 1993), pp. 237–43; Viacheslav Konstantinov, "Jewish Population of the USSR on the Eve of the Great Exodus," *Jews and Jewish Topics in the Soviet Union and Eastern Europe* 3 (16), 1991, pp. 5–23; Mordechai Altshuler, "Socio-demographic Profile of Moscow Jews," ibid., pp. 24–40; Mark Tolts, "The Balance of Births and Deaths Among Soviet Jewry," *Jews and Jewish Topics in the Soviet Union and Eastern Europe* 2 (18), 1992, pp. 13–26; Leonid E. Darsky, "Fertility in the USSR; Basic Trends" (paper presented at European Population Conference, Paris, 1991); Mark Tolts, "Jewish Marriages in the USSR: A Demographic Analysis," *East European Jewish Affairs* 22 (2) (London, 1992); Sidney Goldstein and Alice Goldstein, *Lithuanian Jewry 1993: A Demographic and Sociocultural Profile* (Jerusalem, 1997).

[46]Mark Tolts, "Demographic Trends of the Jews in the Three Slavic Republics of the Former USSR: A Comparative Analysis," in *Papers in Jewish Demography 1993,* ed. S. DellaPergola and J. Even (Jerusalem, 1997), pp. 147–75; Mark Tolts, "The Interrelationship Between Emigration and the Sociodemographic Trends of Russian Jewry," in *Russian Jews on Three Continents,* ed. N. Levin Epstein, Y. Ro'i, and P. Ritterband (London, 1997), pp. 147–76.

[47] Mark Tolts, "Jews in the Russian Republic Since the Second World War: The Dynamics of Demographic Erosion," in International Union for the Scientific Study of Population, *International Population Conference* (Montreal, 1993), vol. 3, pp. 99–111; Evgeni Andreev, "Jews in the Households in Russia," in *Papers in Jewish Demography 1997,* ed. S. DellaPergola and J. Even (Jerusalem, forthcoming).

[48]Israel's Ministry of Interior records the religion-nationality of each person, including new immigrants. Such attribution is made on the basis of documentary evidence supplied by the immigrants themselves and checked by competent authorities in Israel. According to data available from the Interior Ministry's Central Population Register, 90.3 percent of all new immigrants from the USSR during the period October 1989–August 1992 were recorded as Jewish. In 1994 the percent had declined to 71.6. See Israel Central Bureau of Statistics, *Immigration to Israel 1995* (Jerusalem, 1996). See also Sergio DellaPergola, "The Demographic Context of the Soviet Aliya," *Jews and Jewish Topics in the Soviet Union and Eastern Europe,* 3 (16), 1991, pp. 41–56.

wide provisions of Israel's Law of Return (see above) apply to virtually the maximum emigration pool of self-declared Jews and close non-Jewish relatives. Any of the large figures attributed in recent years to the size of Soviet Jewry, insofar as they were based on demographic reasoning, did not relate to the core but to various (unspecified) measures of an enlarged Jewish population. The evidence also suggests that in the FSU, core Jews constitute a smaller share of the total enlarged Jewish population than in some Western countries, such as the United States.

Just as the number of declared Jews evolved consistently between censuses, the number of persons of Jewish descent who preferred not to be identified as Jews was rather consistent too, at least until 1989. However, the recent political developments, and especially the current emigration urge, probably led to greater readiness to declare a Jewish self-identification by persons who did not describe themselves as such in the 1989 census. In terms of demographic accounting, these "returnees" imply an actual net increment to the core Jewish population of the FSU, as well as to world Jewry.

With regard to updating the January 1989 census figure to the end of 1996 for each of the republics of the FSU, Jewish emigration played the major role among the intervening changes. An estimated 71,000, thereof about 62,000 declared Jews, left in 1989, as against 19,300 in 1988, 8,100 in 1987 and only 7,000 during the whole 1982–1986 period. The following migration estimates since 1990 have been compiled from Soviet, Israeli, American, and other sources:[49]

Immigrants to: (thousands)	1990	1991[a]	1992[a]	1993[a]	1994[a]	1995[a]	1996[a]
Israel	185.2	147.8	65.1	66.1	68.1	64.8	58.9
United States	32.7	35.6	46.1	35.9	32.9	24.8	22.0
Elsewhere	10.0	12.0	20.0	14.0	9.0	20.0	24.0
Total	227.9	195.4	131.2	116.0	110.0	109.6	104.9
Of which Jews	200.0	159.0	96.0	80.0	75.0	70.0	60.0

[a]Year of arrival.

These apparently declining emigration figures should not be misconstrued: when compared to the similarly declining Jewish population figures for the FSU, they actually demonstrate a remarkably stable desire to emigrate.

At the same time, the heavy deficit of internal population dynamics continued and even intensified, due to the great aging that is known to have prevailed for

---

[49]Estimates based on Israel Central Bureau of Statistics and HIAS reports. See also Sidney Heitman, "Soviet Emigration in 1990," *Berichte des Bundesinstitut fur Ostwissenschaftliche und internationale studien,* vol. 33, 1991; Tress, "Welfare State Type, Labour Markets and Refugees. . . ."

many decades. In 1993–1994, the balance of recorded vital events in Russia included 2.8 Jewish births versus 30.0 deaths per 1,000 Jewish population; in Ukraine, the respective figures were 4.2 and 35.9 per 1,000; in Belarus, 5.2 and 32.6 per 1,000.[50] These figures imply yearly losses of many thousands to the respective Jewish populations. Aging in the countries of origin was exacerbated by the significantly younger age composition of Jewish emigrants.[51]

On the strength of these considerations, our estimate of the core Jewish population in the USSR (including the Asian regions) was reduced from the census figure of 1,450,500 at the end of 1988/beginning of 1989 to 1,370,000 at the end of 1989, 1,157,500 at the end of 1990, 990,000 at the end of 1991, and 890,000 at the end of 1992.[52] The 1992 estimate, besides considering the intervening changes, also corrected for the past omission of the Tats, also known as Mountain Jews—a group mostly concentrated in the Caucasus area that enjoys fully Jewish status and the prerogatives granted by Israel's Law of Return.

An important new piece of evidence, basically confirming the known trends, became available with the publication of the results of the national microcensus of the Russian republic conducted February 14–23, 1994.[53] The data, based on a 5-percent sample, revealed a Jewish population of about 400,000 plus approximately 8,000 Tats. We thus obtained a total of 408,000, with a range of variation between 401,000 and 415,000, allowing for sampling errors. Apportioning in retrospect for Jewish population changes (decline) between December 31, 1993, the date of our estimate, and February 23, 1994, the date of the microcensus, the central estimate rose to 410,000 at the end of 1993. This figure was only 6 percent higher than the estimate we had independently obtained for the same date

---

[50]Mark Tolts, "Russia's Jewish Population: Emigration, Assimilation and Demographic Collapse," *Jews in Eastern Europe* 3 (31), 1996.

[51]Age structures of the Jewish population in the Russian Federal Republic were reported in Goskomstat SSSR, *Itogi vsesoiuznoi perepisi naseleniia 1970 goda,* vol. 4, table 33 (Moscow, 1973); Goskomstat SSSR, *Itogi vsesoiuznoi perepisi naseleniia 1979 goda,* vol. 4, part 2, table 2 (Moscow, 1989); Goskomstat SSSR, *Itogi vsesoiuznoi perepisi naseleniia 1989 goda* (Moscow, 1991). Age structures of recent Jewish migrants from the USSR to the United States and to Israel appear, respectively, in HIAS, *Statistical Report* (New York, yearly publication) and unpublished annual data kindly communicated to the author; Israel Central Bureau of Statistics, *Immigration to Israel,* Special Series (Jerusalem, yearly publication); Yoel Florsheim, "Immigration to Israel and the United States from the Former Soviet Union, 1992," *Jews in Eastern Europe* 3 (22), 1993, pp. 31–39; Mark Tolts, "Trends in Soviet Jewish Demography Since the Second World War," in *Jews and Jewish Life in Russia and the Soviet Union,* ed. Ya'acov Ro'i (London, 1995), pp. 365–82.

[52]Dr. Mark Tolts of the A. Harman Institute of Contemporary Jewry at the Hebrew University actively contributed to the preparation of FSU Jewish population estimates throughout the present article.

[53]See V. Aleksandrova, "Mikroperepis' naseleniia Rossiiskoi Federatsii," *Voprosy Statistiki,* 1994 (1), p. 37 (Moscow, 1994). See also Mark Tolts, "The Interrelationship Between Emigration and the Socio-Demographic Profile of Russian Jewry," in *Russian Jews on Three Continents,* ed. Noah Levin-Epstein, Paul Ritterband, and Yaakov Ro'i (London, 1996), pp. 147–76.

(385,000), based on our projection of the 1989 census figure of 551,000. After correcting our Russian estimate upward, we obtained a 1993 estimate of 817,000 for the total of the FSU.

Our 1994, 1995, and 1996 estimates were prepared as usual by taking into account for each republic separately all available data and estimates concerning Jewish emigration, births, deaths, and geographical mobility between republics. The total Jewish population for the FSU was estimated at 729,000 in 1994, 660,000 in 1995, and 595,000 at the end of 1996. Of this total, 546,600 lived in the European republics and 48,400 in the Asian republics (see below). The pace of change of Jewish population was significantly different in each republic because of variable propensities to emigrate and different rates of assimilation and natural decrease.

The largest Jewish population in the FSU European parts remained in Russia, currently the fifth-largest in the world. Our end-1996 estimate for Russia was 340,000 (as against census-based estimates of 551,000 for end-1988, and 410,000 for end-1993). Jews in the Ukraine, which in recent years experienced large-scale emigration, were estimated at 155,000, currently the eighth-largest community worldwide (487,300 in 1988). A further 23,000 Jews were estimated to remain in Belarus (112,000 in 1988), and 8,000 in the Republic of Moldova (65,800 in 1988). Based on updated figures from the local national population registers, a combined total of 20,600 were estimated for the three Baltic states of Latvia, Lithuania, and Estonia (versus 39,900 in 1988).[54]

Inconsistencies among recent estimates of the number of Jews in former USSR republics can be explained by any combination of the following five factors: (a) some migration of Jews between the various republics of the former USSR since 1991, especially to the Russian republic; (b) the presence of a proportion of non-Jews higher than previously assumed among the "enlarged" pool of Jewish emigrants from the former USSR, resulting in excessively lowered estimates of the number of Jews remaining there; (c) adoption of a Jewish identification in the most recent official sources of data on the part of persons who declared themselves as belonging to another national (ethnic) group in previous censuses; (d) counting in the Russian microcensus and in the population registers of other republics of some persons whose status is not yet that of émigrés, based on the legal criteria of the country of origin, but is such based on the criteria of the State of Israel or other countries of current residence; (e) some definitive returns to Russia (and other republics) from Israel[55] and other countries of migrants who for various reasons are still registered as residents of the latter. While it is impossible at this stage to establish the respective weight of each of these factors, their

---

[54]Lithuanian Department of Statistics, *Demographic Yearbook 1993* (Vilnius, 1994); "Par Latvijas Republicas cilvekiem," *Latvijas Vestnesim,* 44 (Riga, 1995); Anna Stroi, "Latvia v chelovecheskom izmerenii: etnicheskii aspekt," *Diena* (Riga, 1997); Goldstein and Goldstein, *Lithuanian Jewry 1993.*

[55]Council of Europe, *Recent Demographic Developments in Europe* (Strasbourg, 1996).

impact is quite secondary in the context of overall Jewish population changes. Points (d) and (e) above also indicate the likelihood of some double counts of former-USSR Jews in their country of origin and in the countries they have emigrated to. Consequently, it is entirely possible that our statistical synopsis is overestimated by several thousands.

Other East Europe and Balkans. The Jewish populations in Hungary and Romania and the small remnants in Poland, Bulgaria, the Czech and Slovak republics, and the former Yugoslavia are all reputed to be very overaged and to experience frequent outmarriage. In each of these countries, the recent political transformations have allowed for greater autonomy of the organized Jewish communities and their registered membership. Some Jews or persons of Jewish origin may have come out into the open after years of hiding their identity. But, while the gap between core and enlarged Jewish populations tends to be significant in this region, the general demographic pattern is one of inevitable decline.

The size of Hungarian Jewry—the largest in Eastern Europe outside the FSU—is quite insufficiently known. Overall membership in local Jewish organizations is estimated at about 20,000–25,000. Our core Jewish population estimate of 53,500—as against much higher figures that are periodically circulated—attempts to reflect the declining trend that prevails in Hungary, according to the available indications. The January 1992 census of Romania reported a Jewish population of 9,107. Based on the detailed Jewish community records available there, our estimate for the end of 1996 was 13,000. The numbers of Jews in the Czech Republic and Slovakia were very tentatively estimated at 2,400 and 3,500, respectively, and the estimate for Poland was put at 3,500. In Bulgaria, the December 4, 1992 census reported 3,461 Jews;[56] our 1996 estimate, also reflecting emigration, was 3,100.

The situation in the former Yugoslavia continued to be uneasy, contributing to Jewish population decline. The core Jewish population for the total of the five successor republics, reduced through emigration, was reassessed at about 3,700 at the end of 1996. Of these, roughly 2,000 lived in the territorially shrunken Yugoslavia (Serbia with Montenegro), and 1,300 in Croatia.

The Jewish population of Turkey, where a significant surplus of deaths over births has been reported for several years, was estimated at about 19,000.

ASIA

Israel. At the end of 1996, we estimated the Jewish population of Israel at 4,567,700. A major revision in Israel's figure was introduced following the November 4, 1995, population census. On census day, 4,459,696 Jews were enumerated, 69,700 fewer than the 4,549,500 that were expected according to the cur-

---

[56] *Statistical Yearbook* (Sofia, 1992).

TABLE 5.   ESTIMATED JEWISH POPULATION DISTRIBUTION IN ASIA, END 1996

Country	Total Population	Jewish Population	Jews per 1,000 Population	Accuracy Rating
Israel[a]	5,689,000	4,567,700	802.9	B 1996 X
Azerbaijan	7,594,000	9,500	1.3	C 1996
Georgia	5,442,000	8,600	1.6	C 1996
Kazakhstan	16,820,000	11,000	0.7	C 1996
Kyrgyzstan	4,469,000	2,500	0.6	C 1996
Tajikistan	5,935,000	1,600	0.3	C 1996
Turkmenistan	4,155,000	1,200	0.3	C 1996
Uzbekistan	23,209,000	14,000	0.6	C 1996
Total FSU in Asia[b]	71,262,000	48,400	0.7	
China[c]	1,238,274,000	1,000	0.0	D
India	944,580,000	4,200	0.0	C 1991
Iran	69,975,000	12,500	0.2	C 1986
Iraq	20,607,000	100	0.0	C 1997
Japan	125,351,000	1,000	0.0	C 1993
Korea, South	45,314,000	100	0.0	C 1988
Philippines	69,282,000	100	0.0	C 1988
Singapore	3,384,000	300	0.1	B 1990
Syria	14,574,000	200	0.0	C 1995
Thailand	58,793,000	200	0.0	C 1988
Yemen	15,678,000	200	0.0	B 1996
Other	743,557,000	300	0.0	D
Total other Asia	3,349,279,000	20,200	0.0	
Total[a]	3,426,230,000	4,636,300	1.4	

[a]Total population of Israel: end 1996.
[b]Including Armenia. Not including Turkey and Asian regions of Russian Republic.
[c]Including Hong Kong.

rent update of the Israeli Ministry of Interior's national population register, whose baseline was the previous census of June 4, 1983. Discrepancies between census and population register figures could be due to undercounts or double counts in either the previous or the latest census, and to errors accumulated over the years in the reporting of vital events, migration, and other personal changes to the registrar's office. A major factor in these differences resulted from Israel's Central Bureau of Statistics' (CBS) initial attribution (for the purpose of calculating current population estimates) of a Jewish identification to several thousands of immigrants from the FSU who were later identified as non-Jewish by the Ministry of Interior. The CBS provisional Jewish population estimate for end-1966 was 4,637,400, still based on the 1983 census; reducing that figure by 69,700, we obtained the figure of 4,567,700.[57]

Israel accounts for over 98 percent of all the 4.6 million Jews in Asia, including the Asian republics of the former USSR, but excluding the Asian territories of the Russian Republic and Turkey (see table 5). By the end of 1996, Israeli Jews constituted 35 percent of total world Jewry. Israel's Jewish population grew in 1996 by 87,900, or 2 percent.[58] After reaching growth rates of 6.2 percent in 1990 and 5 percent in 1991, steady population increases of 2–2.5 percent were recorded since 1992. The number of new immigrants in 1996 (70,600) was slightly less than in 1995 (76,400). About 61 percent of Jewish population growth in 1996 was due to the net migration balance; the remaining 39 percent of Jewish population growth reflected natural increase. Moreover, several hundred immigrants from the former USSR and other countries who were previously listed as non-Jews were converted to Judaism and officially registered as Jews.[59]

Former USSR (Asian parts). The total Jewish population in the Asian republics of the former USSR was estimated at 48,400 at the end of 1996. The various ethnic conflicts in the Caucasus area and the fear of Muslim fundamentalism in Central Asia continued to cause concern and stimulated Jewish emigration.[60] Internal identificational and demographic processes were less a factor of attrition among these Jewish populations than was the case in the European republics of the FSU. At the beginning of the 1990s, minimal rates of natural increase still existed among the more traditional sections of these Jewish

---

[57]The official backward population correction was not yet available at the time of this writing, hence our unusual B accuracy rating for Israel in table 5.

[58]Israel Central Bureau of Statistics, *Statistical Abstract of Israel 1997* (Jerusalem, 1997). For a comprehensive review of sociodemographic changes in Israel, see U.O. Schmelz, Sergio DellaPergola, and Uri Avner, "Ethnic Differences Among Israeli Jews: A New Look," AJYB 1990, vol. 90, pp. 3–204. See also Sergio DellaPergola, "Demographic Changes in Israel in the Early 1990s," in *Israel's Social Services 1992–93,* ed. Y. Kop (Jerusalem, 1993), pp. 57–115. We thank the staff of Israel's Central Bureau of Statistics for facilitating compilation of published and unpublished data.

[59]Source for estimate: Israel's Ministry of Religious Affairs.

[60]Israel Central Bureau of Statistics, *Immigration to Israel 1996* (Jerusalem, 1997).

communities, but conditions were rapidly eroding this residual surplus.[61] Reflecting these trends, the largest community remained in Uzbekistan (14,000 in 1996, versus 94,900 at the end of 1988), followed by Kazakhstan (11,000, vs. 19,900 in 1988), Azerbaijan (9,500 vs. 30,800), Georgia (8,600 vs. 24,800), and the balance of the remaining four republics (5,300 vs. 24,000).

Other countries. It is difficult to estimate the Jewish population of Iran, last counted in the 1986 national census.[62] Based on evidence of continuing decline, the 1996 estimate was reduced to 12,500. In other Asian countries with small veteran communities—such as India or several Muslim countries—the Jewish population has tended to decline. The recent reduction was most notable in Syria and Yemen, where Jews were officially allowed to emigrate. Very small Jewish communities, partially of a transient character, exist in several countries of Southeast Asia. With the reunion in 1997 of Hong Kong with mainland China, that separate listing ceased and China's permanent Jewish population was roughly estimated at 1,000, the same as Japan.

AFRICA

Fewer than 105,000 Jews were estimated to remain in Africa at the end of 1996. The Republic of South Africa accounted for 90 percent of total Jews in that continent (see table 6). In 1980, according to a national census, there were about 118,000 Jews among South Africa's white population.[63] Substantial Jewish emigration since then was partially compensated for by Jewish immigration and return migration of former emigrants, but an incipient negative balance of internal changes produced some further attrition. The last official population census, carried out in March 1991, did not provide a reliable new national figure on Jewish population size. The question on religion was not mandatory, and only 65,406 white people declared themselves as Jewish. Assuming that the proportion of Jews who had not stated their religion was the same as that of other whites, an inflated census figure of 91,859 Jews was arrived at.[64] The results of a Jewish-sponsored survey of the Jewish population in the five major South African urban centers, completed—like the census—in 1991, confirmed the ongoing demographic decline.[65] Based on the new evidence, the most likely range of Jewish population size was estimated at 92,000 to 106,000 for 1991, with a central value of

---

[61]Tolts, "The Balance of Births and Deaths. . . ."

[62]Data kindly provided by Dr. Mehdi Bozorghmehr, Von Grunebaum Center for Near Eastern Studies, University of California, Los Angeles.

[63]Sergio DellaPergola and Allie A. Dubb, "South African Jewry: A Sociodemographic Profile," AJYB 1988, vol. 88, pp. 59–140.

[64]Allie A. Dubb, *The Jewish Population of South Africa: The 1991 Sociodemographic Survey* (Cape Town, 1994).

[65]The study was directed by Dr. Allie A. Dubb and supported by the Kaplan Centre for Jewish Studies, University of Cape Town.

TABLE 6. ESTIMATED JEWISH POPULATION DISTRIBUTION IN AFRICA, END 1996

Country	Total Population	Jewish Population	Jews per 1,000 Population	Accuracy Rating
Egypt	63,271,000	200	0.0	C 1993
Ethiopia	56,713,000	100	0.0	C 1995
Morocco	27,021,000	6,100	0.2	B 1995
Tunisia	9,156,000	1,600	0.2	B 1995
Other	61,924,000	100	0.0	D
Total North Africa	218,085,000	8,100	0.0	
Botswana	1,484,000	100	0.1	B 1993
Kenya	27,799,000	400	0.0	B 1990
Namibia	1,575,000	100	0.1	B 1993
Nigeria	115,020,000	100	0.0	D
South Africa	42,393,000	94,000	2.2	B 1991
Zaire	46,812,000	300	0.0	B 1993
Zimbabwe	11,439,000	900	0.1	B 1993
Other	274,123,000	400	0.0	D
Total other Africa	520,645,000	96,300	0.2	
Total	738,730,000	104,400	0.1	

100,000.[66] The latter figure was also suggested as our estimate for 1992. Taking into account the pace of continuing emigration from South Africa to Israel and other Western countries (especially Australia), we projected a decline since 1991 and obtained an estimate of 94,000 for South African Jewry at the end of 1996.

In recent years, the Jewish community of Ethiopia was at the center of an international effort of rescue. In the course of 1991, the overwhelming majority of Ethiopian Jews—about 20,000 people—were brought to Israel, most of them in a dramatic one-day airlift operation. Some of these migrants were non-Jewish members of mixed households. In connection with these events, it was assumed that only a few Jews remained in Ethiopia, but in the subsequent years the small remaining core Jewish population appeared to be larger than previously esti-

[66]Dubb, *The Jewish Population of South Africa.*

mated. Over 3,600 immigrants from Ethiopia arrived in Israel in 1992, 900 in 1993, 1,200 in 1994, 1,300 in 1995, and 1,400 in 1996, including a growing share of non-Jewish immigrants seeking reunification with their Jewish relatives. Although it is possible that more Jews than we know of may appear, wanting to emigrate to Israel, and that more Christian relatives of Jews already in Israel will press for emigration before Israel terminates the family reunification program for such relatives, a conservative estimate of 100 Jews was tentatively suggested for the end of 1996. Small Jewish populations remained in various African countries south of Sahara.

The remnants of Moroccan and Tunisian Jewry tended to shrink slowly through emigration, mostly to France and Canada. The end-1996 estimate was 6,100 for Morocco and 1,600 for Tunisia.[67] As some Jews had a foothold both in Morocco or Tunisia and also in France or other Western countries, their geographical attribution was therefore uncertain.

OCEANIA

The major country of Jewish residence in Oceania (Australasia) is Australia, where 95 percent of the estimated total of nearly 100,000 Jews live (see table 7). In 1996 a total of 79,805 people in Australia described their religion as Jewish, according to the latest national census figures.[68] This represented an increase of 5,419 (7.3 percent) over the 1991 census figure of 74,386 declared Jews, which in turn was 5,303 (7.7 percent) more than the figure reported in the 1986 census.[69] In Australia the question on religion is optional. In 1996, over 25 percent (and in 1991, over 23 percent) of the country's whole population either did not specify their religion or stated explicitly that they had none. This large group must be assumed to contain persons who identify in other ways as Jews, although it is not certain whether Jews in Australia state their religion more or less often than other Australians. In a 1991 survey in Melbourne, where roughly one half of all Australia's Jews live, only less than 7 percent of the Jewish respondents stated they had not identified as Jews in the census.[70] The Melbourne survey actually depicted a very stable community, even if one affected by growing acculturation. Australian Jewry received migratory reinforcements during the last decade, especially from South Africa, the FSU, and Israel. At the same time, there were demographic pat-

---

[67]See George E. Gruen, "Jews in the Middle East and North Africa," AJYB 1994, vol. 94, pp. 438–64; and confidential information obtained through Jewish organizations.
[68]Bernard Freedman, "More Jews," *Australian Jewish News* (Melbourne, July 17, 1997). Thanks are due to Prof. Bill Rubinstein for bringing this article to our attention.
[69]Bill Rubinstein, "Census Total for Jews Up by 7.7 Percent; Big Gains in Smaller States," unpublished report (Geelong, Victoria, 1993).
[70]John Goldlust, *The Jews of Melbourne: A Report of the Findings of the Jewish Community Survey, 1991* (Melbourne, 1993).

TABLE 7.   ESTIMATED JEWISH POPULATION DISTRIBUTION IN OCEANIA, END 1996

Country	Total Population	Jewish Population	Jews per 1,000 Population	Accuracy Rating
Australia	18,057,000	95,000	5.3	B 1996 X
New Zealand	3,602,000	4,500	1.2	C 1991
Other	7,027,000	100	0.0	D
Total	28,686,000	99,600	3.5	

terns with negative effects on Jewish population size, such as strong aging. Taking into account these various factors, we updated our estimate for 1996 to 95,000—substantially more than the official census returns, but less than would obtain by adding the full proportion of those who did not report any religion in the census. The Jewish community in New Zealand was estimated at 4,500.

Dispersion and Concentration

COUNTRY PATTERNS

Table 8 demonstrates the magnitude of Jewish dispersion. The 94 individual countries listed above as each having at least 100 Jews are scattered over all the continents. In 1996, 9 countries had a Jewish population of 100,000 or more; another 4 countries had 50,000 or more; another 25 had more than 5,000; and 56 out of 94 countries had fewer than 5,000 Jews each. In relative terms, too, the Jews were thinly scattered nearly everywhere in the Diaspora. There is not a single Diaspora country where they amounted even to 25 per 1,000 (2.5 percent) of the total population. In most countries they constituted a far smaller fraction. Only three Diaspora countries had more than 10 per 1,000 (1 percent) Jews in their total population; and only 10 countries had more than 5 Jews per 1,000 (0.5 percent) of population. The respective 10 countries were, in descending order of the proportion, but regardless of the absolute number of their Jews: Gibraltar (21.4 per 1,000), United States (21.2), Canada (12.2), France (9.0), Uruguay (7.3), Argentina (5.8), Hungary (5.4), Latvia (5.1), United Kingdom (5.0), and Australia (5.0). Other major Diaspora countries having lower proportions of Jews per 1,000 of total population were Russia (2.3 per 1,000), Ukraine (3.0), Brazil (0.6), South Africa (2.2), and Germany (0.9).

TABLE 8. DISTRIBUTION OF THE WORLD'S JEWS, BY NUMBER AND PROPORTION
(PER 1,000 POPULATION) IN EACH COUNTRY, END 1996

Number of Jews in Country	Jews per 1,000 Population					
	Total	0.0–0.9	1.0–4.9	5.0–9.9	10.0–24.9	25.0+
	Number of Countries					
Total[a]	94	61	22	7	3	1
100–900	32	27	4	—	1	—
1,000–4,900	23	21	2	—	—	—
5,000–9,900	9	2	7	—	—	—
10,000–49,900	17	9	6	2	—	—
50,000–99,900	4	1	1	2	—	—
100,000–999,900	7	1	2	3	1	—
1,000,000 or more	2	—	—	—	1	1
	Jewish Population Distribution (Absolute Numbers)					
Total[a]	13,023,700	404,300	784,500	1,204,600	6,062,600	4,567,700
100–900	10,200	8,100	1,500	—	600	—
1,000–4,900	56,000	48,900	7,100	—	—	—
5,000–9,900	57,800	6,100	51,700	—	—	—
10,000–49,900	342,500	171,200	135,200	36,100	—	—
50,000–99,900	312,500	70,000	94,000	148,500	—	—
100,000–999,900	1,977,000	100,000	495,000	1,020,000	362,000	—
1,000,000 or more	10,267,700	—	—	—	5,700,000	4,567,700
	Jewish Population Distribution (Percent of World's Jews)					
Total[a]	100.0	3.1	6.0	9.2	46.6	35.1
100–900	0.1	0.1	0.0	0.0	0.0	0.0
1,000–4,900	0.4	0.4	0.1	0.0	0.0	0.0
5,000–9,900	0.4	0.0	0.4	0.0	0.0	0.0
10,000–49,900	2.6	1.3	1.0	0.3	0.0	0.0
50,000–99,900	2.4	0.5	0.7	1.1	0.0	0.0
100,000–999,900	15.2	0.8	3.8	7.8	2.8	0.0
1,000,000 or more	78.9	0.0	0.0	0.0	43.8	35.1

[a]Excluding countries with fewer than 100 Jews, with a total of 1,300 Jews. Minor discrepancies due to rounding.

In the State of Israel, by contrast, the Jewish majority amounted to 803 per 1,000 (80.3 percent) in 1996, compared to 810 per 1,000 (81 percent) in 1995—not including the Arab population of the administered areas.

While Jews are widely dispersed throughout the world, they are also concentrated to a large extent (see table 9). In 1996, 97 percent of world Jewry lived in

TABLE 9.   COUNTRIES WITH LARGEST JEWISH POPULATIONS, END 1996

| | | | \% of Total Jewish Population | | | |
| | | Jewish | In the World | | In the Diaspora | |
Rank	Country	Population	%	Cumulative %	%	Cumulative %
1	United States	5,700,000	43.8	43.8	67.4	67.4
2	Israel	4,567,700	35.1	78.9	=	=
3	France	524,000	4.0	82.9	6.2	73.6
4	Canada	362,000	2.8	85.7	4.3	77.9
5	Russia	340,000	2.6	88.3	4.0	81.9
6	United Kingdom	291,000	2.2	90.5	3.4	85.3
7	Argentina	205,000	1.6	92.1	2.4	87.8
8	Ukraine	155,000	1.2	93.3	1.8	89.6
9	Brazil	100,000	0.8	94.1	1.2	90.8
10	South Africa	95,000	0.7	94.8	1.1	91.9
11	Australia	94,000	0.7	95.5	1.1	93.0
12	Germany	70,000	0.5	96.0	0.8	93.8
13	Hungary	53,500	0.4	96.4	0.6	94.5
14	Mexico	40,700	0.3	96.8	0.5	95.0
15	Belgium	31,700	0.2	97.0	0.4	95.3

the 15 countries with the largest Jewish populations, and 79 percent lived in the two largest communities—the United States and Israel. Similarly, ten leading Diaspora countries together comprised nearly 93 percent of the Diaspora Jewish population; three countries (United States, France, and Canada) accounted for 78 percent, and the United States alone for over 67 percent, of total Diaspora Jewry.

CONCENTRATION IN MAJOR CITIES

Intensive international and internal migrations led to the concentration of an overwhelming majority of the Jews in large urban areas. Table 10 provides a ranking of the cities where the largest Jewish populations were found in 1996.[71]

---

[71]Definitions of metropolitan statistical areas vary across countries. Estimates reported here reflect the criteria adopted in each place. For U.S. estimates, see Scheckner, AJYB 1997; for Israeli estimates, see Israel Central Bureau of Statistics, *Population in Localities: Demographic Characteristics by Geographical Divisions, 1995* (Jerusalem, 1997); for Canadian estimates, see Torczyner and Brotman; for other estimates, see A. Harman Institute of Contemporary Jewry.

TABLE 10.   METROPOLITAN AREAS WITH LARGEST JEWISH POPULATIONS, END 1996

Rank	Metro Area[a]	Country	Jewish Population	% Share of World's Jews
1	Tel Aviv[b]	Israel	2,400,000	18.4
2	New York[c]	U.S.	1,937,000	14.9
3	Haifa[b]	Israel	650,000	5.0
4	Los Angeles[d]	U.S.	590,000	4.5
5	Jerusalem[e]	Israel	550,000	4.2
6	Miami-Ft. Lauderdale	U.S.	382,000	2.9
7	Paris	France	310,000	2.4
8	Philadelphia[f]	U.S.	280,000	2.1
9	Chicago	U.S.	263,000	2.0
10	Boston	U.S.	235,000	1.8
11	San Francisco	U.S.	216,000	1.7
12	London	United Kingdom	210,000	1.6
13	Buenos Aires	Argentina	178,000	1.4
14	Washington[g]	U.S.	166,000	1.3
15	Toronto	Canada	166,000	1.3
16	W. Palm Beach-Boca Raton	U.S.	151,000	1.2
17	Be'er Sheva[h]	Israel	143,000	1.1
18	Moscow[i]	Russia	120,000	0.9
19	Baltimore[j]	U.S.	105,000	0.8
20	Montreal	Canada	100,000	0.8

[a]Most metropolitan areas include extended inhabited territory and several municipal authorities around central city. Definitions vary by country.
[b]Area as newly defined in the 1995 Population Census. Including Netanya and Ashod, which previously appeared separately.
[c]Including areas in New Jersey and Connecticut.
[d]Including Orange County, Riverside, San Bernardino, Ventura County.
[e]Adapted from data supplied by Jerusalem Municipality, Division of Strategic Planning and Research.
[f]Including areas in New Jersey and Delaware.
[g]Including areas in Maryland and Virginia.
[h]Central city only. Our estimate from total population data.
[i]Territory administered by City Council.
[j]Including Howard County.

Twenty urban areas worldwide had an estimated population of 100,000 or more Jews. These 20 central places and their suburban and satellite areas together comprised 70 percent of the worldwide Jewish population. Ten of these cities were in the United States, four in Israel,[72] two in Canada, and one each in France, the United Kingdom, Argentina, and Russia. The ten metropolitan areas in the United States included 76 percent of total U.S. Jewry, and the four Israeli major urban areas included 82 percent of Israel's Jewish population.

The extraordinary urbanization of the Jews was evinced even more by the fact that over one half of all world Jewry (7,597,000, or 58.3 percent) lived in only ten large metropolitan areas: New York (including Northern New Jersey), Los Angeles (including Orange, Riverside, and Ventura counties), Miami-Ft. Lauderdale, Philadelphia, Chicago, and Boston in the United States; Paris in France; and Tel Aviv, Haifa, and Jerusalem in Israel.

SERGIO DELLAPERGOLA

---

[72]Following the 1995 population census in Israel, major metropolitan urban areas were redefined. The two cities of Netanya and Ashdod, each with a Jewish population exceeding 100,000, were included in the outer ring of the expanded Greater Tel Aviv area.

Directories
Lists
Obituaries

National Jewish Organizations*

UNITED STATES

COMMUNITY RELATIONS

AMERICAN COUNCIL FOR JUDAISM (1943). PO Box 9009, Alexandria, VA 22304. (703)836–2546. Pres. Alan V. Stone; Exec. Dir. Allan C. Brownfeld. Seeks to advance the universal principles of a Judaism free of nationalism, and the national, civic, cultural, and social integration into American institutions of Americans of Jewish faith. *Issues of the American Council for Judaism; Special Interest Report.*

AMERICAN JEWISH COMMITTEE (1906). The Jacob Blaustein Building, 165 E. 56 St., NYC 10022. (212)751–4000. FAX: (212) 750–0326. Pres. Bruce M. Ramer; Exec. Dir. David A. Harris. Protects the rights and freedoms of Jews the world over; combats bigotry and anti-Semitism and promotes democracy and human rights for all; works for the security of Israel and deepened understanding between Americans and Israelis; advocates public-policy positions rooted in American de-

---

*The information in this directory is based on replies to questionnaires circulated by the editors.

mocratic values and the perspectives of Jewish heritage; and enhances the creative vitality of the Jewish people. Includes Jacob and Hilda Blaustein Center for Human Relations, Project Interchange, William Petschek National Jewish Family Center, Jacob Blaustein Institute for the Advancement of Human Rights, Institute on American Jewish-Israeli Relations. *American Jewish Year Book; Commentary; CommonQuest; AJC Journal; Anti-Semitism World Report.*

AMERICAN JEWISH CONGRESS (1918). Stephen Wise Congress House, 15 E. 84 St., NYC 10028. (212)879–4500. FAX: (212)249–3672. E-mail: pr@ajcongress. org. Pres. Jack Rosen; Exec. Dir. Phil Baum. Works to foster the creative survival of the Jewish people; to help Israel develop in peace, freedom, and security; to eliminate all forms of racial and religious bigotry; to advance civil rights, protect civil liberties, defend religious freedom, and safeguard the separation of church and state; "The Attorney General for the Jewish Community." *Congress Monthly; Judaism; Inside Israel.*

ANTI-DEFAMATION LEAGUE OF B'NAI B'RITH (1913). 823 United Nations Plaza, NYC 10017. (212)885–7700. FAX: (212) 867–0779. Chmn. Howard Berkowitz; Dir. Abraham H. Foxman. Seeks to combat anti-Semitism and to secure justice and fair treatment for all citizens through law, education, and community relations. *ADL on the Frontline; Law Enforcement Bulletin; Dimensions: A Journal of Holocaust Studies; Hidden Child Newsletter; International Reports; Civil Rights Reports.*

ASSOCIATION OF JEWISH COMMUNITY RELATIONS WORKERS (1950). 7800 Northaven Road, Dallas, TX 75230. (214) 369-3313. FAX: (214)373–3186. Pres. Marlene Gorin. Aims to stimulate higher standards of professional practice in Jewish community relations; encourages research and training toward that end; conducts educational programs and seminars; aims to encourage cooperation between community-relations workers and those working in other areas of Jewish communal service.

CENTER FOR JEWISH COMMUNITY STUDIES (1970). Temple University, Center City Campus, 1616 Walnut St., Suite 507,

Philadelphia, PA 19103. (215)204–1459. FAX: (215)204–7784. E-mail: v2026r @vm.temple.edu. Jerusalem office: Jerusalem Center for Public Affairs. Pres. Daniel J. Elazar; Dir. General Zvi Marom; Chmn. Board of Overseers Miriam Schneirov. Worldwide policy-studies institute devoted to the study of Jewish community organization, political thought, and public affairs, past and present, in Israel and throughout the world. Publishes original articles, essays, and monographs; maintains library, archives, and reprint series. *Jerusalem Letter/Viewpoints; Jewish Political Studies Review.*

CENTER FOR RUSSIAN JEWRY WITH STUDENT STRUGGLE FOR SOVIET JEWRY/SSSJ (1964). 240 Cabrini Blvd., #5B, NYC 10033. (212)928–7451. FAX: (212)795–8867. Dir.-Founder Jacob Birnbaum; Chmn. Dr. Ernest Bloch; Student Coord. Glenn Richter. Campaigns for the human rights of the Jews of the former USSR, with emphasis on emigration and Jewish identity; supports programs for needy Jews there and for newcomers in Israel and USA, stressing employment and Jewish education. As the originator of the grassroots movement for Soviet Jewry in the early 1960s, possesses unique archives.

COALITION ON THE ENVIRONMENT & JEWISH LIFE (1993). 443 Park Ave. S., 11th fl., NYC 10016–7322. (212)684–6950, ext. 210. FAX: (212)686–1353. E-mail: coejl @aol.com. Dir. Marc X. Jacobs. A six-year project to promote environmental education, advocacy, and action in the American Jewish community. Sponsored by a broad coalition of Jewish organizations; member of the National Religious Partnership for the Environment. Bi-annual newsletter.

COMMISSION ON SOCIAL ACTION OF RE-FORM JUDAISM (1953, joint instrumentality of the Union of American Hebrew Congregations and the Central Conference of American Rabbis). 838 Fifth Ave., NYC 10021. (212)650–4000. E-mail: csarj@uahc.org. 2027 Massachusetts Ave., NW, Washington, DC 20036. Chmn. Judge David Davidson; Dir. Leonard Fein; Dir. Religious Action Center of Reform Judaism, Rabbi David Saperstein. Policy-making body that relates ethical and spiritual principles of Judaism to social-justice issues; implements resolutions through the Religious Action

Center in Washington, DC, via advocacy, development of educational materials, and congregational programs. *Tzedek V'Shalom (social action newsletter); Chai Impact (legislative update).*

CONFERENCE OF PRESIDENTS OF MAJOR AMERICAN JEWISH ORGANIZATIONS (1955). 110 E. 59 St., NYC 10022. (212) 318–6111. FAX: (212)644–4135. Chmn. Melvin Salberg; Exec. V.-Chmn. Malcolm Hoenlein. Seeks to strengthen the U.S.-Israel alliance and to protect and enhance the security and dignity of Jews abroad. Toward this end, the Conference of Presidents speaks and acts on the basis of consensus of its 55 member agencies on issues of national and international Jewish concern.

CONSULTATIVE COUNCIL OF JEWISH ORGANIZATIONS-CCJO (1946). 420 Lexington Ave., Suite 1733, NYC 10170. (212)808–5437. Pres.'s Ady Steg, Fred Tuckman, and Joseph Nuss; Sec.-Gen. Warren Green. A nongovernmental organization in consultative status with the UN, UNESCO, ILO, UNICEF, and the Council of Europe; cooperates and consults with, advises, and renders assistance to the Economic and Social Council of the UN on all problems relating to human rights and economic, social, cultural, educational, and related matters pertaining to Jews.

COORDINATING BOARD OF JEWISH ORGANIZATIONS (1947). 823 United Nations Plaza, NYC 10017. (212)557–9008. FAX: (212)687-3429. Chmn. David L. Ravich; Exec. Dir. Dr. Harris O. Schoenberg. To promote the purposes and principles for which the UN was created.

COUNCIL OF JEWISH ORGANIZATIONS IN CIVIL SERVICE, INC. (1948). 45 E. 33 St., Rm. 310, NYC 10016. (212)689–2015. FAX: (212)447–1633. Pres. Louis Weiser; 1st V.-Pres. Melvyn Birnbaum. Supports merit system; encourages recruitment of Jewish youth to government service; member of Coalition to Free Soviet Jews, NY Jewish Community Relations Council, NY Metropolitan Coordinating Council on Jewish Poverty, Jewish Labor Committee, America-Israel Friendship League. *Council Digest.*

INSTITUTE FOR PUBLIC AFFAIRS (*see* UNION OF ORTHODOX JEWISH CONGREGATIONS OF AMERICA)

INTERNATIONAL LEAGUE FOR THE REPATRIATION OF RUSSIAN JEWS, INC. (1963). 2 Fountain Lane, Suite 2J, Scarsdale, NY 10583. (914)683–3225. FAX: (914)683–3221. Pres. Morris Brafman; Chmn. James H. Rapp. Helped to bring the situation of Soviet Jews to world attention; catalyst for advocacy efforts, educational projects, and programs on behalf of Russian Jews in the former USSR, Israel, and U.S. Provides funds to help Russian Jewry in Israel and the former Soviet Union.

JEWISH COUNCIL FOR PUBLIC AFFAIRS (formerly NATIONAL JEWISH COMMUNITY RELATIONS ADVISORY COUNCIL) (1944). 443 Park Ave. S., 11th fl., NYC 10016. (212)684–6950. FAX: (212)686–1353. E-mail: jcpa@jon.cjfny.org. Chmn. Steven Schwarz; Sec. Mark Schickman; Exec. V.-Chmn. Lawrence Rubin. National coordinating body for the field of Jewish community relations, comprising 13 national and 122 local Jewish community-relations agencies. Promotes understanding of Israel and the Middle East; supports Jewish communities around the world; advocates for equality and pluralism, and against discrimination, in American society. Through the Council's work, its constituent organizations seek agreement on policies, strategies, and programs for effective utilization of their resources for common ends. *Joint Program Plan for Jewish Community Relations.*

JEWISH LABOR COMMITTEE (1934). Atran Center for Jewish Culture, 25 E. 21 St., NYC 10010. (212)477–0707. FAX: (212) 477–1918. Pres. Lenore Miller; Exec. Dir. Avram B. Lyon. Serves as liaison between the Jewish community and the trade union movement; works with the U.S. andinternational labor movement to combat anti-Semitism, promote intergroup relations, and engender support for the State of Israel and Jews in and from the former Soviet Union; promotes teaching in public schools about the Holocaust and Jewish resistance; strengthens support within the Jewish community for the social goals and programs of the labor movement; supports Yiddish-language and cultural institutions. *Jewish Labor Committee Review; Issues Alert; Alumni Newsletter.*

———, NATIONAL TRADE UNION COUNCIL FOR HUMAN RIGHTS (1956). Atran Center for Jewish Culture, 25 E. 21 St., NYC

10010. (212)477–0707. FAX: (212) 477–1918. Chmn. Sol Hoffman; Exec. Dir. Avram Lyon. Works with the American labor movement in advancing the struggle for social justice and equal opportunity, and assists unions in every issue affecting human rights. Fights discrimination on all levels and helps to promote labor's broad social and economic goals.

JEWISH PEACE FELLOWSHIP (1941). Box 271, Nyack, NY 10960. (914)358–4601. FAX: (914)358–4924. Pres. Rabbi Philip Bentley; Sec. Naomi Goodman; Ed. Murray Polner. Unites those who believe that Jewish ideals and experience provide inspiration for a nonviolent philosophy and way of life; offers draft counseling, especially for conscientious objection based on Jewish "religious training and belief"; encourages Jewish community to become more knowledgeable, concerned, and active in regard to the war/peace problem. *Shalom/Jewish Peace Letter.*

JEWISH WAR VETERANS OF THE UNITED STATES OF AMERICA (1896). 1811 R St., NW, Washington, DC 20009. (202) 265–6280. FAX: (202)234–5662. E-mail: jwv@erols.com. Natl. Exec. Dir. Herb Rosenbleeth; Natl. Commander Jack Berman. Seeks to foster true allegiance to the United States; to combat bigotry and prevent defamation of Jews; to encourage the doctrine of universal liberty, equal rights, and full justice for all; to cooperate with and support existing educational institutions and establish new ones; to foster the education of ex-servicemen, ex-servicewomen, and members in the ideals and principles of Americanism. *Jewish Veteran.*

———, NATIONAL MUSEUM OF AMERICAN JEWISH MILITARY HISTORY (1958). 1811 R St., NW, Washington, DC 20009. E-mail: jwv@erols.com. (202)265–6280. FAX: (202)462–3192. Pres. Edward D. Blatt; Asst. Dir./Archivist Sandor B. Cohen. Documents and preserves the contributions of Jewish Americans to the peace and freedom of the United States; educates the public concerning the courage, heroism, and sacrifices made by Jewish Americans who served in the armed forces; and works to combat anti-Semitism. *Museum News (quarterly newsletter).*

NATIONAL ASSOCIATION OF JEWISH LEGISLATORS (1976). 65 Oakwood St., Albany, NY 12208. (518)527–3353. FAX: (518) 458-8512. E-mail: najl01@aol.com. Exec. Dir. Marc Hiller; Pres. Sen. Richard Cohen, Minn. state senator. A nonpartisan Jewish state legislative network focusing on domestic issues and publishing newsletters. Maintains close ties with the Knesset and Israeli leaders.

NATIONAL CONFERENCE ON SOVIET JEWRY (formerly AMERICAN JEWISH CONFERENCE ON SOVIET JEWRY) (1964; reorg. 1971). 1640 Rhode Island Ave., NW, Suite 501, Washington, DC 20036-3278. (202) 898–2500. fax: (202)898–0822. E-mail: ncsj@access.digex.net. N.Y. office:730 Broadway, 2nd fl., NYC 10003. (212) 780–9500. FAX: (212)780–0888. Chmn. Rabbi Mark N. Staitman; Exec. Dir. Mark B. Levin. Coordinating agency for major national Jewish organizations and local community groups in the U.S., acting on behalf of Jews in the former Soviet Union (FSU); provides information about Jews in the FSU through public education and social action; reports and special pamphlets, special programs and projects, public meetings and forums. *Newswatch; annual report; action and program kits; Wrap-Up Leadership Report.*

———, SOVIET JEWRY RESEARCH BUREAU. Chmn. Rabbi Mark Staitman. Organized by NCSJ to monitor emigration trends. Primary task is the accumulation, evaluation, and processing of information regarding Jews in the FSU, especially those who apply for emigration.

NATIONAL JEWISH COALITION (1985). 415 2nd St., NE, Suite 100, Washington, DC 20002. (202)547–7701. FAX: (202)544–2434. E-mail: njc@njchq.org. Natl. Chmn. Cheryl Halpern; Hon. Chmn. Max M. Fisher, Richard J. Fox, Sam Fox, George Klein, and Amb. Mel Sembler; Exec. Dir. Matt Brooks. Promotes involvement in Republican politics among its members; sensitizes Republican leaders to the concerns of the American Jewish community; promotes principles of free enterprise, a strong national defense, and an internationalist foreign policy. *NJC Bulletin.*

NATIONAL JEWISH COMMISSION ON LAW AND PUBLIC AFFAIRS (COLPA) (1965). 135 W. 50 St., 6th fl., NYC 10020.

(212)641–8992. FAX: (212)641–8197. Pres. Allen L. Rothenberg; Exec. Dir. Dennis Rapps. Voluntary association of attorneys whose purpose is to represent the observant Jewish community on legal, legislative, and public-affairs matters.

NATIONAL JEWISH COMMUNITY RELATIONS ADVISORY COUNCIL (see Jewish Council for Public Affairs)

NATIONAL JEWISH DEMOCRATIC COUNCIL (1990). 503 Capital Court, NE, #300, Washington, DC 20002. (202)216–9060. FAX: (202)544–7645. E-mail: njdconline@aol. com. Chmn. Monte Friedkin; Founding Chmn. Morton Mandel; Exec. Dir. Ira N. Forman. An independent organization committed to strengthening Jewish participation in the Democratic party primarily through grassroots activism. The national voice of Jewish Democrats, NJDC is dedicated to fighting the radical right and promoting Jewish values and interests in the Democratic party. *Capital Communiqué.*

SHALOM CENTER (1983). 7318 Germantown Ave., Philadelphia, PA 19119. (215)247–9700. FAX: (215)247–9703. E-mail: shalomctr@aol.com. (Part of Aleph Alliance for Jewish Renewal.) Exec. Dir. Arthur Waskow. National resource and organizing center for Jewish perspectives on dealing with environmental dangers, unrestrained technology, and corporate irresponsibility. Initiated A.J. Heschel 25th Yahrzeit observance. Trains next generation of *tikkun olam* activists. Holds colloquia on issues like environmental causes of cancer. *New Menorah.*

STUDENT STRUGGLE FOR SOVIET JEWRY, INC. (see Center for Russian Jewry)

UNION OF COUNCILS (formerly UNION OF COUNCILS FOR SOVIET JEWS) (1970). 1819 H St., NW, Suite 230, Washington, DC 20006. (202)775–9770. FAX: (202)775–9776. E-mail: ucsj@ucsj.com; http://www.ucsj.com/ucsj. Pres. Yosef I. Abramowitz; Natl. Dir. Micah H. Naftalin. Its 38 member councils and 100,000 members in the U.S. support and protect Jews in the former Soviet Union (FSU) by disseminating news on their condition; advocacy; publications, educational programs, briefings, and policy analyses. Matches U.S. synagogues to FSU Jewish communities in Yad L'Yad assistance program; operates 7 Human Rights Bureaus to monitor anti-Semitism and ethnic intolerance in FSU, advocate for refuseniks and political prisoners, and seek to advance democracy and rule of law. *Monitor (digest of news and analysis from states of the FSU).*

WORLD CONGRESS OF GAY AND LESBIAN JEWISH ORGANIZATIONS (1980). PO Box 23379, Washington, DC 20026--3379. E-mail: info@wcgljo.org. Pres. Jack Gilbert (London, UK); V.-Pres. Lee Walzer (Washington, DC). Supports, strengthens, and represents over 65 Jewish gay and lesbian organizations across the globe and the needs of gay and lesbian Jews generally. Challenges homophobia and sexism within the Jewish community and responds to anti-Semitism at large. Sponsors regional and international conferences. *The W.C. Digest.*

WORLD JEWISH CONGRESS (1936; org. in U.S. 1939). 501 Madison Ave., 17th fl., NYC 10022. (212) 755–5770. FAX: (212) 755–5883. Pres. Edgar M. Bronfman; Co-chmn. N. Amer. Branch Prof. Irwin Cotler (Montreal) and Evelyn Sommer; Sec.-Gen. Israel Singer; Exec. Dir. Elan Steinberg. Seeks to intensify bonds of world Jewry with Israel; to strengthen solidarity among Jews everywhere and secure their rights, status, and interests as individuals and communities; to encourage Jewish social, religious, and cultural life throughout the world and coordinate efforts by Jewish communities and organizations to cope with any Jewish problem; to work for human rights generally. Represents its affiliated organizations—most representative bodies of Jewish communities in more than 80 countries and 35 national organizations in American section–at UN, OAS, UNESCO, Council of Europe, ILO, UNICEF, and other governmental, intergovernmental, and international authorities. *WJC Report; Bolet'n Informativo OJI; Christian-Jewish Relations; Dateline: World Jewry; Coloquio; Batfutsot; Gesher.*

———, UN WATCH (1993). 1, rue de Varembé, PO Box 191, 1211 Geneva 20, Switzerland. (41–22)734.14.72/3. FAX: (41-22)734.16.13. E-mail: unwatch@unwatch.org. Chmn. Morris B. Abram; Exec. Dir. Michael D. Colson. An affiliate of the World Jewish Congress, UN Watch measures UN performance by the yardstick of that organization's Charter; advocates the non-discriminatory application of the Charter; opposes the use of UN fora to bash Israel and promote anti-Semitism; and seeks to institutionalize at the UN the fight against worldwide anti-Semitism.

CULTURAL

AMERICAN ACADEMY FOR JEWISH RESEARCH (1929). 51 Washington Sq., NYC 10012. (212)998-3550. FAX: (212)678-8947. Pres. Robert Chazan. Encourages Jewish learning and research; holds annual or semiannual meeting; awards grants for the publication of scholarly works. *Proceedings of the American Academy for Jewish Research; Texts and Studies; Monograph Series.*

AMERICAN GATHERING OF JEWISH HOLOCAUST SURVIVORS. 122 W. 30 St., #205. NYC 10001. (212)239-4230. FAX: (212)279-2926. Pres. Benjamin Meed. Dedicated to documenting the past and passing on a legacy of remembrance. Compiles the National Registry of Jewish Holocaust Survivors-to date, the records of more than 100,000 survivors and their families-housed at the U.S. Holocaust Memorial Museum in Washington, DC; holds an annual Yom Hashoah commemoration and occasional international gatherings; sponsors an intensive summer program for U.S. teachers in Poland and Israel to prepare them to teach about the Holocaust. *Together (newspaper).*

AMERICAN GUILD OF JUDAIC ART (1991). PO Box 1794, Murray Hill Station, NYC 10156-0609. (212)889-7581. FAX: (212) 779-9015. Pres. Michael Berkowicz. A membership org. for those with interest in the Judaic arts; serves as a resource center for contemporary Jewish artists and the general public; acts to increase public awareness of Judaic craft and fine art; provides a forum for the exchange of ideas about Judaic art. *Hiddur (newsletter devoted to the Jewish visual arts); Update (members' networking newsletter); Guild Showcase (a marketing magazine supplement).*

AMERICAN JEWISH HISTORICAL SOCIETY (1892). 2 Thornton Rd., Waltham, MA 02154. (617)891-8110. FAX: (617)899-9208. E-mail: ajhs@ajhs.org. Pres. Kenneth J. Bialkin; Dir. Dr. Michael Feldberg. Collects, catalogues, publishes, and displays material on the history of the Jews in America; serves as an informa-

tion center for inquiries on American Jewish history; maintains archives of original source material on American Jewish history; sponsors lectures and exhibitions; makes available audiovisual material. *American Jewish History; Heritage.*

AMERICAN JEWISH PRESS ASSOCIATION (1944). Natl. Admin. Off.: 5307 Marsh Creek Dr., Austin, TX 78759. (512)795-9112. FAX: (512)795-9520. E-mail: ajpamr@aol.com. Exec. Dir. L. Malcolm Rodman; Pres. Debra Rubin. Seeks the advancement of Jewish journalism and the maintenance of a strong Jewish press in the U.S. and Canada; encourages the attainment of the highest editorial and business standards; sponsors workshops, services for members; sponsors annual competition for Simon Rockower awards for excellence in Jewish journalism. *Membership bulletin newsletter; Roster of Members.*

AMERICAN SEPHARDI FEDERATION (1973). 305 7th Ave., Suite 1101, NYC 10001. (212)366-7223. FAX: (212)366-7263. E-mail: sephfed@aol.com. Pres. Leon Levy; Exec. Dir. Salomon Louis Vaz Dias. Representative body of over 350,000 Sephardic Jews in U.S.; part of the World Sephardi Federation. Seeks to preserve and promote Sephardic culture, education, and traditions. Disseminates resource material on all aspects of Sephardic life. Strives to bring a Sephardic agenda and perspective to American Jewish life. *ASF Update Newsletter.*

AMERICAN SOCIETY FOR JEWISH MUSIC (1974). 170 W. 74 St., NYC 10023. (212)874-4456. FAX: (212)874-8605. Pres. Hadassah B. Markson; V.-Pres. Judith Tischler & Martha Novick; Sec. Fortuna Calvo Roth; Bd. Chmn. Rabbi Henry D. Michelman; Treas. Michael Leavitt. Promotes the knowledge, appreciation, and development of Jewish music, past and present, for professional and lay audiences; seeks to raise the standards of composition and performance in Jewish music, to encourage research, and to sponsor performances of new and rarely heard works. *Musica Judaica Journal.*

ASSOCIATION OF JEWISH BOOK PUBLISHERS (1962). c/o Jewish Lights Publishing, PO Box 237, Woodstock, VT 05091. (802) 457-4000. FAX: (802)457-4004. Pres. Stuart M. Matlins; Exec. Dir. Adah

Hirschfeld. As a nonprofit group, provides a forum for discussion of mutual areas of interest among Jewish publishers, and promotes cooperative exhibits and promotional opportunities for members. Membership fee is $85 annually per publishing house.

ASSOCIATION OF JEWISH GENEALOGICAL SOCIETIES (1988). PO Box 26, Cabin John, MD 20818. (301) 365-1395. E-mail: sallyannsack@avotaynu.com. Pres. Dr. Sallyann Amdur Sack. Umbrella organization of more than 70 Jewish Genealogical Societies (JGS) worldwide. Represents organized Jewish genealogy, encourages Jews to research their family history, promotes new JGSs, supports existing societies, implements projects of interest to individuals researching their Jewish family histories. Holds annual conference where members learn and exchange ideas.

ASSOCIATION OF JEWISH LIBRARIES (1965). 15 E. 26 St., Rm. 1034, NYC 10010. (212)725-5359. Pres. Esther Nussbaum; V-Pres. David Gilner. Seeks to promote and improve services and professional standards in Jewish libraries; disseminates Jewish library information and guidance; promotes publication of literature in the field; encourages the establishment of Jewish libraries and collections of Judaica and the choice of Judaica librarianship as a profession; cocertifies Jewish libraries (with Jewish Book Council). *AJL Newsletter; Judaica Librarianship.*

BEIT HASHOAH–MUSEUM OF TOLERANCE OF THE SIMON WIESENTHAL CENTER (1993). 9760 W. Pico Blvd., Los Angeles, CA 90035-4792. (310)553-8403. FAX: (310)553-4521. E-mail: avra@wiesenthal.com. Dean-Founder Rabbi Marvin Hier; Assoc. Dean Rabbi Abraham Cooper; Exec. Dir. Rabbi Meyer May. A unique experiential museum focusing on personal prejudice, group intolerance, struggle for civil rights, and 20th-century genocides, culminating in a major exhibition on the Holocaust. Archives, Multimedia Learning Center designed for individualized research, 6,700-square-foot temporary exhibit space, 324-seat theater, 150-seat auditorium, and outdoor memorial plaza. *Response magazine.*

B'NAI B'RITH KLUTZNICK NATIONAL JEWISH MUSEUM (1957). 1640 Rhode Island Ave., NW, Washington, DC 20036. (202) 857-6583. FAX: (202)857-6609. Dir. Ori Z. Soltes; Asst. Dir. Lisa Rosenblatt. A center of Jewish art and history in the nation's capital, maintains temporary and permanent exhibition galleries, permanent collection of Jewish ceremonial objects, folk art, and contemporary fine art, outdoor sculpture garden and museum shop, as well as the American Jewish Sports Hall of Fame. Provides exhibitions, tours, educational programs, research assistance, and tourist information. *Quarterly newsletter; permanent collection catalogue; temporary exhibit catalogues.*

CENTRAL YIDDISH CULTURE ORGANIZATION (CYCO), Inc. (1943). 25 E. 21 St., 3rd fl., NYC 10010. (212)505-8305. FAX: (212) 505-8044. Mgr. David Kirszencwejg. Promotes, publishes, and distributes Yiddish books; publishes catalogues.

CONFERENCE ON JEWISH SOCIAL STUDIES, INC. (formerly CONFERENCE ON JEWISH RELATIONS, INC.) (1939). Bldg. 240, Rm. 103. Program in Jewish Studies, Stanford University, Stanford, CA 94305-2190. (650)725-0829. FAX: (650)725-2920. E-mail: jss@leland.stanford.edu. Pres. Steven J. Zipperstein; V-Pres. Aron Rodrigue. *Jewish Social Studies.*

CONGREGATION BINA (1981). 600 W. End Ave., Suite 1-C, NYC 10024. (212)873-4261. Pres. Joseph Moses; Exec. V.-Pres. Moses Samson; Hon. Pres. Samuel M. Daniel; Secy. Gen. Elijah E. Jhirad. Serves the religious, cultural, charitable, and philanthropic needs of the Children of Israel who originated in India and now reside in the U.S. Works to foster and preserve the ancient traditions, customs, liturgy, music, and folklore of Indian Jewry and to maintain needed institutions. *Kol Bina.*

CONGRESS FOR JEWISH CULTURE (1948). 25 E. 21 St., NYC 10010. (212)505-8040. FAX: (212)505-8044. Co-pres.'s Prof. Yonia Fain, Dr. Barnett Zumoff. An umbrella group comprising 16 constituent organizations; perpetuates and enhances Jewish creative expression in the U.S. and abroad; fosters all aspects of Yiddish cultural life through the publication of the journal Zukunft, the conferring of literary awards, commemoration of the Holocaust and the martyrdom of the Soviet

Jewish writers under Stalin, and a series of topical readings, scholarly conferences, symposiums, and concerts. *Zukunft.*

ELAINE KAUFMAN CULTURAL CENTER (1952). 129 W. 67 St., NYC 10023. (212) 501–3303. FAX: (212)874–7865. Chmn. Leonard Goodman; Pres. Elaine Kaufman; Exec. Dir. Lydia Kontos. Offers instruction in its Lucy Moses School for Music and Dance in music, dance, art, and theater to children and adults, in Western culture and Jewish traditions. Presents frequent performances of Jewish and general music by leading artists and ensembles in its Merkin Concert Hall and Ann Goodman Recital Hall. The Birnbaum Music Library houses Jewish music scores and reference books. *Kaufman Cultural Center News; bimonthly concert calendars; catalogues and brochures.*

HISTADRUTH IVRITH OF AMERICA (1916; reorg. 1922). 47 W. 34 St., Rm. 609, NYC 10001. (212)629–9443. Pres. Miriam Ostow; Exec. V.-Pres. Rabbi Abraham Kupchik. Emphasizes the primacy of Hebrew in Jewish life, culture, and education; aims to disseminate knowledge of written and spoken Hebrew in N. America, thus building a cultural bridge between the State of Israel and Jewish communities throughout N. America. *Hadoar; Lamishpaha; Tov Lichtov; Hebrew Week; Ulpan.*

HOLOCAUST CENTER OF THE UNITED JEWISH FEDERATION OF GREATER PITTSBURGH (1980). 5738 Darlington Rd., Pittsburgh, PA 15217. (412)421–1500. FAX: (412)422–1996. E-mail: lhurwitz@ujf. net. Pres. Holocaust Comm. Daniel Butler; Bd. Chmn. David Burstin; Dir. Linda F. Hurwitz. Develops programs and provides resources to further understanding of the Holocaust and its impact on civilization. Maintains a library, archive; provides speakers, educational materials; organizes community programs.

HOLOCAUST MEMORIAL CENTER (1984). 6602 West Maple Rd., West Bloomfield, MI 48322. (248)661–0840. FAX: (248) 661–4204. E-mail: info@holocaustcenter.org. Founder & Exec. V.-Pres. Rabbi Charles Rosenzveig. America's first freestanding Holocaust center comprising a museum, library-archive, oral history collection, garden of the righteous, research institute and academic advisory committee. Provides tours, lecture series, teacher training, Yom Hashoah commemorations, exhibits, educational outreach programs, speakers' bureau, computer database on 1,200 destroyed Jewish communities, guided travel tours to concentration camps and Israel, and museum shop. Published *World Reacts to the Holocaust. Newsletter.*

HOLOCAUST MEMORIAL RESOURCE & EDUCATION CENTER OF CENTRAL FLORIDA (1982). 851 N. Maitland Ave., Maitland, FL 32751. (407)628–0555. FAX: (407) 628–1079. E-mail: execdir@holocaustedu.org. Pres. Marilyn Goldman; Bd. Chmn. Tess Wise. An interfaith educational center devoted to teaching the lessons of the Holocaust. Houses permanent multimedia educational exhibit; maintains library of books, videotapes, films, and other visuals to serve the entire educational establishment; offers lectures, teacher training, and other activities. *Newsletter; Bibliography; "Holocaust—Lessons for Tomorrow"; elementary and middle school curriculum.*

HOLOCAUST MUSEUM AND LEARNING CENTER (formerly ST. LOUIS CENTER FOR HOLOCAUST STUDIES) (1977). 12 Millstone Campus Dr., St. Louis, MO 63146. (314)432–0020. Chmn. Michael Litwack; Chmn. Emer. Leo Wolf; Dir. Rabbi Robert Sternberg. Develops programs and provides resources and educational materials to further an understanding of the Holocaust and its impact on civilization; has a 5,000 sq. ft. museum containing photographs, artifacts, and audiovisual displays. *Newsletter for Friends of the Holocaust Museum and Learning Center.*

INTERNATIONAL JEWISH MEDIA ASSOCIATION (1987). U.S.: c/o St. Louis Jewish Light, 12 Millstone Campus Dr., St. Louis, MO 63146. (314)432–3353. FAX: (314)432–0515. E-mail: stlouislgt@aol. com and ajpamr@aol.com. Israel:PO Box 92, Jerusalem 91920. 02–202–222. FAX: 02–513–642. Pres. Robert A. Cohn (c/o St. Louis Jewish Light); Exec. Dir. Malcolm Rodman, 5307 Marsh Creek Dr., Austin, TX 78759-6218. (512)250–2409. FAX: (512)219–5851. Israel Liaison, Jacob Gispan, Lifsha Ben-Shach, WZO Dept. of Info. A worldwide network of Jewish journalists, publications and other media in the Jewish and general media, which seeks to provide a forum for the exchange of materials and ideas and to enhance the status of Jewish media and journalists throughout the world. *IJMA Newsletter; Proceedings of the International Conference on Jewish Media.*

INTERNATIONAL NETWORK OF CHILDREN OF JEWISH HOLOCAUST SURVIVORS, INC. (1981). 3000 NE 145 St., N. Miami, FL 33181–3600. (305)940–5690. FAX: (305)940–5691. E-mail: xholocau@fiu.edu. Pres. Rositta E. Kenigsberg; V.-Pres. Jean Bloch Rosensaft. Links Second Generation groups and individuals throughout the world. Represents the shared interests of children of Holocaust survivors; aims to perpetuate the authentic memory of the Holocaust and prevent its recurrence, to strengthen and preserve the Jewish spiritual, ideological, and cultural heritage, to fight anti-Semitism and all forms of discrimination, persecution, and oppression anywhere in the world. *International Study of Organized Persecution of Children.*

JEWISH BOOK COUNCIL (1946; reorg. 1993). 15 E. 26 St., NYC 10010. (212)532–4949, ext. 297. E-mail: carolynhessel@jewishbooks.org. Pres. Sharon Friedman; Exec. Dir. Carolyn Starman Hessel; Acting Bd. Chmn. Henry Everett. Serves as literary arm of the American Jewish community and clearinghouse for Jewish-content literature; assists readers, writers, publishers, and those who market and sell products. Provides bibliographies, list of publishers, bookstores, libraries, in cooperation with Association of Jewish Libraries. Sponsors National Jewish Book Awards, Jewish Book Month. *Jewish Book Annual; Jewish Book World.*

JEWISH HERITAGE PROJECT (1981). 150 Franklin St., #1W, NYC 10013. (212) 925–9067. Exec. Dir. Alan Adelson. Strives to bring to the broadest possible audience authentic works of literary and historical value relating to Jewish history and culture. Distributor of the film *Lodz Ghetto,* which it developed, as well as its companion volume *Lodz Ghetto: Inside a Community Under Siege.* Grants are not given.

JEWISH MUSEUM (1904, under auspices of Jewish Theological Seminary of America). 1109 Fifth Ave., NYC 10128. (212)423–3200. FAX: (212)423–3232. Dir. Joan H. Rosenbaum; Bd. Chmn.

Robert J. Hurst. Expanded museum reopened in June 1993, featuring permanent exhibition on the Jewish experience. Repository of the largest collection of Judaica–paintings, prints, photographs, sculpture, coins, medals, antiquities, textiles, and other decorative arts–in the Western Hemisphere. Includes the National Jewish Archive of Broadcasting. Tours, lectures, film showings, and concerts; special programs for children; cafe; shop. *Special exhibition catalogues; annual report.*

JEWISH PUBLICATION SOCIETY (1888). 1930 Chestnut St., Philadelphia, PA 19103. (215)564–5925. FAX: (215)564–6640. E-mail: jewishbook@aol.com. Pres. Harold Cramer; Ed.-in-Chief Dr. Ellen Frankel; Dir. of Marketing Mark Levine. Publishes and disseminates books of Jewish interest for adults and children; titles include TANAKH, religious studies and practices, life cycle, folklore, classics, art, history, belles-lettres. *The Bookmark; JPS Catalogue.*

JUDAH L. MAGNES MUSEUM–JEWISH MUSEUM OF THE WEST (1962). 2911 Russell St., Berkeley, CA 94705. (510)549–6950. FAX: (510)849–3673. E-mail: magnesadmin@eb.jfed.org. Pres. Fred Weiss; Acting Dir. Susan Morris. Collects, preserves, and makes available Jewish art, culture, history, and literature from throughout the world. Permanent collections of fine and ceremonial art; rare Judaica library, Western Jewish History Center (archives), Jewish-American Hall of Fame. Changing exhibits, traveling exhibits, docent tours, lectures, numismatics series, poetry award, museum shop. *Magnes News; special exhibition catalogues; scholarly books.*

JUDAICA CAPTIONED FILM CENTER, INC. (1983). PO Box 21439, Baltimore, MD 21208–0439. Voice (1–800)735–2258; TDD (410)655–6767. Pres. Lois Lilienfeld Weiner. Developing a comprehensive library of captioned and subtitled films and tapes on Jewish subjects; distributes them to organizations serving the hearing-impaired, including mainstream classes and senior adult groups, on a freeloan, handling/shipping-charge-only basis. *Newsletter.*

LEAGUE FOR YIDDISH, INC. (1979). 200 W. 72 St., Suite 40, NYC 10023. (212)

787-6675. Pres. Dr. Zuni Zelitch; Exec. Dir. Dr. Mordkhe Schaechter. Encourages the development and use of Yiddish as a living language; promotes its modernization and standardization; publisher of Yiddish textbooks and English-Yiddish dictionaries; most recent book publication: *Yiddish Two: An Intermediate and Advanced Textbook, 1995. Afn Shvel (quarterly).*

LEO BAECK INSTITUTE, INC. (1955). 129 E. 73 St., NYC 10021. (212)744-6400. FAX: (212)988-1305. E-mail: lbi1@lbi.com. Pres. Ismar Schorsch; Exec. Dir. Carol Kahn Strauss. A research, study, and lecture center, museum, library, and archive relating to the history of German-speaking Jewry. Offers lectures, exhibits, faculty seminars; publishes a series of monographs, yearbooks, and journals. *LBI News; LBI Yearbook; LBI Memorial Lecture; LBI Library & Archives News; occasional papers.*

LIVING TRADITIONS (1994). 430 W. 14 St., #514, NYC 10014. (212)691-1272. FAX: (212)691-1657. E-mail: livetrads@aol.com. Pres. Henry Sapoznik; V.-Pres. Lorin Sklamberg. Nonprofit membership organization dedicated to the study, preservation, and innovative continuity of traditional folk and popular culture through workshops, concerts, recordings, radio and film documentaries; clearinghouse for research in klezmer and other traditional music; sponsors yearly weeklong international cultural event, "Yiddish Folk Arts Program/'KlezKamp.' " *Living Traditions (newsletter).*

LOS ANGELES HOLOCAUST MUSEUM & MARTYRS MEMORIAL MUSEUM OF THE HOLOCAUST OF THE JEWISH FEDERATION COUNCIL OF GREATER LOS ANGELES (opened 1978). 6606 Wilshire Blvd., Los Angeles, CA 90036. (213)761-8170. FAX: (213)761-8172. Chmn. Osias G. Goren; Acting Dir./Curator Marcia Reines Josephy. A photo-narrative museum and resource center dedicated to Holocaust history, issues of genocide and prejudice, and curriculum development. *Educational guides; Those Who Dared; Rescuers and Rescued; Guide to Schindler's List.*

MEMORIAL FOUNDATION FOR JEWISH CULTURE, INC. (1964). 15 E. 26 St., Suite 1703, NYC 10010. (212)679-4074. Pres. Rabbi Alexander Schindler; Exec. V.-Pres. Jerry Hochbaum. Through the grants that it awards, encourages Jewish scholarship culture and education; supports communities that are struggling to maintain Jewish life; assists professional training for careers in communal service in Jewishly deprived communities; and stimulates the documentation, commemoration, and teaching of the Holocaust.

MUSEUM OF JEWISH HERITAGE–A LIVING MEMORIAL TO THE HOLOCAUST (1984). One Battery Park Plaza, NYC 10004-1484. (212)968-1800. FAX: (212) 968-1369. Bd. Chmn. Robert M. Morgenthau; Museum Dir. David Altshuler. New York tri-state's principal institution for educating people of all ages and backgrounds about 20th-century Jewish history and the Holocaust. Repository of Steven Spielberg's Survivors of the Shoah Visual History Foundation videotaped testimonies. Core and changing exhibitions. *18 First Place (newsletter); Holocaust bibliography; educational materials.*

NATIONAL FOUNDATION FOR JEWISH CULTURE (1960). 330 Seventh Ave., 21st fl., NYC 10001. (212)629-0500. FAX: (212) 629-0508. E-mail: nfjc@jewishculture.org. Pres. Robert M. Frankel; Exec. Dir. Richard A. Siegel. The leading Jewish organization devoted to promoting Jewish culture in the U.S. Manages the Jewish Endowment for the Arts and Humanities; administers the Council of American Jewish Museums and Council of Archives and Research Libraries in Jewish Studies; offers doctoral dissertation fellowships and grants for documentary films and new plays; coordinates community cultural residencies, local cultural commissions, and regional cultural consortia; organizes conferences, symposia, and festivals in the arts and humanities. *Jewish Cultural News; Plays of Jewish Interest; Jewish Exhibition Traveling Service.*

NATIONAL MUSEUM OF AMERICAN JEWISH MILITARY HISTORY (*see* Jewish War Veterans of the U.S.A.)

NATIONAL YIDDISH BOOK CENTER (1980). 1021 West St., Amherst, MA 01002. (413)256-4900, (800)535-3595. FAX: (413)256-4700. E-mail: yiddish@bikher.org. Founder & Pres. Aaron Lansky. Since 1980 the center has collected 1.4 million Yiddish books for distribution to libraries and readers worldwide; offers innovative English-language programs and produces a quarterly magazine. New permanent home in Amherst, open to the public, features a book repository, exhibits, a bookstore, and a theater. *The Pakn Treger* *(English-language quarterly)*.

ORTHODOX JEWISH ARCHIVES (1978). 84 William St., NYC 10038. (212)797–9000, ext. 73. FAX: (212)269–2843 Dir. Rabbi Moshe Kolodny. Founded by Agudath Israel of America; houses historical documents, photographs, periodicals, and other publications relating to the growth of Orthodox Jewry in the U.S. and related communities in Europe, Israel, and elsewhere. Particularly noteworthy are its holdings relating to rescue activities organized during the Holocaust and its traveling exhibits available to schools and other institutions.

RESEARCH FOUNDATION FOR JEWISH IMMIGRATION, INC. (1971). 570 Seventh Ave., NYC 10018. (212)921–3871. FAX: (212)575–1918. Pres. Curt C. Silberman; Sec. and Coord. of Research Herbert A. Strauss; Archivist Dennis E. Rohrbaugh. Studies and records the history of the migration and acculturation of Central European German-speaking Jewish and non-Jewish Nazi persecutees in various resettlement countries worldwide, with special emphasis on the American experience. *International Biographical Dictionary of Central European Emigrés, 1933–1945; Jewish Immigrants of the Nazi Period in the USA.*

RUSSIAN TELEVISION NETWORK (RTN) (1991). PO Box 3589, Stamford, CT 06905. (203)359–1570. FAX: (203)359–1381. Pres. Mark S. Golub; V.-Pres. Michael Pravin. Devoted to producing daily television programming for the immigrant Jewish community from the former Soviet Union; seen 24 hours a day on Cablevision of Brooklyn and nationally on the International Channel and NJT/National Jewish Television.

SEPHARDIC EDUCATIONAL CENTER (1979). 10808 Santa Monica Blvd., Los Angeles, CA 90025. (310)441–9361. FAX: (310)441–9561. E-mail:sec@primenet.com. Founder & Chmn. Jose A. Nessim, M.D.; World Pres. Jacques Benquesus. Has chapters in the U.S., North, Central, and South America, Europe, and Asia, a spiritual and educational center in the Old City of Jerusalem, and executive office in Los Angeles. Serves as a meeting ground for Sephardim from many nations; sponsors the first worldwide movement for Sephardic youth and young adults. Disseminates information about Sephardic Jewry in the form of motion pictures, pamphlets, and books, which it produces. *Hamerkaz (quarterly bulletin in English).*

SEPHARDIC HOUSE (1978). 2112 Broadway, Suite 200A, NYC 10023. (212)496–2173. FAX: (212)496–2264. E-mail: sephardic-@juno.com. Pres. Morrie R. Yohai; Exec. Dir. Dr. Janice E. Ovadiah. A cultural organization dedicated to fostering Sephardic history and culture; sponsors a wide variety of classes and public programs, film festivals, including summer program in France for high-school students; publication program disseminates materials of Sephardic value; outreach program to communities outside of the New York area; program bureau provides program ideas, speakers, and entertainers; International Sephardic Film Festival every two years. *Sephardic House Newsletter.*

SIMON WIESENTHAL CENTER (1977). 9760 W. Pico Blvd., Los Angeles, CA 90035–4701. (310)553–9036. FAX: (310) 553–2709. Dean-Founder Rabbi Marvin Hier; Assoc. Dean Rabbi Abraham Cooper; Exec. Dir. Rabbi Meyer May. Regional offices in New York, Miami, Toronto, Paris, Jerusalem, Buenos Aires. The largest institution of its kind in N. America, dedicated to the study of the Holocaust, its contemporary implications, and related human-rights issues through education and awareness. Incorporates 185,000-sq.-ft. Beit Hashoah-Museum of Tolerance, library, media department, archives, "Testimony to the Truth" oral histories, educational outreach, research department, international social action, "Page One" (syndicated weekly radio news magazine presenting contemporary Jewish issues). *Response Magazine.*

SKIRBALL CULTURAL CENTER (1996), an affiliate of Hebrew Union College. 2701 N. Sepulveda Blvd., Los Angeles, CA 90049. (310)440–4500. FAX: (310)440–4595. Pres. & CEO Uri D. Herscher; Bd. Chmn. Howard Friedman. Seeks to interpret the Jewish experience and to strengthen American society though a range of cultural programs, including museum exhibitions, children's Discovery Center, concerts, lectures, performances, readings, symposia, film, and educational offerings for adults and children of all ages and backgrounds. through interpretive museum exhibits and programming; museum shop and café. *Oasis magazine; catalogues of exhibits and collections.*

SOCIETY FOR THE HISTORY OF CZECHOSLOVAK JEWS, INC. (1961). 760 Pompton Ave., Cedar Grove, NJ 07009. (973)239–2333. FAX: (973)239-7935. Pres. Rabbi Norman Patz; Sec. Anita Grosz. Studies the history of Czechoslovak Jews; collects material and disseminates information through the publication of books and pamphlets; conducts annual memorial service for Czech Holocaust victims. *The Jews of Czechoslovakia (3 vols.); Review I–VI.*

SOCIETY OF FRIENDS OF TOURO SYNAGOGUE, NATIONAL HISTORIC SHRINE, INC. (1948). 85 Touro St., Newport, RI 02840. (401)847–4794. FAX: (401)847–8121. Pres. Meira Lisman Max; Exec. Dir. B. Schlessinger Ross. Helps maintain Touro Synagogue as a national historic site, opening and interpreting it for visitors; promotes public awareness of its preeminent role in the tradition of American religious liberty; annually commemorates George Washington's letter of 1790 to the Hebrew Congregation of Newport. *Society Update.*

———, TOURO NATIONAL HERITAGE TRUST (1984). 85 Touro St., Newport, RI 02840. (401)847–0810. FAX (401)847–8121. Pres. Bernard Bell; Chmn. Benjamin D. Holloway. Works to establish national education center within Touro compound; sponsors Touro Fellow through John Carter Brown Library; presents seminars and other educational programs; promotes knowledge of the early Jewish experience in this country.

SPERTUS MUSEUM, SPERTUS INSTITUTE OF JEWISH STUDIES (1968). 618 S. Michigan Ave., Chicago, IL 60605. (312)922–9012. FAX: (312)922–6406. Pres. Spertus Institute of Jewish Studies, Dr. Howard A. Sulkin. The largest, most comprehensive Judaic museum in the Midwest with 12,000 square feet of exhibit space and a permanent collection of some 10,000 works reflecting 5,000 years of Jewish history and culture. Also includes the re-designed Zell Holocaust Memorial, permanent collection, changing visual arts and special exhibits, and the children's ARTIFACT Center for a hands-on archaeological adventure. Plus, traveling exhibits for Jewish educators, life-cycle workshops, ADA accessible. *Exhibition catalogues; educational pamphlets.*

SURVIVORS OF THE SHOAH VISUAL HISTORY FOUNDATION (1994). PO Box 3168, Los Angeles, CA 90078–3168. (818)777–7802. FAX: (818)866–0312. Pres. & CEO Dr. Michael G. Berenbaum; Exec. Dir. Ari C. Zev. A nonprofit organization, founded and chaired by Steven Spielberg, dedicated to videotaping and preserving interviews with Holocaust survivors throughout the world. The archive of testimonies will be used as a tool for global education about the Holocaust and to teach racial, ethnic, and cultural tolerance.

UNITED STATES HOLOCAUST MEMORIAL MUSEUM (1980; opened Apr. 1993). 100 Raoul Wallenberg Place, SW, Washington, DC 20024. (202)488–0400. FAX: (202)488–2690. Chmn. Miles Lerman. Federally chartered and privately built, its mission is to teach about the Nazi persecution and murder of six million Jews and millions of others from 1933 to 1945 and to inspire visitors to contemplate their moral responsibilities as citizens of a democratic nation. Opened in April 1993 near the national Mall in Washington, DC, the museum's permanent exhibition tells the story of the Holocaust through authentic artifacts, videotaped oral testimonies, documentary film, and historical photographs. Offers educational programs for students and adults, an interactive computerized learning center, and special exhibitions and community programs. *United States Holocaust Memorial Museum Update (bimonthly); Directory of Holocaust Institutions; Journal of Holocaust and Genocide Studies (quarterly).*

THE WILSTEIN (SUSAN & DAVID) INSTITUTE OF JEWISH POLICY STUDIES (1988). 43 Hawes St., Brookline, MA 02146. (617)232–8710. FAX: (617)264–9264. E-mail: dgordis@lynx.neu.edu. Dir. Dr. David M. Gordis; Chmn. Howard I. Friedman. The Wilstein Institute's West Coast Center in Los Angeles and East Coast Center at Hebrew College in Boston provide a bridge between academics, community leaders, professionals, and the organizations and institutions of Jewish life. The institute serves as an international research and development resource for American Jewry. *Bulletins, various newsletters, monographs, research reports, and books.*

YESHIVA UNIVERSITY MUSEUM (1973). 2520 Amsterdam Ave., NYC 10033–3201. (212)960–5390. FAX: (212)960–5406. E-mail: glickber@aymail.yu.edu. Dir. Sylvia A. Herskowitz. Collects, preserves, and interprets Jewish life and culture through changing exhibitions of ceremonial objects, paintings, rare books and documents, synagogue architecture, textiles, decorative arts, and photographs. Oral history archive. Special events, holiday workshops, live performances, lectures, etc. for adults and children. Guided tours and workshops are offered. *Seasonal calendars; special exhibition catalogues.*

YIDDISHER KULTUR FARBAND–YKUF (1937). 1133 Broadway, Rm. 820, NYC 10010. (212)243–1304. FAX: (212)243-1305. E-mail: mahosu@amc.one. Pres. and Ed. Itche Goldberg. Publishes a bimonthly magazine and books by contemporary and classical Jewish writers; conducts cultural forums; exhibits works by contemporary Jewish artists and materials of Jewish historical value; organizes reading circles. *Yiddishe Kultur.*

YIVO INSTITUTE FOR JEWISH RESEARCH (1925). 555 W. 57 St., Suite 1100, NYC 10019. (212)246–6080. FAX: (212)292-1892. Chmn. Bruce Slovin; Exec. Dir. Tom Freudenheim. Engages in social and cultural research pertaining to East European Jewish life; maintains library and archives which provide a major international, national, and New York resource used by institutions, individual scholars, and the public; trains graduate students in Yiddish, East European, and American Jewish studies; offers continuing education classes in Yiddish language, exhibits, conferences, public programs; publishes books. *Yidishe Shprakh; YIVO Annual; YIVO Bleter; Yedies fun Yivo.*

———, MAX WEINREICH CENTER FOR ADVANCED JEWISH STUDIES (1968). 555 W. 57 St., Suite 1100, NYC 10019. (212)246–6080. FAX: (212)292–1892. Provides advanced-level training in Yiddish language and literature, ethnography, folklore, linguistics, and history; offers guidance on dissertation or independent research; post-doctoral fellowships available.

YUGNTRUF–YOUTH FOR YIDDISH (1964). 200 W. 72 St., Suite 40, NYC 10023. (212)787–6675. FAX: (212)799–1517. Chmn. Dr. Paul Glasser; V-Chmn. Dr. Adina Cimet de Singer; Coord. Brucha Lang. A worldwide, nonpolitical organization for young people with a knowledge of, or interest in, Yiddish; fosters Yiddish as a living language and culture. Sponsors all activities in Yiddish: reading, conversation, and creative writing groups; annual weeklong retreat in Berkshires; non-Hassidic play group; sale of shirts. *Yugntruf Journal.*

ISRAEL-RELATED

THE ABRAHAM FUND (1989). 477 Madison Ave., 4th fl., NYC 10022. (212)303–9421. FAX: (212)935–1834. Chmn. & co-founder Alan B. Slifka; Co-founder Dr. Eugene Weiner; Exec. V.-Pres. Dr. Lee Katz. Fund raising and educational organization established to promote Jewish-Arab coexistence programs in Israel. Programs are developed and managed by both Jews and Arabs in a wide variety of fields, including health, social services, education, the environment, culture, and women's rights. *Quarterly newsletter.*

ALYN–AMERICAN SOCIETY FOR HANDICAPPED CHILDREN IN ISRAEL (1934). 19 W. 44 St., NYC 10036. (212)869–8085. FAX: (212)768–0979. E-mail: alynny @juno.com. Chmn. Simone P. Blum; Hon. Pres. Minette Halpern Brown; Exec. Dir. Joan R. Mendelson. Supports the work of ALYN Hospital, rehabilitation center for severely orthopedically handicapped children, located in Jerusalem, whose aim is to prepare patients for independent living.

AMERICA-ISRAEL CULTURAL FOUNDATION, INC. (1939). 317 Madison Ave., Suite 1605, NYC 10017. (212)557–1600. FAX: (212)557–1611. Bd. Chmn. Isaac Stern; Pres. Vera Stern; Exec. Dir. USA Kathleen Mellon. Supports and encourages the growth of cultural excellence in Israel through grants to cultural institutions; scholarships to gifted young artists and musicians. *Newsletter.*

AMERICA-ISRAEL FRIENDSHIP LEAGUE, INC. (1971). 134 E. 39 St., NYC 10016.

(212)213–8630. FAX: (212)683–3475. E-mail: aifl@nyworld.com. Pres. Mortimer B. Zuckerman; Bd. Chmn. Kenneth J. Bialkin; Sr. Exec. V.-Pres. Stanley A. Urman; Exec. V.-Pres. Ilana Artman. A nonsectarian, nonpartisan organization which seeks to broaden the base of support for Israel among Americans of all faiths and backgrounds. Activities include educational exchanges, tours of Israel for American leadership groups, symposia and public-education activities, and the dissemination of printed information. *Newsletter.*

AMERICAN ASSOCIATES, BEN-GURION UNIVERSITY OF THE NEGEV (1973). 342 Madison Ave., Suite 1224, NYC 10173. (212)687–7721. FAX: (212)370–0686. E-mail: info@aabgu.org. Pres. Kenneth L. Tucker; Bd. Chmn. Harold L. Oshry; Exec. V.-Pres. Kenneth M. Farber. Raises funds for Israel's youngest university, an institution dedicated to providing a world-class higher education and fulfilling David Ben-Gurion's vision to develop the Negev and make Israel a 'light unto the nations' through education, research, and projects that fight hunger, disease, and poverty in nearly 50 countries worldwide. *IMPACT Newsletter; Speaking of Israel radio news service; videos and brochures.*

AMERICAN COMMITTEE FOR SHAARE ZEDEK MEDICAL CENTER IN JERUSALEM, INC. (1949). 49 W. 45 St., Suite 1100, NYC 10036. (212)354–8801. FAX: (212)391-2674. Natl. Pres. & Chmn. Intertnational Board of Governors Menno Ratzker; Chmn. Erica Jesselson; Exec. Dir. Dr. Stuart Tauber. Raises funds for the various needs of the Shaare Zedek Medical Center, Jerusalem, such as equipment and medical supplies, nurses' training, and research; supports exchange program between Shaare Zedek Medical Center and Albert Einstein College of Medicine, NY. *Heartbeat Magazine.*

AMERICAN COMMITTEE FOR SHENKAR COLLEGE IN ISRAEL, INC. (1971). 855 Ave. of the Americas, NYC 10001. (212) 947–1597. FAX: (212)643–9887. E-mail: acfsc@worldnet.att.net. Pres. Steven Boxer; Exec. Dir. Charlotte Fainblatt. Raises funds for capital improvement, research and development projects, laboratory equipment, scholarships, lectureships, fellowships, and library/archives of

fashion and textile design at Shenkar College in Israel, Israel's only fashion and textile technology college. Accredited by the Council of Higher Education, the college is the chief source of personnel for Israel's fashion and apparel industry. *Shenkar News.*

AMERICAN COMMITTEE FOR THE BEER-SHEVA FOUNDATION (1988). PO Box 8578-FDR Sta., NYC 10518. (212) 838-4858. FAX: (212) 838-4858. Bd. Chmn. Sidney Cooperman; Pres. Ron Slevin. U.S. fund-raising arm of the Beer-Sheva Foundation, which funds vital projects to improve the quality of life in the city of Beer-Sheva: nursery schools for pre-K toddlers, residential and day centers for needy seniors, educational programs, facilities and scholarships (especially for new olim, the physically and mentally challenged), parks, playgrounds, and other important projects. Also offers special services for immigrants—heaters, blankets, clothing, school supplies, etc.

AMERICAN COMMITTEE FOR THE WEIZMANN INSTITUTE OF SCIENCE (1944). 51 Madison Ave., NYC 10010. (212)779-2500. FAX: (212)779–3209. E-mail: info@acwis.org. Chmn. S. Donald Sussman; Pres. Albert Willner, M.D.; Exec. V.-Pres. Fran Ginsburg. Through 15 regional offices in the U.S. raises funds, disseminates information, and does American purchasing for the Weizmann Institute in Rehovot, Israel, a world-renowned center of scientific research and graduate study. The institute conducts research in disease, energy, the environment, and other areas; runs an international summer science program for gifted high-school students. *Interface; Weizmann Now; annual report.*

AMERICAN FRIENDS OF ASSAF HAROFEH MEDICAL CENTER (1975). PO Box 749, White Plains, N.Y. 10602-0749. (914)328–2183. FAX: (914)328–2484. Chmn. Kenneth Kronen; Exec. V.-Pres. David Agronin; Treas. Robert Kastin. Support group for Assaf Harofeh, Israel's third-largest government hospital, serving a poor population of over 400,000 in the area between Tel Aviv and Jerusalem. Raises funds for medical equipment, medical training for immigrants, hospital expansion, school of nursing, and school of physiotherapy. *Newsletter.*

AMERICAN FRIENDS OF BAR-ILAN UNIVERSITY (1955). 91 Fifth Ave., Suite 200, NYC 10003. (212)337–1270. FAX: (212)337–1274. Chancellor Rabbi Emanuel Rackman; Chmn. Global Bd. of Trustees Selik Wengrowsky; Pres. Amer. Bd. of Trustees Jane Stern Lebell; Exec. V.-Pres. Gen. Yehuda Halevy. Supports Bar-Ilan University, an institution that integrates the highest standards of contemporary scholarship in liberal arts and sciences with a Judaic studies program as a requirement for graduation. Located in Ramat-Gan, Israel, and chartered by the Board of Regents of the State of NY. *Bar-Ilan News; Bar-Ilan University Scholar.*

AMERICAN FRIENDS OF BETH HATEFUTSOTH (1976). 110 E. 59 St., Suite 4099, NYC 10022. (212)339–6034. FAX: (212)318–6176. Pres. Abraham Spiegel; Chmn. Sam E. Bloch; Exec. Dir. Gloria Golan. Supports the maintenance and development of Beth Hatefutsoth, the Nahum Goldmann Museum of the Jewish Diaspora in Tel Aviv, and its cultural and educational programs for youth and adults. Circulates its traveling exhibitions and provides various cultural programs to local Jewish communities. Includes Jewish genealogy center (DOROT), the center for Jewish music, and photodocumentation center. *Beth Hatefutsoth quarterly newsletter.*

AMERICAN FRIENDS OF HAIFA UNIVERSITY (*see* American Society of the University of Haifa)

AMERICAN FRIENDS OF LIKUD. 218 E. 79 St., NYC 10021-1214. (212) 650-1231. Pres. Jack B. Dweck. Dir. Sharon Elbaum.

AMERICAN FRIENDS OF MERETZ (1988). 114 W. 26 St., Suite 1005, NYC 10001. (212)242–4500. FAX: (212)242–5718. E-mail: afmeretz@aol.com. Pres. Rabbi Israel Dresner; Chmn. Stefi Kirschner; Exec. Dir. Charney V. Bromberg. Promotes the ideals of Meretz-Democratic Israel, the progressive Zionist party dedicated to democracy, human and civil rights, religious pluralism, equality for women and ethnic minorities, and Israeli-Palestinian peace based on mutual recognition and self-determination. Initiates dialogue between Israelis and American Jews on these topics. *Meretz Report.*

AMERICAN FRIENDS OF NEVE SHALOM/WAHAT AL-SALAM (1988). 121 6th Ave., #507, NYC 10013. (212) 226-9246. FAX:

(212) 226-6817. E-mail: afnswas@compuserve.com. Pres. David Matz; V.-Pres. David Hitchcock. Supports this hilltop village, midway between Jerusalem and Tel Aviv, which is home to Jewish Muslim and Christian families who maintain their traditions while respecting and being enriched by those of the others. Democratic, egalitarian, and politically independent, its mission is to exemplify and teach the arts of peace. As a center for conflict resolution, offers unique encounter workshops, university courses, and training for youth and adults. *Biannual newsletters.*

AMERICAN FRIENDS OF RABIN MEDICAL CENTER (1994). 299 Broadway, Suite 1019, NYC 10007. (212) 587–0502. E-mail: afrmcny@jon.cjfny.org. Pres. Sherwood Goldberg. Supports the maintenance and development of this medical, research, and teaching institution in central Israel, which unites the Golda and Beilinson hospitals, providing 12% of all hospitalization in Israel. Department of Organ Transplantation performs 80% of all kidney and 60% of all liver transplants in Israel. Affiliated with Tel Aviv University's Sackler School of Medicine. New Directions Quarterly.

AMERICAN FRIENDS OF RAMBAM MEDICAL CENTER (1969). 850 Seventh Ave., Suite 305, NYC 10019. (212)397–1123. FAX: (212)397–1132. E-mail: 102177.647@compuserve.com. Pres. Michael R. Stoler; Exec. Dir. Linda E. Frankel. Represents and raises funds for Rambam Medical Center (Haifa), an 887-bed hospital serving approx. one-third of Israel's population, incl. the entire population of northern Israel (and south Lebanon), the U.S. Sixth Fleet, and the UN Peacekeeping Forces in the region. Rambam is the teaching hospital for the Technion's medical school. *Quarterly newsletter.*

AMERICAN FRIENDS OF RATZ/CRM (*see* American Friends of Meretz)

AMERICAN FRIENDS OF TEL AVIV UNIVERSITY, INC. (1955). 360 Lexington Ave., NYC 10017. (212)687–5651. FAX: (212)687–4085. Bd. Chmn. Bernard Rapoport; Pres. Robert J. Topchik; Exec. V.-Pres. Jules Love. Promotes higher education at Tel Aviv University, Israel's largest and most comprehensive institution of higher learning. Included in its nine faculties are the Sackler School of

Medicine with its fully accredited NY State English-language program, the Rubin Academy of Music, and 70 research institutes including the Moshe Dayan Center for Middle East & African Studies and the Jaffe Center for Strategic Studies. *Tel Aviv University News; FAX Flash.*

AMERICAN FRIENDS OF THE HEBREW UNIVERSITY (1925; inc. 1931). 11 E. 69 St., NYC 10021. (212)472–9800. FAX: (212) 744–2324. Pres. Keith L. Sachs; Bd. Chmn. Lawrence Newman; Exec. V.-Pres. Adam Kahan. Fosters the growth, development, and maintenance of the Hebrew University of Jerusalem; collects funds and conducts informational programs throughout the U.S., highlighting the university's achievements and its significance. *Hebrew University Today; Scopus Magazine.*

AMERICAN FRIENDS OF THE ISRAEL COMMUNITY DEVELOPMENT FOUNDATION (1990). 119 West 40 St., 14th fl., NYC 10018. (212)944–4884. FAX: (212)840–5206. E-mail: 75222.2142@compuserve. com. Pres. Barry Liben; Exec. Dir. Dina Shalit. Supports the ICDF, whose projects are primarily in Judea, Samaria, and Gaza, areas that have often not been eligible for funding from more established philanthropic agencies. ICDF provides funds for educational programs, community centers, medical clinics and first-aid emergency equipment, synagogues, and colleges, working in direct association with communities that request ICDF's assistance in raising funds, on a project-by-project basis. *Eretz Israel Fund Report (quarterly).*

AMERICAN FRIENDS OF THE ISRAEL MUSEUM (1972). 500 Fifth Ave., Suite 2540, NYC 10110. (212)997–5611. FAX: (212)997–5536. Pres. Judy A. Steinhardt; Exec. Dir. Michele Cohn Tocci. Raises funds for special projects of the Israel Museum in Jerusalem; solicits works of art for permanent collection, exhibitions, and educational purposes. *Newsletter.*

AMERICAN FRIENDS OF THE ISRAEL PHILHARMONIC ORCHESTRA (AFIPO) (1972). 122 E. 42 St., Suite 4507, NYC 10168. (212)697–2949. FAX: (212)697–2943. Pres. Herman Sandler; Exec. Dir. Suzanne K. Ponsot. Works to secure the financial future of the orchestra so that it may continue to travel throughout the world bringing its message of peace and cultural understanding through music. Supports the orchestra's international touring program, educational projects, and a wide array of musical activities in Israel. *Passport to Music (newsletter).*

AMERICAN FRIENDS OF THE OPEN UNIVERSITY OF ISRAEL. 180 W. 80 St., NYC 10024. (212)713–1515. FAX: (212)974–0769. Natl. Chmn. Irving M. Rosenbaum; Exec. V.-Pres. Eric G. Heffler. *Open Letter.*

AMERICAN FRIENDS OF THE SHALOM HARTMAN INSTITUTE (1976). 282 Grand Ave., Englewood, NJ 07631. (201)894–0566. FAX: (201)894–0377. E-mail: afshi@ intac.com. Pres. Richard F. Kaufman; Exec. V.-Pres. Jeffrey M. Snyder; Admin. Dorothy Minchin. Supports the Shalom Hartman Institute, Jerusalem, an institute of higher education and research center devoted to applying the teachings of classical Judaism to the issues of modern life. Founded in 1976 by David Hartman, includes:the Institute for Advanced Judaic Studies with research centers in philosophy, theology, political thought, education, ethics, and Halakhah; the Institute for Judaic Educational Leadership, which focuses on teacher training; and the Institute for Diaspora Education, which offers seminars for rabbis, lay leadership, educators, and communal professionals.

AMERICAN FRIENDS OF THE TEL AVIV MUSEUM OF ART (1974). 133 E. 58 St., Suite 701, NYC 10022-1236. (212)319–0555. FAX: (212)754–2987. Chmn. Uzi Zucker; Exec. Dir. Barbara A. Lax. Raises funds for the Tel Aviv Museum of Art for special projects, art acquisitions, and exhibitions; seeks contributions of art to expand the museum's collection; encourages art loans and traveling exhibitions; creates an awareness of the museum in the USA; makes available exhibition catalogues, monthly calendars, and posters published by the museum.

AMERICAN FRIENDS OF HERZOG HOSPITAL/EZRATH NASHIM–JERUSALEM (1895). 800 Second Ave., 8th fl., NYC 10017. (212)499–9092. FAX:(212)499–9085. E-mail:saraherzog@aol.com. Pres. Rabbi Gilbert Epstein; Exec. Dir. David Cohen. Jerusalem's third-largest hospital (330 beds) and Israel's leading geriatric-psychiatric treatment and research center. Comprehensive in- and out-patient clinics, departments of neuro- and psychogeriatrics, state-of-the-art rehabilitation department, specialized geriatric clinics, and community mental health center treating 16,000 patient visits annually. A teaching hospital affiliated with Hadassah-Hebrew University Medical Center, Bar-Ilan University, Baycrest Center for Geriatric Care (Toronto), and McGill University (Montreal).

AMERICAN-ISRAEL ENVIRONMENTAL COUNCIL (formerly COUNCIL FOR A BEAUTIFUL ISRAEL ENVIRONMENTAL EDUCATION FOUNDATION) (1973). c/o Perry Davis Assoc., 25 W. 45th St., Suite 1405, NYC 10036. (212)575–7530. Co-Pres. Mel Atlas, Edythe Grodnick; Admin. Dir. Donna Lindemann. A support group for the Israeli body, whose activities include education, town planning, lobbying for legislation to protect and enhance the environment, preservation of historical sites, the improvement and beautification of industrial and commercial areas, and sponsoring the CBI Center for Environmental Studies located in Yarkon Park, Tel Aviv. *Yearly newsletter; yearly theme oriented calendars in color.*

AMERICAN ISRAEL PUBLIC AFFAIRS COMMITTEE (AIPAC) (1954). 440 First St., NW, Washington, DC 20001. (202)639–5200. FAX: (202)347–4921. Pres. Melvin Dow; Exec. Dir. Howard A. Kohr. Registered to lobby on behalf of legislation affecting U.S.-Israel relations; represents Americans who believe support for a secure Israel is in U.S. interest. Works for a strong U.S.-Israel relationship. *Near East Report; AIPAC Papers on U.S.-Israel Relations.*

AMERICAN-ISRAELI LIGHTHOUSE, INC. (1928; reorg. 1955). 545 Madison Ave., Suite 600, NYC 10022. (212)838–5322. Pres. Mrs. Leonard F. Dank; Sec. Mrs. Ida Rhein. Provides a vast network of programs and services for blind and physically handicapped persons throughout Israel, to effect their social and vocational integration into the mainstream of their communities. Center of Services for the blind; built and maintains Rehabilitation Center for blind and handicapped persons (Migdal Or) in Haifa.

AMERICAN JEWISH LEAGUE FOR ISRAEL (1957). 130 E. 59 St., NYC 10022. (212)371–1583. FAX: (212)371–3265. Pres. Dr. Martin L. Kalmanson; Exec.

Dir. Judith Struhl. Seeks to unite all those who, notwithstanding differing philosophies of Jewish life, are committed to the historical ideals of Zionism; works independently of class, party, or religious affiliation for the welfare of Israel as a whole. Not identified with any political parties in Israel. Member of World Jewish Congress, World Zionist Organization, American Zionist Movement. *Newsletter.*

AMERICAN PHYSICIANS FELLOWSHIP FOR MEDICINE IN ISRAEL (1950). 2001 Beacon St., Suite 211, Brookline, MA 02146. (617)232–5382. FAX: (617) 739–2616. E-mail: apf@apfmed.org. Pres. Sherwood L. Gorbach, M.D.; Exec. Dir. Donald J. Perlstein. Supports projects that advance medical education, research, and care in Israel and builds links between the medical communities of Israel and N. Amer.; provides fellowships for Israeli physicians training in N. Amer. and arranges lectureships in Israel by prominent N. Amer. physicians; sponsors CME seminars in Israel and N. Amer.; coordinates U.S./Canadian medical emergency volunteers for Israel. *APF News.*

AMERICAN RED MAGEN DAVID FOR ISRAEL, INC. (1940) (a.k.a. ARMDI & Red Magen David). 888 Seventh Ave., Suite 403, NYC 10106. (212)757–1627. FAX: (212)757–4662. E-mail: armdi@juno.com. Natl. Pres. Robert L. Sadoff, M.D.; Exec. V.-Pres. Benjamin Saxe. An authorized tax-exempt organization; the sole support arm in the U.S. of Magen David Adom (MDA), Israel's equivalent to a Red Cross Society; raises funds for the MDA emergency medical, ambulance, blood, and disaster services which help Israel's defense forces and civilian population. Helps to supply and equip ambulances, bloodmobiles, and cardiac rescue ambulances as well as 45 prehospital MDA Emergency Medical Clinics and the MDA National Blood Service Center and MDA Fractionation Institute in Ramat Gan, Israel. *Lifeline.*

AMERICANS FOR A SAFE ISRAEL (AFSI) (1971). 1623 Third Ave., Suite 205, NYC 10128. (212)828–2424. FAX: (212)828–1717. E-mail: afsi@interport.net. Chmn. Herbert Zweibon; Exec. Dir. Helen Freedman. Seeks to educate Americans in Congress, the media, and the public about Israel's role as a strategic asset for the West; through meetings with legislators and the media, in press releases and publications AFSI promotes Jewish rights to Judea and Samaria and the concept of "peace for peace" as an alternative to "territory for peace." *Outpost.*

AMERICANS FOR PEACE NOW (1984). 27 W. 20 St., 9th fl., NYC 10011. (212)645–6262. FAX: (212)645–7355. E-mail: apndc@peacenow.org. Pres. & CEO Debra DeLee; Co-chmn. Ernest Bogen, Mary Ann Stein. Conducts educational programs and raises funds to support the Israeli peace movement, Shalom Achshav (Peace Now), and coordinates U.S. advocacy efforts through APN's Washington-based Center for Israeli Peace and Security. *National Newsletter.*

AMERICANS FOR PROGRESSIVE ISRAEL (1952). 224 W. 35 St., Suite 403, NYC 10001. (212)868–0386. A socialist-Zionist organization historically supporting a just and durable peace between Israel and all its Arab neighbors, including the Palestinian people; works for the national liberation of all Jews; seeks the democratization of Jewish communal and organizational life; promotes dignity of labor, social justice, and a deeper understanding of Jewish culture and heritage. Affiliate of American Zionist Movement and World Union of Mapam, with fraternal ties to Hashomer Hatzair and Kibbutz Artzi Federation of Israel. *Israel Horizons.*

AMERICAN SOCIETY FOR TECHNION–ISRAEL INSTITUTE OF TECHNOLOGY (1940). 810 Seventh Ave., 24th fl., NYC 10019. (212)262–6200. FAX: (212)262–6155. Pres. Irving A. Shepard; Chmn. Ben Z. Sosewitz; Exec. V.-Pres. Melvyn H. Bloom. Supports the work of the Technion-Israel Institute of Technology in Haifa, which trains over 11,000 students in 19 faculties and a medical school, and conducts research across a broad spectrum of science and technology. *Technion USA.*

AMERICAN SOCIETY FOR THE PROTECTION OF NATURE IN ISRAEL, INC. (1986). 28 Arrandale Ave., Great Neck, NY 11024. (212) 398-6750. FAX: (212) 398-1665. E-mail: aspni@aol.com. Cochmn. Edward I. Geffner, Russell Rothman. A nonprofit organization supporting the work of SPNI, an Israeli organization devoted to environmental protection and nature ed-

ucation. SPNI runs 26 Field Study Centers and has 45 municipal offices throughout Israel; offers education programs, organized hikes, and other activities. SPNI News.

AMERICAN SOCIETY FOR YAD VASHEM (1981). 500 Fifth Ave., Suite 1600, NYC 10110-1699. (212)220–4304. FAX: (212) 220–4308. Chmn. Eli Zborowski; Exec. Dir. Selma Schiffer. Development arm of Yad Vashem, Jerusalem, the central international authority created by the Knesset in 1953 for the purposes of commemoration and education in connection with the Holocaust. *Martyrdom and Resistance (newsletter).*

AMERICAN SOCIETY OF THE UNIVERSITY OF HAIFA (formerly AMERICAN FRIENDS OF HAIFA UNIVERSITY) (1972). c/o Lester Schwab Katz & Dwyer, Att.: Robert J. Benowitz, 120 Broadway, Suite 3800, NYC 10271–0071. (212)964–6611. FAX: (212)267–5916. Pres. Paul Amir; Sec./Treas. Robert Jay Benowitz. Promotes, encourages, and aids higher and secondary education, research, and training in all branches of knowledge in Israel and elsewhere; aids in the maintenance and development of Haifa University; raises and allocates funds for the above purposes; provides scholarships; promotes exchanges of teachers and students.

AMERICAN ZIONIST MOVEMENT (formerly AMERICAN ZIONIST FEDERATION) (1939; reorg. 1949, 1970, 1993). 110 E. 59 St., NYC 10022. (212)318–6100. FAX: (212)935–3578. E-mail: staff@azm.com. Pres. Melvin Salberg; Exec. Dir. Karen J. Rubinstein. Umbrella organization for 20 American Zionist organizations and the voice of unified Zionism in the U.S. Conducts advocacy for Israel; strengthens Jewish identity; promotes the Israel experience; prepares the next generation of Zionist leadership. Regional offices in Chicago, Los Angeles, Detroit, South Florida. Groups in Atlanta, Philadelphia, Baltimore, Pittsburgh, Washington, DC. *The Zionist Advocate.*

AMIT (1925). 817 Broadway, NYC 10003. (212)477–4720. FAX: (212)353–2312. Pres. Evelyn Blachor; Exec. Dir. Marvin Leff. The State of Israel's official reshet (network) for religious secondary technological education; maintains innovative children's homes and youth villages in Israel in an environment of traditional Judaism; promotes cultural activities for the purpose of disseminating Zionist ideals and strengthening traditional Judaism in America. *AMIT Magazine.*

AMPAL – AMERICAN ISRAEL CORPORATION (1942). 1177 Avenue of the Americas, NYC 10036. (212)782–2100. FAX: (212)782–2114. E-mail: ampal@aol.com. Pres. Lawrence Lefkowitz; Bd. Chmn. Daniel Steinmetz; CEO Shuki Gleitman. Acquires interests in businesses located in the State of Israel or that are Israel-related. Interests include hotels and leisuretime, real estate, finance, energy distribution, basic industry, high technology, and communications. *Annual report; quarterly reports.*

ARZA – ASSOCIATION OF REFORM ZIONISTS OF AMERICA (1977). 838 Fifth Ave., NYC 10021. (212)650–4280. FAX: (212)517–7968. Pres. Philip Meltzer; Exec. Dir. Rabbi Ammiel Hirsch. Individual Zionist membership organization devoted to achieving Jewish pluralism in Israel and strengthening the Israeli Reform movement. Chapter activities in the U.S. concentrate on these issues and on strengthening American public support for Israel. *Journal of Reform Zionism; ARZA Report.*

BETAR ZIONIST YOUTH ORGANIZATION (1935). 218 E. 79 St., NYC 10021. (212)650–1231. FAX: (212) 650–1413. North American Central Shlicha Sharon Tzur. Organizes youth groups across North America to teach Zionism, Jewish identity, and love of Israel; sponsors summer programs in Israel for Jewish youth ages 14–22; sponsors Tagar Zionist Student Activist Movement on college campuses.

BOYS TOWN JERUSALEM FOUNDATION OF AMERICA INC. (1948). 91 Fifth Ave., Suite 601, NYC 10003. (212)242–1118, (800) 469-2697. FAX: (212)242–2190. E-mail: 74230.3450@compuserve.com. Pres. Michael J. Scharf; Chmn. Josh S. Weston; V.-Chmn. Moshe Linchner; Exec. V.-Pres. Rabbi Ronald L. Gray. Raises funds for Boys Town Jerusalem, which was established in 1948 to offer a comprehensive academic, religious, and technological education to disadvantaged Israeli and immigrant boys from over 45 different coun-

tries, including Ethiopia, the former Soviet Union, and Iran. Enrollment:over 1,000 students in jr. high school, academic and technical high school, and a college of applied engineering. *BTJ Newsbriefs; Your Town Magazine.*

CAMERA – COMMITTEE FOR ACCURACY IN MIDDLE EAST REPORTING IN AMERICA (1983). PO Box 428, Boston, MA 02258. (617)789–3672. FAX: (617)787–7853. Pres./Exec. Dir. Andrea Levin; Chmn. Maxine Laura Wolf. Monitors and responds to media distortion in order to promote better understanding of Middle East events; urges members to alert Israel and the media to errors, omissions, and distortions. *CAMERA Media Report (quarterly); CAMERA on Campus; Action Alerts; Media Directories; Monographs.*

COUNCIL FOR A BEAUTIFUL ISRAEL ENVIRONMENTAL EDUCATION FOUNDATION (*see* American-Israel Environmental Council)

EDUCATION FUND FOR ISRAELI CIVIL RIGHTS AND PEACE (1991). 114 W. 26 St., Suite 1002, NYC 10001. (212)242–4500. FAX: (212)242–5718. E-mail: educfund@aol.com. Pres. Rabbi Israel Dresner; Chmn. Stefi Kirschner; Exec. Dir. Charney V. Bromberg. A forum for addressing the issues of social justice and peace in Israel. Educates about issues related to democracy, human and civil rights, religious pluralism, and equality for women and ethnic minorities; promotes the resolution of Israel's conflict with the Palestinians on the basis of mutual recognition, self-determination, and peaceful coexistence.

EMUNAH OF AMERICA (formerly HAPOEL HAMIZRACHI WOMEN'S ORGANIZATION) (1948). 7 Penn Plaza, NYC 10001. (212)564–9045, (800)368–6440. FAX: (212)643–9731. E-mail: info@emunah. org. Natl. Pres. Dr. Sylvia Schonfeld; Exec. V-Pres. Shirley Singer. Maintains and supports 200 educational and social-welfare institutions in Israel within a religious framework, including day-care centers, kindergartens, children's residential homes, vocational schools for the underprivileged, senior-citizen centers, a college complex, and Holocaust study center. Also involved in absorption of Soviet and Ethiopian immigrants (recognized by Israeli government as an official absorption agency). *Emunah Magazine; Lest We Forget.*

FEDERATED COUNCIL OF ISRAEL INSTITUTIONS—FCII (1940). 4702 15th Ave., Brooklyn, NY 11219. (718)972–5530. Bd. Chmn. Z. Shapiro; Exec. V.-Pres. Rabbi Julius Novack. Central fundraising organization for over 100 affiliated institutions; handles and executes estates, wills, and bequests for the traditional institutions in Israel; clearinghouse for information on budget, size, functions, etc. of traditional educational, welfare, and philanthropic institutions in Israel, working cooperatively with the Israeli government and the overseas department of the Council of Jewish Federations. *Annual financial reports and statistics on affiliates.*

FRIENDS OF THE ISRAEL DEFENSE FORCES (1981). 21 W. 38 St., 5th fl., NYC 10018. (212)575–5030. FAX: (212)575–7815. E-mail: fidf@csi.com. Chmn. Marvin Josephson; Pres. Jay Zises; Natl. Dir. Brig. Gen. Eliezer Hemeli. Supports the Agudah Lema'an Hahayal, Israel's Assoc. for the Well-Being of Soldiers, founded in the early 1940s, which provides social, recreational, and educational programs for soldiers, special services for the sick and wounded, and summer programs for widows and children of fallen soldiers.

GESHER FOUNDATION (1969). 421 Seventh Ave., #611, NYC 10001. (212) 564–0338. FAX: (212)967–2726. Chmn. Marcel Lindenbaum; Exec. V.-Pres. Hillel Wiener. Seeks to bridge the gap between Jews of various backgrounds in Israel by stressing the interdependence of all Jews. Runs encounter seminars for Israeli youth; distributes curricular materials in public schools; offers Jewish identity classes for Russian youth, and a video series in Russian and English on famous Jewish personalities.

GIVAT HAVIVA EDUCATIONAL FOUNDATION, INC. (1966). 114 W. 26 St., Suite 1001, NYC 10001. (212)989–9272. FAX: (212) 989–9840. Chmn. Fred Howard. Supports programs at the Givat Haviva Institute, Israel's leading organization dedicated to promoting coexistence between Arabs and Jews, with 40,000 people participating each year in programs teaching conflict resolution, Middle East studies and languages, and Holocaust studies.

Publishes research papers on Arab-Jewish relations, Holocaust studies, kibbutz life. In the U.S., GHEF sponsors public-education programs and lectures by Israeli speakers. *Givat Haviva News; special reports.*

HABONIM-DROR NORTH AMERICA (1935). 114 W. 26 St., Suite 1004, NYC 10001-6812. (212)255–1796. FAX: (212)929–3459. E-mail: mazkir@lonconnect.net. Mazkirat Tnua Esther Lederman; Shaliach David Lehrer. Fosters identification with progressive, cooperative living in Israel; stimulates study of Jewish and Zionist culture, history, and contemporary society; sponsors summer and year programs in Israel and on kibbutz, 7 summer camps in N. America modeled after kibbutzim, and aliyah frameworks.

HADASSAH, THE WOMEN'S ZIONIST ORGANIZATION OF AMERICA, INC. (1912). 50 W. 58 St., NYC 10019. (212)355–7900. FAX: (212)303–8282. Pres. Marlene Edith Post. Largest women's, largest Jewish, and largest Zionist membership organization in U.S. Founded and funds Hadassah Medical Organization in Jerusalem, as well as Hadassah College of Technology, Hadassah Career Counseling Institute, summer and year-course Young Judaea youth movement programs. U.S. programs: Jewish and health education; leadership training; advocacy on Israel; Zionism and women's issues; and Young Judaea, largest Zionist movement in U.S., including six summer camps. *Hadassah Magazine; Headlines; Update; Hadassah International Newsletter; Medical Update; Kol HaMorot; Pedal Pusher Press.*

——, YOUNG JUDAEA (1909; reorg. 1967). 50 W. 58 St., NYC 10019. (212)303–4575. FAX: (212)303–4572. Natl. Dir. Doron Krakow. Religiously pluralist, politically nonpartisan Zionist youth movement sponsored by Hadassah; seeks to educate Jewish youth aged 8–25 toward Jewish and Zionist values, active commitment to and participation in the American and Israeli Jewish communities; maintains six summer camps in the U.S.; runs both summer and year programs in Israel, and a jr. year program in connection with both Hebrew University in Jerusalem and Ben Gurion University of Negev. College-age arm, Hamagshimim, supports Zionist activity on campuses. *Kol Hat'nua; The Young Judaean; Ad Kahn.*

HASHOMER HATZAIR, SOCIALIST ZIONIST YOUTH MOVEMENT (1923). 114 W. 26 St., Suite 1001, NYC 10001. (212)868-0377. FAX: (212)868-0364. Pres. Gavri Bar-Gil; Natl. Sec. Daniel Perlmutter; Dir. Amos Holtzman. Seeks to educate Jewish youth to an understanding of Zionism as the national liberation movement of the Jewish people. Promotes aliyah to kibbutzim. Affiliated with AZYF and Kibbutz Artzi Federation. Espouses socialist-Zionist ideals of peace, justice, democracy, and intergroup harmony. *Young Guard.*

INTERNS FOR PEACE (NITZANEI SHALOM/ BARA'EM AS'SALAAM/BUDS OF PEACE) (1976). 475 Riverside Dr., 16th fl., NYC 10115. (212)870-2226. FAX: (212)870-2119. Internatl. Dir. Rabbi Bruce M. Cohen; Natl. Dir. Karen Wald Cohen. An independent, nonprofit, nonpolitical educational program training professional community peace workers. In Israel, initiated and operated jointly by Jews and Arabs; over 190 interns trained in 35 cities; over 80,000 Israeli citizens participating in joint programs in education, sports, culture, business, women's affairs, and community development; since the peace accord, Palestinians from West Bank and Gaza training as interns. Martin Luther King Project for Black/Jewish relations. *IFP Reports Quarterly; Guidebooks for Ethnic Conflict Resolution.*

ISRAEL CANCER RESEARCH FUND (1975). 1290 Avenue of the Americas, NYC 10104. (212)969-9800. FAX: (212)969-9822. Pres. Dr. Yashar Hirshaut; Chmn. Leah Susskind; Exec. Dir. Milton Sussman. The largest single source of private funds for cancer research in Israel. Has a threefold mission: to encourage innovative cancer research by Israeli scientists; to harness Israel's vast intellectual and creative resources to establish a world-class center for cancer study; to broaden research opportunities within Israel to stop the exodus of talented Israeli cancer researchers. *Annual Report; Research Awards; Glossary; Newsletter.*

ISRAEL HISTADRUT FOUNDATION (*see* Israel Humanitarian Foundation)

ISRAEL HUMANITARIAN FOUNDATION (formerly ISRAEL HISTADRUT FOUNDATION) (1960). 276 Fifth Ave., Suite 900, NYC 10001. (212)683-5656, (800)443-5699. FAX: (212)213-9233. Pres. Marvin Sirota; Exec. V.-Pres. Stanley J. Abrams. Provides philanthropic support to a network of schools, hospitals, clinics, children's villages, and senior citizen centers in Israel which benefit over 60% of Israel's population. Also supports other philanthropy and educational endeavors in Israel and in the U.S. *Impact; Insights.*

ISRAEL POLICY FORUM (1993). 666 Fifth Ave., 21st fl., NYC 10103. (212)245-4227. FAX: (212)245-0517. E-mail: ipforum@aol.com. Chmn. Michael W. Sonnenfeldt; Exec. V.-Pres. Jonathan Jacoby. A leadership institute that supports the Middle East peace process; publishes educational materials and analysis. *Peace Pulse; Israel Policy Papers; Security Watch.*

THE JERUSALEM FOUNDATION, INC. (1966). 60 E. 42 St., Suite 1936, New York City 10165. (212) 697-4188. FAX: (212) 697-4022. E-mail: jfinc@aol.com. Pres. Michael Neiditch; Chmn. Alvin Einbender. A nonprofit organization devoted to improving the quality of life for all Jerusalemites, regardless of ethnic, religious, or socioeconomic background; has initiated and implemented more than 1,500 projects that span education, culture, community services, beautification, and preservation of the city's historic heritage and religious sites.

JEWISH INSTITUTE FOR NATIONAL SECURITY AFFAIRS (JINSA) (1976). 1717 K St., NW, Suite 800, Washington, DC 20006. (202)833-0020. FAX: (202)296-6452. E-mail: info&jinsa.org. Pres. Norman Hascoe; Exec. Dir. Tom Neumann. A nonprofit, nonpartisan educational organization working within the American Jewish community to explain the link between American defense policy and the security of the State of Israel; and within the national security establishment to explain the key role Israel plays in bolstering American interests. *Security Affairs.*

JEWISH INSTITUTE FOR THE BLIND—JERUSALEM, INC. (1902, Jerusalem). 15 E. 26 St., NYC 10010. (212) 532-4155. FAX: (212) 447-7683. Pres. Rabbi David E. Lapp; Admin. Eric L. Loeb. Supports a dormitory and school for the Israeli blind and handicapped in Jerusalem. *INsight.*

JEWISH NATIONAL FUND OF AMERICA (1901). 42 E. 69 St., NYC 10021. (212)879-9300. FAX: (212)517-3293. E-mail: jnfcomm@aol.com. Pres. Ronald S. Lauder; Exec. V.-Pres. Russell Robinson. The American fund-raising arm of its parent body in Israel—Keren Kayemeth Leisrael, Inc., the official conservation and development agency reclaiming land for afforestation, housing, tourism, recreation, agriculture, infrastructure, and water resource development.

JEWISH PEACE LOBBY (1989). 8604 Second Ave., Suite 317, Silver Spring, MD 20910. (301)589-8764. FAX: (301)589-2722. Pres. Jerome M. Segal. A legally registered lobby promoting changes in U.S. policy vis-a-vis the Israeli-Palestinian conflict. Supports Israel's right to peace within secure borders; a political settlement based on mutual recognition of the right of self-determination of both peoples; a two-state solution as the most likely means to a stable peace. *Washington Action Alerts.*

KEREN OR, INC. JERUSALEM CENTER FOR MULTI-HANDICAPPED BLIND CHILDREN (1956). 350 Seventh Ave., Suite 200, NYC 10001. (212)279-4070. FAX: (212)279-4043. Chmn. Dr. Edward L. Steinberg; Pres. Dr. Albert Hornblass; Exec. Dir. Sheila E. Stein. Funds the Keren-Or Center for Multi-Handicapped Blind Children at 3 Abba Hillel Silver St., Ramot, Jerusalem, housing and caring for over 70 resident and day students who in addition to blindness or very low vision suffer from other severe physical and/or mental disabilities. Students range in age from 1 1/2 through young adulthood. Provides training in daily living skills, as well as therapy, rehabilitation, and education to the optimum level of the individual. *Insights Newsletter.*

LABOR ZIONIST ALLIANCE (formerly FARBAND LABOR ZIONIST ORDER; now uniting membership and branches of Poale Zion–United Labor Zionist Organization of America and American Habonim Association) (1913). 275 Seventh Ave., NYC 10001. (212)366-1194, (212)366-1387. FAX: (212)675-7685. Pres. Daniel Mann. Seeks to enhance Jewish life, culture, and education in U.S.; aids in building State of Israel as a cooperative commonwealth and its Labor movement organized in the Histadrut; supports efforts toward a more democratic society throughout the world; furthers the democratization of the Jewish community in America and the welfare of Jews every-

where; works with labor and liberal forces in America. *Jewish Frontier; Yiddisher Kempfer.*

MACCABI USA/SPORTS FOR ISRAEL (formerly UNITED STATES COMMITTEE SPORTS FOR ISRAEL) (1948). 1926 Arch St., Philadelphia, PA 19103. (215)561-6900. E-mail: maccabi@dca.net. Pres. Robert E. Spivak; Exec. Dir. Barbara G. Lissy. Sponsors U.S. team for World Maccabiah Games in Israel every four years; seeks to enrich the lives of Jewish youth in the U.S., Israel, and the Diaspora through athletic, cultural, and educational programs; develops, promotes, and supports international, national, and regional athletic-based activities and facilities. *SportsScene Newsletter; Gold Medal People Newsletter; commemorative Maccabiah Games journal; financial report.*

MERCAZ USA (1979). 155 Fifth Ave., NYC 10010. (212)533-7800. FAX: (212)533-2601. E-mail: 71262.102@compuserve. com. Pres. Roy Clements, Exec. Dir. Rabbi Robert R. Golub. The U.S. Zionist organization for Conservative/Masorti Judaism; works for religious pluralism in Israel, defending and promoting Conservative/Masorti institutions and individuals; fosters Zionist education and *aliyah* and develops young leadership. *Mercaz News & Views.*

NA'AMAT USA, THE WOMEN'S LABOR ZIONIST ORGANIZATION OF AMERICA, INC. (formerly PIONEER WOMEN/NA'AMAT) (1925). 200 Madison Ave., 21st fl., NYC 10016. (212)725-8010. FAX: (212)447-5187. Natl. Pres.Dina Spector; Exec. Dir. Sheila Guston. Part of the World Movement of Na'amat (movement of working women and volunteers), the largest Jewish women's organization in the world, Na'amat USA helps provide social, educational, and legal services for women, teenagers, and children in Israel. It also advocates legislation for women's rights and child welfare in Israel and the U.S., furthers Jewish education, and supports Habonim Dror, the Labor Zionist youth movement. *Na'amat Woman magazine.*

NATIONAL COMMITTEE FOR LABOR ISRAEL (1923). 275 Seventh Ave., NYC 10001. (212)647-0300. FAX: (212)647-0308. E-mail: laborisrael@jon.cjfny.org. Pres. Jay Mazur; Exec. Dir. Jerry Goodman; Chmn. Trade Union Council Morton Bahr. Brings together diverse groups—

Jews and non-Jews–to build support for Israel and advance closer Arab-Israel ties. Conducts educational and communal activities in the Jewish community and among labor groups to promote better relations with labor Israel. Israel Histadrut Campaign raises funds for youth, educational, health, social, and cultural projects. *NCLI Notebook; occasional background papers.*

NEW ISRAEL FUND (1979). 1625 K St., NW, Suite 500, Washington, DC 20006. (202)223–3333. FAX: (202)659–2789. E-mail: info@nif.org; www.nif.org. New York office:165 E. 56 St., NYC 10022. (212)750–2333. FAX: (212)750–8043. Pres. Franklin Fisher; Exec. Dir. Norman S. Rosenberg. A partnership of Israelis and North Americans dedicated to promoting social justice, coexistence, and pluralism in Israel, the New Israel Fund helps strengthen Israeli democracy by providing grants and technical assistance to the public-interest sector, cultivating a new generation of social activists and educating citizens in Israel and the Diaspora about the challenges to Israeli democracy. *Quarterly newsletter; annual report.*

PEC ISRAEL ECONOMIC CORPORATION (formerly PALESTINE ECONOMIC CORPORATION) (1926). 511 Fifth Ave., NYC 10017. (212)687–2400. Chmn. R. Recanati; Pres. Frank J. Klein; Exec. V.-Pres. James I. Edelson; Treas. William Gold. Primarily engaged in the business of organizing, acquiring interest in, financing, and participating in the management of companies located in the State of Israel or Israel-related. *Annual and quarterly reports.*

PEF ISRAEL ENDOWMENT FUNDS, INC. (1922). 317 Madison Ave., Suite 607, NYC 10017. (212)599–1260. Chmn. Sidney A. Luria; Pres. B. Harrison Frankel; Sec. Harvey Brecher. A totally volunteer organization that makes grants to educational, scientific, social, religious, health, and other philanthropic institutions in Israel. *Annual report.*

PIONEER WOMEN/NA'AMAT (*see* NA'AMAT USA)

POALE AGUDATH ISRAEL OF AMERICA, INC. (1948). 2920 Avenue J, Brooklyn, NY 11210. (718)258–2228. FAX: (718)258–2288. Pres. Rabbi Fabian Schonfeld. Aims to educate American Jews to the values of Orthodoxy and aliyah; supports kib-

butzim, trade schools, yeshivot, moshavim, kollelim, research centers, and children's homes in Israel. *PAI News; She'arim; Hamayan.*

———, WOMEN'S DIVISION OF (1948). Pres. Miriam Lubling; Presidium: Sarah Ivanisky, Tili Stark, Peppi Petzenbaum. Assists Poale Agudath Israel to build and support children's homes, kindergartens, and trade schools in Israel. *Yediot PAI.*

PRO ISRAEL (1990). 17 E. 45 St., Suite 603, NYC 10017. (212)867–0577. FAX: (212)867–0615. E-mail: proisrael@aol.com. Israel office:P.O. Box 31490, Jerusalem 91314, Israel. (02)567-2050. FAX: (02)567-2053. Pres. Dr. Ernest Bloch; Dir. of Admin. Frances Zwickler. Educates the public about Israel and the Middle East; provides support for community development throughout the Land of Israel, particularly in Judea, Samaria, Gaza, and the Golan Heights. Projects include the Ariel Center for Policy Research in Samaria, support for various communities, and a research and information center. Umbrella organization for 7 affiliate groups: in Israel–Aliyah for the Land of Israel Movement, Generals of "Gamla Won't Fall a Second Time," Internatl. Rabbinic Coalition for Israel, IDF Officers for National Strength, Professors for a Strong Israel; in U.S.–American Academics for Israel's Future, Operation Chizuk.

PROJECT NISHMA (1988). 1225 15 St., NW, Washington, DC 20005. (202)462–4268. FAX: (202)462–3892. Cochmn. Theodore R. Mann, Edward Sanders, Henry Rosovsky; Exec. Dir. Thomas R. Smerling. Conducts educational programs on Israeli security and the peace process; arranges military briefings for Jewish leaders; publishes articles by senior Israeli defense and foreign-policy experts; analyzes Israeli and U.S. Jewish opinion; and articulates pragmatic positions on peace and security. Sponsored by over 100 nationally active Jewish leaders from across the country.

RELIGIOUS ZIONISTS OF AMERICA. 25 W. 26 St., NYC 10010. (212)689–1414. FAX: (212)779-3043.

———, BNEI AKIVA OF THE U.S. & CANADA (1934). 25 W. 26 St., NYC 10010. (212)889–5260. FAX: (212)213–3053. Pres. Eric Weisberg; Exec. Dir. Daniel Ehrlich. The only religious Zionist youth movement in North America, serving over 10,000 young people from grade school through graduate school in 16 active regions across the United States and Canada, six summer camps, seven established summer, winter, and year programs in Israel. Stresses communal involvement, social activism, leadership training, and substantive programming to educate young people toward a commitment to Judaism and Israel. *Akivon; Pinkas Lamadrich; Daf Rayonot; Me'Ohalai Torah; Zraim.*

———, MIZRACHI-HAPOEL HAMIZRACHI (1909; merged 1957). 25 W. 26 St., NYC 10010. (212)689–1414. FAX: (212)779–3043. Pres. Dr. Morris L. Green; Exec. V.-Pres. Israel Friedman. Disseminates ideals of religious Zionism; conducts cultural work, educational program, public relations; raises funds for religious educational institutions in Israel, including yeshivot hesder and Bnei Akiva. *Newsletters; Kolenu.*

———, NATIONAL COUNCIL FOR TORAH EDUCATION OF MIZRACHI-HAPOEL HAM'IZRACHI (1939). 25 W. 26 St., NYC 10010. Pres. Rabbi Israel Schorr; Dir. Rabbi Meyer Golombek. Organizes and supervises yeshivot and Talmud Torahs; prepares and trains teachers; publishes textbooks and educational materials; organizes summer seminars for Hebrew educators in cooperation with Torah Department of Jewish Agency; conducts ulpan. *Hazarkor, Chemed.*

SCHNEIDER CHILDREN'S MEDICAL CENTER OF ISRAEL (1982). 130 E. 59 St., Suite 1203, NYC 10022. (212)759–3370. FAX: (212)759–0120. E-mail: mdiscmci@aol.com. Bd. Chmn. H. Irwin Levy; Exec. Dir. Shlomit Manson. Its primary goal is to provide the best medical care to children in the Middle East. *UPDATE Newsletter.*

SOCIETY OF ISRAEL PHILATELISTS (1949). 24355 Tunbridge Lane, Beachwood, OH 44122. (216)292–3843. Pres. Paul Aufrichtig; Journal Ed. Dr. Oscar Stadtler. Promotes interest in, and knowledge of, all phases of Israel philately through sponsorship of chapters and research groups, maintenance of a philatelic library, and support of public and private exhibitions. *The Israel Philatelist; monographs; books.*

STATE OF ISRAEL BONDS (1951). 575 Lexington Ave., #600, NYC 10022. (212)644–2663. FAX: (212)644–3887. E-mail: rothsteinr@aol.com. Bd. Chmn. William Belzberg; Pres. Gideon Patt; Internatl. Chmn. David B. Hermelin; Internatl. Campaign Chmn. Susan Welkers-Volchok; N. Amer. Chmn. Michael Siegal; Natl. Campaign Chmn. Burton P. Resnick. An international organization offering securities issued by the government of Israel. Since its inception in 1951 has secured $18 billion in investment capital for the development of every aspect of Israel's economic infrastructure, including agriculture, commerce, and industry, and for absorption of immigrants.

THEODOR HERZL FOUNDATION (1954). 110 E. 59 St., NYC 10022. (212)339–6000. FAX: (212)318–6176. Chmn. Kalman Sultanik; Dir. of Publications Sam E. Bloch. Offers cultural activities, lectures, conferences, courses in modern Hebrew and Jewish subjects, Israel, Zionism, and Jewish history. *Midstream.*

———, HERZL PRESS. Chmn. Kalman Sultanik; Dir. of Publications Sam E. Bloch. Serves as "the Zionist Press of record," publishing books that are important for the light they shed on Zionist philosophy, Israeli history, contemporary Israel and the Diaspora and the relationship between them. They are important as contributions to Zionist letters and history. *Midstream.*

TSOMET-TECHIYA USA (1978). 185 Montague St., 3rd fl., Brooklyn, NY 11201. (718)596–2119. FAX: (718)858–4074. E-mail: eliahu@aol.com. Central Committee Members:Honey Rackman, Elliot Jager, Melvin D. Shay, Howard B. Weber. Supports the activities of the Israeli Tsomet party, which advocates Israeli control over the entire Land of Israel.

UNITED CHARITY INSTITUTIONS OF JERUSALEM, INC. (1903). 1467 48 St., Brooklyn, NY 11219. (718)633–8469. FAX: (718)633–8478. Chmn. Rabbi Charlop; Exec. Dir. Rabbi Pollak. Raises funds for the maintenance of schools, kitchens, clinics, and dispensaries in Israel; free loan foundations in Israel.

UNITED ISRAEL APPEAL, INC. (1925). 111 Eighth Ave., Suite 11E, NYC 10011. (212)284–6500. FAX: (212)284–6835. Chmn. Shoshana S. Cardin; Exec. V.-

Chmn. Daniel R. Allen. Provides funds raised by UJA/Federation campaigns in the U.S. to aid the people of Israel through the programs of the Jewish Agency for Israel, UIA's operating agent. Serves as link between American Jewish community and Jewish Agency for Israel; assists in resettlement and absorption of refugees in Israel, and supervises flow and expenditure of funds for this purpose. *Annual report; newsletters; brochures.*

UNITED STATES COMMITTEE SPORTS FOR ISRAEL (*see* Maccabi USA/Sports for Israel)

US/ISRAEL WOMEN TO WOMEN (1978). 275 Seventh Ave., 8th fl., New York City 10001. (212) 206-8057. FAX: (212) 206-7031. E-mail: usisrw2w@aol.com. Chmn. Jewel Bellush; Exec. Dir. Joan Gordon. Provides critical seed money for grassroots efforts advocating equal status and fair treatment for women in all spheres of Israeli life; targets small, innovative, Israeli-run programs that seek to bring about social change in health, education, civil rights, domestic violence, family planning, and other spheres of Israeli life. *Newsletters.*

VOLUNTEERS FOR ISRAEL (1982). 330 W. 42 St., NYC 10036-6902. (212)643-4848. FAX: (212)643-4855. E-mail: vol4israel@aol.com. Pres. Rickey Cherner; Natl. Coord. Arthur W. Stern. Provides aid to Israel through volunteer work, building lasting relationships between Israelis and Americans. Affords persons aged 18 and over the opportunity to participate in various duties currently performed by overburdened Israelis on IDF bases and in other settings, enabling them to meet and work closely with Israelis and to gain an inside view of Israeli life and culture. *Quarterly newsletter; information documents.*

WOMEN'S LEAGUE FOR ISRAEL, INC. (1928). 160 E. 56 St., NYC 10022. (212)838-1997. FAX: (212)888-5972. Pres. Harriet Lainer; Exec. Dir. Dorothy Leffler. Maintains centers in Haifa, Tel Aviv, Jerusalem, Nathanya. Projects include Family Therapy and Training Center, Centers for the Prevention of Domestic Violence, Meeting Places (supervised centers for noncustodial parents and their children), DROR (supporting families at risk), Yachdav-"Together" (long-term therapy for parents and children), Cen-

tral School for Training Social Service Counselors, the National Library for Social Work, and the Hebrew University Blind Students' Unit.

WORLD CONFEDERATION OF UNITED ZIONISTS (1946; reorg. 1958). 130 E. 59 St., NYC 10022. (212)371-1452. FAX: (212) 371-3265. Copres. Bernice S. Tannenbaum, Kalman Sultanik, Melech Topiol. Promotes Zionist education, sponsors nonparty youth movements in the Diaspora, and strives for an Israel-oriented creative Jewish survival in the Diaspora. *Zionist Information Views (in English and Spanish).*

WORLD ZIONIST ORGANIZATION-AMERICAN SECTION (1971). 110 E. 59 St., NYC 10022. (212)339-6000. FAX: (212)826-8959. Chmn. Kalman Sultanik. As the American section of the overall Zionist body throughout the world, it operates primarily in the field of aliyah from the free countries, education in the Diaspora, youth and Hechalutz, organization and information, cultural institutions, publications; conducts a worldwide Hebrew cultural program including special seminars and pedagogic manuals; disperses information and assists in research projects concerning Israel; promotes, publishes, and distributes books, periodicals, and pamphlets concerning developments in Israel, Zionism, and Jewish history. *Midstream.*

——, DEPARTMENT OF EDUCATION AND CULTURE (1948). 110 E. 59 St., NYC 10022. (212)339-6001. FAX: (212)826-8959. Renders educational services to boards and schools: study programs, books, AV aids, instruction, teacher-in-training service. Judaic and Hebrew subjects. Annual National Bible Contest; Israel summer and winter programs for teachers and students.

——, ISRAEL ALIYAH CENTER (1993). 110 E. 59 St., 3rd fl., NYC 10022. (212)339-6060. FAX: (212)832-2597. Exec. Dir. N. Amer. Aliyah Delegation, Kalman Grossman. Through 26 offices throughout N. Amer., staffed by *shlichim* (emissaries), works with potential immigrants to plan their future in Israel and processes immigration documents. Through Israel Aliyah Program Center provides support, information, and programming for olim and their families;

promotes long-term programs and fact-finding trips to Israel. Cooperates with Tnuat Aliyah in Jerusalem and serves as American contact with Association of Americans and Canadians in Israel. *The New Aliyon; Daf Kesher.*

YOUTH RENEWAL FUND. 165 E. 56 St., NYC 10022. (212)207-3195. FAX: (212)207-8379. E-mail: yrfny@aol.com. Pres. Samuel L. Katz; Dir. Julie F. Rabinowitz. Provides underprivileged Israeli youth with supplemental educational programs and direct scholarships for additional instruction by qualified teachers in core subjects including math, sciences, and languages. Since 1989, YRF has raised over $2 million which has been put to work in 57 projects throughout Israel and has benefited over 5,500 children. *YRFlash.*

ZIONIST ORGANIZATION OF AMERICA (1897). ZOA House, 4 E. 34 St., NYC 10016. (212)481-1500. FAX: (212)481-1515. E-mail: email@zoa.com. Natl. Pres. Morton A. Klein; Exec. Dir. Bertram Korn, Jr. Strengthens the relationship between Israel and the U.S. through Zionist educational activities that explain Israel's importance to the U.S. and the dangers that Israel faces. Works on behalf of pro-Israel legislation; combats anti-Israel bias in the media, textbooks, travel guides, and on campuses; promotes *aliyah*. Maintains the ZOA House in Tel Aviv, a cultural center, and the Kfar Silver Agricultural and Technical High School in Ashkelon, which provides vocational training for new immigrants. ZOA *Report; Israel and the Middle East: Behind the Headlines.*

OVERSEAS AID

AMERICAN FRIENDS OF THE ALLIANCE ISRAÉLITE UNIVERSELLE, INC. (1946). 420 Lexington Ave., Suite 1733, NYC 10170. (212)808-5437. FAX: (212)983-0094. Pres. Henriette Beilis; Exec. Dir. Warren Green. Participates in educational and human-rights activities of the AIU and supports the Alliance System of Jewish schools, teachers' colleges, and remedial programs in Israel, North Africa, the Middle East, Europe, and Canada. *Alliance Review.*

AMERICAN JEWISH JOINT DISTRIBUTION COMMITTEE, INC.-JDC (1914). 711 Third Ave., NYC 10017-4014. (212)687-6200. FAX: (212)370-5467. E-mail: info@

jdcny.org. Pres. Jonathan Kolker; Exec. V.-Pres. Michael Schneider. Provides assistance to Jewish communities in Europe, Asia, Africa, and the Mideast, including welfare programs for Jews in need. Current concerns include rescuing Jews from areas of distress; helping to meet Israel's social-service needs by developing innovative programs that create new opportunities for the country's most disadvantaged populations. Program expansions emphasize community development in the former Soviet Union and youth activities in Eastern Europe and nonsectarian development and disaster assistance. *Annual report; Fast Facts.*

AMERICAN JEWISH PHILANTHROPIC FUND (1955). 122 E. 42 St., 12th fl., NYC 10168-1289. (212)755-5640. Pres. Charles J. Tanenbaum. Provides resettlement assistance to Jewish refugees primarily through programs administered by the International Rescue Committee at its offices in Western Europe and the U.S.

AMERICAN JEWISH WORLD SERVICE (1985). 989 Avenue of the Americas, 10th Fl., NYC 10018. (212)736-2597. FAX: (212)736-3463. E-mail:jws@jws.org. Chmn. Don Abramson; Pres. Andrew Griffel. Provides nonsectarian, humanitarian assistance and emergency relief to people in need in Africa, Asia, Latin America, Russia, Ukraine, and the Middle East; works in partnership with local nongovernmental organizations to support and implement self-sustaining grassroots development projects; serves as a vehicle through which the Jewish community can express its universal commitment to help those in need. *AJWS Reports (newsletter).*

AMERICAN ORT, INC. (1922). 817 Broadway, NYC 10003. (212)353-5800. FAX: (212)353-5888. E-mail: info@aort.org. Pres. Paul Borman; Bd. Chmn. Murray Koppelman; Exec. V.-Pres. Brian J. Strum. Umbrella organization for all ORT operations in the U.S.; promotes and raises funds for ORT, the world's largest nongovernmental education and training organization, with a global network teaching over 262,000 students in more than 60 countries. In Israel, 100,000 students attend 138 schools and training centers; there are 22 ORT schools and centers in the former Soviet Union; and in the U.S., over 10,000 students are served by ORT's Technical Institutes in Chicago, Los Angeles, and New York, and in Jewish day school programs. *American ORT News, American ORT Update, American ORT Annual Report.*

——, WOMEN'S AMERICAN ORT (1927). 315 Park Ave. S., NYC 10010-3677. (212)505–7700; (800)51-WAORT. FAX: (212)674–3057. E-mail: waort@waort. org. Pres. Ruth S. Taffel; Exec. Dir. Rosina Abramson. Advances the programs and self-help ethos of ORT through membership, fund-raising, and educational activities. Supports 140 vocational schools, junior colleges, and technical training centers in Israel; helps meet the educational needs of Jewish communities in 60 countries; spearheads growing ORT-U.S. school operations in New York, Los Angeles, and Chicago, and associate programs in Miami, Atlanta, and Cleveland. Domestic agenda espouses quality public education, champions women's rights, and promotes a national literacy campaign. *Women's American ORT Reporter; Women's American ORT Annual Report.*

CONFERENCE ON JEWISH MATERIAL CLAIMS AGAINST GERMANY, INC. (1951). 15 E. 26 St., Rm. 906, NYC 10010. (212)696–4944. FAX: (212)679–2126. Pres. Dr. Israel Miller; Exec. V-Pres. & Sec. Saul Kagan. Monitors the implementation of restitution and indemnification programs of the German Federal Republic (FRG) arising from its agreements with West Germany and most recently with united Germany, especially with respect to property lost by Jewish Nazi victims in the territory of the former German Democratic Republic. Administers Hardship and Article 2 Funds for Jewish Nazi victims who received no or only minimal compensation under the original indemnification laws. Also assists needy non-Jews who risked their lives to help Jewish survivors.

HIAS, INC. (HEBREW IMMIGRANT AID SOCIETY) (1880; reorg. 1954). 333 Seventh Ave., NYC 10001–5004. (212)967–4100. FAX: (212)967–4442. E-mail: info@hias. org. Pres. Norman D. Tilles; Exec. V.-Pres. Martin A. Wenick. The international migration agency of the organized American Jewish community, dedicated to assisting persecuted and oppressed people around the world and delivering them to countries of safe haven. Since its founding in 1880, the agency has rescued more than four million people. *Annual report.*

THE JEWISH FOUNDATION FOR THE RIGHTEOUS (1995). 305 7th Ave., 19th fl., NYC 10001. (212)727–9955. FAX: (212)727–9956. E-mail: jfrnyc@worldnet.att.net. Chmn. Harvey Schulweis; Exec. Dir. Stanlee J. Stahl. Provides monthly financial support to 1,400 aged and needy Righteous Gentiles living in 26 countries who risked their lives to save Jews during the Holocaust. The Foundation's education program uses the stories of rescue to teach students about the Holocaust, its relevance for these times, and the significance of altruistic behavior for our society. *Newsletter (3 times a year).*

NORTH AMERICAN CONFERENCE ON ETHIOPIAN JEWRY (NACOEJ) (1982). 132 Nassau St., NYC l0038. (212)752–6340. FAX: (212)980–5294. E-mail: nacoej@aol.com. Pres. Richard Giesberg; Dir. Barbara Ribakove Gordon. Provides programming for Ethiopian Jews in Israel in the areas of education (preschool through college), vocational training, and cultural preservation. Assists Ethiopian Jews remaining in Ethiopia. National speakers bureau offers programs to synagogues, schools, Jewish, and non-Jewish organizations. Exhibits of Ethiopian Jewish artifacts, photos, handicrafts, etc. available. *Lifeline (newsletter).*

RE'UTH WOMEN'S SOCIAL SERVICE, INC. (1937). 130 E. 59 St., NYC 10022. (212)836–1570. FAX: (212)836–1114. Chmn. Ursula Merkin; Pres. Rosa Strygler. Maintains in Israel subsidized housing for self-reliant elderly; old-age homes for more dependent elderly; Lichtenstadter Hospital for chronically ill and young accident victims not accepted by other hospitals; subsidized meals; Golden Age clubs. *Annual dinner journal.*

THANKS TO SCANDINAVIA, INC. (1963). 745 Fifth Ave., Rm. 603, NYC 10151. (212)486–8600. FAX: (212)486–5735. Natl. Chmn. Victor Borge; Pres. Richard Netter. Provides scholarships and fellowships at American universities and medical centers to students and doctors from Denmark, Finland, Norway, and Sweden in appreciation of the rescue of Jews from the Holocaust. Informs Americans and Scandinavians of these singular examples of humanity and bravery; sponsors Danish-American Dialogue on Human Rights program in Denmark for college jrs. and sophomores; instituted fellowship at Hebrew U. in honor of Johan Jorgan Holst; sponsors photographic exhibition. Speakers available on rescue in Scandinavia; also books, videos, and tapes. *Annual report.*

UNITED JEWISH APPEAL, INC. (1939). 111 Eighth Ave., Suite 11E, NYC 10011. (212)284-6500. FAX: (212)284-6835. Natl. Chmn. Richard L. Wexler; Pres. Richard L. Pearlstone; Exec. V.-Pres. Bernard C. Moscovitz. Implements its mission–to rescue the imperiled, care for the vulnerable, and revitalize Jewish life–by raising funds for humanitarian causes and social services at home and abroad through its Annual Campaign with 189 local Jewish federations and a network of 450 independent communities. Serves as the advocate for overseas needs to the American Jewish community; rescues Jews in distress and brings them to Israel, and, through the Jewish Agency, helps them adjust to a new life. UJA funds also help Jews and Jewish communities in 60 countries through the American Jewish Joint Distribution Committee. In recent years, UJA has increased its commitment to Jewish life in America through education and American-Israeli partnership. *Hotline; Annual Report; UJA Press Service.*

RELIGIOUS AND EDUCATIONAL ORGANIZATIONS

AGUDATH ISRAEL OF AMERICA (1922). 84 William St., NYC 10038. (212)797-9000. FAX: (212)269-2843. Pres. Rabbi Moshe Sherer; Exec. V.-Pres. Rabbi Shmuel Bloom; Exec. Dir. Rabbi Boruch B. Borchardt. Mobilizes Orthodox Jews to cope with Jewish problems in the spirit of the Torah; speaks out on contemporary issues from an Orthodox viewpoint; sponsors a broad range of projects aimed at enhancing religious living, education, children's welfare, protection of Jewish religious rights, outreach to the assimilated and to arrivals from the former Soviet Union, and social services. *Jewish Observer; Dos Yiddishe Vort; Coalition.*

——, AGUDAH WOMEN OF AMERICA– N'SHEI AGUDATH ISRAEL (1940). 84 William St., NYC 10038. (212)363-8940. FAX: (212)747-8763. Presidium Aliza Grund, Rose Isbee; Exec. Admin. Gitty Pinter. Organizes Jewish women for philanthropic work in the U.S. and Israel and for intensive Torah education.

——, BOYS' DIVISION–PIRCHEI AGUDATH ISRAEL (1925). 84 William St., NYC 10038 (212)797-9000. Natl. Coord. Rabbi Shimon Grama. Educates Orthodox Jewish children in Torah; encourages sense of communal responsibility. Branches sponsor weekly youth groups and Jewish welfare projects. National Mishnah contests, rallies, and conventions foster unity on a national level. *Leaders Guides.*

——, GIRLS' DIVISION–BNOS AGUDATH ISRAEL (1921). 84 William St., NYC 10038. (212)797-9000. Natl. Dir. Leah Zagelbaum. Sponsors regular weekly programs on the local level and unites girls from throughout the Torah world with extensive regional and national activities. *Kol Bnos.*

——, YOUNG MEN'S DIVISION–ZEIREI AGUDATH ISRAEL (1921). 84 William St., NYC 10038. (212)797-9000, ext. 57. Dir. Rabbi Labish Becker. Educates youth to see Torah as source of guidance for all issues facing Jews as individuals and as a people. Inculcates a spirit of activism through projects in religious, Torah-educational, and community-welfare fields. *Am Hatorah; Daf Chizuk.*

AGUDATH ISRAEL WORLD ORGANIZATION (1912). 84 William St., NYC 10038. (212)797-9000. FAX: (212)269-2843. Chmn. Rabbi Moshe Sherer, Rabbi Yehudah Meir Abramowitz. Represents the interests of Orthodox Jewry on the national and international scenes. Sponsors projects to strengthen Torah life worldwide.

ALEPH: ALLIANCE FOR JEWISH RENEWAL (1963; reorg. 1993). 7318 Germantown Ave., Philadelphia, PA 19119-1720. (215)247-9700. FAX: (215)247-9703. Bd. Chmn. Dr. Sheldon Isenberg; Exec. Dir. R. Daniel Siegel. A multifaceted international organization serving the movement for Jewish renewal, formed out of a merger of P'nai Or Religious Fellowship and the Shalom Center. Activities include creation and dissemination of publications, liturgy, curricula, audio and video tapes; a country retreat center; lay and professional leadership training; spiritual activism on social and environmental issues; and a network of local Jewish renewal communities. *New Menorah (quarterly journal); Pumbedissa (newsletter forum for rabbis and rabbinical students); Or HaDor (newsletter of congregations and havurot affiliated with ALEPH through the Network of Jewish Renewal Communities).*

AMERICAN ASSOCIATION OF RABBIS (1978). 350 Fifth Ave., Suite 3304, NYC 10118. (212)244–3350, (516)244–7113. FAX: (516)244–0779. Pres. Rabbi Jeffrey Wartenberg; Exec. Dir. Rabbi David L. Dunn. An organization of rabbis serving in pulpits, in areas of education, and in social work. *Quarterly bulletin; monthly newsletter; membership directory; sermon manual.*

AMERICAN STUDENTS TO ACTIVATE PRIDE (ASAP/OU COLLEGE AFFAIRS) (1993). 333 7th Ave., 18th fl., NYC 10001. (212)563–4000. FAX: (212)564–9058. E-mail: davidfel@ix.netcom.com. Pres. Zelda Goldsmith; Natl. Dir. Rabbi David Felsenthal; Chmn. Bernard Falk. A spiritual fitness movement of Jewish college students promoting Torah learning and discussion. Supports 100 learning groups at over 65 campuses as well as regional and national seminars and *shabbatonim. Good Shabbos (weekly); Rimon Discussion Guide (monthly); Jewish Student College Survival Guide (yearly).*

ASSOCIATION FOR JEWISH STUDIES (1969). MB 0001, Brandeis University, PO Box 9110, Waltham, MA 02254–9110. (781)736–2981. FAX: (781)736–2982. E-mail: ajs@brandeis.edu. Pres. David Berger; Exec. Sec. Aaron L. Katchen. Seeks to promote, maintain, and improve the teaching of Jewish studies in colleges and universities by sponsoring meetings and conferences, publishing a newsletter and other scholarly materials, aiding in the placement of teachers, coordinating research, and cooperating with other scholarly organizations. *AJS Review; Newsletter.*

ASSOCIATION FOR THE SOCIAL SCIENTIFIC STUDY OF JEWRY (1971). Polisher Research Institute, Philadelphia Geriatric Center, 5301 Old York Rd., Philadelphia, PA 19141–2996. (215)456–2981. FAX: (215)456–2017. E-mail: aglicksm@thunder.ocis.temple.edu. Pres. Allen Glicksman; V.-Pres. Riv-Ellen Prell; Sec.-Treas. Jerome Chanes. Journal Ed. Rela Geffen; Mng. Ed. Egon Mayer; Newsletter Ed.

Gail Glicksman. Arranges academic sessions and facilitates communication among social scientists studying Jewry through meetings, newsletter, and related materials and activities. *Contemporary Jewry; ASSJ Newsletter.*

ASSOCIATION OF HILLEL/JEWISH CAMPUS PROFESSIONALS (1949). c/o Greater Miami Hillel Jewish Student Center, 1100 Stanford Dr., Coral Gables, FL 33146. (305)665–6948. FAX: (305)661–8540. E-mail: jfalick@miami.edu. Pres. Rabbi Jeffrey Falick. Seeks to promote professional relationships and exchanges of experience, develop personnel standards and qualifications, safeguard integrity of Hillel profession; represents and advocates before the Foundation for Jewish Campus Life, Council of Jewish Federations. *Handbook for Hillel Professionals; Guide to Hillel Personnel Practices.*

ASSOCIATION OF ORTHODOX JEWISH SCIENTISTS (1948). 1123 Broadway, Rm. 1010, NYC 10010. (212)229–2340. FAX: (212)691–0573. Pres. Allen J. Bennett, M.D.; Bd. Chmn. Rabbi Nachman Cohen; Exec. Dir. Joel Schwartz. Seeks to contribute to the development of science within the framework of Orthodox Jewish tradition; to obtain and disseminate information relating to the interaction between the Jewish traditional way of life and scientific developments–on both an ideological and practical level; to assist in the solution of problems pertaining to Orthodox Jews engaged in scientific teaching or research. Two main conventions are held each year. *Intercom; Proceedings; Halacha Bulletin; newsletter.*

B'NAI B'RITH HILLEL FOUNDATIONS (*see* HILLEL)

B'NAI B'RITH YOUTH ORGANIZATION (1924). 1640 Rhode Island Ave., NW, Washington, DC 20036. (202)857–6633. FAX: (212)857–6568. Chmn. Youth Comm. Audrey Y. Brooks; Dir. Sam Fisher. Helps Jewish teenagers achieve self-fulfillment and make a maximum contribution to the Jewish community and their country's culture; helps members acquire a greater knowledge and appreciation of Jewish religion and culture. *Shofar; Monday Morning; BBYO Parents' Line; Hakol; Kesher; The Connector.*

CANTORS ASSEMBLY (1947). 3080 Broadway, NYC 10027. (212)678–8834. FAX: (212)662–8989. E-mail: caoffice@jtsa.

edu. Pres. Henry Rosenblum; Exec. Admin. Abraham Shapiro. Seeks to unite all cantors who adhere to traditional Judaism and who serve as full-time cantors in bona fide congregations to conserve and promote the musical traditions of the Jews and to elevate the status of the cantorial profession. *Annual Proceedings; Journal of Synagogue Music.*

CENTER FOR CHRISTIAN-JEWISH UNDERSTANDING (1992). 5151 Park Ave., Fairfield, CT 06432. (203)365-7592. FAX: (203)365-4815. Pres. Dr. Anthony J. Cernera; Exec. Dir. Rabbi Joseph H. Ehrenkranz. An educational and research division of Sacred Heart University; brings together clergy, laity, scholars, theologians, and educators with the purpose of promoting interreligious research, education, and dialogue, with particular focus on current religious thinking within Christianity and Judaism. *Highlights (-tri-annual newsletter).*

CENTRAL CONFERENCE OF AMERICAN RABBIS (1889). 355 Lexington Ave., NYC 10017. (212)972-3636. FAX: (212)692-0819. Pres. Rabbi Simeon J. Maslin; Exec. V.-Pres. Rabbi Paul J. Menitoff. Seeks to conserve and promote Judaism and to disseminate its teachings in a liberal spirit. The CCAR Press provides liturgy and prayerbooks to the worldwide Reform Jewish community. *CCAR Journal: A Reform Jewish Quarterly; CCAR Yearbook.*

CLAL–NATIONAL JEWISH CENTER FOR LEARNING AND LEADERSHIP (1974). 440 Park Ave. S., 4th fl., NYC 10016-8012. (212)779-3300. FAX: (212)779-1009. Pres. Rabbi Irwin Kula; Chmn. Radine Abramson Spier; Exec.V-Chmn. Donna M. Rosenthal. Provides leadership training for lay leaders, rabbis, educators, and communal professionals. A faculty of rabbis and scholars representing all the denominations of Judaism make Judaism come alive, applying the wisdom of the Jewish heritage to reimagine creatively the Jewish community and its institutions. Offers seminars and courses, retreats, symposia and conferences, lecture bureau. Publishes Sacred Days calendar, books, and educational materials. *Sh'ma.*

COALITION FOR THE ADVANCEMENT OF JEWISH EDUCATION (CAJE) (1976). 261 W. 35 St., #12A, NYC 10001. (212)268-4210. FAX: (212)268-4214. E-mail: 500-8447@mcimail.com.; www.caje.org. Chmn. Sylvia Abrams; Exec. Dir. Dr. Eliot G. Spack. Brings together Jews from all ideologies who are involved in every facet of Jewish education and are committed to transmitting the Jewish heritage. Sponsors annual Conference on Alternatives in Jewish Education and Curriculum Bank; publishes a wide variety of publications; organizes shared-interest networks; offers mini grants for special projects; sponsors Mini-CAJEs (one- or two-day in-service programs) around the country; maintains a website for Jewish educators (above). *Bikurim; timely curricular publications; Jewish Education News.*

CONGRESS OF SECULAR JEWISH ORGANIZATIONS (1970). 19657 Villa Dr. N., Southfield, MI 48076. (248)569-8127. FAX: (248)569-5222. E-mail: rifke@earthlink.net. Cochmn. Bobbie Varble, Jeff Zolitor; Exec. Dir. Roberta E. Feinstein. An umbrella organization of schools and adult clubs; facilitates exchange curricula and educational programs for children and adults stressing the Jewish historical and cultural heritage and the continuity of the Jewish people. *New Yorkish (Yiddish literature translations); Haggadah; The Hanuka Festival; Mame-Loshn.*

CONVERSION TO JUDAISM RESOURCE CENTER (1997). 74 Hauppauge Rd., Rm. 53, Commack, NY 11725. (516) 462-5826. E-mail: inform@convert.org. Pres. Dr. Lawrence J. Epstein; Exec. Dir. Susan Lustig. Provides information and advice for people who wish to convert to Judaism or who have converted. Puts potential converts in touch with rabbis from all branches of Judaism.

COUNCIL FOR INITIATIVES IN JEWISH EDUCATION (1991). 15 E. 26 St., Suite 1817, NYC 10010. (212)532-2360. FAX: (212) 532-2646. Founding Chmn. Morton L. Mandel; Bd. Chmn. Lester Pollack; Exec. Dir. Karen A. Barth. An independent, national, not-for-profit organization created to help transform North American Jewish life through Jewish education by developing: lay and professional leadership; strategies for change in partnership with educating institutions, communities, and national organizations; innovative ideas for educational policy and practice; and models of success in Jewish teaching and learning.

COUNCIL FOR JEWISH EDUCATION (1926). 111 Eighth Ave., 11th fl., NYC 10011-5201. (212)529–2000, ext. 1311. FAX: (212)529–2009. Pres. Rabbi Art Vernon; Exec. Sec. Sol Goldman. Fellowship of Jewish education professionals–administrators, supervisors, and teachers in Hebrew high schools and Jewish teachers colleges–of all ideological groupings; conducts annual national and regional conferences; represents the Jewish education profession before the Jewish community; cosponsors, with the Jewish Education Service of North America, a personnel committee and other projects; cooperates with Jewish Agency Department of Education and Culture in promoting Hebrew culture and studies. *Journal of Jewish Education.*

FEDERATION OF JEWISH MEN'S CLUBS (1929). 475 Riverside Dr., Rm. 244, NYC 10115. (212)749–8100. FAX: (212)316–4271. Internatl. Pres. Dr. Stephen H. Davidoff; Exec. Dir. Rabbi Charles E. Simon. Promotes principles of Conservative Judaism; develops family-education and leadership-training programs; offers the Art of Jewish Living series and Yom Hashoah Home Commemoration; sponsors Hebrew literacy adult-education program; presents awards for service to American Jewry. *Torchlight; Hearing Men's Voices.*

FEDERATION OF RECONSTRUCTIONIST CONGREGATIONS AND HAVUROT (*see* JEWISH RECONSTRUCTIONIST FEDERATION)

HILLEL: THE FOUNDATION FOR JEWISH CAMPUS LIFE (formerly B'NAI B'RITH HILLEL FOUNDATIONS) (1923). 1640 Rhode Island Ave., NW, Washington, DC 20036. (202)857–6576. FAX: (202)857–6693. E-mail: info@hillel.org. Chmn. Internatl. Bd. Govs. Edgar M. Bronfman; Chmn. Foundation for Jewish Campus Life Michael B. Rukin; Chmn. B'nai B'rith Hillel Comm. Bert Brown; Pres. & Internatl. Dir. Richard M. Joel. The largest Jewish campus organization in the world, its network of 500 regional centers, campus-based foundations, and affiliates serves as a catalyst for creating a celebratory community and a rich, diverse Jewish life on the campus. *The Hillel Annual Report; On Campus newsletter; Calling Home newsletter; Hillel Now newsletter; The Hillel Guide to Jewish Life on Campus (published with Princeton Review).*

INSTITUTE FOR COMPUTERS IN JEWISH LIFE (1978). 7074 N. Western Ave., Chicago, IL 60645. (312)262–9200. FAX: (312)262–9298. E-mail: rosirv@aol.com. Pres. Thomas Klutznick; Exec. V.-Pres. Dr. Irving J. Rosenbaum. Explores, develops, and disseminates applications of computer technology to appropriate areas of Jewish life, with special emphasis on Jewish education; creates educational software for use in Jewish schools; provides consulting service and assistance for national Jewish organizations, seminaries, and synagogues.

INTERNATIONAL FEDERATION OF SECULAR HUMANISTIC JEWS (1983). 28611 West Twelve Mile Rd., Farmington Hills, MI 48334. (248)476–9532. FAX: (248)476–8509. Co-Chairs Yair Tzaban (Israel), Sherwin Wine (USA). Consists of national organizations in Israel, the United States, Canada, Britain, France, Belgium, Australia, Mexico, Argentina, Uruguay and the countries of the former Soviet Union, involving some 50,000 Jews. The honorary co-chairs are Albert Memmi, well-known French writer and professor of sociology at the University of Paris, and Yehuda Bauer, noted historian and Holocaust scholar at the Hebrew University in Jerusalem. *Newsletter.*

INTERNATIONAL INSTITUTE FOR SECULAR HUMANISTIC JUDAISM (1985). 28611 West Twelve Mile Rd., Farmington Hills, MI 48334. (248)476–9532. FAX: (248)476–8509. Chmn. Rabbi Sherwin T. Wine. Established in 1985 in Jerusalem to serve the needs of a growing movement, its two primary purposes are to commission and publish educational materials and to train rabbis, leaders, teachers, and spokespersons for the movement. The Institute has two offices–one in Israel (Jerusalem) and one in N. America and offers educational and training programs in Israel, N. America, and the countries of the former Soviet Union. The N. American office, located in a suburb of Detroit, offers the Rabbinic Program, the Leadership Program, and the Adult Education Program. *Brochure, educational papers, and projects.*

JEWISH CHAUTAUQUA SOCIETY, INC. (sponsored by NATIONAL FEDERATION OF TEMPLE BROTHERHOODS) (1893). 838 Fifth Ave., NYC 10021. (212)570–0707 or (800)765–6200. FAX: (212)570–0960. E-mail: jcs@uahc.org. Pres. Stephen K. Breslauer; Chancellor/1st V.-Pres. Gary

Rosenthal; Exec. Dir. Douglas E. Barden. Works to promote interfaith understanding by sponsoring accredited college courses and one-day lectures on Judaic topics, providing book grants to educational institutions, producing educational videotapes on interfaith topics, and convening interfaith institutes. A founding sponsor of the National Black/Jewish Relations Center at Dillard University. *Brotherhood.*

JEWISH EDUCATION IN MEDIA (1978). PO Box 180, Riverdale Sta., NYC 10471. (212)362–7633. FAX: (203)359–1381. Pres. Bernard Samers; Exec. Dir. Rabbi Mark S. Golub. Devoted to producing television, film, and video-cassettes for a popular Jewish audience, in order to inform, entertain, and inspire a greater sense of Jewish identity and Jewish commitment. "L'Chayim," JEM's weekly half-hour program, which is seen nationally in 30 million homes on VISN/FAITH and VALUES channel and NJT/National Jewish Television, features outstanding figures in the Jewish world addressing issues and events of importance to the Jewish community.

JEWISH EDUCATION SERVICE OF NORTH AMERICA (JESNA) (1981). 111 Eighth Ave., NYC 10011. (212)284–6950. FAX: (212)284–6951. Pres. Mark Lainer; Exec. V.-Pres. Dr. Jonathan S. Woocher. The Jewish Federation system's educational coordinating, planning, and development agency. Promotes excellence in Jewish education by initiating exchange of ideas, programs, and materials; providing information, consultation, educational resources, and policy guidance; and collaborating with partners in N. America and Israel to develop educational programs. *Agenda: Jewish Education; planning guides on Jewish continuity; JESNA Update; research reports and bulletins.*

JEWISH RECONSTRUCTIONIST FEDERATION (formerly FEDERATION OF RECONSTRUCTIONIST CONGREGATIONS AND HAVUROT) (1954). 7804 Montgomery Ave., Suite 9, Elkins Park, PA 19027. (215)782–8500. E-mail: jrfnatl@aol.com. Pres. Jane Susswein. Exec. Dir. Rabbi Mordechai Liebling. Services affiliated congregations and havurot educationally and administratively; fosters the establishment of new Reconstructionist congregations and fellowship groups. Runs the Reconstruc-

tionist Press and provides programmatic materials. Maintains regional offices in New York, Los Angeles, and Chicago. *The Reconstructionist; Reconstructionism TODAY.*

——, RECONSTRUCTIONIST RABBINICAL ASSOCIATION (1974). Church Rd. and Greenwood Ave., Wyncote, PA 19095. (215)576–5210. FAX: (215)887–5348. E-mail: rraassoc@aol.com. Pres. Rabbi Barbara Penzner; Interim Exec. Dir. Lani Moss. Professional organization for graduates of the Reconstructionist Rabbinical College and other rabbis who identify with Reconstructionist Judaism; cooperates with Jewish Reconstructionist Federation in furthering Reconstructionism in the world. *Newsletters; position papers.*

——, RECONSTRUCTIONIST RABBINICAL COLLEGE (*see* p. 559)

JEWISH TEACHERS ASSOCIATION–MORIM (1931). 45 E. 33 St., Suite 604, NYC 10016. (212)684–0556. Pres. Phyllis L. Pullman; V.-Pres. Ronni David; Sec. Helen Parnes; Treas. Mildred Safar. Protects teachers from abuse of seniority rights; fights the encroachment of anti-Semitism in education; offers scholarships to qualified students; encourages teachers to assume active roles in Jewish communal and religious affairs. *Morim JTA Newsletter.*

KULANU, INC. (formerly AMISHAV USA) (1993). 11603 Gilsan St., Silver Spring, MD 20902. (301)681–5679. FAX: (301) 681–5679. Pres. Jack Zeller; Sec. Karen Primack. Engages in outreach to dispersed Jewish communities around the world who wish to return to their Jewish roots. Current projects include the formal conversion of Shinlung-Menashe tribesmen in India currently practicing Judaism, and supplying materials and rabbis for conversos/marranos in Mexico and Brazil. *Newsletter.*

NATIONAL COMMITTEE FOR FURTHERANCE OF JEWISH EDUCATION (1941). 824 Eastern Pkwy., Brooklyn, NY 11213. (718) 735–0200; (800)33-NCFJE. FAX: (718) 735–4455. Pres. Charles Kupferman; Bd. Chmn. Rabbi Shea Hecht; Chmn. Exec. Com. Rabbi Sholem Ber Hecht. Seeks to disseminate the ideals of Torah-true education among the youth of America; provides education and compassionate care for the poor, sick, and needy in U.S. and

Israel; provides aid to Iranian Jewish youth; sponsors camps and educational functions, family and vocational counseling services, family and early intervention, after-school and preschool programs; maintains schools in Brooklyn and Queens: Yeshivas Kol Yaakov Yehuda-Hadar HaTorah, Machon Chana Women's College, and Mesivta Ohr Torah, Chai-Tots preschool; Ivy League Torah Study Program; Released Time Program of Greater N.Y. *Panorama; Cultbusters; Intermarriage; Brimstone & Fire; Focus; A Life Full of Giving.*

NATIONAL COUNCIL OF YOUNG ISRAEL (1912). 3 W. 16 St., NYC 10011. (212) 929 – 1525. FAX: (212)727 – 9526. E-mail: ncyi@youngisrael.org.; www. youngisrael.org. Pres. Chaim Kaminetzky; Exec. V.-Pres. Rabbi Pesach Lerner. Through its network of member synagogues in N. America and Israel maintains a program of spiritual, cultural, social, and communal activity aimed at the advancement and perpetuation of traditional, Torah-true Judaism; seeks to instill in American youth an understanding and appreciation of the ethical and spiritual values of Judaism. Sponsors rabbinic and lay leadership conferences, kosher dining clubs, and youth programs. *Viewpoint; Divrei Torah Bulletin.*

———, AMERICAN FRIENDS OF YOUNG ISRAEL IN ISRAEL – YISRAEL HATZA'IR (1926). 3 W. 16 St., NYC 10011. (212) 929 – 1525. FAX: (212)727 – 9526. E-mail: ncyi@youngisrael.org. Pres. Meir Mishkoff. Promotes Young Israel synagogues and youth work in Israel; works to help absorb Russian and Ethiopian immigrants.

———, YOUNG ISRAEL DEPARTMENT OF YOUTH AND YOUNG ADULTS ACTIVITIES (reorg. 1981). 3 W. 16 St., NYC 10011. (212)929 – 1525; (800)617 – NCYI. FAX: (212)243 – 1222. Email:youth@youngisrael.org. Chmn. Kenneth Block; Dir. Richard Stareshefsky. Fosters varied program of activities for the advancement and perpetuation of traditional Torah-true Judaism; instills ethical and spiritual values and appreciation for compatibility of ancient faith of Israel with good Americanism. Runs leadership training programs and youth shabbatonim; annual national conference of youth directors; ski week in Canada's Laurentian Moun-

tains and summer programs for teens; Nachala summer program in Israel for Yeshiva H.S. girls and Natzach summer program for Yeshiva H.S. boys. *Torah Kidbits; Shabbat Youth Manual; Y.I. Can Assist You; Synagogue Youth Director Handbook.*

NATIONAL HAVURAH COMMITTEE (1979). 7318 Germantown Ave., Philadelphia, PA 19119 – 1720. (215)248 – 9760. FAX: (215)247 – 9703. E-mail: lauriekatnhl@ compuserve.com. Chmn. Leonard Gordon. A center for Jewish renewal devoted to spreading Jewish ideas, ethics, and religious practices through havurot, participatory and inclusive religious mini-communities. Maintains a directory of N. American havurot and sponsors a weeklong summer institute, regional weekend retreats, and teachers bureau. *Havurah! (newsletter).*

NATIONAL JEWISH CENTER FOR LEARNING AND LEADERSHIP (*see* CLAL)

NATIONAL JEWISH COMMITTEE ON SCOUTING (Boy Scouts of America) (1926). 1325 West Walnut Hill Lane, PO Box 152079, Irving, TX 75015 – 2079. (972)580 – 2000. FAX: (972)580 – 7870. Chmn. Jerrold Lockshin. Assists Jewish institutions in meeting their needs and concerns through use of the resources of scouting. Works through local Jewish committees on scouting to establish Tiger Cub groups (1st grade), Cub Scout packs, Boy Scout troops, and coed Explorer posts in synagogues, Jewish community centers, day schools, and other Jewish organizations wishing to draw Jewish youth. Support materials and resources on request.

NATIONAL JEWISH GIRL SCOUT COMMITTEE (1972). 33 Central Dr., Bronxville, NY 10708. (914)738 – 3986, (718)252 – 6072. FAX: (914)738 – 6752. E-mail: berlw@ aol.com. Chmn. Rabbi Herbert W. Bomzer; Field Chmn. Adele Wasko. Serves to further Jewish education by promoting Jewish award programs, encouraging religious services, promoting cultural exchanges with the Israel Boy and Girl Scouts Federation, and extending membership in the Jewish community by assisting councils in organizing Girl Scout troops and local Jewish Girl Scout committees. *Newsletter.*

NATIONAL JEWISH HOSPITALITY COMMITTEE (1973; reorg. 1993). PO Box 53691,

Philadelphia, PA 19105. (800)745–0301. Pres. Rabbi Allen S. Maller; Exec. Dir. Steven S. Jacobs. Assists persons interested in Judaism–for intermarriage, conversion, general information, or to respond to missionaries. *Special reports.*

OZAR HATORAH, INC. (1946). 1350 Ave. of the Americas, 32nd fl., NYC 10019. (212)582–2050. FAX: (212) 307–0044. Pres. Joseph Shalom; Sec. Sam Sutton; Exec. Dir. Rabbi Biniamine Amoyelle. An international educational network which builds Sephardic communities worldwide through Jewish education.

PARDES PROGRESSIVE ASSOCIATION OF REFORM DAY SCHOOLS (1990). 838 Fifth Ave., NYC 10021–7064. (212)249–0100. FAX: (212)734–2857. E-mail: educate@uahc.org. Pres. Zita Gardner; Chmn. Carol Nemo. An affiliate of the Union of American Hebrew Congregations; brings together day schools and professional and lay leaders committed to advancing the cause of full-time Reform Jewish education; advocates for the continuing development of day schools within the Reform movement as a means to foster Jewish identity, literacy, and continuity; promotes cooperation among our member schools and with other Jewish organizations that share similar goals. *Visions of Excellence (manual).*

P'EYLIM–LEV L'ACHIM (1951). 1034 E. 12 St. Brooklyn, NY 11230. (718)258–7760. FAX: (718)258-4672. E-mail: joskarmel @aol.com. Natl. Dir. Rabbi Joseph C. Karel; Exec. V.-Pres. Rabbi Nachum Barnetsky. Seeks to bring irreligious Jews in Israel back to their heritage. Conducts outreach through ten major divisions consisting of thousands of volunteers and hundreds of professionals across the country.

RABBINICAL ALLIANCE OF AMERICA (Igud Harabonim) (1942). 3 W. 16 St., 4th fl., NYC 10011. (212)242–6420. FAX: (212)255–8313. Pres. Rabbi Abraham B. Hecht; Admin. Judge of Beth Din (Rabbinical Court) Rabbi Herschel Kurzrock. Seeks to promulgate the cause of Torah-true Judaism through an organized rabbinate that is consistently Orthodox; seeks to elevate the position of Orthodox rabbis nationally and to defend the welfare of Jews the world over. Also has Beth Din Rabbinical Court for Jewish divorces,

litigation, marriage counseling, and family problems. *Perspective; Nahalim; Torah Message of the Week; Registry.*

RABBINICAL ASSEMBLY (1900). 3080 Broadway, NYC 10027. (212)280–6000. FAX: (212)749-9166. Pres. Rabbi Seymour L. Essrog; Exec. V.-Pres. Rabbi Joel H. Meyers. The international association of Conservative rabbis; actively promotes the cause of Conservative Judaism and works to benefit *klal yisrael*; publishes learned texts, prayer books, and works of Jewish interest; administers the work of the Committee on Jewish Law and Standards for the Conservative movement; serves the professional and personal needs of its members through publications, conferences, and benefit programs and administers the movement's Joint Placement Commission. *Conservative Judaism; Proceedings of the Rabbinical Assembly; Rabbinical Assembly Newsletter.*

RABBINICAL COUNCIL OF AMERICA, INC. (1923; reorg. 1935). 305 Seventh Ave., Suite 1200, NYC 10001. (212)807-7888. FAX: (212)727-8452. Pres. Rabbi Jacob S. Rubenstein; Exec. V.-Pres. Rabbi Steven M. Dworken. Promotes Orthodox Judaism in the community; supports institutions for study of Torah; stimulates creation of new traditional agencies. *Hadorom; RCA Record; Sermon Manual; Tradition; Resource Magazine.*

SHOMREI ADAMAH/KEEPERS OF THE EARTH (1988). c/o Surprise Lake Camp, 50 W. 17 St., NYC 10011. (212)807–6376. FAX: (212)924–5112. E-mail: shomadam@ aol.com. Exec. Dir. Jordan Dale; Mng. Dir. Laurie Hollin. Promotes understanding that love of nature and protection of the environment are values deeply embedded in Jewish tradition and texts. Runs Jewish environmental educational programs for Jewish day schools, synagogues, community centers, camps and other organized groups. *A Garden of Choice Fruit; Let the Earth Teach You Torah.*

SOCIETY FOR HUMANISTIC JUDAISM (1969). 28611 W. Twelve Mile Rd., Farmington Hills, MI 48334. (248)478–7610. FAX: (248)478–3159. E-mail: info@shj.org. Pres. Rick Naimark; Exec. Dir. M. Bonnie Cousens; Community Development Dir. Stacie Fine. Serves as a voice for Jews who value their Jewish identity and who seek an alternative to conventional Judaism, who reject supernatural authority and affirm the right of individuals to be the masters of their own lives. Publishes educational and ceremonial materials; organizes congregations and groups. *Humanistic Judaism (quarterly journal); Humanorah (quarterly newsletter)*.

TORAH SCHOOLS FOR ISRAEL–CHINUCH ATZMAI (1953). 40 Exchange Pl., NYC 10005. (212)248–6200. FAX: (212)248-6202. Pres. Rabbi Abraham Pam; Exec. Dir. Rabbi Henach Cohen. Conducts information programs for the American Jewish community on activities of the independent Torah schools educational network in Israel; coordinates role of American members of international board of governors; funds special programs of Mercaz Hachinuch Ha-Atzmai B'Eretz Yisroel; funds religous education programs in America and abroad.

TORAH UMESORAH–NATIONAL SOCIETY FOR HEBREW DAY SCHOOLS (1944). 160 Broadway, NYC 10038. (212)227–1000. E-mail: umesorah@aol.com. Bd. Chmn. David Singer; Exec. V.-Pres. Rabbi Joshua Fishman. Establishes Hebrew day schools in U.S. and Canada and provides a full gamut of services, including placement, curriculum guidance, and teacher training. Parent Enrichment Program provides enhanced educational experience for students from less Jewishly educated and marginally affiliated homes through parent-education programs and a monthly magazine, *The Jewish Parent Connection*. Publishes textbooks; runs shabbatonim, extracurricular activities; national PTA groups; national and regional teacher conventions. *Olomeinu–Our World*.

———, NATIONAL ASSOCIATION OF HEBREW DAY SCHOOL ADMINISTRATORS (1960). 1114 Ave. J, Brooklyn, NY 11230. (718)258–7767. Pres. David H. Schwartz. Coordinates the work of the fiscal directors of Hebrew day schools throughout the country. *NAHDSA Review*.

———, NATIONAL ASSOCIATION OF HEBREW DAY SCHOOL PARENT-TEACHER ASSOCIATIONS (1948). 160 Broadway, NYC 10038. (212)227–1000. FAX: (212)406-6934. Natl. PTA Coord. Bernice Brand. Acts as a clearinghouse and service agency to PTAs of Hebrew day schools; organizes parent education courses and

sets up programs for individual PTAs. *Fundraising with a Flair; PTA with a Purpose for the Hebrew Day School.*

———, NATIONAL CONFERENCE OF YESHIVA PRINCIPALS (1956). 160 Broadway, NYC 10038. (212)227–1000. FAX: (212)406-6934. E-mail: umesorah@aol.com. Pres. Rabbi Sholom Skaist; Bd. Chmn. Rabbi Dov Leibenstein; Exec. V.-Pres. Rabbi A. Moshe Possick. Professional organization of elementary and secondary yeshivah/day-school principals providing yeshivah/day schools with school evaluation and guidance, teacher and principal conferences–including a Mid-Winter Curriculum Conference and a National Educators Convention. *Directory of Elementary Schools and High Schools.*

———, NATIONAL YESHIVA TEACHERS BOARD OF LICENSE (1953). 160 Broadway, NYC 10038. (212)227–1000. Exec. V.-Pres. & Dir. Rabbi Joshua Fishman. Issues licenses to qualified instructors for all grades of the Hebrew day school and the general field of Torah education.

UNION FOR TRADITIONAL JUDAISM (1984). 811 Palisade Ave., Teaneck, NJ 07666. (201)801–0707. FAX: (201)801–0449. E-mail: utj@aol.com. Pres. Burton G. Greenblatt; Exec. V.-Pres. Rabbi Ronald D. Price. Through innovative outreach programs, seeks to bring the greatest possible number of Jews closer to an open-minded observant Jewish life-style. Activities include Operation Pesah, the Panel of Halakhic Inquiry, Speakers Bureau, adult and youth conferences, congregational services, and UTJ Internet Education Program. Includes, since 1992, the MORASHAH rabbinic educational fellowship and Neshamah teen program. *Hagahelet (quarterly newsletter); Kosher Nexus (bimonthly newsletter); Cornerstone (journal); Tomeikh Kahalakhah (Jewish legal responsa).*

UNION OF AMERICAN HEBREW CONGREGATIONS (1873). 838 Fifth Ave., NYC 10021–7064. (212)650–4000. FAX: (212)650–4169. E-mail: uahc@uahc.org. Pres. Rabbi Eric H. Yoffie; V.-Pres. Rabbi Lennard R. Thal; Bd. Chmn. Jerome H. Somers. Serves as the central congregational body of Reform Judaism in the Western Hemisphere; serves its approximately 875 affiliated temples and membership with religious, educational, cultural, and administrative programs. *Reform Judaism.*

———, AMERICAN CONFERENCE OF CANTORS (1953). 170 W. 74 St., NYC 10023. (212)874–4762. FAX: (212)874–3527. Pres. Judith K. Rowland; Exec. V.-Pres. Howard M. Stahl; Dir. of Placement Richard Botton; Admin. Asst. Karyn Turner. Members receive investiture and commissioning as cantors at recognized seminaries, i.e., Hebrew Union College–Jewish Institute of Religion, School of Sacred Music, or Jewish Theological Seminary, as well as full certification through HUC-JIR-SSM. Through the Joint Cantorial Placement Commission, the ACC serves Reform congregations seeking cantors and music directors. Dedicated to creative Judaism, preserving the best of the past, and encouraging new and vital approaches to religious ritual, music, and ceremonies. *Koleinu.*

———, COMMISSION ON REFORM JEWISH EDUCATION OF THE UNION OF AMERICAN HEBREW CONGREGATIONS, CENTRAL CONFERENCE OF AMERICAN RABBIS, NATIONAL ASSOCIATION OF TEMPLE EDUCATORS IN ASSOCIATION WITH THE HEBREW UNION COLLEGE-JEWISH INSTITUTE OF RELIGION (1923). 838 Fifth Ave., NYC 10021. (212)650–4110. FAX: (212)650–4129. E-mail: educate@uahc.org. Chmn. Robin L. Eisenberg; Dir. Rabbi Jan Katzen. Long-range planning and policy development for congregational programs of lifelong education; materials concerning Reform Jewish Outreach, Teacher Development and Reform Day Schools; activities administered by the UAHC Department of Education. V'Shinantam; Torah at the Center.

———, COMMISSION ON SOCIAL ACTION OF REFORM JUDAISM (see p. 516)

———, COMMISSION ON SYNAGOGUE MANAGEMENT (UAHC-CCAR) (1962). 838 Fifth Ave., NYC 10021. (212) 650–4040. FAX: (212)650–4239. Chmn. James M. Friedman; Dir. Dale A. Glasser. Assists congregations in management, finance, building maintenance, design, construction, and art aspects of synagogues; maintains the Synagogue Architectural Library.

———, NATIONAL ASSOCIATION OF TEMPLE ADMINISTRATORS (NATA) (1941). PO Box 722, Hartsdale, NY 10530-0722. (914)328–7730. FAX: (914)686–8017. Pres. Fern M. Kamen. Professional organization for UAHC synagogue administrators. Sponsors graduate training in synagogue management with Hebrew Union College; offers in-service training, workshops, and conferences leading to certification; provides NATA Consulting Service, NATA Placement Service for synagogues seeking advice or professional administrators; establishes professional standards. *NATA Journal; Temple Management Manual.*

———, NATIONAL ASSOCIATION OF TEMPLE EDUCATORS (NATE) (1955). 707 Summerly Dr., Nashville, TN 37209–4253. (615)352–6800. FAX: (615)352–7800. E-mail: nateoff@aol.com. Pres. Bini W. Silver; Exec. Dir. Richard M. Morin. Represents the temple educator within the general body of Reform Judaism; fosters the full-time profession of the temple educator; encourages the growth and development of Jewish religious education consistent with the aims of Reform Judaism; stimulates communal interest in and responsibility for Jewish religious education. *NATE NEWS; Compass.*

———, NORTH AMERICAN FEDERATION OF TEMPLE BROTHERHOODS (1923). 838 Fifth Ave., NYC 10021. (212)570–0707. FAX: (212)570-0960. E-mail: nftb@uahc. org. Pres. Stephen K. Breslauer; 1st V.-Pres./JCS Chancellor Gary Rosenthal; Exec. Dir. Douglas Barden. Dedicated to enhancing the world through the ideal of brotherhood, NFTB and its 300 affiliated clubs are actively involved in education, social action, youth activities, and other programs that contribute to temple and community life. Supports the Jewish Chautauqua Society, an interfaith educational project. *Brotherhood magazine.*

———, WOMEN OF REFORM JUDAISM – THE FEDERATION OF TEMPLE SISTERHOODS (1913). 838 Fifth Ave., NYC 10021 – 7064. (212)650–4050. FAX: (212)650–4059. Pres. Judith Silverman; Exec. Dir. Ellen Y. Rosenberg. Serves more than 600 sisterhoods of Reform Judaism; promotes interreligious understanding and social justice; provides funding for scholarships for rabbinic students; founded the Jewish Braille Institute, which provides braille and large-type Judaic materials for Jewish blind; supports projects for Israel; is the women's agency of Reform Judaism, an affiliate of the UAHC; works in behalf of the Hebrew Union College–Jewish Institute of Religion and the World Union for Progressive Judaism. *Notes for Now; Art Calendar.*

———, YOUTH DIVISION AND NORTH AMERICAN FEDERATION OF TEMPLE YOUTH (1939). PO Box 443, Bowen Rd., Warwick, NY 10990. (914)987–6300. FAX: (914)986–7185. E-mail: rjyouth@warwick.net. Dir. Rabbi Allan L. Smith. Dedicated to Jewishly enhancing the lives of the young people of North America's Reform congregations through a program of informal education carried out in UAHC Camp-Institutes (10 camps for grades 2 and up), UAHC/NFTY Israel Programs (summer and semester), NFTY/Junior & Senior High School Programs (youth groups), and Kesher/College Education Department (Reform havurot on campuses).

UNION OF ORTHODOX JEWISH CONGREGATIONS OF AMERICA (1898). 333 Seventh Ave., NYC 10001. (212)563–4000. FAX: (212)564–9058. E-mail: ou@ou.org; ou.org. Pres. Mandell I. Ganchrow, M.D.; Exec. V.-Pres. Rabbi Raphael Butler. Serves as the national central body of Orthodox synagogues; national OU kashrut supervision and certification service; sponsors Institute for Public Affairs; National Conference of Synagogue Youth; National Jewish Council for the Disabled; Israel Center in Jerusalem; Torah Center in the Ukraine; New Young Leadership Division; Pardes; provides educational, religious, and organization programs, events, and guidance to synagogues and groups; represents the Orthodox Jewish community to governmental and civic bodies and the general Jewish community. *Jewish Action magazine; OU Kosher Directory; OU Passover Directory; OU News Reporter; Synagogue Spotlight; Our Way magazine; Yachad magazine; Luach & Limud Personal Torah Study.*

———, INSTITUTE FOR PUBLIC AFFAIRS (1989). 333 Seventh Ave., NYC 10001. (212)613–8123. FAX: (212)564–9058. E-mail: ipa@ou.org. Pres. Mandell I. Ganchrow, M.D.; Chmn. Richard Stone; Dir. Nathan Diament; Dir. Internatl. Affairs & Community Relations Betty Ehrenberg. Serves as the policy analysis, advocacy, mobilization, and program-ming department responsible for representing Orthodox/traditional American Jewry. *IPA Currents (quarterly newsletter).*

———, NATIONAL CONFERENCE OF SYNAGOGUE YOUTH (1954). 333 Seventh Ave., NYC 10001. (212)563–4000. E-mail: ncsy@ou.org. Dir. Rabbi Pinchas Stolper; Exec. Dir. Paul Glasser. Central body for youth groups of Orthodox congregations; provides educational guidance, Torah study groups, community service, program consultation, Torah library, Torah fund scholarships, Ben Zakkai Honor Society, Friends of NCSY, weeklong seminars, Israel Summer Experience for teens and Camp NCSY East Summer Kollel & Michlelet, Teen Torah Center. Divisions include Senior NCSY, Junior NCSY for preteens, Our Way for the Jewish deaf, Yachad for the developmentally disabled, Israel Center in Jerusalem, and NCSY in Israel. *Keeping Posted with NCSY; Darchei Da'at.*

———, WOMEN'S BRANCH (1923). 156 Fifth Ave., NYC 10010. (212)929–8857. Pres. Marilyn Golomb Selber. Umbrella organization of Orthodox sisterhoods in U.S. and Canada, educating women in Jewish learning and observance; provides programming, leadership, and organizational guidance, conferences, conventions, and Marriage Committee. Works with Orthodox Union Commissions and outreach; supports Stern and Touro College scholarships and Jewish braille publications; supplies Shabbat candelabra for hospital patients; NGO representative at UN. *Hachodesh; Hakol.*

UNION OF ORTHODOX RABBIS OF THE UNITED STATES AND CANADA (1902). 235 E. Broadway, NYC 10002. (212)964–6337(8). Dir. Rabbi Hersh M. Ginsberg. Seeks to foster and promote Torah-true Judaism in the U.S. and Canada; assists in the establishment and maintenance of yeshivot in the U.S.; maintains committee on marriage and divorce and aids individuals with marital difficulties; disseminates knowledge of traditional Jewish rites and practices and publishes regulations on synagogal structure; maintains rabbinical court for resolving individual and communal conflicts. *HaPardes.*

UNION OF SEPHARDIC CONGREGATIONS, INC. (1929). 8 W. 70 St., NYC 10023.

(212)873–0300. FAX: (212)724–6165. Pres. Rabbi Marc D. Angel; Bd. Chmn. Alvin Deutsch. Promotes the religious interests of Sephardic Jews; prints and distributes Sephardic prayer books. Annual International Directory of Sephardic Congregations.

UNITED LUBAVITCHER YESHIVOTH (1940). 841–853 Ocean Pkwy., Brooklyn, NY 11230. (718)859–7600. FAX: (718)434-1519. Supports and organizes Jewish day schools and rabbinical seminaries in the U.S. and abroad.

UNITED SYNAGOGUE OF CONSERVATIVE JUDAISM (1913). 155 Fifth Ave., NYC 10010–6802. (212)533–7800. FAX: (212) 353–9439. E-mail: 71263.276@compuserve.com.; www.uscj.org. Pres. Stephen S. Wolnek; Exec. V.-Pres./CEO Rabbi Jerome M. Epstein. International organization of 800 Conservative congregations. Maintains 12 departments and 20 regional offices to assist its affiliates with religious, educational, youth, community, and administrative programming and guidance; aims to enhance the cause of Conservative Judaism, further religious observance, encourage establishment of Jewish religious schools, draw youth closer to Jewish tradition. Extensive Israel programs. *United Synagogue Review; Art/Engagement Calendar; Program Suggestions; Directory & Resource Guide; Book Service Catalogue of Publications.*

———, COMMISSION ON JEWISH EDUCATION (1930). 155 Fifth Ave., NYC 10010. (212)533–7800. FAX: (212)353–9439. Chmn. Dr. Jack Porter; Cochmn. Rabbi Marim Charry; Dir. Rabbi Robert Abramson. Develops educational policy for the United Synagogue of Conservative Judaism and sets the educational direction for Conservative congregations, their schools, and the Solomon Schechter Day Schools. Seeks to enhance the educational effectiveness of congregations through the publication of materials and in-service programs. *Tov L'Horot; Your Child; Shiboley Schechter; Advisories.*

———, COMMISSION ON SOCIAL ACTION AND PUBLIC POLICY (1958). 155 Fifth Ave., NYC 10010. (212)533–7800. FAX: (212)353–9439. Chmn. J.B. Mazer; Dir. Sarrae G. Crane. Develops and implements positions and programs on issues of social action and public policy for the United Synagogue of Conservative Judaism; represents these positions to other Jewish and civic organizations, the media, and government; and provides guidance, both informational and programmatic, to its affiliated congregations in these areas. *HaMa'aseh.*

———, JEWISH EDUCATORS ASSEMBLY (1951). 106–06 Queens Blvd., Forest Hills, NY 11375–4248. (718)268–9452. FAX: (718)520–4369. Pres. Dr. Howard B. Rosenblatt; Exec. Dir. Dr. Hyman J. Campeas. Promotes the vitality of the Conservative movement by encouraging professional growth and development, maintaining professional standards, acting as an advocate for Jewish education, and supporting educators' well-being. Services offered: annual convention, placement service, career services, research grants, and personal benefits. *V'Aleh Ha-Chadashot newsletter.*

———, KADIMA (formerly PRE-USY; reorg. 1968). 155 Fifth Ave., NYC 10010–6802. (212)533–7800. FAX: (212)353-9439. E-mail: youth@uscj.org. Dir. Ari Y. Goldberg. Involves Jewish preteens in a meaningful religious, educational, and social environment; fosters a sense of identity and commitment to the Jewish community and the Conservative movement; conducts synagogue-based chapter programs and regional Kadima days and weekends. *Mitzvah of the Month; Kadima Kesher; Chagim; Advisors Aid; Games;* quarterly *Kol Kadima magazine.*

———, NORTH AMERICAN ASSOCIATION OF SYNAGOGUE EXECUTIVES (1948). c/o Jan Baron, Congregation B'nai Amoona, 324 S. Mason Rd., St. Louis, MO 63141. (314)576–9990. FAX: (324)576–9994. E-mail: bnaiamoona@aol.com. Pres. Jan Baron; Hon. Pres. Ralph B. Kirshbaum. Aids congregations affiliated with the United Synagogue of Conservative Judaism to further the aims of Conservative Judaism through more effective administration (Program for Assistance by Liaisons to Synagogues–PALS); advances professional standards and promotes new methods in administration; cooperates in United Synagogue placement services and administrative surveys. *NAASE Connections Newsletter; NAASE Journal.*

———, UNITED SYNAGOGUE YOUTH OF (1951). 155 Fifth Ave., NYC 10010. (212)533–7800. FAX: (212)353–9439. E-mail: youth@uscj.org. Pres. Adam Rosenthal; Exec. Dir. Jules A. Gutin. Seeks to strengthen identification with Conservative Judaism, based on the personality development, needs, and interests of the adolescent, in a mitzvah framework. *Achshav; Tikun Olam; A.J. Heschel Honor Society Newsletter; SATO Newsletter; USY Program Bank; Hakesher Newsletter for Advisors.*

VAAD MISHMERETH STAM (1976). 4901 16th Ave., Brooklyn, NY 11204. (718)438–4963. FAX: (718)438–9343. Pres. Rabbi David L. Greenfeld. A nonprofit consumer-protection agency dedicated to preserving and protecting the halakhic integrity of Torah scrolls, tefillin, phylacteries, and mezuzoth. Publishes material for laymen and scholars in the field of scribal arts; makes presentations and conducts examination campaigns in schools and synagogues; created an optical software system to detect possible textual errors in stam. Teaching and certifying sofrim worldwide. Offices in Israel, Strasbourg, Chicago, London, Manchester, Montreal, and Zurich. Publishes *Guide to Mezuzah* and *Encyclopedia of the Secret Aleph Beth. The Jewish Quill.*

WASHINGTON INSTITUTE FOR JEWISH LEADERSHIP & VALUES (1988). 11710 Hunters Lane, Rockville, MD 20852. (301) 770-5070. FAX: (301) 770-6365. E-mail: panin@aol.com. Pres. Rabbi Sidney Schwarz; Bd. Chmn. Norman R. Pozez. An educational foundation advancing Tikkun Olam, activism, and civic engagement by American Jews, grounded in Torah and Jewish values. Its flagship program is Panim el Panim:High School in Washington. Also sponsors the Jewish Civic Initiative for communities and day schools and offers leadership training workshops for college and adult audiences. *Jewish Civics: A Tikkun Olam/World Repair Manual; Jewish Civics: Jewish Participation in Public Affairs.*

WOMEN'S LEAGUE FOR CONSERVATIVE JUDAISM (1918). 48 E. 74 St., NYC 10021. (212)628–1600. FAX: (212)772–3507. Pres. Evelyn Seelig; Exec. Dir. Bernice Balter. Parent body of Conservative (Masorti) women's synagogue groups in U.S., Canada, Puerto Rico, Mexico, and Israel; provides programs and resources in Jewish education, social action, Israel affairs, American and Canadian public affairs, leadership training, community service

programs for persons with disabilities, conferences on world affairs, study institutes, publicity techniques; publishes books of Jewish interest; contributes to support of Jewish Theological Seminary of America. *Women's League Outlook magazine; Ba'Olam world affairs newsletter.*

WORLD COUNCIL OF CONSERVATIVE/MASORTI SYNAGOGUES (1957). 155 Fifth Ave., NYC 10010. (212)533–7800, ext. 2014, 2018. FAX: (212)533–9439. Pres. Rabbi Marc Liebhaber; Rabbi of Council, Rabbi Benjamin Z. Kreitman. International representative of Conservative organizations and congregations; promotes the growth and development of the Conservative movement in Israel and throughout the world; supports educational institutions overseas; holds biennial international conventions; represents the world Conservative movement on the Executive of the World Zionist Organization. *World Spectrum.*

WORLD UNION FOR PROGRESSIVE JUDAISM, LTD. (1926). 838 Fifth Ave., NYC 10021. (212)650–4090. FAX: (212)650–4099. E-mail: 5448032@mcimail.com. Pres. Austin Beutel; Exec. Dir. Rabbi Richard G. Hirsch. International umbrella organization of Liberal Judaism; promotes and coordinates efforts of Liberal congregations throughout the world; starts new congregations, recruits rabbis and rabbinical students for all countries; organizes international conferences of Liberal Jews. *World News.*

SCHOOLS, INSTITUTIONS

ACADEMY FOR JEWISH RELIGION (1955). 15 W. 86 St., NYC 10024. (212)875–0540. FAX: (212)875–0541. Pres. Rabbi Shohama Wiener; Dean Rabbi Samuel Barth. The only rabbinical and cantorial seminary in the U.S. at which students explore the full range of Jewish spiritual learning and practice. Graduates serve in Conservative, Reform, Reconstructionist, and Orthodox congregations, chaplaincies, and educational institutions. Programs include rabbinic and cantorial studies in NYC and on/off-campus non-matriculated studies.

ANNENBERG RESEARCH INSTITUTE (*see* CENTER FOR JUDAIC STUDIES)

BALTIMORE HEBREW UNIVERSITY (1919). 5800 Park Heights Ave., Baltimore, MD

21215. (410)578-6900; (888)248-7420. FAX: (410)578-6940. E-mail: bhu@bhu. edu. Pres. Dr. Robert O. Freedman; Bd. Chmn. George B. Hess, Jr . . . Offers PhD, MA, BA, and AA programs in Jewish studies, Jewish education, biblical and Near Eastern archaeology, philosophy, literature, history, Hebrew language, literature, and contemporary Jewish civilization; School of Continuing Education; Joseph Meyerhoff Library; community lectures, film series, seminars. *The Scribe (annual newsletter).*

————, BALTIMORE INSTITUTE FOR JEWISH COMMUNAL SERVICE. (410)578-6932. FAX: (410)578-6940. Dir. Debra S. Weinberg. Trains Jewish communal professionals; offers a joint degree program: an MA from BHU and an MAJE from BHU, an MSW from U. of Maryland School of Social Work, or an MPS in policy sciences from UMBC; MA with Meyerhoff Graduate School and Johns Hopkins U. in nonprofit management.

————, BERNARD MANEKIN SCHOOL OF UNDERGRADUATE STUDIES. Dean Dr. George Berlin. BA program; interinstitutional program with Johns Hopkins University; interdisciplinary concentrations: contemporary Middle East, American Jewish culture, and the humanities; Russian/English program for new Americans; assoc. of arts (AA) degree in Jewish studies.

————, LEONARD AND HELEN R. STULMAN SCHOOL OF CONTINUING EDUCATION. Dean Dr. George Berlin. Noncredit program open to the community, offering a variety of courses, trips, and events covering a range of Jewish subjects.

————, PEGGY MEYERHOFF PEARLSTONE SCHOOL OF GRADUATE STUDIES. Dean Dr. Barry M. Gittlen. PhD and MA programs; MA in Jewish studies; MAJE in Jewish education; PhD in Jewish studies; a double master's degree with an MA from BHU and an MAJE from BHU, an MSW from the University of Maryland School of Social Work, or an MPS in policy sciences from UMBC; MA with Baltimore Institute and Johns Hopkins U. in nonprofit management.

BRAMSON ORT TECHNICAL INSTITUTE (1977). 69-30 Austin St., Forest Hills, NY 11375. (718)261-5800. Dean of Academic Services Barry Glotzer. A two-year Jewish technical college offering certificates and associate degrees in technology and business fields, including accounting, computer, electronics technology, business management, ophthalmic technology, office technology. Extension sites in Manhattan and Brooklyn.

BRANDEIS-BARDIN INSTITUTE (1941). 1101 Peppertree Lane, Brandeis, CA 93064. (805)582-4450. FAX: (805)526-1398. E-mail: bbibci4u@aol.com. Pres. Judge Joseph Wapner; Exec. V.-Pres. Dr. Alvin Mars. A Jewish pluralistic, nondenominational educational institution providing programs for people of all ages:BCI (Brandeis Collegiate Institute), a summer leadership program for college-age adults from around the world; Camp Alonim, a summer Jewish experience for children 8-16; Gan Alonim Day Camp for children in kindergarten to 6th grade; weekend retreats for adults with leading contemporary Jewish scholars-in-residence; Jewish music concerts; Family Days and Weekends, Grandparents Weekends, Elderhostel, Young Adult programs, dance weekends, institute for newly marrieds. *Monthly Updates; BBI Newsletter; BCI Alumni News.*

BRANDEIS UNIVERSITY (1948). 415 South St., Waltham, MA 02254. (781)736-2000. Pres. Jehuda Reinharz; Provost Irving Epstein; Exec. V.-Pres. & CEO Peter B. French; Sr. V.-Pres. of Devel. Nancy Winship. Founded under Jewish sponsorship as a nonsectarian institution offering undergraduate and graduate education. The Lown School is the center for all programs of teaching and research in Judaic studies, ancient Near Eastern studies, and Islamic and modern Middle Eastern studies. The school includes the Department of Near Eastern and Judaic Studies; the Hornstein Program in Jewish Communal Service, a professional training program; the Cohen Center for Modern Jewish Studies, which conducts research and teaching in contemporary Jewish studies, primarily in American Jewish studies; and the Tauber Institute for the study of European Jewry. *Various newsletters, scholarly publications.*

CENTER FOR JUDAIC STUDIES, School of Arts and Sciences, University of Pennsylvania. (Merged with University of Pennsylvania, 1993; formerly Annenberg Research Institute, successor of Dropsie

College.) 420 Walnut St., Philadelphia, PA 19106. (215)238–1290. FAX: (215) 238–1540. Dir. David B. Ruderman. *Jewish Quarterly Review.*

CLEVELAND COLLEGE OF JEWISH STUDIES (1964). 26500 Shaker Blvd., Beachwood, OH 44122. (216)464–4050. FAX: (216)464-5827. Pres. David S. Ariel; Dir. of Student Services Ronald M. Horvat. Provides courses in all areas of Judaic and Hebrew studies to adults and college-age students; offers continuing education for Jewish educators and administrators; serves as a center for Jewish life and culture; expands the availability of courses in Judaic studies by exchanging faculty, students, and credits with neighboring academic institutions; grants bachelor's and master's degrees.

DROPSIE COLLEGE FOR HEBREW AND COGNATE LEARNING (*see* CENTER FOR JUDAIC STUDIES)

FEINBERG GRADUATE SCHOOL OF THE WEIZMANN INSTITUTE OF SCIENCE (1958). 51 Madison Ave., NYC 10010. (212)779–2500. FAX: (212)779–3209. Chmn. Melvin Schwartz; Pres. Robert Asher; Dean Prof. Shmuel Safran. Situated on the Weizmann campus in Rehovot, Israel, provides the school's faculty and research facilities. Accredited by the Council for Higher Education of Israel and the NY State Board of Regents for the study of natural sciences, leading to MSc and PhD degrees.

GRATZ COLLEGE (1895). Old York Rd. and Melrose Ave., Melrose Park, PA 19027. (215)635–7300. FAX: (215)635–7320. Bd. Chmn. William L. Landsburg; Interim Pres. Dr. Ernest M. Kahn. Offers a wide variety of undergraduate and graduate degrees and continuing education programs in Judaic, Hebraic, and Middle Eastern studies. Grants BA and MA in Jewish studies, MA in Jewish education (joint program in special needs education with La Salle U.), MA in Jewish music, MA in Jewish liberal studies, MA in Jewish communal studies, certificates in Jewish communal studies (joint program with U. of Penna. School of Social Work), Jewish education, Israel studies, Judaica librarianship (joint program with Drexel U.), and Jewish music. Joint graduate program with Reconstructionist Rabbinical College in Jewish education and Jewish

music. Netzky Division of Continuing Education and Jewish Community High School. *Various newsletters, annual academic bulletin, scholarly publications, centennial volume, and occasional papers.*

HEBREW COLLEGE (1921). 43 Hawes St., Brookline, MA 02146. (617)232–8710. FAX: (617)264–9264. Pres. Dr. David M. Gordis; Bd. Chmn. Dr. Norman P. Spack. Serves more than 2,000 students in undergraduate and graduate programs, institutes for family and early childhood educators, Jewish music practitioners and other professional educators, and its Center for Adult Jewish Study. Serves youth of Greater Boston through Prozdor high school and overnight Camp Yavneh in Northwood, N.H. Through Wilstein Institute of Jewish Policy Studies engages in research, analysis, and strategic planning in areas of Jewish communal interests. *Hebrew College Today; Leket.*

HEBREW SEMINARY OF THE DEAF (1992). 4435 W. Oakton, Skokie, IL 60076. (847)677-6724; 677–3330. FAX: (847)677–7945. Pres. Rabbi Douglas Goldhamer; Bd. Cochmn. Rabbi William Frankel, Alan Crane. Trains deaf and hearing men and women to become rabbis and teachers for Jewish deaf communities across America. All classes in the 5-year program are interpreted in Sign Language. Rabbis teaching in the seminary are Reform, Conservative, and Reconstructionist.

HEBREW THEOLOGICAL COLLEGE (1922). 7135 N. Carpenter Rd., Skokie, IL 60077. (847)982–2500. FAX: (847)674-6381. E-mail: ssmlhtc@nslsilus.org. Chancellor Rabbi Dr. Jerold Isenberg. An accredited institution of higher Jewish learning which includes a rabbinical school; Fasman Yeshiva High School; Anne M. Blitstein Teachers Institute for Women; Wm. and Lillian Kanter School of Liberal Arts & Sciences; Max Bressler School of Advanced Hebrew Studies. *Or Shmuel; Torah Journal; Likutei P'shatim; Turrets of Silver.*

HEBREW UNION COLLEGE–JEWISH INSTITUTE OF RELIGION (1875). 3101 Clifton Ave., Cincinnati, OH 45220. (513)221–1875. FAX: (513)221–1847. Pres. Sheldon Zimmerman; Chancellor Dr. Alfred Gottschalk; V.-Pres., Admin. & Finance Arthur R. Grant; V.-Pres. Devel. John S.

Borden; Chmn. Bd. Govs. Burton Lehman; Provost Dr. Norman J. Cohen. Academic centers: 3101 Clifton Ave., Cincinnati, OH 45220 (1875), Dean Kenneth Ehrlich. 1 W. 4 St., NYC 10012 (1922), Dean Rabbi Zahara Davidowitz-Farkas. FAX: (212) 388–1720. 3077 University Ave., Los Angeles, CA 90007 (1954), Dean Lewis Barth; FAX: (213)747–6128. 13 King David St., Jerusalem, Israel 94101 (1963), Dean Michael L. Klein; FAX: (972–2)6251478. Prepares students for Reform rabbinate, cantorate, religious-school teaching and administration, communal service, academic careers; promotes Jewish studies; maintains libraries, archives, and museums; offers master's and doctoral degrees; engages in archaeological excavations; publishes scholarly works through Hebrew Union College Press. *American Jewish Archives; Bibliographica Judaica; HUC-JIR Catalogue; Hebrew Union College Annual; Studies in Bibliography and Booklore; The Chronicle; HUC-JIR Annual Report.*

——, AMERICAN JEWISH PERIODICAL CENTER (1957). 3101 Clifton Ave., Cincinnati, OH 45220. (513)221–1875, ext. 294. Dir. Herbert C. Zafren. Maintains microfilms of all American Jewish periodicals 1823–1925, selected periodicals since 1925. *Jewish Periodicals and Newspapers on Microfilm (1957); First Supplement (1960); Augmented Edition (1984).*

——, EDGAR F. MAGNIN SCHOOL OF GRADUATE STUDIES (1956). 3077 University Ave., Los Angeles, CA 90007. (213)749–3424. FAX: (213)747–6128. Dir. Stanley Chyet. Supervises programs leading to PhD (education), DHS, DHL, and MA degrees; participates in cooperative PhD programs with U. of S. Calif.

——, GRADUATE STUDIES PROGRAM. 1 West 4 St. NYC 10012. (212)674–5300, ext. 228. FAX: (212)388–1720. Dean Rabbi Zahara Davidowitz-Farkas; Dir. Kerry M. Olitzky. Offers the DHL (doctor of Hebrew letters) degree in a variety of fields; the MAJS (master of arts in Judaic studies), a multidisciplinary degree; and is the only Jewish seminary to offer the DMin (doctor of ministry) degree in pastoral care and counseling.

——, IRWIN DANIELS SCHOOL OF JEWISH COMMUNAL SERVICE (1968). 3077 University Ave., Los Angeles, CA 90007. (213)749–3424. FAX: (213)747–6128. Dir. Steven J. Windmueller. Offers certificate and master's degree to those employed in Jewish communal services, or preparing for such work; offers joint MA in Jewish education and communal service with Rhea Hirsch School; offers dual degrees with the School of Social Work, the School of Public Administration, the Annenberg School for Communication, and the School of Gerontology of the U. of S. Calif. and with other institutions. Single master's degrees can be completed in 15 months and certificates are awarded for the completion of two full-time summer sessions.

——, JACOB RADER MARCUS CENTER OF THE AMERICAN JEWISH ARCHIVES (1947). 3101 Clifton Ave., Cincinnati, OH 45220. (513)221–1875 ext. 403. FAX: (513)221–7812. Interim Dir. Kevin Proffitt. Promotes the study and preservation of the Western Hemisphere Jewish experience through research, publications, collection of important source materials, and a vigorous public-outreach program. *American Jewish Archives; monographs, publications, and pamphlets.*

——, JEROME H. LOUCHHEIM SCHOOL OF JUDAIC STUDIES (1969). 3077 University Ave., Los Angeles, CA 90007. (213)749–3424. FAX: (213)747–6128. Dir. David Ellenson. Offers programs leading to MA, BS, BA, and AA degrees; offers courses as part of the undergraduate program of the U. of S. Calif.

——, NELSON GLUECK SCHOOL OF BIBLICAL ARCHAEOLOGY (1963). 13 King David St., Jerusalem, Israel 94101. (972)2–6203333. FAX: (972)2–6251478. Dir. Avraham Biran. Offers graduate-level research programs in Bible and archaeology. Summer excavations are carried out by scholars and students. University credit may be earned by participants in excavations. Consortium of colleges, universities, and seminaries is affiliated with the school. Skirball Museum of Biblical Archaeology (artifacts from Tel Dan, Tel Gezer, and Aroer).

——, RHEA HIRSCH SCHOOL OF EDUCATION (1967). 3077 University Ave., Los Angeles, CA 90007. (213)749–3424. FAX: (213)747–6128. Dir. Sara Lee. Offers PhD and MA programs in Jewish and Hebrew education; conducts joint degree programs with U. of S. Calif.; offers courses for Jewish teachers, librarians, and early educators on a nonmatriculating basis; conducts summer institutes for professional Jewish educators.

———, SCHOOL OF EDUCATION (1947). 1 W. 4 St., NYC 10012. (212)674–5300, ext. 228. FAX: (212)388–1720. Dean Rabbi Zahara Davidowitz-Farkas; Dir. Kerry M. Olitzky. Trains teachers and principals for Reform religious schools; offers MA degree with specialization in religious education.

———, SCHOOL OF GRADUATE STUDIES (1949). 3101 Clifton Ave., Cincinnati, OH 45220. (513)221–1875, ext. 230. FAX: (513)221–0321. Dir. Dr. Adam Kamesar. Offers programs leading to MA and PhD degrees; offers program leading to DHL degree for rabbinic graduates of the college.

———, SCHOOL OF JEWISH STUDIES (1963). 13 King David St., Jerusalem, Israel, 94101. (972)2–6203333. FAX: (972)2–6251478. Dean Michael L. Klein; Assoc. Dean Rabbi Shaul R. Feinberg. Offers first year of graduate rabbinic, cantorial, and Jewish education studies (required) for American students; program leading to ordination for Israeli rabbinic students; undergraduate one-year work/study program on a kibbutz and in Jerusalem in cooperation with Union of American Hebrew Congregations; Hebrew Ulpan for Olim; Abramov Library of Judaica, Hebraica, Ancient Near East and American Jewish Experience; Skirball Museum of Biblical Archaeology; public outreach programs (lectures, courses, concerts, exhibits).

———, SCHOOL OF SACRED MUSIC (1947). 1 W. 4 St., NYC 10012. (212)674–5300, ext. 225. FAX: (212)388–1720. Dir. Israel Goldstein. Trains cantors for congregations; offers MSM degree. *Sacred Music Press.*

———, SKIRBALL CULTURAL CENTER (see p. 525)

INSTITUTE OF TRADITIONAL JUDAISM (1990). 811 Palisade Ave., Teaneck, NJ 07666. (201)801–0707. FAX: (201)801–0449. Rector (Reish Metivta) Rabbi David Weiss Halivni; Dean Rabbi Ronald D. Price. A nondenominational halakhic rabbinical school dedicated to genuine faith combined with intellectual honesty and the love of Israel. Graduates receive "yoreh yoreh" smikhah.

JEWISH THEOLOGICAL SEMINARY OF AMERICA (1886; reorg. 1902). 3080 Broadway, NYC 10027–4649. (212)678–8000. FAX: (212)678–8947. Chancellor Dr. Ismar Schorsch; Bd. Chmn. Gershon Kekst. Operates undergraduate and graduate programs in Judaic studies; professional schools for training Conservative rabbis and cantors; the JTS Library; the Ratner Center for the Study of Conservative Judaism; Melton Research Center for Jewish Education; the Jewish Museum; Ramah Camps and the Prozdor high-school honors program. Other outreach activities include the Distance Learning Project, the Lehrhaus Adult Learning Institute, the Finkelstein Institute for Religious and Social Studies, the Havruta Program, and the Wagner Institute lay leadership program. *Academic Bulletin; JTS Magazine; Gleanings; JTS Update.*

———, ALBERT A. LIST COLLEGE OF JEWISH STUDIES (formerly SEMINARY COLLEGE OF JEWISH STUDIES–TEACHERS INSTITUTE) (1909). 3080 Broadway, NYC 10027. (212)678–8826. Dean Dr. Shuly Rubin Schwartz. Offers complete undergraduate program in Judaica leading to BA degree; conducts joint programs with Columbia University and Barnard College enabling students to receive two BA degrees.

———, DEPARTMENT OF RADIO AND TELEVISION (1944). 3080 Broadway, NYC 10027. (212)678–8020. Produces radio and TV programs expressing the Jewish tradition in its broadest sense, including hour-long documentaries on NBC and ABC. Distributes cassettes of programs at minimum charge.

———, GRADUATE SCHOOL OF JTS (formerly INSTITUTE FOR ADVANCED STUDY IN THE HUMANITIES) (1968). 3080 Broadway, NYC 10027-4649. (212)678–8024. FAX: (212)678-8947. E-mail: gradschool@jtsa.edu. Dean Stephen P. Garfinkel; Asst. Dean Bruce E. Nielsen. Programs leading to MA, DHL, and PhD degrees in Judaic studies; specializations include Ancient Judaism, Bible and Ancient Semitic Languages, Interdepartmental Studies, Jewish Art and Material Culture, Jewish education, Jewish history, Jewish literature, Jewish philosophy, Jewish Women's Studies, Liturgy, Medieval

Jewish Studies, Midrash, Modern Jewish studies, Talmud and Rabbinics and Dual Degree Program with Columbia University School of Social Work.

———, H.L. MILLER CANTORIAL SCHOOL AND COLLEGE OF JEWISH MUSIC (1952). 3080 Broadway, NYC 10027. (212)678–8036. FAX: (212)678–8947. Dean Dr. Boaz Tarsi. Trains cantors, music teachers, and choral directors for congregations. Offers full-time programs in sacred music leading to degree of MSM, and diploma of *Hazzan*.

———, JEWISH MUSEUM (see p. 523)

———, LIBRARY OF THE JEWISH THEOLOGICAL SEMINARY. 3080 Broadway, NYC 10027. (212)678–8075. FAX: (212) 678–8998. E-mail: library@jtsa.edu. Librarian Dr. Mayer E. Rabinowitz. Contains one of the largest collections of Hebraica and Judaica in the world, including manuscripts, incunabula, rare books, and Cairo Geniza material. The 320,000-item collection includes books, manuscripts, periodicals, sound recordings, prints, broadsides, photographs, postcards, microform, videos and CD-ROM. Exhibition of items from the collection are ongoing. Exhibition catalogs are available for sale. The Library is open to the public for on-site use (photo identification required). Visit the Library's web site at www.jtsa.edu/library. *Between the Lines.*

———, LOUIS FINKELSTEIN INSTITUTE FOR RELIGIOUS AND SOCIAL STUDIES (1938). 3080 Broadway, NYC 10027. (212)|678–8000 ext. 8576. FAX: (212) 678–8947. E-mail: finkelstein@jtsa.edu. Dir. Rabbi Gerald Wolpe. Since 1938 has maintained an innovative interfaith and intergroup relations program, pioneering new approaches to dialogue across religious lines. Through scholarly and practical fellowship, highlights the relevance of Judaism and other contemporary religions to current theological, ethical, and scientific issues, including the emerging challenge of bioethics.

———, MELTON RESEARCH CENTER FOR JEWISH EDUCATION (1960). 3080 Broadway, NYC 10027. (212)678–8031. E-mail: stbrown@jtsa.edu. Dir. Dr. Steven M. Brown; Admin. Lisa Siberstein-Weber. Develops new curricula and materials for Jewish education; prepares educators through seminars and in-service programs; maintains consultant and supervisory relationships with a limited number of pilot schools; develops and implements research initiatives; sponsors "renewal" etreats. *Gleanings; Courtyard: A Journal of Research and Reflection on Jewish Education.*

———, NATIONAL RAMAH COMMISSION (1947). 3080 Broadway, NYC 10027. (212)678–8881. FAX: (212)749–8251. Pres. Alan H. Silberman; Natl. Dir. Sheldon Dorph. Sponsors an international network of 14 summer camps located in the US, Canada, South America, Russia, and Israel, emphasizing Jewish education, living, and culture; offers opportunities for qualified college students and older to serve as counselors, administrators, specialists, etc., and programs for children with special needs (Tikvah program); offers special programs in U.S. and Israel, including National Ramah Staff Training Institute, Ramah Israel Seminar, Ulpan Ramah Plus, and Tichon Ramah Yerushalayim. Family and synagogue tours to Israel and summer day camp in Israel for Americans.

———, REBECCA AND ISRAEL IVRY PROZDOR (1951). 3080 Broadway, NYC 10027. (212)678–8824. E-mail: prozdor@jtsa.edu. Principal Rabbi Judd Kruger Levingston; Community Advisory Board Chmn. Michael Katz. The Hebrew high school of JTS, offers a program of Jewish studies for day school and congregational school graduates in classical texts, Hebrew, interdisciplinary seminars, training in educational leadership, and classes for college credit. Classes meet one evening a week and on Sundays in Manhattan and at affiliated programs. High School Curricula.

———, RABBINICAL SCHOOL (1886). 3080 Broadway, NYC 10027. (212)678–8817. Dean Rabbi William Lebeau. Offers a program of graduate and professional studies leading to the degree of Master of Arts and ordination; includes one year of study in Jerusalem and an extensive fieldwork program.

———, SAUL LIEBERMAN INSTITUTE FOR TALMUDIC RESEARCH (1985). 3080 Broadway, NYC 10027. (212)678–8994. FAX: (212)678D8947. E-mail: liebinst@jtsa.edu. Dir. Shamma Friedman; Coord. Jonathan Milgram. Engaged in preparing for publication a series of scholarly editions of selected chapters of the Talmud. The following projects support and help disseminate the research:Talmud Text Database; Bibliography of Talmudic Literature; Catalogue of Geniza Fragments.

———, SCHOCKEN INSTITUTE FOR JEWISH RESEARCH (1961). 6 Balfour St., Jerusalem, Israel 92102. (972)2–631288. Dir. Shmuel Glick. Comprises the Schocken collection of rare books and manuscripts and a research institute dedicated to the exploration of Hebrew religious poetry (*piyyut*). *Schocken Institute Yearbook (P'raqim)*.

———, WILLIAM DAVIDSON GRADUATE SCHOOL OF JEWISH EDUCATION (1996). 3080 Broadway, NYC 10027. (212) 678-8030. E-mail: edschool@jtsa.edu. Dean Dr. Aryeh Davidson. Offers master's and doctoral degrees in Jewish education; continuing education courses for Jewish educators and Jewish communal professionals; and programs that take advantage of the latest technology, including distance learning and interactive video classrooms.

MAALOT–A SEMINARY FOR CANTORS AND JUDAISTS (1987). 15 W. Montgomery Ave., Suite 204, Rockville, MD 20850. (301)309–2310. FAX: (301)309–2328. Pres./Exec. Off. David Shneyer. An educational program established to train individuals in Jewish music, the liturgical arts, and the use, design, and application of Jewish customs and ceremonies. Offers classes, seminars, and an independent study program.

MESIVTA YESHIVA RABBI CHAIM BERLIN RABBINICAL ACADEMY (1905). 1605 Coney Island Ave., Brooklyn, NY 11230. (718)377–0777. Exec. Dir. Y. Mayer Lasker. Maintains fully accredited elementary and high schools; collegiate and postgraduate school for advanced Jewish studies, both in America and Israel; Camp Morris, a summer study retreat; Prof. Nathan Isaacs Memorial Library; Gur Aryeh Publications.

NER ISRAEL RABBINICAL COLLEGE (1933). 400 Mt. Wilson Lane, Baltimore, MD 21208. (410)484–7200. FAX: (410)484–3060. Rabbi Yaakov S. Weinberg, Rosh Hayeshiva; Pres. Rabbi Herman N. Neuberger. Trains rabbis and educators for Jewish communities in America and worldwide. Offers bachelor's, master's, and doctoral degrees in talmudic law, as well as teacher's diploma. College has four divisions: Israel Henry Beren High School, Rabbinical College, Teachers Training Institute, Graduate School. Maintains an active community-service division. Operates special programs for Iranian and Russian Jewish students. *Ner Israel Update; Alumni Bulletin; Ohr Hanair Talmudic Journal; Iranian B'nei Torah Bulletin.*

RABBINICAL COLLEGE OF TELSHE, INC. (1941). 28400 Euclid Ave., Wickliffe, OH 44092. (216)943–5300. Pres. Rabbi Mordecai Gifter; V.-Pres. Rabbi Abba Zalka Gewirtz; Rosh Hayeshiva Pres. Rabbi Mordechai Gifter. College for higher Jewish learning specializing in talmudic studies and rabbinics; maintains a preparatory academy including a secular high school, postgraduate department, teacher-training school, and teachers' seminary for women. *Pri Etz Chaim; Peer Mordechai; Alumni Bulletin.*

RECONSTRUCTIONIST RABBINICAL COLLEGE (1968). 1299 Church Rd., Wyncote, PA 19095. (215)576–0800. FAX: (215)576–6143. E-mail: rrcinfo@rrc.edu. Pres. David Teutsch; Bd. Chmn. Jacques G. Pomeranz; Genl. Chmn. Aaron Ziegelman. Coeducational. Trains rabbis and cantors for all areas of Jewish communal life:synagogues, academic and educational positions, Hillel centers, federation agencies, and chaplaincy for hospitals, hospices, and geriatric centers; confers title of rabbi and cantor and grants degrees of Master and Doctor of Hebrew Letters. *RRC Report; Reconstructionist.*

SPERTUS INSTITUTE OF JEWISH STUDIES (1924). 618 S. Michigan Ave., Chicago, IL 60605. (312)922–9012. FAX: (312)922–6406. Pres. Howard A. Sulkin; Bd. Chmn. Barbara Levy Kipper; V.-Pres. for Academic Affairs Byron L. Sherwin. An accredited institution of higher learning offering one doctor of Jewish studies degree; master's degree programs in Jewish studies, Jewish education, Jewish communal service, and human-services administration; plus an extensive program of continuing education. Major resources of the college encompass Spertus Museum, Asher Library, Chicago Jewish Archives, and Spertus College of Judaica Press.

———, SPERTUS MUSEUM (see p. 526)

TOURO COLLEGE (1970). Executive Offices: Empire State Bldg., 350 Fifth Ave., Suite 1700, NYC 10118. (212)643–0700. FAX: (212)643–0759. Pres. Dr. Bernard Lander; Bd. Chmn. Mark Hasten. Chartered by NY State Board of Regents as a non-profit four-year college with Judaic studies, health sciences, business, and liberal arts programs leading to BA, BS, and MA degrees; emphasizes relevance of Jewish heritage to general culture of Western civilization. Also offers JD degree and a biomedical program leading to the MD degree from Technion–Israel Institute of Technology, Haifa.

———, COLLEGE OF LIBERAL ARTS AND SCIENCES. 27–33 W. 23 St., NYC 10010. (212)463–0400. FAX: (212)627–9144. Exec. Dean Stanley Boylan. Offers comprehensive Jewish studies along with studies in the arts, sciences, humanities, and preprofessional studies in health sciences, law, accounting, business, computer science, education, and finance. Women's Division, 160 Lexington Ave., NYC 10016. (212)213–2230. FAX: (212)683–3281. Dean Sara E. Freifeld.

———, JACOB D. FUCHSBERG LAW CENTER (1980). Long Island Campus, 300 Nassau Rd., Huntington, NY 11743. (516) 421–2244. Dean Howard A. Glickstein. Offers studies leading to JD degree.

———, BARRY Z. LEVINE SCHOOL OF HEALTH SCIENCES AND CENTER FOR BIO-MEDICAL EDUCATION (1970). 135 Common Rd., Bldg. #10, Dix Hills, NY 11746. (516)673–3200. Dean Dr. Joseph Weisberg. Along with the Manhattan campus, offers 5 programs: 5-year program leading to MA from Touro and MD from Faculty of Medicine of Technion–Israel Institute of Technology, Haifa; BS/MA–physical therapy and occupational therapy programs; BS–physician assistant and health-information management programs.

———, SCHOOL OF GENERAL STUDIES. 240 E. 123 St., NYC 10021. (212) 722–1575. Dean Stephen Adolphus. Offers educational opportunities to minority groups and older people; courses in the arts, sciences, humanities, and special programs of career studies.

———, TOURO COLLEGE FLATBUSH CENTER (1979). 1277 E. 14 St., Brooklyn, NY 11230. (718)253–7538. Dean Robert Goldschmidt. A division of the College of Liberal Arts and Sciences; options offered in accounting and business, education, mathematics, political science, psychology, and speech. Classes are given on weeknights and during the day on Sunday.

———, GRADUATE SCHOOL OF JEWISH STUDIES (1981). 160 Lexington Ave., NYC 10016. (212)213–2230. FAX: (212)683–3281. Pres. Bernard Lander; Dean Michael A. Shmidman. Offers courses leading to an MA in Jewish studies, with concentrations in Jewish history or Jewish education. Students may complete part of their program in Israel, through MA courses offered by Touro faculty at Touro's Jerusalem center.

———, INSTITUTE OF JEWISH LAW. (516) 421–2244. Based at Fuchsberg Law Center, serves as a center and clearinghouse for study and teaching of Jewish law. Coedits *Dinei Israel* (Jewish Law Journal) with Tel Aviv University Law School.

———, TOURO COLLEGE ISRAEL CENTER. 23 Rehov Shivtei Yisrael, Jerusalem. 2–894–086/088. Assoc. Dean Carmi Horowitz; Resident Dir. Chana Sosevsky. Offers undergraduate courses in business, computer science, and education. Houses the MA degree program in Jewish studies. The Touro Year Abroad Option for American students is coordinated from this center.

———, MOSCOW BRANCH. Oztozhenka #38, Moscow, Russia 119837. Offers BS program in business and BA program in Jewish studies.

UNIVERSITY OF JUDAISM (1947). 15600 Mulholland Dr., Bel Air, CA 90077. (310) 476–9777. FAX: (310)471–1278. Pres. Dr. Robert D. Wexler; V.-Pres. Academic Affairs Dr. Hanan Alexander; Asst. Dean of Students Dr. Jill Landesberg. The College of Arts and Sciences is an accredited liberal arts college for undergraduates offering a core curriculum of Jewish, Western, and non-Western studies, with majors including bioethics (a premedical track in partnership with Cedars-Sinai Medical Center), business, English, Jewish studies, journalism, literature & politics, political science, psychology, and U.S. public policy. Accredited graduate programs in nonprofit business administration (MBA), Jewish education, and psychology with an emphasis on developmental disabilities. The Ziegler School of Rabbinic Studies provides an intensive four-year program with Conservative ordination. Home of the Center for Policy Options, conducting public policy research in areas of concern to the Jewish community, and the Whizin Center for the Jewish Future, a research and programming institute. Offers the largest adult Jewish education program in the U.S., cultural-arts programs, and a variety of outreach services for West Coast Jewish communities. *Bulletin of General Information; University of Judaism Magazine.*

WEST COAST TALMUDICAL SEMINARY (Yeshiva Ohr Elchonon Chabad) (1953). 7215 Waring Ave., Los Angeles, CA 90046. (213)937–3763. FAX: (213)937–9456. Dean Rabbi Ezra Schochet. Provides facilities for intensive Torah education as well as Orthodox rabbinical training on the West Coast; conducts an accredited college preparatory high school combined with a full program of Torah-talmudic training and a graduate talmudical division on the college level. *Torah Quiz; Kovetz Migdal Ohr; Kovetz Ohr HaMigdal.*

YESHIVA TORAH VODAATH AND MESIVTA TORAH VODAATH RABBINICAL SEMINARY (1918). 425 E. 9 St., Brooklyn, NY 11218. (718)941–8000. Bd. Chmn. Chaim Leshkowitz. Offers Hebrew and secular education from elementary level through rabbinical ordination and postgraduate work; maintains a teachers institute and community-service bureau; maintains a dormitory and a nonprofit camp program for boys. *Chronicle; Mesivta Vanguard; Thought of the Week; Torah Vodaath News; Ha'Mesifta.*

———, YESHIVA TORAH VODAATH ALUMNI ASSOCIATION (1941). 425 E. 9 St., Brooklyn, NY 11218. (718)941–8000. Pres. George Weinberger. Promotes social and cultural ties between the alumni and the schools through classes and lectures and fund-raising; offers vocational guidance to students; operates Camp Ohr Shraga; sponsors research fellowship program for boys. *Annual Journal; Hamesivta Torah periodical.*

YESHIVA UNIVERSITY (1886). Main Campus, 500 W. 185 St., NYC 10033–3201. (212)960–5400. FAX: (212)960–0055. Pres. Dr. Norman Lamm; Chmn. Bd. of Trustees David S. Gottesman. In its second century, the nation's oldest and most comprehensive independent university founded under Jewish auspices, with 18 undergraduate and graduate schools, divisions, and affiliates; widespread programs of research and community outreach; publications; and a museum. A broad range of curricula lead to bachelor's, master's, doctoral, and professional degrees. Undergraduate schools provide general studies curricula supplemented by courses in Jewish learning; graduate schools prepare for careers in medicine, law, social work, Jewish education, psychology, Jewish studies, and other fields. It has seven undergraduate schools, seven graduate and professional schools, and four affiliates. *Yeshiva University Review; Yeshiva University Today.*

Yeshiva University has four campuses in Manhattan and the Bronx: Main Campus, 500 W. 185 St., NYC 10033–3201; Midtown Center, 245 Lexington Ave., NYC 10016–4699; Brookdale Center, 55 Fifth Ave., NYC 10003–4391; Jack and Pearl Resnick Campus, Eastchester Rd. & Morris Pk. Ave., Bronx, NY 10461–1602.

Undergraduate schools for men at Main Campus (212)960–5400: Yeshiva College (Bd. Chmn. Jay Schottenstein; Dean Dr. Norman T. Adler) provides liberal arts and sciences curricula; grants BA degree. Isaac Breuer College of Hebraic Studies (Dean Dr. Michael D. Shmidman) awards Hebrew teacher's diploma, AA, BA, and BS. James Striar School of General Jewish Studies (Dean Dr. Michael D. Shmidman) grants AA degree. Yeshiva Program/Mazer School of Talmudic Studies (Dean Rabbi Zevulun Charlop) offers advanced course of study in Talmudic texts and commentaries. Beit Midrash Program (Dean Dr. Michael D. Shmidman) offers diversified curriculum combining Talmud with Jewish studies.

Undergraduate school for women at Midtown Center (212)340–7700: Stern College for Women (Bd. Chmn. Lea Eisenberg; Dean Dr. Karen Bacon) offers liberal arts and sciences curricula supplemented by Jewish studies programs; awards BA, AA, and Hebrew teacher's diploma.

Sy Syms School of Business at Main Campus and Midtown Center (Bd. Chmn. Josh S. Weston; Dean Dr. Harold Nierenberg) offers undergraduate business curricula in conjunction with study at Yeshiva College or Stern College; grants BS degree.

———, ALBERT EINSTEIN COLLEGE OF MEDICINE (1955). Eastchester Rd. & Morris Pk. Ave., Bronx, NY 10461–1602. (718)430–2000. Pres. Dr. Norman Lamm; Chpers. Bd. of Overseers Burton P. Resnick; Dean Dr. Dominick P. Purpura. Prepares physicians and conducts research in the health sciences; awards MD degree; includes Sue Golding Graduate Division of Medical Sciences (Dir. Dr. Anne M. Etgen), which grants PhD degree. Einstein's clinical facilities and affiliates encompass Jack D. Weiler Hospital of Albert Einstein College of Medicine, Jacobi Medical Center, Montefiore Medical Center, Long Island Jewish Medical Center, Beth Israel Medical Center, Catholic Medical Center of Brooklyn and Queens, Bronx-Lebanon Hospital Center, Wyckoff Heights Medical Center, and Rose F. Kennedy Center for Research in Mental Retardation and Human Development. *Einstein; Einstein Today; Einstein Quarterly Journal of Biology and Medicine.*

———, ALUMNI OFFICE, 500 W. 185 St., NYC 10033–3201. (212)960–5373. University Dir. Alumni Affairs Robert R. Saltzman; Dir. Undergraduate Alumni Relations Toby Hilsenrad Weiss. Seeks to foster a close allegiance of alumni to their alma mater by maintaining ties with all alumni and servicing the following associations: Yeshiva College Alumni (Pres. Harry Peters); Stern College for Women Alumnae (Pres. Jan Schechter); Sy Syms School of Business Alumni (Copres. Ofer and Elizabeth Naor); Albert Einstein College of Medicine Alumni (Pres. Dr. Neal Flomenbaum); Ferkauf Graduate School of Psychology Alumni (Pres. Dr. Judith Kaufman); Wurzweiler School of Social Work Alumni (Coord. Lori M. Zimmerman); Rabbinic Alumni (Pres. Rabbi Marc D. Angel); Benjamin N. Cardozo School of Law Alumni (Chmn. Karel Turner). *Yeshiva University Review;*

AECOM Alumni News; Wurzweiler Update; Jewish Social Work Forum.

———, AZRIELI GRADUATE SCHOOL OF JEWISH EDUCATION AND ADMINISTRATION (1945). 245 Lexington Ave., NYC 10016–4699. (212)340–7705. Dir. Dr. Yitzchak S. Handel. Offers MS degree in Jewish elementary and secondary education; specialist's certificate and EdD in administration and supervision of Jewish education. Block Education Program, initiated under a grant from the Jewish Agency's L.A. Pincus Fund for the Diaspora, provides summer course work to complement year-round field instruction in local communities.

———, BELFER INSTITUTE FOR ADVANCED BIOMEDICAL STUDIES (1978). Eastchester Rd. & Morris Pk. Ave., Bronx, NY 10461–1602. (718)430–4106. Dir. Dr. Chester M. Edelmann, Jr. Integrates and coordinates the Albert Einstein College of Medicine's postdoctoral research and training-grant programs in the basic and clinical biomedical sciences. Awards certificate as research fellow or research associate on completion of training.

———, BENJAMIN N. CARDOZO SCHOOL OF LAW (1976). 55 Fifth Ave., NYC 10003–4391. (212)790–0200. Pres. Dr. Norman Lamm; Chmn. Bd. of Dirs. Earle I. Mack; Dean Paul R. Verkuil. Provides innovative courses of study within a traditional legal framework; program includes judicial internships; grants juris doctor (JD) degree. Programs and services include institute for advanced legal studies; center for ethics in the practice of law; legal services clinic; international institute and Israel program; institute of Jewish law; international law and humanrights programs; and other special programs. *Cardozo Law Review; Cardozo Arts and Entertainment Law Journal; Cardozo Women's Law Journal; Cardozo Journal of International and Comparative Law; Cardozo Studies in Law and Literature; Journal of the Copyright Society of the USA; Post-Soviet Media Law and Policy Newsletter; New York Real Estate Reporter.*

———, BERNARD REVEL GRADUATE SCHOOL (1935). 500 W. 185 St., NYC 10033–3201. (212)960–5253. Pres. Dr. Norman Lamm; Chmn. Bd. of Dirs. Mordecai D. Katz; Dean Dr. Arthur

Hyman. Offers graduate programs in Bible, Talmudic studies, Jewish history, and Jewish philosophy; confers MA and PhD degrees. Harry Fischel School for Higher Jewish Studies offers the Revel program during the summer.

———, FERKAUF GRADUATE SCHOOL OF PSYCHOLOGY (1957). Eastchester Rd. & Morris Pk. Ave., Bronx, NY 10461–1602. (718)430–3850. Pres. Dr. Norman Lamm; Chmn. Bd. of Govs. Samson Bitensky; Dean Dr. Lawrence J. Siegel. Offers MA in general psychology; PsyD in clinical and school-clinical child psychology; and PhD in developmental and clinical health psychology. Project for the Study of the Disturbed Adolescent; Psychological and Psychoeducational Services Clinic.

———, (affiliate) RABBI ISAAC ELCHANAN THEOLOGICAL SEMINARY (1896). 2540 Amsterdam Ave., NYC 10033–9986. (212)960–5344. Chmn. Bd. of Trustees Judah Feinerman; V.-Pres. for Administration & Professional Education Rabbi Robert S. Hirt; Dean Rabbi Zevulun Charlop. Leading center in the Western Hemisphere for higher learning in the Orthodox tradition of Judaism. RIETS complex encompasses 15 educational entities and a major service and outreach center with some 20 programs. Grants semikhah (ordination) and the degrees of master of religious education, master of Hebrew literature, doctor of religious education, and doctor of Hebrew literature. Kollelim include Marcos and Adina Katz Kollel (Institute for Advanced Research in Rabbinics) (Dir. Rabbi Hershel Schachter); Kollel l'Horaah (Yadin Yadin) and External Yadin Yadin (Dir. Rabbi J. David Bleich); Ludwig Jesselson Kollel Chaverim (Dir. Rabbi J. David Bleich); Caroline and Joseph S. Gruss Kollel Elyon (Postgraduate Kollel Program) (Dir. Rabbi Aharon Kahn); Caroline and Joseph S. Gruss Institute in Jerusalem (Dir. Rabbi Aharon Lichtenstein).

The seminary sponsors one high school for boys (Manhattan) and one for girls (Queens).

The service arm of the seminary, Max Stern Division of Communal Services (Dir. Rabbi Robert S. Hirt), provides personal and professional service to the rabbinate and related fields, as well as educational, consultative, organizational, and placement services to congregations, schools, and communal organizations around the world; coordinates a broad spectrum of outreach programs, including Center for Jewish Education, Program for the Enhancement of Professional Rabbinics, Kiruv College Outreach Program, and others. Sephardic components are Jacob E. Safra Institute of Sephardic Studies and the Institute of Yemenite Studies; Sephardic Community Program; Dr. Joseph and Rachel Ades Sephardic Outreach Program; Maybaum Sephardic Fellowship Program.

———, PHILIP AND SARAH BELZ SCHOOL OF JEWISH MUSIC (1954). 560 W. 185 St., NYC 10033–3201. (212)960–5353. Dir. Cantor Bernard Beer. Provides professional training of cantors and courses in Jewish liturgical music; maintains a specialized library and conducts outreach; awards associate cantor's certificate and cantorial diploma.

———, (affiliate) YESHIVA OF LOS ANGELES (1977). 9760 W. Pico Blvd., Los Angeles, CA 90035–4701. (213)553–4478. Dean Rabbi Marvin Hier; Bd. Chmn. Samuel Belzberg; Dir. Academic Programs Rabbi Sholom Tendler. Provides Jewish studies program for beginners. Affiliates are high schools, Jewish Studies Institute for Adult Education, and Simon Wiesenthal Center.

———, SIMON WIESENTHAL CENTER (see p. 525)

———, WOMEN'S ORGANIZATION (1928). 500 W. 185 St., NYC 10033–3201. (212) 960–0855. Chmn. Natl. Bd. Dinah Pinczower. Supports Yeshiva University's national scholarship program for students training in education, community service, law, medicine, and other professions, and its development program.

———, WURZWEILER SCHOOL OF SOCIAL WORK (1957). 500 W. 185 St., NYC 10033–3201. (212)960–0800. Pres. Norman Lamm; Chmn. Bd. of Govs. David I. Schachne; Dean Dr. Sheldon R. Gelman. Offers graduate programs in social work and Jewish communal service; grants MSW and DSW degrees and certificate in Jewish communal service. MSW programs are: Concurrent Plan, 2-year, full-time track, combining classroom study and supervised field instruction; Plan for Employed Persons (PEP), for people working in social agencies; Block Education Plan (Dir. Dr. Adele Weiner), which combines summer course work with regular-year field placement in local agencies; Clergy Plan, training in counseling for clergy of all denominations; Center for Professional Training in the Care of the Elderly. *Jewish Social Work Forum.*

———, YESHIVA UNIVERSITY MUSEUM (see p. 527)

SOCIAL, MUTUAL BENEFIT

ALPHA EPSILON PI FRATERNITY (1913). 8815 Wesleyan Rd., Indianapolis, IN 46268–1171. (317)876–1913. FAX: (317)876–1057. E-mail: aepihq@indy. net; www.aepihq.org. Internatl. Pres. Gary A. Shapiro; Exec. V.-Pres. Sidney N. Dunn. International Jewish fraternity active on over 100 campuses in the U.S. and Canada; encourages Jewish students to remain loyal to their heritage and to assume leadership roles in the community; active in behalf of Soviet Jewry, the State of Israel, the United States Holocaust Memorial Museum, Tay Sachs Disease, Mazon:A Jewish Response to Hunger, and other causes. *The Lion of Alpha Epsilon Pi (quarterly magazine).*

AMERICAN ASSOCIATION OF JEWS FROM THE FORMER USSR, INC. (1989). 45 E. 33 St., Suite 3A, New York, NY 10016. (212)779–0383, (516)937–3819. FAX: (212)684–0471, (516)937-3819. Pres. Leonid Stonov; V.-Pres. Inna Arolovich. National not-for-profit mutual-assistance and refugee-advocacy organization, which unites and represents interests of 500,000 Russian-speaking Jewish immigrants from the former Soviet Union. Has chapters in 12 states, Chapter of Struggle Against Anti-Semitism and Xenophobia, Council of Assistance to Veterans Organizations and Club of Intellectuals (House of Scientists) in NYC. Assists newcomers in their resettlement and vocational and cultural adjustment; fosters their Jewish identity and involvement in civic and social affairs; fights anti-Semitism and violation of human rights in the FSU and the U.S. through lobbying and advocacy; provides assistance on social safety net and naturalization for elderly and disabled; advocates in cases of political asylum for victims of anti-Semitism in the FSU. *Chronicle of Anti-Semitism and Nationalism in Republics of the Former Soviet Union (in English, annually); Information Bulletin (in Russian, bimonthly).*

AMERICAN FEDERATION OF JEWS FROM CENTRAL EUROPE, INC. (1938). 570 Seventh Ave., NYC 10018. (212)921–3871. FAX: (212)575–1918. Pres. Fritz Weinschenk; Bd. Chmn. Curt C. Silberman; Exec. Asst. Dennis E. Rohrbaugh. Seeks to safeguard the rights and interests of American Jews of German-speaking Central European descent, especially in reference to restitution and indemnification; through its affiliate Research Foundation for Jewish Immigration sponsors research and publications on the history, immigration, and acculturation of Central European émigrés in the U.S. and worldwide; through its affiliate Jewish Philanthropic Fund of 1933 supports social programs for needy Nazi victims in the U.S.; undertakes cultural activities, annual conferences, publications; member, Council of Jews from Germany, London.

AMERICAN VETERANS OF ISRAEL (1949). 136 E. 39 St., NYC 10016. Pres. Sam Klausner; Sec. Sidney Rabinovich. Maintains contact with American and Canadian volunteers who served in Aliyah Bet and/or Israel's War of Independence; promotes Israel's welfare; holds memorial services at grave of Col. David Marcus; is affiliated with World Mahal. *Newsletter.*

ASSOCIATION OF YUGOSLAV JEWS IN THE UNITED STATES, INC. (1941). 130 E. 59 St., Suite 1202, NYC 10022. (212)371–6891. Pres. Mary Levine; Exec. Off. Emanuel Salom; Treas./V.-Pres. Mirko Goldschmidt. Assists all Jews originally from Yugoslavia; raises funds for Israeli agencies and institutions. *Bulletin.*

BNAI ZION–THE AMERICAN FRATERNAL ZIONIST ORGANIZATION (1908). 136 E. 39 St., NYC 10016. (212)725–1211. FAX: (212)684–6327. Pres. Alan G. Hevesi; Exec. V.-Pres. Mel Parness. Fosters principles of Americanism, fraternalism, and Zionism; offers life insurance and other benefits to its members. The Bnai Zion Foundation supports various humanitarian projects in Israel and the USA, chiefly the Bnai Zion Medical Center in Haifa and homes for retarded children–Maon Bnai Zion in Rosh Ha'ayin and the Herman Z. Quittman Center in Jerusalem.

Also supports building of new central library in Ma'aleh Adumim. In U.S. sponsors program of awards for excellence in Hebrew for high school and college students. Chapters all over U.S. and a new leadership division in Greater N.Y. area. *Bnai Zion Voice; Bnai Zion Foundation Newsletter.*

BRITH ABRAHAM (1859; reorg. 1887). 136 E. 39 St., NYC 10016. (212)725–1211. FAX: (212)684–6327. Grand Master Robert Freeman; Grand Sec. Joseph Levin. Protects Jewish rights and combats anti-Semitism; supports Soviet and Ethiopian emigration and the safety and dignity of Jews worldwide; helps to support Bnai Zion Medical Center in Haifa and other Israeli institutions; aids and supports various programs and projects in the U.S.: Hebrew Excellence Program–Gold Medal presentation in high schools and colleges; Camp Loyaltown; Brith Abraham and Bnai Zion Foundations. *Voice.*

BRITH SHOLOM (1905). 3939 Conshohocken Ave., Philadelphia, PA 19131. (215) 878–5696. FAX: (215) 878–5699. Pres. Saul Cohen; Exec. Dir. Albert Liss. Fraternal organization devoted to community welfare, protection of rights of Jewish people, and activities that foster Jewish identity and provide support for Israel. Through its philanthropic arm, the Brith Sholom Foundation (1962), sponsors Brith Sholom House in Philadelphia, nonprofit senior-citizen apartments; and Brith Sholom Beit Halochem in Haifa, Israel, rehabilitation, social, and sports center for disabled Israeli veterans, operated by Zahal. Chmn. Bennett Goldstein; Exec. Dir. Saundra Laub. *Brith Sholom Digest; monthly news bulletin.*

CENTRAL SEPHARDIC JEWISH COMMUNITY OF AMERICA WOMEN'S DIVISION, INC. (1941). 8 W. 70 St., NYC 10023. (212) 787–2850. Pres. Irma Lopes Cardozo; Treas. Laura Capelluto; Rec. Sec. Esther Shear. Promotes Sephardic culture by awarding scholarships to qualified needy students in New York and Israel; raises funds for hospital and religious institutions in U.S. and Israel. *Yearly Journal.*

FREE SONS OF ISRAEL (1849). 250 Fifth Ave., Suite 201, NYC 10001. (212)725–3690. FAX: (212)725–5874. Grand Master Charles Mackoff; Grand Sec. Richard

Reiner. Oldest Jewish fraternal-benefit order in U.S. Supports the State of Israel; fights anti-Semitism; helps Soviet Jewry. Maintains scholarship fund for members and children of members; insurance fund and credit union; social functions. *Free Sons Reporter.*

JEWISH LABOR BUND (Directed by WORLD COORDINATING COMMITTEE OF THE BUND) (1897; reorg. 1947). 25 E. 21 St., NYC 10010. (212)473–5101. FAX: (212) 473-5102. Sec. Gen. Benjamin Nadel. Coordinates activities of Bund organizations throughout the world and represents them in the Socialist International; spreads the ideas of socialism as formulated by the Jewish Labor Bund; publishes books and periodicals on world problems, Jewish life, socialist theory and policy, and on the history, activities, and ideology of the Jewish Labor Bund. *Unser Tsait* (U.S.); *Lebns-Fragn* (Israel); *Unser Gedank* (Australia).

SEPHARDIC JEWISH BROTHERHOOD OF AMERICA, INC. (1915). 97–45 Queens Blvd., Rm. 610, Rego Park, NY 11374. (718)459–1600. Pres. Bernard Ouziel; Sec. Michael Cohen. A benevolent fraternal organization seeking to promote the industrial, social, educational, and religious welfare of its members. *Sephardic Brother.*

THE WORKMEN'S CIRCLE/ARBETER RING (1900). 45 E. 33 St., NYC 10016. (212) 889–6800. FAX: (212)532–7518. E-mail: wcfriends@aol.com. Pres. Mark Mlotek; Exec. Dir. Robert A. Kaplan. Fosters Jewish identity and participation in Jewish life through Jewish, especially Yiddish, culture and education, friendship, mutual aid, and the pursuit of social and economic justice. Offices are located throughout the U.S. and Canada. Member services include:Jewish cultural seminars, concerts, theater, Jewish schools, children's camp and adult resort, fraternal and singles activities, a Jewish Book Center, public affairs/social action, health insurance plans, medical/dental/legal services, life insurance plans, cemetery/funeral benefits, social services, geriatric homes and centers, and travel services. *The Call.*

ZETA BETA TAU FRATERNITY (1898). 3905 Vincennes Rd., Suite 101, Indianapolis, IN 46268. (317)334–1898. FAX: (317)

334-1899. E-mail: zbt@zbtnational.org. Pres. Ronald J. Taylor, M.D. Oldest and historically largest Jewish fraternity; promotes intellectual awareness, social responsibility, integrity, and brotherhood among over 5,000 undergrads and 110,000 alumni in the U.S. and Canada. Encourages leadership and diversity through mutual respect of all heritages; nonsectarian since 1954. A brotherhood of Kappa Nu, Phi Alpha, Phi Epsilon Pi, Phi Sigma Delta, Zeta Beta Tau. *The Deltan (quarterly magazine).*

SOCIAL WELFARE

AMC CANCER RESEARCH CENTER (formerly JEWISH CONSUMPTIVES' RELIEF SOCIETY, 1904; incorporated as American Medical Center at Denver, 1954). 1600 Pierce St., Denver, CO 80214. (303) 233-6501. FAX: (303)894-8791. Pres./CEO Bob R. Baker; Scientific Dir. Dr. Douglass C. Tormey. A nationally recognized leader in the fight against cancer; employs a three-pronged, interdisciplinary approach that combines laboratory, clinical, and community cancer-control research to advance the prevention, early detection, diagnosis, and treatment of disease. *The Quest for Answers (quarterly).*

AMCHA FOR TSEDAKAH (1990). 9800 Cherry Hill Rd., College Park, MD 20740. (301)937-2600. Pres. Rabbi Bruce E. Kahn. Solicits and distributes contributions to Jewish charitable organizations in the U.S. and Israel; accredits organizations which serve an important tsedakah purpose, demonstrate efficiency and fiscal integrity, and also support pluralism. Contributors are encouraged to earmark contributions for specific organizations; all contributions to General Fund are forwarded to the charitable institutions, as operating expenses are covered by a separate fund. *Newspaper supplement.*

AMERICAN JEWISH CORRECTIONAL CHAPLAINS ASSOCIATION, INC. (formerly NATIONAL COUNCIL OF JEWISH PRISON CHAPLAINS) (1937). 10 E. 73 St., NYC 10021-4194. (212)879-8415. FAX: (212) 772-3977. (Cooperates with the New York Board of Rabbis.) Pres. Rabbi Irving Koslowe. Supports spiritual, moral, and social services for Jewish men and women in corrections; stimulates support of correctional chaplaincy; provides spiritual and professional fellowship for Jewish correctional chaplains; promotes sound standards for correctional chaplaincy; schedules workshops and research to aid chaplains in counseling and with religious services for Jewish inmates. Constituent, American Correctional Chaplains Association. *Chaplains Manual.*

AMERICAN JEWISH SOCIETY FOR SERVICE, INC. (1950). 15 E. 26 St., Rm. 1029, NYC 10010. (212)683-6178. Founder/Chmn. Kenry Kohn; Pres. Arthur Lifson; Exec. Dirs. Carl and Audrey Brenner. Conducts voluntary work-service camps each summer to enable high-school juniors and seniors to perform humanitarian service.

ASSOCIATION OF JEWISH AGING SERVICES (formerly NORTH AMERICAN ASSOCIATION OF JEWISH HOMES AND HOUSING FOR THE AGING) (1960). 316 Pennsylvania Ave., SE, Suite 402, Washington, DC 20003. (202) 543-7500. FAX: (202)543-4090. E-mail: ajas@ajas.org. Pres. Lawrence M. Zippin; Chmn. Harvey Finkelstein. Represents nearly all the not-for-profit charitable homes and housing for the Jewish aging; promotes excellence in performance and quality of service through fostering communication and education and encouraging advocacy for the aging; conducts annual conferences and institutes. *Directory; Membership Handbook.*

ASSOCIATION OF JEWISH CENTER PROFESSIONALS (1918). 15 E. 26 St., NYC 10010-1579. (212)532-4949. FAX: (212) 481-4174. E-mail: ajcp@jcca.org. Pres. Jay R. Roth; V.-Pres. Karen Stern; Exec. Dir. Marilyn Altman. Seeks to enhance the standards, techniques, practices, scope, and public understanding of Jewish Community Center and kindred agency work. *Kesher.*

ASSOCIATION OF JEWISH COMMUNITY ORGANIZATION PERSONNEL (AJCOP) (1969). 14619 Horseshoe Trace, Wellington, FL 33414. (561)795-4853. FAX: (561)798-0358. Pres. Allan Gelfond; Exec. Dir. Louis B. Solomon. An organization of professionals engaged in areas of fundraising, endowments, budgeting, social planning, financing, administration, and coordination of services. Objectives are to develop and enhance professional practices in Jewish communal work; to maintain and improve standards, practices, scope, and public understanding of the field of community organization, as practiced through local federations, national agencies, other organizations, settings, and private practitioners. *Prolog (quarterly newspaper).*

ASSOCIATION OF JEWISH FAMILY AND CHILDREN'S AGENCIES (1972). 3086 State Highway 27, Suite 11, PO Box 248, Kendall Park, NJ 08824-0248. (800) 634-7346. FAX: (732)821-0493. E-mail: ajfca@aol.com. Pres. Jerry Harwood; Exec. V.-Pres. Bert J. Goldberg. The national service organization for Jewish family and children's agencies in the U.S. and Canada. Reinforces member agencies in their efforts to sustain and enhance the quality of Jewish family and communal life. Operates the Elder Support Network for the national Jewish community. *Tachlis (quarterly); Professional Opportunities Bulletin; Executive Digest (monthly).*

BARON DE HIRSCH FUND (1891). 130 E. 59 St., NYC 10022. (212)836-1358. FAX: (212)755-9183. Pres. Seymour W. Zises; Mng. Dir. Lauren Katzowitz. Aids Jewish immigrants in the U.S. and Israel by giving grants to agencies active in educational and vocational fields; has limited program for study tours in U.S. by Israeli agriculturists.

B'NAI B'RITH (1843). 1640 Rhode Island Ave., NW, Washington, DC 20036. (202)857-6600. FAX: (202)857-1099. Pres. Tommy Baer; Exec. V.-Pres. Dr. Sidney Clearfield. International Jewish organization, with affiliates in 55 countries. Offers programs designed to ensure the preservation of Jewry and Judaism: Jewish education, community volunteer service, expansion of human rights, assistance to Israel, housing for the elderly, leadership training, rights of Jews in all countries to study their heritage. *International Jewish Monthly.*

——, ANTI-DEFAMATION LEAGUE OF (see p. 516)

——, HILLEL (see p. 545)

——, KLUTZNICK MUSEUM (see p. 521)

——, YOUTH ORGANIZATION (see p. 543)

CITY OF HOPE NATIONAL MEDICAL CENTER AND BECKMAN RESEARCH INSTITUTE (1913). 1500 E. Duarte Rd., Duarte, CA 91010. (818)359-8111. FAX: (818) 301-8115. E-mail: sphillips@smtplink. coh.org. Pres. and CEO Dr. Charles Balch; Bd. Chmn. Gil N. Schwartzberg. Offers care to those with cancer and other catastrophic diseases, medical consultation service for second opinions, and research programs in genetics, immunology, and the basic life process. *City of Hope Cancer Research Center Report.*

CONFERENCE OF JEWISH COMMUNAL SERVICE (see JEWISH COMMUNAL SERVICE ASSOCIATION OF N. AMERICA)

COUNCIL OF JEWISH FEDERATIONS, INC. (1932). 111 Eighth Ave., Suite 11E, NYC 10011. (212)284-6500. FAX: (212)284-6835. Pres. Dr. Conrad L. Giles; Exec. V.-Pres. Martin Kraar. Provides national and regional services to more than 200 associated federations embracing 800 communities in the U.S. and Canada, aiding in fund-raising, community organization, health and welfare planning, personnel recruitment, and public relations; operates CJF satellite network linking 75 federations throughout North America for conferences, seminars, training, and board meetings; initiated and coordinates the Jewish Online Network, providing E-mail, bulletin board, teleconference, and Internet access services to subscribers. *Directory of Jewish Federations, Welfare Funds and Community Councils; Directory of Jewish Health and Welfare Agencies (biennial); What's New in Federations; annual report.*

INTERNATIONAL ASSOCIATION OF JEWISH VOCATIONAL SERVICES (formerly JEWISH OCCUPATIONAL COUNCIL) (1939). 1845 Walnut St., Suite 608, Philadelphia, PA 19103. (215)854-0233. FAX: (215)854-0212. E-mail: intljvs@aol.com. Pres. Leonard Kulakofsky; Exec. Dir. Dr. Marvin S. Kivitz. Liaison and coordinating body for 26 vocational and family service agencies in the U.S., Israel, and Canada that provide a broad range of counseling, training, job-placement, and rehabilitation services to the Jewish and general community. These services are available to the public as well as to many refugee populations.

INTERNATIONAL COUNCIL ON JEWISH SOCIAL AND WELFARE SERVICES (1961). c/o American Jewish Joint Distribution Committee, 711 Third Ave., NYC 10017. (NY liaison office with UN headquarters.)

(212)687–6200. FAX: (212)370-5467. E-mail: ajjdc@mcimail.com. Chmn. David Cope-Thompson; Exec. Sec. Eli Benson. Provides for exchange of views and information among member agencies on problems of Jewish social and welfare services, including medical care, old age, welfare, child care, rehabilitation, technical assistance, vocational training, agricultural and other resettlement, economic assistance, refugees, migration, integration, and related problems; representation of views to governments and international organizations. Members:six national and international organizations.

JEWISH BRAILLE INSTITUTE OF AMERICA, INC. (1931). 110 E. 30 St., NYC 10016. (212)889–2525. FAX: (212)689–3692. Pres. Selma Shavitz; Exec. V.-Pres. Gerald M. Kass. Provides Judaic materials in braille, talking books, and large print for blind, visually impaired, and reading-disabled; offers counseling for full integration into the life of the Jewish community. International program serves clients in more than 40 countries; sponsors special programs in Israel and Eastern Europe to assist the elderly as well as students. *Jewish Braille Review; JBI Voice; Likutim, Hebrew-language magazine on blindness issues.*

JEWISH CHILDREN'S ADOPTION NETWORK (1990). PO Box 16544, Denver CO 80216–0544. (303)573–8113. FAX: (303) 893–1447. Pres. Stephen Krausz; Exec. Dir. Vicki Krausz. An adoption exchange founded for the primary purpose of locating adoptive families for Jewish infants and children. Works with some 200 children a year, throughout N. Amer., 85–90% of whom have special needs. No fees charged for services, which include birth-parent and adoptive-parent counseling. *Quarterly newsletter.*

JEWISH COMMUNAL SERVICE ASSOCIATION OF N. AMERICA (1899; formerly CONFERENCE OF JEWISH COMMUNAL SERVICE). 3084 State Hwy. 27, Suite 9, Kendall Park, NJ 08824–1657. (732)821–1871. FAX: (732)821–5335. E-mail: jcsana@ aol.com. Pres. Mark Handelman; Exec. Dir. Joel Ollander. Serves as forum for all professional philosophies in community service, for testing new experiences, proposing new ideas, and questioning or reaffirming old concepts; umbrella organization for 7 major Jewish communal

service groups. Concerned with advancement of professional personnel practices and standards. *Concurrents; Journal of Jewish Communal Service.*

JEWISH COMMUNITY CENTERS ASSOCIATION OF NORTH AMERICA (formerly JWB) (1917). 15 E. 26 St., NYC 10010–1579. (212)532–4949. FAX: (212)481–4174. E-mail: info@jcca.org. Pres. Ann Kaufman; Exec. V.-Pres. Allan Finkelstein. Central leadership agency for 275 Jewish Community Centers, YM-YWHAs, and camps in the U.S. and Canada, serving over one million Jews. Provides a variety of consulting services and staff training programs to members, including informal Jewish educational and cultural experiences in Israel. U.S. government-accredited agency for the religious, Jewish educational, and recreational needs of Jewish military personnel, their families, and hospitalized VA patients through JWB Jewish Chaplains Council. JCC Circle; Professional Employment Opportunities; Chaplines; Jewish Educator's Forum.

———, JEWISH WELFARE BOARD JEWISH CHAPLAINS COUNCIL (formerly COMMISSION ON JEWISH CHAPLAINCY) (1940). 15 E. 26 St., NYC 10010–1579. Chmn. Rabbi Matthew H. Simon; Dir. Rabbi David Lapp. Recruits, endorses, and serves Jewish military and Veterans Administration chaplains on behalf of the American Jewish community and the major rab-binic bodies; trains and assists Jewish lay leaders where there are no chaplains, for service to Jewish military personnel, their families, and hospitalized veterans. *CHAPLINES newsletter.*

JEWISH CONCILIATION BOARD OF AMERICA, INC. (A division of the JEWISH BOARD OF FAMILY AND CHILDREN'S SERVICES) (1920). 17 Battery Place, Rm. 615 N, NYC 10004. (212) 425–5051, ext. 3310. FAX: (212)509–9243. Pres. Seymour R. Askin, Jr.; Exec. V.-Pres. Dr. Alan B. Siskind. Offers dispute-resolution services to families, individuals, and organizations. Social-work, rabbinic, and legal expertise is available to individuals and families for conciliation.

JEWISH FAMILY AND CHILDREN'S PROFESSIONALS ASSOCIATION (*see* Jewish Social Services Professionals Association)

JEWISH FUND FOR JUSTICE (1984). 260 Fifth Ave., Suite 701, NYC 10001. (212)

213–2113. FAX: (212)213–2233. E-mail: justiceusa@aol.com. Bd. Chmn. Ronna Stamm; Exec. Dir. Marlene Provizer. A national grant-making foundation supporting efforts to combat the causes and consequences of poverty in the U.S. Provides diverse opportunities for giving, including family and youth endowment funds and the Purim Fund for Women in Poverty; develops educational materials linking Jewish teachings and rituals with contemporary social justice issues; supports Jewish involvement in community-based anti-poverty efforts; and works cooperatively with other denominational and social change philanthropies. *Annual report, newsletter.*

JEWISH FUNDERS NETWORK (1990). 15 E. 26 St., Suite 1038, New York City 10010. (212) 726-0177. FAX: (212) 726-0195. E-mail: jfn@jfunders.org. Chmn. Mark R. Kramer; Exec. Dir. Evan Mendelson. A national membership organization dedicated to advancing the growth and quality of Jewish philanthropy through more effective grant making; brings together individual philanthropists, foundation trustees, and foundation staff to discuss emerging issues, gain expertise in the operational aspects of grant making, explore family dynamics and intergenerational issues of family foundations, and exchange information among peers. *JFN Newsletter.*

JEWISH SOCIAL SERVICES PROFESSIONALS ASSOCIATION (1965). c/o AJFCA, PO Box 248, Kendall Park, NJ 08824-0493. (800)634–7346. FAX: (732)821–0493. E-mail: ajfca@aol.com. Chmn. Alan Goodman. Brings together executives, supervisors, managers, caseworkers, and related professionals in Jewish Family Service and related agencies.Seeks to enhance professional skills, improve personnel standards, further Jewish continuity and identity, and strengthen Jewish family life. Provides a national and regional forum for professional discussion and learning; functions under the auspices of the Association of Jewish Family and Children's Agencies. *Newsletter.*

JEWISH WOMEN INTERNATIONAL (formerly B'NAI B'RITH WOMEN) (1897). 1828 L St., NW, Suite 250, Washington, DC 20036. (202)857–1300. FAX: (202)857–1380. E-mail: jwi@jwi.org. Pres. Randee Lefkow; Exec. Dir. Gail Rubinson. Strengthens the lives of women, children, and families through education, advocacy, and action. Focusing on family violence and the emotional health of children, JWI serves as an agent for change—locally, nationally, and around the world. Offers programs in the United States, Canada, and Israel. *Women's World (quarterly newsletter).*

JWB (*see* Jewish Community Centers Association of North America)

LEVI HOSPITAL (sponsored by B'nai B'rith) (1914). 300 Prospect Ave., Hot Springs, AR 71901. (501)624–1281. FAX: (501) 622–3500. Pres. Dr. Hal Koppel; Admin. Patrick G. McCabe. Offers arthritis treatment, including therapy sessions in large thermal heated pool. Other programs: Levi Life Center, adult inpatient and outpatient psychiatric program, child/adolescent psychiatric clinic, hospice care, home health care, osteoporosis clinic, Levi Rehabilitation Unit, a cooperative effort of Levi and St. Joseph's hospitals (inpatient rehab), and TEAM Rehabilitation Center, a joint venture of Levi and St. Joseph's (outpatient rehab). *The Progress Chart.*

MAZON: A JEWISH RESPONSE TO HUNGER (1985). 12401 Wilshire Blvd., Suite 303, Los Angeles, CA 90025. (310)442–0020. FAX: (310)442–0030. E-mail: mazonmail@aol.com. Bd. Chmn. Mark C. Levy; Sr. Exec. Dir. Irving Cramer. A grant-making and fund-raising organization that raises funds in the Jewish community and provides grants to nonprofit 501(c)(3) organizations which aim to prevent and alleviate hunger in the United States and abroad. Grantees include food pantries, food banks, multi-service organizations, advocacy, education and research projects, and international relief and development organizations. 1997 grants totaled $2 million. *Mazon Newsletter.*

NATIONAL ASSOCIATION OF JEWISH CHAPLAINS (1988). 901 Route 10, Whippany, NJ 07981. (201)884–4800. FAX: (201) 736–9193. Pres. Rabbi Howard Kummer; Natl. Coord. Cecille Asekoff. A professional organization for people functioning as Jewish chaplains in hospitals, nursing homes, geriatric, psychiatric, correctional, and military facilities. Provides collegial support, continuing education, professional certification, and resources for the Jewish community on issues of pastoral and spiritual care. *The Jewish Chaplain.*

NATIONAL COUNCIL OF JEWISH PRISON CHAPLAINS, INC. (*see* American Jewish Correctional Chaplains Association, Inc.)

NATIONAL COUNCIL OF JEWISH WOMEN (1893). 53 W. 23 St., NYC 10010. (212)645-4048. FAX: (212)645-7466. E-mail: ncjwomen@cjf.noli.com. Pres. Nan Rich; Exec. Dir. Susan Katz. Works to improve the lives of women, children, and families in the United States and Israel; strives to insure individual rights and freedoms for all. NCJW volunteers deliver vital services in 500 U.S. communities and carry out NCJW's advocacy agenda through a powerful grassroots network. *NCJW Journal; Washington Newsletter.*

NATIONAL INSTITUTE FOR JEWISH HOSPICE (1985). 8723 Alden Drive, Suite S 148, Los Angeles, CA 90048. (800)446-4448; (213) Hospice (Calif. only). FAX: (201) 816-7321. Pres. Rabbi Maurice Lamm; Exec. Dir. Shirley Lamm. Serves as a national Jewish hospice resource center. Through conferences, research, publications, referrals, and counseling services offers guidance, training, and information to patients, family members, clergy of all faiths, professional caregivers, and volunteers who work with the Jewish terminally ill. *Jewish Hospice Times.*

NATIONAL JEWISH CHILDREN'S LEUKEMIA FOUNDATION (1990). 1310 48 St., Brooklyn, NY 11219. (718)853-0510. FAX: (718)853-7988. E-mail: leukemia@erols. com. Pres./Founder Tzvi Shor. Dedicated to saving the lives of children:bone marrow donor search and matching; harvesting and freezing cells from a baby's umbilical cord for long-term storage and possible future use to replace the traditional bone marrow transplant, for this child or someone with same genetic makeup; Make-A-Dream-Come-True program, granting the wishes of children with leukemia.

NATIONAL JEWISH MEDICAL AND RESEARCH CENTER (formerly NATIONAL JEWISH HOSPITAL/NATIONAL ASTHMA CENTER) (1899). 1400 Jackson St., Denver, CO 80206. (800)222-LUNG. Pres. & CEO Lynn M. Taussig, MD; Bd. Chmn. Meyer Saltzman. The only medical and research center in the United States devoted entirely to respiratory, allergic, and immune system diseases, including asthma, tuberculosis, emphysema, severe allergies, AIDS, and cancer, and autoimmune diseases such as lupus. Dedicated to enhancing prevention, treatment, and cures through research, and to developing and providing innovative clinical programs for treating patients regardless of age, religion, race, or ability to pay. New Directions; *Medical Scientific Update.*

NORTH AMERICAN ASSOCIATION OF JEWISH HOMES AND HOUSING FOR THE AGING (*see* Association of Jewish Aging Services)

UNITED ORDER TRUE SISTERS, INC. (UOTS) (1846). 212 Fifth Ave., NYC 10010. (212)679-6790. Pres. Vivian Walsh; Exec. Admin. Dorothy B. Giuriceo. Charitable, community service, especially home supplies, etc., for indigent cancer victims; supports camps for children with cancer. *Echo.*

WORLD COUNCIL OF JEWISH COMMUNAL SERVICE (1966; reorg. 1994). 711 Third Ave., 10th fl., NYC 10017. (212) 687-6200. FAX: (212)370-5467. Pres. Stephen D. Solender; Assoc. Pres. Zvi Feine; Exec. V.-Pres. Theodore Comet. Seeks to build Jewish community worldwide by enhancing professional-to-professional connections, improving professional practice through interchange of experience and sharing of expertise, fostering professional training programs, and stimulating research. Conducts quadrennial conferences in Jerusalem and periodic regional meetings. *Proceedings of international conferences; newsletters.*

PROFESSIONAL ASSOCIATIONS*

AMERICAN ASSOCIATION OF RABBIS (Religious, Educational)

AMERICAN CONFERENCE OF CANTORS, UNION OF AMERICAN HEBREW CONGREGATIONS (Religious, Educational)

AMERICAN JEWISH CORRECTIONAL CHAPLAINS ASSOCIATION, INC. (Social Welfare)

---

*For fuller listing see under categories in parentheses.

AMERICAN JEWISH PRESS ASSOCIATION (Cultural)

AMERICAN JEWISH PUBLIC RELATIONS SOCIETY (1957). 575 Lexington Ave., Suite 600, NYC 10022. (212)446–5863. FAX: (212)644–6358. Pres. Henry R. Hecker; Treas. Diane Ehrlich. Advances professional status of public-relations practitioners employed by Jewish organizations and institutions or who represent Jewish-related clients, services, or products; upholds a professional code of ethics and standards; provides continuing education and networking opportunities at monthly meetings; serves as a clearinghouse for employment opportunities. *AJPRS Reporter; AJPRS Membership Directory.*

ASSOCIATION OF HILLEL/JEWISH CAMPUS PROFESSIONALS (Religious, Educational)

ASSOCIATION OF JEWISH CENTER PROFESSIONALS (Social Welfare)

ASSOCIATION OF JEWISH COMMUNITY ORGANIZATION PERSONNEL (Social Welfare)

ASSOCIATION OF JEWISH COMMUNITY RELATIONS WORKERS (Community Relations)

CANTORS ASSEMBLY (Religious, Educational)

CENTRAL CONFERENCE OF AMERICAN RABBIS (Religious, Educational)

COUNCIL OF JEWISH ORGANIZATIONS IN CIVIL SERVICE (Community Relations)

INTERNATIONAL JEWISH MEDIA ASSOCIATION (Cultural)

JEWISH CHAPLAINS COUNCIL, JWB (Social Welfare)

JEWISH COMMUNAL SERVICE ASSOCIATION OF N. AMERICA (Social Welfare)

JEWISH EDUCATORS ASSEMBLY, UNITED SYNAGOGUE OF CONSERVATIVE JUDAISM (Religious, Educational)

JEWISH SOCIAL SERVICES PROFESSIONALS ASSOCIATION (Social Welfare)

JEWISH TEACHERS ASSOCIATION–MORIM (Religious, Educational)

NATIONAL ASSOCIATION OF HEBREW DAY SCHOOL ADMINISTRATORS, TORAH UMESORAH (Religious, Educational)

NATIONAL ASSOCIATION OF JEWISH CHAPLAINS (Social Welfare)

NATIONAL ASSOCIATION OF TEMPLE ADMINISTRATORS, UNION OF AMERICAN HEBREW CONGREGATIONS (Religious, Educational)

NATIONAL ASSOCIATION OF TEMPLE EDUCATORS, UNION OF AMERICAN HEBREW CONGREGATIONS (Religious, Educational)

NATIONAL CONFERENCE OF YESHIVA PRINCIPALS, TORAH UMESORAH (Religious, Educational)

NORTH AMERICAN ASSOCIATION OF SYNAGOGUE EXECUTIVES, UNITED SYNAGOGUE OF CONSERVATIVE JUDAISM (Religious, Educational)

RABBINICAL ALLIANCE OF AMERICA (Religious, Educational)

RABBINICAL ASSEMBLY (Religious, Educational)

RABBINICAL COUNCIL OF AMERICA (Religious, Educational)

RECONSTRUCTIONIST RABBINICAL ASSOCIATION (Religious, Educational)

UNION OF ORTHODOX RABBIS OF THE U.S. AND CANADA (Religious, Educational)

WORLD CONFERENCE OF JEWISH COMMUNAL SERVICE (Community Relations)

WOMEN'S ORGANIZATIONS*

AMIT WOMEN (Israel-Related)

BRANDEIS UNIVERSITY NATIONAL WOMEN'S COMMITTEE (1948). PO Box 9110, MS 132, Waltham, MA 02254–9110. (781) 736–4160. FAX: (781)736–4183. Pres. Ellen J. Atlas; Exec. Dir. Joan C. Bowen. A friends-of-the-library organization whose mission is to provide financial support for the Brandeis Libraries; works to enhance the image of Brandeis, a Jewish-sponsored, nonsectarian university. Offers its members opportunity for intellectual pursuit, continuing education, community service, social interaction, personal enrichment, and leadership development. Open to all, regardless of race, religion, nationality, or gender. *Imprint.*

---

*For fuller listing see under categories in parentheses.

EMUNAH WOMEN OF AMERICA (Israel-Related)

HADASSAH, THE WOMEN'S ZIONIST ORGANIZATION OF AMERICA (Israel-Related)

JEWISH WOMEN INTERNATIONAL (Social Welfare)

NA'AMAT USA, THE WOMEN'S LABOR ZIONIST ORGANIZATION OF AMERICA (Israel-Related)

NATIONAL COUNCIL OF JEWISH WOMEN (Social Welfare) UOTS (Social Welfare)

WOMEN OF REFORM JUDAISM–FEDERATION OF TEMPLE SISTERHOODS, UNION OF AMERICAN HEBREW CONGREGATIONS (Religious, Educational)

WOMEN'S AMERICAN ORT, AMERICAN ORT FEDERATION (Overseas Aid)

WOMEN'S BRANCH OF THE UNION OF ORTHODOX JEWISH CONGREGATIONS OF AMERICA (Religious, Educational)

WOMEN'S DIVISION OF POALE AGUDATH ISRAEL OF AMERICA (Israel-Related)

WOMEN'S LEAGUE FOR CONSERVATIVE JUDAISM (Religious, Educational)

WOMEN'S LEAGUE FOR ISRAEL, INC. (Israel-Related)

WOMEN'S ORGANIZATION, YESHIVA UNIVERSITY (Religious, Educational)

YOUTH AND STUDENT ORGANIZATIONS*

AGUDATH ISRAEL OF AMERICA (Religious, Educational)

B'NAI B'RITH YOUTH ORGANIZATION (Religious, Educational)

BNEI AKIVA OF NORTH AMERICA, RELIGIOUS ZIONISTS OF AMERICA (IsraelRelated)

HABONIM-DROR NORTH AMERICA (Israel-Related)

HASHOMER HATZAIR, SOCIALIST ZIONIST YOUTH MOVEMENT (Israel-Related)

HILLEL (Religious, Educational)

KADIMA, UNITED SYNAGOGUE OF CONSERVATIVE JUDAISM (Religious, Educational)

NATIONAL CONFERENCE OF SYNAGOGUE YOUTH, UNION OF ORTHODOX JEWISH CONGREGATIONS OF AMERICA (Religious, Educational)

NATIONAL JEWISH COMMITTEE ON SCOUTING (Religious, Educational)

NATIONAL JEWISH GIRL SCOUT COMMITTEE (Religious, Educational) (Israel-Related)

NORTH AMERICAN ALLIANCE FOR JEWISH YOUTH (1996). 50 W. 58 St., NYC 10019. (212)303–4598. FAX: (212)303–4572. E-mail: dkrakow@aol.com. Chmn. Doron Krakow. Serves the cause of informal Jewish and Zionist education in America; provides a forum for the professional leaders of the major N. American youth movements, camps, Israel programs, and university programs to address common issues and concerns, and to represent those issues with a single voice to the wider Jewish and Zionist community. Sponsors annual Conference on Informal Jewish Education for Jewish youth professionals from across the continent.

NORTH AMERICAN FEDERATION OF TEMPLE YOUTH, UNION OF AMERICAN HEBREW CONGREGATIONS (Religious, Educational)

STUDENT STRUGGLE FOR SOVIET JEWRY–see CENTER FOR RUSSIAN JEWRY (Community Relations)

YOUNG JUDAEA/HASHACHAR, HADASSAH (Israel-Related)

YUGNTRUF–YOUTH FOR YIDDISH (Cultural)

CANADA

B'NAI BRITH CANADA (1875). 15 Hove St., Downsview, ONT M3H 4Y8. (416) 633–6224. FAX: (416)630–2159. E-mail: fdimant@bnaibrith.ca. Pres. Lyle Smordin; Exec. V.-Pres. Frank Dimant. Canadian Jewry's major advocacy and service organization; maintains an office of Government Relations in Ottawa and cosponsors the Canada Israel Committee; makes representations to all levels of government on matters of Jewish concern; promotes humanitarian causes and educational programs, community projects, adult Jewish education, and leadership development; dedicated to the

---

*For fuller listing see under categories in parentheses.

preservation and unity of the Jewish community in Canada and to human rights. *The Jewish Tribune.*

————, INSTITUTE FOR INTERNATIONAL AFFAIRS (1987). Natl. Chmn. Dr. Lawrence Hart; Natl. Dir. Lisa Armony. Identifies and protests the abuse of human rights throughout the world. Monitors the condition of Jewish communities worldwide and advocates on their behalf when they experience serious violations of their human rights. *Institute Report.*

————, LEAGUE FOR HUMAN RIGHTS (1964). Natl. Chmn. Rochelle Wilner; Natl. Dir. Dr. Karen Mock. National volunteer association dedicated to combating racism, bigotry, and anti-Semitism. Educational programs include multicultural antiracist workshops, public speakers, Holocaust education, Media Human Rights Awards; legal and legislative activity includes government submissions, court interventions, monitoring hategroup activity, responding to incidents of racism and anti-Semitism; community liaison includes intergroup dialogue and support for aggrieved vulnerable communities and groups. Canadian distributor of ADL material. *Heritage Front Report: 1994; Anti-Semitism on Campus; Skinheads in Canada; Annual Audit of Anti-Semitic Incidents; Holocaust and Hope Educators' Newsletter; Combatting Hate: Guidelines for Community Action.*

————, NATIONAL FIELD SERVICES DEPARTMENT. Natl. Dir. Pearl Gladman. Services community affordable housing projects, sports leagues, food baskets for the needy; coordinates hands-on national volunteer programming, Tel-Aide Distress Line; responsible for lodge membership; direct-mail campaigns, annual convention and foundation dinners.

CANADIAN FRIENDS OF CALI & AMAL (1944). 7005 Kildare Rd., Suite 14, Cote St. Luc, Quebec, H4W 1C1. (514) 484–9430. FAX: (514)484–0968. Pres. Harry J.F. Bloomfield, QC; Exec. Dir. Fran Kula. Incorporates Canadian Association for Labour Israel (Histadrut) and Canadian Friends of Amal; supports comprehensive health care and education in Israel. Helps to provide modern medical and surgical facilities and the finest vocational, technical education to the Israeli people of all ages.

CANADIAN FRIENDS OF THE HEBREW UNIVERSITY OF JERUSALEM (1944). 3080 Yonge St., Suite 5024, Toronto, ONT M4N 3N1. (416) 485–8000. FAX: (416)485–8565. Pres. Dr. Charles C. Gold; Exec. Dir. Mark Gryfe. Represents the Hebrew University of Jerusalem in Canada; serves as fund-raising arm for the university in Canada; recruits Canadian students and promotes study programs for foreign students at the university; sponsors social and educational events across Canada. *Dateline Jerusalem.*

CANADIAN JEWISH CONGRESS (1919; reorg. 1934). 1590 Dr. Penfield Ave., Montreal, PQ H3G 1C5. (514)931–7531. FAX: (514)931–0548. E-mail: canadianjewishcongress@cjc.ca. Pres. Goldie Hershon; Natl. Exec. Dir. and Genl. Counsel Jack Silverstone. The official voice of Canadian Jewish communities at home and abroad; acts on all matters affecting the status, rights, concerns, and welfare of Canadian Jewry; internationally active on behalf of world Jewry, Holocaust remembrance and restitution; largest Jewish archives in Canada. *National Small Communities Newsletter; DAIS; National Archives Newsletter; regional newsletters.*

ORT CANADA (1948). 3101 Bathurst St., Suite 604, Toronto, ONT M6A 2A6. (416)787–0339. FAX: (416) 787-9420. E-mail: ortcan@pathcom.com. Pres. Kathleen Crook; Admin. Dir. Robyn Raisin; Dir. of Dev. Edna Levitt. Chapters in 11 Canadian cities raise funds for ORT's nonprofit global network of schools, where Jewish students learn a wide range of marketable skills, including the most advanced high-tech professions. *Focus Magazine.*

CANADIAN YOUNG JUDAEA (1917). 788 Marlee Ave., Suite 205, Toronto, ONT M6B 3K1. (416)781–5156. FAX: (416) 787–3100. Natl. Shaliach Ryan Hass; Eastern Region Shaliah Yoram Abrisor; Natl. Exec. Dir. Risa Epstein. Strives to attract Jewish youth to Zionism, with goal of aliyah; educates youth about Jewish history and Zionism; prepares them to provide leadership in Young Judaea camps in Canada and Israel and to be concerned Jews. *The Judaean.*

CANADIAN ZIONIST FEDERATION (1967). 5250 Decarie Blvd., Suite 550, Montreal,

PQ H3X 2H9. (514)486–9526. FAX: (514)483–6392. Pres. Kurt Rothschild; Natl. Sec. Florence Simon. Umbrella organization of distinct constituent member Zionist organizations in Canada; carries on major activities in all areas of Jewish life through its departments of education and culture, aliyah, youth and students, public affairs, and small Jewish communities, for the purpose of strengthening the State of Israel and the Canadian Jewish community. *Canadian Zionist.*

———, BUREAU OF EDUCATION AND CULTURE (1972). Pres. Kurt Rothschild. Provides counseling by pedagogic experts, inservice teacher-training courses and seminars in Canada and Israel; national pedagogic council and research center; distributes educational material and teaching aids; conducts annual Bible contest and Hebrew-language courses for adults; awards scholarships to Canadian high-school graduates studying for one year in Israel.

FRIENDS OF PIONEERING ISRAEL (1950s). 1111 Finch Ave. W., Suite 456, Downsview, ONT M3J 2E5. (416)736–1339. FAX: (416)736–1405. Pres. Joseph Podemsky. Acts as a voice of Socialist-Democratic and Zionist points of view within the Jewish community and a focal point for progressive Zionist elements in Canada; Canadian representative of Meretz; affiliated with Hashomer Hatzair and the Givat Haviva Educational Institute.

HADASSAH–WIZO ORGANIZATION OF CANADA (1917). 1310 Greene Ave., Suite 900, Montreal, PQ H3Z 2B8. (514) 937–9431. FAX: (514)933–6483. Pres. Patricia Joy Alpert; Exec. V.-Pres. Lily Frank. Largest women's volunteer Zionist organization in Canada, located in 43 Canadian cities; dedicated to advancing the quality of life of the women and children in Israel through financial assistance and support of its many projects, day-care centers, schools, institutions, and hospitals. In Canada, the organization promotes Canadian ideals of democracy and is a stalwart advocate of women's issues. *Orah Magazine.*

HASHOMER HATZAIR (1913). 1111 Finch Ave. W., #456, Downsview, ONT M3J 2E5. (416)736–1339. FAX: (416)736–1405. E-mail: cfgh@the-wire.com. Pres. Yehuda Marle; Exec. Off. Mintzy

Clement. Zionist youth movement associated with the Kibbutz Artzi Federation in Israel. Educational activities emphasize Jewish culture and identity as well as the kibbutz lifestyle and values; runs winter and summer camps as well as programs in Israel.

INTERNATIONAL JEWISH CORRESPONDENCE (IJC) (1978). c/o Canadian Jewish Congress, 1590 Dr. Penfield Ave., Montreal, PQ H3G 1C5. (514)931–7531. FAX: (514)931–0548. E-mail: barrys@cjc.ca. Founder-Dir. Barry Simon. Aims to encourage contact between Jews of all ages and backgrounds, in all countries, through pen-pal correspondence. Send autobiographical data and stamped self-addressed envelope or its equivalent (to cover cost of Canadian postage) to receive addresses.

JEWISH IMMIGRANT AID SERVICES OF MONTREAL (JIAS) (1922). 5151 Cote Ste. Catherine Rd., Suite 220, Montreal, PQ H3W 1M6. (514)342–9351. FAX: (514)342–8452. E-mail: jiasmtrl@cjf. noli.com. Pres. Leslie Borshy; Exec. Dir. Bob Luck. Agency for immigration and immigrant welfare and integration.

JEWISH NATIONAL FUND OF CANADA (Keren Kayemeth Le'Israel, Inc.) (1901). 1980 Sherbrooke St. W., Suite 500, Montreal, PQ H3H 1E8. (514)934–0313. FAX: (514)934–0382. Natl. Pres. Naomi Frankenburg; Exec. V.-Pres. Avner Regev. Fund-raising organization affiliated with the World Zionist Organization; involved in afforestation, soil reclamation, and development of the land of Israel, including the construction of roads and preparation of sites for new settlements; provides educational materials and programs to Jewish schools across Canada.

LABOUR ZIONIST ALLIANCE OF CANADA (1909). 272 Codsell Ave., Downsview, ONT. M3H 3X2. (416)630–9444. FAX: (416)636–5248. Pres. Josef Krystal; City Committee Chmn. Montreal–Harry Froimovitch. Associated with the World Labor Zionist movement and allied with the Israel Labor party. Provides recreational and cultural programs, mutual aid, and fraternal care to enhance the social welfare of its membership; actively promotes Zionist education, cultural projects, and forums on aspects of Jewish and Canadian concern.

MIZRACHI ORGANIZATION OF CANADA (1941). 296 Wilson Ave., North York, ONT M3H 1S8. (416)630–9266. FAX: (416)630–2305. Pres. Jack Kahn; Exec. V.-Pres. Rabbi Menachem Gopin. Promotes religious Zionism, aimed at making Israel a state based on Torah; maintains Bnei Akiva, a summer camp, adult education program, and touring department; supports Mizrachi-Hapoel Hamizrachi and other religious Zionist institutions in Israel which strengthen traditional Judaism. *Mizrachi Newsletter; Or Hamizrach Torah Quarterly.*

NATIONAL COMMUNITY RELATIONS COMMITTEE OF CANADIAN JEWISH CONGRESS (1936). 4600 Bathurst St., Willowdale, ONT M2R 3V2. (416)635–2883. FAX: (416)635–1408. E-mail: ncrccjc@ibm. net. Chmn. Hal Joffe; Pres. Goldie Hershon; Dir. Bernie M. Farber. Seeks to safeguard the status, rights, and welfare of Jews in Canada; to combat anti-Semitism, and promote understanding and goodwill among all ethnic and religious groups.

NATIONAL COUNCIL OF JEWISH WOMEN OF CANADA (1897). 118–1588 Main St., Winnipeg, MAN R2V 1Y3. (204)339–9700. FAX: (204)334–3779. E-mail: info @ncjwc.org. Pres. Hinda Simkin; V.-Pres. Gita Arnold, Sharon Allentuck, & Carol Slater. Dedicated to furthering human welfare in the Jewish and general communities, locally, nationally, and internationally; through an integrated program of education, service, and social action seeks to fulfill unmet needs and to serve the individual and the community. *National ByLines.*

STATE OF ISRAEL BONDS (CANADA-ISRAEL SECURITIES, LTD.) (1953). 970 Lawrence Ave. W., Suite 502, Toronto, ONT M6A 3B6. (416)789–3351. FAX: (416)789–9436. Pres. Norman Spector; Bd. Chmn. George A. Cohon. An international securities organization offering interest-bearing instruments issued by the government of Israel. Invests in every aspect of Israel's economy, including agriculture, commerce, and industry. Israel Bonds are RRSP-approved.

Jewish Federations, Welfare Funds, Community Councils

UNITED STATES

ALABAMA

BIRMINGHAM

BIRMINGHAM JEWISH FEDERATION (1936; reorg. 1971); PO Box 130219 (35213); (205)879–0416. FAX: (205)803–1526. Pres. Ronne Hess; Exec. Dir. Richard Friedman.

MOBILE

MOBILE JEWISH WELFARE FUND, INC. (inc. 1966); One Office Park, Suite 219 (36609); (334)343–7197. Pres. Iris Fetterman.

MONTGOMERY

JEWISH FEDERATION OF MONTGOMERY, INC. (1930); PO Box 20058 (36120); (334)277–5820. FAX: (334)277-8383. Pres. Bobby Segall; Admin. Dir. Susan Mayer Bruchis.

ARIZONA

PHOENIX

JEWISH FEDERATION OF GREATER PHOENIX (1940); 32 W. Coolidge, Suite 200 (85013); (602)274–1800. FAX: (602)266–7875. Pres. Elaine Schreiber; Exec. Dir. Arthur Paikowsky.

TUCSON

JEWISH FEDERATION OF SOUTHERN ARIZONA (1946); 3822 East River Rd., Suite 100 (85718); (520)577–9393. FAX: (520)577–0734. Pres. Linda Tumarkin; Exec. Dir. Stuart Mellan.

ARKANSAS

LITTLE ROCK

JEWISH FEDERATION OF ARKANSAS (1911); 2821 Kavanaugh Blvd., Garden Level (72205); (501)663–3571. FAX: (501)663–7286. Pres. Michael Krupitsky; Exec. Dir. Harvey David Luber.

CALIFORNIA

EAST BAY

JEWISH FEDERATION OF THE GREATER EAST BAY (INCLUDING ALAMEDA & CONTRA COSTA COUNTIES) (1917); 401 Grand Ave., Oakland (94610); (510)839-2900. FAX: (510)839-3996. Pres. Jerry Yanowitz; Exec. V.-Pres. Ami Nahshon.

LONG BEACH

JEWISH FEDERATION OF GREATER LONG BEACH AND W. ORANGE COUNTY (1937; inc. 1946); 3801 E. Willow St. (90815); (562)426–7601. FAX: (562)424–3915. Pres. Richard Lipeles; Exec. Dir. Michael S. Rassler.

LOS ANGELES

JEWISH FEDERATION COUNCIL OF GREATER LOS ANGELES (1912; reorg. 1959); 5700 Wilshire Blvd., 2nd fl.(90036); (213)761–8000. FAX: (213)761–8123. Pres. Herbert M. Gelfand; Exec. V.-Pres. John Fishel.

This directory is based on information supplied by the Council of Jewish Federations.

ORANGE COUNTY

JEWISH FEDERATION OF ORANGE COUNTY (1964; inc. 1965); 250 Baker St., Costa Mesa (92626); (714)755–5555. FAX: (714)755–0307. Pres. Joseph Baim; Exec. Dir. Edward Cushman.

PALM SPRINGS

JEWISH FEDERATION OF PALM SPRINGS (1971); 255 El Cielo N., Suite 430 (92262); (619)325–7281. FAX: (619)325–2188. Pres. Barbara Platt; Exec. Dir. Irving Ginsberg.

SACRAMENTO

JEWISH FEDERATION OF THE SACRAMENTO REGION (1948); 2351 Wyda Way. (95825); (916)486–0906. FAX: (916)486–0816. Pres. Bill Slaton; Exec. Dir. Beryl Michaels.

SAN DIEGO

UNITED JEWISH FEDERATION OF SAN DIEGO COUNTY (1936); 4797 Mercury St. (92111–2102); (619)571–3444. FAX: (619) 571–0701. Pres. Rod Stone; Exec. V.-Pres. Stephen M. Abramson.

SAN FRANCISCO

JEWISH COMMUNITY FEDERATION OF SAN FRANCISCO, THE PENINSULA, MARIN, AND SONOMA COUNTIES (1910; reorg. 1955); 121 Steuart St. (94105); (415)777–0411. FAX: (415)495–6635. Pres. Alan E. Rothenberg; Exec. V.-Pres. Wayne Feinstein.

SAN JOSE

JEWISH FEDERATION OF GREATER SAN JOSE (incl. Santa Clara County except Palo Alto and Los Altos) (1930; reorg. 1950); 14855 Oka Rd., Los Gatos (95030); (408)358–3033. FAX: (408)356–0733. Pres. Judy Levin; Exec. Dir. Jon Friedenberg.

SANTA BARBARA

SANTA BARBARA JEWISH FEDERATION (1974); 104 W. Anapamu, Suite A, PO Box 90110 (93190); (805)963–0244. FAX: (805) 963–1124. Pres. Jeri Eigner; Exec. Dir. Judith Stotland.

COLORADO

DENVER/BOULDER

ALLIED JEWISH FEDERATION OF COLORADO (1936); 300 S. Dahlia St., Denver (80222); (303)321–3399. FAX: (303)322–8328. Chmn. Bob Silverberg; Exec. V.-Pres. Steve Gelfand.

CONNECTICUT

BRIDGEPORT

JEWISH CENTER FOR COMMUNITY SERVICES, INC. (1936; reorg. 1981); 4200 Park Ave. (06604–1092); (203)372–6567. FAX: (203) 374–0770. Chmn. Dr. Jeffrey Gross; Pres. & CEO Daniel P. Baker.

DANBURY

THE JEWISH FEDERATION (INCL. N. FAIRFIELD & S. LITCHFIELD COUNTIES IN CONNECTICUT; PUTNAM & N. WESTCHESTER COUNTIES IN NEW YORK) (1945); 105 Newtown Rd. (06810); (203)792–6353. FAX: (203)748–5099. Pres Daniel Wolinsky; Exec. Dir. Rhonda Cohen.

EASTERN CONNECTICUT

JEWISH FEDERATION OF EASTERN CONNECTICUT, INC. (1950; inc. 1970); 28 Channing St., PO Box 1468, New London (06320); (860)442–8062. FAX: (860)443–4175. Pres. Myron Hendel; Exec. Dir. Jerome E. Fischer.

GREENWICH

UJA/FEDERATION OF GREENWICH (1956); 600 W. Putnam Ave. (06830); (203)622–1434. FAX: (203)622–1237. Pres. Geoffrey Thaw; Exec. Dir. Pam Zur.

HARTFORD

JEWISH FEDERATION OF GREATER HARTFORD (1945); 333 Bloomfield Ave., W. Hartford (06117); (860)232–4483. FAX: (860) 232–5221. Pres. Henry M. Zachs; Exec. Dir. Cindy Chazan.

NEW HAVEN

JEWISH FEDERATION OF GREATER NEW HAVEN (1928); 360 Amity Rd., Woodbridge (06525); (203)387–2424. FAX: (203) 387–1818. Pres. Carol Robbins; Exec. Dir. Howard Bloom.

NORWALK

(See Westport)

STAMFORD

UNITED JEWISH FEDERATION (inc. 1973); 1035 Newfield Ave., PO Box 3038 (06905); (203)321–1373. FAX: (203)322–3277. Pres. Robert A. Breakstone; Exec. Dir. Sheila L. Romanowitz.

WATERBURY

JEWISH FEDERATION OF GREATER WATERBURY AND NORTHWESTERN CONNECTICUT,

INC. (1938); 73 Main St. S., Box F, Woodbury (06798); (203)263–5121. FAX: (203) 263–5143. Pres. Dr. Daniel Goodman; Exec. Dir. Robert Zwang.

WESTPORT–WESTON–WILTON–NORWALK

UNITED JEWISH APPEAL/FEDERATION OF WESTPORT–WESTON–WILTON–NORWALK (inc. 1980); 431 Post Road E., Suite 22, Westport (06880); (203)226–8197. FAX: (203)226–5051. Pres. Sandra Lefkowitz; Exec. Dir. Robert Kessler.

DELAWARE

WILMINGTON

JEWISH FEDERATION OF DELAWARE, INC. (1934); 100 W. 10th St., Suite 301 (19801–1628); (302)427–2100. FAX: (302) 427–2438. Pres. Leslie Newman; Exec. V. Pres. Judy Wortman.

DISTRICT OF COLUMBIA

WASHINGTON

UNITED JEWISH APPEAL FEDERATION OF GREATER WASHINGTON, INC. (1935); 6101 Montrose Rd., Rockville, MD 20852; (301)230–7200. FAX: (301)230–7265. Pres. Ivan Michael Schaeffer; Exec. V.-Pres. Ted B. Farber.

FLORIDA

BREVARD COUNTY

JEWISH FEDERATION OF BREVARD (1974); 108-A Barton Ave., Rockledge (32955); (407)636–1824. FAX: (407)636–0614. Pres. Sharon Deligdish.

BROWARD COUNTY

JEWISH FEDERATION OF BROWARD COUNTY (1943; 1968); 8358 W. Oakland Park Blvd., Ft. Lauderdale (33351); (954)748–8400. FAX: (954)748–6332. Pres. Herbert D. Katz; Exec. Dir. Gary N. Rubin.

COLLIER COUNTY

JEWISH FEDERATION OF COLLIER COUNTY (1974); 1250 Tamiami Trail N., Suite 304C, Naples (34102); (941) 263–4205. FAX: (941)263–3813. Pres. William Ettinger.

DAYTONA BEACH
(See Volusia & Flagler Counties)

FT. LAUDERDALE
(See Broward County)

JACKSONVILLE

JACKSONVILLE JEWISH FEDERATION, INC. (1935); 8505 San Jose Blvd. (32217); (904) 448–5000. FAX: (904)448–5715. Pres. Dr. Kenneth Sekine; Exec. V.-Pres. Alan Margolies.

LEE COUNTY

JEWISH FEDERATION OF LEE AND CHARLOTTE COUNTIES (1974); 6237-E Presidential Court, Ft. Myers (33919–3568); (941) 481–4449. FAX: (941)481–0139. Pres. Kenneth Weiner; Exec. Dir. Annette Goodman.

MIAMI

GREATER MIAMI JEWISH FEDERATION, INC. (1938); 4200 Biscayne Blvd. (33137); (305) 576–4000. FAX: (305)573–8115. Pres. Isaac Zelcer; Exec. V.-Pres. Jacob Solomon.

ORLANDO

JEWISH FEDERATION OF GREATER ORLANDO (1949); 851 N. Maitland Ave. (32751); PO Box 941508, Maitland (32794–1508); (407) 645–5933. FAX: (407)645–1172. Pres. Rosalind Fuchs; Exec. Dir. Eric Geboff.

PALM BEACH COUNTY

JEWISH FEDERATION OF PALM BEACH COUNTY, INC. (1962); 4601 Community Dr., W. Palm Beach (33417–2760); (561)478–0700. FAX: (561)478–9696. Pres. Helen G. Hoffman; Exec. V.-Pres. Jeffrey L. Klein.

PINELLAS COUNTY

JEWISH FEDERATION OF PINELLAS COUNTY, INC. (incl. Clearwater and St. Petersburg) (1950; reincorp. 1974); 13191 Starkey Rd., N. Crownpointe, Suite 8, Largo (33773–1438); (813) 530–3223. FAX: (813)531–0221. Pres. Saul Schechter; Exec. Dir. Mark Silverberg.

SARASOTA-MANATEE

SARASOTA-MANATEE JEWISH FEDERATION (1959); 580 S. McIntosh Rd. (34232–1959); (941)371–4546. FAX: (941)378–2947. Pres. Karen Jones Stutz; Exec. Dir. Jan C. Lederman.

TAMPA

TAMPA JCC/FEDERATION (1941); 13009 Community Campus Dr. (33625); (813) 960–1840. FAX: (813)265–8450. Co-Pres. Lili Kaufman, David Scher, Jeffrey Wuliger; Exec. V.-Pres. Howard Borer.

VOLUSIA & FLAGLER COUNTIES

JEWISH FEDERATION OF VOLUSIA & FLA-

GLER COUNTIES, INC. (1980); 733 S. Nova Rd., Ormond Beach (32174); (904)672-0294. FAX: (904)673-1316. Pres. Dr. Richard J. Rhodes; Exec. Dir. Gloria Max.

GEORGIA

ATLANTA

ATLANTA JEWISH FEDERATION, INC. (1905; reorg. 1967); 1440 Spring St., NW (30309-2837); (404)873-1661. FAX: (404)874-7043. Pres. S. Stephen Selig, III; Exec. Dir. David I. Sarnat.

AUGUSTA

AUGUSTA JEWISH FEDERATION (1937); PO Box 15443 (30919); (706)737-8001. FAX: (706)667-8081. Pres. Dr. Michael Rivner; Exec. Dir. Michael Pousman.

COLUMBUS

JEWISH FEDERATION OF COLUMBUS, INC. (1944); PO Box 6313 (31917); (706)568-6668. Pres. Murray Solomon; Sec. Irene Rainbow.

SAVANNAH

SAVANNAH JEWISH FEDERATION (1943); PO Box 23527 (31403); (912)355-8111. FAX: (912)355-8116. Pres. Dr. Richard Bodziner; Exec. Dir. Sharon Gal.

ILLINOIS

CHAMPAIGN-URBANA

CHAMPAIGN-URBANA JEWISH FEDERATION (1929); 503 E. John St., Champaign (61820); (217)367-9872. FAX: (217)367-0077. Pres. Martha Miller; Admin. Dir. Robert S. Silverman.

CHICAGO

JEWISH FEDERATION OF METROPOLITAN CHICAGO/JEWISH UNITED FUND OF METROPOLITAN CHICAGO (1900); Ben Gurion Way, 1 S. Franklin St. (60606-4694); (312)346-6700. FAX: (312)855-2474. Chmn. Barbara Hochberg; Pres. Steven B. Nasatir.

ELGIN

ELGIN AREA JEWISH WELFARE CHEST (1938); 330 Division St. (60120); (847)741-5656. FAX: (847)741-5679. Pres. Robert C. Levine.

PEORIA

JEWISH FEDERATION OF PEORIA (1933; inc. 1947); 2000 Pioneer Pwky., Suite 10B (61615); (309)689-0063. FAX: (309)689-0575. Pres. Dr. Michael Bailie; Exec. Dir. Eunice Galsky.

QUAD CITIES

JEWISH FEDERATION OF QUAD CITIES (incl. Rock Island, Moline, Davenport, Bettendorf) (1938; comb. 1973); 209 18th St., Rock Island (61201); (309)793-1300. FAX: (309)793-1345. Pres. Edward Slivken; Exec. Dir. Ida Kramer.

ROCKFORD

JEWISH FEDERATION OF GREATER ROCKFORD (1937); 1500 Parkview Ave. (61107); (815)399-5497. FAX: (815)399-9835. Pres. James A. Gesmer; Exec. Dir. Marilyn Youman.

SOUTHERN ILLINOIS

JEWISH FEDERATION OF SOUTHERN ILLINOIS, SOUTHEASTERN MISSOURI, AND WESTERN KENTUCKY (1941); 6464 W. Main, Suite 7A, Belleville IL (62223); (618)398-6100. FAX: (618)398-0539. Pres. Dr. Donald Meltzer; Exec. Dir. Steven C. Low.

SPRINGFIELD

SPRINGFIELD JEWISH FEDERATION (1941); 730 E. Vine St. (62703); (217)528-3446. FAX: (217)528-3409. Pres. Theodore R. Le Blang; Exec. Dir. Gloria Schwartz.

INDIANA

EVANSVILLE

EVANSVILLE JEWISH COMMUNITY COUNCIL, INC. (1936; inc. 1964); PO Box 5026 (47716); (812)476-5091. FAX: (812)477-1577. Pres. Susan Shovers; Exec. Sec. Ernest W. Adler.

FORT WAYNE

FORT WAYNE JEWISH FEDERATION (1921); 227 E. Washington Blvd. (46802-3121); (219)422-8566. FAX: (219)422-8567. Pres. Scott Salon; Exec. Dir. Lew Borman.

INDIANAPOLIS

JEWISH FEDERATION OF GREATER INDIANAPOLIS, INC. (1905); 6705 Hoover Rd. (46260-4120); (317)726-5450. FAX: (317) 205-0307. Pres. Charles A. Cohen; Exec. V.-Pres. Harry Nadler.

LAFAYETTE

FEDERATED JEWISH CHARITIES (1924); c/o Hillel, 912 W. State St., W. Lafayette (47906); (317)743-1293. FAX: (765)743-0014. Pres. Leo Weitzman; Finan. Sec. Laura Starr.

MICHIGAN CITY

MICHIGAN CITY UNITED JEWISH WELFARE FUND; c/o Temple Sinai, 2800 S. Franklin St. (46360); (219)874-4477. FAX: (219)874-4190. Co-Chmn. Iris Ourach, Bob Baseman.

NORTHWEST INDIANA

THE JEWISH FEDERATION, INC. (1941; reorg. 1959); 2939 Jewett St., Highland (46322); (219)972-2250. FAX: (219)972-4779. Pres. Ernest Fruehauf; Exec. Dir. Ira Goldberg.

ST. JOSEPH VALLEY

JEWISH FEDERATION OF ST. JOSEPH VALLEY (1946); 105 Jefferson Centre, Suite 804, South Bend (46601); (219)233-1164. FAX: (219)288-4103. Pres. Steven Goldberg; Exec. V.-Pres. Marilyn Gardner.

IOWA

DES MOINES

JEWISH FEDERATION OF GREATER DES MOINES (1914); 910 Polk Blvd. (50312); (515)277-6321. FAX: (515)277-4069. Pres. Robert M. Pomerantz; Exec. Dir. Elaine Steinger.

SIOUX CITY

JEWISH FEDERATION (1921); 815 38th St. (51104-1417); (712)258-0618. FAX: (712) 258-0619. Pres. Michele Ivener; Admin. Dir. Doris Rosenthal.

KANSAS

WICHITA

MID-KANSAS JEWISH FEDERATION, INC. (serving South Central Kansas) (1935); 400 N. Woodlawn, Suite 8 (67208); (316) 686-4741. FAX: (316)686-6008. Pres. Priscilla Cohen; Exec. Dir. Judy Press.

KENTUCKY

CENTRAL KENTUCKY

CENTRAL KENTUCKY JEWISH FEDERATION (1976); 340 Romany Rd., Lexington (40502-2400); (606)268-0672. Pres. Tomás Milch H.; Exec. Dir. Joel H. Eizenstat.

LOUISVILLE

JEWISH COMMUNITY FEDERATION OF LOUISVILLE, INC. (1934); 3630 Dutchmans Lane (40205); (502)451-8840. FAX: (502) 458-0702. Pres. Alfred S. Joseph, III; Exec. Dir. Alan S. Engel.

LOUISIANA

BATON ROUGE

JEWISH FEDERATION OF GREATER BATON ROUGE (1971); 3354 Kleinert, PO Box 80827 (70898); (504) 387-9744. FAX: (504)387-9487. Pres. Dr. Deborah Cavalier.

NEW ORLEANS

JEWISH FEDERATION OF GREATER NEW ORLEANS (1913; reorg. 1977); 3500 N. Causeway Blvd., Suite 1240, Metarie (70002); (504)828-2125. FAX: (504)828-2827. Pres. Hugo Khan; Exec. Dir. Eli Skora.

SHREVEPORT

NORTHERN LOUISIANA JEWISH FEDERATION (1941; inc. 1967); 4700 Line Ave., Suite 117 (71106); (318)868-1200. FAX: (318)868-1272. Pres. Sidney Kent; Exec. Dir. Howard L. Ross.

MAINE

LEWISTON-AUBURN

LEWISTON-AUBURN JEWISH FEDERATION (1947); 74 Bradman St., Auburn (04210); (207)786-4201. Pres. Scott Nussinow.

PORTLAND

JEWISH FEDERATION COMMUNITY COUNCIL OF SOUTHERN MAINE (1942); 57 Ashmont St. (04103); (207)772-1959. FAX: (207) 772-2234. Pres. Larry Waxler; Exec. Dir. David Unger.

MARYLAND

BALTIMORE

THE ASSOCIATED: JEWISH COMMUNITY FEDERATION OF BALTIMORE (1920; reorg. 1969); 101 W. Mt. Royal Ave. (21201); (410) 727-4828. FAX: (410)783-4795. Chmn. Barbara L. Himmerlich; Pres. Darrell D. Friedman.

MASSACHUSETTS

BERKSHIRE COUNTY

JEWISH FEDERATION OF THE BERKSHIRES (1940); 235 East St., Pittsfield (01201); (413)442-4360. FAX: (413)443-6070. Pres. Ellen Silverstein; Exec. Dir. Robert N. Kerbel.

BOSTON

COMBINED JEWISH PHILANTHROPIES OF GREATER BOSTON, INC. (1895; inc. 1961); 126 High St. (02110); (617)457-8500. FAX:

(617)988–6262. Chmn. Michael B. Rukin; Pres. Barry Shrage.

CAPE COD

JEWISH FEDERATION OF CAPE COD (1990); 396 Main St., PO Box 2568, Hyannis (02601); (508)778–5588. FAX: (508)778–9727. Pres. Ernest Smily.

LEOMINSTER

LEOMINSTER JEWISH COMMUNITY COUNCIL, INC. (1939); 268 Washington St. (01453); (617)534–6121. Pres. Dr. Milton Kline; Sec.- Treas. Howard J. Rome.

MERRIMACK VALLEY

MERRIMACK VALLEY JEWISH FEDERATION (Serves Andover, Haverhill, Lawrence, Lowell, Newburyport, and 22 surrounding communities) (1988); 805 Turnpike St., N. Andover (01845–6122); (508)688–0466. FAX: (508)688–1097. Chmn. Jeffrey D. Queen; Acting Exec. Dir. Edward J. Finkel.

NEW BEDFORD

JEWISH FEDERATION OF GREATER NEW BEDFORD, INC. (1938; inc. 1954); 467 Hawthorn St., N. Dartmouth (02747); (508) 997–7471. FAX: (508)997–7730. Co-Pres. Harriet Philips, Patricia Rosenfield; Exec. Dir. Wil Herrup.

NORTH SHORE

JEWISH FEDERATION OF THE NORTH SHORE, INC. (1938); 4 Community Rd., Marblehead (01945); (617)598–1810. FAX: (617)639–1284. Pres. Shepard M. Remis; Exec. Dir. Neil A. Cooper.

SPRINGFIELD

JEWISH FEDERATION OF GREATER SPRINGFIELD, INC. (1925); 1160 Dickinson St. (01108); (413)737–4313. FAX: (413)737–4348. Pres. Gerald B. Berg; Exec. Dir. Joel Weiss.

WORCESTER

WORCESTER JEWISH FEDERATION, INC. (1947; inc. 1957); 633 Salisbury St. (01609); (508)756–1543. FAX: (508)798–0962. Pres. Dr. Robert Honig; Exec. Dir. Meyer L. Bodoff.

MICHIGAN

ANN ARBOR

JEWISH FEDERATION OF WASHTENAW COUNTY/UNITED JEWISH APPEAL (1986); 2939 Birch Hollow Dr. (48108); (313)

677–0100. FAX: (313)677–0109. Pres. Evie Lichter; Exec. Dir. Nancy N. Margolis.

DETROIT

JEWISH FEDERATION OF METROPOLITAN DETROIT (1899); 6735 Telegraph Rd., Suite 30, PO Box 2030, Bloomfield Hills (48303–2030); (248)642–4260. FAX: (248)642–4985. Pres. Robert Naftaly; Exec. V.-Pres. Robert P. Aronson.

FLINT

FLINT JEWISH FEDERATION (1936); 619 Wallenberg St. (48502); (810)767–5922. FAX: (810)767–9024. Pres. Dr. Steve Burton; Exec. Dir. Joel B. Kaplan.

GRAND RAPIDS

JEWISH COMMUNITY FUND OF GRAND RAPIDS (1930); 330 Fuller NE (49503); (616)456–5553. FAX: (616)456–5780. Pres. Charles D. Shapiro; Admin. Dir. Rosalie Stein.

MINNESOTA

DULUTH–SUPERIOR

TWIN PORTS JEWISH FEDERATION (1937); 1602 E. Second St., Duluth (55812); (218)724–8857. FAX: (218)724-2560. Pres. Neil Glazman.

MINNEAPOLIS

MINNEAPOLIS FEDERATION FOR JEWISH SERVICE (1929; inc. 1930); 5901 S. Cedar Lake Rd. (55416); (612)593–2600. FAX: (612)593–2544. Pres. Sanford J. Goldberg; Exec. Dir. Richard Fruchter.

ST. PAUL

UNITED JEWISH FUND AND COUNCIL (1935); 790 S. Cleveland, Suite 201 (55116); (612)690–1707. FAX: (612)690–0228. Pres. James Stein; Exec. Dir. Samuel Asher.

MISSISSIPPI

JACKSON

JACKSON JEWISH WELFARE FUND, INC. (1945); 5315 Old Canton Rd. (39211–4625); (601)956–6215. FAX: (601)956–6260. Pres. Erik Hearon; V.-Pres. Marcy Cohen.

MISSOURI

KANSAS CITY

JEWISH FEDERATION OF GREATER KANSAS CITY MO/KS (1933); 5801 W. 115 St., Overland Park, KS 66211–1824; (913)327–8100.

FAX: (913)327–8110. Pres. Nita R. Levy; Exec. Dir. A. Robert Gast.

ST. JOSEPH

UNITED JEWISH FUND OF ST. JOSEPH (1915); c/o Mrs. Judy Chapnick, 2710 N. 39th Terrace (64506); (816)232–7043. FAX: (816)233-9399. Pres. Mrs. Judy Chapnick; Exec. Sec. Mrs. Beryl Shapiro.

ST. LOUIS

JEWISH FEDERATION OF ST. LOUIS (incl. St. Louis County) (1901); 12 Millstone Campus Dr. (63146); (314)432–0020. FAX: (314) 432–1277. Pres. Nancy Siwak; Exec. V.-Pres. Barry Rosenberg.

NEBRASKA

LINCOLN

LINCOLN JEWISH WELFARE FEDERATION, INC. (1931; inc. 1961); PO Box 67218 (68506); (402)477–4113. FAX: (402)489-1015. Pres. Herb Friedman; Exec. Dir. Karen Sommer.

OMAHA

JEWISH FEDERATION OF OMAHA (1903); 333 S. 132nd St. (68154–2198); (402)334–8200. FAX: (402)334–1330. Pres. Howard Kooper; Exec. Dir. Jan Perelman.

NEVADA

LAS VEGAS

JEWISH FEDERATION OF LAS VEGAS (1973); 3909 S. Maryland Pkwy. (89119–7520); (702)732–0556. FAX: (702)732–3228. Pres. David Dahan; Exec. Dir. Ronni Epstein.

NEW HAMPSHIRE

MANCHESTER

JEWISH FEDERATION OF GREATER MANCHESTER (1974); 698 Beech St. (03104); (603)627–7679. FAX: (603) 627–7963. Pres. Martin Jacobs; Exec. Dir. Richard Friedman.

NEW JERSEY

ATLANTIC AND CAPE MAY COUNTIES

JEWISH FEDERATION OF ATLANTIC AND CAPE MAY COUNTIES (1924); 3393 Bargaintown Rd., Egg Harbor Township (08232–0617); (609)653–3030. FAX: (609)653–8881. Pres. Charles Matison; Exec. V.-Pres. Bernard Cohen.

BERGEN COUNTY

UJA FEDERATION OF BERGEN COUNTY AND NORTH HUDSON (inc. 1978); 111 Kinderkamack Rd., PO Box 4176, N. Hackensack Station, River Edge (07661); (201)488–6800. FAX: (201)488–3962. Pres. Mark Metzger; Exec. V.-Pres. Ron B. Meier.

CENTRAL NEW JERSEY

JEWISH FEDERATION OF CENTRAL NEW JERSEY (1940; merged 1973); 1391 Martine Ave., Scotch Plains (07076); (908)889–5335. FAX: (908)889–5370. Pres. Marilyn Flanzbaum; Exec. V.-Pres. Stanley Stone.

CLIFTON–PASSAIC

JEWISH FEDERATION OF GREATER CLIFTON-PASSAIC (1933); 199 Scoles Ave., Clifton (07012). (973)777–7031. FAX: (973)777–6701. Pres. George Kramer; Exec. V.-Pres. Yosef Y. Muskin.

CUMBERLAND COUNTY

JEWISH FEDERATION OF CUMBERLAND COUNTY (inc. 1971); 629 Wood St., Suite 204, Vineland (08360); (609)696–4445. FAX: (609)696–3428. Pres. James Potter; Exec. Dir. Ann Lynn Lipton.

METROWEST NEW JERSEY

UNITED JEWISH FEDERATION OF METROWEST (1923); 901 Route 10, Whippany (07981–1156); (973)884–4800. FAX: (973) 884–7361. Pres. Murray Laulicht; Exec. V.-Pres. Max L. Kleinman.

MIDDLESEX COUNTY

JEWISH FEDERATION OF GREATER MIDDLESEX COUNTY (org. 1948; reorg. 1985); 230 Old Bridge Tpk., S. River (08882–2000); (732)432–7711. FAX: (732)432–0292. Pres. Roy Tanzman; Exec. V.-Pres. Michael Shapiro.

MONMOUTH COUNTY

JEWISH FEDERATION OF GREATER MONMOUTH COUNTY (1971); 100 Grant Ave., PO Box 210, Deal (07723–0210); (732) 531–6200–1. FAX: (732)531–9518. Pres. William A. Schwartz; Exec. Dir. David A. Nussbaum.

MORRIS–SUSSEX COUNTY

(Merged with MetroWest New Jersey)

NORTH JERSEY

JEWISH FEDERATION OF NORTH JERSEY (1933); One Pike Dr., Wayne (07470–2498); (973)595–0555. FAX: (973)595–1532.

Branch Office: 17–10 River Rd., Fair Lawn (07410–1250); (973)794–1111. FAX: (973) 794–8399. Pres. Sylvia Safer; Exec. Dir. Martin Greenberg.

NORTHERN MIDDLESEX COUNTY
(See Middlesex County)

OCEAN COUNTY
OCEAN COUNTY JEWISH FEDERATION (1977); 301 Madison Ave., Lakewood (08701); (732)363–0530. FAX: (732)363–2097. Pres. Debra Abrahamovic Kay; Admin. Dir. Jill C. Dalin.

PRINCETON MERCER BUCKS
UNITED JEWISH FEDERATION OF PRINCETON MERCER BUCKS (merged 1996); 3131 Princeton Pike, Bldg. 2, Lawrenceville (08648); (609)219–0555. FAX: (609)219–9040. Pres. Eliot Freeman; Exec. Dir. Howard Gases.

SOMERSET COUNTY
JEWISH FEDERATION OF SOMERSET, HUNTERDON & WARREN COUNTIES (1960); 1011 Rt. 22 West, PO Box 6455, Bridgewater (08807); (908)725–6994. FAX: (908)725–9753. Pres. Martin Siegal; Exec. Dir. Daniel A. Nadelman.

SOUTHERN NEW JERSEY
JEWISH FEDERATION OF SOUTHERN NEW JERSEY (incl. Camden, Burlington, and Gloucester counties) (1922); 1301 Springdale Rd., Suite 200, Cherry Hill (08003); (609)751–9500. FAX: (609)751–1697. Pres. Marc Jacobs; Exec. V.-Pres. Stuart Alperin.

NEW MEXICO

ALBUQUERQUE
JEWISH FEDERATION OF GREATER ALBUQUERQUE (1938); 5520 Wyoming Blvd., NE (87109); (505)821–3214. FAX: (505)821–3351. Pres. Dr. Janice Moranz. Exec. Dir. Andrew Lipman.

NEW YORK

ALBANY
(See Northeastern New York)

BUFFALO (INCL. NIAGARA FALLS)
JEWISH FEDERATION OF GREATER BUFFALO, INC. (1903); 787 Delaware Ave. (14209); (716)886–7750. FAX: (716)886–1367. Pres. Irving M. Shuman; Exec. Dir. James M. Lodge.

DUTCHESS COUNTY
JEWISH FEDERATION OF DUTCHESS COUNTY; 110 Grand Ave., Poughkeepsie (12603); (914)471–9811. FAX: (914) 471–0659. Pres. Tomasina Schneider; Exec. Dir. Bonnie Meadow.

ELMIRA
ELMIRA-CORNING JEWISH FEDERATION (1942); Grandview Ave. Ext., PO Box 3087, Elmira (14905); (607)734–8122. FAX: (607) 734–8123. Pres. John Spiegler.

NEW YORK
UJA–Federation of Jewish Philanthropies of New York, Inc. (incl. Greater NY, Westchester, Nassau, and Suffolk counties) (Fed. org. 1917; UJA 1939; merged 1986); 130 E. 59 St. (10022); (212)980–1000. FAX: (212) 836–1778. Pres. Louise B. Greilsheimer; Chmn. Judith Stern Peck; Exec. V.-Pres. Stephen D. Solender.

NORTHEASTERN NEW YORK
UNITED JEWISH FEDERATION OF NORTHEASTERN NEW YORK (1986); Latham Circle Mall, 800 New Loudon Rd., Latham (12110); (518)783–7800. FAX: (518)783–1557. Pres. Dr. Lewis Morrison; Exec. Dir. Jerry S. Neimand.

ORANGE COUNTY
JEWISH FEDERATION OF GREATER ORANGE COUNTY (1977); 68 Stewart Ave., Newburgh (12550); (914)562–7860. FAX: (914)562–5114. Pres. Mona Rieger; Admin. Dir. Joyce Waschitz.

ROCHESTER
JEWISH COMMUNITY FEDERATION OF GREATER ROCHESTER, NY, INC. (1939); 441 East Ave. (14607); (716)461–0490. FAX: (716)461–0912. Pres. Eileen Grossman; Exec. Dir. Lawrence W. Fine.

SCHENECTADY
(See Northeastern New York)

SYRACUSE
SYRACUSE JEWISH FEDERATION, INC. (1918); PO Box 510, DeWitt (13214); (315)445–0161. FAX: (315)445–1559. Pres. David Yaffe; Exec. V.-Pres. Mary Ann Oppenheimer.

TROY
(See Northeastern New York)

ULSTER COUNTY

JEWISH FEDERATION OF ULSTER COUNTY (1951); 159 Green St., Kingston (12401); (914)338–8131. FAX: (914)338–8131. Pres. Dr. Joseph Cohen.

UTICA

JEWISH COMMUNITY FEDERATION OF MO-HAWK VALLEY, NY, INC. (1950; reorg. 1994); 2310 Oneida St. (13501); (315)733-2343. FAX: (315)733-2346. Pres. Ed Kowalsky; Exec. Dir. Barbara Ratner-gantshar.

NORTH CAROLINA

ASHEVILLE

WESTERN NORTH CAROLINA JEWISH FED-ERATION (1935); 236 Charlotte St. (28801); (704)253–0701. FAX: (704)254–7666. Pres. Stan Greenberg; Exec. Dir. Marlene Berger-Joyce.

CHARLOTTE

THE JEWISH FEDERATION OF GREATER CHARLOTTE (1938); 5007 Providence Rd. (28226); (704)366–5007. FAX: (704)365–4507. Pres. Richard Osborne; Exec. Dir. Marvin Goldberg.

DURHAM–CHAPEL HILL

DURHAM–CHAPEL HILL JEWISH FEDERA-TION & COMMUNITY COUNCIL (1979); 3700 Lyckan Pkwy., Suite B, Durham (27707); (919)489–5335. FAX: (919)489–5788. Pres. Dr. Adam Goldstein; Exec. Dir. Elise Light.

GREENSBORO

GREENSBORO JEWISH FEDERATION (1940); 6509C W. Friendly Ave., Guilford Corpo-rate Park (27410-4211); (336)852–5433. FAX: (336)852–4346. Pres. Dr. James U. Adelman; Exec. Dir. Marilyn Forman-Chandler.

RALEIGH

WAKE COUNTY JEWISH FEDERATION (1987); 8210 Creedmoor Rd., Suite 104 (27613); (919)676–2200. FAX: (919)676–2122. Pres. Jim Maass; Exec. Dir. Judah Segal.

OHIO

AKRON

AKRON JEWISH COMMUNITY FEDERATION (1935); 750 White Pond Dr. (44320); (330)869–CHAI (2424). FAX: (330)867–8498. Pres. Gary Rosen; Exec. Dir. Michael Wise.

CANTON

CANTON JEWISH COMMUNITY FEDERATION (1935; reorg. 1955); 2631 Harvard Ave., NW (44709); (330)452–6444. FAX: (330)452–4487. Pres. Sharon Fladen; Exec. Dir. Neil Berro.

CINCINNATI

JEWISH FEDERATION OF CINCINNATI (1896; reorg. 1967); 4380 Malsbary Rd., Suite 200 (45242); (513) 985–1500. FAX: (513)985–1503. Prcs. Harry Davidow; Exec. V.-Pres. Aubrey Herman.

CLEVELAND

JEWISH COMMUNITY FEDERATION OF CLEVELAND (1903); 1750 Euclid Ave. (44115); (216)566–9200. FAX: (216)861–1230. Pres. Sally H. Wertheim; Exec. V.-Pres. Stephen H. Hoffman.

COLUMBUS

COLUMBUS JEWISH FEDERATION (1926); 1175 College Ave. (43209); (614)237–7686. FAX: (614)237–2221. Pres. Ellen Siegel; Exec. Dir. Mitchel Orlik.

DAYTON

JEWISH FEDERATION OF GREATER DAYTON (1910); 4501 Denlinger Rd. (45426); (937)854–4150. FAX: (937)854–2850. Pres. Joseph Bettman; Exec. V.-Pres. Peter H. Wells.

STEUBENVILLE

JEWISH COMMUNITY COUNCIL (1938); 300 Lovers Lane (43952); (614)264–5514. Pres. Curtis L. Greenberg; Exec. Sec. Jennie Bernstein.

TOLEDO

JEWISH FEDERATION OF GREATER TOLEDO (1907; reorg. 1960); 6505 Sylvania Ave., Syl-vania (43560); (419)885–4461. FAX: (419) 885–3207. Pres. Joel Beren.

YOUNGSTOWN

YOUNGSTOWN AREA JEWISH FEDERATION (1935); 505 Gypsy Lane (44504–1314); (330)746–3251. FAX: (330)746–7926. Pres. Louis Epstein; Exec. V.-Pres. Sam Kooper-man.

OKLAHOMA

OKLAHOMA CITY

JEWISH FEDERATION OF GREATER OKLA-HOMA CITY (1941); 710 W. Wilshire, Suite C (73116). (405)848–3132. FAX: (405)848–

3180. Pres. Harriet Carson; Exec. Dir. Edie S. Roodman.

TULSA
JEWISH FEDERATION OF TULSA (1938); 2021 E. 71 St. (74136); (918)495–1100. FAX: (918)495–1220. Pres. Andrew M. Wolov; Exec. Dir. David Bernstein.

OREGON

PORTLAND
JEWISH FEDERATION OF PORTLAND (incl. Northwest Oregon and Southwest Washington communities) (1920; reorg. 1956); 6651 SW Capitol Hwy. (97219); (503)245–6219. FAX: (503)245–6603. Pres. Gayle Romain; Exec. Dir. Charles Schiffman.

PENNSYLVANIA

ALTOONA
FEDERATION OF JEWISH PHILANTHROPIES (1920; reorg. 1940; inc. 1945); 1308 17 St. (16601); (814)944–4072. FAX: (814)944-9874. Pres. William Wallen; Admin. Dir. Maxine Weinberg.

BUCKS COUNTY
(See Jewish Federation of Greater Philadelphia)

ERIE
JEWISH COMMUNITY COUNCIL OF ERIE (1946); 1611 Peach St., Suite 405 (16501–2123); (814)455–4474. FAX: (814)455–4475. Pres. Robert Cohen; Admin. Dir. Cynthia Penman.

HARRISBURG
UNITED JEWISH COMMUNITY OF GREATER HARRISBURG (1941); 3301 N. Front St. (17110); (717)236–9555. FAX: (717)236–8104. Pres. Harvey Fredenberg; Exec. Dir. Jordan Harburger.

JOHNSTOWN
UNITED JEWISH FEDERATION OF JOHNSTOWN (1938); c/o Beth Sholom Cong., 700 Indiana St. (15905); (814)536–6440 (office), (814)539–9891 (home). Pres. Isadore Suchman.

LANCASTER
LANCASTER JEWISH FEDERATION; 2120 Oregon Pike (17601); (717)569–7352. FAX: (717)569–1614. Pres. Robert A. Matlin; Exec. Dir. Paul Spiegal.

PHILADELPHIA
JEWISH FEDERATION OF GREATER PHILADELPHIA (incl. Bucks, Chester, Delaware, Montgomery, and Philadelphia counties) (1901; reorg. 1956); 226 S. 16th St. (19102); (215)893–5600. FAX: (215)546–0349. Pres. Michael R. Belman; Exec. V.-Pres. Howard E. Charish.

PITTSBURGH
UNITED JEWISH FEDERATION OF GREATER PITTSBURGH (1912; reorg. 1955); 234 McKee Pl. (15213); (412)681–8000. FAX: (412) 681–3980. Chmn. David Burstin; Pres. Howard M. Rieger.

READING
JEWISH FEDERATION OF READING, PA., INC. (1935; reorg. 1972); 1700 City Line St. (19604); (610)921–2766. FAX: (610)929–0886. Pres. Sheila Lattin; Exec. Dir. Stanley Ramati.

SCRANTON
SCRANTON-LACKAWANNA JEWISH FEDERATION (1945); 601 Jefferson Ave. (18510); (717)961–2300. FAX: (717)346–6147. Pres. Lois Dubin; Exec. Dir. Seymour Brotman.

RHODE ISLAND

PROVIDENCE
JEWISH FEDERATION OF RHODE ISLAND (1945); 130 Sessions St. (02906); (401) 421–4111. FAX: (401)331–7961. Pres. Edward D. Feldstein; Exec. Dir. Steven A. Rakitt.

SOUTH CAROLINA

CHARLESTON
CHARLESTON JEWISH FEDERATION (1949); 1645 Raoul Wallenberg Blvd., PO Box 31298 (29407); (803)571–6565. FAX: (803) 556–6206. Pres. Mitchell R. Fischbein.

COLUMBIA
COLUMBIA JEWISH FEDERATION (1960); 4540 Trenholm Rd., PO Box 6968 (29206); (803)787–2023. FAX: (803)787–0475. Pres. Edward E. Poliakoff; Exec. Dir. Steven Terner.

GREENVILLE
FEDERATED JEWISH CHARITIES OF GREENVILLE, INC.; PO Box 7016-110 (29606); (864)244–1261. Pres. Dr. Arthur B. Stone.

SOUTH DAKOTA

SIOUX FALLS

JEWISH WELFARE FUND (1938); 510 S. First Ave. (57104); (605)332–3335. FAX: (605) 334–2298. Pres. Laurence Bierman; Exec. Sec. Stephen Rosenthal.

TENNESSEE

CHATTANOOGA

JEWISH COMMUNITY FEDERATION OF GREATER CHATTANOOGA (1931); 3601 Ringgold Rd. (37412); PO Box 8947 (37414); (423)493–0270. FAX: (423)493–9997. Pres. Helen Pregulman; Exec. Dir. Debra Levine.

KNOXVILLE

KNOXVILLE JEWISH FEDERATION, INC. (1939); 6800 Deane Hill Dr. (37919); (423) 693–5837. FAX: (423)694–4861. Pres. Mary Linda Schwartzbart; Exec. Dir. Dr. Bernard Rosenblatt.

MEMPHIS

MEMPHIS JEWISH FEDERATION (incl. Shelby County) (1935); 6560 Poplar Ave. (381)38–3614); (901)767–7100. FAX: (901)767–7128. Pres. Louise Sklar; Exec. Dir. Jeffrey Feld.

NASHVILLE

JEWISH FEDERATION OF NASHVILLE & MIDDLE TENNESSEE (1936); 801 Percy Warner Blvd. (37205); (615)356–3242. FAX: (615) 352–0056. Pres. Stephen Riven; Exec. Dir. Joshua Fogelson.

TEXAS

AUSTIN

JEWISH FEDERATION OF AUSTIN (1939; reorg. 1956); 11713 Jollyville Rd. (78759); (512)331–1144. FAX: (512)331–7059. Pres. Sandy Dochen; Exec. Dir. Barry Silverberg.

DALLAS

JEWISH FEDERATION OF GREATER DALLAS (1911); 7800 Northaven Rd. (75230); (214)369–3313. FAX: (214)369–8943. Pres. Andrea Weinstein; Exec. Dir. Gary Weinstein.

EL PASO

JEWISH FEDERATION OF EL PASO, INC. (1937); 405 Wallenberg Dr. (79912); (915) 584–4437. FAX: (915)584–0243. Pres. Stuart R. Schwartz; Exec. Dir. Larry Harris.

FORT WORTH

JEWISH FEDERATION OF FORT WORTH AND TARRANT COUNTY (1936); 6801 Dan Danciger Rd. (76133); (817)292–3081. FAX: (817)292–3214. Pres. Dr. Michael Korenman; Exec. Dir. Naomi Rosenfield.

GALVESTON

GALVESTON COUNTY JEWISH WELFARE ASSOCIATION (1936); PO Box 146 (77553); (409)763–5241. Pres. Dr. Michael Warren.

HOUSTON

JEWISH FEDERATION OF GREATER HOUSTON (1936); 5603 S. Braeswood Blvd. (770)96–3998); (713)729–7000. FAX: (713)721–6232. Pres. Marvin Woskow; Exec. V.-Pres. Douglas Kleiner.

SAN ANTONIO

JEWISH FEDERATION OF SAN ANTONIO (incl. Bexar County) (1922); 8434 Ahern Dr. (78216); (210)341–8234. FAX: (210)341–2842. Pres. Patricia A. Kalmans; Exec. Dir. Mark Freedman.

WACO

JEWISH FEDERATION OF WACO AND CENTRAL TEXAS (1949); PO Box 8031 (76714–8031); (254)776–3740. Pres. Jeff Wolf; Exec. Sec. Debbie Hersh-Levy.

UTAH

SALT LAKE CITY

UNITED JEWISH FEDERATION OF UTAH (1936); 2416 E. 1700 South (84108); (801) 581–0102. FAX: (801) 581–1334. Pres. Bob Wolff; Exec. Dir. Donald Gartman.

VIRGINIA

RICHMOND

JEWISH COMMUNITY FEDERATION OF RICHMOND (1935); 5403 Monument Ave., PO Box 17128 (23226); (804)288–0045. FAX: (804)282–7507. Pres. Mark B. Sisisky; Exec. Dir. Marsha F. Hurwitz.

TIDEWATER

UNITED JEWISH FEDERATION OF TIDEWATER (incl. Norfolk, Portsmouth, and Virginia Beach) (1937); 5029 Corporate Woods Dr., Suite 335, Virginia Beach (23462–4376); (757)671–1600. FAX: (757)671–7613. Pres. David Brand; Exec. V.-Pres. Mark L. Goldstein.

VIRGINIA PENINSULA

UNITED JEWISH COMMUNITY OF THE VIR-
GINIA PENINSULA, INC. (1942); 2700 Spring
Rd., Newport News (23606); (757)930–
1422. FAX: (757)930–3762. Pres. Ettalea
Kanter; Exec. Dir. Rodney J. Margolis.

WASHINGTON

SEATTLE

JEWISH FEDERATION OF GREATER SEATTLE
(incl. King County, Everett, and Bremer-
ton) (1926); 2031 Third Ave. (98121); (206)
443–5400. FAX: (206)443–0306. Pres. Lucy
Pruzan; Exec. V.-Pres. Michael Novick.

WEST VIRGINIA

CHARLESTON

FEDERATED JEWISH CHARITIES OF
CHARLESTON, INC. (1937); PO Box 1613
(25326); (304)345–2320. FAX: (304)925-
0793. Pres. Stuart May; Exec. Sec. Lee
Diznoff.

WISCONSIN

KENOSHA

KENOSHA JEWISH WELFARE FUND (1938);
600 68th Pl. (53143); (414)697–0300. FAX:
(414)694-4789. Pres. Ben Steverman; Sec.-
Treas. Steven Barasch.

MADISON

MADISON JEWISH COMMUNITY COUNCIL,
INC. (1940); 6434 Enterprise Lane (53719-
1117. (608)278–1808. FAX:(608)278-7814.
Pres. Joel Minkoff; Exec. Dir. Steven H.
Morrison.

MILWAUKEE

MILWAUKEE JEWISH FEDERATION, INC.
(1902); 1360 N. Prospect Ave. (53202); (414)
390–5700. FAX: (414)390–5782. Pres.
Stephen E. Richman; Exec. V.-Pres. Richard
H. Meyer.

CANADA

ALBERTA

CALGARY

CALGARY JEWISH COMMUNITY COUNCIL
(1962); 1607 90th Ave. SW (T2V 4V7);
(403)253–8600. FAX: (403)253–7915. Pres.
Nate Feldman; Exec. Dir. Joel R. Miller.

EDMONTON

JEWISH FEDERATION OF EDMONTON (1954;
reorg. 1982); 7200 156th St. (T5R 1X3);
(403)487–0585. FAX: (403)481–1854.
Pres. Stephen Mandel; Exec. Dir. Lesley
Jacobson.

BRITISH COLUMBIA

VANCOUVER

JEWISH FEDERATION OF GREATER VANCOU-
VER (1932; reorg. 1987); 950 W. 41st Ave.,
Suite 200 (V5Z 2N7); (604)257–5100. FAX:
(604)257–5110. Pres. Dr. Jonathan Berkowitz; Exec. Dir. Drew Staffenberg.

MANITOBA

WINNIPEG

WINNIPEG JEWISH COMMUNITY COUNCIL
(1938; reorg. 1973); 123 Doncaster St., Suite
C300 (R3N 2B2); (204)477–7400. FAX:
(204)477–7405. Pres. Larry Hurtig; Exec.
Dir. Robert Freedman.

ONTARIO

HAMILTON

UJA/JEWISH FEDERATION OF HAMIL-
TON/WENTWORTH & AREA (1932; merged
1971); PO Box 7258, 1030 Lower Lion Club
Rd., Ancaster (L9G 3N6); (905)648–0605.
FAX: (905)648–8350. Pres. Cheryl Green-
baum; Exec. Dir. Patricia Tolkin Eppel.

LONDON

LONDON JEWISH FEDERATION (1932); 536
Huron St. (N5Y 4J5); (519)673–3310. FAX:
(519)673–1161. Pres. Ted Medzon; Exec.
Dir. Hillel Boroditsky.

OTTAWA

JEWISH COMMUNITY COUNCIL OF OTTAWA
(1934); 151 Chapel St. (K1N 7Y2);
(613)789–7306. FAX: (613)789–4593. Pres.
Barbara Farber; Interim Exec. Dir. Mitchell
Bellman.

TORONTO

JEWISH FEDERATION OF GREATER TORONTO
(1917); 4600 Bathurst St., Willowdale (M2R
3V2); (416)635–2883. FAX: (416)631–
5715. Pres. Joseph Steiner; Exec. V.-Pres.
Allan Reitzes.

WINDSOR

JEWISH COMMUNITY FEDERATION (1938);
1641 Ouellette Ave. (N8X 1K9); (519)973–
1772. FAX: (519)973–1774. Pres. Gary
Katz; Exec. Dir. Steven Brownstein.

QUEBEC

MONTREAL

FEDERATION CJA (formerly Allied Jewish
Community Services) (1965); 5151 Cote Ste.
Catherine Rd. (H3W 1M6); (514)735–3541.
FAX: (514)735–8972. Pres. Yoine Gold-
stein; Exec. V.-Pres. Danyael Cantor.

Jewish Periodicals*

UNITED STATES

ALABAMA

SOUTHERN SHOFAR (1990). PO Box 130052, Birmingham, 35213. (205) 595–9255. FAX: (205)595–9256. E-mail: soshofar@aol.com. Lawrence M. Brook. Monthly.

ARIZONA

ARIZONA JEWISH POST (1946). 3812 East River Rd., Tucson, 85718. (520)529–1500. FAX: (520)577–0734. E-mail: 6809162@mcimail.com. Sandra R. Heiman. Fortnightly. Jewish Federation of Southern Arizona.

JEWISH NEWS OF GREATER PHOENIX (1948). 1625 E. Northern Ave., Suite 106, Phoenix, 85020. (602)870–9470. FAX: (602)870–0426. E-mail:jngphx@aol.com. Ed./Pub. Florence Eckstein. Weekly.

CALIFORNIA

CENTRAL CALIFORNIA JEWISH HERITAGE (1914). 7334 Topanga Canyon Blvd., Suite 104, Canoga Park, 91304. (818) 999–9921. FAX: (818) 999-6715. E-mail: brin@lamg.com. Dan Brin. Six times a year. Heritage Group.

HERITAGE-SOUTHWEST JEWISH PRESS (1914). 7334 Topanga Canyon Blvd., Suite 104, Canoga Park, 91304. (818) 999–9921. FAX: (818) 999-6715. E-mail: brin@lamg.com. Dan Brin. Weekly. Heritage Group.

JEWISH BULLETIN OF NORTHERN CALIFORNIA (1946). 225 Bush St., Suite 1480, San Francisco, 94104–4281. (415)263–7200. FAX: (415)263–7223. E-mail: sanfranbul@aol.com. Marc S. Klein. Weekly. San Francisco Jewish Community Publications, Inc.

JEWISH COMMUNITY CHRONICLE (1947). 3801 E. Willow St., Long Beach, 90815. (562)595–5543. FAX:(562)595–5543. E-mail: jchron@net999.com. Harriette Ellis. Fortnightly. Jewish Federation of Greater Long Beach & West Orange County.

JEWISH COMMUNITY NEWS (1976). 14855 Oka Rd., Suite 2, Los Gatos, 95030. (408)358–3033, ext. 31. FAX: (408)356–0733. E-mail: jcn@jfgsj.org. Eileen Goss. Monthly. Jewish Federation of Greater San Jose.

JEWISH JOURNAL OF GREATER LOS ANGELES (1986). 3660 Wilshire Blvd., Suite 204, Los Angeles, 90010. (213)738–7778. FAX: (213)386–9501. E-mail: ab871@lafn.org. Gene Lichtenstein. Weekly.

JEWISH NEWS (1973). 11071 Ventura Blvd., Studio City, 91604. (818)786–4000. FAX: (818)760–4648. Phil Blazer. Monthly.

JEWISH SOCIAL STUDIES: HISTORY, CULTURE, AND SOCIETY (1939). c/o Program in Jewish Studies, Bldg. 240, Rm. 103, Stanford University, Stanford, 94305–2190. (650)725–0829. FAX: (650)725-2920. E-mail: jss@leland.stanford.edu. Steven J. Zipperstein, Aron Rodrigue. Three times a year. Conference on Jewish Social Studies, Inc.

JEWISH SPECTATOR (1935). P.O. Box 8160, Calabasas, 91372D8160. (818)591–7481. FAX: (818)591–7267. E-mail: jewishspec@aol.com. Rabbi Mark Bleiweiss.

---

*The information in this directory is based on replies to questionnaires circulated by the editors. For organization bulletins, see the directory of Jewish organizations.

Quarterly. American Friends of Center for Jewish Living and Values.

LOS ANGELES JEWISH TIMES (formerly B'NAI B'RITH MESSENGER) (1897). 5455 Wilshire Blvd., Suite 903, Los Angeles, 90036. (213)933-0131. FAX: (213)933-8030. E-mail: lajtimes@aol.com. Ed.-in-Chief Joe Bobker; Mng. Ed. Jane Fried. Weekly.

ORANGE COUNTY JEWISH HERITAGE. 24331 Muirlands Blvd., Suite D-347, Lake Forest, 92630. Phone/FAX: (714)837-9564. Stan Brin. Bi-weekly.

SAN DIEGO JEWISH PRESS HERITAGE. P.O. Box 19363, San Diego, 92159D0363. (619)265-0808. FAX: (619)265-0850. Don Harrison. Weekly.

SAN DIEGO JEWISH TIMES (1979). 4731 Palm Ave., La Mesa, 91941. (619)463-5515. FAX: (900) 370-1190. E-mail: jewishtimes@msn.com. Carol Rosenberg. Bi-weekly.

SHALOM L.A. 15301 Ventura Blvd., Suite 500, Sherman Oaks, 91403. (818)783-3090. FAX: (818)783-1104. Meir Doron. Weekly. Hebrew.

TIKKUN: A BIMONTHLY JEWISH CRITIQUE OF POLITICS, CULTURE & SOCIETY (1986). 26 Fell St., San Francisco, 94102. (415) 575-1200. FAX: (415)575-1434. E-mail: tikkun@ncgate.newcollege.edu. Michael Lerner. Bimonthly. Institute for Labor & Mental Health.

WESTERN STATES JEWISH HISTORY (1968). 3111 Kelton Ave., Los Angeles, 90034. (310)475-1415. Prof. William M. Kramer. Quarterly. Western States Jewish History Association.

COLORADO

INTERMOUNTAIN JEWISH NEWS (1913). 1275 Sherman St., Suite 214, Denver, 80203-2299. (303)861-2234. FAX: (303)832-6942. E-mail: ijn@rmii.com. Exec. Ed. Rabbi Hillel Goldberg; Pub. Miriam Goldberg. Weekly.

CONNECTICUT

CONNECTICUT JEWISH LEDGER (1929). 924 Farmington Ave., W. Hartford, 06107. (860)231-2424. FAX: (860)231-2428. E-mail: ctjledger@aol.com. Jonathan S. Tobin. Weekly.

JEWISH LEADER. 28 Channing St., PO Box 1468, New London, 06320. (860)442-7395. FAX: (860)443-4175. Ed. Izzy Schwartz; Mngr. Sidney Schiller. Bi-weekly. Jewish Federation of Eastern Connecticut.

DELAWARE

JEWISH VOICE. 100 W. 10th St., Suite 301, Wilmington, 19801. (302) 427-2100. FAX: (302) 427-2438. E-mail: jewishvoic@aol.com. Faye J. Harris. 22 times per year. Jewish Federation of Delaware.

DISTRICT OF COLUMBIA

B'NAI B'RITH INTERNATIONAL JEWISH MONTHLY (1886, under the name Menorah). 1640 Rhode Island Ave., NW, Washington, 20036. (202)857-6645. FAX: (202)296-1092. E-mail: erozenman@bnaibrith.org. Eric Rozenman. Bi-monthly. B'nai B'rith International.

CAPITAL COMMUNIQUÉ (1991). 503 Capital Ct., NE, Suite 300, Washington, 20002. (202)544-7636. FAX: (202)544-7645. Stephen Silberfarb. Bimonthly. National Jewish Democratic Council.

JEWISH VETERAN (1896). 1811 R St., NW, Washington, 20009-1659. (202)265-6280. FAX: (202)234-5662. E-mail: jwv@erols.com. Tim Clarke, Jr. Bi-monthly. Jewish War Veterans of the U.S.A.

MOMENT (1975). 4710 41 St., NW, Washington, 20016. (202)364-3300. FAX: (202)364-2636. Hershel Shanks. Bimonthly. Jewish Educational Ventures, Inc.

MONITOR (1990). 1819 H Street, NW, Suite 230, Washington, 20006. (202)775-9770. FAX: (202)775-9776.Jason Silberberg. Quarterly. Union of Councils for Soviet Jews.

NEAR EAST REPORT (1957). 440 First St., NW, Suite 607, Washington, 20001. (202)639-5254. FAX: (202) 347-4916. Dr. Raphael Danziger. Fortnightly. Near East Research, Inc.

SECURITY AFFAIRS (1976). 1717 K St., NW, Suite 800, Washington, 20006. (202)833-0020. FAX: (202)296-6452. E-mail: info@jinsa.org. Jim Colbert. Bimonthly. Jewish Institute for National Security Affairs.

WASHINGTON JEWISH WEEK. *See under* MARYLAND

FLORIDA

THE CHRONICLE (1971). 580 S. McIntosh Rd., Sarasota, 34232. (941)371–4546. FAX: (941)378–2947. Barry Millman. Fortnightly. Sarasota-Manatee Jewish Federation.

HERITAGE FLORIDA JEWISH NEWS (1976). PO Box 300742, Fern Park, 32730. (407)834–8787 or 834–8277. FAX: (407)831–0507. E-mail: heritagefl@aol. com. Pub. Jeffrey Gaeser; Assoc. Ed. Chris Allen. Weekly.

JACKSONVILLE JEWISH NEWS (1988). 8505 San Jose Blvd., Jacksonville, 32217. (904)448–5000, (904)262-1971. FAX: (904)448–5715. Susan R. Goetz. Monthly. Jacksonville Jewish Federation.

JEWISH JOURNAL (PALM BEACH-BROWARD-DADE) (1977). 601 Fairway Dr., Deerfield Beach, 33441. (954)698–6397. FAX: (954)429–1207. Andrew Polin; Mng. Ed. Alan Gosh. Weekly. South Florida News-paper Network.

JEWISH PRESS OF PINELLAS COUNTY (-Clearwater-St. Petersburg) (1985). PO Box 6970, Clearwater, 33758-6970; 13191 Starkey Rd., Crownpointe #8, Largo, 33773–1438. E-mail: jptb@aol.com. (813)535–4400. FAX:(813)530–3039. Karen Wolfson Dawkins. Biweekly. Jew-ish Press Group of Tampa Bay (FL), Inc. in cooperation with the Jewish Federa-tion of Pinellas County.

JEWISH PRESS OF TAMPA (1987). PO Box 6970, Clearwater 34618–6970; 13191 Starkey Rd., Crownpointe #8, Largo 33773–1438. (813)871–2332. FAX: (813)530–3039. E-mail: jptb@aol.com. Karen Wolfson Dawkins. Biweekly. Jew-ish Press Group of Tampa Bay (FL), Inc.

PALM BEACH JEWISH TIMES AND BOCA/DEL-RAY JEWISH TIMES (1994). 2240 Wool-bright Rd., #424, Boynton Beach, 33426. (561) 374–7900. FAX: (561) 374–7999. E-mail: 7026474@mcimail.com. Mng. Ed. Boaz Dvir. Weekly.

SHALOM(1994). 8358 W. Oakland Park Blvd., Suite 305, Ft. Lauderdale, 33351. (954)748–8400. FAX: (954) 748-4509.

Ed.-in-Chief Rhonda Roseman-Seriani; Mng. Ed. Elliot Goldenberg. Biweekly. Jewish Federation of Broward County.

GEORGIA

ATLANTA JEWISH TIMES (1925; formerly SOUTHERN ISRAELITE). 1575 Northside Dr., NW, Atlanta, 30318. (404)352–2400. FAX: (404)355–9388. Ed. Neil Rubin; Ed. Emer. Vida Goldgar. Weekly.

JEWISH CIVIC PRESS (1972). 3500 Piedmont Rd., Suite 612, Atlanta, 30305. (404)231–2194. Abner L. Tritt. Monthly.

ILLINOIS

CHICAGO JEWISH NEWS (1994). 2501 W. Pe-terson, Chicago, 60659. (773)728–3636. FAX: (773)728–3734. E-mail: chijew-nes@aol.com. Joseph Aaron. Weekly.

CHICAGO JEWISH STAR (1991). PO Box 268, Skokie, 60076–0268. (847)674–7827. FAX: (847)674–0014. E-mail: chicago-jewish-star@mcimail.com. Ed. Douglas Wertheimer; Assoc. Ed. Gila Wertheimer. Fortnightly.

JEWISH COMMUNITY NEWS (1941). 6464 W. Main, Suite 7A, Belleville, 62223. (618)398–6100. FAX: (618)398–0539. Steve Low. Every other month. Jewish Federation of Southern Illinois.

JUF NEWS & JEWISH GUIDE (1972). One S. Franklin St., Rm. 701G, Chicago, 60606. (312)357–4848. FAX: (312)855–2470. E-mail: aharon@interaccess.com. Aaron Cohen. Monthly (Guide, annually). Jew-ish United Fund/Jewish Federation of Metropolitan Chicago.

INDIANA

ILLIANA NEWS (1976). 2939 Jewett St., Highland, 46322. (219)972–2250. FAX: (219)972–4779. Monthly (except July/ Aug.). Jewish Federation of Northwest Indiana, Inc.

INDIANA JEWISH POST AND OPINION (1935). 238 S. Meridian St., Indianapolis, 46225. (317)927–7800. FAX: (317)927–7807. Ed Stattmann. Weekly.

NATIONAL JEWISH POST AND OPINION (1932). 238 S. Meridian St., Indianapolis, 46225. (317)972–7800. FAX: (317)972–7807. Gabriel Cohen. Weekly.

KANSAS

Kansas City Jewish Chronicle (1920). 7373 W. 107 St., Overland Park, 66212. (913)648–4620. FAX: (913)381–9889. E-mail: kcjchron@aol.com. Rick Hellman. Weekly. Sun Publications.

KENTUCKY

COMMUNITY (1975). 3630 Dutchman's Lane, Louisville, 40205–3200. (502) 451–8840. FAX: (502) 458–0702. E-mail: fedlouky@jon.cjfny.org. Shiela Wallace. Biweekly. Jewish Community Federation of Louisville.

KENTUCKY JEWISH POST AND OPINION (1931). 1551 Bardstown Rd., Louisville, 40205. (502)459–1914. Weekly.

LOUISIANA

JEWISH CIVIC PRESS (1965). 924 Valmont St., New Orleans, 70115. (504)895–8784. FAX: (504) 895–0433. Claire & Abner Tritt, eds. and pubs. Monthly.

JEWISH NEWS (1995). 3500 N. Causeway Blvd., Suite 1240, Metairie, 70002. (504)828–2125. FAX: (504)828–2827. E-mail: jfedrb@aol.com. Marla Shivers. Fortnightly. Jewish Federation of Greater New Orleans.

MARYLAND

BALTIMORE JEWISH TIMES (1919). 2104 N. Charles St., Baltimore, 21218. (410)752–3504. FAX: (410)752–2375. Michael Davis. Weekly.

MODERN JUDAISM (1980). John Hopkins University Press, 2715 N. Charles St., Baltimore, 21218D4363. (410)516D6987. FAX: (410)516D6968. (Editorial address: Center for Judaic Studies, Boston University, 745 Commonwealth Ave., Boston, 02215. (617)353–8096. FAX: (617)353–5441.) Steven T. Katz. Three times a year.

PROOFTEXTS: A JOURNAL OF JEWISH LITERARY HISTORY (1980). Johns Hopkins University Press, 2715 N. Charles St., Baltimore, 21218–4319. (410)516–6987. FAX: (410)516–6968. Editorial address (for contributors): NEJS Dept., Brandeis U., Waltham, MA 02254. Alan Mintz, David G. Roskies. Three times a year.

WASHINGTON JEWISH WEEK (1930, as the National Jewish Ledger). 12300 Twinbrook Pkwy., Suite 250, Rockville, 20852. (301)230–2222. FAX: (301)881–6362. E-mail: wjweek@aol.com. Jonathan Stern. Weekly.

MASSACHUSETTS

AMERICAN JEWISH HISTORY (1893). Two Thornton Rd., Waltham, 02154. (617) 891–8110. FAX: (617)899–9208. E-mail: ajhs@ajhs.org. Marc Lee Raphael. Quarterly. American Jewish Historical Society.

JEWISH ADVOCATE (1902). 15 School St., Boston, 02108. (617)367–9100. FAX: (617)367–9310. E-mail: thejewadv@aol.com. Barbara Rabinovitz. Weekly.

JEWISH CHRONICLE (1927). 131 Lincoln St., Worcester, 01605. (508)752–2512. Sondra Shapiro. Biweekly.

JEWISH GUIDE TO BOSTON & NEW ENGLAND (1972). 15 School St., Boston, 02108. (617)367–9100. FAX: (617)367–9310. Rosie Rosenzweig. Bi-annually. The Jewish Advocate.

THE JEWISH JOURNAL/NORTH OF BOSTON (1976). 201 Washington St., PO Box 555, Salem, 01970. (978)745–4111. FAX: (978)745–5333. E-mail: editorial@jewishjournal.org. Bette W. Keva. Biweekly. Russian section. North Shore Jewish Press Ltd.

THE JEWISH NEWS OF WESTERN MASSACHUSETTS (1945). PO Box 269, Northampton, 01061. (413)582–9870. FAX: (413)582–9847. Kenneth G. White. Biweekly.

METROWEST JEWISH REPORTER (1970). 76 Salem End Rd., Framingham, 01702. (508)872–4808. FAX: (508)879–5856. Marcia T. Rivin. Monthly. Combined Jewish Philanthropies of Greater Boston.

THE PAKN-TREGER (1980). 1021 West St., Amherst, 01002. (800)535–3595. E-mail: jsnybc@worldnet.att.net. (413)535–1007. Jeffrey Sharlet. Quarterly. Yiddish & English. National Yiddish Book Center.

MICHIGAN

DETROIT JEWISH NEWS (1942). 27676 Franklin Rd., Southfield, 48034. (248)354–6060. FAX: (248)354–6069. E-mail: 6819228@mcimail.com. Phil Jacobs. Weekly.

HUMANISTIC JUDAISM (1968). 28611 W. Twelve Mile Rd., Farmington Hills, 48334. (248)478–7610. FAX: (248)478–3159. E-mail: info@shj.org. M. Bonnie

Cousens, Ruth D. Feldman. Quarterly. Society for Humanistic Judaism.

WASHTENAW JEWISH NEWS (1978). 2935 Birch Hollow Dr., Ann Arbor, 48108. (313)971–1800. FAX: (313)677–0109. E-mail: wjna2@aol.com. Susan Kravitz Ayer. Monthly.

MINNESOTA

AMERICAN JEWISH WORLD (1912). 4509 Minnetonka Blvd., Minneapolis, 55416. (612)920–7000. FAX: (612)920–6205. Marshall Hoffman. Weekly.

MISSOURI

KANSAS CITY JEWISH CHRONICLE. See under KANSAS

ST. LOUIS JEWISH LIGHT (1947; reorg. 1963). 12 Millstone Campus Dr., St. Louis, 63146. (314)432–3353. FAX: (314)432–0515. E-mail: stlouislgt@aol.com. Robert A. Cohn. Weekly. St. Louis Jewish Light.

NEBRASKA

JEWISH PRESS (1920). 333 S. 132 St., Omaha, 68154. (402)334–8200. FAX: (402)334–5422. E-mail: jshpress@aol.com. Carol Katzman. Weekly. Jewish Federation of Omaha.

NEVADA

JEWISH REPORTER (1996). 3909 S. Maryland Pkwy., Suite 405, Las Vegas, 89119–7520. (702)732–0556. FAX: (702)732–3228. Rebecca Herren. Bimonthly. Jewish Federation of Las Vegas.

LAS VEGAS ISRAELITE (1965). PO Box 14096, Las Vegas, 89114. (702)876–1255. FAX: (702)364–1009. Michael Tell. Bimonthly.

NEW JERSEY

AVOTAYNU (1985). 155 N. Washington Ave., Bergenfield, 07621. (201)387–7200. FAX: (201)387–2855. E-mail: info@avotaynu. com. Sallyann Amdur Sack. Quarterly.

JEWISH CHRONICLE (1982). 629 Wood St., Suite 204, Vineland, 08360. (609)696–4445. FAX: (609)696–3428. Joyce Baltus. Every other month. The Jewish Federation of Cumberland County.

JEWISH COMMUNITY NEWS. 1086 Teaneck Rd., Teaneck, 07666. (201) 837–8818. FAX: (201) 833–4959. E-mail: jewish-std2@aol.com. Rebecca Kaplan Boroson.

Fortnightly. Jewish Federation of North Jersey and Jewish Federation of Greater Clifton-Passaic.

JEWISH COMMUNITY VOICE (1941). 2393 W. Marlton Pike, Cherry Hill, 08002. (609) 665–6100, ext. 217. FAX: (609) 665–0074. E-mail: jvcheditor@aol. com. Harriet Kessler. Biweekly. Jewish Federation of Southern NJ.

JEWISH HORIZON (1981). 843 St. Georges Ave., Roselle, 07203. (908)245–5775. FAX: (908)245–5599. Fran Gold. Weekly.

JEWISH RECORD (Atlantic City area) (1939). 1525 S. Main St., Pleasantville, 08232. (609)383–0999. Martin Korik. Weekly.

JEWISH STANDARD (1931). 1086 Teaneck Rd., Teaneck, 07666. (201)837–8818. FAX: (201)833–4959. Rebecca Kaplan Boroson. Weekly.

JEWISH STAR (1985). 230 Old Bridge Turnpike, South River, 08882–2000. (732) 432–7711. FAX: (732)432–0292. E-mail: jfgmc@aol.com. Marlene A. Heller. Fortnightly. Jewish Federation of Greater Middlesex County.

JEWISH STATE (1996). 320 Raritan Ave., Suite 203, Highland Park, 08904. (732) 393–0023. FAX: (732)393–0026. E-mail: jewish@castle.net. Ron Ostroff. Weekly.

JEWISH VOICE OF GREATER MONMOUTH COUNTY (1971). 100 Grant Ave., Deal Park, 07723. (732)531–6200. FAX: (732) 531–9518. E-mail: monvoice@-aol.com. Doris Kulman. Monthly. Jewish Federation of Greater Monmouth County and Ocean County Jewish Federation.

JEWISH VOICE & OPINION (1987). 73 Dana Place, Englewood, 07631. (201) 569–2845. FAX: (201)569–1739. Susan L. Rosenbluth. Monthly.

JOURNAL OF JEWISH COMMUNAL SERVICE (1899). 3084 State Hwy. 27, Suite 9, Kendall Pk., 08824–1657. (908)821–1871. FAX: (908)821–5335. E-mail: jcsana@aol.com. Gail Naron Chalew. Quarterly. Jewish Communal Service Association of North America.

METROWEST JEWISH NEWS (1947). 901 Route 10, Whippany, 07981–1157. (201) 887–3900. FAX: (201)887–5999. David Twersky. Weekly. United Jewish Federation of MetroWest.

OPTIONS, THE JEWISH RESOURCES NEWS-
LETTER (1974). Box 311, Wayne, 07474–
0311. (973)694–2327. Betty J. Singer.
Monthly.

NEW MEXICO

NEW MEXICO JEWISH LINK (1971). 5520
Wyoming NE, Albuquerque, 87109.
(505)821–3214. FAX: (505)821–3351. E-
mail: nmjlink@aol.com. Tema Milstein.
Monthly. Jewish Federation of Greater
Albuquerque.

NEW YORK

AFN SHVEL (1941). 200 W. 72 St., Suite
40, NYC, 10023. (212)787–6675.
E-mail: yidleague@aol.com. Mordkhe
Schaechter. Quarterly. Yiddish. League
for Yiddish, Inc.

AGENDA: JEWISH EDUCATION (1949; formerly PEDAGOGIC REPORTER). JESNA,
730 Broadway, NYC, 10003. (212)
529–2000. FAX: (212)529–2009. E-mail:
info@jesna.org. Rabbi Arthur Vernon.
Twice a year. Jewish Education Service of
North America, Inc.

ALGEMEINER JOURNAL (1972). 225 E.
Broadway, NYC, 10002. (212)267–5561.
FAX: (212)267–5624. Gershon Jacobson.
Weekly. Yiddish-English.

AMERICAN JEWISH YEAR BOOK (1899). 165
E. 56 St., NYC, 10022. (212)751–4000.
FAX: (212)751–4017. E-mail: re-
search@ajc.org. David Singer, Ruth R.
Seldin. Annually. American Jewish Com-
mittee.

AMIT (1925). 817 Broadway, NYC, 10003.
(212)477–4720. FAX: (212)353–2312. E-
mail: amitmag@aol.com. Rita Schwalb.
Quarterly. AMIT (formerly AMERICAN
MIZRACHI WOMEN).

AUFBAU (1934). 2121 Broadway, NYC,
10023. (212)873–7400. Voice mail: (212)
579-6578. FAX: (212)496–5736. Mng.
Ed. Tekla Szymanski; Sr. Ed. Monika
Ziegler. Fortnightly. German. New World
Club, Inc.

BUFFALO JEWISH REVIEW (1918). 15 E. Mo-
hawk St., Buffalo, 14203. (716)854–2192.
FAX: (716)854–2198. E-mail: buffjew-
rev@aoc.com. Harlan C. Abbey. Weekly.
Kahaal Nahalot Israel.

THE CALL (1933). 45 E. 33 St., NYC, 10016.
(212)889–6800, ext. 210. FAX: (212)532–
7518. Lorna I. Levy. Quarterly. The
Workmen's Circle/Arbeter Ring.

CATSKILL/HUDSON JEWISH STAR (1991). PO
Box 776 (2793 Route 209 South), Wurts-
boro, 12790. (914)888–4680. FAX: (914)
888–2209. Edith Schapiro. Monthly. Jewish Focus, Inc.

CCAR JOURNAL: A REFORM JEWISH QUAR-
TERLY (formerly JOURNAL OF REFORM JU-
DAISM) (1953). 355 Lexington Ave., NYC,
10017. (212)972–3636. FAX: (212)692–
0819. Ed. Rifat Sonsino. Mng. Ed. Elliot
Stevens. Quarterly. Central Conference of
American Rabbis.

CIRCLE (1943). 15 E. 26 St., NYC,
10010–1579. (212)532–4949. FAX: (212)
481–4174. E-mail: info@jcca.org. Avraham Zimmy Zimberg. Quarterly. Jewish
Community Centers Association of
North America (formerly JWB).

COMMENTARY (1945). 165 E. 56 St., NYC,
10022. (212)751–4000. FAX: (212)751–
1174. E-mail: 103115.2375@compuserve.
com. Ed. Neal Kozodoy; Ed.-at-Large
Norman Podhoretz. Monthly. American
Jewish Committee.

CONGRESS MONTHLY (1933). 15 E. 84 St.,
NYC, 10028. (212)879–4500. Maier
Deshell. Six times a year. American Jew-
ish Congress.

CONSERVATIVE JUDAISM (1945). 3080 Broadway, NYC, 10027. (212)280–6065. FAX:
(212)749–9166. E-mail: apubs@jtsa.edu.
Rabbi Benjamin Edidin Scolnic. Quarterly. Rabbinical Assembly and Jewish
Theological Seminary of America.

FORVERTS (YIDDISH FORWARD) (1897). 45
E. 33 St., NYC, 10016. (212)889–
8200. FAX: (212)684–3949. Mordechai
Strigler. Weekly. Yiddish. Forward Association, Inc.

FORWARD (1897). 45 E. 33 St., NYC, 10016.
(212)889–8200. FAX: (212)447–6406. E-
mail: newsdesk@forward.com. Seth Lip-
sky. Weekly. Forward Newspaper, L.L.C.

HADAROM (1957). 305 Seventh Ave., NYC,
10001. (212)807–7888. FAX: (212)727–
8452. Rabbi Gedalia Dov Schwartz. Annually. Hebrew. Rabbinical Council of
America.

HADASSAH MAGAZINE (1914). 50 W. 58 St.,
NYC, 10019. (212)688–0227. FAX:
(212)446–9521. Alan M. Tigay. Monthly
(except for combined issues of June–July
and Aug.–Sept.). Hadassah, the Women's
Zionist Organization of America.

HADOAR (1921). 47 W. 34 St., Rm. 609, NYC, 10001. (212)629–9443. FAX: (212) 629–9472. Ed. Shlomo Shamir; Lit. Ed. Dr. Yael Feldman. Biweekly. Hebrew. Hadoar Association, Inc., Organ of the Histadruth of America.

ISRAEL HORIZONS (1952). 224 W. 35 St., Rm. 403, NYC, 10001. (212)868–0386. Donald Goldstein. Quarterly. Americans for Progressive Israel.

JBI VOICE (1978). 110 E. 30 St., NYC, 10016. (212)889–2525, (800)433–1531. Dr. Jacob Freid. Ten times a year in U.S. (audiocassettes). English. Jewish Braille Institute of America.

JEWISH ACTION MAGAZINE (1950). 333 Seventh Ave., 20th fl., NYC, 10001. (212)613–8146. FAX: (212)613–8333. E-mail: jaedit@ou.org. Charlotte Friedland. Quarterly. Union of Orthodox Jewish Congregations of America.

JEWISH BOOK ANNUAL (1942). 15 E. 26 St., NYC, 10010. (212)532–4949. Ed. Dr. Philip Miller; Mng. Ed. Dr. Joseph Lowin. Hebrew & English with bibliography in Yiddish. Jewish Book Council.

JEWISH BOOK WORLD (1945). 15 E. 26 St., NYC, 10010. (212)532–4949, ext. 297. FAX: (212)481–4174. Esther Nussbaum. Three times annually. Jewish Book Council.

JEWISH BRAILLE REVIEW (1931). 110 E. 30 St., NYC, 10016. (212)889–2525, (800) 433–1531. Dr. Jacob Freid. 10 times a year in U.S. (braille). English. Jewish Braille Institute of America.

JEWISH CURRENTS (1946). 22 E. 17 St., Suite 601, NYC, 10003–1919. (212)924–5740. FAX: (212)924–5740. Morris U. Schappes. Monthly (July/Aug. combined). Association for Promotion of Jewish Secularism, Inc.

JEWISH EDUCATION NEWS (1980). 261 W. 35 St., Fl. 12A, NYC 10001. (212) 268–4210. FAX: (212)268–4214. E-mail: 500-8447@mcimail.com. Mng. Ed. Roselyn Bell. Tri-annually. Coalition for the Advancement of Jewish Education.

JEWISH FRONTIER (1934). 275 Seventh Ave., 17th fl., NYC, 10001. (212)229–2280. FAX: (212)675–7685. Nahum Guttman. Bimonthly. Labor Zionist Letters, Inc.

JEWISH HERALD (1984). 1689 46 St., Brooklyn, 11204. (718)972–4000. FAX: (718)

972–9400. E-mail: nyjherald.aol.com. Leon J. Sternheim. Weekly.

JEWISH JOURNAL (1969). 11 Sunrise Plaza, Valley Stream, 11580. (516)561–6900. FAX: (516)561–6971. Ed. Paul Rubens; Pub. Harold Singer. Weekly.

JEWISH LEDGER (1924). 2535 Brighton-Henrietta Town Line Rd., Rochester, 14623. (716)427–2434. FAX: (716)427–8521. Barbara Morgenstern. Weekly.

JEWISH OBSERVER (1963). 84 William St., NYC, 10038. (212)797–9000. FAX: (212)269–2843. E-mail: meirf@aol.com. Rabbi Nisson Wolpin. Monthly (except July and Aug.). Agudath Israel of America.

JEWISH OBSERVER OF CENTRAL NEW YORK (1978). PO Box 510, DeWitt, 13214. (315)445–2040. FAX: (315)445–1559. E-mail: jocny@aol.com. Iris Petroff. Biweekly. Syracuse Jewish Federation, Inc.

JEWISH PARENT CONNECTION (1992). 160 Broadway, 4th fl., NYC, 10038. (212)227–1000, ext. 102. FAX: (212)406–6934. E-mail: cyberjpc@aol.com. Mng. Ed. Rabbi Eli Gewirtz; Ed. Joyce Lempel. Bimonthly except for July and August. Torah Umesorah–National Society for Hebrew Day Schools.

JEWISH POST OF NY (1993). 130 W. 29 St., 10th fl., NYC, 10001–5312. (212)967–7313. FAX: (212)967–8321. E-mail: jpostl@gramercy.ios.com. Ed. Gad Nahshon; Pub. & Ed.-in-Chief Henry J. Levy. Monthly. Link Marketing & Promotion, Inc.

JEWISH PRESS (1950). 338 Third Ave., Brooklyn, 11215. (718)330–1100. FAX: (718)935–1215. E-mail: j.press@aol.com. Rabbi Sholom Klass. Weekly.

JEWISH TELEGRAPHIC AGENCY COMMUNITY News Reporter (1962). 330 Seventh Ave., 11th fl., NYC, 10001–5010. (212)643–1890. FAX: (212)643–8498. Ed. Lisa Hostein; Mng. Ed. Ken Bandler. Weekly.

JEWISH TELEGRAPHIC AGENCY DAILY NEWS BULLETIN (1917). 330 Seventh Ave., 11th fl., NYC, 10001–5010. (212)643–1890. FAX: (212)643–8498. Exec. Ed. Mark Joffe; Ed. Lisa Hostein. Daily.

JEWISH TELEGRAPHIC AGENCY WEEKLY NEWS DIGEST (1933). 330 Seventh Ave., 11th fl., NYC, 10001–5010. (212)643–1890. FAX: (212)643–8498. Exec. Ed.

Mark Joffe; Ed. Lisa Hostein; Mng. Ed. Ken Bandler. Weekly.

JEWISH WEEK (1876; reorg. 1970). 1501 Broadway, NYC, 10036–5503. (212)921–7822. FAX: (212)921–8420. E-mail: editor@jewishweek.org. Gary Rosenblatt. Weekly.

JEWISH WORLD (1965). 1104 Central Ave., Albany, 12205. (518)459–8455. FAX: (518)459–5289. Laurie J. Clevenson. Weekly.

JOURNAL OF JEWISH EDUCATION (formerly JEWISH EDUCATION) (1929). 111 Eighth Ave., NYC, 10011-5201. (212) 529–2000. FAX: (212)529–2009. Dr. Bernard Ducoff. Three times a year. Council for Jewish Education.

JOURNAL OF REFORM JUDAISM. See CCAR JOURNAL

JTS MAGAZINE (formerly MASORET) (1991). 3080 Broadway, NYC, 10027. (212)678-8950. FAX: (212)864-0109. E-mail: joginsberg@jtsa.edu. Johanna R. Ginsberg. Three times a year. Jewish Theological Seminary.

JUDAISM (1952). 15 E. 84 St., NYC, 10028. (212)360–1586. FAX: (212)249–3672. Editor's address: Kresge Col., U. of California, Santa Cruz, CA, 95064. (408)459–2566. FAX: (408)459–4424. E-mail: judaism@cats.ucsc.edu. Prof. Murray Baumgarten. Quarterly. American Jewish Congress.

KASHRUS FAXLETTER–THE MONTHLY KOSHER UPDATE (1990). PO Box 204, Brooklyn, 11204. (718)336–8544. FAX: (718)336–8550. Rabbi Yosef Wikler. Monthly. Kashrus Institute.

KASHRUS MAGAZINE–THE PERIODICAL FOR THE KOSHER CONSUMER (1980). PO Box 204, Brooklyn, 11204. (718)336–8544. FAX: (718)336–8550. Rabbi Yosef Wikler. Five times per year (February, April, June, September, December). Kashrus Institute.

KOL HAT'NUA (VOICE OF THE MOVEMENT) (1975). c/o Young Judaea, 50 W. 58 St., NYC, 10019. (212)303–4576. FAX: (212)303–4572. E-mail: joshofrane@aol.com. Josh Ofrane. Quarterly. Hadassah Zionist Youth Commission–Young Judaea.

KULTUR UN LEBN–CULTURE AND LIFE (1960). 45 E. 33 St., NYC, 10016. (212)889–6800. FAX: (212)532–7518. E-mail: wcfriends@aol.com. Joseph Mlotek. Quarterly. Yiddish. The Workmen's Circle.

LAMISHPAHA (1963). 47 W. 34 St., Rm. 609, NYC, 10001–3012. (212)629–9443. FAX: (212)629–9472. Dr. Vered Cohen-Raphaeli. Illustrated. Monthly (except July and Aug.). Hebrew. Histadruth Ivrith of America.

LIKUTIM (1981). 110 E. 30 St., NYC, 10016. (212)889–2525. Joanne Jahr. Two times a year in Israel (print and audiocassettes). Hebrew. Jewish Braille Institute of America.

LILITH–THE INDEPENDENT JEWISH WOMEN'S MAGAZINE (1976). 250 W. 57 St., #2432, NYC, 10107. (212)757–0818. FAX: (212)757–5705. E-mail: lilithmag@aol.com. Susan Weidman Schneider. Quarterly.

LONG ISLAND JEWISH WORLD (1971). 115 Middle Neck Rd., Great Neck, 11021. (516)829–4000. FAX: (516)829–4776. E-mail: lijeworld@aol.com. Jerome W. Lippman. Weekly.

MANHATTAN JEWISH SENTINEL (1993). 115 Middle Neck Rd., Great Neck, 11021. (212)244–4949. FAX: (212)244–2257. E-mail: lijeworld@aol.com. Jerome W. Lippman. Weekly.

MARTYRDOM AND RESISTANCE (1974). 500 Fifth Ave., Suite 1600, NYC, 10110–1699. (212)220–4304. FAX: (212)220–4308. E-mail: yadvashem.org. Ed. Dr. Harvey Rosenfeld; Ed.-in-Chief Eli Zborowski. Bimonthly. International Society for Yad Vashem.

MIDSTREAM (1954). 110 E. 59 St., NYC, 10022. (212)339–6040. FAX: (212)318–6176. Joel Carmichael. Nine times a year. Theodor Herzl Foundation, Inc.

NA'AMAT WOMAN (1926). 200 Madison Ave., Suite 2120, NYC, 10016. (212)725–8010. FAX: (212)447–5187. Judith A. Sokoloff. Five times a year. English-Yiddish-Hebrew. Na'amat USA, the Women's Labor Zionist Organization of America.

OLOMEINU–OUR WORLD (1945). 5723 18th Ave., Brooklyn, 11204. (718)259–1223.

FAX: (718)259-1795. Rabbi Yaakov Fruchter, Rabbi Nosson Scherman. Monthly. English-Hebrew. Torah Umesorah—National Society for Hebrew Day Schools.

PASSOVER DIRECTORY (1923). 333 Seventh Ave., NYC, 10001. (212)563-4000. FAX: (212)564-9058. Charlotte Friedland. Annually. Union of Orthodox Jewish Congregations of America.

PROCEEDINGS OF THE AMERICAN ACADEMY FOR JEWISH RESEARCH (1920). 51 Washington Sq. South, NYC, 10012-1075. (212)998-3550. FAX: (212)995-4178. Dr. Nahum Sarna. Annually. English-Hebrew-French-Arabic-Persian-Greek. American Academy for Jewish Research.

PS: THE INTELLIGENT GUIDE TO JEWISH AFFAIRS. (1993) PO Box 48, Mineola, 11501-0048. (516)487-3758. FAX: (516)829-1248. E-mail: psreports@compuserve.com. Murray Polner, Adam Simms. Fortnightly.

RCA RECORD (1953). 305 Seventh Ave. NYC, 10001. (212)807-7888. FAX: (212)727-8452. Rabbi Mark Dratch. Quarterly. Rabbinical Council of America.

REFORM JUDAISM (1972; formerly DIMENSIONS IN AMERICAN JUDAISM). 838 Fifth Ave., NYC, 10021. (212)650-4240. Aron Hirt-Manheimer. Quarterly. Union of American Hebrew Congregations.

THE REPORTER (1972). 500 Clubhouse Rd., Vestal, 13850. (607)724-2360. FAX: (607)724-2311. E-mail: treporter@aol.com. Marc S. Goldberg. Weekly. Jewish Federation of Broome County, Inc.

THE REPORTER (1966). 315 Park Ave. S., NYC, 10010. (212)505-7700. FAX: (212)674-3057. Aviva Patz. Quarterly. Women's American ORT, Inc.

RESPONSE: A CONTEMPORARY JEWISH REVIEW (1967). 114 W. 26th St., Suite 1004, NYC, 10001-6812. (212)620-0350. FAX: (212)929-3459. E-mail: response@panix. com. David R. Adler, Michael R. Steinberg, Chanita Baumhaft. Quarterly. Response Magazine, Inc.

RUSSIAN FORWARD (1995). 45 E. 33rd St., NYC, 10016. (212)889-8200, ext. 1450. FAX: (212)684-3949. Vladimir Yedidovick. Weekly.

SH'MA (1970). c/o CLAL, 440 Park Ave. South, 4th fl., NYC, 10016-8012. (212) 779-3300. FAX: (212)779-1009. Sr. Eds. Irving Greenberg, Harold M. Schulweis; Ed. Nina Beth Cardin. Biweekly (except June, July, Aug.). CLAL—The National Jewish Center for Learning and Leadership.

SYNAGOGUE LIGHT AND KOSHER LIFE (1933). 47 Beekman St., NYC, 10038. (212)227-7800. Rabbi Meyer Hager. Quarterly. The Kosher Food Institute.

TRADITION (1958). 305 Seventh Ave., NYC, 10001. (212)807-7888. FAX: (212)727-8452. Rabbi Emanuel Feldman. Quarterly. Rabbinical Council of America.

UNITED SYNAGOGUE REVIEW (1943). 155 Fifth Ave., NYC, 10010. (212)533-7800. FAX: (212)353-9439. E-mail: 71263. 276@compuserve.com. Lois Goldrich. Semiannually. United Synagogue of Conservative Judaism.

UNSER TSAIT (1941). 25 E. 21 St., 3rd fl., NYC, 10010. (212)475-0055. Bimonthly. Yiddish. Jewish Labor Bund.

VOICE OF THE DUTCHESS JEWISH COMMUNITY (1989). 110 Grand Ave., Poughkeepsie, 12603. (914)471-9811. FAX: (914)471-0659. E-mail: bj@jon.cjfny.org. Business off.:500 Clubhouse Rd., Vestal, 13850. (607)724-2360. FAX: (607)724-2311. Marc S. Goldberg, Sandy Gardner. Monthly. Jewish Federation of Dutchess County, Inc.

WOMEN'S LEAGUE OUTLOOK MAGAZINE (1930). 48 E. 74 St., New York, 10021. (212)628-1600. FAX: (212)772-3507. E-mail: wleague74@aol.com. Jessica Gribetz. Quarterly. Women's League for Conservative Judaism.

WORKMEN'S CIRCLE CALL. See THE CALL

THE WYOMING VALLEY JEWISH REPORTER (formerly WE ARE ONE) (1995). 500 Clubhouse Rd., Vestal, 13850. (607)724-2360. FAX: (607)724-2311. E-mail: treporter@aol.com. Marc S. Goldberg. Every other week. Wilkes-Barre Jewish Community Board.

YEARBOOK OF THE CENTRAL CONFERENCE OF AMERICAN RABBIS (1890). 355 Lexington Ave., NYC, 10017. (212)972-3636. FAX: (212)692-0819. Rabbi Elliot L. Stevens. Annually. Central Conference of American Rabbis.

YIDDISH (1973). Queens College, NSF 350, 65–30 Kissena Blvd., Flushing, 11367. (718)997–3622. Joseph C. Landis. Quarterly. Queens College Press.

DI YIDDISHE HEIM (1958). 770 Eastern Pkwy., Brooklyn, 11213. (718)735–0458. Rachel Altein, Tema Gurary. Twice a year. English-Yiddish. Neshei Ub'nos Chabad-Lubavitch Women's Organization.

YIDDISHE KULTUR (1938). 1133 Broadway, Rm. 820, NYC, 10010. (212)243–1304. FAX: (212)243–1305. E-mail: mahosu@ame.onl. Itche Goldberg. Bimonthly. Yiddish. Yiddisher Kultur Farband, Inc.–YKUF.

DOS YIDDISHE VORT (1953). 84 William St., NYC, 10038. (212)797–9000. Joseph Friedenson. Monthly. Yiddish. Agudath Israel of America.

YIDDISHER KEMFER (1900). 275 Seventh Ave., NYC, 10001. (212)675–7808. FAX: (212) 675–7685. Adele Grubart. Monthly. Yiddish. Labor Zionist Letters.

YIDISHE SHPRAKH (1941). 555 W. 57 St., Suite 1100, NYC, 10019. (212)246–6080. FAX: (212) 292–1892. Dr. Mordkhe Schaechter. Irregularly. Yiddish. YIVO Institute for Jewish Research, Inc.

YIVO ANNUAL (1946). 555 W. 57 St., Suite 1100, NYC, 10019. (212)246–6080. FAX: (212)292–1892. Lisa R. Epstein. Annually. YIVO Institute for Jewish Research, Inc.

YIVO BLETER (1931). 555 W. 57 St., Suite 1100, NYC, 10019. (212)246–6080. FAX: (212)292–1892. David E. Fishman, Abraham Nowersztern. Biannually. Yiddish. YIVO Institute for Jewish Research, Inc.

YOUNG ISRAEL VIEWPOINT (1952). 3 W. 16 St., NYC, 10011. (212)929–1525, ext. 113. FAX: (212)727–9526. E-mail: chana@youngisrael.org. Chana Chechik. Quarterly. National Council of Young Israel.

YOUNG JUDAEAN (1910). 50 W. 58 St., NYC, 10019. (212)303–4579. FAX: (212)303–4572. Deborah Neufeld. Bimonthly. Hadassah Zionist Youth Commission.

YUGNTRUF: YIDDISH YOUTH MAGAZINE (1964). 200 W. 72 St., Suite 40, NYC, 10023. (212)787–6675. FAX: (212)799–

1517. Elinor Robinson. Two to four times a year. Yiddish. Yugntruf Youth for Yiddish.

ZUKUNFT (THE FUTURE) (1892). 25 E. 21 St., NYC, 10010. (212)505–8040. FAX: (212)505–8044. Yonia Fain. Quarterly. Yiddish. Congress for Jewish Culture.

NORTH CAROLINA

AMERICAN JEWISH TIMES OUTLOOK (1934; reorg. 1950). PO Box 33218, Charlotte, 28233–3218. (704)372–3296. FAX: (704)377–9237. E-mail: geri@pop.vnet.net. Geri Zhiss. Monthly. The Blumenthal Foundation.

CHARLOTTE JEWISH NEWS (1978). 5007 Providence Rd., Charlotte, 28226. (704) 366–5007. FAX: (704) 365–4507. Suzanne Cannon. Monthly (except July). Jewish Federation of Greater Charlotte.

OHIO

AKRON JEWISH NEWS (1929). 750 White Pond Drive, Akron, 44320. (330)869–2424. FAX: (330)867–8498. Toby Liberman. Fortnightly. Akron Jewish Community Federation.

AMERICAN ISRAELITE (1854). 906 Main St., Rm. 508, Cincinnati, 45202. (513)621–3145. FAX: (513)621–3744. Phyllis R. Singer. Weekly.

AMERICAN JEWISH ARCHIVES (1948). 3101 Clifton Ave., Cincinnati, 45220. (513) 221–1875. FAX: (513)221–7812. E-mail: aja@fuse.net. Abraham J. Peck. Semiannually. Jacob Rader Marcus Center, American Jewish Archives, HUC-JIR.

CLEVELAND JEWISH NEWS (1964). 3645 Warrensville Center Rd., Suite 230, Cleveland, 44122. (216)991–8300. FAX: (216)991–2088. Cynthia Dettelbach. Weekly. Cleveland Jewish News Publication Co.

INDEX TO JEWISH PERIODICALS (1963). PO Box 18570, Cleveland Hts., 44118. (216) 381–4846. FAX: (216)381–4321. Lenore Pfeffer Koppel. Annually. Available in book and CD-ROM form.

JEWISH JOURNAL (1987). 505 Gypsy Lane, Youngstown, 44504–1314. (330)744–7902. FAX: (330)746–7926. E-mail: bf379@yfn.ysu.edu. Sherry Weinblatt. Biweekly (except July/Aug.). Youngstown Area Jewish Federation.

OHIO JEWISH CHRONICLE (1922). 2862 Johnstown Rd., Columbus, 43219. (614)337-2055. FAX: (614)337-2059. Roberta Keck. Weekly.

STARK JEWISH NEWS (1920). 2631 Harvard Ave. NW, Canton, 44709. (330)452-6444. FAX: (330)452-4487. E-mail: cantonjcf@aol.com. Carol Tulgan. Monthly. Canton Jewish Community Federation.

STUDIES IN BIBLIOGRAPHY AND BOOKLORE (1953). 3101 Clifton Ave., Cincinnati, 45220. (513)221-1875. FAX: (513)221-0519. Herbert C. Zafren. Irregularly. English-Hebrew-etc. Library of Hebrew Union College-Jewish Institute of Religion.

TOLEDO JEWISH NEWS (1951). 6505 Sylvania Ave., Sylvania, 43560. (419)885-4461. FAX: (419)885-8627. Laurie Cohen. Monthly. Jewish Federation of Greater Toledo.

OKLAHOMA

TULSA JEWISH REVIEW (1930). 2021 E. 71 St., Tulsa, 74136. (918)495-1100. FAX: (918)495-1220. Ed Ulrich. Monthly. Jewish Federation of Tulsa.

OREGON

BRIDGES: A JOURNAL FOR JEWISH FEMINISTS AND OUR FRIENDS (1990). PO Box 24839, Eugene, 97402. (541)935-5720. FAX: (541)935-5720. E-mail: ckinberg@pond.net. Mng. Ed. Clare Kinberg. Semiannually.

JEWISH REVIEW (1959). 506 SW Sixth Ave., Suite 606, Portland, 97204. Edit.:(503) 227-7464. FAX:(503) 227-7438. Adv.: (503) 684-2677. FAX: (503) 620-3433. E-mail: jreview@teleport.com. Paul Haist. Regular column in Russian. Fortnightly. Jewish Federation of Portland.

PENNSYLVANIA

COMMUNITY REVIEW (1925). 3301 N. Front St. Annex, Harrisburg, 17110. (717)236-9555. FAX: (717)236-2552. E-mail: communityreview@redrose.nt. Carol L. Cohen. Fortnightly. United Jewish Community of Greater Harrisburg.

CONTEMPORARY JEWRY (1974, under the name JEWISH SOCIOLOGY AND SOCIAL RESEARCH). Gratz College, Old York Rd. & Melrose Ave., Melrose Park, 19027. (215) 635-7300. FAX: (215) 635-7320. E-mail: rela1@aol.com. Ed. Rela Mintz Geffen; Mng. Ed. Egon Mayer. Annually. Association for the Social Scientific Study of Jewry.

JERUSALEM LETTER/VIEWPOINTS (1978). 1616 Walnut St., Suite 507, Philadelphia, 19103. (215)204-1459. FAX: (215)204-7784. Mark Amiel. 24 times a year. Jerusalem Center for Public Affairs.

JEWISH CHRONICLE OF PITTSBURGH (1962). 5600 Baum Blvd., Pittsburgh, 15206. (412)687-1000. FAX: (412)687-5119. E-mail: pittjewchr@aol.com. Joel Roteman. Weekly. Pittsburgh Jewish Publication and Education Foundation.

JEWISH EXPONENT (1887). 226 S. 16 St., Philadelphia, 19102. (215)893-5700. FAX: (215)546-3957. Bertram Korn, Jr. Weekly. Jewish Federation of Greater Philadelphia.

JEWISH POLITICAL STUDIES REVIEW (1989). 1616 Walnut St., Suite 507, Philadelphia, 19103. (215)204-1459. FAX: (215)204-7784. Mark Amiel. Twice yearly. Jerusalem Center for Public Affairs.

JEWISH QUARTERLY REVIEW (1910). 420 Walnut St., Philadelphia, 19106. (215) 238-1290. FAX: (215)238-1540. E-mail: jqr@mail.cjs.upenn.edu. Ed. David M. Goldenberg; Mng. Ed. Bonnie L. Blankenship. Quarterly. Center for Judaic Studies, University of Pennsylvania.

NEW MENORAH (1978). 7318 Germantown Ave., Philadelphia, 19119-1793. (215) 247-9700. FAX: (215)247-9703. Dr. Arthur Waskow. Quarterly. Aleph: Alliance for Jewish Renewal.

RECONSTRUCTIONISM TODAY (1993). 1299 Church Rd., Wyncote, 19095. (215)887-1988. FAX: (215)877-5348. E-mail: jrfnatl@aol.com. Lawrence Bush. Quarterly. Jewish Reconstructionist Federation.

THE RECONSTRUCTIONIST (1934). 1299 Church Rd., Wyncote, 19095-1898. (215) 576-0800. FAX: (215)576-6143. E-mail: jrcrav@aol.com. Rabbi Richard Hirsh. Semiannually. Reconstructionist Rabbinical College.

SCRANTON FEDERATION REPORTER (1994). 500 Clubhouse Rd., Vestal, NY, 13850. (607)724-2360. FAX: (607)724-2311. E-mail: treporter@aol.com. Marc S. Goldberg. Biweekly. Scranton-Lackawanna Jewish Federation.

RHODE ISLAND

JEWISH VOICE OF RHODE ISLAND (1973). 130 Sessions St., Providence, 02906. (401) 421–4111. FAX: (401)331–7961. E-mail: jvoice@aol.com. Jane S. Sprague. Monthly. Jewish Federation of Rhode Island.

RHODE ISLAND JEWISH HERALD (1930). P.O.Box 6063, Providence, 02940. (401)724–0200. FAX: (401)726–5820. Tara V. Lisciandero, Sara Wise. Weekly. Herald Press Publishing Company.

RHODE ISLAND JEWISH HISTORICAL NOTES (1954). 130 Sessions St., Providence, 02906. (401)331–1360. Judith Weiss Cohen. Annually. Rhode Island Jewish Historical Association.

SOUTH CAROLINA

CHARLESTON JEWISH JOURNAL. 1645 Wallenberg Blvd., Charleston, 29407. (803)571–6565. FAX: (803)556–6206. Eileen Chepenik. Monthly. Charleston Jewish Federation.

TENNESSEE

HEBREW WATCHMAN (1925). 4646 Poplar Ave., Suite 232, Memphis, 38117. (901)763–2215. FAX: (901)763–2216. Herman I. Goldberger. Weekly.

OBSERVER (1934). 801 Percy Warner Blvd., Nashville, 37205. (615)356–3242, ext. 237. FAX: (615)352–0056. E-mail: nashobserv@aol.com. Judith A. Saks. Biweekly (except July). Jewish Federation of Nashville.

SHOFAR. PO Box 8947, Chattanooga, 37414. (423)493–0270, Ext. 12. FAX: (423) 493–9997. E-mail: shofar@jcfgc.com. Rachel Schulson. Monthly. Jewish Federation of Greater Chattanooga.

TEXAS

JEWISH HERALD-VOICE (1908). PO Box 153, Houston, 77001–0153. (713)630–0391. FAX: (713)630–0404. E-mail: joexhk@aol.com. Jeanne Samuels. Weekly.

JEWISH JOURNAL OF SAN ANTONIO (1973). 8434 Ahern, San Antonio, 78213. (210)

341–6963. FAX: (210)342–8098. Barbara Richmond. Monthly (11 issues). Jewish Federation of San Antonio.

TEXAS JEWISH POST (1947). 3120 S. Freeway, Fort Worth, 76110. (817)927–2831. FAX: (817)429–0840. 11333 N. Central Expressway, Suite 213, Dallas, 75243. (214)692–7283. FAX: (214)692–7285. Jimmy Wisch. Weekly.

VIRGINIA

RENEWAL MAGAZINE (1984). 5029 Corporate World Dr., Suite 225, Virginia Beach, 23462. (757)671–1600. FAX: (757)671–7613. E-mail: ujft@ujft.com. Reba Karp. Quarterly. United Jewish Federation of Tidewater.

SOUTHEASTERN VIRGINIA JEWISH NEWS (1959). 5029 Corporate World Dr., Suite 225, Virginia Beach, 23462. (757)671–1600. FAX: (757)671–7613. E-mail: ujft@ujft.com. Reba Karp. 22 issues yearly. United Jewish Federation of Tidewater.

WASHINGTON

JEWISH TRANSCRIPT (1924). 2041 Third Ave., Seattle, 98121. (206)441–4553. FAX: (206)441–2736. E-mail: jewishtran@aol.com. Donna Gordon Blankinship. Fortnightly. Jewish Federation of Greater Seattle.

WISCONSIN

WISCONSIN JEWISH CHRONICLE (1921). 1360 N. Prospect Ave., Milwaukee, 53202. (414)390–5888. FAX: (414)271–0487. E-mail: milwaukeej@aol.com. Andrew Muchin. Weekly. Milwaukee Jewish Federation.

INDEXES

INDEX TO JEWISH PERIODICALS (1963). PO Box 18570, Cleveland Hts., OH 44118. (216)381–4846. FAX: (216)381–4321. Lenore Pfeffer Koppel. Annually. Available in book and CD form.

NEWS SYNDICATES

JEWISH TELEGRAPHIC AGENCY, INC. (1917). 330 Seventh Ave., 11th fl., NYC, 10001–5010. (212)643–1890. FAX: (212)643–8498. Mark J. Joffe, Lisa Hostein. Daily.

CANADA

CANADIAN JEWISH HERALD (1977). 17 Anselme Lavigne, Dollard des Ormeaux, PQ H9A 1N3. (514)684-7667. FAX: (514) 684-7667. Dan Nimrod. Irregularly. Dawn Publishing Co., Ltd.

CANADIAN JEWISH NEWS (1971). 205-1500 Don Mills Rd., North York, ONT M3B 3K4. (416)391-1836. FAX: (416)391-0829 (Adv.); (416)391-1836. FAX: (416)391-0829. Mordechai Ben-Dat. 50 issues per year. Some French.

CANADIAN JEWISH OUTLOOK (1963). 6184 Ash St., #3, Vancouver, BC V5Z 3G9. (604)324-5101. FAX: (604)325-2470. Henry M. Rosenthal. Eight times per year. Canadian Jewish Outlook Society.

DAIS (formerly INTERCOM) (1985). 1590 Ave. Dr. Penfield, Montreal, PQ H3G 1C5. (514)931-7531. FAX: (514)931-0548. E-mail: mikec@cjc.ca. Mike Cohen. Three times annually. Canadian Jewish Congress.

DIALOGUE (1988). 1590 Ave. Dr. Penfield, Montreal, PQ H3G 1C5. (514)931-7531. FAX: (514)931-3281. E-mail: rebeccar@cjc.ca. Rebecca Rosenberg. Annually. French-English. Canadian Jewish Congress, Quebec Region.

JEWISH FREE PRESS (1990). 8411 Elbow Dr., SW, Calgary, Alberta T2V 1K8. (403)252-9423. FAX: (403)255-5640. Judy Shapiro. Fortnightly.

JEWISH POST & NEWS (1987). 117 Hutchings St., Winnipeg, MAN R2X 2V4. (204)694-3332. FAX: (204)694-3916. E-mail: jewishp@pangea.ca. Matt Bellan. Weekly.

JEWISH STANDARD (1930). 77 Mowat Ave., Suite 016, Toronto, ONT M6K 3E3. (416)537-2696. FAX: (416)789-3872. Julius Hayman; Mng. Ed. Michael Hayman. Fortnightly.

JEWISH TRIBUNE (1950). 15 Hove St., North York, ONT M3H 4Y8. (416)633-6224. FAX: (416)630-2159. Daniel Horowitz. Fortnightly.

JEWISH WESTERN BULLETIN (1930). 873 Beatty St., Suite 203, Vancouver, BC V6B 2M6. (604)689-1520. FAX: (604)689-1525. E-mail: rwolk@istav.ca. Assoc. Eds. Howard Fluxgold, Peter Caufield; Pub. Andrew Buerger. Weekly. Anglo-Jewish Publishers Ltd.

JOURNAL OF PSYCHOLOGY AND JUDAISM (1976). 1747 Featherston Dr., Ottawa, ONT K1H 6P4. (613)731-9119. Reuven P. Bulka. Quarterly. Center for the Study of Psychology and Judaism.

OTTAWA JEWISH BULLETIN (1954). 151 Chapel St., Ottawa, ONT K1N 7Y2. (613)789-7306. FAX: (613)789-4593. Myra Aronson. Biweekly. Ottawa Jewish Bulletin Publishing Co. Ltd.

SHALOM (1975). 1515 S. Park St., Suite 305, Halifax, NS, B3J 2LA. (902)422-7491. FAX: (902)425-3722. E-mail: ajc.halifax@ns.sympatico.ca. Jon M. Goldberg. Quarterly. Atlantic Jewish Council.

LA VOIX SÉPHARADE (1976). 4735 Chemin de la Cote St. Catherine Rd., Montreal, PQ H3W 1M1. (514)733-4998, (514)733-8696. FAX: (514)733-3158. Perla Serfaty-Garzon. Bimonthly (five times a year). French and occasional Spanish and English. Communauté Sépharade du Québec.

WINDSOR JEWISH FEDERATION (1942). 1641 Ouellette Ave., Windsor, ONT N8X 1K9. (519)973-1772. FAX: (519)973-1774. Exec. Dir. Steven Brownstein. Three times a year. Windsor Jewish Federation.

THE WORLD OF LUBAVITCH (1980). 770 Chabad Gate, Thornhill, ONT L4J 3V9. (905)731-7000. FAX: (905)731-7005. Rabbi Moshe Spalter. Bimonthly. English-Hebrew. Chabad Lubavitch of Southern Ont.

Obituaries: United States*

BERGER, ELMER, rabbi, organization executive; b. Cleveland, Ohio, May 27, 1908; d. Long Boat Key, Fla., Oct. 5, 1996. Educ.: U. Cincinnati; Hebrew Union College (rabbinic ord.). Rabbi: Temple Beth Jacob, Pontiac, Mich., 1932–36; Temple Beth El, Flint, Mich., 1936–42. In 1943 joined Amer. Council for Judaism—a group founded in 1942 to oppose Zionism and the founding of a Jewish state in then Palestine—serving as exec. dir. 1943–55, and exec. v.-pres., 1955–67. Pres., Amer. Jewish Alternatives to Zionism, 1968 until his death. Au.: *The Jewish Dilemma* (1945); *A Partisan History of Judaism* (1951); *Who Knows Better, Must Say So* (1955); *Judaism or Jewish Nationalism* (1957); *Memoirs of an Anti-Zionist Jew* (1976); articles in Encycl. Britannica Yearbook and other publications.

BERMAN, PHILIP I., business executive, philanthropist; b. Pennsburg, Pa., June 28, 1915; d. Allentown, Pa., Nov. 26, 1997. Served U.S. Marine Corps, WW II. Following successful careers in trucking and heavy equipment fields, went on to expand a department store in Allentown into a 14-store chain, Hess's Department Stores Inc., serving as chairman. Also chairman, Hess Brothers Inc., a real estate company. Bd. mem., Philadelphia Museum of Art, 1980–89, chmn. 1989

on; a major supporter and donor of art from his and his wife Muriel's collection. Active in numerous civic, cultural, and business associations. Major benefactor: Hebrew University of Jerusalem; Jewish Publication Society; Amer. Jewish Committee; Hadassah Medical Org.; City of Jerusalem (gifts of outdoor sculpture). Recipient: Hon. doctorates: Ursinus Coll., Lehigh U., Hebrew U., and many other honors.

BERNSTEIN, HENRY C., communal professional; b. NYC, Mar. 15, 1903; d. Orlando, Fla., Nov. 29, 1997. Educ.: St. John's Coll. (LLB). Exec. dir. and exec. v.-pres., UJA of Greater N.Y., 1940–70; mem. natl. UJA exec. com. and campaign cabinet, 1949–.

BERNSTEIN, IRVING, communal professional; b. NYC, Aug. 9, 1921; d. Scarsdale, N.Y., Dec. 10, 1997. Educ.: CCNY; Teachers Coll., Columbia U. Served U.S. Air Force, WW II. High-school teacher, NYC, 1946; social worker, NYC welfare dept., 1947. Joined UJA staff 1948: field rep., Midwest region, 1948–50; West Coast regional dir., 1950–62; natl. asst. exec. v.-chmn., 1962–71; exec. v.-chmn., 1971–83. Mem.: exec. com., U.S. Holocaust Memorial Council; bd. govs., Jewish Agency; bd. regents, Internatl. Center

---

*Including American Jews who died between July 1, 1996 and December 31, 1997.

for Univ. Teaching of Jewish Civilization, Jerusalem; bd. advisers (chmn.), Brandeis U. Hornstein Prog. for Graduate Studies in Jewish Communal Service; adv. council, Center for Modern Jewish Studies; exec. com., Natl. Jewish Conf.; Commission on Econ. Growth of Israel; adv. bd., Natl. Jewish Family Center; bd., Jerusalem Coll. Technology; exec. com. bd., JDC; bd. govs. (assoc. mem.), Hebrew U.; bd.: United Israel Appeal; Amer. Jewish Com. Inst. on Israel-Diaspora Relations; Amer. Technion Soc.; Amer. Assoc. Ben-Gurion U.; Medical Development for Israel; Natl. Soc. Fundraising Execs. Au.: *Living UJA History.*

BUERGER, CHARLES, publisher; b. Pittsburgh, Pa., Oct. 23, 1938; d. Baltimore, Md., Nov. 8, 1996. Educ.: Carnegie Mellon U. Worked in the printing business in New Jersey until 1972,when he moved to Baltimore to work with his mother at the *Baltimore Jewish Times,* a paper founded by his grandfather, David Alter, in 1919. Subsequently became publisher of the paper and of five other Jewish weekly newspapers across N. America (*Atlanta Jewish Times, Detroit Jewish News, Palm Beach Jewish Times, Boca Raton-Delray Beach Jewish Times,* and the *Western Jewish Bulletin,* Vancouver, B.C., Canada) as well as three glossy lifestyle magazines. Active in various civic and Jewish organizations, incl. the Associated (Baltimore Federation), Baltimore Jewish Council, Baltimore Hebrew University, United Way, Meals on Wheels, Baltimore Symphony Orch., and the Baltimore Museum of Art. Recipient: Smolar Award for Jewish journalism; Amer. J. Com. Humanitarian Award; Baltimore Zionist District Award; Meals on Wheels Straus Award; and other honors.

EDEL, (JOSEPH) LEON, professor, author; b. Pittsburgh, Pa., Sept. 9, 1907; d. Honolulu, Hawaii, Sept. 5, 1997. Served U.S. Army, WW II. Educ.: McGill U.; U. Paris (LittD). Writer, journalist, 1932–43; dir. press agency, U.S. zone, Germany, 1945–47. Joined NYU faculty 1950: prof. of English, 1955–66; Henry James Prof. of English and Amer. Letters, 1966–73. Citizens Prof. of English, U. Hawaii, 1971–78; visiting prof., Toronto, Princeton, Harvard, Indiana, and other insts. Au.: *The Henry James Biography* (5 vols.,

1953–73); 2-vol. revised ed., *The Life of Henry James* (1977); 1-vol. abridged ed., *Henry James: A Life* (1985); ed. or co-ed. of critical works on James as well as ed. of papers of Edmund Wilson and au. of biogs. of Willa Cather and Henry Thoreau, and other works. Mem.: PEN Amer. Center (pres., 1957–59); Natl. Inst. Arts and Letters (sec. 1965–67); Authors Guild (mem. of Council, pres. 1969–71); Hawaii Lit. Arts Council (pres. 1978–79); fellow, Amer. Acad. Arts and Sciences; and other orgs. Recipient: Pulitzer Prize and National Book Award, 1963, for second and third vols. of James biog.; elected mem. Amer. Acad. Inst. of Arts and Letters, 1972; recipient its Gold Medal for biog. 1976; and other honors.

FARKAS, RUTH LEWIS, business executive, communal worker; b. NYC, Dec. 20, 1906; d. NYC, Oct. 18, 1996. Educ.: NYU (BA, EdD); Columbia U. (MA). Psych. tutor, Fed. of Jewish Philanthropies, 1941–45; instr., NYU School of Educ., 1949–55; pres., Dolma Realty Corp., Fort Lauderdale, Fla., 1955–70; associated with Alexander's Dept. Stores, founded by her husband, George, 1955–72, as personnel consult. and community relations dir., as well as dir. and mem. exec. com.; major supporter, Pres. Richard Nixon's reelection campaign; appointed U.S. ambassador to Luxembourg, 1973–76; personnel and community relations consult., 1977 on. Active on boards of many orgs., incl.: NYU, NYU Medical Center, NYU Graduate School of Social Work; Beth Abraham Health Svcs.; Beth Israel Medical Center; Montefiore Hosp.; women's div. Albert Einstein Medical Coll.; Center for the Study of the Presidency. Mem.: NY State Women's Council; US Comm. UNESCO; President's Comm. on Handicapped; pres. Role Found.; v.-pres. Maferr Found. Recipient: Grand Cross Order of Merit, Luxembourg; Cordier Fellow, Columbia U. School of Internatl. Affairs; and other honors.

FISHBEIN, JACK, editor, publisher; b. Chicago, Ill., Oct. 12, 1912; d. Chicago, Ill., July 17, 1996. Educ.: Northwestern U. Reporter, *Chicago Tribune* and *Chicago American;* joined staff of *The Sentinel,* a Jewish weekly magazine, in 1936; became co-owner in 1943, serving as both publisher and editor, and sole owner in 1982. Founding mem., Amer. Jewish Press Assoc.; mem., Soc. Professional Journalists. Recipient: Smolar Award for editorial writing and numerous other honors.

FLACKS, PAUL, businessman, communal professional; b. Dayton, Ohio, Apr. 22, 1921; d. Dayton, Ohio, Dec. 4, 1997. Served US Army, WWII. Retail businessman, Dayton, until early 1970s; pres., Zionist Org. of Amer. district, Dayton. Dir., public affairs, Zionist Org. of Amer., 1972–77; exec. dir. and CEO, later exec. v.-pres., 1977–93. Pub. and ed., *Focus,* Middle East information svc., 1993–. Mem.: Conf. of Presidents of Major Jewish Orgs.; del., several Zionist Congresses.

GANCHOFF, MOSHE, cantor; b. Odessa, Russia, Dec. 15, 1904; d. NYC, Aug. 11, 1997; in U.S. since 1913. Studied privately with cantors in Toledo, Ohio, where he grew up, and in New York. Started as cantor of the Hunts Point Jewish Center in the Bronx in 1928; as his reputation grew, he served a succession of congregations in Brooklyn. In 1944 he succeeded David Roitman at Cong. Shaare Zedek in Manhattan—regarded as "the Carnegie Hall of Jewish music"—where he remained until 1956. Founding faculty mem., Hebrew Union College School of Sacred Music, 1951–1972; popular cantor at Grossingers' Catskills resort for High Holy Days and Passover, 1955–mid '70s. International concert artist, composer, and host of a weekly radio program on WEVD for 25 years.

GEBINER, BENJAMIN, communal professional; b. Rovno, Poland, June 25, 1898; d. Manhasset, N.Y., Feb. 7, 1997; in U.S. since 1921. Educ.: Rovno gymnasium; univs. of Odessa and Kiev; Workmen's Circle Teachers Seminary; Brooklyn Law School. Teacher: Bedford Ave. Talmud Torah, Brooklyn, 1923–25; various Workmen's Circle schools, 1925–34; founding exec. dir., Jewish Labor Com., 1934–35; gen. sec., Jewish Socialist Verband and ed., *Der Wecker,* 1935–37; asst. gen. sec., Workmen's Circle, 1937–63; gen. sec. and mng. ed., WC periodical *The Friend,* until retiring in 1970; prof., Jewish studies, Queens Coll., 1970–84. Prolific author of articles in the *Forward* and other Yiddish and English publications; lecturer; commentator on radio station WEVD, 1950–72. Active in Jewish Labor

Com., World Jewish Culture Cong., UJA, ORT, Israel Bonds, Jewish Professors Org., and the Forward Assoc.

GERSTEIN, LOUIS C., rabbi; b. Brooklyn, N.Y., Mar. 25, 1918; d. Kiryat Ono, Israel, Oct. 6, 1996. Educ.: NYU (BA, MA, PhD); Jewish Theol. Sem. of Amer. (rabbinic ord.). Asst. and assoc. rabbi, Shearith Israel, the Spanish and Portuguese Cong. of N.Y., 1942–1955; succeeded Dr. David de Sola Pool in 1956 as sr. rabbi, serving in that post until 1988 and as rabbi emer. thereafter. Lect., philosophy and religion: JTSA School of Jewish Studies, Cantorial School, Women's Inst.; NYU; C.W. Post Coll. Mem.: Rabbinical Assembly exec. council, placement comm. (v.-chmn.), and membership com.; exec. bd. NY Bd. of Rabbis (1943–53); exec. bd., Religion in Amer. Life; exec. bd., Amer. Friends of Touro Synagogue; Central Sephardic Comm. Chaplain: NYC civil defense corps; Jewish Teachers Assoc. Au.: *Conception of God in Maimonides and Thomas Aquinas* (1947) and *Faith in Our Times* (1948).

GINSBERG, ALLEN, poet; b. Newark, N.J., June 3, 1926; d. NYC, Apr. 5, 1997. Educ.: Columbia U. With the publication in 1956 of *Howl and Other Poems,* became the first and leading poetic voice of the "Beat Generation" of writers and a guru to the "flower children" (a term he coined) of the 1960s counterculture. An advocate of mysticism, anarchism, and the use of psychedelic drugs, he was a strong presence in the anti-Vietnam, free speech, and sexual liberation movements; was later active on behalf of environmental, antinuclear, and other causes; taught Buddhist meditation at Naropa Inst. in Colorado; in his last years taught English at Brooklyn Coll. Among his published works of poetry: *Kaddish and Other Poems* (1961), *Planet News: 1961–67* (1968), *The Fall of America: Poems of These States, 1965–1971* (1973; National Book Award winner), *Mind Breaths* (1978), *Collected Poems 1947–80* (1985), *Snapshot Poetics* (1993), and *Cosmopolitan Greetings: Poems 1986–1992* (1995). Also published several volumes of prose. Mem.: Amer. Inst. of Arts and Letters (inducted 1974).

GOTTESMAN, ESTHER G., communal worker; b. NYC, ?, 1898; d. Palm Beach, Fla., Oct. 1, 1997. Educ.: New York U.

Widow of Benjamin Gottesman, banker and investment manager. Mem., natl. bd., Hadassah, for 64 years, during which she served as v.-pres. and treas. and as chairwoman of *Hadassah Newsletter* (overseeing its change to *Hadassah Magazine*), Hadassah Israel Education Services, educ. dept. (responsible for publication of *Great Ages and Ideas of the Jewish People*), and other positions. Mem.: United Israel Appeal bd., World Zionist Org. Actions Com., bd. of dirs. of New York's Bd. of Jewish Education; natl. v.-pres., Amer. Assoc. for Jewish Education.

GOULD, NATHAN, communal professional; b. Chicago, Ill., Aug. 22, 1913; d. NYC, Nov. 10, 1997. Served U.S. Army, WW II. Free-lance writer and ed., public relations consult., 1946–49; joined Women's American ORT in 1950 as public relations dir., soon becoming exec. dir. and later exec. v.-pres., serving for 40 years. Credited with building Women's American ORT into a mass membership org. with a strong sense of mission. Initiated ORT technical and vocational programs in U.S., Russia, Latin Amer., and N. Africa. Mem., central bd., World ORT Union; the ORT Technical Inst. in Buenos Aires named in his honor in 1982.

ILUTOVICH, LEON; communal professional; b. Odessa, Russia, Apr. 8, 1914; d. NYC, Feb. 15, 1997; in U.S. since 1947. Educ.: Warsaw U. (law and polit. sci.). Sec., political com. representing Polish Jewry, 1937; sec. gen., General Zionist Org. of Poland, 1938–39; spent WW II years in Japan and China and served as Far East rep. of the Jewish Agency for Palestine. Asst. dir., Palestine Bureau, and dir. and ed., Zionist Information Service, New York, 1948–52; asst. exec. dir., Zionist Org. of Amer., 1952–64, exec. dir., 1964–78, and natl. exec. v.-chmn., 1978–. Mem.: Zionist Actions Com.; exec. of the World Union of General Zionists; exec. com., Amer. Zionist Council; delegate to many Zionist congresses; v.-pres., Fed. of Polish Jews.

KANE, IRVING, businessman, communal worker; b. Kiev, Russia, Jan. 14, 1908; d. Palm Beach, Fla., Mar. 22, 1997; in U.S. since 1913. Educ.: Case Western Reserve U. Private practice of law; pres. and co-owner, Hospital Specialty Co. (retired 1952). Pres., Cleveland Jewish Community Council; natl. chmn., AIPAC; pres.,

Council of Jewish Feds.; chmn., Natl. Jewish Community Relations Advisory Council; hon. v.-chmn., Amer. Jewish Joint Distribution Com. Also active in behalf of Amer. J. Com., Amer. ORT Found., Amer. Friends of Hebrew U.

KATZKI, HERBERT, communal professional; b. Elizabeth, N.J., (?), 1908; d. NYC, Aug. 3, 1997. Educ.: New York U. Joined staff of Amer. Jewish Joint Distribution Com. 1936; assigned to JDC headquarters in Paris 1939; named sec., JDC's Eur. Exec. Council, 1940; after closure of JDC Paris office, one day before entry of Nazi troops into the city helped to establish new Eur. HQ in Lisbon, then opened office in Marseilles to assist refugees in unoccupied zone of France. Joined US Army in Jan. 1944, assigned as rep. of U.S. War Refugee Bd. and special attache to U.S. embassies in Ankara and Bern; JDC country dir. for Germany, 1946–50, heading vast relief program for concentration camp survivors and displaced persons; named asst. dir.-gen. in 1951 and deputy dir.-gen. in 1965; reassigned to N.Y. office of JDC in Dec. 1967; elected asst. exec. v.-chmn., Dec. 1967; assoc. exec. v.-pres. 1976; retired 1979. Recipient: Paul Baerwald Award for Education for Social Service (shared with his wife, a refugee specialist); JDC's Ma'asim Tovim Award; and other honors.

KEMELMAN, HARRY, teacher, mystery writer; b. Boston, Mass., Nov. 24, 1908; d. Marblehead, Mass., Dec. 15, 1996. Educ.: Boston U., Harvard U. Teacher: Boston public schools, 1935–41; evening div., Northeastern U., 1938–41; chief job analyst, Boston Port, 1942–49; free-lance writer, 1949–on; instr., Franklin Inst. and Boston State Coll., 1960s. Mem.: Authors League, Mystery Writers Assoc. Au.: a series of 11 mystery novels featuring a small-town rabbi, David Small, as the unconventional sleuth: *Friday the Rabbi Slept Late* (1964); *Saturday the Rabbi Went Hungry* (1966); *Sunday the Rabbi Stayed Home* (1969); *Monday the Rabbi Took Off* (1972); *Tuesday the Rabbi Saw Red* (1973); *Wednesday the Rabbi Got Wet* (1976); *Thursday the Rabbi Walked Out* (1978); *Someday the Rabbi Will Leave* (1985); *One Fine Day the Rabbi Bought a Cross* (1987); *The Day the Rabbi Resigned* (1992); and *That Day the Rabbi Left Town* (1996). Other published works: *The Nine Mile Walk* (1967), *Commonsense in Education* (1970), and *Conversations with Rabbi Small* (1981). Recipient: Edgar Allan Poe Award (Mystery Writers of Amer.); Faith and Freedom Communications Award.

KLEIN, JUDITH WEINSTEIN, psychotherapist; b. Chicago, Ill., Nov. 11, 1947; d. Berkeley, Calif., Aug. 9, 1996. Educ.: U. Calif.-Berkeley, Stanford U., Wright Institute (PhD). An authority on ethnic self-esteem who developed a national reputation for her use of "ethnotherapy" as a treatment for self-hatred and alienation. Au.: *Jewish Identity and Self-Esteem,* based on research conducted for the American Jewish Committee; articles in professional journals.

KRESH, PAUL, publicist, writer, record producer; b. NYC, Dec. 3, 1919; d. NYC, Jan. 13, 1997. Educ.: Columbia U., CCNY. Publicity writer, JWB, 1941–45; publicity dir., Amer. ORT Fed., 1945–46; asst. publicity dir., Council of Jewish Feds., 1946–47; acct. exec., Nathan C. Belth Assoc., 1947–50; asst. publicity dir. and motion picture coord., UJA, 1950–59; PR dir., Union of Amer. Hebrew Congs., and ed., *American Judaism,* 1959–67; v.-pres., Spoken Arts Records, 1967–71; recording dir., Caedmon Records, 1971–72; PR dir., UJA Greater N.Y., 1972–74; creative dir., UJA-Fed. Campaign, 1974–81; communications consult., 1981 on; publicist, Richard Cohen Assoc., 1988–90; contributing ed., N.Y. *Jewish Week,* 1990 on. Producer: dozens of recordings of Amer. poets reading their own works and other spoken-arts recordings; several radio series, incl. "Adventures in Judaism" (1960s); "World of Jewish Music" (1982–83); scriptwriter: several documentary films, mostly on Jewish subjects, incl. *The Day the Doors Closed* (1965), *Broken Sabbath* (1974), *Commitment* (1976), and *On the Brink of Peace* (1980); music reviewer and critic: *Stereo Review* and *American Record Guide, N.Y. Times, High Fidelity,* and other pubs. Au.: *The Power of the Unknown Citizen* (1969), *Isaac Bashevis Singer: The Magician of West 86th Street* (1979), *Isaac Bashevis Singer: The Story of a Storyteller* (1984), and *An American Rhapsody: The Story of George Gershwin* (1988); ed.: *American Judaism Reader* (1967). Recipient: Armstrong Award,

Emmy Award, Golden Eagle Award, Internatl. TV and Film Festival Award, and other honors.

KRESSYN, MIRIAM, actress, entertainer; b. Bialystok, Poland, Mar. 4, 1912; d. NYC, Oct. 27, 1996; in U.S. since 1924. Educ.: Northeastern U., New England Conservatory of Music. One of the most popular artists in the Yiddish theater for over 60 years, often co-starring with her husband, Seymour Rechtzeit, with whom she also hosted radio programs for some 40 years on WEVD, and TV programs. Taught Yiddish theater at Queens Coll.; authored or adapted a number of plays, incl. *Broome St. in America, Anna Lucasta, The Jester,* and *Raisins and Almonds.* Recipient: Yiddish theater Goldie Award.

LEHMANN, MANFRED RAPHAEL, business executive, communal worker; b. Stockholm, Sweden, Aug. 28, 1922; d. (?), May 30, 1997; in U.S. since (?). Educ.: John Hopkins U.; Yeshiva U. (DHL). Pres., Inter-Govt. Philatelic Corp., Lehmann Traing Corp. Mem.: global bd. trustees, Bar-Ilan Univ.; bd. dirs., Bernard Revel Graduate School, Yeshiva U.; bd., Likud USA; bd., Jerusalem Reclamation Project; bd. govs., United Israel Institutes; founder and benefactor, Young Israel of Lawrence-Cedarhurst, N.Y. Au.: numerous scholarly articles on archaeology and biblical topics.

LIMAN, ARTHUR LAWRENCE, lawyer; b. NYC, Nov. 5, 1932; d. NYC July 17, 1997. Educ.: Harvard U., Yale U. (LLB). Asst. US atty., S. Dist. NY, 1961–63; special assist., US atty., 1965. With law firm of Paul, Weiss, Rifkind, Wharton & Garrison, 1957–61 and 1963–; partner, 1966–. Regarded as one of the best trial lawyers of his day, his corporate clients incl. Time-Warner, Pennzoil, CBS, and Calvin Klein; individual clients incl. notable financial figures Robert L. Vesco, Dennis B. Levine, Michael Milken, and John Zaccaro. Chief counsel: NY state special comm. on inmate uprising at Attica state prison, 1972; US Senate comm. investigating the Iran-Contra affair, 1987. Founder and chmn. for 25 years, Legal Action Center; pres., Legal Aid Soc. Served on various govt. comms. Mem.: bd. overseers, Harvard U.; council of trustees, Amer. Friends of Hebrew U. Fellow: Amer. Coll. Trial Lawyers, Amer.

Bar Found. Recipient: Proskauer Award, NY UJA-Federation; Judge Learned Hand Human Relations Award, Amer. Jewish Com.

LINCHNER, ALEXANDER S., rabbi, communal professional; b. NYC, August 8, 1908; d. Jerusalem, Israel, June 4, 1997. Educ.: Yeshivah Torah Vodaath, Brooklyn; Yeshivah, Radin, Poland (1930–33). English studies teacher and principal, Torah Vodaath, Brooklyn, in the '30s and '40s. Founded Boys Town Jerusalem, 1949; thereafter served officially, in Jerusalem, as dean, in the U.S. as v.-chmn. of the bd. of the U.S. Boys Town Found., and unofficially as the inspiration and guiding spirit of the institution, which combines Torah studies with vocational/technical training.

MILLER, RUTH RATNER, business executive, civic leader; b. Cleveland, Ohio, Dec. 1, 1925; d. Cleveland, Ohio, Nov. 26, 1996. Educ.: Case Western Reserve U. (PhD). Lect., educ. psych., Case Western Reserve U., 1969–74; dir., community development and later, dir., public health and welfare, City of Cleveland. Pres., Tower City Center, a complex of buildings built by her family's Forest City Enterprises, a natl. real estate developer; unsuccessful cand. for Congress, 1980; del., UN World Conf. on the Decade of Women, Nairobi, 1985. Bd. mem.: U.S. Holocaust Memorial Museum; Natl. Jewish Coalition; trustee: Cleveland State U.; Western Reserve Hist. Soc. Recipient: Human Relations Award, Amer. J. Com.; Disting. Community Service Award, Brandeis U.; State of Israel David Ben-Gurion Award; named by *Cleveland Magazine* one of the city's most influential women.

MINTZ, JEROME R., professor; b. Brooklyn, N.Y., Mar. 29, 1930; d. Bloomington, Ind., Nov. 22, 1997. Educ.: Brooklyn Coll., CUNY, Indiana Univ.(PhD). Instr., Ohio State U., 1961–62; prof., anthropology and Jewish studies, Indiana U., 1962–; curator, Mediterranean ethnology, Indiana U. Museum; exec. bd. mem., Soc. for Anthropology of Visual Communication. Au.: *Legends of the Hasidim* (1968); *The Anarchists of Casas Viejas* (1983); *Hasidic People: A Place in the New World* (1992), winner of a 1993 National Jewish Book Award; *Carnival Song and Society: Gossip, Sexuality and Creativity in Andalusia* (1997), and articles in various periodicals; producer of six films about tradition and change in Andalusia, Spain. Recipient: Natl. Endowment for the Humanities fellowship, 1986.

PATAI, RAPHAEL, anthropologist, writer; b. Budapest, Hungary, Nov. 22, 1910; d. Tucson, Arizona, July 20, 1996; in U.S. since 1947. Educ.: U. Budapest (PhD); Rabbinical Sem., Budapest (rabbinic ord.); Hebrew University, Jerusalem (PhD). Instr., Hebrew lang., Hebrew U., 1938–42; exec. sec., Haifa Technion, 1942–43; research fellow, ethnology, Hebrew U., 1943–47; research dir., Palestine Inst. Folklore and Ethnology, 1944–48; prof.: Dropsie Coll., Phila., 1948–57; Fairleigh-Dickinson U., 1966–76; visiting lect.: Princeton U., U. Pa., New School for Social Research, Columbia U., Brooklyn Coll., NYU, Ohio State; research dir., Herzl Inst., 1956–71, and ed., Herzl Press, 1957–71. Fellow: Amer. Anthropological Assoc.; mem., Council of Amer. Folklore Societies. Au.: More than 3 dozen books on Jewish and Arab culture, history, politics, psychology, and folklore, incl. *A Study in Palestinian Folklore* (1936); *Man and Earth in Hebrew Custom, Belief and Legend* (1942–43); *Man and Temple in Ancient Jewish Myth and Ritual* (1947, 1967); *Israel Between East and West* (1953); *Cultures in Conflict* (1958, 1961); *Golden River to Golden Road: Society, Culture and Change in the Middle East* (1962, 1969); *Hebrew Myths* (with Robert Graves) (1964); *The Hebrew Goddess* (1967, 1978); *The Myth of the Jewish Race* (with Jennifer Patai Wing) (1975); *The Seed of Abraham: Jews and Arabs in Contact and Conflict* (1983); *The Jews of Hungary: History, Culture, Psychology* (1996). Ed.: *Complete Diaries of Theodor Herzl* (1960); *Studies in Biblical and Jewish Folklore* (with F. Utley and D. Noy) (1960); *Encycl. of Zionism and Israel* (1971), and other works. Recipient: Viking Fund fellowship; Columbia U. Bureau of Applied Social Research fellowship; Bialik Prize, Tel Aviv Municipality, 1936; Jewish Book Award, 1975, 1976; Anisfield Wolf Award, 1975.

RABB NORMAN, business executive, communal worker; b. Boston, Mass., Sept. 13, 1905; d. W. Palm Beach, Fla., May 4, 1997. Educ.: Harvard Coll. Served U.S. Navy, WW II. V.-pres. and dir., Stop and Shop supermarket chain, 1929–59; v.-

chmn., 1959–65. One of 8 founding trustees of Brandeis U. in 1948; bd.sec., later bd. chmn., 1961–67, the period of the univ.'s greatest expansion; with family members, supported construction of Graduate Center. Founding pres., Boston chap., Amer. Jewish Com., and natl. v.-pres. and hon. gov.; v.-pres. and hon. life trustee, Combined Jewish Philanthropies; mem. bd. delegates, UAHC; trustee or bd. mem.: Boston U., UIA, Hebrew Coll., Temple Adath Israel, Temple Emanuel of Palm Beach, and other orgs. Recipient: hon. doctorate, Brandeis U. and other honors.

RICE, JAMES P., communal executive; b. Cleveland, Ohio, Mar. 6, 1913; d. Chicago, Ill., Oct. 25, 1997. Educ.: Western Reserve Univ. Began career as social worker in the 1930s; joined Amer. Jewish Joint Distrib. Com. in 1945, serving as overseas field rep. in Europe, helping to resettle displaced persons, and as JDC liaison to UN High Commissioner for Refugees in Geneva, until 1955; exec. dir., HIAS, 1955–66; exec. v.-pres., Jewish Federation/Jewish United Fund of Chicago, 1966–79. Consult.: natl. UJA, Chicago Fed. legacy and endowment com.; v.-pres.: Thanks to Scandinavia, Amer. ORT Fed.; adv. bd. mem., Albert Einstein Peace Prize Found.; mem. exec. com., Citizens Com. on the Juvenile Court.

ROSENBAUM, SAMUEL, cantor; b. NYC, June 11, 1919; d. Rochester, N.Y., Mar. 23, 1997. Educ.: New York U.; Herzliah Hebrew Teachers Coll.; private study with Cantors Jacob Beimel and Adolph Katchko. Cantor, Temple Beth El, Rochester, N.Y., 1946–87; emer. thereafter. Composer and/or librettist of oratorios, solo, and choral works; lecturer on Jewish music, culture, and folklore. A founder and past pres. of the Cantors Assembly (Conservative) and its exec. v.-pres.,1959–; helped to win four landmark court cases gaining recognition for cantors as clergy. Au.: four religious school textbooks, *A Yiddish Word Book for English Speaking People,* and *Mahzor 101;* transls. of Yiddish poetry and folk songs; managing ed., Cantors Assembly's *Journal of Synagogue Music;* consult., Prayer Book Press. Recipient: 1st hon. Doctor of Music degree, Jewish Theol. Sem., and other honors.

ROSENSAFT, HADASSAH BIMKO, dentist, communal worker; b. Sosnowiec, Poland, Aug. 26, 1912; d. NYC, Oct. 3, 1997; in U.S. since 1958. Educ.: U. of Nancy, France. Practiced dentistry in Sosnowiec from 1935 until deportation to Auschwitz in Aug. 1943, where her parents, husband, and small son were sent to the gas chambers. Both there and in Bergen-Belsen, where she was interned from Nov. 1944 until liberation in Apr. 1945, she worked in infirmaries and was credited with saving many lives. Admin. of hospital at Bergen-Belsen and v.-chmn., Jewish com. of displaced persons camp, 1945–47; head of the health dept. of the Central Jewish Com. in the British zone of Germany, 1945–47, and v.-chmn. of the council of the Central Jewish Com., 1947–50. Remarried and with a child, moved to Switzerland in 1950. Hon. pres., World Fed. of Bergen-Belsen Survivors, 1975–97; mem., President's Com. on the Holocaust, 1978–79; served two terms as mem., U.S. Holocaust Memorial Council (1980–94). Chmn., archives and library com. and mem. exec. com. and content com., U.S. Holocaust Memorial Museum, 1980–94. Lecturer and writer on the Holocaust. Recipient: hon. doctorate, Hebrew Union Coll.-Jewish Inst. of Religion.

ROSENWALD, WILLIAM, investment executive, philanthropist; b. Chicago, Ill., Aug. 19, 1903; d. NYC, Oct. 31, 1996. Educ.: MIT, Harvard U., London School of Economics. Joined Sears, Roebuck, the company headed by his father, Julius, in 1928, serving as a director 1934–1938; in 1935 began career as private investor; founder, chmn., Amer. Securities Corp., 1946 on. Beginning in 1930s, devoted himself to rescue of Jews in Europe, incl. bringing to U.S. and settling 300 family members. Active in a number of orgs. aiding Jews in distress: Amer. Jewish Joint Distribution Com. beginning 1935 (mem. exec. com. 1941 to early '90s; hon. v.-pres.); v.-chmn., Natl. Coord. Com. for Refugees from Germany; organizer and 1st pres. of Natl. Refugee Service, predecessor of Hebrew Immigrant Aid Soc. (HIAS), 1939–44; hon. pres., United Service for New Americans, another HIAS predecessor, 1946–54; life mem., HIAS bd. dirs., 1954 on. One of three signatories of agreement creating national UJA in 1939, natl. chmn. 1941–55, genl. chmn.

1955, 1956, 1957, and life trustee. Also active in UJA of Greater N.Y. (1st pres., N.Y. UJA-Federation joint campaign, 1974–77); Amer. J. Com. (mem. exec. com. starting 1935, chmn. natl. advisory com., v.-pres., hon. v.-pres.); Fed. of J. Philanthropies of NY; Council of Jewish Federations and Welfare Funds; N.Y. Philharmonic; Tuskegee Inst. (trustee, 1935–76). Mem.: Council on Foreign Relations; NY state com. on displaced persons; Council on Foreign Relations; hon. life trustee, Chicago Museum of Science and Industry. Recipient: hon. doctorates from Hebrew Union Coll. and Tuskegee Inst. and numerous org. awards.

ROSTEN, LEO CALVIN (Leonard Q. Ross), author; b. Lodz, Poland, Apr. 11, 1908; d. NYC, Feb. 19, 1997; in U.S. since 1911. Educ.: U. Chicago (BA, PhD); London School of Economics. Night-school teacher of English to new immigrants, 1932–34; public lect., 1932–35; research asst., polit. sci., U. Chicago, 1934–35; fellow, Social Sci. Research Council, 1935–36; researcher, President's com. on admin. management, 1936; motion picture writer, 1937; dir., Carnegie Corp. motion picture research project, 1939; Rockefeller Found. grantee for study of Hollywood, 1940; consult., Natl. Defense Adv. Comm. and Office for Emergency Management, 1941; deputy dir., Office of War Information, and chief, motion pictures div., 1942–44; special consult., War Dept., 1945–47; researcher, Rand Corp., late 1940s; special edit. adviser, *Look* magazine, starting 1949; lect. in political science at Yale, Columbia, U. Calif.-Berkeley, and other insts. Au.: Dozens of works of fiction and nonfiction, most notably *The Education of H*Y*M*A*N K*A*P*L*A*N* (1937), based on his experience teaching immigrants, in which he created one of the classic comic characters in 20th-cent. Amer. lit., and *The Joys of Yiddish,* 1968. Other works incl. *The Return of H*Y*M*A*N K*A*P*L*A*N* (1959); *Captain Newman, M.D.* (1961); *O K*A*P*L*A*N! My K*A*P*L*A*N!* (1976); mystery novels *Silky* (1979), and *King Silky* (1980); and *The Joys of Yinglish* (1989). Also co-authored or authored numerous screenplays.

SAGAN, CARL EDWARD, astronomer, author; b. Brooklyn, N.Y., Nov. 9, 1934; d. Seat-

tle, Wash., Dec. 20, 1996. Educ.: U. Chicago (BA, MA, PhD). Postdoc. fellowship, U. Calif.-Berkeley, 1960–62; teaching and research in genetics, Stanford U. School of Medicine, 1962–63; staff mem., Smithsonian Astrophysical Observatory, and asst. prof., astronomy, Harvard U., 1963–68; dir., Cornell U.'s Laboratory for Planetary Studies, from 1968, and prof. astronomy and space sciences from 1971. His 1980 public TV series *Cosmos* reached an estimated 400 million viewers. Au.: more than 600 scientific papers and popular articles and more than a dozen books, incl. *Cosmos* (companion to TV series); *The Cosmic Connection: An Extraterrestrial Perspective* (1973); *Other Worlds* (1975); *The Dragons of Eden: Speculations on the Evolution of Human Intelligence* (1977; Pulitzer Prize winner); and a best-selling science-fiction novel, *Contact* (1984). Recipient: Public Welfare Medal (Natl. Acad. of Sciences); the NASA Medal for Distinguished Public Service (twice); and many other honors.

SCHWARCZ, ERNEST, professor; b. Zemplen Agard, Hungary, Aug. 26, 1921; d. Flushing, N.Y., Aug. 26, 1997; in U.S. since 1957. Educ.: U. Budapest (PhD); Rabbinical Seminary of Budapest (rabbinic ord.). Instr., philosophy, U. Vienna, 1948–50; founder and principal, Mt. Scopus College, Melbourne, Australia, 1950–57; joined Queens College (N.Y.) faculty in 1959 as instr.; prof. of philosophy, 1970, and dean, School of Genl. Studies, until 1992; founder, Center for Jewish Studies, of which he remained an active fellow until his death; chmn.: Queens Black-Jewish People to People Project and Adult Collegiate Education. Au.: articles on education in prof. journals; co-author, books on Amer. education and the learning process.

SERWER-BERNSTEIN, BLANCHE L., psychologist, author; b. NYC, July 13, 1911; d. NYC, May 11, 1997. Educ.: Barnard Coll., Columbia U. (MA), City Coll. of NY (MS), NYU (PhD), Jewish Theol. Sem. of Amer. (BHL). Clinical psychologist in private practice, 1957–97; sr. lect. and research assoc., City U. of NY, 1960–66; visiting lect. and research assoc., Harvard U., 1966–69; prof., Boston U., 1969–75. Active in behalf of ELEM/Youth in Distress, Givat Haviva, and Interns for Peace. Au.: *Let's Steal the Moon* (1970); *In the Tradition of Moses and Mohammed* (1994). Recipient: Givat Haviva Leadership Award, 1997.

SHANKER, ALBERT, teacher, labor union official; b. NYC, Sept. 14, 1928; d. NYC, Feb. 22, 1997. Educ.: U. Illinois; Columbia U. Teacher, NYC elem. and jr. high schools, 1952–59; field rep., Amer. Fed. Teachers and N.Y. Teachers Guild (succeeded by United Fed. Teachers), 1960–63; pres., United Fed. Teachers (NYC), 1964–86; pres., Amer. Fed. Teachers (Washington, DC), 1974 on; sr. v.-pres., AFL-CIO exec. council, 1973 on; exec. v.-pres., NY State United Teachers, 1972–78. A combative leader during 1967–68 battle in NYC over decentralization and community control, he led the 85,000-member UFT in strikes against the city to protect teachers' rights, for which he went to jail twice. As pres. of 900,000-mem. AFT, became known as a champion of rigorous educ. standards, his views widely disseminated through weekly paid column in the Sunday *N.Y. Times*. V.-pres.: NY State AFL-CIO; NYC Central Labor Council; sec., Jewish Labor Com.; hon. v.-chmn., Amer. Trade Union Council for Histadrut; mem. exec. com., Workers Defense League; bd. mem., numerous orgs.

SHULMAN REBECCA, communal worker; b. Vienna, Austria-Hungary, Oct. 10, 1896; d. NYC, Mar. 30, 1997; in U.S. since 1899. Educ.: Hunter Coll. Nurse-social worker, NYC; associated with Hadassah starting 1924: natl. bd. mem., 1932 on; chairwoman various coms., incl. Natl. Child Welfare, Jewish Natl. Fund, and Hadassah Medical Org.; delegate to World Zionist Cong., 1929, 1933, 1935, 1937, and 1946; natl. sec., v.-pres., and other offices; natl. pres., 1953–56. A lifelong Zionist, in the years prior to the establishment of Israel, her home was a center of activity for Abba Eban, David Ben-Gurion, and other leaders of the new state. In 1954, helped to establish Amer. wing at Israel Museum with gift of 12 paintings by Amer. artists.

STAMPFER, JUDAH L., professor, writer; b. Jerusalem, Palestine, Nov. 11, 1923; d. NYC, Oct. 4, 1996; in U.S. since (?). Educ.: U. Chicago (BA); Teachers Coll., Columbia U. (MS); Yeshiva U. (rabbinic ord.); Harvard U. (PhD). Asst. rabbi,

Harvard U. and Brandeis U., 1950–51; rabbi, Dover, NH, 1951–52; Hillel rabbi, U. Manitoba, Can., 1952–55; teaching fellow, Harvard U., 1955–59; asst. prof., later prof., English lit. and Jewish studies, State U. of N.Y. at Stony Brook, 1960–97. Au.: *Jerusalem Has Many Faces* (poetry, 1950); *Saul Myers* (novel).

TEMKIN, SEFTON, professor, lawyer; b. Manchester, England, June 7, 1917; d. Manchester, England, Dec. 20, 1996; in U.S. since 1959. Educ.: Liverpool Inst., Liverpool U. (law degree and MA in hist.), Hebrew Union Coll. (doctorate). Secy., Anglo-Jewish Assoc., London, 1943–51; practiced law as a barrister until moving to U.S. Co-ed., *Topham's Company Law* and contrib. to *Halbury's Laws of England.* Active in Jewish affairs as rep. on Bd. of Deputies from West London Syn., and columnist and features writer for London *Jewish Chronicle.* In U.S.: instr.: U. Cincinnati, Boston U.; assoc. prof., Judaic studies, State U. New York-Albany, 1970–85. Mng. ed., *Jewish Social Studies.* Au.: *The New World of Reform* (1974); *Isaac Mayer Wise: Shaping American Judaism* (1992); contrib.: *American Jewish Year Book* and *Encyclopedia Judaica,* of which he was also an editor.

TRILLING, DIANA, critic, author; b. NYC, July 21, 1905; d. NYC, October 23, 1996. Educ.: Radcliffe Coll. Fiction critic, *The Nation,* 1941–49; free-lance essayist and critic, 1949 on, appearing primarily in *Partisan Review* and *The Nation,* as well as in *American Scholar, New Leader,* the *New Yorker, Harper's,* and other publications. With her husband, Lionel, was a member of the influential "New York intellectuals," a circle that flourished in the 1930s-1950s. Published 3 collections of essays: *Reviewing the Forties* (1948), *Claremont Essays* (1965), and *We Must March My Darlings* (1977). Au. also of *Mrs. Harris: The Death of the Scarsdale Diet Doctor* (1981) and *Beginning of the Journey: The Marriage of Diana and Lionel Trilling* (1993). Ed.: *Uniform Edition of the Works of Lionel Trilling* and other works. Fellow: Amer. Acad. Arts and Sciences.

TROBE, HAROLD, communal professional; b. Pittsburgh, Pa., Jan. 4, 1914; d. Gainesville, Fla., June 24, 1996. Educ.: U. Pittsburgh, Columbia U. School of Social Work. Joined Amer. Jewish Joint Distribution Com. in 1944 as overseas field representative in Lisbon, Portugal, from where he succeeded in sending two shiploads of refugees to Palestine; served in Czechoslovakia in 1945 and in Milan in 1946 assisting displaced persons; JDC dir. in Italy, 1952–57; dir. gen., HIAS, for Europe and N. Amer., 1957–62, and for Latin Amer., 1962–66; from 1966 until retirement in 1980, worked for JDC in Israel.

TWERSKY, ISADORE (Yitzhak), professor, rabbi; b. Boston, Mass., Oct. 9, 1930; d. Boston, Mass., Oct. 12, 1997. Educ.: Harvard U. (BA, MA, PhD); Rabbi Isaac Elchanan Theol. Sem. (ord.). Joined Harvard faculty after completing his doctorate in 1956, teaching Hebrew and Jewish hist.; in 1965 succeeded his mentor, Harry A. Wolfson, as Nathan Littauer Prof. of Hebrew Literature and Philosophy; chmn., dept. of Near Eastern langs. and lit.; founding dir., Harvard Center for Jewish Studies, 1978–93. Widely credited with making Harvard a more comfortable place for observant Jews and for expanding its Jewish studies program. As the Talner rebbe, descended from a Hassidic dynasty that has its roots in Chernobyl, Ukraine, he served as spiritual leader of Beth David Cong. and Maimonides School in Brookline. Mem.: bd. govs., Hebrew U.; fellow, Amer. Acad. for Jewish Research; visiting prof., Yeshiva U., Hebrew U. Au.: *Introduction to the Code of Maimonides (Mishne Torah)* (1981 National Jewish Book Award), *A Maimonides Reader*, and other works.

ULLMANN, IRMA, philanthropist; b. Hamburg, Germany, (?), 1905; d. White Plains, N.Y., Nov. 4, 1996; in U.S. since 1926. Widow of metals and commodities trader Siegfried Ullmann (d. 1965), she continued the philanthropic work she had begun with her husband through the Ullmann Family Found. Major benefactor: Yeshiva U., Albert Einstein Coll. Medicine, Amer. Soc. for Technion-Israel Inst. of Technology, Weizmann Inst. of Science, Hadassah Hosp. (Jerusalem), Lichtenstadter Hosp. for the Chronically Ill (Israel), UJA-Fed. of N.Y.

WAXMAN, RUTH B., editor; b. Jaffa, Palestine, Feb. 22, 1916; d. Great Neck, N.Y., Oct. 18, 1996; in U.S. since 1920. Educ.: U. Chicago (BA, PHD). Instr., comp. lit.: U. Chicago, Adelphi U., Long Island U.

(C.W. Post campus), SUNY at Stony Brook; frequent lect. on the role of women in the synagogue; ed., *Judaism: A Quarterly Journal of Jewish Life and Thought*, 1972–94. Chmn., publications com. and bd. mem., United Synagogue of Conservative Judaism, 1972–96. Co-au. (with Robert Gordis): *Faith and Reason* (1973).

WEINSTEIN, LEWIS H., lawyer, communal worker; b. Arany, Lithuania, Apr. 10, 1905; d. Boston, Mass., Oct. 23, 1996; in U.S. since 1906. Educ.: Harvard Coll., Harvard Law School. Served US Army, WW II. Partner, Rome, Weinstein & Wolbarsht, 1930–45; asst. corp. counsel, city of Boston, 1934–35; genl. counsel, Boston Housing Auth., 1938–45, where he helped shape first urban renewal legislation in U.S.; partner, Foley, Hoag, and Eliot, 1946–93. Lect., Harvard Law School, 1960–76; sr. visiting lect., city planning, MIT, 1961–68. Mem.: Mass. State Emergency Housing Com.; Pres. Kennedy's and Pres. Johnson's Exec. Coms. on Equal Opportunity in Housing; fellow: Amer. Bar Found., Amer. Coll. Trial Lawyers. Boston Jewish activity: Combined Jewish Philanthropies (trustee, pres.); Hebrew Teachers Coll. (trustee, pres.); Jewish Community Council, Beth Israel Hosp., Hebrew Rehab. Center for the Aged, Bureau of Jewish Educ., Temple Mishkan Tefila. National offices: chmn.: Natl. Community Relations Advisory Council, 1960–64; Conf. of Presidents of Major Amer. Jewish Orgs., 1963–65; pres., Council of Jewish Federations, 1965–66; chmn., Amer. Jewish Conf. on Soviet Jewry, 1968–70; served on natl. boards of JWB, JDC, Amer. Jewish Hist. Soc., and other bodies; mem. bd. overseers, Brandeis U.'s Florence Heller Grad. School and Lown Center for Contemporary Jewish Studies. Au.: numerous articles in genl. and prof. pubs. and two books: *MASA: Odyssey of an American Jew* and *My Life at the Bar: Six Decades as Lawyer, Soldier, Teacher and Pro Bono Activist*. Recipient: U.S. Army Legion of Merit; Bronze Star with Oak Leaf Cluster; chevalier, French Legion of Honor; Croix de Guerre with Palm; military medal, Pope Pius XII; Heritage Award, Yeshiva U.; Roosevelt Day Award, Amers. for Democratic Action; and many other honors.

WEISGALL, HUGO DAVID, composer, conductor, teacher; b. Ivancice, Bohemia, Oct. 13, 1912; d. Manhasset, N.Y., Mar. 11, 1997; in U.S. since 1920. Educ.: Peabody Conservatory, Curtis Inst., private composition study with Roger Sessions, Johns Hopkins U. (PhD in comp. lit.). Served U.S. Army, WW II. Conductor (in Baltimore): Har Sinai Temple Choir, 1931–42; "Y" Alliance Orch., 1935–42; String Symph., 1936–38; Natl. Youth Admin. Orch., 1940–41. During wartime army service in Europe: asst. military attaché, govts.-in-exile, 1945–46; cultural attaché, Amer. embassy, Prague, 1946–47; guest conductor: London Symph., London Philharmonic, BBC Symph., Belgian Natl. Radio Orch. Instr., composition, Cumington School of Arts (Mass.), 1948–51. In Baltimore: dir.: Inst. of Musical Arts, 1949, and Hilltop Music Co., 1951–56; lect., music, Johns Hopkins U., 1952–56; conductor, Chizuk Amuno choir and chorus, 1958–59. In New York: a founder and chmn. of faculty, Cantors Inst., Jewish Theol. Sem. of Amer., 1952 on; instr., Juilliard School, 1957–69; disting. prof. of composition, Queens Coll., 1960–83. Pres., Amer. Music Center, 1964–73; assoc., Lincoln Center Fund, 1965–68; composer in residence, Amer. Acad. in Rome, 1966–67. Composer: some instrumental and chamber music but chiefly vocal music in modern, atonal style, incl. song cycles, one-act operas, and full-length operas. *Six Characters in Search of an Author* (1959), *Nine Rivers from Jordan* (1968), and *Esther* (1993) premiered at the N.Y. City Opera; other works incl. the operas *The Tenor* (1948–50), *The Stronger* (1952), *Athaliah* (1964), and *Will You Marry Me?* (1987), and *Tekiatot: Rituals for Rosh Hashannah,* for orchestra. Mem.: ASCAP; Amer. Acad. of Arts and Letters. Recipient: Amer. Inst. Arts and Letters Award; 3 Guggenheim fellowships, and other honors

Calendars

SUMMARY JEWISH CALENDAR, 5758–5762 (Oct. 1997–Aug. 2002)

HOLIDAY	5758 (1997)	5759 (1998)	5760 (1999)	5761 (2000)	5762 (2001)
Rosh Ha-shanah, 1st day	Th Oct. 2	M Sept. 21	Sa Sept. 11	Sa Sept. 30	T Sept. 18
Rosh Ha-shanah, 2nd day	F Oct. 3	T Sept. 22	S Sept. 12	S Oct. 1	W Sept. 19
Fast of Gedaliah	S Oct. 5	W Sept. 23	M Sept. 13	M Oct. 2	Th Sept. 20
Yom Kippur	Sa Oct. 11	W Sept. 30	M Sept. 20	M Oct. 9	Th Sept. 27
Sukkot, 1st day	Th Oct. 16	M Oct. 5	Sa Sept. 25	Sa Oct. 14	T Oct. 2
Sukkot, 2nd day	F Oct. 17	T Oct. 6	S Sept. 26	S Oct. 15	W Oct. 3
Hosha'na' Rabbah	W Oct. 22	S Oct. 11	F Oct. 1	F Oct. 20	M Oct. 8
Shemini 'Azeret	Th Oct. 23	M Oct. 12	Sa Oct. 2	Sa Oct. 21	T Oct. 9
Simhat Torah	F Oct. 24	T Oct. 13	S Oct. 3	S Oct. 22	W Oct. 10
New Moon, Heshwan, 1st day	F Oct. 31	T Oct. 20	S Oct. 10	S Oct. 29	W Oct. 17
New Moon, Heshwan, 2nd day	Sa Nov. 1	W Oct. 21	M Oct. 11	M Oct. 30	Th Oct. 18
New Moon, Kislew, 1st day	S Nov. 30	Th Nov. 19	T Nov. 9	T Nov. 28	F Nov. 16
New Moon, Kislew, 2nd day		F Nov. 20	W Nov. 10		
Hanukkah, 1st day	W Dec. 24	M Dec. 14	Sa Dec. 4	F Dec. 22	M Dec. 10
New Moon, Tevet, 1st day	M Dec. 29	Sa Dec. 19	Th Dec. 9	W Dec. 27	Sa Dec. 15
New Moon, Tevet, 2nd day	T Dec. 30	S Dec. 20	F Dec. 10		S Dec. 16
Fast of 10th of Tevet	Th Jan. 8 (1998)	T Dec. 29	S Dec. 19	F Jan. 5 (2001)	T Dec. 25

	1998			1999			2000			2001			2002		
New Moon, Shevat	W	Jan.	28	M	Jan.	18	Sa	Jan.	8	Th	Jan.	25	M	Jan.	14
Hamishshah-'asar bi-Shevat	W	Feb.	11	M	Feb.	1	Sa	Jan.	22	Th	Feb.	8	M	Jan.	28
New Moon, Adar I, 1st day	Th	Feb.	26	T	Feb.	16	S	Feb.	6	F	Feb.	23	T	Feb.	12
New Moon, Adar I, 2nd day	F	Feb.	27	W	Feb.	17	M	Feb.	7	Sa	Feb.	24	W	Feb.	13
New Moon, Adar II, 1st day							T	Mar.	7						
New Moon, Adar II, 2nd day							W	Mar.	8						
Fast of Esther	W	Mar.	11	M	Mar.	1	M	Mar.	20	Th	Mar.	8	M	Feb.	25
Purim	Th	Mar.	12	T	Mar.	2	T	Mar.	21	F	Mar.	9	T	Feb.	26
Shushan Purim	F	Mar.	13	W	Mar.	3	W	Mar.	22	Sa	Mar.	10	W	Feb.	27
New Moon, Nisan	Sa	Mar.	28	Th	Mar.	18	Th	Apr.	6	S	Mar.	25	Th	Mar.	14
Passover, 1st day	Sa	Apr.	11	Th	Apr.	1	Th	Apr.	20	S	Apr.	8	Th	Mar.	28
Passover, 2nd day	S	Apr.	12	F	Apr.	2	F	Apr.	21	M	Apr.	9	F	Mar.	29
Passover, 7th day	F	Apr.	17	W	Apr.	7	W	Apr.	26	Sa	Apr.	14	W	Apr.	3
Passover, 8th day	Sa	Apr.	18	Th	Apr.	8	Th	Apr.	27	S	Apr.	15	Th	Apr.	4
Holocaust Memorial Day	Th	Apr.	23	T	Apr.	13	T	May	2	F	Apr.	20*	T	Apr.	9
New Moon, Iyar, 1st day	S	Apr.	26	F	Apr.	16	F	May	5	M	Apr.	23	F	Apr.	12
New Moon, Iyar, 2nd day	M	Apr.	27	Sa	Apr.	17	Sa	May	6	T	Apr.	24	Sa	Apr.	13
Israel Independence Day	Fr	May	1*	W	Apr.	21	W	May	10	Sa	Apr.	28†	W	Apr.	17
Lag Ba-'omer	Th	May	14	T	May	4	T	May	23	F	May	11	T	Apr.	30
Jerusalem Day	S	May	24	F	May	14*	F	June	2*	M	May	21	F	May	10*
New Moon, Siwan	T	May	26	S	May	16	S	June	4	W	May	23	S	May	12
Shavu'ot, 1st day	S	May	31	F	May	21	F	June	9	M	May	28	F	May	17
Shavu'ot, 2nd day	M	June	1	Sa	May	22	Sa	June	10	T	May	29	Sa	May	18
New Moon, Tammuz, 1st day	W	June	24	M	June	14	M	July	3	Th	June	21	M	June	10
New Moon, Tammuz, 2nd day	Th	June	25	T	June	15	T	July	4	F	June	22	T	June	11
Fast of 17th of Tammuz	S	July	12	Th	July	1	Th	July	20	S	July	8	Th	June	27
New Moon, Av	F	July	24	W	July	14	W	Aug.	2	Sa	July	21	W	July	10
Fast of 9th of Av	S	Aug.	2	Th	July	22	Th	Aug.	10	S	July	29	Th	July	18
New Moon, Elul, 1st day	Sa	Aug.	22	Th	Aug.	12	Th	Aug.	31	S	Aug.	19	Th	Aug.	8
New Moon, Elul, 2nd day	S	Aug.	23	F	Aug.	13	F	Sept.	1	M	Aug.	20	F	Aug.	9

*Observed Thursday, a day earlier, to avoid conflict with the Sabbath.

†Observed Thursday, two days earlier, to avoid conflict with the Sabbath.

CONDENSED MONTHLY CALENDAR
(1997–2000)

1997, Jan. 9–Feb. 7]　　　　SHEVAṬ (30 DAYS)　　　　[5757

Civil Date	Day of the Week	Jewish Date	SABBATHS, FESTIVALS, FASTS	PENTATEUCHAL READING	PROPHETICAL READING
Jan. 9	Th	Shevaṭ 1	New Moon	Num. 28:1–15	
11	Sa	3	Wa-'era'	Exod. 6:2–9:35	Ezekiel 28:25–29:21
18	Sa	10	Bo'	Exod. 10:1–13:16	Jeremiah 46:13–28
23	Th	15	Ḥamishah 'asar bi-Shevaṭ		
25	Sa	17	Be-shallaḥ (Shabbat Shirah)	Exod. 13:17–17:16	Judges 4:4–5:31 _Judges 5:1–31_
Feb. 1	Sa	24	Yitro	Exod. 18:1–20:23	Isaiah 6:1–7:6; 9:5–6 _Isaiah 6:1–13_
7	F	30	New Moon, first day	Num. 28:1–15	

Italics are for
Sephardi Minhag.

1997, Feb. 8 – Mar. 9] ADAR I (30 DAYS) [5757

Civil Date	Day of the Week	Jewish Date	SABBATHS, FESTIVALS, FASTS	PENTATEUCHAL READING	PROPHETICAL READING
Feb. 8	Sa	Adar I 1	Mishpaṭim; New Moon, second day	Exod. 21:1 – 24:18 Num. 28:9 – 15	Jeremiah 34:8 – 22 *Jeremiah 33:25 – 26*
15	Sa	8	Terumah	Exod. 25:1 – 27:19	I Kings 5:26 – 6:13
22	Sa	15	Teẓawweh	Exod. 27:20 – 30:10	Ezekiel 43:10 – 27
Mar. 1	Sa	22	Ki tissa'	Exod. 30:11 – 34:35	I Kings 18:1 – 39 *I Kings 18:20 – 39*
8	Sa	29	Wa-yaḵhel (Shabbat Sheḵalim)	Exod. 35:1 – 38:20 Exod. 30:11 – 16	II Kings 12:1 – 17 *II Kings 11:17 – 12:17* I Samuel 20:18, 42
9	S	30	New Moon, first day	Num. 28:1 – 15	

Italics are for Sephardi Minhag.

Civil Date	Day of the Week	Jewish Date	SABBATHS, FESTIVALS, FASTS	PENTATEUCHAL READING	PROPHETICAL READING
Mar. 10	M	Adar II 1	New Moon, second day	Num. 28:1–15	
15	Sa	6	Peḳude	Exod. 38:21–40:38	I Kings 7:51–8:21 *I Kings 7:40–50*
20	Th	11	Fast of Esther	Exod. 32:11–14 Exod. 34:1–10 (morning and afternoon)	Isaiah 55:6–56:8 (afternoon only)
22	Sa	13	Wa-yiḳra' (Shabbat Zakhor)	Levit. 1:1–5:26 Deut. 25:17–19	I Samuel 15:2–34 *I Samuel 15:1–34*
23	S	14	Purim	Exod. 17:8–16	Book of Esther (night before and in the morning)
24	M	15	Shushan Purim		
29	Sa	20	Ẓaw (Shabbat Parah)	Levit. 6:1–8:36 Num. 19:1–22	Ezekiel 36:16–38 *Ezekiel 36:16–36*
Apr. 5	Sa	27	Shemini (Shabbat Ha-ḥodesh)	Levit. 9:1–14:47 Exod. 12:1–20	Ezekiel 45:16–46:18 *Ezekiel 45:18–46:15*

Italics are for Sephardi Minhag.

1997, Apr. 8 – May 7] NISAN (30 DAYS) [5757

Civil Date	Day of the Week	Jewish Date	SABBATHS, FESTIVALS, FASTS	PENTATEUCHAL READING	PROPHETICAL READING
Apr. 8	T	Nisan 1	New Moon	Num. 28:1–15	
12	Sa	5	Tazria'	Levit. 12:1–13:59	II Kings 4:42–5:19
19	Sa	12	Mezora' (Shabbat Ha-gadol)	Levit. 14:1–15:33	Malachi 3:4–24
21	M	14	Fast of Firstborn		
22	T	15	Passover, first day	Exod. 12:21–51 Num. 28:16–25	Joshua 5:2–6:1, 27
23	W	16	Passover, second day	Levit. 22:26–23:44 Num. 28:16–25	II Kings 23:1–9, 21–25
24	Th	17	Ḥol Ha-mo'ed, first day	Exod. 13:1–16 Num. 28:19–25	
25	F	18	Ḥol Ha-mo'ed, second day	Exod. 22:24–23:19 Num. 28:19–25	
26	Sa	19	Ḥol Ha-mo'ed, third day	Exod. 33:12–34:26 Num. 28:19–25	Ezekiel 37:1–14
27	S	20	Ḥol Ha-mo'ed, fourth day	Num. 9:1–14 Num. 28:19–25	
28	M	21	Passover, seventh day	Exod. 13:17–15:26 Num. 28:19–25	II Samuel 22:1–51
29	T	22	Passover, eighth day	Deut. 15:19–16:17 Num. 28:19–25	Isaiah 10:32–12:6
May 3	Sa	26	Aḥare mot	Levit. 16:1–18:30	Amos 9:7–15 *Ezekiel 22:1–16*
4	S	27	Holocaust Memorial Day		
7	W	30	New Moon, first day	Num. 28:1–15	

Italics are for Sephardi Minhag.

1997, May 8 – June 5] **IYAR (29 DAYS)** [5757

Civil Date	Day of the Week	Jewish Date	SABBATHS, FESTIVALS, FASTS	PENTATEUCHAL READING	PROPHETICAL READING
May 8	Th	Iyar 1	New Moon, second day	Num. 28:1–15	
10	Sa	3	Ķedoshim	Levit. 19:1–20:27	Ezekiel 22:1–19 *Ezekiel 20:2–20*
12	M	5	Israel Independence Day		
17	Sa	10	Emor	Levit. 21:1–24:23	Ezekiel 44:15–31
24	Sa	17	Be-har	Levit. 25:1–26:2	Jeremiah 32:6–27
25	S	18	Lag Ba-'omer		
31	Sa	24	Be-ḥuķķotai	Levit. 26:3–27:34	Jeremiah 6:19–17:14
June 4	W	28	Jerusalem Day		

*Italics are for
Sephardi Minhag.*

1997, June 6 – July 5] SIWAN (30 DAYS) **[5757**

Civil Date	Day of the Week	Jewish Date	SABBATHS, FESTIVALS, FASTS	PENTATEUCHAL READING	PROPHETICAL READING
June 6	F	Siwan 1	New Moon	Num. 28:1–5	
7	Sa	2	Be-midbar	Num. 1:1–4:20	Hosea 2:1–22
11	W	6	Shavuʻot, first day	Exod. 19:1–20:23 Num. 28:26–31	Ezekiel 1:1–28 3:12
12	Th	7	Shavuʻot, second day	Deut. 15:19–16:17 Num. 28:26–31	Habbakuk 3:1–19 *Habbakuk 2:20–3:19*
14	Sa	9	Naso'	Num. 4:21–7:89	Judges 13:2–25
21	Sa	16	Be-Haʻalotekha	Num. 8:1–12:16	Zechariah 2:14–4:7
28	Sa	23	Shelaḥ lekha	Num. 13:1–15:41	Joshua 2:1–24
July 5	Sa	30	Korah; New Moon, first day	Num. 16:1–18:32 Num. 28:9–15	Isaiah 66:1–24 *Isaiah 66:1–24* I Samuel 20:18, 42

Italics are for Sephardi Minhag.

1997, July 6 – Aug. 3]   TAMMUZ (29 DAYS)   [5757

Civil Date	Day of the Week	Jewish Date	SABBATHS, FESTIVALS, FASTS	PENTATEUCHAL READING	PROPHETICAL READING
July 6	S	Tammuz 1	New Moon, second day	Num. 28:1–15	
12	Sa	7	Ḥukkat	Num. 19:1–22:1	Judges 11:1–33
19	Sa	14	Balak	Num. 22:2–25:9	Micah 5:6–6:8
22	T	17	Fast of 17th of Tammuz	Exod. 32:11–14 Exod. 34:1–10 (morning and afternoon)	Isaiah 55:6–56:8 (afternoon only)
26	Sa	21	Pineḥas	Num. 25:10–30:1	Jeremiah 1:1–2:3
Aug. 2	Sa	28	Maṭṭot, Mas'e	Num. 30:2–36:13	Jeremiah 2:4–28 3:4 *Jeremiah 2:4–28 4:1–2*

Italics are for Sephardi Minhag.

1997, Aug. 4 – Sept. 2]   AV (30 DAYS)   [5757

Civil Date	Day of the Week	Jewish Date	SABBATHS, FESTIVALS, FASTS	PENTATEUCHAL READING	PROPHETICAL READING
Aug. 4	M	Av 1	New Moon	Num. 28:1 – 15	
9	Sa	6	Devarim (Shabbat Ḥazon)	Deut. 1:1 – 3:22	Isaiah 1:1 – 27
12	T	9	Fast of 9th of Av	Morning: Deut. 4:25 – 40 Afternoon: Exod. 32:11 – 14 Exod. 34:1 – 10	(Lamentations is read the night before) Jeremiah 8:13 – 9:23 (morning) Isaiah 55:6 – 56:8 (afternoon)
16	Sa	13	Wa-Ethannan (Shabbat Naḥamu)	Deut. 3:23 – 7:11	Isaiah 40:1 – 26
23	Sa	20	ʿEḳev	Deut. 7:12 – 11:25	Isaiah 49:14 – 51:3
30	Sa	27	Re'eh	Deut. 11:26 – 16:17	Isaiah 54:11 – 55:5
Sept. 2	T	30	New Moon, first day	Num. 28:1 – 15	

Italics are for Sephardi Minhag.

ELUL (30 DAYS)

Civil Date	Day of the Week	Jewish Date	SABBATHS, FESTIVALS, FASTS	PENTATEUCHAL READING	PROPHETICAL READING
Sept. 3	W	Elul 1	New Moon, second day	Num. 28:1–15	
6	Sa	4	Shofeṭim	Deut. 16:18–21:9	Isaiah 51:12–52:12
13	Sa	11	Ki teẓe'	Deut. 21:10–25:19	Isaiah 54:1–10
20	Sa	18	Ki tavo'	Deut. 26:1–29:8	Isaiah 60:1–22
27	Sa	25	Niẓẓavim, Wa-yelekh	Deut. 29:9–30:20	Isaiah 61:10–63:9

Italics are for Sephardi Minhag.

Civil Date	Day of the Week	Jewish Date	SABBATHS, FESTIVALS, FASTS	PENTATEUCHAL READING	PROPHETICAL READING
Oct. 2	Th	Tishri 1	Rosh Ha-shanah, first day	Gen. 21:1–34 Num. 29:1–6	I Samuel 1:1–2:10
3	F	2	Rosh Ha-shanah, second day	Gen. 22:1–24 Num. 29:1–6	Jeremiah 31:2–20
4	Sa	3	Ha'azinu (Shabbat Shuvah)	Deut. 32:1–52	Hosea 14:2–10 Micah 7:18–20 Joel 2:15–27 *Hosea 14:2–10* *Micah 7:18–20*
5	S	4	Fast of Gedaliah	Exod. 32:11–14 Exod. 34:1–10 (morning and afternoon)	Isaiah 55:6–56:8 (afternoon only)
11	Sa	10	Yom Kippur	Morning: Levit. 16:1–34 Num. 29:7–11 Afternoon: Levit. 18:1–30	Isaiah 57:14–58:14 Jonah 1:1–4:11 Micah 7:18–20
16	Th	15	Sukkot, first day	Levit. 22:26–23:44 Num. 29:12–16	Zechariah 14:1–21
17	F	16	Sukkot, second day	Levit. 22:26–23:44 Num. 29:12–16	I Kings 8:2–21
18	Sa	17	Ḥol Ha-mo'ed, first day	Exod. 33:12–34:26 Num. 29:17–22	Ezekiel 38:18–39:16
19–21	S–T	18–20	Ḥol Ha-mo'ed, second to fourth days	S Num. 29:20–28 M Num. 29:23–31 T Num. 29:26–34	
22	W	21	Hosha'na' Rabbah	Num. 29:26–34	
23	Th	22	Shemini 'Aẓeret	Deut. 14:22–16:17 Num. 29:35–30:1	I Kings 8:54–66
24	F	23	Simḥat Torah	Deut. 33:1–34:12 Gen. 1:1–2:3 Num. 29:35–30:1	Joshua 1:1–18 *Joshua 1:1–9*
25	Sa	24	Be-re'shit	Gen. 1:1–6:8	Isaiah 42:5–43:10 *Isaiah 42:5–21*
31	F	30	New Moon, first day	Num. 28:1–15	

Italics are for
Sephardi Minhag.

Civil Date	Day of the Week	Jewish Date	SABBATHS, FESTIVALS, FASTS	PENTATEUCHAL READING	PROPHETICAL READING
Nov. 1	Sa	Heshwan 1	Noaḥ; New Moon, second day	Gen.　6:9–11:32 Num. 28:9–15	Isaiah 66:1–24
8	Sa	8	Lekh lekha	Gen. 12:1–17:27	Isaiah 40:27–41:16
15	Sa	15	Wa-yera'	Gen. 18:1–22:24	II Kings 4:1–37 *II Kings 4:1–23*
22	Sa	22	Ḥayye Sarah	Gen. 23:1–25:18	I Kings 1:1–31
29	Sa	29	Toledot	Gen. 25:19–28:9	I Samuel 20:18–42

Italics are for Sephardi Minhag.

1997, Nov. 30 – Dec. 29]   KISLEW (30 DAYS)   [5758

Civil Date	Day of the Week	Jewish Date	SABBATHS, FESTIVALS, FASTS	PENTATEUCHAL READING	PROPHETICAL READING
Nov. 30	S	Kislew 1	New Moon	Num. 28:1–15	
Dec. 6	Sa	7	Wa-yeẓe'	Gen. 28:10–32:3	Hosea 12:13–14:10 *Hosea 11:7–12:12*
13	Sa	14	Wa-yishlaḥ	Gen. 32:4–36:43	Hosea 11:7–12:12 *Obadiah 1:1–21*
20	Sa	21	Wa-yeshev	Gen. 37:1–40:23	Amos 2:6–3:8
24–26	W–F	25–27	Ḥanukkah, first to third days	W Num. 7:1–17 Th Num. 7:18–29 F Num. 7:24–35	
27	Sa	28	Mi-keẓ; Ḥanukkah, fourth day	Gen. 41:1–44:17 Num. 7:30–35	Zechariah 2:14–4:7
28	S	29	Ḥanukkah, fifth day	Num. 7:36–47	
29	M	30	New Moon, first day; Ḥanukkah, sixth day	Num. 28:1–15 Num. 7:42–47	

Italics are for Sephardi Minhag.

1997, Dec. 30–Jan. 27, 1998] ṬEVET (29 DAYS) [5758

Civil Date	Day of the Week	Jewish Date	SABBATHS, FESTIVALS, FASTS	PENTATEUCHAL READING	PROPHETICAL READING
Dec. 30	T	Ṭevet 1	New Moon, second day; Ḥanukkah, seventh day	Num. 28:1–15 Num. 7:48–53	
31	W	2	Ḥanukkah, eighth day	Num. 7:54–8:4	
Jan. 3	Sa	5	Wa-yiggash	Gen. 44:18–47:27	Ezekiel 37:15–28
8	Th	10	Fast of 10th of Ṭevet	Exod. 32:11–14 Exod. 34:1–10 (morning and afternoon)	Isaiah 55:6–56:8 (afternoon only)
10	Sa	12	Wa-yeḥi	Gen. 47:28–50:26	I Kings 2:1–12
17	Sa	19	Shemot	Exod. 1:1–6:1	Isaiah 27:6–28:13 29:22–23 *Jeremiah 1:1–2:3*
24	Sa	26	Wa-'era'	Exod. 6:2–9:35	Ezekiel 28:25–29:21

*Italics are for
Sephardi Minhag.*

1998, Jan. 28 – Feb. 26]   SHEVAṬ (30 DAYS)   [5758

Civil Date	Day of the Week	Jewish Date	SABBATHS, FESTIVALS, FASTS	PENTATEUCHAL READING	PROPHETICAL READING
Jan. 28	W	Shevaṭ 1	New Moon	Num. 28:1–15	
31	Sa	4	Bo'	Exod. 10:1–13:16	Jeremiah 46:13–28
Feb. 7	Sa	11	Be-shallaḥ (Shabbat Shirah)	Exod. 13:17–17:16	Judges 4:4–5:31 *Judges 5:1–31*
11	W	15	Hamishah-'asar bi-Shevaṭ		
14	Sa	18	Yitro	Exod. 18:1–20:23	Isaiah 6:1–7:6; 9:5–6 *Isaiah 6:1–13*
21	Sa	25	Mishpatim (Shabbat Sheḳalim)	Exod. 21:1–24:18 Exod. 30:11–16	II Kings 12:1–17 *II Kings 11:17–12:17*
26	Th	30	New Moon, first day	Num. 28:1–15	

Italics are for
Sephardi Minhag.

Civil Date	Day of the Week	Jewish Date	SABBATHS, FESTIVALS, FASTS	PENTATEUCHAL READING	PROPHETICAL READING
Feb. 27	F	Adar 1	New Moon, second day	Num. 28:1–15	
28	Sa	2	Terumah	Exod. 25:1–27:19	I Kings 5:26–6:13
Mar. 7	Sa	9	Teẓawweh (Shabbat Zakhor)	Exod. 27:20–30:10 Deut. 25:17–19	I Samuel 15:2–34 *I Samuel 15:1–34*
11	W	13	Fast of Esther	Exod. 32:11–14 Exod. 34:1–10 (morning and afternoon)	Isaiah 55:6–56:8 (afternoon only)
12	Th	14	Purim	Exod. 17:8–16	Book of Esther (night before and in the morning)
13	F	15	Shushan Purim		
14	Sa	16	Ki tissa'	Exod. 30:11–34:35	I Kings 18:1–39 *I Kings 18:20–39*
21	Sa	23	Wa-yaḳhel, Peḳude (Shabbat Parah)	Exod. 35:1–40:38 Num. 19:1–22	Ezekiel 36:16–38 *Ezekiel 36:16–36*

Italics are for Sephardi Minhag.

1998, Mar. 28 – April 26] NISAN (30 DAYS) [5758

Civil Date	Day of the Week	Jewish Date	SABBATHS, FESTIVALS, FASTS	PENTATEUCHAL READING	PROPHETICAL READING
Mar. 28	S	Nisan 1	Wa-yikra'; New Moon (Shabbat Ha-hodesh)	Levit. 1:1 – 5:26 Num. 28:9 – 15 Exod. 12:1 – 20	Ezekiel 45:16 – 46:18 *Ezekiel 45:18 – 46:15* *Isaiah 66:1, 23*
Apr. 4	Sa	8	Ẓaw (Shabbat Ha-gadol)	Levit. 6:1 – 8:36	Malachi 3:4 – 24
10	F	14	Fast of Firstborn		
11	Sa	15	Passover, first day	Exod. 12:21 – 51 Num. 28:16 – 25	Joshua 5:2 – 6:1, 27
12	S	16	Passover, second day	Levit. 22:26 – 23:44 Num. 28:16 – 25	II Kings 23:1 – 9, 21 – 25
13	M	17	Ḥol Ha-mo'ed, first day	Exod. 13:1 – 16 Num. 28:19 – 25	
14	T	18	Ḥol Ha-mo'ed, second day	Exod. 22:24 – 23:19 Num. 28:19 – 25	
15	W	19	Ḥol Ha-mo'ed, third day	Exod. 34:1 – 26 Num. 28:19 – 25	
16	Th	20	Ḥol Ha-mo'ed, fourth day	Num. 9:1 – 14 Num. 28:19 – 25	
17	F	21	Passover, seventh day	Exod. 13:17 – 15:26 Num. 28:19 – 25	II Samuel 22:1 – 51
18	Sa	22	Passover, eighth day	Deut. 15:19 – 16:17 Num. 28:19 – 25	Isaiah 10:32 – 12:6
23	Th	27	Holocaust Memorial Day		
25	Sa	29	Shemini	Levit 9:1 – 11:47	I Samuel 20:18 – 42
26	S	30	New Moon, first day	Num. 28:1 – 15	

Italics are for Sephardi Minhag.

1998, Apr. 27 – May 25]　　　IYAR (29 DAYS)　　　[5758

Civil Date	Day of the Week	Jewish Date	SABBATHS, FESTIVALS, FASTS	PENTATEUCHAL READING	PROPHETICAL READING
Apr. 27	M	Iyar 1	New Moon, second day	Num. 28:1–15	
May 1	F	5	Israel Independence Day*		
2	Sa	6	Tazria', Mezora'	Levit. 12:1–15:33	II Kings 7:3–20
9	Sa	13	Aḥare mot, Kedoshim	Levit. 16:1–20:27	Amos 9:7–15 *Ezekiel 20:2–20*
14	Th	18	Lag Ba-'omer		
16	Sa	20	Emor	Levit. 21:1–24:23	Ezekiel 44:15–31
23	Sa	27	Be-har, Be-ḥukkotai	Levit. 25:1–27:34	Jeremiah 6:19–17:14
24	S	28	Jerusalem Day		

*Observed Apr. 30, to avoid conflict with the Sabbath.

*Italics are for
Sephardi Minhag.*

1998, May 26 – June 24]   SIWAN (30 DAYS)   [5758

Civil Date	Day of the Week	Jewish Date	SABBATHS, FESTIVALS, FASTS	PENTATEUCHAL READING	PROPHETICAL READING
May 26	T	Siwan 1	New Moon	Num. 28:1–15	
30	Sa	5	Be-midbar	Num. 1:1–4:20	Hosea 2:1–22
31	S	6	Shavu'ot, first day	Exod. 19:1–20:23 Num. 28:26–31	Ezekiel 1:1–28 3:12
June 1	M	7	Shavu'ot, second day	Deut. 15:19–16:17 Num. 28:26–31	Habbakuk 3:1–19 *Habbakuk 2:20–3:19*
6	Sa	12	Naso'	Num. 4:21–7:89	Judges 13:2–25
13	Sa	19	Be-ha'alotekha	Num. 8:1–12:16	Zechariah 2:14–4:7
20	Sa	26	Shelaḥ lekha	Num. 13:1–15:41	Joshua 2:1–24
24	W	30	New Moon, first day	Num. 28:1–15	

Italics are for Sephardi Minhag.

1998, June 25 – July 23]　　TAMMUZ (29 DAYS)　　[5758

Civil Date	Day of the Week	Jewish Date	SABBATHS, FESTIVALS, FASTS	PENTATEUCHAL READING	PROPHETICAL READING
June 25	Th	Tammuz 1	New Moon, second day	Num. 28:1–15	
27	Sa	3	Ḳoraḥ	Num. 16:1–18:32	I Samuel 11:14–12:22
July 4	Sa	10	Ḥuḳḳat	Num. 19:1–22:1	Judges 11:1–33
11	Sa	17	Balaḳ	Num. 22:2–25:9	Micah 5:6–6:8
12	S	18	Fast of 17th of Tammuz	Exod. 32:11–14 Exod. 34:1–10 (morning and afternoon)	Isaiah 55:6–56:8 (afternoon only)
18	Sa	24	Pineḥas	Num. 25:10–30:1	Jeremiah 1:1–2:3

Italics are for
Sephardi Minhag.

1998, July 24 – Aug. 22]   AV (30 DAYS)   [5758

Civil Date	Day of the Week	Jewish Date	SABBATHS, FESTIVALS, FASTS	PENTATEUCHAL READING	PROPHETICAL READING
July 24	F	Av 1	New Moon	Num. 28:1–15	
25	Sa	2	Maṭṭot, Masʻe	Num. 30:2–36:13	Jeremiah 2:4–28 3:4 *Jeremiah 2:4–28 4:1–2*
Aug. 1	Sa	9	Devarim (Shabbat Ḥazon)	Deut. 1:1–3:22	Isaiah 1:1–27
2	S	10	Fast of 9th of Av	Morning: Deut. 4:25–40 Afternoon: Exod. 32:11–14 Exod. 34:1–10	(Lamentations is read the night before) Jeremiah 8:13–9:23 (morning) Isaiah 55:6–56:8 (afternoon)
8	Sa	16	Wa-etḥannan (Shabbat Naḥamu)	Deut. 3:23–7:11	Isaiah 40:1–26
15	Sa	23	ʻEkev	Deut. 7:12–11:25	Isaiah 49:14–51:3
22	Sa	30	Re'eh; New Moon, first day	Deut. 11:26–16:17 Num. 28:9–15	Isaiah 66:1–24 *Isaiah 66:1–24 I Samuel 20:18, 42*

Italics are for Sephardi Minhag.

1998, Aug. 23 – Sept. 20]   ELUL (29 DAYS)   [5758

Civil Date	Day of the Week	Jewish Date	SABBATHS, FESTIVALS, FASTS	PENTATEUCHAL READING	PROPHETICAL READING
Aug. 23	S	Elul 1	New Moon, second day	Num. 28:1–15	
29	Sa	7	Shofeṭim	Deut. 16:18–21:9	Isaiah 51:12–52:12
Sept. 5	Sa	14	Ki teze'	Deut. 21:10–25:19	Isaiah 54:1–55:5
12	Sa	21	Ki tavo'	Deut. 26:1–29:8	Isaiah 60:1–22
19	Sa	28	Niẓẓavim	Deut. 29:9–30:20	Isaiah 61:10–63:9

Italics are for
Sephardi Minhag.

Civil Date	Day of the Week	Jewish Date	SABBATHS, FESTIVALS, FASTS	PENTATEUCHAL READING	PROPHETICAL READING
Sept. 21	M	Tishri 1	Rosh Ha-shanah, first day	Gen. 21:1–34 Num. 29:1–6	I Samuel 1:1–2:10
22	T	2	Rosh Ha-shanah, second day	Gen. 22:1–24 Num. 29:1–6	Jeremiah 31:2–20
23	W	3	Fast of Gedaliah	Exod. 32:11–14 Exod. 34:1–10 (morning and afternoon)	Isaiah 55:6–56:8 (afternoon only)
26	Sa	6	Wa-yelekh (Shabbat Shuvah)	Deut. 31:1–30	Hosea 14:2–10 Micah 7:18–20 Joel 2:15–27 *Hosea 14:2–10* *Micah 7:18–20*
30	W	10	Yom Kippur	Morning: Levit. 16:1–34 Num. 29:7–11 Afternoon: Levit. 18:1–30	Isaiah 57:14–58:14 Jonah 1:1–4:11 Micah 7:18–20
Oct. 3	Sa	13	Ha'azinu	Deut. 32:1–52	II Samuel 22:1–51
5	M	15	Sukkot, first day	Levit. 22:26–23:44 Num. 29:12–16	Zechariah 14:1–21
6	T	16	Sukkot, second day	Levit. 22:26–23:44 Num. 29:12–16	I Kings 8:2–21
7–10	W–Sa	17–20	Ḥol Ha-mo'ed	W Num. 29:17–25 Th Num. 29:20–28 F Num. 29:23–31 Sa Exod. 33:12–34:26 Num. 29:26–34	Ezekiel 38:18–39:16
11	S	21	Hosha'na' Rabbah	Num. 29:26–34	
12	M	22	Shemini 'Aẓeret	Deut. 14:22–16:17 Num. 29:35–30:1	I Kings 8:54–66
13	T	23	Simḥat Torah	Deut. 33:1–34:12 Gen. 1:1–2:3 Num. 29:35–30:1	Joshua 1:1–18 *Joshua 1:1–9*
17	Sa	27	Be-re'shit	Gen. 1:1–6:8	Isaiah 42:5–43:10 *Isaiah 42:5–21*
20	T	30	New Moon, first day	Num. 28:1–15	

Italics are for Sephardi Minhag.

1998, Oct. 21 – Nov. 19]   ḤESHWAN (30 DAYS)   [5759

Civil Date	Day of the Week	Jewish Date	SABBATHS, FESTIVALS, FASTS	PENTATEUCHAL READING	PROPHETICAL READING
Oct. 21	W	Ḥeshwan 1	New Moon, second day	Num. 28:1 – 15	
24	Sa	4	Noaḥ	Gen. 6:9 – 11:32	Isaiah 54:1 – 55:5 *Isaiah 54:1 – 10*
31	Sa	11	Lekh lekha	Gen. 12:1 – 17:27	Isaiah 40:27 – 41:16
Nov. 7	Sa	18	Wa-yera'	Gen. 18:1 – 22:24	II Kings 4:1 – 37 *II Kings 4:1 – 23*
14	Sa	25	Ḥayye Sarah	Gen. 23:1 – 25:18	I Kings 1:1 – 31
19	Th	30	New Moon, first day	Num. 28:1 – 15	

Italics are for
Sephardi Minhag.

1998, Nov. 20 – Dec. 19]   KISLEW (30 DAYS)   [5759

Civil Date	Day of the Week	Jewish Date	SABBATHS, FESTIVALS, FASTS	PENTATEUCHAL READING	PROPHETICAL READING
Nov. 20	F	Kislew 1	New Moon, second day	Num. 28:1–15	
21	Sa	2	Toledot	Gen. 25:19–28:9	Malachi 1:1–2:7
28	Sa	9	Wa-yeẓe'	Gen. 28:10–32:3	Hosea 12:13–14:10 *Hosea 11:7–12:12*
Dec. 5	Sa	16	Wa-yishlaḥ	Gen. 32:4–36:43	Hosea 11:7–12:12 *Obadiah 1:1–21*
12	Sa	23	Wa-yeshev	Gen. 37:1–40:23	Amos 2:6–3:8
14–18	M–F	25–29	Ḥanukkah, first to fifth days	M Num. 7:1–17 T Num. 7:18–29 W Num. 7:24–35 Th Num. 7:30–41 F Num. 7:36–47	
19	Sa	30	Mi-keẓ; New Moon, first day; Ḥanukkah, sixth day	Gen. 41:1–44:17 Num. 28:9–15 Num. 7:42–47	Zechariah 2:14–4:7 *Zechariah 2:14–4:7* *Isaiah 66:1, 24* *I Samuel 20:18, 42*

Italics are for
Sephardi Minhag.

1998, Dec. 20 – Jan. 17, 1999] ṬEVET (29 DAYS) [5759

Civil Date	Day of the Week	Jewish Date	SABBATHS, FESTIVALS, FASTS	PENTATEUCHAL READING	PROPHETICAL READING
Dec. 20	S	Ṭevet 1	New Moon, second day; Ḥanukkah, seventh day	Num. 28:1–15 Num. 7:48–53	
21	M	2	Ḥanukkah, eighth day	Num. 7:54–8:4	
26	Sa	7	Wa-yiggash	Gen. 44:18–47:27	Ezekiel 37:15–28
29	T	10	Fast of 10th of Ṭevet	Exod. 32:11–14 Exod. 34:1–10 (morning and afternoon)	Isaiah 55:6–56:8 (afternoon only)
Jan. 2	Sa	14	Wa-yeḥi	Gen. 47:28–50:26	I Kings 2:1–12
9	Sa	21	Shemot	Exod. 1:1–6:1	Isaiah 27:6–28:13 29:22–23 *Jeremiah 1:1–2:3*
16	Sa	28	Wa-’era’	Exod. 6:2–9:35	Ezekiel 28:25–29:21

Italics are for Sephardi Minhag.

1999, Jan 18 – Feb. 16]   **SHEVAṬ (30 DAYS)**   **[5759**

Civil Date	Day of the Week	Jewish Date	SABBATHS, FESTIVALS, FASTS	PENTATEUCHAL READING	PROPHETICAL READING
Jan. 18	M	Shevaṭ 1	New Moon	Num. 28:1–15	
23	Sa	6	Bo'	Exod. 10:1–13:16	Jeremiah 46:13–28
30	Sa	13	Be-shallaḥ (Shabbat Shirah)	Exod. 13:17–17:16	Judges 4:4–5:31 *Judges 5:1–31*
Feb. 1	M	15	Hamishah-'asar bi-Shevaṭ		
6	Sa	20	Yitro	Exod. 18:1–20:23	Isaiah 6:1–7:6; 9:5–6 *Isaiah 6:1–13*
13	Sa	27	Mishpaṭim (Shabbat Sheḳalim)	Exod. 21:1–24:18 Exod. 30:11–16	II Kings 12:1–17 *II Kings 11:17–12:17*
16	T	30	New Moon, first day	Num. 28:1–15	

Italics are for Sephardi Minhag.

1999, Feb. 17 – Mar. 17]   ADAR (29 DAYS)   [5759

Civil Date	Day of the Week	Jewish Date	SABBATHS, FESTIVALS, FASTS	PENTATEUCHAL READING	PROPHETICAL READING
Feb. 17	W	Adar 1	New Moon, second day	Num. 28:1–15	
20	Sa	4	Terumah	Exod. 25:1–27:19	I Kings 5:26–6:13
27	Sa	11	Teẓawweh (Shabbat Zakhor)	Exod. 27:20–30:10 Deut. 25: 17–19	I Samuel 15:2–34 *I Samuel 15:1–34*
Mar. 1	M	13	Fast of Esther	Exod. 32:11–14 Exod. 34:1–10 (morning and afternoon)	Isaiah 55:6–56:8 (afternoon only)
2	T	14	Purim	Exod. 17:8–16	Book of Esther (night before and in the morning)
3	W	15	Shushan Purim		
6	Sa	18	Ki tissa' (Shabbat Parah)	Exod. 30:11–34:35 Num. 19:1–22	Ezekiel 36:16–38 *Ezekiel 36:16–36*
13	Sa	25	Wa-yaḵhel, Peḵude (Shabbat Ha-ḥodesh)	Exod. 35:1–40:38 Exod. 12:1–20	Ezekiel 45:16–46:18 *Ezekiel 45:18–46:15*

Italics are for Sephardi Minhag.

1999, Mar. 18 – April 16]   NISAN (30 DAYS)   [5759

Civil Date	Day of the Week	Jewish Date	SABBATHS, FESTIVALS, FASTS	PENTATEUCHAL READING	PROPHETICAL READING
Mar. 18	Th	Nisan 1	New Moon	Num. 28:1 – 15	
20	Sa	3	Wa-yiḳra'	Levit. 1:1 – 5:26	Isaiah 43:21 – 44:23
27	Sa	10	Ẓaw (Shabbat Ha-gadol)	Levit. 6:1 – 8:36	Malachi 3:4 – 24
31	W	14	Fast of Firstborn		
Apr. 1	Th	15	Passover, first day	Exod. 12:21 – 51 Num. 28:16 – 25	Joshua 5:2 – 6:1,27
2	F	16	Passover, second day	Levit. 22:26 – 23:44 Num. 28:16 – 25	II Kings 23:1 – 9, 21 – 25
3	Sa	17	Ḥol Ha-mo'ed, first day	Exod. 33:12 – 34:26 Num. 28:19 – 25	Ezekiel 37:1 – 14
4	S	18	Ḥol Ha-mo'ed, second day	Exod. 13:1 – 16 Num. 28:19 – 25	Ezekiel 45:16 – 46:18
5	M	19	Ḥol Ha-mo'ed, third day	Exod. 22:24 – 23:19 Num. 28:19 – 25	
6	T	20	Ḥol Ha-mo'ed, fourth day	Num. 9:1 – 14 Num. 28:19 – 25	
7	W	21	Passover, seventh day	Exod. 13:17 – 15:26 Num. 28:19 – 25	II Samuel 22:1 – 51
8	Th	22	Passover, eighth day	Deut. 15:19 – 16:17 Num. 28:19 – 25	Isaiah 10:32 – 12:6
10	Sa	24	Shemini	Levit. 9:1 – 11:47 Num. 28:19 – 25	II Samuel 6:1 – 7:17 *II Samuel 6:1 – 19*
13	T	27	Holocaust Memorial Day		
16	F	30	New Moon	Num. 28:19 – 25	

*Italics are for
Sephardi Minhag.*

1999, Apr. 17–May 15]   IYAR (29 DAYS)   [5759

Civil Date	Day of the Week	Jewish Date	SABBATHS, FESTIVALS, FASTS	PENTATEUCHAL READING	PROPHETICAL READING
Apr. 17	Sa	Iyar 1	Tazria', Mezora'; New Moon, second day	Levit. 12:1–15:33 Num. 28:9–15	Isaiah 66:1–24
21	W	5	Israel Independence Day		
24	Sa	8	Ahare mot, Kedoshim	Levit. 16:1–20:27	Amos 9:7–15 *Ezekiel 20:2–20*
May 1	Sa	15	Emor	Levit. 21:1–24:23	Ezekiel 44:15–31
4	T	18	Lag Ba-'omer		
8	Sa	22	Be-har, Be-hukkotai	Levit. 25:1–27:34	Jeremiah 16:19–17:14
14	F	28	Jerusalem Day*		
15	Sa	29	Be-midbar	Num. 1:1–4:20	I Samuel 20:18–18:42

*Observed May 13, to avoid conflict with the Sabbath.

Italics are for Sephardi Minhag.

1999, May 16 – June 14]   SIWAN (30 DAYS)   [5759

Civil Date	Day of the Week	Jewish Date	SABBATHS, FESTIVALS, FASTS	PENTATEUCHAL READING	PROPHETICAL READING
May 16	S	Siwan 1	New Moon	Num. 28:1 – 15	
21	F	6	Shavu'ot, first day	Exod. 19:1 – 20:23	Ezekiel 1:1 – 28, 3:12
22	Sa	7	Shavu'ot, second day	Deut. 15:19 – 16:17 Num. 28:26 – 31	Habbakuk 3:1 – 19 *Habbakuk 2:20 – 3:19*
29	Sa	14	Naso'	Num. 4:21 – 7:89	Judges 13:2 – 25
June 5	Sa	21	Be-ha'alotekha	Num. 8:1 – 12:16	Zechariah 2:14 – 4:7
12	Sa	28	Shelaḥ lekha	Num. 13:1 – 15:41	Joshua 2:1 – 24
14	M	30	New Moon, first day	Num. 28:1 – 15	

Italics are for Sephardi Minhag.

1999, June 15–July 13] TAMMUZ (29 DAYS) [5759

Civil Date	Day of the Week	Jewish Date	SABBATHS, FESTIVALS, FASTS	PENTATEUCHAL READING	PROPHETICAL READING
June 15	T	Tammuz 1	New Moon, second day	Num. 28:1–15	
19	Sa	5	Ḳoraḥ	Num. 16:1–18:32	I Samuel 11:14–12:22
26	Sa	12	Ḥukḳat, Balaḳ	Num. 19:1–25:9	Micah 5:6–6:8
July 1	Th	17	Fast of 17th of Tammuz	Exod. 32:11–14 Exod. 34:1–10 (morning and afternoon)	Isaiah 55:6–56:8 (afternoon only)
3	Sa	19	Pineḥas	Num. 25:10–30:1	Jeremiah 1:1–2:3
10	Sa	26	Maṭṭot, Masʿe	Num. 30:2–36:13	Jeremiah 2:4–28 3:4 *Jeremiah 2:4–28 4:1–2*

Italics are for Sephardi Minhag.

1999, July 14 – Aug. 12] AV (30 DAYS) [5759

Civil Date	Day of the Week	Jewish Date	SABBATHS, FESTIVALS, FASTS	PENTATEUCHAL READING	PROPHETICAL READING
July 14	W	Av 1	New Moon	Num. 28:1 – 15	
17	Sa	4	Devarim (Shabbat Ḥazon)	Deut. 1:1 – 3:22	Isaiah 1:1 – 27
22	Th	9	Fast of 9th of Av	Morning: Deut. 4:25 – 40 Afternoon Exod. 32:11 – 14 Exod. 34:1 – 10	(Lamentations is read the night before) Jeremiah 8:13 – 9:23 (morning) Isaiah 55:6 – 56:8 (afternoon)
24	Sa	11	Wa-etḥannan (Shabbat Naḥamu)	Deut. 3:23 – 7:11	Isaiah 40:1 – 26
31	Sa	18	'Ekev	Deut. 7:12 – 11:25	Isaiah 49:14 – 51:3
Aug. 7	Sa	25	Re'eh	Deut. 11:26 – 16:17	Isaiah 54:11 – 55:5
12	Th	30	New Moon, first day	Num. 28:1 – 15	

Italics are for Sephardi Minhag.

1999, Aug. 13–Sept. 10]   ELUL (29 DAYS)   [5759

Civil Date	Day of the Week	Jewish Date	SABBATHS, FESTIVALS, FASTS	PENTATEUCHAL READING	PROPHETICAL READING
Aug. 13	F	Elul 1	New Moon, second day	Num. 28:1–15	
14	Sa	2	Shofeṭim (Shabbat Ḥazon)	Deut. 16:18–21:9	Isaiah 51:12–52:12
21	Sa	9	Ki teẓe'	Deut. 21:10–25:19	Isaiah 54:1–10
28	Sa	16	Ki tavo'	Deut. 26:1–29:8	Isaiah 60:1–22
Sept. 4	Sa	23	Niẓẓavim, Wa-yelekh	Deut. 29:9–30:20	Isaiah 61:10–63:9

Italics are for
Sephardi Minhag.

Civil Date	Day of the Week	Jewish Date	SABBATHS, FESTIVALS, FASTS	PENTATEUCHAL READING	PROPHETICAL READING
Sept. 11	Sa	Tishri 1	Rosh Ha-shanah, first day	Gen. 21:1–34 Num. 29:1–6	I Samuel 1:1–2:10
12	S	2	Rosh Ha-shanah, second day	Gen. 22:1–24 Num. 29:1–6	Jeremiah 3:2–20
13	M	3	Fast of Gedaliah	Exod. 32:11–14 Exod. 34:1–10 (morning and afternoon)	Isaiah 55:6–56:8 (afternoon only)
18	Sa	8	Ha'azinu (Shabbat Shuvah)	Deut. 32:1–52	Hosea 14:2–10 Micah 7:18–20 Joel 2:15–27 *Hosea 14:2–10* *Micah 7:18–20*
20	M	10	Yom Kippur	Morning: Levit. 16:1–34 Num. 29:7–11 Afternoon: Levit. 18:1–30	Isaiah 57:14–58:14 Jonah 1:1–4:11 Micah 7:18–20
25	Sa	15	Sukkot, first day	Levit. 22:26–23:44 Num. 29:12–16	Zechariah 14:1–21
26	S	16	Sukkot, second day	Levit. 22:26–23:44 Num. 29:12–16	I Kings 8:2–21
27-30	M-Th	17–20	Ḥol Ha-mo'ed	M Num. 29:17–25 T Num. 29:20–28 W Num. 29:23–31 Th Num. 29:26–34	
Oct. 1	F	21	Hosha'na' Rabbah	Num. 29:26–34	
2	Sa	22	Shemini 'Aẓeret	Deut. 14:22–16:17 Num. 29:35–30:1	I Kings 8:54–66
3	S	23	Simḥat Torah	Deut. 33:1–34:12 Gen. 1:1–2:3 Num. 29:35–30:1	Joshua 1:1–18 *Joshua 1:1–9*
9	Sa	29	Be-re'shit	Gen. 1:1–6:8	I Samuel 20:18–42
10	S	30	New Moon, first day	Num. 28:1–15	

Italics are for Sephardi Minhag.

Civil Date	Day of the Week	Jewish Date	SABBATHS, FESTIVALS, FASTS	PENTATEUCHAL READING	PROPHETICAL READING
Oct. 11	M	Ḥeshwan 1	New Moon, second day	Num. 28:1–15	
16	Sa	6	Noaḥ	Gen. 6:9–11:32	Isaiah 54:1–55:5 *Isaiah 54:1–10*
23	Sa	13	Lekh lekha	Gen. 12:1–17:27	Isaiah 40:27–41:16
30	Sa	20	Wa-yera'	Gen. 18:1–22:24	II Kings 4:1–37 *II Kings 4:1–23*
Nov. 6	Sa	27	Ḥayye Sarah	Gen. 23:1–25:18	I Kings 1:1–31
9	T	30	New Moon, first day	Num. 28:1–15	

Italics are for Sephardi Minhag.

1999, Nov. 10 – Dec. 9]   KISLEW (30 DAYS)   [5760

Civil Date	Day of the Week	Jewish Date	SABBATHS, FESTIVALS, FASTS	PENTATEUCHAL READING	PROPHETICAL READING
Nov. 10	W	Kislew 1	New Moon, second day	Num. 28:1 – 15	
13	Sa	4	Toledot	Gen. 25:19 – 28:9	Malachi 1:1 – 2:7
20	Sa	11	Wa-yeze'	Gen. 28:10 – 32:3	Hosea 12:13 – 14:10 *Hosea 11:7 – 12:12*
27	Sa	18	Wa-yishlah	Gen. 32:4 – 36:43	Hosea 11:7 – 12:12 *Obadiah 1:1 – 21*
Dec. 4	Sa	25	Wa-yeshev; Hanukkah, first day	Gen. 37:1 – 40:23 Num. 7:1 – 17	Zecharia 2:14 – 4:7
5 – 8	S – W	26 – 29	Hanukkah, second to fifth days	S Num.7:18 – 29 M Num.7:24 – 35 T Num.7:30 – 41 W Num. 7:36 – 47	
9	Th	30	New Moon, first day; Hanukkah, sixth day	Num. 28:1 – 15 Num. 7:42 – 47	

Italics are for
Sephardi Minhag.

1999, Dec. 10–Jan. 7, 2000]   ȚEVET (29 DAYS)   [5760

Civil Date	Day of the Week	Jewish Date	SABBATHS, FESTIVALS, FASTS	PENTATEUCHAL READING	PROPHETICAL READING
Dec. 10	F	Ṭevet 1	New Moon, second day; Ḥanukkah, seventh day	Num. 28:1–15 Num. 7:42–47	
11	Sa	2	Miḳeẓ; Ḥanukkah, eighth day	Gen. 41:1–44:17 Num. 7:54–8.4	I Kings 7:40–50
18	Sa	9	Wa-yiggash	Gen. 44:18–47:27	Ezekiel 37:15–28
19	S	10	Fast of 10th of Ṭevet	Exod. 32:11–14 Exod. 34:1–10 (morning and afternoon)	Isaiah 55:6–56:8 (afternoon only)
25	Sa	16	Wa-yeḥi	Gen. 47:28–50:26	I Kings 2:1–12
Jan. 1	Sa	23	Shemot	Exod. 1:1–6:1	Isaiah 27:6–28:13 29:22–23 *Jeremiah 1:1–2:3*

Italics are for Sephardi Minhag.

SELECTED ARTICLES OF INTEREST IN RECENT VOLUMES OF THE AMERICAN JEWISH YEAR BOOK

American Jewish Fiction Turns Inward, 1960–1990	Sylvia Barack Fishman 91:35–69
American Jewish Museums: Trends and Issues	Ruth R. Seldin 91:71–113
Anti-Semitism in Europe Since the Holocaust	Robert S. Wistrich 93:3–23
Counting Jewish Populations: Methods and Problems	Paul Ritterband, Barry A. Kosmin, and Jeffrey Scheckner 88:204–221
Current Trends in American Jewish Philanthropy	Jack Wertheimer 97:3–92
The Demography of Latin American Jewry	U.O. Schmelz and Sergio DellaPergola 85:51–102
Ethiopian Jews in Israel	Steven Kaplan and Chaim Rosen 94:59–109
Ethnic Differences Among Israeli Jews: A New Look	U.O. Schmelz, Sergio DellaPergola, and Uri Avner 90:3–204
The Impact of Feminism on American Jewish Life	Sylvia B. Fishman 89:3–62
Israeli Literature and the American Reader	Alan Mintz 97:93–114
Israelis in the United States	Steven J. Gold and Bruce A. Phillips 96:51–101
Jewish Experience on Film—An American Overview	Joel Rosenberg 96:3–50
Jewish Identity in Conversionary and Mixed Marriages	Peter Y. Medding, Gary A. Tobin, Sylvia Barack Fishman, and Mordechai Rimor 92:3–76

OBITUARIES

Index